KU-560-532

RIDEOUT'S
PRINCIPLES OF LABOUR LAW

AUSTRALIA AND NEW ZEALAND
The Law Book Co. Ltd.
Sydney : Melbourne : Perth

CANADA AND U.S.A.
The Carswell Company Ltd.
Agincourt, Ontario

INDIA
N. M. Tripathi Private Ltd.
Bombay
and
Eastern Law House Private Ltd.
Calcutta and Delhi
M.P.P. House
Bangalore

ISRAEL
Steimatzky's Agency Ltd.
Jerusalem : Tel Aviv : Haifa

MALAYSIA : SINGAPORE : BRUNEI
Malayan Law Journal (Pte.) Ltd.
Singapore

PAKISTAN
Pakistan Law House
Karachi

RIDEOUT'S PRINCIPLES
OF
LABOUR LAW

by

ROGER W. RIDEOUT, LL.B., Ph.D.

of Gray's Inn, Barrister
Professor of Labour Law,
University College London

with

JACQUELINE C. DYSON, LL.M.

of the Inner Temple, Barrister,
Lecturer in Law, University College London

FOURTH EDITION

LONDON
SWEET & MAXWELL
1983

First Edition 1972
Second Edition 1976
Third Edition 1979
Fourth Edition 1983

Published in 1983 by
Sweet & Maxwell Ltd. of
11 New Fetter Lane, London
and printed in Scotland

British Library Cataloguing in Publication Data
Rideout, Roger W.
  Rideout's Principles of labour law.—4th ed.
  1. Labor laws and legislation—England
  I. Title
  344.204′1   KD3009

  ISBN 0–421–296100
  ISBN 0–421–296208 Pbk

All rights reserved.
No part of this publication may be
reproduced or transmitted, in any form
or by any means, electronic, mechanical,
photocopying, recording or otherwise, or
stored in any retrieval system of any
nature, without the written permission
of the copyright holder and the publisher,
application for which shall be made to
the publisher.

©
R. W. Rideout
1983

FOR MY FATHER

FOR MY FATHER

PREFACE TO THE FOURTH EDITION

The time had come substantially to rewrite this textbook. It is intended that it should remain primarily a textbook the aim of which is to explain the law to degree students studying labour law for the first time. The book is not primarily concerned, however, with first principles but aims to bring the student up to a level of practising competence. It is not an encyclopedia nor is it designed materially to instruct the competent academic.

Much individual labour law has changed, even since the third edition. This change is not confined to, nor even primarily concerned with, the content of the law. Labour law has developed, not always deliberately, some peculiar features. It is generally agreed that far too many decisions are reported. This excess is made the more significant by the insistence of the Court of Appeal that most of what comes before industrial tribunals involves questions of fact or broad bands of discretion upon which they are expected to act as "industrial juries." In consequence, all writers are forced to select decisions to illustrate trends. These trends may be towards the development of rules, but, in matters within the jurisdiction of industrial tribunals, are more likely to indicate directions of judicial thought.

That such thought has changed radically in the 12 years of what might be called "modern labour law" is common knowledge. Codes of practice as sources of procedural rules have given way to broad considerations of equity. In turn subjective reasonableness has appeared to go too far and obvious efforts to shift the balance have been made more recently by the E.A.T. This movement has its counterpart not only in the approach to the identification and assessment of reasons for action but also in associated areas. Again it is common knowledge that the concepts of the law of contract have been found surprisingly capable of adaptation to fit in to an informal contract, regulating a relationship most of which depends on non-contractual sources and attitudes.

There is, however, another side of labour law, from which other writers to various extents excuse themselves. The comparison of the judicial approach to the individual employee and the individual trade unionist is a fascinating one. The approach of the E.A.T. and, to some extent, the Court of Appeal in individual labour law is sharply at odds with the attitude of the Court of Appeal when dealing with industrial action. In those "collective" areas the student can see to what a marked degree United Kingdom legislation, and, indeed, the question of State intervention, remains in the experimental stage. The authors of this book continue to have not the slightest hesitation in presenting the whole area of the employment of labour as a single study. Comparison is instructive just because the law is not uniform in its approach to the different, and largely artificial compartments too often selected for isolated study.

The outcome of these considerations is that most of the consideration of individual employment law has been replanned and rewritten. This is parti-

vii

cularly true of the chapters on the Contract of Employment, Unfair Dismissal, Redundancy and Discrimination. The chapter on trade union internal affairs has also been rewritten to introduce a new approach. In addition, so much new material has been introduced in other areas, particularly the consideration of industrial action, that only the outline of former editions remains.

Finally, it has become common for books of this nature to present for consideration substantial extracts from major judgments. Many such extracts have been produced for the first time in this edition.

It is hoped, however, that all these changes, which have led to a much longer work, will not have detracted from the readability of earlier editions.

The original author would like to thank Mrs. Dyson for joining him in this project and for greatly improving the chapter on liability for injury at work. His thanks are also due especially to Brian Bercusson of Queen Mary College who can be described as a constant source of inspiration. We would both like to express our deep appreciation of the vast amount of work done on yet another edition by Miss Lisa Goulding who has produced all the new typescript and read the galleys. This is probably the last edition for which she will perform this invaluable service so it is fair to couple with this renewed thanks for similar work on the second and third editions.

R. W. RIDEOUT
J. C. DYSON

UNIVERSITY COLLEGE LONDON
March 1983

PREFACE TO THE FIRST EDITION

Some years ago, when I first thought of writing this book, it appeared that Industrial Law, as it was then generally called, had changed from its initial conception as surely as that conception differed from the law of Master and Servant which had preceded it. The work of the great pioneer textbook writer, Sir William Mansfield Cooper, had for some time contained chapters which seemed to the ordinary student of little relevance. It had begun to be evident that we would even relegate such matters as the Truck Acts to a less significant place than they had enjoyed in earlier years. Mansfield Cooper's single final chapter on trade unions obviously called for expansion, since this aspect occupied at least a third part of most degree courses.

It was also clear that this was only the beginning. No other aspect of law, save perhaps Restitution, has changed and expanded at such a pace in recent years. The Industrial Relations Act 1971, revolutionary and unexpected as it may be, is only the greatest step in this process. It may be, indeed, that this development has now partly outstripped the concept of this book. Labour Law is in the process of being divided into ever more specialised fragments which themselves look like growing to the size of the former whole. No doubt the, presently common, single course will give place to separate courses on some of these subdivisions. It seems to me, however, that the need for a general textbook will always remain so that the student setting out to study Labour Law, may see the different aspects of it in the context of each other. For this reason, also, I have sought to include all the aspects which commonly form the general study whether or not the purist would deem them part of Labour Law.

The passage of the Industrial Relations Act 1971 interrupted the preparation of this book when it was almost complete. At this time it feels as if we have lived for a long time with the Act, whereas, of course, there are yet no judicial comments available on any part of its vast implications. I have thought it right, therefore, to include relatively substantial comment upon the common law relating to wrongful dismissal and to the economic torts. Much of this material is obsolescent, but it is not obsolete. It is bound to have a significant influence on the development of the application of this Act and others which will inevitably follow. In time the space occupied by Chapter 17 will be occupied by the vastly expanded matter of Chapter 18, but it does not seem wise, in a general textbook, to speculate too widely upon the nature of the unknown.

It would be pleasant, perhaps, if the exposition of Labour Law could be halted until it had settled into new and defined lines. The pause would be a lengthy, even indefinite, one. This book is offered, primarily to the student, in the hope that it will help to indicate some firm ground of study at this time.

I am indebted to a number of my colleagues for their comments, help and interest. I would like particularly to thank Mr. Peter Birks, Fellow of Brasenose College, Oxford, and Dr. W. E. Butler, Reader in Comparative

Law at University College London, for sparing much of their overloaded time to read the manuscript. The many valuable suggestions that they made have been incorporated, as have those of Dr. D. Prentice and others. I am also grateful for the help of various people at the Department of Employment and the Department of Health and Social Security. In some instances their assistance was given in other contexts and I hope they will not mind it being used also here. Finally, I would like to take this opportunity of affirming the enormous general debt I owe to Professor G. W. Keeton.

I have borrowed, directly or by sub-delegation, extensively the secretarial aid available to my more senior colleagues. Despite my handwriting the results they have produced have been of the highest degree of accuracy. Especially my thanks are due in this respect to Miss Mary Hoppen, Miss Gillian Hoxley, Mrs. Judy Berndt, Miss Rosemary Komlosi and Miss Loreley Teulon. Nevertheless so many additions were made before the submission of the typescript that I took the silence of my publishers for despair. Their patience, and that of their printers, astounds me. They have prepared the Tables of Cases and Statutes.

For all the shortcomings of this work and for any error I take full responsibility.

R. W. RIDEOUT

UNIVERSITY COLLEGE LONDON
February 1972

CONTENTS

	page
Preface to the Fourth Edition	vii
Preface to the First Edition	ix
Table of Cases	xvii
Table of Social Security Commissioners' Decisions	lxiii
Table of Statutes	lxv
Table of Statutory Instruments	lxxv
Table of Abbreviations	lxxvii

1. FORMS OF ENGAGEMENT OF LABOUR	1
The Significance of Classification	1
The Definition of Service—Employment	4
The control test	4
The organisation test	6
Multiple factor tests	7
Other Sub-Divisions of the Supply of Labour	14
Office holders	15
Workers	16
Crown servants	17
Merchant seamen	18
Apprentices	20
Special Categories of Employment	22
Women and young persons	22
The disabled	23
Unenforceable and Illegal Contracts	24

2. THE CONTRACT OF EMPLOYMENT	27
Judicial Contract Making	27
Sources of Terms and Conditions	28
Express written or oral terms	29
Incorporation of collective agreements	31
Incorporation of other documents	41
The statutory statement of terms and conditions of employment	42
Implication of terms	46
Particular Contractual Terms	53
The wage-work element—work	53
The wage-work element—wages	59
The obligation to maintain the essentials of a working relationship	69

xi

2. THE CONTRACT OF EMPLOYMENT—*cont.*
  Confidentiality in employment 73
  Acquisition of knowledge on behalf of an employer 88
  Work for others 92
  Obedience to reasonable orders 93
  Exercise of reasonable care 96
  Accounting 97
  Indemnification 99

3. INDIVIDUAL STATUTORY RIGHTS AFFECTING THE COURSE OF
  EMPLOYMENT 100
  Guarantee Payments 101
  Maternity Rights 104
  Paid and Unpaid Time Off Work 111
  Unpaid time for union activities 114
  Public duties 115
  Time off upon redundancy 116
  Time off for ante-natal care 117
  Inadmissible Reasons and Action Short of Dismissal 117
  Suspension From Work on Medical Grounds 122
  Protection Against Insolvency of an Employer 123
  Payments from company assets 124
  Statutory Protection of Wage 125
  The Truck Acts 125
  Associated legislation 131
  Attachment of earnings 132

APPENDIX: QUALIFICATIONS TO CLAIM STATUTORY
  EMPLOYMENT PROTECTION 134
  Employment 134
  Age limits 134
  Time for making the claim 135
  The requirement for continuous employment 137
  Employment in Great Britain 152
  Fixed term contracts 154
  Miscellaneous exclusions 154
  Estoppel so as to create a qualification 155

4. TERMINATION OF EMPLOYMENT 156
  Repudiatory Breach 157
  Date of Termination of Employment 165
  Wrongful Dismissal—The Common Law 169
  Termination for cause 169
  Dismissal with due notice 170
  Statutory minimum notice 172
  Specific Enforcement 173
  Frustration 177
  Death 179
  Dissolution of Partnership and Winding up of a Company 180

5. UNFAIR DISMISSAL 182
   Dismissal 183
   The Standard of Fairness 192
   Reasons for Dismissal 195
   Sufficiency of the Reason 201
   Procedural Fairness 205
   Specific Procedural Heads 215
     Warning and consultations 216
     Enquiries and hearings 223
     Appeal 226
   Statutory Provision for Particular Situations 227
     Pressure to dismiss 228
     Dismissal relating to trade union membership or
         activities—interim procedure 228
     Union membership agreements 230
     Dismissal in connection with industrial action .. 242
     Redundancy 247
     Pregnancy 250
     Transfer of undertakings 251
     Other special situations 253
   Remedies 254
     Reinstatement or re-engagement 254
     The basic award 256
     Compensation 257

6. REDUNDANCY COMPENSATION 263
   Qualifications to Claim 264
   Dismissal 265
   Misconduct excluding the right to redundancy compensation . 268
   "Redundancy" 269
   Alternative Offers 281
     The concept of consensual variation 281
     Alternative offer as a statutory defence 287
     The trial period 293
   Procedure for Dealing with Redundancy 295
   Amount of Redundancy Payment 300

7. DISCRIMINATION IN EMPLOYMENT 303
   The Equal Pay Act 303
     The concept of equality 303
     "Like work" 306
     Job evaluation 311
     Genuine material difference 312
     Exclusions 317
     Rectification of discriminatory collective agreements . 318
   Race and Sex Discrimination 319
     The definition of discrimination 320
     The burden of proof 321
     Direct discrimination 324
     Indirect discrimination 329

7. DISCRIMINATION IN EMPLOYMENT—*cont.*
    Application to employment   335
    Exclusions   338
  Remedies   342

8. COLLECTIVE INDUSTRIAL RELATIONS   345
  Local and National Bargaining   346
  State Intervention   349
    Wages councils   350
    The Central Arbitration Committee   356
    Conciliation and arbitration   363
    The Advisory, Conciliation and Arbitration Service   364
    Recognition of trade unions   366
  The Response of the Law   370

9. INTERNAL TRADE UNION AFFAIRS   384
  Organisational Legislation Position   384
    The definition of a trade union   384
    The status of a trade union   386
    The legality of trade unions and their agreements   390
    Amalgamation with other industrial organisations   393
    The political fund   395
  Trade Unions and Their Members   399
    The contractual approach   399
    Admission to membership   401
    The Bridlington Agreement   409
    Resignation and repudiation   415
    Discipline   416
    The judicial approach   421
  Trade Union Government   439
    The attitude of the courts   439
    Union office and elections   441
    Services and benefits   446

10. INDUSTRIAL ACTION   449
  Introduction   449
  "Right to Strike"   450
  The History of Legal Control   452
  The Contractual Position of Industrial Action   454
  Tort Liability   468
    Conspiracy   468
    Inducement to breach of contract   471
    Interference with contract   477
    Intimidation   479
    Other civil liability   482
  Legislative Intervention   485
    General considerations   485
    The provision of State benefits   486
    Criminal sanctions   490
    Statutory immunity from civil liability   492

10. INDUSTRIAL ACTION—*cont.*
    The scope of immunity   514
    The Labour Injunction   520
    Picketing   522
    Special and Emergency Provisions   532

11. PROTECTING HEALTH AND SAFETY AT WORK   535
    Introduction   535
    Safety legislation in general   536
    The Health and Safety at Work Act 1974   538
    Enforcement   547
    Civil Liability for Breach of Statutory Duty   552
    Principles   552
    The obligation to fence   555

APPENDIX: HEALTH AND SAFETY AT WORK ETC. ACT 1974,
    SCHEDULE 1   566

12. CIVIL LIABILITY FOR INJURY AT WORK   568
    The Forms of Liability   568
    Historical development   568
    Present position   569
    Proof   571
    Elements of Liability   573
    Foresight   573
    The duty of care   575
    Causation   583
    Remoteness   588
    Defences   589
    Volenti non fit injuria   589
    Contributory negligence   592
    Limitation of Action   594
    Vicarious Liability   597

13. INDUSTRIAL INJURY BENEFIT   614
    Benefits   615
    Industrial disablement   616
    "Arising out of and in the course of employment" 618
    Causation   628
    Prescribed diseases   630
    Claims   631

    Index   635

TABLE OF CASES

AEI Cables Ltd. *v.* McLay [1980] I.R.L.R. 84 ....198, 199
APAC *v.* Kirvin Ltd. [1978] I.R.L.R. 318 298
ARW Transformers Ltd. *v.* Cupples (1977) I.T.R. 355; [1977] I.R.L.R. 228...........312, 315
Abbots and Stanley *v.* Wesson-Glynwed Steels Ltd. [1982] I.R.L.R. 51 222
Abbot *v.* Sullivan [1952] 1 K.B. 189; [1952] I.T.R. 133; 96 S.J. 119; [1952] 1 All E.R. 226;
    sub nom. Abbott *v.* Sullivan and Isett (Cornporters Committee Members),
    Transport and General Workers Union, Platt *v.* Port of London Authority [1951]
    2 Lloyd's Rep. 573; affirming [1951] 1 Lloyd's Rep. 283 ....424, 431
Abernethy *v.* Hutchinson (1825) 1 H. & T.W. 28; 3 L.J. (o.s.) Ch. 209; 47 E.R. 1313,
    L.C. 73
Abernethy (L.) *v.* Mott, Hay and Anderson [1974] I.C.R. 323; 118 S.J. 294; [1974]
    I.T.R. 251; 16 K.I.R. 277; [1974] I.R.L.R. 213; C.A.; affirming [1973] I.T.R. 228 280
Acrow (Automation) Ltd. *v.* Rex Chain Belt Incorporated [1971] 1 W.L.R. 1676 478
Adams *v.* Sankey (G.K.N.) [1980] I.R.L.R. 416, E.A.T. 168
——— *v.* Union Cinemas Ltd. [1939] 3 All E.R. 136; 83 S.J. 564, C.A. 171
——— *v.* Zub (Charles) Associates Ltd. [1978] I.R.L.R. 551, E.A.T. 188
Addis *v.* The Gramophone Co. Ltd. [1909] A.C. 488; 78 L.J.K.B. 1122; 101 L.T. 466;
    [1908–10] All E.R. Rep. 1, H.L. 176, 177
Adsett *v.* K. and L. Steelfounders and Engineers [1953] 1 W.L.R. 773; 97 S.J. 419; [1953]
    2 All E.R. 320; 51 L.G.R. 418, C.A.; affirming [1953] 1 W.L.R. 137; 97 S.J. 49;
    [1953] 1 All E.R. 97n.; 51 L.G.R. 99 539
Advocate (Lord) *v.* De Rosa [1974] I.C.R. 480; [1974] 1 W.L.R. 946; [1974] 2 All E.R.
    849; [1974] I.T.R. 357; (1974) 16 K.I.R. 425; *sub nom.* De Rosa *v.* Barrie (John)
    (Contractor) (1974) 118 S.J. 479; *sub nom.* Advocate (Lord) *v.* De Rosa and
    Barrie (John) (Contractor) [1974] I.R.L.R. 215, H.L., reversing [1973] I.C.R.
    553 146
African Association Ltd. and Allen, *Re* [1910] 1 K.B. 396; 79 L.J.K.B. 259; 102 L.T. 129;
    26 T.L.R. 234, D.C. 171
Agnew *v.* Munro (1891) 28 S.L.R. 335; 2 White 611 524
Agreement between the Scottish Daily Newspapers Society and its Members, *Re* noted in
    (1971) 34 M.L.R. 575 492
Ainsworth *v.* Glass Tubes & Components Ltd. [1977] I.C.R. 347; [1977] I.R.L.R. 74,
    E.A.T. 306
Air Canada *v.* Lee [1978] I.C.R. 1202; (1978) 13 I.T.R. 347; [1978] I.R.L.R. 392 293
Airfix Footwear *v.* Cope [1978] I.C.R. 1210; [1978] I.R.L.R. 396; (1978) 13 I.T.R. 513,
    E.A.T. 12, 14
Albion Shipping Agency *v.* Arnold [1982] I.C.R. 22; [1981] I.R.L.R. 525 314
Alexander *v.* McMillan [1969] I.T.R. 171 144
Alidair Ltd. *v.* Taylor [1978] I.C.R. 445; (1977) S.J. 758, *sub nom.* Taylor *v.* Alidair
    (1978) 13 I.T.R. 180; [1978] I.R.L.R. 82, C.A.; affirming [1977] I.C.R.
    446..199, 218, 219
Allen *v.* Aeroplane and Motor Aluminium Castings Ltd. [1965] 1 W.L.R. 1244; (1965)
    109 S.J. 629; [1965] 3 All E.R. 377, C.A. 573
——— *v.* Flood [1898] A.C. 1, H.L.; reversing *sub nom.* Flood *v.* Jackson [1895] 2 Q.B. 21
    468, 479, 481, 482
——— *v.* Robles, Compagnie Parisienne de Garantie, Third Party [1969] 1 W.L.R. 1193;
    (1969) 113 S.J. 484; [1969] 3 All E.R. 154; [1969] 2 Lloyd's Rep. 61, C.A. 164
——— *v.* Scott (Thomas) & Son (Bakers) Ltd. [1983] I.R.L.R. 11 112
——— *v.* Thorn Electrical Industries; Griffin *v.* Metropolitan Police District Receiver
    [1968] 1 Q.B. 487; [1967] 3 W.L.R. 858; 111 S.J. 496; 2 K.I.R. 853; [1967] 2 All
    E.R. 1137, C.A. 34
Allen and Son *v.* Coventry [1980] I.C.R. 9; [1979] I.R.L.R. 399, E.A.T. 147
Allied Ironfounders Ltd. *v.* Macken [1971] I.T.R. 109, D.C. 301

xvii

Allinson v. General Council of Medical Education and Registration [1894] 1 Q.B. 750, C.A.; previous proceedings (1892) 8 T.L.R. 784, C.A.; affirming (1892) 8 T.L.R. 727, D.C. 433

Allman v. Rowland [1977] I.C.R. 201 146

Amalgamated Engineering Union v. Minister of Pensions and National Insurance [1963] 1 W.L.R. 441; (1963) 107 S.J. 195; [1963] 1 All E.R. 864 .... 5, 9

Amalgamated Society of Boilermakers, Shipwrights, Blacksmiths & Structural Workers v. Wimpey (George) (M.E. & C.) (1977) 12 I.T.R. 215; [1977] I.R.L.R. 95, E.A.T. 299

Amalgamated Society of Railway Servants v. Osborne [1910] A.C. 87; 79 L.J.Ch. 87; 101 L.T. 787; 26 T.L.R. 177; 54 S.J. 215; [1908–10] All E.R. Rep. 368, H.L.; affirming [1909] 1 Ch. 163, C.A. 396

Amalgamated Textile Workers Union v. Shilogh Spinners Ltd. C.A.C. No. 80/139 60

American Cyanamid Co. v. Ethicon Ltd. [1975] A.C. 396; [1975] 2 W.L.R. 316; (1975) 119 S.J. 136; [1975] 1 All E.R. 504; [1975] F.S.R. 101; [1975] R.P.C. 513, H.L.; reversing [1974] F.S.R. 312, C.A. 521

Annamunthodo v. Oilfield Workers' Trade Union [1961] A.C. 945; [1961] 3 W.L.R. 650; (1961) 105 S.J. 706; [1961] 3 All E.R. 621 .... 431, 432, 437

Archer v. Cheshire & Northwich Building Society [1976] I.R.L.R. 424, E.A.T.; reversing [1976] I.R.L.R. 281 197

Argyll (Duchess) v. Argyll (Duke) [1967] Ch. 302; [1965] 2 W.L.R. 790; [1965] 1 All E.R. 611 79

Armour v. Skeen [1977] I.R.L.R. 310; 1977 J.C. 15; 1977 S.L.T. 71 552

Arnold v. Beecham Group Ltd. [1982] I.R.L.R. 307 311

—— v. Harrington (Thomas) Ltd. [1969] 1 Q.B. 312; [1967] 3 W.L.R. 852; (1967) 111 S.J. 412; [1967] 2 All E.R. 866; (1967) 2 K.I.R. 493, D.C. 276

Ashburton (Lord) v. Pape [1913] 2 Ch. 469; 82 L.J.Ch. 527; 109 L.T. 381; 57 S.J. 644; [1911–13] All E.R. Rep. 708; sub nom. Ashburton (Lord) v. Nocton (1913) 29 T.L.R. 623, C.A. 81

Associated Newspapers Group Ltd. v. Flynn (1970) 114 S.J. 930; (1970) 10 K.I.R. 17 504

—— v. Wade [1979] I.C.R. 664; [1979] 1 W.L.R. 697; (1979) 123 S.J. 250; [1979] I.R.L.R. 201, C.A. 479, 484, 506

Association of Scientific, Technical and Managerial Staffs v. Hawker Siddeley Aviation Ltd. [1977] I.R.L.R. 418 .... 296, 297

Association of Westinghouse Salaried Employees v. Westinghouse Electric Corporation 348 U.S. 437 (1955) 381

Atkinson v. Lindsay (George) and Co. [1980] I.R.L.R. 196 219

—— v. Tress Engineering Co. Ltd. [1976] I.R.L.R. 245 306

Att.-Gen. v. Cape (Jonathan) Ltd.; Att.-Gen. v. Times Newspapers [1976] Q.B. 752; [1975] 3 W.L.R. 606; (1975) 119 S.J. 696; [1975] 3 All E.R. 484 81

Att.-Gen. (Guyana) v. Nobrega [1969] 3 All E.R. 1604, P.C. 18

Att.-Gen. (New South Wales) v. Perpetual Trustee Co. Ltd. [1955] A.C. 457; [1955] 2 W.L.R. 707; 99 S.J. 233; [1955] 1 All E.R. 846, P.C.; affirming (1952) 85 C.L.R. 237 16

Attwaters v. Courtney (1841) Car. & M. 51, N.P. 21

Attwood v. Lamont [1920] 3 K.B. 571; 90 L.J.K.B. 121; 124 L.T. 108; 36 T.L.R. 895; 65 S.J. 25; [1920] All E.R. Rep. 55 .... 84, 87

Ault (G.D.) (Isle of Wight) Ltd. v. Gregory (1967) K.I.R. 590 146

Australian Workers' Union v. Bowen (No. 2) (1948) 77 C.L.R. 601 436

Automatic Woodturning Co. v. Stringer [1957] A.C. 544, H.L.; reversing in part and affirming in part [1956] 1 W.L.R. 138; (1956) 100 S.J. 109; [1956] 1 All E.R. 327; (1956) 54 L.G.R. 103, C.A.; reversing in part and affirming in part [1955] 1 W.L.R. 971 576

Axe v. British Domestic Appliances [1973] I.C.R. 133; [1973] I.T.R. 126, N.I.R.C. 248, 249

Aynsworth v. Wood (1728) Sess. Cas. K.B. 84; 93 E.R. 85; 1 Barn. K.B. 312 21

Ayub v. Vauxhall Motors Ltd. [1978] I.R.L.R. 428 .... 220, 221

B.P. Chemicals Ltd. v. Joseph [1980] I.R.L.R. 55, E.A.T. 134

B.S.M. (1257) Ltd. v. Secretary of State for Social Services [1978] I.C.R. 894 13

Baddeley *v.* Granville (Earl of) (1887) 19 Q.B.D. 423; 56 L.J.Q.B. 501; 57 L.T. 268; 51
    J.P. 822; 36 W.R. 63; 3 T.L.R. 759, D.C. 25, 589
Bailey *v.* Amey Roadstone Corporation Ltd. [1977] I.R.L.R. 299 229
—— *v.* B.P. Oil (Kent Refinery) Ltd. [1980] I.C.R. 642; [1980] I.R.L.R. 287, C.A.;
    reversing [1979] I.R.L.R. 150, E.A.T. 192, 208, 209, 215, 216, 219
Bailey (N.G.) and Co. Ltd. *v.* Preddy [1971] 1 W.L.R. 796; (1971) 115 S.J. 366; [1971] 3
    All E.R. 225; (1971) 10 K.I.R. 265; [1971] I.T.R. 136, D.C. 302
Baker *v.* Hopkins (T.E.) & Son Ltd.; Ward *v.* Same [1959] 1 W.L.R. 966; (1959) 103 S.J.
    812; [1959] 3 All E.R. 225, C.A.; affirming [1958] 1 W.L.R. 993 588
—— *v.* Snell [1908] 2 K.B. 825; 77 L.J.K.B. 1090; 99 L.T. 753; 24 T.L.R. 811; 52 S.J.
    681; [1908–10] All E.R. Rep. 398; 21 Cox C.C. 716, C.A. 610
—— *v.* White's Window and General Cleaning Co. Ltd. *The Times*, March 1, 1962 587
Bakers' Union *v.* Clarks of Hove. *See* Clarks of Hove *v.* Bakers' Union.
Ball *v.* Johnson [1971] T.R. 147; 47 T.C. 155; 50 A.T.C. 178 127
Ballard *v.* Ministry of Defence [1977] I.C.R. 513, C.A. 556
Bandey *v.* Penn [1968] 1 W.L.R. 670; (1968) 112 S.J. 354; [1968] 1 All E.R. 1187n.;
    (1968) K.I.R. 261, D.C. 148
Banerjee *v.* City and East London Area Health Authority [1979] I.R.L.R. 147,
    E.A.T. 200, 204
Bank voor Handel en Scheepraart N.V. *v.* Slatford [1953] 1 Q.B. 248; [1951] 2 T.L.R.
    755; (1951) 95 S.J. 546; [1951] 2 All E.R. 779; 31 A.T.C. 535 6
Banner *v.* Sutcliffe Speakman and Co. [1972] I.R.L.R. 7 249
Barber *v.* Manchester Regional Hospital Board [1958] 1 W.L.R. 181; (1958) 122 J.P.
    124; (1958) 102 S.J. 140; [1958] 1 All E.R. 322 37
Barclay *v.* Crittal (Richard) (Electrical) [1978] I.T.R. 173 302
Barkway *v.* South Wales Transport Co. Ltd. [1950] A.C. 185; (1950) 66 T.L.R. (Pt. 1)
    597; (1950) 114 J.P. 172; (1950) 94 S.J. 128; [1950] 1 All E.R. 392, H.L.; reversing
    [1949] 1 K.B. 54, C.A. 579
Barley *v.* Amey Roadstone Corporation Ltd. (No. 2) [1978] I.C.R. 190, E.A.T. 257
Barratt   *v.*   National   Coal   Board   [1978]   I.C.R.   1101,
    E.A.T. 36
Barratt Developments (Bradford) Ltd. *v.* Union of Construction Allied Trades and
    Technicians [1978] I.C.R. 319; (1977) 12 I.T.R. 478; [1977] I.R.L.R. 403, E.A.T. 296
Barry *v.* Murphy (D.) & Son Ltd. [1967] I.T.R. 134; (1966) 2 K.I.R. 187 144
Barthorpe *v.* Exeter Diocesan Board of Finance [1979] I.C.R. 900; (1979) 123 S.J. 585,
    E.A.T. 15
Basted *v.* Pell Footwear [1978] I.R.L.R. 117 301
Batty *v.* Monks (1865) 12 L.T. 832 21
Bauman *v.* Hulton Press Ltd. [1952] W.N. 556; [1952] 2 All E.R. 1121 57
Baxter *v.* Burfield (1747) 2 Stra. 1266; 1 Bott 6th ed. 542; 93 E.R. 1172 20
—— *v.* Central Electricity Generating Board [1965] 1 W.L.R. 200; [1964] 2 All E.R. 815
    570, 581, 603
Bayley *v.* Manchester, Sheffield and Lincolnshire Ry. (1872) L.R. 7 C.P. 415 ....598, 606
Beal *v.* Beecham Group Ltd. [1981] I.R.L.R. 127; affirmed [1982] I.R.L.R. 192 112
Beaverbrook Newspapers Ltd. *v.* Keys [1978] I.C.R. 582; [1978] I.R.L.R. 34, C.A. 506
Beer *v.* Wheeler (1965) 109 S.J. 133; reversed (1965) 109 S.J. 457, C.A. 578
Beeston *v.* Collyer (1827) 2 C. & P. 607, N.P.; subsequent proceedings 4 Bing. 309 171
Beetham *v.* Trinidad Cement Co. Ltd. [1960] A.C. 132; [1960] 2 W.L.R. 77; 104 S.J. 49;
    [1960] 1 All E.R. 274, P.C. 499, 501
Beloff *v.* Pressdram Ltd. [1973] 1 All E.R. 241; [1973] F.S.R. 33; [1973] R.P.C. 765 5
Bennett *v.* Chemical Construction (G.B.) Ltd. [1971] 1 W.L.R. 1571; (1971) 115 S.J.
    550; [1971] 3 All E.R. 822; 12 K.I.R. 4, C.A. 572
Bentley *v.* Craven (1853) 18 Beav. 75; 52 E.R. 29 98
Bents Brewery Ltd. *v.* Hogan [1945] 2 All E.R. 570 .... 74, 499
Bessenden Properties Ltd. *v.* Corness [1974] I.T.R. 128; [1973] I.R.L.R. 365, N.I.R.C.;
    affirmed [1974] I.R.L.R. 338, C.A. 249
Bevan Harris Ltd. *v.* Gair [1981] I.R.L.R. 520 ....203, 208
Bex *v.* Securicor Transport Ltd. [1972] I.R.L.R. 68 281
Bickley (J.& S.) Ltd. *v.* Washer [1977] I.C.R. 425; (1977) 12 I.T.R. 137, E.A.T. 302
Billings (A.C.) & Sons Ltd. *v.* Riden [1958] A.C. 240; [1957] 3 W.L.R. 496; (1958) 101
    S.J. 645; [1957] 3 All E.R. 1, H.L.; affirming [1957] 1 Q.B. 46, C.A. 588

Birch v. National Union of Railwaymen [1950] Ch. 602; (1950) 66 T.L.R. 1223; (1950)
    S.J. 384; [1950] 2 All E.R. 253 .... 398, 399
Bird v. British Celanese Ltd. [1945] K.B. 336; 114 L.J.K.B. 184; 172 L.T. 260; 109 J.P.
    170; 61 T.L.R. 316; [1945] 1 All E.R. 488; 43 L.G.R. 199, C.A. 25, 129, 455
——— v. O'Neal [1960] A.C. 907; [1960] 3 W.L.R. 584; (1960) 104 S.J. 725; [1960] 3 All
    E.R. 254, P.C. 527
Birk v. Royal West of England Residential School for the Deaf [1976] I.R.L.R. 326 337
Birmingham City District Council v. Beyer [1978] 1 All E.R. 910; (1977) 12 I.T.R. 409;
    [1977] I.R.L.R. 211; (1977) 8 Build. L.R. 83, E.A.T. 119
Black v. Carricks (Caterers) Ltd. [1980] I.R.L.R. 448, C.A. 575
Blackall v. National Union of Foundry Workers (1923) 39 T.L.R. 431 424
Blackman v. Post Office [1974] I.C.R. 151; [1974] I.T.R. 122; [1974] I.R.L.R. 46,
    N.I.R.C. 374, 447
Bloomfield v. Springfield Hosiery Finishing Co. Ltd. [1972] I.C.R. 91; [1972] 1 W.L.R.
    386; (1971) 116 S.J. 141; [1972] 1 All E.R. 609; 12 K.I.R. 175; [1972] I.T.R. 89,
    N.I.R.C. 246
Blue Star Ship Management Ltd. v. Williams [1978] I.C.R. 770; [1979] I.R.L.R. 16;
    (1978) 13 I.T.R. 282, E.A.T. 236
Boardman v. Phipps [1967] 2 A.C. 46; [1966] 3 W.L.R. 1009; (1966) 110 S.J. 853; [1966]
    3 All E.R. 721, H.L.; affirming [1965] Ch. 992, C.A.; affirming [1964] 1 W.L.R.
    993 82
Bohon-Mitchell v. Common Professional Examination Board and Council of Legal
    Education [1978] I.R.L.R. 525 332
Bolt v. Moss (William) & Sons (1966) 110 S.J. 385 591
Bonsor v. Musicians Union [1956] A.C. 104; [1955] 3 W.L.R. 788; (1955) 99 S.J. 814;
    [1955] 3 All E.R. 518, H.L.; reversing [1954] Ch. 479; affirming *The Times*, April
    18, 1953 .... 387, 419, 421, 424, 426, 428, 430
Booth & Co. (International) Ltd. v. National Enterprise Board [1978] 3 All E.R. 624 553
Boothman v. British Northrop 13 K.I.R. 112, C.A. 592
Boson v. Sandford (1690) 2 Salk 440; 91 E.R. 382; *subsequent* proceedings (1690) 1
    Show. 101 569
Boston Deep Sea Fishing Co. Ltd. v. Ansell (1888) 39 Ch.D. 339; 59 L.T. 345,
    C.A. 61, 69, 98, 156, 163, 169, 170, 196
Boulting v. Association of Cinematograph, Television and Allied Technicians [1963] 2
    Q.B. 606; [1963] 2 W.L.R. 529; (1963) 107 S.J. 133; [1963] 1 All E.R. 716, C.A.;
    affirming *The Times*, March 23, 1962 .... 404, 493
Bound v. Lawrence [1892] 1 Q.B. 226; 61 L.J.M.C. 21; 65 L.T. 844; 56 J.P. 118; 40 W.R.
    1; 8 T.L.R. 1; 36 S.J. 11, C.A. 127
Bouzourou v. Ottoman Bank [1930] A.C. 271; 99 L.J.P.C. 166; 142 L.T. 535, P.C. 95
Bovey v. Board of Governors of the Hospital for Sick Children [1978] I.C.R. 934; (1978)
    13 I.T.R. 416; [1978] I.R.L.R. 241, E.A.T.; affirming [1977] I.R.L.R. 417 106
Bowater v. Rowley Regis Corporation [1944] K.B. 476; 113 L.J.K.B. 427; 170 L.T. 314;
    108 J.P. 163; 60 T.L.R. 356; [1944] 1 All E.R. 465, C.A. 590
Bowater Containers Ltd. v. McCormack [1980] I.R.L.R. 50, E.A.T. 204
Bowes and Partners v. Press [1894] 1 Q.B. 202; 63 L.J.Q.B. 165; 38 S.J. 56; 70 L.T. 116;
    58 J.P. 280; 42 W.R. 340; 10 T.L.R. 55; 9 R. 302, C.A. 94, 95
Boyle v. Kodak Ltd. [1969] 1 W.L.R. 661; (1969) 113 S.J. 382; [1969] 2 All E.R. 439;
    (1969) 6 K.I.R. 427, H.L.; reversing (1967) 3 K.I.R. 28, C.A. 577, 578, 585
Boynton v. Willment Bros. Ltd. [1971] 1 W.L.R. 1625; 115 S.J. 673; [1971] 3 All E.R.
    624; 11 K.I.R. 397, C.A.; reversing (1970) 114 S.J. 972 539
Brace v. Calder [1895] 2 Q.B. 253; 64 L.J.Q.B. 582; 72 L.T. 829; 59 J.P. 693; 11 T.L.R.
    450; 14 R. 473, C.A. 180, 181
Bradford v. Robinson Rentals Ltd. [1967] 1 W.L.R. 337; (1967) 111 S.J. 33; [1967] 1 All
    E.R. 267; 1 K.I.R. 486; [1966] C.L.Y. 8283 588
Braham v. Lyons (J.) & Co. Ltd. [1962] 1 W.L.R. 1048; (1962) 106 S.J. 588; [1962] 3 All
    E.R. 281; 60 L.G.R. 453, C.A. 580
Braithwaite v. Electrical, Electronics and Telecommunications Union—Plumbing Trades
    Union (1969) 113 S.J. 305; [1969] 2 All E.R. 859; (1969) 6 K.I.R. 169, C.A. 436
Brandy v. Owners of S.S. Raphael [1911] A.C. 413, H.L.; affirming [1911] 1 K.B. 376.
    C.A. 18
Brassington v. Cauldon Wholesale Ltd. [1978] I.C.R. 405; [1977] I.R.L.R. 479, E.A.T. 119
Breach v. Epsylon Industries Ltd. [1976] I.C.R. 316; [1976] I.R.L.R. 180, E.A.T. 58

Breen v. Amalgamated Engineering Union [1971] 2 Q.B. 175; [1971] 2 W.L.R. 742; (1971) 115 S.J. 203; (1971) 2 K.I.R. 120; [1971] 1 All E.R. 1148, C.A. 408, 429, 430, 433, 434, 442, 444, 445

Brekkes Ltd. v. Cattel [1972] Ch. 105; [1971] 2 W.L.R. 647; (1972) 115 S.J. 10; [1971] 1 All E.R. 1031 .... 479, 482

Brennan (J.) and Ging (B.) v. Ellward (Lancs.) Ltd. [1976] I.R.L.R. 378, E.A.T. 120

Brimelow v. Casson [1924] 1 Ch. 302; 93 L.J.Ch. 256; 130 L.T. 725; 68 S.J. 275; [1923] All E.R. Rep. 40 .... 476, 500

Brintons Ltd. v. Turvey [1905] A.C. 230; 74 L.J.K.B. 474; 92 L.T. 578; 53 W.R. 641; 21 T.L.R. 444; 49 S.J. 445; 7 W.C.C. 1, H.L.; affirming [1904] 1 K.B. 328, C.A. 617

Bristol Channel Ship Repairers v. O'Keefe [1977] 2 All E.R. 258; [1978] I.C.R. 691; [1977] I.R.L.R. 13, E.A.T. 226

Bristol Garage (Brighton) Ltd. v. Lowen [1979] I.R.L.R. 86, E.A.T. 27, 49, 50

Bristol Ship Repairers Ltd. v. Lewis [1977] I.R.L.R. 13 216

British Actors Equity Association v. Goring [1977] I.C.R. 393, C.A.; reversed [1978] I.C.R. 791, H.L. 426, 428, 441

British Aircraft Corporation Ltd. v. Austin [1978] I.R.L.R. 332, E.A.T. 71, 72

British Airways Engine Overhaul Ltd. v. Francis [1981] I.C.R. 278; [1981] I.R.L.R. 9, E.A.T. 120

British Broadcasting Corporation v. Dixon; same v. Constanti [1979] I.C.R. 281; [1979] 2 W.L.R. 647; [1979] I.R.L.R. 114; sub nom. Dixon v. British Broadcasting Corporation; Constanti v. British Broadcasting Corporation [1979] Q.B. 546; (1978) 122 S.J. 713; [1979] 2 All E.R. 112, C.A.; affirming [1978] I.C.R. 357 .... 139, 154

—— v. Hearn [1977] I.C.R. 685 .... 499, 504, 507, 508, 520

British Building and Engineering Appliances Ltd. v. Dedman. See Dedman v. Building and Engineering Appliances Ltd.

British Home Stores v. Burchell (Note) [1980] I.C.R. 303; sub nom. British Home Stores v. Birchell (1978) 13 I.T.R. 560; [1978] I.R.L.R. 379, E.A.T. 193, 198, 199

British Labour Pump v. Byrne [1979] I.C.R. 347; [1979] I.R.L.R. 94, E.A.T. 209, 211

British Leyland (U.K.) Ltd. v. Ashraf [1978] I.C.R. 979; (1978) 13 I.T.R. 500; [1978] I.R.L.R. 330, E.A.T. 184

—— v. McQuilken [1978] I.R.L.R. 245, E.A.T. 37, 188

—— v. Powell [1978] I.C.R. 83 308

British Leyland Cars Ltd. and General and Municipal Workers Union Award No. 80/65 370

British Midland Airways Ltd. v. Lewis [1978] I.C.R. 782; (1978) 13 I.T.R. 327, E.A.T. 200

British Motor Trade Association v. Salvadori [1949] Ch. 556; [1949] L.J.R. 1304; (1949) 65 T.L.R. 44; [1949] 1 All E.R. 208 473

British Railways Board v. Herrington [1972] A.C. 877; [1972] 2 W.L.R. 537; (1972) 116 S.J. 178; [1972] 1 All E.R. 749, H.L.; affirming [1971] 2 Q.B. 107, C.A.; affirming (1970) 214 E.G. 561 612

British Railways Board v. Liptrot [1969] 1 A.C. 136; [1967] 3 W.L.R. 770; (1967) 111 S.J. 516; [1967] 2 All E.R. 1072; (1967) 3 K.I.R. 257, H.L.; affirming [1966] 2 Q.B. 353; [1966] 2 W.L.R. 841; (1966) 110 S.J. 185; [1966] 2 All E.R. 247; (1966) 1 K.I.R. 187; [1966] C.L.Y. 5092, C.A. 557, 558

—— v. Natarajan [1979] I.C.R. 326; (1978) S.J. 861; [1979] 2 All E.R. 794; [1979] I.R.L.R. 45, E.A.T. 324

British Reinforced Concrete Co. Ltd. v. Lind (1917) 86 L.J.Ch. 486; 116 L.T. 243; 33 T.L.R. 170 88

British Syphon Co. Ltd. v. Homewood (No. 2) [1956] 1 W.L.R. 1190; (1956) 100 S.J. 633; [1956] 2 All E.R. 897; [1956] R.P.C. 225, 330 .... 53, 89

Broadbent v. Crisp [1974] I.C.R. 248; [1974] 1 All E.R. 1052; [1974] I.T.R. 147; (1973) 16 K.I.R. 168, N.I.R.C. 17, 385

Brodie v. Startrite Engineering Co. Ltd. [1976] I.R.L.R. 101 306

Bromby and Hoare Ltd. v. Evans [19721] I.C.R. 113 279

Brook Bros. (Petroleum) Ltd. v. Preece [1974] I.C.R. 231, N.I.R.C. 259

Broome v. D.P.P. [1974] A.C. 587; [1974] I.C.R. 84; [1974] 2 W.L.R. 58; (1973) 118 S.J. 50; [1974] 1 All E.R. 314; [1974] I.R.L.R. 26; sub nom. Hunt v. Broome [1974] Crim.L.R. 311, H.L.; affirming [1973] 1 Q.B. 691, D.C. 527, 529

Brown v. Amalgamated Union of Engineering Workers (Engineering Section) [1976] I.C.R. 147; (1975) 119 S.J. 709 .... 442, 445

—— v. Hall Advertising [1978] I.R.L.R. 246, E.A.T. 218
—— v. Mills (John) and Co. Ltd. (1970) 114 S.J. 149; (1970) 8 K.I.R. 702, C.A. 579
—— v. Rolls Royce Ltd. [1960] 1 W.L.R. 210; (1960) 104 S.J. 207; [1960] 1 All E.R. 577;
   1960 S.C. (H.L.) 22; 1960 S.L.T. 119, H.L.; affirming 1958 S.C. 600 579
—— v. Southall & Knight [1980] I.C.R. 617; [1980] I.R.L.R. 130, E.A.T.............. 158, 192
—— v. Sugar Manufacturing Co. Ltd. [1967] I.T.R. 213 185
Browning v. Crumlin Valley Collieries Ltd. [1926] 1 K.B. 522; 95 L.J.K.B. 711; 134 L.T.
   603; 90 J.P. 201; 42 T.L.R. 323; [1926] All E.R. Rep. 132; 24 L.G.R. 302 61
Brydon v. Stewart (1855) 2 Macq. 30 568
Buck v. English Electric Co. Ltd. [1977] I.C.R. 629, [1977] 1 W.L.R. 806; [1978] 1 All
   E.R. 271 ....595, 596, 597
—— v. Everard (Edward) Ltd. [1968] I.T.R. 328, D.C. 271
Buckingham v. Surrey and Hants Canal Co. (1882) 46 L.T. 885; 46 J.P. 774,
   D.C. 171
Buckland v. Guildford Gas, Light and Coke Co. [1949] 1 K.B. 410; (1949) 113 J.P. 44;
   (1949) 93 S.J. 41; [1948] 2 All E.R. 1086; (1948) 47 L.G.R. 75 612
Buckley v. National Union of General and Municipal Workers [1967] 3 All E.R. 767;
   (1967) 112 S.J. 292; (1967) 4 K.I.R. 277 448
Buckoke v. Greater London Council [1970] 1 W.L.R. 1092; (1970) 114 S.J. 269; [1970] 2
   All E.R. 193; (1970) 68 L.G.R. 543; affirmed [1971] 1 Ch. 655, C.A. 93
Budgen and Co. v. Thomas [1976] I.C.R. 344; [1976] I.R.L.R. 174; (1976) 19 Man.Law
   7, E.A.T. 207, 224, 226
Bull v. Pitney-Bowes Ltd. [1967] 1 W.L.R. 273; (1967) 111 S.J. 32; [1966] 3 All E.R. 384;
   (1966) 1 K.I.R. 342 86
Bullock v. Merseyside County Council [1979] I.C.R. 79; [1979] I.R.L.R. 33; (1978) 77
   L.G.R. 333, C.A.; affirming [1978] I.C.R. 419 140
—— v. Power (G. John) (Agencies) [1956] 1 W.L.R. 171; (1956) 100 S.J. 131, [1956] 1
   All E.R. 498; (1956) 54 L.G.R. 116, C.A. 558
Burn v. National Amalgamated Labourers' Union [1920] 2 Ch. 364; 89 L.J.Ch. 370; 123
   L.T. 411; 64 S.J. 570; 18 L.G.R. 449 424
Burnett v. British Waterways Board [1973] 1 W.L.R. 700; (1973) 117 S.J. 203; [1973] 2
   All E.R. 631; [1973] 2 Lloyd's Rep. 137, C.A.; affirming [1972] 1 W.L.R. 1329 591
Burns v. Terry (Joseph) & Sons Ltd. [1951] 1 K.B. 454; [1951] 1 T.L.R. 349; (1951) 114
   J.P. 613; (1951) 94 S.J. 837; [1950] 2 All E.R. 987; (1950) 49 L.G.R. 161, C.A. 562
Burroughs Machines Ltd. v. Timmoney [1977] I.R.L.R. 404 ....38, 46
Burrows v. Ace Caravan Co. (Hull) Ltd. [1972] I.R.L.R. 4 222
Burton v. British Railways Board [1982] I.R.L.R. 116 .... 304, 317, 318, 329, 342
Burton, Allton and Johnson Ltd. v. Peck [1975] I.C.R. 193; [1975] I.R.L.R. 87 184
Burton Group Ltd. v. Smith [1977] I.R.L.R. 351, E.A.T. 34
Bushell v. Secretary of State for the Environment [1981] A.C. 75; [1980] 3 W.L.R. 22;
   (1980) 124 S.J. 168; [1980] 2 All E.R. 608; (1980) 40 P. & C.R. 51; (1980) 78
   L.G.R. 269; [1980] J.P.L. 458, H.L.; reversing (1979) 123 S.J. 605, C.A.;
   reversing (1977) 122 S.J. 110 211
Byers v. Head Wrightson & Co. Ltd. [1961] 1 W.L.R. 961; (1961) 105 S.J. 569; [1961] 2
   All E.R. 538; (1961) 59 L.G.R. 385 578

Cadbury Ltd. v. Doddington [1977] I.C.R. 982, E.A.T. 257
Callow (F.E.) (Engineers) v. Johnson [1971] A.C. 335; [1970] 3 W.L.R. 982; (1970) 114
   S.J. 846; [1970] 3 All E.R. 639, (1970) 10 K.I.R. 35, H.L.; affirming [1970] 2 Q.B.
   1, C.A. 556, 559, 561
Camden Exhibition and Display Ltd. v. Lynott [1966] 1 Q.B. 555; [1965] 3 W.L.R. 763;
   (1965) 109 S.J. 473; [1965] 3 All E.R. 28, C.A. 44
Camden Nominees v. Slack (or Forcey) [1940] Ch. 352; 109 L.J..Ch. 231; 163 L.T. 88; 56
   T.L.R. 445; 84 S.J. 256; [1940] 2 All E.R. 1 476
Camellia Tanker S.A. v. International Transport Workers' Federation [1976] I.C.R. 274;
   [1976] I.R.L.R. 183, 190; [1976] 2 Lloyd's Rep. 546, C.A. 472, 517
Cameron v. Royal London Ophthalmic Hospital [1941] 1 K.B. 350; 110 L.J.K.B. 225;
   165 L.T. 138; 105 J.P. 16; 57 T.L.R. 105; 84 S.J. 683; [1940] 4 All E.R. 439. 128
Camilla M., The. See Star Ship Transport Corp. of Monrovia v. Slater.
Capper Pass Ltd. v. Lawton [1977] Q.B. 852; [1977] I.C.R. 83; [1977] 2 W.L.R. 26;
   [1977] 2 All E.R. 11; (1976) 11 I.T.R. 316, E.A.T. 306, 308, 309

Carling v. N.U.G.M.W. [1973] I.C.R. 267; [1973] I.T.R. 307, N.I.R.C. 445
Carlson v. Hotel West Ltd. [1950] 2 W.W.R. 129 610
Carmarthenshire County Council v. Lewis [1955] A.C. 549; [1955] 2 W.L.R. 517; (1955)
    119 J.P. 230; (1955) 99 S.J. 167; [1955] 1 All E.R. 565; (1955) 53 L.G.R. 230,
    H.L.; affirming [1953] 1 W.L.R. 1439 574
Carr v. Mercantile Produce Co. Ltd. [1949] 2 K.B. 601; [1949] L.J.R. 1597; (1949) 113
    J.P. 488; (1949) 93 S.J. 588; [1949] 2 All E.R. 531; (1949) 47 L.G.R. 642, D.C. 561
—— v. Russell (Alexander) Ltd. [1976] I.T.R. 39; [1976] I.R.L.R. 220; affirming [1975]
    I.R.L.R. 49 432
Carroll v. Barclay (Andrew) & Sons Ltd. [1948] A.C. 477; [1948] L.J.R. 1490, (1948) 64
    T.L.R. 384; (1948) 2 All E.R. 386; 1948 S.C. (H.L.) 100; 1948 S.L.T. 464, H.L.;
    affirming [1947] S.C. 411 562
Carron v. Pullman Spring-Filled Co. Ltd. [1967] I.T.R. 650 301
Carron Co. v. Robertson [1967] I.T.R. 484 289
Carter v. Law Society, The [1973] I.C.R. 113; (1973) 117 S.J. 166, N.I.R.C. 17, 385
—— v. Wiltshire County Council [1979] I.R.L.R. 331 119
Cartledge v. Jopling (E.) & Sons [1963] A.C. 758; [1963] 2 W.L.R. 210; (1963) 107 S.J.
    73; [1963] 1 All E.R. 341; [1963] 1 Lloyd's Rep. 1, H.L.; affirming [1962] 1 Q.B.
    189, C.A. 594
Cartwright v. Sankey (G.K.N.) Ltd. (1972) 116 S.J. 433; (1972) 12 K.I.R. 453; reversed
    (1973) 14 K.I.R. 349, C.A. 539
Cassidy v. Ministry of Health [1951] 2 K.B. 343; [1951] 1 T.L.R. 539; (1951) 95 S.J. 253;
    [1951] 1 All E.R. 574, C.A. 6
Caswell v. Powerr Duffryn Associated Collieries Ltd. [1940] A.C. 152; 108 L.J.K.B. 779;
    161 L.T. 374; 55 T.L.R. 1004; 83 S.J. 976; [1939] 3 All E.R. 722................ 569, 592
—— v. Worth (1856) 5 E. & B. 849; 26 L.T.(o.s.) 216; 20 J.P. 54; 2 Jur.(N.S.) 116; 4
    W.R. 231; 119 E.R. 697; sub nom. Casswell v. Worth 25 L.J.Q.B. 121 569
Cavanagh v. Ulster Weaving Co. [1960] A.C. 145; [1959] 3 W.L.R. 262; 103 S.J. 581;
    [1959] 2 All E.R. 745; [1959] 2 Lloyd's Rep. 165, H.L. 569, 571, 579
Cawthorn & Sinclair Ltd. v. Hedger [1974] I.C.R. 146; [1974] I.T.R. 171; [1974]
    I.R.L.R. 49, N.I.R.C. 260
Central de Kaap Gold Mines, Re (1899) 69 L.J.Ch. 18; 7 Mans. 82 61
Century Insurance Co. Ltd. v. Northern Ireland Road Transport Board [1942] A.C. 509;
    111 L.J.P.C. 138; 167 L.T. 404; [1942] 1 All E.R. 491, H.L. 601, 605
Chadwick v. Pioneer Private Telephone Ltd. [1941] 1 All E.R. 522 5
Chakki v. United Yeast Co. Ltd. [1982] I.C.R. 140...177, 179
Champion (A.W.) v. Scoble [1967] I.T.R. 411 276
Chant v. Aquaboats Ltd. [1978] I.C.R. 643; [1978] 3 All E.R. 102, E.A.T. 120
Chaplin v. Frewin (Leslie) (Publishers) Ltd. [1966] Ch. 71; [1966] 2 W.L.R. 40; (1966)
    S.J. 871; [1965] 3 All E.R. 764, C.A., reversing [1966] Ch. 71 ....24, 25
Chapman v. Goonvean & Rostowrack China Clay Co. Ltd. [1973] I.C.R. 310; [1973] 1
    W.L.R. 678; (1973) 117 S.J. 416; [1973] 2 All E.R. 1063; [1974] I.T.R. 379; 14
    K.I.R. 382, C.A.; affirming [1973] I.C.R. 50................................270, 273, 278
Chappell v. Cooper; Player v. Bruguiere [1980] 1 W.L.R. 958; (1979) 124 S.J. 544; [1980]
    2 All E.R. 463, C.A. 596
Chappell v. Times Newspapers Ltd. [1975] I.C.R. 145; [1975] 1 W.L.R. 482; (1975) 119
    S.J. 82; [1975] 2 All E.R. 233; [1975] I.R.L.R. 90; 18 Man.Law. 5,
    G.A. 174, 448, 460, 465, 486, 495
Charles v. Science Research Council (1977) 121 I.T.R. 208, E.A.T. 223
—— v. Smith (S.) & Sons (England) Ltd. [1954] 1 W.L.R. 451; (1954) 98 S.J. 146; [1954]
    1 All E.R. 499; (1954) 52 L.G.R. 187 563
Charlton v. The Forrest Printing Ink Co. [1980] I.R.L.R. 331...........................574, 578
Chawner v. Cummings (1846) 8 Q.B. 311; 15 L.J.Q.B. 161; 6 L.T.(o.s.) 364; 10 J.P. 229;
    10 Jur. 454; 115 E.R. 893 129
Cheall v. Apex [1982] I.R.L.R. 91...411, 423, 428, 430
—— v. Vauxhall Motors Ltd. [1979] I.R.L.R. 253 119
Cherry v. International Alloys Ltd. [1961] 1 Q.B. 136; [1960] 3 W.L.R. 568; (1960) 104
    S.J. 782; [1960] 3 All E.R. 264; (1960) 58 L.G.R. 307, C.A. 557, 558
Chesham Shipping Ltd. v. Rowe [1977] I.R.L.R. 391, E.A.T. 48
Chowdhary v. Gillot [1947] W.N. 267; (1947) 63 T.L.R. 569; [1947] 2 All E.R. 541 601
Chrystie v. Rolls Royce (1971) Ltd. [1976] I.R.L.R. 336, E.A.T. 227

Churchman v. Joint Shop Stewards Committee of the Port of London [1972] I.C.R. 222;
    [1972] 1 W.L.R. 1094; (1972) 116 S.J. 617; [1972] 3 All E.R. 603; (1972) 13 K.I.R.
    123, C.A.; reversing *The Times*, June 13, 1972, N.I.R.C. 492
Claisse v. Hostettor, Stewart and Keydrill Ltd. [1978] I.C.R. 812; (1978) 13 I.T.R. 389,
    E.A.T. 153, 154
Clard v. Eley (IMI) Kynock Ltd. [1982] I.R.L.R. 418 334
Clarke v. Ferrie [1926] N.I. 1 424
—— v. Holmes (1862) 7 H. & N. 937; 8 Jur.(N.S.) 992; 158 E.R. 751; *sub nom.* Holmes v.
    Clarke (1862) 31 L.J.Ex. 356; 9 L.T. 178, 10 W.R. 405 589
—— v. National Union of Furniture Trade Operatives, *The Times*, October 18, 1957 407
Clarke and Powell v. Eley (I.M.I. Kynoch) Ltd. [1982] I.R.L.R. 482 .... 331, 334
—— v. Rotax Aircraft Equipment Ltd. [1975] I.C.R. 440; [1975] 1 W.L.R. 1570; (1975)
    119 S.J. 679; [1975] 3 All E.R. 794, C.A. 257
Clarke Chapman—John Thompson Ltd. v. Walters [1972] 1 W.L.R. 378; (1971) 116 S.J.
    36; [1972] 1 All E.R. 614; (1971) 12 K.I.R. 166; [1972] I.C.R. 83; [1972] I.T.R. 96,
    N.I.R.C. 246
Clarks of Hove v. Bakers' Union [1978] I.C.R. 1076; [1978] 1 W.L.R. 1207; [1979] 1 All
    E.R. 152; (1978) 13 I.T.R. 356; *sub nom.* Bakers' Union v. Clarks of Hove [1978]
    I.R.L.R. 366; (1978) 122 S.J. 643; C.A.; reversing [1977] I.C.R. 838 .....296, 298, 299
Clarkson v. Modern Foundries Ltd. [1957] 1 W.L.R. 1210; (1957) 101 S.J. 960; [1958]
    1 All E.R. 33 578
Clarkson International Tools Ltd. v. Short [1973] I.C.R. 191; (1973) 14 K.I.R. 400;
    [1973] I.T.R. 185; [1973] I.R.L.R. 90, N.I.R.C. 206, 208, 221, 247
Clay v. Crump (A.J.) & Sons Ltd. [1964] 1 Q.B. 533; [1963] 3 W.L.R. 866; (1963) 107
    S.J. 664; [1963] 3 All E.R. 687, C.A. 584
Clay Cross (Quarry Services) Ltd. v. Fletcher [1979] I.C.R. 47; [1978] 1 W.L.R. 1429;
    (1978) 122 S.J. 776; [1979] 1 All E.R. 474; [1978] 3 C.M.L.R. 1; [1978] I.R.L.R.
    361; C.A.; reversing [1977] I.C.R. 868 314
Clayton v. Gothorp [1971] 1 W.L.R. 999; (1971) 115 S.J. 266; [1971] 2 All E.R. 1311;
    [1971] T.R. 103; (1971) 69 L.G.R. 389; (1971) 47 T.C. 168 127
Clemens v. Richards (Peter) Ltd. [1977] I.R.L.R. 332, E.A.T. 104
Close v. Steel Company of Wales Ltd. [1962] A.C. 367; [1961] 3 W.L.R. 319; (1961) 105
    S.J. 856; [1962] 2 All E.R. 953; (1962) 59 L.G.R. 439, H.L. affirming [1960]
    2 Q.B. 299, C.A. 560, 561, 563
Clyde Pipeworks Ltd. v. Foster [1978] I.R.L.R. 313, E.A.T. 226, 249
Coates and Venables v. Modern Methods and Materials Ltd. [1982] I.C.R. 763; [1982]
    3 All E.R. 946 [1982] I.R.L.R. 318, C.A. 465
Cockcroft v. Trendsetter Furniture Co. [1973] I.R.L.R. 6 217
Coco v. Clark (A.N.) (Engineers) Ltd. [1968] F.S.R. 415; [1969] R.P.C. 41 ....74, 80
Coleman v. Magnet Joinery Ltd. [1975] I.C.R. 46; [1975] K.I.L.R. 139; [1974] I.R.L.R.
    343, C.A.; affirming [1974] I.C.R. 25 255
—— v. Skyrail Oceanic Ltd. [1981] I.C.R. 864 334
Coleman (D.A.) v. Baldwin (S. and W.) Ltd. [1977] I.R.L.R. 342, E.A.T. 55, 190
Collier v. Sunday Referee Publishing Co. Ltd. [1940] 2 K.B. 647; 109 L.J.K.B. 974; 164
    L.T. 10; 57 T.L.R. 2; 84 S.J. 538; [1940] 4 All E.R. 234 ....57, 58
Collins v. Nats (Scotland) Ltd. [1967] I.T.R. 423 140
Coltness Iron Co. Ltd. v. Sharp [1938] A.C. 90; 106 L.J.P.C. 142; 157 L.T. 394; 53
    T.L.R. 978; [1937] 3 All E.R. 593, H.L. 538
Colvilles Ltd. v. Devine [1969] 1 W.L.R. 475; (1969) 113 S.J. 287; [1969] 2 All E.R. 53;
    (1969) 6 K.I.R. 333, H.L. 572
Commercial Plastics Ltd. v. Vincent [1965] 1 Q.B. 623; [1964] 3 W.L.R. 820; (1964) 108
    S.J. 599; [1964] 3 All E.R. 546; C.A.; affirming (1964) 108 S.J. 484 ....85, 88
Commission for Racial Equality v. Associated Newspapers Group Ltd. [1978] 1 W.L.R.
    905; (1978) 122 S.J. 281; [1978] 3 All E.R. 419, C.A. 343
Commission of the European Communities v. U.K. [1982] I.R.L.R. 333 311
Compton v. McClure [1975] I.C.R. 378; (1975) 18 Man.Law. 100 608
Construction Industry Training Board v. Leighton [1978] 2 All E.R. 723; [1978] I.R.L.R.
    60; *sub nom.* Leighton v. Construction Industry Training Board [1978] I.C.R. 577,
    E.A.T.   44
—— v. Labour Force (1970) 114 S.J. 704; [1970] 3 All E.R. 220; [1970] I.T.R. 290;
    (1970) 9 K.I.R. 269, D.C. 9, 31

Conway v. Queen's University of Belfast [1981] I.R.L.R. 137; [1980] 9 N.I.J.B.,
    N.I.C.A. 322
—— v. Wade [1909] A.C. 506; 78 L.J.K.B. 1025; 101 L.T. 248; 25 T.L.R. 779; 53 S.J.
    754; [1908–10] All E.R. Rep. 344, H.L. 470, 499, 503, 504, 505, 508
—— v. Wimpey (George) & Co. [1951] W.N. 27; [1951] 1 T.L.R. 215; (1951) 94 S.J. 823;
    [1951] 1 All E.R. 56, C.A. 610, 611, 612
—— v. Wright (Matthew) and Nephew Ltd. [1977] I.R.L.R. 89, E.A.T. 432
Cook v. Linnell (Thomas) and Sons Ltd. [1977] I.C.R. 770; (1977) 12 I.T.R. 330; [1977]
    I.R.L.R. 132, E.A.T. 201
Cooper v. British Steel Corporation [1975] I.C.R. 454; (1975) 119 S.J. 743; [1975] I.T.R.
    137; [1975] I.R.L.R. 308; (1975) 18 Man.Law. 98 261
—— v. Wandsworth Board of Works (1863) 14 C.B.(N.S.) 180; 2 New Rep. 31; 32
    L.J.C.P. 185; 8 L.T. 278; 9 Jur.(N.S.) 1155; 11 W.R. 646; 143 E.R. 414 429
Cope v. Nickel Electro [1980] C.L.7 1268 594
Copson v. Eversure Accessories Ltd. [1974] I.C.R. 636; [1975] K.I.L.R. 61; sub nom.
    Copson & Trahearn v. Eversure Accessories [1974] I.T.R. 406; [1974] I.R.L.R.
    247, N.I.R.C. 260
Coral Leisure Group Ltd. v. Barnett [1981] I.C.R. 503; (1981) 125 S.J. 374; [1981]
    I.R.L.R. 204, E.A.T. 25, 26
Corby v. Morrison [1980] I.C.R. 564; [1980] I.R.L.R. 218, E.A.T. 25
Corn v. Weir's Glass (Hanley) Ltd. (L. Bates, Third Party) [1960] 1 W.L.R. 577; (1960)
    104 S.J. 447; [1960] 2 All E.R. 300, C.A. 556
Corner v. Buckinghamshire County Council (1978) 13 I.T.R. 421; (1978) 77 L.G.R. 268;
    [1978] I.C.R. 836; [1978] I.R.L.R. 320, E.A.T. 115
Cort (Robert) and Son Ltd. v. Charman [1981] I.C.R. 816; [1981] I.R.L.R. 437,
    E.A.T. 164, 169
Corton House Ltd. v. Skipper [1981] I.C.R. 307; [1981] I.R.L.R. 78, E.A.T. 140
Cory Lighterage Ltd. v. Transport and General Workers' Union [1973] I.C.R. 339;
    [1973] 1 W.L.R. 792, C.A.; upholding [1973] I.C.R. 339, C.A.; affirming in part
    and on other grounds [1973] I.C.R. 197 ....482, 500
Costain Civil Engineering Ltd. v. Draycott [1977] I.C.R. 335; [1977] I.R.L.R. 17,
    E.A.T. 153
Cotter v. National Union of Seamen [1929] 2 Ch. 58; 98 L.J.Ch. 323; 141 L.T. 178; 73
    S.J. 206; 45 T.L.R. 352; [1929] All E.R. Rep. 342, C.A. 421
Courtaulds Northern Textiles Ltd. v. Andrew [1979] I.R.L.R. 84, E.A.T. 46, 70, 72
Covell v. Scamell (1910) 103 L.T. 535, D.C. 180
Cowen v. Haden Carrier Ltd. [1982] I.R.L.R. 225 overruled on other grounds (1982)
    I.R.L.R. 314 270
Cox v. Wildt Mellor (Bromley) Ltd. (1978) 13 I.T.R. 465; [1978] I.C.R. 736; [1978]
    I.R.L.R. 157, E.A.T. 249
Cox (W.E.) Toner (International) Ltd. v. Crook [1981] I.C.R. 823; [1981] I.R.L.R. 443,
    E.A.T. 157, 164, 189
Cranleigh Precision Engineering Ltd. v. Bryant [1965] 1 W.L.R. 1293; (1965) 109 S.J.
    830; [1964] 3 All E.R. 289; [1966] R.P.C. 81.............................74, 77, 78, 82, 88
Crazy Prices (Northern Ireland) Ltd. v. Hewitt [1980] I.R.L.R. 396, N.I.C.A. 499
Crockford v. Furse Electrical Installations Ltd. (1973) 224/203 249
Crofter Hand Woven Harris Tweed Association v. Veitch [1942] A.C. 435; affirming
    [1940] S.C. 141 ....469, 470, 477, 500
Crook v. Derbyshire Stone Ltd. [1956] 1 W.L.R. 432; (1956) 100 S.J. 302; [1956] 2 All
    E.R. 447 ....606, 607
Crookhall v. Vickers-Armstrong Ltd. [1955] 1 W.L.R. 659; (1955) 99 S.J. 401; [1955]
    2 All E.R. 12; (1955) 53 L.G.R. 407 578
Cross v. British Iron, Steel and Kindred Trades Association [1968] 1 W.L.R. 494; (1968)
    111 S.J. 944; [1968] 1 All E.R. 250, C.A. 448
—— v. Redpath Dorman Long (Contracting) Ltd. [1978] I.C.R. 730, E.A.T. 600
Crown v. Bentley Engineering Co. Ltd. (361/212) 144
Crown Agents for Overseas Governments & Administration v. Lawal [1979] I.C.R. 103;
    [1978] I.R.L.R. 542, E.A.T. 168
Cruickshank v. Hobbs [1977] I.C.R. 725, E.A.T. 249, 295, 468
Cuckson v. Stones (1858) 1 E. & E. 248; 28 L.J.Q.B. 25; 32 L.J.(O.S.) 242; 5 Jur.(N.S.)
    337; 7 W.R. 134; 120 E.R. 902 62

Cullen v. Creasey Hotels (Limbury) Ltd. [1980] I.C.R. 236; [1980] I.R.L.R. 59, E.A.T. 105
Cuming v. Hill (1819) 3 B. & Ald. 59; 106 E.R. 585 20
Curran v. Neill (William) and Son (St. Helens) Ltd. [1961] 1 W.L.R. 1069; (1961) 105 S.J. 526; [1961] 3 All E.R. 108, C.A. 554
Curry v. Harlow District Council [1979] I.C.R. 769; [1979] I.R.L.R. 269, E.A.T. 237
Cutter v. Powell (1795) 6 T.R. 320; 101 E.R. 573 61

Daily Mirror Newspapers Ltd. v. Gardner [1968] 2 Q.B. 762; [1968] 2 W.L.R. 1239; (1968) 112 S.J. 271; [1968] 2 All E.R. 163, C.A. 473, 475, 476, 477, 481
Dale v. I.R.C. [1954] A.C. 11; [1953] 3 W.L.R. 448; (1953) 97 S.J. 538; [1953] 2 All E.R. 671; [1953] T.R. 269; [1953] 46 R. & I.T. 513; (1953) 34 T.C. 468, (1953) 32 A.T.C. 294, H.L.; reversing [1952] Ch. 704, C.A.; reversing [1951] Ch. 893 15
Daley v. Allied Suppliers Ltd. [1983] I.C.R. 90; [1983] I.R.L.R. 14 10
—— v. Radnor (1973) 117 S.J. 321; (1973) 226 E.G. 619 130
—— v. Strathclyde Regional Council [1977] I.R.L.R. 414 103
Dalgleish v. Kew House Farm Ltd. [1982] I.R.L.R. 251 42
Dallow Industrial Properties Ltd. v. Else [1967] 2 Q.B. 449; [1967] 2 W.L.R. 1352; (1967) 111 S.J. 255; [1967] 2 All E.R. 30; (1967) 2 K.I.R. 253, D.C. 147
Daniels v. Whetstone Entertainments Ltd. (1962) 106 S.J. 284; [1962] 2 Lloyd's Rep. 1, C.A. 610
Darlington Forge Ltd. v. Sutton [1968] I.T.R. 196 302
Davidson v. Handley Page Ltd. (1945) L.J.K.B. 81; 172 L.T. 138; 61 T.L.R. 178, 89 S.J. 118; [1945] 1 All E.R. 235, C.A. 573
—— v. Pilley [1979] I.R.L.R. 275, E.A.T. 26
Davie v. New Merton Board Mills [1959] A.C. 604; [1959] 2 W.L.R. 331; (1959) 103 S.J. 177; [1959] 1 All E.R. 346; (1959) 2 Lloyd's Rep. 587; H.L.; affirming [1958] 1 Q.B. 210, C.A.; reversing [1957] 2 Q.B. 368 ....569, 570, 581, 582
Davies v. British Insulated Callendar's Cables Ltd. (1977) 121 S.J. 203; The Times, February 15, 1977 596
Davies v. Davies (1887) 36 Ch.D. 359; 56 L.J.Ch. 962; 58 L.T. 209; 36 W.R. 86; 3 T.L.R. 839, C.A. 88
—— v. G.K.N. Birwelco (Uskside) Ltd. [1976] I.R.L.R. 82 220
—— v. Pullman Spring Filled Co. Ltd. [1967] I.T.R. 247 141
Davis v. Carew-Pole [1956] 1 W.L.R. 833; (1956) 100 S.J. 510; [1956] 2 All E.R. 524...404, 432
Davis v. St. Mary's Demolition & Excavation Co. [1954] 1 W.L.R. 592; (1954) 98 S.J. 217; [1954] 1 All E.R. 578 612
Davis Contractors Ltd. v. Fareham U.D.C. [1959] A.C. 696; [1956] 3 W.L.R. 37; (1956) 100 S.J. 378; [1956] 2 All E.R. 145; (1956) 54 L.G.R. 289, H.L.; affirming (1955) 1 Q.B. 302, C.A. 177
Davis (E. & J.) Transport Ltd. v. Chattaway [1972] I.C.R. 267 267
Dawkins v. Antrobus (1881) 17 Ch.D. 615; 44 L.T. 557; 29 W.R. 511, C.A.; affirming (1879) 41 L.T. 490 436
Dealey v. British Rail Engineering Ltd. [1980] I.R.L.R. 147 42
Deane v. Craik, The Times, March 16, 1962; The Guardian, March 16, 1962 34
Deaway Ltd. v. Calverley [1973] I.C.R. 546; [1973] 3 All E.R. 776; [1973] I.T.R. 562, N.I.R.C. 181
Decro Wall International S.A. v. Practitioners in Marketing Ltd. [1971] 1 W.L.R. 361; (1970) 115 S.J. 171; [1971] 2 All E.R. 216, C.A. 161, 176
Dedman v. British Building and Engineering Appliances Ltd. [1974] I.C.R. 53; [1974] 1 W.L.R. 171; (1973) 117 S.J. 938; [1974] 1 All E.R. 520; [1974] I.T.R. 100; (1973) 16 K.I.R. 1; [1973] I.R.L.R. 379, C.A.; affirming [1973] I.C.R. 82, N.I.R.C. 136, 137
De Dohse v. R. (1886) 66 L.J.Q.B. 422n.; 2 T.L.R. 114, H.L. 18
Deeley v. British Rail Engineering Ltd. [1980] I.R.L.R. 147, C.A.; reversing [1979] I.R.L.R. 5, E.A.T. 49, 50
De Francesco v. Barnum (1889) 43 Ch.D. 165; 59 L.J.Ch. 151; 6 T.L.R. 59; sub nom. Francesco v. Barnum (1889) 62 L.T. 40; 54 J.P. 420; 38 W.R. 187 24
—— v. —— (1900) 45 Ch.D. 430; 60 L.J.Ch. 63; 63 L.T. 438; 39 W.R. 5; 6 T.L.R. 463 ... 174

Defrenne (Gabrielle) v. Société Anonyme Belge de Navigation Aérienne (SABENA)
(No. 43/75 [1976] I.C.R. 547; [1976] 2 C.M.L.R. 98; [1976] E.C.R. 455 318
—— v. —— (No. 149/77) [1978] E.C.R. 1365; [1978] 3 C.M.L.R. 312 304
Delanair v. Mead [1976] I.C.R. 552; [1976] I.R.L.R. 340, E.A.T. 279
Denham v. Midland Employers' Mutual Assurance Ltd. [1955] 2 Q.B. 437; [1955] 3
W.L.R. 84; (1955) S.J. 417; [1955] 2 All E.R. 561; [1955] 1 Lloyd's Rep. 467,
C.A.; affirming [1955] 1 Lloyd's Rep. 245 600
Denmark Productions Ltd. v. Boscobel Productions Ltd. [1969] 1 Q.B. 699; [1968] 3
W.L.R. 841; (1968) 112 S.J. 761; [1968] 3 All E.R. 513, C.A.; affirming in part
(1967) 111 S.J. 715 .... 176, 179
Denning v. Secretary of State for India (1920) 37 T.L.R. 138 18
Dennis (A.R.) and Co. Ltd. v. Campbell [1976] I.C.R. 465; [1976] 3 W.L.R. 501; (1976)
120 S.J. 690; [1977] 1 All E.R. 138 93
—— v. —— [1978] Q.B. 365; [1978] I.C.R. 862; [1978] 2 W.L.R. 429; (1977) 121 S.J.
790; [1978] 1 All E.R. 1215 26
Depledge v. Pye Telecommunications Ltd. [1981] I.C.R. 82; [1980] I.R.L.R. 390,
E.A.T. 114
De Stempel v. Dunkels (1938) L.T. 85; 54 T.L.R. 289; 82 S.J. 51; [1938] 1 All E.R. 238,
C.A.; affirmed (1939) 55 T.L.R. 655, H.L. 171
Devis (W.) & Sons Ltd. v. Atkins [1977] A.C. 931; (1978) 13 I.T.R. 71; [1977] I.C.R.
662; [1977] 3 W.L.R. 214; (1977) 121 S.J. 512; [1977] I.R.L.R. 314; (1978) 8
Build. L.R. 57, H.L.; affirming (1976) 12 I.T.R. 12; [1977] I.C.R. 377; [1977] 2
W.L.R. 70; [1977] 2 All E.R. 321, C.A. 196, 197, 208, 216, 256, 257, 261
Devon County Council v. Cook (1977) 12 I.T.R. 347; [1977] I.R.L.R. 188,
E.A.T. 183, 184
Devonald v. Rosser & Sons [1906] 2 K.B. 728; 95 L.T. 232; 22 T.L.R. 682; 50 S.J. 616,
C.A. 57
Deyong v. Shenburn [1946] 1 K.B. 227; 115 L.J.K.B. 262; 174 L.T. 129; 62 T.L.R. 193;
99 S.J. 139; [1946] 1 All E.R. 226, C.A. 97
Dhami v. Top Spot Night Club [1977] I.R.L.R. 231, E.A.T. 148
Dickson v. Flack [1953] 2 Q.B. 464; [1953] 3 W.L.R. 571; (1953) 97 S.J. 586; [1953] 2 All
E.R. 840; (1953) 51 L.G.R. 515, reversing; [1953] 1 W.L.R. 196, C.A. 562
Dimes v. Grand Junction Canal Co. (1852) H.L.Cas. 759, H.L. 435
Din v. Carrington Viyella Ltd. [1982] I.C.R. 256; [1982] I.R.L.R. 281, E.A.T. 328
Distillers Co. (Biochemicals) Ltd. v. Times Newspapers Ltd. [1975] Q.B. 613; [1974] 3
W.L.R. 728; (1974) 118 S.J. 864; [1975] 1 All E.R. 41 81
Distillers Co. Ltd. v. Gardner [1982] I.R.L.R. 47 198
Dixon v. Stenor Ltd. [1973] I.C.R. 157; [1973] I.R.L.R. 28; [1973] I.T.R. 141, N.I.R.C. 167
Dixon and Shaw v. West Ella Developments Ltd. [1978] I.C.R. 856; (1978) 13 I.T.R.
235; [1978] I.R.L.R. 151, E.A.T. 118, 120
Donaghey v. Boulton & Paul Ltd. [1968] A.C. 1; [1967] 3 W.L.R. 829; (1967) 111 S.J.
517; [1967] 2 All E.R. 1014; (1967) 2 K.I.R. 787, H.L.; reversing in part sub nom.
Donaghey v. O'Brien (P.) & Co. [1966] 1 W.L.R. 1170, C.A. 554, 599
Donoghue v. Stevenson [1932] A.C. 562; 101 L.J.P.C. 119; 147 L.T. 281; 48 T.L.R. 76
S.J. 396; 37 Com.Cas. 850, H.L. 573
Donnelly v. Feniger and Blackburn Ltd. [1973] I.C.R. 68, [1973] I.T.R. 134, [1973]
I.R.L.R. 26; N.I.R.C. 258
Donovan v. Invicta Airways Ltd. [1970] 1 Lloyd's Rep. 486 affirming [1969] 2 Lloyd's
Rep. 413 .... 46, 70
Donovan v. Laing, Wharton and Down Construction Syndicate [1893] 1 Q.B. 629; 63
L.J.Q.B. 25; 68 L.T. 512; 57 J.P. 583; 41 W.R. 455; 9 T.L.R. 313; 37 S.J. 324;
4 R. 317, C.A. 602
Dooley v. Cammell Laird and Co. Ltd. and Mersey Insulation Co. [1951] 1 Lloyd's Rep.
271 575
Dorman Long & Co. Ltd. v. Carroll (1945) 173 L.T. 141; 61 T.L.R. 501; 89 S.J. 382;
[1945] 2 All E.R. 567; 44 L.G.R. 5, D.C. 283
Doughty v. Turner Manufacturing Co. Ltd. [1964] 1 Q.B. 518; [1964] 2 W.L.R. 240; 108
S.J. 53; [1964] 1 All E.R. 98, C.A. 588
Doyle v. White City Stadium [1935] 1 K.B. 110; 104 L.J.K.B. 140; 152 L.T. 32; 78 S.J.
601; [1934] All E.R. Rep. 252, C.A. 24
Drake v. Morgan [1978] I.C.R. 56; [1977] Crim.L.R. 739; (1977) 121 S.J. 743 440

Drew v. St. Edmundsbury Borough Council [1980] I.C.R. 513; [1980] I.R.L.R. 459,
    E.A.T. 119
Driver v. Willett (William) (Contractors) Ltd. [1969] 1 All E.R. 665 584
Dudfield v. Ministry of Works (1964) 108 S.J. 118.. 18, 32
Dugdale v. Kraft Foods Ltd. [1977] I.C.R. 48; [1977] 1 W.L.R. 1288; (1979) 11 I.T.R.
    309; [1977] All E.R. 454, E.A.T.; Industrial Tribunal rehearing [1977] I.R.L.R.
    60 ....306, 307, 309, 310
Duke v. Reliance Systems Ltd. [1982] I.R.L.R. 347 ....33, 50
Dunlop Ltd. v. A.S.T.M.S. Award No. 82/17 359
Dunn v. Pochin (Contractors) Ltd. [1982] I.R.L.R. 449 210
—— v. R. [1896] 1 Q.B. 116; 65 L.J.Q.B. 279; 73 L.T. 695; 60 J.P. 117; 44 W.R. 243; 12
    T.L.R. 101; 40 S.J. 129, C.A. 18
Dunning (A.J.) and Sons (Shop Fitters) Ltd. v. Jacomb [1973] I.C.R. 448; [1973] I.T.R.
    453; (1973) 15 K.I.R. 9; [1973] I.R.L.R. 206, N.I.R.C. 217
Duport Steels Ltd. v. Sirs [1980] I.C.R. 161; [1980] 1 W.L.R. 142; (1980) 124 S.J. 133,
    [1980] 1 All E.R. 529; [1980] I.R.L.R. 116, H.L.; reversing [1980] I.R.L.R.
    112..509, 513, 520
Dutton v. Bailey (C.H.) Ltd. 3 I.T.R. 355; [1968] 2 Lloyd's Rep. 122 273
—— v. Hawker Siddeley Aviation Ltd. [1978] I.C.R. 1057; [1978] I.R.L.R. 390,
    E.A.T. 116
Dyer v. Munday [1895] 1 Q.B. 742; 64 L.J.Q.B. 448; 72 L.T. 448; 59 J.P. 276; 43 W.R.
    440; 11 T.L.R. 283; 14 R. 306, C.A. 610

Earl v. Slater and Wheeler (Airlyne) [1972] I.C.R. 508; [1973] 1 W.L.R. 51; (1973) 117
    S.J. 14; [1973] 1 All E.R. 145; [1973] I.T.R. 33; (1972) 13 K.I.R. 319; [1972]
    I.R.L.R. 115; N.I.R.C.; affirming [1972] I.T.R. 387 .... 196, 206, 209, 217, 257, 261
Early (Charles) & Marriott (Witney) v. Smith. See Snoxell and Davies v. Vauxhall
    Motors; Early (Charles) & Marriott (Witney) v. Smith & Ball.
Easson v. L. & N.E. Railway Co. Ltd. [1944] 2 K.B. 421; 113 L.J.K.B. 449; 170 L.T.
    234; 60 T.L.R. 280; 88 S.J. 143; [1944] 2 All E.R. 425, C.A. 571
East v. Beavis Transport [1969] 1 Lloyd's Rep. 302; (1969) 119 New L.J. 486, C.A. 607
East African Airways Corporation v. Foote [1977] I.C.R. 776, E.A.T. 199
East Hertfordshire District Council v. Boyten (K.) [1977] I.R.L.R. 347, E.A.T. 225
East Lindsey District Council v. Daubney [1977] I.C.R. 566; (1977) 12 I.T.R. 359; [1977]
    I.R.L.R. 181, E.A.T. 222
Eastham v. Newcastle United F.C. Ltd. [1964] Ch. 413; (1963) 3 W.L.R. 574; (1963) 107
    S.J. 574; [1963] 3 All E.R. 139 83
Eaton v. Nuttall [1977] 1 W.L.R. 549; [1977] 3 All E.R. 1131; [1977] I.C.R. 272; [1977]
    I.T.R. 197; [1977] I.R.L.R. 71; (1977) 121 S.J. 353, E.A.T. 310, 311
—— v. R.K.B. (Furmston) Ltd. [1972] I.C.R. 273; (1972) 13 K.I.R. 170; [1972] I.T.R.
    348, N.I.R.C. 292
Eaves v. Morris Motors Ltd. [1961] 2 Q.B. 385; [1961] 3 W.L.R. 657; (1961) 105 S.J. 610;
    [1961] 3 All E.R. 233; (1961) 59 L.G.R. 466, C.A.; reversing [1961] 1 W.L.R.
    511..558, 561
Ebbs v. Whitson (James) and Co. Ltd. [1952] 2 Q.B. 877; [1952] 1 T.L.R. 1428; (1952) 96
    S.J. 375; [1952] 2 All E.R. 192; (1952) 50 L.G.R. 563, C.A. 554
Edmonds (B.J.) v. Computer Services (South-West) Ltd. [1977] I.R.L.R. 359,
    E.A.T. 310
Edwards v. Halliwell [1950] W.N. 537; (1950) 94 S.J. 803; [1950] 2 All E.R. 1064,
    C.A. 421
—— v. National Coal Board [1949] 1 K.B. 704; (1949) 65 T.L.R. 430; (1949) 93 S.J. 337;
    [1949] 1 All E.R. 743, C.A. 538
—— v. Skyways [1964] 1 W.L.R. 349; (1964) 108 S.J. 279; [1964] 1 All E.R.
    494..30, 34, 35, 375
—— v. Society of Graphical and Allied Trades [1971] Ch. 354; [1970] 3 W.L.R. 713;
    (1970) 114 S.J. 618; [1970] 3 All E.R. 689; (1970) 8 K.I.R. 1, C.A.; varying [1970]
    1 W.L.R. 379 ....93, 94, 370, 391, 400, 412, 415, 426, 430, 431
—— v. West Herts Group Management Committee [1957] 1 W.L.R. 415; (1957) 121 J.P.
    212; (1957) 101 S.J. 190; [1957] 1 All E.R. 541; [1957] S.L.T. 1971 97
Edwards and the National Federation of Insurance Workers, decision of registrar,
    January 21, 1949 397

Egg Stores (Stamford Hill) Ltd., The v. Leibovici [1977] I.C.R. 260 [1977] I.C.R. 260; (1976) 11 I.T.R. 289; [1976] I.R.L.R. 376, E.A.T. 178, 179

Electrical, Electronic, Telecommunication and Plumbing Union v. Times Newspapers [1980] Q.B. 585; [1980] 3 W.L.R. 98; (1979) 124 S.J. 31; [1980] 1 All E.R. 1097 ... 389

Electrochrome Ltd. v. Welsh Plastics Ltd. [1968] 2 All E.R. 205 611

Electrolux Ltd. v. Hutchinson [1977] I.C.R. 252; (1976) 12 I.T.R. 40; (1976) 120 S.J. 818; [1976] I.R.L.R. 410, E.A.T. 309

Elegbede v. Wellcome Foundation Ltd., The [1977] I.R.L.R. 383 250

Ellen v. Topp (1851) 6 Ex. 424; 20 L.J.Ex. 241; 17 L.T.(o.s.) 52; 15 Jur. 451; 155 E.R. 609 21

Elliott v. Liggens [1902] 2 K.B. 84; 71 L.J.K.B. 483; 87 L.T. 29; 50 W.R. 524; 18 T.L.R. 514; 4 W.C.C. 11, D.C. 62

Elliott Bros. (London) Ltd. v. Colverd [1979] I.R.L.R. 92, E.A.T. 218

Ellis v. Brighton Co-operative Society [1976] I.R.L.R. 419 447

Emerald Construction Co. v. Lowthian [1966] 1 W.L.R. 691; (1966) 110 S.J. 226; [1966] 1 All E.R. 1013; (1966) 1 K.I.R. 200; C.A. 473, 477, 479

Emmerson v. Commissioners of Inland Revenue [1977] I.R.L.R. 458 115

Employment Appeals Tribunal Practice Direction, March 3, 1978 136

Enderby Town Football Club v. Football Association [1971] Ch. 591; [1970] 3 W.L.R. 1021; (1970) 114 S.J. 827; [1971] 1 All E.R. 215, C.A.; petition for leave to appeal to House of Lords dismissed 404, 439

England v. Bromley London Borough Council [1978] I.C.R. 1, E.A.T. 311

Esso v. Harper's Garage (Stourport) Ltd. [1968] A.C. 269; [1967] 2 W.L.R. 871; (1967) 111 S.J. 174; [1967] 1 All E.R. 699; H.L.; reversing in part [1966] 2 Q.B. 514...83, 84

Esso Petroleum Co. Ltd. v. Kingswood Motors (Addlestone) Ltd. [1974] Q.B. 142; (1973) 3 W.L.R. 780; (1973) 117 S.J. 852; [1973] 3 All E.R. 1057; [1973] C.M.L.R. 665 478

Esterman v. National and Local Government Officers Association [1974] I.C.R. 625; (1974) 118 S.J. 596; [1975] K.I.L.R. 179 .... 400, 417, 425, 427, 428, 442

European Chefs (Catering) Ltd. v. Currell (1971) I.T.R. 37, D.C. 276

Evans v. Elemeta Holdings Ltd. [1982] I.C.R. 323; [1982] I.R.L.R. 143 .... 205, 253

—— v. National Union of Printing, Bookbinding and Paper Workers [1938] 4 All E.R. 51 428

Evans and Morgan v. A.B. Electronic Components Ltd. [1981] I.R.L.R. 111, E.A.T. 249

Evenden v. Guildford City Association Football Club [1975] Q.B. 917; [1975] I.C.R. 367; [1975] 3 W.L.R. 95; [1975] I.R.L.R. 213; 18 Man.Law. 92, C.A.; reversing [1974] I.C.R. 554 .... 43, 155

Everest (J.F.), (Executors of) v. Cox [1980] I.C.R. 415, E.A.T. 292

Everwear Candlewick Ltd. v. Isaac [1974] I.C.R. 525; [1974] 3 All E.R. 24; [1974] I.T.R. 334; (1974) 17 K.I.R. 70, N.I.R.C. 258

Express Lift Co. Ltd. v. Bowles (F.L.) [1977] I.C.R. 474; (1976) 12 I.T.R. 71; [1977] I.R.L.R. 99, E.A.T. 49, 50

Express Newspapers Ltd. v. McShane [1980] A.C. 672; [1980] I.C.R. 42; [1980] 2 W.L.R. 89; (1979) 124 S.J. 30; [1980] 1 All E.R. 65; [1980] I.R.L.R. 35, H.L.; reversing [1979] I.C.R. 210, C.A. 506

F.T.A.T.U. v. Modgill; P.E.L. v. Modgill [1980] I.R.L.R. 142, E.A.T. 374

Faithful v. Admiralty, The Times, January 24, 1964; The Guardian, January 24, 1964 357

Faramus v. Film Artistes' Association [1964] A.C. 925; [1964] 2 W.L.R. 126; (1964) S.J. 13; [1964] 1 All E.R. 25, H.L.; affirming [1963] 2 Q.B. 527; [1963] 2 W.L.R. 504; (1963) 107 S.J. 93; [1963] 1 All E.R. 636, C.A.; reversing The Times, June 2, 1962 .... 391, 400, 404, 405, 407

Farmer v. Wilson (1900) 69 L.J.Q.B. 496; 82 L.T. 546; 64 J.P. 486, 16 T.L.R. 309; 44 S.J. 363; 19 Cox C.C. 502, D.C. 525

Farnworth Finance Facilities v. Attryde [1970] 1 W.L.R. 1053; (1970) 114 S.J. 354; [1970] 2 All E.R. 774, C.A. 164

Farrow v. Wilson (1869) L.R. 4 C.P. 744; 38 L.J.C.P. 326; 20 L.T. 810; 18 W.R. 43 179

Farthing v. Ministry of Defence [1980] I.R.L.R. 402, C.A. 315

Fenton v. Thorley and Co. [1903] A.C. 443; 72 L.J.K.B. 787; 89 L.T. 314; 52 W.R. 81; 19 T.L.R. 684; 5 W.C.C. 1, H.L. 617

Ferguson Ltd. v. O'Gorman [1937] I.R. 620 525

Ferguson (M.J.) v. Dawson (John) and Partners (Contractors) Ltd. [1976] I.R.L.R.
  346.. 4, 52
Field v. Jeavons (E.E.) and Co. Ltd. [1965] 1 W.L.R. 996; (1965) 109 S.J. 312; [1965]
  2 All E.R. 162, C.A. 570, 574
Financial Techniques (Planning Service) Ltd. v. Hughes [1981] I.R.L.R. 32, C.A. 42, 52, 191
Finch e v. Oake [1896] 1 Ch. 409; 65 L.J.Ch. 324; 73 L.T. 716; 60 J.P. 309; 12 T.L.R. 156;
  40 S.J. 224, C.A. 415, 416
Firman v. Ellis; Ince v. Rogers; Dawn v. Harvey; Pheasant v. Smith (Tyres) Ltd. [1978]
  Q.B. 886; [1978] 3 W.L.R. 1; (1978) 122 S.J. 147; [1978] 2 All E.R. 851, C.A.;
  affirming (1977) 121 S.J. 606 597
Fisher v. Dick (W.B.) and Co. Ltd. (1938) 82 S.J. 952; [1938] 4 All E.R. 467 171
—— v. Jackson [1891] 2 Ch. 84; 60 L.J.Ch. 482; 64 L.T. 782; 7 T.L.R. 358 15
—— v. Port of London Authority [1962] 1 W.L.R. 234; [1962] 1 All E.R. 458 543
—— v. York Trailer Co. Ltd. [1979] I.C.R. 834; [1979] I.R.L.R. 386, E.A.T. 158, 192
Fitzgerald v. Hall, Russell & Co. Ltd. [1970] A.C. 984; [1969] 3 W.L.R. 868; (1969) 113
  S.J. 899; [1969] 3 All E.R. 1140; (1969) 3 K.I.R. 263; [1970] I.T.R. 1; 1970 S.C. 1,
  H.L.; reversing 1969 S.C. 50 ....141, 142, 143, 144
Ford v. Warwickshire County Council [1983] 1 All E.R. 753; [1982] I.R.L.R. 246,
  H.L...141, 143
Ford Motor Co. Ltd. v. Amalgamated Union of Engineering and Foundry Workers
  [1969] 2 Q.B. 303; [1969] 1 W.L.R. 339; (1969) 113 S.J. 203; [1969] 2 All E.R.
  481; (1969) 6 K.I.R. 50...373, 379
Forgings and Presswork Ltd. v. McDougall [1974] I.C.R. 532; [1974] I.R.L.R. 243,
  N.I.R.C. 191
Forman Construction Ltd. v. Kelly [1977] I.R.L.R. 468, E.A.T...................226, 295, 297
Forster v. National Amalgamated Union of Shop Assistants, Warehousemen & Clerks
  [1927] 1 Ch. 539; 96 L.J.Ch. 141; 137 L.T. 86; 43 T.L.R. 199; 71 S.J. 105; [1927]
  All E.R. Rep. 618..397, 398
Forsyth v. Fry's Metals Ltd. [1971] I.R.L.R. 243 229
Foss v. Harbottle (1843) 2 Hare 461; 67 E.R. 189 421
Foster Clark's Indenture Trusts, Re, Loveland v. Horscroft [1966] 1 W.L.R. 125; (1966)
  110 S.J. 108; [1966] 1 All E.R. 43 180
Fowler v. Commercial Timber Co. Ltd. [1930] 2 K.B. 1; 99 L.J.K.B. 529; 143 L.T. 391;
  [1930] All E.R. Rep. 224, C.A. 180
—— v. Kibble [1922] 1 Ch. 487; 91 L.J.Ch. 353; 126 L.T. 566; 38 T.L.R. 271; 66 S.J. 267;
  [1922] All E.R.Rep. 626, C.A. 524, 525
Fox v. Wright (C.) (Farmers) Ltd. [1978] I.C.R. 98, E.A.T. 301
Franchi v. Franchi [1967] R.P.C. 149 76
Francis v. Municipal Councillors of Kuala Lumpur [1962] 1 W.L.R. 1411; (1962) 106 S.J.
  833; [1962] 3 All E.R. 633, P.C. 175, 176
Fraser v. Evans [1969] 1 Q.B. 349; [1968] 3 W.L.R. 1172; (1968) 112 S.J. 805; [1969]
  1 All E.R. 8, C.A.; reversing The Times, September 26, 1968 81
Freud v. Bentalls Ltd. [1982] I.R.L.R. 443 213
Froom v. Butcher [1976] Q.B. 286; [1975] 3 W.L.R. 379; (1975) 119 S.J. 613; [1975] 3 All
  E.R. 520; [1975] R.T.R. 518; [1975] 2 Lloyd's Rep. 478, C.A.; reversing [1974]
  1 W.L.R. 1297 594
Fuller v. Bowman (Stephanie) (Sales) Ltd. [1977] I.R.L.R. 7 292
Fyfe & McGrouther Ltd. v. Byrne [1977] I.R.L.R. 29, E.A.T. 188

G.W.K. Ltd. v. Dunlop Rubber Co. Ltd. (1926) 42 T.L.R. 376; on appeal (1926) 42
  T.L.R. 593, C.A. 473
Gale (B.G.) Ltd. v. Gilbert [1978] I.C.R. 1149; (1978) 13 I.T.R. 547; [1978] I.R.L.R.
  453, E.A.T. 183
Gallagher v. Post Office [1970] 3 All E.R. 712; (1970) 9 K.I.R. 78...................18, 37, 49, 50
Gannon v. Firth (J.C.) Ltd. [1976] I.R.L.R. 415 192
Gardner (F.C.) Ltd. v. Beresford [1978] I.R.L.R. 63, E.A.T. 70, 188
Garland v. British Rail Engineering [1981] 2 C.M.L.R. 542, H.L.; affirming sub nom.
  Garland v. British Rail Engineering; Turton v. MacGregor Wallcoverings;
  Roberts v. Cleveland Area Health Authority [1979] I.C.R. 558; [1979] 1 W.L.R.
  754; [1979] I.R.L.R. 244; (1979) 123 S.J. 300; [1979] 2 All E.R. 1163, C.A.;
  reversing [1978] I.R.L.R. 8, E.A.T. 341

—— v. —— [1982] I.R.L.R. 111 329
Garner v. Grange Furnishing Ltd. [1977] I.R.L.R. 206, E.A.T. 188
Garrard v. Southey (A.E.) & Co. [1952] 2 Q.B. 174; [1952] 1 T.L.R. 630; (1952) 96 S.J.
    166; [1952] 1 All E.R. 597 .... 600, 602
Garratt v. Burghart (1828) 3 C. & P. 581 21
Garret v. Taylor (1620) Cro.Jac. 567; 2 Roll.Rep. 162; 79 E.R. 485 480
Gartside v. Outram (1856) 26 L.J.Ch. 113; 28 L.T.(o.s.) 120; 3 Jur.(N.S.) 39; 5 W.R. 35 73
Gascol Conversions Ltd. v. Mercer [1974] I.C.R. 420; (1974) 118 S.J. 219; [1974] I.T.R.
    282; [1975] K.I.L.R. 149; [1974] I.R.L.R. 155, C.A. 29, 35, 36, 44,
                                                                        284, 285, 302, 373, 374
Gayle v. Wilkinson (John) & Sons (Saltley) Ltd. and Transport and General Workers'
    Union [1978] I.C.R. 154; [1977] I.R.L.R. 208, E.A.T. 236
Gaynor v. Allen [1959] 2 Q.B. 403; [1959] 3 W.L.R. 221; (1959) 123 J.P. 413; (1959) 103
    S.J. 677; [1959] 2 All E.R. 644 577
Gee v. Pritchard (1818) 2 Swans. 402 429
General & Municipal Workers' Union v. Wailes Dove Bitumastic Ltd. [1977] I.R.L.R.
    45 295
General & Municipal Workers' Union (Managerial, Administrative, Technical and
    Supervisory Association Section) v. British Uralite [1979] I.R.L.R. 409, 413 299
General Aviation Services (U.K.) Ltd. v. Transport and General Workers' Union [1976]
    I.R.L.R. 224, H.L.; affirming [1975] I.C.R. 276, C.A.; reversing [1974] I.C.R. 35;
    [1973] I.R.L.R. 355, N.I.R.C. 495, 497, 504
General Cleaning Contractors Ltd. v. Christmas [1953] A.C. 180; [1953] 2 W.L.R. 6;
    (1953) 97 S.J. 7; [1952] 2 All E.R. 1110; (1952) 51 L.G.R. 109, H.L.; affirming
    [1952] 1 K.B. 141, C.A.; affirming in part and reversing in part [1951] W.N.
    294 .... 225, 574, 579
General Rolling Stock, Co., Re (1866) L.R. 1 Eq. 346; 35 Beav. 207; 12 Jur.(N.S.) 44, 55
    E.R. 874 180
Genower v. Ealing, Hammersmith and Hounslow Area Health Authority [1980]
    I.R.L.R. 297, E.A.T. 190
Genys v. Matthews [1966] 1 W.L.R. 758; (1966) 110 S.J. 332; [1965] 3 All E.R. 24; [1965]
    2 Lloyd's Rep. 449 612
George v. Beecham Group [1977] I.R.L.R. 43 256
Gibb v. United Steel Companies Ltd. [1957] 1 W.L.R. 668; (1957) 101 S.J. 393; [1957]
    2 All E.R. 110 .... 5, 600, 601
Gibson v. British Transport Docks Board [1982] I.R.L.R. 228 210
—— v. Lawson [1891] 2 Q.B. 545; 61 L.J.M.C. 9; 65 L.T. 573; 55 J.P. 485; 7 T.L.R. 650;
    17 Cox C.C. 354 524
Gilbert v. Goldstone Ltd. [1977] I.C.R. 36; [1977] 1 All E.R. 423, E.A.T. 187
Gill v. Andrews (Harold) (Sheepbridge) Ltd. [1974] I.C.R. 294; [1974] I.T.R. 219; [1975]
    K.I.L.R. 71; [1974] I.R.L.R. 109, N.I.R.C. 260
Gillies v. Daniels (Richard) and Co. Ltd. [1979] I.R.L.R. 457, E.A.T. 188
Ginty v. Belmont Building Supplies Ltd. [1959] 1 All E.R. 414 585
Glacier Metal Co. Ltd. v. Dyer [1974] 3 All E.R. 21; [1974] I.R.L.R. 189, N.I.R.C. 185
Gledhow Autoparts Ltd. v. Delaney [1965] 1 W.L.R. 1366; (1965) 109 S.J. 571; [1965]
    3 All E.R. 288, C.A. 84
Glynn v. Keele University [1971] 1 W.L.R. 487; (1970) 115 S.J. 173; [1971] 2 All E.R.
    89 430
Goldsoll v. Goldman [1915] 1 Ch. 292; 84 L.J.Ch. 228; 112 L.T. 494; 59 S.J. 188
    [1914–15] All E.R. Rep. 257, C.A. previous proceedings [1914] 2 Ch. 603 88
Goodwin (H.) Ltd. v. Fitzmaurice [1977] I.R.L.R. 393, E.A.T. 230
Gorman v. London Computer Training Centre [1978] I.C.R. 394, [1978] I.R.L.R. 22,
    E.A.T. 248
Gould v. Stuart [1896] A.C. 575; 65 L.J.P.C. 82; 75 L.T. 110; 12 T.L.R. 595, P.C. 18
Gouriet v. Union of Post Office Workers [1978] A.C. 435; [1977] 3 W.L.R. 300; (1977)
    121 S.J. 543; [1977] 3 All E.R. 70, H.L.; reversing [1977] Q.B. 729, C.A. 491
Gozney v. Bristol Trade and Provident Society [1909] 1 K.B. 901; 78 L.J.K.B. 616; 100
    L.T. 669; 25 T.L.R. 370; 53 S.J. 341, C.A. 391
Grace and Anderson v. Northgate Group, The [1972] I.R.L.R. 53 281
Grant v. Australian Knitttng Mills Ltd. [1936] A.C. 85; 105 L.J.P.C. 6; 154 L.T. 18; 52
    T.L.R. 38; 79 S.J. 815, P.C. 573

—— v. Secretary of State for India (1877) 2 C.P.D. 445; 46 L.J.Q.B. 681; 37 L.T. 188; 25 W.R. 848 18
Gray Dunn and Co. Ltd. v. Edwards [1980] I.R.L.R. 23, E.A.T. 209, 225, 374, 432, 447
Great Western Railway Co. v. Bater [1922] A.C. 1; 91 L.J.K.B. 472; 127 L.T. 170; 38 T.L.R. 448; 66 S.J. 365, 8 Tax Cas. 231, H.L. 15
Greater London Council v. Farrar [1980] I.C.R. 266; [1980] 1 W.L.R. 608; (1979) 124 S.J. 412 317
Green v. Broxtowe District Council [1977] I.C.R. 241; [1977] I.R.L.R. 34; (1976) 12 I.T.R. 90; [1970] 1 All E.R. 694, E.A.T. 311
Greenhalgh v. Executors of James Mills Ltd. [1973] I.R.L.R. 78 215
Gregory v. Ford [1951] 1 All E.R. 121 .... 93, 99
Greig v. McAlpine (Sir Alfred) & Son (Northern) Ltd. [1979] I.R.L.R. 372 .... 206, 247
Gresham Life Assurance Society, Re, Ex p. Penney (1872) 8 Ch. App. 446; 42 L.J.Ch. 183; 28 L.T. 150; 21 W.R. 186 405
Grieg v. Community Industry; Greig v. Ahern [1979] I.C.R. 356; [1979] I.R.L.R. 158, E.A.T. 328
Griffiths v. Arch Engineering Co. (Newport) Ltd. [1968] 3 All E.R. 217 .... 575, 576
Griggs v. Duke Power Company 401 U.S. 424 (1971) 313
Grogan v. British Railways Board (E.A.T.) (unreported) 119
Groves v. Wimborne (Lord) [1898] 2 Q.B. 402; 67 L.J.Q.B. 862; 79 L.T. 284; 47 W.R. 87; 14 T.L.R. 493; 42 S.J. 633, C.A. 553
Gunton v. Richmond-upon-Thames London Borough Council [1980] I.C.R. 755; [1980] 3 W.L.R. 714; (1980) 124 S.J. 792; [1980] 3 All E.R. 577; [1980] I.R.L.R. 321; (1980) 79 L.G.R. 241, C.A. 160, 161, 163, 192
Gylbet v. Fletcher (1629) Cro.Car. 179; 79 E.R. 757 21

Hadden Ltd. v. Cowen [1982] I.R.L.R. 315 .... 57, 94
Hadmor Productions Ltd. v. Hamilton [1981] I.C.R. 690; [1981] 3 W.L.R. 139; (1981) 125 S.J. 288; [1981] 2 All E.R. 724; [1981] I.R.L.R. 210, C.A.; leave to appeal granted [1981] 1 W.L.R. 1128 ....482, 509, 517, 518
Hamish Armour (Receiver of Barry Staines) v. Association of Scientific, Technical and Managerial Staffs [1979] I.R.L.R. 24, E.A.T. 298, 299
Hancke v. Hooper (1835) 7 C. & P. 81 20
Hancock v. British Road Services [1973] I.R.L.R. 42 199
Handley v. Mono (H.) Ltd. [1979] I.C.R. 147; [1978] I.R.L.R. 534, E.A.T. 316
Hannam v. Bradford Corporation [1970] 1 W.L.R. 937; (1970) 114 S.J. 414, [1970] 2 All E.R. 690; (1970) 68 L.G.R. 498, C.A. 433
Hanson v. Wood [1968] I.T.R. 14; (1967) 3 K.I.R. 231, D.C. 267
Hare v. Murphy Bros. [1974] I.C.R. 603; (1974) 118 S.J. 596; [1974] 3 All E.R. 940; [1975] K.I.L.R. 31; [1974] I.R.L.R. 342; [1975] I.T.R. 1, C.A.; affirming [1973] I.C.R. 331; [1973] I.T.R. 458; (1973) 16 K.I.R. 57, N.I.R.C. 179, 191
Harman v. Flexible Lamps Ltd. [1980] I.R.L.R. 418, E.A.T. 177
Harmer v. Cornelius (1858) 5 C.B.(N.S.) 236; 28 L.J.C.P. 85; 32 L.T.(o.s.) 62; 22 J.P. 724; 4 Jur.(N.S.) 1110; 6 W.R. 749; 141 E.R. 94 .... 96, 170
Harris v. Cardiff Channel Dry Docks and Pontoon Co. Ltd. [1969] I.T.R. 266; [1969] 1 Lloyd's Rep. 407, D.C. 144
Harris (Ipswich) Ltd. v. Harrison [1978] I.C.R. 1256; [1978] I.R.L.R. 382, E.A.T. 223
Hart v. Aldridge (1774) 1 Cowp. 54; 98 E.R. 964; sub nom. Anon. (1774) Lofft 493 5
—— v. Riversdale Mill Co. [1928] 1 K.B. 176; 96 L.J.K.B. 691; 137 L.T. 364; 91 J.P. 135; 43 T.L.R. 396; 71 S.J. 407, C.A.; previous proceedings [1927] 1 K.B. 624, D.C. 129, 130
Hart (R.N.) v. Marshall (A.R.) & Sons (Bulwell) Ltd. [1977] I.C.R. 539; [1977] 1 W.L.R. 1067; [1978] 2 All E.R. 413; (1977) 121 S.J. 677; (1977) 12 I.T.R. 190; [1977] I.R.L.R. 61, E.A.T. 178
Harvey v. O'Dell (R.G.) (Galway) Ltd. (Third Party) [1958] 2 Q.B. 78; [1958] 2 W.L.R. 473; (1958) 102 S.J. 196; [1958] 1 All E.R. 657; [1958] 1 Lloyd's Rep. 273 ....97, 99, 607
Haseltine Lake & Co. v. Dowler [1981] I.C.R. 222; [1981] I.R.L.R. 25, E.A.T. 191
Hawker Siddeley Power Engineering Ltd. v. Rump [1979] I.R.L.R. 425 .... 271, 284
Hawkins v. Ross (Ian) Castings Ltd. [1970] 1 All E.R. 180 593
Hawley v. Fieldcastle and Co. Ltd. [1982] I.R.L.R. 223 10

Hay v. Dowty Mining Equipment Ltd. [1971] 3 All E.R. 1136 587
Haynes v. Harwood [1935] 1 K.B. 146; 104 L.J.K.B. 63; 152 L.T. 121; 51 T.L.R. 100; 78
    S.J. 801, C.A. 574
Hazell (Quinton) Ltd. v. Earl (W.C.) [1976] I.R.L.R. 296, E.A.T. 215
Hazell's Offset Ltd. v. Luckett (1977) 12 I.T.R. 298; [1977] I.R.L.R. 430, E.A.T. 228
Hearn v. British Broadcasting Corporation [1977] I.C.R. 685 .... 502, 503
Heath v. Longman (J.F.) (Salesman) Ltd. [1973] I.C.R. 407; [1973] 2 All E.R. 1228;
    [1973] I.T.R. 427; (1973) 14 K.I.R. 569; [1973] I.R.L.R. 214, N.I.R.C. 245, 467, 488
Heathcote v. North Western Electricity Board (1973) 258/174 248
Heaton's Transport (St. Helens) v. Transport and General Workers' Union; Craddock
    Brothers v. Same; Panalpina Services v. Same [1973] A.C. 15; [1972] I.C.R. 308;
    [1972] 3 W.L.R. 431; (1972) 116 S.J. 598; [1972] 3 All E.R. 101; (1972) 14 K.I.R.
    48; [1972] I.R.L.R. 25, H.L.; reversing [1972] 3 W.L.R. 73, C.A.; reversing
    [1972] I.C.R. 285 ....371, 389, 477, 495
Hebden v. Forsey & Son [1973] I.C.R. 607; [1973] I.T.R. 656; (1973) 15 K.I.R. 161;
    [1973] I.R.L.R. 344, N.I.R.C. 178
Henderson v. Masson Scott Thrissell Engineering [1974] I.R.L.R. 98, N.I.R.C. 227
Hepworth Manufacturing Co. Ltd. v. Ryott [1920] 1 Ch. 1; 89 L.J.Ch. 69; 122 L.T. 135;
    36 T.L.R. 10; 64 S.J. 19; [1918–19] All E.R. Rep. 1019, C.A. 25, 85
Herton v. Blaw Knox Ltd. (1968) 112 S.J. 963; 6 K.I.R. 35 587
Hewitson v. Anderton Springs (1972) 13 K.I.R. 197; [1972] I.T.R. 391; [1972] I.R.L.R.
    56 217
Hewitt v. Bonvin [1940] 1 K.B. 188; 109 L.J.K.B. 223; 161 L.T. 360; 56 T.L.R. 43; 83
    S.J. 869, C.A. 495
Hewlett v. Allen [1894] A.C. 383, H.L.; affirming [1892] 2 Q.B. 662 .... 128, 129
Hiles v. Amalgamated Society of Woodworkers [1968] Ch. 440; [1967] 3 W.L.R. 896;
    (1967) 111 S.J. 603; [1967] 3 All E.R. 70; (1967) 3 K.I.R. 179, ... 428, 430
Hill v. Parsons (C.A.) & Co. Ltd. [1972] 1 Ch. 305; [1971] 3 W.L.R. 995; (1971) 115 S.J.
    868; [1971] 3 All E.R. 1345, C.A. 58, 69, 170, 172, 174, 466
Hillingdon Area Health Authority v. Kauders [1979] I.C.R. 472; [1979] I.R.L.R. 197,
    E.A.T. 150
Hilti (Great Britain) Ltd. v. Windridge [1974] I.C.R. 352; [1974] I.T.R. 197; [1974]
    I.R.L.R. 53, N.I.R.C. 258, 260
Himpfen v. Allied Records Ltd. [1978] I.C.R. 684; [1978] 3 All E.R. 891; (1978) 13
    I.T.R. 201; [1978] I.R.L.R. 154, E.A.T. 234, 235, 236
Hindes v. Supersine Ltd. [1979] I.C.R. 517; [1979] I.R.L.R. 343, E.A.T. 289, 292
Hindle v. Birtwhistle [1897] 1 Q.B. 192; 66 L.J.Q.B. 173; 76 L.T. 159; 61 J.P. 70; 45
    W.R. 207; 13 T.L.R. 129; 41 S.J. 171; 18 Cox C.C. 508, D.C. 560
—— v. Percival Boats Ltd. [1969] 1 W.L.R. 174; (1969) 113 S.J. 13; [1969] 1 All E.R.
    836; (1968) 6 K.I.R. 462; [1969] I.T.R. 86, C.A. Petition for appeal to the House
    of Lords refused [1969] 1 W.L.R. C.A. 182, 276, 277, 279, 281
—— v. Porritt (Joseph) & Sons Ltd. [1970] 1 All E.R. 1142 559
Hitchcock v. Post Office [1980] I.C.R. 100, E.A.T. 11, 13
Hivac Ltd. v. Park Royal Scientific Instruments Ltd. [1946] Ch. 169; 115 L.J.Ch. 241; 174
    L.T. 422; 62 T.L.R. 231; 90 S.J. 175; (1946) 2 All E.R. 350, C.A. 92, 93
Hobbs v. Royal Arsenal Co-operative Society Ltd. (1930) 144 L.T. 10; 23 B.W.C.C. 254,
    C.A. 9
Hobson v. Park Brothers Ltd. (1973) 258/102 249
Hodges v. Webb [1920] 2 Ch. 70; 89 L.J.Ch. 273; 123 L.T. 80; 36 T.L.R. 311; [1920] All
    E.R. Rep. 447 480
Hodgson v. NALGO [1982] 1 W.L.R. 130; (1971) 116 S.J. 56; [1972] 1 All E.R. 15 421
Holland v. London Society of Compositors (1924) 40 T.L.R. 440 .... 34, 35, 36, 375
Holliday v. National Telephone Co. [1899] 2 Q.B. 392; 68 L.J.Q.B. 1016; 81 L.T. 252; 47
    W.R. 658; 15 T.L.R. 483, C.A. 583
Hollies v. Principal Patterns and Engineering Co. [1973] I.R.L.R. 165 249
Hollister v. National Farmers' Union [1979] I.C.R. 542; [1979] I.R.L.R. 238, C.A.;
    reversing [1978] I.C.R. 712; [1978] I.R.L.R. 161, E.A.T. 199, 204, 222, 224
Home Counties Dairies v. Skilton [1970] 1 W.L.R. 526; (1970) 114 S.J. 107; [1970] 1 All
    E.R. 1227; (1970) 8 K.I.R. 691, C.A. 86, 87
—— v. Woods [1977] I.C.R. 463; (1976) 11 I.T.R. 322; [1977] 1 All E.R. 869, E.A.T. 236
Home Office v. Robinson [1981] I.R.L.R. 524 154

Honeywill and Stein Ltd. *v.* Larkin Bros. (London's Commercial Photographers) Ltd. [1934] 1 K.B. 191; 103 L.J.K.B. 74; 150 L.T. 71; 50 T.L.R. 56; [1933] All E.R. Rep. 77 583
Hoover Ltd. *v.* Forde [1980] I.C.R. 239, E.A.T. 227
Horan *v.* Hayhoe [1904] 1 K.B. 288; 73 L.J.K.B. 133; 90 L.T. 12; 68 J.P. 102; 52 W.R. 231; 20 T.L.R. 118, 48 S.J. 117, D.C. 20
Hornby *v.* Close (1867) L.R. 2 Q.B. 153; 8 B. & S. 175; 36 L.J.M.C. 43; 15 L.T. 563; 31 J.P. 148; 15 W.R. 336; 10 Cox C.C. 393 390
Horne *v.* LEC Refrigeration Ltd. [1965] 2 All E.R. 898 ....564, 565, 585
Horrigan *v.* Lewisham London Borough Council [1978] I.C.R. 15, E.A.T. 52, 55, 271, 282, 284
Horsey *v.* Dyfed County Council [1982] I.R.L.R. 395 ....325, 326
Horsley Smith & Sherry Ltd. *v.* Dutton [1977] I.C.R. 594; (1977) 12 I.T.R. 351; [1977] I.R.L.R. 172, E.A.T. 195
Horwood *v.* Millar's Timber and Trading Co. Ltd. [1917] 1 K.B. 305; 86 L.J.K.B. 190; 115 L.T. 805; 33 T.L.R. 86; 61 S.J. 114; [1916–17] All E.R. Rep. 847, C.A. 174, 176
Houghton *v.* Hackney Borough Council (Note) (1961) 3 K.I.R. 615; [1961] C.L.Y. 5929 571
Howgate *v.* Fane Acoustics Ltd. [1981] I.R.L.R. 161, E.A.T. 168
Hubbard *v.* Pitt [1976] Q.B. 142; [1975] I.C.R. 308; [1975] 3 W.L.R. 201; (1975) 119 S.J. 393; [1975] 3 All E.R. 1, C.A.; affirming on different grounds [1975] I.C.R. 77; [1975] 2 W.L.R. 254; (1974) 118 S.J. 791; [1975] 1 All E.R. 1056 ....521, 523, 526
Hudson *v.* Fuller Shapcott [1970] I.T.R. 266 185
Hughes *v.* Gwynedd Area Health Authority [1978] I.C.R. 161; [1977] I.R.L.R. 436, E.A.T. 105
—— *v.* Lord Advocate [1963] A.C. 837; [1963] 2 W.L.R. 779; (1963) 107 S.J. 232; (1963) 1 All E.R. 705; 1963 S.C. (H.L.) 31; 1963 S.L.T. 150, H.L.; reversing 1961 S.C. 310 588
Hugh-Jones *v.* St. John's College Cambridge [1979] I.C.R. 848; (1979) 123 S.J. 603, E.A.T. 342
Hulland Gravel Co. Ltd. *v.* Secretary of State for Employment and Productivity [1969] I.T.R. 110 300
Hunt *v.* British Railways Board [1979] I.R.L.R. 379, E.A.T. 189
—— *v.* Broome. *See* Broome *v.* D.P.P.
—— *v.* Great North Railway Co. [1891] 1 Q.B. 601; 60 L.J.Q.B. 216; 64 L.T. 418; 55 J.P. 470, D.C. 128
Hunter *v.* Smith's Dock Co. Ltd. [1968] 1 W.L.R. 1865; (1968) 112 S.J. 963; [1968] 2 All E.R. 81; (1968) 5 K.I.R. 113; [1968] 1 Lloyd's Rep. 354, D.C. Petition for leave to the House of Lords allowed 141, 142
Huntley *v.* Thornton [1957] 1 W.L.R. 321; (1957) 101 S.J. 171; [1957] 1 All E.R. 234 ....406, 471, 504, 519
Hurley *v.* Mustoe [1981] I.C.R. 490; (1981) 125 S.J. 374; [1981] I.R.L.R. 208, E.A.T. ... 334
Hussein *v.* Saints Complete House Furnishers [1979] I.R.L.R. 337 332
Hutchinson *v.* Westward Television Ltd. [1977] I.C.R. 279; (1976) 12 I.T.R. 125; [1977] I.R.L.R. 69, E.A.T. 342
—— *v.* York, Newcastle & Berwick Ry. Co. (1850) 5 Exch. 343; 6 Ry. & Can. Cas. 580; 19 L.J.Ex. 296; 15 L.T.(o.s.) 230; 14 Jur. 837; 155 E.R. 150 568
Hilton *v.* Burton (Thomas) (Rhodes) Ltd. [1961] 1 W.L.R. 705; (1961) 105 S.J. 322; [1961] 1 All E.R. 74 605
Hynds *v.* Spillers French Baking Ltd. 1974 S.L.T. 191, [1974] I.T.R. 261; [1974] I.R.L.R. 281, N.I.R.C. 238
Hyett *v.* Great Western Rail Co. [1948] 1 K.B. 345; [1947] L.J.R. 1243; 177 L.T. 178; 63 T.L.R. 411; 91 S.J. 434; [1947] 2 All E.R. 264, C.A. 588

I.P.C. Business Press Ltd. *v.* Greig [1977] I.C.R. 858; (1977) 12 I.T.R. 148, E.A.T. 168
ITT Components (Europe) Ltd. *v.* Kolah (Y.) [1977] I.C.R. 740; [1977] I.R.L.R. 53, E.A.T. 139, 140
Iceland Frozen Foods Ltd. *v.* Jones [1982] I.R.L.R. 439 ....202, 206
Ilkiw *v.* Samuels [1963] 1 W.L.R. 991; (1963) 107 S.J. 680; [1963] 2 All E.R. 879, C.A. 598, 606

Imperial Chemical Industries Ltd. *v.* Shatwell [1965] A.C. 656; [1964] 3 W.L.R. 329; (1964) 108 S.J. 578; [1964] 2 All E.R. 999; H.L.; reversing *The Guardian*, July 17, 1963; [1963] C.L.Y. 2377, C.A. 589, 590, 591

Imperial Metal Industries (Kynoch) Ltd. *v.* Amalgamated Union of Engineering Workers (Technical, Administrative and Supervisory Section) [1979] I.C.R. 23; [1979] 1 All E.R. 847; [1978] I.R.L.R. 407; C.A. 398

Industrial Rubber Products Ltd. *v.* Gillon [1977] I.R.L.R. 389; [1977] 13 I.T.R. 100, E.A.T. 204

Inglefield *v.* Macey (1967) 2 K.I.R. 146; (1967) 117 New L.J. 101 570

Initial Services Ltd. *v.* Putterill [1968] 1 Q.B. 396; [1967] 3 W.L.R. 1032; (1967) 111 S.J. 541; [1967] 3 All E.R. 145; (1967) 2 K.I.R. 863. Petition for leave to appeal to the House of Lords dismissed. 81

Inner London Education Authority *v.* Nash [1979] I.C.R. 229; (1978) 122 S.J. 860; (1978) 77 L.G.R. 398; [1979] I.R.L.R. 29, E.A.T. 105

Innes *v.* Wylie (1844) 1 Car. & K. 257 432

International Computers Ltd. *v.* Kennedy [1981] I.R.L.R. 28, E.A.T. 191

Ipswich Tailors' Case (1614) 11 Co. Rep. 53a; 77 E.R. 1218; *sub nom.* Ipswich Tailors *v.* Sherring (1614) 1 Roll.Rep. 4; *sub nom.* Ipswich Clothworkers Cas. (1614) Godb. 252 405

Iqbal *v.* London Transport Executive (1974) 16 K.I.R. 329 609

Irwin *v.* White, Tompkins & Courage Ltd. [1964] 1 W.L.R. 387; (1964) 108 S.J. 154; [1964] 1 All E.R. 545; (1964) 62 L.G.R. 256, H.L. 556, 560

Island Records Ltd., *Ex p.* [1978] Ch. 122; [1978] 3 W.L.R. 23; (1978) 122 S.J. 298; (1978) 3 All E.R. 824; [1978] F.S.R. 505, C.A. 484

Isle of Wight Tourist Board *v.* Coombes [1976] I.R.L.R. 413 ....70, 188, 337

Jackson *v.* Barry Ry. Co. [1893] 1 Ch. 238; 68 L.T. 472; 9 T.L.R. 90, 2. R. 207, C.A. 434

—— *v.* General Accident Fire and Life Assurance Co. Ltd. [1976] I.R.L.R. 338, E.A.T. 219

—— *v.* Hayes, Candy and Co. Ltd. (1938) 160 L.T. 112; 82 S.J. 952; [1938] 4 All E.R. 587 177

James *v.* Hepworth & Grandage Ltd. [1968] 1 Q.B. 94; [1967] 3 W.L.R. 178; (1968) 111 S.J. 232; [1967] 2 All E.R. 829; (1967) 2 K.I.R. 809, C.A. 578, 587

—— *v.* James (1872) 41 L.J.Ch. 353 76

—— *v.* Waltham Holy Cross U.D.C. [1973] I.C.R. 398; [1973] I.T.R. 467; (1973) 14 K.I.R. 576; [1973] I.R.L.R. 202, N.I.R.C. 224

Janata Bank *v.* Ahmed [1981] I.C.R. 791; [1981] I.R.L.R. 457, C.A. 97

Jarman *v.* Pollard (E.) and Co. Ltd. [1967] I.T.R. 406 185

Jefford *v.* Gee [1970] 2 Q.B. 130; [1970] 2 W.L.R. 702; (1970) 114 S.J. 206; [1970] 1 All E.R. 1202; [1970] 1 Lloyd's Rep. 107 257

Jeffrey *v.* Scott (Laurence) & Electromotors Ltd. [1977] I.R.L.R. 466, E.A.T. 236

Jenkins *v.* Kingsgate (Clothing Productions) Ltd. [1981] I.C.R. 715; [1981] 1 W.L.R. 1485; (1981) 125 S.J. 587; [1980] 1 C.M.L.R. 81; [1980] I.R.L.R. 6, E.A.T.; [1981] I.C.R. 592; [1981] 1 W.L.R. 972; (1981) 125 S.J. 442; [1981] 2 C.M.L.R. 24; [1981] I.R.L.R. 228, European Ct. 312, 314, 317

Jeremiah *v.* Ministry of Defence. *See* Ministry of Defence *v.* Jeremiah.

Jobling *v.* Associated Dairies [1981] 3 W.L.R. 155; (1981) 125 S.J. 481; [1981] 2 All E.R. 752, H.L.; affirming [1981] Q.B. 389, C.A. 613

Joel *v.* Cammell Laird (Ship Repairers) [1969] I.T.R. 206......................................35, 284

Johnson *v.* Beaumont (A.H.) [1953] 2 Q.B. 184; [1953] 2 W.L.R. 1153; (1953) 97 S.J. 389; [1953] 2 All E.R. 106; [1953] 1 Lloyd's Rep. 546 600

—— *v.* Cross [1977] I.C.R. 872; (1977) T.R. 151, E.A.T. 267

—— *v.* Nottinghamshire Combined Police Authority [1974] I.C.R. 170; [1974] 1 W.L.R. 358; (1973) 118 S.J. 166; [1974] 1 All E.R. 1082; [1974] I.R.L.R. 20; [1974] I.T.R. 164, C.A.; affirming [1973] I.T.R. 411, N.I.R.C. 274, 278, 308

—— *v.* Rea Ltd. [1962] 1 Q.B. 373; [1961] 1 W.L.R. 1400; (1961) 105 S.J. 867; [1961] 3 All E.R. 816; [1961] 2 Lloyd's Rep. 243, C.A. 576

—— *v.* Stone (J.) & Co. (Charlton) Ltd. [1961] 1 W.L.R. 849; (1961) 105 S.J. 209; [1961] 1 All E.R. 869; (1961) 59 L.G.R. 344 563

Johnson Matthey Metals Ltd. *v.* Harding (1978) 13 I.T.R. 407; [1978] I.R.L.R. 248, E.A.T. 226

Johnston and Gunn v. St. Cuthberts Co-operative Association Ltd. (1969) I.T.R. 137 292
Jolliffe v. Willmett & Co. (1970) 114 S.J. 619; [1971] 1 All E.R. 478 599
Jolly v. Spurlings [1967] I.T.R. 157; (1966) 2 K.I.R. 184 141
Jones v. Associated Tunnelling Co. Ltd. [1981] I.R.L.R. 477, E.A.T.............33, 35, 38, 44,
                                                                          48, 50, 52, 282
—— v. Aston Cabinet Co. Ltd. [1973] I.C.R. 292; (1973) 14 K.I.R. 413; [1973] I.T.R.
        356, N.I.R.C. 292
—— v. Lee and Guilding [1980] I.C.R. 310; (1979) 123 S.J. 785; (1979) 78 L.G.R. 213;
        [1980] I.R.L.R. 67, C.A. 42
—— v. Lionite Specialities (Cardiff) Ltd. (1961) 105 S.J. 1082, C.A.; reversing (1961)
        105 S.J. 468 578
—— v. Liverpool Corporation & Liverpool Polytechnic [1974] I.R.L.R. 55; [1974]
        I.T.R. 33, N.I.R.C. 191
—— v. Manchester Corporation [1952] 2 Q.B. 852; [1952] 1 T.L.R. 1589; (1952) 116 J.P.
        412; [1952] 2 All E.R. 125, C.A. 99
—— v. Secretary of State for Social Services [1972] A.C. 944; [1972] 2 W.L.R. 210;
        (1971) 116 S.J. 57; [1972] 1 All E.R. 145, H.L.; reversing [1970] 1 Q.B. 477, C.A.;
        affirming [1969] 2 W.L.R. 647, D.C. 632
—— v. Sherman (H.) Ltd. [1979] I.T.R. 63 267
—— v. Smith (William) (Poplar) Ltd. [1969] I.T.R. 317 140
Jowett v. Bradford (Earl of) (No. 2) [1978] I.C.R. 431; [1978] I.R.L.R. 16; (1978) 13
        I.T.R. 141, E.A.T...202, 219
Jupiter General Insurance Co. Ltd. v. Shroff (Ardeshir Bomanji) [1937] 3 All E.R. 67,
        P.C. 156, 169

K. v. Raschen (1878) 38 L.J. 38; sub nom. K. v. R. (1878) 4 J.P. 264 170
Kallinos v. London Electric Wire Ltd. [1980] I.R.L.R. 11, E.A.T. 158
Kavanagh v. Hiscock [1974] Q.B. 600; [1974] I.C.R. 282; [1974] 2 W.L.R. 421; (1974)
        118 S.J. 98; [1974] 2 All E.R. 177; (1974) 16 K.I.R. 31, [1974] I.R.L.R. 121;
        [1974] Crim.L.R. 255, D.C. 527, 529
Kay v. I.T.W. [1968] 1 Q.B. 140; [1967] 3 W.L.R. 695; (1967) 111 S.J. 351; [1967] 3 All
        E.R. 22; (1967) 3 K.I.R. 18, C.A. 570, 607, 608, 625
Kearney v. Waller (Eric) Ltd. [1967] 1 Q.B. 29; [1966] 2 W.L.R. 208; (1966) 110 S.J. 13;
        [1965] 3 All E.R. 352 585
—— v. Whitehaven Colliery Co. [1893] 1 Q.B. 700; 62 L.J.M.C. 129; 68 L.T. 690; 57 J.P.
        645; 41 W.R. 594; 9 T.L.R. 402; 4 R. 388, C.A. 25, 87, 131
Kelly v. Dale (John) Ltd. [1965] 1 Q.B. 185; [1964] 3 W.L.R. 41; (1965) 108 S.J. 218,
        [1964] 2 All E.R. 497; (1964) 62 L.G.R. 331 565
—— v. National Society of Operative Printers' Assistants (1915) 84 L.J.K.B. 2236; 113
        L.T. 1055; 31 T.L.R. 632; 59 S.J. 716; [1914–15] All E.R. Rep. 576,
        C.A. 387, 388, 427
—— v. Upholstery and Cabinet Works (Amesbury) Ltd. [1977] I.R.L.R. 91 247
Kenmir Ltd. v. Frizzell [1968] 1 W.L.R. 329; [1968] 1 All E.R. 414; [1968] I.T.R. 159;
        (1968) 3 K.I.R. 240, D.C. 147
Kenyon v. Darwen Cotton Manufacturing Co. Ltd. [1936] 2 K.B. 193; 105 L.J.K.B. 342;
        154 L.T. 553; 52 T.L.R. 294; 80 S.J. 147, C.A. 128
Keppel Bus Co. Ltd. v. Sa'ad Bin Ahmed [1974] 1 W.L.R. 1082; (1974) 118 S.J. 531;
        [1974] 2 All E.R. 700; (1974) 17 K.I.R. 90; [1974] R.T.R. 504, P.C. 609
Keys v. Shoefayre Ltd. [1978] I.R.L.R. 467 96
Khanna v. Ministry of Defence [1981] I.C.R. 653; [1981] I.R.L.R. 331, E.A.T. 322
Khanum v. Mid-Glamorgan Area Health Authority [1979] I.C.R. 40; (1978) 13 I.T.R.
        303; [1978] I.R.L.R. 215, E.A.T. 215
Kingston and Richmond Area Health Authority v. Kaur [1981] I.C.R. 631; [1981]
        I.R.L.R. 337, E.A.T. 333
Kirby v. Manpower Services Commission [1980] I.C.R. 420; [1980] 1 W.L.R. 725; (1980)
        124 S.J. 326; [1980] 3 All E.R. 334; [1980] I.R.L.R. 229, E.A.T. 337
Kirkby v. Taylor [1910] 1 K.B. 529; 79 L.J.K.B. 267; 102 L.T. 184; 74 J.P. 143; 26 T.L.R.
        246, D.C. 20
Kirkham v. National Society of Printers, Graphical and Media Personnel [1981] I.R.L.R.
        244 403

Knight v. Leamington Spa Courier Ltd. [1961] 2 Q.B. 253; [1961] 3 W.L.R. 79; (1961)
   105 S.J. 465; [1961] 2 All E.R. 666; (1961) 59 L.G.R. 374, C.A. 564
—— v. Wall (Howard) Ltd. [1938] 4 All E.R. 667 623
Kodeeswaren (Chelliah) v. Att.-Gen. of Ceylon [1970] 2 W.L.R. 456; (1969) 114 S.J. 87,
   P.C. 18
Kolatsis v. Rockware Glass Ltd. [1974] I.C.R. 580; [1974] 3 All E.R. 555; [1974]
   I.R.L.R. 240, N.I.R.C. 143
Kolfor Plant Ltd. v. Wright [1982] I.R.L.R. 311 .... 107, 108
Kooragang Investments Ltd. v. Richardson & Wrench Ltd. [1981] 3 W.L.R. 493; [1981]
   3 All E.R. 64, P.C. 605, 609
Kores Manufacturing Co. Ltd. v. Kolok Manufacturing Co. Ltd. [1959] Ch. 108; [1958]
   2 W.L.R. 858; [1958] 102 S.J. 362; [1958] 2 All E.R. 65; [1958] R.P.C. 200, C.A.;
   affirming [1957] 1 W.L.R. 1012 83
Koufos v. Czarnikow (C.) Ltd. [1969] 1 A.C. 350; [1967] 3 W.L.R. 1491; (1967) 111 S.J.
   848, [1967] 3 All E.R. 686; [1967] 2 Lloyd's Rep. 457, H.L.; affirming sub nom.
   Czarnikow (C.) v. Koufos [1966] 2 Q.B. 695, C.A.; reversing (1966) 110 S.J.
   287 96
Kraft Foods Ltd. v. Fox [1978] I.C.R. 311; (1978) 13 I.T.R. 96; [1977] I.R.L.R. 431,
   E.A.T. 261
Kunick (Philip) v. Smyth (unreported) 92

Ladbroke Racing Ltd. v. Arnott [1979] I.R.L.R. 192, E.A.T. 220, 221
Laffin and Callaghan v. Fashion Industries (Hartlepool) Ltd. [1978] I.R.L.R. 448,
   E.A.T. 249
Laing (John) & Son Ltd. v. Best [1968] I.T.R. 3 96
Lake v. Essex County Council [1979] I.C.R. 577; (1979) 77 L.G.R. 708; [1979] I.R.L.R.
   241, C.A.; reversing [1978] I.C.R. 657; (1977) 76 L.G.R. 341; (1978) 13 I.T.R. 1;
   [1978] I.R.L.R. 24, E.A.T. 47, 49, 56, 72
Lamb v. Evans [1893] 1 Ch. 218; 62 L.J.Ch. 404; 68 L.T. 131; 41 W.R. 405; 9 T.L.R. 87;
   2 R. 189, C.A. 75
Land and Wilson v. West Yorkshire Metropolitan County Council [1981] I.C.R. 334;
   [1981] I.R.L.R. 87, C.A.; reversing [1979] I.C.R. 452; (1979) 123 S.J. 283; (1979)
   77 L.G.R. 676; [1979] I.R.L.R. 174, E.A.T..... 29, 34, 54, 140, 171, 186, 190, 285, 375
Lane v. Norman (1891) 61 L.J.Ch. 149; 66 L.T. 83; 40 W.R. 268 436
Lang (Charles) and Sons Ltd. v. Aubrey (B.) [1978] I.C.R. 168; [1977] I.R.L.R. 335,
   E.A.T. 195
Langston v. Amalgamated Union of Engineering Workers (No. 2) [1974] I.C.R. 510;
   (1974) 118 S.J. 660; (1968) 17 K.I.R. 74; sub nom. Langston v. Amalgamated
   Union of Engineering Workers (Engineering Section) and Chrysler United
   Kingdom [1974] I.R.L.R. 182, N.I.R.C. 57, 167, 177
Larkin v. Long [1915] A.C. 814; 84 L.J.P.C. 201; 113 L.T. 337; 31 T.L.R. 405; 59 S.J.
   455; [1914–15] All E.R. Rep. 469, H.L. 500, 501
Latimer v. A.E.C. Ltd. [1953] A.C. 643; [1953] 3 W.L.R. 259; (1953) 117 J.P. 387;
   (1953) 97 S.J. 486; [1953] 2 All E.R. 449; (1953) 51 L.G.R. 457, H.L.; affirming
   [1952] 2 Q.B. 701, C.A.; varying [1952] 1 T.L.R. 507 577
Launchbury v. Morgans. See Morgans v. Launchbury.
Lavery v. Plessey Telecommunications Ltd. [1982] I.R.L.R. 180 .... 107, 108
Lawlor v. Union of Post Office Workers [1965] Ch. 712; [1965] 2 W.L.R. 579; (1965) 108
   S.J. 879; [1965] 1 All E.R. 353 .... 430, 438, 439
Lawrence v. Newham London Borough Council [1978] I.C.R. 10; [1977] I.R.L.R. 396,
   E.A.T. 28, 29, 50
Laws v. London Chronicle (Indicator Newspapers) Ltd. [1959] 1 W.L.R. 698; (1959) 103
   S.J. 470; [1959] 2 All E.R. 285, C.A. 53, 93, 159, 243, 456
Leach v. Standard Telephones and Cables Ltd. [1966] 1 W.L.R. 1392; (1966) 110 S.J.
   465; [1966] 2 All E.R. 523; (1966) 1 K.I.R. 27 585
Leadbitter v. Hodge Finance Ltd. [1982] 2 All E.R. 167 595
Leall v. APEX [1982] I.R.L.R. 102 211
Learoyd v. Brook [1891] 1 Q.B. 431; 60 L.J.Q.B. 373; 64 L.T. 458; 55 J.P. 265; 39 W.R.
   480; 7 T.L.R. 236 21
Leary v. National Union of Vehicle Builders [1971] Ch. 34; [1970] 3 W.L.R. 434; [1970]
   2 All E.R. 713; (1970) 9 K.I.R. 137 .... 432, 436, 437, 445

Lee v. Barry High Ltd. [1970] 1 W.L.R. 1549; (1970) 114 S.J. 825; [1970] 3 All E.R.
1041; (1970) 9 K.I.R. 187; [1971] T.R. 3, C.A. 145
—— v. Nottinghamshire County Council. See Nottinghamshire County Council v. Lee.
—— v. Showman's Guild of Great Britain [1952] 2 Q.B. 329; [1952] 1 T.L.R. 1115;
(1952) 96 S.J. 296; [1952] 1 All E.R. 1175, C.A. 404, 424, 427, 430, 438
Leech v. Gartside (1885) 1 T.L.R. 391 128
Lees v. Greaves (Arthur) (Lees) Ltd. [1974] I.C.R. 501; (1975) 2 All E.R. 393; [1974]
I.T.R. 91; [1975] K.I.L.R. 37; [1974] I.R.L.R. 93, C.A.; reversing [1973] I.C.R.
90, N.I.R.C. 167
Leesh River Tea v. British India Steam Navigation Co. Ltd. [1967] 2 Q.B. 250; [1966] 3
W.L.R. 642; (1966) 110 S.J. 633; [1966] 3 All E.R. 593; [1966] 2 Lloyd's Rep. 193,
C.A.; reversing [1966] 1 Lloyd's Rep. 450 604
Leigh v. National Union of Railwaymen [1970] Ch. 326; [1970] 2 W.L.R. 60; (1970) 113
S.J. 852; [1969] 3 All E.R. 1249; (1969) 8 K.I.R. 629 .... 438, 444
Leonard v. Simo Securities [1972] 1 W.L.R. 80; (1971) 115 S.J. 911; [1971] 3 All E.R.
1318, C.A.; reversing (1971) 115 S.J. 811 196
Lesney Products and Co. Ltd. v. Nolan [1977] I.C.R. 235; (1976) 12 I.T.R. 6; [1977]
I.R.L.R. 77, C.A. 274, 275, 278
Letts (Charles) and Co. Ltd. v. Howard [1982] I.R.L.R. 248 .... 209, 212
Lewis Shops v. Wiggins [1973] I.C.R. 335; [1974] I.T.R. 55; (1974) 14 K.I.R. 528; [1973]
I.R.L.R. 205; N.I.R.C.; reversing sub nom. Wiggins (F.) v. Lewis Shops Group,
The [1973] I.R.L.R. 114 218
Leyland Shipping Co. v. Norwich Union Fire Insurance Society [1918] A.C. 350; 87
L.J.K.B. 395; 118 L.T. 120; 34 T.L.R. 221; 62 S.J. 307; [1918–19] All E.R. Rep.
443; 14 Asp. M.L.C. 258, H.L.; affirming [1917] 1 K.B. 873 584
Lifeguard Assurance v. Zadrozny (J.J.) (1977) 12 I.T.R. 141; [1977] I.R.L.R. 56,
E.A.T. 247
Liff v. Peasley [1980] 1 W.L.R. 781; (1979) 124 S.J. 360; [1980] 1 All E.R. 623, C.A. 596
Limpus v. London General Omnibus Co. (1862) 1 H. & C. 526; 32 L.J.Ex. 34; 7 L.T.
641; 27 J.P. 147; 11 W.R. 149; 158 E.R. 993; 9 Jur.(N.S.) 333; previous
proceedings (1861) 2 F. & F. 640 605
Line v. White (C.E.) and Co. [1969] I.T.R. 336, D.C. 273
Lipton (L.) Ltd. v. Marlborough [1979] I.R.L.R. 179, E.A.T. 184
Lister v. Romford Ice and Cold Storage Co. [1957] A.C. 555; [1957] 2 W.L.R. 158;
(1957) 121 J.P. 98; (1957) 101 S.J. 106; [1957] 1 All E.R. 125; [1956] 2 Lloyd's
Rep. 505, H.L.; affirming [1956] 2 Q.B. 180 .... 49, 97, 98, 99
Lister & Co. v. Stubbs (1890) 45 Ch.D. 1; 59 L.J.Ch. 570; 63 L.T. 75; 38 W.R. 548; 6
T.L.R. 317, C.A. 98
Littlewoods Organisation Ltd. v. Harris [1977] 1 W.L.R. 1472; (1977) 121 S.J. 727;
[1978] 1 All E.R. 1026, C.A. 83
Liverpool Area Health Authority (Teaching) Central & Southern District v. Edwards
[1977] I.R.L.R. 471, E.A.T. 222
Liverpool City Council v. Irwin [1976] Q.B. 319; [1975] 3 W.L.R. 663; (1975) 119 S.J.
612; [1975] 3 All E.R. 658; (1975) 74 L.G.R. 21; (1975) 31 P. & C.R. 34, C.A.;
varied [1977] A.C. 239, H.L. 50, 52
Liverpool Taxi Owners' Association, Re. See R. v. Liverpool Corporation, ex p.
Liverpool Taxi Fleet Operators' Association.
Lloyd v. Brassey [1969] 2 Q.B. 98; [1969] 2 W.L.R. 310; (1969) 112 S.J. 984; [1969] 1 All
E.R. 382; (1969) 5 K.I.R. 393, C.A.; reversing [1968] 2 Q.B. 832, D.C. 146, 148
Lloyde v. West Midlands Gas Board [1971] 1 W.L.R. 749; (1971) 115 S.J. 227; [1971]
2 All E.R. 1240, C.A. 571
Loats v. Maple (1903) 88 L.T. 288 178
Lock v. Baker (1851) 18 L.T.(o.s.) 81 21
Logabax Ltd. v. Titherley (R.H.) [1977] I.C.R. 369; (1977) 12 I.T.R. 158; [1977]
I.R.L.R. 97, E.A.T. 189
Logan v. G.U.S. Transport Ltd. [1969] I.T.R. 287 146
Loman and Henderson v. Merseyside Transport Service Ltd. (1968) 3 I.T.R. 108 ..... 31, 373
London Borough of Barnet v. Nothman. See Nothman Barnet London Borough Council.
London Borough of Merton v. Gardiner. See Merton London Borough Council v.
Gardiner.
London Borough of Redbridge v. Fisherman. See Redbridge London Borough Council
v. Fisherman.

London County Council v. Cattermoles (Garages) Ltd. [1953] 1 W.L.R. 997; (1953) 97
S.J. 505; [1953] 2 All E.R. 582; 1953 S.L.T. 185, C.A. 607
London Passenger Board v. Upson [1949] A.C. 155; [1949] L.J.R. 238; (1949) 93 S.J. 40;
[1949] 1 All E.R. 60; (1949) 65 T.L.R. 9; (1949) 47 L.G.R. 333, H.L.; affirming
[1947] K.B. 930, C.A.; affirming on different grounds (1947) 176 L.T. 356 553
London Transport Executive v. Clarke [1981] I.C.R. 355; (1981) 125 S.J. 306; [1981]
I.R.L.R. 166, C.A.; reversing [1980] I.C.R. 532, E.A.T. 158, 163, 192
Lonrho Ltd. v. Shell Petroleum Co. Ltd. [1981] 3 W.L.R. 33; (1981) 125 S.J. 429; [1981]
2 All E.R. 456; H.L.; affirming (1981) 125 S.J. 255, C.A.; affirming [1981]
Com.L.R. 6 484
Losinska v. Civil and Public Services Association [1976] I.C.R. 473, C.A. 445
Lotus Cars Ltd. v. Sutcliffe and Stratton [1982] I.R.L.R. 381 301
Low (Wm.) & Co. v. MacCuish [1979] I.R.L.R. 458, E.A.T. 199
Lowndes v. Specialist Heavy Engineering Ltd. [1977] I.C.R. 1; (1976) 8 Build.L.R. 76,
E.A.T. 208, 209, 213
Lovelidge v. Anselm Odling & Sons Ltd. [1967] 2 Q.B. 351; [1967] 2 W.L.R. 585; (1967)
111 S.J. 132; [1967] 1 All E.R. 459; (1969) 2 K.I.R. 6 ....558, 563
Lucas v. Lucas [1943] P. 68 18
—— v. Mason (1875) L.R. 10. Exch. 251; 44 L.J.Exch. 145; 33 L.T. 13; 39 J.P. 663; 23
W.R. 924 495
Lumley v. Gye (1853) 2 E. & B. 216; 22 L.J.Q.B. 463; 17 Jur. 827; 1 W.R. 432; 18 E.R.
749 472
—— v. Wagner [1852] 1 De G.M. & G. 604; 21 L.J.Ch. 898; 19 L.T.(o.s.) 264; 16 Jur.
871; 42 E.R. 687, L.C. 176
Lyford v. Turquand (Liquidator of G. A. Sprott) [1966] I.T.R. 544; [1966] 1 K.I.R.
736 301
Lyons (J.) & Sons v. Wilkins [1896] 1 Ch. 811; 65 L.J.Ch. 601; 74 L.T. 358; 60 J.P. 325;
45 W.R. 19; 12 T.L.R. 278; 40 S.J. 372, C.A.; subsequent proceedings [1899] 1 Ch.
255, C.A. 453, 521, 523, 527

M. & S. Drapers Ltd. (A. Firm) v. Reynolds [1957] 1 W.L.R. 9; (1957) 101 S.J. 44;
[1956] 3 All E.R. 814, C.A. 84, 85
McArdle v. Andmac Roofing [1967] 1 W.L.R. 356; (1967) 111 S.J. 37; [1967] 1 All E.R.
583, C.A.; varying in part, affirming in part [1966] 3 All E.R. 241 ....541, 570, 580,
584, 603
Macarthys v. Smith [1981] Q.B. 180; [1980] I.C.R. 672; [1980] 3 W.L.R. 929; (1980) 124
S.J. 808; [1981] 1 All E.R. 111; [1980] 2 C.M.L.R. 217; [1980] I.R.L.R. 209,
C.A. 306
McCabe v. Ninth District Council of the County of Lanark [1973] I.R.L.R. 75 226
McCafferty v. Metropolitan Police Receiver [1977] I.C.R. 799; [1977] 1 W.L.R. 1073;
(1977) 121 S.J. 678; [1977] 2 All E.R. 756, C.A. 595, 596
McCaffrey v. Jeavons (E.E.) & Co. Ltd. [1967] I.T.R. 636 .... 96, 281
McCall v. Castleton Crafts [1979] I.R.L.R. 218 ....219, 223
McCartney v. Kellogg International Corporation (unreported) 144
McClelland v. Northern Ireland General Health Services Board [1957] 1 W.L.R. 594;
(1957) 101 S.J. 355; [1957] 2 All E.R. 129; [1957] N.I. 100, H.L.; reversing [1956]
N.I. 127 ....171, 175
McConnell v. Bolik [1979] I.R.L.R. 422, E.A.T. 26
McCormick v. Horsepower Ltd. [1981] I.C.R. 535; [1981] 1 W.L.R. 993; (1981) 125 S.J.
375; [1981] 2 All E.R. 746; [1981] I.R.L.R. 217, C.A.; affirming [1980] I.C.R.
278, E.A.T. 242, 489
McCulloch (R.H.) Ltd. v. Moore [1968] 1 Q.B. 360; [1967] 2 W.L.R. 1366; (1967) 111
S.J. 213; [1967] 2 All E.R. 290, (1967) 2 K.I.R. 160, D.C. 54
McDonald v. South Cambridgeshire R.D.C. [1973] I.C.R. 611; [1973] I.T.R. 557; [1973]
I.R.L.R. 308, N.I.R.C. 168
—— v. Twiname (John) [1953] 2 Q.B. 304; [1953] 3 W.L.R. 347; (1953) 97 S.J. 505;
[1953] 2 All E.R. 589, C.A. 20
McGhee v. National Coal Board [1973] 1 W.L.R. 1; (1973) 116 S.J. 967, [1972] 3 All
E.R. 1008; (1972) 13 K.I.R. 471, H.L.; reversing 1972 S.L.T. (Notes) 61 578
MacGregor Wallcoverings Ltd. v. Turton [1978] I.C.R. 5410 332
McGuiness v. Key Markets Ltd. (1973) 13 K.I.R. 249..593, 594

Machray v. Stewarts and Lloyds Ltd. [1965] 1 W.L.R. 602; (1965) 109 S.J. 270; [1964]
  3 All E.R. 716 578
McInnes v. Onslow-Fane [1978] 1 W.L.R. 520; (1978) 122 S.J. 844; [1978] 3 All E.R.
  211..407, 429
Mack Trucks (Britain) Ltd., Re [1967] 1 W.L.R. 780; (1967) 111 S.J. 435; [1967] 1 All
  E.R. 977 181
Mackay v. Dick (1881) 6 App.Cas. 251; 29 W.R. 541, H.L. 163
—— v. Ozonair Engineering Co. Ltd. (1981) 131 New L.J. 481 564
Maclaughlan v. Paterson (Alexander) Ltd. [1968] I.T.R. 251 277
Maclea v. Essex Line Ltd. (1933) 45 Ll.L.Rep. 254 ....33, 51
McLean v. Workers Union, The (1929) 1 Ch. 602; 98 L.J.Ch. 293; 141 L.T. 83; 73 S.J.
  190; 45 T.L.R. 256; [1929] All E.R. Rep. 468 430
MacLelland v. National Union of Journalists; Mills v. National Union of Journalists
  [1975] I.C.R. 116 442
Macleod v. Rostron (John) & Sons [1972] I.T.R. 144, N.I.R.C. 146
McLoughlin v. O'Brian [1982] 2 W.L.R. 982 575
Maclure, Ex p., Re English & Scottish Marine Insurance Co. (1870) L.R. 5 Ch. App.
  737; 39 L.J.Ch. 685; 23 L.T. 685; 18 W.R. 1123, C.A. 57
McManus v. Crickett (1800) 1 East 106; 102 E.R. 43 568
McMath v. Rimmer Bros. (Liverpool) Ltd. [1962] 1 W.L.R. 1; (1962) 106 S.J. 110; [1961]
  3 All E.R. 1154; (1962) 60 L.G.R. 116, C.A. 585
McPhail v. Gibson [1977] I.C.R. 42, E.A.T. 218
McPhee v. General Motors Ltd. (1970) 8 K.I.R. 885 593
McShane v. Express Newspapers Ltd. [1979] I.R.L.R. 79 506
McWilliams v. Arrol (Sir William) & Co. Ltd. [1962] 1 W.L.R. 295; (1962) 106 S.J. 218;
  1962 S.C. 70; 1962 S.L.T. 121; [1962] 1 All E.R. 623, H.L.; affirming 1961 S.C.
  134...577, 578, 587, 594
Maher v. Fram Gerrard Ltd. [1974] I.C.R. 31; (1973) 117 S.J. 911; [1974] 1 All E.R. 449;
  [1974] I.T.R. 36; (1973) 16 K.I.R. 62, N.I.R.C. 184
Maidment v. Cooper and Co. (Birmingham) Ltd. [1978] I.C.R. 1094; (1978) 13 I.T.R.
  458; [1978] I.R.L.R. 462, E.A.T. 311
Mailway (Southern) Ltd. v. Willsher [1978] I.C.R. 511; (1977) 122 S.J. 79; [1978]
  I.R.L.R. 322, E.A.T. 12
Malone v. Metropolitan Police Commissioner [1979] Ch. 344; [1979] 2 W.L.R. 700;
  (1979) 69 Cr.App.R. 168; sub nom. Malone v. Commissioner of Police for the
  Metropolis (1979) 123 S.J. 303; sub nom. Malone v. Commissioner of Police of the
  Metropolis (No. 2) [1979] 2 All E.R. 620 81
Malloch v. Aberdeen Corporation [1971] 1 W.L.R. 1578; (1971) 115 S.J. 756; [1971]
  2 All E.R. 1278; 1971 S.C. 85, H.L. 15
Managers (Holborn) Ltd. v. Hohne (1977) 12 I.T.R. 379; [1977] I.R.L.R. 230,
  E.A.T. 55, 95
Manders v. Showman's Guild of Great Britain The Times, November 4, 1966 424
Manning v. Wale (R. and H.) (Export) Ltd. [1979] I.C.R. 433, E.A.T. 260
Mansfield Hosiery Mills Ltd. v. Bromley (M.) [1977] I.R.L.R. 301, E.A.T. 221
Manubens v. Leon [1919] 1 K.B. 208; 88 L.J.K.B. 311; 120 L.T. 279; 35 T.L.R. 94; 63
  S.J. 102; [1918–19] All E.R. Rep. 792, D.C. 177
Marbe v. Edwardes (George) (Daly's Theatre) Ltd. [1928] 1 K.B. 269; 96 L.J.K.B. 980;
  138 L.T. 51; 43 T.L.R. 809; [1927] All E.R. Rep. 253, C.A. 57
Marchant v. Earley Town Council [1979] I.C.R. 891; [1979] I.R.L.R. 311, E.A.T. 195
Marcusfield (A. & B.) v. Melhuish [1977] I.R.L.R. 484, E.A.T. 301
Margolis v. Burke 53 N.Y.S. 2d 157 (1945) 422
Marina Shipping Ltd. v. Laughton [1982] 1 All E.R. 481 512
Maris v. Rotherham Corporation [1974] I.C.R. 435; [1974] 2 All E.R. 776; [1974] I.T.R.
  288; (1974) 16 K.I.R. 466; [1975] I.R.L.R. 147, N.I.R.C. 261
Market Investigations v. Minister of Social Security [1969] 2 Q.B. 173; [1969] 2 W.L.R.
  1; (1968) 112 S.J. 905; [1968] 3 All E.R. 732..9, 11
Marley Tile Co. Ltd. v. Johnson [1982] I.R.L.R. 75 ....52, 53
—— v. Shaw [1980] I.C.R. 72; (1979) 123 S.J. 803; [1980] I.R.L.R. 25, C.A.; reversing
  [1978] I.C.R. 828; (1978) 13 I.T.R. 257; [1978] I.R.L.R. 238, E.A.T. 120, 121,
                                                                                                    230, 424

Marriot v. Oxford and District Co-operative Society (No. 2) [1970] 1 Q.B. 186; [1969]
    3 W.L.R. 984; (1969) 113 S.J. 655; [1969] 3 All E.R. 1126; (1969) 7 K.I.R. 219;
    [1969] I.T.R. 377, C.A.; reversing [1969] 1 W.L.R. 254, D.C. 186, 282, 285, 286
Marshall v. English Electric Co. Ltd. (1945) 173 L.T. 134; 109 J.P. 145; 61 T.L.R. 379; 89
    S.J. 315 [1945] 1 All E.R. 633; 43 L.G.R. 275, C.A. 173
—— v. Gotham Co. Ltd. [1954] A.C. 360; [1954] 2 W.L.R. 812; (1954) 98 S.J. 268;
    [1954] 1 All E.R. 937, H.L.; affirming [1953] 1 Q.B. 167, C.A.....................538, 539
—— v. Harland and Wolff Ltd. [1972] I.C.R. 101; [1972] 1 W.L.R. 899; (1972) 116 S.J.
    484; [1972] 2 All E.R. 715; [1972] I.T.R. 150; [1972] 1 R.L.R. 90, N.I.R.C. 178
Marshall (Thomas) (Exports) Ltd. v. Guinle [1979] Ch. 227; [1979] F.S.R. 208; [1978]
    I.C.R. 905; [1978] 3 W.L.R. 116; (1978) 122 S.J. 295; [1978] 3 All E.R. 193; [1978]
    I.R.L.R. 174...157, 158, 466
Marrison v. Bell [1939] 2 K.B. 187; 108 L.J.K.B. 481; 160 L.T. 276; 103 J.P. 135; 55
    T.L.R. 475; 83 S.J. 176; [1939] 1 All E.R. 745; 37 L.G.R. 257, C.A. 61, 63, 64
Martin v. B.S.C. Footwear (Supplies) Ltd. [1978] I.R.L.R. 95 250
—— v. Scottish Transport and General Workers' Union [1952] W.N. 142; [1952]
    1 T.L.R. 677; (1952) 96 S.J. 212; [1952] 1 All E.R. 691; 1952 S.C. 92; 1952 S.L.T.
    224, H.L.; affirming 1951 S.C. 129...406, 407, 436
—— v. Solus Schall [1979] I.R.L.R. 1, E.A.T. 45
—— v. Yorkshire Imperial Metals Ltd. [1978] I.R.L.R. 440, E.A.T. 220, 221
Mason v. Provident Clothing and Supply Co. Ltd. [1913] A.C. 724; 82 L.J.K.B. 1153;
    109 L.T. 449; 29 T.L.R. 727, 57 S.J. 739; [1911–13] All E.R. Rep. 400, H.L.;
    reversing [1913] 1 K.B. 65, C.A. 79, 84
—— v. Williams and Williams and Turton (Thomas) & Sons [1955] 1 W.L.R. 549; (1955)
    99 S.J. 338; [1955] 1 All E.R. 808 ....570, 572
—— v. Wimpey Waste Management Ltd. [1982] I.R.L.R. 454 262
Massey v. Crown Life Assurance Co. [1978] I.C.R. 590; [1978] 1 W.L.R. 676; (1978) 122
    S.J. 791; [1978] 2 All E.R. 576; (1978) 13 I.T.R.S; [1978] I.R.L.R. 31, C.A. 4, 13
Matthews v. Kuwait Bechtel Corporation [1959] 2 Q.B. 57; [1959] 2 W.L.R. 702; (1959)
    103 S.J. 393; [1959] 2 All E.R. 345, C.A. 573
Meade v. Haringey London Borough Council [1979] I.C.R. 494; [1979] 1 W.L.R. 637;
    (1979) 123 S.J. 216, [1979] 2 All E.R. 1016; (1979) 77 L.G.R. 577, C.A. 484
Meadows v. Stanbury (J.) Ltd. [1970] I.T.R. 57 146
Meadows (C.) v. Faithfull Overalls [1977] I.R.L.R. 330 102
Mears v. Safecar Security Ltd. [1982] I.R.L.R. 183; affirming [1981] I.C.R. 409; [1981]
    I.R.L.R. 99, E.A.T... 45, 51, 63
Meek v. Allen (J.) Rubber Co.; Same v. Secretary of State for Employment [1980]
    I.R.L.R. 21, E.A.T..285, 294
—— v. Port of London Authority [1918] 1 Ch. 415; affirmed [1978] 2 Ch. 97, C.A. 33
Melon v. Powe (Hector) Ltd. (1980) 124 S.J. 827; [1981] 1 All E.R. 313; [1981] I.C.R.
    43; [1980] I.R.L.R. 477, H.L.; affirming [1980] I.R.L.R. 80, Ct. of Session;
    reversing [1978] I.R.L.R. 258, E.A.T..149, 150, 151
Menzies v. Smith & McLaurin Ltd. [1980] I.R.L.R. 180, E.A.T. 113
Mercia Rubber Mouldings v. Lingwood [1974] I.C.R. 256; [1974] I.R.L.R. 82,
    N.I.R.C. 184
Meridian Ltd. v. Gomersall [1977] I.C.R. 597; (1977) 121 T.R. 323; [1977] I.R.L.R. 425,
    E.A.T. 218
Meriton v. Hornsby (1747) 1 Ves. Sen. 48, 27 E.R. 883 21
Merrington v. Ironbridge Metal Works (1952) 117 J.P. 23; [1952] 2 All E.R. 1101 589
Mersey Dock and Harbour Co. v. Verrinder [1982] I.R.L.R. 152.......................524, 526
Mersey Docks and Harbour Board v. Coggins and Griffith (Liverpool) Ltd. [1947] A.C.
    1; 115 L.J.K.B. 465; 175 L.T. 270; 62 T.L.R. 533; [1946] 2 All E.R. 345, H.L.;
    affirming [1945] K.B. 301..600, 601, 602, 603
Merseyside and North Wales Electricity Board v. Taylor [1975] I.C.R. 185; (1975) 119
    S.J. 272; [1975] I.T.R. 52; [1975] I.R.L.R. 60 215
Merton London Borough Council v. Gardiner [1980] I.R.L.R. 302, E.A.T.; affirmed
    [1981] Q.B. 269 150
Methven and Musiolik v. Cow Industrial Polymers Ltd. [1980] I.R.L.R. 289; sub nom.
    Methven v. Cow Industrial Polymers Ltd. [1980] I.C.R. 463; (1980) 124 S.J. 374,
    C.A.; affirming [1979] I.C.R. 613 314
Meyer Dunmore International Ltd. v. Rogers [1978] I.R.L.R. 167, E.A.T. 220
Middleton v. Fowler (1698) 1 Salk 282; 91 E.R. 247 568

Midland and Low Moor Iron and Steel Co. Ltd. *v.* Cross [1965] A.C. 343; [1964]
    3 W.L.R. 1180; (1964) 108 S.J. 938; (1964) 63 L.G.R. 81; [1964] 3 All E.R. 752,
    H.L.; affirming [1964] 2 W.L.R. 1365, D.C. 559, 563
Midland Cold Storage Ltd. *v.* Steer [1972] Ch. 630; [1972] 3 W.L.R. 700; (1972) 116 S.J.
    783; [1972] 3 All E.R. 941; [1972] I.C.R. 435; (1972) 13 K.I.R. 286,
    N.I.R.C. 385, 386, 389, 520
—— *v.* Turner [1972] I.C.R. 230; (1972) 116 S.J. 783; [1972] 3 All E.R. 773,
    N.I.R.C. 389, 501, 522
Midland Counties District Bank Ltd. *v.* Attwood [1905] 1 Ch. 357; 74 L.J. Ch. 286; 92
    L.T. 360; 21 T.L.R. 175; [1904–7] All E.R. Rep. 648; 12 Mans. 20 180
Midland Electric Manufacturing Co. Ltd. *v.* Kanji [1980] I.R.L.R. 185, E.A.T. 184
Midland Plastics Ltd. *v.* Till [1983] I.C.R. 118; [1983] I.R.L.R. 9 ....246, 466
Midland Foot Comfort Centre Ltd. *v.* Moppett [1973] I.C.R. 219; *sub nom.* Midland
    Foot Comfort Centre Ltd. *v.* Richmond [1973] 3 All E.R. 294 ....248, 270
Millar *v.* Taylor (1769) 4 Burr. 2303; 98 E.R. 201 81
Millard *v.* Serck Tubes Ltd. [1969] 1 W.L.R. 211; (1969) 112 S.J. 924; [1969] 1 All E.R.
    598; (1968) 5 K.I.R. 389, C.A. 561
Miller *v.* Executors of Graham (John C.) [1978] I.R.L.R. 309, E.A.T. 197
—— *v.* Thornton (Harry) (Lollies) Ltd. [1978] I.R.L.R. 430 103
Minards *v.* Courtaulds Ltd. [1967] I.T.R. 219 141
Minister of Social Security *v.* Amalgamated Engineering Union [1967] 1 A.C. 725; [1967]
    2 W.L.R. 516; (1967) 111 S.J. 33; [1967] 1 All E.R. 210, H.L.; affirming *sub nom.*
    R. *v.* Deputy Industrial Injuries Commissioner, *ex p.* Amalgamated Engineering
    Union, *Re* Dowling [1967] 1 Q.B. 202, C.A. 619, 623, 632
Ministers of United Methodist Church, Employment of, *Re* (1912) 107 L.T. 143; 56 S.J.
    687; 28 T.L.R. 539; 6 B.W.C.C.N.1 16
Ministry of Defence *v.* Jeremiah [1980] Q.B. 87; [1980] I.C.R. 13; [1979] 3 W.L.R. 857;
    (1979) 123 S.J. 735; [1979] 3 All E.R. 833; [1979] I.R.L.R. 436, C.A.; affirming
    [1978] I.C.R. 984; (1978) 122 S.J. 642; [1978] I.R.L.R. 402, E.A.T. 326, 327, 328,
                                                                                                          337, 343
Mirza *v.* Ford Motor Co. Ltd. [1981] I.C.R. 757, C.A. 557
Mitchell *v.* Old Hall Exchange and Palantine Club Ltd., The [1978] I.R.L.R. 160,
    E.A.T. 202
—— *v.* Westin (W.S.) Ltd. [1965] 1 W.L.R. 297; (1965) 109 S.J. 49; [1965] 1 All E.R.
    657; (1965) 63 L.G.R. 219, C.A. 564
Moberly *v.* Commonwealth Hall (University of London) [1977] I.C.R. 791; [1977]
    I.R.L.R. 176, E.A.T. 322
Mole Mining Ltd. *v.* Jenkins (H.G.) [1972] I.C.R. 282; [1972] I.T.R. 340 301
Monarch Electric Ltd. *v.* McIntyre [1968] N.I. 163, C.A. 142, 144
Moncrieff (D.G.) (Farmers) *v.* MacDonald [1978] I.R.L.R. 112; (1978) 13 I.T.R. 222,
    E.A.T. 201
Monie *v.* Coral Racing Ltd. [1980] I.C.R. 109; [1980] I.R.L.R. 464, C.A.; affirming
    [1979] I.C.R. 254; [1979] I.R.L.R. 54, E.A.T. 198, 199, 227
Monk *v.* Redwing Aircraft Co. Ltd. [1942] 1 K.B. 182; 111 L.J.K.B. 277; 166 L.T. 42; 58
    T.L.R. 94; [1942] 1 All E.R. 133, C.A. 176
Montreal Locomotive Works Ltd. *v.* Montreal and Att.-Gen. for Canada [1947]
    1 D.L.R. 161 9
Moon *v.* Homeworthy Furniture (Northern) Ltd. [1977] I.C.R. 117; [1976] I.R.L.R. 298,
    E.A.T. 201, 204, 248, 280
Moorcock, The (1889) 14 P.D. 64 ....45, 48
Mordecai *v.* Beatus (Jacob) Ltd. (1975) 18 Man.Law. 34, [1975] I.R.L.R. 170 35
Morgan *v.* Fry [1968] 2 Q.B. 710; [1968] 3 W.L.R. 506; (1968) 112 S.J. 671; [1968] 3 All
    E.R. 452; (1968) 5 K.I.R. 275; *sub nom.* Morgan *v.* Fry, Crispin, Crone, Harrall,
    Mehegan and Bilson [1968] 2 Lloyd's Rep. 82, C.A.; reversing in part [1967]
    3 W.L.R. 65. Petition for appeal to House of Lords allowed. 243, 244,
                            455, 456, 457, 458, 459, 475, 480, 481, 482, 500, 517
Morgans *v.* Launchbury [1973] A.C. 127; [1972] 2 W.L.R. 1217; (1972) 116 S.J. 396;
    [1972] 2 All E.R. 606; [1972] R.T.R. 406; [1972] 1 Lloyd's Rep. 483, H.L.;
    reversing *sub nom.* Launchbury *v.* Morgans [1971] 2 Q.B. 245; [1971] 2 W.L.R.
    602; (1970) 115 S.J. 96; [1971] 1 All E.R. 642; [1971] 1 Lloyd's Rep. 197; [1971]
    R.T.R. 97, C.A. 495, 598, 599
Moriarty *v.* Regents Garage [1921] 1 K.B. 423, reversed [1921] 2 K.B. 766, C.A. 61

Morison v. Moat (1851) 9 Hare 241; 20 L.J.Ch. 513; 18 L.T.(o.s.) 28; 15 Jur. 787; 68
 E.R. 492; affirmed (1852) 21 L.J.Ch. 248 73
Morleys of Brixton Ltd. v. Minott [1982] I.R.L.R. 270 200
Morren v. Swinton and Pendlebury Borough Council [1965] 1 W.L.R. 576; [1965] 2 All
 E.R. 349; (1965) 63 L.G.R. 288, D.C. 6
Morris v. Martin (C.W.) & Sons Ltd. [1966] 1 Q.B. 716; [1965] 3 W.L.R. 276; (1965) 109
 S.J. 451; [1965] 2 All E.R. 725; [1965] 2 Lloyd's Rep. 63, C.A. 604
—— v. West Hartlepool Steam Navigation Ltd. [1956] A.C. 552; [1956] 1 W.L.R. 177;
 (1956) 100 S.J. 129; [1956] 1 All E.R. 385; [1956] 1 Lloyd's Rep. 76, H.L.;
 reversing [1954] 2 Lloyd's Rep. 507, C.A. 579
Morris (Herbert) Ltd. v. Saxelby [1916] 1 A.C. 688, H.L.; previous proceedings [1915]
 2 Ch. 57 .... 79, 84
Morrish v. Henlys (Folkestone) [1973] I.C.R. 482; [1973] 2 All E.R. 137; [1973] I.T.R.
 167, N.I.R.C. 72, 95
Morton Sundour Fabrics Ltd. v. Shaw (1967) 2 K.I.R. 1; [1966] C.L.Y. 4472, D.C. 183,
 184, 265, 267
Mourton v. Poulter [1930] 2 K.B. 183 612
Mulholland v. Bexwell Estates Co. [1950] W.N. 502; (1950) 66 T.L.R. (Pt. 2) 764; (1950)
 94 S.J. 671 .... 171, 172
Mullard v. Ben Line Steamers Ltd. [1970] 1 W.L.R. 1414; (1970) 114 S.J. 570; (1970) 9
 K.I.R. 111; [1971] 2 All E.R. 424; [1970] 2 Lloyd's Rep. 121, C.A.; reversing
 [1969] 2 Lloyd's Rep. 631 593
Mulvenna v. Admiralty 1926 S.C. 824 18
Murphy v. Birrell (A.) & Sons Ltd. [1978] I.R.L.R. 458, E.A.T. 144
Mustad (O.) & Son v. Allcock (S.) & Co. and Dosen. See Mustad (O.) & Son v. Dosen.
—— v. Dosen [1964] 1 W.L.R. 109n.; [1963] R.P.C. 41; sub nom. Mustad (O.) & Son v.
 Allcock (S.) & Co. and Dosen [1963] 3 All E.R. 416, H.L. 76, 78

N.W.L. Ltd. v. Woods; N.W.L. Ltd. v. Nelson [1979] I.C.R. 867; [1979] 1 W.L.R. 1294;
 (1979) 123 S.J. 751; [1979] 3 All E.R. 614; [1979] I.R.L.R. 478; [1980] 1 Lloyd's
 Rep. 1, H.L.; affirming [1979] I.C.R. 321, C.A. 499, 501,
 502, 504, 505, 506
Nagle v. Feilden [1966] 2 Q.B. 633; [1966] 2 W.L.R. 1027; (1966) 110 S.J. 286; [1966]
 1 All E.R. 689, C.A. 58, 83, 303, 392, 404, 405, 413, 477, 482
Nash v. Ryan Plant International Ltd. [1977] I.C.R. 560; (1977) 121 S.J. 374; [1978] 1 All
 E.R. 492; (1977) 12 I.T.R. 336, E.A.T. 265
Nassé v. Science Research Council; Vyas v. Leyland Cars. See Science Research Council
 v. Nassé; Leyland Cars v. Vyas.
National Coal Board v. England [1954] A.C. 403; [1954] 2 W.L.R. 400; (1954) 98 S.J.
 176; [1954] 1 All E.R. 546, H.L.; varying [1953] 1 Q.B. 724, C.A. 591
—— v. Galley [1958] 1 W.L.R. 16; (1958) 102 S.J. 31; [1958] 1 All E.R. 91,
 C.A. 35, 466
—— v. Hughes (1959) 109 L.J. 526 94
—— v. Sherwin [1978] I.C.R. 700; [1978] I.R.L.R. 122, E.A.T. 310
National Heart and Chest Hospitals Board of Governors v. Nambiar [1981] I.C.R. 441;
 [1981] I.R.L.R. 196, E.A.T. 168
National Insurance Act 1911, Re [1912] Ch. 563; 82 L.J.Ch. 8, 107 L.T. 643; 28 T.L.R.
 579; 6 B.W.C.C.N. 3 16
National Sailors' and Firemen's Union v. Reed [1926] Ch. 536; 95 L.J.Ch. 192; 135 L.T.
 103; 42 T.L.R. 513; [1926] All E.R. Rep. 381 533
National Union of General and Municipal Workers v. Gillian [1946] K.B. 81; 115
 L.J.K.B. 43; 174 L.T. 8; 62 T.L.R. 46; 89 S.J. 543; [1945] 2 All E.R. 593,
 C.A. 387
National Union of Gold, Silver and Allied Trades v. Albury Bros. [1979] I.C.R. 84;
 (1978) 122 S.J. 662; [1978] I.R.L.R. 504, C.A.; affirming [1978] I.C.R. 62,
 E.A.T. 295, 368
National Union of Tailors & Garment Workers v. Ingram (Charles) & Co. Ltd. [1977]
 I.C.R. 530; [1978] 1 All E.R. 1271; (1977) 12 I.T.R. 285; [1977] I.R.L.R. 147,
 E.A.T. 295, 368
National Union of Teachers v. Avon County Council [1978] I.C.R. 626; (1977) 76
 L.G.R. 403; [1978] I.R.L.R. 55, E.A.T. 297

National Vulcan Engineering Insurance Group Ltd. v. Wade [1979] Q.B. 132; [1978] I.C.R. 800; [1978] 3 W.L.R. 214; (1978) 122 S.J. 470; [1978] 3 All E.R. 121; [1978] I.R.L.R. 225, (1978) 13 I.T.R. 212, C.A.; reversing [1977] I.C.R. 455, E.A.T. 312, 315, 333

Navarro v. Moregrand Ltd. [1951] W.N. 335; [1951] 2 T.L.R. 674; (1951) S.J. 367, C.A.; reversing (1951) 157 E.G. 247 607

Navy, Army & Air Force Institutes v. Varley [1977] I.C.R. 11; [1977] 1 W.L.R. 149; (1976) S.J. 84; [1977] 1 All E.R. 840; [1976] I.R.L.R. 408; (1976) 11 I.T.R. 328, E.A.T. 305

Neepsend Steel & Tool Corporation v. Vaughan [1972] I.C.R. 278; [1972] 3 All E.R. 725; [1972] I.T.R. 371, N.I.R.C. 267

Nelson v. British Broadcasting Corp. [1977] I.C.R. 649; (1977) 121 T.R. 273; [1977] I.R.L.R. 148, C.A. 270

—— v. —— (No. 2) [1980] I.C.R. 110; (1979) 123 S.J. 552; [1979] I.R.L.R. 346, C.A. 261, 270

Newell v. Gillingham Corporation (1941) 165 L.T. 184; [1941] 1 All E.R. 552; 39 L.G.R. 191 170

Newlin Oil Co. Ltd. v. Trafford [1974] I.T.R. 324; [1974] I.R.L.R. 205, N.I.R.C. 146

Newman (R.S.) Ltd., Re, Raphael's Claim [1916] 2 Ch. 309; 85 L.J.Ch. 625; 115 L.T. 134; 60 S.J. 585; H.B.R. 129, C.A. 57, 177

Newsham v. Dunlop Textiles (No. 2) [1969] I.T.R. 268, D.C. 141

Nicoll v. Falcan Airways [1962] 1 Lloyd's Rep. 245 172

Nicholls v. Austin (Leyton) Ltd. [1946] A.C. 493; 115 L.J.K.B. 329; 175 L.T. 5; 62 T.L.R. 320; 90 S.J. 628; [1946] 2 All E.R. 628; 44 L.G.R. 287, H.L. 574

Nightingale v. Biddle Bros. Builders Ltd. (1967) 3 K.I.R. 481 167

Noble v. Gold (David) & Sons (Holdings) Ltd. [1980] I.C.R. 543; [1980] I.R.L.R. 253, C.A. 317

Noble v. Southern Ry. Co. [1940] A.C. 583; 109 L.J.K.B. 509; 164 L.T. 1; 56 T.L.R. 613; 86 S.J. 464; [1940] 2 All E.R. 383; 33 B.W.C.C. 176, H.L. 623

Nohar v. Granitstone (Galloway) Ltd. [1974] I.C.R. 273; [1974] I.T.R. 155, N.I.R.C. 260

Nokes v. Doncaster Amalgamated Collieries [1940] A.C. 1014; 109 L.J.K.B. 865; 163 L.T. 343; 56 T.L.R. 988; 85 S.J. 45; [1940] 3 All E.R. 549, H.L............173, 252, 600

Nolan v. Dental Manufacturing Co. Ltd. [1958] 1 W.L.R. 936; (1958) 102 S.J. 619; [1958] 2 All E.R. 449 587

Nordenfelt v. Maxim Nordenfelt Guns and Ammunition Co. Ltd. [1894] A.C. 535; 71 L.T. 489; 10 T.L.R. 636; [1891–4] All E.R. Rep. 1; 11 R.1, H.L.; affirming [1893] 1 Ch. 630, C.A. 83, 390

Norris v. Southampton City Council [1982] I.C.R. 177 179

North v. Pavleigh Ltd; Skeet v. Carr Mills Clothing Co. [1977] I.R.L.R. 461 ....101, 102

North East Coast Ship Repairers v. Secretary of State for Employment [1978] I.C.R. 755; (1978) 122 S.J. 348; [1978] I.R.L.R. 149; (1978) 13 I.T.R. 251, E.A.T. 272

North East Midlands Co-operative Society Ltd. v. Allen [1977] I.R.L.R. 212, E.A.T. 247

North Riding Garages v. Butterwick [1967] 2 Q.B. 56; [1967] 2 W.L.R. 571; (1967) 111 S.J. 72; [1967] 1 All E.R. 644; (1967) 1 K.I.R. 782; [1966] C.L.Y. 4474, D.C. 276

North Western Salt Co. Ltd. v. Electrolytic Alkali Co. Ltd. [1914] A.C. 461; 83 L.J.K.B. 530; 110 L.T. 852; 30 T.L.R. 313; 58 S.J. 338; [1914–15] All E.R. Rep. 752, H.L. 83

Norton v. Canadian Pacific Steamships Ltd. [1961] 1 W.L.R. 1057; (1961) 105 S.J. 442; [1961] 2 All E.R. 785; [1961] 1 Lloyd's Rep. 569, C.A. 570

Norton Tool Co. Ltd. v. Tewson [1972] I.C.R. 501; [1973] 1 W.L.R. 45; (1973) 117 S.J. 33; [1973] 1 All E.R. 183; (1972) 13 K.I.R. 328; [1973] I.T.R. 23, N.I.R.C. ...258, 259

Nothman v. Barnet London Borough Council [1979] I.C.R. 111; [1979] 1 W.L.R. 67; (1978) 123 S.J. 64; [1979] 1 All E.R. 142; (1978) 77 L.G.R. 89; [1979] I.R.L.R. 35, H.L.; affirming [1978] I.C.R. 336, C.A.; reversing [1977] I.R.L.R. 398, E.A.T. 134

Nottingham v. Aldridge [1971] 2 Q.B. 739; [1971] 3 W.L.R. 1; (1971) 115 S.J. 328; [1971] 2 All E.R. 751; (1971) 10 K.I.R. 252; [1971] R.T.R. 242; [1971] 1 Lloyd's Rep. 424...599, 607

Nottinghamshire Area Health Authority v. Gray (No. 2) (1981) E.A.T. 163/81 140

Nottinghamshire County Council v. Lee [1980] I.C.R. 635; (1980) 78 L.G.R. 568; sub nom. Lee v. Nottinghamshire County Council [1980] I.R.L.R. 284, C.A.; reversing [1979] I.C.R. 818 280

Nova Plastics Ltd. v. Froggatt [1982] I.R.L.R. 146...92, 93

Nu-Swift International Ltd. *v.* Mallison [1979] I.C.R. 157; [1978] I.R.L.R. 537, E.A.T. 105

O'Brien *v.* Associated Fire Alarms Ltd. [1968] 1 W.L.R. 1916; (1968) 112 S.J. 232; [1969] 1 All E.R. 93; (1969) 3 K.I.R. 223, C.A. 50, 51, 55, 95, 271, 281
—— *v.* Sim-Chem Ltd. [1980] I.C.R. 573; [1980] 1 W.L.R. 1011; (1980) 124 S.J. 560; [1980] 3 All E.R. 132; [1980] I.R.L.R. 373, H.L.; reversing [1980] I.C.R. 429, C.A.; reversing [1979] I.C.R. 13 311
O'Conell *v.* Jackson [1972] 1 Q.B. 270; [1971] 3 W.L.R. 463; (1971) 115 S.J. 742; [1971] 3 All E.R. 129; [1972] R.T.R. 51, C.A. 594
Oddy *v.* Transport Salaried Staffs Association [1973] I.C.R. 524; [1973] 3 All E.R. 610; [1973] I.T.R. 533, N.I.R.C. 374, 447
O'Grady *v.* Saper (M.) Ltd. [1940] 2 K.B. 469; 109 L.J.K.B. 785; 163 L.T. 165; 56 T.L.R. 913; 84 S.J. 501; [1940] 3 All E.R. 527, C.A. 62, 63
O'Hare *v.* Rotaprint [1980] I.C.R. 94; *sub nom.* O'Hare and Rutherford *v.* Rotaprint [1980] I.R.L.R. 47, E.A.T. 204, 278, 280, 281
Ojutiku and Oburoni *v.* Manpower Services Commission [1982] I.R.L.R. 418 .... 333, 340
Open University, The *v.* Triesman [1978] I.C.R. 524; [1978] I.R.L.R. 114, E.A.T. 154
O'Reilly *v.* Imperial Chemical Industries [1955] 1 W.L.R. 1155; (1955) 99 S.J. 778; [1955] 3 All E.R. 382; C.A.; reversing [1955] 1 W.L.R. 839 .... 601, 602
—— *v.* National Rail and Tramway Appliances Ltd. [1966] 1 All E.R. 499 591
Orman *v.* Saville Sportswear Ltd. [1960] 1 W.L.R. 1055; (1960) 104 S.J. 212; [1960] 3 All E.R. 105 62
Ormrod *v.* Crosville Motors Services Ltd. [1953] 1 W.L.R. 1120; (1953) 97 S.J. 570; [1953] 2 All E.R. 753, C.A.; affirming [1953] 1 W.L.R. 409 599
Osborne *v.* Amalgamated Society of Railway Servants [1910] A.C. 87; 79 L.J.Ch. 87; 101 L.T. 787; 26 T.L.R. 177; 54 S.J. 215; [1908–10] All E.R. Rep. 368; H.L.; affirming [1909] 1 Ch. 163, C.A.; subsequent proceedings [1911] 1 Ch. 540, C.A. 385, 391, 396
Ottoman Bank *v.* Chakarian [1930] A.C. 277; 99 L.J.P.C. 97; 142 L.T. 465, P.C. 95
Overseas Tankship (U.K.) Ltd. *v.* Miller Steamship Co. Pty (The Wagon Mound (No. 2) [1967] 1 A.C. 617, [1966] 3 W.L.R. 498, (1966) 110 S.J. 447; [1966] 2 All E.R. 709; [1966] 1 Lloyd's Rep. 657, P.C. reversing [1963] 1 Lloyd's Rep. 402 588
—— *v.* Morts Dock and Engineering Co. (The Wagon Mound) (1961) A.C. 388; [1961] 2 W.L.R. 126; 105 S.J. 85; [1961] 1 All E.R. 404; [1961] 1 Lloyd's Rep. 1, P.C.; reversing [1959] 2 Lloyd's Rep. 697 588
Owen *v.* Crown House Engineering Ltd. [1973] I.C.R. 511; [1973] 3 All E.R. 618; [1973] I.T.R. 539; (1973) 16 K.I.R. 67; [1973] I.R.L.R. 233, N.I.R.C. 448
Owen and Briggs *v.* James [1982] I.C.R. 377; [1982] I.R.L.R. 502; affirming [1981] I.R.L.R. 133 .... 323, 324
Oxley (Graham) Tool Steels Ltd. *v.* Firth [1980] I.R.L.R. 135, E.A.T. 188, 189

P.B.D.S. (National Carriers) Ltd. *v.* Filkins [1979] I.R.L.R. 356, C.A. 506
Page One Records Ltd. *v.* Britton [1967] 1 W.L.R. 157; (1968) 111 S.J. 944; *sub nom.* Page One Records Ltd. *v.* Britton (Trading as "The Troggs") [1967] 3 All E.R. 822 176
Palmanor *v.* Cedron [1978] I.C.R. 1008; (1978) 13 I.T.R. 450; [1978] I.R.L.R. 303, E.A.T. 47, 70
Pambakian *v.* Brentford Nylons Ltd. [1978] I.C.R. 665; (1978) 122 S.J. 177; E.A.T. 152
Panesar *v.* Nestlé Co. Ltd. [1980] I.C.R. 144; [1980] I.R.L.R. 64, C.A. 333
Papparis *v.* Fulton (Charles) & Co. Ltd. [1981] I.R.L.R. 104, E.A.T. 137
Paris *v.* Stepney Borough Council [1951] A.C. 367; [1951] 1 T.L.R. 25; (1951) 115 J.P. 22; (1951) 94 S.J. 837; [1951] 1 All E.R. 42; (1951) 49 L.G.R. 293; (1951) 84 Ll.L.Rep. 525, H.L.; reversing [1950] 1 K.B. 320, C.A. 576, 579
Park *v.* Wilsons & Clyde Coal Co. Ltd. 1928 S.C. 121; affirmed 1929 S.C. 38 6
Parke *v.* Daily News Ltd. [1962] Ch. 927; [1962] 3 W.L.R. 566; (1962) 106 S.J. 704; [1962] 2 All E.R. 929 125
Parker *v.* Belfast Steamship Co. Ltd. (unreported) 249
—— *v.* Clifford Dunn Ltd. [1979] I.C.R. 463; [1979] I.R.L.R. 56, E.A.T. 207, 209, 432

Parkers Bakeries Ltd. *v.* Palmer (1976) 12 I.T.R. 111; [1977] I.R.L.R. 215, E.A.T. 49, 201, 220

Parry *v.* Holst & Co. Ltd. [1978] I.T.R. 317 281

Parsons (Albert J.) & Sons Ltd. *v.* Parsons [1979] I.C.R. 271; [1979] I.R.L.R. 117; [1979] F.S.R. 254, C.A.; affirming [1978] I.C.R. 456, E.A.T. 13

Parsons (C.A.) & Co. Ltd. *v.* McLoughlin [1978] I.R.L.R. 65, E.A.T. 208, 220

Parvin *v.* Morton Machine Co. Ltd. [1952] A.C. 515; [1952] 1 T.L.R. 682; (1952) 116 J.P. 211; (1952) 96 S.J. 212; [1952] 1 All E.R. 670; 1952 S.C. (H.L.) 9; 1952 S.L.T. 201, H.L.; affirming 1950 S.C. 371 .... 556, 557

Patterson (J.) *v.* Bracketts (Messrs.) [1977] I.R.L.R. 137, E.A.T. 197

Powley *v.* Bristol Siddeley Engines [1966] 1 W.L.R. 729; (1966) 110 S.J. 369; [1965] 3 All E.R. 612; [1965] C.L.Y. 1637 577

Payne *v.* Electrical Trades Union, *The Times*, April 14, 1960 .... 432, 433

Payzu *v.* Hannaford [1918] 2 K.B. 348; 87 L.J.K.B. 1017; 119 L.T. 282; 82 J.P. 216; 34 T.L.R. 442; [1918–19] All E.R. Rep. 961, D.C. 171

Peake *v.* Automotive Products Ltd. [1978] Q.B. 233; [1977] I.C.R. 968; [1977] 3 W.L.R. 853; (1977) 121 S.J. 644; [1978] 1 All E.R. 106; [1977] I.R.L.R. 365; (1977) 12 I.T.R. 428; C.A.; reversing [1977] Q.B. 780; [1977] I.C.R. 480; [1977] 2 W.L.R. 751; (1977) 121 S.J. 222; (1977) 12 I.T.R. 259; [1977] I.T.L.R. 105, E.A.T. 325, 326, 327, 328, 336

Pearce *v.* Armitage (1950) 83 Ll.L.Rep. 361 580

—— *v.* Landsdowne (1893) 62 L.J.Q.B. 441; 69 L.T. 316; 57 J.P. 760, D.C. 128

—— *v.* Stanley-Bridges Ltd. [1965] 1 W.L.R. 931; (1965) 109 S.J. 472; [1965] 2 All E.R. 594, C.A. 560, 561

Pearlberg *v.* Varty [1972] 1 W.L.R. 534; (1972) 116 S.J. 335; [1972] 2 All E.R. 6; [1972] T.R. 5; (1972) 48 T.C. 14, H.L.; affirming [1971] 1 W.L.R. 728, C.A.; affirming [1970] T.R. 25 430

Pearson *v.* Jones (William) Ltd. [1967] 1 W.L.R. 1140; (1967) 111 S.J. 603; [1967] 2 All E.R. 1062; (1967) 3 K.I.R. 49, D.C.; affirming (1966) 2 K.I.R. 190 302

Pedersen *v.* Camden London Borough [1981] I.C.R. 674; [1981] I.R.L.R. 173, C.A. 30, 58

Penman *v.* Fife Coal Co. Ltd., The [1936] A.C. 45; 104 L.J.P.C. 74; 153 L.T. 261; 51 T.L.R. 494; 79 S.J. 478, H.L. 128

Penn *v.* Ward (1835) 2 Cr.M. & R. 338; 4 Dowl. 215; 1 Gale 189; 5 Tyr. 975; 4 L.J.Ex. 304, 150 E.R. 146 21

Penprase *v.* Manders Bros. Ltd. [1973] I.R.L.R. 167 .... 192, 200

Pepper *v.* Webb [1969] 1 W.L.R. 514; (1969) 113 S.J. 186; [1969] 2 All E.R. 216; (1969) 6 K.I.R. 109, C.A. 93

Pepper & Hope *v.* Daish [1980] I.R.L.R. 13, E.A.T. 32, 50

Perera *v.* Civil Service Commission [1980] I.C.R. 699; [1980] I.R.L.R. 233, E.A.T.; affirmed [1982] I.R.L.R. 147 .... 324, 330

Performing Right Society Ltd. *v.* Mitchell & Booker (Palais de Danse) Ltd. [1924] 1 K.B. 762; 93 L.J.K.B. 306; 131 L.T. 243; 40 T.L.R. 308; 68 S.J. 539 .... 5, 605

Pergamon Press Ltd., *Re* [1971] Ch. 388; [1970] 3 W.L.R. 792; (1970) 114 S.J. 569; [1970] 3 All E.R. 535, C.A.; affirming [1970] 1 W.L.R. 1075; (1970) 114 S.J. 354; [1970] 2 All E.R. 449 409

Perkins (Dorothy) Ltd. *v.* Dance [1977] I.R.L.R. 226, E.A.T. 307

Petrie *v.* MacFisheries Ltd. [1940] 1 K.B. 258; 109 L.J.K.B. 263; 161 L.T. 408; 104 J.P. 40; 56 T.L.R. 119; 83 S.J. 959; [1939] 4 All E.R. 281; 38 L.G.R. 44, C.A. 28, 62

Pettersson *v.* Royal Oak Hotel Ltd. [1948] N.Z.L.R. 136 .... 609, 610

Phillips *v.* Alhambra Palace Co. [1901] 1 K.B. 59; 70 L.J.Q.B. 26; 83 L.T. 431; 49 W.R. 223; 17 T.L.R. 40; 45 S.J. 81, D.C. 180

—— *v.* Britannia Hygienic Laundry Co. Ltd. [1923] 2 K.B. 832; 93 L.J.K.B. 5; 129 L.T. 777; 39 T.L.R. 530; 68 S.J. 102; [1923] All E.R. Rep. 127; 21 L.G.R. 709, C.A. 553

—— *v.* Clift (1859) 4 H. & N. 168; 28 L.J.Ex. 153; 32 L.T.(o.s.) 282; 23 J.P. 120; 5 Jur.(N.S.) 74; 7 W.R. 295; 157 E.R. 801 21

Photo Production Ltd. *v.* Securicor Transport Ltd. [1980] A.C. 827; [1980] 2 W.L.R. 283; (1980) 124 S.J. 147; [1980] 1 All E.R. 556; [1980] 1 Lloyd's Rep. 545, H.L.; reversing [1978] 1 All E.R. 556, C.A. 159

Pickering *v.* Kingston Mobile Unit [1978] I.R.L.R. 102 249

Piddington v. Bates; Robson v. Ribton-Turner [1961] 1 W.L.R. 162; (1961) 105 S.J. 110;
[1960] 3 All E.R. 660, D.C. 528
Pillinger v. Manchester Area Health Authority [1979] I.R.L.R. 430, E.A.T. 215, 216
Pirelli v. Faber (Oscar) & Partners [1983] 2 W.L.R. 6 594
Plowman (G.W.) & Son Ltd. v. Ash [1964] 1 W.L.R. 568; (1964) 108 S.J. 216; [1964]
2 All E.R. 10, C.A. 84, 86
Pointon v. University of Sussex [1974] I.R.L.R. 119 306
Poland v. Parr and Sons [1927] 1 K.B. 236 609
Portec (U.K.) Ltd. v. Mogenson [1976] I.C.R. 396; [1976] 3 All E.R. 565; [1976] I.T.R.
137; [1976] I.R.L.R. 209, E.A.T. 153
Porter v. Bandbridge Ltd. [1978] I.C.R. 943; [1978] 1 W.L.R. 1145; (1978) 122 S.J. 592;
(1978) 13 I.T.R. 340; [1978] I.R.L.R. 271, C.A. 137
Post Office v. Crouch. See Post Office v. Union of Post Office Workers.
—— v. Roberts [1980] I.R.L.R. 347, E.A.T. 72
—— v. Strange [1981] I.R.L.R. 515 ....117, 226, 227
—— v. Union of Post Office Workers. [1974] I.C.R. 378; [1974] 1 W.L.R. 89; (1973) 118
S.J. 182; [1974] 1 All E.R. 229; [1974] I.T.R. 136; [1974] I.R.L.R. 22, H.L.;
affirming sub nom. Post Office v. Crouch [1973] I.C.R. 366, C.A.; reversing sub
nom. Post Office v. Ravyts, N.I.R.C.; reversing sub nom. Ravyts v. Post Office
[1972] I.T.R. 242 119
—— v. Waddell (G.A.) [1977] I.R.L.R. 344, E.A.T. 134
Potters-Ballotini v. Weston-Baker [1977] R.P.C. 202, C.A. 74, 78, 85
Poulton v. London and South Western Ry. (1867) L.R. 2 Q.B. 534 604
Poussard v. Spiers & Pond (1876) 1 Q.B.D. 410; 45 L.J.Q.B. 621; 34 L.T. 572; 40 J.P.
645; 24 W.R. 819 ....159, 178
Power Packing Casemakers v. Faust [1981] I.C.R. 484; [1981] I.R.L.R. 120,
E.A.T. 244, 246, 460, 465
Powers and Villiers v. Clarke (A.) and Co. (Smethwick) Ltd. [1981] I.R.L.R. 483,
E.A.T. 248
Powley v. Bristol Siddeley Engines [1966] 1 W.L.R. 729; (1966) 110 S.J. 369; [1965] 3 All
E.R. 612; [1965] C.L.Y. 1637 577
Powrmatic Ltd. v. Bull (I.R.) [1977] I.C.R. 469; (1977) 12 I.T.R. 204; [1977] I.R.L.R.
144, E.A.T. 260, 262
Pratt v. Cook, Son & Co. (St. Pauls) Ltd. [1940] A.C. 437; 109 L.J.K.B. 293; 162 L.T.
243; 104 J.P. 135; 56 T.L.R. 363; 84 S.J. 167; [1940] 1 All E.R. 410; 38 L.G.R.
125, H.L. 131
Price v. Civil Service Commission [1978] I.C.R. 2; [1977] 1 W.L.R. 1417; (1977) 121 S.J.
558; [1978] 1 All E.R. 1228; (1977) 12 I.T.R. 482; [1977] I.R.L.R. 291, E.A.T.;
[1976] I.R.L.R. 405 ....330, 332
—— v. Gourley Bros. [1973] I.R.L.R. 11 200
—— v. Mouat (1862) 11 C.B.(N.S.) 508; 142 E.R. 895 94
Priddle v. Dibble [1978] I.C.R. 148; [1978] 1 W.L.R. 895; [1978] 1 All E.R. 1058; (1977)
122 S.J. 486, E.A.T. 199
Priestley v. Fowler (1837) 3 M. & W. 1; Murp. & H. 305; 7 L.J. Ex. 42; 1 Jur. 987; 150
E.R. 1030 568
Prince Albert v. Strange (1849) 1 Mac. & G. 25 73
Printers and Finishers Ltd. v. Holloway (Practice Note) [1965] 1 W.L.R. 1; (1965) 108
S.J. 521; [1964] 3 All E.R. 54n. 79, 82
Pritchard v. Clay (James) Ltd. [1926] K.B. 238; 95 L.J.K.B. 107; 134 L.T. 244; 90 J.P.
15; 42 T.L.R. 139; 70 S.J. 266, 28 Cox C.C. 122, D.C. 130
Pritchard-Rhodes Ltd. v. Boon and Milton [1979] I.R.L.R. 19, E.A.T. 267
Property Guards Ltd. v. Taylor and Kershaw [1982] I.R.L.R. 175 254
Prudential Assurance Co. Ltd. v. Lorenz (1971) 11 K.I.R. 78 484
Punton v. Ministry of Pensions and National Insurance [1963] 1 W.L.R. 186; (1963) 106
S.J. 1010; [1963] 1 All E.R. 275; C.A. 489
Punton and Croxford v. Ministry of Pensions and National Insurance [1964] 1 W.L.R.
226; (1964) 108 S.J. 34; [1964] 1 All E.R. 448, C.A.; affirming [1963] 1 W.L.R.
1176 631
Putsman v. Taylor [1927] 1 K.B. 741; 96 L.J.K.B. 726; 137 L.T. 291; 43 T.L.R. 392;
[1927] All E.R. Rep. 356, C.A. 87
Puttick v. Wright (John) and Sons (Blackwell) Ltd. [1972] I.C.R. 457; [1972] I.T.R. 438,
N.I.R.C. 267

Qualcast (Wolverhampton) Ltd. v. Haynes [1959] A.C. 743; [1959] 2 W.L.R. 510; (1959) 103 S.J. 310; [1959] 2 All E.R. 38, H.L.; reversing [1958] 1 W.L.R. 225, C.A. 576, 577, 578
Quinn v. Burch Brothers Builders Ltd. [1966] 2 Q.B. 370; [1966] 2 W.L.R. 1017; (1966) 110 S.J. 214; [1966] 2 All E.R. 283; (1966) 1 K.I.R. 9, C.A.; affirming [1966] 2 Q.B. 370 .... 573, 586
—— v. Green (J.W.) (Painters) [1966] 1 Q.B. 509; [1965] 3 W.L.R. 1301; (1965) 109 S.J. 830; [1965] 3 All E.R. 785; [1965] C.L.Y. 360, C.A. 585
—— v. Leathem [1901] A.C. 495; 70 L.J.P.C. 76; 85 L.T. 289; 65 J.P. 708; 50 W.R. 139; 17 T.L.R. 749; [1900–3] All E.R. Rep. 1, H.L. 453, 468, 469, 477, 478
Quintos v. National Smelting Co. Ltd. [1961] 1 W.L.R. 401; (1961) 105 S.J. 152; [1961] 1 All E.R. 630, C.A.; varying [1960] 1 W.L.R. 217 558

R. v. Barnsley Licensing Justices, ex p. Barnsley and District Licensed Victuallers' Association [1960] 2 Q.B. 167; [1960] 3 W.L.R. 305; (1960) J.P. 359; (1960) 104 S.J. 583; [1960] 2 All E.R. 703; [1960] 58 L.G.R. 285, C.A.; affirming [1959] 2 Q.B. 276, D.C. 433, 435
—— v. Barnsley Metropolitan Borough Council, ex p. Hook [1976] 1 W.L.R. 1052; (1976) 120 S.J. 182; [1976] 3 All E.R. 452; (1976) 74 L.G.R. 493, C.A. 408
—— v. British Broadcasting Corporation, ex p. Lavelle [1982] I.R.L.R. 404 16
—— v. Bunn (1872) 12 Cox C.C. 316 453
—— v. Central Arbitration Committee ex p. Deltaflow [1978] I.C.R. 534, [1977] I.R.L.R. 486, D.C. 36, 359, 373
—— v. Central Arbitration Committee, ex p. Hy-Mac Ltd. [1979] I.R.L.R. 461, D.C. ... 319
—— v. D'Alberquerque, ex p. Bresnahan [1966] 1 Lloyd's Rep. 69; (1966) 116 New L.J. 585, D.C. 625
—— v. Deputy Industrial Injuries Commissioner, ex p. Amalgamated Engineering Union, Re Dowling. See Minister of Social Security v. Amalgamated Engineering Union.
—— v. ——, ex p. Moore [1965] 1 Q.B. 456; [1965] 2 W.L.R. 89; (1965) 108 S.J. 1030; [1965] 1 All E.R. 81, C.A.; affirming (1965) 108 S.J. 380, D.C. 632
—— v. Druitt (1867) 10 Cox C.C. 592 453
—— v. Duffield (1851) 5 Cox C.C. 404 453
—— v. Gaming Board for Great Britain, ex p. Benaim and Khaida [1970] 2 Q.B. 417; [1970] 2 W.L.R. 1009, (1970) 114 S.J. 266; [1970] 2 All E.R. 528, C.A. 430
—— v. Industrial Court, ex p. A.S.S.E.T. [1965] 1 Q.B. 377; [1964] 3 W.L.R. 680; (1964) 108 S.J. 691; [1964] 3 All E.R. 130, D.C. 358
—— v. Industrial Injuries Commissioner, ex p. Langley [1976] I.C.R. 36, D.C. 631
—— v. Jones (John); R. v. Tomlinson; R. v. Warren; R. v. O'Shea; R. v. Carpenter; R. v. Llywarch [1974] I.C.R. 310; (1974) 118 S.J. 277; (1974) 59 Cr.App.R. 120; [1974] I.R.L.R. 117; [1974] Crim.L.R. 663, C.A. 524, 525
—— v. Lincoln's Inn Benchers (1825) 4 B. & C. 855; 7 Dow. & Ry. K.B. 351; 107 E.R. 1277 405
—— v. Liverpool Corporation, ex p. Liverpool Taxi Fleet Operators' Association [1972] 2 Q.B. 299; [1972] 2 W.L.R. 1262; (1972) 116 S.J. 201; (1972) 71 L.G.R. 387; sub nom. Liverpool Taxi Owners' Association, Re [1972] 2 All E.R. 589, C.A. 430
—— v. McKenzie [1892] 2 Q.B. 519 524
—— v. National Insurance Commissioners, ex p. East [1976] I.C.R. 206, C.A. 620
—— v. —— ex p. Maiden (Herbert) (unreported) 633
—— v. —— ex p. Michael [1977] I.C.R. 121; [1977] 1 W.L.R. 109; [1977] 2 All E.R. 420, C.A. 624, 625
—— v. —— ex p. Viscusi [1974] 1 W.L.R. 646; (1974) 118 S.J. 346; [1974] 2 All E.R. 724; (1974) 16 K.I.R. 197, C.A. 632, 633
—— v. National Insurance (Industrial Injuries) Commissioner, ex p. Richardson [1958] 1 W.L.R. 851; (1958) 102 S.J. 563; [1958] 2 All E.R. 689, D.C. 629
—— v. Smith (1837) 8 C. & P. 153 21
—— v. Surgeons' Co. (Master) 2 Burr. 892; 97 E.R. 621 405
—— Swan Hunter Shipbuilders Ltd. [1982] 1 All E.R. 264; [1981] I.C.R. 831 ... 541, 542, 581
—— v. Tempest (1902) 86 L.T. 585; 66 J.P. 472; 18 T.L.R. 433; sub nom. R. v. Tamworth JJ.; ex p. Clarke, (1902) 46 S.J. 360, D.C. 433

—— v. Thames Magistrates' Court, ex p. Polemis [1974] 1 W.L.R. 1371; (1974) 118 S.J. 734; [1974] 2 All E.R. 1219; [1974] 2 Lloyd's Rep. 16, D.C. 421

—— v. Welch (1853) 2 E. & B. 357; 1 C.L.R. 319; 22 L.J.M.C. 145; 21 L.T.(o.s. 127; 17 J.P. 553; 17 Jur. 1007; 118 E.R. 800; sub nom. R. v. Birmingham JJ. (1853) 1 W.R. 368 57

R.S. Components v. Irwin [1973] I.C.R. 535; [1974] 1 All E.R. 41; (1973) 15 K.I.R. 191; [1973] I.T.R. 569; [1973] I.R.L.R. 239, N.I.R.C.; reversing [1973] I.T.R. 404 ..... 203, 206, 216

Racal Communications v. Pay Board [1974] I.C.R. 590; [1974] 1 W.L.R. 1149; (1974) 118 S.J. 564; [1974] 3 All E.R. 263; [1974] I.R.L.R. 209 359

Radford v. National Society of Operative Printers, Graphical and Media Personnel [1972] I.C.R. 484; (1972) 116 S.J. 695...423, 430, 439

Rand (Joseph) v. Craig [1919] 1 Ch. 1; 88 L.J.Ch. 45; 119 L.T. 751; 35 T.L.R. 8; 63 S.J. 39, C.A. 605

Randall v. Post Office [1977] I.R.L.R. 346; (1977) 12 I.T.R. 451, E.A.T. 134

Rands v. McNeil [1955] 1 Q.B. 253; [1954] 3 W.L.R. 905; (1954) 98 S.J. 851; [1954] 3 All E.R. 593, C.A. 578

Rank Xerox (U.K.) Ltd. v. Goodchild [1979] I.R.L.R. 185, E.A.T. 226

Ranson v. Collins (G. & W.) [1978] I.C.R. 765, E.A.T. 204, 278, 280

Rashid v. Inner London Education Authority [1977] I.C.R. 157; (1976) 11 I.T.R. 215, E.A.T. 141, 143

Rasool v. Hepworth Pipe Co. Ltd. (No. 1) [1980] I.C.R. 495; [1980] I.R.L.R. 88, E.A.T. 158, 163, 192

—— v. —— (No. 2) [1980] I.R.L.R. 137, E.A.T. 219, 246, 462

Ratcliffe v. Dorset County Council [1978] I.R.L.R. 191 116

Rath v. Cruden Construction Ltd. [1982] I.R.L.R. 9 122

Reading v. Att.-Gen. [1951] A.C. 507; [1951] 1 T.L.R. 480; (1951) 95 S.J. 155; [1951] 1 All E.R. 617; H.L.; affirming [1949] 2 K.B. 232, C.A.; affirming [1948] 2 K.B. 268 98

Ready Case Ltd. v. Jackson [1981] I.R.L.R. 312, E.A.T. 168, 185

Ready Mixed Concrete (South East) v. Minister of Pensions and National Insurance [1968] 2 Q.B. 497; [1968] 2 W.L.R. 775; [1968] 1 All E.R. 433; (1968) 4 K.I.R. 132. ....4, 6, 7, 8, 11, 13, 28, 173, 385, 601

Reary v. North Eastern Co-operative Society Ltd. (1978) 111 I.R.L.R. 12 223

Redbridge London Borough Council v. Fisherman [1978] I.C.R. 569; (1978) 76 L.G.R. 408; [1978] I.R.L.R. 69, E.A.T. 30, 93

Redland Roof Tiles v. Harper [1977] I.C.R. 349, E.A.T. 307

Reigate v. Union Manufacturing Co. (Ramsbottom) [1918] 1 K.B. 592; 87 L.J.K.B. 724; 118 L.T. 479; [1918–19] All E.R. Rep. 143, C.A. 48

Reilly v. Hogan 32 N.Y.S. 2d 864 (1942) 422

—— v. R. [1934] A.C. 176; 103 L.J.P.C. 41; 150 L.T. 384; 50 T.L.R. 212, P.C. 18

Rely-a-Bell Burglar and Fire Alarm Co. Ltd. v. Eisler [1926] Ch. 609; 95 L.J.Ch. 345; 135 L.T. 286; 70 S.J. 669 83

Rennison (E.) and Son v. Minister of Social Security (1970) 114 S.J. 952; (1970) 10 K.I.R. 65 14

Retarded Children's Aid Society Ltd. v. Day [1978] I.C.R. 437; [1978] 1 W.L.R. 763; (1977) 122 S.J. 385; [1978] I.R.L.R. 128, C.A. 208, 218

Reuters Telegram Co. v. Byron (1874) 43 L.J.Ch. 661 76

Reynolds v. Shipping Federation Ltd. [1924] 1 Ch. 28; 93 L.J.Ch. 70; 130 L.T. 341; 39 T.L.R. 710; 68 S.J. 61; [1923] All E.R. Rep. 383 ....234, 391, 469

Rice v. Scottish Legal Life Assurance Society [1976] I.R.L.R. 330 305

Richards v. Highway Ironfounders (West Bromwich) Ltd. [1955] 1 W.L.R. 1049; (1955) 99 S.J. 580; [1955] 3 All E.R. 205; (1955) 53 L.G.R. 641, C.A. 539

Richardson v. Colne Fishery Co. (1897) 77 L.T. 501 21

—— v. Koefod [1969] 1 W.L.R. 1812; [1969] 3 All E.R. 1264; C.A. 171

—— v. Stephenson Clarke Ltd. [1969] 1 W.L.R. 1695; (1969) 113 S.J. 873; [1969] 3 All E.R. 705 577

Ridge v. Baldwin [1964] A.C. 40; [1963] 2 W.L.R. 935; (1964) 127 J.P. 295; (1964) 107 S.J. 313; [1963] 2 All E.R. 66; (1964) 61 L.G.R. 369; H.L.; reversing [1963] 1 Q.B. 539; [1962] 2 W.L.R. 716; (1963) 126 J.P. 196; 106 S.J. 111; [1962] 1 All E.R. 834; (1962) 60 L.G.R. 229; [1962] C.L.Y. 2317, C.A.; affirming [1961] 2 W.L.R. 1054.. 15, 16, 408, 429, 432

Rigby v. British Steel Corporation [1973] I.C.R. 160; [1973] I.T.R. 191; [1973] I.R.L.R.
    241, N.I.R.C. 247, 248
—— v. Connol (1880) 14 Ch.D. 482; 49 L.J.Ch., 328; 42 L.T. 139; 28 W.R. 650;
    [1874–80] All E.R. Rep. 592 429
Riley v. Tesco Stores; Riley v. Greater London Citizens' Advice Bureaux [1980] I.C.R.
    323; [1980] I.R.L.R. 103, C.A.; affirming [1979] I.C.R. 223, E.A.T. 137
Riordan v. War Office [1961] 1 W.L.R. 210; [1960] 3 All E.R. 774n., C.A.; affirming
    [1959] 1 W.L.R. 1046 18
Riverstone Meat Co. Pty Ltd. v. Lancashire Shipping Co. Ltd. [1961] A.C. 807; [1961]
    2 W.L.R. 269; (1961) 105 S.J. 148; [1961] 1 All E.R. 495; [1961] 1 Lloyd's Rep.
    57, H.L.; reversing [1960] 1 Q.B. 536, C.A.; reversing [1959] 1 Q.B. 74 581
Roadburg (M.) v. Lothian Regional Council [1976] I.R.L.R. 283 336
Robb v. Green [1895] 2 Q.B. 315; 64 L.J.Q.B. 593; 73 L.T. 15; 59 J.P. 695; 44 W.R. 25;
    11 T.L.R. 517; 39 S.J. 653; 14 R. 580, C.A. 75
—— v. Leon Motor Services Ltd. [1978] I.C.R. 506; [1978] I.R.L.R. 26, E.A.T.;
    reversing [1977] I.R.L.R. 245 230
Roberts v. Cleveland Area Health Authority; sub nom. Garland v. British Rail
    Engineering; Turton v. MacGregor Wallcoverings; Roberts v. Cleveland Area
    Health Authority [1979] I.C.R. 558; [1979] 1 W.L.R. 754; [1979] I.R.L.R. 244;
    (1979) 123 S.J. 300; [1979] 2 All E.R. 1163, C.A.; affirming sub nom. Roberts v.
    Cleveland Area Health Authority [1977] I.R.L.R. 401, E.A.T. 341
—— v. Dorman Long & Co. Ltd. [1953] 1 W.L.R. 942; (1953) 97 S.J. 487; [1953] 2 All
    E.R. 428; (1953) 51 L.G.R. 476, C.A. 587
—— v. Dorothea Slate Quarries [1948] W.N. 246; [1948] L.J.R. 1409; (1948) 92 S.J. 513;
    [1948] 2 All E.R. 201, H.L.; affirming (1947) 176 L.T. 541, D.C. 617
—— v. Smith (1857) 2 H. & N. 213; 26 L.J.Ex. 319; 19 L.T.(o.s.) 167; 3 Jur.(N.S.) 469; 5
    W.R. 581; 157 E.R. 89 568
Robertson v. Minister of Pensions [1949] 1 K.B. 227; [1949] L.J.R. 323; (1949) 64 T.L.R.
    526; (1949) 92 S.J. 603; [1948] 2 All E.R. 767 18
Robinson v. British Island Airways Ltd. [1978] I.C.R. 304; [1977] I.R.L.R. 477; (1977)
    13 I.T.R. 111, E.A.T. 275, 276
—— v. Crompton Parkinson Ltd. [1978] I.C.R. 401; [1978] I.R.L.R. 61, E.A.T. 70
—— v. Post Office [1974] 1 W.L.R. 1176; (1973) 117 S.J. 915; [1974] 2 All E.R. 737;
    (1973) 16 K.I.R. 12, C.A. 577
Rodwell v. Thomas [1944] K.B. 596; 114 L.J.K.B. 6; 171 L.T. 278; 60 T.L.R. 431; [1944]
    1 All E.R. 700 .... 18, 37, 38
Roe v. Minister of Health; Woolley v. Same [1954] 2 Q.B. 66; [1954] 2 W.L.R. 915;
    (1954) 98 S.J. 319; [1954] 2 All E.R. 131, C.A.; affirming [1954] 1 W.L.R. 128 575
Roebuck v. National Union of Mineworkers (Yorkshire Area); O'Brien v. Same [1977]
    I.C.R. 573 ....427, 428, 430, 433
—— v. —— (No. 2) [1978] I.C.R. 676 435
Rogers v. Booth (1937) 156 L.T. 487; 53 T.L.R. 741; 81 S.J. 418; [1937] 2 All E.R. 751;
    30 B.W.C.C. 188, C.A. 16
Rolls Royce Ltd. v. Walpole [1980] I.R.L.R. 343, E.A.T. 203
Ronbar Enterprises v. Green [1954] 1 W.L.R. 815; (1954) 98 S.J. 369; [1954] 2 All E.R.
    266, C.A. 87
Rookes v. Barnard [1964] A.C. 1129; [1964] 2 W.L.R. 269; (1964) 108 S.J. 93; [1964]
    1 All E.R. 367; [1964] 1 Lloyd's Rep. 28, H.L.; reversing [1963] 1 Q.B. 623; [1962]
    3 W.L.R. 260; (1962) 106 S.J. 371; [1962] 2 All E.R. 579; [1962] C.L.Y. 3063,
    C.A.; restoring [1961] 3 W.L.R. 438 .... 34, 40, 243, 375, 456,
                                                            457, 479, 480, 481, 482, 498, 500, 514, 516, 517, 518
Rose v. Plenty [1975] I.C.R. 430; [1976] 1 W.L.R. 141; [1976] I.R.L.R. 60; (1976) 119
    S.J. 592; [1976] 1 All E.R. 97; (1976) 18 Man.Law. 148; [1976] 1 Lloyd's Rep. 263,
    C.A. 598, 604, 605, 608, 611, 612
Ross v. Associated Portland Cement Manufacturers Ltd. [1964] 1 W.L.R. 768; (1964)
    108 S.J. 460; [1964] 2 All E.R. 452; (1964) 62 L.G.R. 513, H.L. 578, 585, 587
Rothwell v. Association of Professional, Executive, Clerical and Computer Staff and the
    Trades Union Congress [1976] I.C.R. 211; [1975] I.R.L.R. 375 410
Routh v. Jones [1947] 1 All E.R. 179; affirmed [1947] W.N. 205; 91 S.J. 354; [1947] 1 All
    E.R. 758, C.A. 84
Rowe v. Radio Rentals Ltd. [1982] I.R.L.R. 177 ....226, 227
Royal Naval School v. Hughes [1979] I.R.L.R. 383, E.A.T. 208

Royle v. Dredging and Construction Co. Ltd. [1966] I.T.R. 233; (1966) 1 K.I.R. 104 94
—— v. Globtik Management Ltd. [1977] I.C.R. 552, E.A.T. 153
Rubel Bronze & Metal Co. and Vos. Re [1918] 1 K.B. 315; 87 L.J.K.B. 466; sub nom.
    Vos v. Rubel Bronze & Metal Co. Ltd. (1918) 118 L.T. 348; 34 T.L.R. 171 ... 69, 170
Russell v. Amalgamated Society of Carpenters & Joiners [1910] 1 K.B. 506; 79 L.J.K.B.
    507; 102 L.T. 119; 26 T.L.R. 228; 54 S.J. 213, C.A.; affirmed [1912] A.C. 421; 81
    L.J.K.B. 619; 106 L.T. 433; 28 T.L.R. 276; 56 S.J. 342; [1911–13] All E.R. Rep.
    550..388, 391
—— v. Norfolk (Duke) (1949) 65 T.L.R. 225; (1949) 93 S.J. 132; [1949] 1 All E.R. 109,
    C.A.; affirming [1948] 1 All E.R. 488..430, 432
Ryan v. Cooke and Quinn [1938] I.R. 512 529

S. and U. Stores Ltd. v. Wilkes [1974] I.C.R. 645; [1974] 3 All E.R. 401; [1974] I.T.R.
    415; [1975] K.I.L.R. 117; [1974] I.R.L.R. 283, N.I.R.C. 302
Sadler v. Henlock (1855) 4 E. & B. 570; 3 C.L.R. 760; 24 L.J.Q.B. 138; 24 L.T.(o.s.)
    233; 1 Jur.(n.s.) 677; 3 W.R. 181; 119 E.R. 209 9
Sagar v. Ridehalgh (H.) and Son Ltd. [1931] 1 Ch. 310; 100 L.J.Ch. 220; 144 L.T. 480; 95
    J.P. 42; 47 T.L.R. 189; 29 L.G.R. 421, C.A. 32, 33, 51, 129, 130
Saggers v. British Railways Board [1977] I.R.L.R. 166 238
Sainsbury (J.) Ltd. v. Savage. See Savage v. Sainsbury (J.) Ltd.
St. Ann's Board Mill Co. Ltd. v. Brien [1973] I.C.R. 444; [1973] I.T.R. 463; [1973]
    I.R.L.R. 309, N.I.R.C. 196
Salsbury v. Woodland [1970] 1 Q.B. 324; [1969] 3 W.L.R. 29; (1969) 113 S.J. 327; [1969]
    3 All E.R. 863, C.A. 583
Salt v. Power Plant Co. Ltd. [1936] 3 All E.R. 322, C.A. 172
Saltman Engineering Co., Ferotel and Monarch Engineering Co. (Mitcham) v. Campbell
    Engineering Co. [1963] 3 All E.R. 413n.; 65 R.P.C. 203, C.A. 76, 77, 78
Sanders v. Neale (Ernest A.) Ltd. [1974] I.C.R. 565; [1974] 3 All E.R. 327; [1974] I.T.R.
    395; [1975] K.I.L.R. 77; [1974] I.R.L.R. 236, N.I.R.C..................163, 168, 204, 280
Santer v. National Graphical Association [1973] I.C.R. 60; (1972) 14 K.I.R. 193 424,
                                                                                426, 428, 436
Sarrent v. Central Electricity Generating Board [1976] I.R.L.R. 66; (1975) 18 Man.Law
    112 ....235, 236
Satchwell Sunvic Ltd. v. Secretary of State for Employment [1979] I.R.L.R. 455,
    E.A.T. 104
Saunders v. Richmond-upon-Thames London Borough Council [1978] I.C.R. 75; (1977)
    12 I.T.R. 488; [1977] I.R.L.R. 362, E.A.T. 322, 336
—— v. Scottish National Camps Association Ltd. [1980] I.R.L.R. 174, E.A.T.; affirmed
    [1981] I.R.L.R. 277 ....199, 203
Savage v. British India Steam Navigation Co. Ltd. (1930) 46 T.L.R. 294 ....156, 169, 172
—— v. Sainsbury (J.) Ltd. [1981] I.C.R. 1; [1980] I.R.L.R. 109, C.A.; affirming [1979]
    I.C.R. 96; [1978] I.R.L.R. 479, E.A.T. 168
Savoia v. Chiltern Herb Farms Ltd. [1982] I.R.L.R. 166; affirming [1981] I.R.L.R. 65,
    E.A.T. 190, 197, 261
Savory v. Holland & Hannen & Cubitts (Southern) Ltd. [1964] 1 W.L.R. 1158; (1964)
    108 S.J. 479; [1964] 3 All E.R. 18, C.A..601, 602
Saxton v. National Coal Board (1970) 8 K.I.R. 893; [1970] I.T.R. 196...........283, 301, 302
Scala Ballroom (Wolverhampton) Ltd. v. Ratcliffe [1958] 1 W.L.R. 1057; (1958) 102 S.J.
    758; [1958] 3 All E.R. 220, C.A.; affirming The Times, July 30, 1958 ....470, 506
Schmidt v. Austicks Bookshops Ltd. [1978] I.C.R. 85; [1977] I.R.L.R. 360,
    E.A.T. 326, 336, 337
—— v. Secretary of State for Home Affairs [1969] 2 Ch. 149; [1969] 2 W.L.R. 337; (1969)
    133 J.P. 274; (1969) 113 S.J. 16; [1969] 1 All E.R. 904, C.A.; affirming (1968) 112
    S.J. 863 408
Schwalb v. Fass (H.) & Son Ltd. (1946) 175 L.T. 345; 90 S.J. 394 539
Science Research Council v. Nassé; Leyland Cars v. Vyas; sub nom. Nassé v. Science
    Research Council; Vyas v. Leyland Cars [1980] A.C. 1028, H.L.; affirming [1979]
    Q.B. 144; [1978] 3 W.L.R. 754; (1978) 122 S.J. 593; [1978] 3 All E.R. 1196; (1978)
    13 I.T.R. 367; [1978] I.R.L.R. 352, C.A.; reversing [1978] I.C.R. 777 324
Scorer v. Seymour Jones [1966] 1 W.L.R. 1419; (1966) 110 S.J. 526; [1966] 3 All E.R.
    347; (1966) 1 K.I.R. 303, C.A. 88

Scott v. Avery (1856) 5 H.L.Cas. 811; (1856) 25 L.J.Ex. 308; 28 L.T.(o.s.) 207;
    2 Jur.(N.S.) 815; 4 W.R. 746; 10 E.R. 1121, H.L. 438
—— v. London Dock Co. (1865) 3 H. & C. 596; 5 New Rep. 420; 34 L.J.Ex. 220; 13 L.T.
    148; 11 Jur.(N.S.) 204, 13 W.R. 410; 159 E.R. 665 571
Scott, Brownrigg and Turner v. Dance [1977] I.R.L.R. 141, E.A.T. 153
Scott Packing and Warehousing Co. Ltd. v. Paterson [1978] I.R.L.R. 166, E.A.T. 199
Scottish Co-operative Wholesale Society Ltd. v. Lloyd [1973] I.C.R. 137; [1973] I.T.R.
    178; [1973] I.R.L.R. 93, N.I.R.C. 217, 257, 259, 260
Scottish Special Housing Association v. Cooke [1979] I.R.L.R. 264, E.A.T. 199
—— v. Linnen [1979] I.R.L.R. 265, E.A.T. 224
Seaboard World Airlines Inc. v. Transport and General Workers Union [1973] I.C.R.
    458; [1973] I.R.L.R. 300, N.I.R.C. 53, 90, 449, 461
Secretary of State for Employment v. ASLEF (No. 2) [1972] 2 Q.B. 455; [1972] I.C.R.
    19; [1972] 2 W.L.R. 1370; (1972) 116 S.J. 467; [1972] 2 All E.R. 949; (1972) 13
    K.I.R. 1, C.A.; affirming [1972] 2 Q.B. 443; [1972] I.C.R. 7; [1972] 2 W.L.R.
    1362; (1972) 116 S.J. 333, 434; [1972] 2 All E.R. 853, N.I.R.C. 27, 40, 54,
                                  56, 70, 71, 94, 243, 283, 449, 460, 534
—— v. Doulton Sanitaryware [1981] I.C.R. 477; [1981] I.R.L.R. 365, E.A.T. 104
—— v. Globe Elastic Thread Co. [1980] A.C. 506; [1979] I.C.R. 706; [1979] 3 W.L.R.
    143; (1979) 123 S.J. 504; [1979] 2 All E.R. 1077; [1979] I.R.L.R. 327, H.L.;
    reversing [1979] Q.B. 183, C.A.; affirming [1978] Q.B. 86, E.A.T. 155
—— v. Newbold and Joint Liquidators of David Armstrong (Catering Services) Ltd.
    [1981] I.R.L.R. 305, E.A.T. 150
—— v. Rooney [1977] I.C.R. 440; (1976) 12 I.T.R. 117, E.A.T. 146
—— v. Swain (John) and Son Ltd. [1981] I.R.L.R. 303 166
—— v. Wilson [1978] I.C.R. 200; [1978] 1 W.L.R. 568; (1977) S.J. 791; [1978] 3 All E.R.
    137; [1977] I.R.L.R. 483; (1978) 13 I.T.R. 191, E.A.T. 124
—— v. Woodrow (John) and Sons (Builders) Ltd. [1983] I.R.L.R. 11...................257, 302
Seide v. Gillette Industries Ltd. [1980] I.R.L.R. 427, E.A.T. 328
Selby v. Plessey Co. Ltd.; The [1972] I.R.L.R. 36..248, 249
Selz (Charles) Ltd.'s Application, Re (1953) 71 R.P.C. 158 89
Semtex v. Gladstone [1954] 1 W.L.R. 945; (1954) 98 S.J. 438; [1954] 2 All E.R. 206 97
Sexton v. Scaffolding (Great Britain) Ltd. [1953] 1 Q.B. 153; [1952] 2 T.L.R. 986; (1952)
    96 S.J. 850; [1952] 2 All E.R. 1085; 51 L.G.R. 41, C.A.; reversing [1952] W.N.
    343 579
Seymour v. Barber and Heron Ltd. [1970] I.C.R. 65, D.C. 144
—— v. British Airways Board [1983] I.C.R. 148; [1983] I.R.L.R. 55; (1983) 80 L.S.Gaz.
    157 24
Shakespeare v. Blundell (C.L. and H.L.) Ltd. [1966] I.T.R. 458; (1966) 1 K.I.R. 508 271
Shanks v. Plumbing Trades Union (unreported, November 15, 1967) 445
Shaw v. Garden King Frozen Foods [1975] I.R.L.R. 98 249
Sheet Metal Components Ltd. v. Plumridge [1974] I.C.R. 373; [1974] I.T.R. 238; [1974]
    I.R.L.R. 86, N.I.R.C..283, 295
Sheffield v. Oxford Controls Co. Ltd. [1979] I.C.R. 396; [1979] I.R.L.R. 133, E.A.T. 192
Shenton v. Smith [1895] A.C. 229; 64 L.J.P.C. 119; 72 L.T. 130; 43 W.R. 637; 11 R. 375,
    P.C. 18
Sherard v. Amalgamated Union of Engineering Workers [1973] I.C.R. 421; [1973]
    I.R.L.R. 188; affirming [1973] I.C.R. 421...426, 442, 499, 504
Sheridan v. Durkin (1967) 111 S.J. 112; (1966) 117 New L.J. 74 576
Shields v. Coomes (E.) (Holdings) Ltd. [1978] I.C.R. 1159; [1978] 1 W.L.R. 1408; [1978]
    I.T.R. 473; [1978] I.R.L.R. 263; (1978) 122 S.J. 592; [1979] 1 All E.R. 456, C.A.
                                  309, 310, 311, 312, 314, 317, 329
Shields Furniture Ltd. v. Goff [1973] I.C.R. 187; [1973] 2 All E.R. 653; [1973] I.T.R.
    233, N.I.R.C...283, 286, 293
Shirlaw v. Southern Foundries (1926) Ltd. See Southern Foundries (1926) Ltd. v.
    Shirlaw.
Short v. Henderson (J. & W.) Ltd. (1946) 174 L.T. 417; 1945 S.C. 155 6
Sick and Funeral Society of St. John's Sunday School, Galcar, Re [1973] Ch. 51; [1972]
    2 W.L.R. 962; (1972) 116 S.J. 355; [1972] 2 All E.R. 439 415
Silk v. Merrick (1809) 2 Comp. 31 9
Silvester v. National Union of Printing, Bookbinding and Paper Workers (1966) New
    L.J. 1489; (1966) 1 K.I.R. 679; [1966] C.L.Y. 12198...........................422, 424, 436

Simmonds v. Dowty Seals Ltd. [1978] I.R.L.R. 211, E.A.T. 29, 30, 52, 271, 284
Simmons v. Hoover Ltd. [1977] Q.B. 284; [1977] I.C.R. 61; [1976] 3 W.L.R. 901; [1977]
    1 All E.R. 775, E.A.T. 243, 269, 454, 465, 486
Simpson v. Dickinson [1972] I.C.R. 474; (1972) 13 K.I.R. 336; [1973] I.T.R. 40,
    N.I.R.C. 292
—— v. Kodak Ltd. [1948] 2 K.B. 184, (1948) 92 S.J. 271 359
—— v. Norwest Holst Southern Ltd. [1980] 1 W.L.R. 968; (1980) 124 S.J. 313; [1980]
    2 All E.R. 471, C.A. 595, 596
—— v. Roneo (1972) 13 K.I.R. 199; (1972) I.T.R. 404; [1972] I.R.L.R. 5 248
Sinclair v. Neighbour [1967] 2 Q.B. 279; [1967] 2 W.L.R. 1; (1967) 110 S.J. 808; [1966]
    3 All E.R. 988; (1966) 1 K.I.R. 451, C.A. 69, 156, 169, 170
Singh v. British Steel [1974] I.R.L.R. 131..34, 375
—— v. Higgs and Hill Ltd. [1977] I.C.R. 193 280
—— v. London Country Bus Services Ltd. [1976] I.T.R. 131; [1976] I.R.L.R. 176,
    E.A.T. 220
—— v. Rowntree Mackintosh Ltd. [1979] I.C.R. 554; [1979] I.R.L.R. 199, E.A.T. 333
Skyrail Oceanic Ltd. (Trading as Goodmos Tours) v. Coleman [1980] I.C.R. 596; [1980]
    I.R.L.R. 226, E.A.T. 343
Smart v. Tyrer. See Tyrer v. Smart.
Smith v. Austin Lifts Ltd. [1959] 1 W.L.R. 100; (1959) 103 S.J. 73; [1959] 1 All E.R. 81;
    [1958] 2 Lloyd's Rep. 583, H.L. 575, 580
—— v. Avana Bakeries Ltd. [1979] I.R.L.R. 423, E.A.T. 158
—— v. Baker (Charles) & Sons [1891] A.C. 325; 60 L.J.Q.B. 683; 65 L.T. 467; 55 J.P.
    660; 40 W.R. 392; 7 T.L.R. 697, H.L. 96, 589
—— v. Blandford Gee Cementation Co. Ltd. [1970] 3 All E.R. 154; (1970) 8 K.I.R.
    1107, D.C. 600
—— v. Chesterfield and District Co-operative Society Ltd. [1953] 1 W.L.R. 370; (1953)
    97 S.J. 132; [1953] 1 All E.R. 447; (1953) 51 L.G.R. 194, C.A. 561
—— v. Davies (A.) and Co. (Shopfitters) Ltd. (1968) 5 K.I.R. 320 570
—— v. Hayle Town Council [1978] I.C.R. 996; (1978) 122 S.J. 642; (1978) 74 L.G.R. 52,
    C.A.; affirming [1978] I.R.L.R. 413, E.A.T. 118, 230
—— v. Leech Brain Co. Ltd. [1962] 2 Q.B. 405; [1962] 2 W.L.R. 148; (1962) 106 S.J. 77;
    [1961] 3 All E.R. 1159 588
—— v. Martin and Kingston-upon-Hull Corporation [1940] A.C. 955 606
—— v. National Coal Board [1967] 1 W.L.R. 871; (1967) 111 S.J. 455; [1967] 2 All E.R.
    593; (1967) 3 K.I.R. 1, H.L.; reversing sub nom. Westwood v. National Coal
    Board [1966] 1 W.L.R. 682, C.A. 575
—— v. Thomasson (1891) 62 L.T. 68 524
—— v. Vange Scaffolding and Engineering Co. Ltd. [1970] 1 W.L.R. 733; (1970) 114 S.J.
    148; [1970] 1 All E.R. 249; (1970) 8 K.I.R. 709 ....570, 603
—— v. Wimpey (George) & Co. [1972] 2 Q.B. 329; [1972] 2 W.L.R. 1166; (1972) 116
    S.J. 314; [1972] 2 All E.R. 723; (1972) 12 K.I.R. 345, C.A. 4
Smith (H.W.) (Cabinets) Ltd. v. Brindle [1973] I.C.R. 12; [1972] 1 W.L.R. 1653; [1973]
    1 All E.R. 230; (1973) K.I.R. 203; [1973] I.T.R. 69; [1972] I.R.L.R. 125, C.A.;
    reversing (1972) 13 K.I.R. 195, N.I.R.C. 167
Smith, Kline and French Laboratories Ltd. v. Coates [1977] I.R.L.R. 220, E.A.T. 260
Snoxell and Davies v. Vauxhall Motors; Early (Charles) & Mariott (Witney) v. Smith
    and Ball [1978] Q.B. 11; [1977] 3 W.L.R. 189; (1977) 121 S.J. 353; [1977] 3 All
    E.R. 770; [1977] I.C.R. 700; [1977] 1 C.M.L.R. 487; (1977) 12 I.T.R. 235; [1977]
    I.R.L.R. 123, E.A.T. 315
Sood v. G.E.C. Elliott Process Automation Ltd. [1980] I.C.R. 1; [1979] I.R.L.R. 416,
    E.A.T. 112, 113
Sorrell v. Smith [1925] A.C. 700; 94 L.J.Ch. 347; 133 L.T. 370; 41 T.L.R. 529; 69 S.J.
    641; [1925] All E.R. Rep. 1..469, 474
South Wales Miners' Federation v. Glamorgan Coal Co. Ltd. [1905] A.C. 239; 74
    L.J.K.B. 525; 92 L.T. 710; 53 W.R. 593; 21 T.L.R. 441; [1904–7] All E.R. Rep.
    211, H.L.; affirming [1903] 2 K.B. 545, C.A. 468, 476
Southern Electricity Board v. Collins [1970] 1 Q.B. 83; [1969] 3 W.L.R. 147; (1970) 113
    S.J. 425; [1969] 2 All E.R. 1166; (1969) 6 K.I.R. 516; [1969] I.T.R. 277,
    D.C. 144
Southern Foundries (1926) Ltd. v. Shirlaw [1940] A.C. 701; affirming [1939] 2 K.B. 206;
    [1939] 2 All E.R. 113 ....49, 171, 423

Southwood Hostel Management Committee v. Taylor [1979] I.C.R. 813; [1979] I.R.L.R.
    397, E.A.T. 150
Spain v. Arnott (1817) 2 Stark. 256 93
Spanlite Structures Ltd. v. Jarrett (G.) [1973] I.C.R. 465; [1973] I.T.R. 511; (1973) 16
    K.I.R. 79; [1973] I.R.L.R. 280, N.I.R.C. 150
Sparrow v. Fairey Aviation Co. [1964] A.C. 1019; [1962] 3 W.L.R. 1210; (1962) 106 S.J.
    875; [1962] 3 All E.R. 706; (1962) 62 L.G.R. 379, H.L.; affirming [1962] 1 Q.B.
    161; [1961] 3 W.L.R. 855; (1961) 105 S.J. 665; [1961] 3 All E.R. 452; (1961) 59
    L.G.R. 507, C.A.; affirming [1961] 1 W.L.R. 844; [1961] All E.R. 216; (1961) 59
    L.G.R. 340.. 558, 563
Spring v. National Amalgamated Stevedores and Dockers Society [1956] 1 W.L.R. 585;
    (1956) 100 S.J. 401; [1956] 2 All E.R. 221; [1956] 1 Lloyd's Rep. 331 .....410, 411, 422
Square Grip Reinforcement Co. Ltd. v. MacDonald, 1968, S.L.T. 65 472
Squibb United Kingdom Staff Association v. Certification Officer [1978] I.C.R. 115;
    [1977] I.R.L.R. 355, E.A.T.; reversed [1979] I.C.R. 235, C.A. 386
Squire v. Bayer and Co. Ltd. [1901] 2 K.B. 299; 70 L.J.K.B. 705; 85 L.T. 247; 65 J.P.
    629; 49 W.R. 557; 17 T.L.R. 492; 45 S.J. 503, D.C. 129
Stagecraft Ltd. v. Minister of National Insurance, 1952 S.C. 288 5
Stanley v. Concentric (Pressed Products) Ltd. (1971) 11 K.I.R. 260, C.A. 554
Stannard, Gent, Halsey and Field v. Dexion Ltd. [1966] I.T.R. 274; (1966) 1 K.I.R.
    113 94
Stapley v. Gypsum Mines Ltd. [1953] A.C. 663; [1953] 3 W.L.R. 279; [1953] 97 S.J. 486;
    [1953] 2 All E.R. 478, H.L.; reversing [1952] 2 Q.B. 575............................. 584, 590
Stapp v. The Shaftesbury Society [1982] I.R.L.R. 326 168
Star Sea Transport Corp. of Monrovia v. Slater; Camilla M., The [1979] 1 Lloyd's Rep.
    26; [1978] I.R.L.R. 507; (1978) 122 S.J. 745; C.A. 502, 503, 504, 506
Staton v. National Coal Board [1951] 2 T.L.R. 674 .... 606, 607
Staveley Iron and Chemical Co. Ltd. v. Jones [1956] A.C. 627; [1956] 2 W.L.R. 479;
    (1956) 100 S.J. 130; [1956] 1 All E.R. 403; [1956] 1 Lloyd's Rep. 65, H.L.;
    affirming [1956] 1 Q.B. 474, C.A.. 590, 592
Steel v. Cammell, Laird Ltd. [1905] 93 L.T. 357 617
—— v. Union of Post Office Workers [1978] I.C.R. 181; [1978] 1 W.L.R. 64; (1977) 121
    S.J. 575; [1978] 2 All E.R. 504; [1977] I.R.L.R. 288; [1978] I.R.L.R. 198,
    E.A.T.. 332, 333
Steele v. South Wales Miners' Federation [1907] 1 K.B. 361; 76 L.J.K.B. 333; 96 L.T.
    260; 23 T.L.R. 228; 51 S.J. 190 396
Stepek (J.) v. Hough [1974] I.C.R. 352; [1973] I.T.R. 516, N.I.R.C. 258
Stephen v. Stewart [1944] 1 D.L.R. 305; [1943] 3 W.W.R. 580; 59 B.C.R. 410 422
Stephen (Harold) and Co. v. Post Office [1977] 1 W.L.R. 1172; (1977) 121 S.J. 707;
    [1978] 1 All E.R. 939, C.A.. 491, 521
Stepney Cast Stone Co. Ltd. v. Macarthur [1979] I.R.L.R. 181, E.A.T. 134
Sterling Engineering Co. v. Patchett [1955] A.C. 534; [1955] 2 W.L.R. 424; (1955) 99 S.J.
    129; (1955) 1 All E.R. 369; (1955) 72 R.P.C. 50, H.L.; reversing (1953) 71 R.P.C.
    61, C.A.; restoring (1953) 70 R.P.C. 184 88
Stevenson v. Golden Wonder Ltd. [1977] I.R.L.R. 474, E.A.T. 226
—— v. Teesside Bridge and Engineering Ltd. (1970) 114 S.J. 907; [1971] 1 All E.R. 296;
    [1971] I.T.R. 44; (1971) 10 K.I.R. 53, D.C. 40, 51, 95, 271
—— v. United Road Transport Union [1977] I.C.R. 893; [1977] 2 All E.R. 941,
    C.A. 430, 431, 446
Stevenson, Jordan & Harrison v. Macdonald & Evans [1952] 1 T.L.R. 101; (1952) 69
    R.P.C. 10, C.A.; reversing in part (1951) 68 R.P.C. 190 6
Stock v. Jones (Frank) (Tipton) [1978] I.C.R. 347; [1978] 1 W.L.R. 231; (1978) 13 I.T.R.
    289; (1978) 122 S.J. 109; [1978] 1 All E.R. 948, H.L; affirming [1977] I.C.R. 976,
    C.A. 246
Stocker v. Norprint Ltd. (1971) 115 S.J. 58; (1971) 10 K.I.R. 10, C.A...............586, 593
Stokes v. Guest, Keen and Nettlefold (Bolts and Nuts) Ltd. [1968] 1 W.L.R. 1776; (1968)
    112 S.J. 821; (1968) 5 K.I.R. 401 576
Stone v. Charrington and Co. Ltd. [1977] I.C.R. 248; (1977) 12 I.T.R. 255, E.A.T. 229
—— v. Taffe [1974] 1 W.L.R. 1575, (1974) 118 S.J. 863; [1974] 3 All E.R. 1016,
    C.A. 604, 608, 609
Stott v. Gamble [1916] 2 K.B. 504 476

Strange (S.W.) Ltd. v. Mann [1965] 1 W.L.R. 629; (1965) 109 S.J. 352; [1965] 1 All E.R.
 1069 285
Stratford (J.T.) & Son Ltd. v. Lindley [1965] A.C. 307; [1964] 3 W.L.R. 541; (1964) 108
 S.J. 636; [1964] 3 All E.R. 102; [1964] 2 Lloyd's Rep. 133, H.L.; reversing [1965]
 A.C. 269, C.A.; restoring (1965) 108 S.J. 137 .... 243, 455, 456, 474, 475,
 477, 481, 499, 504, 513, 515, 517
Strick v. Swansea Tin-Plate Co. (1887) 36 Ch.D. 558; 57 L.J.Ch. 438; 57 L.T. 392; 35
 W.R. 831 388
Stringer v. Automatic Woodturning Co. See Automatic Woodturning Co. v. Stringer.
Summers (John) v. Frost [1955] A.C. 740; [1955] 2 W.L.R. 825; (1955) 99 S.J. 257; [1955]
 1 All E.R. 870; (1955) L.G.R. 329; H.L.; affirming [1954] 2 Q.B. 21, C.A. 557,
 560, 562
Sumner v. Henderson (William) & Sons Ltd. [1963] 1 W.L.R. 823; (1963) 107 S.J. 436;
 [1963] 2 All E.R. 712n.; [1963] 1 Lloyd's Rep. 537, C.A.; setting aside [1964]
 1 Q.B. 450; [1963] 2 W.L.R. 330; (1963) 107 S.J. 74; [1963] 1 All E.R. 408; (1963)
 61 L.G.R. 233; [1962] 2 Lloyd's Rep. 435 582
Sun and Sand Ltd. v. Fitzjohn [1979] I.C.R. 268; [1979] I.R.L.R. 154, E.A.T. 257
Superlux v. Plaisted, The Times, December 12, 1958, C.A. 97
Sutcliffe v. Hawker Siddeley Aviation Ltd. [1973] I.C.R. 560; [1974] I.T.R. 58 (1973) 16
 K.I.R. 85; [1973] I.R.L.R. 304, N.I.R.C. 96, 186, 264, 271
Sutton v. Att.-Gen. (1923) 39 T.L.R. 295; 67 S.J. 422, H.L. 18
Swain v. West (Butchers) Ltd. (1936) 80 S.J. 973; [1936] 3 All E.R. 261, C.A. 90
Swaine v. Wilson (1889) 24 Q.B.D. 252; 59 L.J.Q.B. 76; 62 L.T. 309; 54 J.P. 484; 38
 W.R. 261; 6 T.L.R. 121, C.A. 391
Sweetlove v. Redbridge and Waltham Forest Area Health Authority [1979] I.C.R. 477;
 [1979] I.R.L.R. 195, E.A.T. 255
System Floors (U.K.) Ltd. v. Daniel [1981] I.R.L.R. 475, E.A.T. 44

T.B.A. Industrial Products Ltd. v. Morland [1982] I.R.L.R. 331 168
T.W.U.A. v. Lincoln Mills 353 U.S. 448 (1957) 381
Taff Vale Ry. Co. v. Amalgamated Society of Railway Servants [1901] A.C. 426; 70
 L.J.K.B. 905n.; 83 L.T. 474; 50 W.R. 44; 44 S.J. 714; reversed [1901] 1 K.B. 170,
 C.A.; restored [1901] A.C. 434, H.L. 387, 388, 390, 453, 469, 492
Talke Fashions Ltd. v. Amalgamated Society of Textile Workers and Kindred Trades
 [1977] I.C.R. 833; [1978] 1 W.L.R. 558; (1977) 122 S.J. 263; [1978] 2 All E.R. 649;
 [1977] I.R.L.R. 309, E.A.T. 297
Tarleton v. M'Gawley (1793) 1 Peake 270 480
Tarmac Roadstone Holdings Ltd. v. Peacock [1973] I.C.R. 273; [1973] 1 W.L.R. 594;
 (1973) 117 S.J. 186; [1973] 2 All E.R. 485; (1973) 14 K.I.R. 277; [1973] I.T.R.
 300; [1973] I.R.L.R. 157, C.A. 301, 302
Tarrant v. Webb (1856) 18 C.B. 797; 25 L.J.C.P. 261; 27 L.T.(o.s.) 202; 20 J.P. 711; 4
 W.R. 640; 139 E.R. 1584 568
Taylor v. Caldwell (1863) 3 B. & S. 826; 2 New Rep. 198; 32 L.J.Q.B. 164; 8 L.T. 356; 27
 J.P. 710; 11 W.R. 726; 122 E.R. 309 179
—— v. Co-operative Retail Services Ltd. [1982] I.R.L.R. 354 236
—— v. Kent County Council [1969] 2 Q.B. 560; [1969] 3 W.L.R. 156; 113 S.J. 425; [1969]
 2 All E.R. 1080; (1969) 6 K.I.R. 524; (1969) 67 L.G.R. 483; [1969] I.T.R. 294,
 D.C. 290
—— v. Rover Co. Ltd. [1966] 1 W.L.R. 1491; [1966] 2 All E.R. 181................572, 582, 588
—— v. Sims and Sims [1942] 2 All E.R. 375 590
Taylorplan Catering (Scotland) Ltd. v. McInally [1980] I.R.L.R. 53, E.A.T. 224
Taylor's Cater Inns Ltd. v. Minister of Labour [1966] I.T.R. 242; (1966) 1 K.I.R.
 106...167, 177
Teesside Times Ltd. v. Drury [1980] I.C.R. 338; (1979) 124 S.J. 80; [1980] I.R.L.R. 72,
 C.A.; affirming [1978] I.C.R. 822; [1978] 13 I.T.R. 298, E.A.T. 147
Terrapin Ltd. v. Builders Supply Co. (Hayes) Ltd. [1967] R.P.C. 375 77
Tesco Group of Companies (Holdings) Ltd. v. Hill [1977] I.R.L.R. 63, E.A.T. 227
Tesco Stores Ltd. v. Edwards [1977] I.R.L.R. 120 550
Tesco Supermarkets Ltd. v. Natrass [1972] A.C. 153; [1971] 2 W.L.R. 1166; (1971) 115
 S.J. 285; [1971] 2 All E.R. 127; (1971) 69 L.G.R. 403, H.L.; reversing [1971]
 1 Q.B. 133 552

Thomas v. Quartermaine (1887) 18 Q.B.D. 685 589
Thomas & Betts Manufacturing Co. Ltd. v. Harding [1978] I.R.L.R. 213, E.A.T;
    affirmed [1980] I.R.L.R. 255 250
Thomas (Richard) & Baldwins Ltd. v. Cummings [1955] A.C. 321; [1955] 2 W.L.R. 293;
    (1955) 99 S.J. 94; [1955] 1 All E.R. 285, H.L; reversing [1953] 2 Q.B. 95, C.A. 564
Thompson v. British Channel Ship Repairers and Engineers (1970) 114 S.J. 167; (1970) 8
    K.I.R. 687; [1970] 1 Lloyd's Rep. 105, C.A.; affirming (1969) 113 S.J. 382; [1969]
    6 K.I.R. 510; [1969] I.T.R. 262; [1969] 1 Lloyd's Rep. 407, D.C. 144
—— v. Brown [1981] 1 W.L.R. 744; (1981) 125 S.J. 377; [1981] 2 All E.R. 296, H.L. 596,
                                                                                             597
—— v. National Coal Board [1982] I.C.R. 15 569
—— v. Priest (Lindley) Ltd. [1978] I.R.L.R. 99 102
Thomson v. Eaton Ltd. [1976] I.C.R. 336 .... 463, 467
Thomson (D.C.) & Co. v. Deakin [1952] Ch. 646; [1952] 2 T.L.R. 105; [1952] 2 All E.R.
    361, C.A.; affirming [1952] 1 T.L.R. 1397 .... 54, 472, 473, 474
Thorndyke v. Bell Frist (North Central) Ltd. [1979] I.R.L.R.1 332
Throsby v. Imperial College of Science and Technology. See British Broadcasting
    Corporation v. Dixon.
Thurogood v. Van Den Berghs and Jurgens Ltd. [1951] 2 K.B. 537; [1951] 1 T.L.R. 557;
    (1951) 96 S.J. 317; (1951) 49 L.G.R. 504; sub nom. Thorogood v. Van Den
    Berghs and Jurgens Ltd. (1951) 115 J.P. 237; [1951] 1 All E.R. 682,
    C.A. 556
Tidman v. Aveling Marshall Ltd. [1977] I.C.R. 506; (1977) 12 I.T.R. 290; [1977]
    I.R.L.R. 218, E.A.T. 257
Times Newspapers Ltd. v. O'Regan [1981] I.C.R. 637; [1977] I.R.L.R. 101,
    E.A.T. 137, 448
Timex Corporation v. Thomson [1981] I.R.L.R. 522 200
Titmus & Titmus Ltd. v. Rose and Watts [1940] 162 L.T. 304; 56 T.L.R. 337; 84 S.J. 61;
    [1940] 1 All E.R. 599 21
Todd v. British Midland Airways [1978] I.C.R. 959; (1978) 122 S.J. 661; (1978) 13 I.T.R.
    553; [1978] I.R.L.R. 370, C.A. 52, 153
—— v. Kerrich (1852) 8 Exch. 151; 22 L.J.Ex. 1; 20 L.T.(o.s.) 101; 17 J.P. 490; 17 Jur.
    119; 155 E.R. 1298 172
Tomlinson v. Evans (Dick) "U" Drive Ltd. [1978] I.C.R. 639; [1978] I.R.L.R. 77,
    E.A.T. 25, 26, 87
Toppin v. Feron (1909) 43 I.L.T.R. 190 527
Torquay Hotel Co. Ltd. v. Cousins (1969) 2 Ch. 106; [1969] 2 W.L.R. 289; (1968) 113
    S.J. 52; [1969] 1 All E.R. 522; (1969) 6 K.I.R. 15, C.A.; affirming [1968] 3
    W.L.R. 540 .... 475, 476
Toronto Power Co. v. Paskwan [1915] A.C. 734; (1915) 84 L.J.P.C. 148; (1915) 113 L.T.
    253, P.C. 577
Torr v. British Railways Board [1977] I.C.R. 785; [1977] I.R.L.R. 184 254
Tracey v. Zest Equipment Co. Ltd. [1982] I.R.L.R. 268 184
Transport and General Workers' Union v. Courtenham Products Ltd. [1977] I.R.L.R.
    8 295
—— v. Dyer (Andrew) (1976) 12 I.T.R. 113; [1977] I.R.L.R. 93, E.A.T. (Scotland);
    affirming [1976] I.R.L.R. 358 .... 296, 368
—— v. Nationwide Haulage Ltd. [1978] I.R.L.R. 143 296
Treacy v. Corcoran (1874) I.R. 8 C.L. 40 61
Treganowan v. Knee (Robert) & Co. [1975] I.C.R. 405; (1975) 119 S.J. 490; [1975]
    I.T.R. 121; [1975] I.R.L.R. 247, D.C.; affirming [1975] I.R.L.R. 112 216
Tremain v. Pike [1969] 1 W.L.R. 1556; (1969) 113 S.J. 812; [1969] 3 All E.R. 1303;
    (1969) 7 K.I.R. 318 576
Trend v. Chiltern Hunt Ltd. [1977] I.C.R. 612; (1977) 12 I.T.R. 180; [1977] I.R.L.R. 66,
    E.A.T. 228, 261
Trevethan v. Stirling Metals Ltd. [1977] I.R.L.R. 416 103
Trevillion v. Hospital of St. John and St. Elizabeth, The [1973] I.R.L.R. 176,
    N.I.R.C. 283
Triplex Safety Glass Co. Ltd. v. Scorah [1938] 1 Ch. 211; 107 L.J. Ch. 91; 157 L.T. 576;
    157 L.T. 576; 54 T.L.R. 90; S.J. 982; 55 R.P.C. 21 88
Truelove v. Hall (Matthew) Mechanical Services Ltd. [1978] I.T.R. 65 301
Trusler (I.T.J.) v. Lummus Co., The [1972] I.R.L.R. 35 248

Trust Houses Forte Hotels Ltd. *v.* Murphy [1977] I.R.L.R. 186, E.A.T. 192
Tsoukka *v.* Potomac Restaurants Ltd. [1968] I.T.R. 259 301
Tucker *v.* British Museum Trustees (1967) 112 S.J. 70; affirming *The Times*, April 22,
    1967 15
——— *v.* Secretary of State for Employment 312/88 (1975) 300
Tunnel Holdings Ltd. *v.* Woolf [1976] I.C.R. 387; [1976] I.T.R. 75 168
Turner *v.* Goldsmith (1891) 1 Q.B. 544; 60 L.J.Q.B. 247; 64 L.T. 301; 39 W.R. 547;
    7 T.L.R. 233, C.A. 57
——— *v.* Kean (D.T.) [1978] I.R.L.R. 110 183
——— *v.* Mason (1845) 14 M. & W. 112; 2 Dow. & L. 898; 14 L.J.Ex. 311; 5 L.T.(o.s.) 97;
    153 E.R. 411..53, 90
——— *v.* Sawdon [1901] 2 K.B. 653; 70 L.J.K.B. 897; 85 L.T. 222; 49 W.R. 712; 17 T.L.R.
    45, C.A...57, 58, 59
Turley *v.* Allders Deparment Stores Ltd. [1980] I.C.R. 66; [1980] I.R.L.R. 4, E.A.T. 325
Turriff Construction Ltd. *v.* Bryant [1976] I.T.R. 292 ....36, 44
Turton *v.* MacGregor Wallcoverings; *sub nom.* Roberts *v.* Cleveland Area Health
    Authority; Garland *v.* British Rail Engineering; MacGregor Wallcoverings *v.*
    Turton [1979] I.C.R. 558; [1979] 1 W.L.R. 754; [1979] I.R.L.R. 244; (1979) 123
    S.J. 300; [1979] 2 All E.R. 1163, C.A.; reversing Turton *v.* MacGregor
    Wallcoverings [1977] I.R.L.R. 249 341
Turvey *v.* Cheney (C. W.) and Son Ltd. [1979] I.C.R. 341; [1979] I.R.L.R. 105, E.A.T. 293
Tyne and Clyde Warehouses *v.* Hamerton [1978] I.C.R. 661; (1978) 13 I.T.R. 66,
    E.A.T. 13
Tyrer *v.* Smart [1979] 1 W.L.R. 113; (1978) 123 S.J. 65; [1979] 1 All E.R. 321; [1979]
    S.T.C. 34; [1978] T.R. 443; (1978) 52 T.C. 533; *sub nom.* Smart *v.* Tyrer [1979]
    I.R.L.R. 121, H.L.; reversing [1978] 1 W.L.R. 415, C.A. 127

UBAF Bank Ltd. *v.* Davis [1978] I.R.L.R. 442, E.A.T. 262
Uddin *v.* Associated Portland Cement Manufacturers Ltd. [1965] 2 Q.B. 582; [1965]
    2 W.L.R. 1183; (1965) 109 S.J. 313; [1965] 2 All E.R. 213; (1965) 63 L.G.R. 241,
    C.A.; affirming [1965] 2 Q.B. 15 573
Umar *v.* Plaistar Ltd. [1981] I.C.R. 727, E.A.T. 150
Under Water Welders & Repairers Ltd. and S.B.C. (Under Water) Ltd. *v.* Street and
    Longthorne [1967] 1 Lloyd's Rep. 364; [1967] F.S.R. 194; [1968] R.P.C. 498;
    (1968) 117 New L.J. 547 76
Union of Construction, Allied Trades and Technicians *v.* Ellison Carpentry Contractors
    Ltd. [1976] I.R.L.R. 398 296
——— *v.* Rooke (H.) and Son Ltd. [1978] I.C.R. 818; (1978) 122 S.J. 229; (1978) 13 I.T.R.
    310; [1978] I.R.L.R. 204, E.A.T. 296
Union of Shop, Distributive and Allied Workers *v.* Sketchley Ltd. [1981] I.C.R. 644;
    [1981] I.R.L.R. 291, E.A.T. 369
United Biscuits (U.K.) Ltd. *v.* Fall [1979] I.R.L.R. 110 ....507, 509
——— *v.* Young [1978] I.R.L.R. 15, E.A.T. 316
United Kingdom Atomic Energy Authority *v.* Claydon [1974] I.C.R. 128; [1974] I.T.R.
    185; (1973) 16 K.I.R. 94; [1974] I.R.L.R. 6, N.I.R.C. 271
University Council of the Vidyodaya University of Ceylon *v.* Silva [1965] 1 W.L.R. 77;
    (1965) 108 S.J. 896; [1964] 3 All E.R. 865, P.C. 16
Universe Tankships Inc. of Monrovia *v.* International Transport Workers Federation
    [1981] I.C.R. 129, C.A.; reversed [1982] 2 All E.R. 67, H.L. 483, 505

Vacher *v.* London Society of Compositors [1913] A.C. 107; 82 L.J.K.B. 232; 107 L.T.
    722; 29 T.L.R. 73; 57 S.J. 75; [1911–13] All E.R. Rep. 241, H.L.; affirming [1912]
    3 K.B. 547, C.A. 493
Vandyke *v.* Fender (Sun Insurance Office, Third Party) [1970] 2 Q.B. 292; [1970] 2
    W.L.R. 929; (1970) 114 S.J. 205; [1970] 2 All E.R. 335; (1970) 8 K.I.R. 854;
    [1970] R.T.R. 236; [1970] 1 Lloyd's Rep. 320; C.A.; reversing [1969] 3 W.L.R.
    217..606, 626
Vaughan *v.* Weighpack [1974] I.C.R. 261; [1974] I.T.R. 226; (1974) 16 K.I.R. 233; [1974]
    I.R.L.R. 105, N.I.R.C. 258

Vaux and Associated Breweries *v.* Ward (1969) 113 S.J. 920; (1969) 7 K.I.R. 308, D.C. 276

Veness *v.* Dyson, Bell and Co.; *The Times*, May 25, 1965; *The Guardian*, May 25, 1965 70

Vickers Ltd. *v.* Smith [1977] I.R.L.R. 11, E.A.T. 202, 219

Videan *v.* British Transport Commission [1963] 2 Q.B. 650; [1963] 3 W.L.R. 374; (1963) 107 S.J. 458; [1963] 2 All E.R. 860, C.A. 574

Vine *v.* National Dock Labour Board [1957] A.C. 488; [1957] 2 W.L.R. 106; (1957) 101 S.J. 86; [1956] 3 All E.R. 939; [1956] 2 Lloyd's Rep. 567, H.L.; reversing in part [1956] 1 Q.B. 658; [1956] 2 W.L.R. 311; (1956) S.J. 73; [1956] 1 All E.R. 1; [1955] 2 Lloyd's Rep. 531 ....11, 15, 175, 446

Vinnyey *v.* Star Paper Mills Ltd. [1965] 1 All E.R. 175 578

Virdee *v.* E.C.C. Quarries Ltd. [1978] I.R.L.R. 295 321

Vokes Ltd. *v.* Bear [1974] I.C.R. 1; [1974] I.T.R. 85; (1973) 15 K.I.R. 302; [1973] I.R.L.R. 363, N.I.R.C. 216, 250, 263

Waddington *v.* Leicester Council for Voluntary Services [1977] I.C.R. 266; [1977] W.L.R. 544; (1976) 121 S.J. 84; [1977] I.R.L.R. 32; (1976) 12 I.T.R. 65, E.A.T. 310

Wagon Mound, The. *See* Overseas Tankship (U.K.) Ltd. *v.* Morts Dock and Engineering Co. (The Wagon Mound).

—— (No. 2). *See* Overseas Tankship (U.K.) Ltd. *v.* Miller Steamship Co. Pty.

Walker *v.* Bletchley Flettons Ltd. [1937] 1 All E.R. 170 560

—— *v.* British Guarantee Association (1852) 18 Q.B. 277; 21 L.J.Q.B. 257; 19 L.T.(o.s.) 87; 16 J.P. 582; 16 Jur. 885; 118 E.R. 104 96

—— *v.* Crystal Palace Football Club [1910] 1 K.B. 87; 79 L.J.K.B. 229; 101 L.T. 645; 26 T.L.R. 71; 54 S.J. 65; 3 B.W.C.C. 53, C.A. 5

—— *v.* Wedgwood (Josiah) and Sons Ltd. [1978] I.C.R. 744; (1978) 13 I.T.R. 271; [1978] I.R.L.R. 105, E.A.T. 188, 189

Walkley *v.* Precision Forgings Ltd. [1979] 1 W.L.R. 606; (1979) 123 S.J. 354; [1979] 2 All E.R. 548, H.L.; reversing [1978] 1 W.L.R. 1228, C.A. 596

Wallace *v.* Guy (E.J.) Ltd. [1973] I.C.R. 117; (1972) 14 K.I.R. 124; [1973] I.T.R. 154; [1973] I.R.L.R. 175, N.I.R.C. 206

—— *v.* South Eastern Education and Library Board [1980] I.R.L.R. 193, N.I.C.A. 322

Wallwork *v.* Fielding [1922] 2 K.B. 66; 91 L.J.K.B. 568; 127 L.T. 131; 86 J.P. 133; 38 T.L.R. 441; 66 S.J. 366; [1922] All E.R. Rep. 298; 20 L.G.R. 618, C.A. 455

Ward *v.* Barclay Perkins and Co. Ltd. [1939] 1 All E.R. 287 172

—— *v.* Bradford Corporation (1971) L.G.R. 27 226

—— *v.* Tesco Stores Ltd. [1976] 1 W.L.R. 810; (1976) 120 S.J. 550; [1976] 1 All E.R. 219; [1976] I.R.L.R. 92 572

Ward, Lock & Co. *v.* Operative Printers' Assistants' Society (1906) 22 T.L.R. 327, C.A.
524, 525, 526

Ware and De Freville *v.* Motor Trade Association [1921] 3 K.B. 40; 90 L.J.K.B. 949; 125 L.T. 265; 37 T.L.R. 213; 65 S.J. 239, C.A. 493

Warner Brother Pictures Inc. *v.* Nelson [1937] 1 K.B. 209; 106 L.J.K.B. 97; 155 L.T. 538; 53 T.L.R. 14; 80 S.J. 855; [1936] 3 All E.R. 160 176

Warren *v.* Henlys Ltd. [1948] W.N. 449; [1948] 2 All E.R. 935; 92 S.J. 706 610

Wass (W. and J.) Ltd. *v.* Binns [1982] I.R.L.R. 283 211

Waterman *v.* Fryer [1922] 1 K.B. 499; 91 L.J.K.B. 315; 126 L.T.316; 38 T.L.R. 87; 66 S.J. 108; [1921] All E.R. Rep. 582; 20 L.G.R. 691, D.C. 21

Watling (N.C.) and Co. Ltd. *v.* Richardson [1978] I.C.R. 1049; [1979] I.T.R. 333; [1978] I.R.L.R. 255, E.A.T. 202, 219, 249

Watson *v.* Smith (1941) 57 T.L.R. 552; 85 S.J. 316; [1941] 2 All E.R. 725 444

Watt *v.* Hertfordshire County Council [1954] 1 W.L.R. 835; (1954) 118 J.P. 377; (1954) 98 S.J. 372; [1954] 2 All E.R. 368; (1954) 52 L.G.R. 383, C.A.; affirming [1954] 1 W.L.R. 208 577

Watts, Watts Co. *v.* Steeley (1968) 3 I.T.R. 363; [1968] 2 Lloyd's Rep. 179, D.C. 276

Wayne Tank and Pump Co. *v.* Employers' Liability Corporation [1974] Q.B. 57; [1973] 3 W.L.R. 483; (1973) 117 S.J. 564; [1973] 3 All E.R. 825; [1973] 2 Lloyd's Rep. 237, C.A.; reversing [1972] 2 Lloyd's Rep. 141 584

Wearing *v*. Pirelli Ltd. [1977] I.C.R. 90; [1977] 1 W.L.R. 48; [1977] 1 All E.R. 339;
 [1977] I.R.L.R. 36, H.L. 560
Weaver *v*. Tredegar Iron and Coal Co. Ltd. [1940] A.C. 955; 109 L.J.K.B. 621; 164 L.T.
 231; 56 T.L.R. 813; 84 S.J. 586; [1940] 3 All E.R. 157 ....606, 607, 629
Weavings *v*. Kirk and Randall [1904] 1 K.B. 213; 73 L.J.K.B. 77; 89 L.T. 577; 68 J.P. 91;
 52 W.R. 209; 20 T.L.R. 152; 6 W.C.C. 95, C.A. 543
Webb *v*. Rose cited (1769) 4 Burr. 2303 81
Webster *v*. United Kingdom 7806/77 [1981] I.R.L.R. 480 240
Weddel (W.) & Co. Ltd. *v*. Tepper [1980] I.C.R. 286; [1979] 124 S.J. 80; [1980] I.R.L.R.
 96, C.A. 198, 199
Weevsmay *v*. Kings [1977] I.C.R. 244, E.A.T. 302
Weinberger *v*. Inglis [1919] A.C. 606, H.L.; affirming [1918] 1 Ch. 517, C.A. ...303, 405, 408
Welsh (B.) *v*. Associated Steel and Tools Co. Ltd. [1973] I.R.L.R. 111 222
Wessex Dairies Ltd. *v*. Smith [1935] 2 K.B. 80; 104 L.J.K.B. 484; 153 L.T. 185; 51
 T.L.R. 439; [1935] All E.R. Rep. 75 75
Westall Richardson Ltd. *v*. Roulson [1954] 1 W.L.R. 905; [1954] 98 S.J. 423; [1954] 2 All
 E.R. 448 5
Western Excavating (E.C.C.) Ltd. *v*. Sharp [1978] Q.B. 761; [1978] I.C.R. 221; [1978]
 2 W.L.R. 344; (1977) 121 S.J. 814; [1978] 1 All E.R. 713; (1978) 13 I.T.R. 132,
 C.A.; reversing [1978] I.R.L.R. 27, E.A.T. 47, 70, 71, 73, 165, 187,
                         188, 337, 464
Westwick *v*. Theodor (1875) L.R. 10 Q.B. 224; 44 L.J.Q.B. 110; 32 L.T. 696; 39 J.P.
 646; 23 W.R. 620 21
Westwood *v*. Post Office [1974] A.C. 1; [1973] 3 W.L.R. 287; (1973) 117 S.J. 600; [1973]
 3 All E.R. 184; (1973)15 K.I.R. 113, H.L.; reversing [1973] 1 Q.B. 591; [1973]
 2 W.L.R. 135; (1972) 117 S.J. 15; [1973] 1 All E.R. 283; (1973) 14 K.I.R. 96,
 C.A. 573, 593
Wetherall (Bond St., W.1) *v*. Lynn [1978] I.C.R. 205; (1978) 1 W.L.R. 200; (1977) 122
 S.J. 94; (1977) 13 I.T.R. 87; [1977] I.R.L.R. 333, E.A.T. 46, 70, 157, 187
Wheeler *v*. New Merton Board Mills Ltd. [1933] 2 K.B. 669; 1034 L.J.K.B. 17; 149 L.T.
 587; 49 T.L.R. 574; [1933] All E.R. Rep. 28; 26 B.W.C.C. 230, C.A. 25, 589
White *v*. British Sugar Corporation Ltd. [1977] I.R.L.R. 121 340
—— *v*. Kuzych [1951] A.C. 585; [1951] 2 T.L.R. 277; (1951) 95 S.J. 527; [1951] 2 All
 E.R. 435, P.C.; reversing [1950] 4 D.L.R. 187; affirming [1949] 4 D.L.R.
 662 ....434, 439
—— *v*. London Transport Executive [1981] I.R.L.R. 261, E.A.T. 190
—— *v*. Pressed Steel Fisher Ltd. [1980] I.R.L.R. 176, E.A.T. 113
—— *v*. Riley [1921] 1 Ch.1; 89 L.J.Ch. 628; 124 L.T. 168; 36 T.L.R. 849; 64 S.J. 725;
 [1920] All E.R. Rep. 371 500
White (Arthur) (Contractors) *v*. Tarmac Civil Engineering [1967] 1 W.L.R. 1508; (1967)
 111 S.J. 831; [1967] 3 All E.R. 568, H.L.; reversing *sub nom*. Spalding *v*. Tarmac
 Civil Engineering [1966] 1 W.L.R. 156, C.A. 600
Whiterod *v*. Safety Fast Ltd. (1975) COIT 306/96 148
Whittaker *v*. Minister of Pensions and National Insurance [1967] 1 Q.B. 156; [1966]
 3 W.L.R. 1090; (1966) 110 S.J. 924; [1966] 3 All E.R. 531; (1966) K.I.R. 669 6
Whitwood Chemical Co. Ltd. *v*. Hardman [1891] 2 Ch. 416; 60 L.J.Ch. 428; 64 L.T. 716;
 39 W.R. 433; 7 T.L.R. 325, C.A. 176
Wigan Borough Council *v*. Davies [1979] I.C.R. 411; [1979] I.R.L.R. 127, E.A.T. 46,
                             70, 156
Wigan Case (1869) 21 L.T. 122; 1 O'M. & H. 188 495
Wilkins *v*. Cantrell and Cochrane (G.B.) Ltd. [1978] I.R.L.R. 483, E.A.T. 464, 466
Willard *v*. N.U.P.B.P.W., *The Times*, May 29, 1938 433
Williams *v*. Butlers Ltd. [1975] I.C.R. 208; [1975] 1 W.L.R. 946; (1975) 119 S.J. 368;
 [1975] 2 All E.R. 889; [1975] I.R.L.R. 120; (1975) 18 Man.Law. 8, D.C. 128, 129
—— *v*. Compair Maxam Ltd. [1982] I.R.L.R. 83 .... 194, 203, 211, 213, 215,
                 221, 222, 225, 247, 249, 295, 297, 431
—— *v*. Grimshaw (1967) 112 S.J. 14; (1967) 3 K.I.R. 610 571
—— *v*. National Theatre Board Ltd. [1981] I.C.R. 248; [1981] I.R.L.R. 5,
 E.A.T. 247
—— *v*. North's Navigation Collieries (1899) Ltd. [1906] A.C. 136; 75 L.J.K.B. 334; 94
 L.T. 447; 70 J.P. 217; 54 W.R. 485; 22 T.L.R. 372; 50 S.J. 343; H.L.; reversing
 [1904] 2 K.B. 44, C.A. 128

—— v. Port of Liverpool Stevedoring Co. Ltd. [1956] 1 W.L.R. 551; 100 S.J. 381; [1956]
    2 All E.R. 69; [1956] 1 Lloyd's Rep. 541 593
—— v. Western Mail & Echo Ltd. [1980] I.C.R. 366; [1980] I.R.L.R. 222,
    E.A.T. 466
Williamson v. National Coal Board [1970] I.T.R. 43 291
Williamson (J.W.) v. Alcan (U.K.) Ltd. [1977] I.R.L.R. 303, E.A.T. 197, 224
Willment Bros. Ltd. v. Oliver [1979] I.C.R. 378; [1979] I.R.L.R. 393, E.A.T. 260
Wilson v. Maynard Shipbuilding Consultants A.B. [1978] Q.B. 665; [1978] I.C.R. 376;
    [1978] 2 W.L.R. 466; (1977) 121 S.J. 792; [1978] 2 All E.R. 78; (1978) 13 I.T.R.
    23; [1977] I.R.L.R. 491, C.A.; reversing (1976) 11 I.T.R. 303, E.A.T. 52, 63, 153
—— v. Merry (1868) L.R. 1 Sc. & Div. 326; 19 L.T. 30, 32 J.P. 675, H.L. 568, 569
—— v. Racher [1974] I.C.R. 428; (1974) 16 K.I.R. 212; [1974] I.R.L.R. 114, C.A. 93
—— v. Tyneside Cleaning Co. [1958] 2 Q.B. 110; [1958] 2 W.L.R. 900; (1958) 102 S.J.
    380; [1958] 2 All E.R. 265, C.A. 569, 580
—— v. Uccelli (1929) 45 T.L.R. 395 177
—— v. Underhill House School Ltd. (1977) 12 I.T.R. 165; [1977] I.R.L.R. 475, E.A.T.   275
Wilson (Joshua) and Bros. Ltd. v. Union of Shop, Distributive and Allied Workers
    [1978] I.C.R. 614; [1978] 3 All E.R. 4; (1978) 13 I.T.R. 229; [1978] I.R.L.R. 120,
    E.A.T. 368
Wilsons and Clyde Coal Co. Ltd. v. English [1938] A.C. 57; 106 L.J.P.C. 117; 157 L.T.
    406; 53 T.L.R. 944; 81 S.J. 700; [1937] 3 All E.R. 628, H.L. 569
Wiltshire County Council v. National Association of Teachers in Further and Higher
    Education and Guy [1980] I.C.R. 455; [1980] I.R.L.R. 198; (1980) 78 L.G.R. 445;
    C.A.; affirming [1978] I.C.R. 968, E.A.T. 154
Wiltshire Police Authority v. Wynn [1980] I.C.R. 401; reversed [1981] Q.B. 95, C.A. 13
Winnett v. Seamarks Bros. Ltd. [1978] I.C.R. 1240; (1978) I.R.L.R. 387, E.A.T. ...119, 446
Winter v. Cardiff Rural District Council [1950] W.N. 193; (1950) J.P. 234; [1950] 1 All
    E.R. 819; (1950) 49 L.G.R. 1, H.L. 580
—— v. Deepsawin Garages Ltd. [1969] I.T.R. 162 147
Winterhalter Gastronom Ltd. v. Webb [1973] I.C.R. 245; [1973] I.T.R. 313; [1973]
    I.R.L.R. 120, N.I.R.C. 217
Wishart v. National Coal Board [1974] I.C.R. 460; [1974] I.T.R. 320, N.I.R.C. 144
Withers v. Flackwell Heath Football Supporters' Club [1981] I.R.L.R. 307, E.A.T. 12
—— v. Perry Chain Co. Ltd. [1961] 1 W.L.R. 1314; (1961) 105 S.J. 648; [1961] 3 All
    E.R. 676; (1961) 59 L.G.R. 496, C.A. 575, 578
Wolfe v. Matthews (1882) 21 Ch.D. 194; 51 L.J.Ch. 833; 47 L.T. 158; 30 W.R. 838 388
Wolstenholme v. Amalgamated Musicians' Union; Wolstenholme v. Ariss [1920] 2 Ch.
    403; 89 L.J.Ch. 395; 123 L.T. 741, 64 S.J. 585; 84 J.P. 266..........................427, 432
Wood v. Freeloader Ltd. [1977] I.R.L.R. 455 ....27, 70, 188, 337
—— v. Kettering Co-operative Chemists Ltd. [1978] I.R.L.R. 438, E.A.T. 223
—— v. Leeds Area Health Authority (Training) [1974] I.C.R. 535; [1974] I.R.L.R. 204;
    (1974) I.T.R. 352, N.I.R.C. 17
Woodford v. Smith [1970] 1 W.L.R. 806; (1970) 114 S.J. 245; [1970] 1 All E.R. 1091n. ... 404
Woodhouse v. Brotherhood (Peter) [1972] 2 Q.B. 520; [1972] 3 W.L.R. 215; (1972) 116
    S.J. 467; [1972] 3 All E.R. 91; [1972] I.C.R. 186; (1972) 13 K.I.R. 45, C.A.;
    reversing on first appeal [1972] 1 W.L.R. 401, N.I.R.C. 148
Woods v. W.M. Car Services (Peterborough) Ltd. [1981] I.C.R. 666; [1981] I.R.L.R.
    347; subsequent proceedings [1982] I.R.L.R. 315.. 72, 94
Worringham v. Lloyds Bank Ltd. (No. 69/80) [1981] I.C.R. 558; [1981] 1 W.L.R. 950;
    (1981) 125 S.J. 442; [1981] 2 All E.R. 434; [1981] 2 C.M.L.R. 1 [1981] I.R.L.R.
    178, European Ct.; [1980] 1 C.M.L.R. 293, C.A.; reversing [1979] I.C.R. 174,
    E.A.T. 318, 341
Worthington Pumping Engine Co. v. Moore (1902) 19 T.L.R. 84; 20 R.P.C. 41 90
Wragg (Thomas) and Sons Ltd. v. Wood [1976] I.C.R. 313 292
Wright v. Dunlop Rubber Co. Ltd. (1972) 12 K.I.R. 255, C.A.; affirming (1972) S.J. 336;
    (1971) 11 K.I.R. 311...539, 573, 576
Writers' Guild of Great Britain v. British Broadcasting Corporation [1974] I.C.R. 234;
    [1974] 1 All E.R. 574, N.I.R.C.; previous proceedings [1973] I.R.L.R. 342,
    N.I.R.C. 17
Wrottesley v. Regent Street Florida Restaurant [1951] 2 K.B. 277; [1951] 1 T.L.R. 338;
    (1951) 115 J.P. 185; (1951) 95 S.J. 139; [1951] 1 All E.R. 566; (1951) 49 L.G.R.
    369, D.C. 301

Wyatt v. Kreglinger & Ferneau [1933] 1 K.B. 793; 102 L.J.K.B. 325; 148 L.T. 521; 49
 T.L.R. 264; [1933] All E.R. Rep. 349, C.A. 86
Wylie v. Dee & Co. (Menswear) Ltd. [1978] I.R.L.R. 103 340

Yetton v. Eastwoods Froy Ltd. [1966] 1 W.L.R. 104, (1966) 111 S.J. 32; [1966] 3 All
 E.R. 353; (1966) 1 K.I.R. 469 177
Yewens v. Noakes (1880) 6 Q.B.D. 530; 50 L.J.Q.B. 132, 44 L.T. 128; 45 J.P. 468; 28
 W.R. 562; 1 Tax Cas. 260, C.A. 4
York and Reynolds v. College Hosiery Co. Ltd. [1978] I.R.L.R. 53 101
Yorkshire Miners' Association v. Howden [1903] 1 K.B. 308; 72 L.J.K.B. 176; 88 L.T.
 134; 19 T.L.R. 193; 47 S.J. 237, C.A.; affirmed [1905] A.C. 256 388
Young v. Box (Edward) & Co. Ltd. [1951] 1 T.L.R. 789, C.A. 611
—— v. Canadian Northern Ry. Co. [1931] A.C. 83 .... 36, 285
—— v. Carr Fasteners Ltd. [1979] I.C.R. 844; [1979] I.R.L.R. 420, E.A.T. 113
—— v. Ladies Imperial Club [1920] 2 K.B. 523; 89 L.J.K.B. 563; 123 L.T. 191; 36 T.L.R.
 392; 64 S.J. 374, C.A. 432
—— v. Thomas (F.) and Co. Ltd. [1972] I.R.L.R. 40 217
—— v. United Kingdom, The [1981] I.R.L.R. 408 413
Young and James v. United Kingdom 7601/76 [1981] I.R.L.R. 480 240
Young & Woods Ltd. v. West [1980] I.R.L.R. 201, C.A. 3, 11, 13

Zarb and Samuels v. British & Brazilian Produce Co. (Sales) Ltd. [1978] I.R.L.R. 78,
 E.A.T. 151
Zarezynska v. Levy [1979] I.C.R. 184; [1979] 1 W.L.R. 125; (1978) 122 S.J. 776; [1979]
 1 All E.R. 814; [1978] I.R.L.R. 532, E.A.T. 328
Zucker v. Astrid Jewels Ltd. [1978] I.C.R. 1088; (1978) 13 I.T.R. 568; [1978] I.R.L.R.
 385, E.A.T. 121

Wyatt v. Kreglinger & Fernau [1933] 1 K.B. 793; [1933] 1 K.B. 325; 149 L.T. 521; 39 30
— v. L.B. &S.I. [1955] A.E.R. 9; ...; C.A. 50
Wyllie v. Dee & Co. (Menswear) Ltd. [1978] I.R.L.R. 103 146

Yetton v. Eastwoods Froy Ltd. [1966] 1 W.L.R. 104; (1966) 110 S.J. 52; [1966] 3 All
    E.R. 353; [1966] 1 K.I.R. 469 127
Yewens v. Noakes (1880) 6 Q.B.D. 530; 50 L.J.Q.B. 132; 44 L.T. 128; 45 J.P. 468; 28
    W.R. 562; 45 J.P.Tax Cas. 260; C.A. 6
York and Reynolds v. College Hosiery Co. Ltd. [1978] I.R.L.R. 53 101
Yorkshire Miners' Association v. Howden [1905] 1 K.B. 803; 74 L.J.K.B. 176; 91 L.T.
    738; 19 T.L.R. 194; 47 S.J. 197; C.A.; affirmed [1905] A.C. 256 288
Young (Edward) & Co. Ltd. [1951] 1 T.L.R. 790; C.A. 101
    — v. Canadian Northern Ry. Co. [1931] A.C. 83 .... 30, 281
    — v. Carr Fasteners Ltd. [1979] I.C.R. 844; [1979] I.R.L.R. 420; E.A.T. 118
    — v. Ladies Imperial Club [1920] 2 K.B. 523; 89 L.J.K.B. 563; 123 L.T. 191; 36 T.L.R.
    769; 64 S.J. 374; C.A. 432
    — v. Thomas (Herbert) Co. Ltd. [1927] I.R.L.R. 41 217
    — v. United Kingdom (The) [1981] I.R.L.R. 408 113
Young and James v. United Kingdom [1977] I.C.R. [1981] E.U. R.580 280
Young & Woods Ltd. v. West [1980] I.R.L.R. 201; C.A. 5, 11, 13

Zarb and Samuels v. British & Brazilian Produce Co. (Sales) Ltd. [1978] I.R.L.R. 78;
    E.A.T. 151
Zarczynska v. Levy [1979] I.C.R. 184; [1979] 1 W.L.R. 125; [1979] 123 S.J. 216; [1979]
    1 All E.R. 814; [1979] I.R.L.R. 532; E.A.T. 178
Zucker v. Astrid Jewels Ltd. [1978] I.C.R. 1088; [1979] 13 I.T.R. 568; [1978] I.R.L.R.
    385; E.A.T. 221

TABLE OF SOCIAL SECURITY COMMISSIONERS' DECISIONS

C.I. 27/49 ... 618
C.I. 29/49 ... 617, 618
C.I. 39/49 ... 618
C.I. 51/49 ... 620
C.I. 114/49 ... 618
C.I. 148/49 ... 626
C.I. 120/49 ... 628
C.I. 182/49 ... 626
C.I. 257/49 ... 617
C.I. 5/50 ... 620
C.I. 83/50 ... 618
C.I. 88/50 ... 630
C.I. 125/50 ... 618
C.I. 172/50 ... 618
C.I. 334/50 ... 630
C.I. 374/50 ... 628
C.S. 221/49 ... 65
C.S. 414/50 ... 631
C.S.I. 3/49 ... 624
C.S.I. 6/49 ... 628
C.S.I. 21/49 ... 618
C.W.I. 20/49 ... 66
R(G) 3/54 ... 65
R(G) 3/62 ... 632
R(I) 70/50 ... 618
R(I) 9/51 ... 626
R(I) 14/51 ... 619, 628
R(I) 21/51 ... 626
R(I) 47/51 ... 618
R(I) 49/51 ... 628
R(I) 52/51 ... 617
R(I) 62/51 ... 624
R(I) 63/51 ... 623
R(I) 65/51 ... 628
R(I) 79/51 ... 626
R(I) 8/52 ... 624
R(I) 10/52 ... 627
R(I) 31/52 ... 618
R(I) 34/52 ... 622
R(I) 49/52 ... 618
R(I) 62/52 ... 624
R(I) 63/52 ... 630
R(I) 71/52 ... 621
R(I) 72/52 ... 624
R(I) 78/52 ... 622
R(I) 1/53 ... 626
R(I) 11/53 ... 628
R(I) 32/53 ... 622
R(I) 34/53 ... 622
R(I) 46/53 ... 621
R(I) 54/53 ... 618
R(I) 59/53 ... 626

R(I) 71/53 ... 630
R(I) 90/53 ... 620
R(I) 3/54 ... 624
R(I) 11/54 ... 628
R(I) 52/54 ... 623
R(I) 53/54 ... 624
R(I) 72/54 ... 625
R(I) 75/54 ... 630
R(I) 13/55 ... 65
R(I) 18/55 ... 627
R(I) 36/55 ... 622, 624
R(I) 7/56 ... 617
R(I) 11/56 ... 623
R(I) 31/56 ... 617, 618
R(I) 41/56 ... 621
R(I) 48/56 ... 625
R(I) 53/56 ... 624
R(I) 36/57 ... 626
R(I) 4/58 ... 628
R(I) 12/58 ... 618
R(I) 16/58 ... 626
R(I) 21/58 ... 620
R(I) 1/59 ... 627
R(I) 38/59 ... 624
R(I) 46/59 ... 628
R(I) 17/60 ... 628
R(I) 8/61 ... 622
R(I) 16/61 ... 629
R(I) 20/61 ... 627
R(I) 43/61 ... 618
R(I) 3/62 ... 627
R(I) 4/62 ... 618
R(I) 2/63 ... 619, 630
R(I) 3/63 ... 620
R(I) 10/63 ... 616
R(I) 17/63 ... 621
R(I) 1/64 ... 620
R(I) 7/66 ... 628
R(I) 13/66 ... 621, 622, 624
R(I) 2/67 ... 627
R(I) 3/67 ... 619, 621, 630
R(I) 4/67 ... 624, 627
R(I) 5/67 ... 626
R(I) 6/67 ... 632
R(I) 1/68 ... 628
R(I) 2/68 ... 621, 624, 625
R(I) 13/68 ... 622, 626
R(I) 1/70 ... 622
R(I) 3/71 ... 626
R(I) 4/71 ... 632
R(I) 2/72 ... 632
R(I) 3/72 ... 620

R(I) 1/73 633
R(I) 4/73 623
R(I) 7/73 617
R(I) 16/75 620
R(S) 18/35 66
R(S) 69/50 66
R(S) 9/51 67
R(S) 11/51 66
R(S) 24/51 66
R(S) 13/52 66
R(S) 24/52 66
R(S) 34/52 66
R(S) 2/53 67
R(S) 9/53 66
R(S) 16/54 65
R(S) 8/55 65
R(S) 17/55 66
R(S) 1/58 65
R(S) 4/60 65
R(S) 7/60 .... 65, 66
R(S) 10/61 66

R(U) 20/27 488
R(U) 19/51 488
R(U) 17/52 487
R(U) 41/56 489
R(U) 24/57 487
R(U) 25/57 488
R(U) 18/58 489
R(U) 21/59 488
R(U) 12/60 488
R(U) 5/61 487
R(U) 3/62 .... 487, 489
R(U) 15/62 631
R(U) 11/63 488
R(U) 23/64 487
R(U) 1/65 488
R(U) 4/65 489
R(U) 5/66 489
R(U) 3/69 .... 488, 489
R(U) 1/70 487
R(U) 7/71 630
R(U) 8/71 487

TABLE OF STATUTES

1700 Act of Settlement (12 & 13 Will. 3, c. 2) 23

1800 Unlawful Combinations of Workmen Act (39 & 40 Geo. 3, c. 106) 452

1802 Preservation of the Health and Morals of Apprentices and others employed in Cotton and Other Mills and Cotton and Other Factories Act (42 Geo. 3, c. 73) 536

1831 Truck Act (1 & 2 Will. 4, c. 37)...............126–127, 128, 129, 130, 131, 349
 s. 3 128
 s. 9 130
 s. 23 129
 s. 24 129
 s. 25 127

1870 Apportionment Act (33 & 34 Vict. c. 34) 61
 s. 2 61

1871 Trade Union Act (34 & 35 Vict. c. 31) 349, 384, 387, 388, 390, 391
 s. 3 ....391, 392, 404, 426
 s. 4 426
 s. 9 493
 s. 23 384

1875 Explosives Act (38 & 39 Vict. c. 17) 566
 ss. 30–32, 80, 116–121 566

 Conspiracy and Protection of Property Act (38 & 39 Vict. c. 32).........................453, 525
 s. 3 491
 s. 4 ....458, 491
 s. 5 ....458, 491, 533
 s. 7 ....453, 523, 524, 525
  (2) 528
  (4) 528

 Employers and Workmen Act (38 & 39 Vict. c. 90) 21
 s. 5 21
 s. 12 21

1876 Trade Union Amendment Act (39 & 40 Vict. c. 22) 387, 393
 s. 16 387

1878 Factory and Workshop Act (41 & 42 Vict. c. 16) 537

1882 Boiler Explosions Act (45 & 46 Vict. c. 22) 566

1887 Truck Amendment Act (50 & 51 Vict. c. 46)—
 s. 2 127
 s. 11 130

 Coal Mines Regulation Act (50 & 51 Vict. c. 58)—
 s. 13(1) 131

1890 Boiler Explosions Act (53 & 54 Vict. c. 35) 566

1891 Factory and Workshop Act (54 & 55 Vict. c. 75) 131

1894 Merchant Shipping Act (57 & 58 Vict. c. 60) 19, 491

1896 Conciliation Act (59 & 60 Vict. c. 30).........................349, 363

 Truck Act (59 & 60 Vict. c. 44)...........................129, 130
 s. 1 130
 s. 2 25
 s. 3 129
 s. 4 130

1897 Workmen's Compensation Act (60 & 61 Vict. c. 37) 614

1901 Factory and Workshops Act (1 Edw. 7, c. 22) 131

1902 Shops Clubs Act (2 Edw. 7, c. 21) 132

1906 Alkali, etc., Works Regulations Act (6 Edw. 7, c. 14) 566

 Trade Disputes Act (6 Edw. 7, c. 47)...........453, 488, 492, 493, 500, 525, 527
 s. 1 ....469, 518
 s. 2 ....525, 527
  (2) 523
 s. 3 ....477, 514, 517, 525
 s. 4 493
  (1)(2)........................ 492–493
 s. 5(3) 504

1909 Revenue Act (9 Edw. 7, c. 43) ... 566
 s. 11 566

1913 Trade Union Act (2 & 3 Geo. 5, c. 30)..............396, 397, 398, 399
 s. 1 ....384, 396
 s. 2 384
 s. 3(1) 396
  (b) 398
 s. 5(1) 398

1914 Bankruptcy Act (4 & 5 Geo. 5, c. 59)—
 s. 33 123

1917 Trade Union (Amalgamation) Act (7 & 8 Geo. 5, c. 24) 393

1918 Trade Boards Act (8 & 9 Geo. 5,
         c. 32)..........................350, 352
1919 Anthrax Prevention Act (10 & 11
         Geo. 5, c. 23) 566
      Police Act (9 & 10 Geo. 5, c. 46)
                                    490, 533
      Checkweighing in Various Indus-
         tries Act (9 & 10 Geo. 5,
         c. 51) 131
      Industrial Court Act (9 & 10
         Geo. 5, c. 69) 356
         Pt. I 357
         s. 2 363
      Electricity Supply Act (9 & 10
         Geo. 5, c. 69)—
         s. 31 491
      Sex Disqualification (Removal)
         Act (9 & 10 Geo. 5, c. 71) ... 303
1920 Emergency Powers Act (10 & 11
         Geo. 5, c. 55) 533
      Employment of Women, Young
         Persons and Children Act
         (10 & 11 Geo. 5, c. 65) 23,
                                    317, 566
         s. 1 22
1922 Celluloid and Cinematograph
         Film Act (12 & 13 Geo. 5,
         c. 35) 566
1923 Explosives Act (13 & 14 Geo. 5,
         c. 17) 566
1926 Public Health (Smoke Abate-
         ment) Act (16 & 17 Geo. 5,
         c. 43) 566
1927 Trade Union Act (17 & 18 Geo.
         5, c. 22) 533
1928 Petroleum (Consolidation) Act
         (18 & 19 Geo. 5, c. 32) 566
1933 Children and Young Persons Act
         (23 & 24 Geo. 5, c. 12)—
         s. 18(1) 22
1934 Law Reform (Miscellaneous Pro-
         visions) Act (24 & 25 Geo.
         5, c. 41)—
         s. 1 594
      Incitement to Disaffection Act
         (24 & 25 Geo. 5, c. 56)—
         s. 1 491
1936 Hours of Employment (Conven-
         tions) Act (26 Geo. 5 &
         Edw. 8, c. 22) 23, 317, 566
         s. 5 566
      Petroleum (Transfer of Licences)
         Act (26 Geo. 5 & Edw. 8,
         c. 27) 566
1937 Hydrogen Cyanide (Fumigation)
         Act (1 Edw. 8 & 1 Geo. 6,
         c. 45) 566
1938 Holidays with Pay Act (1 & 2
         Geo. 6, c. 70) 354

1940 Societies (Miscellaneous Provi-
         sions) Act (3 & 4 Geo. 6,
         c. 19)—
         s. 6 393
1942 Restoration of Pre-War Trade
         Practices Act (5 & 6 Geo. 6,
         c. 9) 382
1944 Disabled Persons (Employment)
         Act (7 & 8 Geo. 6, c. 10) 23, 24
         s. 7 23
         s. 9 23
            (5) 24
         s. 11 24
         s. 12 24
1945 Ministry of Fuel and Power Act
         (8 & 9 Geo. 6, c. 19) 566
         s. 1(1) 566
      Law Reform (Contributory
         Negligence) Act (8 & 9 Geo.
         6, c. 41) 569, 592
         s. 1 593
1946 Coal Industry Nationalisation
         Act (9 & 10 Geo. 6, c. 59) ... 566
         s. 42(1)(2) 566
1948 Radioactive Substances Act (11
         & 12 Geo. 6, c. 37) 566
         s. 5(1)(a) 566
      Law Reform (Personal Injuries)
         Act (11 & 12 Geo. 6, c. 41)
                                    568, 569
      Agricultural Wages Act (11 & 12
         Geo. 6, c. 47) 352
1950 Shops Act (14 Geo. 6, c. 28) 23
      Restoration of Pre-War Trade
         Practices Act (14 & 15 Geo.
         6, c. 9) 382
1951 Alkali, etc., Works Regulation
         (Scotland) Act (14 & 15
         Geo. 6, c. 21) 566
      Fireworks Act (14 & 15 Geo. 6,
         c. 58) 567
1952 Agriculture (Poisonous Sub-
         stances) Act (15 & 16 Geo. 6
         & 1 Eliz. 2, c. 60) 567
1953 Emergency Laws (Miscellaneous
         Provisions) Act (1 & 2 Eliz.
         2, c. 47) 567
         s. 3 567
      Post Office Act (1 & 2 Eliz. 2,
         c. 36)—
         s. 58 491
1954 Mines and Quarries Act (2 & 3
         Eliz. 2, c. 70) 23, 547, 567
         s. 124(2) 22
         s. 151 567
         s. 160 22
         s. 187 131
         Sched. V 131
1955 Aliens' Employment Act (4 & 5
         Eliz. 2, v. 18)—
         s. 1 23

1956 Agriculture (Safety, Health and
    Welfare Provisions) Act (4
    & 5 Eliz. 2, c. 49)........537, 567
    Restrictive Trade Practices Act
    (4 & 5 Eliz. 2, c. 68) 81, 475, 492
    s. 6(1)(10) 492
1957 Occupiers' Liability Act (5 & 6
    Eliz. 2, c. 31) 612
1958 Disabled Persons (Employment)
    Act (6 & 7 Eliz. 2, c. 33)—
    s. 2 23
    Dramatic and Musical Perfor-
    mers' Protection Act (6 & 7
    Eliz. 2, c. 44) 484
1959 Highways Act (7 & 8 Eliz. 2,
    c. 74) 528
1960 Payment of Wages Act (8 & 9
    Eliz. 2, c. 37) 127
1961 Factories Act (9 & 10 Eliz. 2,
    c. 34)...........127, 131, 340, 538,
    540, 543, 546, 554, 555,
    556, 565, 567, 570, 585
    Pt. II 556
    Pt. VI 317
    ss. 4, 7 567
    s. 12 555
    s. 13...........................555, 556
    s. 14.... 538, 553, 556, 558, 559, 561
    (1) 557
    s. 15 564
    s. 16 564
    s. 76 562
    s. 86 30
    s. 87(1) 22
    s. 89 22
    s. 93 340
    s. 135 ....131, 567
    s. 167 22
    s. 183 131
    Sched. VI 131
    Family Allowances and National
    Insurance Act (10 Eliz. 2,
    c. 6)—
    s. 2 619
    Public Health Act (9 & 10 Eliz. 2,
    c. 64)—
    s. 73 567
1962 Pipe-lines Act (c. 58) 567
    ss. 20–26, 33, 34, 42,
    Sched. 5 567
1963 Offices, Shops and Railway Pre-
    mises Act (c. 41)..........537, 567
    s. 23 575
    Limitation Act (c. 47) 594
    Contracts of Employment Act
    (c. 49) 153, 172, 263
    s. 4 42
    Sched. 1, para. 7 456
1964 Trade Union (Amalgamations,
    etc.) Act (c. 24) 393
    Emergency Powers Act (c. 38) ... 533

1964 Police Act (c. 48) 533
    s. 48 16
    s. 53(1) 491
1965 Trade Disputes Act (c. 48) 457,
    515, 516
    Nuclear Installations Act (c.
    57) 567
    ss. 1, 3–6, 22, 24, Sched. 2 567
    Redundancy Payments Act
    (c. 62) 100, 102, 146,
    182, 186, 263, 264, 266,
    269, 276, 278, 287
    s. 1 ....273, 275, 308
    (2)(b) 279
    s. 2(2)...........................291, 456
    (3) 290
    (4) 290
    s. 3(2)(a)(b) 293
    (c) 293
    (3) 294
    (5)...........................293, 294
    (8) 293
    s. 10...........................244, 459
    (1)(4) 244, 459
    s. 13............................146, 149
    (1) 147
    s. 37 456
1967 Companies Act (c. 81)—
    s. 16 362
1968 Trade Descriptions Act (c. 29)—
    s. 37(1) 552
    Civil Evidence Act (c. 64)—
    s. 11. 571
    Race Relations Act (c. 71) 319
    s. 3(1) 256
1969 Mines and Quarries (Tips) Act
    (c. 10) 567
    ss. 1–10 567
    Employer's Liability (Defective
    Equipment) Act (c. 37) 582
    s. 1 582
    (2) 583
    Family Law Reform Act
    (c. 46)—
    s. 1 24
    s. 9 24
    Employer's Liability (Compul-
    sory Insurance) Act (c.
    57)...............573, 593, 599, 613
1970 Merchant Shipping Act (c.
    36)............................ 19, 491
    Equal Pay Act (c. 41) 22, 30,
    291, 304, 305, 306, 307,
    308, 309, 310, 311, 313,
    314, 316, 317, 320, 321,
    329, 333
    s. 1(1)–(4) 304–305
    (1) 329
    (2) 313
    (3)...................310, 312, 313,
    314, 315, 316, 317, 329,
    333, 338

1970 Equal Pay Act—*cont.*
    s. 1(4).....306, 307, 308, 309 310, 326
      (13) 316
    s. 2(4) 135
    s. 3 ....317, 318, 360
    s. 3(4) 319
    ss. 4, 5 319
    s. 6(1) 318
      (*b*) 318
1971 Monies Management Act (c.
    20).................................... 567
  Attachment of Earnings Act
    (c. 32) 132
    s. 1 132
    s. 3 132
    s. 4 132
    s. 6 133
    s. 7 133
    s. 12 133
    s. 14 133
    s. 15 133
    Sched. 3, paras. 5, 6 133
          para. 7 133
  Industrial Relations Act (c.
    72)..................... 17, 18, 43, 119,
        182, 186, 204, 207, 231, 240,
        245, 254, 350, 355, 360,
        364, 367, 371, 373, 378,
        384, 385, 389, 390, 391,
        392, 393, 394, 396, 405,
        415, 431, 460, 461, 481,
        491, 492, 493, 500, 518,
        520, 526, 533, 534
    s. 18(2)(3) 378
      (4).........................378–379
      (5) 379
    s. 24(6) 207
    s. 26 467
    s. 33(4) 463
    s. 34(1) 375
    ss. 44–60 367
    s. 65(2) 405, 445
      (8)(*a*) 431
    s. 75 389
    s. 124(1) 356
    s. 128 ....466, 515
    s. 132 516
      (2) 518
      (4) 520
    s. 133 491
    s. 134 529
      (1) 529
    s. 136 520
    ss. 138–145 534
    s. 169 493
    Sched. 3, para. 38 353
    Sched. 9 493
  Immigration Act (c. 77) 23
1972 Superannuation Act (c. 11) 145
  Employment Medical Advisory
    Service Act (c. 28) 567
    ss. 1, 6, Sched. 1 567

1972 Children Act (c. 44)—
    s. 1 22
  Contracts of Employment Act
    (c. 53) 30, 244, 459
  National Insurance Act (c. 57)—
    s. 5(2)(*b*) 617
  European Communities Act
    (c. 68)—
    s. 2 313
1973 Employment of Children Act
    (c. 24)—
    s. 1 22
  Statute Law (Repeals) Act
    (c. 39) 21
    Sched. 2 127
1974 Health and Safety at Work, etc.,
    Act (c. 37)............ 112, 535–552
    Pt. I 546
    s. 1 367
    ss. 2–8 ....551, 553
    ss. 2–9 546
    s. 2 ....541, 543, 547
      (1)........................540, 541
      (2)........................540, 541
        (*a*) 541
        (*c*) 541
      (7) 549
    s. 3 542
      (1) 542
      (2) 542
      (3) 542
    s. 4 ....540, 543
      (3) 543
    s. 5 544
    s. 6 ....544, 545
    s. 7 543
    s. 8 544
    s. 14 554
    s. 15(3)(*a*) 546
      (6) 546
    s. 16............................547, 576
      (5)(6) 547
    s. 17 547
    s. 18(2) 549
    s. 20 550
    s. 21 551
    s. 22 551
    s. 24................................550, 551
    s. 25 550
    s. 28(8) 548
    s. 33 551
    s. 36................................544, 552
    s. 37 552
    s. 47 553
    s. 50 546
    s. 53 540
    Sched. 1............................566–567
    Sched. 3 546
  Merchant Shipping Act (c. 43)—
    s. 19(2) 20
      (3) 20

1974 Rehabilitation of Offenders Act
(c. 53) 254
Trade Union and Labour Relations Act (c. 52)............. 17, 21,
40, 92, 136, 186, 350, 355,
368, 375, 385, 389, 391,
392, 396, 467, 468, 488,
493, 501, 516, 518
s. 1 390
(1) 390
s. 2 .... 389, 390, 421
(1) 390
(a) 392
s. 2(5)................... 391, 392, 406
s. 5 392
(5) 392
s. 6(8)........................ 193, 196
s. 7 415
s. 13 .... 239, 497, 498, 512,
513, 514, 516, 517, 522,
532
(1) 516, 518
(a) 498
(b) 499
(2) 499, 516, 517, 518
(3) 516, 517
(4) 469, 499, 518
s. 14(1) 493
(2) 522
s. 15 .... 511, 513, 522, 526, 530, 532
(1)(b) 511
s. 16 .... 175, 392, 466, 522
s. 17 522
s. 18 .... 373, 378
s. 18(1) 31
(4) 32, 40
s. 19 512
(3) 501
s. 28(1) 385
s. 29 .... 501–502, 508, 509, 510
(1) 368, 369, 504
(a) 503
(5) 501
s. 30 .... 231, 386
(1) 17, 21, 385
(a) 17
(b) 17
(2) 385
Sched. 1, para. 6(8) 202
para. 8............. 244, 459
Sched. 3, para. 9(2) 353
(3) 355
para. 10(3) 393
Sched. 4 390
1975 Social Security Act (c. 14) 105,
486, 488, 625
Pt. II, Chap. V 630
s. 7 625
s. 17(1)(a)(ii) 65
s. 19(1) 486, 487
(2)(b) 488
s. 20(2) 67

1975 Social Security Act—cont.
s. 20(4) 486
s. 22(6)(a) 487
s. 50(1) 616
(2) 615
(3) 619, 629
s. 52 625
s. 53 625
s. 55 .... 619, 629, 630
s. 59 616
s. 60(1) 616
(3) 616
s. 61 616
s. 63 616
s. 67 615
(2) 615
ss. 76–78 616
s. 90(1) 616
(2)(a) 616
(b) 616
s. 104 634
Sched. 4, Pt. 1 105
Limitation Act (c. 54) 595
Sex Discrimination Act (c.
65) 117, 256, 313, 315,
320, 321, 322, 326, 332,
333, 335, 336, 337, 338,
340, 341, 342, 343
Pt. II 342
s. 1(1)(b)....................... 313, 330
(i) 330, 331
(ii)(iii) 330
s. 3 337
(4) 326
s. 4 335
(2) 336
s. 5(1) 325
(3) 326
s. 6 .... 329, 335–336
(1) 329
(a) 338
(b) 329
(c) 338
(2)–(5) 329
(2) 336
(4).......................... 332, 340
s. 7 .... 338–339, 340
(1)(f) 340
(2)(b) 340
s. 8 329
(3) 335
s. 12 403
ss. 14, 16 333
s. 21(1) 23
s. 37 342
s. 38 343
s. 42 343
s. 43 342
s. 51 340
s. 55 565
s. 63 342
s. 64 342

1975 Sex Discrimination Act—*cont.*
 s. 65 342
 s. 66(4) 342
 s. 67(2) 344
 s. 70 344
 s. 71 344
 s. 74 321
 s. 75 344
 ss. 82(1), 85 336
 Employment Protection Act
  (c. 71) 43, 61, 100,
   106, 116, 186, 256, 295,
   355, 357, 360, 363, 547
 ss. 1–3 349
 s. 1(2) 365
 s. 2 365
 s. 3(1)(*b*) 357
 s. 4 365
  (3) 355
 s. 5 365
 s. 6 366
  (1)(*a*) 340
  (4)(5) 366
 s. 7 394
 s. 10 ....355, 356
 ss. 11–16 .... 41, 350, 367
 s. 11 355
 s. 16 350
 ss. 17–21 350
 s. 17 367
  (1) 360
  (2) 360
 s. 19 361
  (4) 362
 s. 20(1) 362
 s. 21(1) 362
  (3) 362
 s. 39 105
 s. 71 254
 s. 89 353
 s. 92 366
 s. 99 ....247, 298, 367
 s. 99(1) 386
  (9) 247
 s. 101 ....123, 247, 265
 s. 111 486
 s. 121(7) 18
 s. 126 368
 s. 126A 501
 Sched. 9 354
 Sched. 11 ....350, 359, 360, 373
  para. 1(*a*) 359
  (*b*) 359
 Sched. 16, Pt. III, para. 13 467
  Pt. IV, para. 10 394,
   395, 398
1976 Trade Union and Labour Relations Act (c. 7) 392, 516
 s. 1 405
 s. 3(3)(4) 231
 s. 16 384
 Fatal Accidents Act (c. 30) 594

1976 Supplementary Benefits Act
  (c. 71)—
 s. 8 490
 Sched. 1, paras. 23, 26 490
 Race Relations Act (c. 74) 117,
  313, 320, 321, 322, 325, 335, 336,
   338, 340, 342, 343
 s. 3(4) 325
 s. 4 ....335, 336
  (1)(*a*)(*b*)(*c*) 339
 s. 5 339–340
 s. 11 403
 ss. 13, 15 333
 s. 29 343
 s. 33 343
 s. 34 342
 s. 41 342
 s. 54 342
 s. 55 342
 s. 56 342
 s. 57(4) 342
 s. 58(2) 344
 s. 61 344
 s. 62 344
 s. 65 321
 s. 66 344
 s. 75 336
 s. 78(1) 336
1977 Patents Act (c. 37) 90–92
 s. 39 .... 90–91, 92
 s. 42 ....25, 91
 s. 42(3) 91
 s. 43(3) 91
 Unfair Contract Terms Act
  (c. 50) 591
 s. 2(1) 591
1978 Employment Protection (Consolidation) Act (c. 44) 21,
  100–102, 106, 107, 108, 114,
  118, 119, 123, 132, 145, 172,
  195, 197, 201, 246, 254,
   255, 261, 269, 287
 Pt. III 104
 Pt. V 253
 s. 1 ....30, 42
  (1) 138
  (4)(*c*) 44
 s. 3(1) 102
 s. 11 45
  (9) 135
 ss. 12–18 61
 s. 12 101
  (2) 103
  (*b*) 101
 s. 13 102
  (2)(*b*) 103
 s. 14(4) 264
 s. 15(3) 103
  (4) 103
 s. 16(1) 104
  (2) 104
 s. 17(2) 135

1978 Employment Protection (Consolidation) Act—*cont.*

s. 18 104
s. 19(1) 122
   (2) 123
s. 20 123
s. 21 123
s. 22 123
s. 23(1) 118
   (2A) 118
s. 24 121
   (2) 135
s. 25 122
s. 26 122
s. 26A 122
s. 27 .... 111, 115, 123
   (1) 113, 114
     (a) 112, 113
   (2) 112, 113
   (3) 114
   (6) 114
s. 28 .... 114, 115
   (2) 115
   (3) 115
s. 29 115
   (2) 269
   (4) 115
s. 30(2) 135
s. 31 .... 116, 123
   (2) 116
   (5)–(7) 116
   (9) 116
s. 31A 117, 135
s. 33(3) 109, 138
   (b) 104
   (c) 105
   (3A) 108
   (4) 251
   (5) 105
s. 34(1) 105
   (2) 105
s. 35(1) 105
   (4) 105
s. 36 .... 105, 110
   (2) 135
s. 37 105
s. 39(1) 105
s. 40 111
   (3) 105
s. 41 111
s. 45(1) 106
   (2) 106
   (4) 107
s. 47(1) 108
   (2) 108
   (3) 109
   (5)(6) 109
s. 49 .... 166, 172
   (4) 172
s. 50 173
s. 53 209
   (2) 166

1978 Employment Protection (Consolidation) Act—*cont.*

s. 53(3)(c) 233
   (5) 135
s. 54(2) 21
s. 55 .... 166, 183, 185
   (2)(a) 73
     (c) 73
   (3) 267
   (4)–(7) 166
   (4) 135
   (6)(7) 167
s. 56 .... 110, 111
ss. 57–60 245
s. 57 197
   (1) 200
   (b) 110, 253
   (3) 193, 196, 201, 210, 253
s. 58 .... 229, 230, 248, 256
   (1) 135, 228, 234
   (c) 233
s. 58(3)–(11), (13) 231–233
   (3)(b) 233
   (c) 234
   (3A)–(3E) 118
s. 58A 232, 233–234
s. 59 .... 118, 138, 248
s. 60 .... 105, 106
   (1)(a)(b) 250
s. 61 251
s. 61 110
   (2) 251
s. 62 .... 244, 245–246, 467
s. 63 .... 18, 228
s. 64(1)(a) 137, 166
   (b) 134
   (3) 135, 229
s. 64A 166
s. 67(4) 137
   (8) 135
s. 68 254
s. 69 .... 174, 254
   (5) 255
   (6) 255
s. 70 255
s. 71(2) 256
s. 73 256
   (2) 256
   (3) 166
   (7) 197
s. 74 257
   (3) 259
   (4) 259
   (6) 261
s. 75 256
   (1) 256
   (7) 256
s. 76A 228
ss. 77–79 229
s. 77(2) 229
   (3) 229
   (5)(6) 229

1978 Employment Protection (Consolidation) Act—*cont.*
s. 78 230
s. 81 266
    (2) 269–270
        (b) 270
    (4) 138, 264
s. 82(2) 268, 269
    (3) 287
    (5)(6)(7) 287, 288
s. 84(1)–(3) 294
    (1) 145, 252, 288, 289
    (2) 147
    (3)–(6) 288–289, 294
s. 85 .... 185, 267
s. 86 111
s. 88(1) 266
    (2) 266
    (3) 267
    (4) 267
s. 89(1) 267
    (3) 266
    (4) 266
    (5)(a) 266
        (c) 267
s. 90(1) 135, 167
s. 91(2) 268, 270
s. 92 269
s. 93 180
    (1) 265
s 94 .... 149, 252
    (1)(2) 294
    (4) 288
s. 98(1) 302
ss. 99–107 295
s. 101 265
    (1) 135
    (2) 136
s. 102 302
s. 104(3) 300
    (7) 300
s. 106 300
    (3) 300
s. 108(4) 300
s. 121 123
s. 122 123
    (4) 123
s. 123(1)(2) 124
    (3)(5) 124
s. 124 124
    (2) 135
s. 126(1) 124
s. 138 154
    (1) 264
s. 140 .... 25, 155
    (1) 30
s. 141 152
    (2) 102
s. 142(1) 154
s. 143(1) 101, 138
    (2) 138
    (3)(4) 138

1978 Employment Protection (Consolidation) Act—*cont.*
s. 144 154
    (2) 102
s. 145 .... 102, 154
s. 146(1) 102
s. 151 138
s. 153(1) 21, 119
    (4) 150
Sched. 2 110
    para. 2(2) 108
    para. 5 109
    para. 6(2) 110
        (4) 109
Sched. 3 173
    para. 14 102
Sched. 4 300
    para. 4 302
Sched. 6 300
Sched. 13 .... 138, 145, 151, 152
    para. 1(2) 139
    para. 3 140
    para. 4 .... 139, 140
    para. 5 .... 139, 151
    para. 6 139
    para. 7 139
    para. 9 ..... 140, 142, 143
        (1)(b) 143
        (c) 143, 144
        (d) 143
    para. 11(1) 145
        (2) 145
    para. 12 145
    para. 15(1) 145
        (2)(3) 145
    para. 24 449
        (1) 242, 462
Sched. 14, paras. 1, 2 301
    paras. 4–6 301
    para. 8(1)(c) 302
        (3) 166

Civil Liability (Contribution) Act
    (c. 47) 584, 597
1979 Wages Councils Act (c. 12) 349,
        351, 352, 354
    s. 5 355
    s. 12 .... 351, 355
    s. 14 354
        (5)–(7) 354
    s. 15 356
    Sched. 1, para. 3 355
    Sched. 2, para. 1(2)–(4) 354
1980 Companies Act (c. 22)
    s. 2A 595
    s. 74 124
Social Security (No. 2) Act
    (c. 39)—
    s. 6 490
Employment Act (c. 42) 106, 197,
        208, 228, 237, 402, 416,
        485, 510, 529, 530, 532

1980 Employment Act—*cont.*
      s. 1 ....439, 444
      s. 2 444
      s. 3 366
      s. 4 ..... 232, 237, 242, 366, 401, 402
      s. 6 .... 193, 196, 201, 208, 209
      s. 7 237
      s. 8 239
      s. 8(1) 138
          (2) 154
      s. 9 ....197, 257
          (5) 256
      s. 10 261
      s. 11 103
          (2) 108
      s. 12 107
      s. 13 117
      s. 16 513
          (1) 530
          (2) 532
      s. 17 513
          (2) 510, 513, 530
          (3) 510–511, 512, 513, 517
          (4) 510, 511, 512, 513, 517
          (5) 510, 511, 512, 530
          (6) 511
          (8) 517
      s. 19................................ 41, 367
      s. 97 257
      Sched. 2 517
1980 Limitation Act (c. 58) 594, 597
      s. 11................................594, 595
      s. 12................................594, 595
      s. 13 594
      s. 14 595
          (2) 595
          (7) 595
      s. 33 595

1982 Social Security and Housing Be-
      nefits Act (c. 24).......43, 67, 615
      s. 1 615
      s. 5(1) 615
      s. 39 615
      Employment Act (c. 46).....238, 245,
                  246, 372, 450, 493, 495,
                       501, 506, 510, 513
      s. 1 362
      s. 3 ....231, 232
      s. 4 258
      s. 5 ....228, 238
      s. 6 ....229, 261
      s. 9 ....118, 122, 245, 467
      s. 10...........................135, 228
      s. 12(7) 484
      s. 13(4) 484
      s. 14 ....239, 513
      s. 15........................486, 493, 497
      s. 15(2)(*b*) 372
      s. 15(3)–(6) 494
      s. 15(3) 495
      s. 15(4) 372
      s. 16 486
      s. 18 501
          (2) 506
          (*a*) 501
          (*b*) 499
          (6) 17
      Sched. 2.................101, 122, 137,
                          138, 139, 172
      Sched. 2, para. 4 123
          paras. 16–19 228
      Sched. 3, para. 1 166
          para. 8 357
          paras. 19, 20 135
          Pt. II, para. 13(3) ... 501
      Sched. 4........................499, 516

TABLE OF STATUTORY INSTRUMENTS

1897 Truck Act 1896 (Exempted Persons in Cotton Weaving Industry) Order (S.R. & O. 1897 No. 299) 130

1938 Operations at Unfenced Machinery Regulations (S.R. & O. 1938 No. 641) 564

Aerated Water Manufacture (Overtime) Regulations (S.R. & O. 1938 No. 727) ... 22

Laundries (Overtime) Regulations (S.R. & O. 1938 No. 728) 22

Chocolates and Sugar Confectionery (Overtime) Regulations (S.R. & O. 1938 No. 1245) 22

Biscuit Manufacture (Overtime) Regulations (S.R. & O. 1938 No. 1528) 22

1939 Bread, Flour, Confectionery and Sausage Manufacture (Overtime) Regulations (S.R. & O. 1939 No. 509) 22

Dyeing and Cleaning (Overtime) Regulations (S.R. & O. 1939 No. 642) 22

Ice Cream (Overtime) Regulations (S.R. & O. 1939 No. 857) 22

1946 Disabled Persons (Designated Employments) Order (S.R. & O. 1946 No. 1257) 24

Disabled Persons (Standard Percentage) Order (S.R. & O. 1946 No. 1258) 23

1948 Building (Safety, Health and Welfare) Regulations (S.R. & O. 1948 No. 1145)—
reg. 29(4) 586

1949 Disabled Persons (Special Percentage) (No. 1) Order (S.R. & O. 1949 No. 236) ... 24

1967 Unemployment and Sickness Benefit Regulations (S.I. 1967 No. 330)—
reg. 11 67

1971 Employers' Liability (Compulsory Insurance) Commencement Order (S.I. 1971 No. 1116) 613

1971 Employers' Liability (Compulsory Insurance) General Regulations (S.I. 1971 No. 1117) 613

National Insurance (Industrial Injuries) Hospital In-Patients Regulations (S.I. 1971 No. 1440) 616

1972 Raising of the School Leaving Age Order (S.I. 1972 No. 444) 22

Immigration (Revocation of Employment Restrictions) Order (S.I. 1972 No. 1647) 23

1975 Rehabilitation of Offenders Act 1974 (Exceptions) Order (S.I. 1975 No. 1023) 254

Occupational Pension Schemes (Certification of Employments) Regulations (S.I. 1975 No. 1927)—
reg. 4 367

1976 Industrial Relations (Northern Ireland) Order—
Arts. 20–41 253
Art. 22(1)(b) 253
(10) 253

1977 Safety Representatives and Safety Committees Regulations (S.I. 1977 No. 500)—
reg. 3(1) 547
(2) 548
reg. 6 548
reg. 7 549
(2) 549
reg. 8 547
reg. 9 549
reg. 11 549

Employment Protection (Recoupment of Unemployment and Supplementary Benefit) Regulations (S.I. 1977 No. 674) 262

1979 Employment Protection (Handling of Redundancies) Variation Order (S.I. 1979 No. 958) 296

1980 Companies (Directors' Reports) (Employment of Disabled Persons) Regulations (S.I. 1980 No. 1160) 24

1980 Funds for Trade Union Ballots
       Regulations (S.I. 1980 No.
       1252) 444
      Supplementary Benefit (Trade
       Disputes and Recovery from
       Earnings) Regulations (S.I.
       1980 No. 1641) 490
1981 Transfer of Undertakings (Pro-
       tection of Employment)
       Regulations (S.I. 1981 No.
       1794) 146, 151, 152, 251,
               252, 253, 298, 381–383
       reg. 4 ....152, 181

1981 Transfer of Undertakings (Pro-
       tection of Employment)
       Regulations—cont.
       reg. 5 ....173, 251–252
       reg. 5 251–252
       reg. 6(6) 298
           (7) 298
       reg. 7 252
       reg. 8 253
       reg. 9 382
       reg. 10....................298, 367
       reg. 12 253
       reg. 26 253

TABLE OF ABBREVIATIONS

STATUTES

TULRA	Trade Union and Labour Relations Act 1974
E.P.A.	Employment Protection Act 1975
E.P.C.A.	Employment Protection (Consolidation) Act 1978
E.A. 1980	Employment Act 1980
E.A. 1982	Employment Act 1982

COURTS, TRIBUNALS, INSTITUTIONS, ETC.

ACAS	Advisory Conciliation and Arbitration Service
C.A.C.	Central Arbitration Committee
C.I.R.	Commission on Industrial Relations
E.A.T.	Employment Appeal Tribunal
I.L.O.	International Labour Organisation
I.T.	Industrial Tribunal
N.I.R.C.	National Industrial Relations Court

BOOKS

Davies and Freedland—*Labour Law: Text and Materials* (Weidenfeld and Nicolson) (1979 + supp. 1980)
Elias Napier and Wallington—*Labour Law Cases and Materials* (Butterworth) (1980)
Freedland—*The Contract of Employment* (Oxford University Press) (1976)
Hepple and O'Higgins—*Encyclopedia of Labour Relations Law* (Sweet and Maxwell)

NOTE

Throughout this book, even where the context suggests otherwise, where both male and female might be affected reference is made to males. This is intended to be the opposite of discriminatory since it was discovered at an early stage that conscious effort to refer to the most likely sex was itself discriminatory by implication.

CHAPTER 1

FORMS OF ENGAGEMENT OF LABOUR

THE SIGNIFICANCE OF CLASSIFICATION

IT is clear that the terms and conditions under which one person may do work for another will vary almost infinitely. This variation is seldom the result of random selection of alternatives by one or both of the parties. The jobbing gardener and the contract draftsman derive the characteristics of their engagement from the fact that it is uneconomic for a single employer with too little work of the kind to employ one man full time. The unusual position of the "temporary" whether working as secretary, nurse or in some other job may be an irritant to regular employees engaged in the same work. It may derive from economic necessity, but the convenience of the worker is often more relevant than that of the person for whom the work is done. The desire of one, or sometimes both, parties for a particular form of engagement is rarely irrational. Indeed the reasons for the choice may make it a customary one for an entire trade. One of the oldest subsisting examples of this type arises in the Sheffield cutlery trade where the craftsman is often a "small master" originally employing members of his family but dependent on another for working premises and for marketing of the product. The "lump" in the construction industry is a wholly different, though now customary, form of self-employment not necessarily associated with craft skills nor linked to a single contractor. This form appears to stem from the economic advantage of the worker operating in small gangs desiring to support neither the older nor the infirm worker but dependent on the hard work and mutual understanding of its members to earn high bonus or overtime payments. Inevitably such a group tends to select the work from which the maximum earnings can be obtained leaving less remunerative work to those who prefer the security of employment. The contractor may or may not see advantage to himself in the arrangement. The practice is now so widespread that he probably has little choice in many instances if he is to get the work done.

Even within those arrangements which clearly involve contracts of service the incidents of employment will vary almost as greatly as the variation between employment and self-employment. Sometimes these variations are pure tradition of which the best known and most widespread involve the "staff status" once afforded to white collar occupations. Such a type incorporates important legal consequences such as the contractual right to payment during sickness, the expectation of overtime work without extra payment and, in the past at least, separate canteen facilities. Such class distinction is breaking down but has been a feature of employment in Britain since the industrial revolution. One has only to recollect the marked differences, almost certainly amounting to contractual rights, between the nursery and the domestic staffs of a great nineteenth century household to realise how long such distinctions have existed and in what diverse situations. Sometimes distinct rights and obligations are conferred as rules of law rather than arising from the parties' own arrangements. Merchant seamen afford a marked and long standing example of such regulation.

1

It is thus possible to select almost any characteristic of the engagement of labour and find some types that reveal it, some that do not, and then to find that the degree of possession or lack of it varies within each group. Nor is it possible to be certain for any length of time which set of characteristics should be the most significant to distinguish one group from another. Legislation now so frequently intervenes in the rights of employees that lines of distinction are obliterated or made less prominent. Larger legislative policy, of which the most notable example is the development of social security provision, may alter the significant features of major divisions. "Control" as a feature of employment may have served very well whilst the law was primarily concerned to determine the incidence of vicarious liability. It may remain a characteristic division but lose its significance as a rational line of distinction if the incidence of legal advantage comes to depend more on the lack of economic independence because of the introduction of national insurance benefits available to some workers but denied to others.

It is pointless to base arguments on the semantics of the labels attached. Legislation normally conceals the difficulty of defining employment by expressing it as engagement under a "contract of service." This term, like "servant," is merely a different, perhaps more acceptable, name for the same category. "Employer," usually used as a counterpart to "employee," is often used as a neutral word applicable to all engagers of labour. The words do not matter, although for obvious reasons the reader will find it useful to adopt terms which are commonly accepted as conveying a certain connotation. The real problem is that the variation in the content of the labour relationship just remarked upon means that any attempt to force the whole spectrum of such relationship into a few categories is bound to be based on selection of a few characteristics alleged to be dominant but whose appearance is so much a matter of degree that the decision as to whether they exist to a sufficient extent to justify a particular classification will often appear artificial.

Despite this it is an unjustified academic luxury to reject the attempt to define the major division of work into "employment" and "self-employment" (or whatever alternative words may seem more appropriate) as a meaningless exercise.[1] Two different reasons force such a definition on all who would study labour law. In the first place this distinction has been used throughout all labour legislation and social security legislation since the 1940s to determine the conferment of one benefit or another. The employee (or, if you like, he who is subject to a contract of service) will enjoy, and the self-employed will not, *inter alia*: national insurance unemployment benefit, industrial injury and disablement benefit; the right to statutory redundancy compensation; the right to complain of unfair, as distinct from wrongful, termination of the contract for his labour; the right, in certain circumstances, to complain of detrimental action short of such termination; the right to statutory guarantee payments; (if a woman) the right to maternity pay and return to employment after maternity leave; and, in certain cases, the right to preference over other creditors on the insolvency of an employer. All these rights will, of course, have a correlative effect on the other party to the contract whom we may, for convenience, call the employer. Conversely the person who works under any other sort of contract, whom we may call self-employed even if these words taken out of that context

---

[1] See Davies and Freedland, *Labour Law: Text and Materials*, pp. 456 *et seq.*

mean nothing, is liable to pay national insurance contribution at a lower rate; is not subject to deduction of income tax at source and is generally thought to benefit from an advantageous treatment of his reasonable expenses when assessed for such tax. In the past there have even been attached different rights and obligations in respect of his safety at work.

The second justification for seeking a distinction is the undoubted fact that, for all the variety, guidelines for such a distinction do exist. Supply anyone you meet in the street with a few basic facts about a labour situation and in at least 90 per cent. of such situations he will accurately express an opinion on whether the workers involved are employed or self-employed. The variety of forms of engagement on which we have remarked, almost inevitably because of its extent, only produces serious doubt in a small proportion of cases. The sub-postmaster who doubles up in his own stationery business may be pushed into one or other category without anyone feeling very satisfied that it is the right one. The same may be true of classifying the social survey worker or the company director. Left to itself, however, the distinction between employed and self-employed has rightly been regarded by the legislature as a sufficiently clearly defined peg on which to hang a great array of important consequences.

Unfortunately the very growth of those consequences has meant that many seek one or other status for the economic advantages which it will confer. It is not possible, therefore, to consign the fringe of cases to the inevitable difficulty of drawing a single line through such a wide variety. The line seems clear to the man in the street simply because he makes assumptions based on a few known facts and his knowledge of the normal working of industry. If extra facts are added, the emphasis placed on certain of these facts changes and the normal assumptions of the industry changes then the conclusion may be different. The apparent certainty may appear as merely the product of those assumptions and not at all as the inevitable outcome of legal rules. The words chosen by judges with a lawyer's yearning for a rational test may turn out to have been chosen because the width of their meaning allows them to explain, rather than define, an uncertain situation. The massive legislative structure founded upon the distinction may, as the Phelps Brown Committee on the Construction Industry in 1965 discovered,[2] turn out to hang on nothing but the will of the parties to the normal industrial relationship to sustain it. The reader is likely to find, therefore, that the classification of employment or self-employment selected as the one all-important division in the labour field cannot provide any degree of certainty in this fringe area of untypical situations. It may even be possible to give more or less emphasis to certain characteristics so as to induce the most favourable categorisation.

The significance of employment, as against other working arrangements, was demonstrated in *Young and Woods Ltd.* v. *West*.[3] The Court of Appeal decided that the claimant was an employee and thus entitled to claim a remedy for unfair dismissal despite an agreement between himself and his employer that he should be treated as self-employed. Ackner L.J. pointed out that this false designation, which had been accepted by the Inland Revenue, had resulted in a tax advantage of some £500 over five years simply as a result of assessment under Schedule D instead of Schedule E. The statement of facts in the *All*

---

[2] Cmnd. 3714 (1965).
[3] [1980] I.R.L.R. 201.

England Report of *Ready Mixed Concrete (South East) Ltd.* v. *Minister of Pensions and National Insurance*[4] indicates some of the considerable anticipated advantages from the deliberate alteration of the relationship in that case.

> "It was considered that not only would the scheme further the policy of keeping and [sic] making and selling of concrete separate from its delivery but also that the scheme would benefit the group by stimulating speedy and efficient cartage, the maintenance of trucks in good condition, and the careful driving thereof, and would benefit the owner driver by giving him an incentive to work for a higher return without abusing the vehicle in a way which often happened if an employee were given a bonus scheme related to the use of his employer's vehicle."[5]

Unfortunately the apparent immediate economic and psychological advantages may tempt workers to accept the far less protected status of self-employment persuading themselves that prospective disadvantages will not materialise. In *M. J. Ferguson* v. *John Dawson and Partners (Contractors) Ltd.*[6] the plaintiff had stumbled and fallen off an unguarded flat roof whilst engaged in throwing scaffold boards to the ground below. The question whether he was entitled to the £30,387 awarded by the court of first instance depended solely on whether he was employed or self-employed. Megaw L.J. said:

> "It is conceded by the defendants that if the plaintiff was employed under a contract of service, they were, subject only to the issue as to 'appreciate time,' under a duty to the plaintiff; they failed to carry out that duty; and that failure was the cause of the accident. But, say the defendants, the plaintiff was employed under a contract for services: he was 'self employed'; he owed a statutory duty to himself to take the statutory precautions.[7] It was for him, under the regulations, not for the defendants, to ensure that the guard rail was erected. The defendants were under no such duty."

In view of the fact that the learned judge is here able to use "employed" in two different senses it is unfortunate that the distinction between service and services should have loomed so large in case and statute law. In the light of this importance one might have expected the legislature to assign to one category or the other with much greater precision than is in fact apparent the admittedly wide variety of work situations.

THE DEFINITION OF SERVICE—EMPLOYMENT

Nineteenth-century courts were obviously dominated by the belief that if there were said to be more than a single factor determining the distinction the discretion in borderline cases would be revealed. What they did not acknowledge was that the search for a single critical factor in so wide a variety of situations was bound, if it produced any result, to lead to selection of a factor of such generality as to be largely meaningless in any borderline case. In practice this would permit a similar, if not more extensive, discretion.

The control test

The single factor selected by the courts as the characteristic of employment was control of the manner of doing the work.[8] This was still being cited as the

---

[4] [1968] 2 Q.B. 497; [1968] 1 All E.R. 433.
[5] See also *Massey* v. *Crown Life Assurance Co.* [1978] I.C.R. 590.   [6] [1976] I.R.L.R. 346.
[7] *Smith* v. *Wimpey Bros.* [1972] 2 Q.B. 329.   [8] *Yewens* v. *Noakes* (1880) 6 Q.B. 530.

sole test, in 1957, subject only to modification to refer to the right of control rather than its reality.[9] Despite this longevity, however, the courts had never been unaware of the unreality of a single test. In 1774[10] Lord Mansfield had said that if "a man lived in his own house and took in work for different people, it would be strong ground to say that he was not a journeyman of any particular master." Subsequently in the twentieth century the courts often admitted that they were talking of degrees of control without suggesting any guidelines to decide in which direction one degree or another pointed.[11] As early as 1910, however,[12] Fletcher Moulton L.J. had commented on the difficulty of establishing a single definitive characteristic. As expressions of the control test became more vague[13] it became apparent that many situations generally recognised as involving self-employment would fit within it. When Vaisey J. in *Westall Richardson Ltd.* v. *Roulson*[14] spoke of balancing control against independence he revealed clearly that there was no sharp distinction between the many types of labour relationship which might be called employment and those which might be called self-employment. In so doing, however, he helped to destroy confidence in control as the test.

It now appears that this loss of confidence was not justified and that control does remain the most significant single factor determining the distinction. It is as difficult to imagine employment without the right to control the work as it is to imagine the contract of employment lacking an obligation to obey reasonable instructions. The one is, of course, the source of the other. On the one hand it is obvious that the reality of control will never be total. An employment which evinced no freedom from control would be pointless since it would require constant supervision. On the other hand it is equally obvious that the more specialised and skilled the job, or the more trusted the employee, the less will control be apparent.[15] Each employment contains an area of discretion within which the employee may act. That area may be so wide that there is little chance of the employee stepping outside of it so as to encounter the reality of control. Nevertheless the consultant surgeon or the airline pilot who does perform his work in an unacceptable manner will usually be subject to control. If he is not so he may reasonably be thought to show signs of independence such as to justify regarding him as self-employed.

It is, however, equally obvious that as the reality of control shades off into non-existence an attempt to draw a line at some point in this process alone will not produce a satisfactory distinction between service and independence. We have seen that many different considerations induce people to opt for one

---

[9] *Gibb* v. *United Steel Co. Ltd.* [1957] 1 W.L.R. 668. As late as 1967 the 5th edition of Batt, *Master and Servant*, p. 8 also advanced control as the sole test.

[10] *Hart* v. *Aldridge* (1774) 1 Cowp. 54.

[11] *Performing Right Society Ltd.* v. *Mitchell and Booker* [1924] 1 K.B. 762; *Chadwick* v. *Pioneer Private Telephone Ltd.* [1951] 1 All E.R. 522; *A.E.U.* v. *Minister of Pensions and National Insurance* [1963] 1 W.L.R. 441; *Stagecraft Ltd.* v. *Minister of National Insurance*, 1952 S.C. 288.

[12] *Walker* v. *Crystal Palace Football Club* [1910] 1 K.B. 87 at p. 93.

[13] See, *e.g. Performing Right Society Ltd.* v. *Mitchell and Booker* [1924] 1 K.B. 762 where McCardie J. said " . . . the final test, if there be a final test, and certainly the test to be generally applied, lies in the nature and degree of detailed control over the person alleged to be a servant."

[14] [1954] 1 W.L.R. 905.

[15] See *Beloff* v. *Pressdram Ltd.* [1973] 1 All E.R. 241.

relationship or another. It must be true, therefore, that each relationship has a number of characteristics the prominence of which is as variable as the working environment. So it was that assertion of the single element of control gave way to consideration of numerous characteristics from a balance of which the classification might be made. Some of the early attempts at a multi-factor test are noticeably unsuccessful. In *Short* v. *J. and W. Henderson Ltd.*[16] Lord Thankerton repeated a list first mentioned in 1928.[17]

"(a) the master's power of selection of his servant; (b) the payment of wages or other remuneration; (c) the master's right to control the method of doing the work, and (d) the master's right of suspension or dismissal."

Apart from control it is clear that one has only to substitute for "remuneration" the word "payment" and for "dismissal" "termination" and one is talking of an independent contractor. In *Morren* v. *Swinton and Pendlebury Borough Council*[18] Lord Parker C.J. was only able to draw from this attempt the conclusion that control did not stand alone, although it is now clear that he went too far when he said that accordingly its absence could be little if any use as a test.

The organisation test

It is submitted that the "organisation" or "integration" test primarily propounded by Denning L.J., as he then was, would have been far more successful had he allowed it to be seen as a multi-factor test and not tried to present it as a single decisive characteristic. In *Stevenson, Jordan and Harrison Ltd.* v. *Macdonald and Evans*[19] he said:

"One feature which seems to run through the instances is that, under a contract of service, a man is employed as part of a business, and his work done as an integral part of the business; whereas, under a contract for services, his work, although done for the business, is not integrated into it but is only accessory to it."

This test was applied in a few cases.[20] But in *Ready Mixed Concrete (South East) Ltd.* v. *Minister of Pensions*[21] MacKenna J. said of it:

"This raises more questions than I know how to answer. What is meant by being 'part and parcel of an organisation'? Are all persons who answer this description servants? If only some are servants, what distinguishes them from the others if it is not their submission to orders?"

This criticism is, of course, true. "Organisation" is as lacking in precision as "employment." Nevertheless it is possible, by using another word, that Denning L.J. might have explained a point he clearly saw but failed to elucidate. Employment is distinguished from self-employment simply by its greater *degree* of organisation. "Organisation" is control first and foremost but, as MacKenna J. said:

---

[16] (1946) 174 L.T. 417 at p. 421.
[17] *Park* v. *Wilsons and Clyde Coal Co. Ltd.*, 1928 S.C. 121.
[18] [1965] 2 All E.R. 349.
[19] [1952] 1 T.L.R. 101.
[20] See, *e.g. Cassidy* v. *Ministry of Health* [1951] 2 K.B. 343; *Whittaker* v. *Minister of Pensions* [1967] 1 Q.B. 156; *Bank voor Handel en Scheepvaart N.V.* v. *Slatford* [1953] 1 Q.B. 248.
[21] [1968] 2 Q.B. 491.

"Control includes the power of deciding the thing to be done, the way in which it shall be done, the means to be employed in doing it, the time when, and the place where it shall be done."

Several of these decisions can be taken by the contractor of the self-employed but:

"All these aspects of control must be considered in deciding whether the right exists in sufficient degree to make one party the master and the other his servant. The right need not be unrestricted. 'What matters is lawful authority to command, so far as there is scope for it.'"

In other words, the employer seeks to control the situation and all aspects of control—not just control of the manner of the work—are relevant to determine whether he does so. He who fits in to that controlled situation is likely to be employed.

Multiple factor tests

The organisation inherent in employment is indicated by many factors other than control. Whether Denning L.J. meant to include these is not apparent from his broad generalisation but it is submitted that elements such as coming within holiday and pension schemes and working fixed hours in common with the bulk of other workers are elements of the organisation typical of employment and much less normally encountered in self-employment. In the *Ready Mixed Concrete* case MacKenna J. freed the definition from a single generalised test. The fact situation was, however, unusual and it may be much less easy to apply the more complex process envisaged by MacKenna J. to the normal situation where evidence of the incidents of the relationship is less complete than it was in that case. The employer had deliberately set out to produce clear evidence of the existence of a contract for services rather than a contract of service. To this end he had produced numerous versions of a lengthy draft contract each of which had been submitted to the Minister of Pensions to support the contention that the drivers engaged under the contract were self-employed. Each had been rejected and the resulting dispute was referred, under the peculiar procedure laid down in national insurance legislation, to a single judge of the Queen's Bench Division sitting as the final appellate court.

MacKenna J. laid down three basic tests.

"(i) There must be a wage or other remuneration. Otherwise there will be no consideration and without consideration no contract of any kind. The servant must be obliged to provide his own work and skill. Freedom to do the job either by one's own hands, or by another's is inconsistent with a contract of service though a limited or occasional power of delegation may not be."

If we ignore the first sentence of this quotation as leading up the wrong path it looks as if the learned judge has brought to light a characteristic at least as significant as control. Like control it will normally have to be implied from surrounding circumstances. MacKenna J. subjects it to the same sort of quantitative test as control by saying that some right to delegate is not inconsistent with employment. Common experience suggests that an absence of the right to delegate is not inconsistent with self-employment, but the contract will rarely make express provision as to delegation. The problem in practice, therefore, will be to know how much to imply. The danger will be that the answer is readily seen to be likely to be influenced by a preceding decision that the relationship is, or is not, one of employment. That will often be the only available support for the implication of any provision relating to delegation. It is probably because of the difficulty of arriving at a conclusion as to delegation without a simultaneous, or earlier, decision as to the relationship which deterred the courts from using this test before the *Ready Mixed* case and which explains the absence of any effective application of it since then.

The second test adopted by MacKenna J. is the control test. But, as we have seen, it adopts a concept of control far wider than that confined to the manner of doing the work.

Thirdly, the learned judge proposed to seek provisions inconsistent with the contract of service. He quite correctly demonstrated that some aspects of the contract might appear as the principal purpose thereof and indicate that the parties were, for instance, not so much interested in obtaining or providing service as erecting a building or transporting goods. This difference of purpose will be discovered most often from one or more provisions pointing to a contract other than a contract of service. As with the other two tests such indications of inconsistency are not necessarily fatal.

There is, however, a weakness in the reasoning. The importance of inconsistencies can surely only be judged relative to those provisions which support the conclusion that the contract is one of service, yet the judgment makes no provision for such a balancing of provisions nor does MacKenna J. at any stage consider the weight of the factors in the case before him which pointed to employment. His actual assessment is as follows:

"It is now time to state my conclusion, which is that the rights conferred and the duties imposed by the contract between Mr. Latimer and the company are not such as to make it one of service. It is a contract of carriage.

I have shown earlier that Mr. Latimer must make the vehicle available throughout the contract period. He must maintain it (and also the mixing unit) in working order, repairing and replacing worn parts when necessary. He must hire a competent driver to take his place if he should be for any reason unable to drive at any time when the company requires the services of the vehicle. He must do whatever is needed to make the vehicle (with a driver) available throughout the contract period. He must do all this, at his own expense, being paid a rate per mile for the quantity which he delivers. These are obligations more consistent, I think, with a contract of carriage than with one of service. The ownership of the assets, the chance of profit and the risk of loss in the business of carriage are his and not the company's.

If (as I assume) it must be shown that he has freedom enough in the performance of those obligations to qualify as an independent contractor, I would say that he has enough. He is free to decide whether he will maintain the vehicle by his own labour or that of another, and, if he decides to use another's, he is free to choose whom he will employ and on what terms. He is free to use another's services to drive the vehicle when he is away because of sickness or holidays, or indeed at any other time when he has not been directed to drive himself. He is free again in his choice of a competent driver to take his place at these times, and whoever he appoints will be his servant and not the company's. He is free to choose where he will buy his fuel or any other of his requirements, subject to the company's control in the case of major repairs. This is enough. It is true that the company are given special powers to ensure that he runs his business efficiently, keeps proper accounts and pays his bills. I find nothing in these or any other provisions of the contract inconsistent with the company's contention that he is running a business of his own. A man does not cease to run a business on his own account because he agrees to run it efficiently or to accept another's superintendence.

A comparison of Mr. Latimer's profits with the wages earned by men who are admittedly the company's servants confirms my conclusion that his status is different, that he is, in the words of the judgment in *Silk's* case, a 'small businessman,' and not a servant."

Subsequent courts have purported to find much assistance in the reference to "small businessman" as the obverse of employee. No doubt this is true. If we speak of the self-employed that term conjures up no very clear picture of a group of characteristics. A man with a ladder, a van and a yard, however, looks like a small businessman. This concept had been derived from the judgment of Lord Wright in *Montreal Locomotive Works Ltd.* v. *Montreal and Att.-Gen. for Canada*[22] when four indicia based on such a distinction were suggested. They were; control, ownership of tools, chance of profit, risk of loss.

One of the clearest examples of the application of the *Ready Mixed Concrete* test occurs in the judgment of Cooke J. in *Market Investigations Ltd.* v. *Minister of Social Security*.[23]

"It is apparent that the control which the company had the right to exercise in this case was very extensive indeed. It was in my view so extensive as to be entirely consistent with Mrs. Irving's being employed under a contract of service. The fact that Mrs. Irving had a limited discretion when she should do the work was not in my view inconsistent with the existence of a contract of service. For examples of a servant having such a discretion, see *Hobbs* v. *Royal Arsenal Co-operative Society Ltd.* and *Amalgamated Engineering Union* v. *Minister of Pensions and National Insurance*. Nor is there anything inconsistent with the existence of a contract of service in the fact that Mrs. Irving was free to work for others during the relevant period. It is by no means a necessary incident of a contract of service that the servant is prohibited from serving any other employer. Again, there is nothing inconsistent with the existence of a contract of service in the master having no right to alter the place or area within which the servant has agreed to work. So far as concerns practical limitations on a master's power to give instructions to his servant, there must be many cases where such practical limitations exist. For example, a chauffeur in the service of a car hire company may, in the absence of radio communication, be out of reach of instructions for long periods.

I therefore turn to the second question, which is whether, when the contract is looked at as a whole, its nature and provisions are consistent or inconsistent with its being a contract of service. Counsel for the company points first to the fact that Mrs. Irving was appointed on each occasion to do a specific task at a fixed fee. He points to the fact that the company's officers were of the opinion that they could not have dismissed Mrs. Irving in the middle of an assignment. He says that these factors are most consistent with the conception of a contract for services than a contract of service.

As to the first factor, appointment to do a specific task at a fixed fee, I do not think that this is inconsistent with the contract being a contract of service. See, for example, *Sadler* v. *Henlock*. As to the right of dismissal, it is necessary to distinguish between a right of dismissal for breach and a right of dismissal irrespective of breach. It is noticeable that as regards the right of dismissal for breach, the Minister's finding is somewhat cautiously worded; it relates to what the company's

---

[22] [1947] 1 D.L.R. 161 at p. 169.
[23] [1969] 2 Q.B. 173. See also *Construction Industry Training Board* v. *Labour Force* [1970] 3 All E.R. 220.

officers thought and not to what the provisions of the contract were. In the absence of some special term either expressed in the contract or to be implied from particular circumstances, I should have thought that certain types of breach might well justify dismissal of an interviewer, even in the middle of an assignment. I cannot see on what ground the right to dismiss in the middle of an assignment is said to be entirely excluded in this case; but assuming that it is, that fact does not in my view assist the company in establishing that the contract is a contract for services and not a contract of service. Even in a contract for services a breach by one party which goes to the root of the contract will entitle the other party to terminate it.

Then counsel for the company says that the fact that the contract makes no provision for time off, sick pay and holidays, suggests that it is not a contract of service. I cannot accept that this is a test which is of great assistance in the present case. The fact that the contract makes no provision for time off is merely a reflection of the fact that there are no specified hours of work. I have already dealt with this. The fact that there is no provision for sick pay and holidays is merely a reflection of the fact that the contract is of very short duration. If a man engages himself as an extra kitchen hand at a hotel for a week in the holiday season, there will be no provision for sick pay and holidays, but the contract will almost certainly be a contract of service.

The company then refer to the fact that Mrs. Irving's work was performed under a series of contracts, each for a specific survey. They say that the relationship of master and servant is normally conceived of as a continuous relationship, and that the fact that there is a series of contracts is more consistent with those contracts being contracts for services than contracts of service. For my part, I doubt whether this factor can usefully be considered in isolation. It must, I think be considered in connection with the more general question whether Mrs. Irving could be said to be in business on her own account as an interviewer. In considering this more general question I take into account the fact that Mrs. Irving was free to work as an interviewer for others, though I think it is right to say that in this case there is no finding that she did so. I also take into account the fact that in her work as an interviewer Mrs. Irving would, within the limits imposed by her instructions, deploy a skill and personality which would be entirely her own. I can only say that in the circumstances of this case these factors are not in my view sufficient to lead to the conclusion that Mrs. Irving was in business on her own account. The opportunity to deploy individual skill and personality is frequently present in what is undoubtedly a contract of service. I have already said that the right to work for others is not inconsistent with the existence of a contract of service. Mrs. Irving did not provide her own tools or risk her own capital, nor did her opportunity of profit depend in any significant degree on the way she managed her work.

Taking all the factors into account and giving full weight, I hope, to the persuasive arguments of counsel for the company, I am clearly of opinion that on the facts of this case the Minister was right in concluding that Mrs. Irving was employed by the company under a series of contracts of service, and the appeal accordingly must fail."

It may be noted that since the courts identify employment with a particular contract the factors considered relevant to the definition must exist between the parties to that contract. In *Hawley* v. *Fieldcastle and Co. Ltd.* [23a] it was held that a person placed under a government-sponsored Work Experience Programme was not an employee because the necessary elements of control of recruitment,

---

[23a] [1982] I.R.L.R. 223 (I.T.). See also *Daley* v. *Allied Suppliers Ltd.* [1983] I.C.R. 90 (E.A.T.).

the work to be done, discipline, termination and remuneration were missing from the relationship with the company. This result may be said to depend on an impressive list of missing elements. The decision in *Vine* v. *National Dock Labour Board*[23b] indicates that the character of employment will not always be destroyed because a third party controls some of its features.

Despite the fact that ever since the judgment in the *Ready Mixed Concrete* case courts have always considered a multiplicity of factors, there is still apparent a tendency to try to present these as constituting a single test. In *Young and Woods Ltd.* v. *West*[24] Stephenson L.J. approved a statement of Cooke J. in the *Market Investigations* case that:

". . . the fundamental test to be applied is this: 'Is the person who has engaged himself to perform the services performing them as a person in business on his own account?' If the answer is 'yes' then the contract is a contract for services. If the answer is 'no' then the contract is a contract of service."

It will be seen at a glance that this is not a test at all. All it does is to substitute for "self-employed" the words "in business on his own account." Otherwise it states the obvious. Nevertheless there are signs that the classification "small businessman" is usually the head under which are gathered MacKenna J.'s inconsistent elements. So Slynn J. in *Hitchcock* v. *Post Office*[25]:

"We accept, as Mr. Carr quite rightly has accepted, that there is here a substantial measure of control which relates to the conduct of the Post Office's business. It might be, if there were no other factors present, that that control would be sufficient to make the contract one of service rather than for services. But there are other factors present. The question in this case, it seems to us, is really whether the control which does exist is such that it prevents the contract from being one for services rather than of service. Accordingly we must look at the matter as a whole. We consider here that great importance has to be attached to the fact that the applicant provided the premises and a certain amount of the equipment at his own expense. The sub-post office came into what was his general store. It was a part of his own business. Moreover it is clear that even though, apparently, he chose to spend a great deal of his working week doing the sub-post office work at this particular premises himself, he had the right to delegate, and did in fact delegate. At the other two offices, we have been told, he delegated on virtually a full-time basis; but even at Springfield Road there was some delegation. In addition it seems to us that on the terms set out in the rules he was obliged to be no more than responsible for the conduct of the office. He may have chosen either to do it himself or to supervise it; if he did not, then at most he was responsible for the performance of the duties. It was for him to decide whether to do it himself or whether to employ someone else to do it, as long as he retained the responsibility. We do not feel that the provision as to his giving notice if he is to be absent for more than three days is in any way inconsistent with his right to appoint other people to carry out the duties of the sub-post office. Moreover it seems to us that even though there may be less chance of making profit, or risk of loss than in many businesses, there was still here the chance of profit and the risk of loss. If the population of the village had suddenly increased, and if the applicant by the way in which he ran the sub-post office attracted people to come to that office rather than, perhaps, go to some other

---

[23b] [1957] A.C. 488.
[24] [1980] I.R.L.R. 201.
[25] [1980] I.C.R. 100.

sub-post office in the same area, then his income under the method of payment adopted would be increased. On the other hand, if, by the way that he ran the business, he drove people away, or if the population moved away to new houses in another area, he would run the risk of loss seen against the background of the capital investment which he had been required to put into the running of the sub-post office. It is true that, here, part of the payment made to him was for the use of the premises and part was for his own services. We have considered carefully Mr. Slater's suggestion that this is a contract which is really severable in the way indicated by MacKenna J. It does not seem to us here that, even though there was this double element in the payment, even though there is the obligation to provide the premises and to do the work, it is right to sever the matter in the way which has been suggested. In our view, the essential position was that the applicant, although under control as to the way in which much of the work was done, was carrying on business on his own account. The economic reality of it was that this was his shop, his premises, and it was he who was conducting this sub-post office business even if on behalf of the Post Office. We do not consider that it can be said that he, although doing work for them, was so integrated into their business that he became a servant. The position of a head postmaster who is a full-time employee of the Post Office, and who provides no premises, no employees of his own, seems to us to be entirely different. The very fact here that the applicant was carrying on this business with employees of his own seems to us to indicate very strongly that he was not employed under a contract of service. We do not consider that the element of control here—which, as the industrial tribunal found, is not so much of a managerial nature but is connected with the protection of the Post Office's own property and public interest—is such as to prevent this being a contract for services in the generally understood sense. Nor do we think that the fact that the applicant did carry on long hours here, and signed a certificate to say that he was working for more than 18 hours a week in the sub-post office—which had for him consequences in relation to National Insurance—means that he is to be treated as a servant. Nor do we think that the fact than an ex gratia payment was made in respect of his pension, or the fact that although he did not get holiday or sickness pay he was able to qualify for a payment in lieu to enable him to employ other people to carry out the business, makes his position one of a servant."

In *Withers* v. *Flackwell Heath Football Supporters Club*[26] Bristow J. in the E.A.T. suggested that an "elementary lay approach" might be to suppose the employee was asked whether he was his own boss. As he said, this makes the ultimate test on whose business the employee is engaged. There would be no harm in this if the concept of a small businessman was merely used to give a clearer picture of the self-employed. In some cases, however, it seems to have been allowed to give undue weight to particular elements.[27] In other cases such a concept is clearly inappropriate to the facts.[28] It is suggested that in most cases evocative labels would be better omitted. If in defining employment we are looking for a relationship organised and controlled by him who engages the worker then that must be determined by consideration of as much fact as we have. The obverse is not necessarily that of a small businessman. As MacKenna

---

[26] [1981] I.R.L.R. 307.

[27] *Mailway (Southern) Ltd.* v. *Willsher* [1978] I.C.R. 511; *Airfix Footwear* v. *Cope* [1978] I.R.L.R. 396.

[28] *Wiltshire Police Authority* v. *Wynn* [1980] I.C.R. 401; *Albert J. Parsons and Sons Ltd.* v. *Parsons* [1979] I.C.R. 271.

J., said it is any other type of relationship. The same open-ended enquiry into factors pointing in such a direction is necessary.

There is no doubt that the modern test is impressionistic. That being so it works best when impressions are freely formed. Anomalous as it seems, the *Ready Mixed* test is in most danger where the facts are similar to that case and reveal careful drafting of the contract. This is because such drafting will emphasise certain aspects and conceal inconsistencies. A wide ranging view of the actual facts such as occurred in *Hitchcock* v. *The Post Office* is likely to be clouded by such emphasis.

It is against this background that the development of the importance of what the parties say about the nature of their contract may be viewed with some disquiet. In the *Ready Mixed Concrete* case the court stated that the parties' own label would be irrelevant unless there was a doubt as to the rights and duties for which the parties wish to provide. In *Massey* v. *Crown Life Assurance Co.*[29] Lord Denning M.R., with whom the remainder of the Court of Appeal agreed, whilst agreeing that the parties could not alter the nature of a clear relationship by putting upon it an incorrect label, went a little further than this in doubtful cases when he said:

> "On the other hand, if the parties' relationship is ambiguous and is capable of being one or the other, then the parties can remove that ambiguity, by the very agreement itself which they make with one another."[30]

It does not seem entirely clear that this is what MacKenna J. meant. What he had said was that the parties' label would not necessarily be ineffective but might resolve a doubt as to the *terms and conditions* which were intended. Sir Douglas Frank sitting as a Deputy Judge of the Queen's Bench Division appears to have taken Lord Denning's proposition a little further in *B.S.M. (1257) Ltd.* v. *Secretary of State for Social Services*[31] when he decided that the parties' own label is effective even if some terms are more appropriate to the other relationship so long as those other terms are not inconsistent with that label. The Court of Appeal returned to the point in *Young and Woods Ltd.* v. *West*[32] in which a skilled sheet metal worker had chosen to go on the company's books as self-employed. No tax or National Insurance contributions were deducted from his earnings and he did not receive holiday or sickness benefit. Stephenson L.J. pointed out that some of the remarks of Lord Denning M.R. elsewhere in the *Massey* judgment might be read to mean that wherever there was an agreement to assume a particular relationship the parties must accept it. He did not accept this interpretation, saying:

> "It must be the court's duty to see whether the label correctly represents the true legal relationship between the parties. . . ."

The court acknowledged that this might mean that a party could enjoy the benefits of a particular relationship under an unchallenged agreement but effectively alter that relationship when it became inconvenient by invoking the

---

[29] [1978] I.C.R. 590.
[30] In *Tyne and Clyde Warehouses* v. *Hamerton* [1978] I.C.R. 661 the E.A.T. correctly applied this principle despite misstating it on p. 664.
[31] [1978] I.C.R. 894.
[32] [1980] I.R.L.R. 201.

correct legal position. The answer to this in the court's opinion was that when the true position was decided it would be for those who had wrongly acted on the contrary assumption to take steps to recoup the advantages improperly enjoyed.

It is suggested that the courts have now reached a point where they are prepared to decide the issue as between two alternatives. These may not always, though they will usually, be employment or managing a small business. Instead of adopting a step by step approach they will be inclined immediately to face the question of which alternative is most strongly supported by the available factors. It follows that control as a factor will be bound to change its nature because the courts will be looking rather for control of an undertaking indicating self-employment, and its absence, rather than control by another of the manner of work, as indicating employment. Regularity of the relationship, despite the somewhat unexpected outcome of the *Airfix Footwear* case, is likely to appear as a new factor simply because it tends not to be a characteristic of self-employment. The parties' own attitude is clearly established as a major element when, as will often be the situation in cases coming to the courts, the answer is uncertain.

OTHER SUB-DIVISIONS OF THE SUPPLY OF LABOUR

It will have been noted that though statutes conferring rights on employees tend to refer to those under a contract of service and the courts often speak of defining the contract of employment the effect of broadening the enquiry from control to a consideration of almost any element has been to concentrate as much on the practice as on the contract.[33] The courts nowadays are much nearer to defining the employment relationship than the contract of service. In consequence there seems little value in implying contractual provisions from a fact situation so that the fact situation can then be classified. Nowhere is the advantage of a single stage more apparent than in the numerous usually highly informal situations which fall within the general heading of labour-only subcontracting.

More technical considerations of contract may have to be invoked in some situations, however, in order to emphasise similarities with normal employment and reduce the significance of other factors such as the short term nature of the relationship. The casual employee, for instance, might well be confused with the self-employed were it not possible to see his relationship merely as a fleeting form of what is usually more prolonged and indefinite. A few special categories of working arrangement are either not open to this explanation or give rise to policy considerations necessitating alteration of the normal conclusion.

Office-holders

It was probably policy that gave rise to the oldest subsisting of these divisions. The policy considerations have subsequently been extended almost generally so that the classification of office-holder has lost most of its significance. Its main

---

[33] This concentration reduces the chance of deliberate alteration of the relationship. See *E. Rennison and Son* v. *Minister of Social Security* (1970) 10 K.I.R. 65.

advantage at the present time is that it confers at common law a right to specific performance. Previously it alone had carried an implied right to a fair hearing before dismissal.[34] Application of this classification was always confused by the fact that the term "office" clearly has a recognised popular meaning although it is not entirely clear what that meaning is. Sometimes in the nineteenth century it appears that it suited the policy of the courts to differentiate between workers on the basis of such a popular meaning.[35] The classification as office-holder conferred significant rights to natural justice and reinstatement to those whom the courts thought should be conceded a status above the run-of-the-mill servant. Rather unexpectedly, this line of thought was resurrected by Lord Wilberforce in *Malloch* v. *Aberdeen Corporation*.[36] His decision was that the system of registration of school teachers pertaining in Scotland conferred upon them an office. No one seems to have thought that a similar system of registration in the docks should have had a similar effect in *Vine* v. *National Dock Labour Board*.[37] His Lordship went further, however, to suggest the existence of a class of public employees who, as a matter of public policy, might be said to possess a status entitling them to a hearing before dismissal.

In these circumstances it is not surprising that the common law did not attempt to define the characteristics of an office-holder. In *Great Western Railway* v. *Bater*[38] Rowlatt J., for the purposes of the law of taxation, defined an office as "a subsisting, permanent, substantive position, which had an existence independently from a person who filled it, which went on and was filled in succession by successive holders." "Permanence" here is used only in the sense of a possible succession of holders. It does not distinguish "temporary" appointments. In *Dale* v. *I.R.C.*[39] it was considered too obvious for argument that a trustee was an office-holder, although not only his term but the office itself is temporary. Nevertheless Rowlatt J.'s is not a satisfactory definition since many successive offices are held by employees who are not themselves regarded as office-holders. *Dale's* case did support the view that an employee could simultaneously be an office-holder and this was also the conclusion of the E.A.T. in *Barthorpe* v. *Exeter Diocesan Board of Finance*.[40] In that instance a lay reader of the Anglican church paid a monthly stipend was held to possess both an ecclesiastical office and a contract of employment. This decision both clarifies and confuses the case law.

There is no doubt that the concept of office holding has, *inter alia*, been used as a rag bag for those who were not self-employed but equally were not regarded as possessing contracts of employment. A policeman, for instance, was said[41] to be an office-holder because:

"His authority is original, not delegated, and is exercised at his own discretion by virtue of the office; he is a ministerial officer exercising statutory rights independent of contract. The essential difference is recognised in the fact that the relation-

---

[34] See *Ridge* v. *Baldwin* [1964] A.C. 40.
[35] See, *e.g. Fisher* v. *Jackson* [1891] 2 Ch. 84; *cf. Tucker* v. *British Museum Trustees* (1967) 112 S.J. 70.
[36] [1971] 1 W.L.R. 1578.
[37] [1957] A.C. 488.
[38] [1923] K.B. 266 at p. 274.
[39] [1954] A.C. 11.
[40] [1979] I.C.R. 900.
[41] *Att.-Gen. for New South Wales* v. *Perpetual Trustee Co. Ltd.* [1955] A.C. 457 at p. 489.

ship to the Government is not in ordinary parlance defined as that of servant and master."[42]

Almost the same words would be used of the ministerial officers of a church who have normally been regarded as office-holders.[43] So far, at least as employment law is concerned, it is submitted that it is not the presence of a successive position but the absence of a contract which is decisive. Otherwise vast numbers of employees, such as the head of a University department in *University Council of the Vidyodaya University of Ceylon* v. *Silva*[44] would be both employees and office-holders. In that case the Privy Council held that whatever the name given to the job the holder of it was an employee and not an office-holder.

If lawyers find it convenient to have a name for everything the term office-holder will serve well enough for those who fit neither into the category of employed or self-employed. There seems, however, no justification for applying it to an employee. It does not really suggest that there is some status attaching to school teachers in Scotland and lay readers in England which attaches neither to the Vice-Chancellor of a University nor the Convenor of shop stewards. It may even do harm to suggest that the common law recognition of a right to natural justice and reinstatement is somehow more inherent than the statutory right of employees to those benefits. For this reason the decision of Woolf J. in the Queen's Bench Division in *R.* v. *B.B.C., ex parte Lavelle*[44a] may prove unwelcome. In that case the employee sought the prerogative order of certiorari to review a decision to dismiss on the ground of a failure of natural justice. It was held that the prerogative orders were not an appropriate remedy in private actions but that natural justice should apply wherever the employment contained any element of public service, statutory support, office or status.

Workers

Apart from the obvious specialised categories introduced for statutory purposes the law does not usually find it necessary to categorise others. It did not even define the self-employed until it was found useful to ascertain the existence of a contract of employment by comparison. As we have seen, the self-employed have now been cast in the guise of small businessmen and their characteristics of independence and capital risk emphasised. The critics of such loose generalisation are currently more numerous than the supporters but it is probably true to say that if we are to have widespread categories they cannot be defined precisely without thereby failing to achieve their purpose. The Industrial Relations Act 1971, for instance, sought to distinguish "worker" from employee. The definition it adopted is continued, though for much more limited purposes, in the Trade Union and Labour Relations Act 1974.[45]

---

[42] See also *Ridge* v. *Baldwin* [1964] A.C. 40. The Police Act 1964, s.48 rendered the police authority vicariously liable for the tortious acts of a policeman.

[43] *Re National Insurance Act 1911* [1912] Ch. 563; *Re Employment of Ministers of United Methodist Church* (1912) 107 L.T. 143; *Rogers* v. *Booth* [1937] 2 All E.R. 751.

[44] [1965] 1 W.L.R. 77.

[44a] [1982] I.R.L.R. 404

[45] s.30(1). See Employment Act 1982, s.18(6).

"'Worker' means an individual regarded in whichever (if any) of the following capacities is applicable to him, that is to say, as a person who works or normally works or seeks to work

(*a*) under a contract of employment; or

(*b*) under any other contract . . . whereby he undertakes to perform personally any work or services for another party to the contract who is not a professional client of his; or

(*c*) in employment under or for the purposes of a government department . . . otherwise than in the police service."

It seems clear that the intention was to cover any person while he was himself available to work. The term is obviously wider than that of "employee" which is comprehended solely within sub-paragraph (*a*).[46] In *Broadbent* v. *Crisp*[47] however, the N.I.R.C. chose to place the words "perform personally" in a contractual, rather than a factual, context. In that case a collector for a firm of football pool promoters was held to be a worker. The decision is no doubt right but the court felt it necessary to examine the implied obligations of his contract to ascertain from the significant degree of control exercised a contractual commitment to personal service. If this emphasis is followed in future cases it will restrict the term "worker" to employees and a fringe of situations close to employment.

It seems somewhat doubtful if the category was intended even to exclude the scriptwriters involved in *Writer's Guild of Great Britain* v. *British Broadcasting Corporation*.[48] It is true that they had no contractual obligation to produce any result at all. There seems no reason, however, why those who themselves work should not fall within a class allowed, for instance, to form trade unions simply because they are under a contract which envisages, but does not compel, that work. The wording of sub-paragraph (*b*) would, nonetheless, seem to produce both these results and clearly demonstrates the need not only for the courts but also for draftsmen to cease to measure categories by reference to the contract alone rather than the relationship.

Crown servants

The distinction between public and private sector employment is simply stated and normally results in reliable classification of types. Within the public sector, however, there exists a marked lack of precision as to the distinction between Crown servants, civil servants and the employees of public corporations. Clearly one may be a Crown servant without being a civil servant.[49] It is suggested that there is good reason to argue that the disabilities the common law has attached to Crown servants may be unjustified in the case of those who are not civil servants. Nevertheless, in *Gallagher* v. *The Post Office*,[50] Brightman J., although avoiding any decision on the point, appeared to think it doubtful whether a Crown servant possesses a contract of service. The balance of authority, however, favours the view that there is a contract of employment in

---

[46] See *Carter* v. *Law Society* [1973] I.C.R. 113.

[47] [1974] I.C.R. 248.

[48] [1974] I.C.R. 234.

[49] *Wood* v. *Leeds Area Health Authority* [1974] I.C.R. 535.

[50] [1970] 3 All E.R. 712. The question was avoided in *Dudfield* v. *Ministry of Works* (1964) 108 S.J. 118.

such cases.[51] The provisions of the 1971 legislation clearly discounted the former view. Whether this is so or not it was, at common law, largely unenforceable by him since he could neither bring an action for wrongful dismissal nor sue for wages due to him.[52]

A number of reasons were advanced as to why this should be so. It was said that the right of the Crown to dismiss at pleasure rested originally in an implied term to that effect.[53] If this were so it would suggest that an express term to the contrary would override the implication, and this was plainly not so.[54] It may be, however, that the right of the Crown could be abrogated by a strong statutory implication[55] which lends support to the contention that its exercise was a matter of the prerogative.[56] A third possible explanation, akin to this, is that the right was a matter of public policy.[57] This is, however, unsatisfactory simply because there is no overriding reason of policy why the Crown should have had the right to avoid the payment of wages in lieu of notice, by which any difficulty about continued employment could have been resolved.

In *Reilly* v. *R*.[58] Lord Atkin could see no reason why the Crown should not be bound if it expressly contracted for a fixed period, dismissal to be only for cause, but there has been no development in the common law of this method of limitation of the right.[59]

Under the Industrial Relations Act 1971,[60] Crown servants received a right, equal with other employees, to bring an action for unfair dismissal, the only reservation being that a Minister of the Crown can certify that any dismissal took place in the interests of national security, and the industrial tribunal must then dismiss the case.[61]

Merchant seamen

Certain occupations and certain types of employee are subject to peculiar legal incidents. It is not feasible in a general textbook to deal separately with every class of employment which reveals characteristics radically different from those generally attributed to the relationship. The reader must remember that, in a sense, no generalised statement is applicable to every circumstance of every employment from bricklayer to docker and from production line operative to works manager. Some classes are, however, so radically different that generalisations derived from other employments are actually misleading. Prob-

---

[51] *Brandy* v. *Owners of S.S. Raphael* [1911] A.C. 413; *Sutton* v. *Att.-Gen.* (1923) 39 T.L.R. 294; *Reilly* v. *The King* [1934] A.C. 176; *Kodeeswaran* v. *Att.-Gen. of Ceylon* [1970] 2 W.L.R. 456; *Att.-Gen. for Guyana* v. *Nobrega* [1969] 3 All E.R. 1604. But the Employment Protection Act 1975, s.121(7), skirts the issue.

[52] *Mulvenna* v. *Admiralty*, 1926 S.C. 842; *Lucas* v. *Lucas* [1943] P. 68; *cf.* dicta in *Kodeeswaran* v. *Att.-Gen. of Ceylon* [1970] 2 W.L.R. 456.

[53] *Dunn* v. *R.* [1896] 1 Q.B. 116, *per* Lord Herschell. See also *Shenton* v. *Smith* [1895] A.C. 229; *Gould* v. *Stuart* [1896] A.C. 575; *Riordan* v. *War Office* [1961] 1 W.L.R. 210.

[54] *Shenton* v. *Smith* [1895] A.C. 229; *Dunn* v. *R., supra; Denning* v. *Secretary of State for India* (1920) 37 T.L.R. 138; *Rodwell* v. *Thomas* [1944] K.B. 596 at p. 602; *cf. Reilly* v. *R.* [1934] A.C. 176.

[55] *Gould* v. *Stuart* [1896] A.C. 575, P.C.

[56] *Grant* v. *Secretary of State for India* (1877) 37 L.T. 188.

[57] *De Dohsé* v. *R.* (1866) 2 T.L.R. 114; *Dunn* v. *R., supra, per* Lord Esher M.R. and Kay J.

[58] [1934] A.C. 179; see also Denning J. in *Robertson* v. *Minister of Pensions* [1949] 1 K.B. 227.

[59] See Margaret Cowan, "Contracts with the Crown" (1965) 18 C.L.P. 153.

[60] "Crown servants are not entitled, however, to statutory redundancy payments, statutory minimum periods of notice or a written statement of terms and conditions of employment."

[61] See now Employment Protection (Consolidation) Act 1978, s.63.

ably the most obvious of these is merchant seamen.[62] The following very brief statement is intended to act only as an example of the type of differences which will be encountered.

The Merchant Shipping Act 1894 required the master of every ship, except a ship of 80 tons or less exclusively engaged in trading between the ports of the United Kingdom, to enter into a written contract of service with each member of the crew in a form approved by the Board of Trade and signed by both master and seamen. In practice this was normally in the form of "articles of association" the one form being signed by all the crew. The contract required to set out the nature of the voyage and, as far as possible, its intended duration, or the duration of the engagement and the places to which it applied, as well as details of the crew and their respective tasks and any regulations as to conduct, fines, short allowance of provisions or other lawful punishment approved by the Board of Trade and adopted by the parties. In the case of foreign-going vessels the agreement had to be signed in the presence of a marine superintendent who had to ascertain that each seaman understood its purport and then had to attest the signature. In practice it was also necessary for a person seeking employment on a British ship in this country to be registered under the "Established Service Scheme," by which he was normally allocated to a ship. He might be disciplined under the scheme, even to the point of de-registration.

The Merchant Shipping Act 1970 attempts a much needed reform of this procedure. It abolishes the formalities of signing-on. The "articles" are replaced by a "crew agreement" which must be written and signed by each crew member, but without the formality of ensuring that it is understood or the presence of a marine superintendent. The form of agreement must be approved by the Minister but may differ from ship to ship. Specified ships or particular descriptions of seamen may be exempt from the requirement. Ministerial regulations may set out details of the method of discharge, but otherwise the parties are left to their common law, and now, statutory remedies, except where the contract is frustrated by wreck, or in the absence of agreement to the contrary where a ship registered in the United Kingdom is sold outside the United Kingdom. In these two cases compensation of the equivalent of a maximum of two months' wages is payable, unless the seaman unreasonably refuses to obtain available alternative employment.

The old "discharge book" still exists but the Department of Trade and Industry has indicated that it will no longer contain the adverse marking "DR" (declines report) which would accompany the seaman into any job he sought. A seaman is to be given an account of wages due 24 hours before discharge. A properly adjusted account must be provided at the time of the discharge, or within seven days thereof, when the balance of the wages becomes due. A seaman may lose all right to wages where, in the event of wreck or loss, he does not make reasonable efforts to save his ship. Failure in his duties permits termination of the contract, or a fine for certain offences,[63] but the Minister for

---

[62] See thesis for Cambridge Ph.D. by J. S. Kitchen, *Law Relating to Merchant Seamen and Oil Rig Workers*.

[63] The offence of misconduct endangering a ship or persons on board is punishable by a fine not exceeding £400 (Merchant Shipping Act 1974, s.19(2)). S.30 of the 1970 Act creates criminal offences arising from continued or concerted disobedience or neglect of duty, but the criminal offences of wilful disobedience of a lawful command relating to the operation of the ship or its equipment and of absence without leave at the time of sailing have been abolished (Merchant Shipping Act 1974, s.19(3)).

Trade and Industry is given power to establish ship's disciplinary committees in place of the master's powers of discipline, although the master will retain the power of arrest (which is made statutory) for offences connected with the safety of the ship. No provision is made for representation at the hearings before these committees, nor for a right to appeal from a finding. In July 1974 the Secretary for Trade announced his intention to establish working groups to examine rules of discipline for sea-going employment in merchant ships and in fishing vessels with particular reference to the framework of authority required in modern conditions.

Apprentices

Although formal apprenticeship has become less important throughout this century and noticeably so in the last 20 years, the system still merits some explanation of the peculiar legal provisions that attach to it. Technically a contract of apprenticeship does not give rise to the relationship of employer and employee.[64] Some of the principal incidents of such a relationship at common law do, however, attach to that of apprenticeship, the most obvious of which is vicarious liability.[65]

The contract of apprenticeship, properly so called, must be entered into by written indenture and an oral contract is not enforceable as such, though it may constitute a valid contract of service.[66] For this reason the growing practice in certain trades of teaching the craft on an informal basis to those sometimes known as "improvers" will result in such persons being under ordinary contracts of service.[67]

Because a contract of apprenticeship will be considered both necessary and beneficial to him it will bind a minor but it may be repudiated by him within a reasonable time after he attains the age of 18. It is for this reason common for the parent or guardian of the apprentice to undertake that he will complete the apprenticeship.[68] The rights of the master are personal and the apprentice is not bound, unless the contract so provides, to serve his successor or personal representatives.[69]

A number of the terms said to be implied into the contract of apprenticeship would, today, normally be considered out of date. There is, for instance, an implied term to provide an apprentice with medicines and medical attendance[70] but this, like the implied duty to provide lodging, will only apply where the apprentice enters the master's household, in which event the master would be precluded from claiming the cost of such lodging.[71] There is also said to be a

---

[64] *Horan* v. *Hayhoe* [1904] 1 K.B. 288.

[65] See Atiyah, *Vicarious Liability*, p. 72; Batt, *Master and Servant* (5th ed.), p. 603; *Hancke* v. *Hooper* (1835) 7 C.&P. 81.

[66] *McDonald* v. *Twiname (John)* [1953] 2 Q.B. 304 at p. 313; *Kirkby* v. *Taylor* [1910] 1 K.B. 529.

[67] In the construction industry about 45 per cent. of so-called apprentices have no indentures.

[68] See *Cuming* v. *Hill* (1819) 3 B. & Ald. 59—guarantor liable to compensate for non-completion.

[69] *Baxter* v. *Burfield* (1747) 2 Stra. 1266.

[70] *R.* v. *Smith* (1837) 8 C. & P. 153.

[71] *Attwaters* v. *Courtney* (1841) Car. & M. 51; *Garratt* v. *Burghart* (1828) 3 C. & P. 581.

right moderately to chastise the apprentice[72] but all that remains of this today is a tacit acceptance of a somewhat more severe control that one would normally apply to employees.

If the master abandons the business to which the apprentice was bound the apprenticeship is at an end because its essential nature has gone.[73] In the absence of a contrary stipulation the dissolution of a firm to which an apprentice was attached is a breach of contract, so that it is usual to bind the apprentice to one of the partners.[74] On the other hand no such result will follow from movement of the business or some non-fundamental change in its character.[75] Otherwise the apprentice is contractually bound to serve out the term of his apprenticeship and not, during that time, to attach himself to anyone else.[76]

As an apprentice may not by notice terminate his contract, so a master may not, in the normal way, dismiss an apprentice even for what would amount to cause in an ordinary contract of employment.[77] There are, however, some grounds which will justify termination of the contract.[78] The provisions of the Employment Protection (Consolidation) Act 1978 apply to contracts of apprenticeship.[79] The definition of employee in unfair dismissal legislation does not expressly so refer to apprenticeship. It seems clear from the reference to apprenticeship in the 1974 Act that it was intended to be included.[80]

A master seeking to enforce the contract of apprenticeship is in a difficult position but he may sue an adult apprentice for breach, or the guarantor for compensation. He may not sue a minor apprentice because of the now outdated theory that the master is in a quasi-parental position. Where, as would normally be the case, no premium, or a premium of less than £25 has been paid, the master might have brought proceedings under the Employers and Workmen Act 1875.[81] A magistrates' court then had the wide general powers available under the Act and might, additionally, order the apprentice to perform the contract and even imprison him for 14 days at a time for failure to comply with the order. There is now no method of specific enforcement.

The principal advocates of the continuation of apprenticeship at the present time are the craft unions who frequently use requirements in their rule books that applicants for membership should have served, or be serving, an apprenticeship, often before a certain age, to regulate entry to the union and, where there is a closed shop, to the trade.

Special Categories of Employment

In a number of other cases particularised rules have been applied to the employment of certain persons in certain occupations.

---

[72] *Gylbert* v. *Fletcher* (1629) Cro.Car. 179; *Penn* v. *Ward* (1835) 2 Cr.M.' & R. 338.
[73] *Ellen* v. *Topp* (1851) 6 Ex. 424.
[74] *Titmus* v. *Rose and Watts* [1940] 1 All E.R. 599.   [75] *Batty* v. *Monks* (1865) 12 L.T. 832.
[76] *Richardson* v. *Colne Fishery Co.* (1897) 77 L.T. 501; *Aynsworth* v. *Wood* (1728) Sess.Cas. K.B. 84; *Meriton* v. *Hornsby* (1747) 1 Ves.Sen. 48.
[77] *Waterman* v. *Fryer* [1922] 1 K.B. 499.
[78] *Waterman* v. *Fryer, supra*—perverse refusal to learn; *Learoyd* v. *Brook* [1891] 1 Q.B. 431— apprentice's conduct destroying purpose of instruction: *Westwick* v. *Theodor* (1875) L.R. 10 Q.B.D. 224; *Phillips* v. *Clift* (1859) 4 H. & N. 168—neglect of duties if habitual and serious or a danger to the master; *Lock* v. *Baker* (1851) 17 L.T. (o.s.) 81—habitual loose living.
[79] s.153(1). See particularly, s.142 relating to fixed term contracts.
[80] TULRA 1974, s.30(1). See Employment Protection (Consolidation) Act 1978, s.54(2).
[81] ss.5 and 12. Repealed by the Statute Law Reform Act 1973.

The minimum age at which children may be employed at all is 13.[82] Those under school leaving age[83] may not be employed in a ship registered in the United Kingdom nor in any factory, mine or transport, nor in any other industrial undertaking unless only members of the same family are employed there.[84] The Secretary of State has power to regulate the employment of children under school leaving age in entertainment.[85] Local authorities may require information concerning children's employment and may prevent the employment of a child in unsuitable ways, times or periods even though this is not otherwise unlawful.

Women and young persons

Employment of both women and young persons in factories for more than nine hours a day (10 if the factory is working a five-day week), or 48 hours a week, exclusive of meals and rest intervals, is forbidden. For all workers under 16 the weekly limit is 44 hours.[86] The daily spread of work must not exceed 11 hours (12 in a five-day week), to begin no earlier than 7 a.m. for workers under 16, nor later than 6 p.m. for them and 8 p.m. for women and young persons.[87] Unless the work of a male young person over the age of 16 is vital to the continuous employment of men with whom he is working, in which case he may work a continuous spell of five hours, women and young persons may not work a spell of more than four-and-a-half hours without at least a half-hour break. If a 10-minute break is permitted during the spell it may be increased to five hours.

It is permissible to increase these maximum hours where the pressure of work in the factory demands it, but in no such case shall more than 100 overtime hours annually be permitted, and they shall not be at the rate of more than six hours in any week, nor for more than 25 weeks in the year. Even then, the maximum working day may not exceed 10 hours, spread over 12 hours.[88] The Secretary of State may permit an increase in these maxima in special circumstances.[89]

Women and young persons may not be employed outside the factory during meal or rest intervals, or outside the period of employment, save, if over the age of 16, in a shop, in which case the employment counts as employment in the factory. Except for defined exceptions those under 18 may not be employed at night.[90]

---

[82] Children and Young Persons Act 1933, s.18(1) as amended by the Children Act 1972, s.1.

[83] Currently 16. See Raising of the School Leaving Age Order 1972 (S.I. 1972 No. 444).

[84] Factories Act 1961, s.167; Mines and Quarries Act 1954, ss.124(2) and 160; Employment of Women, Young Persons and Children Act 1920, s.1.

[85] Employment of Children Act 1973, s.1.   [86] Factories Act 1961, s.87(1).

[87] One p.m. on Saturday, or such other short day as the Secretary of State shall prescribe if satisfied that the exigencies of the trade require it.

[88] Ibid. s.89.

[89] Such special regulations have been made for a number of industrial processes including: Aerated Water (S.R. & O. 1938 No. 727); Biscuit Manufacture (S.R. & O. 1938 No. 1528); Bread and Flour Confectionery and Sausage Manufacture (S.R. & O. 1939 No. 509); Chocolates and Sugar Confectionery (S.R. & O. 1938 No. 1245); Dyeing and Cleaning (S.R. & O. 1929 No. 642); Ice-Cream Manufacture (S.R. & O. 1939 No. 857); Laundering (S.R. & O. 1938 No. 728). But see Equal Pay Act 1970.

[90] A period of 11 consecutive hours including those between 10 p.m. and 5 a.m.—Women, Young Persons and Children Act 1920, Hours of Employment (Conventions) Act 1936. The provisions limiting hours of work for women are not to be affected by legislation for equal opportunities, although they will be kept under review.

The Mines and Quarries Act 1954 continues the prohibition on women and young persons working below ground and also limits their hours of employment above ground.[91]

The Shops Act 1950 contains a very detailed set of provisions concerning the hours of shop assistants, their half-holidays, meal times and over-time, which were inspired by the exceptionally long, continuous periods of work expected at one time in the retail trades where shop-keepers tended to wait for each other to close for the day. At the time of going to press the Government has announced proposals to relax these requirements.

An alien may not hold public office[92] nor be employed in the civil service without certification.[93] Neither these nor any other restrictions on employment of aliens applies, however, to the nationals of States members of the European Economic Community.[94] Any non-patrial, as defined by the Immigration Act 1971, may have restrictions placed on his right to accept or change employment when he is given leave to enter the country.

The disabled

Apart from statutory domination of the law relating to safety at work and the more recent anti-discrimination legislation, statute law has not, in the United Kingdom, played a significant role in the direct imposition upon either employer or employee of social obligations. The Disabled Persons (Employment) Act 1944 and associated legislation, is, however, one of the few examples of such legislation.

A disabled person is one who, on account of injury, disease, or congenital deformity is substantially handicapped in obtaining or keeping employment, or in undertaking work on his own account, of a kind which apart from that injury, disease or deformity, would be suited to his age, experience and qualifications. Such a person may, after his disability has continued for 12 months[95] apply for registration as disabled.[96] An employer of 20 or more employees (which includes apprentices) is required to employ a percentage of disabled persons and, where he does not currently attain to that quota, to allocate vacancies for that purpose. The employer is required not to take into his employment other than a disabled person if immediately after such engagement the quota would not be met.[97] The general quota is currently 3 per cent.[98] There is power to fix special percentages for specified industries but this power has only been used in relation to crews of British ships where the percentage is 0.1.[99] The Minister may issue a permit in a particular case, which may be subject to conditions, entitling an employer who would otherwise be bound to engage a disabled person to avoid the obligation where it appears to the Minister that it would be expedient to do so having regard to the nature of the work for which the

---

[91] But see the amendment in Sex Discrimination Act 1975, s.21(1).
[92] Act of Settlement 1700.
[93] Aliens Employment Act 1955, s.1.
[94] Immigration (Revocation of Employment Restrictions) Order 1972 (S.I. 1972 No. 1647).
[95] Disabled Persons (Employment) Act 1958, s.2.
[96] Disabled Persons (Employment) Act 1944, s.7.
[97] *Ibid*. s.9 subject to certain exceptions.
[98] Disabled Persons (Standard Percentage) Order 1946 (S.R. & O. 1946 No. 1258).
[99] Disabled Persons (Special Percentage) (No. 1) Order 1949 (S.R. & O. 1949 No. 236).

applicant desires to engage and the qualifications and suitability for the work of any available registered disabled person, or if he is satisfied that there are insufficient such persons available.[1]

The 1944 Act contains a very early example of partial protection from dismissal[2] of a registered disabled person if his dismissal would produce a failure to meet the quota. No particular sanctions are provided and the prohibition on dismissal does not operate where the employer has reasonable cause for dismissal. This aspect of the protection of the disabled has, therefore, clearly been overtaken by the provision of general remedies for unfair dismissal but, more significantly, its very existence in this attenuated and easily avoidable form reveals the major weakness of the legislation which seems to have been founded on pious hopes rather than the provision of effective enforcement procedures. Apart from being largely unpoliced and ineffective, some of the provisions of the legislation appear not only condescending but almost detrimental. Nowhere is this more apparent than in the Disabled Persons (Designated Employments) Order 1946[3] which reserves to the disabled alone employment as lift and car park attendants.

In what appears to have been an effort either to introduce a spark of life into the implementation of the obligation or, at least, to appear to be endeavouring to do so, the annual returns of all companies which are required to attach to their balance sheets a directors' report must, from September 1, 1980, include in that report a statement as to the policy applied during the financial year to which the report relates as to the employment of disabled people.[4]

UNENFORCEABLE AND ILLEGAL CONTRACTS

In contracts of persons under the age of 18[5] are, prima facie, unenforceable. Although a minor may enforce his own contract of employment, he is bound by that contract only if it is, on balance, beneficial to him even if some of the terms are disadvantageous.[6] The common law rule applies to any contractual arrangement for work regardless of whether it is one properly defined as employment.[7] There is no doubt that in some of the earlier cases the courts were looking for a benefit over and above the monetary return that the minor received for his work. This element may, however, have been considered simply because it arose from the type of engagement that tended to be litigated. Had it not been expanded there would be considerable room to doubt whether many of the more humdrum employments were beneficial overall. It seems that the courts will now tend to take the wage into account as a beneficial factor.[8] In consequence it is likely that employment containing no exceptionally burdensome obligations upon the employee will be considered beneficial. To all intents and

---

[1] Disabled Persons (Employment) Act 1944, s.11.

[2] *Ibid.* s.9(5). See *Seymour* v. *British Airways Board* [1983] I.R.L.R. 55 (E.A.T.).

[3] S.R. & O. 1946 No. 1257 made under the Disabled Persons (Employment) Act 1944, s.12.

[4] Companies (Directors' Report) (Employment of Disabled Persons) Regulations 1980 (S.I. 1980 No. 1160).

[5] Family Law Reform Act 1969, ss.1 and 9.

[6] *De Francesco* v. *Barnum* (1889) 43 Ch.D. 165.

[7] *Doyle* v. *White City Stadium* [1935] 1 K.B. 110; *Chaplin* v. *Leslie Frewin (Publishers) Ltd.* [1966] Ch. 71.

[8] *Chaplin* v. *Leslie Frewin (Publishers) Ltd., supra.*

purposes, therefore, this form of protection of minors does not apply in the law of employment. For this reason the suggestion of the Law Commission in 1982 that minors might well be placed in the same contractual position as adults, may well be regarded as feasible.

So far as the contract of employment is concerned it is important to distinguish two degrees of illegality. One degree affects merely a particular term leaving the remainder of the contract enforceable. An agreement by an employee that his employer may make deductions by way of fine from his wages contrary to the Truck Acts and not in accordance with section 2 of the Truck Act 1896 is illegal and void.[9] An attempt to agree to waive a breach of statutory duty would, similarly, be void.[10] Although not normally referred to as illegal, terms which deprive an employee of certain statutory rights, such as the right to claim for an unfair dismissal, are declared void by the statute granting the right.[11]

There is, however, a higher degree of illegality which destroys the entire contract because it taints the purpose thereof. A contract contrary to public policy is totally illegal. All immoral contracts are contrary to public policy.[12] The same result, incidentally, will follow if removal of the affected term destroys the consideration for, or the mutuality of, the contract.[13] The clearest example of the operation of this principle in recent years concerns employment wholly or partly remunerated in a way which operates as a fraud upon the Revenue. In fact practices such as this are far more widespread than the number of reported cases suggests.[14] In *Tomlinson* v. *Dick Evans U Drive Ltd.*[15] an employee received £15 of a weekly wage in cash without deduction of tax. The arrangement was held illegal and its effect was to destroy the entire contract so as to deprive the "employee" of that status. Although ignorance of the law is no excuse so that the failure of the parties to realise the illegality of what they were doing will not prevent invalidity, where the contract is *ex facie* lawful the issue will be whether the party relying on the contract subjectively knew of the intended illegality.[16] In *Corby's* case the E.A.T. concluded that an employee who had received an untaxed £5 per week in excess of basic pay must have known of the purpose of this payment and its illegality. In two earlier cases, however, the same court was prepared to accept the employee's innocence as validating the contract.[17]

It appears surprising that the general unwillingness of the courts to sever truly illegal provisions, as distinct from those declared by statute to be void led to the conclusion in *Tomlinson* v. *Dick Evans U Drive Ltd.*[18] that an illegal contract of

---

[9] *Kearney* v. *Whitehaven Colliery Co.* [1893] 1 Q.B. 700; see also *Bird* v. *British Celanese Ltd.* [1945] K. B. 336.

[10] *Baddeley* v. *Earl of Granville* (1887) 19 Q.B.D. 423; *Wheeler* v. *New Merton Board Mills Ltd.* [1933] 2 K.B. 669.

[11] See, *e.g.* Employment Protection (Consolidation) Act 1978, s.140; Patents Act 1977, s.42.

[12] *Coral Leisure Group Ltd.* v. *Barnett* [1981] I.C.R. 503.

[13] As in a contract of employment containing servile incidents—*Hepworth Manufacturing Co.* v. *Ryott* [1920] 1 Ch. 1.

[14] See *Clandestine employment: a problem of our times*: Raffaele de Grazia (1980) 119 *International Labour Review* in which it is estimated that the annual income through all forms of clandestine employment in the U.K. is some £10,000 million or 7.5 per cent. of G.N.P.

[15] [1978] I.C.R. 639.

[16] *Corby* v. *Morrison* [1980] I.C.R. 564.

[17] *Davidson* v. *Pilley* [1979] I.R.L.R. 275; *McConnell* v. *Bolik* [1979] I.R.L.R. 422.

[18] [1978] I.C.R. 639.

employment could not give rise to any statutory rights derived from that employment. Hepple and O'Higgins[19] suggest that the severity of this rule should be moderated wherever the illegal element of the contract does not have to be disclosed as a necessary part of the claim. It is not clear, however, whether the learned editors consider that this can produce much significant effect without a considerable extension of severance. Modern statutory employment rights tend to be restricted to those under a contract of service. Since the existence of such a contract is a matter of jurisdiction it cannot be waived. The legality or otherwise of the contract is an essential part to the claim.

A more profitable area of moderation has been developed by the courts by way of a distinction between purpose and effect. A contract the purpose of which is illegal is void, but a contract for a proper purpose which is being performed illegally is not. Sometimes the absence of a connection between the illegalities and the contract is obvious.[20] In other cases the illegality may have entered more inseparably into the contractual relationship. In *Coral Leisure Group Ltd.* v. *Barnett*,[21] for instance, the employer pleaded the illegality of the contract as a defence to the claim against him on the ground that one of the duties of the employee was to procure prostitutes for clients. The court held that the contract was not for an immoral purpose so far as the employee was concerned.

The courts will, apparently, endeavour to avoid allowing a valid contract of employment to be invoked so as to effect the purpose of an illegal contract. In *A. R. Dennis and Co. Ltd.* v. *Campbell*[22] an action was brought against an employee, upon the duties contained in his contract of employment, to recover damages for permitting unauthorised credit to a customer of a betting shop. The Court of Appeal held that the loss arose from an illegal wagering contract. It declined to award even nominal damages for breach of duty arising from the contract of employment on the ground that this would give effect to a void transaction.

---

[19] *Encyclopedia of Labour Relations*, 1–107/1.
[20] *McConnell* v. *Bolik* [1979] I.R.L.R. 422.
[21] [1981] I.C.R. 503.
[22] [1979] I.C.R. 862.

CHAPTER 2

THE CONTRACT OF EMPLOYMENT

JUDICIAL CONTRACT MAKING

THE legal incidents of employment derive from two main sources; contract and statute. Because of the increasing intervention of statute to confer rights and obligations on the parties to the contract of employment *inter se* it is not uncommon to suggest that the relationship is moving away from contract towards status.[1] Professor Sir Otto Kahn-Freund demonstrated[2] that this was to use the term "status" so loosely as to mean only that the relationship was not purely contractual. He pointed out that the legal systems of many Continental Western European countries would avoid the possibility of such confusion by making it clear that a contract could well embody rules of law taking precedence over the agreement of the parties. The relationship would, nonetheless, contain far too much freedom to fix terms and conditions to be regarded as one of status. English common law, obsessed with the idea that all terms of the contract have to be the product of agreement, has habitually supposed that, agreement to exist when policy has suggested incorporating a particular incident in the contract. In the last 20 years the Court of Appeal has gone a long way to reduce the need to "prove" the fiction in terms of necessity and to substitute an assumption based on reasonableness. Nevertheless the courts still pretend that the parties would have agreed to what the courts consider reasonable. Occasionally this pretence leads the courts to misconstrue the supposed consent of the parties and to impose a term they would not have agreed to.[3] More often the supposition of agreement is not demonstrably wrong but owes more to conceptions of the standard contents of a contract of employment than to any examination of the mind of the parties.[4] One wonders whether Miss Wood or Mrs. Cohen,[5] having had time to think about it, would really have agreed that their spare time relationship constituted a breach of the obligations in a contract of employment. In the light of the apparent consent of both to the relationship there can be little pretence that the parties had not been saddled with terms imposed upon them by the law.

The courts are normally permitted a great deal of room in which to create a contract of employment to their liking by the surprising degree of informality in the creation of the majority of employment relationships.

---

[1] See the author's article (1966) 19 C.L.P. 111.

[2] (1967) 30 M.L.R. 635.

[3] See, *e.g. Bristol Garage (Brighton) Ltd.* v. *Lowen* [1979] I.R.L.R. 86.

[4] *e.g.* it seems unlikely that employers would agree to a term which made all industrial action a breach of contract such as was implied on scarcely concealed grounds of policy in *Secretary of State for Employment* v. *ASLEF* [1972] 2 Q.B. 455. Such policy, however, would not have favoured the alternative conclusion that both parties accepted intermittent industrial action as part of the normal pattern of the relationship.

[5] *Wood* v. *Freeloader Ltd.* [1977] I.R.L.R. 455.

SOURCES OF TERMS AND CONDITIONS

Although a considerable number of contracts of employment are reduced to writing, it would be rare to find such a one which contained all the contractual terms and conditions applicable to the employment concerned.[6] It has, moreover, always been the case that the vast majority of contracts of employment are unwritten in the sense of being presented as a formal written contract. Since 1963 statute has required that every employee (save a small number of categories who do not qualify under the legislation) should receive a written statement of certain terms and conditions of employment. Even this statement will not normally be regarded as a written contract and, probably more often than not, it will merely refer to other written sources of terms such as collective agreements. The contractual terms and conditions of employment have, therefore, to be collected from a number of extra-contractual sources, both written and unwritten. The most important of these sources in general are:

(a) express written or oral statements of terms and conditions;
(b) relevant collective agreements;
(c) other documents which may or may not have been formulated after discussion or negotiation between employer and employee such, for instance, as works rule books, statements of pension schemes and, possibly, notices posted at the place of work[7];
(d) the statutorily required statement of terms and conditions of employment;
(e) implication by statutory provision such, for instance, as the terms of a Wages Council order[8];
(f) implication according to the ordinary rules of common law, which source will also comprehend trade customs;
(g) implication of established common law terms of employment considered characteristic of employment as a whole.

A confusingly loose nomenclature is adopted to describe the process of collecting terms from these sources in which the concept of implication is invoked far too generally. An excellent example of the misuse of this term occurred in the judgments of both an industrial tribunal and the E.A.T. in *Lawrence* v. *Council of the London Borough of Newham*.[9] The complainant, in pursuit of a remedy for alleged unfair dismissal, sought to establish that her contract contained a term permitting her to bring her young child to work with her. The employer had agreed that she could do this when she was engaged, provided that the child did not interfere with her work. The child was then aged four months. As it grew up and began to crawl around the school where the complainant worked as a cleaner, several accidents occurred. Both tribunals discussed the original permission as a possible implied term but it is quite clear that, though oral, it was, if anything, an express term. Had it been so viewed it is

---

[6] Even the many leaved contracts current in *Ready Mixed Concrete (South-East) Ltd.* v. *Minister of Pensions and National Insurance* [1968] 2 Q.B. 497, did not and, indeed, were not intended to, achieve this comprehensiveness.

[7] See, *e.g. Petrie* v. *Mac Fisheries Ltd.* [1940] 1 K.B. 258.

[8] These will be dealt with as appropriate in the text and nothing further will be said of them at this point.

[9] [1978] I.C.R. 10.

suggested that it might have been easier for both tribunals to accept that if the permission was contractual it was, nonetheless, conditional and that the condition not having been met the permission could be withdrawn without breach. Instead, both tribunals held that the permission was not contractual. This achieved the same result but, it is submitted, is less satisfactory in the light of the probability that both parties would have been surprised to learn immediately after making the contract that the complainant had no right to bring her child to work with her.

It is submitted that there is little point, save as a description of fact, to distinguish between written and unwritten terms. In *Gascol Conversions Ltd.* v. *Mercer*[10] the decision of the Court of Appeal that a local agreement could not be "implied" into the contract depended in part on its view that the contract was written and signed. The rule that an implied term cannot override an express term would apply equally to an oral express term such as that in *Lawrence* v. *Borough of Newham*[11] so that the suggestion that there is some vital difference between written and oral contracts is, in this respect, misleading.[12] It is as misleading to apply the same concept of implication to those terms derived by the common law rules for detecting implied terms, as to those terms derived from extraneous documents, such as collective agreements. The question of whether the latter are to be given individual contractual effect does not depend on considerations of business efficacy, but rather on the fact that the source exists and the particular provision is appropriate to an individual contract of employment. Ideally, therefore, it would be desirable if the term "express" were applied to clearly specified contractual provisions, written or oral; the term "implied" were confined to terms which did not depend on the existence of a written source appropriate to affect the individual relationship of employment but which were extracted from the unexpressed presumed intention of the parties; and some such concept as "incorporation by reference" were used to explain the adhesion to the contract of extraneous documents. The student must be aware, however, that the judgments of tribunals and courts almost always adopt more misleading nomenclature. The possibility of this judicial confusion leading to incorrect conclusions is not great but over-frequent resort to supposed implication gives an artificial effect to some of the devices which then have to be adopted to explain the decision. This is particularly apparent when the courts seek to explain the effect of collective agreements.[13]

(a) Express written or oral terms

Implication may not override

Little need be said about express terms in the contract of employment. In *Gascol Conversions Ltd.* v. *Mercer*[14] the employee had received a document described in its heading as a contract of employment and had signed a receipt which itself described the document as a contract. In fact the document was

[10] [1974] I.C.R. 420.
[11] *Supra*.
[12] The E.A.T. demonstrated this lack of difference in *Simmonds* v. *Dowty Seals* [1978] I.R.L.R. 211.
[13] See, *e.g. Land and Wilson* v. *W. Yorks M.C.C.* [1979] I.C.R. 452 (E.A.T.).
[14] *Supra*.

intended to satisfy the requirements of the Contracts of Employment Act 1972,[15] and need have been no more than a non-contractual statement of contractual terms. Since, however, it was described and accepted as a contract the Court of Appeal had no hesitation in attaching to it the usual attributes of a written, signed contract. It follows from what has been said, however, that a signature to what is merely a receipt for a non-contractual instrument will not turn it into a contract. Nor indeed does the presence or absence of a signature have more than evidential value in this situation. Express oral terms cause different problems not least because they are confused with implied terms and because evidence on which to base interpretation is less clear. Clearly an express oral term may be inserted at an interview.[15a]

Interpretation

Although an express contract cannot be varied by implication it must be remembered that an express written term can be varied by an express oral term.[16] The contract can, of course, be interpreted, and such interpretation may take into account the same considerations of subsequent conduct or of reasonableness as would be relevant to a decision as to whether a term should be implied. It is, for instance, not uncommon for an employer to describe certain payments as "ex gratia." In *Edwards* v. *Skyways*,[17] Megaw J. said that that term did not necessarily convey an absence of contractual obligation. Its interpretation in any given case would seem likely, therefore, to depend upon subsequent conduct. If payment had been intermittent the inference that there was no obligation would be supported. Consistent payment would not prove an obligation but would afford strong evidence which might be fortified in the outcome by application of the doctrine of estoppel. Such factors as the frequency with which such payments were encountered in the industry would also affect the reasonableness of one or other interpretation.

Void terms

There are, however, some limitations on what may validly be contained in an express contract. Certain terms are expressly prohibited by statute.[18] In other cases,[19] statute permits the rectification of express terms in conflict with either statutory obligations or statutorily implied terms. Contractual terms at variance with certain statutory rights may be regarded as ineffective. So, for instance, a term in a contract of employment purporting to authorise an unfair dismissal such as by stating that the contract might be terminated if the employee was, on a single occasion, late by one minute could be so regarded by an industrial tribunal.[20] Since the jurisdiction to hear a complaint of unfair dismissal depends

---

[15] Now the Employment Protection (Consolidation) Act 1978, s.1.
[15a] *e.g. London Borough of Redbridge* v. *Fishman* [1978] I.C.R. 569. Such a term may displace a written source as in *Hawker Siddeley Power Engineering Ltd.* v. *Rump* [1979] I.R.L.R. 425.
[16] *Simmonds* v. *Dowty Seals* [1978] I.R.L.R. 211.
[17] [1964] 1 W.L.R. 349. See also *Pedersen* v. *London Borough of Camden* [1981] I.C.R. 674 (C.A.).
[18] See, *e.g.* the Truck Acts, pp. 125–131, *infra*; Factories Act 1961, s.86.
[19] *e.g.* the Equal Pay Act 1970.
[20] Employment Protection (Consolidation) Act 1978, s.140(1).

on the establishment of a dismissal and, in the case of constructive dismissal this can only exist if it can be shown that the employer has broken the contract of employment, an intriguing academic question arises as to whether all statutory provisions conferring rights upon the employer do not amount to an attempt to contract out of the employee's statutory protection from unfair dismissal. The question of the fairness of the term will never arise if the existence of the term prevents the employee from establishing a constructive dismissal. No contract can oust the jurisdiction of the courts and so, though the parties might be bound by an interpretation clause in a contract they would not be bound by an incorrect statement of the law, as for instance if the contract incorrectly described itself as a contract of employment.[21]

(b) Incorporation of collective agreements

As we shall see (*infra*, p. 375) an agreement between one or more trade unions and an employer, or employers' association, regarding conditions of employment or negotiating procedures—commonly referred to as a collective agreement—is regarded in the United Kingdom, prima facie, as having no contractual enforceability as between the parties.[22] Save as regards industrial peace clauses there is nothing to prevent the parties indicating a contrary intention. Statutory provisions to the contrary exist but departure from the normal rule is uncommon.

Simple observation will establish that, on the other hand, considerable portions of the contract of employment are derived from provisions contained in collective agreements. Rates of pay, for instance, are collectively negotiated in most cases where unions are recognised for any bargaining purposes. It is at once obvious that the law will have to accept that the resultant agreement becomes at some time the source of the contractual obligation to pay that wage. Such an obligation is very likely to operate as an agreed variation of the previously existing wage rate. Although wage rates are the most obvious term to be incorporated from collective agreements many other important conditions derive from the same source. Indeed, wherever unions agree any matter which, to be effective, must confer rights or impose obligations upon individual employees it is likely to be the intention that the employer should be bound to the individual to honour that agreement. So far as the central policies of trade unions are concerned it is usually true that there is an equally strong intention that the individual employee member should be bound to observe the agreement.[23]

On the other hand, it is a matter of common understanding that individual rights will not be derived from certain aspects of collective agreements. Few people would expect an individual employee to be able to bring a successful action to compel an employer to adhere to a recognition agreement or a closed

---

[21] See *Construction Industry Training Board* v. *Labour Force Ltd.* [1970] 3 All E.R. 220.

[22] See Trade Union and Labour Relations Act 1974, s.18(1).

[23] The court in *Loman and Henderson* v. *Merseyside Transport Service Ltd.* (1968) 3 I.T.R. 108 totally confused the separate aspects of the non-enforceability of a collective agreement as between the parties to it and the enforceability of its provisions when incorporated into individual contracts of employment. In that case it was held incorrectly that a statement that a local agreement was intended to be binding in honour alone must mean that provisions of the agreement could not be implied into the contract of employment.

shop agreement. Implication of a restriction upon the freedom to take industrial action—the "peace clause"—is now regulated by statute.[24]

The choice by the courts of which, if any, principle of implication to apply and what conclusion to draw from it will probably be a matter of policy. It is, for instance, very likely that in an industrial tribunal both lay members will desire to emphasise the binding effect of collective agreements on individuals. They are not particularly interested in how a lawyer justifies such a conclusion so long as he does so. If he chooses to adopt the "agency" approach it may be that the lay members will feel most satisfied since it has about it an air of authority which both, for different reasons, will find satisfying. The "custom and practice" explanation will strike a chord with both and will suit the lawyer who may see considerable difficulties in the agency approach but who finds that "custom and practice" is not far removed from policy since it is likely to be the policy of the law to give effect to the wishes of those who collectively regulate industry. In some ways, therefore, an examination of the basis for incorporation of collective agreements in individual contracts is an exercise in *ex post facto* explanation of a desired result rather similar to that of manipulating the rules of statutory interpretation.

Mutual acceptance

The most common ground of implication is evidence of acceptance by both parties. In the surprisingly unreported case of *Dudfield* v. *Ministry of Works*[25] it was held that contractual incorporation of one agreement should not be deduced from habitual acceptance of previous agreements. The decision in *Pepper and Hope* v. *Daish*[25a] that an employee has a contractual right to an annual pay rise because such an expectation is reasonable must be regarded as of doubtful validity. That case might have been decided on the narrower ground that an employee has a contractual right to participate in a rise negotiated for his class. The wider ground upon which the judgment is based raises, however, unanswerable problems of unilateral variation in economically bad years.

We are considering in each case whether there is evidence of acceptance of the particular agreement in question. Acceptance by the employer causes little problem in practice. It is likely that aspects of an agreement burdensome to him will necessitate some relatively immediate and directly related action on his part. Acceptance by the employee cannot be so convincingly demonstrated because it must often be implied from indirectly related conduct. Bearing in mind that the employee will, in many instances, have nothing better than constructive knowledge of the alleged term, care must be taken in seeking to apply by analogy the reasoning in *Sagar* v. *Ridehalgh*.[26] This decision that an employee was bound by a term of which he had no knowledge simply because he had accepted the job ought, it is submitted, to be confined to the type of well established custom and practice that was there under consideration. In that context the decision is acceptable, if only on the basis of a form of constructive knowledge. The collective agreement, however, may seek to impose a new and unestablished obligation. If the court feels the need to resort to acceptance

---

[24] Trade Union and Labour Relations Act 1974, s.18(4).
[25] (1964) 108 S.J. 118.
[25a] [1980] I.R.L.R. 13
[26] [1931] 1 Ch. 301.

rather than agency it may well be because it is seeking to impose that obligation on one who is not a union member, and may even be opposed to acceptance. Courts will, however, be tempted to use an argument based on a form of custom, namely: that evidence of widespread acceptance of the agreement should be taken as evidence of acceptance by an individual. The temptation is one of policy since it is obviously desirable that individual employees should not be exempt from generally accepted obligations.[27]

The other major problem facing the courts is from what evidence they should imply acceptance. Most often such evidence will be in the form of a failure to object. Despite the existence of a well-established contractual principle that silence is not to be deemed to indicate acceptance it is clear that much of the content of the contract of employment is the product of tacit acceptance. Nevertheless the very upsurge of the implied term has led the courts to warn against too facile an assumption that one who continues to work without protest thereby accepts new conditions proposed by the other even though he knows of the proposal.[28] The judgment in *Jones* v. *Associated Tunnelling Co. Ltd.* shows a clear realisation, and rejection, of the temptation to assume acceptance so as to overcome the problem of incorporating the many collectively agreed provisions which will not produce any positive response from the employees to whom they apply.

It is submitted, however, that this decision is also an early indication of judicial withdrawal from previous signs of readiness to regard employees as bound by collective agreements. This raises a much wider issue as to the extent of an employee's knowledge of any source of evidence of terms of the contract. The decision in the *Jones* case does not assist greatly to resolve this problem save that if variation may be said to require consent based on knowledge the initial consent to terms should not be derived more readily from an assumed knowledge. In *Sagar* v. *Ridehalgh and Son Ltd.*[29] lack of an employee's knowledge of a trade custom was not regarded as a barrier to its implication. In *Duke* v. *Reliance Systems Ltd.*[29a] Browne-Wilkinson J. continued his insistence on knowledge as a prerequisite of consent and said that even recognised custom and practice cannot be a basis for unilateral implication unless it is shown that the practice is drawn to the attention of the employee or has been followed without exception for a considerable period.

Agency

An alternative, and deceptively attractive, explanation is that the trade union is acting as agent for those for whom it bargains. The deceptiveness of this approach lies in its artificiality. If we are talking of a true agency as the law understands it incorporation of collective agreements is likely to be partial and confused. If we are inventing a concept of agency applicable to industrial relations will the courts be free to invoke it wherever it produces a "reasonable" result? The significance of this choice will be appreciated if we consider whether employees who are not union members are bound by the collective agreement

---

[27] See *Meek* v. *Port of London Authority* [1918] 1 Ch. 415; *cf. Maclea* v. *Essex Lines* (1933) 45 Ll.L.Rep. 254.
[28] *Jones* v. *Associated Tunnelling Co. Ltd.* [1981] I.R.L.R. 477, *per* Browne-Wilkinson J.
[29] [1931] 1 Ch. 310.
[29a] [1982] I.R.L.R 347.

in the same way as if they were members. If they are not, a potentially chaotic contractual differentiation will result. It is easy in industrial relations terms to say that they are bound because they are part of the bargaining unit for which the union is recognised.[30] But this is to invent an agency imposed without the agreement of the principals. Would that peculiar agency hold good even despite express rejection by a principal? The lawyer might have no difficulty in visualising a presumption of agency allowing any individual to opt out.[31] The expert in industrial relations would see no principle compelling him to agree to such an option. If the agency theory is adopted it must be understood therefore to raise far more problems for the courts to resolve than it answers.

Originally the agency doctrine gained a foothold in situations where bargaining on a specific issue for a small group of employees was involved.[32] The actual judgments in these cases, however, did not use language which confined the application of the doctrine to that aspect of the facts of the case and the unwise concession of the point in *Rookes* v. *Barnard*[33] certainly did not involve so limited a view. In *Allen* v. *Thorn Electrical Industries Ltd.*[34] the Court of Appeal held that a contract existed to pay a collectively agreed increase in wages which was due to be paid as soon as administratively possible but which never had been paid because of the call of the then Prime Minister[35] for a wage standstill. Such a contract could only exist on the assumption that it derived from the agency of the union which negotiated its terms.

These judgments and indeed those in *Singh* v. *British Steel* and *Land and Wilson* v. *West Yorkshire M.C.C.*[36] provide only circumstantial support for the application of agency to general collective bargaining. They do, however, reveal a creeping tendency towards acceptance of such a doctrine against which stands very little directly contrary authority. Brian Napier[37] makes a gallant attempt to reject "agency" on the grounds of good sense and with the single authority of Lush J. in *Holland* v. *London Society of Compositors*.[38] In that case a member of a provincial trade union brought an action to enforce an agreement between his union and its London based counterpart that he would be received into membership of the latter when he moved to London. The agreement was clearly designed to benefit individuals but the learned judge held that the unions must, nevertheless, be regarded as acting for their own interests and not those of individual members. It is difficult to resist acceptance of agency as totally as this and all this decision may mean is that in that instance the unions intended an arrangement between themselves alone. A scarcely more acceptable solution is that adopted by Arnold J. in *The Burton Group Ltd.* v. *Smith*.[39] In that judgment it was said that there was no reason why an agency should not be created between the union and its members but such an agency would not be

---

[30] At least one court has rejected this extension; see *Land* v. *West Yorkshire M.C.C.* [1979] I.C.R. 452 (E.A.T.). Confirmed on other grounds [1981] I.R.L.R. 87 (H.L.).
[31] *Singh* v. *British Steel Corporation* [1974] I.R.L.R. 131.
[32] *Deane* v. *Craik*, *The Times*, March 16, 1962; *Edwards* v. *Skyways Ltd.* [1964] 1 W.L.R. 349.
[33] [1963] 1 Q.B. 623.
[34] [1968] 1 Q.B. 487.
[35] On July 20, 1966.
[36] *Supra*.
[37] Elias, Napier and Wallington, *Labour Law Cases and Materials*, Chap. 5, p. 407.
[38] (1924) 40 T.L.R. 440.
[39] [1977] I.R.L.R. 351.

implied simply from the fact of union membership. Agency would only exist where a specific agency had been created. It is however clear from the cases cited that agency has been seriously entertained by the courts on a wider basis than that adumbrated by Arnold J. What is not clear is that any court save that in *Holland's* case which rejected agency and *Edwards* v. *Skyways* which was dealing with the classic confined agency situation really understood itself to be talking of agency save in a rather loose popular sense. The lawyer who sees grave, if not insuperable, problems arising from any widespread application of the strict legal doctrine will have difficulty persuading laymen of this. They often see agency merely as a way of ensuring that the individual is bound by the agreements of his union. A warning that we might find unions charged with breach of warranty of authority may serve to curb such enthusiasm.

Express inclusion—the statutory statement

In *National Coal Board* v. *Galley*[40] the contract of employment declared that the employee "will serve the Board as regularly as the state of trade and interruptions from accidents or repairs to its mines and works or the non-arrival of wagons or general holidays will from time to time permit and that [his] wages shall be regulated by such national agreement and the county wages agreement for the time being in force and that this contract of service shall be subject to these agreements and to any other agreements relating to or in connection with or subsidiary to the wages agreement and to statutory provisions for the time being in force affecting the same." Such a provision undoubtedly incorporates the agreements to which it refers avoiding the doubts raised by the previous two explanations of incorporation. On the other hand it is not likely to be encountered commonly in contracts of employment for the simple reason that few will be sufficiently reduced to writing to include such a statement. There is, however, at hand a source of express incorporation likely to produce the same effect in a large proportion of cases. This source is the statutory statement of terms and conditions of employment. As we have seen, unless it is developed to constitute a contract in itself[41] such a statement is not conclusive of the contents of the contract. Theoretically therefore, an employee could argue that the statement that he was bound by the terms of the collective agreement on a given matter was incorrect in that he had never accepted the agreement. In practice the statement, by avoiding the need to invoke custom and practice and by supplying evidence of acceptance, removes the two principal uncertainties of the acceptance theory of incorporation. It is submitted, therefore, that the effect of a statutory statement to the effect that certain terms and conditions of employment are governed by the relevant collective agreements will, in practice, be difficult to eliminate.[42] The reference in a statutory statement to a collective agreement will also, presumably, overcome any difficulty that may be felt about lack of knowledge by the employee of the term to be incorporated.[43] This position also has suffered from the increasing reluctance to assume acceptance varying the contract demonstrated by the decision in *Jones* v.

---

[40] [1958] 1 W.L.R. 16 at p.19.
[41] See *Gascol Conversions Ltd.* v. *Mercer* [1974] I.C.R. 420.
[42] See the detailed and precise discussion of this point by an industrial tribunal in *Mordecai* v. *Jacob Beatus Ltd.* [1975] I.R.L.R. 170.
[43] See *Joel* v. *Cammell Laird (Ship Repairers)* [1969] I.T.R. 206.

Associated Tunnelling. It may now only be arguable when the term sought is one affecting everyday working practices so that the employee might be assumed to have considered it.

This effect of the statutory statement is, however, very significantly limited in that the requirements applicable to that statement cover those aspects of the contract where it is most obvious in common sense that clauses of collective agreements will be incorporated into the contract of employment. It may help, therefore, to remove the need for the lawyer to develop technical explanations of what is obvious to everyone else. It may, as the decision in *Gascol Conversions* v. *Mercer* demonstrates, serve to resolve doubts as to which of two or more contradictory collective agreements is to be incorporated. No better than any other of the theories of incorporation we have discussed will it serve to resolve the question of which aspects of a collective agreement are apt to be incorporated.

Even when there is evidence to support the incorporation of collective agreements, problems may arise in deciding whether local or national agreements take priority. In the past the courts seem to have been over influenced by their supposed status to give priority to national agreements.[43a] In *Barratt* v. *N.C.B.*[43b] the E.A.T. was clearly aware of the significance of local agreements even if they were so informal that they could best be referred to as arrangements.

Choice of clauses for incorporation

No area of the law has ever developed so rapidly as has labour law in the past 20 years. The lawyer will instinctively apply his normal technique of seeking case authority over a considerable period of time but must be more readily conscious in this than in any other subject that what to him is a relatively short period of time may have rendered a point of an earlier judgment almost useless. Earlier, for instance, we discussed the case of *Holland* v. *London Society of Compositors* as the only clear authority against the agency theory. The plain truth is that whatever the authority of Lush J. it is unlikely that his views in this area would now serve to withstand any movement of thought towards acceptance of agency based, for instance, on a policy of giving legal effect to the fact of the regulatory function of collective agreements.

In the same way there is little point in continuing to regard *Young* v. *Canadian Northern Railway Co.*[44] as a useful authority on the appropriateness of a collective clause for incorporation into the contract of employment. That decision was to the effect that a wages agreement was not adapted for incorporation in a contract of service. Professor Lord Wedderburn in the first edition of his great pioneering rationalisation of labour law[45] asked the question whether an agreement that women packers should only be required to hammer nails of a certain maximum length could become part of their contracts of employment. At the time it seemed to many, probably including Lord Wedderburn himself, that the answer should be in the negative. It is suggested that the

---

[43a] *e.g. Turriff Construction Ltd.* v. *Bryant* [1976] I.T.R. 292; *R.* v. *C.A.C., ex parte Deltaflow* [1978] I.C.R. 534.
[43b] [1978] I.C.R. 1101.
[44] [1931] A.C. 83.
[45] *The Worker and the Law* (1st ed., 1965).

massive spread of the contract is now likely to have absorbed such a clause. Those who litigated the issue of inclusion of procedural safeguards before discipline of an employee in *Barber* v. *Manchester Regional Hospital Board*[46] might well now be advised that such incorporation was not worth resisting.[47]

The argument has moved on to the consideration for inclusion of aspects which once would not have been thought to give rise to such a possibility. In *British Leyland (UK) Ltd.* v. *McQuilken*[48] the actual decision was, however, still against the inclusion of the provision as a contractual term. The employer and the majority of unions represented among the workforce had agreed a procedure to deal with reorganisation involving redundancies. Part of the agreement provided that employees would be interviewed to establish lists of those desiring retraining and those desiring redundancy. Later the employer changed the policy and offered either retraining or transfer to another site. The appellant was never interviewed under the terms of the original agreement and eventually left the employment because of the prevailing uncertainty about his future. He claimed a constructive dismissal and the question arose, therefore, whether the failure to interview him constituted a breach of contract such as to entitle him to leave. Lord McDonald in the Scottish E.A.T. said:

> "In our opinion in the present case the terms of the agreement between the appellants and the unions did not alter the respondents individual contract of employment. That agreement was a long term plan, dealing with policy rather than the rights of the individual employees under their contracts of employment."

This decision is obviously based on broad impressions of the type of provision involved. It must be for the reader to decide whether anything is added to the authority of such a decision by the more precise reasoning adopted in the earlier case of *Gallagher* v. *The Post Office*.[49] At the time of Gallagher's recruitment the Post Office recognised two trade unions including what was then called the Guild of Telephonists. An agreement stated this fact as a preliminary matter and Gallagher was told by his training supervisor that he was free to join either trade union. Subsequently the Post Office withdrew recognition from the Guild which Gallagher had joined. He brought an action alleging that this withdrawal constituted a breach of his contract of employment. In deciding that the statement concerning recognition was not incorporated into individual contracts the court conducted a careful survey of the nature of the various parts of the agreement and also invoked the doctrine of business efficacy to conclude that there was no necessity for such a term to be included in the contract. Brightman J. added:

> "In my judgment, counsel for the Post Office was correct when he submitted that all the terms and conditions of the employment of the first plaintiff are contained on pages 2, 3 and 4 of CS 1, and that the second paragraph of page 1 is no more than a glimpse of the fairly obvious, namely that the Post Office intended to discuss matters with the relevant trade union before seeking to alter the terms and conditions of anyone's employment. If the paragraph was intended to bind the Post

---

[46] [1958] 1 W.L.R. 181.
[47] The same reserve may not have overtaken the decision in *Rodwell* v. *Thomas* [1944] 1 K.B. 596 concerning a circular on disciplinary procedure.
[48] [1978] I.R.L.R. 245.
[49] [1970] 3 All E.R. 712.

Office, as part of the contract of employment, to indefinite recognition of particular trade unions, I cannot think that the paragraph would have been placed ambiguously on page 1 instead of in its proper place on pages 2, 3 or perhaps 4. Nor do I think that such vague language as 'appropriate staff associations' would have been adopted when it would have been child's play to have specified the relevant trade union and to have stated that recognition of that union would not be withdrawn during the currency of the contract of employment."

This careful explanation has led one commentator,[50] Patrick Elias, to deduce that the court did not reject the possibility of the inclusion of such a provision.

Even at its simplest the consideration must involve the two separate aspects of

(a) the nature of the clause under consideration
(b) the way in which the parties have framed the clause.

In the older case of *Rodwell* v. *Thomas*[51] the matter involved concerned disciplinary procedure for serious offences other than those that might give rise to criminal proceedings. There can be no doubt that whereas "recognition" is essentially collective and, therefore, might be said to raise a prima facie assumption against incorporation, "discipline" has an individual connotation. The procedure had, however, been incorporated in a Treasury circular to government departments. This was held to indicate that it was intended to be a matter "disposed of by give and take" and not to be subject to the rigidity of enforceable contractual rights. It is doubtful whether such a distinction would now be so readily thought to exclude a highly relevant individual element from the contract of employment.

Interpretation of incorporated provisions

Once a collective agreement has come into being and an appropriate clause from that agreement has been incorporated into the individual contract it will retain its contractual status until properly amended or removed from the contract. What happens to the collective agreement ceases to be relevant. The parties may, of course, have agreed that properly negotiated amendments to a collective agreement will have the effect of amending the individual contracts. The decision in *Jones* v. *Associated Tunnelling Co. Ltd.* (*supra*) must cast doubt on whether such amendment will automatically occur as a result of such a statement in the statutory statement of terms and conditions of employment. Unless otherwise agreed, a unilateral act—such as the employer's rejection of the agreement—will not affect the individual contract. This situation raises a fascinating problem for the courts. Very commonly when implying terms into the contract of employment they are, as we have seen, in the habit of leaving themselves room to manoeuvre by framing the term in general—often rather meaningless—terms such as "trust and confidence." When extracting a term from a definite source, however, the source itself suggests that all that should be implied is the precise form of words used. In *Burroughs Machines Ltd.* v. *Timmoney*[52] the employer had been a member of the Allied Employers'

---

[50] Elias, Napier and Wallington, *Labour Law Cases and Materials*, p. 126.
[51] [1944] 1 K.B. 596.
[52] [1977] I.R.L.R. 404.

National Federation. This Federation had negotiated with the Confederation of Shipbuilding and Engineering Unions a Guarantee of Employment Agreement which provided *inter alia* that "in the event of dislocation of production in a federated establishment as a result of an industrial dispute in that or any other federated establishment the operation of the period of the guarantee shall be automatically suspended." After the agreement had been made and the applicant had become employed the employer terminated his membership of the Employers' Federation. An industrial tribunal found that this unilateral action could not alter the contract of employment and that the employee remained contractually entitled to receive the guarantee payment under the terms incorporated from the agreement. The tribunal held, however, that the provision for suspending the payment in terms only applied to federated establishments and could not be invoked by the employer after he had ceased to be federated. In the Inner House of the Court of Session the Lord President Emslie said:

"We are only concerned in this case with the contract of employment of an employee, engaged during the company's membership of the Employers' Federation, who completed his qualifying service with them for entitlement to the guaranteed week, and who remained in their service thereafter both before and after their resignation from the Federation. In his case we are to interpret that contract between the respondent and his individual employer and in our opinion it is clear that by the reference in that contract to the guaranteed week provisions in the National Agreement, the employer offered and the employee accepted employment on certain interdependent terms and conditions. The 'guaranteed week' provision in favour of the employee was clearly and explicitly conditioned by acceptance by the employee of the provision in clause 5(1)(c) in favour of the employer, at least in the event of dislocation of production due to industrial dispute in the employer's premises. Any other reading of the contract would involve in the event which happened the virtual deletion of a term which is expressly made a condition of the concession of the 'guaranteed week.' Such a construction of the contract is also in accord with common sense and what must have been understood by the respondent and by the company by the importation by reference into his contract of employment, of the essentials of the Guarantee of Employment Agreement of July 1965.

In our opinion it is clear that, whatever else may have been included in that agreement, so far as the respondent was concerned qualifying service with the company would and did give him a right to the guarantee at least so long as he remained in their service, on condition that the company could lay him off without pay if there was dislocation of production in the premises in which they employed him attributable, *inter alia*, to an industrial dispute there. That was the plain import of the respondent's contract of employment before February 24, 1973 and we can conceive of no colourable reason why, for the purposes of the guarantee and its corresponding condition, during the currency of the contract of employment, it was necessary in a question between the respondent and the company arising out of an industrial dispute in the respondent's place of work, for the company to be a member of the federation or for the federation to exist. In a question between the respondent and the company, once he was entitled to the guarantee, there could be no plausible purpose to be served that we can see by any alleged requirement that when a dislocation of production occurred in the premises in which the respondent was employed as the result of an industrial dispute there, the company must be a member of an undissolved federation in order to have the right to exact, for that reason, the price stipulated for the guarantee. The contract of employment of the respondent, as we see it, must be understood to have included essentially the provision of a guaranteed week coupled with a corresponding right to suspend it in the event of the relevant industrial trouble emerging at the respondent's place of work.

In our opinion the tribunal erred in thinking that clause 5(1) of the National Agreement must be deemed to have been incorporated word for word in the contract of employment of the respondent and we are content to know that we are not placed in the position of endorsing a construction of the provisions governing the guaranteed week in the respondent's contract of employment which has the thoroughly unsatisfactory, if not startling, consequences of the result reached by the Tribunal. In the result we hold that the company was not in breach of contract when they laid the respondent off without pay on August 28, 1974."

In *Stevenson* v. *Teesside Bridge and Engineering Ltd.*[52a] the court was prepared to deduce the existence of a mobility term from the provisions of a collective agreement for payment for travelling time.

The "peace clause"

Statute has occasionally intervened in the process of incorporation. The legislature which enacted the Trade Union and Labour Relations Act 1974 obviously felt that even at that date the courts showed some facility for giving contractual effect to collective agreements by incorporation in the contract of employment. It determined to protect collectively agreed limitations upon the freedom to take industrial action from such development. It provided[53]:

". . . any terms of a collective agreement (whether made before or after the commencement of this section) which prohibit or restrict the right of workers to engage in a strike or other industrial action, or have the effect of prohibiting or restricting that right, shall not form part of any contract between any worker and the person for whom he works unless the collective agreement—

(a) is in writing; and
(b) contains a provision expressly stating that those terms shall or may be incorporated in such a contract; and
(c) is reasonably accessible at his place of work to the worker to whom it applies and is available for him to consult during working hours; and
(d) is one where each trade union which is a party to the agreement is an independent trade union;

and unless the contract with the worker expressly or impliedly incorporates these terms in the contract."

This caution is obviously the outcome of the over-readiness to concede incorporation of such a clause in *Rookes* v. *Barnard*.[54] It must not be taken to suggest that without such special protection it would be at all likely that an essentially collective matter would be so incorporated without some clear indication of intention so to do. The real problem is, no doubt, that such intention—which may well alter the balance of the decision—is in the nature of things likely to be that of the employer to which the employee is deemed to consent.

Collective awards

A number of statutes going back to the early part of the century incorporate into contracts of employment the awards of certain official bodies participating

---

[52a] [1971] 1 All E.R. 296.
[53] Trade Union and Labour Relations Act 1974, s.18(4).   [54] [1964] A.C. 1129.

in industrial relations. The classic example is the incorporation of the award of the relevant Wages Council. When what appeared to be the same device was applied to unilateral applications for recognition[55] the reaction of the adjudicating agency—the Central Arbitration Committee—was, for our purposes, most interesting. It took the view that it was entirely inappropriate, even impracticable, to imply such a collective obligation into individual contracts and that it could not have been the intention of the legislature to allow the ultimate enforcement of such an award to depend upon a High Court injunction. This approach, despite the fact that it incurred a certain amount of criticism for lack of a spirit of adventure is, it is submitted, correct. It is one thing to provide a system of general statutory awards and then to incorporate them. It is entirely another to suggest that statute has intended to incorporate all the uncertainties—and most especially the partial coverage—of a collective agreement.

(c) Incorporation of other documents

Incorporation of documents other than collective agreements into the contract of employment is even less settled. This is not because such documents are infinitely diverse (since the uncertainty is general), nor because they are not the result of agreement between representatives of the employees and the employers since on occasion (as is often the case with a works rule book) the contents of the document will have been the subject of negotiation. The greater uncertainty is probably because most such documents are more likely to be concerned with matters not apt for incorporation in the contract of employment. As we shall see, even a works rule book which is directly applicable to the individual employment is more likely to be regarded as a set of variable instructions than as constituting contractually enforceable provisions.

It is indeed in the case of the rule book that there now exist the clearest statements of general principle upon contractual enforceability. In *Secretary of State for Employment* v. *Associated Society of Locomotive Engineers and Firemen (No.* 2)[56] the issue relevant to this discussion was whether the railwaymen who were engaged in a "work to rule" were thereby acting in breach of their contracts of employment. The rules to which the employees claimed they were adhering were contained in a book of detailed instructions relating more or less closely to their everyday work. The precedential value of the judgments on this issue is somewhat marred by the fact that a number of the rules were obviously out of date whilst others were framed in terms not readily referable to contractual provisions. Lord Denning M.R. in the Court of Appeal dealt most clearly with the point; holding that the rules did not constitute contractual terms. Subsequently, however, he implied that they might acquire a somewhat similar effect by the fact that they were standing instructions on how the work was to be done. As such it follows that the employee would be contractually bound to obey them because of an implied term in every contract that lawful (or reasonable) orders would be obeyed. The effect then is that the rules could be freely altered by the employer without the consent of the employee who at any given time would be bound to obey the rules then in force.

This aspect of the judgment should be applied cautiously. So-called rule books are various in their nature. Some of them amount to something more

---

[55] Employment Protection Act 1975, ss.11–16 repealed by the Employment Act 1980, s.19.
[56] [1972] 2 Q.B. 455.

akin to an employee's handbook containing, for example, information on pension rights, rules of procedure in the case of absence due to sickness or other cause, a list of disciplinary offences and the disciplinary and grievance procedure and the employer's safety policy. Some of these matters must be referred to in the statutory statement of terms and conditions of employment. Some of them, such as the safety policy, are plainly not contractual, whilst others, such as the disciplinary procedure, may well be.

One of the most common documentary sources of terms and conditions of employment is the letter of appointment, which, in turn, may be considered in conjunction with the advertisement for applicants. This source is particularly strong since it arises at the start of the contract and so does not have to overcome the barrier of conscious acceptance recently erected to defeat variation.[56a]

No clear propositions can be formulated to cover the whole field of such documents.[56b] Clearly the decision on when to incorporate them wholly or partially into the contract involves elements similar to common law implication in that the presumed intention of both parties must be sought. On the other hand, the issue is not one purely of implication and business efficacy would prove too rigid a test. It is probable that the test in reality in these cases is one of what it would be reasonable to expect to have contractual status and what is non-contractual either because it is more reasonably regarded as a changeable instruction or because it is by its form or position or content not thought of as contractual. In *Jones* v. *Lee and Guilding*[57] "conditions of tenure" specifying a right of appeal from disciplinary decisions had been issued to a headmaster upon appointment. These conditions expressly envisaged that subsequently prepared "rules of management" would amend them. Such rules were never prepared. The Court of Appeal held that the "conditions" were incorporated. Lord Denning M.R. said that as they had been given to the employee for his protection management would be estopped from denying their validity.

(d) The statutory statement of terms and conditions of employment

Terms required to be stated

The statement of terms and conditions of employment first required by section 4 of the Contracts of Employment Act 1963[58] requires written notice specifying the following matters to be sent to any employee under a contract normally involving not less than 16 hours employment per week and who has been continuously employed by the same employer for 13 weeks (excepting civil servants, registered dock workers and the husband or wife of the employer).[59] No statement is required where terms do not differ from those of a previous employment with the same employer which ended not more than six months before. Provision must be included for:

[56a] See, *e.g. Deeley* v. *British Rail Engineering Ltd.* [1980] I.R.L.R. 147; *Dalgleish* v. *Kew House Farm Ltd.* [1982] I.R.L.R 251.

[56b] A good example of such documentary terms is contained in *Financial Techniques Ltd.* v. *Hughes* [1981] I.R.L.R. 32.

[57] [1980] I.C.R. 310 (C.A.).

[58] Now the Employment Protection (Consolidation) Act 1978, s.1.

[59] No statement is required where terms do not differ from those of a previous employment with the same employer which ended not more than six months before.

(a) Identifying the parties.
(b) The date on which the period of continuous employment began stating whether any employment with a previous employer counts as part of the period of continuous employment with the present employer and, if so, the date when the continuous period began.

The statement shall contain the following particulars of the terms of employment as at a specified date, not more than one week before the statement is given:

(a) The scale or rate of remuneration or the method of calculating the remuneration;
(b) The intervals at which remuneration is paid (that is, whether weekly or monthly or by some other period);
(c) Any terms and conditions relating to hours of work (including any terms and conditions relating to normal working hours);
(d) Any terms and conditions relating to:
   (i) entitlement to holidays, including public holidays, and holiday pay (the particulars given being sufficient to enable the employee's entitlement, including any entitlement to accrued holiday pay on the termination of employment, to be precisely calculated);
   (ii) incapacity for work due to sickness or injury, including any provisions for sick pay (this is now extended by the terms of the Social Security and Housing Benefits Act 1982 which introduces a Statutory Sick Pay scheme. Regulations made under this Act require an employer to make it clear to the employee how and when he wants notification of incapacity to be given);
   (iii) pensions and pension schemes, with the exception of statutory pension schemes which require such information to be given to new employees;
(e) The length of notice which the employee is obliged to give and entitled to receive to determine his contract of employment;
(f) The title of the job which the employee is employed to do.

The provision in relation to continuous employment in (a) was inserted by the Employment Protection Act 1975. In view of the complexity of statutory provisions as to continuity, compliance with the requirement is likely to be difficult in some cases. It is worth pointing out that a misstatement to the employee's disadvantage would be ineffective as an attempt to contract out of statutory requirements. An error in the employee's favour, however, might be held to effect an estoppel.[60]

In addition the Employment Protection Act 1975 added a requirement that the statement should contain a note specifying any disciplinary rules applicable to the employee, or refer to a reasonably accessible document containing such rules. The same Act amended two further requirements, first introduced by the Industrial Relations Act 1971, so as to provide for notification, by description or otherwise, of a person to whom the employee can apply if he is dissatisfied with any disciplinary decision, or where he seeks redress of any employment grievance, and the manner in which such application should be made. An explana-

---

[60] *Evenden* v. *Guildford City Association Football Club* [1975] Q.B. 917.

tion of any further steps in such procedures where they exist, or reference to a reasonably accessible document explaining them, must also be included.[61]

The requirement that the statement shall specify the job title will be a significant advantage in the law of redundancy. It should be noted that what is required is not a job description. The more detailed the "title" the more restrictive of movement within the contract it is likely to prove. The main disadvantages to the employer of a generalised statement would seem to be that employees may fear a loss of status if lumped together in broad categories.

As has already been said, instead of setting out the details of these matters in the statement, the statement itself may refer to other documents available for inspection by the employee during normal working hours and containing the requisite information. Amendments must be notified in the same way within four weeks of the date of coming into effect of the amendment but, as we have also seen, it is possible to avoid this requirement by making reference to future documents.[62]

Non-contractual nature

The statutory statement of terms and conditions of employment is not a contract despite a statement to the contrary by Lord Denning M.R. as early as 1965.[63] As Lord Parker C.J. said in *Turriff Construction Ltd.* v. *Bryant*[64] the statement is only evidence of the terms of the contract. For this reason it is better to regard Lord Denning's subsequent judgment in *Gascol Conversions Ltd.* v. *Mercer*[65] as confined to the situation in that case in which the document issued to comply with the statute was expressly described as a contract and for which the employee had signed a receipt itself referring to the statement as a contract. In *System Floors (UK) Ltd.* v. *Daniel*[66] Browne-Wilkinson J. held an industrial tribunal wrong to consider a statement for which the employee had signed a receipt to be anything more than a unilateral declaration of the employer's views, one of which was evidently a mistake.

Despite this clearly correct view it might be thought that the usual position in which there is likely to be an absence of better evidence contradicting the statement would make it a very significant source of contractual obligation in practice. Browne-Wilkinson J. in *Jones* v. *Associated Tunnelling Co. Ltd.*[67] was at pains to discount the negative effect of an employee's silence when faced with a written statement of terms. The statement in that case was, in fact, a second issue intended to vary the employee's contract so as to impose an obligation on the employee to work anywhere in the United Kingdom. The learned judge held that in the absence of supporting evidence that the terms have been agreed the statement itself cannot be compelling evidence of a variation. The implication of continuing to work without objection to the new statement would, in his

---

[61] Employment Protection (Consolidation) Act 1978, s.1(4)(c).
[62] An industrial tribunal, when considering the adequacy of the statement was held to have no power to declare the meaning of the contract nor to rectify a manifest error; *Construction Industry Training Board* v. *Leighton* [1978] 2 All E.R. 723.
[63] *Camden Exhibition and Display Ltd.* v. *Lynott* [1965] 3 All E.R. 28.
[64] [1967] I.T.R. 292 and see *Systems Floors (U.K.) Ltd.* v. *Daniel* [1981] I.R.L.R. 475.
[65] [1974] I.C.R. 420.
[66] [1981] I.R.L.R. 475 (E.A.T.).
[67] [1981] I.R.L.R. 477.

view, not be strong in the case of anything but matters of immediate practical effect.

Although this decision only applies in terms of variation, which the courts are reluctant to imply too readily, it must cast doubt on the suggestions that the loose references to wide-ranging documentary evidence often contained in original statements will have sweeping incorporative effect. Even the decision in *Martin* v. *Solus Schall*[67a] must be viewed with caution. It was held in that case that a statement that the employee "will be expected to work such overtime as is necessary to ensure continuity of service" must be regarded as a contractual obligation since otherwise the provision would be meaningless. It can clearly be seen that this conclusion does not follow from the premise. The relevant question must be whether there is evidence that the term was accepted as contractual.

Extent of jurisdiction to rectify the statement

The power of an industrial tribunal to rectify a written statement relates closely to the question of implied terms since most commonly the tribunal will be asked to consider whether a term not stated elsewhere should or should not be included. This function received extensive consideration by the Court of Appeal in *Mears* v. *Safecar Security Ltd.*[68] where the question was whether the written statement should contain an obligation to pay wages during sickness. Stephenson L.J.:

"But without departing from the majority view of the facts and the inferences to be drawn from them, I am of opinion that when, in exercising its statutory jurisdiction under s.11, an Industrial Tribunal has to imply and insert missing terms, it is not tied to the requirements of the test propounded by Lord Justice Scrutton and Lord Justice MacKinnon, a test for commercial contracts which goes back to *The Moorcock*, but can and should consider all the facts and circumstances of the relationship between the employer and employee concerned, including the way in which they had worked the particular contract of employment since it was made, in order to imply and determine the missing term which ought to have been particularised by the employer and so to complete the contract.

And that was, I think, the view of the Employment Appeal Tribunal. In rejecting the term included by the Industrial Tribunal and preferring a different term they were, in my judgment, looking at the problem confronting them in that way and acting within their statutory powers and upon evidence which justified their preference. The Industrial Tribunal have stated (paragraph 1) that they would welcome authoritative guidance on 'problems over implied terms which are, on the authorities, of considerable difficulty in the modern employment context,' and in the hope of giving it I shall amplify that given by the Employment Appeal Tribunal in the judgment of Mr. Justice Slynn and what I have already said about s.11 and its application to this case.

The section enables the employee who has not received any statement, or a complete statement, of the terms of his employment to require the Industrial Tribunal to state them for him. When all the specified terms have been agreed, either expressly or by necessary implication, there is no problem for the Industrial Tribunal in stating any that have not been stated by the employer. But when one or more of the specified terms have not been agreed, even by necessary implication,

---

[67a] [1979] I.R.L.R. 1.
[68] [1982] I.R.L.R. 183.

the Industrial Tribunal may nevertheless have to state it for them. That is a possibility which I shall discuss later. But in a case where as here there are two alternatives—sick pay or no sick pay (I leave out the sub-division of the second alternative into sick pay gross and sick pay reduced by benefits received)—it is in the highest degree unlikely that neither has been agreed and the Industrial Tribunal's task is the simpler task of deciding which of the two terms has been agreed."

(e) Implication of terms

Scope of the implied term

It is not uncommon to find courts and tribunals speaking of the "implication" in the contract of employment of collective agreements and other similar extraneous sources. There is no right or wrong about the use of these words but it is confusing. The "incorporation," as we have called it, of such sources raises a wholly different type of consideration from that produced by less well documented evidence. The difference largely stems from the fact that a written source will provide a form of words open to interpretation but restricting the scope of the resultant term. As we have seen[69] the flexibility allowed by the process of interpretation may be surprisingly wide. Finally, however, the courts may accept or reject incorporation. If they accept it only a view of the form accepted by the parties can be imposed. Implication, as the word is used here, allows the courts to test any wording they choose for inclusion in the contract. More often than not the supposed term is framed so widely that the words used are almost meaningless and the courts rarely discuss the detail that will be necessary to adapt the term to the particular circumstances. The situation under consideration is generalised to a degree which provides a precedent for a vast range of future applications. This is particularly true of the modern development of an implied duty of trust and confidence which has greatly increased the implied obligations of the employer which were, until recently, heavily outweighed by the implied obligations of the employee. If, for example, the issue concerns abusive admonition of an employee by management it is rare to find the courts relying on an implied obligation to treat the employee courteously—which is a loose enough term in all conscience.[70] Even when offered the opportunity to make an obviously logical but limited implication they will be inclined to favour the wider generalisation which cannot be faulted simply because it can mean much or little as justice appears to demand. In Wetherall (Bond St., W.1) v. Lynn,[71] for instance, the employee who was in a position of some authority was admonished by his superior in the presence of his subordinates. It is submitted that it is wholly logical to say that if an employer places an employee in a position where the latter is expected to exercise authority there must be an implied obligation on the employer not to undermine that authority. In the instant case, however, the courts preferred the popular modern concept of a contractual duty to sustain "trust and confidence."[72] The facts in Courtaulds Northern Textiles Ltd. v. Andrew[73] show how confusing such loose

---

[69] Burroughs Machines Ltd. v. Timmoney [1977] I.R.L.R. 404, supra, p. 39.
[70] But see Donovan v. Invicta Airlines Ltd. [1969] 2 Lloyd's Rep. 413.
[71] [1978] I.C.R. 205.
[72] Wigan Borough Council v. Davies [1979] I.C.R. 411 affords a rare example of the E.A.T. resorting to a more narrow purpose-built implication.
[73] [1979] I.R.L.R. 84.

language may be. The employer sought to counter an allegation of destruction of trust and confidence by alleging that the manager who had used the derogatory remark did not have the impression of the employee that that remark suggested. The loss of confidence relied on by the court in that case if it existed at all, was that of the employee. A groundless suggestion that a foreman of considerable experience was incompetent might reasonably be taken by the employee to destroy the basis of his working relationship.

It would be wrong, however, to suggest that the courts are using shorthand terms because they cannot be bothered to be precise. It is true that the contract of employment is not now, and possibly has never been, subject to the normal contractual rule that a term will fail for uncertainty. Consequently the courts rarely trouble with certainty when implying terms.[74] No doubt the courts are aware of the discretion that they acquire by the formulation of substantially meaningless implied terms. The real reason for the use of loose phraseology is, it is suggested, the fact that in answering the question whether a contract has been broken the courts are, and have always been, aware that in most cases an answer will be of no value unless the breach can simultaneously be shown to be a serious one. This is why lack of courtesy is unattractive and destruction of trust and confidence the more rewarding enquiry. It was just as true when the common law preferred to speak of breach of the contractual duty of fidelity when considering a minor breach of confidence. This inherent tendency to use the language of repudiatory breach from the start is clearly apparent in the judgment of Slynn J. in the E.A.T. in *Palmanor Ltd*. v. *Cedron*.[75] The employee was engaged as a barman at a London night club. The manager thought he had reported for duty late and, when the employee pointed out that it was his late turn, abused him; telling him if he did not like the abuse he could leave and continuing to abuse him as he left. The court was concerned to show not only that it was considering conduct which was not only beyond the bounds of reasonableness and a breach of contract but also a repudiatory breach. Accordingly it framed the question as one of a general contractual obligation not to behave intolerably.

"We have considered anxiously the words used in the decision of this industrial tribunal, because the decision of the Court of Appeal in *Western Excavating* v. *Sharp* was not given until after the tribunal had come to their determination. The tribunal's words which to us appear to be important are that the various matters to which they referred 'rendered this conduct which entitled the [employee] to treat himself as dismissed' under the paragraph of the Schedule. It can be said, as Mr. Jarvis in his attractive and persuasive argument has said, that this is doing no more than asking the question, was this reasonable conduct? Mr. Jarvis points to another reference in the decision of the industrial tribunal where Mr. Owide is said to have acted unreasonably. On the other hand it is clear from the judgment of Lord Denning M.R. that there may be cases where conduct is sufficiently serious to entitle an employee to leave at once. Certainly Lawton L.J. gave instances of the kind of behaviour on the part of an employer which would be regarded as so intolerable that an employee could not be expected to put up with it. It seems to us that in a case of this kind the tribunal is required to ask itself the question whether the conduct was so unreasonable, that it really went beyond the limits of the contract. We observe that in the course of the argument on behalf of the employee,

---

[74] But see *Lake* v. *Essex County Council* [1979] I.C.R. 577.
[75] [1978] I.C.R. 1008.

it was submitted that the treatment that he was accorded was a repudiation of the contract.

We consider here that the industrial tribunal has not been shown to have failed to ask themselves the right question—that they have, reading their decision as a whole, approached the matter in the right way and have considered whether the behaviour of Mr. Owide was really so intolerable that the employee could not be expected to stay. It is to be observed that this is not simply a case, like some of the cases which have been cited to us, where merely abusive language was used. Mr. Jarvis has cited a number of cases where foul language was used and yet that was held not to justify dismissal. We attach importance to the fact that what Mr. Owide said, after the employee had sought to argue with him that he had no right to speak like that, was 'If you don't like it, you can go,' and 'I can talk to you any way I like'; and then he added further abusive language. Moreover, the employee . . . also contends that he was told . . . . 'I'll make sure you don't get another job anywhere in London.'

Moreover it seems to us that although it is quite right that in these cases tribunals have to be careful not to attach too great importance to words used in the heat of the moment or in anger, as was stressed in *Chesham Shipping Ltd.* v. *Rowe* nonetheless there comes a time when the language is such that even if the person using it is in a state of anger, an employee cannot be expected to tolerate it."

The present writer doubts, therefore, whether it can truthfully be said in relation to the contract of employment that "the implication of terms in contracts . . . is an activity cautiously undertaken."[76]

Discovering the intention of the parties

The courts do, however, like to present the process as one of scientific enquiry. Primarily, since they are dealing with contract, they insist that they are looking for the intention of the parties.[77] This common law view that every implication must be justified by presumed intent is not shared by many continental systems. Lord Denning M.R. has departed from it and argued for its rejection.[78] Nevertheless English courts still commonly adopt reasoning based on the assumption of intention. In one form or another the parties are supposed to have been likely to agree had they been asked whether they intended to incorporate the term in question. A fascinating extension of this approach was made in *Jones* v. *Associated Tunnelling Co. Ltd.*[78a] in which the E.A.T., in effect, regarded the parties, having failed to agree, as being imagined to be told that there must be a term covering the place of work and, supposedly, eventually reaching a compromise agreement.

Business efficacy

One or more of a number of theoretical tests for implication may be invoked. The business efficacy test was defined by Bowen L.J. in *The Moorcock*.[79]

". . . what the law desires to effect by the implication is to give such business efficacy to the transaction as must have been intended at all events by both parties who are business men."

---

[76] Elias, Napier and Wallington, *Labour Law: Cases and Materials*, p. 416.
[77] See *Reigate* v. *Union Manufacturing Co.* [1918] 1 K.B. 592 at 605–606.
[78] Lord Denning, *The Discipline of the Law* (Butterworth).
[78a] [1981] I.R.L.R. 477.
[79] (1889) 14 P.D. 64.

The test is often invoked in employment cases.[80] It would undoubtedly explain most, if not all the generally implied common law terms which a bare 20 years ago tended to be regarded as forming the substance of the "rights and duties of master and servant." It is suggested that as it was formulated it was meant to be applied as a rule of necessity. Certainly this is how it was applied by the majority of the House of Lords in *Lister* v. *Romford Ice and Cold Storage Ltd.* although it is arguable that their view of the result of such application is wrong.[81] It is clear that the reaction to the decision in that case, stopping just short of contrary legislation, demonstrated that necessity might well have been thought to require elimination of the obligation on an employee to indemnify his employer for breach of his contractual duty of care. In *Bristol Garage* v. *Lowen*[82] the court also mistook the necessity of implying a qualification upon the express obligation to make up cash deficiencies when it alleged that no one would accept an obligation to make up deficiencies caused by the dishonesty of others.[83] All this demonstrates, however, is a factual mistake in the evidence. Brightman J. applied the rule correctly and strictly when deciding in *Gallagher* v. *Post Office*[84] that business efficacy did not demand the incorporation of a recognition agreement.

Obvious consensus

The test put foward by MacKinnon L.J. in *Shirlaw* v. *Southern Foundries Ltd.*,[85] though also based on presumed intent, appears not to contain the element of necessity since its application could undoubtedly be supported by evidence of actual intention. He said:

"Prima facie that which in any contract is left to be implied and need not be expressed is something so obvious that it goes without saying; so that if, while the parties were making their bargain an officious bystander were to suggest some express provision for it in their agreement, they would testily suppress him with a common 'Oh, of course!' "

This invites consideration of the proper conclusions to be drawn from the facts as they existed at the time of engagement and it is commonly used in employment law in such situations.[86] There is, however, no reason why this test should not also be used to determine the existence of a consensual variation to an existing contract.

Reasonableness

There is, however, a serious weakness in the function of either of these tests. They can reveal whether or not there should be a term covering a situation but

---

[80] See, *e.g. Express Lift Co. Ltd.* v. *Bowles* [1977] I.C.R. 474; *Bristol Garage (Brighton)* v. *Lowen* [1979] I.R.L.R. 86.

[81] [1957] A.C. 555.   [82] *Supra*.

[83] The author still has in his possession a considerable quantity of false coin which, as a bus conductor, he was required by his contract of employment to replace with coin of the realm from his own wages. Indeed in *Bristol* v. *Lowen* it was almost certainly intended that the obligation should be without qualification so as to discourage "forecourt conspiracies." The facts in *Parker's Bakeries Ltd.* v. *Palmer* [1977] I.R.L.R. 215 provide clear evidence that the assumption in *Bristol* v. *Lowen* was wrong.

[84] [1970] 2 All E.R. 112.   [85] [1939] 2 K.B. 206 at 227.

[86] *e.g. Lake* v. *Essex County Council* [1979] I.C.R. 577; *Deeley* v. *British Rail Engineering Ltd.* [1980] I.R.L.R. 147.

they cannot define with any precision the content of such a term. In order to produce that result they must be assisted by some written source such as existed in *Gallagher* v. *The Post Office*,[87] or by other evidence. Unless the evidence is unusually clear and unchallenged a choice must be made.[88] That choice will depend on considerations of reasonableness, as is clearly demonstrated by the judgment of Lord Denning M.R. in *O'Brien* v. *Associated Fire Alarms Ltd.*[88a]

It is possible to contend that such tests as business efficacy are used by the courts to decide whether there should be a term covering the situation. Reasonableness is then applied to determine the detail of such a term. The language used by Browne-Wilkinson J. in *Jones* v. *Associated Tunnelling Co. Ltd.*[89] certainly supports the existence of such a tidy distinction. In the light of the assumption there made that there must be provision as to the place of work it is possible to see the judgment of Lord Denning M.R. in *O'Brien* v. *Associated Fire Alarms Ltd.*,[99] in such a light. There are, however, clear indications that the courts adopt reasonableness as the test for implication. Lord Denning in *O'Brien's* case did not suggest he was using this standard only to fill in the details. He has repeatedly said that reasonableness is the basis on which the courts operate to imply terms. Despite the fact that the House of Lords decisively rejected this as the basis for implication in *Liverpool City Council* v. *Irwin*,[91] Lord Denning has advanced that very judgment as authority for the proposition. Apart from the fact that judges other than Lord Denning openly invoke reasonableness[92] it is almost impossible to find a case where the courts have used the business efficacy or "Oh, of course!" tests to arrive at other than a conclusion the court obviously considered reasonable. In *Irwin's* case itself it is difficult to say that business efficacy necessitates the maintenance of a lift to a ninth storey flat, highly convenient as such a facility may be. Was not the House of Lords at pains to deny the obvious, namely: that it had concluded that business practice demanded a reasonable provision? We have already suggested that since a proper application of business efficacy in *Bristol Garage* v. *Lowen*[93] would have led to the opposite conclusion it is not likely that the court could have regarded the implied qualification as necessary. Rather was it decided that such a qualification would be reasonable.

It is not possible to prove that those courts which invoke either of the two or more formal tests to reach reasonable conclusions are more influenced by the latter conclusion but it is significant that there seems to be only one recently reported case in which the court applied business efficacy to reach a conclusion it manifestly considered unreasonable. In *Express Lift Co. Ltd.* v. *Bowles*[94] the E.A.T. refused to imply a reasonable qualification upon the obligation to work

---

[87] *Supra.*

[88] As in *Deeley* v. *British Rail Engineering, supra*; *O'Brien* v. *Associated Fire Alarms Ltd.* [1968] 1 W.L.R. 1916.

[88a] *Supra.*

[89] [1981] I.R.L.R. 477. The same judge, in *Duke* v. *Reliance Systems Ltd.* [1982] I.R.L.R. 347 stated that terms could only be implied on the basis of custom and practice or business efficiency.

[90] *Supra.*

[91] [1977] A.C. 329.

[92] *e.g. Lawrence* v. *London Borough of Newham* [1978] I.C.R. 10; *Pepper and Hope* v. *Daish* [1980] I.R.L.R. 13.

[93] [1979] I.R.L.R. 86.

[94] [1977] I.C.R. 474.

anywhere in the United Kingdom on the ground that the contract could work perfectly well without any limitation.

Evidence of intention

Whatever test is nominally, or actually, invoked it will be necessary to seek evidence of what the implied term should be. Apart from incorporation of source documents the most common evidence derives from what may loosely be called "custom and practice." This is not necessarily, nor probably usually, to be found in trade customs since that would be to suggest a far more restricted source of evidence than is in fact used. Trade practice may, of course, be valuable evidence as such. It would be unrealistic to discuss the implication of terms as to mobility in the construction industry, for instance, without acknowledging the existence of a standard practice of requiring mobility from site to site. Similarly the existence of a well-established custom may serve to overcome barriers to reasonable implication such as the lack of knowledge of the alleged term by one of the parties.[95] In industrial relations terms "custom and practice" means, however, nothing much more than an understanding based on precedent and it is in this sense that the courts—and more particularly industrial tribunals—increasingly apply it to determine the content of the contract of employment.

A custom is quite likely to begin life in response to the need to settle an individual dispute or deal with an unforeseen need. The next time another individual finds himself in a similar position the earlier precedent will be cited. Apart from the natural tendency to defend one's decision by adoption of such a precedent the fact that it had previously been considered reasonable and has worked in practice will seem to justify its adoption. On the third occasion it is likely no one will even pause to consider what solution should be adopted. By then practice has become established and if subsequently the courts are considering the situation in a contractual context there is already considerable evidence to support the argument that employees to whom the situation may apply are contractually entitled to the customary solution. A very simple example occurred in *O'Brien* v. *Associated Fire Alarms Ltd.*[96] where the habit of only working in Liverpool was taken as one factor in the implication of a contractual term that that was the place of work.

The process of gathering evidence in order to imply terms was extensively considered by the Court of Appeal in *Mears* v. *Safecar Security Ltd.*[97] Stephenson L.J.:

> ". . . there is nothing in those authorities which prevents the court from looking at the way the parties acted for the purpose of ascertaining what that term was. Commonsense suggests that their subsequent conduct is the best evidence of what they had agreed orally but not reduced to writing, though it is not evidence of what any written terms mean; and Mr. Tabachnik has put before us binding authority for that common sense view.

---

[95] *Sagar* v. *H. Ridehalgh and Son Ltd.* [1931] 1 Ch. 310; *Maclea* v. *Essex Line Ltd.* (1933) 45 Ll.L.Rep. 254.
[96] [1968] 1 W.L.R. 1916; compare *Stevenson* v. *Teesside Bridge and Engineering Ltd.* [1971] 1 All E.R. 296.
[97] [1982] I.R.L.R. 183.

. . . In *Wilson* v. *Maynard Shipbuilding* this court held that where one cannot ascertain from the terms of the contract itself what was agreed about a relevant term (in that case the place where under his contract an employee ordinarily works), one may look at what has happened and what the parties have done under the contract during the whole contemplated period of the contract for the limited purpose of ascertaining what that term is: see *per* Lord Justice Megaw at page 493, applied in *Todd* v. *British Midland Airways* [1978] I.R.L.R. 370, where Lord Denning, Master of the Rolls, said (at 371) that in considering the particular question where the parties have agreed that an employee should ordinarily work, the court gets less help from the terms of the contract than from the conduct of the parties and the way they have been operating the contract. See also what Sir David Cairns said at page 372.

But in *Wilson's* case the court was applying a more general principle stated by Lord Wilberforce in *Liverpool City Council* v. *Irwin* that in order to complete a contract which is partly but not wholly stated 'it is necessary to take account of the actions of the parties and the circumstances.' That case was cited not only to the Court of Appeal in *Wilson's* case and in *Ferguson* v. *Dawson & Partners* but to the Employment Appeal Tribunal in the instant case. As was pointed out in *Ferguson's* case by Lords Justices Megaw and Browne in deciding whether an oral and only partially expressed agreement was a contract of service or a contract for services, the court was not merely entitled but bound to take into account what was done under the contract, not to construe the contract but to infer what its terms were. . . ."

The difficulty the courts are faced with is inevitable in any such system of implication. There can be no precise rules to enable them to determine when a practice, particularly an individual habit, has become a contractual obligation. For obvious reasons, however, the fact that one person does something, albeit repeatedly, is far less compelling evidence of an agreement that it shall be done than is a similar practice copied by numerous people. So, in *Horrigan* v. *Lewisham London Borough Council*[98] the court declined to imply a contractual obligation from the fact that a particular employee had regularly worked overtime for ten years. On the other hand, a carefully worked out system applied generally and held out as an inducement may be implied despite a unilateral statement denying its contractual effect. In *Financial Techniques Ltd.* v. *Hughes*[99] this was the decision of the Court of Appeal concerning a profit-sharing scheme which contained a provision that a shortfall against target in one quarter should be carried forward to the next quarter but should not be capable of being set off against a bonus due on the previous quarter. In *Jones* v. *Associated Tunnelling Co. Ltd.*[1] Browne-Wilkinson J. made no pretence to discover the actual intention of the parties but adopted a term neither had mentioned as the "lowest common denominator" of agreement. Such an approach clearly leads to the production of generally applicable terms.

In view of the frequency with which the contract of employment is varied, it is important to bear in mind that such a contract will usually carry with it all the terms applicable before variation save those which are inconsistent with that variation.[2] Even if a wholly new contract is entered into, it will often be reasonable to imply into it many of the terms applicable to the former contract

---

[98] [1978] I.C.R. 15. Compare *Simmonds* v. *Dowty Seals Ltd.* [1978] I.R.L.R. 211.
[99] [1981] I.R.L.R. 32.
[1] [1981] I.R.L.R. 477.
[2] *Marley Tile Co. Ltd.* v. *Johnson* [1982] I.R.L.R. 75 (C.A.).

and not inconsistent with the new relationship. It may be, however, that the adoption of a particular form to incorporate a term in a previous contract will lead to the conclusion that the absence of that form in the new contract precludes any implication that such a term should continue to apply.[3] We turn now to consider, in detail, some of the most important terms which are usually implied into all normal contracts of employment.

PARTICULAR CONTRACTUAL TERMS

(a) The wage-work element—work

Extent of commitment

The employer, according to some lawyers, has a contractual duty to do the whole of the work defined in the contract giving his total ability to it. He may not excuse incomplete performance. So, in the course of argument in *Seaboard World Airlines Inc.* v. *Transport and General Workers Union*[4] Sir John Donaldson in the National Industrial Relations Court said:

"These contracts normally would provide for the performance of broadly specified types of work for a specified period of working hours. It would not be a breach of contract by the employers to ask the clerical employees to do clerical work of any kind within those times. The fact that their actual work load increased over the working day because business improved would not be a ground for saying that the employers were in breach of contract. It might be a ground for the employee saying to the employers, 'Well now, look, this job is getting a good deal harder. I am producing a good deal more. You ought to pay me an increased wage.' But there is no question of breach of contract in the employers asking the employee to do the work. It is what he has contracted to do. If the employee is unwilling to do the increased amount of work for the wage which he is being paid, his right then as an individual is to give notice terminating his contract and find another job."

In relation to the actual nature of the job the decision in *British Syphon Co. Ltd.* v. *Homewood*[5] appears to demonstrate the same absolute quality of the legal theory. The conclusion that the patent invention which the employee had developed in his own time and which it was not part of his job to develop nonetheless belonged to his employer was explained in the light of the fact that he could not be in a position where he was able to decline to give his employer his best advice on the ground that he had committed the benefits of that advice elsewhere.

The decision in *Turner* v. *Mason*[6] is frequently criticised for the severity of the decision that a domestic servant whose contract was to be on call 24 hours of the day was not entitled to time off to visit her dying mother. It may be pointed out, however, that in all three of these situations, the employee's duties were assumed to be widely defined. There is little doubt that courts at the present time would seek to modify the severity of any such absolute doctrine, as did the court in *Laws* v. *London Chronicle (Indicator Newspapers Ltd.)*[7] by holding

---

[3] *Marley Tile Co. Ltd.* v. *Johnson, supra.*
[4] [1973] I.C.R. 458.
[5] [1956] 1 W.L.R. 1190 the outcome of which would now be considerably affected by the Patents Act 1977, s.39.
[6] (1845) 14 M. & W. 112.
[7] [1959] 1 W.L.R. 698.

that the breach was not of such severity to justify dismissal or by regarding the job definition as more or less narrow; but the basic principle that the contract of employment does not contain a let-out clause on moral grounds is unquestionable.

Nevertheless if the employee fails to do what he has contracted to do, for whatever reason, he commits a breach of contract. For this reason if for no other there must be grave doubts as to the correctness of the approach adopted by all three members of the Court of Appeal in *Secretary of State for Employment* v. *ASLEF*[8] that the employee is under a duty "not wilfully to disrupt his employer's undertaking." If the employee is under a contractual obligation to do a job, or to do it at a particular time or in a particular place failure to comply with that obligation is a breach of contract however good the reason. Conversely if an employee is under no such contractual duty the existence of a wrong motive for failing to go beyond the scope of his duty should be irrelevant. Those who contend, therefore, that there is in fact an implied duty on both parties to co-operate with each other, whether they be right or wrong, are ridding the ASLEF principle of its insupportable element of motive.

Co-operation

It is, however, necessary to discuss whether the contract which has failed to specify a work obligation sufficient to meet the needs of the employer can be bolstered by a general obligation to co-operate in the sense of active assistance. It is submitted that it cannot and that the Court of Appeal in the *ASLEF* case was correct to reject this suggestion by Sir John Donaldson at first instance. Although, like several other implied terms in the contract of employment, it is the fashion to resort not only to generalisations but to shortened versions of them, the duty to co-operate must be confined to co-operation in the carrying out of the contractual obligations. Otherwise it would impose upon the employee the intolerable burden of obeying an instruction which had not been issued. There are several reported examples of the courts refusing to go so far.[9]

Job content

The contract of employment is often very precise concerning the extent of the work obligation. Most commonly such precision stems from the incorporation into it of relatively precise job definitions for different grades of worker contained in collective agreements. Trade unions are correct from their point of view in pursuing a policy of careful definition since the more general is the job description the more scope the employer has for movement of the employee from one job to another without the need to receive the consent of the employee to any change of contract. Nevertheless, such precise job definition may cause the union problems if at a later stage it wishes to negotiate a change unless the union can establish that the individual employee not only has a contractually defined obligation but also a contractual obligation to accept negotiated change. In *Land and Wilson* v. *West Yorkshire Metropolitan County*

---

[8] [1972] 2 Q.B. 455.
[9] See *D.C. Thomson and Co. Ltd.* v. *Deakin* [1952] 2 All E.R. 361; *McCulloch Ltd.* v. *Moore* [1968] 1 Q.B. 360.

Council[10] the appellants were employed as full-time firemen but were also subject to a "retained" system under which they were liable to additional duties on call. This system was unpopular with most firemen and their union successfully negotiated the phasing out of the practice. A minority, including the appellants, wished to keep the system and refused to accept their employers' offer of new contracts which excluded it. The employer gave notice that the retained element would be discontinued. While continuing their whole time duties the appellants claimed for unfair dismissal in respect of these part-time duties. The E.A.T. holding that the nature of the *single* contract was fundamentally altered by the withdrawal of this element indicated how, in normal circumstances, union members may be regarded as bound by a form of implied agency to accept such negotiated changes.

> ". . . where a variation of, or a termination of, an existing contract is to be made based upon a collective agreement such a change can only be binding upon individuals if it is accepted individually or if they were collectively represented at the time the change was agreed upon. If the applicants had still been members of the Fire Brigades Union in October 1976 none of us would have found any difficulty in this case. That, in our view, makes it all the more necessary, where one is dealing with a small unit . . . where the job description tends to be wide precisely because to run a small unit one has to have flexibility, that it should be pointed out to employees, if it is not apparent that they understand this . . . that the ambit of the obligation in the contract of employment may very well be wider than the particular duties upon which the person concerned is normally engaged."[11]

Much will depend on what the courts consider to be the reasonable expectations of the parties in circumstances where jobs are not defined with precision. In *Coleman* v. *S. and W. Baldwin*[12] the claimant was acting manager and one of his duties was the buying of greengrocery. Subsequently he agreed to relinquish the position of acting manager but retained the job of buying greengrocery until that too was removed and he was wholly engaged in routine administration. It was held that removal of a substantial proportion of his contractual work without the substitution of new duties amounted to a breach of contract.

This, of course, is really an example of filling gaps by implication and this is the primary method by which the courts control the parties' definition of job content. In a number of cases the "surrounding circumstances," usually meaning what has happened in practice, will substantially affect a decision based on the reasonableness of implying one term as against another.[13] Nevertheless the courts are usually prepared to test such practices to discover whether they do suggest the acceptance of an obligation. So, in *Managers (Holborn) Ltd.* v. *Hohne*[14] a practice of working in one place did not exclude a contractual obligation to undertake a reasonable move to another. The practice, over 10 years, of working overtime almost every working day was, in *Horrigan* v. *Lewisham London Borough Council*[15] not permitted to establish a contractual obligation to do so. The courts are obviously anxious not to allow an operational

---

[10] [1979] I.C.R. 452 (E.A.T.).
[11] The Court of Appeal overruled this decision on the ground that the contract contained two separate work obligations [1981] I.C.R. 334.
[12] [1977] I.R.L.R. 342.
[13] See, *e.g. O'Brien* v. *Associated Fire Alarms Ltd.* [1969] 1 All E.R. 93.
[14] [1977] I.R.L.R. 230.
[15] [1978] I.C.R. 15.

practice to become a contractual obligation, and on such occasions will often resort to one of the "necessity" tests of implication rather than to considerations of reasonableness. Whereas the "business efficacy" or "Oh! of course" test can be used to achieve no more than is reasonable, it can, and in these instances does provide a much more positive rejection of an alleged implication. So in *Lake* v. *Essex County Council*[16] in which a part-time school teacher claimed that her contract impliedly required her to spend some time at home marking work and preparing lessons for the next day, Geoffrey Lane L.J. said:

> "It seems to me that that term, at least arguably, was void for uncertainty. It was certainly impossible of application. But are these circumstances circumstances in which it is justifiable to imply a term at all? If Lord Justice Mackinnon's officious bystander had asked Mrs. Lake and the Essex County Council this question: 'Is Mrs. Lake contractually required to work such hours out of school time as may be necessary to prepare her work so that if she does not do so she can be dismissed?' neither would have replied either testily or otherwise: 'Of course.' "

Not only are the courts able to exert considerable influence on the job content by implying contractual terms to fill gaps, or rejecting contractual obligation despite a long continued practice, but, even where the parties have taken some care to define the obligations, the courts may interpret them. In *Secretary of State for Employment* v. *ASLEF*[17] the management of British Railways had issued in written form a lengthy set of working instructions. Lord Denning M.R. said:

> "These rules are to be construed reasonably. They must be fitted in sensibly the one with the other. They must be construed according to the usual course of dealing and to the way they have been applied in practice. When the rules are so construed the railway system, as we all know, works efficiently and safely. But if some of those rules are construed unreasonably, as, for instance, the driver takes too long examining his engine or seeing that all is in order, the system may be in danger of being disrupted. It is only when they are construed unreasonably that the railway system grinds to a halt. It is, I should think, clearly a breach of contract first to construe the rules unreasonably, and then to put that unreasonable construction into practice."

Though this is undoubtedly correct there may be differing views as to the reasonableness of a construction of an ambiguous rule depending upon whether one is a passenger wanting a quick safe journey, a member of management wanting efficiency or an individual employee wanting to ensure that if something goes wrong he can show what was expected of him. Suppose, for instance, that a railway guard is required to take steps to ensure that all carriage doors are securely closed before the train leaves the station. In normal working he may well look down the line of carriages from the rear of the train but he may contend that in reality he is taking something of a personal risk in order to co-operate with management in keeping the train on time. He may not be all that sure, should one of the doors open as the train leaves the station, that it will be agreed that the normal operation was so obviously reasonable as to constitute the correct procedure.

The process of interpretation is nonetheless one in which the parties will instinctively indulge and the courts no doubt are right to apply it to avoid the

---

[16] [1979] I.R.L.R. 241.
[17] [1972] 2 Q.B. 455.

burdensome effects of a rigid approach to construction. In *Hadden Ltd.* v. *Cowen*,[17a] for example, an obligation upon the employee to undertake anything within his capability was constructively limited to his ability within the particular skill for which he had been engaged.

In practice, therefore, the work obligation will virtually never be sufficiently precisely defined to avoid the possibility of dispute. In practice, however, relatively few disputes arise, either because bargaining representatives for the employees have ensured that obligations likely to cause dispute have been defined or because a practice of working inevitably develops which is not questioned. When a dispute does arise it is apparent that the Courts have considerable discretion by way of "reasonable" interpretation or the generous or cautious implication, or rejection, of a term.

The obligation to provide work

The reciprocal obligation upon the employer in return for the obligation of the employee to be available to perform his contractual duty is the obligation to pay wages—not the obligation to provide work. Almost as the courts enunciated a lack of inherent obligation upon the employer to provide work, however,[18] exceptions were established[19] and doubts expressed as to the validity of the basic proposition.[20] Somewhat surprisingly the doubts did not lead to any marked amount of litigation. It is sometimes suggested that this absence of apparent dispute owes much to the work of joint negotiation. Certainly in potentially the most prolific area—that of payment by results involving many forms of piece work—provision by agreement of minimum guarantee rates prevented the debate, not because the rates were necessarily adequate payment or long continued but because it was then clear that such payment was the limit of the employer's obligation.[21] If *Turner* v. *Sawdon* is taken still to establish a basic rule of no obligation there is authority for each of the following exceptions:

   (i) A duty exists to offer work where remuneration depends wholly[22] or perhaps partially[23] on the piece or on commission payments;
   (ii) In special cases it may be considered to be understood that part of the consideration is the opportunity to gain publicity or experience[24];
   (iii) Point (ii) is capable of extension if such understandings can be read into the element of consideration. Donaldson J. did so in *Langston* v. *A.U.E.W.* (*No.* 2)[25] on the ground that a chance of overtime was part of

---

[17a] [1982] I.R.L.R. 315.
[18] See *Turner* v. *Sawdon* [1901] 2 K.B. 653.
[19] *Devonald* v. *Rosser and Sons* [1906] 2 K.B. 728.
[20] *Re Rubel Bronze and Metal Co. and Vos* [1918] 1 K.B. 315 at pp. 324–325.
[21] See: Freedland, *The Contract of Employment* (O.U.P. 1976), p. 24.
[22] *R.* v. *Welch* (1853) 2 E. & E. 357; *Devonald* v. *Rosser and Sons* [1906] 2 K.B. 728; *Turner* v. *Goldsmith* (1891) 1 Q.B. 544.
[23] *Re Rubel Bronze and Metal Co. and Vos* [1918] 1 K.B. 315; *Bowman* v. *Hulton Press Ltd.* [1952] 2 All E.R. 1121 but compare *Ex parte Maclure* (1870) L.R. 5 Ch. App. 737; *Re Newman Ltd., Raphael's Claim* [1916] 2 Ch. 309.
[24] *Marbé* v. *George Edwardes (Daly's Theatre) Ltd.* [1928] 1 K.B. 269; *Collier* v. *Sunday Referee Publishing Co. Ltd.* [1940] 2 K.B. 647.
[25] [1974] I.C.R. 510.

the consideration and that chance depended on attendance at the place of work. Lord Denning M.R. had earlier said in the same case[26]:

"We have repeatedly said in this court that a man has a right to work which the courts will protect: see *Nagle* v. *Feilden* and *Hill* v. *C.A. Parsons and Co. Ltd.* I would not wish to express any decided view, but simply to state the argument which could be put foward for Mr. Langston. In these days an employer, when employing a skilled man, is bound to provide him with work. By which I mean that a man should be given the opportunity of doing his work when it is available and he is ready and willing to do it. A skilled man takes a pride in his work. He does not do it merely to earn money. He does it so as to keep himself busy, and not idle. Tax his skill, and to improve it. To have the satisfaction which comes of a task well done."[26a]

In the same way the decisions in *Coleman* v. *S. and W. Baldwin*[26b] and *Pedersen* v. *London Borough of Camden*[26c] that it may be a breach of contract to deprive an employee of a substantial portion of his job depends largely on the view that employees do not work for wages alone but also for the satisfaction derived from a particular job.

As Dr. Freedland points out[27] this is an acknowledgement of a social duty upon the employer but it can also be adapted to fit the argument that fulfilment of the expectation is part of the consideration for the contract.

It would appear that courts are beginning to have doubts as to whether a society which more clearly understands the advantages of having a job to do can continue to support the existence of a basic proposition in the terms laid down in *Turner* v. *Sawdon*. In *Collier* v. *Sunday Referee Publishing Co. Ltd.*[28] Asquith J. distinguished that decision partly on the ground that the plaintiff, having been engaged to fill the specific office of chief sub-editor of a defined Sunday newspaper, was contractually entitled to the work that gave that office its particular character. The E.A.T. drew this point to the attention of the tribunal to whom it referred for reconsideration the decision in *Breach* v. *Epsylon Industries Ltd.*[29] The employee was, in 1972, employed "in the capacity of chief engineer." In 1974 some of the company's engineering activities were transferred to Canada and the employee was given no work to do as chief engineer. His solicitors informed the employer that he would treat this as a repudiation of the contract for which he would claim redundancy payment. An industrial tribunal, following *Turner* v. *Sawdon*, held that his claim failed since the employer had no obligation to provide work. Remitting the case Phillips J. said:

"*Turner* v. *Sawdon and Co.* is a decision of the Court of Appeal. It is binding upon us and it was binding upon the industrial tribunal. However, it appears from the judgments in that case, and in particular from the observations of Stirling L.J., that there may well be cases which are exceptions to the general rule and where it can be said that from the nature of the employment, the circumstances in which it has to be

---

[26] [1974] I.C.R. 180 at 190.
[26a] That Lord Denning's remarks amount to misuse of his own earlier concept of a "right to work" is clearly demonstrated by Professor B. A. Hepple in (1981) 10 I.L.J. 65 where at least three different uses of the term are discussed.
[26b] *Supra.*
[26c] [1981] I.C.R. 674.
[27] *The Contract of Employment* (O.U.P.), pp. 26–27.
[28] [1940] 2 K.B. 647.
[29] [1976] I.C.R. 316.

served, and so on, there is indeed an obligation on the part of the employer to provide work. The line is a difficult one to draw. It may be said that the underlying thought in *Turner* v. *Sawdon* is somewhat out of date and old fashioned now; that fact, if it be a fact, cannot invalidate the binding effect of that decision, but it may within limits lead to the consequence that a consideration of the facts will more easily lead to the conclusion that the case is one where there is such an obligation to provide work."

In the light of an obviously increasing willingness to recognise the existence in a particular case of a right to be given work it is suggested that to say even so much as that the basic rule of *Turner* v. *Sawdon* stands subject to exceptions may be misleading. It is suggested that the position would be more nearly correctly stated if it were said that the Courts would be sympathetic to an argument in favour of further development of exceptions to the proposition that there is no implied obligation to provide work. This may be a preliminary to total abolition of the former rule.

(b) The wage-work element—wages

Lawyers are apt to talk of the obligation to pay wages as if all wages were of a single kind or, at least, as if any differences did not fundamentally affect other aspects of employment. As Davies and Freedland point out[30]:

". . . the form of the wage-work bargain can be both a source and an expression of social differentiation between certain types of workers . . . This poses a problem for the labour law and social security law system, which has to decide how far it will permit the employer by means of a low security payment system to transfer economic risks from himself to the employee and via the employee to the social security function of the state itself."

Forms of remuneration

Whether the payment of a salary (normally expressed as an annual sum and paid in monthly instalments) is a cause or an effect it is undoubtedly the most obvious sign of an attitude to the employment of "staff" wholly different from the attitude to "production workers." It goes hand in hand with many other symbols of a greater reliance upon what common law judges would call the essential characteristic of mutual trust and confidence such as the absence of a requirement to clock in or account so rigorously for absence due to sickness. It undoubtedly helps to produce a greater understanding of job security in both parties to which the common law has lent its support by way, for instance, of a readiness to imply more favourable notice rights. If one compares the salary earner with the opposite extreme—the worker wholly remunerated by piece rates—one can see clearly the difference the system both recognises and encourages in day to day control of the quantity and quality of work. It is almost inconceivable that it would be suggested to the salary earner that his earnings should be reduced during a period when work was slack. Without the intervention of collective agreement the piece worker automatically suffers such a reduction.

Trade unions have accordingly been at pains to negotiate agreements for minimum rates of earnings for those who would otherwise be subjected to this

---

[30] *Labour Law: Texts and Materials* (Weidenfeld and Nicolson 1979), p. 263.

form of insecurity. The National Labour Agreement for the Furniture Manufacturing Trade[31] provides:

> "a scheme of Payment by Results, approved by the appropriate Union, may apply to individual workers or to a group of workers or to a department of a factory or to a whole factory.
>   Every scheme shall be subject to the following provisions:
> (a) No worker shall receive as wages for a normal working week less than the wages to which he or she would be entitled as the appropriate time worker's rate and allowances under this Agreement.
> (b) The scheme shall provide for the appropriate time worker's rate and allowances being paid for time lost in the factory caused by lack of materials, faulty materials, alteration of design or other causes beyond the control of the worker."

Not every protective clause is as clear as this and it may be necessary for the lawyer to consider the effect of alternative interpretations upon the security which is the purpose of such agreements. In *Amalgamated Textile Workers Union* v. *Shiloh Spinners Ltd.*[32] the union had entered into an agreement with the British Textile Employers' Association dated December 1, 1978 which provided that

> "No full time employee who competently undertakes the full normal duties, workload and production level expected of a capable adult shall be paid less than £39.62. . . ."
> "A fully competent Winder shall be defined as any Winder who is normally engaged upon a full complement of spindles or ends."

The employer sought to pay less than the minimum rate to any winder who, though accepting a normal complement of spindles, did not operate them. The C.A.C. accepted the argument of the union that though the agreement allowed for reduction in the case of an employee who, for reasons of incapacity or some other reason, undertook less than the full complement, it would make nonsense of a minimum clause that the minimum should not apply where an expected level of production was not maintained. The union pointed out that in such a case the employer would possess normal disciplinary powers.

A basic absence of security of earnings arises in the case of the hourly paid worker. This is a considerably more numerous type than is often realised since many systems apparently of weekly payment are merely multiples of hourly pay. In these situations the protection most commonly sought by agreement is the specification of a basic number of hours (usually 40) which comprise the working week.

In an excellent note Davies and Freedland[33] explain a relatively modern attempt to combine supervision over the amount of production with security of wages by effectively transferring control from the payment of wages to the disciplinary procedure. In a measured day work system production targets are fixed. A fixed payment system is applied and the enforcement of the targets is carried out by either the disciplinary or the disputes and grievances procedure.

---

[31] Para. 15, revised to April 1980.
[32] C.A.C. No. 80/139.
[33] At p. 275.

Unfortunately, as Davies and Freedland point out, this tends to destroy the direct link between negotiations about pay and productivity upon which trade unions base their bargaining techniques.

It was partly because of a recognition that insecurity of wages bore unequally on the working population that the legislature took a small step towards protection in the Employment Protection Act 1975[34] by the introduction of statutory guarantees.

Apportionment of wages

A termination by employee breach or by frustration or some similar event other than by proper notice may raise a problem of the right to apportion the wages due. The normal rule of contract is that if there is a single contract covering a period of service failure to complete the period results in total failure of consideration so that no wages are due.[35] The same result will follow in respect of the period not completed if each period of calculation—*e.g.* weeks or months—is regarded as a separate contractual period.[36] On the other hand, payment at say an hourly rate at the end of each week or month will entitle the employee to be paid for each complete (hourly) unit.[37]

Many writers contend that the effect of the Apportionment Act 1870 is that even the remuneration due for an uncompleted unit can be apportioned between the part of the unit completed and the part not worked.[38] Paul Matthews[39] has convincingly argued, however, that this conclusion based on *Moriarty* v. *Regents Garage*[40] involves a misconception of the meaning of the word "salary."[41] Matthews shows that the legislative use of the word salaries was intended to refer to remuneration for public office where the emoluments are payable to a successor in title.[42] He submits that the very considerable number of cases since 1870 which have ignored the possibility of apportionment of wages correctly assumed that the Act was not intended to permit such apportionment.[43]

The effect of sickness upon wages

In *Browning* v. *Crumlin Valley Collieries Ltd.*[44] Greer J. said "the consideration for work is wages, and the consideration for wages is work." The common law, however, has not developed the law relating to payment of wages according to this principle. In *Marrison* v. *Bell*[45] Scott L.J. said:

---

[34] Now the Employment Protection (Consolidation) Act 1978, ss.12–18.

[35] *Cutter* v. *Powell* (1795) 6 T.R. 320.

[36] *e.g. Boston Deep Sea Fishing Co. Ltd.* v. *Ansell* (1888) 39 Ch.D. 339.

[37] *Re Central de Kaap Gold Mines* (1899) 69 L.J. Ch. 18.

[38] Glanville Williams (1941) 57 L.Q.R. 373 at 382; Freedland at 132–133; Treitel, *Law of Contract* (5th ed.), 620–622.

[39] "Salaries in the Apportionment Act 1870" (1982) 2 *Legal Studies* 302.

[40] [1921] 1 K.B. 423.

[41] Section 2 of the 1870 Act provides "All rents, annuities [which includes salaries and pensions] dividends, and other periodical payments in the nature of income . . . shall, like interest on money lent, be considered as accruing from day to day, and shall be apportionable in respect of time accordingly."

[42] See, *e.g. Treacy* v. *Corcoran* (1874) I.R. 8 C.L. 40.

[43] See *Salton* v. *New Beeston Cycle Co.* [1899] 1 Ch. 775 at 776–777.

[44] [1926] 1 K.B. 522.

[45] [1939] 2 K.B. 187.

". . . under a contract of service, irrespective of the question of the length of notice provided by that contract, wages continue through sickness and incapacity from sickness to do the work contracted for until the contract is terminated by a notice by the employer in accordance with the terms of the contract."

The headnote of the case reported this proposition of law as:

"Illness of a servant, which, while it lasts, incapacitates him for the performance of his duties, but is not so long-continued or so serious as to terminate the contract of service, does not at common law suspend his right to wages under the contract."

This inspired the defendants in both *O'Grady* v. *M. Saper Ltd.*[46] and *Petrie* v. *MacFisheries Ltd.*[47] to bring actions for unpaid wages alleged to be due for periods of absence from work through sickness although, in both cases, their contracts precluded, or limited, such right. Atkinson J. said[48]:

"I think the Court of Appeal meant that. . . where there is nothing in the contract, expressed or implied, to the contrary, the consideration for wages is not the actual doing of the work contracted for, but the readiness and willingness, if of ability, to do the work."

The headnote in *O'Grady* v. *Saper*[49] was also incorrect. It reads:

"*Held*, the facts proved showed by implication that there was no agreement that the respondent should be paid wages while absent through illness and he was not entitled to recover."

In fact what was shown was that a course of conduct implied a term that the respondent was *not* to be paid wages during sickness. In *Petrie's* case the employee had received express notice to this effect.

Pilcher J. in *Orman* v. *Saville Sportswear Ltd.* said[50]:

"Where the written terms of the contract of service are silent as to what is to happen in regard to the employee's rights to be paid whilst he is absent from work due to sickness, the employer remains liable to continue paying so long as the contract is not determined by proper notice, except where a condition to the contrary can properly be inferred from all the facts and the evidence in the case. If the employer . . . seeks to establish an implied condition that no wages are payable, it is for him to make it out."

Freedland[51] demonstrates that this development resulted from a failure to apply a vital qualification in the early case of *Cuckson* v. *Stones*.[52] What was involved in that case was a 10 year service contract incorporating an additional element of instruction. Illness temporarily interrupted the service. The employee, therefore, had a peculiar security of tenure and never ceased to conduct some of his functions. In *Elliott* v. *Liggens*[53] moreover, Darling J. assumed that statutory provision for compensation for injury at work had been made on the assumption that the employee would otherwise have no contrac-

---

[46] [1940] 3 All E.R. 527.
[47] [1940] 1 K.B. 258.
[48] *Petrie* v. *MacFisheries, supra*, at 270.
[49] *Supra*.
[50] [1960] 1 W.L.R. 1055 at 1064.
[51] At p. 109.
[52] (1858) 1 E. & E. 240.
[53] [1902] 2 K.B. 840.

tual right to wages. The point made by Scott L.J. in *Marrison* v. *Bell*[54] that provision of statutory benefit should not replace a contractual right only begs the question whether such a right exists.

However this may be, it is not easy to see how, at the present time, courts would, on the basis of reasonableness, imply into the contract of employment a term that no wages should be payable during sickness. Labour law develops fast. Twenty years ago the opposite argument might well have been advanced on the basis of business efficacy relying on the fact that normal business practice was to make express contractual provision in respect of those not enjoying "staff" status which virtually eliminated the common law rule. It is the possibility of introducing a variable implication which causes doubts about the alteration of emphasis attempted by Slynn J. in *Mears* v. *Safecar Security Ltd.*[55] The Court of Appeal however, strongly affirmed the basis of the obligation in implication rather than presumption. It was there pointed out that the Common Law had virtually[56] established a rebuttable presumption that wages were payable during sickness. The E.A.T. had suggested that no such presumption was justifiable. Slynn J., in a passage approved by the Court of Appeal, said:

> "The implication to be drawn in a case where a man is employed on a daily basis may be different from one to be drawn in a case where a man is employed for a fixed term of years, such as five or 10 years, as has been referred to in some of the cases. It seems to us on the basis of what was said by MacKinnon L.J. in *O'Grady* v. *Saper* that it is also permissible on occasions to look at what the parties did during the performance of the contract. We, of course, recognise the dangers which are inherent in such a course, because evidence of what the parties did is generally inadmissible evidence in construing the terms of contract, but in *Wilson* v. *Maynard Shipbuilding Consultants Ab* Megaw L.J. having regard to the general rule, said: 'There would seem, however, to be an exception to the strictness of that doctrine where there must be a relevant term, but what that term is cannot be ascertained otherwise than by looking at what the parties did.'
>
> That seems to us to be in accordance with what was said in *O'Grady* v. *Saper*, and so it seems to us that, contrary to the approach of the Industrial Tribunal in this case, and contrary to the approach which we understand Pilcher J. to have taken, the right approach is to ask, on all the facts and circumstances of the case to which it is proper to have regard, what term is to be implied. One does not begin by assuming the term as to payment is to be implied unless the employer displaces it. On the facts of the present case it is clear that nothing was said at the time when the contract was made, but the Industrial Tribunal were quite satisfied that had the employer been asked he would have said that no wages would be paid to an employee like Mr. Mears if he was away ill. He would, on the findings of the Tribunal, have said that it was their policy not to pay. We understand that to mean also that it was their practice not to pay. There was evidence that Mr. Mears, who was ill some six months after he began working, did not ask for any payment—did not, apparently, send in the sort of sick notes regularly from the beginning which one would have expected had he considered that he was entitled to his wages. He was told by his colleagues that he would not get any sick pay from the company.
>
> It seems to us, accordingly, in this case, if one adopts the approach which we consider it is right to adopt in these cases, that here the term to be implied into this contract is that wages would not be paid during periods of absence during sickness.

[54] [1939] 1 All E.R. 745.
[55] [1981] I.C.R. 409.
[56] [1982] I.R.L.R. 183.

In our judgment the Industrial Tribunal in the present case erred in their approach and they refused to imply a term which really ought to have been implied."

Stephenson L.J. only felt the need to add:

"Where, as here, the Tribunal is searching for the right term to imply relating to the payment of wages during absence through sickness and are left by lack of material in doubt about that particular term, the doubt will be resolved in favour of the employee by *Marrison* v. *Bell* as interpreted in the authorities ending with this case. When the missing term relates to payment of wages during periods of absence through sickness, the Tribunal must approach the search for the missing term by considering all the facts and circumstances, including the subsequent conduct of the parties, and only if they do not indicate what that term is or must be, should the Tribunal assume that it is a term that wages should be paid during those periods and determine that that is the term of which particulars ought to be included."

One of the most powerful sources of such implication would be normal practice in comparable situations. If it would now be considered unacceptable to imply into the contracts of non-staff employees the substantial absence of such pay provision that was once standard practice why should it be any more reasonable for the future to imply the provision for six or 12 weeks' full pay that is now quite common? The E.A.T. judgment supposes that as practice develops so will the contractual implication. The danger is that if the law picks up and implies existing practice, such practice may appear hallowed by such acceptance. When practice alone justifies implication by what subsequent actions will it be possible to imply variation?

Examples of contractual sick pay schemes

Unlike many of the situations in which implied terms operate it is usual for the contract of employment to make some express provision for wages during sickness. In 1977, for instance, 94 per cent. of men in non-manual occupations and 74 per cent. of men in manual occupations were covered by such schemes.[57] A similar percentage of non-manual women were covered but only 58 per cent. of manually employed women.

In the past most such schemes have required the employee to produce independent written evidence—normally by way of a doctor's certificate—within three days or so of the onset of incapacity. There is normally relatively little supervision at this stage but as the period of sickness lengthens the more likely it will be that a system of checks by way of sick-visiting and required medical examinations will apply. Correspondingly, payment will be reduced and eventually become either non-existent or nominal. A nominal payment will often be used in conjunction with a holding list designed to retain contact with the employee as such whilst avoiding the expensive obligation of paying a living wage. Some schemes pick up from the national insurance system methods of limiting abuse of the benefit by providing a discretion to terminate payment in face of specified offences.

A report in 1979[58] stated that flat rate payments (usually associated with contributory schemes) had virtually died out. In linking payment to a percen-

---

[57] Report on a Survey of Occupational Sick Pay Schemes (D.H.S.S. 1977).
[58] IDS: *Guide to Sick Pay and Absence*. See a more cautious statement in IDS Study No. 283 (Feb. 1983).

tage of wages many schemes took account of bonus payments and shift allowances, recognising that payment at basic rates would involve substantial reduction of earnings. Most schemes limit payment to a defined period which is still often longer for clerical than for manual staff. The length of such period will often increase with service. A qualifying period of employment is often required, particularly for manual workers.

Statutory requirements for employer provision

This somewhat haphazard provision by way of common law contract and collective agreement poses, but does not answer, the question of the extent to which the employer should be required to assume the cost of sickness and injury, at least some of which will be directly attributable to the employment. We shall deal with industrial injury benefit when considering compensation for injury at work by negligence, breach of safety requirements and accident.[59] It is appropriate at this point, however, briefly to consider the outline of national insurance provision for sickness benefit which, in practice, provides the short term element in such State provision.[60]

Incapacity

Sickness benefit is available for any day of incapacity for work. Since April 1983 this has applied only after an initial period of eight weeks in which, under the Statutory Sick Pay scheme the employer assumes the obligation to make payments. An employee suffering from one of a number of specified diseases or bodily or mental disablement will be deemed to be incapable for work.[61] Otherwise it is for the claimant to establish his incapacity. The common practice, which we have seen adopted by private schemes, of medical certification is usually acceptable but is not regarded as conclusive.[62]

In questioning such evidence the claimant's record showing, for example, persistent claims during holiday periods may be taken into account.[63] If they are so considered, the reports must be shown to him on the grounds of natural justice.[64] Capacity for part-time work will defeat the claim.[65] Alcoholism is a disease although its incidence may itself lead to a disqualification. Diseases associated with pregnancy lead to qualification in the normal way[66] but disablement by pregnancy alone has been the subject of some dispute. Calvert suggests that the better view is that expressed in decision R(G) 3/54 that if pregnancy does indeed produce disablement sickness benefit may be claimed.[67]

A person is incapable for work if, having regard to his age, education, experience, state of health and other personal factors, there is no work or type of work which he can reasonably be expected to do. It seems reasonable to

---

[59] Infra, p. 614.
[60] Sickness benefit is available only for a maximum of 168 days without requalification.
[61] Social Security Act 1975, s.17(1)(a)(ii).
[62] R(I) 13/55. But a claimant with a medical certificate may reasonably abstain from work until the question is decided—R(S) 8/55—and it is the normal practice to accept a medical certificate rather than to refer the question of incapacity to a tribunal.
[63] R(S) 16/54, and see R(S) 4/60.
[64] R(S) 1/58.
[65] R(S) 7/60.
[66] C.S. 221/49.
[67] Calvert, Social Security Law (2nd ed.), pp. 210–211.

conclude that during relatively short periods of illness attention should be paid primarily to incapacity to perform his usual work. As time goes on the claimant may reasonably be expected to seek and obtain other work for which he is capable.[68] By "work," in this connection, is meant remunerative work, that is to say, either gainful self-employment or work for which an employer would be willing to pay.[69] It follows that sickness benefit is not payable because of a diminution of earning power, but only for its total reduction or a reduction to a negligible amount.[70] It is possible that there might be such a reduction of earning power as applied to work one might reasonably be expected to do whilst yet leaving open avenues of work one might not reasonably be expected to pursue. If the claimant pursued such an "unreasonable" avenue he would be disentitled by his earnings from sickness benefit even though technically incapable of work. In the case of a woman who could only use one hand and was helped in housework by her two daughters, the local employment officer did not consider that, having regard to "the general set-up of industry in the local area" she could usefully fill any job in either factory or household. She was held incapable for work.[71] The position of a married woman capable of housework was further explained in a case where the claimant admitted that she was able to do housework in a small flat and to cook for her husband. It was stated that:

". . . the question whether a person is incapable of work . . . must be approached in the light of all the facts, including the amount of work that it is decided that she is able to do, taken in conjunction with the medical evidence. . . . It is perhaps necessary to add that in order to prove that a woman is incapable of work it is not enough to show that she is not capable of doing remunerative work in addition to the work of her own household or that work which she is capable of doing will not be sufficiently remunerative to enable her to support herself."

So far as male claimants are concerned it has been held that supervision of a small farm, without doing any manual work, may show capacity,[72] unless the amount is small, the bulk being done by someone else.[73] A newsvendor who merely kept the accounts and employed two boys to deliver the papers was held incapable.[74] Performance of one hour's work a day is not so trifling that it can be disregarded.[75]

Not infrequently, a claimant may carry on work intermittently. In this case it is open to him to show that on particular days he was incapable of work. An estimate will then be made of the number of days worked.[76] Normally, days of attendance at a hospital will be counted as days of incapacity,[77] and it may be that the nature of the treatment received on those days makes it impossible to work on the days in between.[78] More complicated problems may arise where the incapacity is partly the result of the claimant's position and partly of

---

[68] R(S) 7/60.
[69] R(S) 11/51.
[70] R(S) 13/52.
[71] R(S) 17/55.
[72] R(S) 34/52.
[73] R(S) 24/52.
[74] R(S) 10/61.
[75] R(S) 18/35.
[76] R(S) 9/53.
[77] C.W.I. 20/49; R(S) 69/50.
[78] R(S) 24/51.

extraneous circumstances, as in the case of a disabled man with one leg who was unable to go to work because of a heavy snow fall. He was held incapable because the immediate circumstances were beyond his control. It was said that it would be otherwise if a conveyance upon which he was dependent had broken down.

A person who is not incapable of work may be deemed to be incapable of work by reason of some specific disease or bodily or mental disablement for any day on which either:

(a) (i) he is under medical care in respect of such a disease or disablement,

(ii) it is certified by a registered medical practitioner that by reason of such disease or disablement he should abstain from work, and

(iii) he does not work; or

(b) he is excluded from work on the certificate of a Medical Officer for Environmental Health and is under medical observation by means of his being a carrier, or having been in contact with, a case of infectious disease.[79]

Disqualification

A person may be disqualified from receiving sickness benefit for a period not exceeding six weeks if he has become incapable of work through his own misconduct.[80] "Misconduct" is taken to include yielding to an addiction such as alcoholism, or, presumably drugs, if it is not involuntary.[81]

Disqualification may be imposed for failure without good cause to attend for, or submit to, medical or other examination or treatment, as may be required in accordance with regulations, or to observe any prescribed rules of behaviour. Care has to be exercised in the application of this provision because different people respond in different ways to the opportunity of treatment. It is, therefore, expressly provided that the disqualification shall not apply to any failure to attend for, or submit to, vaccination or inoculation of any kind or to attend for, or submit to, a surgical operation other than one of a minor character, refusal of which is considered by the determining authority to be reasonable. Generally the onus of establishing good cause is on the claimant. The genuine conscientious beliefs of a Christian Scientist have been held to be good cause for refusing treatment.[82-84]

The statutory sick pay scheme

Short term sickness provision imposes a considerable administrative burden on the State. Largely to alleviate this the Social Security and Housing Benefits Act 1982 introduces (with effect from April 1983) a scheme whereby much of this burden is transferred to the employer. In the first instance the employer of any employee, whether full or part time, paying national insurance class I

---

[79] Unemployment, Sickness and Invalidity Regulations, reg. 3(1).

[80] Social Security Act 1975, s.20(2). Unemployment and Sickness Benefit Regulations, S.I. 1967 No. 330, reg. 11.

[81] R(S) 2/53. Expressly excluded from this disqualification are venereal disease and pregnancy in a married woman or a woman separated from her husband.

[82-84] R(S) 9/51.

contributions will be liable to pay sickness benefit for the first eight weeks of sickness absence in any one period of sickness or in total in any tax year. There is no minimum qualifying period of employment. Employers will be liable to deduct income tax and national insurance contributions from these payments and may recoup the net amount paid to the employee by deducting those amounts from sums due by way of national insurance contribution (and taxation if national insurance contributions are inadequate).

Married women and widows who opted out of full national insurance contribution when this option was still open qualify nevertheless for such payments. On the other hand there are excluded from the scheme: those over pensionable age; those who earn less than a specified weekly minimum; pregnant women whose first day of absence is within 11 weeks of the expected date of confinement; and those employed on contracts for 12 weeks or less. No payment is due if the incapacity is for three days or less or *begins* on a day when the employee is in any event workless because of a trade dispute (unless the employee can prove that he was not participating in, or directly interested in, that dispute).

Earnings bands for each of which a fixed amount of benefit will be payable have been established. For most wage earners the significant point is that the highest band includes all those currently earning over £60 per week and provides for a flat rate benefit of £40.25 per week. (These rates are subject to periodic review.) There is no addition for dependants. No benefit is payable for the first three days of incapacity save as regards a subsequent period not separated from the first by more than two weeks. At the end of the annual eight week maximum for payment under the scheme transfer to the national insurance sickness scheme is automatic without any waiting days.

Subject to the exception of some defined groups all employees under the age of 65 for men and 60 for women who are absent from work due to sickness for four or more days are within the Statutory Sick Pay scheme. A day of sickness is defined as a day on which the employee is incapable, because of a specific disease or disablement, of doing work he can reasonably be expected to do under his contract of employment. The four day qualifying period of incapacity for work may include Saturdays and Sundays. Sick pay only has to be given under the scheme for such days as are "qualifying days." Normally these will be all days on which the employee would have worked had he not been sick but the employer and employee may agree to specify qualifying days so long as there is at least one in each week. If there is no contrary agreement but the employee would not normally work on any day in a week, Wednesday of that week will be deemed a qualifying day. No payment is due for the first three qualifying days in any period of absence unless that period of incapacity is separated from a previous period of incapacity of more than three qualifying days by less than 14 calendar days.

If an employer disputes the employee's entitlement to sick pay the employee may ask for the reasons in writing and may ultimately apply to the local D.H.S.S. office for a formal decision on his entitlement. There is an appeal available to either employer or employee from the decision of the insurance officer to a local appeal tribunal and from thence to a Social Security Commissioner.

The employee may be asked by his employer to produce any reasonable evidence in support of his entitlement. It would presumably be unreasonable for the employer to demand a medical certificate for a period of absence of less than seven calendar days since medical practitioners are entitled to make a charge for certificates in such cases. Most employers will cover short periods by asking for "self certification" but they are free to adopt any other system of control they choose. The employer can ask for notification of absence (as distinct from evidence) by any method and within any period. The employer must, however, make full details of his rules available to the employee. If an employee is late in notifying sickness and the employer is not satisfied of good reason for the delay the employer may withhold SSP for the same number of qualifying days as are involved in the delay. Payment under the scheme lasts for a maximum of eight weeks in any single period or on aggregate in each tax year but days on which payment is withheld do not count as part of this period. Payment is not due to an employee whose average earnings are less than a specified minimum. The amount of payment depends on three stated levels of earnings but the top level is considerably lower than the national average so that it will include the majority of employees. An employer may count any sickness payment he makes, whether or not under contract, towards the satisfaction of his statutory liability. He may recoup the amount of his statutory liability whether or not it is paid as such or as part of a private scheme from his monthly payments of National Insurance contributions. If these are not sufficient the excess may be recouped from PAYE income tax.

(c) The obligation to maintain the essentials of a working relationship

Trust and confidence

We have previously referred to the recent development of what is effectively a new term common to all employment. Typically, it is expressed in terms of broad generality as the duty to maintain trust and confidence. The existence of an essential element of this nature was not entirely unsuspected. The common law had rendered it as "breach of the confidential relationship" in 1888.[85] It was then and subsequently used as a test of whether a breach amounted to repudiation as precluding further satisfactory continuation of the relationship[86] and as late as 1971[87] Sachs L.J. referred to continuation of trust and confidence as justification for the unusual course of ordering specific performance of the contract. As a test of the viability of the employment relationships it may have had the appearance of useful adaptability to suit the seriousness of particular offences in different employment situations.[88] It offered no real standard since the court usually decided that the offence was sufficiently serious to justify an assumption of destruction of trust and confidence rather than undertaking the pointless task of seeking evidence of such destruction. The present writer has not, however, been able to find any common law decision before 1970 where the maintenance of trust and confidence was considered to constitute a term of the contract of employment. It is logical to deduce that if trust and confidence is essential to the continuation of the relationship then business efficacy would

---

[85] *Boston Deep Sea Fishing and Ice Co.* v. *Ansell* (1888) 39 Ch.D. 339.
[86] See, *e.g. Re Rubel Bronze and Metal Co. and Vos* [1918] 1 K.B. 315; *Sinclair* v. *Neighbour* [1967] 2 Q.B. 279.
[87] *Hill* v. *C. A. Parsons and Co. Ltd.* [1971] 3 W.L.R. 995.
[88] See, *e.g. Pepper* v. *Webb* [1969] 1 W.L.R. 514.

lead to an implied obligation to maintain it. It is, however, not clear how the common law would have dealt with such a situation since it tended only to cite the concept in those situations where the personal or confidential nature of the employment might be said to give rise to some special degree of trust.

Unreasonable behaviour

The existence of a contractual obligation to maintain the working relationship does not seem to have sprung from the common law, nor even from rationalisation of Lord Denning's obligation not wilfully to disrupt the undertaking[89] into a duty to co-operate.[90] Indeed it does not seem to have commenced its new life as a term of general implication at all. One of the earliest cases to apply it was *Isle of Wight Tourist Board* v. *Coombes*.[91] Bristow J. said:

> "The relationship between somebody in the position of the director of this board and his personal secretary must be one of complete confidence. They must trust each other; they must respect each other."

This is very close to the partial recognition by the common law of a duty of courtesy[92] and it seems that similar considerations of the special nature of the employment prompted the decision in *Wetherall (Bond St., W.1)* v. *Lynn*.[93] In *Courtaulds Northern Textiles Ltd.* v. *Andrew*[94] it may well be that the court was influenced by the relative seniority of the employee but the concept was treated as of general application. Destruction of "trust and confidence" is really no more than a technical sounding name for intolerable behaviour the existence of which destroys the ability to work together. The situation can derive from abuse[95]; failure to support an employee in a position of authority[96]; false and baseless accusations of dishonesty[97]; and deliberate discrimination against an employee.[98]

The courts have not shown themselves committed to formulating in any precise terms the contractual obligation which may be said to comprehend this type of behaviour. It is very noticeable that the category is most commonly applied to the conduct of the employer. Employee conduct having the same effect is more readily covered by well-established obligations and it can be said that this most recent development of the implied term goes a long way to redress the imbalance of the common law which had concentrated on developing positive obligations for the employee. In *Western Excavating (E.C.C.) Ltd.* v. *Sharp*[99] Lawton L.J. was content to leave the repudiatory breach to gut reaction rather than precise definition.

---

[89] *Secretary of State for Employment* v. *ASLEF (No. 2)* [1972] 2 Q.B. 455.

[90] See Freedland, *The Contract of Employment* (O.U.P.); *Wood* v. *Freeloader Ltd.* [1977] I.R.L.R. 455—an industrial tribunal decision containing, not surprisingly, a highly advanced view of the obligation to maintain co-operation.

[91] [1976] I.R.L.R. 413.

[92] Compare, *Veness* v. *Dyson, Bell and Co.*, *The Times*, May 25, 1965—no duty to treat personal secretary with courtesy—and *Donovan* v. *Invicta Airways Ltd.* [1970] 1 Lloyd's Rep. 486; affirming [1969] 2 Lloyd's Rep. 413.

[93] [1978] I.C.R. 205.   [94] [1979] I.R.L.R. 84.

[95] *Palmanor* v. *Cedron* [1978] I.C.R. 1008.

[96] *Wigan Borough Council* v. *Davies* [1979] I.C.R. 411.

[97] *Robinson* v. *Crompton Parkinson Ltd.* [1978] I.C.R. 401.

[98] *F. C. Gardner Ltd.* v. *Beresford* [1978] I.R.L.R. 63.

[99] [1978] Q.B. 761; [1978] I.C.R. 221.

"For the purpose of this judgment, I do not find it either necessary or advisable to express any opinion as to what principles of law operate to bring a contract of employment to an end by reason of an employer's conduct. Sensible persons have no difficulty in recognising such conduct when they hear about it. Persistent and unwanted amorous advances by an employer to a female member of his staff would, for example, clearly be such conduct; and for a chairman of an industrial tribunal in such a case to discuss with his lay members whether there had been a repudiation or a breach of a fundamental term by the employer would be for most lay members a waste of legal learning."

In *British Aircraft Corporation Ltd.* v. *Austin*[1] the search by Phillips J. for a term to break was easily satisfied in the failure to take reasonable care but he went out of his way to add:

. . . if employers do behave in a way which is not in accordance with good industrial practice to such an extent—and this is how it was put in that case—that the situation is intolerable or the situation is that the employee really cannot be expected to put up with it any longer, it will very often be the case, perhaps not always but certainly very often be the case, that by behaving in that way the employers have behaved in breach of contract because it must ordinarily be an implied term of the contract of employment that employers do not behave in a way which is intolerable or in a way which employees cannot be expected to put up with any longer. That is an aside, and we certainly do not wish Industrial Tribunals to guide themselves otherwise than in accordance with the judgment in *Weston Excavating (E.C.C.) Ltd.* v. *Sharp*."

Co-operation

To find a comprehensive term to cover this mass of circumstances is a rather pointless exercise for such a term will follow, rather than lead to, the conclusion that a breach of contract has occurred. The difficulty of formulating any general principle is clearly demonstrated by the history of the development of the supposed duty of co-operation which might seem to afford the best expression of a comprehensive term. In *Secretary of State for Employment* v. *ASLEF (No.* 2)[2] Lord Denning M.R. had been careful to say:

"Now I quite agree that a man is not bound positively to do more for his employer than his contract requires. He can withdraw his goodwill if he pleases. But what he must not do is wilfully to obstruct the employer as he goes about his business."

As soon, however, as an attempt was made to apply this principle it became clear that it was nonsense. The example of the chauffeur deliberately missing the train which Lord Denning advanced rested not on such a contractual duty but on the duty to obey an instruction—albeit an implied instruction. Either the employee has done all that is required of him by his contract or he has not. If he has not he will be in breach of some existing contractual obligation such as to obey reasonable instructions. If he has observed his contract then the imposition of an obligation not wilfully by that observance to disrupt the undertaking must require him to go beyond the contract. Donaldson J. had said as much when the case had been before the N.I.R.C. and several commentators pointed out that the explanation lay in the fact that the law was actually ready to

---

[1] [1978] I.R.L.R. 332.
[2] [1972] 2 Q.B. 455.

recognise a positive duty on both parties to co-operate in the employment venture.[3] This comes very close to saying that the parties must behave reasonably towards each other. To that extent the new obligation eliminates the need to search for and define a breach of contract. It may be objected that this is a major step in judicial creativity since there is no longer any real need to ask what the parties intended. The courts have decided that they intended that they should each behave reasonably. All the apparently defined common law terms are now to be tested by this since, for instance, an order precisely within the terms of the contract may constitute a breach of contract by being intolerable. *Morrish* v. *Henlys (Folkestone) Ltd.*[4] which came to this conclusion was decided before such development had taken place using the flexibility which we have seen to be almost inevitable in any judicial process of construction of so imprecise an instrument as the contract of employment. If there are those who feel that the English law of contract might benefit from the introduction of a principle that the contract should be carried out in good faith they will find the foundation for such a principle here.

The extent to which this type of implication can be pushed raises the question whether the time has not come at which implication might be limited within the boundaries of certainty as suggested in *Lake* v. *Essex County Council.*[5] In *Woods* v. *W.M. Car Services (Peterborough) Ltd.*[6] Browne-Wilkinson J. in the E.A.T., whilst declining to upset a tribunal decision that none of the employer's actions amounted to a repudiatory breach, stated that had it been left to the E.A.T. to make an initial decision it would have concluded that a position with which an employee could not be expected to put up amounted to a breach of the employer's obligation not to conduct himself in a manner calculated or likely to destroy or seriously damage trust and confidence. In that case the employer had made a series of proposals to change the terms of employment, to each of which the employee had objected. Each of which having been withdrawn, was followed by another. The object was to induce the employee to accept change of her contract. The policy behind this approach is expressed in the following extract:

> "In our view it is clearly established that there is implied in a contract of employment a term that the employers will not, without reasonable and proper cause, conduct themselves in a manner calculated or likely to destroy or seriously damage the relationship of confidence and trust between employer and employee: *Courtaulds Northern Textiles Ltd.* v. *Andrew*. To constitute a breach of this implied term, it is not necessary to show that the employer intended any repudiation of the contract: the Tribunals' function is to look at the employer's conduct as a whole and determine whether it is such that its effect, judged reasonably and sensibly, is such that the employee cannot be expected to put up with it: see *BAC Ltd.* v. *Austin* and *Post Office* v. *Roberts*. The conduct of the parties has to be looked at as a whole and its cumulative impact assessed: *Post Office* v. *Roberts*.
>
> We regard this implied term as one of great importance in good industrial relations. Quite apart from the inherent desirability of requiring both employer and employee to behave in the way required by such a term, there is a more technical reason for its importance. The statutory right of an employee who ceases

---

[3] See Freedland, *The Contract of Employment*, p. 27.
[4] [1973] 2 All E.R. 137.
[5] [1978] I.C.R. 657.
[6] [1981] I.C.R. 666.

to be employed to complain that he has been unfairly dismissed is wholly dependent on his showing that he has been 'dismissed.' In the ordinary case, where an
employer in fact dismisses the employee (*i.e.* cases falling within section 55(2)(a)
and (b)) this normally presents no difficulty. The difficulty arises in cases of
constructive dismissal falling within section 55(2)(c) where the employee has
resigned due to the behaviour of the employer. As is well known, there used to be
conflicting decisions as to whether, in order to constitute constructive dismissal,
the conduct of the employer had to amount to a repudiation of the contract at
common law or whether it was sufficient if the employer's conduct was, in lay
terms, so unreasonable that an employee could not be expected to put up with it. In
Western Excavating (E.C.C.) Ltd. v. *Sharp* this conflict was resolved in favour of
the view that the conduct of the employer had to amount to repudiation of the
contract at common law. Accordingly, in cases of constructive dismissal, an
employee has no remedy even if his employer has behaved unfairly, unless it can be
shown that the employer's conduct amounts to a fundamental breach of the
contract."

Although the Court of Appeal[6a] reversed the decision of the E.A.T. that the
employer had destroyed trust and confidence—Watkins L.J. even suggesting
that the employee had behaved unreasonably—no doubt was cast on this
statement of principle.

(d) Confidentiality in employment

The basis of the duty

The Report of the Law Commission on Breach of Confidence in 1981[7] states
that the law of confidentiality has its foundations in equity. Such a foundation is,
however, very flimsy. A line of eighteenth century cases relied on protection of
property whilst in *Abernethy* v. *Hutchinson*[8] and *Morison* v. *Moat*[9] the jurisdiction is founded in contract. If one excludes *Prince Albert* v. *Strange*[10] as a
somewhat unsatisfactory decision only *Gartside* v. *Outram*[11] has a clear equitable basis. Thereafter there was virtually no development of anything save the
contractual foundation applied to the employment relationship. It is, however,
certainly true to say that "property, contract, bailment, trust, fiduciary relationship, good faith, unjust enrichment, have all been claimed, at one time or
another, as the basis of judicial intervention" and "the result is that the answer
to many fundamental questions remains speculative."[12] It is, however, true also
that quite a number of these fundamental questions are not particularly applicable to the law of employment. For instance, employment is clearly a relationship to which confidentiality applies so that there is no need to concern
ourselves with a discussion of what principles if any define such relationships.

It is also true that, though most modern development of protection of
confidence has been based on equitable principles, the law of employment

---

[6a] [1982] I.R.L.R. 413.
[7] Cmnd. 8388.
[8] (1825) 3 L.J. Ch. 209.
[9] (1851) 9 Hare 241.
[10] (1849) 1 Mac. & G. 25.
[11] (1856) 26 L.J. Ch. 113.
[12] Gareth Jones, "Restitution of Benefits Obtained in Breach of Another's Confidence" (1970)
86 L.Q.R. 463.

continues to be firmly based on the supposition of a term in the contract of employment.[13] The Law Commission point out, therefore, that though there is no doubt as to the existence of jurisdiction to enforce confidence it is not clear how any particular issue will be decided since, for instance, it is impossible to say whether equitable or tort principles will be used.[14] It is suggested that in the law of employment any differences caused by a contractual approach are likely to be less significant than appears probable at first sight. In most cases the contractual duty of confidentiality will arise by way of implication. Whatever the courts may say, implication of terms in the contract of employment is most likely to be founded on the court's view of what is reasonable.[15] The details of the obligation are, therefore, likely to be much the same as they would be had they been derived from the more recently developed line of equitable reasoning.[16] The infinite variety of contract that may exist in employment will, of course, give rise to the possibility of some specific statement in the contract which the courts interpret as varying the normal implication. A striking example of this variation appears in *Potters-Ballotini* v. *Weston-Baker*[17] in which the express contractual term limited the continuation of the duty of confidentiality to one year from the end of the employment relationship. The Law Commission also point out that contract could extend the duty to non-disclosure of information that was already public. The difference between interpreting the contract and implying a term into it must, therefore, be appreciated. In normal circumstances it is unlikely that the courts would imply into the contract of employment a duty of confidentiality limited to one year from the end of the employment relationship or extending to information which the Law Commission describe as "in the public domain."[18]

It is submitted, therefore, that it is correct to examine the normal employment obligation on the basis of what the courts will consider it reasonable to impose so that the fact that it is imposed through the contract of employment will not normally significantly alter its content from that derived from equitable concepts.

Fidelity

It is often said that the employee's obligation to respect the confidentiality of information which is the property of his employer springs from the general duty of faithful service. In practice it is dangerous to construe a general obligation by implication from an even more loosely phrased generalisation just because the latter is so widely stated as to be capable of encompassing the former.

The duty faithfully to serve will impose obligations in respect of information to which consideration of the confidentiality of that information is not relevant. The duty of faithful service, however, must cease with the ending of the contract of employment. The duty imposed by confidentiality, whether it be contractual or equitable, obviously does not.

---

[13] See, *e.g. Bents Brewery Ltd.* v. *Hogan* [1945] 2 All E.R. 570. This case, interestingly, indicates a difference in effect between contractual and equitable sources.
[14] Cmnd. 8388, para. 5.2.
[15] See, *e.g.* Roskill J. in *Cranleigh* v. *Bryant* [1965] 1 W.L.R. 1293 at 1320.
[16] See Megarry J. in *Coco* v. *A. N. Clark (Engineering) Ltd.* [1969] R.P.C. 41.
[17] [1977] R.P.C. 202.
[18] See, *e.g.* Cmnd. 8388, para. 3.7.

Nowhere are these distinctions clearer than in the judgment of Maugham L.J. in *Wessex Dairies Ltd.* v. *Smith*.[19] The employee had, during his employment, solicited his employer's customers to transfer their custom to him upon the termination of his employment. It is, of course, true that he might thereby have made use of a list of customers to which confidentiality was attached. Had his actions taken place after his employment had ended this would have been the only obligation which might have been used against him—assuming the express clause in his contract concerning acting contrary to his former employer's interests to be void as in unreasonable restraint of trade. As it was, however, there was no need for the Court of Appeal to consider this aspect so that its comments about termination of the obligation do not apply to the duty of confidentiality.

Maugham L.J. said:

"Hawkins J. said in *Robb* v. *Green* that in a contract of service, and in the absence of any stipulation to the contrary, there is an implied obligation that the servant will honestly and faithfully serve his master; that he will not abuse his confidence in matters appertaining to his service; and that he will, 'by all reasonable means in his power, protect his master's interests in respect to matters confided to him in the course of his service.' This is somewhat vague; I do not quite know what is meant by the words 'matters confided to him.' For myself I prefer the more general implication stated thus by A.L. Smith L.J. 'I think that it is a necessary implication which must be engrafted on such a contract that the servant undertakes to serve his master with good faith and fidelity. That is what was said in the case of *Lamb* v. *Evans* and I entirely agree with it.' The Lord Justice then asked himself whether the defendant in *Robb* v. *Green* acted with good faith and fidelity. The same question has to be answered in the present case. In dealing with it certain considerations should not be left out of sight. First, after the employment terminates, the servant may, in the absence of special stipulation, canvass the customers of the late employer, and further he may send a circular to every customer. On the other hand, it has been held that while the servant is in the employment of the master he is not justified in making a list of the master's customers, and he can be restrained, as he was in *Robb* v. *Green*, from making such a list, or if he has made one, he will be ordered to give it up. But it is to be noted that in *Robb* v. *Green* the defendant was not restrained from sending out circulars to customers whose names he could remember. Another thing to be borne in mind is that although the servant is not entitled to make use of information which he has obtained in confidence in his master's service he is entitled to make use of the knowledge and skill which he acquired while in that service, including knowledge and skill directly obtained from the master in teaching him his business. It follows, in my opinion, that the servant may, while in the employment of the master, be as agreeable, attentive and skilful as it is in his power to be to others with the ultimate view of obtaining the benefit of the customers' friendly feelings when he calls upon them if and when he sets up business for himself. That is, of course, where there is no valid restrictive clause preventing him doing so.

In this case the question is whether the defendant acted with fidelity when, on the Saturday afternoon in question and perhaps on the previous days of the week, in going his round he informed the customers that he would cease on Saturday to be in the employment of the plaintiffs, that he was going to set up business for himself, and would be in a position to supply them with milk. He was plainly soliciting their custom as from Saturday evening. In my opinion that was a deliberate as it was a

---

[19] [1935] 2 K.B. 80.

successful canvassing at a time when the defendant was under an obligation to serve the plaintiffs with fidelity."

Information capable of confidentiality

The first thing to appreciate is that there is no major difference between the concept of a trade secret and that of confidential information. A contract referring to disclosure of trade secrets is most likely to be regarded as referring to confidential information divulged in the course of a normal working relationship. Unless the contract were to make it clear that it envisaged an unusual meaning of "trade secret" that description would tend to be regarded as subject to the same limitations as confidentiality.

The information must be secret

The most significant of the limitations is that referred to by the Law Commission as excluding information in the public domain. This defence to a claim for breach of confidence seems to stem from the early cases of *James* v. *James*[20] and *Reuters Telegram Co.* v. *Byron*.[21] The leading case is now *Saltman Engineering Co. Ltd.* v. *Campbell Engineering Co. Ltd.*[22] which can be cited for the proposition that the information alleged to be confidential must not be something which is public property and public knowledge. In *Mustad* v. *Allcock*[23] this was applied to exclude from the duty of confidentiality a process which the plaintiff had himself registered as a patent.

In *Saltman's* case Lord Greene M.R. also said that the information "must have the necessary quality of confidence about it." The recipient must have a reason to be aware that the information is communicated to him in confidence. Such belief will often derive from the circumstances of the communication. It follows, therefore, that if information spreads there may come a point when recipients have no reason to believe it to be communicated in confidence.[23a]

Secrecy is not often likely to be absolute. In *Franchi* v. *Franchi*[24] Cross J. said that the fact that there were other people who knew the alleged secret would not necessarily deprive it of that character in the hands of the plaintiff. "It must be a question of degree depending on the particular case, but if relative secrecy remains, the plaintiff can still succeed."

Triviality

The question arises whether there exists some objective test in addition to that of non-public—or "secret"—character. The better opinion seems to be that there is not.[25] In *Under Water Welders and Repairers Ltd.* v. *Street and Longthorne*[26] Buckley J. said:

---

[20] (1872) 41 L.J. Ch. 353.
[21] (1874) 43 L.J. Ch. 661.
[22] [1963] 3 All E.R. 413n.
[23] [1963] 2 All E.R. 416.
[23a] *Sun Printers Ltd.* v. *Westminster Press Ltd.* [1982] I.R.L.R. 292 (C.A.).
[24] [1967] R.P.C. 149.
[25] See Cmnd. 8388, para. 4.15.
[26] [1968] R.P.C. 498.

"The fact that some new invention or some new process may be one which, when someone looks at it, is found to provide a self-evident solution for some problem—it may be a very simple solution once it has been recognised—does not mean that that is not something which may merit protection as being a secret process or something of that nature or a process which the person operating it is not entitled to protect by a certain degree of confidentiality."

In *Cranleigh Precision Engineering Ltd.* v. *Bryant*[27] one of the pieces of information involved concerned the right type of clamping strip to hold together the inner and outer walls of a portable swimming pool. Roskill J. said:

"I think the knowledge that this particular clamping strip was the right type of plastic clamping strip to use for this particular purpose, coupled with the knowledge of how to define to a plastics manufacturer what was required for this particular purpose and that a plastics manufacturer could readily supply this particular form of strip, is and was a trade secret of the plaintiff's."

The "spring-board" test

The conjunction of these various principles gives rise to an obvious problem. If confidentiality can be attached to anything, however trivial, provided it is "relatively secret" we must be prepared to draw the definition of the "thing" which is confidential with some care. We might for instance be forced to ask at what point the gathering and arrangement of public information constitutes a separate thing to which confidentiality may be attached.

The courts have sought to provide an answer for this problem in the so-called "spring-board doctrine." This doctrine was first propounded in *Terrapin Ltd.* v. *Builders' Supply Co. (Hayes) Ltd.*[28]

Roxburgh J.:

". . . The brochures would not enable anybody to see exactly how the unit was constructed. They would give the general idea, but not the details. The dismantling [of a unit] would, of course, enable any competent carpenter to see exactly how the building was constructed. 'And,' says Mr. Aldous [counsel for the defendants], 'that publication discharges the confidential obligation.'

Frankly he admitted that there is no suggestion of such a doctrine in any reported case. I go further and say that it is inconsistent with the principles stated by Lord Greene in Saltman's case.

As I understand it, the essence of this branch of the law, whatever the origin of it may be, is that a person who has obtained information in confidence is not allowed to use it as a spring-board for activities detrimental to the person who made the confidential communication, and spring-board it remains even when all the features have been published or can be ascertained by actual inspection by any member of the public. The brochures are certainly not equivalent to the publication of the plans, specifications, other technical information and know-how. The dismantling of a unit might enable a person to proceed without plans or specifications, or other technical information, but not, I think, without some of the know-how, and certainly not without taking the trouble to dismantle. I think it is broadly true to say that a member of the public to whom the confidential information had not been imparted would still have to prepare plans and specifications. He would probably*

---

[27] [1965] 1 W.L.R. 1293.
[28] The judgment was delivered in 1959 but not fully reported until [1967] R.P.C. 375. It is discussed by the Law Commission–Cmnd. 8388 at paras. 4.24 *et seq.* from which the quotation is taken.

have to construct a prototype, and he would certainly have to conduct tests. Therefore, the possessor of the confidential information still has a long start over any member of the public. *The design may be as important as the features*. It is, in my view, inherent in the principle upon which the *Saltman* case rests that the possessor of such information must be placed under a special disability in the field of competition in order to ensure that he does not get an unfair start; *or, in other words, to preclude the tactics which the first defendants and the third defendants and the managing director of both of those companies employed in this case."* (Emphasis added.)

It will be noted that Roxburgh J. derives this principle from *Saltman* v. *Campbell*.[29] Under agreement with Saltman the second plaintiffs prepared drawings for the manufacture of dies from which leather punches were to be made. An order for the manufacture of these dies was placed with the third plaintiff who, however, asked the defendants to undertake the work. The defendants used the drawings also to make dies to manufacture leather punches on their own account. Notwithstanding that they could have bought one of the plaintiff's punches and from it designed the necessary die the defendants were held to have used confidential information. The substance of the information was public but in order to use it it had to be developed.

The spring-board doctrine was confirmed by Roskill J. in *Cranleigh Precision Engineering Ltd.* v. *Bryant*.[30] It contains, however, a very serious difficulty. If the restraint imposed on the recipient of the spring-board is maintained he will be at a disadvantage over the rest of the "public domain" who have the same information without resort to the spring-board. On the other hand, to allow the use of the spring-board immediately the information had become publicly available would be to confer a special advantage on the possessor of the spring-board just because he had that spring-board whilst everyone else had to reach that position by application of thought or some other process. The Law Commission[31] suggests that the restraint imposed on the recipient of a spring-board might last only long enough to afford the rest of the public a chance to catch up. Not surprisingly it describes this as "somewhat speculative."[32] Nevertheless the idea of a limited period of protection would conform with the proposition that the thing to which confidence attaches should be carefully defined. If the actual information is in the public domain then the confidentiality only applies to that which confers the spring-board advantage. In due course that will simply cease to exist because the advantage will be overtaken by the public opportunity.

Third party intervention

In *Cranleigh* Roskill J. distinguished *Mustad* partly on the ground that the "public domain" defence did not apply if a third party, rather than the plaintiff, had disclosed the information before the person to whom the plaintiff had confided it did so. Again it is difficult to see why that confidant should be restricted when the rest of the public are free to use the information because

---

[29] (1948) [1963] 3 All E.R. 413n.
[30] [1965] 1 W.L.R. 1293.
[31] Para. 4.31.
[32] But see *Potters-Ballotini* v. *Weston-Baker* [1977] R.P.C. 202.

they can acquire it without the fetter of confidence. This situation would not arise if the information has leaked to the "public domain" only by way of breach of confidence and subsequent recipients of it might reasonably assume that it was confidential.[33] Obviously, however, such constructive knowledge of confidentiality will rapidly be exhausted once the information is in the public domain.

Personal knowledge, skill and experience

A further problem of definition of what it is that is confidential is particularly significant in the circumstances of employment. It would obviously be inequitable to impose upon a person a restriction upon the use of information which is part of the inevitable store of knowledge, skill or experience which every person builds up. In fact it is at this point that there might have been some danger of the contractual base of confidentiality in employment producing a conclusion different than that of the equitable base of other confidentiality situations. The doctrine of restraint of trade is readily available to avoid a contractual term which would impose such a limit upon an employee.[34] It would no doubt have been possible for a similar application of public policy to have limited the equitable principle in the same way. Such a limitation might, however, turn out to be only partial since it could be argued that it was reasonable for an employer to place some restraint on expertise gained solely in his employ. It would seem better, therefore, to distinguish such personal information as belonging to its possessor and not capable of being fettered by an obligation of confidentiality alleged to be owed to one who was never in possession of the knowledge. In other words the process of gathering and assimilating the knowledge, turning it into skill and experience, makes it a thing different from any of its sources. In *Printers and Finishers Ltd.* v. *Holloway*[35] the manager of a flock printing factory, whilst still employed as such, had conveyed obviously confidential information to another manufacturer in the same field. After his dismissal by the plaintiffs he entered into the employment of that other manufacturer. The plaintiffs sought to restrain him from disclosing to his new employer information relating to the plaintiffs' manufacturing methods.
Cross J. said:

"What is asked for here however, goes far beyond any relief granted in any case which was cited to me. The plaintiffs are saying, in effect: 'True it is that other flock printers use plant and machinery similar to ours and that as we did not trouble to exact any covenant from him not to do so Holloway was entitled to go and work for a trade competitor who uses such plant and machinery. Nevertheless we are entitled to prevent him from using for the benefit of his new employers his recollection of any features of our plant, machinery or process which are in fact peculiar to us.' If this is right then, as it seems to me, an ex-employee is placed in an impossible position. One naturally approaches the problem in this case with some bias in favour of the plaintiffs, because [the first defendant] has shown himself unworthy of their trust; but to test their argument fairly one must take the case of an employee who has been guilty of no breach of contract. Suppose such a man to

---

[33] *Duchess of Argyll* v. *Duke of Argyll* [1967] Ch. 302.
[34] *Herbert Morris Ltd.* v. *Saxelby* [1916] 1 A.C. 688; *Mason* v. *President Clothing and Supply Company Ltd.* [1913] A.C. 724.
[35] [1965] 1 W.L.R. 1.

be told by his new employers that at this or that stage in the process they encounter this or that difficulty. He may say to himself: 'Well, I remember that on the corresponding piece of machinery in the other factory such-and-such a part was set at a different angle or shaped in a different way'; or again, 'When that happened we used to do this and it seemed to work,' 'this' being perhaps something which he had been taught when he first went to the other factory, or possibly an expedient which he had found out for himself by trial and error during his previous employment.

Recalling matters of this sort is, to my mind, quite unlike memorising a formula or list of customers or what was said (obviously in confidence) at a particular meeting. *The employee might well not realise that the feature or expedient in question was in fact peculiar to his late employer's process and factory; but even if he did, such knowledge is not readily separable from his general knowledge of the flock printing process and his acquired skill in manipulating a flock printing plant.*" (Emphasis added.)

Such a distinction can also be explained, both in the field of contract and of equitable obligation, as an aspect of the rule that the recipient of the information must have actual or constructive knowledge of its confidential character. This would not apply to a contrary express contractual provision but, as has been said, it is clearly likely to form part of the content of any implied term. Cross J. said:

"I do not think that any man of average intelligence and honesty would think that there was anything improper in [the employee] putting his memory of particular features of his late employer's plant at the disposal of his new employer."

Once that is conceded the necessary realisation of confidentiality cannot be present.

Notice and acceptance

Megarry J. said in *Coco* v. *A.N. Clark (Engineers) Ltd.*[36] that the obligation of confidence only attaches to information the recipient actually or constructively knows to be conveyed to him in confidence. The Law Commission did not commit itself on whether this was a correct statement of the law but seemed to favour the view that it was and, certainly, that it should be. This principle is likely to apply equally to a contractual duty as to an equitable obligation. It is unlikely that the contract will specify particular information or otherwise define its scope than by using words such as "trade secrets" or "confidential information." This will inevitably extend the obligation only to what the courts will recognise as such and that recognition is likely to be confined to what a reasonable person would assume to be confidential.

The Law Commission[37] point out that in principle it makes little difference whether one asks what a reasonable man would appreciate or whether the test is one of implied acceptance of an obligation. In the field of employment, assuming that the obligation continues to be founded on implied contract, we can say that the limit of the employee's acceptance of the obligation to treat information as confidential is what would reasonably be recognised as such. If we removed contract as the base the equitable base would attain the same result by reference to an obligation extending to what a reasonable man would consider to be communicated in confidence.

---

[36] [1969] R.P.C. 41.
[37] Cmnd. 8388, para. 6.8.

Either way it can readily be seen that the problem of personal knowledge which we have just discussed can be answered by the application of the test of actual or constructive notice. The reasonable employee would not consider the sources from which he had built up knowledge and experience as confidential.

The public interest

Finally, the question arises whether equity or reasonable contractual implication can permit an exception to the obligation of confidentiality on the ground that the public interest in disclosure overrides that of maintaining the confidential nature of the disclosure. In *Initial Services Ltd.* v. *Putterill*[38] a former manager had disclosed to a newspaper information obtained during his employment which was said to reveal a price-fixing arrangement entered into by his former employer and not registered under the Restrictive Trade Practices Act 1956. Lord Denning M.R. took the view that there would be a defence to breach of confidence in disclosure of any misconduct which ought, in the public interest, to be disclosed provided the disclosure was made to one who had a proper interest to secure it. In some cases such a proper interest could be so general as to justify disclosure to the Press. Subsequently, in *Fraser* v. *Evans*[39] Lord Denning extended this proposition beyond misconduct to anything of which the public interest might require disclosure. In *Distillers Co. (Biochemicals) Ltd.* v. *Times Newspapers Ltd.*[40] Talbot J. indicated that it would not be sufficient to show that there was a public interest in disclosure. It would have to be shown that it overrode the public interest in maintaining confidentiality.

An unexpected twist was given to this largely unexceptionable point by Lord Widgery C.J. in *Attorney-General* v. *Jonathan Cape Ltd.*[41] He took the view that the duty of confidentiality must be supported by proof that the balance of public interest was in favour of non-disclosure. It seems unlikely that this suggestion can be supported otherwise than in the circumstances of that case involving attempts to restrain publication of the Crossman Diaries where it may have been correct to begin with an assumption of a public interest in disclosure. It is suggested that no such initial assumption would be justified in most employment cases.

Information obtained by unlawful means

The employee is clearly under an obligation not to disclose information communicated to him in confidence. It would be a ludicrous position if he was free of the duty should he break in to his employer's premises after hours and dishonestly acquire that information. There are cases which have impressed such information with a duty of confidentiality because of the improper means of obtaining it.[42] Nevertheless the Law Commission[43] concluded that it is very doubtful to what extent, if at all, information becomes impressed with an

---

[38] [1968] 1 Q.B. 396.
[39] [1969] 1 Q.B. 349.
[40] [1975] Q.B. 613.
[41] [1976] Q.B. 752.
[42] *Webb* v. *Rose* cited (1769) 4 Burr. 2303; *Millar* v. *Taylor* (1769) 4 Burr. 2303; *Lord Ashburton* v. *Pape* [1913] 2 Ch. 469; *Malone* v. *Metropolitan Police Commissioner* [1979] Ch. 344.
[43] Cmnd. 8388, para. 4.10.

obligation of confidence by reason solely of the reprehensible means by which it has been acquired. The solution, in the case of employment, however, may lie in the next few words of the Commission's conclusion in which it is suggested that the obligation might be more clear if a special relationship existed between the persons alleged to owe the confidence. Thus far it seems that such relationships have not extended beyond the fiduciary relationship which existed in *Boardman* v. *Phipps*[44] and *Cranleigh Precision Engineering Co. Ltd.* v. *Bryant*.[45] It is submitted that in these cases the recipient of the information was not under a duty of confidence. He could not be since the information had not come to him from the person claiming to possess it. The duty there was to disclose the information to the person claiming it. On the other hand, that duty must contain as a corollary the obligation not previously or subsequently to that disclosure to destroy the value of the information by disclosure to others. We shall see that it is extremely doubtful whether an employee in normal circumstances is under a duty to disclose to his employer information coming into his possession relevant to his employment. The effect of this may be that senior management, research workers and the like can be said to be in a special relationship imposing confidentiality in respect of information acquired improperly, whereas other employees are under no such duty.

Protection of confidentiality after the employment relationship ends

Confidentiality attaches to the information in question. Both equity and contractual implication, therefore, will continue to afford protection whilst the information retains its character as confidential. It has often been pointed out that as applied to the contract of employment this raises the possibility of arguing that though the employment relationship may end, and with it the aspects of contract relating to the performance of work, aspects of the contract of employment may never be terminated, at least without the agreement of both parties. It is suggested that such a concept is not that difficult to apply and is to be preferred to the only alternative which would be that the contractual source of confidentiality should give place to an equitable source when the work obligation ceased.

Nevertheless, employers frequently insert into contracts of employment express terms restrictive of the employee's freedom to seek other employment. There is no doubt that the purpose of these restrictive covenants is, in part, to add to the protection of confidential information upon the ending of employment. The explanation is a practical one. It is extremely difficult to monitor and check the flow of information between an employer and his employee. By far the best way of restricting confidential information is to ensure that such a relationship does not arise, at least where it would involve an employer with an interest in acquiring the confidential information. Prevention of this nature has the added advantage that it will also prevent the potential employer obtaining the benefit of personal knowledge and skill such as passed in *Printers and Finishers Ltd.* v. *Holloway*.[46] Whatever the law may say, the employer in whose service such skills are learned may well feel that he has an interest which he is entitled to protect.

---

[44] [1967] 2 A.C. 46.
[45] [1965] 1 W.L.R. 1293.
[46] [1965] 1 W.L.R. 1.

The restrictive covenant is an express term to which none of the issues we have been discussing in connection with protection of confidentiality apply, save the question of the effect of the public interest. Apart from interpretation of the covenant the principal issue before the courts is that of the validity of the intended restriction.

The doctrine of restraint of trade

The jurisdiction to avoid an unreasonably wide provision is based upon the view that freedom of trade is a matter of public policy.[47] It seems that, whereas upholding the validity of the restraint is a matter of contract and only available to the parties thereto, destruction of the restraint, in the interests of public policy, is open to any third party whose right to exercise or benefit from that freedom is "vitally affected."[48]

The doctrine of restraint of trade has many facets[49] and very different policy considerations affect, for example, the application of the doctrine as between the vendor and the purchaser of a business. Even in that situation it is incorrect to suppose that all restraints are regarded as basically reasonable, as was implied by Lord Haldane L.C. when he stated that the parties were the best judges of what was reasonable.[50] The question of reasonableness is always one for the court.[51]

In the leading case of *Esso Petroleum Co. Ltd.* v. *Harper's Garage (Stourport) Ltd.*,[52] the House of Lords recast this aspect of the subject and incidentally tried to explain why an express covenant should be construed so strictly whilst, during employment, freedom is so severely restricted by implication. It was said that the implied term is justified as a means of securing the worker's absorption into the employment, whilst the express term, operative after employment, secures his sterilisation.[53] Lord Morris said that if the law is to "uphold freedom to contract and also to uphold freedom to trade, a certain adjustment is necessary." So in some contracts, like those between vendor and purchaser, the consideration of the freedom of contract will be stronger, whereas, in employment, the maintenance of freedom of trade will be the primary factor.

In *Nordenfelt* v. *Maxim Nordenfelt Guns and Ammunition Co. Ltd.*,[54] Lord Macnaghten had taken the view that any agreement interfering with individual freedom to trade came within the doctrine. If this were so it would always be necessary to prove the reasonableness of such a restraint, because it is clear that

---

[47] The basis of the jurisdiction in public policy is, however, not often apparent in the decisions of the courts. In *The Littlewoods Organisation Ltd.* v. *Harris* [1978] 1 All E.R. 1026, for example, the Court of Appeal said that where a contract could be construed so as to be valid—as for instance by confining its application to the U.K.—it should be so construed.

[48] Wilberforce J. in *Eastham* v. *Newcastle United F.C. Ltd.* [1964] Ch. 413.

[49] See for instance, *Nagle* v. *Feilden* [1966] 2 Q.B. 633 and (1967) 30 M.L.R. 389.

[50] *North Western Salt Co. Ltd.* v. *Electrolytic Alkali Co. Ltd.* [1914] A.C. 461 at 471.

[51] *Kores Manufacturing Co. Ltd.* v. *Kolok Manufacturing Co. Ltd.* [1959] Ch. 108, *per* Jenkins L.J. In this case the Court of Appeal left open the question of whether an agreement between two employers restricting the work opportunities of their employees should be judged by the stricter standards normally applicable to agreements between employers and employees.

[52] [1968] A.C. 269.

[53] In the light of this it goes too far to say that an express covenant operative during employment is necessarily binding—*Rely-a-Bell Burglar and Fire Alarm Co. Ltd.* v. *Eisler* [1926] Ch. 609. The decision would depend on whether it went beyond "absorption."

[54] [1894] A.C. 535.

when the presumption of unreasonableness applies the onus falls on the party seeking to set up the validity of the restraint.[55] In the *Esso* case, however, the House of Lords made plain its view that there are classes of agreement where restriction is normal and necessary. To them the doctrine does not apply so that the question of proof of reasonableness never arises. The implication in the contract of service is one of these classes. It may be that a restrictive clause in a collective agreement, if intended to be contractually enforceable, would be regarded in the same light.[56] Possibly, an express restriction in a contract of service, even where it had effect after the termination of that service, could in some circumstances be regarded as normal and necessary.

If, as will continue to be more usual, the express covenant is considered to be within the doctrine of restraint, the party alleging its validity must show that it is a reasonable method of protecting property without undue restriction of freedom.[57] Once it has been shown that it is reasonable as between the parties a presumption is raised that it is reasonable as regards the public interest. The party denying the validity of the restriction may seek to rebut this presumption.[58] Rebuttal will, however, be a difficult task at that stage.

The general test of reasonableness between the parties is whether the restraint is necessary to protect the proprietary interests of the employer, or whether it operates largely as a restraint upon competition.[59] The protection of property must not be unreasonably extensive in area, time or subject-matter, or in relation to the interest of the employee in the maintenance of his freedom. The matter is relatively simple when the property is plainly identifiable as a trade secret and the restriction is designed to prevent the employee using it. It becomes progressively more difficult as the proprietary right shades off into general aspects of the business and the restriction affects the employee's own abilities. In *Morris & Co. Ltd.* v. *Saxelby*[60] the House of Lords had to consider the case of an employee who, on leaving school, had entered the company's drawing office and had risen eventually to become head of one of its departments. He had covenanted not to engage in business similar to that of the company for seven years after leaving its employment. The business of the company involved the manufacture of travelling cranes, pulley-blocks and other lifting machinery and the restriction applied to the whole of the United Kingdom. The House emphasised that its effect would be to deprive the defendant of the power to use the specialised skills which were his sole stock-in-trade, and concluded that the covenant was void because it amounted to a protection against competition.

---

[55] *Mason* v. *Provident Clothing and Supply Co. Ltd.* [1913] A.C. 724; *Morris (Herbert) Ltd.* v. *Saxelby* [1916] 1 A.C. 688; *Attwood* v. *Lamont* [1920] 3 K.B. 571; *G. W. Plowman & Son Ltd.* v. *Ash* [1964] 1 W.L.R. 568. The contrary view stated by Hodson L.J. in *M. & S. Drapers Ltd.* v. *Reynolds* [1957] 1 W.L.R. 9 may be an attempt to overcome the difficulty of proof that might arise if all restrictive agreements were so affected and, if this is so, its purpose has been achieved by the *Esso* decision.

[56] See Cronin and Grime, *Labour Law*, p. 333, n.7.

[57] See Evershed J. in *Routh* v. *Jones* [1947] 1 All E.R. 179 at 181; citing Younger L.J. in *Attwood* v. *Lamont* [1920] 3 K.B. 571 at 590.

[58] This chronological process does not mean that public interest is of secondary importance in all cases. In the *Esso* case the interest of the parties was considered only as an aspect of public interest.

[59] *M. & S. Drapers Ltd.* v. *Reynolds* [1957] 1 W.L.R. 9. *cf. Gledhow Autoparts Ltd.* v. *Delaney* [1965] 1 W.L.R. 1366.   [60] [1916] 1 A.C. 688.

A similar point was taken, more recently, in *Commercial Plastics Ltd.* v. *Vincent.*[61] The plaintiffs' business consisted wholly or mainly in manufacturing thin plastic sheeting, of which they held about 20 per cent. of the United Kingdom market. In the specialised manufacture of this sheeting for use in the production of adhesive tape they were pre-eminent; holding about 80 per cent. of the market and taking care to protect the secrecy of their recent discoveries in that field. The defendant primarily worked in connection with this specialised field, and he had covenated "not to seek employment with any of our competitors in the P.V.C. calendering field for at least one year after leaving our employ." Pearson L.J. said:

"Secondly, there is the fact that, although the plaintiffs required protection only for their trade secrets of confidential information relating to the production of sheeting for tape, they took protection in their restrictive provision for the whole P.V.C. calendering field. That would be likely to cause great hardship to the defendant, because his experience for his last three years with I.C.I. had been, and his experience in his employment with the plaintiffs was expected to be exclusively or almost exclusively in the P.V.C. calendering field. He would be barred from making use of his skill and aptitude and general knowledge in that field, and that would be detrimental both to his interests and to the public interest."

The restraint may operate not only upon the employee's own knowledge but may prevent him from using more easily identifiable property of his own, such as a stage name.[62] Similar considerations would apply to a personal reputation. It must be remembered that restrictions on the employee's property only strengthen, they do not make, his case. Essentially his case lies in his freedom to offer himself for work. Many of the aspects so far discussed arose in what was unfortunately only an interim application in the case of *Potters-Ballotini* v. *Weston-Baker.*[63] The plaintiffs had been the sole manufacturers of ballotini in the United Kingdom. The three defendants who were very senior employees of the plaintiff, whilst still in that employment and unknown to the plaintiff raised a large loan and constructed a factory for the manufacture of ballotini which was alleged to be remarkably similar to that of the plaintiff. There was a covenant in their contract restraining them for one year after the end of employment from using information obtained in the course of employment.

The Court of Appeal pointed out that the defendants could not be restrained from using general knowledge. There would be great difficulty in deciding which parts of the information were confidential and which parts simply knowledge and an uncertain injunction should not be issued. In addition the court pointed out that a spring-board does not last for ever and possibly should not be the subject of long term protection. Finally the contractual protection had only one month to run and it was arguable that the effect of the equitable protection of confidence could be said to be limited to one year by the contractual limitation. Damages were, therefore, the appropriate remedy.

Considerable difficulty has been experienced by the courts in dealing with covenants which seek to protect against the solicitation of customers. In *M. & S. Drapers Ltd.* v. *Reynolds,*[64] the issue was clouded by the fact that some of the

[61] [1965] 1 Q.B. 623.
[62] *Hepworth Manufacturing Co. Ltd.* v. *Ryott* [1920] 1 Ch. 1.
[63] [1977] R.P.C. 202.
[64] *Supra.*

customers had belonged to the employee before he entered the plaintiffs' employment. So it was considered unreasonable to restrict him in the use of his own property. More open to question is the decision of the Court of Appeal in *G.W. Plowman & Son Ltd.* v. *Ash*.[65] The covenant was to the effect that the employee should not "canvass or solicit . . . any farmer or market gardener who shall at any time during the employment of the employee hereunder have been a customer of the employer." It was, therefore, not confined to the employee's own district, nor to customers existing at the commencement of the employment. Harman L.J. said that in covenants restricting solicitation of customers, as distinct from those dealing with the carrying on of a business, the extent of the area of the restriction was not normally relevant. If this is so, and there is added, not only acceptance of property in one's customers, but also in potential customers, the restraint must come very close to operating upon competition.

All the members of the Court of Appeal reasserted the continuing interest in former customers who might return in *Home Counties Dairies* v. *Skilton*.[66] The judgment of Salmon L.J. suggested that that rather nominal interest survives, even if the customer moves from the area covered by the business. Cross L.J. saw the difficulty of distinguishing legitimate trade connections and protection from competition, but suggested that the line between the legitimate and the occasional case where there was nothing to protect was so difficult to draw that the benefit of doubt should be given in favour of the validity of the covenant which could be seen to have been carefully drawn for a legitimate purpose. As some stress was laid in all the judgments on the flagrant nature of the breach it may well be dangerous to give the views expressed in this case too much general application. Certainly the decision leans a long way in favour of freedom of contract. It may be wrong to be astute to devise hypothetical situations in which a restraint would prove unduly burdensome to an employee, but it is on borderlines such as this that the policy behind the doctrine of restraint of trade should be the most obvious consideration.

If the line of thought in the *Esso* case continues, it is likely that the courts will find themselves more often forced to consider the second objection based on contravention of the public interest. The danger in this is that views as to the nature of the public interest are likely to vary from time to time. The leading case on this aspect of the doctrine is *Wyatt* v. *Kreglinger and Ferneau*,[67] in which the Court of Appeal held that a pension agreement was entirely void because a condition that the pensioner should not take any employment in the wool trade, which provided the consideration for the pension, was unreasonably wide and void. The decision was extensively criticised at the time, mainly on the ground that, with the employment position as it was in 1933, it could hardly be said to be contrary to the public interest that a man of 60 should be excluded from working in any trade in return for a pension. It was followed, however, in *Bull* v. *Pitney-Bowes Ltd.*,[68] in which Thesiger J. pointed out that the basis of the criticism had disappeared. It appears that if this is the correct approach an agreement may

---

[65] [1964] 1 W.L.R. 568.
[66] [1970] 1 W.L.R. 526.
[67] [1933] 1 K.B. 793.
[68] [1967] 1 W.L.R. 273.

sometimes be void and sometimes valid according to such extraneous considerations as the state of the economy.

It may be observed that the contract as a whole will usually survive the invalidity of a restrictive covenant. In the case of a contract of employment there is plenty of other consideration on both sides.[69] A similar question of severance arises, however, as to the fate of a restraint which is justifiable in part only. Such a situation should be distinguished from that which arose in *Home Counties Dairies* v. *Skilton*.[70] The terms of the restraint were loosely worded and it was pointed out that if construed literally it would not only prevent the milk-roundsman accepting other employment as such but would also prevent him working in a grocer's shop which sold butter and cheese. The court did not need to sever these wide aspects but held instead that it could take account of the intention of the parties that they were not included.

When the meaning of the covenant is established it may still appear that only a part of it is too wide. It can be argued that the valid part can be severed from the invalid and enforced. The modern rule is that such severance is only permissible where the unreasonable element forms a separate part of the agreement, trivial to the main issue, and such that its removal will not affect the nature of the agreement. Unfortunately it is obvious that this statement is an attempt at a composite resolution of a number of decisions and that, as such, it is sufficiently imprecise to be open to wide or narrow application as the court sees fit. In the leading case of *Attwood* v. *Lamont*,[71] Lord Sterndale M.R., was almost equally imprecise. He said:

> "I think, therefore, that it is still the law that a contract can be severed if the severed parts are independent of one another and can be severed without the severance affecting the meaning of the part remaining. . . . I think it clear that if the severance of a part of the agreement gives it a meaning and object different in kind and not only in extent, the different parts of it cannot be said to be independent."

Younger L.J.'s test was even more imprecise: "[Severance is] permissible in a case where the covenant is not really a single covenant but is in effect a combination of several distinct covenants . . . where the severance can be carried out without the addition or alteration of a word . . . "

At first instance, in *Putsman* v. *Taylor*,[72] the test was applied mechanically, but in *Attwood* v. *Lamont* itself it was held impossible to sever from the agreement descriptions of trades beyond those that it was reasonable to protect, on the ground that this would alter the nature of the covenant from a general restraint on competition to a restraint protective of a proprietary interest.

In *Ronbar Enterprises* v. *Green*,[73] in a contract akin to the sale of goodwill, the words "or similar to" preceding the description of the business in question

---

[69] The same is normally true of illegal methods of payment of wages: *Kearney* v. *Whitehaven Colliery Co.* [1893] 1 Q.B. 700; see N. S. Marsh, "Severance of Illegality in Contract" (1948) 64 L.Q.R. 230, 347 at 351. But it must be borne in mind that almost the only undertaking of the employer in ordinary circumstances is the obligation to pay wages, so that if all such payments were void the contract might fail. Other forms of illegality, however, may destroy the enforceability of the contract or the right of the employee to invoke statutory protection. See, *e.g. Tomlinson* v. *Dick Evans "U" Drive Ltd.* [1978] I.C.R. 639.

[70] *Supra.*

[71] [1920] 3 K.B. 571.

[72] [1927] 1 K.B. 637.

[73] [1954] 1 W.L.R. 815.

were severed on the ground that this did not alter the nature of the agreement. Even if this is true it can hardly be said that they formed a separate part of the agreement.[74] In *Commercial Plastics Ltd.* v. *Vincent*,[75] Pearson L.J., implied that if a blue pencil cannot be used effectively severance is not possible, for he says: "the subject of severance was mentioned, but it cannot be contended that there are any words to be struck out or that this provision may be construed as two provisions."

Some authorities take the view that it is almost impossible to succeed in an argument for severance at the present time on the ground that, even if the blue pencil can be used, it must not be used in such a way as to turn a "general restraint" (which is really only another name for an unreasonably wide restraint) into a "protective [or permissible] restraint." Others contend that there is still room for the approach adopted in *Goldsoll* v. *Goldman*,[76] in which the court severed all restraint outside the United Kingdom and all reference to dealing in real, as distinct from imitation, jewellery, and enforced the remainder of the agreement. In the light of the uncertainty that must remain, there must be some sympathy for the draftsman who resorted to the impermissible device of adding to the covenant the cautious words, "so far as the law allows."[77]

(e) Acquisition of knowledge on behalf of an employer

The common law

In *Cranleigh Precision Engineering Co. Ltd.* v. *Bryant*[78] the plaintiff's managing director had acquired a patent directly relevant to the plaintiffs' products and had used it for his own purposes. Undoubtedly he was under a duty to disclose the information thus acquired but it seems clear that that duty only arose because of the fiduciary relationship which he had as a director. An employee ordinarily is not in a fiduciary relationship. Nevertheless, there is no doubt that at common law an employee is under a duty to disclose to his employer information relevant to what the employee is employed to do. This is certainly true of information which the employee has discovered; *a fortiori* it would seem to apply to similar information which he derives from other sources unless, of course, a duty of confidentiality exists between the employee and that other source.

In *British Reinforced Concrete Co. Ltd.* v. *Lind*[79] the defendant employee was employed in the plaintiffs' drawing office to work out designs and calculations for tenders for supporting roofs of mines. While doing this he worked out a method more satisfactory than that used by his employer. Eve J. held that as the plaintiff was employed to work out solutions to this problem he was bound to

---

[74] The decision in *Scorer* v. *Seymour Jones* [1966] 1 W.L.R. 1419, that it was permissible to sever the excessive radius of five miles so as to restrict the area of restraint to the town where the employee had worked, seems open to doubt.

[75] [1965] 1 Q.B. 623.

[76] [1915] 1 Ch. 292.

[77] *Davies* v. *Davies* (1887) 36 Ch.D. 359.

[78] [1965] 1 W.L.R. 1293.

[79] (1917) 116 L.T. 243. See also *Triplex Safety Glass Co. Ltd.* v. *Scorah* [1938] 1 Ch. 211; *Sterling Engineering Co. Ltd.* v. *Patchett* [1955] A.C. 534.

offer the best solution he could devise. His employer was, therefore, entitled to secure the details of the new method.

This line of reasoning was developed further in *British Syphon Co. Ltd.* v. *Homewood*[80] where the defendant, while in charge of the plaintiffs' design and development department, designed and patented an improved form of soda-water syphon. Roxburgh J. held that he was employed to give his employer his best service in the broad field of design related to his employer's undertaking. It is clear that, conversely, at common law an invention in the employee's time which does not impinge on what he is employed to do and does not use confidential information would remain the property of the inventor.[81] It is only fair to point out that the judgment of Roxburgh J. in the *British Syphon* case raises some problems. The learned judge said:

> "It is common ground that the defendant had not been expressly asked to design any new method of dispensing soda water by a low-pressure system or any other system, and that he had not been asked to give any advice in relation to any such problem. This is the circumstance which, as far as I can see, differentiates this case from all that have gone before. . . . He was employed to give the plaintiffs technical advice in relation to the design or development of anything connected with any part of the plaintiffs' business. No particular problem had been put before him, but if, and as often as, any problem of that kind was put before him, it was his duty to be ready to tender his advice and to assist in any matter of design or development. He was paid to stand by in that respect. He had other functions, but those are not material to the present case.
>
> Would it be consistent with good faith, as between master and servant, that he should in that position be entitled to make some invention in relation to a matter concerning a part of the plaintiffs' business and either keep it from his employer, if and when asked about the problem, or even sell it to a rival and say: 'Well, yes, I know the answer to your problem, but I have already sold it to your rival'? In my judgment, that cannot be consistent with a relationship of good faith between a master and a technical adviser. It seems to me that he has a duty not to put himself in a position in which he may have personal reasons for not giving his employer the best advice which it is his duty to give if and when asked to give it.
>
> He has a duty to be free from any personal reason for not giving his employer the best possible advice. *A fortiori*, it seems to me that he is not entitled to put himself into the position of being able to say: 'You retained me to advise you, and I will tell you what I advise you. Do it this way, but you will have to buy the method from your rival, because I have just sold it to him, having invented it yesterday.' That seems to me to be reasoning which, in the absence of authority, makes it right and proper for me to decide that this invention (which, in my judgment, plainly relates to and concerns the business of the plaintiffs, namely, the distribution of soda water to the public in containers of a satisfactory character), if made during a time during which the chief technician is standing by under the terms of his employment, must be held to be in equity the property of the employer. Accordingly, my decision is for the plaintiffs."

It is apparent, therefore, that the common law bears particularly severely on more senior employees, research workers and those with a wider remit, since it is they to whom the implied obligation will most significantly extend. Nevertheless, it is less clear than may once have been the case that an employer can say that he purchases the whole potential of an employee who has no special

---

[80] [1956] 1 W.L.R. 1190.
[81] *Re Selz Ltd.'s Application* (1953) 71 R.P.C. 158.

position within a given area. This is what Sir John Donaldson thought in *Seaboard World Airlines Inc.* v. *Transport and General Workers Union*[82] and it is depressingly reminiscent of the reasoning in *Turner* v. *Mason*.[83] Logically the approach of Roxburgh J. would mean that an employer would acquire inventions and patents belonging to any employee at the time of his engagement if they were within the field of his employment. As early as 1903[84] it has been said that it did not follow that the obligation was so extensive in all cases. The employee in no special position and not expected to make discoveries may not be subject to any obligation to disclose them if made. Nevertheless the cases cited are considered to represent the current state of the common law as to information in the hands of an employee who can be expected to be in a position to acquire such information. The only reservation that seems to have been made concerns information which would affect the interests of a fellow employee. In *Swain* v. *West (Butchers) Ltd.*[85] the court appeared very willing to construe a contract so as to include even such an obligation. It would appear that many employees engaged in management might be regarded as under an implied obligation to disclose information about other employees on exactly the same basis as explains their obligation to disclose other information namely; that that is among the things for which they are paid.

The Patents Act 1977

It may be considered an astounding feat that the common law should have been able to produce so many of the detailed obligations of confidentiality by way of contractual implication. It would be surprising if such judicial invention, fraught with historical undertones, should produce a wholly satisfactory practical outcome.

The common law in this respect has been largely replaced by the provisions of the Patents Act 1977. In part this Act was a response to the effect of the normal common law term upon employees with a widely defined obligation. In part also it was intended to deal with a problem arising from the employer's use of freedom of contract to impose upon employees who were likely to make discoveries express obligations of even greater scope. The most senior employees might reasonably be said to accept such an obligation in return for their remuneration but the obligation at common law extended to all types of information and so might easily include unspectacular but useful ideas which could be said to be within the scope of virtually any employee. It is, moreover, true to say that no employee could claim possession of an idea derived from, or as a development upon, his employer's property. This would include an improvement upon any piece of information which the employee had received in confidence.

Statute defines the property rights in an invention as between the employer and employee as follows:

39.—(1) Notwithstanding anything in any rule of law, an invention made by an

---

[82] [1973] I.C.R. 458.
[83] (1845) 14 M. & W. 112.
[84] *Worthington Pumping Engine Co.* v. *Moore* (1903) 20 R.P.C. 41 at 48.
[85] [1936] 3 All E.R. 261.

employee shall, as between him and his employer, be taken to belong to his employer for the purposes of this Act and all other purposes if—

    (a) it was made in the course of the normal duties of the employee or in the course of duties falling outside his normal duties, but specifically assigned to him, and the circumstances in either case were such that an invention might reasonably be expected to result from the carrying out of his duties; or

    (b) the invention was made in the course of the duties of the employee and, at the time of making the invention, because of the nature of his duties and the particular responsibilities arising from the nature of his duties he had a special obligation to further the interests of the employer's undertaking.

(2) Any other invention made by an employee shall, as between him and his employer, be taken for those purposes to belong to the employee.

This extends to joint inventions but not to inventions of others to which the employee has merely contributed advice or assistance.[86]

This leaves a lot of questions unanswered. The first ground of obligation requires that the employment should be such that an invention, but not *the* invention, might reasonably be expected to result from carrying out his duties. The duties of more senior employees, as we have said, may be very wide. The invention, it is said, must be made in the course of normal duties. This presumably refers not to the contractual duties but to those that it is normal for the employee to perform within the contract. Again, however, it may be difficult in the case of more senior employees to say which duties which they sometimes perform are "normal." The second limb imposes the obligation in respect of inventions made in the course of duty, and not "normal" duty. It is arguable, therefore, that this refers to contractual duties and such an interpretation is the more likely since it will be to the contract that the courts are likely to look to see whether a special obligation arises. It is clear that the courts are left free to decide when to imply such a special obligation from the nature of the duties. It should be noted, however, that it must be possible to imply such an obligation. An express statement of such an obligation in circumstances which would not otherwise support its implication will not satisfy the test.

An employer would be free by contract to define the employee's duty of confidentiality widely so as to catch as large an area as possible in which the employee's inventions were developments upon such confidential information.[87] Otherwise it is not only impossible for there to be a valid term in the contract of employment diminishing the employee's rights as defined in section 39; but also the employee may not validly dispose of his invention by any advance contract to his employer or to anyone else at the request of the employer. Section 42 provides that no such contract may diminish the rights of an employee in inventions made by him after the date of the contract. An employee is, therefore, free to dispose of inventions he has already made even to his employer.

Even there, however, the employee is protected from disposing of his invention for an inadequate return. When the employee assigns, or grants an exclusive licence over, his *patented* invention to his employer, he may apply to the court or the Comptroller who may decide that the benefit derived by the employee from the assignment or grant is inadequate in relation to the benefit derived by the employer and that it is just to increase that benefit.

---

[86] s.43(3).
[87] s.42(3).

Where the employee's *patented* invention vests in the employer under section 39 a similar application may be made. In that case, however, the court or Comptroller must be satisfied that the patent is of outstanding benefit to the employer having regard to the size and nature of the employer's undertaking and that by reason of those facts it is just that the employee should be compensated. In either case compensation shall be such as will secure for the employee a fair share of the benefit the employer has derived, or may reasonably be expected to derive, from the patent or from any further dealing with it.[88] In both cases, however, the jurisdiction may be excluded where a relevant collective agreement (within the meaning of the Trade Union and Labour Relations Act 1974) provides for compensation in respect of inventions of the same description to employees of the same description. The collective agreement in question must be one by or on behalf of a trade union to which the employee belongs and which is in force at the time of making the invention.

(f) Work for others

It is clear that an employee who worked for another during the time he was employed would be in breach of his obligation to be available to work for his first employer.

The duty to serve faithfully, from which springs the contractual basis of the obligations we have just considered, does not, however, in normal circumstances prevent an employee working for another in his own time, even if that other should be in competition with the first employer. A decision which was often misunderstood to have the opposite effect was reached by the Court of Appeal in *Hivac Ltd.* v. *Park Royal Scientific Instruments Ltd.*[89] Careful reading of the judgment of Lord Greene M.R. and Morton L.J. reveals clearly that the injunction to prevent five employees working for a rival manufacturer on Sundays was granted to prevent a clear risk that the primary employer's confidential information would thereby be passed to the rival. The examples invoked in the judgment of Lord Greene are those relative to trade secrets. In the unreported decision of *Philip Kunick Ltd.* v. *Smyth* the N.I.R.C., in 1973, confirmed this view but made it conditional upon there being no conflict of interest and no damage to the first employer. It is difficult to discover a basis for these conditions. The conflict of interest which undoubtedly existed in *Hivac* was not the basis of the decision and it is not correct to suppose that where there is a conflict of interest there will inevitably be a risk to confidentiality. All the employee has to transfer may be his own accumulated experience and expertise. Nevertheless the idea that part-time work *substantially* detrimental to the primary employer may be a "breach of trust . . . contrary to the implied term of loyal service" appeared again in *Nova Plastics Ltd.* v. *Froggatt.*[90]

The degree of detriment may affect the decision whether to grant an injunction but it cannot feasibly have any relevance to the existence of a breach of contract. It seems to be clear from this judgment that the element of rivalry is not sufficient in itself, although on the face of it this would seem of greater logical relevance than the degree of damage.

---

[88] s.41.
[89] [1946] Ch. 169—the decision was upon an interlocutory application.
[90] [1982] I.R.L.R. 146 (E.A.T.).

In practice, however, the issue is likely to produce a more simple solution than these rather unsatisfactory authorities suggest. Any employee who is in a more than ordinary situation of trust is likely by working for a rival to endanger confidence and so to fall within the actual decision in *Hivac*. Such an employee not working for a rival is unlikely to cause substantial damage and so will be free. An employee who is unlikely to possess confidential information, like the odd job man in *Nova Plastics*, is neither likely to endanger confidentiality or cause substantial damage even if, as in that case, he does work for a rival. The reader must wait patiently for light to be shed on further possibilities by the tea lady who, by careless talk in the hospital canteen where she cleans in the evening, reveals a serious health hazard at her primary workplace.

(g) Obedience to reasonable orders

Refusal, without justification, to obey a reasonable order within the scope of the contract of service is a breach of that contract,[91] although, as in all other classes of breach, the refusal may not be so fundamental a rejection of the contract as to justify rescission by way of dismissal.[92] It may be that what is often accepted as an obvious reason for dismissal in practice (for instance, swearing at the foreman) would present the common law with some problem of sufficiency.[93] That problem might often be resolved by demonstrating that the act which appeared to be the reason for the dismissal was only a method of indicating a refusal to obey a reasonable order. Most often the problem has been avoided in the past because the employer has exercised his undoubted right to terminate the contract by a payment of wages in lieu of notice. In *Pepper* v. *Webb*[94] the court, although not making the distinction very clearly, appears to have accepted the right to dismiss as arising from the refusal of an order (or possibly a prolonged process of breakdown of relations) rather than the bad language used.

Some textbooks state the duty as one to obey *lawful* orders. Not all lawful, nor all reasonable, orders need be obeyed if they are beyond the contractual duty. A servant is certainly under no duty to obey unlawful orders[95] but it is submitted that this is merely an extreme example of an order outside the scope of his contract.[96] Even if the contract appeared to encompass such unlawful work the term conveying such appearance would presumably be void. It is

---

[91] The cases range in time from *Spain* v. *Arnott* (1817) 2 Stark. 256, to *Pepper* v. *Webb* [1969] 1 W.L.R. 514. See also the facts in *Edwards* v. *Society of Graphical and Allied Trades* [1971] Ch. 354.

[92] *Callo* v. *Brouncker* (1831) 4 Car. & P. 518. It is worth noting that in *Laws* v. *London Chronicle Ltd.* [1959] 1 W.L.R. 698 the court distinguished between an order to comply with the contract and advice to do so.

[93] But see *Wilson* v. *Racher* [1974] I.C.R. 428.

[94] *Supra.*

[95] *Gregory* v. *Ford* [1951] 1 All E.R. 121. Atiyah, *Vicarious Liability*, p. 246 points out that an order to drive an uninsured vehicle will not now involve the driver in committing an offence unless he has knowledge of the facts. It is submitted that the order would still be unreasonable. See *Buckoke* v. *Greater London Council* [1970] 1 W.L.R. 1092, where the court in its discretion, declined to interfere with discipline in the Fire Brigade. The order was considered not unreasonable. See also *A. R. Dennis and Co. Ltd.* v. *Campbell* [1976] I.C.R. 465.

[96] In *London Borough of Redbridge* v. *Fishman* [1978] I.C.R. 569, the reference to reasonable instruction was made in terms of the duties the employee was engaged to undertake and other custom and practice of the profession.

logical to suppose that the refusal is only justified so far as the unreasonableness extends. The servant is bound to obey any reasonable aspects of the order. In support of this proposition Wedderburn cites the county court decision in *National Coal Board* v. *Hughes*.[97] Miners had refused to work a coal face at all because the method of so doing envisaged by the overman was, allegedly, dangerous. Judge Harding said that to justify the refusal to work they would have to show that there was no method of working the face with reasonable safety. This proposition arises from the generality of their refusal. It is not to be supposed that an employee is under any duty to suggest what would be reasonable. He is entitled to refuse an unreasonable order and to wait for another order to be given.

An employee is not obliged to be accommodating and helpful.[98] He is entitled to construe the terms of his contract strictly and to refuse to move outside that construction. In *Price* v. *Mouat*[99] the court refused to disturb the finding of a jury that one employed as a lace-buyer was not bound to obey an order to card lace. In *Woods* v. *W.M. Car Services Ltd.*[99a] Watkins L.J. thought that persistent refusal to accommodate the reasonable requests of an employer for change of terms might itself be unreasonable. It seems, however, that he was thinking of unreasonableness in the sense of rendering dismissal fair rather than as constituting a breach of contract. Cronin and Grime[1] suggest that a servant hired generally is subject to orders to do any work at all. It is not denied that such an obligation is possible, but it is suggested that in practice such width would have to be expressed. The implication would otherwise be that a general servant was restricted to the scope of his foreseeable skills and, at its most extensive, to the industry into which he had contracted.[2]

In almost all modern industrial conditions this must, at some time, raise the question of the extent to which restrictions imposed by an employee's trade union may provide a justification for him to refuse to obey an order of his employer. In *Bowes and Partners* v. *Press*[3] a trade union had given employers notice that its members would refuse to descend the mine in the same cage as that occupied by non-unionists. On the day the notice expired a non-union employee entered the cage and the union members refused to go down with him. The manager declined to send the cage down a second time to take them to work. The same thing happened on three successive days. The court held that the employer was entitled to substantial damages for the refusal of the unionists to go to work, and that he was not obliged to seek to mitigate that damage by allowing them to go to work on their own terms when they were ready to do so. The principle that the master was not bound to take steps that he ordinarily would not be expected to take is, no doubt, sound.

The significance of such distinctions as these is, of course, much diminished

---

[97] (1959) 109 L.J. 526; Wedderburn, *Cases and Materials*, p. 89.
[98] See *Secretary of State for Employment* v. *ASLEF* [1972] 2 Q.B. 443.
[99] (1862) 11 C.B. (N.S.) 508. The facts of *Edwards* v. *Society of Graphical and Allied Trades* [1971] Ch. 354 reveal a similar demarcation refusal. See also *Royle* v. *Dredging and Construction Co. Ltd.* [1966] I.T.R. 233.
[99a] [1982] I.R.L.R. 413.
[1] *Labour Law*, pp. 54–55.
[2] See *Stannard, Gent, Halsey and Field* v. *Dexion Ltd.* [1966] I.T.R. 274. See also *Hadden Ltd.* v. *Cowen* [1982] I.R.L.R. 315.
[3] [1894] 1 Q.B. 202.

now that most dismissal cases are dealt with on the basis of what is fair. It is most unlikely that a tribunal would hold fair a dismissal on such facts.[4]

The practical scope of this decision is further diminished today by the fact that now an employer would not be regarded as entitled strictly to regulate every aspect of the conduct of his employees upon his premises, unless special circumstances, such as the requirements of security, dictated the need to do so. If it is supposed that the employer in *Bowes'* case would normally have raised and lowered the cage several times to take all the men to work, their motive for deciding to descend in one cage rather than another would be no concern of his. There would be no implication that he could order them to choose one cage rather than another. There is no reason why restrictive practices, dictated by a trade union, should not impliedly be accepted by an employer so as to become part of the contract of employment, upon which the employed union member, at least, could rely.

The employer's orders may relate to the place at which the job is to be done so that it is necessary, often on flimsy evidence, to decide what geographical scope the parties contemplated. In *Bouzourou* v. *Ottoman Bank*[5] a Christian employee was held bound to obey an order to work at a branch of the bank situated in Asia Minor, despite the hostility of the Turkish authorities to Christians. In *Ottoman Bank* v. *Chakarian*,[6] however, an Armenian, who had escaped while under sentence of death imposed by the Turks, and had subsequently been recognised by the Turkish authorities, was held not obliged to remain at work in Istanbul. It is sometimes said that the difference between the decisions is that between a general danger and a specific personal risk. It is more likely that at some point a risk of either type becomes of such a high degree that to take it can no longer be considered to be part of the contract of service. The position of this point will, of course, depend on the nature of the work contemplated by the contract. A professional espionage agent, a film stunt man, or Lord Bramwell's famous example of the lion-tamer, all contract high personal risks which it would be a breach of contract for them to reject.

An employee may be required to move from place to place so far as such movement can be said to be contemplated by his contract. When this contemplation is a matter of implication the outcome will depend to some extent on the reasonableness of the inclusion of such a requirement. In *O'Brien* v. *Associated Fire Alarms Ltd.*[7] the Court of Appeal held that men whose homes were in Liverpool, and who had been hired in Liverpool, could impliedly be under an obligation to work anywhere in the Liverpool area, but not beyond it, and certainly not in Barrow-in-Furness. In a number of industries collective agreements either provide for transferability or permit the payment of wages for travelling time, disturbance allowance and the like, so that transferability may be implied.[8] By implication from collective agreements into the individual contract a requirement of mobility will arise, although greater care may have to

---

[4] In *Morrish* v. *Henlys (Folkestone) Ltd.* [1973] 2 All E.R. 137, an employee was held to have been unfairly dismissed when the reason was his refusal to accede to a request to falsify his record of amounts of petrol used in order to cover a discrepancy in the quantities used from the pumps.

[5] [1930] A.C. 271.

[6] [1930] A.C. 277.

[7] [1968] 1 W.L.R. 1916. Compare *Managers (Holborn) Ltd.* v. *Hohne* [1977] I.R.L.R. 230.

[8] *Stevenson* v. *Teesside Bridge and Engineering Ltd.* [1971] 1 All E.R. 296.

be taken in such mobility situations in deducing exactly how wide such movement is intended to be.[9]

There is no reason why an employer with a right to give an order must be taken to have done so. He may be considered to have waived his right to give an order by making a request instead. In such a case refusal to comply with the request would not amount to a breach of the contract.[10]

(h) Exercise of reasonable care

The duty of reasonable care is generally thought of as lying within the law of tort and, so far as it concerns the employer's duty towards his employee, is always treated as such. There is no doubt, however, that a comparable—almost identical—contractual duty does exist.[11] The reason for choosing to proceed in tort is apparently explicable on the ground that the basis for the assessment of damages may be more beneficial[12] and that there may be procedural advantages in such matters as greater ease in securing the production of documents. It is surprising, therefore, to find that, though a question of the servant's breach of a duty of care to his master could be pursued in tort, such actions are normally founded on contract.

That an action against an employer in contract might have substantial advantages was, however, indicated by O'Connor J. in *Wright* v. *Dunlop Rubber Co. Ltd.*[13] The learned judge, having held that the employers had not created the danger and were under no duty in tort to protect an employee from dangers created by third parties, held that discharge of the duty imposed by the contract of employment did require that, at a certain stage, the employers should take reasonable steps to take note of warnings they had received of the dangerous qualities of the materials used.

The servant's duty apparently arises from his warranty of competence to do the job for which he is engaged. Such a warranty would usually be implied and might be limited if the servant disclosed his incompetence in certain respects. In *Harmer* v. *Cornelius* Willes J. said[14]:

> "It may be, that, if there is no general and no particular representation of ability and skill, the workman undertakes no responsibility. If a gentleman, for example, should employ a man who is known to have never done anything but sweep a crossing, to clean or mend his watch, the employer probably would be held to have incurred all risks himself."

---

[9] See *McCaffrey* v. *E. E. Jeavons & Co. Ltd.* [1967] I.T.R. 636, where, it is submitted, the Divisional Court was wrong to assume that the collective agreements in the construction industry permitted movement anywhere in the United Kingdom. In *Sutcliffe* v. *Hawker Siddeley Aviation Ltd.* [1973] I.C.R. 560, however, the contract quite clearly required such mobility.

[10] *John Laing & Son Ltd.* v. *Best* [1968] I.T.R. 3. The matter is significant in industrial disputes when an action based on inducement of breach of contract will not arise if, in the light of union opposition, the employer does not give the critical order.

[11] *Smith* v. *Charles Baker & Sons* [1891] A.C. 325. The contractual duty is similarly limited to the taking of reasonable care: *Walker* v. *British Guarantee Association* (1852) 18 Q.B. 277.

[12] See *Koufos* v. *C. Czarnikow Ltd.* [1969] 1 A.C. 350.

[13] (1972) 11 K.I.R. 311, *affirmed* (1973) 13 K.I.R. 255 (C.A.); and see *Keys* v. *Shoefayre Ltd.* [1978] I.R.L.R. 467.

[14] (1858) 5 C.B. (N.S.) 236 at p. 246.

In modern circumstances it is probable that there will be no such warranty where the employee's job is altered during employment. Either the employee will merely undertake to attempt the task, or the employer, having retrained the man, will act on the faith of his observations and there will be no room to say that the employee warrants a competence which the employer already accepts.

The servant's duty of care arises from his contractual duty of service, whilst that of the master arises from his control of the situation. Different methods of enforcement may be natural. Though this may be so the results of the difference are in some cases surprising. In general the law of tort imposes no duty to refrain from causing pecuniary loss whilst it is plain that a servant is liable for such loss in a contractual claim for an indemnity.[15]

In *Lister's* case the argument was advanced that whilst a servant might warrant that he possessed a particular skill he did not warrant that he would use it. As Viscount Simonds tersely asked: "Of what advantage to the employer is his servant's undertaking that he possesses skill unless he undertakes also to use it?" It is clear, as his Lordship observed, that "possess" and "exercise" are conjoint forms of expressing the same obligation. There may be a question, however, as to the extent of the care that the servant has undertaken to show, since it is usually correct to say that he does not warrant to display care in activities outside the scope of his employment.[16]

The duty of the servant extends to taking reasonable care of his master's property if it is entrusted to him. In *Superlux* v. *Plaisted*[17] the defendant had been in charge of a team of vacuum-cleaner salesmen and he negligently allowed 14 of the cleaners to be stolen from his van. Willmer J. said: " . . . Mr. Plaisted was in a responsible position and owed a duty to exercise reasonable care to safeguard the equipment left in his charge and to guard against the possibility of theft."[18]

On the other hand, in *Deyong* v. *Shenburn*[19] an employer was held not to be liable for the loss of goods belonging to an employee stolen from a dressing-room; du Parcq L.J. pointed out that there had been no bailment.

(i) Accounting

An employee is under a duty to account to his employer for all money and property received in the course of his employment. It is typical of the un-

---

15 *Lister* v. *Romford Ice and Cold Storage Co. Ltd.* [1957] A.C. 555. This was relied upon by the Court of Appeal in *Janata Bank* v. *Ahmed* [1981] I.R.L.R. 457.

16 It was on this point that McNair J. distinguished *Lister's* case in *Harvey* v. *R. G. O'Dell Ltd.* [1958] 2 Q.B. 78—storekeeper asked to transport worker to a job on the storekeeper's motor-bicycle—Atiyah, *op. cit.*, criticises this decision on the ground that it would not be unreasonable to ask a storekeeper to drive a car and to expect him to do it with care. This, it is submitted, misses the point of the nature of his duty. The storekeeper does not warrant that he can drive a car at all and so no action founded upon a contractual undertaking can arise, however reasonable it might have been if that undertaking had been given. The master can claim a contribution from the storekeeper if the act is done negligently since they are then joint tortfeasors. This contribution might be 100 per cent. so as to produce the same result as contractual indemnity. See also *Semtex* v. *Gladstone* [1954] 1 W.L.R. 945.

17 [1958] C.L.Y. 195; *The Times*, December 12, 1958.

18 It is suggested that it should not be assumed from this that it is for the servant to prove that he did use reasonable care.

19 [1946] 1 K.B. 227; *Edwards* v. *West Herts Group Hospital Management Committee* [1957] 1 W.L.R. 415.

certainty of detail that surrounds a number of these implied obligations that this particular duty is explained sometimes in term of agency[20] and sometimes as if the employee were a constructive trustee, having made a secret profit. In the leading case of *Boston Deep-Sea Fishing and Ice Co.* v. *Ansell*[21] Bowen L.J. necessarily linked it to the duty of fidelity, and the whole Court of Appeal thought that it was necessary, in order to justify the dismissal of the director for breach of the duty, that a loss of confidence should be shown in addition to the fact of retention of a secret profit. In that case the defendant had been the managing director of the plaintiff company. He was also a shareholder in a company which supplied ice to the plaintiffs and he received a bonus on his shares in respect of such supplies, the orders for which he placed. He also received commission in respect of other contracts which he placed on behalf of the plaintiff company with other companies. His dismissal was held to be justified.

It is doubtful how far this principle should extend where there is no fiduciary relationship. In *Reading* v. *Att.-Gen.*,[22] the plaintiff, whilst serving as a sergeant with the British Army in Egypt, was approached by certain persons who asked him to accompany lorries engaged in smuggling goods through military check-points and, by wearing his uniform, to imply that they had authority to pass unsearched. He received substantial sums of money for this, but was eventually detected by reason of his manner of living on the proceeds. The Crown took possession of the money in his bank accounts and he brought an unsuccessful action to reclaim it. The House of Lords approved the formulation of the duty by Denning J. at first instance. He had explained that to constitute a breach of contract the real source of the profit must be the assets the employee, as such, controls, the facilities he enjoys, or the position he occupies, and that the duty to account will not apply if these merely provide an opportunity to profit, as distinct from playing a prominent part in the production of the profit. Denning J. had regarded the case as not disclosing a fiduciary relationship but Asquith L.J. had been prepared to find that such a fiduciary position arises when a servant acquires from his employment a position of authority enabling him to gain a benefit. The employer can confiscate this benefit because of the fiduciary position.

It may be that if the profit made by the employee produces further profit he must account for the total. The authority of *Lister & Co.* v. *Stubbs*,[23] is to the contrary. It was there held by the Court of Appeal that a profit made upon a profit arising from a bribe was not recoverable. Since this was a decision of Lindley, Cotton and Bowen L.JJ. it must be treated with great respect. The decision over-emphasises the aspect of a personal action over that of a tracing action *in rem*. The decision is frequently justified on the basis of a supposed distinction between a bribe and other forms of profit. It is suggested that such a distinction is not only unjustifiable but unworkable and that, with the development of the principle of unjust enrichment, *Lister* v. *Stubbs* would not be followed.

---

[20] See, *e.g. Bentley* v. *Craven* (1853) 18 Beav. 75.
[21] (1888) 39 Ch.D. 339.
[22] [1951] A.C. 507.
[23] (1890) 45 Ch.D. 1.

(j) Indemnification

Either party to the contract of employment is under a duty to indemnify the other for loss or expense occasioned in the course of employment.[24] "Course of employment" in this context is construed strictly and not in the manner adopted for determination of the existence of vicarious liability.[25] An employer who has been held to be vicariously liable for the tort of his servant may not always be able to claim an indemnity. A similar strictness in the case of the duty of the employer to indemnify produces the proposition that there is no such duty where employer and employee are joint tortfeasors.[26] It seems to be correct to say that the duty to indemnify extends to the consequences of all torts and is not simply another way of saying that the parties owe each other a duty of care.[27]

The *Lister* case has raised the problem of the survival of the duty of an employee to indemnify his employer in the light of the common practice of insurance against loss and damage caused by employees. In some situations the employee himself may be able to claim the benefit of the insurance, particularly in the case of road traffic insurance, where anyone driving the vehicle with the consent of the owner may be covered.[28]

In *Gregory* v. *Ford*[29] a court of first instance held that since an employer impliedly warranted not to require an employee to perform an unlawful act, it was an implied undertaking in the contract that a policy of insurance, required by law, would be taken out. It could, accordingly, be said that the employer had undertaken to insure himself and not to claim an indemnity.[30] In the *Lister* case Denning L.J. had contended that wherever insurance could reasonably be expected to exist there should be implied a term that the employer would insure, and bear the liability without seeking an indemnity. The majority of the House of Lords (Lords Radcliffe and Somervell dissenting) held that business efficacy, which is not always a reliable test of implication in the case of a contract of employment, did not require such implication.

A committee was set up to deal with the implications of the *Lister* case. As an outcome of its report[31] all the members of the British Insurance Association entered into a more precise agreement than had hitherto existed to the effect that they would not enforce their rights of subrogation in an employer's liability policy, except where there was evidence of collusion or wilful misconduct on the part of the employee. A number of other insurance organisations also entered into a similar agreement. As a result employers are not likely, in ordinary circumstances, to be forced by their insurers to bring an action to enforce their rights to an indemnity.

---

[24] *Lister* v. *Romford Ice and Cold Storage Co. Ltd.* [1957] A.C. 555.

[25] *Harvey* v. *R. G. O'Dell Ltd.* [1958] 2 Q.B. 78.

[26] *Jones* v. *Manchester Corporation* [1952] 2 Q.B. 852.

[27] Atiyah, *Vicarious Liability*, pp. 422 *et seq.*; Batt, *Master and Servant* (5th ed.), pp. 210 and 227. Does the duty extend to the economic torts?

[28] Such a right did not exist in the *Lister* case because, although the employee was a lorry driver, the accident took place on a private road and liability was met by the employer's general insurers.

[29] [1951] 1 All E.R. 121.

[30] The employee does not now commit an offence if he drives his employer's vehicle without knowledge that it is not insured.

[31] See (1959) 22 M.L.R. 652.

CHAPTER 3

INDIVIDUAL STATUTORY RIGHTS AFFECTING THE COURSE OF EMPLOYMENT

THE Employment Protection (Consolidation) Act 1978 contains a number of statutory employment rights additional to those which may be derived from the individual contract. In the case of some of these, and most particularly those involving maternity rights, the right to guarantee payments and the right to time off work, it might well be thought that the best vehicle for ensuring that the employee possessed these benefits was the voluntary collective agreement. There is no doubt that most of these benefits can be dealt with by the normal process of collective bargaining and that, in many cases, they are so dealt with. It may be asked, therefore, why a trade union movement which has always pursued a policy of independence from legislative assistance (as distinct from legislative protection) should seek such legislation as this. Superficially it might be seen as a gift to all employees whether organised or not of the hard-won benefits of collective bargaining. In seeking to answer these objections, it must be borne in mind that this is not the first legislation to which they apply. The Redundancy Payments Act 1965 had obvious similarities.[1] In that case it may well be that the trade union movement had little option but to accept such legislation. The social and economic problems of mass dismissal were becoming very noticeable. Voluntary collective bargaining had, overall, made relatively little provision for redundancy payments. Although the Redundancy Payments Act 1965 was followed by a very considerable upsurge of voluntary redundancy agreements, it appears in retrospect that had it not been for this legislation major injustice would have occurred to large numbers of redundant employees. No similar point can be made concerning the Employment Protection Act 1975. There are, however, a large number of reasons why the fears inherent in the objections raised above are not likely to mature. Although there is considerable evidence from other countries that legislative gifts of this nature tend to be followed by legislative restrictions upon trade union activities, there is no particular reason why the two should be connected. Nor does it seem likely that the 1978 Act will in any way detract from the field available for voluntary collective bargaining. Rather, the reverse may happen. Although large numbers of collective agreements already provide for guarantee payments the same is not true of such benefits as are provided in the case of maternity. The legislative provisions are likely, therefore, to have the double effect of inspiring the development of collective agreements either in areas where such matters are already dealt with, to improve upon the statutory minima, or, alternatively, to perform the same function of bettering the statutory provisions even where there have been no collectively agreed arrangements previously. It is just possible that a different type of collective agreement may emerge from this process of building upon legislative provisions. It seems likely that if one is contemplating, as it were, amending a piece of legislation the language used in

---

[1] The provisions of this Act are re-enacted in the Consolidation Act of 1978.

the collective agreement would tend to become very much more precise than it has been in the past.

The following are the principal statutory protective rights available to the employee:

(a) The right to guarantee pay for periods of absence of work whilst employed;
(b) The right to maternity pay and maternity leave;
(c) The right to paid and unpaid time off work;
(d) The right in certain circumstances to complain of action short of dismissal;
(e) Certain rights upon the insolvency of an employer;
(f) Entitlement to compensation upon dismissal for redundancy;
(g) The right to claim in respect of unfair dismissal.

The last two merit consideration in separate chapters. In all cases the rights are only available upon the establishment of certain qualifications which, to save deviation from consideration of the content of the employment relationship, are considered in an appendix to this chapter.

GUARANTEE PAYMENTS

The Act confers a right to a guarantee payment upon any employee with at least one month's employment ending the day before that in respect of which the payment is claimed,[2] who, throughout a day during any part of which he would normally be required to work in accordance with his contract of employment, is not provided with work for one of two wide-ranging reasons.[3] The first of these is that there has been a diminution in the requirements of the employer's business for work of the kind which the employee is employed to do. The similarity between this provision and the definition of "redundancy" will be apparent. The 1978 Act is in effect providing a benefit for a temporary redundancy. On the other hand it must be carefully noted that the Act refers to an absence of requirement for work and not, as in the redundancy provisions to an absence of requirement for employees to do the work. The second reason is defined as "any other occurrence affecting the normal working of the employer's business in relation to work of the kind which the employee is employed to do."[4] There has been little litigation upon the meaning of this provision but in one case[5] an industrial tribunal had to consider a situation in which the employer had posted a notice setting out the annual holidays to which his employees were entitled. On this notice May 23 and 24 were set out as "unpaid holidays." These two days were Jewish holidays which those who held a controlling interest in the company strictly observed. The industrial tribunal held that the two were days on which the applicant employees would normally work since there was nothing in the contract of employment to exclude them. In the view of the tribunal, however, there was no entitlement to guarantee

---

[2] s.143(1). As amended by the Employment Act 1982, Sched. 2. Special provision is made for short term contracts.
[3] s.12. See industrial tribunal decision in York v. College Hosiery Co. Ltd. [1978] I.R.L.R. 53.
[4] s.12(2)(b).
[5] North v. Pavleigh Ltd. [1977] I.R.L.R. 461.

payments under the Act since there was no suggestion of any diminution in the requirements of the business nor absence of work because of an "occurrence" affecting the normal working of the business. Although this reveals the possibility of gaps in even so general a definition as that contained in the section, some issue may be taken with the decision. If the employer had decided to close his factory permanently there would inevitably have been a redundancy. In other words, the requirement for employees would have ceased or diminished just because he himself no longer required them. There is no reason why exactly the same view should not be taken of a temporary diminution in requirements for work at the whim of an employer.

This benefit, which is available to all employees except dock workers,[6] share fishermen,[7] those employed outside Great Britain[8] and those employed by a husband or wife[9] is not available if the workless day occurs in consequence of a strike, lock-out or other industrial action involving any employee of his employer or of an associated employer.[10] The employer has also, as it were, a defence to a claim in two provisions of section 13. The employee is not entitled to a guarantee payment in respect of a workless day if his employer has offered to provide alternative work for that day which is suitable in all the circumstances, whether or not it is work which the employee is under his contract employed to perform, and the employee has unreasonably refused that offer. This is parallel to the defence originally provided by the Redundancy Payments Act 1965. It is suggested that some care should be taken, however, in applying decisions under the earlier Act. It would seem quite likely that industrial tribunals would be inclined to hold that during a period of purely temporary redundancy the employee might be expected to be rather more accommodating in his readiness to take alternative work than would be the case where the performance of that alternative work would continue indefinitely. It has been held[11] that an offer of work upon a different day does not constitute an offer of alternative work within this provision.

The second situation provided for is one where the employee does not comply with reasonable requirements imposed by his employer with a view to ensuring that his services are available. There seems no reason to suppose that this provision was intended only to apply to requirements within the employee's contract of employment, although it is not clear whether such a contractual requirement should be regarded automatically as reasonable. In another industrial tribunal case[12] the claim arose out of the failure of the heating system at the place of employment because the oil to operate it had run out. The employer had arranged for oil to arrive by 9.30 a.m. He was notified of a slight delay which was likely to mean that the oil would not arrive until 9.45 a.m. Employees were asked to wait in the canteen where they were supplied with

---

[6] s.145.
[7] s.144(2).
[8] s.141(2).
[9] s.146(1).
[10] s.3(1). In *Thompson* v. *Priest (Lindley) Ltd.* [1978] I.R.L.R. 99 an industrial tribunal held that a trade dispute need not be the sole factor. Since then "trade dispute" has been replaced by the words "strike, lock-out or other industrial action," Employment Act 1982, Sched. 3, para. 14.
[11] *North* v. *Pavleigh Ltd., supra.*
[12] *Meadows* v. *Faithfull Overalls Ltd.* [1977] I.R.L.R. 330.

tea. They voted to go home when the oil did not arrive at the expected time. In fact the oil arrived just after 10 a.m. The industrial tribunal held that the employees had failed to comply with a reasonable requirement within what is now section 13(2)(*b*). It pointed out that they had been supplied with information about the delay and that it had been made clear that there would be no pay if the workforce went home.

In each period of 13 consecutive weeks the employee is entitled to a maximum of five days of guaranteed payment.[13] If the employee normally works less than five days in a week under his contract of employment then he will only be entitled to payment for that lesser number of days.[14] This reduction, however, does not apply in any case where an employee's contract has been varied or a new contract has been entered into in connection with a period of short-time working. In such a case the number of days of payment will be governed by the original contract.[15] It remains to be seen how industrial tribunals interpret this provision. At face value, it would appear not to refer to a situation where there is a standing contract which provides for a reduction in the working week in certain circumstances. In such a case it would seem possible to hold that the situation before the reduction took effect constituted the normal contractual requirement and the reduced week an abnormal situation. This would, of course, have the effect of entitling the employee to rely upon the pre-reduction situation to govern his entitlement. It is suggested, however, that difficulties might occur in applying this view if the reduction had continued over a considerable period of time. The position was considered by an industrial tribunal in *Trevethan* v. *Stirling Metals Ltd.*[16] A regular night shift worker worked four shifts between 8 p.m. and 6.30 a.m. Day shift workers worked five eight-hour shifts per week. The night shift worker was laid off on four isolated days and paid the statutory maximum guarantee payment of £6.60 per day. On the fifth day of lay-off he was refused a statutory payment on the ground that he had used his statutory entitlement for that quarter. An industrial tribunal held that his entitlement was limited to four days. This decision is obviously correct because the statute provides[17] that where a period of employment straddles midnight then only the day in which the major part of that employment occurs shall be counted as a day of employment.

Some support for the proposition that a permanent alteration does not fall within the provisions of section 15(4) is obtained from the industrial tribunal decision in *Daley* v. *Strathclyde Regional Council.*[18] In that case, night shift cleaners had been employed on five eight-hour shifts a week. As an alternative to redundancy this was reduced to one week of five eight-hour shifts and one week of four eight-hour shifts, alternating. One trade union did not agree to this and its members claimed guarantee payments for the alternate Fridays. The industrial tribunal held that the agreement meant that those days were days on which they were not normally required to work. The change was a permanent one, and therefore did not, presumably, fall within the meaning of a section

---

[13] s.15(3), as amended by Employment Act 1980, s.11.
[14] As to what amounts to normal work, see *Miller* v. *Harry Thornton* (*Lollies*) *Ltd.* [1978] I.R.L.R. 430 (I.T.).
[15] s.15(4).
[16] [1977] I.R.L.R. 416.
[17] s.12(2).
[18] [1977] I.R.L.R. 414.

which refers to an alteration "in connection with a period of short-time working."[19] In both cases the tribunal's decision that the new arrangement had been accepted appears to be open to question but this matter is discussed elsewhere.

From the amount of the statutory entitlement there is to be deducted any contractual remuneration paid to the employee in respect of a workless day.[20] This obviously excludes such payments as a trade union might make for unemployment since they would not be remuneration. The statute indicates[21] that contractual remuneration is, in fact, only intended to cover remuneration derived from the claimant's contract of employment. It is unlikely that this would cover such things as sick pay for a day when the employee's colleagues were laid off and he would have been laid off but for the fact that he was already off work, sick. The most likely source of deduction of contractual remuneration, therefore, will be that which derives from a contractual undertaking by the employer himself to pay some form of guaranteed wage during the period of lay-off. This in turn is, of course, likely to derive from a collective agreement. It follows from this that the provision in section 18, whereby an exemption order can be obtained in respect of collectively agreed guarantee provisions, is of little value since the collectively agreed amount will be deducted from the statutory amount in any event. There would, however, be some advantage in obtaining an exemption order if, for instance, the collective agreement provided for six weeks of guarantee pay during a year. If it so happened that six weeks of lay-off occurred during a single quarter, then only five days of statutory guarantee would be eliminated by that agreement, and the statutory guarantee could be claimed for the remaining three quarters of the year. The effect of an exemption order, however, would be to eliminate all statutory payment.

A complaint may be presented to an industrial tribunal, normally within three months of any day on which a guarantee payment is alleged to be due, that the employer has failed to pay the whole or part of the payment. If the tribunal finds the claim well founded it must order the employer to pay the amount due.[22]

MATERNITY RIGHTS

An employee with not less than two years' continuous employment[23] who is absent from work wholly or partly because of pregnancy or confinement is entitled, under Part III of the Act, to maternity payment and to return to work.[24] These rights only arise if she continues to be employed (whether or not she actually is at work) until immediately before the beginning of the eleventh week before the expected week of confinement.[25]

The further conditions for a valid claim for the two maternity benefits for which the statute provides are that the employee should inform her employer,

---

[19] See also Clemens v. Peter Richards Ltd. [1977] I.R.L.R. 332.

[20] s.16(2).

[21] s.16(1).

[22] s.17.

[23] s.33(3)(b).

[24] s.33(1).

[25] s.33(3)(b). This means no more than being under a contract of employment; Satchwell Sunvic Ltd. v. Secretary of State for Employment [1979] I.R.L.R. 455; Secretary of State for Employment v. Doulton Sanitaryware [1981] I.C.R. 477.

in writing, at least 21 days before her absence begins or, if this is not reasonably practicable, as soon as is reasonably practicable, that she will be, or is, absent from work wholly or partly because of pregnancy or confinement and, in the case of the right to return to work, that she intends to return to work with her employer.[26] This information is not in itself to be construed as a resignation by the employee.[26a] In addition, she must, if requested by her employer to do so, produce for his inspection a certificate from a registered medical practitioner or a certified midwife indicating the expected week of her confinement.[27] An employee who terminates her own employment or who is dismissed before the beginning of the eleventh week before the expected week of confinement will normally lose her claim under these provisions unless the dismissal is for a reason falling within section 60.[28]

Maternity payment

The first of the two statutory maternity entitlements is to pay for a period not exceeding in aggregate six weeks during which the employee is absent from work wholly or partly because of pregnancy or confinement.[29] The employee is not entitled to maternity pay before the beginning of the eleventh week before the expected week of confinement and the six-week period of payment is to be the first six weeks of absence after the beginning of that eleventh week.[30] In *Inner London Education Authority* v. *Nash*[30a] a majority of the E.A.T., the legal chairman dissenting, held that the statute impliedly confers on the employee a right to decide when to commence leave which no contractual provision can override. The amount of the maternity pay is nine-tenths of a week's pay reduced by the amount of maternity allowance payable for the week under Part 1 of Schedule 4 to the Social Security Act 1975, whether or not the employee is in fact entitled to the whole or any part of such an allowance.[31] Any contractual remuneration paid to the employee in respect of a day within the payment period can be set off against the statutory entitlement.[32] Provided the employee is entitled to the payment the entire amount of this maternity payment is refunded to the employer[33] from a Maternity Pay Fund[34] which is itself funded by an increase in the employer contribution under the Social Security Act 1975 payable in respect of all employees, male and female.[35] Complaint may be made to an industrial tribunal, normally within three months of the last day of the payment period, that an employer has failed to pay the whole or any part of the amount due.[36]

---

[26] s.33(3)(*c*). As to what is reasonably practicable see *Nu-Swift International Ltd.* v. *Mallison* [1978] I.C.R. 157.
[26a] *Hughes* v. *Gwynedd Area Health Authority* [1978] I.C.R. 161.
[27] s.33(5).
[28] See *infra.*
[29] s.34(1).
[30] s.34(2).
[30a] [1979] I.C.R. 229
[31] s.35(1). If the employee has two employments the whole of the maternity allowance may be deducted from each in turn. *Cullen* v. *Creasey Hotels (Limburg) Ltd.* [1980] I.C.R. 236.
[32] s.35(4).
[33] s.39(1).
[34] s.37; Employment Protection Act 1975, s.39.
[35] s.40(3).
[36] s.36.

Right to return

The second of the statutory maternity rights is the right for the employee to return to work at the conclusion of the statutorily permitted period of absence. Section 45(1) provides that the employee has a right to return to work with her original employer or his successor at any time before the end of the period of 29 weeks, beginning with the week in which the date of confinement falls, in the job in which she was employed under the original contract of employment, and on terms and conditions not less favourable than those which would have been applicable to her if she had not been so absent. If the employee also had a contractual right to return she may take advantage of whichever of the statutory or contractual right is in any particular respect the more favourable. The E.A.T. held, however, in *Bovey* v. *Board of Governors of the Hospital for Sick Children*[37] that this did not mean that statutory and contractual rights could be intermingled in any favourable permutation. Nevertheless, this provision has an effect not anticipated by the legislation in 1978, accustomed as it was to the concept of statutory provisions steadily improving the rights of the employee. Many employees will now possess contractual statements of terms and conditions of employment indicating that their maternity rights are as stated in either the 1975 and 1978 Acts. Employees who reject any attempt to reissue these statements amending the reference to the Employment Act 1980 will be entitled to rely on the contractually entrenched and more beneficial provisions of the earlier legislation.

It is suggested that it may be assumed that the use of the word "original" means that the employee who has accepted a suitable alternative offer of employment—made in a situation where she cannot adequately continue to perform her original work or such continuous performance would be a breach of a statutory obligation (see 1978 Act, s.60)—is entitled to return to the job she had before the acceptance of such an alternative. The Act states specifically that "terms and conditions not less favourable than those which would have been applicable to her if she had not been so absent" means, as regards seniority, pension rights and other similar rights, that the period or periods of employment prior to the employee's absence shall be regarded as continuous with her employment following that absence.[38] In fact, there is rather more to be said on the subject than this. It is provided that for purposes of calculating continuity for statutory entitlement such as redundancy payment and entitlement to claim unfair dismissal, the period of absence for maternity reasons shall count as a period of continuous employment provided that the employee returns in accordance with the statutory right contained in section 45(1). So we may say that for many statutory entitlements the period before the absence, the period of the absence and the period following return to work all count towards the entitlement. For the purpose of many purely contractual rights section 45(2) ensures that rights similar to seniority and pension rights shall continue where the employee left them when she left work because of her impending maternity. There is of course no reason why the period of absence should not also be included if the contracting parties agree. In the case of all rights other than those specifically mentioned the effect of section 45(1) is to entitle the employee to

---

[37] [1978] I.C.R. 934.
[38] s.45(2).

their continuing accrual throughout the period of absence. It is not at all clear that these statutory provisions are necessary in most cases. In most cases, it will be unlikely (or at least unwise) for the employer to attempt to terminate the contract of employment. If the employee does not do so either before or after the eleventh week preceding the expected week of confinement, then the contract subsists throughout. It would follow that employment is continuous not only for statutory purposes, but also at common law.[38a] Unless the working of the contract made it clear that rights only accrued while the employee was at work, as distinct from being in employment, all other rights would continue to accrue throughout the absence period. It seems possible, for instance, that an employee absent for maternity reasons but possessing a subsisting contract of employment might in certain circumstances be able to argue that the wording of her contract entitled her, for instance, to sickness benefit during that period should she fall ill for some reason not connected with her pregnancy.

Exclusions

The basic right to return to her original employment is now subject to four significant limitations[38b]:

(i) An employer of five employees or less (the Act does not indicate whether this is to include part-time employees) is relieved of the obligation wherever he can show that it is not reasonably practicable to reinstate the absent employee, whatever the reason and whether or not he has, or offers, suitable alternative employment.

(ii) An employer of more than five employees who can show that it is not reasonably practicable *by reason of redundancy* to reinstate the employee is relieved of the obligation either if there is no suitable available vacancy in his own employment or that of any associated employer or successor or, if there is such suitable alternative, one such vacancy is offered and unreasonably rejected.

(iii) An employer of more than five employees who can show that it is not reasonably practicable, for a reason other than redundancy, to reinstate the employee is relieved of the obligation provided that he does offer a suitable alternative which is unreasonably rejected.

(iv) All employers are relieved of the obligation to reinstate if the employee fails, within 14 days of receipt of their intermediate enquiry referred to below, to indicate her continuing intention to return.

A suitable alternative is one in which the work to be done under the new contract is of a kind which is both suitable in relation to the employee and appropriate for her to do in the circumstances and the terms and conditions are not less favourable to her than if she had returned under her original contract.[39] Because the absence of a suitable alternative under (ii) above means that the employer needs to make no offer at all it is probably the employer in these circumstances who will be seeking to show that alternatives are unsuitable,

---

[38a] But see *Lavery* v. *Plessey Telecommunications Ltd.* [1982] I.R.L.R. 180; *Kolfor Plant Ltd.* v. *Wright* [1982] I.R.L.R. 311.

[38b] Employment Protection (Consolidation) Act 1978, s.45(4) as amended by the Employment Act 1980, s.12.

[39] Employment Protection (Consolidation) Act 1978, s.45(4).

whereas under (iii) it will be the employee seeking her original job or compensation who will wish to justify rejection of an offer on the ground that it is not suitable.

It is provided[40] that in a redundancy situation under (ii) above failure to offer a suitable alternative that is available will operate as an unfair dismissal. In fact this provision only brings the redundancy situation in line with all other failures to comply with the unrelieved obligation to reinstate. All count as a dismissal and apparently, therefore complaint has to be made of unfair dismissal. This enables the tribunal to limit the right of return both by the statutory preconditions and by the fact that reasonable grounds for refusal to re-employ may be pleaded.[41] It seems to follow that despite the rather complicated provisions just discussed an employer who simply refuses to reinstate will only have to show that it was reasonable for him so to do. Suppose for instance that during the absence of a part-time employee who has qualified to exercise maternity rights the (large) employer decides to upgrade her job to full-time status. Suppose further that she is unwilling herself to undertake the full-time work. She is not redundant and the employer is, therefore, under an obligation to offer her suitable alternative employment or to reinstate her. If he does neither he faces a claim for unfair dismissal but only has to show that his decision to upgrade the job was a reasonable one and that he behaved reasonably in offering the job to her. If he has no alternative to offer he is relieved of all other liability. This appears to make nonsense of the careful provisions of the Act. The obvious solution is to hold that the statute confers an absolute right refusal of which leads to automatic unfairness. Unfortunately for this argument the Act could easily have so provided but it does not do so. The employee seems to have the worst of both worlds because it has been held[41a] that a failure to satisfy the statutory conditions for an entitlement to return to work disentitles the employee to any remedy for unfair dismissal, notwithstanding that the contract subsists until the employer terminates it by his refusal to reinstate.

At any time later than 49 days from the expected date of confinement the employer may make an intermediate enquiry in writing of the employee as to whether she still intends to return to work. The enquiry must notify her that if she does not indicate such continuing intention within 14 days she will forfeit her right to return.[41b] The employee must exercise her right to return to work by written notification to her original employer or, if appropriate, his successor, at least 21 days before the date on which she proposes to return.[42] The employer may postpone such a return for not more than four weeks from that notified day of return provided that he informs the employee before that notified day of return and furnishes her with specified reasons for the postponement.[43]

The employee may extend the permitted period of 29 weeks' absence from the week of confinement, once, for a maxiumum of four weeks upon production of a certificate from a registered medical practitioner stating that by reason

---

[40] *Ibid.* Sched. 2, para. 2(2).
[41] *Lavery* v. *Plessey Telecommunications Ltd.* [1982] I.R.L.R. 180.
[41a] *Lavery* v. *Plessey Communications Ltd.* [1982] I.R.L.R. 180; *Kolfor Plant Ltd.* v. *Wright* [1982] I.R.L.R. 311.
[41b] Employment Act 1980, s.11(2) inserting a new s.33(3A) into Employment Protection (Consolidation) Act.
[42] s.47(1).
[43] s.47(2).

of disease or bodily or mental disablement she will be incapable of work on the notified day of return or, if no such date has been notified, the expiration of the permitted period of 29 weeks.[44] Certain provisions are made to deal with circumstances such as the existence of industrial action which makes it unreasonable to expect the employee to return to work on the notified day.[45]

Dismissal during absence

It is provided[46] that if in any proceedings arising out of a failure to permit an employee to return to work the employer shows that the reason for the failure is that the employee is redundant and that the employee was in fact dismissed or, had she continued to be employed by him, would have been dismissed, by reason of redundancy at some earlier date during her absence than the notified day of return but falling after the beginning of the eleventh week before the expected week of confinement, then for the purposes of "the statutory right to a redundancy payment" the employee shall be treated as having been dismissed with effect from that earlier date. Her continuity of employment will only run to that earlier date. It will be observed that this provision clearly anticipates that an employee who has already been dismissed for redundancy may nonetheless exercise her right to seek to return to work at the completion of her absence for reasons connected with her pregnancy. The fact that she has been dismissed at some earlier date, therefore, will apparently not deprive her of the chance of a suitable available vacancy upon the expiration of her statutory permitted period of absence. It also appears that the substitution of an earlier date than the date of return cannot be made if the employee has remained in employment without dismissal until the notified day of return even if the employer can show that she could have been dismissed for redundancy at an earlier date. The substitution provision only applies, in other words, to two situations: that in which the employee has actually been dismissed at an earlier date and that in which she has for some reason not continued in employment and so could not be dismissed at the earlier date when it became apparent that she was redundant.

Surprisingly little provision is made for dismissal, for any other reason than redundancy, during the permitted period of absence. It is briefly provided[47] that any cessation of the contract of employment after the beginning of the eleventh week before the expected week of confinement will not affect the employee's right to return to work. It is also provided that, should she bring any proceeding for unfair dismissal based upon this earlier dismissal compensation will be assessed without regard to her right to return to work but, if she does exercise her right to return to work, it shall be upon the condition that she repays any compensation in respect of such dismissal if the employer so requests.[48] No provision is made, however, for a situation in which, for instance, facts are discovered during the employee's absence which justify a dismissal and she is so dismissed. She would appear to be able to exercise her right to work within the statutory provisions. It would seem from the fact that the employee's remedy is

---

[44] s.47(3).
[45] s.47(5) and (6).
[46] Sched. 2, para. 5.
[47] s.33(3).
[48] Sched. 2, para. 6(4).

for unfair dismissal that the employer would be entitled to refuse to reinstate her and to defend his refusal in any subsequent tribunal proceedings by arguing the earlier substantial reason for dismissal. This would not seem to cause a problem in respect of section 56. This section provides that where an employee who is entitled to return to work is not permitted to return to work, her rights in respect of unfair dismissal and redundancy payment shall apply as if she had been employed until the notified day of return. All this seems to mean is that an employee who has been dismissed on an earlier date would not be out of time in making a claim for unfair dismissal within three months of her notified day of return. It also seems to mean that she could not claim that any compensation should begin earlier than that notified day of return but this does not appear to be unfair since it can be shown that she would not have been at work during that period in any case.

There is a very ambiguous provision in Schedule 2,[49] the best interpretation of which seems to be that any attempt to dismiss an employee during the period after she has notified the employer of her specific intention to return to work, but before she actually does return to work, will be totally ineffective as a dismissal. Strictly read, the sub-paragraph might appear actually to deprive such an employee of her right to return to work by suggesting that the dismissal must be deemed to have occurred after her return to work, but that cannot be the correct interpretation.

Replacements

It will often be the case that an employer has had to replace an employee absent by reason of these maternity provisions. It is provided in the Act of 1978[50] that if, upon engaging such an employee, the employer informs the employee in writing that his or her employment will be terminated upon the return to work of another employee who is or will be absent wholly or partly because of pregnancy or confinement and the employer does actually dismiss the temporary replacement in order to make it possible to give work to the other employee then these facts constitute a substantial reason for dismissal within the meaning of section 57(1)(b). This does not mean that such a dismissal is necessarily fair. Given the existence of a deemed substantial reason, it will still be necessary for the employer to show that it was reasonable in all the circumstances for him to terminate the employment of the temporary replacement. This provision has lost much of its significance however by reason of the extension of the period of employment necessary to qualify to make a claim for unfair dismissal from 26 to 52 weeks.

Complaint to tribunal

An employee may complain to an industrial tribunal within three months beginning with the last day of the period of payment of maternity pay that her employer has failed to pay her the whole or any part of the maternity pay to which she is entitled.[51] Provision is made for an employee who has taken all reasonable steps other than proceedings to enforce the award of an industrial tribunal to secure her maternity payment, or for an employee whose employer

---

[49] para. 6(2).
[50] s.61.
[51] s.36.

is insolvent to claim payment from the Secretary of State.[52] The Secretary of State may seek to secure the amount so paid from the employer if satisfied that the employer's default is without reasonable excuse.[53] Section 54 makes it clear that an employee who is not permitted to return to work in accordance with the statutory rights may substantiate her claim in an ordinary proceeding for unfair dismissal. Either the failure to allow her to return will constitute a dismissal or she will have been dismissed at some earlier date. In every case where the employee has acquired a right to return to work, whether or not she has been dismissed during her absence, it is provided[54] that she is to be treated as having been continuously employed until "dismissed" on the notified day of return. The reason for the "dismissal" will be the reason for which she was denied the right to return.

PAID AND UNPAID TIME OFF WORK

Paid time off

An employer is required to permit an employee who is an official of an independent trade union recognised by the employer for bargaining purposes to take paid time off work for certain specific purposes.[55] The first of these purposes is to carry out those duties of his as such an official which are concerned with industrial relations between his employer and an associated employer, and their employees. An official is defined in the ACAS Code of Practice (Para. 4) as an employee who has been elected or appointed in accordance with the rules of the union to be a representative of all or some of the union's members in a particular company and workplace. This would appear not to apply to a person merely elected or appointed the delegate to a conference outside the workplace. If, however, a workers' representative were to wish to go to such a conference, being an official, his right to paid leave would depend on the rest of the statutory definition.

The Act does not, as it might have done, use the words "connected with." It may be thought that the words "concerned with" require a closer affinity to industrial relations. Although the heads of industrial relations are numerous, it seems reasonable to suggest from the language used in the Code of Practice that the matter in issue should fall directly within one such head rather than be a by-product of something in the list. The Code itself (Para. 13) states that an official's duties are those duties pertaining to his or her role in the jointly agreed procedures or customary arrangements for collective bargaining and grievance handling. It then lists six specific sub-headings including: collective bargaining with appropriate levels of management; meetings with other lay officials or full-time officers on matters concerned with industrial relations between his employer and the employees; appearing on behalf of constituents before an outside official body dealing with industrial relations matters concerning the employer, and interviews with and on behalf of constituents on grievance and disciplinary matters concerning them and their employer. It seems to be generally accepted that to this list should be added the duties of a safety

---

[52] s.40.
[53] s.41.
[54] ss.56 and 86.
[55] s.27.

representative under the Health and Safety at Work, etc., Act 1974. Even with this addition, the list would appear to be closely linked with the basic concepts of industrial relations.

Matters connected with industrial relations

The question of what falls within the scope of matters connected with industrial relations duties was considered in *Beal* v. *The Beecham Group Ltd.* [56] in relation to the not unusual situation in which officials normally negotiate on a plant basis but wish to co-ordinate a policy covering a group of companies. In this instance the Group was divided into two sub-groups containing five and six divisions respectively. The sub-groups were divided for industrial relations purposes into common interest groups, and it was at that level that collective bargaining was carried on. The extent of the unions' negotiating rights varied considerably between these common interest groups. Officials sought paid time off to attend a meeting of the National Advisory Committee for the Beecham Group "to enable representatives . . . to discuss matters of an industrial relations nature and to plan a co-ordinated strategy."

The E.A.T. held that it would be unduly restrictive to interpret "concerned with industrial relations between" employers and their employees to exclude this function. The duties of a trade union official are not limited to bargaining and the precise terms of a recognition agreement. Although the employer was not required to deal with the N.A.C. the meeting in question was concerned with industrial relations. The meeting did not involve a mere exchange of information and, even had it done so, it might still have been concerned with industrial relations. The actual decision in *Sood* v. *G.E.C. Elliott Process Automation Ltd.* [57-58] that an exchange of information was not within the permission does not mean that such a function can never be more than purely educative. The facts of each case would have to be looked at to see whether the processes of industrial relations were involved. Moreover, a co-ordinated approach is a legitimate objective and is not, therefore, too remote to constitute a duty.

The Court of Appeal confirmed this. O'Connor L.J. said

> "[The provisions of the ACAS Code of Practice, para. 13] which expressly are not comprehensive show that the code envisages that what is a union meeting may well be concerned with industrial relations. The code uses collective bargaining in a restricted sense as it separates matters of grievance and discipline, but it shows that what may be called preparatory work and explanatory work by officials may well be in fulfilment of duties concerned with industial relations.
>
> Mr. Field submitted that as the SEM CIG only had representational recognition, and as there were also invited representatives from Products and a non-accredited representative, the NAC meeting could not be a duty for the Technicians' Representatives within s.27(1)(a). Like the E.A.T., I cannot accept this submission. I am not concerned with the position of the SEM representatives, but only with the respondents and if they were attending to enable them to carry out their duties concerned with industrial relations I do not think it matters who else was there. Such factors may well be relevant under s.27(2).
>
> Finally, Mr. Field submitted that as the NAC had no negotiating function with

---

[56] [1981] I.R.L.R. 127 (E.A.T.); [1982] I.R.L.R. 192 (C.A.). See also *Allen* v. *Thomas Scott and Son (Bakers) Ltd.* [1983] I.R.L.R. 11.
[57-58] [1980] I.C.R. 1.

the employers—indeed no function at all with the employers—attending its meetings could not be for the purpose of enabling the official to carry out his duties concerned with industrial relations. Once it is recognised that preparatory work falls within the discharge of duties concerned with industrial relations, then one looks to see if the preparatory work had some direct relevance to an industrial relations matter, and if so, it qualifies under s.27(1)(a). As I have said, attending the NAC to exchange information would not have that direct relevance but to determine policies nationally may well be directly relevant, depending upon what the policies are. The agenda and minutes of the meeting show that some at least of the policies were concerned with industrial relations matters that were to go into the 1979 wage claim.

It follows that in my judgment when the respondents attended the NAC meeting it was for the purpose of enabling them to carry out their duties concerned with industrial relations.

It must be remembered that time off under s.27(1) is subject to, and in accordance with, subsection (2). This is the safeguard for employers against any attempt by a union to dress up what is an activity to make it look like a duty concerned with industrial relations. So too it is under subsection (2) that the question has to be decided whether it was reasonable for the respondents to seek time off with pay for the NAC meeting in addition to their accepted CIG meeting."

Training

The second main purpose for which paid time off may be claimed is to undergo training in aspects of industrial relations relevant to the carrying out of the duties of the official concerned with industrial relations and approved by the Trades Union Congress or the independent trade union of which the employee is an official. This does not have the effect which might at first sight seem to be intended. There is nothing to stop an employer giving time off for his own courses. In *White* v. *Pressed Steel Fisher Ltd.*[59] the E.A.T. held that it did not follow that an employers' course was not adequate because it had not been approved by a trade union. Furthermore, the existence of an adequate course offered by the employer might provide a reasonable ground for refusing time off to attend a course approved by a trade union.

On the question of permissible training, the Code suggests two main areas: (1) initial basic training as soon as possible after the official is elected or appointed; (2) further training relevant to any special responsibilities or necessary to meet special circumstances. It is necessary to consider the nature of the officials' duties in deciding whether the course is one which it is reasonable to permit him to attend.[60]

Reasonable limits may be placed on the amount of time; the purposes for which; the occasions on which; and any conditions subject to which time off may be taken.[61] It is, of course, impossible to specify all the considerations which may justify such limits. The Code of Practice sets out quite a number in reasonably general terms. These include the operational requirements of the business; safety considerations; the obligations of the industry or service;

---

[59] [1980] I.R.L.R. 176.
[60] *Sood* v. *G. E. C. Elliott Ltd.* [1981] I.R.L.R. 127 (E.A.T.); [1982] I.R.L.R. 192 (C.A.); *Menzies* v. *Smith and McLaurin Ltd.* [1980] I.R.L.R. 180. Compare *Young* v. *Carr Fasteners Ltd.* [1979] I.C.R. 844.
[61] s.27(2).

accordance with agreed procedures and consistency with wider agreements; arrangements, where necessary, for other employees to cover the work; and the convenience of the times. Some of these enter into areas of great difficulty in terms of industrial relations. Manning agreements are not uncommon in certain areas of industry. In such areas there is little doubt that the employer will seek trade union agreement to refrain from requiring a replacement for an absent official. Although such agreement may at first sight seem reasonable, there are many reasons why, for instance, a trade union should resist any attempt to establish the fact that the machinery can be run with fewer employees than a manning agreement specifies. So far as the actual purpose for which the time is required is concerned it does not follow that the right is established as soon as it can be shown that the matter is concerned with the industrial relations duties of the official. The existence of an established procedure or an agreed solution to a problem may mean that it is reasonable for an employer to refuse paid time off so that an official may take part in an unofficial procedure or seek a different solution.[62]

Pay

Where an official is permitted to take time off under this section, then the employer is required to pay him the amount of remuneration he would receive for the work he would ordinarily have been doing during that time as if he had worked for the whole of that time.[63] If the employee's remuneration for that work varies with the amount of work done, then he must receive an amount calculated by reference to the average hourly earnings for the work. This formula uses actual pay and not the notion of a normal week's pay. It appears to follow, therefore, that if time off is permitted during what would normally be overtime working, the employee is entitled to remuneration at the premium rate for that time off. Any contractual remuneration paid to the employee in respect of the time off may be set off against the statutory entitlement.[64]

An employee who is an official of an independent trade union recognised by the employer may present a complaint to an industrial tribunal that his employer has failed to permit him to take time off as required by the section or to pay him the whole or part of any amount so required to be paid.[65] This is, in fact, the only formal method provided by the Act for resolving any dispute as to the right of an official to time off or the reasonableness of any conditions to be attached to that right. It is perhaps unfortunate for the operation of this statutory provision that the effect of this is that any doubts can only finally be resolved by a refusal to grant the time off or the pay and resort to what is usually seen in this country as an adversary procedure.

Unpaid time for union activities

An employee who is a member of an independent recognised trade union has a right[66] to unpaid time off during working hours for the purpose of taking part

---

[62] *Depledge* v. *Pye Telecommunications Ltd.* [1981] I.C.R. 82.
[63] s.27(3).
[64] s.27(6).
[65] s.27(1).
[66] s.28.

in any activity of the union of which he is a member or for which he is acting as a representative, excluding activities which themselves consist of industrial action, whether or not in contemplation or furtherance of a trade dispute.

This latter exclusion clearly is not intended to exclude from the right unpaid time off to organise industrial action.[67] Again, the amount of time off which an employee is to be permitted to take, the purposes for which, the occasions on which, and any conditions subject to which this unpaid time off may be so taken, must be those that are reasonable in all the circumstances, having regard to the Code of Practice issued by the Advisory Conciliation and Arbitration Service.[68]

Public duties

An employee is also entitled to unpaid time off for certain public duties. These are listed in section 29 of the Employment Protection (Consolidation) Act 1978 as:

(a) A Justice of the Peace;
(b) A member of the local authority;
(c) A member of any statutory tribunal;
(d) A member of, in England and Wales, a Regional Health Authority or Area Health Authority, or in Scotland, a Health Board;
(e) A member of, in England and Wales, the managing or governing body of an educational establishment maintained by a Local Education Authority, or, in Scotland, a School or College Council, or the governing body of a central institution of a College of Education; or
(f) A member of, in England and Wales, a Water Authority, or, in Scotland, River Purification Board.

In this instance, the legislation provides within itself certain guidelines to determine the reasonableness of the amount of time, the occasions on which, and any conditions subject to which such time off may be so taken.[69] These guidelines require again that these elements shall be reasonable in all the circumstances, but continue by directing attention in particular to:

(a) how much time off is required for the performance of the duties of the office or as a member of the body in question, and how much time off is required for the performance of the particular duty;
(b) how much time off the employee has already been permitted under this section or sections 27 and 28;
(c) the circumstances of the employer's business and the effect of the employee's absence on the running of that business.

It is unlikely that this degree of specification adds anything to the general requirement of reasonableness in the preceding section. In *Emmerson* v. *Commissioners of Inland Revenue*[70] an industrial tribunal dealt with the question of the amount of time off to which the leader of the opposition on the Portsmouth Council was entitled. Civil service regulations applicable to his

---

[67] s.28(2).
[68] s.28(3).
[69] s.29(4). The I.T. may not itself insert conditions—*Corner* v. *Buckinghamshire County Council* [1978] I.C.R. 836.
[70] [1977] I.R.L.R. 458.

employment allowed him 18 days' paid leave per year for such duties. Those regulations also provided that further special leave without pay might be granted. Since 1973 he had taken the 18 days' paid leave per year as an ordinary member of the Council. When he was elected leader of the opposition in May 1976 he applied for additional unpaid leave but his application was refused. The industrial tribunal held that this refusal amounted to a failure to allow reasonable time off and decided that a reasonable total would be 30 days. The tribunal accepted that his duties as leader of the opposition of the Council would involve more than that 30 days but that such a period constituted a reasonable balance between his needs and the needs of the employer.[71] The tribunal largely dismissed the contention that it was unreasonable for him to require more than the permitted 18 days on the ground that he was the only training officer in the district since it suggested that his absence could be dealt with by the appointment of a deputy. The entitlement is to time off and not to a re-arrangement of time only.[72]

Time off upon redundancy

There is one further provision in the Employment Protection (Consolidation) Act as to time off which has already been noted. An employee with two years' continuous service who is given notice of dismissal by reason of redundancy is entitled before the expiration of his notice to be allowed by his employer reasonable time off work in order to look for new employment or make arrangements for training for future employment.[73] This entitlement is to paid time off of up to two-fifths of a week's pay.[74] The right only applies to an employee who on the date on which the notice is due to expire or would expire had he received the proper statutory minimum period of notice would have had two years' continuous service with that employer.[75] An employee may present a claim to an industrial tribunal within three months of the day on which it is alleged the paid time off should have been permitted that the employer has unreasonably refused such entitlement. The tribunal may award payment equal to the amount of any entitlement.[76]

It seems, from the way section 31 of the Employment Protection (Consolidation) Act 1978 is drafted, that the right is to reasonable time off work and that the limitation on the amount of pay to which the employee is entitled does not qualify this basic right. In other words, an employee is entitled to reasonable time off in excess of two-fifths of a week although this extra entitlement may be unpaid. The problem about this interpretation, however, would seem to be that no sanction exists since a tribunal may only award the amount of pay to which the employee would have been entitled had he been allowed the time off.

---

[71] This idea of balancing the needs of employer and employee was also adopted in *Ratcliffe* v. *Dorset County Council* [1978] I.R.L.R. 191.
[72] *Ratcliffe* v. *Dorset County Council, supra.*
[73] Now Employment Protection (Consolidation) Act 1978, s.31. It is not a necessary precondition that an employee should supply details of the appointments he will keep—*Dutton* v. *Hawker Siddeley Aviation Ltd.* [1978] I.C.R. 1057.
[74] s.31(9).
[75] s.31(2).
[76] s.31(5)–(7).

Time off for ante-natal care

In addition to any contractual rights in this respect an employee who is pregnant and who has, on the advice of a doctor, midwife or registered health visitor, made an appointment to attend for ante-natal care has the right not unreasonably to be refused paid time off during working hours to enable her to keep the appointment. In the case of appointments after the first one, the employer is entitled to request a certificate of pregnancy and documentary evidence of the appointment. The employee is entitled to complain to an industrial tribunal within three months of the date of the appointment of an unreasonable refusal of time off and the tribunal may order payment of the amount which would have been due had permission been granted.[76a]

INADMISSIBLE REASONS AND ACTION SHORT OF DISMISSAL

Sooner or later any system of protection of employment against unacceptable forms of dismissal faces the question whether there are not some reasons which cannot be permitted as a justifiable ground for termination of the relationship. Almost certainly foremost among such considerations will be trade union activities. It is here that an employee's clash with his employer is most likely to be considered, if not inevitable, at least excusable. It is here too that the employer is most likely to have underlying reasons which have nothing to do with the individual, as an employee, for seeking to rid himself of an active trade union organiser or representative. In some countries the issue is dealt with by conferring on the trade union representative a blanket protection from dismissal regardless of the reason put forward to justify the termination of employment. This has the obvious disadvantage of placing him in a privileged position not always necessary to protect him from discrimination. On the other hand it eliminates the very real risk that an employer may be able to rid himself of a troublesome union representative on some trumped-up charge of misconduct relative to his employment.

United Kingdom law affords protection to all employees regardless of their status in the relevant independent union. Inevitably, therefore, it must be confined to protection against dismissal only for defined reasons. Such protection is only available if the action is by reason of membership, or intended membership, of an independent trade union, non-membership of any trade union or the activities of an independent trade union. It is, of course, true that action short of dismissal could lead to a claim for unlawful discrimination under the Sex Discrimination Act 1975 or the Race Relations Act 1976. It seems probable that the difficulty involved in any extension of the grounds of complaint lies in the wide divergence in the severity of action falling within so broad a category. That some action short of dismissal is severe enough to be akin to dismissal is, however, apparent. The facts of *The Post Office* v. *Strange*[77] illustrate this point. Compulsory disciplinary transfer of the employee from night shift to day duties for two years would entail a loss of pay of at least £3,000. In that case the employee left his employment and successfully claimed an unfair constructive dismissal. It may well be said that the requirement that one

---

[76a] s.31A inserted by Employment Act 1980, s.13.
[77] [1981] I.R.L.R. 515.

should forfeit one's job before a remedy is available for unfair disciplinary action short of dismissal affords less than a satisfactory remedy even assuming that it will be possible for the employee to show that the action involves the repudiatory breach necessary to establish constructive dismissal.

So far as dismissal is concerned these prohibited reasons, no longer called "inadmissible reasons," are contained in the Employment Protection (Consolidation) Act 1978,[78] and will be dealt with at page 228 below. We shall also see that selection for redundancy will also be considered to constitute an unfair dismissal if mainly for such a reason.[79]

The provision for a remedy in respect of action short of dismissal is likewise based on the same specified reasons[80] subject to alteration of the wording to indicate that whereas dismissal will be a response to the activities in question action short of dismissal is as likely to be designed to prevent or deter such action. A difference existed until 1982 in that whereas dismissal for refusal to join a trade union was confined to refusal to join an independent union the remedy for action short of dismissal extends to refusal to join any trade union. It should be borne in mind that neither set of provisions extends to pressure to enforce a valid union membership agreement.[81] Nevertheless it may seem surprising that an employer who has not entered into a union membership agreement should be absolutely prevented from lending support to recognised unions by way of action short of dismissal (which might, for instance, involve no more than seeking to move a dissenter to another department).

Proof

The protection on these grounds both from dismissal and from action short of dismissal is available irrespective of length of service. In neither case is the employer likely to concede that the true reason is an inadmissible reason. He is most likely to assert some other reason. In any event the initial burden of proving an inadmissible reason is upon the employee.[82] On the other hand, if the counter reason which the employer is likely to advance fails to convince the tribunal that situation will go a long way to establishing the likelihood of the correctness of the employee's allegation. The tribunal is looking for evidence of the principal reason. It will not be enough for the employee merely to demonstrate the existence of some anti-union bias. In practice, therefore, there is no doubt that employees do have difficulty in refuting the primacy of an admissible reason which the employer can show to have existed.[83]

Action short of dismissal

Since there is no attempt to define "action short of dismissal" in either statutory provision it is clear that any positive act by the employer which affects the claimant is included.

Penalisation of an employee by denying him access to normal union facilities or procedures is within the scope of action short of dismissal. Whilst there is a

---

[78] As amended by the Employment Act 1982, s.9.
[79] Employment Protection (Consolidation) Act 1978, s.59; see *infra*, p. 248.
[80] *Ibid.* s.23(1).
[81] *Ibid.* ss.23(2A); 58(3A–3E) as amended.
[82] *Smith* v. *Hayle Town Council* [1978] I.C.R. 996 (C.A.) Denning M.R. dissenting.
[83] *Dixon and Shaw* v. *West Ella Developments Ltd.* [1978] I.C.R. 856.

difference between action short of dismissal involving an element of detriment and failure actively to facilitate union activities the House of Lords in *Post Office* v.*Crouch*[84] held that an employer must tolerate minor infringements of his strict legal rights. In that case denial of facilities enjoyed by the members and officials of one union to the members and officials of another was considered to constitute "discrimination against a worker." There seems no reason why the outcome of the earlier provisions of the Industrial Relations Act 1971 should differ in this respect from the application of the word "action" which must include discrimination. In *Cheall* v. *Vauxhall Motors Ltd.*[85] the plaintiff was denied union representation when his employer discovered that his union had been ordered to return him to another by the T.U.C. Disputes Committee. This was held to amount to penalisation because of union membership.

"Action" is defined[86] as including omission unless the context otherwise requires. Clearly there is no such contextual requirement in either section with which we are here concerned. A failure to promote for instance would, therefore, constitute action short of dismissal. There is some doubt as to whether "action" includes a threat of action.[87] Elsewhere the Act expressly refers both to taking, and threatening to take, industrial action. If "action" did not include threats then nor, presumably, would union "activities" with the odd result that the employer could make threats with impunity whilst the employee could not claim protection for threats as part of union activities.[88]

Activities of a . . . trade union

The most difficult issues relating to the scope of the protection concern the second head of "activities of an independent trade union." These are only protected if taken at an appropriate time and that is, in turn, defined as a time outside working hours or, by agreement with or consent of the employer, within working hours. Originally some doubt was expressed as to whether the provisions were intended to authorise a trespass as by allowing meetings outside working hours on the employer's premises without the employer's consent.

It is surprising that whereas taking part in industrial action is expressly excluded from the definition of union activity for the purpose of provisions relating to permitted time off work no mention is made of this exclusion in relation to inadmissible reasons for dismissal or action short of dismissal. In *Drew* v. *St. Edmondsbury Borough Council*[89] Slynn J. pointed out that the legislature could not have intended to include industrial action in union activities which would constitute an inadmissible reason for dismissal in view of the specific statutory provisions referring to dismissal for industrial action. Earlier the same judge had pointed to difficulty in distinguishing between the activities of an independent trade union and industrial action.[90] No doubt he

---

[84] [1974] I.C.R. 378.
[85] [1979] I.R.L.R. 253 (I.T.).
[86] Employment Protection (Consolidation) Act 1978, s.153(1).
[87] Compare *Brassington* v. *Cauldon Wholesale Ltd.* [1978] I.C.R. 405 (E.A.T.) with *Grogan* v. *British Railways Board* (E.A.T.) (unreported)—followed in *Carter* v. *Wiltshire County Council* [1979] I.R.L.R. 331 (I.T.).
[88] In *City of Birmingham District Council* v. *Beyer* [1977] I.R.L.R. 211, resort to deceit to obtain employment was held not to be a trade union activity.
[89] [1980] I.C.R. 513.
[90] *Winnett* v. *Seamarks Bros. Ltd.* [1978] I.C.R. 1240.

had in mind such devices as mandatory union meetings in working hours which may be intended to disrupt production. In view of his later remarks and those of Phillips J.[91] it may be stated with some certainty that industrial action is not a protected union activity but that it is a question of fact for the tribunal whether what is done amounts to industrial action.

It is difficult to define what essential element may turn an activity into a trade union activity. In *Chant* v. *Aquaboats Ltd.*[92] the employee had organised a petition in respect of the safety of a machine. He had taken his draft petition to the local union officer for vetting. Three days later he was dismissed, allegedly for slow work. It was held that he was acting as an individual spokesman for his fellow workers and that what he did was not a union activity. On the other hand in *Brennan* v. *Ellward (Lancs.) Ltd.*[93] it was held to be too wide to say that the activities must be those of an authorised representative. The E.A.T. gave recruiting of union members by existing rank and file members during lunch breaks as an obvious union activity. In *Dixon and Shaw* v. *West Ella Developments Ltd.*[94] the E.A.T. sought to define the characteristics of trade union activity by pointing out that the provision did not say "activities of a trade union." So it was said to be strongly arguable that to contact one's union representative with a complaint about safety constituted a trade union activity. The difference between the situation in this case and that in *Chant* is that the individual sought to transfer his complaint to the normal industrial relations machinery operated by the union whereas in *Chant* the complaint remained an individual one outside that system. This seems to suggest that there is an area, admittedly not defined with precision, in which it is commonly acknowledged trade unions normally operate various procedures. Resort to that type of procedure in such a situation is likely to be regarded as a union activity. It is the conjunction of use of trade union procedures to deal with trade union type problems which creates a trade union activity. Such procedures are, however, themselves loosely defined. A union official may present a safety complaint to an employer in much the same way as an individual. The official's action is a union procedure because he is acting as a union official and not an individual. His action may be unauthorised but nonetheless he uses an authority to make the approach inherent in his office. It is correct to conclude from this that in doubtful cases it is more likely that a union official will be regarded as undertaking a union activity than will an individual pursuing the same end. The official, provided he acts as such, implies that the union machinery is functioning. An example of the lengths to which this can be taken is contained in *British Airways Engine Overhaul Ltd.* v. *Francis.*[95] An aircraft component worker who had been a A.U.E.W. shop steward for some three years was instructed to try to get a statement published in the local Press expressing the dissatisfaction of those she represented with the union's actions to secure equal pay. She succeeded in having such a statement published and was reprimanded by her employer for making a public statement requiring his permission. The E.A.T. held that an

---

[91] See, *e.g. Brennan* v. *Ellward (Lancs.) Ltd.* [1976] I.R.L.R. 378; *Marley Tile Co. Ltd.* v. *Shaw* [1978] I.R.L.R. 238 overruled on other grounds [1980] I.C.R. 72.
[92] [1978] I.C.R. 643 (E.A.T.).
[93] *Supra.*
[94] [1978] I.C.R. 856.
[95] [1981] I.C.R. 278.

industrial tribunal was entitled to regard hers as a union activity. In *Marley Tile Co. Ltd.* v. *Shaw*[96] both Goff and Stephenson L.JJ. expressed doubts as to whether the action of an individual in calling a meeting to protest at his non-recognition by the employer as a shop steward was a union activity. The difficulty lay in the fact that not only was the individual's action not positively authorised by the union but might be said to have been positively unauthorised since consultation and negotiation procedures would normally be used between the union and the employer to deal with disputes over such recognition. The method of protest adopted by Shaw might, therefore, be seen as a private ventilation of grievances.

Employer consent during working hours

In the *Marley Tile* case[97] the E.A.T. had upheld the view of the industrial tribunal[98] that employer consent to union activities in working hours could be implied and that the existence of a normal bargaining and industrial relations system might be sufficient to imply such consent. In overruling the finding that such consent could be implied in the instant case the Court of Appeal did not deny the possibility of implied consent. The Court felt that such consent could not be implied from the employer's silence when the activity in question was an interference with production wholly unincorporated into the normal industrial relations machinery. This leaves entirely open the situations in which consent can be implied for some unusual or unexpected activity. In between the decisions of the E.A.T. and the Court of Appeal in this case the E.A.T. had considerably extended the concept of implied consent in *Zucker* v. *Astrid Jewels Ltd.*[99] The Court was prepared to imply consent to certain union activities from the fact that they were normal human conduct which might be expected in any employment situation. For example, few employers would seek to deny that they consented to their employees talking to each other during a tea break on any matter which the employees chose. The tea break, therefore, is likely to be a time during working hours when the employer might be taken to have consented to employees discussing the advantages, or otherwise, of union membership. This is the essential element of an effort to recruit union members and the E.A.T. obviously did not think that consent to a particular activity should vary by reference to the purpose of that activity. Alternatively the E.A.T. took the view that not all the time during which an employee is on the employer's premises is "working hours." A tea-break is not a time when an employee is required to be at work and, therefore, it may be unnecessary to require an employer's consent to the use of such time for union activities.

Where it can be shown that the primary reason for dismissal is a specified reason the dismissal is automatically unfair. Where action short of dismissal is alleged to have been taken for such a reason the employee may complain to an industrial tribunal normally within three months of the taking of such action or the last of a series of such actions.[1] The employer is not entitled to put forward

---

[96] [1980] I.C.R. 72.
[97] *Supra.*
[98] [1978] I.R.L.R. 238.
[99] [1978] I.C.R. 1088.
[1] Employment Protection (Consolidation) Act 1978, s.24.

union pressure as a defence.[2] The tribunal may award compensation in such amount as it considers just and equitable having regard both to the loss sustained and the fact that the right has been infringed. Loss includes the loss of a benefit which might reasonably have been expected but for the action, but is subject to the normal common law duty on the claimant to mitigate his loss. The compensation may be reduced where the action is caused or contributed to by any action of the complainant.[3] If the complaint alleges that the purpose of the action was to compel the claimant to be or become a member of a trade union, either the employer or the complainant may join a union or other person as a party claiming that the employer was induced to take the action by pressure imposed by industrial action or threats thereof, the employer may join the pressuriser and seek contribution from him towards the compensation awarded. Alternatively an award may be made wholly against the pressuriser.[4]

It must be borne in mind, in all these provisions that the claimant will be expected to bring his proof clearly within one of the specified heads. The courts have shown themselves sympathetic to the conduct of established trade union practices in developing wide interpretations of union activity and employer consent. A similar sympathy seems to have prompted the narrow view of dismissal for union membership taken in *Rath* v. *Cruden Construction Ltd.*[5] The claimant was a member of UCATT. During less than 52 weeks' employment pressure was brought upon him to join the T.G.W.U. and he was eventually dismissed for failing to do so. The E.A.T. held that an industrial tribunal was entitled to take the view that dismissal was not because of membership of UCATT (which would have constituted an inadmissible reason) but because of refusal to join the T.G.W.U. which was an independent union so that such refusal did not then constitute an inadmissible reason for purposes of unfair dismissal, even in the absence of a union membership agreement.

SUSPENSION FROM WORK ON MEDICAL GROUNDS

We have seen that at common law absence from work because of illness may not affect the employee's right to wages. An employer who suspends an employee for any reason not regarded as affecting that employee's willingness to work may be obliged to continue payment of wages depending on what provision is implied or expressed in the contract.[5a]

In certain cases statute, statutory instrument or recommendation may have the effect of requiring an employer to suspend an employee on medical grounds. It is obviously considered unfair to the employee that in such a circumstance his contract of employment might exclude his right to continuing wages during that period of suspension. It is, accordingly, provided[6] that in such circumstances the suspended employee is entitled to up to 26 weeks' remuneration while so suspended. Any period during which he is actually incapable of work by reason of disease or bodily or mental disablement is, however,

---

[2] *Ibid.* s.25.
[3] *Ibid.* s.26.
[4] *Ibid.* s.26 as amended by the Employment Act 1982, s.9.
[5] [1982] I.R.L.R. 9.
[5a] *Supra*, p. 61.
[6] s.19(1). These provisions apply to employees with at least one month's employment ending the day before the first day of claim. (Employment Act 1982, Sched. 2).

excluded from the operation of the right.[7] The entitlement is also inoperative in respect of any period during which his employer has offered to provide him with suitable alternative work (even though not within his contractual obligation) which the employee has unreasonably refused, or during which the employee does not comply with reasonable requirements imposed by his employer with a view to ensuring that his services are available.[8]

The amount of remuneration is a week's pay for each week of suspension. Any contractual remuneration actually paid by the employer to the employee goes in discharge of the statutory entitlement and vice versa.[9] Complaint of non-payment may be made, normally within three months of the day to which the claim relates, to an industrial tribunal which may award the amount due.[10]

PROTECTION AGAINST INSOLVENCY OF AN EMPLOYER

It is provided that certain amounts due to an employee under the provisions of the Employment Protection (Consolidation) Act 1978 shall have priority over other debts in the same way as arrears of wages under section 33 of the Bankruptcy Act 1914.[11] These are amounts in respect of:

(a) a guarantee payment;
(b) remuneration in respect of a period of suspension on medical grounds;
(c) payment for time off work for officials of trade unions engaged in matters concerned with industrial relations or training in aspects thereof under section 27;
(d) payment for time-off to look for work under section 31;
(e) remuneration under a protective award arising out of interim proceedings on a claim for unfair dismissal for trade union activities under section 101 of the Employment Protection Act 1975.

In addition to this priority, an employee may make application in writing to the Secretary of State that his employer is insolvent owing, on the date of the insolvency or of the termination of employment, whichever is later, the whole or any part of any of a number of specified debts. These are[12]:

(a) arrears of pay in respect of one or more (but not more than eight) weeks;
(b) payment due for the statutorily required minimum period of notice;
(c) holiday pay accrued due in the previous 12 months up to a maximum of six weeks' pay;
(d) a basic award of compensation in respect of an unfair dismissal;
(e) any reasonable sum by way of reimbursement of the whole or part of any fee or premium paid by an apprentice or articled clerk;
(f) any amount due in respect of any of the items given priority under section 121 up to the equivalent of eight weeks' pay.[13]

---

[7] s.19(2).
[8] s.20.
[9] s.21.
[10] s.22.
[11] s.121.
[12] s.122. As amended by Employment Act 1982, Sched. 2 para. 4.
[13] s.122(4).

The Secretary of State shall, if satisfied of the basis of the claim, pay the amount due out of the Redundancy Fund up to whatever is the current maximum amount fixed for each weekly payment or in a proportionate part thereof.

In addition the Secretary of State may similarly pay out of the Redundancy Fund any sum in his opinion payable in respect of unpaid payments due from an insolvent employer in respect of an occupational pension scheme. These contributions may be either those due on the employer's own account or on behalf of an employee. This latter situation will only arise where an equal sum has been deducted from the pay of the employee by way of contribution.[14] Certain maxima are specified as to the amount of such payments.[15] The application in writing must come, in this case, from persons competent to act in respect of the scheme.

Where an application is made to the Secretary of State in respect of any of these payments he may require the employer to provide him with such information as he may reasonably require to determine whether the application is well founded. He may also require any person having custody or control of any relevant records or other documents to produce such documents for examination.[16]

Any applicant may, within three months of the decision of the Secretary of State, complain to an industrial tribunal that the Secretary of State has failed to pay the whole or any part of the amount claimed to be due.[17] The industrial tribunal may make a declaration that the Secretary of State ought to make the payment specified in the declaration. Broadly speaking, when the Secretary of State has made any such payment he is subrogated to the rights of the claimant against the employer.

It has been held with reference to a claim for wages due during a period of notice that the claim against the Secretary of State cannot be better than would have been the right against the insolvent employer. The Secretary of State is, accordingly, entitled to the benefit of a contractual set-off.[18]

Payments from company assets

Section 74 of the Companies Act 1980 extends the powers of a company to include provision for the benefit of employees or former employees of the company or any of its subsidiaries in connection with cessation or transfer of the whole or part of the undertaking. The power may be exercised notwithstanding that it is not in the best interests of the company. The power may be exercised only by a resolution of the directors if authorised by the memorandum or articles or, if not so authorised, by an ordinary resolution of the company. The memorandum or articles may, however, require exercise by a special resolution of the company with more than a simple majority. In effect the memorandum or articles can be so drafted as effectively to exclude the exercise since the section

---

[14] s.123(1) and (2).
[15] See s.123(3) and (5).
[16] s.126(1).
[17] s.124.
[18] *Secretary of State for Employment* v. *Wilson* [1978] I.C.R. 200. There seems no reason why a similar principle should not apply to all the payments specified.

goes on to provide that any other requirements of the memorandum or articles must be satisfied before the payment is made.

On a winding up the liquidator may make the payments so authorised out of assets available to shareholders after the discharge of all the company's liabilities. If made before a winding up the payment may only be made out of profits available for the payment of a dividend. So creditors of the company may not be prejudiced.

These provisions replace the rule in *Parke* v. *Daily News Ltd.*[19] that such payments were not in the best interests of the company and so could not be made.

STATUTORY PROTECTION OF WAGES

Statutory fixing and regulation of wages has usually been carried out on general economic grounds rather than in the interests of individual wage earners. Even the Truck Acts, which appear to be the prime example of protection of the individual in this respect were, to a considerable extent, motivated by a desire to reduce the power of the small employer to undercut the larger by paying low effective wages. Most recently, with wages as the dominant factor in production costs, and thus in the regulation of the economy, the State has been compelled, in one way or another, to attempt to control the rate of increase. Within this broad approach the detailed purposes sought to be achieved by wage regulation vary considerably. It may be that, in future, purposes not so far sought after will be pursued as, for example, the planned re-organisation of industry by the manipulation of wage levels, thus breaking down the effect of free market factors such as supply and demand.

(a) The Truck Acts

In the agricultural economy that preceded the industrial revolution payment in kind was a normal, and even a beneficial, system of remuneration. Indeed, it operated upon both parties in that payment for the use of the land might be made in service to the lord, who in turn might pay for certain service in goods. It is not surprising that some of this system should have appeared in the early factories. It is even less surprising when one considers that, in the developing urban areas, organised supply of consumer goods was not an obvious feature, and money might be less useful than the goods themselves.

Even as these reasons declined others might have taken their place. There is, for instance, no reason why an employer should not buy essential goods cheaply in bulk and sell them to his workers at a discount, eliminating the retailers' profit. In fact the beneficent aspects of the system did not predominate. Two main types of truck[20] developed:

(a) Payment in the goods produced at the factory. Unlike the former agricultural truck the specialisation of production meant that the worker could not utilise the goods he received but had to exchange them for cash. The goods themselves tended to be over-valued in relation to the

---

[19] [1962] Ch. 927.

[20] "Truck" in this sense means much the same as barter. Its only survival in modern usage appears to be in the expression, "I will have no truck with him."

market, especially in times of depressed markets and over-production. In any event the worker had no access even to the market that did exist and was forced to exchange the goods at such price as he could obtain locally. The more "kindly" employer might help things along by arranging with a third party, like a local publican, to redeem the goods, probably below the value that he himself had placed on them, and the publican, in turn, would put an even lower value on them in his transaction with the workers.[21]

(b) Payment in token coins exchangeable at "tommy shops" only. The employer might himself run such a shop, or he might, as it were, let the franchise. In either case, however, the advantages of buying in bulk were rarely passed on, and often, because of the monopoly enjoyed the shopkeeper practised the utmost dishonesty in exchanging the coins.

The truck system tended to favour the small employer, for no very obvious reason save that he could more easily and economically make such arrangements. As is not uncommonly the case, economic reasons came to the aid of philanthropy and it was the support of the larger industrial interests that got the first general Truck Act through the unreformed parliament of 1831. As a matter of history there must be some doubt to what extent the Truck Acts destroyed the truck system and to what extent it died of its own inherent defects. Sir Otto Kahn-Freund has pointed out[22] that there is clear evidence that the system continued well into the second half of the nineteenth century and that even the introduction of inspection as a means of enforcement in 1887 did not wholly eradicate it. He adds, however;

> "The Truck Acts and other protective legislation began to be effectively enforced when membership in trade unions gave the workers the strength to insist on the maintenance of legal standards,"

thereby suggesting that the truck system was ultimately destroyed rather than that it withered away. One is bound to wonder whether, so far as the truck system is concerned it is not in fact true to say that it is largely the product of the early industrial revolution which took a long time to die out. It must be admitted that it is too clumsy a system to survive to any marked degree in any developed industrial economy. To the extent that the Truck Acts serve any useful purpose today, that purpose lies largely in the regulation of deductions from pay that, later in the nineteenth century, became part of their function. Payment in kind has probably reverted to its original position as only likely where it would benefit the worker.

The Truck Act 1831 was a culmination by way of general prohibition of a series of specific measures which had attempted, usually ineffectively, to regulate the truck system in various trades. It provides that wages shall be paid in the current coin of the realm and that any provision of a contract of employment to which the Act applies specifying any other manner of payment,

---

[21] The publican was apt to be helpful in such matters. He would, for instance, allow a commission to the employer who would pay the wages due in his public-house. Many devices have been employed to prevent wages reaching home. At the beginning of this century the wives of Welsh miners would go to the colliery to meet the men. The men, therefore, took their wives' shoes to work on Fridays.

[22] *Labour and the Law* (2nd ed.) p. 8.

or the place or manner in which the money shall be spent, shall be void. The Act is, in many respects, badly drafted, but the definition of wages[23] reveals a scope that it might be as well to regard as a general definition:

". . . any money or other thing had or contracted to be paid, delivered or given as a recompense, reward or remuneration for any labour done or to be done, whether within a certain time or to a certain amount, or for a time or an amount uncertain, shall be deemed and taken to be the 'wages' of such labour."[24]

"Coin" now includes banknotes but does not include cheques or other modern methods of avoiding the manual transfer of large sums of money. An extremely cautious amendment of this narrowly restrictive provision was produced by the Payment of Wages Act 1960. This provides that in certain situations to which truck or related legislation would apply, an employee may, in writing, request payment of the whole or part of his wages direct to a bank account, or by postal or money order, or cheque, and that the employer may validly agree to this. Such request or agreement may be cancelled at any time upon four weeks' notice in writing by the appropriate party. Without such request an employer may, in respect of such workers, only pay by postal or money order if he has reasonable ground to believe that his employee is absent from the proper or usual place of payment in order to carry out the duties of his employment, or on account of his being ill or injured. The need for individual written request, in the light of the fact that banking is not a developed habit among manual workers, has ensured that rarely will enough applications come forward to make organisation of a separate system worthwhile. It may be that the change would have more chance of being successful if it could be introduced by collective agreement.

The Act of 1831 applied to "artificers" but did not define that term. Its scope was extended in 1887[25] to all workmen, as defined in that Act, as amended.[26] Substantially, therefore, subject to express exceptions, the Acts apply to manual employees.[27]

The question is whether the employee is really and substantially engaged to perform manual labour or whether the manual part of the work is only incidental to the more intellectual aspect of his employment.[28] The distinction is

---

23 s.25.
24 No definition could avoid all difficulties. See *Ball* v. *Johnson* [1971] T.R. 147 and *Clayton* v. *Gothorp* [1971] 1 W.L.R. 999 on payment of a bonus for obtaining qualifications. In *Smart* v. *Tyrer* [1978] I.R.L.R. 132 it was held that a share system was not a benefit arising out of employment (and, presumably, therefore, not wages) but rather an inducement to employees to enter into a closer relationship with the company.
25 Truck Amendment Act 1887, s.2.
26 *Ibid.* This section was amended by Sched. 2 of the Statute Law (Repeals) Act 1973 to include a definition of "workman." The expression "workman" does not include a seaman or a domestic or menial servant but means any other person who, being a labourer, a servant in husbandry, journeyman, artificer, handicraftsman, miner, or otherwise engaged in manual labour, whether under the age of 18 years or above that age, has entered into or works under a contract with an employer, whether the contract be made before or after the passing of this Act, be express or implied, oral or in writing, and be a contract of service or a contract personally to execute any work or labour.
27 See Redgrave's *Health and Safety in Factories*.
28 *Bound* v. *Lawrence* [1892] 1 Q.B. 226. It must be noted that the meaning of the term "manual labour" in the definition of a factory for the purposes of the Factories Act 1961, is not the same as that applied in the Truck Acts and the case law is not interchangeable.

largely artificial. It is not intended to enter into a discussion of the quantity of case law on the subject, but the impossibility of devising any comprehensive rule will emerge from the decision that a man who spent half his time superintending the operation of looms was nonetheless a manual worker[29] whilst the guard of a freight train was not.[30]

Most of the remainder of the truck legislation affects, not so much the method of payment, as the amount. In *Williams* v. *North's Navigation Collieries*[31] the House of Lords held that an employer could subtract nothing, except the deductions expressly permitted by the Acts, without offending against the requirement that the *whole of the wages due* should be paid, and paid in coin. In *Kenyon* v. *Darwen Cotton Manufacturing Co. Ltd.*[32] workers, after a long period of trade depression, agreed to help finance the company by purchasing shares which were paid for eventually by deduction from their wage packets. The Court of Appeal held that this understanding amounted to an agreement that a part of the wages should be paid in shares and that such an agreement was void. It was said that section 3 of the 1831 Act made it clear that the payment must be final and absolute and not subject to any agreement with the employer as to what the employee should do with it afterwards.

Though such a restriction may still be essential to protect the unorganised worker it may have some oddly restrictive effects. In *Penman* v. *The Fife Coal Co. Ltd.*[33] the plaintiff had agreed in writing that his employers should deduct from his wages each week the rent which his father owed to them. Lord MacMillan adopted a remark of Bowen L.J.[34] that the "employer cannot, for the purposes of compliance with the statute, be both payer and payee." *Hewlett's* case, which Lord Wright described[35] as going to the limit of what is permissible in a liberal construction of the Act, must, therefore, be regarded as permitting deductions only in situations where the employer wholly divests himself of a direct interest in the sum deducted, paying it to a third party on behalf of, and, probably necessarily, for the direct benefit of the employee. In that case a weekly deduction was made and paid to the employees' sick and accident club. The House of Lords disregarded the strict construction of the Act in favour of consideration of its purpose, and held that such a deduction was merely a payment diverted to the employees' agent.[36]

It is this decision which is said to be the basis of the authority for the "check-off," whereby union dues are deducted by the employer from the wage packet and paid to the union. If it is so, then it should be noted that operation of the check-off does not, as is often supposed, require the written agreement of the employees involved, although the fact of it operating as a new term in the

---

[29] *Leech* v. *Gartside* (1885) 1 T.L.R. 391.

[30] *Hunt* v. *Great Northern Railway Co.* [1891] 1 Q.B. 601. A similar conclusion might be reached from the decisions in *Pearce* v. *Landsdowne* (1893) 57 J.P. 760—potman living at a public-house was a domestic servant—and *Cameron* v. *Royal London Ophthalmic Hospital* [1941] 1 K.B. 350—stoker in hospital boiler house a domestic servant, apparently because private houses have central heating systems.

[31] [1906] A.C. 136.

[32] [1936] 2 K.B. 193. Compare note 5 *supra*.

[33] [1936] A.C. 45.

[34] In *Hewlett* v. *Allen* [1894] A.C. 383.

[35] *Penman* v. *The Fife Coal Co. Ltd.*, *supra*.

[36] *Hewlett* v. *Allen* was applied and *Penman* v. *The Fife Coal Co.* distinguished in *Williams* v. *Butlers Ltd.* [1975] I.C.R. 208.

contract of employment will, of course, necessitate agreement in some form. In some instances the employer retains a portion of the sum so collected as payment for the service he renders. It is suggested that this, strictly speaking, places the deduction outside the *Hewlett* principle, and that it would be better if the whole amount were paid to the union and the employer paid separately for the work of collection. If a deduction is permissible in this way then a contractual limitation upon the manner in which permission to make it may be withdrawn is valid.[37]

The courts have drawn a distinction between a deduction from wages earned and a method of calculation of wages due, such as by the payment of a reduced rate for bad work. In *Sagar* v. *Ridehalgh and Son Ltd.*[38] the Court of Appeal held that the trade custom of deduction for bad work was a method of calculating the amount of the wages due for that type of work. Lawrence L.J. expressed himself as unable to agree either with the argument that the standard prices fixed in the "Uniform List of Prices," collectively agreed between employers and employees' trade unions, were payable whether the work was well or badly done, subject only to a right to sue in contract for damages for careless work, or with the argument that there was no contract price for bad work.

A similar line of argument may be applied in relation to the right to suspend an employee without pay. In *Bird* v. *British Celanese Ltd.*[39] the plaintiff had been suspended for two days without pay under a well established practice known to him. Scott L.J. said:

> "Under the suspense clause the right to wages ceases and the wages are not earned, and no deduction can be made from wages which are not payable. . . . The clause operates in accordance with its terms; the whole contract is suspended, in the sense that the operation of the mutual obligations of both parties is suspended; the workman ceases to be under any present duty to work, and the employer ceases to be under any consequential duty to pay."

The 1831 Act did permit a valid written agreement for stoppage of wages to pay the real value of any medicine or medical attendance, fuel, material, tools or implements, for use in the employee's trade, the rent of a tenement let to the employee, or food prepared on the premises and consumed there by the employee.[40] In addition, deduction of sums from wages is permitted where the money is to be used for the education of the employee's children.[41]

More specifically, the Truck Act 1896 provides regulations for the imposition of fines and the making of deductions for bad work. Fines may be imposed provided:

(i) the terms of the contract are constantly displayed where they can easily be read and copied by the persons concerned, and the actual contract is in writing, signed by the workman;

(ii) the contract specifies[42] the acts or omissions leading to a fine and the amount, or method of calculating the amount, of the fine;

---

[37] *Williams* v. *Butlers Ltd., supra.*
[38] [1931] 1 Ch. 310, following *Hart* v. *Riversdale Mill Co.* [1928] 1 K.B. 176. See also *Chawner* v. *Cummings* (1846) 8 Q.B. 311.
[39] [1945] K.B. 336.
[40] s.23. The scope of this is now restricted by s.3 of the 1896 Act.
[41] s.24.
[42] On the meaning of "specifies," see *Squire* v. *Bayer and Co. Ltd.* [1901] 2 K.B. 299.

    (iii) the act or omission causes, or is likely to cause, damage to the employer or interruption or hindrance to his business;

    (iv) the amount of the fine is fair and reasonable, having regard to all the circumstances of the case;

    (v) written particulars of the acts or omissions, and the amount of the fine, are supplied to the employee on each occasion when a deduction or payment of a fine is made.[43]

Similarly conditions apply to deductions for bad work and, with modifications, to deductions for the use or supply of materials, tools or machines, standing room, light, heat or other things to be done or provided by the employer in relation to the work.

These special provisions for making deductions and fines have undoubtedly resulted in a less liberal application of the exception to the Act of 1831 which was developed in *Sagar* v. *Ridehalgh* and *Hart* v. *Riversdale*.[44] So, in *Pritchard* v. *James Clay Ltd.*[45] a moulder of iron pipes was employed on piece-work rates, being paid an agreed price, according to the type of defect, for anything other than a normal pipe. It was held that this was "an ingenious attempt to get round the Act which does not succeed," although, on the *Sagar* principle, it should not have been considered to infringe the 1831 Act.

The offending provisions of the contract of employment are a nullity. This may affect other aspects of the contract which cannot be severed from them. In *Daley* v. *Radnor*[46] the employee had orally agreed to rent certain premises from his employer at £10 per week, to be deducted from his wages. When he was wrongfully dismissed three years later the employee claimed £1,570 as an improper deduction under the Truck Act 1831. He was held entitled to recover and the employer's counterclaim for rent under a tenancy agreement failed on the ground that such an agreement was not severable from the void agreement for deduction from wages.

It is a criminal offence for an employer to enter into a contract in breach of the Truck Acts, or to break a term of an existing contract in breach of the Acts.[47] The fine can be avoided if the employer can show that the breach was committed by his agent without his knowledge or negligence. Wages Inspectors operate under the Acts and may examine the employer's books and bring prosecutions. Fewer than one prosecution a year is brought at present.

For a breach of the 1831 Act, that is to say, for failure to pay in coin or for failure to pay the whole wages due, the employee may, by an action for debt, recover wages due over the previous six years. If the breach is of the 1896 Act, as by making a deduction or fine not in compliance with that Act, a similar action may be brought but only within six months of the breach. There is no right to set off the value of goods supplied, or any other claim, in either case, but if, under the 1896 Act, the employee has consented to or acquiesced in the

---

[43] s.1.

[44] *Supra.* s.1 of the 1896 Act exceptionally applies to shop-assistants but, by 1897, S.R. & O. No. 299 exemption from the whole of the 1896 Act was granted to all branches of the cotton weaving industry in Lancashire, Cheshire, Derbyshire and the West Riding of Yorkshire, which explains why the decisions in these two cases rested on the 1831 Act alone.

[45] [1926] K.B. 238.

[46] (1973) 117 S.J. 321.

[47] Truck Act 1831, s.9; Truck Amendment Act 1887, s.11; Truck Act 1896, s.4.

deduction he can only recover compensation for the excess over what the court thinks would have been a just and reasonable deduction.[48]

(b) Associated legislation

There may now be considerable doubt as to whether the machinery of the Truck Acts need be retained, although some of the restrictions on fines and deductions might be preserved. The same doubts apply to most of the minor legislation associated with this type of wage control.

The requirements of the Checkweighing in Various Industries Act 1919 may provide a useful job for the union branch secretary. Large sections of the industries to which it applied are now nationalised or in the hands of large companies and there would seem little reason to fear that the weighing of the "quantity of mineral gotten," or of other goods handled, in those cases where this determines the wage to be paid, would be conducted in an improper fashion. The Act itself extends to iron and steel manufacture, loading and unloading of cargo in vessels, chalk and lime quarrying and the manufacture of cement. It follows a pattern laid down for coal mining in 1887[49] whereby employees whose pay is determined by quantity of mineral or weight of material may appoint, at their own expense by way of deduction from their wages, a checkweigher and a deputy to check the tare weight of containers and the weight of material. Employers must afford such a person every facility to do this job, but the checkweigher must not interfere with the ordinary working of the place, nor is his absence a reason to stop the weighing. The checkweigher may be removed by a court of summary jurisdiction on the complaint of the employer. The Act requires that where such an agreement exists payment must be for the amount of material actually produced. An agreement to check every twentieth container, and pay nothing for it if it contained more than a certain percentage of dirt, has been held illegal. Such illegality, like that imposed by the Truck Acts, does not vitiate the whole contract.[50] No use has been made of the power by regulation to extend the 1919 Act to other industries.

The "Particulars Clause" of the Factories Act 1961,[51] applies only to textile factories and, again, no use has been made of the power to extend it by regulation. Orders defining classes of work for which particulars of the work involved and the wages therefor must be given under earlier legislation[52] are continued in force[53] and include felt hat making, laundering, and work in shipyards, iron and steel foundries and a number of less significant industrial processes. These provisions require the occupier of a factory to cause particulars of piece-rates and work to be given to the worker in writing when the work is given out, or to be posted in the workroom. The Act prohibits divulgence of such rates as a trade secret. In a number of the trades covered outworkers are included in the statutory requirements. This legislation could easily be absorbed

---

[48] 15 years' arrears of wages were recovered in *Pratt* v. *Cook Son & Co.* (*St. Pauls*) *Ltd.* [1940] A.C. 437 because this breach of the 1831 Act was then regarded as a specialty debt for which the period of limitation was then 20 years.

[49] Coal Mines Regulation Act 1887, s.13(1). See now Mines and Quarries Act 1954, s.187 and Sched. V.

[50] *Kearney* v. *Whitehaven Colliery Co. Ltd.* [1893] 1 Q.B. 700.

[51] s.135.

[52] Factory and Workshops Acts 1895 and 1901.

[53] Factories Act 1961, s.183 and Sched. VI.

into the type of notification required by the Employment Protection (Consolidation) Act 1978.

The Shop Clubs Act 1902 attempts to regulate one form of fringe benefit which it defines as any club or society for providing benefits to workmen in connection with a workshop, factory, dock, shop or warehouse. The Act makes it an offence for an employer to impose, as a condition of employment, a requirement that a workman shall discontinue membership of a friendly society, or join any friendly society other than a shop-club or thrift fund. Such clubs or funds must be registered with the Registrar of Friendly Societies after having satisfied him that they afford the workman substantial benefits at the expense of the employer, over and above that made up of contributions from the workman. They must be of a permanent character and must not annually or periodically divide their funds. The workman, on leaving the employment, must have the option of remaining a member (without the continued right to take part in the management of the club or fund), or receiving his share of the funds. It must be shown that at least 75 per cent. of the workmen to be covered by the club or fund desire its establishment. As Wedderburn notes,[54] by 1966 occupational pension schemes numbered some 65,000, covering over 12 million workers, yet membership of certified shop-clubs numbers only about 24,000.

(c) Attachment of earnings

The law relating to the attachment of earnings has been consolidated in the Attachment of Earnings Act 1971. Attachment orders may be made by the High Court to secure payments under a High Court maintenance order; by a county court for county court, or High Court, maintenance orders, a judgment debt over £5 or under an administration order; or by a magistrates' court for a magistrates' court maintenance order, the payment of any sum adjudged to be paid by a conviction and any sum required to be paid by a legal aid contribution order.[55] Generally speaking it is the creditor who is empowered to make the application but the debtor himself may apply to a magistrates' court or, in respect of maintenance payments, to the High Court or a county court. Where a creditor applies it must appear that the debtor has failed to make at least one required payment. In the case of maintenance orders the failure must be by reason of the debtor's wilful refusal or culpable neglect unless, of course, the application is from the debtor.[56]

Where an application is made to a county court to secure the payment of a judgment debt the court may, in the light of the debtor's other debts, make, together with the attachment order or alone, an order for the administration of his estate.[57] The county court, however, will have no such jurisdiction if the total of the debts exceeds the county court limit, presently of £500.

An attachment order, which may incorporate a number of debts, instructs the employer to make periodic deductions from the debtor's earnings at such times as the order requires or the court allows and to pay the amounts deducted to the specified collecting officer. The order must specify a rate of protected earnings below which, in the opinion of the court, the earnings actually paid to the

---

[54] *The Worker and the Law* (2nd ed.) p. 232.
[55] s.1.
[56] s.3.
[57] s.4.

employee should not fall. The collecting officer is normally the county court registrar or a magistrates' clerk or an officer of the High Court.[58] The employer is under a duty to comply with the order seven days after receipt unless, within 10 days, he notifies the court that the person is not in his employment. On every occasion on which he deducts he may also deduct 5p for his administrative expenses. He must, on each occasion, give the debtor a written statement of the total deduction.[59] Where, because of the operation of the protected earnings level, it is not possible to deduct the whole amount due then, except in the case of judgment debts or payments under an administration order, the backlog must be made up subsequently.[60] If an employer is faced with more than one attachment order he must deal with them in order of priority dependent on the dates they were made.[61] The employer, the debtor or the creditor may apply to the court to determine what constitutes "earnings."

The order is directed to a particular employer and not to whoever may be employing the debtor from time to time. It, therefore, lapses if the debtor ceases to be in that employment (or, presumably, if he was not in that employment when the order was first served) but it may be redirected by the court to any other person appearing to be the employer. The court will give notice to an employer when an order ceases to have effect or the amount of the debt has been paid. Seven days after this notice the employer will become liable to pay the unreduced wages to the employee again.[62]

Where a court has power to make, or has made, an order it may require the person appearing to it to be the employer to furnish specified particulars of the debtor's actual and anticipated earnings.[63] Failure to comply will render the employer liable to a fine of £25. Of much more significance is the requirement that every person who becomes the debtor's employer and knows of the order, and by which court it was made, must notify the court within seven days of this fact and of the actual or anticipated earnings of the debtor.[64]

---

[58] s.6.
[59] s.7.
[60] Sched. 3, paras. 5 and 6.
[61] Sched. 3, para. 7.
[62] s.12.
[63] s.14.
[64] s.15.

QUALIFICATIONS TO CLAIM STATUTORY EMPLOYMENT PROTECTION

(a) Employment

All the rights conferred by employment protection legislation are confined to those under a contract of service.[1]

(b) Age limits

Claims for redundancy payment and unfair dismissal may only be made by those within an upper age limit. In the case of redundancy payment claims the age limit is simply expressed as 65 for a man and 60 for a woman. (There is an additional provision applicable to redundancy and largely affecting calculation of benefit that no account shall be taken of any period of employment before the applicant attains the age of 18).

In the case of unfair dismissal the upper age limit is somewhat concisely expressed so as to debar an employee who

> ". . . on or before the effective date of termination attained the age which, in the undertaking in which he was employed, was the normal retiring age for an employee holding the position which he held, or, if a man, attained the age of 65, or, if a woman, attained the age of 60."[2]

In *London Borough of Barnet* v. *Nothman*[3] the House of Lords, by a majority, affirmed the decision of the Court of Appeal that the proper interpretation of this provision was that the existence of a normal retirement age overrode the specific age provision. Only when there was no normal retirement age did the specific age limits apply. Mrs. Nothman was therefore qualified, although she was 63, because there was a normal retirement age of 65. The normal retiring age is that at which employees usually retire[4] taking into account both the contractual position and the position in practice[5]; it is not necessarily the same as the pensionable age and alterations in qualifications under a pension scheme do not, therefore, necessarily affect continuation of statutory entitlements.[6]

The age disqualification does not apply to a claim for unfair dismissal if the reason for the dismissal was that the employee:

(i) was, or proposed to become, a member of an independent trade union; or

(ii) had taken or proposed to take, part at any appropriate time in the activities of an independent trade union; or

---

[1] See, *supra*, pp. 4–14 for discussion of the definition of employment.

[2] Employment Protection (Consolidation) Act 1978, s.64(1)(*b*).

[3] [1979] I.C.R. 111.

[4] *Post Office* v. *Waddell* [1977] I.R.L.R. 344.

[5] *Randall* v. *Post Office* [1977] I.R.L.R. 346.

[6] *Stepney Cast Stone Co. Ltd.* v. *Macarthur* [1979] I.R.L.R. 181. But see *B.P. Chemicals Ltd.* v. *Joseph* [1980] I.R.L.R. 55.

(iii) had refused, or proposed to refuse, to become or remain a member of a trade union.[7]

(c) Time for making the claim

The following limitation periods apply to the presentation of a claim in actions in industrial tribunals.

* *Unfair dismissal*—3 months from the effective date of termination.[8]

Redundancy payments—6 months from the relevant date of termination unless within that time the employee has presented the claim to his employer in writing.[9-10]

* *Maternity payment*—3 months from last day of the payment period.[11]

Guarantee payment—3 months from the date for which the payment is due.[12]

* *Payment during suspension on medical grounds*—3 months from the date for which the payment is due.[13]

* *Action short of dismissal for the purpose of interfering with union activity or membership*—3 months from the day, or last of the days, on which the action complained of occurred.[14]

* *Time off work*—3 months from the date when failure to comply with the statutory requirement occurred.[15]

* *Failure of Secretary of State to make payments arising from employee's redundancy*—3 months from date of communication of decision.[16]

Written statement of reasons for dismissal—at any time during the employment or within the time permitted for a complaint of unfair dismissal.[17]

Written statement of terms of employment and itemised pay statements—at any time during the employment or within 3 months from the date on which the employment ceased.[18]

Equal pay claims—any time before the expiration of six months after the applicant has left the employment in question.[19]

---

[7] s.64(3). These reasons were previously described in the legislation as "inadmissible reasons." They are now deprived of this shorthand title and referred to as reasons "specified in section 58(1)." See Employment Act 1982, Sched. 3, paras. 19 and 20. They have significance elsewhere in the law and will in this book be referred to collectively as "trade union membership or activities."

[8] Employment Protection (Consolidation) Act 1978, s.67(2). See also Employment Act 1982, s.10.

[9] Employment Protection (Consolidation) Act 1978, s.101(1).

[10] The reference to "effective date" and "relevant date" is defined respectively in sections 55(4) and 90(1). They are discussed at, *infra*, p. 165. The two dates are *not* subject to notional extension so as to affect the limitation period to include a statutory period of notice which has not actually been given. Where notice is given, there will be a presumption that the date of termination is the date of expiry of the notice but this will be rebutted by the commonly specified provision for immediate termination. See p. 168.

[11] Employment Protection (Consolidation) Act 1978, s.36(2).

[12] Employment Protection (Consolidation) Act 1978, s.17(2).

[13] Employment Protection (Consolidation) Act 1978, s.22(2).

[14] Employment Protection (Consolidation) Act 1978, s.24(2).

[15] Employment Protection (Consolidation) Act 1978, ss.30(2), and 31A.

[16] Employment Protection (Consolidation) Act 1978, s.124(2).

[17] Employment Protection (Consolidation) Act 1978, s.53(5).

[18] Employment Protection (Consolidation) Act 1978, s.11(9).

[19] Equal Pay Act 1970, s.2(4).

Sex and Race Discrimination—3 months from the act of discrimination.
Non-discrimination notices—within six weeks of the issue of the notice.

Appeals

* *Appeals against Improvement and Prohibition Notices issued under the Health and Safety at Work, etc., Act*—within 21 days from the date of service upon the appellant of the notice in question.
* *Appeals from failure of Secretary of State to pay redundancy or maternity benefit on employer's insolvency or failure to comply with order to pay*—3 months from date of communication of Secretary of State's decision.
* *Appeal from failure of Secretary of State to pay redundancy or maternity rebate to employer*—3 months from date of communication of Secretary of State's decision.
* *Appeal from rejection by Secretary of State of application for payment upon an employer's insolvency*—3 months from date of communication of Secretary of State's decision.

Appeals to the employment appeal tribunal

In all cases, within 42 days of the date on which the document recording the decision or order appealed against was sent to the appellant.[20]

Extension of time limits

In the case of claims for redundancy payment there is power to extend the time limit by up to a further six months if the tribunal is satisfied that it is just and equitable that the employee should receive a redundancy payment.[21] The same test is applied to anti-discrimination legislation. In all the situations marked with an asterisk, there is power to extend the time limit indefinitely for such time as the tribunal considers reasonable if the tribunal is satisfied that it was not reasonably practicable for the complaint to have been presented within the permitted time. The principles governing what is to be regarded as reasonably practicable laid down in *British Building and Engineering Appliances Ltd.* v. *Dedman*[22] continue to be applicable. In this case Lord Denning M.R. stated the proper approach thus:

> "If in the circumstances the man knew or was put on inquiry as to his rights, and as to the time limit, then it was 'practicable' for him to have presented his complaint within the [appropriate time], and he ought to have done so. But if he did not know and there was nothing to put him on inquiry, then it was 'not practicable' and he should be excused. But what is the position if he goes to skilled advisers and they make a mistake? The English court has taken the view that the man must abide by their mistake.
>
> Summing up, I would suggest that in every case the tribunal should inquire into the circumstances and ask themselves whether the man or his advisers were at fault in allowing the [time limit] to pass by without presenting the complaint. If he was not at fault, nor his advisers—so that he had just cause or excuse for not presenting his complaint within [that time]—then it was 'not practicable' for him to present it within that time. The court then has a discretion to allow it to be

---

[20] E.A.T. Practice Direction, March 3, 1978.
[21] Employment Protection (Consolidation) Act 1978, s.101(2).
[22] [1974] I.C.R. 53.

presented out of time, if it thinks it right to do so. But, if he was at fault, or his advisers were at fault, in allowing the [time limit] to slip by, he must take the consequences."

The reference to "skilled advisers" for a long time caused a distinction to be made between "professional" and other advice. In *Riley* v. *Tesco Stores Ltd.*[23] however, the Court of Appeal rejected the distinction, holding that ignorance or mistake as an excuse for delay must be examined in the light of any explanation or advice so as to determine whether the ignorance or mistake was reasonable. No rigid rule is applicable to the status of the adviser. The test of reasonableness is applied both to the claimant and his adviser. The claimant, therefore, cannot seek to excuse delay by asserting that his adviser behaved unreasonably.[24]

The *Dedman* test has, in fact, survived amendment of the statutory provision applicable at that time by the subsequent inclusion of the word "reasonable." In *Porter* v. *Bandbridge Ltd.*[25] two members of the Court of Appeal expressly supported the view that the judgments in *Dedman* had been based on the understanding that the requirement of reasonableness should be implied. Ormrod L.J. dissented on the ground that introduction of the word reasonable gave rise to a significant distinction between a situation in which the claimant did not know, as a matter of law, that a claim could be made and that in which the claimant knew of the availability of the claim but not of the existence of the time limit. The practical effect of the test was, however, acknowledged to have been affected by the extension from four weeks to three months of the limitation period for unfair dismissal claims. In *Times Newspapers Ltd.* v. *O'Regan*[26] union negotiation to secure reinstatement of the dismissed employee broke down. Earlier, the claimant had discussed with the union the possibility of presenting a claim to an industrial tribunal but she thought the time limit only ran from the end of negotiations and did not file her claim until then. It is suggested that there will be many situations in which presentation of a claim might reasonably be thought to hamper negotiations so justifying a delay until the conclusion of those negotiations.

A claim for unfair dismissal may be made during a period of notice of dismissal given by the employer[27] even if the complainant is working out that notice, but a complaint in respect of a *constructive* dismissal may only be presented after the employee has left the employment.

(d) The requirement for continuous employment

A number of statutory rights only accrue after a minimum qualifying period of continuous employment. These periods are as follows:

Unfair dismissal—normally one year.[28]

There is an industrial tribunal decision[29] to the effect that this includes dismissal on grounds of pregnancy. Where an employer does not, at

---

[23] [1980] I.C.R. 323.
[24] *Papparis* v. *Charles Fulton and Co. Ltd.* [1981] I.R.L.R. 104.
[25] [1978] I.C.R. 943.   [26] [1977] I.R.L.R. 101.
[27] Employment Protection (Consolidation) Act 1978, s.67(4).
[28] Employment Protection (Consolidation) Act 1978, s.64(1)(*a*) as amended by Employment Act 1982, Sched. 2.
[29] See [1979] I.R.L.R. 217.

any time during the appropriate period, employ more than 20 people the qualifying period of continuous employment to support a claim for unfair dismissal is two years.[30]

An employee dismissed on medical grounds by reason of a statutory requirement may claim after one month of continuous service. An employee dismissed for an inadmissible reason connected with trade union membership or activities or by reason of incorrect selection for redundancy[31] need satisfy no preliminary qualifying period of employment.

Redundancy—two years.[32]

Maternity pay—two years.[33]

Guarantee payment—one month ending with the last day before the day of the claim.[34]

Payment for suspension on medical grounds—one month ending with the last day before the beginning of the period of suspension.[35]

Guarantee payments and payment for medical suspension are not available to an employee under a fixed term contract for three months or less or to an employee engaged for a specific task which is not expected to last for more than three months unless, in either case, the employee has actually been continuously employed for more than three months.[36]

An employee is entitled to a written statement of terms of employment not later than 13 weeks after the beginning of his period of employment.[37] There would seem no reason to suppose that this right is limited to cases where these weeks have been weeks of continuous employment nor even that the employment is still continuing, although it is unlikely in practice that statements will be given to former employees who have left their employment before the expiry of the 13 week period without receiving the statement.

The period of continuous employment is also material in the calculation of the amount of statutory entitlement to redundancy payment, calculation of the amount of the basic award in claims for unfair dismissal and calculation of the minimum statutory entitlement to notice of termination of the contract of employment.

Calculation of continuous employment

The rules for calculating the period of continuous employment are contained in the Employment Protection (Consolidation) Act 1978, Sched. 13,[37a] and the

---

[30] Employment Act 1980, s.8(1).

[31] Employment Protection (Consolidation) Act 1978, s.59.

[32] Employment Protection (Consolidation) Act 1978, s.81(4) as amended by Employment Act 1982, Sched. 2.

[33] Employment Protection (Consolidation) Act 1978, s.33(3).

[34] Employment Protection (Consolidation) Act 1978, s.143(1) as amended by Employment Act 1982, Sched. 2. An exception to this qualification exists when the employee is engaged under a fixed term contract for three months or less or for a specific task likely to take no more than three months unless the employment actually continues beyond three months.

[35] Employment Protection (Consolidation) Act 1978, s.143(2) as amended by Employment Act 1982, Sched. 2.

[36] Employment Protection (Consolidation) Act 1978, s.143(3) and (4) as amended by Employment Act 1982, Sched. 2.

[37] Employment Protection (Consolidation) Act 1978, s.1(1). There is evidence to suggest that there is widespread failure to comply with this requirement.

[37a] s.151; Sched. 13 is amended by the Employment Act 1982, Sched. 2.

period is calculated week by week and compiled in months and years. Basically, each week during which there is in existence a contract of employment which would normally involve employment for 16 hours or more counts as a week of continuous employment[37b] whether the employee is actually at work in any part of that week or not.[38] It follows that periods of absence from work by reason, for instance, of sickness or pregnancy will count as periods of continuous employment without reliance on any other provision so long as the contract of employment has not been terminated either by the employer or the employee. The only exception to this rule is that weeks on strike do not count for continuity even if there is in existence a contract of employment. The beginning of the period of continuous employment is deemed to be postponed by the number of days which do not count.[39]

A period of employment outside Great Britain counts for purposes of continuity.[40]

The need for a contract providing for 16 hours employment per week is reduced in the following circumstances:

(i) If an employee has once had such a contract but this has been reduced to a contract normally involving employment for more than eight hours but less than 16, so long as that reduction does not last more than 26 weeks at a time.[41]

(ii) If the employee has been continuously employed for a period of five years under a contract normally involving more than eight hours employment.[42]

(iii) So far as any particular right is concerned, if the employee has once qualified for the right in question and has not subsequently had a week in which he has a contract normally involving both less than eight hours employment and actual employment of less than 16 hours.[43]

In such a situation not only is the right retained but the entire period covered is to be regarded as one of continuous employment. In ascertaining the number of contractual hours of employment in any week averaging over any number of weeks is not permitted unless that is the proper way to decide what the contract normally requires.[44]

Reckonable hours

A considerable number of issues arise as to the hours that are to be reckoned which it is not possible to deal with fully in the space available.

(i) Hours of employment with the same employer but under two separate contracts probably should be added together. There is no reported decision clearly on this point but in *Throsby* v. *Imperial College*[44a] the

---

[37b] Para. 4.

[38] So far as redundancy is concerned the period of calculation begins on the employee's 18th birthday.

[39] Employment Act 1982, Sched. 2.

[40] Para. 1(2).

[41] Para. 5.

[42] Para. 6.

[43] Para. 7.

[44] *ITT Components (Europe) Ltd.* v. *Kolah* [1977] I.C.R. 740.

[44a] [1978] I.C.R. 357.

E.A.T; and in *Land* v. *West Yorkshire MCC*[44b] the Court of Appeal accepted the existence of two employments. It would be highly undesirable that the question of qualification should depend on a decision as to whether these were employments under two separate contracts or under one contract divided into two parts.

(ii) Where an employee works the requisite number of hours but his contract is for a lesser number of hours it is suggested that the better view of paragraph 3 is that there is qualification. The decision in *ITT Components (Europe) Ltd.* v. *Kolah*,[45] sometimes cited for the contrary view, is better regarded as a refusal to accept an averaging of weekly hours actually worked. It would be very unsatisfactory if the number of hours actually worked which will often by implication form the contractual hours should not only be precluded from doing so by express provision but that such nominal provision should have a disqualifying effect.[45a]

(iii) The requirement in paragraph 4 that the contract "involves" hours of work was regarded by the E.A.T. in *Kolah* as having the same effect as a requirement that the contract should so provide. This is in line with provisions relating to redundancy compensation which have been held to exclude all but overtime compulsory on both sides.

This leaves unanswered the question of what is normal employment in relation to employees on call.[45b]

Interruptions

Even if there is at some period no contract of employment, or no contract sufficient of itself to produce continuous employment, provision is made for certain periods of interruption of employment to count as if they were periods covered by a contract.[46] Though the paragraph is headed "Periods in which there is no contract of employment" it also applies to a gap created by any contract inadequate in itself to create continuous employment.[46a]

The periods are:

(i) Up to 26 weeks without a sufficient contract where the employee is incapable of work in consequence of sickness or injury. It follows that the employee must resume a sufficient contract with the employer in the first week in which he does again become capable of work. It has been held, however, that "capable of work" means capable of the work he was previously engaged to perform.[47]

(ii) Up to 26 weeks absence wholly or partly because of pregnancy and confinement.

(iii) The whole of the statutorily permitted absence for maternity provided the employee returns to her former employer in accordance with the statutory provisions.

[44b] [1979] I.C.R. 452 (E.A.T.).

[45] [1977] I.C.R. 740.

[45a] *Corton House Ltd.* v. *Skipper* [1981] I.R.L.R. 78.

[45b] Compare *Bullock* v. *Merseyside C.C.* [1979] I.C.R. 79 where a part-time fireman could count 102¼ hours on call, with the unreported E.A.T. decision in *Notts AHA* v. *Gray (No. 2)* (1981) E.A.T. 163/81 in which a doctor on call but rarely required was held not entitled to count such hours.

[46] Para. 9.

[46a] See *Jones* v. *William Smith (Poplar) Ltd.* [1969] I.T.R. 317—Industrial Tribunal.

[47] *Collins* v. *Nats (Scotland) Ltd.* [1967] I.T.R. 423.

It will be noted that (iii) will absorb (ii) but that (ii) is available for example to the woman who does not qualify by two years continuous employment for the statutory maternity rights. On the other hand (ii) does not cover the period of maternity after confinement. Very often, of course, the contract will subsist during such absences so that there will be no need to rely on these provisions.

(iv) Any period of absence from work will count as a period of continuous employment if it is:

   (a) on account of a temporary cessation of work, or
   (b) in circumstances such that, by arrangement or custom, the employee is regarded as continuing in the employment of his employer for all or any purposes.

The provision in (a) refers to a temporary cessation of work. It is obvious that such a period might still be covered by a contract of employment so that it will only be necessary to resort to this provision where there is no subsisting contract or the contract does not qualify the employment as continuous under the general provisions.[48] A distinction may be drawn, as we shall see, between a temporary cessation and a permanent cessation. In *Rashid* v. *Inner London Education Authority*[49] the E.A.T. held that a cessation was permanent apparently because employment ended at the conclusion of each school term. The Court of Appeal followed this decision in *Ford* v. *Warwickshire County Council*.[49a] The first mentioned provision is designed to deal precisely with situations where the employment has ended. The question it asks is whether that ending is temporary or permanent. This question is largely one of fact but the basis for examination of the facts has been the subject of considerable judicial comment. In *Minards* v. *Courtaulds Ltd.*[50] it was said that the only test of the temporary nature of cessation was that when it began its end must have been foreseeable. In *Davies* v. *Pullman Spring Filled Co. Ltd.*[51] this approach was followed and several successive breaks, one of three months, were discounted. But, in *Hunter* v. *Smith's Dock Co. Ltd.*[52] the Divisional Court held that all the circumstances must be looked at after the event and, in the light of this hindsight, the tribunal must decide, in general and non-technical terms, whether the cessation had been temporary. So it may be that although it can then be seen that the break was in fact only a temporary one, it was originally intended to be permanent.[53] This was undoubtedly an attempt to free the legislation from the adjunctive rules, sometimes concealing the original statutory principles, that courts and tribunals were developing at that time. It does, however, very considerably broaden the utility of the sub-paragraph, to the point where it might have swallowed the other two aspects of paragraph 9, had it not been restricted in other ways.

The First Division of the Court of Session attempted such a limitation, based on the scope of the meaning of "cessation of work," in the decision in *Fitzgerald*

---

[48] *Jolly* v. *Spurlings* [1967] I.T.R. 157.
[49] [1977] I.C.R. 157.
[49a] [1982] I.R.L.R. 246. It was overruled by the House of Lords [1983] 1 All E.R. 753.
[50] [1967] I.T.R. 219.
[51] [1967] I.T.R. 247.
[52] [1968] 1 W.L.R. 1865; approved by the House of Lords in *Fitzgerald* v. *Hall, Russell & Co. Ltd.* [1970] A.C. 984, *infra*.
[53] *Newsham* v. *Dunlop Textiles (No. 2)* [1969] I.T.R. 268.

v. *Hall, Russell & Co. Ltd.*[54] The court based its judgment on the important decision of the Chief Justice of Northern Ireland in *Monarch Electric Ltd.* v. *McIntyre*[55] and rejected the reasoning on this point in *Hunter* v. *Smith's Dock Co. Ltd.*[56] The appellant had been discharged on November 28, 1962, due to a shortage of work. He was re-engaged on January 21, 1963. He was ultimately dismissed for redundancy in December 1967. During the claimant's lay-off in 1962–63, the employer had continued operations on a reduced basis.

There appear to be four possible interpretations of "cessation of work":

(i) Has the work of the employer ceased, *i.e.* has the employer ceased operations in that factory or a section of it?

(ii) Is there no work available for the employee, *i.e.* has the employer been unable to provide work?

(iii) Is no work made available for the employee, *i.e.* does the employer fail to make work available, even though he has it to offer?

(iv) Is the employee, for any reason, not performing his work, *e.g.* because he has, off his own bat, taken a holiday?

The Scottish court preferred the first of these interpretations saying that what was meant was not a cessation of the employee's work but of the work on which he was engaged (*i.e.* welding). The Lord President quoted a passage from the *Monarch* case in which Lord MacDermott C.J. had said:

> "One must look at the cessation from the point of view of the employers who conduct the work and of what is happening at the place of work. An employee can lose his job without any cessation in that sense. Orders may have fallen away and he may have become surplus to requirements; or he may have been dismissed because his performance had become unsatisfactory; or he may simply have taken French leave and gone on holiday. In such a case there has been a cessation of work on the part of the employee, but not in my opinion a cessation of work within the meaning of paragraph [9 of Schedule 13 of the 1978 Act]."

Only Lord Guest supported this view in the House of Lords. Like Lord Cameron in the Court of Session, he could see no justification for placing "his" before the word "work" in the sub-paragraph. Like both the Scottish and Northern Ireland courts, all the members of the House of Lords were concerned to prevent the voluntary quitter from returning and claiming to disregard his absence, so all of them excluded the fourth alternative. The majority[57] held that the employer must have temporarily ceased to make work available for the claimant. They did not, however, make it clear whether this could be a voluntary act on the part of the employer or whether it must be because he had no work to offer. To put it another way; can there be a "temporary cessation" where termination of a contract occurs for any reason, provided the employer takes the initiative in bringing about the termination and thus the lack of availability of work or must there be a potential redundancy? It appears from *Kolatsis* v. *Rockware Glass Ltd.*[58] that any absence which both parties regard as appropriate, as distinct from a unilateral absenteeism, may be considered.

---

[54] [1970] A.C. 984.

[55] [1968] N.I. 163. Northern Ireland possesses its own Redundancy Payments Act not differing materially from that in Great Britain.

[56] *Supra.*

[57] Lords Upjohn and Morris gave the two major judgments.

[58] [1974] I.C.R. 580.

The meaning of "temporary" was considered by the House of Lords in *Ford* v. *Warwickshire County Council*.[58a] The appellant entered into a contract each September to teach at a college of further education until the end of the academic year in the following July. The Court of Appeal had held that this was a permanent cessation since the appellant agreed that at the expiry of each contract she would have no further right to work. Lord Diplock said:

"My Lords, since para. 9 only applies to an interval of time between the coming to an end of one contract of employment and the beginning of a fresh contract of employment, the expression 'absent from work,' where it appears in para. 9(1)(*b*), (*c*) and (*d*), must mean not only that the employee is not doing any actual work for his employer but that there is no contract of employment subsisting between him and his employer that would entitle the latter to require him to do any work. So in this context the phrase 'the employee is absent from work on account of a temporary cessation of work' as descriptive of a period of time, as it would seem to me, must refer to the interval between (1) the date on which the employee who would otherwise be continuing to work under an existing contract of employment is dismissed because for the time being his employer has no work for him to do, and (2) the date on which work for him to do having become again available he is re-engaged under a fresh contract of employment to do it; and the words 'on account of a temporary cessation of work' refer to the reason why the employer dismissed the employee, and make it necessary to inquire what the reason for the dismissal was. The fact that the unavailability of work had been foreseen by the employer sufficiently far in advance to enable him to anticipate it by giving to the employee a notice to terminate his contract of employment that is of sufficient length to satisfy the requirements of s.49 of the Act (which may be as long as 12 weeks) cannot alter the reason for the dismissal or prevent the absence from work following on the expiry of the notice from being 'on account of a temporary cessation of work.' . . .

My Lords, I am quite unable to be persuaded that para. 9(1) is *not* applicable to cases where a contract of employment for a fixed term has expired and on expiry has not been renewed by the employer, in exactly the same way as it is applicable to contracts of employment of indefinite duration which are terminated by the employer by notice. One looks to see what was the reason for the employer's failure to renew the contract on the expiry of its fixed term and asks oneself the question: was that reason 'a temporary cessation of work,' within the meaning of that phrase in para. 9(1)(*b*)? . . .

From the fact that there is no work available for the employee to do for the employer during the whole of the interval between the end of one fixed-term contract of employment and the beginning of the next, and that this was the reason for his non-employment during that interval, it does not necessarily follow that the interval constitutes a '*temporary* cessation of work.' In harmony with what this House held in *Fitzgerald's* case, para. 9(1)(*b*), in cases of employment under a succession of fixed-term contracts of employment with intervals in between, requires one to look back from the date of the expiry of the fixed-term contract in respect of the non-renewal of which the employee's claim is made over the whole period during which the employee has been intermittently employed by the same employer, in order to see whether the interval between one fixed-term contract and the fixed-term contract that next preceded it was short in duration relative to the combined duration of those two fixed-term contracts during which work had continued, for the whole scheme of the Act appears to me to show that it is in the sense of 'transient,' i.e. lasting only for a relatively short time, that the word 'temporary' is used in para. 9(1)(*b*)."

[58a] *Supra.*

In *Seymour* v. *Barber and Heron Ltd.*[59] the Divisional Court said that, as a question of fact, 31 weeks was a substantial period to count as temporary cessation in the case of a weekly paid man. The case was remitted to the tribunal for consideration of this question.[60]

(v) Schedule 13, paragraph 9(1)(c) of the 1978 Act provides that periods of absence from work in circumstances such that, by arrangement or custom, the employee is regarded as continuing in the employment of his employer for all or any purposes may be counted as periods of employment.

In *Barry* v. *D. Murphy & Son Ltd.*[62] a casual worker was habitually laid off from time to time for periods varying from a few days to two or three weeks. When new work came along, a member of the firm would contact him and he would be expected to start work at short notice. The majority of the tribunal held that this was a customary arrangement within this provision; the minority member took the view that the claimant was engaged for short periods, rather than being laid off from time to time. The better opinion seems to be that the arrangement cannot be retrospective.[63]

In *Southern Electricity Board* v. *Collins*[64] Lord Parker C.J. said that a collective agreement allowing for transfer from one Electricity Board to another and providing for continuity of employment in the sense of maintaining accrued benefits was not the type of agreement contemplated by the paragraph, which, in his view, referred to cases where an employer lent his workman to another for a short period with the understanding and intention that the employee would return to work with the lender. This example is more akin to temporary cessation. There seems little reason to suppose that paragraph 9(c) is limited in this way. An employee lent to work for another may continue in the employment of the lender or be effectively transferred, depending on the facts. Subjection to the orders of the borrower, though it might transfer vicarious liability, is clearly not the test for transfer of the contractual relationship.[65] In *Wishart* v. *N.C.B.*[66] a variation of the Southern Electricity Board situation occurred in which the "transferred" employee retained his pension and mem-

---

[59] [1970] I.T.R. 65.
[60] In *Monarch Electric* v. *McIntyre* [1968] N.I. 163 it was held that there could be a "temporary cessation" where the return was to an associate employer. In *Fitzgerald's* case (*supra*) Lord Cameron had said that an absence of 26 weeks should be regarded as the maximum permissible period. In *Crown* v. *Bentley Engineering Co. Ltd.* (361/212) an industrial tribunal counted an absence of two years followed by return to an associated employer as a "temporary cessation."
[61] *Thompson* v. *Bristol Channel Ship Repairers and Engineers Ltd.* [1969] I.T.R. 262, *affirmed* (1970) 8 K.I.R. 687 (C.A.); *Harris* v. *Cardiff Channel Dry Docks and Pontoon Co. Ltd.* [1969] I.T.R. 266.
[62] [1967] I.T.R. 134: in *McCartney* v. *Kellogg International Corporation*, C.O.I.T. unreported, 226/223, 8/24/76 a tribunal held that an employee moving from site to site, with short breaks, but always for the same employer was continuously employed.
[63] *Southern Electricity Board* v. *Collins, infra; Murphy* v. *A. Birrell and Sons Ltd.* [1978] I.R.L.R. 458.
[64] [1970] 1 Q.B. 83.
[65] See *Alexander* v. *McMillan* [1969] I.T.R. 171.
[66] [1974] I.C.R. 460.

bership with the transferor employer. Such membership was expressly limited
to employees and it was, accordingly, held on the facts that, by custom and
arrangement, employment was continuous with the transferor. In *Lee* v. *Barry
High Ltd.*[67] a deed of apprenticeship allowed for transfer but provided that the
apprenticeship, though transferred, should be treated as the same. The apprenticeship was transferred twice. The Court of Appeal held that each employer
must be treated as separate for the purposes of the Act. There was, therefore,
no arrangement for absence from one while being instructed by the other.

   (vi) A week does not count for the purpose of computing continuity of
        employment if the employee takes part in a strike in any part of that
        week.[68] In all other cases save that of weeks of lock-out the effect of
        discounting a week would be irretrievably to break the continuity of
        employment so that computation would have to start afresh on resump-
        tion of work. It is provided, however, that this consequence does not
        follow a week in which there is a strike or lock-out.[69] The period of
        interruption is deducted from the beginning of the period of employ-
        ment.

The Schedule contains a number of more particular provisions:

   (i) Where in the case of a redundancy an employee accepts alternative
       employment which has the effect of his not being dismissed by reason of
       the operation of section 84(1) any interval between the two jobs is
       treated as a period of continuous employment.[70]
  (ii) Where an employee's previous contract is renewed or he is re-engaged
       by the same or another employer in circumstances where he would
       otherwise be treated as continuously employed but a redundancy pay-
       ment is made then no account shall be taken of any time before the
       relevant date for that payment so far as redundancy rights are con-
       cerned.[71]
 (iii) For the purpose of qualification by 26 weeks' continuous employment to
       claim for unfair dismissal or the calculation of the basic award the period
       between the actual date of termination of the contract and the date
       deemed to be the effective date of termination by adding the statutorily
       required period of notice will be regarded as a period of continuous
       employment.[72]

Transfer of business

Prima facie the employment to which Schedule 13 of the 1978 Act refers is
employment with a single employer.[73] The Schedule provides for several
exceptional cases where employment with two or more different employers
may be considered continuous. These cases are:

---

[67] [1970] 1 W.L.R. 1549.
[68] Para. 15(1).
[69] Para. 15(2) and (3).
[70] Para. 11(2).
[71] Para. 12. Similar provision is made in respect of payment under the Superannuation Act
1972.
[72] Para. 11(1).
[73] See *Lee* v. *Barry High Ltd.* [1970] 1 W.L.R. 1549.

(a) where a trade business or undertaking is transferred from one person to another;

(b) where under Act of Parliament a contract of employment with a body corporate is modified so as to substitute some other body corporate as the employer;

(c) where on the death of an employer the employee is taken into the employment of personal representatives or trustees of the deceased;

(d) where there is a change of employing partners, personal representatives or trustees;

(e) where an employee is taken into the employment of an associated employer of his previous employer.

We will here discuss in detail only the first and last of these special cases.

The original provision in the Redundancy Payments Act 1965[74] specifically included the transfer of a part of the business. The same is true of the latest provision made to satisfy the requirements of an EEC Directive guaranteeing continuation of the accrued rights of transferred employees.[75] In practice the courts have insisted that to satisfy this extension the part of a business must also be transferred as a going concern. They concluded, therefore, that the section transferred must have been operating as a separate business before the transfer.[76] The 1981 Regulations add to the express mention of transfer of part of a business the words "so long as the part is transferred as a business." Although this is probably meant to represent the outcome of the judicial approach to partial transfer these words appear to open up the possibility not considered by the courts that a part which had not been carried on as a business could be transferred in order to run it as a separate business.

If any one of the exceptions applies there will be continuity of employment notwithstanding a change in the nature of the job the employee undertakes. In *Lord Advocate* v. *De Rosa*[77] Viscount Dilhorne sought to justify this conclusion by reference to a consensual variation of one and the same contract; it is very unlikely, however, that a variation of contract could encompass a change of the parties to the contract. The majority of the House of Lords preferred to reach the conclusion more simply by separating the concept of transfer of business from that of a suitable alternative offer in considering continuity in a redundancy situation.

The provisions for continuity spanning a transfer are not capable of extension to cover an intervening period of non-employment. At one time it was held that the two periods must abut precisely.[78] This application of the rule could operate harshly in a redundancy situation where the previous employer had given notice to terminate employment on Friday so that the employee was not actually in

---

[74] s.13.

[75] Transfer of Undertakings (Protection of Employment) Regulations 1981, *infra*, p. 151.

[76] *Macleod* v. *John Rostron and Sons Ltd.* (N.I.R.C.) (1972) I.T.R. 144; *Meadows* v. *J. Stanbury Ltd.* [1970] I.T.R. 57; *G. D. Ault Ltd.* v. *Gregory* (1967) 3 K.I.R. 590 followed in *Newlin Oil Co. Ltd.* v. *Trafford* [1974] I.T.R. 324 (N.I.R.C.); *Secretary of State* v. *Rooney* [1977] I.T.R. 177.

[77] [1974] I.C.R. 480. This decision was not cited in the contrary judgment of O'Connor J. in *Allman* v. *Rowland* [1977] I.C.R. 201 which must, therefore, be regarded as incorrect. In *Lloyd* v. *Brassey* [1969] 2 Q.B. 98 Lord Denning had incidentally referred to the employee keeping the same job.

[78] *Logan* v. *G.U.S. Transport Ltd.* [1969] I.T.R. 287.

employment again until the Monday—the transfer having taken place during the interval. So far as redundancy rights were concerned this situation was covered by later statutory provision.[79] The problem has, however, been solved more generally by the decision of the Court of Appeal in *Teesside Times Ltd.* v. *Drury*.[80] The Receiver of the former employer reached agreement for the transfer of its business and before the final transfer informed the employees that their employment terminated forthwith. The Board of the transferee company resolved to dismiss the general manager of the transferor company and argued that his brief period of employment by it was not continuous since he had not been employed by the transferor at the time of the transfer. The members of the Court of Appeal differed in their method of arriving at the conclusion that the two periods of employment were continuous. Stephenson L.J. took the view that transfer did not take place at a precise moment but extended over a period of time. Goff L.J. did not agree with this. Eveleigh L.J. took the view that there was a period of employment and that all that was necessary was for the two periods to abut. A small gap at the end of a week in which there had been sufficient employment for continuity purposes would not, in his view, operate to break continuity. All of them, however, concluded that, as continuity was measured by the week, one week with sufficient employment followed by another in which a contract existed which would normally produce sufficient employment represented no break in continuity.

In *Allen and Son* v. *Coventry*[81] it was held that the transfer to one partner of the entire equity of the partnership could amount to transfer of the business. It must be carefully noted that this situation differs from that of transfer of control of a company by means of shareholding. In the latter case there is no transfer of the business from one person to another.[82] In such a case, of course, employment by the same company will normally remain unbroken so that there is no need to make special provision for continuity.

Authority upon what is meant by transfer of a business appears to begin with the English decision in *Dallow Industrial Properties Ltd.* v. *Else*[83] and the Scottish decision in *Rencoole (Joiner and Shopfitters) Ltd.* v. *Hunt*.[84] In the former Diplock L.J. said:

> "In order to come within section 13(1) of the Act of 1965 there must be a change of ownership, not merely in an asset of a business as in this case, but a change of ownership in the combination of operations carried on by the trader or by the non-trading body of persons, and there can only be a change of ownership in a business or part of a business . . . if what is transferred is a separate and self-contained part of the operations of the transferor in which assets, stock-in-trade and the like are engaged, or the corresponding expression which would apply to a body of persons which was carrying on operations not for profit."

The tendency to seek a single critical element such as the transfer of goodwill was resisted in *Kenmir Ltd.* v. *Frizzell*[85] although it was said that the presence or absence of this element would be strong evidence. Widgery J. said:

---

[79] Now the Employment Protection (Consolidation) Act 1978, s.84(2).
[80] [1980] I.C.R. 338.
[81] [1980] I.C.R. 9.
[82] See, *e.g. Winter* v. *Deepsawin Garages Ltd.* [1969] I.T.R. 162 (I.T. only).
[83] [1967] 2 Q.B. 449.
[84] (1967) S.L.T. 218.
[85] [1968] 1 W.L.R. 329.

"In the end the vital consideration is whether the effect of the transaction was to put the transferee in possession of a going concern the activities of which he could carry on without interruption."

Lord Denning M.R. took up this reference to transfer of a going concern in *Lloyd* v. *Brassey*.[86] The subject matter of the business was farming, in the transfer of which goodwill does not tend to play a significant part. Very often, indeed, the farmland is held on a lease and this factor had prompted Lord Parker C.J. to follow his own earlier decision[87] and to conclude that the essence of the transaction was simply the transfer of a lease. Though there was some difference in the Court of Appeal on what exactly was the nature of the business all the members agreed that sale of the farm and buildings, the new owner intending to continue the same type of farming, would constitute a transfer of the business. Salmon L.J. proposed that two questions be asked of the reasonable man, namely; what was the nature of the business before the transfer and what was the nature of the business after the transfer. Even so useful a concept as "going concern" can be perverted by treating it as if it constituted the statutory requirement. In *Dhami* v. *Top Spot Night Club*[88] for instance, the E.A.T. suggested that a deliberate termination of contracts of employment might mean that the whole complex of activities had not been transferred.[89]

The most significant of the authorities is, however, *Woodhouse* v. *Peter Brotherhood Ltd.*[90] The transferor employers were manufacturers of large diesel engines. They sold one of their factories to the transferees who took on almost all the previous employees. Those employees continued to operate the same machines but after the completion of four or five large diesel engines for the former employers they were engaged in the manufacture of spinning machines, compressors and steam turbines. There was no transfer of goodwill or restriction on competition, no transfer of business name, and no transfer of customers or the benefit of contracts. The N.I.R.C. held that the object of the legislation was to avoid prejudice to an employee by change in ownership of the business. This, in the opinion of Sir John Donaldson involved the transfer of the whole working environment. In his view only if failure to transfer the goodwill effected no change in that environment would it prevent the conclusion that there had been a transfer of the business. Inevitably concentration on the business of the employee rather than that of the employer produced a fundamentally different result. The Court of Appeal firmly returned to the former concept of the employer's business. Lord Denning asked the questions proposed by Salmon L.J. in *Lloyd* v. *Brassey*[91]:

"It seems to me that this factory is quite different from the farm in *Lloyd* v. *Brassey*. In that case there was the same business being carried on both before and after the transfer. Here it was a different business. I would ask a similar question to that asked by Salmon L.J. in *Lloyd* v. *Brassey*: if anyone had been asked prior to August 1965: 'What business is being carried on in the factory at Sandiacre?,' his answer would have been 'The manufacture of diesel engines.' And if he had been

---

86 [1969] 2 Q.B. 98.
87 *Bandey* v. *Penn* [1968] 1 W.L.R. 670.
88 [1977] I.R.L.R. 231.
89 More obviously incorrect is the tribunal decision in *Whiterod* v. *Safety Fast Ltd.* (1975) COIT. 306/96 that a business which is not independently viable is not a going concern.
90 [1972] I.C.R. 196.
91 [1969] 2 Q.B. 98.

asked the same question in January 1966, his answer would have been 'The manufacture of spinning machines, compressors and steam turbines.' If he had been asked 'Is it the same business?'; he would have said 'No. The manufacture of diesel engines has now gone to Manchester. All that is being done at Sandiacre is the manufacture of spinning machines etc.' True the same men are employed using the same tools: but the business is different.

That is how the majority of the tribunal looked at it. The Industrial Court looked at it differently. They seem to have asked themselves the question; was there a change in the working environment of the men? It seems to me that that was not the right question. The statute requires the tribunal to see whether there was a transfer of the 'business' of the employer. So you look at the nature of the business of the employer and not at the actual work being done by the men. Looking at it in that way, I am quite satisfied that in 1965 Crossleys did *not* transfer their business at Sandiacre to Peter Brotherhood Ltd. They took it off to Manchester. They only transferred the physical assets to Peter Brotherhood Ltd. The result is that, as from 1965, the men were employed in a different business, namely, that of Peter Brotherhood Ltd.: and are only entitled from Peter Brotherhood to redundancy payment for the period of their service with Peter Brotherhood. So I think the majority of the tribunal were right. I would therefore allow the appeal and restore their decision."

Up to this point the reader may reasonably have assumed that the business was comprised of the essential elements of producing goods or services and marketing them. This is true, but the industrial tribunal which first heard the case of *Melon* v. *Hector Powe Ltd.* and whose decision was subsequently upheld by both the Court of Session and the House of Lords gave the package an unexpectedly limited content.[92] The transferor employer had manufactured suits for their own retail outlets, and for one other retailer, at two factories. The factory at Dagenham supplied the factory at Blantyre with all its requirement of cloth save that used in products for the other retailer. Decisions as to apportionment of work were made at Dagenham. Due to a decline in demand the Blantyre factory was sold to another company which, apart from finishing off work in hand, did not intend to limit its customers in the same way. The employees with the exception of the general manager were taken on by the transferee and subsequently claimed redundancy compensation from the transferor. The Redundancy Payments Act 1965[93] provides that where a business or part of a business is transferred employees who continue to work for the transferee shall be treated as if their contracts had been varied by agreement rather than terminated by dismissal. The Court of Session and the House of Lords concluded that there had been no transfer of business. The clearest example of the reasoning of these two courts is contained in the judgment of Lord Emslie in the Court of Session:

"[I]n looking at what happened on and after the take-over as the result of the contract [the industrial tribunal] were, it seems to me, quite entitled to notice that in considering whether or not to take over the Blantyre factory Executex clearly had in mind the necessity of guaranteeing continuity of work there until such time as they had established themselves as manufacturers of suits and clothing for all comers. They were entitled, too, not to ignore the facts that before the take-over

---

[92] [1978] I.R.L.R. 258 (E.A.T.); [1980] I.R.L.R. 80—Court of Session [1980] I.R.L.R. 477 (H.L.).
[93] s.13. Now, The Employment Protection (Consolidation) Act 1978, s.94.

the main function of the Blantyre factory was the production of made-to-measure suits, and that the business of Executex at Blantyre was, at least after 31.8.77, to be the manufacture of garments of a quality different from those formerly made there by Hector Powe."

Both higher courts carefully avoid the inference that it would have been wrong to hold that the business was the making and selling of suits. Very few transfers of companies with established and limited custom are likely to operate to transfer that custom. Indeed it may be the loss of such custom that precipitates the transfer. The employee is quite likely to know what customers his employer serves but he is unlikely to appreciate that absence of any change in either his environment or the product has nonetheless resulted in a change in the nature of the business. The issue may be defined as a question of fact for the tribunal but that cannot permit a tribunal to apply an incorrect definition of business to the facts. It is submitted that there is a considerable case for legislation effectively to reverse the permission given in *Melon's* case to apply a narrow technical definition having no connection with any logical purpose of continuity and which is likely to exclude most transfers from providing continuity of employment. It cannot be pretended that this complexity is tolerable when it is borne in mind that an employee who is retained when the business is not transferred will lose his accumulated redundancy entitlement against his former employer if he neglects to claim within six months.

Associated employers

There will be continuity of employment where the employee enters into the employment of an associated employer of his former employer without a gap otherwise operating to break continuity. Originally the reference was to an associated *company* and the definition covered situations in which one company was a subsidiary of another or both were subsidiaries of a third.[94]

The amended definition says that:

". . . any two employers are to be treated as associated if one is a company of which the other (directly or indirectly) has control or if both are companies of which a third person (directly or indirectly) has control . . . "[95]

In *London Borough of Merton* v. *Gardiner*[96] the E.A.T. confirmed that the organisation subject to control must be an incorporated company. It concluded, therefore, that periods of employment by various local authorities could not be said to give rise to continuity even if one controlled the other. The mere provision of financial support was said not to amount to control in *Southwood Hostel Management Committee* v. *Taylor*[97] where two bodies funded by the Home Office were held not thereby to become associated employers. The E.A.T. said that control involved direction of the operation and not simply making its conduct possible. In *Umar* v. *Pliastar Ltd.*[97a] Browne-Wilkinson J. in

---

[94] See *Spanlite Structures Ltd.* v. *Jarrett* [1973] I.C.R. 465.

[95] Employment Protection (Consolidation) Act 1978, s.153(4).

[96] [1980] I.R.L.R. 302, overruling its earlier decision in *Hillingdon Area Health Authority* v. *Kauders* [1979] I.C.R. 472.

[97] [1979] I.C.R. 813.

[97a] [1981] I.C.R. 727. The same conclusion was reached by Bristow J. in the E.A.T. in *Secretary of State* v. *Newbold* [1981] I.R.L.R. 305. In (1982) 11 I.L.J. 190 John Bowers points out that

the E.A.T. expressly stated that "control" referred to "the normal legal concept of control by control of voting." This appears to be contrary to the implication in the cases just cited and also to the decision in *Zarb and Samuels* v. *British and Brazilian Produce Co. (Sales) Ltd.*[98] The learned judge, however, limited the decision in *Zarb* to a situation in which it was necessary to decide whether when two or more people together could exercise voting control they were, *de facto*, likely to do so.

Total transfer of employee rights

The Transfer of Undertakings (Protection of Employment) Regulations 1981[99] also affect continuity for the purpose of transfer of statutory rights. They, however, extend beyond this to effect a transfer of contractual rights in the situations to which they apply.[1]

The reference in the United Kingdom regulations to the transfer of an undertaking, to which alone the substantive provisions apply, does not include an effective transfer by way of a change in control of the company's shares. Though this is by far the most common method of transferring a business in the United Kingdom its exclusion from both the Directive and the Regulations should not give rise to many problems. In such a case the legal entity which constitutes the employer does not change. Consequently there will normally be no change in the contract—let alone a termination—and no break in continuity for the purpose of statutory rights. The operation of the Regulations extends only to the transfer of undertakings in the nature of "commercial ventures'" (which may lead to the conclusion that any transfer from the public to the private sector is not included). It is also expressly stated that where a part of an undertaking is transferred it is only covered if transferred "as a business." This seems likely to have the effect of incorporating all the limitations on transfer of business inherent in the application of Schedule 13 unless it could be argued that it could be taken to include something which, though not a separate business before transfer, was intended to be operated as such afterwards. Unless this rather strained construction is placed upon the Regulations it seems likely that they will be equally affected by the narrow view of transfer taken in *Melon* v. *Hector Powe Ltd.*[2]

"Hiving-down"

Assuming that the Regulations do include the transfer of statutory rights[3] it appears, therefore, that the Regulations will not extend the general effect of Schedule 13 in this respect. The principal effect may be to close one of the major loopholes in the operation of Schedule 13 which is opened by the practice of "hiving-down" which is a device peculiarly attractive to British receivers. Under the practice the receiver of an insolvent company transfers the assets to an

---

if this approach is correct the "niceties" of "corporate incarnation" will go a long way to frustrate the reasonable expectations of employees who cannot be expected to know the state of the shareholding.

[98] [1978] I.R.L.R. 78.
[99] Enacted in alleged pursuance of EEC Council Directive 77/187.
[1] Para. 5.
[2] [1981] I.C.R. 43.
[3] See Rideout (1982) 35 C.L.P. 239.

intermediate owner which is usually a wholly-owned subsidiary of the insolvent company. The insolvent company retains the liabilities which will include the accumulated statutory rights of the employees, for instance, to redundancy payment. The intermediate company is then in a position to continue the business of the insolvent company, pending an ultimate sale, without assuming its liabilities. This arrangement provides a more attractive package for a potential purchaser. The rights of employees whom he does not wish to continue to employ and who are dismissed by the insolvent company before the final sale will attach to the purchase price or become a charge upon the central fund under the statutory provisions protecting an employee in the event of the employer's insolvency. It is even possible under Schedule 13[4] that the rights of employees who are retained would not be transferred to the ultimate purchaser since the transfer of business was between him and the intermediate company which did not transfer any employees.

Had the normal provisions of the Regulations operated they would have closed this gap completely. The transfer of business to the intermediary would have constituted a transfer of business which would automatically have transferred the contractual and statutory rights of the insolvent company's employees regardless of any purported contractual relation. The process would have repeated itself upon the transfer of business to the ultimate purchaser. The United Kingdom government was persuaded that this would deprive hiving-down of its most attractive element and make it considerably more difficult to dispose of an insolvent company as a going concern. Accordingly Regulation (4) provides that where there is such an intermediate transfer to a wholly-owned subsidiary the transfer for the purposes of the Regulations will be deemed to occur only upon the disposal by the intermediary of the assets (or the achievement of independence by the subsidiary). This means that the rights only of those still in employment of the insolvent at that date will be transferred. The ultimate purchaser's advantage of being able to decide in advance of purchase which employees he wishes to engage and ensuring that the rest are not a charge upon him is preserved. On the other hand the further possibility that employees who are engaged by the ultimate purchaser will not enjoy continuity is eliminated. The Regulations, however, bristle with practical problems. As we are talking of transfer of a business rather than the property it seems it may, for instance, be impossible to decide what is the date of transfer.

Collective aspects of the employment relationship

The Regulations also contain provisions for transferring recognition and collective agreements as well as for consultation preceding the transfer. These are dealt with respectively at pp. 382 and 298 below.

(e) Employment in Great Britain

Because the statutory qualification requirements have been consolidated from legislation passed at different times some of them contained detailed differences between one right and another which otherwise seem to have no purpose. This is true of the provisions relating to the requirement for employment to be in Great Britain.[5]

---

[4] See *Pambakian* v. *Brentford Nylons Ltd.* [1978] I.C.R. 665.
[5] Employment Protection (Consolidation) Act 1978, s.141.

(i) The statutory right to statements of terms and conditions of employment and the minimum notice provisions which stem from the Contracts of Employment Act 1963 do not apply during any period when the employee is engaged in work wholly or mainly outside Great Britain unless the employee ordinarily works in Great Britain and the work outside Great Britain is for the same employer.

(ii) The statutory rights to an itemised pay statement, to written reasons for dismissal, guarantee payments, protection from action short of dismissal, time off work, maternity pay and leave, protection from unfair dismissal and protection upon insolvency of an employer do not apply to employment where under his contract of employment the employer ordinarily works outside Great Britain.

(iii) The statutory right to payment upon redundancy does not apply to an employee who is outside Great Britain on the relevant date unless under his contract he ordinarily worked in Great Britain or, conversely, to an employee who under his contract ordinarily works outside Great Britain unless on the relevant date he is in Great Britain in accordance with instructions given to him by his employer.[6]

But a person employed to work on board a ship registered in the United Kingdom shall be regarded as one who under his contract ordinarily works in Great Britain unless the employment is wholly outside Great Britain or he is not ordinarily resident in Great Britain.[7]

In *Portec (U.K.) Ltd.* v. *Mogensen*[8] the E.A.T. had held that the second of these provisions applied to everyone who ordinarily worked under a contract of employment outside Great Britain even if that person also ordinarily worked under that contract inside Great Britain. This decision was overruled by the Court of Appeal in *Wilson* v. *Maynard Shipbuilding Consultants Ab.*[9] The court said that a person could not ordinarily be working both inside and outside Great Britain. Since one venue had to be selected the question was not simply what happened in practice, it must be ascertained from the contract where the base was to be. Subsequently this test was applied by Lord Denning M.R.[10] but Eveleigh L.J. doubted that it had great significance since, in his view, it was only intended to exclude those who worked almost exclusively outside Great Britain. In *Scott, Brownrigg and Turner* v. *Dance*[11] the E.A.T. said that in cases where employment was of brief duration "ordinary course" would have to be established by reference to the contract, the circumstances under which it was entered into and what could reasonably be contemplated at that time.

It is for the employee in this, as in every other case, to prove his qualification. In *Claisse* v. *Hostetter, Stewart and Keydrill Ltd.*[12] the E.A.T. held that he failed to do so when his place of employment—a floating oil rig in the North Sea—moved across national boundaries so that it was impossible to say whether or not it was ordinarily in Great Britain. In *Todd* v. *British Midland Airways*

---

[6] See *Costain Civil Engineering Ltd.* v. *Draycott* [1977] I.C.R. 335.
[7] See *Royle* v. *Globtik Management Ltd.* [1977] I.C.R. 552.
[8] [1976] I.C.R. 396.
[9] [1978] I.C.R. 376.
[10] *Todd* v. *British Midland Airways Ltd.* [1978] I.C.R. 959.
[11] [1977] I.R.L.R. 141.
[12] [1978] I.C.R. 812.

Ltd.,[13] however, Lord Denning M.R. pointed out that the base is not necessarily at the same location as one normally works. The base in *Claisse's* case is most likely to have been the port from which the rig was administered.

(f) Fixed term contracts

The right to claim an unfair dismissal upon the expiration of the term of a fixed term contract for a period of one year or more[14] may be excluded by a written agreement to that effect between the employer and the employee entered into at any time before the expiration of that term. The right to claim a redundancy payment may, similarly, be excluded provided that the fixed term is for two years or more.

A fixed term requires a defined beginning and a defined ending. A contract to terminate on the happening of a future uncertain event is not a fixed term contract. But in *Wiltshire County Council* v. *N.A.T.F.H.E.*[15] employment for an academic year was held to be for a fixed term, notwithstanding that the obligation to teach might end earlier, so long as the contractual obligations would continue. A fixed term contract is not confined to one that cannot properly be terminated before the expiration of the term. Provision for earlier termination by notice of a fixed term will not destroy its character as such.[16]

Despite the introduction in 1963 of the statutory concept of continuity of employment it was held in *The Open University* v. *Triesman*[17] that when deciding whether a fixed term was for the necessary one or two years one must look only at the current contractual period. It follows, therefore, that an exclusion claim inserted in the very common case of a fixed term contract for three years, renewal thereafter for a year at a time, will cease to be effective to exclude a claim for unfair dismissal if the contract is terminated at the end of any year succeeding the first three.

It should be noted that the exclusions only refer to termination at the end of a fixed term. Dismissal for any reason during the course of a term will not be effected by the exclusion clause.

(g) Miscellaneous exclusions

Employees of the Crown are excluded from claiming in respect of statutory statements of terms and conditions (though they may claim an itemised pay statement), minimum notice rights and the right to redundancy payment. None of the statutory rights applies to the armed forces.[18]

A number of specific detailed exclusions apply to seamen,[19] shore fishermen[20] and dock workers.[21] Statutory remedies for unfair dismissal are not available to the police or, it seems, to prison officers.[22]

---

[13] [1978] I.C.R. 959.
[14] Employment Act 1980, s.8(2) amending Employment Protection (Consolidation) Act 1978, s.142(1).
[15] [1980] I.C.R. 455.
[16] *British Broadcasting Corporation* v. *Dixon* [1979] I.C.R. 281.
[17] [1978] I.C.R. 524.
[18] Employment Protection (Consolidation) Act 1978, s.138.
[19] Employment Protection (Consolidation) Act 1978, s.144.
[20] Employment Protection (Consolidation) Act 1978, s.144.
[21] Employment Protection (Consolidation) Act 1978, s.145.
[22] *Home Office* v. *Robinson* [1981] I.R.L.R. 524.

Apart from these exclusions any agreement to exclude or limit the operation of statutory employment protection rights or to preclude any person from presenting a complaint or otherwise bringing proceedings before an industrial tribunal is void[23] subject to some specified exceptions mostly concerned either with closed shop agreements or settlements effected through a conciliation officer.

(h) Estoppel so as to create a qualification

It is provided that the statutory statement of terms and conditions of employment shall state whether any employment with a previous employer counts as part of the employee's continuous period of employment, and, if so, specify the date when the continuous period of employment began. Following the decision of the Court of Appeal in *Evenden* v. *Guildford City A.F.C.*[24] it had been assumed that such a statement, if incorrect but advantageous to the employee, would operate as an estoppel. The practice had developed, for instance, of agreeing with trade unions upon a takeover to make such advantageous statements of continuity so as to confer upon transferred employees an additional statutory benefit. In *Secretary of State for Employment* v. *Globe Elastic Thread Ltd.*,[25] however, the House of Lords overruled the Court of Appeal in *Evenden's* case and held that jurisdiction could not be conferred by an estoppel. An industrial tribunal had no jurisdiction in cases where an employee had insufficient continuous employment to qualify to claim a statutory benefit and could not acquire such jurisdiction from a misstatement of fact. The House, nevertheless, pointed out that this would not necessarily prevent estoppel operating upon a claim upon the contract. Since contractual estoppel is not, like equitable estoppel, confined to the purpose of a shield against action, the implication is that an employee might rely on the incorrect statement to found an action for damages. In the case in point it might be argued that these damages should include the amount of the redundancy payment which the express statement of continuity had led the employee to believe he would receive.

---

[23] Employment Protection (Consolidation) Act 1978, s.140.
[24] [1975] I.C.R. 367; [1975] Q.B. 917.
[25] [1979] I.C.R. 706.

CHAPTER 4

TERMINATION OF EMPLOYMENT

THE answer to the question of how the lawyer should regard termination of employment depends upon the answer, as yet unclear, to another deeper problem. This second question is whether the employment relationship is only a matter of contract. Some commentators in the past have called the alternative to contract "status" only to be reminded[1] that it is misleading to use a technical term, such as status, as a shorthand way of defining a more general situation whose only single characteristic is that it is not wholly contractual. It is undoubtedly true that we delude ourselves as much by suggesting that contractual principles (or even alleged exceptions to those principles) are wholly appropriate to employment as by suggesting that it has become (or has always been) a form of status. With increasing momentum in recent years in the United Kingdom incidents have been introduced common to all employment which do not stem from contract and which serve to make more obvious the fact that in any society, but most obviously in an industrial society, the relationship does not rest primarily on agreement, nor contain true examples of consideration, but rather rests on economic dependence.

The lawyer who seeks to regulate this relationship by contractual concepts may provide for, and even foster, changes in it by way of implied obligations. The recently enunciated implied duty of mutual co-operation, for instance, is an attempt to restate the relationship as one of interdependence. Possibly the common law recognised the situation as partly governed by non-contractual relationship[2] when it declined specifically to enforce it and, more obviously so, when it took the view that the proper test of the repudiatory character of a breach was its tendency to destroy essential trust and confidence.[3] Certainly the court in *Pepper* v. *Webb*[4] was more concerned with the fact that a steady deterioration had destroyed the relationship than in isolating any single breach necessary to explain the termination in contractual language. Partly because of the statutory demand that a claim for constructive dismissal should be supported by a repudiatory breach tribunals dealing with unfair dismissal are forced on occasion to turn the breakdown of trust and confidence into breach of an implied term.[5] But it is suggested that the use of implied terms in this way is normally only a necessary cloak for a decision based on the irretrievable breakdown of the relationship.

---

[1] See, *e.g.* Kahn-Freund, "A Note on Status and Contract in British Labour Law" (1967) 3 M.L.R. 635.

[2] *Boston Deep Sea Fishing and Ice Co.* v. *Ansell* (1888) 39 Ch.D. 339; *Savage* v. *British India Steam Navigation Co.* (1930) 46 T.L.R. 294; *Jupiter General Insurance Co. Ltd.* v. *Shroff* [1937] 3 All E.R. 67.

[3] See also *Sinclair* v. *Neighbour* [1967] 2 Q.B. 279.

[4] [1969] 1 W.L.R. 514.

[5] *Wetherall (Bond St., W.1)* v. *Lynn* [1977] I.C.R. 205; *Wigan Borough Council* v. *Davies* [1979] I.C.R. 411.

REPUDIATORY BREACH

It would appear that it is the inevitable confusion caused by forcing the facts of breakdown into the appearance of repudiatory breach that has led to the wholly artificial difficulty of explaining why a repudiatory breach of a contract which is not specifically enforceable should sometimes terminate the contract and at other times require acceptance before having this effect. The conclusion that a repudiatory breach terminates the contract of employment depends for its apparent logic on the assumption that a repudiatory breach is inevitably a repudiation of the entire contractual obligation. This assumption is fortified by using destruction of essential trust and confidence as the test for the repudiatory nature of breach of any essential obligation. If every repudiatory breach of necessity destroys the trust and confidence without which the employment relationship cannot exist then it must follow that every such breach is a rejection of the entire contract. A moment's thought will reveal that this is not so in practice. Any selection of constructive dismissal cases will reveal a number of situations in which, despite what the courts found to be a repudiatory breach, it would have been well within the bounds of feasibility for the employee to have elected to continue the relationship. The same conclusion would be reached by examining cases of employer reaction to substantial breaches by the employee.

The proposition, formerly adhered to, that a repudiatory breach of the contract of employment is effective to terminate the contract without the need for acceptance of the repudiation by the "innocent" party contains two instances of illogicality. The second is revealed by Megarry V.-C. in *Thomas Marshall (Exports) Ltd.* v. *Guinle*[6] in which an employee sought to rely on his own repudiatory breach to terminate the contract and, in the process, his express duty of fidelity. The learned Vice-Chancellor pointed out that since, characteristically, the contract of employment is not capable of specific performance it can hardly be an objection to its existence that that remedy is not available. That being so there is no objection to the continuation of a contractual obligation carrying with it a remedy in damages where one party has indicated that he does not intend to honour his obligations and the law has admitted that he cannot be compelled to do so. There is, however, a difficulty in accepting the *Guinle* decision and reverting to the proposition that in employment, as in contract generally, a repudiatory breach does not terminate the contract until it is accepted. The difficulty arises because many repudiatory breaches obviously terminate the relationship of employer and employee. If the employee walks out without notice indicating an intention not to return is it realistic to say that the contractual obligation subsists and, if so, for how long? The problems are even more acute if it is the employer who commits such a breach. It is inconceivable that in either case the innocent party should be able indefinitely to extend the contractual obligation so as to claim continuing damages; yet to adopt a solution such as suspension of obligations only until the guilty party could properly have terminated the contract would be a fiction.

It has been pointed out[7] that some aspects of the contract of employment, such as covenants in reasonable restraint of trade, do not cease to be operative

---

[6] [1979] Ch. 227.
[7] F. P. Davidson 31 N.I.L.Q. 339—There is some support for the point in *W. E. Cox Toner (International) Ltd.* v. *Crook* [1981] I.C.R. 823.

for a considerable time after termination of the relationship. The duty of confidentiality probably never ceases. But even if this meant that there could be developed a principle that repudiatory breach operated to terminate only the wage/work obligation it would not solve many of the practical problems. It has to be admitted that, whatever a repudiatory breach of the contract of employment does to the contract, a breach which does indicate an intention not to continue the employment relationship must be taken to have ended the wage/work aspect within a relatively short time after the breach.

In the judicial confusion following the decision in *Guinle* some courts developed a concept of different types of repudiatory breach. The confusion is most apparent in the opposed decisions of the E.A.T. at the end of 1979.[8] Slynn J. attempted to resolve the conflict in *Brown* v. *Southall and Knight*[9] saying:

> "We do not think that there is any one absolute rule either way; that is to say, either that there is always automatic determination if a fundamental breach or a repudiation occurs on the one hand; or, on the other hand, there is always an option and there must always be an acceptance by the employee before the employer can dismiss. It seems to us that different rules are applicable to a case where an employer dismisses in the sense that he 'sends away' . . . or an employee goes away, than to cases where a repudiation of a contract of some other kind is alleged. In the former case it seems to us that the 'sending away' may or may not be a breach of contract. On the authorities it seems to us that the employee cannot refuse to be sent away. . . . The sending away amounts to a termination . . . whether or not it is accepted. In other cases it may be that an acceptance is often required. If, for an example, the repudiation is said to consist of a failure to carry out the work to be done with the requisite skill it may be there that the employer can elect. He has to accept the repudiation before the contract comes to an end. If he does, it is he who determines the contract."

It is not surprising that the arch-protagonist of fundamental breach should have supported this in *London Transport Executive* v. *Clarke*.[10] Lord Denning M.R.:

> "It is over 50 years ago now that I studied in depth the common law relating to the discharge of contract by breach or by incapacity or by repudiation. The result is to be found in *Smith's Leading Cases* (13th ed.) (1929), vol. II, pp. 45–46. I adhere to what I then said. All I would say is that nowadays some people seem to think that a contract is never discharged by a breach—no matter how fundamental—unless it is accepted by the other side. That is a great mistake. It is the result of the modern phraseology about 'repudiatory breach.' A repudiation by words only, saying that he will not perform a future obligation—an anticipatory breach—is, of course, a thing 'writ in water.' It is as nothing unless and until it is accepted. But a repudiatory breach is better described as a 'fundamental breach' or a 'breach going to the root of the contract.' Such a breach may well lead to the discharge of a contract without any need for acceptance. The classic instance is where a singer genuinely fell ill and could not attend the rehearsals. Her incapacity discharged the theatre from further performance, without any talk of acceptance. It would be just the

---

[8] *Smith* v. *Avana Bakeries Ltd.* [1979] I.R.L.R. 423; *Kallinos* v. *London Electric Wire Ltd.* [1980] I.R.L.R. 11 on the one hand and *Fisher* v. *York Trailer Co. Ltd.* [1979] I.C.R. 834; *Rasool* v. *Hepworth Pipe Co. Ltd.* [1980] I.C.R. 495 on the other. The effect of the majority decision of the Court of Appeal in *London Transport Executive* v. *Clarke* [1981] I.C.R. 355 is, as Dunn L.J. said, to overrule the first two of these decisions.

[9] [1980] I.C.R. 617.

[10] [1981] I.C.R. 355.

same if she had not really been ill but had pretended to be ill and thus been guilty of a breach going to the root of the contract. Again the contract would be discharged without any talk of acceptance. That is clear from the illuminating judgment of Blackburn J. in *Poussard* v. *Spiers & Pond*.

If we put anticipatory breach on one side, these actual breaches can be divided at common law into three categories. I will illustrate the position from some modern cases. First, in *Laws* v. *London Chronicle (Indicator Newspapers) Ltd.*, the managing director at a business meeting said to the lady representative: 'You stay where you are.' She did not do so but walked out of the room. Till then she had been a good employee. She was dismissed. Her conduct was a breach of her contract of employment, but it did not go to the root of the contract such as to justify her dismissal. The company were liable in damages for wrongful dismissal. Second, in *Pepper* v. *Webb*, the lady of the house asked the head gardener to put some plants in the greenhouse. He said he was not going to do it. The master of the house went out and said to him: 'The job will only take half-an-hour. Why make all this fuss about it?' The head gardener said: 'I couldn't care less about your bloody greenhouse and your sodding garden.' It was a breach going to the root of the contract. It gave the master an option whether to dismiss him or not. He elected to dismiss him. It was justifiable. The master was not liable for wrongful dismissal. Third, but if the head gardener had just walked off and got another job, it would be a breach which discharged the contract of employment without any need for acceptance. If the head gardener had disliked his new job and came back after a fortnight, the master would have been entitled to say: 'You gave up your job here. I cannot have you back now.' "

In fact the doctrine of duality of repudiation does not conflict with the destruction of fundamental breach by the House of Lords in *Photo Production Ltd.* v. *Securicor Transport Ltd.*[11] The breach which is said automatically to terminate the contract of employment is obviously a breach of clearly defined terms of the contract and not merely of some supposed underlying purpose. It may be possible to select the types of breach which will be placed in this category by reference to such an underlying purpose but that does not seem to raise any objection. What the alleged distinction does not explain is why certain unilateral repudiation should be permitted this extended effect in the law of employment merely because, in practice, one party insists that it should do so. It will not have escaped the reader's notice that Lord Denning M.R., in the first paragraph of the above quotation, uses an example of frustration and not of repudiatory breach. The law is prepared to concede automatic termination arising from extraneous circumstances rendering the performance impossible. For obvious reasons it hesitates to include in that category circumstances for which one of the parties is responsible, let alone circumstances created for the deliberate purpose of avoiding the contract. The very fact that frustration can cancel all obligations whereas fundamental repudiation must leave the guilty party liable for the breach indicates the essentially different approach. The fallacy is also apparent as soon as it is realised that the dual repudiation doctrine is often unnecessary to achieve the purpose of those advocating it. They agree that the lesser form of repudiatory breach will give the innocent party an option to terminate. If he does not exercise the option, however, he will be held to have waived the breach. We do not, therefore, need to embark on some artificial categorisation of two types of repudiatory breach. The innocent party must

---

[11] [1980] A.C. 827.

either accept or reject the repudiation; he cannot adopt a compromise position by alleging non-acceptance and yet, for instance, asserting his right to cease payment of wages. This, as we shall see, is the argument put forward by Buckley L.J. in *Gunton* v. *Richmond-upon-Thames London Borough Council.*[12] Shaw L.J., dissenting, in that case pointed out the practical snag. There is a category of repudiation as to which the innocent party cannot in practice choose to waive the breach since he must either vainly knock upon a closed door until he starves or goes out of business, or take action which must amount to acceptance. As Shaw L.J. put it:

> "In the face of this plain intimation that he would not be permitted to perform his erstwhile functions, the plaintiff understandably and sensibly kept away from the college. He regarded himself as dismissed de facto; but not, as thereafter became apparent, de jure. On February 11, 1976, the plaintiff issued a writ, by which he claimed a declaration:
>
> > 'that the purported termination of his appointment as registrar and clerk to the governors of the college is illegal, ultra vires and void and that the plaintiff at all material times has been and remains registrar and clerk to the governors of the college.'
>
> In seeking this form of relief, the plaintiff ventured into a vexed area of the common law. It is trite enough that the wrongful repudiation of a contract does not, in general, determine the contract. It is for the innocent party to decide whether he will treat the contract as at an end and seek redress by way of damages, or whether he will regard the contract as still subsisting and call for performance in accordance with the contractual terms. In the sphere of employment this basic exposition of the law is not easy or possible to reconcile with the realities of life. While damages as a universal remedy for breach of contract may generally serve to redress the injury done to the injured party, it may not always in itself be an adequate remedy. Specific performance in lieu of, or as an adjunct to, damages may be both necessary and appropriate to give that party his due. It is therefore practical and legitimate to give the party not in default the option of treating the contract as still subsisting notwithstanding the repudiation by the other party; if he elects to treat the contract as still subsisting he may seek and obtain those supplemental or auxiliary remedies which serve more effectively to compensate him or to provide him with a fulfilment of his expectations under the contract. This practical basis for according an election to the injured party has no reality in relation to a contract of service where the repudiation takes the form of an express and direct termination of the contract in contravention of its terms. I would describe this as a *total* repudiation which is at once destructive of the contractual relationship. There may conceivably be a different legal result where the repudiation is oblique and arises indirectly as, for example, where the employer seeks to change the nature of the work required to be done or the times of employment; but I cannot see how the undertaking to employ on the one hand, and the undertaking to serve on the other can survive an out-and-out dismissal by the employer or a complete and intended withdrawal of his service by the employee. It has long been recognised that an order for specific performance will not be made in relation to a contract of service. Therefore, as it seems to me, there can be no logical justification for the proposition that a contract of service survives a total repudiation by one side or the other. If the only real redress is damages, how can its measure or scope be affected according to whether the contract is regarded as still subsisting or as at an end? To preserve the bare contractual relationship is an empty formality. The servant who

---

[12] [1980] I.C.R. 755.

is wrongfully dismissed cannot claim his wage for services he is not given the opportunity of rendering; and the master whose servant refuses to serve him cannot compel that servant to perform his contracted duties. In this context remedies and rights are inextricably bound together. It is meaningless to say that the contract of service differs from other contracts only in relation to the availability of remedies in the event of breach. The difference is fundamental, for there is no legal substitute for voluntary performance."

Buckley L.J. in the majority in *Gunton's* case surveyed the cases and detected a change of opinion signalled by the judgment in *Decro Wall International SA* v. *Practitioners in Marketing Ltd.*[13] He continued:

"Why should the doctrine operate differently in the case of contracts of personal service from the way in which it operates in respect of other contracts? I for my part can discover no reason why it should do so in principle. It cannot be because the court will not decree specific performance of a contract of personal service, for there are innumerable kinds of contract which the court would not order to be specifically enforced, to which the doctrine would undoubtedly apply. For similar reasons it cannot, in my opinion, be because a contract of personal service involves a relationship of mutual confidence, or because the obligations of a master and a servant are mutually dependent upon co-operation between the parties. If one party to a contract of personal service were to repudiate it before the time for performance had arrived, there would be no breach of contract until the time for performance and no cause of action until then, unless the innocent party chose to create one by accepting the repudiation. I can only conclude that the doctrine does apply to contracts of personal service as it applies to the generality of contracts.

However, cases of wrongful dismissal in breach of a contract of personal service have certain special features. In the first place, as the term 'wrongful dismissal' implies, they always occur after the employment has begun and so involve an immediate breach by the master of his obligation to continue to employ the servant. Secondly, a wrongful dismissal is almost invariably repudiatory in character; it is very rarely that there can be any expectation that the master will relent and take the servant back into his service under the contract. Thirdly, the servant cannot sue in debt under the contract for remuneration in respect of any period after the wrongful dismissal, because the right to receive remuneration and the obligation to render services are mutually interdependent. [It will be observed that both Shaw and Buckley L.JJ. mis-state this obligation.] Fourthly, the servant must come under an immediate duty to mitigate his damages and so almost invariably must be bound to seek other employment in fulfilment of that obligation; it would be very rarely that he could expect to find other employment, or could mitigate his damages in any other way, which would leave him free to return to his original employer's service at any moment, should the original employer relent. It follows, in my view, that at least as soon as the servant finds, and enters into, other employment he must put it out of his power to perform any continuing obligations on his part to serve his original employer. At this stage, if not earlier, the servant must, I think, be taken to have accepted his wrongful dismissal as a repudiatory breach leading to a determination of the contract of service.

Finally, in a case of wrongful dismissal in the absence of special circumstances the damages recoverable on the footing of an accepted repudiation must, I think, be as great as, and most probably greater than, any damages which could be recovered on the footing of an affirmation of the contract by the innocent party and of the contract consequently remaining in operation. So, as was recognised in the *Decro-Wall* case and in *Ivory* v. *Palmer* a wrongfully dismissed servant really has,

---

[13] [1971] 1 W.L.R. 361.

in the absence of special circumstances, no option but to accept the master's repudiation of the contract.

It consequently seems to me that, in the absence of special circumstances, in a case of wrongful dismissal the court should easily infer that the innocent party has accepted the guilty party's repudiation of the contract. I do not think, however, that it is impossible that in some cases incidental or collateral terms might cause the injured party to want to keep the contract on foot.

In the present case the plaintiff has accepted the repudiation. He did so at the trial, if not earlier.

Where a servant is wrongfully dismissed, he is entitled, subject to mitigation, to damages equivalent to the wages he would have earned under the contract from the date of dismissal to the end of the contract. The date when the contract would have come to an end, however, must be ascertained on the assumption that the employer would have exercised any power he may have had to bring the contract to an end in the way most beneficial to himself; that is to say, that he would have determined the contract at the earliest date at which he could properly do so: see *McGregor on Damages* (13th ed.) (1972), paras. 884, 886 and 888.

If a master, who is entitled to dismiss a servant on not less than three months' notice, wrongfully purports to dismiss the servant summarily, the dismissal, being wrongful, is a nullity and the servant can recover as damages for breach of contract three months' remuneration and no more, subject to mitigation; that is to say, remuneration for the three months following the summary dismissal. If the master wrongfully purports to dismiss the servant on a month's notice and continues to employ him and pay him during that month, no breach occurs until the servant is excluded from his employment at the end of the month, in which case he would be entitled, subject to mitigation, to damages equivalent to three months' remuneration from the date of exclusion. If the master were to pay the servant one month's remuneration in lieu of notice and were to exclude him from his employment forthwith, there would be an immediate breach of the contract by the master; the servant would be entitled to three months' remuneration by way of damages, but would have to give credit for the one month's remuneration paid in lieu of notice.

Suppose, however, that the master were to dismiss the servant summarily or on a month's notice, and the facts were such as to justify the view that the servant did not accept the master's repudiation of the contract until the end of 10 weeks from the servant's exclusion from his employment. In such a case, if I am right in supposing acceptance of a repudiation to be requisite in master and servant cases, the master would be guilty of a breach of contract continuing de die in diem for refusing to offer the servant employment from the date of exclusion down to the date of acceptance, and thereafter for damages on the basis of a wrongful repudiation of the contract. Could the servant properly claim damages under the second head in relation to a period of three months from the date of acceptance as well as damages under the first head in relation to the 10-week period? In my judgment, he clearly could not. His cause of action would have arisen when he was wrongfully excluded from his employment. The subsequent acceptance of the repudiation would not create a new cause of action, although it might affect the remedy available for that cause of action. The question must, I think, be for how long the servant could have insisted at the date of the commencement of his cause of action upon being continued by the master in his employment.''

So Buckley L.J. purports to resolve the major problem raised by a need for acceptance of any repudiation of the contract of employment namely that contractual obligations could be perpetuated indefinitely by non-acceptance despite the termination of the relationship and the practical lack of avail of the refusal to accept. Buckley L.J.'s argument is logically unsound in that if an employee is *ready* to work he is entitled under the continuing contract to wages and not merely to damages. It is only acceptance of the terminating effect of the breach which can convert the claim to damages. Apart from this it is difficult to see why acceptance, which must be an act of will, should be inferred from mitigation, which is a duty enjoined by the law. Finally, even if the solution were supportable it would do nothing to resolve the practical difficulty of deciding the precise date on which the contract is terminated.[14] Dunn L.J. attempted to deal with some of these difficulties, and in particular the last of them, in *London Transport Executive* v. *Clarke*[15]:

> "On analysis the dismissal may in many cases be regarded as an acceptance by the employer of a repudiation by conduct on the part of the employee, so that it is the dismissal which terminates the contract and not the conduct: see *Rasool* v. *Hepworth Pipe Co. Ltd.* In *Sanders* v. *Ernest A. Neale Ltd.,* the National Industrial Relations Court held that the contract was terminated by the dismissal of the employee by the employers. Sir John Donaldson, having cited *Mackay* v. *Dick* said,
>
> > 'Applying the *Mackay* v. *Dick* principle to a contract of employment, it seems to us that the fact that the servant has not rendered the service would be no obstacle to suing for wages if it was the employer's act which produced this state of affairs. It being admitted that a wrongful dismissal does not prevent a servant from so suing, there must be some other explanation. The obvious, and indeed the only, explanation is that the repudiation of a contract of employment is an exception to the general rule. It terminates the contract without the necessity for acceptance by the injured party.'
>
> In my judgment the proposition was too widely stated. The facts of the case show that because the employees had refused to give an undertaking to resume normal working, the employers had refused them admission to the factory and had subsequently dismissed them. The employers had treated the refusal to give the undertaking as a repudiation of the contract which they had accepted by giving notice of dismissal. The decision as opposed to its ratio may therefore be supported on that ground. It matters not in considering the question of termination whether at common law the employers were ultimately found to be entitled to regard the conduct of the employees as a repudiation, or whether the dismissal was subsequently held to be unfair. This is in accordance with the general principle that contracts of employment are not terminated unless and until the repudiation is accepted as in *Boston Deep Sea Fishing and Ice Co.* v. *Ansell.*
>
> But there may be cases in which there has been no repudiation by the employee, and the employer has given notice of dismissal either in accordance with the terms of the contract or in breach of them: see *Gunton* v. *Richmond-upon-Thames London Borough Council* and the cases there cited. Such cases where the employee has no option but to accept the notice I would regard as an exception to the general rule as stated in the *Boston Deep Sea Fishing* case. In these cases the contract is terminated by the notice of the employer. To hold otherwise might, in some circumstances, enable the employer to take advantage of his own wrong where the employer gives notice within the statutory period after which an employee can claim compensation for unfair dismissal, although notice under the contract would have enabled him to do so."

---

[14] *Infra*, p. 167.
[15] [1981] I.C.R. 355.

Unfortunately, as the learned Lord Justice himself admits, this resolution does not deal with any situation in which acceptance of repudiation must be implied.

In *Robert Cort and Son Ltd.* v. *Charman*[16] Slynn J. held that even if the contract continues for some purposes following a repudiatory breach the employee cannot insist upon being employed. His rights from the date of effective repudiation cease to be rights to employment and become rights to damages. It may therefore be concluded that that date is the date of effective termination of his employment. The point was also considered by Browne-Wilkinson J. in *W. E. Cox Toner (International) Ltd.* v. *Crook.*[17] The respondent had been censured for unauthorised absence and warned that if he did not take steps to rectify the situation (by which it was presumably meant that he should not repeat the conduct) his Directorship would be terminated. He repudiated the allegations but on October 2, 1979, the Board of Directors indicated that they stood by them. On January 31, 1980, the respondent's solicitors informed the Board that unless the allegations were unreservedly withdrawn their client would resign and claim a constructive dismissal. On February 6, 1980, solicitors for the company again indicated that the allegations would not be withdrawn and the respondent resigned on March 3, 1980. The E.A.T. held that the act of repudiation had occurred seven months before the respondent purported to accept the repudiation and he must, therefore, be taken to have affirmed the contract. The judgment of the E.A.T. states:

> "It is accepted by both sides (as we think rightly) that the general principles of the law of contract apply to this case, subject to such modifications as are appropriate to take account of the factors which distinguish contracts of employment from other contracts. Although we were not referred to cases outside the field of employment law, our own researches have led us to the view that the general principles applicable to a repudiation of contract are as follows. If one party ('the guilty party') commits a repudiatory breach of the contract, the other party ('the innocent party') can choose one of two courses: he can affirm the contract and insist on its further performance or he can accept the repudiation, in which case the contract is at an end. The innocent party must at some stage elect between these two possible courses: if he once affirms the contract, his right to accept the repudiation is at an end. But he is not bound to elect within a reasonable or any other time. Mere delay by itself (unaccompanied by any express or implied affirmation of the contract) does not constitute affirmation of the contract; but if it is prolonged it may be evidence of an implied affirmation: *Allen* v. *Robles.* Affirmation of the contract can be implied. Thus, if the innocent party calls on the guilty party for further performance of the contract, he will normally be taken to have affirmed the contract since his conduct is only consistent with the continued existence of the contractual obligation. Moreover, if the innocent party himself does acts which are only consistent with the continued existence of the contract, such acts will normally show affirmation of the contract. However, if the innocent party further performs the contract to a limited extent but at the same time makes it clear that he is reserving his rights to accept the repudiation or is only continuing so as to allow the guilty party to remedy the breach, such further performance does not prejudice his right subsequently to accept the repudiation: *Farnworth Finance Facilities Ltd.* v. *Attryde.*
>
> It is against this background that one has to read the short summary of the law

---

[16] [1981] I.C.R. 816.
[17] [1981] I.C.R. 823.

given by Lord Denning MR in the *Western Excavating* case. The passage 'moreover, he must make up his mind soon after the conduct of which he complains: for, if he continues for any length of time without leaving, he will lose his right to treat himself as discharged' is not, and was not intended to be, a comprehensive statement of the whole law. As it seems to us, Lord Denning was referring to an obvious difference between a contract of employment and most other contracts. An employee faced with a repudiation by his employer is in a very difficult position. If he goes to work the next day, he will himself be doing an act which, in one sense, is only consistent with the continued existence of the contract, he might be said to be affirming the contract. Certainly, when he accepts his next pay packet (*i.e.* further performance of the contract by the guilty party) the risk of being held to affirm the contract is very great. Therefore, if the ordinary principles of contract law were to apply to a contract of employment, delay might be very serious, not in its own right but because any delay normally involves further performance of the contract by both parties. It is not the delay which may be fatal but what happens during the period of the delay."

It is impossible to pretend that the law upon the effect of a repudiatory breach of the contract of employment is clear. It is suggested that two majority decisions of the Court of Appeal ought to be accepted as establishing the proposition that the contract of employment is not in a special position but that no repudiatory breach will terminate the contract unless accepted. It is suggested that Buckley L.J. is correct to say that voluntary acts inconsistent with the continuation of the contract must amount to implied acceptance. On the other hand it is less clear that an employee forced to look for another job and even, having found it, to accept it, should be regarded as having impliedly accepted the repudiation or that, while the contract continues following employer repudiation, there is only a right to damages. In practice, however, the most important matter still to be resolved is the fixing of a date for termination of the employment.

DATE OF TERMINATION OF EMPLOYMENT

The Common Law had had no real cause to consider the question of the precise date of dismissal. Limitation periods were sufficiently long to allow very little chance of a claim being made out of time and the "old" principle of automatic termination following a repudiatory breach in practice allowed the courts to assume that the contract ended when the working relationship ended. The introduction of employee protection legislation raised a number of new problems. Originally the limitation period in which to make a claim for unfair dismissal was four weeks from the "effective date" thereof. Even the longer period of three months which, as we have seen[18] now applies to this and many other statutory rights throws up a number of situations where claims are made on the borderline of permissible time necessitating precise fixing of the date of dismissal. Assessment of redundancy compensation and of the basic award for unfair dismissal may require the fixing of a firm date of termination if there is doubt whether the employment has lasted for any number of complete years.

For the purposes of unfair dismissal statute speaks of the "effective date of termination" which it defines, rather unhelpfully, thus:

---

[18] *Supra*, p. 135.

"(4) In this Part the effective date of termination—

(*a*) in relation to an employee whose contract of employment is terminated by notice, whether given by his employer or by the employee, means the date on which that notice expires;

(*b*) in relation to an employee whose contract of employment is terminated without notice, means the date on which the termination takes effect; and

(*c*) in relation to an employee who is employed under a contract for a fixed term, where that term expires without being renewed under the same contract, means the date on which that term expires.[19]

(5) Where the contract of employment is terminated by the employer and the notice required by section 49 to be given by an employer would, if duly given on the material date, expire on a date later than the effective date of termination (as defined by subsection (4)) then, for the purposes of sections 53(2), 64(1)(*a*), 64A and 73(3) and paragraph 8(3) of Schedule 14, the later date shall be treated as the effective date of termination in relation to the dismissal.

(6) Where the contract of employment is terminated by the employee and—

(*a*) the material date does not fall during a period of notice given by the employer to terminate that contract; and

(*b*) had the contract been terminated not by the employee but by notice given on the material date by the employer, that notice would have been required by section 49 to expire on a date later than the effective date of termination (as defined by subsection (4)),

then, for the purposes of sections 64(1)(*a*), 64A and 73(3) and paragraph 8(3) of Schedule 14, the later date shall be treated as the effective date of termination in relation to the dismissal.

(7) "Material date" means—

(*a*) in subsection (5), the date when notice of termination was given by the employer or (where no notice was given) the date when the contract of employment was terminated by the employer; and

(*b*) in subsection (6), the date when notice of termination was given by the employee or (where no notice was given) the date when the contract of employment was terminated by the employee."[20]

In relation to redundancy the same statute speaks of "the relevant date" which, save for certain specialised provisions, it substantially defines in similar terms.[21] In essence, therefore, these dates are either the expiry of notice or the date on which termination of the contract takes effect. This general rule is subject to an exception which for some purposes substitutes a notional date of the end of the minimum statutory period of notice wherever the actual notice would expire earlier than that date. This concession applies however only to:

(i) Calculation of the period of employment needed before entitlement to a written statement of terms of employment;

(ii) Calculation of the period of employment needed before entitlement to a claim for unfair dismissal or for redundancy;

(iii) Calculation of the period of employment for the purpose of determining

---

[19] Employment Protection (Consolidation) Act 1978, s. 55.
[20] Subsections (5) to (7) substituted by Employment Act 1982, Sched. 3, para. 1.
[21] s.90(1). This does not include the provisions in subsections (6) and (7) above.

the quantum of the basic award for unfair dismissal or for statutory redundancy compensation.[21a]

The concession does not, for instance, extend the "effective" or "relevant" date of termination beyond the actual date or date of expiry of actual notice for the purpose of validating a claim which would otherwise be out of time.

It will be appreciated that the statutory provisions assume that there is a date of termination of the contract but do not provide any formula (save in the case of the concession of a notional date) by which such a date can be fixed.

The "old" common law principle of the automatic effect of a repudiatory breach was invoked in the early days of the operation of the statutory redundancy payments scheme. The President of Industrial Tribunals in practice had to assume the role of producing consistent principles. In *Taylor's Caters Inns Ltd.* v. *Minister of Labour,*[22] he took the view that payment of wages in lieu of notice constituted payment of agreed damages for summary dismissal without cause.[23] From this proposition Sir Diarmaird Conroy concluded that the (wrongful) dismissal was effective at the date when the employee left work. The effect of this decision is at least consistent with the later decision in *Nightingale* v. *Biddle Bros. Ltd.*[24] that where there was indeed a summary dismissal with no payment in lieu of notice the contract was terminated when the employee left work.

In *H. W. Smith (Cabinets) Ltd.* v. *Brindle*[25] the Court of Appeal held that notice of dismissal given before the coming into force of the statutory provisions for unfair dismissal but expiring after that date had the effect of terminating the employment within the period of operation of those provisions. The facts of the case indicate, however, that it had been the original intention that the employee should work out her notice and that the employer, having changed his mind, had substituted leave of absence rather than purporting to terminate the contract. The Court of Appeal, by a majority, confirmed the view that it had meant generally to provide for a presumption of employment continuing during an unworked period of notice in *Lees* v. *Arthur Greaves (Lees) Ltd.*[26] Such a presumption will be rebutted by evidence of an agreement that employment should terminate earlier than the ending of the notice period, though the courts will apparently lean against implying such an agreement. The clear indication by the employer of a unilateral intention to terminate the contract at some earlier date despite the payment of wages in lieu of notice will also rebut the presumption.[27] Under pressure to avoid a voluntary leaving before expiry of the employer's notice depriving an employee of a claim for redundancy payment

---

[21a] See *Secretary of State for Employment* v. *John Swain and Son Ltd.* [1981] I.R.L.R. 303.

[22] [1966] I.T.R. 242.

[23] The only clear statement of this principle existing at that time was contained in Fridman: *The Modern Law of Employment*, p. 471. The cases there cited do not, upon examination, appear to be authority for the proposition but such a principle seems to have been accepted in *Langston* v. *A.U.E.W. (No. 2)* [1974] I.C.R. 510. If the employer has no duty to provide work then it would seem difficult to construe the carrying out by him of his obligation to pay wages as a breach of contract. It seems unlikely, moreover, that if an employer defaulted on his undertaking to pay the wages due in lieu of notice the employee would be under a duty to mitigate.

[24] (1967) 3 K.I.R. 481.

[25] [1973] I.C.R. 12.

[26] [1974] I.C.R. 501.

[27] *Dixon* v. *Stenor Ltd.* [1973] I.C.R. 157.

the courts have also been prepared to imply a consensual variation of the date of termination.[28] It is clear that these conclusions depended on the assumption that one party can unilaterally terminate the contract.[28a]

In *Adams* v. *G.K.N. Sankey*,[29] Slynn J. appeared inclined to lay down a somewhat rigid rule concerning the difference between summary dismissal with payment in lieu and dismissal with notice paid in lieu. But in *Chapman* v. *Letherby and Christopher Ltd.*[30] the issue was made one of intention without the need for such a rule. The claimant was dismissed by letter written on February 27, 1980, and received by him the following day. The letter stated that employment would terminate on May 10, 1980. It also stated that the claimant was entitled to nine weeks' notice and would be paid his retainer of £18 per week during the period in lieu of notice. The claimant presented a complaint of unfair dismissal on July 7, 1980. The E.A.T. held that the tribunal was wrong to conclude that it was bound to construe a letter referring to payment in lieu of notice as producing an immediate termination of the contract. The question was what was the intention of the employer as to terminating the contract. In the instant case the employer on the one hand clearly gave 10 weeks' notice terminating on May 10. On the other hand he had referred to a payment in lieu of notice. A reasonable employee would conclude that his employment ended on May 10, even if he had cause to wonder why he was then being paid in lieu of notice. In *T.B.A. Industrial Products Ltd.* v. *Morland*[30a] the notice originally given to the employee clearly indicated that his employment was to end some two months later. At the same time the employee was informed that he might be allowed to leave early and he did do so after being given permission. The Court of Appeal, by a majority, held that there was no indication of any alteration of the original date of termination[30b] and confirmed that the cause of the termination was the original notice. In *Stapp* v. *The Shaftesbury Society*,[31] however, the employer was considered by the Court of Appeal effectively to have substituted immediate termination for an earlier intention that the employment should continue during a period of notice.

On the other hand, the legislation refers only to dates of determination and does not commit itself to what it is that has to be terminated. It could readily be argued that since the effective date of termination was defined in reference to dismissal which was in turn defined as applying to termination of the contract it must have been the legislative intention to refer to the effective date of termination of the contract. In *Robert Cort and Son Ltd.* v. *Charman*,[35] Browne-Wilkinson J. did not seek to challenge this. He held instead that, despite the controversy over the effect of repudiation, there was no doubt that if

---

[28] *Tunnel Holdings Ltd.* v. *Woolf* [1976] I.C.R. 387; *Ready Case Ltd.* v. *Jackson* [1981] I.R.L.R. 312. See also *I.P.C. Business Press Ltd.* v. *Greig* [1977] I.C.R. 859.
[28a] See *Sanders* v. *Ernest A. Neale Ltd.* [1974] I.C.R. 565.
[29] [1980] I.R.L.R. 416.
[30] [1981] I.R.L.R. 440.
[30a] [1982] I.R.L.R. 331.
[30b] [1977] I.C.R. 859.
[31] [1982] I.R.L.R. 326.
[32] *J. Sainsbury Ltd.* v. *Savage* [1981] I.C.R. 1; *McDonald* v. *South Cambridgeshire R.D.C.* [1973] I.C.R. 611; *Crown Agents for Overseas Governments, etc.* v. *Lawal* [1979] I.C.R. 103.
[33] [1981] I.C.R. 441.
[34] *Howgate* v. *Fane Acoustics Ltd.* [1981] I.R.L.R. 161.

work was not performed because one party insisted that the obligation was at an end further performance of the contract was impossible and it could be said that it had effectively been terminated. As he pointed out, such certainty is necessary if limitation periods are to be strictly enforced. This conclusion is, it is submitted with respect, sensible. It does, however, obliquely raise the problem again of the conclusion to be drawn when a period of notice is given and paid for but not worked but it is made clear that employment is to end at the conclusion of the period of notice. "Effectively" the contract may be said to have ended yet such a situation will still raise a presumption of continuing employment.

Pursuit of an internal appeal against terminaton will not have the effect of extending the effective date of dismissal beyond that originally intended.[32] It has been made clear that this rule means that an employee may have to file a claim for unfair dismissal even though it appears that his employment is continuing. In *Board of Governors of the National Heart and Chest Hospitals* v. *Nambiar*[33] it was held that dismissal occurs when it is notified even if full salary is maintained pending appeal and further proceedings, which in the instant case spread over 10 months. On the other hand, if the appeal is successful it avoids the decision to dismiss and the employment will be continuous.[34]

WRONGFUL DISMISSAL—THE COMMON LAW

The right of one party to terminate the contract of employment without the consent of the other was accepted by common law courts in two wholly different sets of circumstances.

A sufficiently serious breach of contract is regarded as a repudiation of contractual obligations, either totally or partially, which, according to which of the views previously discussed is preferred, either ends the contract automatically or entitles the party not in breach to accept the repudiation as terminating the contract. *Turner* v. *Mason*[36] established that termination depended, not on any moral or equitable right, but on a strictly contractual approach. The sufficiency of the breach also depends on a theoretical assessment and not on the actual consequences.[37]

Termination for cause

Single acts in breach of contract have often been considered sufficient to amount to repudiation at common law.[38] On the other hand many instances of repudiation arise from a series of breaches of contract where no single breach may be sufficiently serious to amount to repudiation but the combination of which does so.[39] There is the possibility of difficulty arising in such a situation since it might be argued that failure to act by the imposition of any discipline following previous breaches in the series amounted to waiver of that particular breach. There do not, however, seem to be any reported cases where it has been seriously suggested that the mere failure to act upon a breach which would not

---

[35] [1981] I.C.R. 816 (E.A.T.).

[36] (1845) 14 M. & W. 112.

[37] *Savage* v. *British India Steam Navigation Co.* (1930) 46 T.L.R. 294.

[38] See, *e.g. Savage* v. *British India Steam Navigation Co., supra; Sinclair* v. *Neighbour* [1967] 2 Q.B. 279; *Jupiter General Insurance Co. Ltd.* v. *Shroff Ardeshir Bomanyi* [1937] 3 All E.R. 67; *Boston Deep Sea Fishing and Ice Co. Ltd.* v. *Ansell* (1888) 39 Ch.D. 339.

[39] See, *e.g. Pepper* v. *Webb* [1969] 1 W.L.R. 514.

in itself amount to repudiation indicates waiver. It is suggested, therefore, that in order to accumulate breaches *at common law* there will not normally be any need expressly to indicate that they remain on the record so long as there is no converse indication that they have been waived.[40]

The repudiatory nature of the breach will, of course, depend on the type of service to be rendered. The nature of the work of a personal secretary, for instance, will suggest that actions of his superiors which might be overlooked by other employers will constitute repudiatory breaches of his contract. The courts normally ask whether the breach is incompatible with the contract of service so as to preclude "further satisfactory continuance of the relationship."[41] As has been said in Chapter 2 this is sometimes rendered as loss of essential trust and confidence.[42] There is no harm in this as a test if it is merely a way of assessing whether one who has reacted to the breach by regarding the relationship as at an end is justified. It must not be taken to indicate an inevitable consequence where neither party desires the end of the relationship since the supposed test has no objective validity. To construe the breach as indicating that the contract breaker must so desire would be a fiction.

Dismissal with due notice

The existence of a repudiatory breach justifies dismissal without notice which common law courts refer to as summary dismissal. In many cases where dismissal is regarded as morally (and statutorily) "justified," however, no such breach has occurred. This is, for instance, true of dismissal for redundancy or dismissal following a long period of absence through illness or injury. It is probable that the same applies to many situations of dismissal for incompetence. If the employee has warranted his competence, as when he applies for and is appointed to a job requiring a particular skill, failure to show that level of competence will amount to a breach of contract or even to misrepresentation justifying rescission. But if the employer has, in a sense, taken a risk; as where he promotes an employee to a different post in which it can only be said that the employee agrees to do his best, it is submitted that there will be no such breach.[43] In other cases the employer may deem it in the interests of his undertaking that he should sever relationships with a particular employee. In *Newell* v. *Gillingham Corporation*,[44] for instance, the plaintiff apprentice was a registered conscientious objector although the court obviously had doubts as to whether such a description was the correct one. His support for the German cause in the second world war, which at the relevant time was at a somewhat critical stage for this country, produced considerable irritation among those who worked with him and he was dismissed. His actions were held not to justify dismissal of an apprentice since the purpose of that contract was instruction and he had not rendered that impossible. Although the irritation had been inspired

---

[40] This conclusion is facilitated by the fact that if the breach is not in itself repudiatory and given that it is most uncommon to claim damages for minor breaches of the contract of employment the absence of an action is explicable for reasons other than an intention to waive the breach.

[41] *Sinclair* v. *Neighbour* [1967] 2 Q.B. 279; *Re Rubel Bronze and Metal Co. and Voss* [1918] 1 K.B. 315.

[42] *Boston Deep Sea Fishing and Ice Co.* v. *Ansell* (1888) 39 Ch.D. 339. See Sachs L.J. in *Hill* v. *C. A. Parsons and Co. Ltd.* [1972] 1 Ch. 305.

[43] See *Harmer* v. *Cornelius* (1858) 5 C.B. (N.S.) 236; *K.* v. *Raschen* (1878) 38 L.J. 38.

[44] [1941] 1 All E.R. 552.

deliberately it is by no means clear that there would have been a repudiatory breach had he been an ordinary employee.

In cases where it is necessary to terminate the relationship despite the absence of a breach of contract, the common law solution is to regard a term permitting unilateral termination upon a period of notice as so necessary as to justify its implication unless expressly excluded.[45]

The idea that a contract of service might, by implication, be terminated on the giving of reasonable notice was first accepted in *Beeston* v. *Collyer*.[46] The concept seems to have sprung from discussion as to whether a yearly hiring terminated automatically at the end of the year or whether notice in advance of the termination was required.[47] The law of employment had taken over the yearly hiring from the agricultural economy which flourished before the industrial revolution. In that economy it had been customary to regard the hiring of labour as operative from Michaelmas to Michaelmas. Even in 1882 Grose J. was prepared to refer to the normal presumption of a yearly hiring capable of displacement by a term implied by custom,[48] and in 1950 Parker J. said[49] " . . . it is old law that an employment, an engagement, for an indefinite period is what is called a general hiring for a year unless something is shown to the contrary." It was easy to rebut the presumption and in this century it has never been a practicable alternative to termination by notice. In 1910, for instance, Lord Alverstone C.J. said.[50] "The general principle applicable to contracts of service is that, in the absence of misconduct or of grounds specified in the contract, the engagement can only be terminated after reasonable notice." In that case the contract stated that save for certain specified grounds of summary dismissal it should be terminable in the absolute discretion of the employer. It was held that this discretion could only be exercised after proper notice. In *De Stempel* v. *Dunkels*[51] the Court of Appeal used the ordinary rules of contractual implication to conclude that the parties to the contract could not have intended otherwise than that the contract should be terminable by notice. It was left to Lord Denning M.R. in *Richardson* v. *Koefod*[52] finally to assert the presumption of terminability by notice and to discard that of the yearly hiring. "The time has now come," he said, "to state explicitly that there is no presumption of a yearly hiring. In the absence of express stipulation, the rule is that every contract of service is determinable by reasonable notice."

It appears that it will only be possible to displace the presumption of a right to terminate upon reasonable notice by very strong words. In *McClelland* v. *Northern Ireland General Health Services Board*[53] both Lords Oaksey and

---

[45] The Court of Appeal in *Land and Wilson* v. *West Yorkshire M.C.C.* [1981] I.C.R. 334 was prepared to concede a right to terminate one of two separate jobs under a single contract by adequate notice.

[46] (1827) 2 C. & P. 607.

[47] See Cronin and Grime, *Labour Law* (Butterworth 1970). This book is now out of print and, obviously, out of date but it did contain some very useful leads to further thought.

[48] *Buckingham* v. *Surrey and Hants Canal Co.* (1882) 46 L.T. 885.

[49] *Mulholland* v. *Bexwell Estates Co. Ltd.* (1950) 66 T.L.R. (Pt. 2) 764.

[50] *Re African Association Ltd. and Allen* [1910] 1 K.B. 396. See also *Payzu* v. *Hannaford* [1918] 2 K.B. 348.

[51] [1938] 1 All E.R. 238. See also *Fisher* v. *W. B. Dick and Co. Ltd.* [1938] 4 All E.R. 467; *Adams* v. *Union Cinemas Ltd.* [1939] 3 All E.R. 136 at 143.

[52] [1969] 1 W.L.R. 1812.

[53] [1957] 1 W.L.R. 594. See also *Southern Foundries (1926) Ltd.* v. *Shirlaw* [1940] A.C. 701.

Goddard, in the majority, stated that a contract of service said to be permanent and pensionable could be terminated by notice. They did not look with favour on the decision in *Salt* v. *Power Plant Co. Ltd.*[54] that use of the word "permanent" indicated that the contract was not capable of termination by notice.

Statutory minimum notice

The question of the length of notice that will be considered reasonable is now best approached from the statutory provision of minimum notice rights first introduced in 1963 and contained as amended in the Employment Protection (Consolidation) Act 1978.[55] The minimum notice required to be given by an employer to terminate the employment of an employee with one month or more of continuous employment is one week if the period of continuous employment is less than two years. If the period of continuous employment is two years or more the minimum period of notice is one week for each completed year up to a maximum of 12 weeks. The Contracts of Employment Act 1963 broke the principle of reciprocity and since then the minimum period of notice required to be given by an employee with more than one month continuous employment is one week, whatever his length of service. These periods replace any contractual provision for shorter periods but a party may waive his right or accept payment in lieu. It is quite clear that these statutory minimums can be extended both in favour of the employee and of the employer's right to receive notice. There seems no reason to suppose that they cannot be extended by normal common law implication. Custom has often been used as the basis for such implication and it is largely this that has given the common law on notice its peculiarly status-conscious aspect. In *Todd* v. *Kerrick*[56] for instance it was held that a governess could not be treated as a mere menial entitled only to the customary one month's notice available to domestic servants because she enjoyed a different position and status in the family and society.[57] In *Nicoll* v. *Falcon Airways*[58] an airline pilot was held entitled to six months' notice and in *Savage* v. *British India Steam Navigation Co. Ltd.*[59] it was suggested that the master of an ocean-going steamship could be entitled to six months' notice. Lord Denning M.R. in *Hill* v. *C. A. Parsons and Co. Ltd.*[60] concluded that the position of a draughtsman justified him granting the right to six months' notice—a deliberately exaggerated period but no less dependent on concepts of status. The common law did not so extensively examine the notice entitlement of the manual workers because they rarely considered it worthwhile to bring claims for wrongful dismissal, least of all in a court from which a published report might emerge. It was generally assumed, however, that the practice of dismissing with wages for the next pay period established the

---

[54] [1936] 3 All E.R. 322; *cf. Ward* v. *Barclay Perkins and Co. Ltd.* [1939] 1 All E.R. 287.
[55] s.49. A contract for a fixed term of one month or less under which an employee has served continuously for three months is converted into an indefinite contract. Employment Protection (Consolidation) Act 1978, s.49(4) as amended by the Employment Act 1982, Sched. 2.
[56] (1852) 8 Exch. 151.
[57] In *Mulholland* v. *Bexwell Estates Co.* (1950) 66 T.L.R. (Pt. 2) 764 the "general manager" of three companies was considered in reality to hold a comparatively lowly position and to be entitled only to three months' notice.
[58] [1962] 1 Lloyd's Rep. 245.
[59] [1930] 46 T.L.R. 294.
[60] [1972] 1 Ch. 305.

implication of a right to notice corresponding to such pay periods. It was this assumption which, in *Marshall* v. *English Electric Co. Ltd.*[61] enabled the Court of Appeal to hold that suspension of an hourly paid worker could be treated as dismissal on an hour's notice. There is no doubt that implication of such periods of notice would not be countenanced today even if the statutory minimum periods did not exist. On the other hand there is nothing to suggest that common law courts if left to themselves would now extend these minima by implication in the case of most manual employees.

Statute now confers on the employee entitled to notice, not exceeding one week more than the statutory minimum,[62] certain rights during the minimum statutory period.[63] If the employee is ready and willing to work or is incapable of work through sickness or is absent from work in accordance with his contractual holiday rights he is entitled to be paid the average hourly rate if he has normal working hours or not less than a week's pay for each week of notice if there are no normal working hours. The same rights apply where it is the employee who gives notice, but in that case only for the period of notice required by statute of an employee and from the time when the employee leaves the service of the employer in accordance with the notice. Any amount paid to such an employee under a sick pay scheme will go towards meeting this liability. The right to payment during notice ceases if the employer rightfully treats a breach of contract by the employee during the notice period as terminating the contract. If the employee breaks the contract during the notice period then any payment made by him in respect of a period after that breach will go to mitigate damages for the breach.

SPECIFIC ENFORCEMENT

Whatever the fate of the former common law principle that repudiation automatically terminates the contract of employment no doubt has been cast on its source. The contract of employment is regarded as establishing a personal relationship which cannot be the subject of an order for specific performance. The personal nature of the contract has been recognised in a number of respects, the most notable of which is the establishment of the rule that the contract of employment is not assignable.[64] To the argument that the personal quality of the relationship was more obvious to nineteenth century judges thinking of their own domestic servants than to a modern industrialist thinking of the workers on a mass production line common law courts would probably answer that though less apparent it is nonetheless a reality. This reality is derived from the supposition of a mutual trust and confidence upon which more, rather than less, emphasis has been placed in recent years. When we were examining the definition of employment the proposition was advanced that an element of discretion existed in all employment. Of course the same might be said about wide areas of self-employment where contracts to produce a particu-

---

[61] [1945] 1 All E.R. 633.
[62] Employment Protection (Consolidation) Act 1978, s.50.
[63] *Ibid.* Sched. 3.
[64] See *Nokes* v. *Doncaster Amalgamated Collieries* [1940] A.C. 1014; *Ready Mixed Concrete (South East) Ltd.* v. *Minister of Pensions* [1968] 1 Q.B. 497. But see now Employment Protection (Transfer of Undertakings) Regulations 1981, para. 5, p. 251, *infra.*

lar result would be regarded as open to specific enforcement if the nature of the breach left the element of confidence in the ability of the worker unimpaired. Why then should it be said that specific performance is never available as a remedy for breach of the contract of employment even if trust and confidence are unimpaired? It was this line of argument that the majority of the Court of Appeal pursued in *Hill* v. *C. A. Parsons and Co. Ltd.*[65] where trade union pressure rather than any fault of either party had induced the breach. Sachs L.J. in particular, pointed out that none of the reasons usually advanced to explain the non-availability of the remedy were present in the facts of the case. In *Chappell* v. *Beaverbrook Newspapers Ltd.*[66] the Court of Appeal fully considered this decision and concluded that it had depended on the unusual circumstance of the continuing existence of trust and confidence. The court suggested that facts such as to justify an order for specific performance would rarely recur. It seems, therefore, that even if it were to be concluded that refusal of specific performance did depend on absence of trust and confidence that element would be regarded as of extreme fragility so easily broken that only in the most unusual circumstances of breach could it be said to survive. The question arises whether Stamp L.J. in the minority in *Hill* v. *Parsons,* was correct to rest refusal of specific performance on the willingness of either party to continue the relationship. The existence of such unwillingness regardless of the reason must threaten a relationship based on co-operation. There is, in practice, little possibility of a common law court seeking to impose an employment relationship on an unwilling party. The very fact that one party has purported to terminate the contract almost inevitably suggests an unwillingness to continue it even, as Stamp L.J. pointed out, on the facts in *Hill* v. *Parsons.* So one must conclude that though the impossibility of re-establishing trust and confidence may have a satisfying appearance of a logical explanation what really justifies the inevitability of the denial of specific performance is recognition that employment involves elements which depend on a personal willingness to continue the relationship. The other explanations which have from time to time been advanced[67] and the usual principle of reciprocity which denies specific performance to one party if it is not available to the other are, it is submitted, similarly useful explanations of a conclusion based on much less articulate assumptions. Accordingly little is to be gained by seeking, as did the majority in *Hill* v. *Parsons,* gaps in such explanations. Criticism of the statement that employment is a personal relationship is merely a semantic quibble. What matters in practice is that common law courts are unlikely to be persuaded that the indefinite relationship of employment can be established at their order.

Statutory provisions relating to enforcement

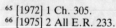

Despite this, after some initial hesitation industrial tribunals have been given the power to order reinstatement or re-engagement.[68] As this power is operated in practice, however, it tends to confirm rather than deny the inevitability of the common law rule. The Act itself recognises that even if such an order is made

---

[65] [1972] 1 Ch. 305.
[66] [1975] 2 All E.R. 233.
[67] *Hopwood* v. *Millar's Timber and Trading Co. Ltd.* [1917] 1 K.B. 305—imposition of a system of villeinage; *De Francesco* v. *Barnum* (1900) 45 Ch.D. 430 at 438—public policy.
[68] See now, Employment Protection (Consolidation) Act 1978, s.69.

the penalty for non-compliance is simply enhanced compensation. Industrial tribunals seldom make such an order unless the employer indicates that he is willing to obey. The availability of the statutory remedy, therefore, appears to recognise the persuasive effect of an order whilst acknowledging what the common law has always accepted.[69]

For different reasons the common law's denial of specific enforcement has received statutory support[70] in the rule that:

"No court shall, by way of

(a) an order for specific performance or specific implementation of a contract of employment, or
(b) an injunction or interdict restraining a breach or threatened breach of such a contract

compel an employee to do any work or attend at any place for the doing of any work."

Presumably, though the draftsman was reluctant to say "impose the relationship of employment" this is what he meant. There could be no order for specific performance of the contract short of the obligation actually to do the work. The principle of reciprocity has not been denied and would enable this statutory provision to be invoked to deny an order for specific performance against an employer.

Exceptions where specific enforcement available

Despite the existence of some examples of acceptance by common law courts of the availability of specific enforcement of the contract[71] it is submitted that the correct rule is that the remedy is not available save, possibly, in two fringe areas.

The decision of the House of Lords in *Vine* v. *National Dock Labour Board*[72] suggests that the courts may declare a purported termination to be a nullity if, in fact, neither party has validly acted to repudiate the contract. In that case a dock worker registered under the former dock labour scheme, was given seven days' notice of de-registration by a committee of his local dock labour board. His appeal to a tribunal established under the scheme failed and he sought a declaration that the action of the committee was *ultra vires* and void on the ground that the local board had no jurisdiction to delegate its statutory disciplinary powers. Viscount Kilmuir L.C. accepting this argument, said:

". . . it follows from the fact that the plaintiff's dismissal was invalid, that his name was never validly removed from the register and he continued in the employ of the National Board. This is an entirely different situation from the ordinary master and servant case; there, if the master wrongfully dismisses the servant, either summarily or by giving insufficient notice, the employment is effectively terminated, albeit in breach of contract. Here the removal of the plaintiff's name from the register being, in law, a nullity, he continued to have the right to be

---

[69] See Williams and Lewis: "The Aftermath of Tribunal Reinstatement and Re-engagement" *DE Research Paper No. 23* (June 1981).
[70] Trade Union and Labour Relations Act 1974, s.16.
[71] *McClelland* v. *Northern Ireland General Health Services Board* [1957] 1 W.L.R. 594; *Francis* v. *Municipal Councillors of Kuala Lumpur* [1962] 1 W.L.R. 1411.
[72] [1957] A.C. 488.

treated as a registered dock worker with all the benefits which by statute, that status conferred on him."

Care should be taken in the application of this decision, however. So far as this account has gone the facts were repeated in *Francis* v. *Municipal Councillors of Kuala Lumpur*[73] but the Privy Council refused a declaration. Logical as would seem to be the decision to declare a nullity non-existent it may be that common law courts will not do so unless they can be persuaded that it has operated to deprive the plaintiff of something more than employment alone.

The second exception to permit the specific enforcement of negative covenants not to work for another is supported by a much stronger line of authority starting with the decision in *Lumley* v. *Wagner*[74] and for long regarded as established by *Warner Brothers Pictures Inc.* v. *Nelson.*[75] It is submitted that Stamp J. was wrong in *Page One Records Ltd.* v. *Britton*[76] to suggest that the cases rested on a different contractual position since this would require acceptance of the idea that specific performance can be expressly contracted for.[77] Stamp J. also appears to have been wrong to suggest that *Lumley's* case could be distinguished from the general principle of non-enforceability because the defendant then could have enforced the only obligation of the plaintiff which was to pay remuneration so that the plaintiff, in turn, was entitled to enforce the obligation to serve.[78] The obligation to pay remuneration cannot be enforced and it makes no difference to the principle that a single payment is due for service so that damages will secure its equivalent. Nevertheless the validity of the *Lumley* principle has been doubted[79] and in *Page One Records Ltd.* v. *Britton*[80] its application was confined to situations where it was realistic to suppose that the prospects of the covenanter in other occupations than those closed to him by the covenant would be substantially as attractive as those offered by employment under the contract containing the covenant.

Damages

In almost every case of breach of the contract of employment the only remedy available in common law courts is the action for damages.[81] Neither punitive nor exemplary damages are available for a breach of contract.[82] The common law does not recognise any property right in employment and accordingly damages for breach of contract by the employer are confined to the amount of remuneration that would have been earned had the contract been carried out, that is to say, had the contract been terminated by the proper contractual period of notice together with any remuneration, including holiday pay, accrued due. This is subject to the normal common law duty to mitigate

[73] *Supra.*
[74] (1852) 1 De G.M. & G. 604.
[75] [1937] 1 K.B. 209.
[76] [1967] 1 W.L.R. 157.
[77] See *Horwood* v. *Millar's Timber and Trading Co. Ltd.* [1917] 1 K.B. 305.
[78] See *Monk* v. *Red Wing Aircraft Co. Ltd.* [1942] 1 K.B. 182.
[79] *Whitwood Chemical Co. Ltd.* v. *Hardman* [1891] 2 Ch. 416, *per* Lindley L.J.
[80] [1967] 1 W.L.R. 157.
[81] *Denmark Productions Ltd.* v. *Boscobel Productions Ltd.* [1969] 1 Q.B. 699; *Decro Wall International S.A.* v. *The Practitioners in Marketing Ltd.* [1971] 1 W.L.R. 361 at 370.
[82] *Addis* v. *The Gramophone Co. Ltd.* [1909] A.C. 488.

damages for breach of contract.[83] Loss of fringe benefits may be taken into account only if they are expressed in monetary terms as part of the periodic wage. So in *Addis* v. *The Gramophone Co. Ltd.*[84] the chance to earn a commission was so expressed and an estimate of the commission allowed as part of the damages. However, where there is a basic salary and fringe benefits exist independently they are not normally taken into account.[85] The same principle applies to compensation for loss of board and lodging[86] and to the opportunity to earn tips even if provided for in the contract.[87]

It is this method of assessing damages which permits termination of the contract immediately with payment of wages in lieu of notice. If there is an obligation only to pay wages there are strong grounds for contending that such a termination is a complete fulfilment of the contract, but this conclusion would run into problems if the common law accepted the wider existence of an obligation to provide work. Dismissal with wages in lieu of notice might then constitute a breach of that obligation for which, however, there would be no substantial remedy. The more commonly held view seems to be that payment of wages in lieu of notice is the payment of liquidated damages for summary dismissal in breach of contract.[88] If the newly emergent principle that a repudiatory breach does not automatically terminate the contract before acceptance were to become established without reservation, however, this view could produce some problems since refusal of the wages in lieu of notice might become an established way of indicating non-acceptance of the repudiation.

FRUSTRATION

In *Davis Contractors Ltd.* v. *Fareham U.D.C.*[89] frustration was described in the following terms:

> "Frustration occurs whenever the law recognises that without default of either party a contractual obligation had become incapable of being performed because the circumstances in which the performance is called for would render it a thing radically different from that which was undertaken by the contract."

One of the largely unexplored difficulties is to decide on the degree of impossibility of performance that is necessary to establish frustration. In *Harman* v. *Flexible Lamps Ltd.*[90] it was said that where a contract is, like the contract of employment, terminable by a relatively short period of unilateral notice there was little necessity for the doctrine in any event. In *Chakki* v. *United Yeast Co. Ltd.*[91] the strength of this point was noted. The court went on

---

[83] See, *e.g. Yetton* v. *Eastwoods Froy Ltd.* [1966] 1 W.L.R. 104.

[84] *Supra.*

[85] *Re R. S. Newman Ltd.* [1916] 2 Ch. 309; *Jackson* v. *Hayes, Candy and Co. Ltd.* [1938] 4 All E.R. 587.

[86] *Wilson* v. *Uccelli* (1929) 45 T.L.R. 395.

[87] *Manubens* v. *Lean* [1919] 1 K.B. 208.

[88] Freedman: *Modern Law of Employment* at p. 471 categorically stated this though none of the three cases cited by him in support of the proposition offers any authority for it. This view was, however, relied on by Sir Diarmaird Conroy in *Taylors Cater Inns Ltd.* v. *The Minister of Labour* [1966] I.T.R. 242 and receives support from the judgments of the Court of Appeal in *Langston* v. *A.U.E.W.* (*No.* 2) [1974] I.C.R. 510.

[89] [1956] A.C. 696, *per* Lord Radcliffe.

[90] [1980] I.R.L.R. 418 (E.A.T.).

[91] [1982] I.C.R. 140 (E.A.T.).

to talk of the need to consider the "reasonableness" of finding a temporary replacement for an employee serving a prison sentence.

Frustration operates automatically. The fact that the employer has taken no steps to end the contract is not conclusive although it is strong evidence tending to show that the employer did not regard the circumstances as constituting frustration.[92]

The most usual circumstance alleged to produce a frustration in the contract of employment is that of illness. In *Poussard* v. *Spiers & Pond*[93] the plaintiff had been engaged to sing the chief part in an opera. She fell ill and was replaced by a substitute who had insisted on engagement for a month. The plaintiff was ready to return after missing only four performances. In the special circumstances the court was prepared to hold that this was a sufficient frustrating event. This decision was distinguished in *Loats* v. *Maple*[94] which concerned a three-year contract to employ a jockey who had sustained a broken thigh and collar bone which incapacitated him for part of a season. Wright J. considered that such a risk was within the contemplation of the contract and that, therefore, a partial incapacitation of this kind had not destroyed the fundamental purpose of the contract. In *Marshall* v. *Harland and Wolff Ltd.*[95] a shipyard fitter had been absent from work for 18 months because of illness and was still incapacitated when he was dismissed owing to the closure of the shipyard. The court formulated the following test of frustration[96]:

> "Was the employee's incapacity, looked at before the purported dismissal of such a nature, or did it appear likely to continue for such a period, that further performance of his obligations in the future would either be impossible or would be a thing radically different from that undertaken by him and accepted by the employer under the agreed terms of his employment?"

In *Hebden* v. *Forsey & Son*[97] this test was adopted in a case where the employee had stopped work in March 1971 and, although fit to return to work in July, had stayed away sick with the permission of the employer until he had recovered from a second operation in August 1972. The court held that after the first operation there was little doubt it would be possible for him to return to work in the future. Throughout his absence he remained in regular contact with his employer and in such circumstances the court concluded that the employer's remedy, if he thought that the period of incapacity was becoming too prolonged, would have been to have given notice to terminate the contract. The absence of any move by the employer to terminate the contract during a period of incapacity was, in the view of the court, a powerful indication that the contractual relationship survived.

It appears to be clear from the sickness cases that the determination of the existence of frustration does not have to be a matter of speculation based on the situation at the onset of the disability. As a disabling circumstance develops

---

[92] *The Egg Stores (Stamford Hill) Ltd.* v. *Leibovici* [1977] I.C.R. 260; *Hart* v. *A. R. Marshall and Sons (Bulwell) Ltd.* [1977] I.C.R. 539.
[93] (1876) 1 Q.B.D. 410.
[94] (1903) 88 L.T. 288.
[95] [1972] I.C.R. 101.
[96] At 106.
[97] [1973] I.C.R. 607.

circumstances may be sufficient at some point in that development to create a frustration.[98]

There are, of course, numerous occurrences, other than illness of an employee, which may frustrate a contract of employment. In *Taylor* v. *Caldwell*,[99] from which the doctrine sprang, a music hall which had been hired out for certain concerts was accidentally destroyed by fire and the contract of hire was held thereby to have been frustrated. Had another hall not been available this, in turn, would have frustrated contracts to appear in the concerts. Detention of a ship by a hostile power upon the outbreak of war has been held to be an event frustrating the seamen's contracts of employment. So has internment, or call-up for military service, provided, in all these cases, that the interruption is likely to be so lengthy as fundamentally to alter the nature of the contract.

The law does not recognise self-induced frustration. A party responsible for the allegedly frustrating event will not be able to rely on it to excuse performance of his contractual obligations. Harman L.J. said in *Denmark Productions Ltd.* v. *Boscobel Productions Ltd.*[1]:

> "The frustrating event is something outside the control of the parties—a war, a famine, a flood or some event of that sort—so that if the parties had thought to provide for it they would at once have agreed that on its happening the contract must come to an end. I have never heard the doctrine applied to an event such as this which depends on the action of one of the parties in connection with the contractual duty of the other of them to a third party."

In *Hare* v. *Murphy Brothers Ltd.*[2] the Court of Appeal considered this point in relation to a sentence of imprisonment. Lord Denning M.R. pointed out that no question had ever been raised as to the possibility that sickness was brought on by the fault of the employee. In his view the important factor was the unforeseen nature of the alleged frustrating event. Notwithstanding this decision of the Court of Appeal, in *Norris* v. *Southampton City Council*[3] Kilner Brown J. declined on this ground to regard imprisonment as a frustrating event.

DEATH

It appears that the death of either the employee, or of the employer, terminates the contract of service. Fridman[4] suggests that, in the latter case, termination will only occur if there was a personal relationship (meaning one specially personal, rather than merely partaking of the personal nature of all contracts of employment). Willes J. referring to personal considerations as the foundation of the contract in *Farrow* v. *Wilson*,[5] appears to have been using that term in its general application to all employment relationships. On the other hand, what Willes J. thought of as a reality is now recognised, normally, as a fiction. It may, therefore, be asked whether the rule should be so general. In practice the

---

[98] *Chakki* v. *United Yeast Co. Ltd.* [1982] I.C.R. 140 following *Egg Stores (Stamford Hill) Ltd.* v. *Leibovici* [1977] I.C.R. 260.

[99] (1863) 3 B. & S. 826.

[1] [1969] 1 Q.B. 699 at 756.

[2] [1974] I.C.R. 603.

[3] [1982] I.C.R. 177. Compare *Chakki* v. *United Yeast Co. Ltd.* [1982] I.C.R. 140 (E.A.T.).

[4] *The Modern Law of Employment*, p. 473.

[5] (1869) L.R. 4 C.P. 744.

argument is academic. The corporations which are responsible for most of the impersonal nature of employment do not die. Where the individual "boss" is the employer there will probably be sufficient of a personal relationship to justify continuation of the rule. A meaningful distinction could only be made if the rule were to be confined to categories of employees like domestic servants. It has been provided, since 1965, that in the case of a claim to redundancy payment, the death of the employer shall count as dismissal even if, by the other provisions relating to redundancy, it would not do so.[6]

DISSOLUTION OF PARTNERSHIP AND WINDING UP OF A COMPANY

A contract of service with a partnership should provide for the effect upon it of a dissolution of the partnership. In the absence of an express, or otherwise implied, provision, where the employee is the servant of the partnership and not of an individual partner, dissolution will operate as a breach of contract of service and not as an effective termination of it.[7]

A contract of apprenticeship, because of the element of personal instruction, will be dissolved by such an event. The effect of lesser changes, such as the introduction of a new partner or the retirement of an old one cannot be stated generally. Theoretically, the change of employers should suggest the offer of a new contract to the employee. In *Phillips* v. *Alhambra Palace Co.*[8] Kennedy J. suggested that the answer would turn on the personal quality of the contract. Batt[9] takes the view that all partnership changes, unless special provision is made in the contract, or they are accepted by the employee, will operate as a breach of contract of service.

In *Brace* v. *Calder*[10] the Court of Appeal held that the retirement of two of the partners operated as a dismissal of the firm's manager.

An order for compulsory winding up of a limited company operates as a notice of dismissal.[11] It had been thought that the same was true of such an appointment in a voluntary winding up[12] although this was doubted where the voluntary winding up was with a view to reorganisation.[13] In *Re Foster Clark's Indenture Trusts*[14] there occurred what is now known as a hiving down by which a receiver appointed by a debenture holder transferred the business of the company to one of its wholly-owned subsidiaries. Plowman J. quoted opinions of commentators to the effect that an appointment of a receiver would only determine contracts if it was an appointment by the court. He said

> "At first sight there seems to be no very good reason in principle why an appointment out of court of a receiver who is agent of the company should determine contracts of employment and the two passages which I have cited . . . suggest that such an appointment does not have that effect."

---

[6] See now Employment Protection (Consolidation) Act 1978, s.93.
[7] *Covell* v. *Scamell* (1910) 103 L.T. 535.
[8] [1901] 1 K.B. 59.
[9] *Master and Servant* (5th ed.), pp. 106 *et seq*.
[10] [1895] 2 Q.B. 253.
[11] *Re General Rolling Stock Co.* (1866) L.R. 1 Eq. 346.
[12] *Fowler* v. *Commercial Timber Co. Ltd.* [1930] 2 K.B. 1.
[13] *Midland Counties District Bank Ltd.* v. *Attwood* [1905] 1 Ch. 357.
[14] [1966] 1 W.L.R. 125.

The learned judge held that, however that might be, there could be no doubt that the sale of the business as a going concern even to a subsidiary must have the effect of terminating the contracts of employment because the employing company no longer had a business in which to employ people. So far as this latter conclusion is concerned the analogy with the partnership case of *Brace* v. *Calder*[15] is clearly incorrect. It might be argued that an employer who deprived himself of the ability to offer work committed a repudiatory breach of contract but such an action cannot amount to a termination save as the inevitable result (under the "old" rule) of that breach. The basis of the partnership decision is wholly different. The new partnership is a thing different in character from the old. The old no longer exists and so there must have been a termination of its contracts of employment. So far as this aspect of the decision is concerned it would in any case seem to have been supplanted by the provisions of Regulation 4 of the Transfer of Undertakings (Protection of Employment) Regulations 1981[16] which not only envisage a situation in which the employees may temporarily remain in the employment of their original employer but have the effect, ultimately, of transferring their contracts of employment to the eventual acquirer of the business.

So far as the general principle is concerned that the voluntary appointment of a receiver does not automatically terminate the contracts of employment Pennycuick J. applied (without detailed discussion) Plowman J.'s dictum in *Re Mack Trucks (Britain) Ltd.*[17] on the basis there stated that the receiver was acting as agent of the company and not as a principal. This had the useful effect of maintaining continuity of employment.

In *Deaway Ltd.* v. *Calverley*[18] Sir John Donaldson sitting then in the N.I.R.C. but with a reputation as one of the great commercial judges suggested that the whole matter might be simplified. He pointed out that the distinction ought to be between receivers on insolvency (whether voluntarily appointed or not) on the one hand and receivers who carry on the business. But he then said that the employee should not be at the mercy of such technicalities. In his view the receiver should be regarded as employing as the receiver of the company and not in his personal capacity. There had been no transfer of the business and the receiver always acted expressly on behalf of the company. It is not clear to what extent this can be applied to a receiver appointed by the court but it is submitted that it makes good sense that the law should endeavour to produce rules which can be understood by those to whom they apply. There is enough in the situation of a transfer of business already which leaves the employee uncertain who is employing him without the niceties of legal logic adding to it. If Sir John Donaldson did intend a single rule to apply to all receivers it is suggested that this authority should be followed.

---

[15] [1895] 2 Q.B. 253.
[16] S.I. 1981 No. 1794.
[17] [1967] 1 W.L.R. 780.
[18] [1973] I.C.R. 546.

CHAPTER 5

UNFAIR DISMISSAL

THE common law offered no security of employment. The contract could be terminated for no reason and the only compensation available was the equivalent of wages for a short period. Nevertheless this position survived until 1971, alleviated only by a statutory concession to the pressing social problem of multiple dismissals for redundancy. Even here no security was afforded by the Redundancy Payments Act 1965 which accepted the prerogative of management to decide when a redundancy existed and merely enhanced the compensation available for loss of a job. As the decision in *Hindle* v. *Percival Boats Ltd.*[1] demonstrated it was still open to an employer in a redundancy situation to avoid even this consequence by dismissing for some other reason unless, improbably, it could be shown that he did not genuinely believe that reason. No doubt it was the pressing need to offer job protection at least recognisably comparable to that of other Western European countries that induced the enactment in 1971 of the provisions of the Industrial Relations Act establishing a statutory system of remedies for unfair dismissal. This system, after an uncertain start, has somewhat improved the available compensation for an improper dismissal. It has totally altered the concept of justification for dismissal so that there now exists a vastly extended range of causes of complaint. It also totally removed the defence that, however insubstantial the cause, adequate notice had been given. It substantially failed to ensure return of the unfairly dismissed to employment, however, and many would contend that in relation to other industrial countries the available compensation is so low as to afford little deterrent to the employer determined to rid himself of the obligations of employment. It would, however, be exaggerated criticism to say that the statutory system did not substantially improve the position of the employee but radically altered the foundation on which he held his job. Whereas formerly it was common to regard dismissal as a legal right of management it is now an action which almost every management, regardless of the existence of trade union objection, hesitates to take. Conversely, it was equally exaggerated to suggest that even at the height of its current effectiveness between 1975 and, say, 1978 the system made it so difficult to dismiss that it was wise to hesitate to engage employees. It is suggested that relative to comparable industrial countries the effectiveness of the system in those years was not such as to justify the reduction in that effectiveness that followed 1978 both as a result of changed judicial attitudes and of legislative amendment. To a considerable extent the job protection available in this country is only tolerable because it is in practice supported by trade union power. It must follow that in sections of industry where that power does not exist United Kingdom standards fall below those of a number of Continental European countries in this respect.

---

[1] [1969] 1 W.L.R. 174.

DISMISSAL

Assuming that the employee satisfies the qualifying preconditions examined in
the Appendix to Chapter 3 it is for him to prove, unless the point is conceded,
that the circumstances in which his contract came to an end satisfy the statutory
definition of dismissal.[2] This definition covers three distinct forms of termination of the contract of employment.

Employer-initiated termination

   (a) The contract under which the employee is employed by the employer is
       terminated by the employer, whether it is so terminated by notice or
       without notice.

This aspect embodies the popular concept of an employer-initiated termination. Nevertheless it does give rise to a few problems. It may occasionally have
to be decided whether the words or the action taken amount to a dismissal.
There are a number of reported examples of the use of ambiguous words but the
best working test was laid down by the E.A.T. in *Turner* v. *D. T. Kean*.[3] The
employee had been instructed by his employer not to use the company's van
outside working hours and had been lent £275 to enable him to buy himself a
car. His employer discovered the van outside a country club of which he was a
member and the employee the part-time doorman. Obviously having lost his
temper the employer, among other things, said to the employee "That's it,
you're finished with me." Phillips J. said:

> "In our judgment the test which has to be applied in cases of this kind is along these
> lines. Were the words spoken those of dismissal, that is to say, were they intended
> to bring the contract of employment to an end? What was the employer's inten-
> tion? In answering that a relevant, and perhaps the most important question is how
> would a reasonable employee, in all circumstances, have understood what the
> employer intended by what he said and did? Then in most of these cases, and in this
> case, it becomes relevant to look at the later events following the utterance of the
> words and preceding the actual departure of the employee . . . . A word of caution
> is necessary because in considering later events it is necessary to remember that a
> dismissal or resignation, once it has taken effect, cannot be unilaterally withdrawn.
> Accordingly, as it seems to us, later events need to be scrutinised with some care in
> order to see whether they are genuinely explanatory of the acts alleged to con-
> stitute dismissal, or whether they reflect a change of mind. If they are in the former
> category they may be valuable as showing what was really intended."

This test was held, however, only to apply where the words are ambiguous.
Where there is no ambiguity and the words are understood in a certain sense
there is no room for consideration of what a reasonable person might have
understood.[4]

Notice of termination has at common law been held to require some precision
of date and time. This led to the formulation of a distinction between a mere
warning of an impending decision to dismiss and notice of dismissal.[5] A warning

[2] Now contained in the Employment Protection (Consolidation) Act 1978, s.55.
[3] [1978] I.R.L.R. 110.
[4] *B. G. Gale Ltd.* v. *Gilbert* [1978] I.C.R. 1149.
[5] *Morton Sundour Fabrics Ltd.* v. *Shaw* (1967) 2 K.I.R. 1; *Devon County Council* v. *Cook*
[1977] I.R.L.R. 188.

of an impending decision on dismissal has, moreover, been held[6] not to constitute a repudiatory breach such as to justify the employee in leaving and claiming constructive dismissal.[7] It is important, however, to avoid defining a warning as any imprecise notice of impending termination despite the fact that this was the source of the rule in *Morton Sundour*. In *Maher* v. *Fram Gerrard Ltd.*[8] the N.I.R.C. made it clear that notice of dismissal would constitute a dismissal however imprecise.

It is clear that the fact that an employee asks to be dismissed[9] or is willing to accept dismissal[10] does not prevent satisfaction of the statutory definition. On the other hand these situations may be distinguished from that in which the employee effectively asks for and is given permission to leave.[11] There is a third situation which has caused more difficulty which involves agreement, or apparent agreement, that upon the happening of a certain event the contract will terminate. In *British Leyland (U.K.) Ltd.* v. *Ashraf*[12] the employee was allowed five weeks' unpaid leave to return to his native Pakistan to visit his mother who was seriously ill. In accordance with established company practice he was required to sign a document which stated that "no further extension will be considered" and which also made it clear that if the employee failed to return to work by a specified date his contract would be terminated. The E.A.T. held that the resulting termination was the outcome of agreement and did not, therefore, constitute a dismissal within the definition. Clearly this must be construed very narrowly. In *Ashraf* itself the E.A.T. indicated that the agreement might be regarded as effective because it was the price paid for a concession distinct from the incidents of employment. It stated that the imposition of such a term in a contract of employment without such a link would not be regarded as giving rise to agreed termination. This indicates an adherence to the need to support variation of contract by fresh consideration which is rare in the law of employment. Even where a concession had been made subject to a condition backed by the sanction of termination a subsequent decision of the E.A.T. in *Midland Electric Co. Ltd.* v. *Kanji*[13] indicated a reluctance to imply an agreement to vary the normal method of termination of employment. The court was able to conjure a distinction between the words "your contract will terminate on that date" used in *Ashraf* and "the Company will consider that you have terminated your employment." It is submitted that the distinction owes a good deal to the persuasive skill of counsel but more to a desire to avoid following *Ashraf* if possible. The possibility of *Ashraf* opening up any significant gap in the availability of the remedies for unfair dismissal was finally removed by the decision in *Tracey* v. *Zest Equipment Co. Ltd.*[13a] that the exception should be confined to the facts of that case.

A further difficulty emerging from the apparently straightforward concept of dismissal by the employer is one which was foreseen by the legislature at its

---

[6] *Devon County Council* v. *Cook, supra*.

[7] See, *infra*, p. 187.

[8] [1974] I.C.R. 31.

[9] *Mercia Rubber Mouldings Ltd.* v. *Lingwood* [1974] I.C.R. 256.

[10] *Burton, Allton and Johnson Ltd.* v. *Peck* [1975] I.C.R. 193.

[11] *L. Lipton Ltd.* v. *Marlborough* [1979] I.R.L.R. 179.

[12] [1978] I.C.R. 979.

[13] [1980] I.R.L.R. 185.

[13a] [1982] I.R.L.R. 268.

inception. If notice of dismissal has been given by an employer but the employee of his own initiative leaves before that notice expires the contract has been terminated by that leaving and not by the action of the employer. Legislative provisions in relation both to claims for redundancy payment and unfair dismissal provide that there will be deemed to be a dismissal where an employee under notice from his employer, himself gives notice to his employer of his desire to leave on a date earlier than the date on which the employer's notice is due to expire.[14] The development of the two rights from different statutory sources has, however, given rise to significant differences of detail between them. Whereas, in the case of a claim for unfair dismissal, the employee's rights are preserved at whatever point in his period of notice he gives notice or leaves and regardless of his employer's consent to that leaving, in the case of a claim to redundancy payment the right is only preserved if the employee actually gives notice *in writing*[15] during the minimum statutory period of notice to which he is entitled. Even then the claim is subject to objection by the employer and possible apportionment of the payment.[16] It is, therefore, not improbable that a notice to leave early will be ineffective to satisfy the requirements of the redundancy provisions but most unlikely that such a notice would fail to satisfy those of the unfair dismissal provisions. If, for any reason, the notice to leave early were invalid the employee's right might still be capable of preservation. In *Hudson* v. *Fuller Shapcott*[17] an industrial tribunal held that the acceptance of the notice to leave early by the employer might be regarded as a consensual variation of the date of dismissal. This view was subsequently accepted by the N.I.R.C.[18] In *Ready Case Ltd.* v. *Jackson*[19] it was held that an industrial tribunal was entitled to attribute to the words "you can piss off" the quality of an agreement to vary the original date of termination. It could also be contended that where the employer's notice amounted to a repudiatory breach an employee's subsequent leaving constituted a constructive dismissal. This, however, would not arise in the normal early leaving situation since, to constitute a constructive dismissal, the employee would have to leave almost immediately upon receipt of the employer's notice and the circumstances would have to show that he did so in protest at the breach of contract and not, for instance, because he had found other employment.

Expiry of fixed term

(b) Where under that contract he is employed for a fixed term that term expires without being renewed under the same contract.

The definition of a fixed term contract has already been considered.[20]

Constructive dismissal

(c) The employee terminates that contract with or without notice, in circumstances (apart, in the case of a redundancy payment claim, from

---

[14] Employment Protection (Consolidation) Act 1978, ss.55 and 85.
[15] See, *e.g. Brown* v. *Sugar Manufacturing Co. Ltd.* [1967] I.T.R. 213.
[16] See, *e.g. Jarman* v. *E. Pollard and Co. Ltd.* [1967] I.T.R. 406.
[17] [1970] I.T.R. 266.
[18] *Glacier Metal Co. Ltd.* v. *Dyer* [1974] 3 All E.R. 21.
[19] [1981] I.R.L.R. 312 (E.A.T.).
[20] *Supra*, p. 154.

an employer lock-out) such that he is entitled to terminate it without notice by reason of the employer's conduct.

The group of situations comprehended within heading (c) has come to be commonly called constructive dismissal. This concept has a strange history. It was incorporated in the Redundancy Payments Act 1965 for the obvious reason that, without it, an employer might have appeared able, with impunity, to force an employee to leave his employment without the employer terminating the contract. The Industrial Relations Act 1971, introducing a remedy for unfair dismissal, however, did not include this heading and it was made clear in debate that this was no oversight but that the government did not intend to extend the right for unfair dismissal to an employee who left in such circumstances. Nevertheless, in *Sutcliffe* v. *Hawker Siddeley Aviation Ltd.*[21] Sir John Donaldson in the N.I.R.C. described as "academic pedantry" the suggestion that the statutory concept of dismissal for the purpose of claims for unfair dismissal was not intended to include this situation. He pointed out that the then unchallenged effect of a repudiatory breach of the contract would be that the contract was automatically terminated. Accordingly it could be argued that, at common law, where an employee left in response to a repudiatory breach by the employer it was the employer who had terminated the contract. With the increasing doubt as to the correctness of this view of repudiatory breach it would not now be so easy to deduce a constructive dismissal from common law doctrines but the view in *Sutcliffe's* case, to which objection could not then be taken, served its turn until statute made express provision for it in 1974. Incidentally, whilst common law was the support for the doctrine of constructive dismissal there could be no question but that the action of the employer had to constitute a repudiatory breach of the contract and that the response of the employee must demonstrably be to that breach. As we shall see these conclusions continue to be applied to the purely statutory concept. It may be observed that it is feasible to contend that this form of constructive dismissal is not "constructive" at all. If, indeed, the employer has indicated by his repudiatory breach his rejection of all contractual obligations then he has actually—not constructively—terminated the contract. This view was adopted by the Court of Appeal in *Marriot* v. *The Oxford and District Co-operative Society Ltd.* (*No.* 2)[22] to avoid what was then the effect of the additional requirement for a constructive dismissal under the Redundancy Payments Act 1965 that the employee must leave without notice.[23]

Some of the problems were eliminated by the introduction in the Trade Union and Labour Relations Act 1974 of statutory provision for complaint of unfair constructive dismissal in similar terms to that applicable to redundancy payment but without the requirement that the employee should leave without notice.[24] Not only did this free the courts to develop new ideas about repudiation but it also allowed them to speculate on what was meant by the requirement

---

[21] [1973] I.C.R. 560.

[22] [1970] 1 Q.B. 186. See also *Land and Wilson* v. *West Yorkshire M.C.C.* [1981] I.R.L.R. 87 (C.A.).

[23] This requirement, which has now disappeared from the statutory definition, is difficult to explain since it seems to envisage a situation where in order to terminate the contract the employee has to indicate his acceptance of the repudiation, *i.e.* the modern view of the effect of repudiation.

[24] This requirement was also removed from the redundancy provisions by the E.P.A. 1975.

that the employer's action should be such as to "entitle" the employee to terminate the contract "without notice." In *Gilbert* v. *Goldstone Ltd.*[25] the E.A.T. accepted the proposition that entitlement might be governed not only by breach of the contract but also by an employer's unreasonable conduct. With hindsight it is difficult to understand the support that this extension enjoyed at the time since the conclusion of the Court of Appeal in *Western Excavating (E.C.C.) Ltd.* v. *Sharp*[26] that, without more, the word "entitled" must mean "having a legal right" appears unarguable. The qualification that the employee needs to be entitled to leave *without notice* seems conclusive. Nevertheless, it may be said in support of the "heresy" that to limit complaints of constructive dismissal to breaches of contract is to tie a new statutory remedy to the older rules of the common law. If the employee has a right to complain of unreasonable termination why should he be forced to get his case off the ground by complaining of a breach of contract? If his statutory rights cannot be excluded by contract how is it that they can be effectively excluded by a contractual provision that prevents the action of the employer from constituting a breach of contract? The effect of the test in *Gilbert* v. *Goldstone* would have been to eliminate subsequent inquiry into the reasonableness of the dismissal since that issue would already have been determined by the decision that there was a constructive dismissal.[27]

The decision of the Court of Appeal in *Western Excavating (E.C.C.) Ltd.* v. *Sharp*[28] firmly established constructive dismissal as arising only from a repudiatory breach. As a result of a disciplinary suspension without pay Sharp was short of money and sought an advance of accrued holiday pay. His request was refused on the ground that company policy was not to make holiday payments save for holidays. In order to secure his holiday pay and thus solve his immediate financial problems Sharp left his employment. Subsequently he claimed to have been unfairly constructively dismissed. The industrial tribunal and the E.A.T., founding themselves on the test of unreasonable conduct, upheld his complaint, but the Court of Appeal reversed this decision. Lord Denning M.R. said:

> "The new test of 'unreasonable conduct' of the employer is too indefinite by far: it has led to acute difference of opinion between the members of tribunals . . . It is better to have the contract test of the common law. It is more certain: as it can well be understood by intelligent laymen under the direction of a legal chairman . . . . I would adopt the reasoning of the considered judgment of the Employment Appeal Tribunal in *Wetherall (Bond St., W.1) Ltd.* v. *Lynn*[28]:
>
> > 'Parliament might well have said, in relation to whether the employer's conduct had been reasonable having regard to equity and the substantial merits of the case, but it neither laid down that special statutory criterion or any other. So, in our judgment, the answer can only be, entitled according to law, and it is to the law of contract that you have to look.' "

In the result the certainty that Lord Denning envisaged did not materialise. Our study of the implication of terms[29] will have revealed how relatively easy it

---

[25] [1977] I.C.R. 36.
[26] [1978] I.C.R. 221.
[27] See p. 201, *infra*.
[28] [1978] I.C.R. 205 at p. 211.
[29] See Chap. 2.

is to turn an unreasonable action into a breach of contract by implying an obligation not to commit such an unreasonable act. The more meaningless the alleged term the more discretion is afforded to discover a breach giving rise to unfair dismissal.[30] Nowhere is this more apparent than in the use that has been made of an alleged obligation to sustain mutual trust and confidence.[31]

Correct application of the principle in *Western Excavating Ltd.* v. *Sharp*[32] however, involves some limitation upon this discretion. Lord Denning made it quite clear that "entitlement" referred to the concept of a repudiatory breach. The breach must be sufficiently serious to justify the employee in treating the contract as at an end. There is little doubt that some earlier reported decisions, not only of industrial tribunals, failed to consider this requirement. It was, however, emphasised in *Walker* v. *Josiah Wedgwood and Sons Ltd.*[33] in which a series of incidents, such as failure to consult the works manager over the appointment of a subordinate and instructing him to pay increases to his subordinates when his own increase was withheld, were considered not indicative of any sufficiently serious breach to amount to repudiation. Although interspersed with examples of acceptance of apparently less serious breaches this insistence seems to have found support from most subsequent judgments.[34] It is nonetheless true to say that by the process of taking particular breaches and applying to them a generalised description such as 'destruction of trust and confidence' it is still possible to make relatively minor breaches look serious, especially when fortified by the fact that continuation of the relationship is, indeed, impossible because the employee has walked out. In *Garner* v. *Grange Furnishing Ltd.*[35] for instance, the E.A.T. allowed a series of incidents to amount to repudiation and added that conduct making it impossible for the employee to stay is plainly repudiatory.

There is no doubt that the need to act upon a repudiatory breach to establish constructive dismissal has led to a considerable increase in judicial attention to the development of implied terms in the contract of employment. As we have seen this raises some very complex considerations haphazard and ill-formulated discussion of which could make the contract of employment a virtually unworkable method of controlling the relationship of employment. Davies and Freedland[36] cite the judgment in *British Leyland (U.K.) Ltd.* v. *McQuilken*[37] and pose the question whether discussion of the implication of a collectively agreed scheme of redundancy into individual contracts of employment was an appropriate way to decide whether a constructive dismissal had occurred. A clause in this agreement provided that employees affected by reorganisation

---

[30] Early signs of this development were observed by Patrick Elias writing in (1978) 87 I.L.J. 100.

[31] For some extreme examples of the application of implied terms see: *Fyfe and McGrouther Ltd.* v. *Byrne* [1977] I.R.L.R. 29; *Wood* v. *Freeloader Ltd.* [1977] I.R.L.R. 455; *Isle of Wight Tourist Board* v. *Coombes* [1976] I.R.L.R. 413; *Gardner Ltd.* v. *Beresford* [1978] I.R.L.R. 63.

[32] *Supra.*

[33] [1978] I.C.R. 744.

[34] See, *e.g. Adams* v. *Charles Zub Associates Ltd.* [1978] I.R.L.R 551; *Gillies* v. *Richard Daniels and Co. Ltd.* [1979] I.R.L.R. 457; *Graham Oxley Tool Steels Ltd.* v. *Firth* [1980] I.R.L.R. 135.

[35] [1977] I.R.L.R. 206.

[36] At p. 340.

[37] [1978] I.R.L.R. 245.

would be interviewed to discover whether they desired retraining or dismissal for redundancy. Subsequently the employer changed his plans, and employees were told they would have the option of transfer to other locations or retraining. Uncertainty continued as to the precise fate of individuals and McQuilken eventually left the employment without ever having been interviewed. The Scottish E.A.T. discussed the doctrine of constructive dismissal and concluded that the collective agreement was a long term policy plan not incorporated into individual contracts of employment. It is apparent from the judgment that had it decided otherwise it would have found great difficulty in avoiding a decision that a constructive dismissal had occurred, notwithstanding its ultimate conclusion that the real reason which caused McQuilken to leave was uncertainty about his future.

The difficulty in avoiding complexity of this type is that it is not clear from the statutory definition how closely the reason for the termination must relate to the employer's conduct. All the statute says is that termination must take place in circumstances such that the employee is entitled to terminate. The courts have, however, tended to insist on a closer relationship than those words would necessarily imply. This is particularly apparent in the judgment in *Walker* v. *Josiah Wedgwood and Sons Ltd.*[38] where Arnold J. in the E.A.T., said:

> "The question has been whether it is sufficient merely to act in such a way as to indicate that the contractual relationship will not be continued, or whether it is necessary to do more than that, namely to indicate that the reason why it will not be continued is the conduct of the employers which is regarded as unjustified by the employee."

The court expressed surprise at the absence of authority on this but relied on some remarks in *Logabax Ltd.* v. *Titherley*[39] to assist it in reaching the conclusion that:

> ". . . . it is at least a requisite that the employee should leave because of the breach of the employer's relevant duty to him, and that this should demonstrably be the case. It is not sufficient, we think, if he merely leaves. . . . And secondly, we think it is not sufficient if he leaves in circumstances which indicate some ground for his leaving other than the breach of the employer's obligation to him."

The second more general aspect of this proposition has, in turn, received little attention but its more specific application in the rule that it must be clear from the circumstances or the employee's own action that he has responded promptly to the breach is, it is submitted, generally accepted by industrial tribunals and the E.A.T.[40] The modification in *Graham Oxley Tool Steels Ltd.* v. *Firth*[41] that it is enough if the only reasonable conclusion must be that the employer appreciated that the employee's leaving was an objection to his breach of contract does not detract from the value of the general principle from which the rule derives. In *W. E. Cox Toner (International) Ltd.* v. *Crook*[42] Browne-Wilkinson J. said that mere continuation at work, though some evidence, would not be conclusive of affirmation and an employee who made his objection clear

---

[38] [1978] I.C.R. 744 at p. 751.
[39] [1977] I.R.L.R. 369.
[40] See, *e.g. Hunt* v. *British Railways Board* [1979] I.R.L.R. 379.
[41] [1980] I.R.L.R. 135.
[42] [1981] I.C.R. 823 (E.A.T.).

would not be taken to have affirmed. In *Genower* v. *Ealing, etc., Area Health Authority*[42a] it was pointed out that though a constructive dismissal occurs it may be held to be a fair dismissal if the circumstances cause the tribunal to consider the employer's breach of contract a reasonable action.[43]

Unilateral variation as constructive dismissal

It is normal for the courts to treat as constructive dismissal the common situation in which an employer, for one reason or another, offers the employee a job different from that which he is by contract obliged to do. As students who have absorbed the principles of the contract of employment frequently point out this situation appears to be one in which the contract has been terminated by the employer. It is fair to reply that this may not always be as obvious as it looks. In *White* v. *London Transport Executive*[44] the employee was employed as a waitress. Subsequently she assisted the manager of the social centre and was paid a supervisor's rate. When the manager left she was appointed to that position on a probationary basis. The probation was not successful and she was offered alternative employment as a waitress. It seems that the E.A.T. thought that her contract was as assistant to the manager since it held that failure to reinstate her in that job was a very small breach. With respect, it is suggested that it was a very large breach, however reasonable it might then have been considered to be. Apart from that, however, it is clear that had she been offered reinstatement at that level the employee could not have complained that removal from a probationary post was a termination of contract by the employer. The proper questions, as the judgment reveals, would have been directed to alleged repudiatory factors such as a possible contractual obligation to conduct periodic appraisal.

In *Land and Wilson* v. *West Yorkshire M.C.C.*[45] the Court of Appeal refused to regard withdrawal of one aspect of the job as a repudiatory breach on the ground that the contract of employment contained two separate elements and that it was necessary to imply a right to terminate one without affecting the other. This is likely to prove an exceptional case. More normally the elimination of a significant part of an employee's duties will be regarded as a repudiatory breach.[46]

To treat all cases of rejection of alternative offers as constructive dismissal might seem to avoid a number of difficult questions which might arise if some were argued as dismissal. In many such circumstances the employer might respond that when making the alternative offer he had taken no decision not to continue the former employment if the offer was rejected. On the other hand, if he could put forward this contention it would also remove the existence of the repudiatory breach necessary to found a constructive dismissal.

The employee must be careful not to presume an anticipatory breach. In *Haseltine Lake and Co.* v. *Dowler*[47] the employee left employment after

---

[42a] [1980] I.R.L.R. 297.

[43] A number of other decisions supporting this were collected in the judgment of the Court of Appeal in *Savoia* v. *Chiltern Herb Farms Ltd.* [1982] I.R.L.R. 166.

[44] [1981] I.R.L.R. 261.

[45] [1981] I.C.R. 334.

[46] See *Coleman* v. *S. and W. Baldwin Ltd.* [1977] I.R.L.R. 342 (E.A.T.).

[47] [1981] I.C.R. 222. See also *International Computers Ltd.* v. *Kennedy* [1981] I.R.L.R. 28.

numerous intimations that if he did not do so he would eventually be dismissed. The E.A.T. held that the employer had not committed himself to a date for dismissal so no question arose that he would inevitably be in breach. In *Financial Techniques (Planning Service) Ltd.* v. *Hughes*[48] the employee resigned without notice before he had otherwise intended to do so, claiming that he was entitled to do so by reason of the employer's refusal to comply with a scheme of bonus payment. The Court of Appeal held that action in support of one point of view during a genuine dispute as to the meaning of the contract did not constitute an anticipatory breach. Templeman L.J., however, was of the opinion that a party who insisted on the correctness of his view might be guilty of such a breach. In the light of these decisions it is apparent that the employee may have difficulty in selecting the right time to leave since he may neither go too early nor leave it too late.

It may be argued that even if it is accepted that there is no real justification for treating such cases as constructive dismissal there is no real harm in doing so. This is almost certainly correct in practice. In theory it is possible to point out that in a case of constructive dismissal the employer does not have to establish a reason to rebut the presumption that it is unfair. In practice such a presumption virtually exists in cases of established constructive dismissal and the employer will have to work hard to prove the reasonableness of the dismissal so that the question becomes one only of the order in which the issues are considered.

"Constructive resignation"

If the original common law explanation for constructive dismissal is correct then it is possible to contend that an employee who commits a repudiatory breach of the contract of employment himself thereby terminates the contract. Any subsequent act of the employer apparently dismissing the employee can be said merely to be a recognition of this termination. Because it is immediately obvious that this argument, if accepted, could destroy the application of remedies for unfair dismissal in a large number of cases of dismissal for cause courts and tribunals have been very reluctant to draw such an apparently logical conclusion. In *Hare* v. *Murphy Bros.*[49] the first major decision to raise the point, the N.I.R.C. held that an employee sentenced to 12 months' imprisonment had terminated his own contract by making performance impossible. The Court of Appeal preferred to rest its decision on frustration.[50] Whilst this case was awaiting decision by the Court of Appeal the N.I.R.C. distinguished its own decision in a way that leaves the problem open even in the light of recent changes in the effect of repudiatory breach. In *Forgings and Presswork Ltd.* v. *McDougall*[51] it said that the employee in *Hare* had left the employer no option but to regard the contract as at an end. If, as seems inevitable, courts must continue to accept that there are some repudiatory acts, such as walking out, which do of themselves terminate the contract the question becomes one of which acts are to be placed in this category. Many breaches can either be

---

[48] [1981] I.R.L.R. 32.
[49] [1973] I.C.R. 331 affirmed on other grounds [1974] I.C.R. 603. See also *Jones* v. *Liverpool Corporation* [1974] I.T.R. 33.
[50] See p. 179, *supra*.
[51] [1974] I.C.R. 532.

regarded as not repudiatory at all[52] or sufficient only to raise the employer's option to terminate. Acts which are classified as conclusive rejection of the contract, however, must logically be regarded as termination by the party committing the act. The effect of this discretion so to classify a breach is clearly seen in *Gannon* v. *J. C. Firth Ltd.*[53] Nineteen employees had walked out during their shift leaving a high pressure steam vessel switched on. When they reported for work next day they found the entrance locked and were told there was no work for them. The following day they were told their employment was ended. It was held that they had terminated their own contracts. Subsequent cases which form the basis of the modern rule as to repudiation[54] have all expressly or implicitly rejected this decision. But if the rationalisation by Slynn J. in *Brown* v. *Southall and Knight*[55] is correct it is not wrong in principle but only in the sense that it classified as conclusive a repudiation which clearly the other party could have overlooked. The possibility of *Gannon* v. *Firth* "resignations" continuing to be recognised from time to time will only disappear if one accepts the argument of Buckley L.J. in *Gunton* v. *London Borough of Richmond*[56] that no repudiation, however apparently conclusive, terminates the contract until accepted.

Forced resignation as dismissal

One situation has consistently been recognised as giving rise to dismissal notwithstanding that it does not fit neatly into any of the three statutory categories. An employee who resigns as a result of being given an option either to do so or be dismissed is usually said to have been constructively dismissed.[57] In *Sheffield* v. *Oxford Controls Co. Ltd.*[58] the E.A.T. insisted that for this rule to apply the causal connection between the threat of dismissal and the resignation must be shown. In that case the threat of dismissal if the employee did not resign had been made but the employee then negotiated terms upon which he left voluntarily.

THE STANDARD OF FAIRNESS

We now turn to consideration of the standard by which the tribunals determine the fairness of a dismissal once the reason is established. Before we proceed a word of warning is appropriate. The reader, if he is a lawyer, will no doubt be looking for rules. If he has read previous sections of this book he may be becoming used to the idea that much of labour law is a matter of trends rather than rules. Nowhere is this more so than in the application of the test of fair dismissal. In *Bailey* v. *B.P. Oil (Kent Refinery) Ltd.*[59] Lawton L.J. delivering the judgment of the Court of Appeal said:

---

[52] As in *Trust Houses Forte Hotels Ltd.* v. *Murphy* [1977] I.R.L.R. 186.
[53] [1976] I.R.L.R. 415.
[54] See, *e.g. Fisher* v. *York Trailer Co. Ltd.* [1979] I.C.R. 834; *Rasool* v. *Hepworth Pipe Co. Ltd.* [1980] I.C.R. 495; *Brown* v. *Southall and Knight* [1980] I.C.R. 617; *London Transport Executive* v. *Clarke* [1980] I.C.R. 532.
[55] *Supra*, p. 158.
[56] [1980] 3 All E.R. 577.
[57] See *Penprase* v. *Mander Bros. Ltd.* [1973] I.R.L.R. 167. An industrial tribunal decision.
[58] [1979] I.C.R. 396.   [59] [1980] I.C.R. 642.

"The relevant statutory provisions contain no reference to procedures agreed with trade unions. Every employee in a relevant employment has the right not to be unfairly dismissed by his employer. In determining whether the dismissal was fair or unfair in a case such as this, the employer has to show what was the reason for the dismissal and that the reason related to the conduct of the employee, as in this case it did. The all important provision is para. 6(8)[60] which is in these terms: ' . . . the determination of the question whether the dismissal was fair or unfair, having regard to the reason shown by the employer, shall depend on whether the employer can satisfy the Tribunal that in the circumstances (having regard to equity and the substantial merits of the case) he acted reasonably in treating it as a sufficient reason for dismissing the employee.' This wording, which is clear and unambiguous, requires the Tribunal, which is the one which hears the evidence, not the one which hears the legal argument, to look at every aspect of the case. The employer must show that he acted fairly and reasonably—and whether he did will depend upon what the employee was known, or had been proved, to have done, the circumstances in which the misconduct occurred and his behaviour when found out and asked for an explanation. Each case must depend upon its own facts. In our judgment it is unwise for this Court or the Employment Appeal Tribunal to set out guidelines, and wrong to make rules and establish presumptions for Industrial Tribunals to follow or take into account when applying para. 6(8). An example will show why guidelines can mislead. In most unfair dismissal cases Industrial Tribunals are likely to be critical, and justly so, of an employer who has dismissed a man without giving him an opportunity of explaining why he did what he did; but cases can occur when instant dismissal, without any opportunity for explanation being given, would be fair, as for example when on the shop floor a worker was seen by the works manager and others to stab another man in the back with a knife. The dismissal in such a case would not be any the less fair because the employers did not follow a disciplinary procedure agreement with a number of trade unions containing the kind of provisions which are under consideration in this appeal. In most cases, if not all, a failure to comply with such an agreement would be a factor to be taken into account; but the weight to be given to it would depend on the circumstances. An Industrial Tribunal should not base its decision on reasoning to the effect that because there has been a failure to comply, the dismissal must have been unfair."

If the E.A.T. can only consider error of law but should not lay down guidelines and is wrong to seek to establish rules we must expect a good deal of inconsistency in the approach of industrial tribunals which is only likely to be checked by the application of concepts of good industrial practice. Even the guidelines which do exist, and in particular the Code of Practice, are likely increasingly to be regarded as outdated. So, for instance, we shall come to the decision in *British Home Stores* v. *Burchell*[61] which is often taken as the basic statement of the test of fair procedure. Yet it does not lay down a set of stages through which the procedure ought to go. Rather it says that the employer must have a reason in which he may reasonably sustain belief because it is established by reasonable and appropriate enquiry. It is apparent that among the effects of such an approach is the enshrinement of current standards as the measure of fairness. That is to say, the law may be in danger of following rather than leading.

The reader will find in the subsequent pages that this abdication from rule-making is a very recent development. The N.I.R.C. was considerably more

---

[60] Now Employment Protection (Consolidation) Act 1978, s.57(3) as amended by Employment Act 1980, s.6.
[61] [1978] I.R.L.R. 379.

inclined to rely on what, at the very least, were firm guidelines. The E.A.T. under the Presidency of Phillips J., though anxious to point out that supposed rules were all merely guidance in the application of the overriding standard of fairness, nevertheless maintained such guidance. It seems doubtful whether a system of legal regulation can be sustained on the basis of the guidance given by Lawton L.J., and the policy of producing guidelines will, no doubt, be reasserted.

Browne-Wilkinson J. in *Williams* v. *Compair Maxam Ltd.*[62] sought to establish a new standard of review. He said:

"In considering whether the decision of an Industrial Tribunal is perverse in a legal sense, there is one feature which does not occur in other jurisdictions where there is a right of appeal only on a point of law. The Industrial Tribunal is an industrial jury which brings to its task a knowledge of industrial relations both from the viewpoint of the employer and the employee. Matters of good industrial relations practice are not proved before an Industrial Tribunal as they would be proved before an ordinary court; the lay members are taken to know them. The lay members of the Industrial Tribunal bring to their task their expertise in a field where conventions and practices are of the greatest importance. Therefore in considering whether the decision of an Industrial Tribunal is perverse, it is not safe to rely solely on the common sense and knowledge of those who have no experience in the field of Industrial Relations. A course of conduct which to those who have no practical experience with industrial relations might appear unfair or unreasonable, to those with specialist knowledge and experience might appear both fair and reasonable: and vice versa.

For this reason, it seems to us that the correct approach is to consider whether an Industrial Tribunal, properly directed in law and properly appreciating what is currently regarded as fair industrial practice, could have reached the decision reached by the majority of this Tribunal. We have reached the conclusion that it could not.

In law therefore the question we have to decide is whether a reasonable Tribunal could have reached the conclusion that the dismissal of the applicants in this case lay within the range of conduct which a reasonable employer could have adopted. It is accordingly necessary to try to set down in very general terms what a properly instructed Industrial Tribunal would know to be the principles which, in current industrial practice, a reasonable employer would be expected to adopt.

In this case, with the possible exception of early warning, none of the principles of good industrial relations practice which we have sought to state was observed. So far as warning is concerned, the majority of the Industrial Tribunal took the view that the work force were in general aware that further redundancies were in the offing and that the extra four weeks salary offset any unfairness. Although we would not ourselves agree with this view, it is not by itself so manifestly wrong as to be termed perverse.

We must add a word of warning. For the purpose of giving our reasons for reaching our exceptional conclusion that the decision of the Industrial Tribunal in this case was perverse, we have had to state what in our view are the steps which a reasonable and fair employer at the present time would seek to take in dismissing unionised employees on the ground of redundancy. We stress two points. First, these are not immutable principles which will stay unaltered for ever. Practices and attitudes in industry change with time and new norms of acceptable industrial relations behaviour will emerge. Secondly the factors we have stated are *not* principles of law, but standards of behaviour. Therefore in future cases before this

---

[62] [1982] I.R.L.R. 83.

Appeal Tribunal there should be no attempt to say that an Industrial Tribunal which did not have regard to or give effect to one of these factors has misdirected itself in law. Only in cases such as the present where a genuine case for perversity on the grounds that the decision flies in the face of commonly accepted standards of fairness can be made out, are these factors directly relevant. They are relevant only as showing the knowledge of industrial relations which the industrial jury is to be assumed as having brought to bear on the case they had to decide."

This is to acknowledge that the question of law remains whether a reasonable employer would be expected to behave in the way the facts of the case reveal. The question is to be answered by reference to standards currently regarded as fair industrial practice. Those standards, which will change from time to time, form, as it were, guidelines by which a tribunal is to judge the fairness of the action. A tribunal which ignores those guidelines may be said to have acted perversely and an appeal tribunal may overturn its decision as an error of law.

REASONS FOR DISMISSAL

Statement of reasons

In the first two of the three statutory definitions of dismissal discussed above, the employee with six months' continuous employment is entitled, on request, to be supplied by his employer, within 14 days of that request, with a written statement giving particulars of the reasons for his dismissal. The statement is admissible in evidence in any proceedings.[63] The statement can refer to other documents but it must contain the essential reasons for dismissal and be such that anyone who sees it can know from it why the employee was dismissed.[64] In *Marchant* v. *Earley Town Council*[65] the E.A.T. clouded the effect of its decision in *Horsley Smith* by holding that a statement which was inadequate was not unreasonably so, where it referred to a previous letter which did offer an adequate explanation. Despite the generality of the obligation, however, the statutory remedy of complaint to an industrial tribunal will only succeed if it can be shown that the employer unreasonably *refused* to supply the statement. The Scottish E.A.T. has held that delay beyond the 14-day limit does not of itself constitute an unreasonable refusal.[66]

The statutory right to a written statement is obviously designed to assist the presentation of an employee's case to a tribunal by enabling him to know in advance upon what ground he may base a complaint as to the insufficiency of the reasons for dismissal. In practice the employer will be bound in such proceedings by what he has stated in the written reasons since a tribunal is almost certain to consider that reliance on some reason not there stated renders the dismissal unfair. In fact such a view is not always supportable in theory. It rests on the proposition that the employee would not have had an adequate opportunity to counter an unstated allegation. He may, of course, have had such an opportunity; the allegation in question merely having been omitted from the subsequent written statement.

---

[63] Employment Protection (Consolidation) Act 1978, s.53(3).
[64] *Horsley Smith and Sherry Ltd.* v. *Dutton* [1977] I.C.R. 594.
[65] [1979] I.C.R. 891.
[66] *Charles Lang and Sons Ltd.* v. *Aubrey* [1978] I.C.R. 168.

Apart from its evidential value and its tendency to crystallise the reasons that will be relied on, the written statement has no effect on the decision whether a dismisal is fair or unfair. This decision will depend primarily on consideration of the reasons as a justification for dismissal and, secondly, the procedure adopted for that dismissal. We will discuss firstly the issue arising from consideration of the reasons.

Reasons existing at the time of dismissal

The most important principle of all concerning the advancement of reasons to justify dismissal is that established by the House of Lords in *Devis and Sons Ltd.* v. *Atkins*[67] which, on this point, merely confirmed a rule generally accepted since the decision of the N.I.R.C. in *Earl* v. *Slater and Wheeler (Airlyne) Ltd.*[68] Whereas the common law permits a dismissal to be justified by facts only discovered after the dismissal[69] the statutory concept of unfair dismissal, which Phillips J. in the E.A.T. in *Devis* v. *Atkins* described as the concept of "dismissal contrary to statute" permits only consideration of the reason for the dismissal. Viscount Dilhorne said:

> ". . . it is to be observed that the paragraph does not require the tribunal to consider whether the complainant in fact suffered any injustice by being dismissed. If it had, then I see no reason to suppose that evidence subsequently discovered of the complainant's misconduct (acquired after the dismissal) would not have been relevant to that question and admissible . . . paragraph 6(8)[70] requires the determination of the question whether the dismissal was unfair 'having regard to the reason shown by the employer' to depend on whether in the circumstances the employer had acted 'reasonably in treating it as a sufficient reason for dismissing the employee.'
>
> 'It' must refer to the reason shown by the employer and to the reason for which the employee was dismissed. Without doing very great violence to the language I cannot construe this paragraph as enabling the tribunal to have regard to matters of which the employer was unaware at the time of dismissal and which therefore cannot have formed part of his reason or reasons for dismissing an employee."

In other words, legislation fixes a point of time for the assessment of fairness.[71] This serves to emphasise the point made by Phillips J. that the statutory concept has no necessary connection with common law concepts nor, indeed, with some broad abstract concept of justice. In *Devis* v. *Atkins* the House of Lords was very concerned that the decision was to compensate an employee whom subsequent events established had got his just desserts. The decision in *St. Ann's Board Mill Co. Ltd.* v. *Brien*[72] reveals that it can equally serve to protect an employer whom subsequent discoveries reveal to have acted on incorrect assumptions.[73]

---

[67] [1977] I.C.R. 662.　　　　　　　　　　　　　　　　[68] [1972] I.C.R. 508.

[69] *Boston Deep Sea Fishing and Ice Co.* v. *Ansell* (1888) 39 Ch.D. 339; *Cyril Leonard and Co. Ltd.* v. *Simo Securities Trust Ltd.* [1972] 1 W.L.R. 80.

[70] Of TULRA. Now Employment Protection (Consolidation) Act 1978, s.57(3) as amended by Employment Act 1980, s.6.

[71] This point may occasionally be difficult to determine. See "effective date of dismissal," *supra*, p. 165.

[72] [1973] I.C.R. 444.

[73] It must be noted, however, that though for convenience of exposition the concepts of substantive and procedural fairness are here treated separately the one aspect may allow the

The practical cause of concern to the House of Lords in *Devis* v. *Atkins* has been removed. It was that a decision that a dismissal was unfair because the employer could not plead in justification facts discovered later might be regarded as unjust if those very facts revealed that the employee was undeserving of compensation. As we shall see[74] it has always been possible to reduce the compensation awarded by taking into account the contribution of the employee to his own dismissal.[75] This could not be said to be so, however, when the potentially contributory conduct was unknown at the time of the dismissal. The Employment Act 1980[76] inserted an additional provision into the Employment Protection (Consolidation) Act 1978 allowing such factors to be taken into account in deciding the extent to which it would be just and equitable to reduce the compensation awarded.

The need to show a reason

The legislative scheme envisages a two stage consideration. The employer is required to show firstly what was the reason, or principal reason, and that it was one of the specified reasons or "some other substantial reason of a kind such as to justify the dismissal of an employee from the position he held."[77] In practice these provisions do not operate in precisely the terms in which they are stated. It is not necessary to isolate a single reason as the sole or primary reason.[78] In practice, tribunals look for all the reasons, however numerous, which contributed to the decision to dismiss.[79] In *Savoia* v. *Chiltern Herb Farms Ltd.*[79a] the Court of Appeal held that the employer did not have to confine himself to reasons directly applicable to the employee but could put forward as reasons all surrounding facts such as the attitude of others of his employees. This, of course, must be correct since it would be impossible to plead reorganisation, for example, without such latitude. Equally the suggestion that there is some standard by which to test the sufficiency of a reason before it can be advanced as such is not adopted by tribunals. It would indeed be difficult for them to do so since the specified heads of reasons are so broad as to be almost meaningless. They cover:

   (a) capability or qualifications of the employee for performing work of the kind which he was employed by the employer to do;
   (b) conduct of the employee;
   (c) redundancy of the employee;
   (d) the need to avoid contravention of a statutory duty or restriction which would occur if employment continued.

---

court to modify the effect of the other so as to arrive at what it considers overall justice. In *Williamson* v. *Allcan Ltd.* [1978] I.C.R. 104, for example, it was pointed out that an employer who had time to reverse a decision justified at the point of time it was made might be held to have behaved unfairly if he did not take that opportunity.

[74] *Infra*, p. 261.
[75] Employment Protection (Consolidation) Act 1978, s.73(7).
[76] s.9.
[77] Employment Protection (Consolidation) Act 1978, s.57.
[78] Though the tribunal is required to indicate which reasons it considers predominant: *Archer* v. *Cheshire and Northwich Building Society* [1976] I.R.L.R. 424.
[79] See, *e.g. Patterson* v. *Bracketts* [1977] I.R.L.R. 137; *Miller* v. *Executors of John C. Graham* [1978] I.R.L.R. 309.
[79a] [1982] I.R.L.R. 166.

The employer must establish as a fact that he did believe in the existence of a reason for dismissal and that that belief was supported by reasonable grounds established by such investigation as was reasonable.[80] It is suggested that though this and the question of whether it was reasonable to dismiss on such a ground will normally be considered together there may, in some cases, be advantage in considering the establishment of a reason as a separate stage. Very often the reasons which may be advanced are not in doubt and if there is any argument it simply concerns which of them the employer did in fact rely on. In *Monie* v. *Coral Racing Ltd.*,[81] however, it seems that the Court of Appeal made an unnecessarily difficult problem out of the case which would have been much simpler had the actual reason for the dismissal first been determined. In the circumstances of the case it was apparent that one of two employees had stolen £1,750 from the employer's safe. There was no evidence that they had combined to do so. The responsible director decided that as he could not establish, by reasonable inquiry, which of the two was guilty he would dismiss both. When one of them appealed it was apparent that the managing director who heard the appeal saw the difficulty in formulating the reason for both dismissals as theft and substituted failure to operate the authorised cash control system. The appellant had undoubtedly so failed but the Court of Appeal, it is submitted entirely consistently with principle, held that a new reason could not be validly substituted on appeal. Left, therefore, with the originally stated reason a number of earlier cases appeared to hold that suspicion could not justify dismissal.[82] The reason for the dismissal could not have been theft since it was known that that reason did not apply to one of those dismissed. It has accordingly been suggested that the Court of Appeal was wrong to attempt to distinguish these earlier cases on the ground that in them there was only a suspicion whereas in *Monie* the theft had undoubtedly occurred. It is submitted that this is, indeed, the wrong ground for distinction since it would justify the dismissal of everyone upon whom suspicion might reasonably be cast so long only as the offence had been committed by someone. In other words, the Court of Appeal seems to be saying that an employer can assert his belief in a reason which exists as a fact rather than a reason which he has established in his mind by enquiry. Both these qualifications on the mere statement of a reason are obvious attempts to seem to be imposing some realistic means of checking the accuracy of the employer's statement. It is submitted, however, that only the first of them has this effect. It is suggested that had the Court of Appeal asked the question whether suspicion alone can be a substantial ground for dismissal it would, in accordance with established principle, have been bound to conclude that a suspicion established as the reason which the employer had in his mind following reasonable inquiry may be presented as a "substantial reason" within the residuary category.[83] The second stage of enquiry as to whether dismissal was a reasonable response to mere suspicion would then be seen to involve no problem of principle.

---

[80] *W. Weddel & Co. Ltd.* v. *Tepper* [1980] I.C.R. 286. See for an example of the effect of this, *The Distillers Company Ltd.* v. *Gardner* [1982] I.R.L.R. 47.

[81] [1980] I.C.R. 109.

[82] *British Home Stores Ltd.* v. *Burchell* [1978] I.R.L.R. 379; *W. Weddel & Co.* v. *Tepper* [1980] I.C.R. 286.

[83] See now *AEI Cables Ltd.* v. *McLay* [1980] I.R.L.R. 84.

The process of establishing a reason does not involve establishing its sufficiency as a justification for fair dismissal. It is suggested that the legislative intention must have been that anything falling within the "specific" headings of "misconduct" or "incapacity" suffices as a reason. That being so there can be no case for applying a different test to "any other substantial reason." If it were otherwise there would develop a wholly artificial process of presenting reasons as within the more specific heads in order to avoid enquiry as to their sufficiency under the heading of "any other substantial reason."[84]

The purpose of the stage at which the employer establishes the reason for the dismissal is no more than to ascertain that the employer genuinely believed the reason advanced. In *Alidair Ltd.* v. *Taylor*[85] the Court of Appeal said that so long as there did exist in the employer's mind such a genuine belief it was immaterial that, as a matter of fact, no such ground existed. The Court of Appeal also adopted, in *W. Weddel and Co. Ltd.* v. *Tepper*[86] a statement of the matters which must be established at this stage.[87]

These are:

(a) that the employer did believe the ground;
(b) that he had it in mind as a reasonable ground; and
(c) that he had carried out such investigation as was reasonable.

It is submitted that the third requirement is a vital element in ascertaining the existence of such a reason in the employer's mind.

A failure to carry out such reasonable inquiry means that the facts which could only be established thereby cannot be held by the employer to be established in his mind.[88] Similarly, therefore, if the inquiry can only establish a suspicion the employer's actions must be judged on the basis of such suspicion and not as if the suspected facts actually existed.[89]

Effectively this means that there is no objective standard by which to reject any reasons which may be put forward. This has meant that the employer is free to invoke his prerogative of deciding on any reason for dismissal. This, it is true, is then tested for reasonableness but, as we shall see, that stage has until recently been largely subjective.[90]

There are only a handful of cases that appear to go against this and suggest that there are some facts which cannot constitute reasons for dismissal.[91] In

---

[84] See *Priddle* v. *Dibble* [1978] I.C.R. 148; *Hollister* v. *National Farmers' Union* [1978] I.C.R. 712.

[85] [1978] I.C.R. 445.

[86] [1980] I.C.R. 286.

[87] These had earlier been put forward in *British Home Stores Ltd.* v. *Burchell* [1978] I.R.L.R. 279; see also *Scottish Special Housing Association* v. *Cooke* [1979] I.R.L.R. 264.

[88] *Hancock* v. *British Road Services* [1973] I.R.L.R. 43; *Wm. Low and Co. Ltd.* v. *MacCuish* [1979] I.R.L.R. 458. *cf. AEI Cables Ltd.* v. *McLay* [1980] I.R.L.R. 84.

[89] *Monie* v. *Coral Racing Ltd.* [1980] I.C.R. 109.

[90] *Hollister* v. *National Farmers' Union* [1978] I.R.L.R. 712—Reorganisation; *Saunders* v. *Scottish National Camps Association Ltd.* [1980] I.R.L.R. 174, Court of Session [1981] I.R.L.R. 277—the fact that the employee was a homosexual leading to the employer's assumption that he was a danger to children; *Scott Packing and Warehousing Co. Ltd.* v. *Paterson* ([1978] I.R.L.R. 166; *East African Airways Corporation* v. *Foote* [1977] I.C.R. 776—Africanisation).

[91] Apart, of course from the statutorily excluded reasons relating to union membership and activities.

Penprase v. *Manders Bros. Ltd.*[92] it was held that age could not of itself be a reason for dismissal and in *Price* v. *Gourley Brothers*,[93] a desire to reduce costs by replacing a highly paid employee with one on a lower rate was held not to afford a substantial reason. It is submitted that these must now be regarded as displaced by the test in *Weddell* v. *Tepper*.[94] The decisions in *Banerjee* v. *City and East London Area Health Authority*[95] and *British Midland Airways Ltd.* v. *Lewis*[96] which are sometimes cited as examples of insubstantial reasons are simply cases where, on the evidence, the employer could not have been said reasonably to believe in the reason he advanced. In *Morleys of Brixton Ltd.* v. *Minott*[96a] it was held that since the purpose was to ascertain what reason was in the employer's mind and not whether that reason existed as a fact it was of no consequence that the employer's reason derived from a confession extracted in breach of the judges' rules.

So long therefore as the reason alleged is "substantiated" the employer is not likely to fail to meet this stage of the claim. If he does the failure is most likely to stem from an inability to establish which of a number of potential reasons was the one relied on. Since there is nothing in practice to prevent reliance upon a number of reasons his problem is less a real obstacle than a matter of technique. A good example of lack of technique occurred in *Timex Corporation* v. *Thomson*.[97] The company had reorganised three management posts into two, for both of which engineering qualifications were requested. The applicant was the only one of three employees who held the posts not to possess such qualifications. The applicant was selected for redundancy but the employer maintained that the selection had also been influenced by the fact that his job performance was, in some ways, unsatisfactory. It would obviously have been open to the tribunal to find that the reason for the dismissal was redundancy—incompetence and lack of qualification merely being the reasons for selection. The tribunal might still have come to the conclusion that the dismissal was unfair on the ground that the employee should have been given an opportunity to counter the allegations of unsatisfactory performance in the knowledge that they were a basis for his selection for dismissal. The tribunal held, however, that though there was a redundancy situation the employer had failed to satisfy it that this, rather than unsatisfactory performance, was the real reason for the dismissal. Browne-Wilkinson J. in the E.A.T. said:

> "Even where there is a redundancy situation, it is possible for an employer to use such a situation as a pretext for getting rid of an employee he wishes to dismiss. In such circumstances the reason for the dismissal will not necessarily be redundancy. It is for the Industrial Tribunal in each case to see whether, on all the evidence, the employer has shown them what was the reason for the dismissal, that being the burden cast on the employer by section 57(1) of the Act. . . . The Industrial Tribunal was entitled to hold that they were not satisfied as to the reason for dismissal. On this basis the employer's defence to the claim failed at the first hurdle and a finding of unfair dismissal followed of course."

---

[92] [1973] I.R.L.R. 167.
[93] [1973] I.R.L.R. 11.
[94] *Supra.*
[95] [1979] I.R.L.R. 147.
[96] [1978] I.C.R. 782.
[96a] [1982] I.R.L.R. 270.
[97] [1981] I.R.L.R. 522.

SUFFICIENCY OF THE REASON

The standard of sufficiency

Since almost any reason can be put forward, provided that it can be shown to have existed in the mind of the employer and to have been the reason on which he acted, that reason is to be assessed to determine whether the employer was acting reasonably in treating it as a sufficient reason for dismissal. As we shall see, this question also involves consideration of the procedure adopted in dealing with the situation. We will return to that aspect later. The statutory test contained in the Employment Protection (Consolidation) Act 1978[98] was amended[99] in an attempt to eliminate the burden of proof which the 1978 provision had clearly placed on the employer. In the process, however, it appears accidentally to have transposed the dependence of reasonableness upon equity and the substantial merits of the case. The 1980 amendment states that:

". . . the determination of the question whether the dismissal was fair or unfair, having regard to the reason shown by the employer, shall depend on whether in the circumstances (including the size and administrative resources of the employer's undertaking) the employer acted reasonably or unreasonably in treating it as a sufficient reason; and *that question* [Author's italics] shall be determined in accordance with equity and the substantial merits of the case."

It seems unlikely, however, that the grammatical quibble that this could be said to leave the question of the employer's reasonableness at large conferring instead upon the court an overall power to apply considerations of equity will be taken up. For all practical purposes it may continue to be assumed that the employer's reasonableness must be established by reference to equity and the substantial merits of the case.[1]

Equally it seems unlikely that the formal removal of the burden of proof from the employer will, in practice, impose it on the employee. The employer will still need to bring evidence to establish the reason and his belief in it. The employee will find it easy to raise a question of reasonableness wherever there is the faintest chance of such a contention succeeding. If the employer produced no evidence to counter this he might still in theory succeed on the ground that the employee also had failed to prove unreasonableness. In practice, however, such a course is almost impossible to conceive. The employer will be advised to bring evidence to demonstrate the reasonableness of his action and this will, as before, become the ground on which the claim is fought.

In numerous decisions the E.A.T. has said that it is not the task of the tribunal to decide whether, in its independent view, the decision to dismiss was reasonable, but whether a reasonable employer could take that view.[2] Despite the fact that such a formulation could confer considerable discretion upon tribunals—there being no objectivity about what is reasonable—tribunals have

---

[98] Employment Protection (Consolidation) Act 1978, s.57(3).
[99] Employment Act 1980, s.6.
[1] The academic discussion may be pursued if the reader so wishes by considering the effect of the change on the judgment in *Moncrieff (Farmers)* v. *MacDonald* [1978] I.R.L.R. 112.
[2] See, *e.g. Moon* v. *Homeworthy Furniture (Northern) Ltd.* [1976] I.R.L.R. 298; *Parkers Bakeries Ltd.* v. *Palmer* [1977] I.R.L.R. 215; *Cook* v. *Thomas Linnell and Sons Ltd.* [1977] I.C.R. 770.

been overruled so often on this point that it is fair to say that they are being asked not to pass judgment on harshness or leniency. The question remains, however, how far are they to control the more obviously unreasonable decisions.

Davies and Freedland[3] describe as the extreme of judicial abdication from the role of applying substantive justice the statement in *Vickers Ltd.* v. *Smith*[4] that the tribunal should only find management's decision unfair where "It was so wrong, that no sensible or reasonable management could have arrived at the decision." In *Jowett* v. *Earl of Bradford (No.* 2)[5] the E.A.T. suggested that this extremely narrow view—which would confer a prerogative on management to judge the reasons for dismissal subject only to the limit of arbitrariness—was an attempt to help tribunals to understand the correct approach. The E.A.T. said, however, that it would not have been wrong to follow such a guideline and not to follow it would very likely result in the tribunal going wrong. Phillips J. in *N. C. Watling and Co. Ltd.* v. *Richardson*[6] effectively substituted a far less restrictive approach which is likely to become standard. He said:

"In reaching this conclusion we have not forgotten Miss Stanger's submission based on *Vickers Ltd.* v. *Smith*. In particular, she relied upon that case as authority for the proposition that no employee can succeed in a claim such as the present unless the industrial tribunal is satisfied that no reasonable management could have arrived at the decision at which the management in fact arrived. It appears from the submissions in this case, and submissions which we have heard in other cases, that *Vickers Ltd.* v. *Smith* has given rise to certain misunderstandings: see also *Mitchell* v. *Old Hall Exchange and Palatine Club Ltd.* It does not seem to us that the terms of the judgment itself, in *Vickers* v. *Smith*, properly understood, justify submissions which are often made in reliance upon it. The confusion results from stating without explanation that a dismissal is fair unless the case is one where the employer has acted in a way in which no reasonable employer would have acted. In fact, and in law, this is accurate enough; but so stated, without understanding the background, it can, particularly to laymen, seem to suggest an inordinately high standard. It should always be remembered that in all cases of unfair dismissal, and whatever the authorities say, it is necessary to take as a starting point the words of paragraph 6(8) of Schedule 1 to the Trade Union and Labour Relations Act 1974 . . .

The difficulty is that the words can be applied in practice in more than one way. One view—now rejected in the authorities, and to be regarded as heretical—is that all the industrial tribunal has to do is say to itself, reciting the words of paragraph 6(8), 'Was the dismissal fair or unfair?'; that having done that it has arrived at an unappealable decision; and that in answering that question it is not required to apply any standard other than its own collective wisdom. What the authorities, including *Vickers Ltd.* v. *Smith*, have decided is that in answering that question the industrial tribunal, while using its own collective wisdom is to apply the standard of the reasonable employer; that is to say, the fairness or unfairness of the dismissal is to be judged not by the hunch of the particular industrial tribunal, which (though rarely) may be whimsical or eccentric, but by the objective standard of the way in

---

[3] p. 356.
[4] [1977] I.R.L.R. 11. In *Iceland Frozen Foods Ltd.* v. *Jones* [1982] I.R.L.R. 439 Browne-Wilkinson J. suggested that tribunals would do well not to direct themselves by reference to this case.
[5] [1978] I.C.R. 431.
[6] [1978] I.C.R. 1049. This approach was approved by the E.A.T. in *Iceland Frozen Foods Ltd.* v. *Jones* [1982] I.R.L.R. 439.

which a reasonable employer in those circumstances, in that line of business, would have behaved. It has to be recognised that there are circumstances where more than one course of action may be reasonable. In the case of redundancy, for example, and where selection of one or two employees to be dismissed for redundancy from a larger number is in issue, there may well be and often are cases where equally reasonable, fair, sensible and prudent employers would take different courses, one choosing A, another B and another C. In those circumstances for an industrial tribunal to say that it was unfair to select A for dismissal, rather than B or C, merely because had they been the employers that is what they would have done, is to apply the test of what the particular industrial tribunal itself would have done and not the test of what a reasonable employer would have done. It is in this sense that it is said that the test is whether what has been done is something which 'no reasonable management would have done.' In such cases, where more than one course of action can be considered reasonable, if an industrial tribunal equates its view of what itself would have done with what a reasonable employer would have done, it may mean that an employer will be found to have dismissed an employee unfairly although in the circumstances many good and fair employers would have done as that employer did." It follows that if a tribunal is not to substitute its own view there will often be not one but a range of reasonable employer reactions.

Common practice

In applying this test the courts and tribunals are likely to apply an intuitive test of their own as to what a reasonable employer might do. The trouble with such a test is that it tends to have regard to what employers commonly do. Rather like the standard of common practice in the law of negligence it is difficult to reverse this trend without saying that most employers are acting unreasonably.[7] The effect of this form of reference is clear in the following passage from the judgment of Lord MacDonald in the E.A.T. in *Saunders* v. *Scottish National Camps*.[8] An industrial tribunal had held fair the dismissal of an employee at a children's holiday camp on the ground that he was a homosexual. Lord Mac-Donald said that it had been argued that the tribunal had assumed

> "in the teeth of the evidence, that homosexuals created a special risk to the young. This does less than justice to their finding which is that a considerable proportion of employers would take the view that the employment of a homosexual should be restricted particularly when required to work in proximity and contact with children. Whether this view is scientifically sound may be open to question but there was clear evidence from the psychologist that it exists as a fact."[9]

The scope that even this wider permission to interfere leaves to management is seen at its most extreme when it is applied to the less clearly defined reasons which we brought together under the heading "Some other substantial reason." In *R.S. Components Ltd.* v. *Irwin*[10] the employers had for some time been

---

[7] Even in *Williams* v. *Compair Maxam Ltd.* [1982] I.R.L.R. 83 it was this standard that was applied to judge the reasonableness of procedure.

[8] [1980] I.R.L.R. 174; Court of Session [1981] I.R.L.R. 277.

[9] Alternatively in *Rolls Royce Ltd.* v. *Walpole* [1980] I.R.L.R. 343 it was said, again by the E.A.T., that it might be meaningful to ask whether the employer had satisfied the tribunal that his response was in the range of reasonable responses. This has the advantage of asking not so much "can this response be regarded as reasonable?" as "what other responses were available?" See also *Bevan Harris Ltd.* v. *Gair* [1981] I.R.L.R. 520.

[10] [1973] I.C.R. 535.

worried about members of their sales staff who joined other companies and
solicited former customers on behalf of their new employers. Employees were
asked to sign an agreement to accept a new restrictive covenant forbidding such
solicitation within 12 months of leaving that employment. Four of the sales staff
who refused to do so were dismissed and one of them made this claim for unfair
dismissal. The common law would have considered such a cause to be inadequate since no breach of contract by the employee had occurred. The industrial
tribunal considered the reason not capable of comprehension within the statutory list. As we have seen, and as the N.I.R.C. subsequently held, this is
incorrect. The tribunal had made it clear that had it decided otherwise it would
have considered the dismissal fair and the N.I.R.C. accordingly substituted
such a finding indicating quite clearly that it shared that view.
Brightman J. said:

> ". . . it is not difficult to imagine a case where it would be essential for employers
> embarking, e.g., on a new technical process, to invite existing employees to agree
> to some reasonable restriction on their use of the knowledge they acquire of the
> new technique; and where it would be essential for the employer to terminate, by
> due notice, the services of an employee who was unwilling to accept such a
> restriction . . . It would be unfortunate for the development of industry if an
> employer were unable to meet such a situation without infringing or risking
> infringement of rights conferred by the Industrial Relations Act 1971."

Since the test is not what is essential but what is reasonable it is difficult to decide
at what, if any, point the tribunal would be in a position to judge that the
employer had acted unreasonably. Similarly in *Industrial Rubber Products Ltd.*
v. *Gillon*[11] it was held reasonable for an employer to withdraw a pay increase in
excess of that allowed by the voluntary pay policy then suggested by the
government.

   Although there must be evidence to support the employer's contention that
there is a good reason for reorganisation[12] once that is forthcoming there seems
very little to stand in the way of the conclusion that it is reasonable to
reorganise. Indeed if the reason is redundancy the tribunals rarely even ask this
question.[13] They are usually content to accept the decision of the employer and
merely to inquire whether that decision does lead to a reduction in requirement.[14] The only question left is whether, given the existence of the reason,
there is any alternative to dismissal. If not, dismissal may be regarded as fair.[15]
In the leading case of *Hollister* v. *National Farmers Union*[16] the Court of Appeal
adopted the common practice of combining consideration of the existence of a
reason and its sufficiency. Lord Denning M.R. indicated clearly that consideration of the reasonableness of the decision was made from the point of view of
business interest.

> "The question which is being discussed in this case is whether the reorganisation of
> the business which the National Farmers' Union felt they had to undertake in 1976,

---

[11] [1977] I.R.L.R. 389.
[12] *Bannerjee* v. *City and East London Area Health Authority* [1979] I.R.L.R. 147.
[13] *Sanders* v. *Ernest A. Neale Ltd.* [1974] I.C.R. 565; *Moon* v. *Homeworthy Furniture
(Northern) Ltd.* [1977] I.C.R. 117.
[14] *Ranson* v. *G. W. Collins Ltd.* [1978] I.C.R. 765; *O'Hare* v. *Rotaprint Ltd.* [1980] I.C.R. 94,
infra, p. 280.
[15] *Bowater Containers Ltd.* v. *McCormack* [1980] I.R.L.R. 50.
[16] [1979] I.C.R. 542.

coupled with Mr. Hollister's refusal to accept the new agreement, was a substantial reason of such a kind as to justify the dismissal of the employee. Upon that there have only been one or two cases. One we were particularly referred to was *Ellis* v. *Brighton Co-operative Society Ltd.* where it was recognised by the court that reorganisation of business may on occasion be a sufficient reason justifying the dismissal of an employee. They went on to say, at p. 420, 'Where there has been a properly consulted-upon reorganisation which, if it is not done, is going to bring the whole business to a standstill, a failure to go along with the new arrangements may well—it is not bound to, but it may well—constitute some other substantial reason.'

Certainly, I think everyone would agree with that. But in the present case Arnold J. expanded it a little so as not to limit it to where it came absolutely to a standstill but to where there was some sound, good business reason for the reorganisation. I must say I see no reason to differ from Arnold J.'s view on that. It must depend on all the circumstances whether the reorganisation was such that the only sensible thing to do was to terminate the employee's contract unless he would agree to a new arrangement."

Good practice

A single recent case contradicting this trend might be passed by were it not for the obvious intention of Browne-Wilkinson J. that the trend should thereby be reversed. In *Evans* v. *Elemeta Holdings Ltd.*[17] a new general manager decided to issue employees with new contracts whereby, in return for double the nationally agreed pay increase, employees would undertake on request to work unlimited overtime on any weekday evening and up to four hours on Saturdays without any premium on the hourly rate. The claimant refused to accept these new terms and was dismissed. It is possible that such a "reorganisation" would, under the established trend, have been regarded as so unusual as not to attract the almost automatic sufficiency attached to most reorganisations. The judgment of the E.A.T., however, had to go further than this in order to find a ground on which to overrule the industrial tribunal which had held that the new contract was not unreasonable or oppressive and, accordingly, that it was unreasonable for the employee to reject it. The applicant's representative argued that it was proper to require the tribunal to consider whether, as a matter of commercial need, the employer was justified in his decision. The E.A.T. was not prepared to go this far in intervening in management. Instead it deftly turned consideration from the normal view of the needs of the business to that of the reasonable reactions of the employee. It might be said that its conclusion that the dismissal was unfair amounts to a decision that a reasonable employer cannot expect an employee to accept conditions which are unreasonable from his point of view. There can be no doubt of the substantial effect this line of reasoning, if pursued, will have on the insidious growth of self-justifying management decision.

PROCEDURAL FAIRNESS

For convenience of exposition the subject of unfair dismissal has here been divided into a consideration of the sufficiency of the reasons and adequacy of

---

[17] [1982] I.C.R. 323.

the procedure. It is, however, wrong to consider the sufficiency of the reason as a separate question from the adequacy of the procedure.[17a] We shall see that the nature of the offence may have a substantial influence on the type of procedure considered fair. We have already seen that while, on the one hand, industrial tribunals and courts are willing to desert the formal rules of the common law as epitomised in the terms of the contract in search of "justice"[18] they have not really attempted to seek to balance the notion of fairness. The effect of allowing an almost free hand to the employer to select his reasons and then judging the sufficiency of these reasons in the light of the employer's business necessity totally excludes consideration of the reasonableness of the employee's reaction in the light of his need to retain employment. It is, of course, management and not the employee who must run the undertaking but it is arguable that even allowing for this there is a great deal more room to balance the needs of employer and employee. This imbalance is more pronounced in certain circumstances, of which "re-organisation" or redundancy is the most obvious.

The courts have, whether consciously or not, tended to achieve a greater degree of balance of interest by introducing an emphasis, more marked formerly than now, on the need to adopt a procedure which, in the hands of the reasonable, would be most likely to produce a just result.[19]

Procedure as a substantive requirement

At one time the emphasis was so great that it was often possible effectively to separate the substance of the justification for dismissal from the procedure adopted to consider that substance. The leading case representing this development is *Earl* v. *Slater and Wheeler (Airlyne) Ltd.*[20] in which Sir John Donaldson said:

> "The employers' establishment is certainly not large. We were told that there were between 40 and 50 shop floor and between 15 and 27 management employees—but it hardly ranks as 'very small.' However, whether or not it is 'very small,' the principles of conduct should be the same, size being only relevant to the need for formality. Accordingly, the employee is fully entitled to rely upon paragraph 132, [of the Code of Industrial Relations Practice] which provides that the disciplinary procedure should 'give the employee the opportunity to state his case and the right to be accompanied by his employee representative.' So far as representation is concerned, the employers neither knew nor had any reason to know that the employee had recently become a member of a trade union, but the procedure which they operated contravened the code of practice in that, in the circumstances of the employee's case, it did not give him the opportunity to state his case.
>
> But quite apart from the Code of Practice, good industrial relations depend upon management not only acting fairly but being manifestly seen to act fairly. This did not happen in the case of the employee. Granted that his work had been unsatisfactory over a long period and that he had been told that it must improve,

---

[17a] *Iceland Frozen Foods Ltd.* v. *Jones* [1982] I.R.L.R. 439.

[18] *e.g. cf. Wallace* v. *Guy Ltd.* [1973] I.C.R. 117 and *R.S. Components Ltd.* v. *Irwin* [1973] I.C.R. 535.

[19] In *Greig* v. *Sir Alfred McAlpine & Son (Northern) Ltd.* ([1979] I.R.L.R. 372) an industrial tribunal were not content to insist on the procedure but proposed to consider evidence of whether it had led to a rational and objective application of criteria.

[20] [1972] I.C.R. 508. See also *Clarkson International Tools Ltd.* v. *Short* [1973] I.C.R 191.

the fact remains that the decisive matters leading to his dismissal were all discovered whilst he was absent due to sickness. He was unable to satisfy the tribunal that he had any answer to these complaints, but the employers did not know this when they dismissed him and they took no steps to find out. Whilst we do not say that in all circumstances the employee must be given an opportunity of stating his case, the only exception can be the case where there can be no explanation which could cause the employers to refrain from dismissing the employee. This must be a very rare situation. The employee's case was far removed from this. The manner of his dismissal cannot possibly be justified, notwithstanding the fact that if a proper procedure had been adopted, he would still have been dismissed and would then have been fairly dismissed."

The industrial tribunal, surprisingly at so early a stage in the development of the law, had adopted what would now be considered the modern view.

"Whilst we accept that management in this case must be held to have fallen far short of the standard procedure which is to be expected, and do not at the hearing appear to have implemented any proper grievance procedure even since the Act [of 1971] came into force, we feel that what we have got to decide is not whether they acted in accordance with natural justice, or with the procedure advised in the Code of Practice, but whether the result was in all respects fair in accordance with the definition or directions contained in section 24(6) of the Act . . . The tribunal has no inherent jurisdiction, but is confined to the jurisdiction conferred upon us by the statute. That jurisdiction is confined to deciding whether a dismissal was fair or unfair, not according to whether the procedure adopted was fair, but according to whether in all the circumstances it is properly found by us that the employers acted reasonably or unreasonably in treating the allegations made and accepted by us as a sufficient reason for dismissal. If we are right in that view, reading the subsection in question, then we do not think it is open to us to hold that this was an unfair dismissal merely because of the procedure adopted. If that procedure had in fact led to any conceivable injustice, then it would be inequitable to dismiss the claim, but although the procedure was such that it is wide open to criticism, we do not think that in all the circumstances it led to injustice."

The N.I.R.C., however, asserted the separate significance of procedure.

"With respect to the tribunal, we think that it erred in holding that an unfair procedure which led to injustice is incapable of rendering unfair a dismissal which would otherwise be fair. The question in every case is whether the employer acted reasonably or unreasonably in treating the reason as sufficient for dismissing the employee and it has to be answered with reference to the circumstances known to the employer at the moment of dismissal.

If an employer thinks that his accountant may be taking the firm's money, but has no real grounds for so thinking and dismisses him for this reason, he acts wholly unreasonably and commits the unfair industrial practice of unfair dismissal, notwithstanding that it is later proved that the accountant had in fact been guilty of embezzlement. Proof of the embezzlement affects the amount of the compensation, but not the issue of fair or unfair dismissal."

This approach certainly appears to have been accepted in 1976 in *Budgen and Co.* v. *Thomas* where an interview at the enquiry stage was held not to make up for the absence of a hearing.[21]

---

[21] [1976] I.C.R. 344. This decision was said in *Parker* v. *Clifford Dunn Ltd.* [1979] I.C.R. 463 to indicate too rigid a view of procedural requirements.

This, it is submitted, is a much more extreme view than that of Viscount Dilhorne in *W. Devis and Sons Ltd.* v. *Atkins*[22] which is sometimes said to support it. All he said there was the obvious, namely that an unfair procedure might render unfair a decision which would have been fair had the proper procedure been adopted. Indeed the House of Lords was most anxious in that case that the employee should not as a result of considerations akin to fair procedure receive a better deal than the substance of his position justified. From this decision stems the marked increase in insistence that procedural irregularities should not serve to prevent fair dismissal for substantial offences but it is suggested that an element of that feeling had been present for much longer in the false but widely utilised concept of gross misconduct.[23]

Procedure as an equitable guideline

It happens that the attack on the predominance of procedure, first mounted through this or a similar but less emotively named concept[24] was made soon after the E.A.T. emerged to replace the N.I.R.C.[25] The point is probably only significant in that a change of personnel facilitated the introduction of a number of developments which were already on foot. It is just likely, however, that the change was inspired by the introduction of the basic award which meant that there could not be a finding of unfairness without an award of compensation. Indeed, as Davies and Freedland said,[26] the E.A.T. itself "went through a phase when it elaborated the notion of procedural justice in relation to all sorts of categories of dismissal."

In *Retarded Children's Aid Society Ltd.* v. *Day*[27] the Court of Appeal reversed the decision of the E.A.T. which had held that there was a heavy burden on an employer who had dismissed for misconduct without a warning. The Court of Appeal was prepared to assume that the industrial tribunal, having described the case as "very special," had been prepared to overlook the absence of a warning.

Subsequently a number of decisions have held that in particular circumstances procedural defects could be overlooked. Perhaps the most startling of these is that in *The Royal Naval School* v. *Hughes*[28] because there the reason had nothing to do with the protection of the employee but took into account only the convenience of the small employer. The basis of the decision that reasonableness may vary with the size of the employer was enshrined in the amended test embodied in the Employment Act 1980.[29] It is suggested, however, that whereas the quality of the reason may be altered by the size of the undertaking, that can scarcely be a reasonable excuse for lapses in procedure.[30]

By far the most common ground for permitting departures from procedure

---

[22] [1977] A.C. 931 at 955.
[23] See, *infra*, p. 220.
[24] The door existed in the Code of Practice and had been pushed ajar by the rare N.I.R.C. decision like that in *Clarkson International Tools Ltd.* v. *Short* [1973] I.C.R. 191.
[25] *Lowndes* v. *Specialist Heavy Engineering Ltd.* [1977] I.C.R. 1; *C. A. Parsons Ltd.* v. *McLoughlin* [1978] I.R.L.R. 65.
[26] p. 365.
[27] [1978] I.C.R. 437; See also *Bailey* v. *B.P. Oil* [1980] I.C.R. 642.
[28] [1979] I.R.L.R. 383.
[29] s.6.
[30] But see *Bevan Harris Ltd.* v. *Gair* [1981] I.R.L.R. 520.

has been that there is no evidence to suggest that the decision would have been different had a more satisfactory procedure been adopted.[31] The process of excusing observance of procedure shows some signs of itself developing sub-rules.[32] In *Gray Dunn and Co. Ltd.* v. *Edwards*[33] there had been a refusal to hear witnesses as to the fitness to work of an employee who admitted drinking two pints of beer contrary to the disciplinary rules of the employer which stated that summary dismissal would result from being under the influence of alcohol. It was said that the test for the permissibility of omitting a hearing was whether, on balance of probabilities, the same course would have been taken had a proper procedure been adopted and whether dismissal would have been considered reasonable whatever the evidence might have revealed.[34]

In *Charles Letts and Co. Ltd.* v. *Howard*[35] it was suggested that failure to provide an opportunity for a hearing would only be excused if the employer could show that the result would inevitably have been the same but in *Lowndes* v. *Specialist Heavy Engineering Ltd.*[36] the industrial tribunal had reached the conclusion that the employee had become incapable of doing his job properly and concluded that "even if the procedures had been meticulously followed the result would have been no different; he would still have been dismissed. Phillips J. said:

> "If an industrial tribunal concludes that there has been a failure in procedure (as they did in the present case) it might seem reasonable for them to go on to consider, in a case such as the present, the question whether it would have made any difference had the proper procedure been followed. If the answer is 'no,' it seems an affront to common sense to say that nonetheless the complainant has been unfairly dismissed. Yet it is said, and can often with justice be said, that to inquire whether, had the fair procedure been adopted, it would have made any difference, may involve looking into matters which occurred after the date of dismissal, or, though occurring before the date of dismissal, were unknown to the employer, and therefore in either case outside the ambit of paragraph 6(8).[37] This presents a real difficulty. Thus, in the present case Mr. Rees says of the employers that, quoting Sir John Donaldson in *Earl* v. *Slater & Wheeler (Airlyne) Ltd.*:

> > 'They thus acted on the basis of a reason which, so far as they then knew, might or might not be sufficient, according to whether he could or could not offer an adequate explanation.'

> We know now that the employee could offer no explanation of his incompetence; but the employers could not have known that, if questioned, he might not have given some unexpected explanation, for example, recently diagnosed ill-health. These are strong logical difficulties in the way of the decision; yet, as we have said, it seems to us that this was a very strong case indeed from the employers' point of view. Here was a man of whom the industrial tribunal could, obviously correctly, say that the employers could not "possibly be expected to keep a man"—such as

---

[31] *Lowndes* v. *Specialist Heavy Engineering Co.* [1977] I.C.R. 1; *Bailey* v. *B.P. Oil (Kent Refinery) Ltd.* [1980] I.C.R. 642 *Parker* v. *Clifford Dunn Ltd.* [1979] I.C.R. 463.

[32] *Parker* v. *Clifford Dunn Ltd.*, *supra*; *British Labour Pump* v. *Byrne* [1979] I.C.R. 347.

[33] [1980] I.R.L.R. 23.

[34] For a consideration of the undesirable effects of this watering down of procedural requirements see Elias; "Fairness in Unfair Dismissal" (1981) 10 I.L.J. 201 at 215.

[35] [1976] I.R.L.R. 248.

[36] [1977] I.C.R. 1.

[37] Now Employment Protection (Consolidation) Act 1978, s.53 as amended by Employment Act 1980, s.6.

the employee—"who had, not deliberately, but through incapacity caused them so much trouble and so much financial loss." Where logic and common sense conflict there is usually an explanation, if one can find it.

It seems to us that the trouble arises in part from the form of the industrial tribunal's decision which finds that there was a failure in procedure, in effect saying that this gives rise to a prima facie case of unfair dismissal. . . . They go on, as an aid to answering that question, to consider whether it would have made any difference if the correct procedure had been followed, and, for powerful reasons, conclude that it would not, and that had the procedures been meticulously followed the result would have been no different. It seems to us that what the tribunal is there really saying is that, not forgetting that the correct procedure was not followed, they are satisfied that the employers have discharged the onus placed upon them under paragraph 6(8). In our judgment they were right about that. The case is not one where, in order to reach that conclusion, it was necessary to pray in aid some subsequent event or discovery subsequently made. The circumstances, they are saying, were so egregious that dismissal was justified, despite the failure in procedure, and no injustice was done. Again we agree. . . .

We would not wish anything in this judgment to be taken to encourage the view that failures in procedure can be lightly disregarded or ordinarily lead to any conclusion other than that the consequent dismissal was unfair. Normally that conclusion would be correct. But there are exceptions. They are easy enough to recognise when encountered, although it is not so easy to marshal them logically in terms of paragraph 6(8)."

Even Browne-Wilkinson J., who, it is submitted, has revealed a lack of addiction to this principle, was prepared to confirm its continued general applicability in *Gibson* v. *British Transport Docks Board*[38] and *Dunn* v. *Pochin (Contractors) Ltd.*[39] In the first of these cases, however, he indicated that the approach should be adopted with caution:

"There are cases where there has been a failure of procedure in which it has been held that the failure to follow the correct procedure does not automatically render the dismissal unfair if the Tribunal is satisfied that even if the correct procedure had been followed it would not have altered the result, *i.e.* the employers would have reached the same conclusion, even if they had followed the right procedures. In our view, that approach has to be adopted with considerable caution. It is of obvious application where the departure in procedure is a slight one. Where there is a major procedural error, the dangers of an Industrial Tribunal speculating and guessing as to the outcome become substantial. In this case there was no need to speculate or guess because it is clear that the Tribunal could not and did not come to the conclusion that the result would have been the same if the procedure had been correct, *i.e.* if each case had been considered individually. It is clear that it was not established that the same result would have followed if the employers had considered each case individually. What the majority of the Industrial Trubunal in this case has done is to seek to take the principle one step further. They say, notwithstanding the fact that there has been a fundamental error and notwithstanding the fact that it has been shown that that fundamental error might have affected the decision of these employers, even so we, the Industrial Tribunal, consider that even if the matter had been considered individually, dismissal would still have been fair.

In our view, that is not an approach which is permissible under s.57(3) of the Act. Under that section, as unamended, the employer has to satisfy the Tribunal

---

[38] [1982] I.R.L.R. 228.
[39] [1982] I.R.L.R. 449.

that in the circumstances, having regard to equity and the substantial merits of the case, he (that is to say the employer) acted reasonably in treating it (that is to say the reason) as a sufficient reason for dismissing the employee. The whole tenor of the law on this section is that the Tribunal is not to substitute its view of what was fair for the employers, but to look at the actual decision of the employer and see if that decision fell within the band of conduct which a reasonable employer might have adopted. It seems to us that the course taken by the Tribunal in this case departs from that approach. They are not, on the evidence, assessing what the employers would have done; they are assessing whether, if the employers had rightly treated the cases individually, a decision to dismiss would have been fair, even though these employers would not in these circumstances have dismissed. In our judgment, that is not a permissible approach to the section. We therefore cannot accept that the decision of the Industrial Tribunal that the dismissals were fair is correct."

In W. and J. Wass Ltd. v. Binns[40] the Court of Appeal strongly re-asserted the principle of lack of prejudice as established on a balance of probabilities. The decision, it is suggested, demonstrates the unsatisfactory nature of the enquiry since Sir George Baker, in the minority, was able to conclude that on the facts it could not be said that the employee would probably still have been dismissed had he had a proper hearing. It is difficult, therefore, to see how the case satisfies Waller L.J.'s requirement that the facts should be exceptional.

Though it may be "an affront to common sense" to hold the dismissal unfair for absence of a procedure which is unlikely to have made a difference such an affront has not deterred the courts from applying natural justice to trade union discipline nor to substantial areas of public law.[41] The requirements of natural justice vary in severity but were not, until recently, excluded on the ground that the result would have been the same without them. Whatever the effect of the change of emphasis on natural justice in other areas of law there are two principal dangers in the course approved by the E.A.T. in relation to unfair dismissal. The more general is that however unlikely it may seem, there is rarely clear evidence at the time of the dismissal that there is nothing that can alter the decision.[42] The task is easier when dealing with redundancy.[43] Nevertheless Williams v. Compair Maxam Ltd.[44] casts doubt on the possibility of deciding that nothing said would alter the decision. More often than not the employer, like the union disciplinary committee, will conclude that the case is cut and dried. If he is lucky it will transpire at the hearing the industrial tribunal conducts for him that it appears that he was right. Quite apart from the academic point that this is, in a sense, a "subsequently discovered fact," there is the real danger that extraneous matters the employee might have raised in a hearing before his employer to explain his conduct will not appear relevant to the issue before the tribunal. One must ask, therefore, whether it is safe to decide that the evidence given at such a hearing makes it clear that the evidence which would have been given to the employer would not have altered his decision. This, it is submitted, is very clear in the situation that arose in British Labour Pump Co. Ltd. v. Byrne.[45] One of the company's employees had been

---

[40] [1982] I.R.L.R. 283.
[41] But see now Cheall v. APEX [1982] I.R.L.R. 102, infra, p. 412.
[42] But see Bushell v. Secretary of State for the Environment [1981] A.C. 75.
[43] Abbotts and Standley v. Wessen Glynwed Steels Ltd. [1982] I.R.L.R. 51.
[44] [1982] I.R.L.R. 83.   [45] [1979] I.C.R. 347.

stopped by the police. They were suspicious about the origins of some castings they found in his car and informed his employer. The employers dismissed him and a chargehand for dishonesty. During the enquiry it became apparent that a number of employees were involved. In response to an invitation from the managing director several of them voluntarily made statements about their involvement. The applicant in this case, who was a shop steward, said that he had been involved but only technically. It proved difficult to secure the attendance of a full time union official, as recommended by the Code of Practice, at a subsequent interview and the convenor of shop stewards attended, in his view as an observer. Byrne stated that he was aware of the theft and stood to get a share of the proceeds but he had not otherwise participated. He and a number of other employees who had been involved were dismissed. The unease felt by the industrial tribunal about the fact that the failure to secure representation had resulted in a failure to put the whole case for Byrne is clear from the following passage from the judgment of Slynn J. on appeal.

"In deciding whether they were satisfied by the employers that they had behaved reasonably in regarding the reason for dismissing the employee as sufficient and whether they had handled the matter in a reasonable way, the industrial tribunal considered first what they called the procedural aspect of the matter. They said that they fully sympathised with the employers who had unearthed dishonesty. They recognised that it is important for employers to discover dishonesty which has occurred. It is particularly difficult, they recognised, for employers to deal with it once the police are involved in the investigation. There is no doubt that the tribunal was sympathetic to the situation in which the employers found themselves. On the other hand the tribunal were disturbed about a number of features of the case. They thought that the employers ought to have had more regard to the fact that the employee was a shop steward. They felt that Mr. Garner's initial reaction in telephoning the union to see if a senior official could attend was the right one; but unfortunately in the last resort no full time official was present. The tribunal felt that had it been possible for a full time official to be able to attend, to make representations on behalf of the employee, it might have led to his suspension rather than to his dismissal until the matter had been gone into more fully. Moreover they were troubled that at this inquiry there had not been a detailed examination of the employee's role. They felt that his particular involvement had not been investigated at all. He had not been asked to explain what he meant by saying that he was technically involved. He had not been asked whether there was anything he wanted to say in mitigation of what appeared to be a very serious charge. The tribunal said that the matter could have been examined further. Finally, they were troubled about the fact that there had not been held a disciplinary committee to consider the matter in accordance with the employers' rules. They thought that the second meeting between Mr. Garner and the employee, at which Mr. Trotman and also the convenor of shop stewards were present, had not really been in accordance with the employers' practice. They thought that there should have been present, in accordance with the rules, the divisional head, the company secretary or the general manager, whereas it appeared that it was Mr. Garner who was really taking the decisions himself."

The tribunal concluded that the failure by the employer to enquire sufficiently into the employee's part in the offence rendered the dismissal unfair. The tribunal applied the test of whether the result would *inevitably* have been the same had the proper procedure been followed.[46] The E.A.T. reduced this to a

---

[46] See *Charles Letts and Co. Ltd.* v. *Howard* [1976] I.R.L.R. 248.

"balance of probabilities" test. It concluded that the decision of the tribunal could properly be presented as a feeling that the employer had failed to satisfy it that on balance of probabilities there would have been a dismissal after a proper hearing.

It is presumably an affront to common sense to demand that where justice has been done it should, nonetheless, manifestly be seen to be done, but it is for this purpose that such a rule is applied. This, it is submitted, is brought home more clearly when the more specific danger of the absence of an opportunity to put forward mitigating circumstances is examined. In *Lowndes'* case it may have been obvious that there had been a series of damaging acts of negligence. It may be that the employer could and would have reasonably decided that he could not risk his business further. It may be, however, that a hard luck story would have persuaded him to impose discipline short of dismissal. Are we to say that because an employer, having heard the hard luck story, could reasonably have dismissed an employee he is acting reasonably in closing his mind by not listening to the hard luck story? If *Lowndes* is right the answer is "yes." If that is so we have added another management prerogative to that of choosing the reason for dismissal and destroyed the employee's second line of protection against the freedom of the employer to advance virtually any reason for dismissal. In *Byrne's* case, for example, management would have only needed to take procedural steps a little further in order to have justified the conclusion that whatever Byrne had said they acted reasonably to protect themselves from the type of cover up conspiracy in which he was involved.

The point must not be overdone. There are relatively few situations to which the reasoning in *Lowndes* would apply. There is undoubtedly a presumption that failure to follow procedure, in particular by affording an adequate hearing, renders the dismissal unfair. The question is, whether, if procedure is the only real protection for the employee, there should be any weakening of the demand for it to be properly applied.

In *Williams* v. *Compair Maxam Ltd.*[47] Browne-Wilkinson J. in the E.A.T., dealing with a claim regarding total absence of procedures to select employees for redundancy, pointed out that the test of fairness must be applied in relation to each employee. He paid no attention, however, to the question whether the end result was fair. Indeed it is apparent that the presentation of the case before him had not adduced evidence which would have enabled him to reach any conclusion on that question. Instead he contended that whilst it was established that the proper standard was not what the tribunal would have done, objectivity could be achieved by requiring adherence to the accepted practice of good industrial relations:

> "The second point of law, particularly relevant in the field of dismissal for redundancy, is that the Tribunal must be satisfied that it was reasonable to dismiss each of the applicants on the grounds of redundancy. It is not enough to show simply that it was reasonable to dismiss *an* employee; it must be shown that the employer acted reasonably in treating redundancy 'as a sufficient reason for dismissing *the* employee,' *i.e.* the employee complaining of dismissal. Therefore, if the circumstances of the employer make it inevitable that some employee must be dismissed, it is still necessary to consider the means whereby the applicant was selected to be

---

[47] [1982] I.R.L.R. 83. See also *Freud* v. *Bentalls Ltd.* [1982] I.R.L.R. 443.

the employee to be dismissed and the reasonableness of the steps taken by the employer to choose the applicant, rather than some other employee, for dismissal.

In law therefore the question we have to decide is whether a reasonable Tribunal could have reached the conclusion that the dismissal of the applicants in this case lay within the range of conduct which a reasonable employer could have adopted. It is accordingly necessary to try to set down in very general terms what a properly instructed Industrial Tribunal would know to be the principles which, in current industrial practice, a reasonable employer would be expected to adopt. This is not a matter on which the chairman of this Appeal Tribunal feels that he can contribute much, since it depends on what industrial practices are currently accepted as being normal and proper. The two lay members of this Appeal Tribunal hold the view that it would be impossible to lay down detailed procedures which *all* reasonable employers would follow in *all* circumstances: the fair conduct of dismissals for redundancy must depend on the circumstances of each case. But in their experience, there is a generally accepted view in industrial relations that, in cases where the employees are represented by an independent union recognised by the employer, reasonable employers will seek to act in accordance with the following principles.

1. The employer will seek to give as much warning as possible of impending redundancies so as to enable the union and employees who may be affected to take early steps to inform themselves of the relevant facts, consider possible alternative solutions and, if necessary, find alternative employment in the undertaking or elsewhere.

2. The employer will consult the union as to the best means by which the desired management result can be achieved fairly and with as little hardship to the employees as possible. In particular, the employer will seek to agree with the union the criteria to be applied in selecting the employees to be made redundant. When a selection has been made, the employer will consider with the union whether the selection has been made in accordance with those criteria.

3. Whether or not an agreement as to the criteria to be adopted has been agreed with the union, the employer will seek to establish criteria for selection which so far as possible do not depend solely upon the opinion of the person making the selection but can be objectively checked against such things as attendance record, efficiency at the job, experience, or length of service.

4. The employer will seek to ensure that the selection is made fairly in accordance with these criteria and will consider any representations the union may make as to such selection.

5. The employer will seek to see whether instead of dismissing an employee he could offer him alternative employment.

The lay members stress that not all these factors are present in every case since circumstances may prevent one or more of them being given effect to. But the lay members would expect these principles to be departed from only where some good reason is shown to justify such departure. The basic approach is that, in the unfortunate circumstances that necessarily attend redundancies, as much as is reasonably possible should be done to mitigate the impact on the work force and to satisfy them that the selection has been made fairly and not on the basis of personal whim."

It is, of course, possible to criticise this standard of fair procedure for exactly the same reason that we have criticised the effect upon the sufficiency of reasons of adoption of commonly accepted practice as the reference point. The justification for both is that there is no objectively correct and immutable standard of fairness either of cause or procedure. The choice is between that which a tribunal might prefer and that accepted by employers in practice. If, as has been said by the E.A.T. and the Court of Appeal consistently, the tribunal is not to substitute its own judgment for that of a reasonable employer it would seem logical that the standard of the reasonable employer should determine the fairness of dismissal both as to cause and procedure. On the other hand it is not the fact that these standards will change from time to time which need cause concern but rather that the courts will be forced to accept practices which they do not consider to ensure fairness. Again, the law will follow, and not lead, the development of fair procedure. It may be that the E.A.T. would have liked to go further to take account of this but this would have involved the presentation of rules of law as to fair procedure which it has repeatedly been told by the Court of Appeal[48] is not its function. The only other source of resort to an objective standard which is available, therefore, is that of good industrial relations practice which may, at least, displace the subjectivity into which the requirement of fair procedure has declined.

The decline in the importance of procedural safeguards, if it survives the *Compair Maxim* decision, must not be allowed to appear out of proportion to its importance. It is a decline relative only to the initial predominance of such requirements. Procedure continues in most cases to be a very important factor in determining the fairness of dismissal and there is no sign of any reduction in the breadth of elements that may compose required procedure. Its width and importance is plainly shown in *Pillinger* v. *Manchester Area Health Authority*[49] which, without it, might have become one of the cases which held dismissal on grounds of reorganisation to be fair. The applicant had been promoted from Grade 2 to Grade 2S. A committee reviewing staff structures ruled that the work only justified employment in Grade 2 and the applicant was dismissed. It was held that though diminution of available funds was a factor to be taken into account the employer should have explained to the employee the reason for the proposed change. Such a process might well have brought to light misapprehensions about the employee's work and, in an appropriate case, might have made possible consideration of reversion to the previous grade.[50]

SPECIFIC PROCEDURAL HEADS

It is convenient to consider procedural requirements in the most commonly invoked categories. Most of these derive from suggestions made in the Code of Practice first issued under the Industrial Relations Act 1971.[51] It has been made clear that this Code is merely a set of guidelines which is neither exhaustive nor compulsory. In *Lewis Shops Group* v. *Wiggins*[52] the N.I.R.C. said that the requirements boiled down to a general standard of fair play. Similar considerations have tempted some legal chairmen of tribunals to refer to the standard as that of "natural justice."[53] There is no doubt that requirements may be added to

---

[48] *e.g. Bailey* v. *B.P. Oil (Kent Refinery) Ltd.* [1980] I.C.R. 642, *supra*, p. 193.

[49] [1979] I.R.L.R. 430.

[50] On this last point see, however, *Merseyside Electricity Board* v. *Taylor* [1975] I.C.R. 185, D.C.; *Quinton Hazell Ltd.* v. *Earl* [1976] I.R.L.R. 296.

[51] Reissued as ACAS Code of Practice 1: Disciplinary Practice and Procedures in Employment (1977).

[52] [1973] I.C.R. 335.

[53] *Greenhalgh* v. *Executors of James Mills Ltd.* [1973] I.R.L.R. 78; *Khanum* v. *Mid-Glamorgan Area Health Authority* [1979] I.C.R. 40.

the code especially when, as in the case of redundancy or sickness, the matter is not one of discipline, and consultation with the employee is regarded as the most appropriate procedure.[54]

Relevance of contract

Procedural requirements are not linked to the terms of the contract of employment. One element that has not been included in any requirement of fair procedure is that of giving a period of notice of termination.[55] Employers often feel that tribunals will react more sympathetically to them if they have given notice but there is no logical, or legal, reason why this should be so. A dismissal is no more or less unfair because time has been allowed for it to take effect.[56] It is most important that the separation of procedural requirements and contractual expectations should be maintained. It is, of course, true that much of the disciplinary procedure which is applied, and subsequently held to be fair, does form part of the contract of employment. On the other hand, if departure from an agreed procedure is considered not to be unfair the fact that it was incorporated into the contract of employment will make no difference.[57] Similarly, statutory procedural requirements may actually impose on the employer an obligation he is under no contractual duty to accept exactly as rejection by the employee of non-contractual duties may, in some circumstances furnish a reason for dismissal.[58] In *Vokes Ltd.* v. *Bear*[59] the employer was considered to have acted unfairly in not seeking alternative employment for a redundant employee.[60] Although there is no doubt that this decision is not considered to lay down any rule of general application it is clear that where an employer did make an offer which was considered reasonable the employee who unreasonably rejected it, despite the absence of any contractual obligation to accept, would have considerably less chance of success in a claim for unfair dismissal.

(a) Warning and consultations

The introduction of a "guideline" that warnings should precede dismissal for other than the more serious offences derived from the inclusion in the original Code of Practice of an indication that such would be regarded as good industrial relations practice. The current version of this guidance states[61]:

> "Often supervisors will give informal warnings for the purpose of improving conduct when employees commit minor infringements of the established standards of conduct. However, where the facts of a case appear to call for disciplinary action, other than summary dismissal, the following procedure should normally be observed:

---

[54] In *Bristol Ship Repairers Ltd.* v. *Lewis* [1977] I.R.L.R. 13 it was said that the tribunal should be satisfied as to who took the decision and how it was arrived at.

[55] *Treganowan* v. *Robert Knee and Co. Ltd.* [1975] I.C.R. 405; *Devis and Sons Ltd.* v. *Atkins* [1977] I.C.R. 377 (C.A.), *per* Cairns L.J.

[56] The suggestion by Waller L.J. in *Devis* v. *Atkins*, *supra*, that an offer of money might be a factor in making a peremptory dismissal fair is equally without logical foundation.

[57] *Bailey* v. *B.P. Oil (Kent Refinery) Ltd.* [1980] I.C.R. 642 (C.A.).

[58] See *R.S. Components Ltd.* v. *Irwin* [1973] I.C.R. 535, *supra*, p. 204.

[59] [1974] I.C.R. 1.

[60] See also *Pillinger* v. *Manchester A.H.A.*, *supra*.

[61] ACAS Code No. 1 (1977) para. 12.

(a) In the case of minor offences the individual should be given a formal oral warning or if the issue is more serious, there should be a written warning setting out the nature of the offence and the likely consequences of further offences. In either case the individual should be advised that the warning constitutes the first formal stage of the procedure.

(b) Further misconduct might warrant a final written warning which should contain a statement that any recurrence would lead to suspension or dismissal or some other penalty, as the case may be.

(c) The final step might be disciplinary transfer, or disciplinary suspension without pay (but only if these are allowed for by an express or implied condition of the contract of employment), or dismissal, according to the nature of the misconduct. Special consideration should be given before imposing disciplinary suspension without pay and it should not normally be for a prolonged period."

Both the earlier and the current statements of good practice refer to warnings in terms of dismissal for misconduct. The intention is clearly that it will normally be reasonable to afford an opportunity to rectify an error. It was argued in early cases, however, that the suggestion was confined to cases of misconduct. There would be no difficulty at the present time in dealing with such a contention by pointing out that the code was only guidance. In *Winterhalter Gastronom Ltd.* v. *Webb*[62] in which the employee had been dismissed for incompetence, Sir John Donaldson preferred a reasoned extension of the purpose of warnings of misconduct.

"There are many situations in which a man's apparent capabilities may be stretched when he knows what is demanded of him; many do not know they are capable of jumping the five-barred gate until the bull is close behind them."

This line of reasoning provided strong support for the early tendency to require prior warnings and other procedures despite the obvious sufficiency of the cause for dismissal.[63] The purpose of a warning may, however, be stated more widely as designed to enable the employee to appreciate the risk he runs. In *A. J. Dunning and Sons (Shopfitters) Ltd.* v. *Jacomb*[64] the tribunal had taken what Sir John Donaldson characterised as a procedural, rather than a substantive, view of the need for a warning and had held that the absence of a specific indication of possible dismissal necessarily made the preliminaries to ultimate dismissal inadequate. A similar approach had produced a number of decisions laying down such sub-rules for adequate warnings.[65] The N.I.R.C. held, however, that no such rigid view of the need for a warning was justified.

"We have no doubt at all that had the tribunal taken the question of warning into account not as a matter of procedure, but as going to the basic sufficiency of the reasons which moved the employers to dismiss him, they must have come to the conclusion that this was a case where an employee, occupying a responsible position, had known over a relatively long period of time that his inability to get on with clients was placing his job in jeopardy. They must also have concluded that

---

[62] [1973] I.C.R. 245. See also *Scottish Co-operative Wholesale Society Ltd.* v. *Lloyd* [1973] I.C.R. 137.

[63] *e.g. Earl* v. *Slater Wheeler (Airlyne) Ltd.* [1972] I.C.R. 508.

[64] [1973] I.C.R. 448.

[65] *e.g. Hewittson* v. *Anderton Springs* [1972] I.R.L.R. 56; *Cockroft* v. *Trendsetter Furniture Co.* [1973] I.R.L.R. 6; *Young* v. *F. Thomas and Co. Ltd.* [1972] I.R.L.R. 40.

bearing in mind the fact that he continued to have difficulties with the clients notwithstanding this knowledge, he was incapable of changing his attitude to clients in such a way as would enable him to serve the true interests of his employers. That he tried to serve these interests is not, of course, in question; he was a most loyal employee. It was a constitutional inability on his part to do so which caused the difficulties."

It is, of course, open to tribunals to continue to hold that the words of the supposed warning do not, in the circumstances, convey the necessary understanding of risk to the employee. This is the reason for the decision in *Meridian Ltd.* v. *Gomersall*.[66] The fact that that decision does not by coming to this conclusion on the particular facts re-establish the general proposition that a warning must be precise was made clear by the E.A.T. in *Elliott Bros. (London) Ltd.* v. *Colverd*.[67]

The courts do not always bother to spell out clearly the nature of the realisation which will suffice as a warning[68] but there are a number of examples where the circumstances were considered a substitute for an explicit warning.[69] In *McPhail* v. *Gibson*[70] the court disapproved of the development of any subcategory of employees who, by reason of seniority, were deemed to know of their obligations. The constant danger of applications of broad conceptions of the purpose of requirements to produce such sub-rules and categories of sufficiency is apparent in the passage from the judgment of Bristow J. in *Alidair Ltd.* v. *Taylor*[71]:

"In our judgment there are activities in which the degree of professional skill which must be required is so high, and the potential consequences of the smallest departure of that high standard are so serious, that one failure to perform in accordance with those standards is enough to justify dismissal. The passenger-carrying airline pilot, the scientist operating the nuclear reactor, the chemist in charge of research into the possible effects of, for example, thalidomide, the driver of the Manchester to London express, the driver of an articulated lorry full of sulphuric acid, are all in the situation in which one failure to maintain the proper standard of professional skill can bring about a major disaster."

This line of reasoning is a clear example of what Davies and Freedland[72] reveal as the choice between seeking to guarantee justice by a set of formal rules and the "substantive" approach favoured by all the more recent decisions. This latter approach cannot, however, be isolated from the former because of the innate tendency of lawyers to attach to the idea of substantive justice qualifying rules. The decision of the Court of Appeal in *Retarded Children's Aid Society Ltd.* v. *Day*[73] is generally regarded as signalling the demise of the procedural approach. A house-father of a home for retarded people was dismissed not only for punishing a person aged 34 with a mental age of seven contrary to estab-

---

[66] [1977] I.C.R. 597.
[67] [1979] I.R.L.R. 92.
[68] *e.g.* Lord Denning M.R. in *Retarded Children's Aid Society* v. *Day* [1978] I.C.R. 437 at 442.
[69] *e.g. Lewis Shops* v. *Wiggins* [1973] I.C.R. 335; *Brown* v. *Hall Advertising Ltd.* [1978] I.R.L.R. 246.
[70] [1977] I.C.R. 42.
[71] [1978] I.C.R. 445—the passage was approved by the Court of Appeal.
[72] At pp. 354–371.
[73] [1978] I.C.R. 437.

lished rules but for refusing to acknowledge that he should not do so. There was a noticeable lack of proper procedure but, as Lord Denning M.R. put it, the tribunal concluded that it was no good the employee remaining because he thought he knew better than anyone else, and if he went on, would break the rules again.

The Master of the Rolls acknowledged the reasonableness and good sense of a rule requiring a warning before dismissal for a first offence.

> "You should warn him that, if it happens again, it would be an offence for which he should be dismissed. It is true that in this case this was not done. There was no initial warning given. He was dismissed on the instant. But nevertheless that is not a rule which has to be applied in every case. In some cases it may be proper and reasonable to dismiss at once, especially with a man who is determined to go on in his own way."

In *Alidair Ltd.* v. *Taylor*[74] the Court of Appeal, not on this occasion differing from the E.A.T., held that the employer's honest and reasonable belief in the incompetence of an airline pilot would override the adverse effect of an inadequate inquiry procedure. Yet again the Court of Appeal adopted the same approach in *Bailey* v. *B.P. Oil (Kent Refinery) Ltd.*[75] in which the claimant had been dismissed for certifying that his own absence was due to sickness when, in fact, he was on holiday in Majorca. The E.A.T. held the dismissal unfair on the ground that the agreed procedure required a union official to be informed of any proposed dismissal. The Court of Appeal confirmed its previous view that though failure to follow procedure is a factor to be taken into account the weight to be given to that defect depends on the circumstances and adherence to procedure is not a condition precedent to a fair dismissal.

Inevitably there are growing signs of acceptance of this attitude at earlier stages. The Scottish E.A.T. on *McCall* v. *Castleton Crafts*[76] held fair a dismissal without formal warning for persistently dealing in the goods of other manufacturers despite clear knowledge of express prohibition and a number of oral warnings. In *Rasool* v. *Hepworth Pipe Co. Ltd. (No. 2)*[77] the English E.A.T. was prepared to overlook the absence of consultation with a full-time union official before dismissal of a shop steward where such consultation would serve no other purpose than to place the shop steward in a preferential position. Davies and Freedland[78] point out that in the case of redundancy the reason was often held almost conclusive of the fairness of dismissal not because of a desire to achieve overall justice so much as because in the law relating to redundancy is enshrined the idea of management prerogative in which the tribunals are reluctant to intervene.[79] Those authors point out that even this attitude is giving place to enquiry.[80]

---

[74] [1978] I.C.R. 445.
[75] [1980] I.C.R. 642.
[76] [1979] I.R.L.R. 218.
[77] [1980] I.R.L.R. 137.
[78] At pp. 357–359.
[79] See *Vickers Ltd.* v. *Smith* [1977] I.R.L.R. 11; *Jackson* v. *General Accident Fire and Life Assurance Co. Ltd.* [1976] I.R.L.R. 338.
[80] See *Jowett* v. *Earl of Bradford (No. 2)* [1978] I.C.R. 431; *Watling and Co. Ltd.* v. *Richardson* [1978] I.R.L.R. 255 but see the Court of Session in *Atkinson* v. *George Lindsay and Co.* [1980] I.R.L.R. 196.

Gross misconduct

Even when the procedural approach was at its highest there were situations in which the cause was regarded as so obviously sufficient that a warning was unnecessary. This led to acceptance of a classification of "gross misconduct" as overriding procedure and, particularly, as justifying a dismissal without warning; although it is hard to reconcile such an exception with the function of warnings. If it is conceded, as most lawyers would concede, that "gross misconduct" is nothing more than legal shorthand for a serious offence justifying summary dismissal it can be seen that this classification is really nothing more than tribunals and the E.A.T. expressing the same desire to by-pass technicalities in favour of a concept of justice that characterises the decisions we have just considered. It is not an entirely novel device for a lawyer to cloak such a desire with the appearance of a technical explanation. It is suggested that if it can be said that the Court of Appeal has rid the law of technical unfairness it will be possible to dispense with "gross misconduct" as an escape clause. The apparent self-justifying appearance of the concept as a term of art gave rise to sub-rules which threatened to impose the very technicality from which the courts desired to escape.

The concept of gross misconduct, and indeed its principal consequence of excluding the requirement of warning, can be traced back to the embodiment in the code of dismissal procedure itself of a procedural escape clause. Having propounded the basic fairness of the requirement of a warning (originally said to apply to misconduct alone) the framers of that code at once realised that there would be offences to which such a requirement would be regarded by employers as inappropriate. To the question, how far does this exception extend, the non-lawyer may be content to answer that it will be obvious in any given set of circumstances when a procedural requirement is inappropriate because of the obvious justification for summary dismissal in the severity of the offence. By trained instinct, however, the lawyer seeks rules to guide himself and others. So the point was approached where categories of "gross misconduct" were sufficiently clearly established to be pleaded as such. Dishonesty, including clocking offences, and fighting at work were commonly accepted as such.[81] In *Martin* v. *Yorkshire Imperial Metals Ltd.*[82] the E.A.T. lent more than credence to the idea that the class of gross misconduct might be established by the employer's own act in conveying to his employees that he so regarded certain action.

Since then, however, rather as with technical unfairness, the courts appear to have been trying to talk themselves out of the worst consequences of assigning to gross misconduct the status of a term of art. They have said that gross misconduct cannot be created by employer designation of acts that are plainly not so[83]; that summary dismissal is not justified for fighting unless there are other circumstances such as the existence of a clear prohibition or actual danger[84]; and, finally, in *C. A. Parsons and Co. Ltd.* v. *McLoughlin*[85] the E.A.T. stated clearly that gross misconduct is nothing more than serious

---

[81] *e.g. Singh* v. *London Country Bus Services Ltd.* [1976] I.T.R. 131; Parkers Bakeries v. *Palmer* [1977] I.R.L.R. 215; *Davies* v. *GKN Birwells (Uskside) Ltd.* [1976] I.R.L.R. 82.
[82] [1978] I.R.L.R. 440. See also *Ayub* v. *Vauxhall Motors Ltd.* [1978] I.R.L.R. 428. (I.T.).
[83] *Ladbroke Racing Ltd.* v. *Arnott* [1979] I.R.L.R. 192.
[84] *Meyer Dunmore International Ltd.* v. *Rogers* [1978] I.R.L.R. 167.
[85] [1978] I.R.L.R. 65.

misconduct. This re-naming of the concept does nothing to destroy its ability to create separate rules. With the developing readiness to treat a compelling reason as capable of overriding procedural irregularities, however, it seems that the escape route by way of misconduct has quietly disappeared.

Advance warning

A good example of this tendency being nipped in the bud is provided by what may be called the "standing warning" theory. In *Martin* v. *Yorkshire Imperial Metals Ltd.*[86] the existence of clear notification that interference with a safety device would lead to dismissal without prior warning was considered to be a material factor in rendering such a dismissal fair. In *Ayub* v. *Vauxhall Motors Ltd.*[87] it was held that no reasonable employer would consider that sleeping during a night shift justified summary dismissal, despite the existence of clear indications in that case that it was not an isolated occurrence. Nevertheless, it was said that different considerations would have applied had the employers put up a notice saying that sleeping would be regarded as a dismissable offence. The Court did not explain how it was that something a reasonable employee would not do becomes reasonable because of advance notice that it would be done. The E.A.T. acknowledged the lack of foundation in the later case of *Ladbroke Racing Ltd.* v. *Arnott*[88] and held unfair a dismissal without warning notwithstanding prior notification that such action would be taken. Like any other aspect of unfair dismissal the question of the need for a warning can only be answered by consideration of numerous factors such as the seriousness of the offence; the likelihood that a warning will prevent repetition (which will not only include the attitude of the employee but also his past record) and the reasonableness of providing an opportunity for reform. If this last point is thought to be affected by the employee's appreciation of the way in which his offence will be treated it must surely equally be affected by the employee's likely acceptance of the reasonableness of that appreciation. The cases dealing with what management or specialist employees may appreciate were all based on the courts' view of what would be a reasonable expectation. It is submitted, therefore, that advance warning of a course of conduct should only be allowed to replace warning after the act has once been committed if the advance warning is itself reasonable.

A more profitable line of development from the view that warnings are relevant to the reasonable understandings of an employee has led to a realisation that the word "warning" is itself only one way of describing the process of bringing about such an understanding. In non-disciplinary circumstances exactly the same process is better described as consultation.

The cases holding that warning may be equally necessary in the case of dismissal for redundancy[89] are not so much developing warnings for different purposes as pointing out that it is reasonable to indicate to an employee the risks that face him as soon as may otherwise be reasonable after they are first

---

[86] [1978] I.R.L.R. 440.
[87] [1978] I.R.L.R. 428.
[88] [1979] I.R.L.R. 192.
[89] *e.g. Clarkson International Tools* v. *Short* [1973] I.C.R. 191; *Mansfield Hosiery Mills Ltd.* v. *Bromley* [1977] I.R.L.R. 301; *Williams* v. *Compair Maxam Ltd.* [1982] I.R.L.R. 83.

apparent to the employer. It is of no significance whether this is done by
"consultation" or "warning." It is unfortunate[90] that the introduction of a
statutory obligation to consult recognised trade unions before redundancy[91]
should have concealed the possibility that this may simply be the obvious way of
carrying out consultation with those affected by a collective dismissal and led to
the wholly artificial discussion of whether absence of statutory consultation
makes dismissal unfair. Professor Wallington makes this point very clearly[92]:

> "Consultation is a process dfferent in kind both to a disciplinary hearing and to a
> disciplinary warning; it essentially entails warning an employee of what is likely to
> happen and giving him (or his union) an opportunity to make representations. It is
> particularly relevant in a case where the employee is sick, or in a reorganisation or
> redundancy."

The present writer would only differ from this in suggesting that consultation
involves both a type of hearing and of warning. In *Hollister* v. *National Farmers
Union*[93] Lord Denning quoted from the 1972 Code of Practice:

> "Consultation means jointly examining and discussing problems of concern to both
> management and employees. It involves seeking mutually acceptable solutions
> through a genuine exchange of views and information."[94]

It is the element of problem solving, rather than of explanation or defence
which adapts consultation as the counterpart to warning in non-disciplinary
cases where the "problem" is not simply whether there will be an improvement.

Consultation in sickness

In the case of dismissal for sickness though the employer will normally be
entitled to accept the evidence of a medical practitioner as to the facts of the
sickness[95] the employee is entitled to a discussion upon the question whether
the only solution is dismissal.[96]

Support following warning

In cases where the purpose of the warning is to encourage improvement it
may be reasonable to expect provision of training to overcome the fault.[97] A
warning may be useless without the opportunity to improve.

Form and duration of warning

The Code of Practice talks of oral and written warnings and it has become
common for disciplinary procedures to embody the separate stages of oral and
written warning. The preceding discussion will have revealed that there is (save

---

[90] As the judgment in *Williams* v. *Compair Maxam Ltd.*, *supra*, indicated.
[91] *Infra*, p. 296.
[92] Elias Napier and Wallington, at p. 591.
[93] [1979] I.C.R. 542.
[94] A good example of the court seeking an opportunity to solve the problem of redundancy
appears in *Abbots and Stanley* v. *Wesson-Glynwed Steels Ltd.* [1982] I.R.L.R. 51.
[95] *Liverpool Area Health Authority, etc.* v. *Edwards* [1977] I.R.L.R. 471.
[96] *East Lindsey District Council* v. *Daubney* [1977] I.C.R. 566.
[97] *Burrows* v. *Ace Caravan Co. (Hull) Ltd.* [1972] I.R.L.R. 4; *Welsh* v. *Associated Steel and
Tools Co. Ltd.* [1973] I.R.L.R. 111 (Both I.T. only).

for evidentiary purposes) no magic in this.[98] It has also become standard practice to provide that a warning shall have a limited active life.[99] It is not clear whether cancellation of the warning should be regarded as wiping the slate clean. Certainly it must indicate to a reasonable employee that he is regarded as having responded to the purpose of the warning. It is, however, possible to imagine a case where a long series of warnings, all of them "cancelled" before the next successive offence, nevertheless justified ultimate dismissal.[1] The test remains one of overall reasonableness and is not supplanted by supposed rules about cancellation of warnings.

Repetition of offence

Surprisingly no attention has been paid to the possibility of arguing that if a warning is considered reasonable the commission of an entirely different offence should not constitute the requisite ground for dismissal. Such a situation occurred in a case cited by Elias Napier and Wallington[2] in which a funeral worker had been summarily dismissed for carelessly delivering the wrong body to the deceased's home.[3] He had previously been orally warned for wearing brown shoes at a funeral. Probably because this was regarded as not sufficiently significant to be a contributory factor the dismissal was held fair on the basis of the final offence alone. If the sole reason for disciplinary warning was to afford an opportunity to improve there would be something to be said for disregarding earlier, but unexhausted, warnings of different offences. If the purpose is more to place the employee on notice that his job is at risk then the present practice of paying little or no attention to any difference in the nature of disciplinary offences appears to be the correct one.

Absence of "procedure" for issuing warnings

There is no rule that a warning should be preceded by a hearing.[4] The feeling, apparent at times in both employees and employers that it should, stems from the fact that warnings are now often regarded, in themselves, as a form of discipline. If that is so then, as a matter of good industrial relations practice, it may well be that an employee who raises an objection to accepting a warning should be heard. It is possible that if the fairness of a dismissal rested upon the validity of a preceding warning an employee who had not been heard before the issue of that warning would be able to show that it would not have been issued had he been allowed to contest it.

(b) Enquiries and hearings[5]

As "warning" is a useful word to denote a wider process making an employee aware of his obligations, so "hearing" is not necessarily confined to being

---

[98] *McCall* v. *Castleton Crafts Ltd.* [1979] I.R.L.R. 218.
[99] This too depends on the suggestion in the Code (para. 19) that good practice would involve such cancellation.
[1] See *Charles* v. *Science Research Council* (1977) 121 I.T.R. 208.   [2] At p. 595.
[3] *Reay* v. *North Eastern Co-operative Society Ltd.* (1978) 111 I.R.L.I.B. 12.
[4] *Wood* v. *Kettering Co-operative Chemists Ltd.* [1978] I.R.L.R. 438.
[5] There is nothing to prevent a hearing in the fact that it may involve discussion of issues which are the subject of criminal charges on which the employee is awaiting trial. *Harris (Ipswich) Ltd.* v. *Harrison* [1978] I.C.R. 1256.

indicative only of some process of answering a charge.[6] In *Williamson* v. *Alcan (U.K.) Ltd.*[7] the process of permitting an employee likely to be dismissed for sickness to express his views was properly treated in the same light as a hearing. This example also makes the point that the process of inquiry to establish the true facts and the process of hearing in which the employer discusses the course of action appropriate to these facts may shade off into each other. On the facts of the case the decision in *Budgen and Co.* v. *Thomas*[8] that the presence of the employee at an enquiry does not replace the need for a hearing may be correct. If of general application, however, that decision has been held to represent too strict a view of procedural requirements. Both enquiry and hearing must serve the purpose of fairness. So an enquiry is said not to be necessary if the facts are clear and any attempt to suggest that they are otherwise or can be explained away would be likely to be disbelieved.[9]

On the other hand, it is considerably less easy to envisage cases of disciplinary dismissal where the absence of the chance of a hearing could be excused than it is to envisage absence of need for a warning. In the early case of *James* v. *Waltham Holy Cross U.D.C.*[10] the N.I.R.C. said:

> "This duty of fairness both to the employee and to the business is the only general rule. All else is but a particular application of that general rule. Thus in the field of conduct there are at least two types of case in which it may be reasonable exceptionally to dismiss without giving the employee an opportunity of offering an explanation. The first is that in which the employee, as part of the conduct complained of, states in terms why he is adopting that attitude. If it is clear that this is the employee's considered view, not merely the result of a passing emotion, there can be no point in giving him an opportunity of re-stating a view, the expression of which led to the decision to dismiss him. But even so, an employer should be slow to conclude that an opportunity to reflect and a subsequent opportunity to explain could in no circumstances produce a changed situation in which dismissal would be unnecessary. The second is that in which an employee's conduct is of such a nature that, whatever the explanation, his continued employment is not in the interests of the business. In such a case it is not unfair to dismiss without giving the employee an opportunity for explanation, although even in such a case many employers would rightly afford such an opportunity in order that the employee may have no possible excuse for feeling aggrieved."

Jointly agreed procedures

A more common question before tribunals concerns not the absence of an aspect of procedure but the departure from a specific procedure, often agreed with trade unions. The obverse of this is whether to follow an agreed procedure

---

[6] It is submitted, therefore, that Lord Denning M.R. in *Hollister* v. *National Farmers Union* [1979] I.C.R. 542 did not unjustifiably confuse hearing and consultation. Doubts about the desirability of lessening the apparent need for such a process which that case raises stem rather from the psychological point that "consultation" obviously appeared less essential to the protection of an individual than it would if the word "hearing" had been used. It suffered a similar reduction of emphasis in *Taylorplan Catering (Scotland) Ltd.* v. *McInally* [1980] I.R.L.R. 53.

[7] [1977] I.R.L.R. 303.

[8] [1976] I.C.R. 344.

[9] *Scottish Special Housing Association* v. *Linnen* [1979] I.R.L.R. 265.

[10] [1973] I.C.R. 398.

raises something like a presumption of fairness. In *East Hertfordshire District Council* v. *Boyten*[11] Forbes J. in the E.A.T. said:

"When one comes to consider what an employer has to show . . . it is quite clear he has to show that he acted reasonably. It is perfectly possible to imagine a situation where, if an employer considering a disciplinary matter followed a code of procedure which was unfair, it could be said, and has been said in other cases, that he acted unreasonably. But this is not a case where the employer is following a code of procedure of his own devising or unassisted by others. This is a case where the employer was following a code of procedure laid down and agreed by both sides of the industry. It is in effect the bible on what should happen in these circumstances. As was pointed out in the course of the argument, it may be extremely difficult for an employer if he does not follow the agreed procedure laid down, because it may be said in those circumstances that in not following an agreed code of procedure he is in fact acting unreasonably because that code was one which in the context of industrial relations had been agreed between both sides of industry. It appears to us that in looking at this matter the industrial tribunal wholly overlooked the question that what they were really deciding was whether the employer acted reasonably. We cannot find it possible to say, in a case of this character, at any rate, that an employer, in following such an agreed procedure, could be said to be acting unreasonably. Of course there may be an argument that the code could be improved, or that greater safeguards could be included. But that is not the point of this case. The point is that there is a code, carefully agreed between the parties, and, in the way we look at it, it is not for an industrial tribunal, or, indeed, this Appeal Tribunal to rewrite an agreed code of that kind which has been hammered out by both sides of industry. No employer, it seems to us, should be accused of acting unreasonably in those circumstances, if that employer follows a code which has been arrived at in that way. In our view the industrial tribunal wholly misdirected themselves about this. Had they directed their minds to the correct point they could not possibly have come to any other conclusion than that the employer was acting reasonably in this case."

In this light it can be seen that the standard of good industrial relations practice referred by Browne-Wilkinson J. in *Williams* v. *Compair Maxam Ltd.* will, in practice, be an agreed standard or its equivalent. That being so much of the apparent danger of hallowing "standard practice" disappears. Nevertheless, the interests of the trade union either in agreeing the procedure or operating it in a particular case is not always in line with the interest of the particular employee involved. In the present writer's experience, for instance, trade unions often have a stronger objection to violence on the shop floor than has management. Just as the assumption in *Gray Dunn and Co. Ltd.* v. *Edwards*[12] that there is no need for the accused employee to be present throughout the hearing if his union representatives are present, so too there may be aspects of agreed procedure which fail to ensure sufficient fairness to the individual. The danger of producing a presumption that the good industrial relations practice of adhering to agreements is fair is that it will produce some of the same effects as the principle of "best practice" in the law of negligence. The reason for the doctrine is much the same. To hold that the procedure is unfair is to say that the union has agreed to an unfair procedure and even possibly that standard practice is unfair.[13]

---

[11] [1977] I.R.L.R. 347.
[12] [1980] I.R.L.R. 23.
[13] Compare the judgment of Lord Reid in *General Cleaning Contractors Ltd.* v. *Christmas* [1953] A.C. 180.

Napier[14] points out that if an employer's failure to observe the procedural requirements of the Code of Practice may be taken into account so too should his observance of the exhortation in that Code to establish agreed procedures. With respect, however, the logic of this argument seems to be based on a false premise. The early cases may have suggested following the Code for its own sake. Later cases, however, have allowed the general concept of fairness to override the Code. By agreeing a procedure with the unions, the employer is, of course, establishing his own Code and logically it should be judged by the same overall standard of fairness. In practice, however, whatever logic may suggest, tribunals are prepared to question the fairness of unilateral procedures but are not at all happy about passing judgment on agreed procedures.

It is submitted that there is an urgent need to provide guidance on the purpose of these interrelated stages of procedure but that such guidance will only be possible when the courts themselves are clear as to that purpose. It is suggested that there is an urgent need to re-emphasise the point in *Budgen Ltd.* v. *Thomas*[15] wherever a disciplinary charge is involved that the purpose of a hearing is to afford an opportunity to the employee adequately to defend himself and that similarly significant purposes attach to a process of consultation where that is the appropriate means of arriving at a decision.[16]

(c) Appeal

The Code of Practice states that a disciplinary procedure should provide a right of appeal and specify the procedure to be followed. It also emphasises the value of the external stages of a grievance procedure or independent arbitration. One of the problems, in practice, is that appeal to a member of the same management group may not be thought to produce the impartial judgment that is generally thought necessary to make an appeal worthwhile. The E.A.T. has noticed this point but, since purely internal procedures are normal in British industrial relations, it is unwilling to do more than accept that they are satisfactory provided there is no evidence that the person hearing the appeal failed to appear to act impartially.[17]

A failure to follow the proper appeal procedure is no more necessarily unfair than failure in any other aspect of procedure.[18] It is very likely to constitute a breach of contract and may in itself be sufficient to establish a constructive dismissal.[19] But even if it does this will not inevitably render the dismissal unfair. On the other hand, failure to follow properly an appeal procedure is likely to raise a presumption that a dismissal is unfair.[20] Appeal procedures are,

---

[14] Elias Napier and Wallington: *Labour Law: Cases and Materials*, at p. 586.
[15] [1976] I.C.R. 344.
[16] See *Bristol Channel Ship Repairers* v. *O'Keefe* [1978] I.C.R. 691. Compare, *Clyde Pipeworks Ltd.* v. *Foster* [1978] I.R.L.R. 313. On the question whether the statutory requirement to consult recognised trade unions before dismissal for redundancy see *Forman Construction Ltd.* v. *Kelly* [1977] I.R.L.R. 468.
[17] *Johnson Matthey Metals Ltd.* v. *Harding* [1978] I.R.L.R. 248.
[18] See, *e.g. Stevenson* v. *Golden Wonder Ltd.* [1977] I.R.L.R. 474; *Ward* v. *Bradford Corporation* (1971) L.G.R. 27; *Rowe* v. *Radio Rentals Ltd.* [1982] I.R.L.R. 177.
[19] *Post Office* v. *Strange* [1981] I.R.L.R. 515.
[20] *Rank Xerox (UK) Ltd.* v. *Goodchild* [1979] I.R.L.R. 185—failure to permit representation; *McCabe* v. *9th District Council of County of Lanark* [1973] I.R.L.R. 75. But see *Rowe* v. *Radio Rentals Ltd., supra.*

however, much more susceptible to the argument that absence or defect in them would not have affected the outcome than are other procedural stages. It is also true that the application of this principle to appeal procedures is less open to objection than, for instance, the absence of a hearing. By its nature, the process of enquiry by an industrial tribunal will tend to reveal more reliably the sort of issues that would have been raised on appeal.[21] The appeal must produce evidence to overturn an initial decision and it is likely to be much clearer what that evidence will be than that a hearing has brought forward all the issues likely to affect the initial decision.

It is well known that in practice, internal disciplinary appeals are often conducted by those who have been to some extent involved in the preceding disciplinary process. In *Rowe* v. *Radio Rentals Ltd.*[22] Browne-Wilkinson J. in the E.A.T. said that contact with those who had made the initial decision was almost inevitable and such persons were often required to give evidence at the hearing. Total separation of functions was, therefore, impossible. What was required was evidence that the appeal had been fair and just.

The question whether a satisfactory appeal can cure previous defects arises in many areas of the law. The view generally is that if there is a preceding material defect the function of an appeal is to discover that defect and reverse the previous decision or refer it back for reconsideration. In *Henderson* v. *Masson Scott*[23] however, it was held that an appeal operating by way of a complete rehearing could cure defects in the initial hearing. In *Monie* v. *Coral Racing Ltd.*[24] the E.A.T. extended this to entitle an appeal which in fact was conducted as a rehearing to advance and validate new grounds for dismissal. The Court of Appeal[25] overruled this but there are so many reasons in the facts of that case in favour of that decision of the Court of Appeal that it is not possible to say that its judgment has any general effect on the power of an appeal to rectify defects. It is clear, however, that whether it operates as a rehearing or not an appeal is not capable of producing a valid initial finding and so cannot validate an *ultra vires* decision.[26]

Failure by an employee to use an appeal cannot affect the fairness of his dismissal[27] though it may amount to a failure on his part to mitigate his loss.[28] Where an appeals procedure is in existence, however, the E.A.T.[29] said that it was highly desirable that its existence should be brought to the notice of the employee.

STATUTORY PROVISION FOR PARTICULAR SITUATIONS

In certain cases, all relating to the reason for dismissal, Statute has made special provision for the fairness or unfairness of dismissal. It follows that where such provision applies normal considerations of reasonableness do not enter into

---

[21] See *Rowe* v. *Radio Rentals Ltd.*, *supra*.
[22] [1982] I.R.L.R. 177.
[23] [1974] I.R.L.R. 98.
[24] [1979] I.C.R. 254.
[25] [1980] I.R.L.R. 464.
[26] *Post Office* v. *Strange* [1981] I.R.L.R. 515.
[27] *Chrystie* v. *Rolls Royce (1971) Ltd.* [1976] I.R.L.R. 336.
[28] *Hoover Ltd.* v. *Forde* [1980] I.C.R. 239.
[29] *Tesco Group of Companies (Holdings) Ltd.* v. *Hill* [1977] I.R.L.R. 63.

consideration and, most obviously, procedural sufficiency or defect is irrelevant. It must be remembered, however, that if the special provisions do not apply the normal test of fairness may be applied to the facts.

(a) Pressure to dismiss

In deciding upon the reason for the dismissal and the reasonableness of a dismissal based upon it pressure exercised by any person on the employer to dismiss the employee by calling, organising, procuring or financing a strike or other industrial action or threatening to do so is to be disregarded.[30] If this is the only reason, therefore, the employer has no defence to a claim[31] and indeed even if it is one among more principal reasons the disclosure of it would jeopardise the success of an argument that other reasons were sufficient. There seems no reason, however, why an employee's conduct in provoking trade union opposition should not be considered as contributing to his dismissal subject to a doubt as to whether such contribution must be deliberate.

The Employment Act 1980 introduced a new provision[32] since extended and now allowing the employer or the complainant to join as a party to the proceedings any trade union or person who has applied pressure on an employer to dismiss an employee because the latter was not a member of any trade union or of a particular trade union. If the request is made before the hearing begins joinder must be allowed. Any award of compensation may be made wholly against the person so joined or partly against him and partly against the employer as the tribunal considers just and equitable. This provision will not have any effect on pressure to comply with a union membership agreement operating within statutorily permitted limits since no successful unfair dismissal claim will result from such a dismissal.[33]

(b) Dismissal relating to trade union membership or activities—interim procedure

Three reasons for dismissal were formerly statutorily designated inadmissible reasons.[34] They are that the employee:

(a) was, or proposed to become a member of an independent trade union;
(b) had taken, or proposed to take, part at any appropriate time in the activities of an independent trade union; or
(c) had refused or proposed to refuse, to become or remain a member of a trade union.[35]

Save where a union membership agreement is properly applied dismissal principally because of one of these reasons is automatically unfair. Complaint

---

[30] Employment Protection (Consolidation) Act 1978, s.63. See *Trend* v. *Chiltern Hunt Ltd.* [1977] I.C.R. 612.

[31] *Hazells Offset Ltd.* v. *Luckett* [1977] I.R.L.R. 430.

[32] Employment Protection (Consolidation) Act 1978, s.76A, as amended by Employment Act 1982, s.5.

[33] Under the Employment Act 1982, s.10 a union membership requirement in a subcontract is void. Pressure to observe it is, therefore, comprehended within the above principle.

[34] This term has now been removed from the relevant provisions (E.A. 1982, Sched. 2, paras. 16–19).

[35] Employment Protection (Consolidation) Act 1978, s.58(1). The meaning of these has been examined, pp. 118–122, *supra*.

can be made without any need to serve a qualifying period of employment and is not subject to restrictions on the employee's age.[36] In the case of dismissal alleged to be unfair for any of the reasons covered by section 58 of the 1978 Act[37] there exists a statutory procedure enabling the employee to claim interim relief.[38] This relief is available upon a complaint of unfair dismissal for any of the above three reasons. This has been extended to a claim regarding any statutory exception to the enforceability of a union membership agreement. An application must be made to an industrial tribunal within seven days immediately following the effective date of termination. Before the end of that period in cases other than those involving dismissal for non-compliance with a union membership agreement there must also be presented a written certificate signed by an official of the trade union of which the employee was, or proposed to become, a member, authorised by that union to act for this purpose. The certificate must state that on the date of the dismissal the employee was, or had proposed to become, a member of the union and that there appear to be reasonable grounds for supposing that the reason or principal reason for dismissal was one alleged in the complaint.[39] The certificate will be invalid if it does not meet these requirements, but a valid certificate may be amended at the hearing so as to rectify a mistake. A valid certificate cannot be revoked by the official who signed it.[40]

A tribunal composed of one member only, selected from the panel of chairmen, must determine the application as soon as practicable and must, at least seven days before the hearing, give the employer a copy of the application and certificate together with notice of the date, time and place of the hearing.[41]

If, on hearing the application, it appears to the tribunal likely that on a full hearing it will be held that the complainant is by reason of the amended section 58 regarded as having been unfairly dismissed the tribunal must announce its findings and explain to both parties (if present) the powers the tribunal has under this procedure.[42] The employer (if present) must then be asked whether he is willing to reinstate the applicant or, failing reinstatement, to re-engage him on terms and conditions not less favourable than those applicable to his previous job.[43] If the employer is willing to reinstate the employee the tribunal shall make an order to that effect. If the employer is willing to re-engage and states the terms and conditions upon which he is willing to do so, the employee must be asked whether he is willing to accept the job on those conditions. If he is the appropriate order will be made. If he is not willing and the tribunal considers his refusal reasonable then an order will be made for the continuation of his contract of employment. This latter order will also be made if the employee fails to attend,[44] or if the employer is unwilling to reinstate or re-engage.

An order for the continuation of the contract of employment is an order that the contract shall continue in force until the determination or settlement of the

---

[36] *Ibid.* 1978, s.64(3).
[37] See Employment Act 1982, s.6.
[38] Employment Protection (Consolidation) Act 1978, ss.77–79.
[39] s.77(2).
[40] *Stone* v. *Charrington and Co. Ltd.* [1977] I.C.R. 248.
[41] s.77(3). See *Bailey* v. *Amey Roadstone Corporation Ltd.* [1977] I.R.L.R. 299.
[42] As to the considerations to be taken into account in determining the likelihood of a successful claim see *Forsyth* v. *Fry's Metals Ltd.* [1971] I.R.L.R. 243.
[43] s.77(5) and (6).
[44] Presumably in such a situation a prima facie case will have been made out.

complaint for the purposes of pay or other benefit derived from the employment, seniority, pension and similar matters and continuity of employment.
The order itself must specify the amount to be paid by way of pay and this
amount shall be that which the employee could reasonably have expected to
earn for the appropriate period. So far as concerns the amount falling due after
the order, payment is due on the normal pay days. Any payment actually made
under the contract and any lump sum received by the employee on dismissal
shall be set off against the amount due.[45]

It is for the employee to prove that the reason for the dismissal was one of
those specified by section 58.[46] If the tribunal only has jurisdiction because the
reason is one so specified it is inevitable that the applicant will have to establish
the existence of the jurisdiction. If the tribunal otherwise has jurisdiction it
seems a little surprising that the employer should be relieved of his normal
burden to prove a reason by the allegation of an inadmissible reason. It seems
inconceivable that if the employee fails to establish an inadmissible reason the
employer should succeed notwithstanding the latter's inability to establish any
other reason. In *Marley Tile Co.* v. *Shaw*[47] in which the Court of Appeal
confirmed the decision upon the burden of proof, the employee lacked the
necessary qualifying period of employment to sustain an ordinary claim for
unfair dismissal. The reference in *Smith* v. *Hayle*[48] to his need to establish an
exception is, therefore, applicable.

(c) Union membership agreements

Types of closed shop

Before we examine the meaning of the legal concept of union membership
agreement it is advisable to consider briefly what practices fall within the scope
of the popular concept of a closed shop. The two most commonly used
categories of closed shop are "pre-entry" and "post-entry." A pre-entry closed
shop requires an employee to belong to a particular union before he is
employed. In this way it allows the trade union to regulate entry into the trade.
Types within this category range from what McCarthy[49] called the "labour
supply shop" to situations in which the union limits the number, and may even
control the selection, of apprentices and requires all skilled employees to be
drawn from those apprentices. The decline in apprenticeship has rendered this
last type very much less common but many examples exist of similar restrictions
upon promotion of those who are union members. The post-entry closed shop
seeks only to ensure that those who are employed become union members.
Entry to the trade is regulated by the employer and the market. Both main
categories seek to secure trade union solidarity. Such solidarity may be seen
from a number of different points of view. At its lowest it ensures that union

---

[45] s.78.
[46] *Smith* v. *Hayle Town Council* [1978] I.C.R. 996; *Goodwin Ltd.* v. *Fitzmaurice* [1977]
I.R.L.R. 393. In *Robb* v. *Leon Motor Services Ltd.* [1978] I.C.R. 506 the E.A.T. held that
transfer to less desirable work was not a response to a steward's trade union activities but his
"over enthusiasm" in carrying them out.
[47] [1980] I.C.R. 72.
[48] *Supra.*
[49] W.E.J., now Lord, McCarthy, *The Closed Shop in Britain* (Blackwell).

discipline will be a meaningful sanction. In the eyes of most union officials this is only a side effect and the principal purpose of the closed shop is to lend support to collective bargaining by preventing the employer either appealing to a considerable number of non-unionists or weakening the effect of any industrial action by relying on non-unionists not to participate.

The so called agency shop introduced into British legislation by the Industrial Relations Act 1971 but still to be found in the practice of some trade unions[50] is, in these terms, a half-way house. It does not ensure union solidarity since it allows employees freely to opt out of membership and support. In practice it may well tend to produce such solidarity since it breaks through the apathy of doing nothing and by forcing a decision to pay money either as union dues or in lieu thereof will normally induce the decision to enjoy the benefits of union membership rather than nothing.

Within the categories the actual agreement may take many forms. At their lowest these will be mere informal understandings. Some of these are sufficiently informal to permit one party to deny the existence of a closed shop agreement. An employer may, for instance, merely undertake to do his best to ensure that all employees join the appropriate union. Arguments as to whether these arrangements are truly closed shop agreements depend on the definition adopted. The legislature has, therefore, preferred to ask whether in practice they result in a requirement that employees shall join the union. In other words, their legal effectiveness depends on the degree to which the employer, whether or not under pressure from the union, applies them.

Enforcement of union membership agreements

As we have seen[51] action short of dismissal designed to induce membership of a union may be the subject of a claim before an industrial tribunal unless, and to the extent that, such a requirement is covered by a valid union membership agreement. A union membership is defined as[52] an agreement or arrangement which

"(a) is made by or on behalf of, or otherwise exists between, one or more independent trade unions and one or more employers or employers' association; and
 (b) relates to employees of an identifiable class; and
 (c) has the effect in practice of requiring the employees for the time being of the class to which it relates (whether or not there is a condition to that effect in their contract of employment) to be or become a member of the union or one of the unions which is or are parties to the agreement or arrangement or of another specified independent trade union."

Section 58 of the Employment Protection (Consolidation) Act 1978[53] extends the validity of such agreements so as to render fair dismissals in accordance therewith.

"(3) Subject to the following provisions of this section, the dismissal of an employee by an employer shall be regarded for the purposes of this Part as having been fair if—

---

[50] *e.g.* The Lock and Metal Workers' agreements.
[51] *Supra*, p. 118.
[52] TULRA 1974, s.30 as amended by Trade Union and Labour Relations (Amendment) Act 1976, s.3(3) and (4).
[53] As amended by Employment Act 1982, s.3.

(*a*) it is the practice, in accordance with a union membership agreement, for employees of the employer who are of the same class as the dismissed employee to belong to a specified independent trade union, or to one of a number of specified independent trade unions; and

(*b*) the reason (or, if more than one, the principal reason) for the dismissal was that the employee was not, or had refused or proposed to refuse to become or remain, a member of a union in accordance with the agreement; and

(*c*) the union membership agreement had been approved in relation to employees of that class in accordance with section 58A through a ballot held within the period of five years ending with the effective date of termination."

This permission is subject to a number of exceptions which have been amended and extended by subsequent Acts. The current full version of such exceptions is contained in the amendments introduced by section 3 of the Employment Act 1982.

"(4) Subsection (3) shall not apply if the employee genuinely objects on grounds of conscience or other deeply-held personal conviction to being a member of any trade union whatsoever or of a particular trade union.

(5) Subsection (3) shall not apply if the employee—

(*a*) has been among those employees of the employer who belong to the class to which the union membership agreement relates since before the agreement had the effect of requiring them to be or become members of a trade union, and

(*b*) has not at any time while the agreement had that effect been a member of a trade union in accordance with the agreement.

(6) Subsection (3) shall not apply if—

(*a*) the union membership agreement took effect after 14th August 1980 in relation to the employees of the employer who are of the same class as the dismissed employee, and

(*b*) the employee was entitled to vote in the ballot through which the agreement was approved in accordance with section 58A or, if there have been two or more such ballots, in the first of them, and

(*c*) the employee has not at any time since the day on which that ballot was held been a member of a trade union in accordance with the agreement.

(7) Subsection (3) shall not apply if the dismissal was from employment in respect of which, at the time of the dismissal, either—

(*a*) there was in force a declaration made on a complaint presented by the employee under section 4 of the Employment Act 1980 (unreasonable exclusion or expulsion from trade union), or

(*b*) proceedings on such a complaint were pending before an industrial tribunal,

unless the employee has at any time during the period beginning with the date of the complaint under section 4 and ending with the effective date of termination been, or failed through his own fault to become, a member of a trade union in accordance with the union membership agreement.

(8) In any case where neither subsection (4) nor subsection (7) has the effect of displacing subsection (3) and the employee—

(*a*) holds qualifications which are relevant to the employment in question,

(*b*) is subject to a written code which governs the conduct of those persons who hold those qualifications, and

(c) has—

    (i) been expelled from a trade union for refusing to take part in a strike or other industrial action, or

    (ii) refused to become or remain a member of a trade union,

subsection (3) shall not apply if the reason (or, if more than one, the principal reason) for his refusal was, in a case falling within paragraph (c)(i), that his taking the action in question would be in breach of the code or, in a case falling within paragraph (c)(ii), that if he became, or as the case may be remained, a member he would be required to take part in a strike, or other industrial action, which would be in breach of that code.

(10) For the purposes of subsections (3) and (7) the reference to the time of the dismissal shall, in a case where the dismissal was with notice, be construed as a reference to the time when the notice was given.

(11) For the purposes of subsection (7) an employee shall be taken to have failed through his own fault to become a member of a trade union only if the tribunal is satisfied that the fact that he is not a member is attributable to his failure to apply (or re-apply) for membership or to his failure to accept an offer of membership.

(13) Where the reason, or one of the reasons, for the dismissal of an employee was—

    (a) his refusal, or proposed refusal, to comply with a requirement (whether or not imposed by his contract of employment or in writing) that, in the event of his failure to become or his ceasing to remain a member of any trade union or of a particular trade union or of one of a number of particular trade unions, he must make one or more payments; or

    (b) his objection, or proposed objection (however expressed) to the operation of a provision (whether or not forming part of his contract of employment or in writing) under which, in the event mentioned in paragraph (a), his employer is entitled to deduct one or more sums from the remuneration payable to him in respect of his employment;

that reason shall be treated as falling within sub-sections (1)(c) and (3)(b)."

The ballot provisions referred to have likewise been amended and the current provisions governing the validity of a ballot are as follows:

"58A.—(1) Subject to the following provisions of this section, a union membership agreement shall be taken for the purposes of section 53(3)(c) to have been approved in relation to the employees of any class of an employer if a ballot has been held on the question whether the agreement should apply in relation to them and either—

    (a) not less than 80 per cent. of those entitled to vote, or

    (b) not less than 85 per cent. of those who voted, voted in favour of the agreement's application.

(2) Subsection (1)(b) shall not apply if the agreement—

    (a) has not previously been approved in accordance with this section in relation to the employer's employees of the class in question, and

    (b) came into force in relation to them after 14th August 1980.

(3) The persons entitled to vote in a ballot under this section, in relation to the application of a union membership agreement to the employees of any class of an employer, shall be all those employees who belong to that class and who—

    (a) in the case of a ballot in which votes may only be cast on one day, are in the employment of the employer on that day; or

    (b) in any other case, are in that employment on the qualifying day.

(4) "Qualifying day" means the day specified as such by the person conducting the ballot; but no day shall be specified which—

(a) falls after the last of the days on which votes may be cast in the ballot; or
(b) is so long before that date as to be unreasonable in relation to that ballot.

(5) A ballot under this section shall be so conducted as to secure that, so far as reasonably practicable, all those entitled to vote—

(a) have an opportunity of voting, and of doing so in secret; and
(b) in a case which does not fall within subsection (3)(a), know, before they cast their votes, which day has been specified as the qualifying day.

(6) in determining for the purposes of subsection (3) whether a person belongs to a class of employees, any restriction of the class by reference to membership (or objection to membership) of a trade union shall be disregarded.

(7) An agreement shall not be taken for the purposes of section 58(3) (c) to have been approved through a ballot of the employees of any class of an employer if since it was held another ballot of those employees has been held under this section and both—

(a) less than 80 per cent. of those entitled to vote, and
(b) less than 85 per cent. of those who voted, voted in favour of the agreement's application.

(8) Subsection (7) shall not affect the determination in any case of the question whether the condition in subsection (2)(a) is satisfied."

The common law regards a closed shop agreement as normally not constituting an unreasonable restraint of trade.[54] This degree of validity, however, scarcely raises an issue since the agreement will normally be regarded as not intended to have contractual effect[55] or likely to be incorporated in the individual contract of employment.[56] The employer will be free to act upon it to refuse to employ a non-member initially but this is simply because, subject to the prohibitions on sex and race discrimination, an employer is free to choose whom he employs.

Once an employee is engaged the provisions of section 58(1) will apply to protect him from dismissal for non-membership of any union immediately and without the need to serve a qualifying period of continuous employment. In order to justify dismissal the employer will have to prove the dismissal to be in accordance with a valid union membership agreement, the practice of observing it and the fact that the employee in question was not a member of the designated union. In *Himpfen* v. *Allied Records Ltd.*[57] the E.A.T. pointed out that although in theory an employer could make any such agreement that he wished with any union that he wished that agreement would not be enforceable until the practice of observing it was established. In a sense, therefore, the initial consent of the bulk of the work-force to the operation of the agreement is required. In that case the employer was unable to show that the agreement was operational since about half the employees were members of another trade

---

[54] *Reynolds* v. *Shipping Federation Ltd.* [1924] 1 Ch. 28.
[55] See *ante*, p. 347.
[56] See *supra*, p. 28.
[57] [1978] I.C.R. 684.

union. In fact the principal reason for the decision in this case goes further than this to require the employer to give reasonable notice of a change in his requirements before enforcing it. Arnold J. said:

> "The question is whether reasonable notice was given of what we think was a state of affairs inconsistent with that which had earlier been represented; reasonable notice, that is, not as that phrase is often used by lawyers as meaning notice of a reasonable length, but notice given in a reasonable manner, such as a thoughtful, caring employer would consider to be a sensible way of communicating the departure to the workforce. Now we think that this is inconsistent with the earlier position because we regard the language which had been used, indicating a freedom of choice of union, to mean not only that the employees were at liberty to belong to any union which they wished to belong to, but also as indicating that the workpeople were at liberty not to belong to any union to which they did not wish to belong provided at least that they belonged to some independent union. The only reference in the agreement to the future employment of the workpeople being involved with their choice of union is in the short phrase in paragraph 2 of the agreement, 'membership of the union shall be a condition of employment' couched, as we have indicated, in somewhat equivocal terms and finding its place in a document which apparently is couched in legally provided language and certainly is not so simple as to be obvious and stand out clearly as an indication of the impact of that particular passage. We do not think that merely to post upon the notice board without comment, without direction, without emphasis, without selection, the text of this agreement was a reasonable way in which to bring to the notice of the workforce that that which had been represented to be the state of affairs existing between the management and the employees was no longer so.
>
> On June 8 a letter was written to each employee. That letter was not couched in legal language. That letter was one which being in the hands of each of the employees could be studied conveniently, comfortably at leisure, and it, in two places, stated that membership of the union had been made by the agreement a condition of employment with the employers, and moreover, at one of those points, this was demonstrated to be a legally enforceable condition. We think that the writing of that letter was a reasonable notice of the new developments, a reasonable notice therefore that the state of affairs earlier represented down to May 18, was no longer one which obtained."

It is submitted that although in *Himpfen's* case there had been an express representation of the employees' freedom to join any trade union this statement need not be confined to an estoppel thus induced. The situation preceding the introduction of a union membership agreement will always constitute a representation of the existence of different requirements. *Himpfen's* case is, therefore, authority for the fact that no such agreement can be enforced without the type of notification discussed or without a response which indicates substantial acceptance.

The degree of acceptance is not clearly defined. The earlier version of the requirements for enforceability states that all the employees of the affected class should in practice be required to join the union. In *Sarvent* v. *C.E.G.B.*[58] an industrial tribunal held that this rendered unenforceable an agreement which was operated loosely so as not to compel a small minority of dissenters to join the union. The existence of this form of leniency is by no means uncommon, and the decision in *Sarvent*, had it been followed, would have either invalidated

---

[58] [1976] I.R.L.R. 66.

large numbers of closed shop agreements or forced upon the unions a strict application of agreements which most of them would not have considered desirable. The amendment omitting the specific reference to all the employees does not compel a different conclusion to that reached in *Sarvent* but in *Home Counties Dairies* v. *Woods*[59] the E.A.T. held that reference to the existence of a practice of requiring employees to join the union indicated the need to show the existence of a general state of affairs and not necessarily a uniform condition. In *Himpfen's* case the E.A.T. rendered this as a practice of requiring "almost all" the employees to join. The acceptance of some non-compliance is also apparent in the decision to consider it sufficient a practical requirement that it had been agreed that management would tell all new employees that they were expected to join the union.[60]

In *Taylor* v. *Co-operative Retail Services Ltd.*[61] the Court of Appeal held that a practice of adherence could be said to exist notwithstanding that ten per cent. of employees were not union members and, in addition, many of the employees had not been members of the union for long.

In *Gayle* v. *John Wilkinson and Sons*[62] the employer acted on the incorrect assurance of the shop steward that an employee was not a union member. The resulting dismissal was held to be fair. On the other hand, in *Blue Star Ship Management Ltd.* v. *Williams*[63] a differently constituted E.A.T., without referring to *Gayle's* case, required the employer to prove the non-membership as a fact. Since we are here dealing with a statutory presumption of fairness the honest belief of the employer which is sufficient to sustain the reasonableness of his action in other dismissal situations is scarcely relevant. On the other hand the words "the reason . . . was that the employee was not a member" on which Phillips J. relied in *Blue Star* are just as capable of referring to the reason in the mind of the employer, whether that reason is right or wrong in fact.

Procedure

The E.A.T. has twice clearly expressed the view that strict compliance with the terms of the union membership agreement must be shown. In *Jeffry* v. *Laurence Scott and Electromotors Ltd.*[64] the employer had omitted the third stage of considering the dismissal which involved discussion with full time officials of the Employers Association and the union. This was done because it had become clear that the union would not moderate its requirement of dismissal. Phillips J. however, reasoned that though the employee was not a party to the agreement the statutory provision was an exception to his normal protection and he was entitled to rely on the provisions of a procedure designed to ensure proper consideration of the issues. It is, however, difficult to see why this requirement should be more strict than that applicable to ordinary dismissal procedure. As in those cases, statute here defines a reason for dismissal and, therefore, no more provides an exception than in any other case unless, indeed, it could be said that, by designating dismissal fair, it requires no procedure at all.

---

[59] [1977] I.C.R. 463.
[60] *Gayle* v. *John Wilkinson and Sons (Saltley) Ltd.* [1978] I.C.R. 154.
[61] [1982] I.R.L.R. 354.
[62] *Supra*.
[63] [1978] I.C.R. 770.
[64] [1977] I.R.L.R. 466.

In adhering to Phillips J.'s decision, Arnold J. in *Curry* v. *Harlow District Council*[65] clearly leaves the way open for a modification of the strictness of the requirement so as to require only compliance with aspects of the agreement essential to a proper consideration. It is a very short step then to the conclusion that, if in the view of the tribunal, proper consideration has been given to the issues the employee has no reason to complain. Any other view appears rather strange in the light of the fact that it is quite clear from the words of the statute that if the agreed procedures are inadequate to ensure proper consideration the requirements have, nevertheless, been satisfied by observance of these procedures and the dismissal is fair.

Circumstances in which union membership agreements are unenforceable

Five situations are now defined by statute in which a union membership agreement cannot be relied upon to render fair the dismissal of an employee who is not a member of the specified union. They are:

(a) If the employee genuinely objects on grounds of conscience or other deeply held personal conviction to being a member of any trade union whatsoever, or of a particular trade union.

(b) If the employee has belonged to a class to which the agreement applies (disregarding any definition of that class by reference to trade union membership) since before the agreement became effective and has not since that time been a union member in accordance with the agreement; or, where a ballot is required, has not been a union member in accordance with the agreement since the date on which the ballot was held.

(c) If an agreement taking effect after the coming into force of section 7 of the Employment Act 1980 has not been approved within five years by 80 per cent. of the class to which it applies (or subsequently 85 per cent. of those actually voting) (disregarding any definition of that class by reference to union membership) in a ballot of all employees in that class.

(d) The employee has made a complaint of unreasonable exclusion or expulsion from the union under section 4 of the Employment Act 1980.

(e) The employee holds qualifications relevant to the employment in question and is subject to a written code which governs the conduct of those persons who hold those qualifications and has refused to become or remain a member of a trade union or has been expelled from a trade union for refusing to take part in industrial action. This exception only applies if the principal reason for the industrial action would be a breach of the code or if the failure to retain union membership was because he would be required to take part in industrial action in breach of the code.

At the time of writing virtually nothing is clear about the likely application or effect of these provisions. Doubt as to whether ballots are required to give effect to amended agreements has been overtaken by legislative extension of the ballot requirement to validate agreements at periodic intervals. Most questions are certain to arise, however, concerning the protection for those with deeply held personal convictions leading to objection to membership even of a particular trade union. The protection which this provision in the 1980 Act replaced

---

[65] [1979] I.C.R. 769.

had covered only religious objection. This was not in practice significantly narrower than protection on grounds of conscience. In *Hynds* v. *Spillers French Baking Ltd.*[66] the Scottish N.I.R.C. had held that conscience for this purpose must be regarded as requiring a broadly religious basis as contrasted with personal feeling or intellectual creed.[67] It may seem surprising, for example, that a member of management could rely on an irrational, though genuine, belief in Divine guidance but could not rely on reasoned arguments about conflict of duty. There was no certainty that to replace the reference to religious objection with a reference to conscience would extend the categories of those employees excepted from an obligation to join a trade union. There can be no such doubts about the scope of "deeply held personal conviction." In any event the Code of Practice on Closed Shop Agreements and Arrangements clearly suggests that an objection to strike action based on a professional ethic in turn depending, for instance, on considerations of the maintenance of safety would be capable of constituting such a conviction. It remains to be seen how far such objections will be permitted in practice. The establishment of such a conviction will however, render the dismissal automatically unfair.

Compensation

The compensation available for a dismissal contrary to these provisions—that is to say, for union membership, non-membership or activities where the dismissal is unprotected by a valid union membership agreement is regulated by the Employment Act 1982.[68] There is a minimum basic award of £2,000 subject to reduction on grounds of the complainant's conduct prior to dismissal. In the light of the fact that in 1980 (the latest year for which full figures are available) only just over 12 per cent. of claimants for unfair dismissal received compensation of £2,000 or more and the mean award was less than £600 it seems difficult to justify the imposition of such a minimum save as an attack upon the operation of the closed shop. Where the claimant applies for an order for reinstatement or re-engagement the tribunal may make a "special award," in addition to basic and compensatory awards, of 104 times a week's pay up to a maximum of £20,000, or £10,000, whichever is the greater. The special award is subject to reduction on the grounds of the complainant's conduct prior to dismissal. Where an order for reinstatement or re-engagement is made but not complied with and the employer fails to satisfy the tribunal that it is not reasonably practicable for him to comply, the amounts of the special award are increased to a multiple of 158 or £15,000.

The provisions for application by employer or complainant to join as a party to the action a trade union or other person (*sic*) who has induced the dismissal by industrial action or threat thereof apply equally to claims for unfair dismissal under these provisions. A trade union might, therefore, be ordered to pay the whole amount of the compensation for demanding dismissal under an invalid union membership agreement or a valid agreement to which a valid exception applied in the instant case.

---

[66] 1974 S.L.T. 191; [1974] I.T.R. 261.
[67] The statement in *Saggers* v. *British Railways Board* [1977] I.R.L.R. 166 that this must not be taken to mean that all conscientious objection is necessarily based on religion is not, as some commentators suppose, a contradiction of this, but rather an affirmation.
[68] ss.4 and 5.

Union membership agreements in supply contracts

Any union membership term in a contract for the supply of goods or services is void in so far as it purports to require that the whole, or part, of the work is to be done by persons who are, or are not, members of a particular trade union. A statutory duty is owed to the supplier of goods or services, or any other person who may be adversely affected, not, on grounds of union membership, to exclude that person's name from any list of approved suppliers or of those from whom tenders may be invited. A similar duty is owed to any other party to the contract, or any other person who may be adversely affected, not on such a ground to terminate a contract of supply of goods or services. It is also a breach of a newly created statutory duty to the person concerned, or any other person who may be adversely affected, on grounds of union membership to exclude a person from an invitation to tender or to fail to permit such a person to tender or otherwise to determine not to enter into a contract with such a person for the supply of goods or services. Those inducing breaches of this duty or the inclusion of one of the above mentioned terms in a contract lose any immunity granted by statute to individuals contemplating or furthering a trade dispute.[69] It is not difficult to see how a determined court could have avoided such statutory immunity and breach of statutory duty does not require the use of illegal means[70] anyway, since neither of those actions necessarily falls only under one of the specified heads of protected action.

Statutory protection from tort liability otherwise provided by section 13 of TULRA 1974 is not available in certain situations relevant to the imposition of closed shop provisions on sub-contractors where any person has induced another to break a contract of employment, interfered with the performance of such a contract or threatened so to do or has threatened that a contract of employment will be broken or that inducement to breach or interference will be applied by the person so threatening. The conditions in which such immunity is removed are:

(i) that the effect of the action is to interfere, or be reasonably likely to interfere, with the supply of goods or services, whether or not under contract;

(ii) that one of the reasons for doing the act is that work in connection with that supply is, or is likely to be, done by employees of an employer other than the employer subject to the contract of employment who are not union members, or who are members of trade unions or of a particular trade union.[71]

These provisions concerning pressure on contractors represent, it is submitted, a massive response to a wholly one-sided view of a problem. On the one hand it can be said to be wholly illegitimate for a union to use its organised strength with one employer to compel another, whose employees do not themselves desire unionisation, to force his employees into membership of that union as the price of staying in business. A few years ago a notorious example of this occurred when the Society of Lithographic Artists, Designers and

---

[69] Employment Act 1982, s.14.
[70] See, *infra*, p. 474.
[71] Employment Act 1982, s.14 replacing the narrower provisions of Employment Act 1980, s.8.

Engravers sought by such means to organise small, and almost entirely non-union "art shops." Modern techniques meant that art work done in these shops could be prepared for printing without an application of the older craft skills of the Society's members.

Whatever may be thought of the merits of this example of an attempt to sustain union membership and influence, there are, on the other hand, many situations where trade unions can be said to have a legitimate interest in controlling the undesirable practices of small contractors. In 1968 the Phelps Brown Committee on the Supply of Labour in the Construction Industry[72] reported on some of the shortcomings of labour only sub-contracting in that industry. There can be little doubt that similar practices exist, doubtless in less widespread form, in other industries. It may, of course, be said that unions can seek to control these practices without seeking to impose a closed shop, but it is rather more difficult to say how this can be achieved. The small contractor is in a strong position to resist union attempts to establish a bargaining structure. It does not follow, however, that the lack of desire for such representation among his workforce is motivated by reasons of which public policy would approve. A trade union's desire to enforce standards of safety or to make sure that terms and conditions of employment which it has established with other employers are not undercut by sub-standard terms adopted by non-union firms can scarcely be said to be reprehensible.

It is submitted, therefore, that more thought needs to be given to both sides of this problem before some rather more careful drafting produces a more balanced provision.

International conventions

Finally an employee may seek a remedy for dismissal because of the operation of closed shop provisions before the European Court of Human Rights under Article 11 of the European Convention of Human Rights and Fundamental Freedoms which provides that everyone has a right to freedom of association with others, including the right to form and join trade unions. It is arguable that this involves a correlative right not to associate and it was on this that the claimants relied in *Young and James* v. *The United Kingdom* and *Webster* v. *U.K.*[73]

The applicants, who did not allege a religious objection, which alone at this time would have excused them, had refused to join the appropriate railway union and had, accordingly, been dismissed by British Rail. In all three cases, at the time employment began, there was no requirement for a British Rail employee to be a member of a specified trade union. The union membership agreement had been revived in 1975 following repeal of the 1971 Act. The applicants claimed that enforcement of the legislative provision that dismissal in accordance with a union membership agreement was fair interfered with their freedom of thought, conscience, expression and association under Articles 9, 10, 11 and 13 of the European Human Rights Convention. The European Court of Human Rights by 18 votes to three decided that there had been a breach of Article 11 and, accordingly, did not consider the possibility of breach

---

[72] Cmnd. 3714.
[73] Applications numbered 7601/76 and 7806/77 [1981] I.R.L.R. 480.

of the other Articles. The majority held that the requirement to join a particular union which had not existed when they were engaged amounted to an infringement of the employee's right to join an association of their choice—the sanction of dismissal, being, for practical purposes, compulsive. They also held that compulsion to join a particular union contrary to the employees' convictions was an infringement of the freedom guaranteed by Article 11. The majority did not finally decide whether the positive freedom of association necessarily included the negative freedom not to associate. On the assumption that it did not, however, they concluded that the freedom to associate involved an element of freedom of choice which must imply some limit on the power to compel membership of a particular union. In their view a compulsive threat of dismissal involving loss of livelihood directed at those engaged before the introduction of the requirement struck at the very substance of the guaranteed freedom of choice.

In the view of the majority the suggestion that the applicants could form any association they chose, provided they also joined the specified union, in no way altered the degree of compulsion to join the specified union even if it was true that such action would not have led to their expulsion from the railway union. This compulsion in reality reduced any freedom to join another association to one of no practical value. They also added that Article 11 was part of a pattern of protection of freedom of thought, conscience and expression and this whole pattern was threatened by compulsion to join an association against one's convictions. Even if the applicants were in a minority it did not follow that the majority could insist that restriction of their freedom was necessary to protect the rights and freedoms of others. "Necessary" means more than advantageous and there was no evidence that the absence of power to compel membership of those with connections like those of the applicants would have prevented the railway unions striving for protection of the interests of their members. Even had there been such evidence a balance must be struck to avoid the majority acting unfairly to the minority.

Seven members of the Court went further to hold that the positive freedom necessarily involved the correlative negative freedom not to join an association. Any attempt to compel membership regardless of its compulsive effect would, therefore, be an infringement of that aspect of the guarantee contained in the Convention.

Presumably the difference between imposing the obligation on existing employees and imposing it on those seeking employment as a condition of engagement envisaged by the majority lies in the fact that the latter retain the freedom to seek other employment. It is easy to see, however, arguments that such freedom is itself insubstantial where a single employer controls access to all but a very small part of an industry. The Convention, however, does not guarantee freedom to select a particular trade and it remains to be seen, therefore, how far the scope of this decision can be extended to protect other than existing non-union employees. The opinion of the seven concurring members would extend protection against any attempt at compulsion whatever the effectiveness of its sanction and would, therefore, cover applicants for employment.

"Trade union freedom," they said, "involves freedom of choice; it implies that a person has a choice as to whether he will belong to an association or not and that, in the former case he is able to choose the association. However, the possibility of choice, an indispensable component of freedom of association, is in reality non-existent where there is a trade union monopoly of the kind encountered in the present case."

An extra legal remedy exists for employees dismissed as a result of expulsion from or refusal of admission to a trade union where a union membership agreement operates. The T.U.C. in 1976 set up an Independent Review Committee for such cases primarily to replace the former statutory machinery[74] allowing individuals to make claims against trade unions for arbitrary or unreasonable exclusion or expulsion.[75]

(d) Dismissal in connection with Industrial Action

Brian Bercusson has pointed out that the law relating to strikes, lock-outs and other industrial action is virtually certain to be unsatisfactory whilst lawyers pursue their normal function of locating what they regard as the essential characteristics of such action and moulding the law around those characteristics. The trouble is that lawyers do not begin with a clear sheet but with the preconception that they are discussing the contract of employment. So the definition of "strike"[76] selects three characteristics, namely: *a concerted cessation of work* designed *to compel* any person to accept or not to accept *terms or conditions affecting employment*.[77] Bercusson points out that experts in industrial relations accept at least two other major characteristics, namely:

  (a) A strike is a temporary stoppage in which there is no intention to terminate the contract of employment;
  (b) A strike is, in practice, normally produced by a managerial act of taking the employees concerned off the clock. Stoppages of work in which the employees do not leave the premises are not regarded in industrial relations practice as strikes.

It is not surprising, therefore, that if the present legal position of strike action is based on consideration of only a few of a larger number of factors there is plenty of scope for discussion of different legal approaches which would acknowledge other characteristics. In a number of the United States, for instance, job protection is offered to the employee who takes industrial action in protest against what are regarded as illegitimate methods or aims of the employer (unfair labour practices). No such security is afforded to the striker who seeks improved terms and conditions. It follows that the law could be used to further a variety of policies. Protection of official, as compared to unofficial strikes would tend to lend support to the central organisation of trade unions. Distinction between constitutional and unconstitutional strikes would emphasise the effectiveness of collectively agreed procedure, and so on.

Not only shall we find the approach of English law remarkably unsophisticated in this respect but we shall also find it tending to generalisation. So, for

---

[74] Now substantially re-enacted in the Employment Act 1980, s.4.
[75] For survey of the work of this Committee from 1976 to 1978 see Davies and Freedland: *Labour Law: Text and Materials*, pp. 548–557.
[76] Employment Protection (Consolidation) Act 1978, Sched. 13, para. 24(1).
[77] "Concerted" implies the necessity of a common purpose: *M'Cormick* v. *Horsepower Ltd.* [1981] I.C.R. 535 (C.A.).

instance, all industrial action is likely to be treated in a similar fashion. Even without Lord Denning's obligation not wilfully to disrupt the undertaking[78] most industrial action will be regarded as amounting to a repudiatory breach of contract. Statute has picked this up and incorporated it into a peculiar exception to the jurisdiction of industrial tribunals over unfair dismissal, thereby completely ignoring the sort of considerations suggested above. It may be asked whether by assuming termination to be the legitimate outcome of strikes, and probably of other industrial action, the law is paying any attention to the expectations of the parties. It may also be asked why the law should suppose all industrial action to produce the same consequence. In *Laws* v. *The London Chronicle (Indicator Newspapers) Ltd.*[79] the Court of Appeal was prepared to regard disobedience to an instruction indicated by a form of withdrawal of labour as not intended as a terminating event. It may be asked why, even if the common law was unable or unwilling to recognise the different consequences of industrial action, statute should not have allowed scope for such consideration.

The common law

Until 1963 there existed a largely unchallenged assumption that the common law regarded a strike as a termination of employment by the employee.[80] Donovan L.J. first seriously questioned this assumption in the Court of Appeal in *Rookes* v. *Barnard*.[81] He pointed out that neither party regarded the contract (by which he may have meant the relationship) as ended and that serious legal consequences would arise from strict application of the idea of termination. Lord Devlin supported this view in the House of Lords[82] as did Lord Denning M.R. in *J. T. Stratford and Son Ltd.* v. *Lindley*.[83] The report of the Royal Commission on Trade Unions, etc.,[84] clearly proceeded on the assumption that the earlier view was correct and said that it had reason to believe that the judges disavowed the views attributed to them. That this was true of Lord Denning was made clear by him in *Morgan* v. *Fry*[85] where he said that whereas logical legal reasoning would hold that a strike was necessarily a breach of contract constituting a refusal to be available for work during the subsistence of the contract, such could not be the law since it would conflict with the right to strike.

In *Simmons* v. *Hoover Ltd.*[86] Phillips J. categorically reaffirmed the common law position. He said:

> ". . . bearing in mind the many changes in the law of industrial relations which have occurred since the decision in *Morgan* v. *Fry*, we do not feel that we are bound by that case to hold that the effect of a strike, whether preceded by a proper strike notice or not, is to prevent the employer from exercising the remedy which in our

---

[78] *Secretary of State for Employment* v. *ASLEF* (*No. 2*) [1972] 2 Q.B. 455.

[79] [1959] 1 W.L.R. 698.

[80] As we have seen there might be some conceptual difficulty now in such an assumption, although realisation of the need to show acceptance by the employer of the repudiation might, oddly enough, contribute to an understanding of management's part in defining a strike.

[81] [1963] 1 Q.B. 623.

[82] [1964] A.C. 1129.

[83] [1965] A.C. 307.

[84] Cmnd. 3623 (1968).

[85] [1968] 2 Q.B. 710.

[86] [1977] I.C.R. 61.

judgment he formerly enjoyed at common law to dismiss the employee for refusing to work. We accept, of course, that in most cases men are not dismissed when on strike; that they expect not to be dismissed; that the employers do not expect to dismiss them, and that both sides hope and expect one day to return to work. Sometimes, however, dismissals do take place, and in our judgment they are lawful. The Trade Union and Labour Relations Act 1974, in paragraph 8 of Schedule 1 seems to have recognised that fact. No doubt problems can arise, when a man on strike is dismissed—for example, in connection with a claim for a redundancy payment or for compensation for unfair dismissal. But these are matters which are easily dealt with by legislation; indeed, as we have pointed out, so far as unfair dismissal is concerned that has already been done. As to the effect of the dismissal of a man on strike on his entitlement to a redundancy payment, that matter has also received attention in section 10 of the Redundancy Payments Act 1965, to which we shall turn in a moment. If in the result the present statutory answers are judged to be unsatisfactory, they are easily corrected by legislation. It would, in our judgment, be far more unsatisfactory to seek to achieve a particular result by distorting the underlying law relating to employer and employee. Similarly, problems relating to continuity of employment can be, and to some extent have been, regulated by statute; see Contracts of Employment Act 1972. We have considered whether any conclusions can be drawn about the legal effect of a strike upon a contract of employment from the terms of this, and other, statutes. There is obviously a limit to the usefulness of this exercise, but some indication of how the law was generally regarded before the decision in *Morgan* v. *Fry* is to be found in the language used in section 10(1) and (4) of the Redundancy Payments Act 1965. In each case the assumption seems to be that participation in a strike, or exclusion by a lock-out, is or may be repudiatory conduct entitling the employer to dismiss the employee, or the employee to terminate the contract, without notice.

We do not accept Mr. Sedley's submission that, if the contract of employment was not suspended, nonetheless the employee's action in going on strike was not repudiatory of the contract. It seems to us to be plain that it was, for here there was a settled, confirmed and continued intention on the part of the employee not to do any of the work which under his contract he had engaged to do; which was the whole purpose of the contract. Judged by the usual standards, such conduct by the employee appears to us to be repudiatory of the contract of employment. We should not be taken to be saying that all strikes are necessarily repudiatory, though usually they will be. For example, it could hardly be said that a strike of employees in opposition to demands by an employer in breach of contract by him would be repudiatory. But what may be called a "real" strike in our judgment always will be."

Although much other industrial action will also involve a breach of contract it does not follow that this is true of all industrial action—provided there is no implied obligation not wilfully to disrupt. It may well be that there are forms of working to rule which are not more than a strict application of the rules as properly construed. In *Power Packing Casemakers* v. *Faust*[87] the E.A.T. held that "other industrial action" as applied in section 62 of the Employment Protection (Consolidation) Act 1978 would include a withdrawal of voluntary overtime notwithstanding that no breach of contract was involved.

Unfair dismissal

In 1971 dismissal of those engaged in strikes or other irregular industrial action was declared fair unless one or more employees was selected for

---

[87] [1981] I.C.R. 484.

dismissal from among a larger number of strikers and the reason for the selection was an inadmissible reason. This provision underwent a number of changes over the years, not all of them as a result of relevant considerations. The concept of irregular industrial action involving a breach of contract was abandoned in 1974 and in the haste to repeal the 1971 Act it seems that the word "irregular" was deleted from this provision without very clear realisation that this would render fair dismissal regardless of the absence of any breach of contract. There is no reason why such a breach should be considered a relevant factor in determining the law in relation to industrial action. Nevertheless it does point out sharply the different practical consequences of different types of industrial action to which, however, a common legal consequence is assigned and it certainly throws in doubt the explanation by the N.I.R.C. of the provision as a means whereby the employer can avoid the ruin of his business.[88]

The provision that dismissal on account of industrial action should be fair was changed to a provision that an industrial tribunal should not have jurisdiction to decide upon the fairness of a dismissal for this reason. In 1975 even the reason itself disappeared and the provision which became section 62 of the Employment Protection (Consolidation) Act 1978 merely referred to dismissal where, at the date of the dismissal, the employee was taking part in industrial action or the employer was conducting a lock-out. The reference to prohibited reasons for discrimination among those concerned was dropped in favour of a general prohibition on selective dismissal regardless of the reason.

Section 62 was further amended by the Employment Act 1982[89] and the current provision is as follows:

(1) The provisions of this section shall have effect in relation to an employee (the "complainant") who claims that he has been unfairly dismissed by his employer where at the date of dismissal—

(a) the employer was conducting or instituting a lock-out, or
(b) the complainant was taking part in a strike or other industrial action.

(2) In such a case an industrial tribunal shall not determine whether the dismissal was fair or unfair unless it is shown—

(a) that one or more relevant employees of the same employer have not been dismissed, or
(b) that any such employee has, before the expiry of the period of three months beginning with that employee's date of dismissal, been offered re-engagement and that the complainant has not been offered re-engagement.

(3) Where it is shown that the condition referred to in paragraph (b) of subsection (2) is fulfilled, the provision of sections 57 to 60 shall have effect as if in those sections for any reference to the reason or principal reason for which the complainant was dismissed there were substituted a reference to the reason or principal reason for which he has not been offered re-engagement.

(4) In this section—

(a) "date of dismissal" means—
(i) where the employee's contract of employment was terminated by notice, the date on which the employer's notice was given, and
(ii) in any other case, the effective date of termination;

---

[88] *Heath* v. *J. F. Longman Ltd.* [1973] 2 All E.R. 1228.
[89] s.9.

  (*b*) "relevant employees" means—

     (i) in relation to a lock-out, employees who were directly interested in the dispute in contemplation or furtherance of which the lock-out occurred, and

     (ii) in relation to a strike or another industrial action, those employees at the establishment who were taking part in the action at the complainant's date of dismissal;

    "establishment," in sub-paragraph (ii), meaning that establishment of the employer at or from which the complainant works and

  (*c*) any reference to an offer of re-engagement is a reference to an offer (made either by the original employer or by a successor of that employer or an associated employer) to re-engage an employee, either in the job which he held immediately before the date of dismissal or in a different job which would be reasonably suitable in his case.

Interpretation of the provisions

It should be noted that it is not always clear whether the employees are taking part in industrial action. In *Rasool* v. *Hepworth Pipe Co. Ltd. (No. 2)*[90] participation in a union meeting was held to be a union activity but not to constitute industrial action even though the employer had expressly warned his employees that no permission had been given for them to attend the union meeting. On the other hand, as we have seen, the fact that the action is in breach of an employee's obligations does not mean that it does not constitute industrial action.[91] It is not even clear when industrial action may be said to have ended. In *Bloomfield* v. *Springfield Hosiery Finishing Co. Ltd.*[92] the N.I.R.C., with considerable perception of the industrial relations realities of the matter, regarded strikes as part of the process of industrial relations and concluded that, for the purposes of continuity of employment, a strike could be said still to be in progress even though the employer had dismissed the strikers because of their action. On the other hand, in *Clarke Chapman—John Thompson Ltd.* v. *Walters*[93] it was said that a strike was at an end when the employees are ready to return to work, even though they have not yet been taken back.[93a]

The provisions added to the section by the Employment Act 1982 were designed to overcome the effect of the decision in *Stock* v. *Jones (Frank) (Tipton) Ltd.*[94] that an employer could only claim protection from any decision as to unfair dismissal if he had dismissed all those who had ever taken part in the strike in question regardless of whether some of them had returned to their jobs by the time of the dismissal. It had also appeared that an unconscious re-employment of one of the strikers some time after the dismissal would offend the provision in the 1978 Act concerning subsequent re-engagement.

In fact, however, the amendments afford the employer more scope than is necessary to overcome this problem. The prohibition on selection is stated to cover the "relevant employees." These are defined as those employees who were taking part in the action at the date of the complainant's dismissal. The effect of this is to allow the employer to select a point of time when he may

---

[90] [1980] I.R.L.R. 137.
[91] *Power Packing Casemakers* v. *Faust* [1981] I.C.R. 484.
[92] [1972] I.C.R. 91.   [93] [1972] 1 W.L.R. 378.
[93a] A threat of action, however, does not constitute the start of industrial action—*Midland Plastics Ltd.* v. *Till* [1983] I.R.L.R. 9.
[94] [1978] I.C.R. 347 (H.L.).

dismiss all those still on strike. Inevitably this will tend to mean in some cases that a hard core who remain on strike may be dismissed without remedy. The employer is also entitled to dismiss strikers at one establishment but not at another.

It should be noted that if the employer does dismiss strikers he can still claim the protection of the section even though he does not re-engage all of them in their previous jobs. It is provided that re-engagement means the offer of any job reasonably suitable in the particular employee's case. So in *Williams* v. *National Theatre Board Ltd.*[95] it was held that an offer of re-engagement to one striker on condition that he should be regarded as under a second warning did not entitle him to claim an unfair dismissal. The E.A.T. did not hold this condition suitable. It held that suitability only extended to consideration of the nature of the job. If this decision is correct it entitles the employer selectively to impose discriminatory conditions upon re-engagement regardless of their unreasonableness, provided only that they do not affect the job content. Finally, after three months, the employer is now to be released from any obligation not selectively to re-engage.

(e) Redundancy

Some idea of the changes of emphasis—even of presumption—which occur throughout the area of unfair dismissal decisions is apparent from the fact that in *Lifeguard Assurance Ltd.* v. *Zadrozny*[96] it had been said that though it was not correct to say that a dismissal for redundancy is always fair a tribunal should not lightly find dismissal for this reason to be unfair. It is submitted, however, that this never did apply to a dismissal for redundancy which has some other obviously unfair element.[97] The most likely, and probably the most problematical, such element, it is suggested, is the absence of consultation prior to the redundancy. There was considerable support for the view that absence of the statutorily required consultation is a factor in assessing reasonableness of individual dismissals.[98] The leading case on this issue is now *Williams* v. *Compair Maxam Ltd.*,[99] That case declares that redundancy *selection* will be unfair if standard industrial relations procedures are not applied. There would seem to be no reason why the comment in the judgment about the reasons for the requirement of consultations should not apply even where the issue of selection within a particular class arises. Of the statutory requirement for prior consultation the court said:

> "Breach of s.99 does not confer any legal rights other than those conferred by s.101: see s.99(9). But in our judgment it does show an approach by the legislature to the correct handling of redundancies where there is a recognised union which echoes what we have said is current good practice: *i.e.* early warning, consultation with the union, a pre-ordained basis of selection for redundancy. Moreover it reflects the view expressed above that departure from any of these principles is only justifiable in special circumstances."

---

[95] [1981] I.C.R. 248 (E.A.T.). [96] [1977] I.R.L.R. 56 (E.A.T.).

[97] See, *e.g. Clarkson International Tools Ltd.* v. *Short* [1973] I.C.R. 191; *Rigby* v. *British Steel Corporation* [1973] I.C.R. 160; *Greig* v. *Sir Alfred McAlpine and Son (Northern) Ltd.* [1979] I.R.L.R. 372.

[98] *North East Midlands Co-operative Society Ltd.* v. *Allen* [1977] I.R.L.R. 212; *Kelly* v. *Upholstery and Cabinet Works (Amesbury) Ltd.* [1977] I.R.L.R. 91.

[99] [1982] I.R.L.R. 83 (E.A.T.) see, *supra*, p. 213.

A tribunal, however, has no power to investigate the reasonableness of the employer's decision to declare a redundancy.[1]

There is no reason why claims for redundancy payment and unfair dismissal should not be combined.[2] In *Midland Foot Comfort Centre Ltd.* v. *Moppett*[3] both claims succeeded by application of the statutory presumption available in both instances since the employer failed to appear to prove that the reason was not redundancy or to show that there was a substantial reason for the dismissal.

Special provision is made for dismissal for redundancy where it is shown that the circumstances constituting the redundancy applied equally to one or more other employees in the same undertaking who held similar positions and who have not been dismissed. It is obvious that many cases of redundancy involve reduction of one or more of a larger number of employees holding similar positions. Section 59 provides that such a selective redundancy must be regarded as unfair if the reason, or principal reason, is within one of the three heads formerly called "inadmissible reasons" and specified in section 58 in connection with trade union activities or if the selection for dismissal is in contravention of a customary arrangement or agreed procedure departure from which is not justified by any special reason.

In deciding on such contravention, account need only be taken of employees in the same undertaking who hold similar positions. In *Axe* v. *British Domestic Appliances*[4] it was held that where employees are in the same grade of employment, even though they may receive a different rate of pay, owing, for instance, to a sex differential, the employees in question are in a similar position. Other factors may, however, lead to a different decision. In *Simpson* v. *Roneo*[5] an inspector who specialised in security equipment was held not to be in a similar position to a general inspector of mechanical equipment, even though both worked in the same section of assembly work. A tribunal has held[6] that where a company is selecting "labourers" to be made redundant it must select them on a company-wide basis and not merely from the particular section where the redundancy is thought to be necessary. It has been pointed out[7] that the distinction may properly be made between skilled and unskilled since the greater flexibility of unskilled jobs entitles a tribunal to consider a wider class.

In *Powers'*[7] case a driver's mate working in the transport section was selected on a "last-in, first-out" procedure which was applied only in that section. The tribunal did point out, however, that selecting specialists on a departmental basis would be reasonable. Differences in work expectation, rather than actual skill, may be held to justify dismissal of one group rather than of certain employees from two or more groups.[8]

Where companies have customary arrangements or agreed procedures relating to redundancy, they will, apparently, be required to follow them reasonably

---

[1] *Moon* v. *Homeworthy Furniture (Northern) Ltd.* [1977] I.R.L.R. 117.

[2] See *Gorman* v. *London Computer Training Centre* 1978] I.C.R. 394.

[3] [1973] I.C.R. 219; *sub nom. Midland Foot Comfort Centre Ltd.* v. *Richmond* [1973] 3 All E.R. 294. See also *Rigby* v. *British Steel Corporation, supra.*

[4] [1973] I.C.R. 133.   [5] [1972] I.R.L.R. 5.

[6] *Heathcote* v. *North Western Electricity Board* (1973) 258/174. Tribunals differ on this— *Trusler* v. *The Lummus Co.* [1972] I.R.L.R. 35.

[7] *Powers and Villiers* v. *A. Clarke and Co. (Smethwick) Ltd.* [1981] I.R.L.R. 483.

[8] *Selby* v. *The Plessey Co. Ltd.* [1972] I.R.L.R. 36.

closely.[9] In *Evans and Morgan* v. *A.B. Electronic Components Ltd.*[10] it was pointed out that it would be difficult for a claimant successfully to contend that the agreed procedure was unfair to him since to depart from it would involve automatic unfairness to others. Where there is no customary procedure, there are considerable indications that tribunals will tend to imply the well known practice of selecting for redundancy on a last-in, first-out basis.[11] It seems necessary, however, to be able to infer that this standard practice is a customary procedure in the firm in question. That is to say, there is no general assumption that a "last-in, first-out" principle applies customarily throughout industry.

Where, however, it is not possible to find any customary or agreed procedure, the "last-in, first-out" principle may be used to form the basis of a decision that dismissal which does not accord with this principle is unfair under the general provisions as to reasonableness in all circumstances.[12] Where the tribunal relies upon this general provision it will, obviously, take into account all the relevant factors as in an ordinary case of unfair dismissal. In *Cruickshank* v. *Hobbs*[13] selection of those who had been on strike was held reasonable. In *Parker* v. *Belfast Steamship Company Ltd.*[14] no customary practice existed and the tribunal held that the "last-in, first-out" principle was not of such general application as to make it necessarily a customary arrangement. The employer had tried to select for redundancy those who would suffer least hardship and in particular had decided to give preference to young married men with families. It was held that this system was fair.[15] In such situations it is also reasonable for an employer to seek to retain the most qualified of the possible candidates for redundancy. In *Hobson* v. *The Park Brothers Ltd.*[16] selection of an older and more senior manager for redundancy was held fair and reasonable because the younger man had better marketing techniques, results and a preference for head office work. In *Crockford* v. *Furse Electrical Installations Ltd.*[17] two older more senior men were selected for redundancy because the younger men were better equipped to be retained. In both cases unavailing efforts had been made to find other work for the redundant men.[18] The significance of this last mentioned element must be emphasised in the light of the decision in *Williams* v. *Compair Maxam Ltd.*[19] that the employer is not entitled to apply purely subjective and unexaminable tests of the needs of the business.

---

[9] *Axe* v. *British Domestic Appliances Ltd.*, *supra*; *Selby* v. *The Plessey Co. Ltd.* [1972] I.R.L.R. 36. But see *Banner* v. *Sutcliffe Speakman and Co.* [1972] I.R.L.R. 7. Conversely, adherence to agreed criteria cannot be challenged on the ground that the criteria are unfair— *Clyde Pipeworks Ltd.* v. *Foster* [1978] I.R.L.R. 313.

[10] [1981] I.R.L.R. 111.

[11] See *Hollies* v. *Principal Patterns and Engineering Co.* [1973] I.R.L.R. 165.

[12] See *Bessenden Properties Ltd.* v. *Corness* [1974] I.T.R. 128, where it was held that the "customary" did not refer to a normal custom but was confined to something so well known, certain and clear as to be implied in procedure.

[13] [1977] I.C.R. 725.

[14] Unreported. But see *Shaw* v. *Garden King Frozen Foods* [1975] I.R.L.R. 98. As to standard of proof, see *Cox* v. *Wildt Mellor (Bromley) Ltd.* [1978] I.C.R. 736.

[15] cf. *Pickering* v. *Kingston Mobile Unit* [1978] I.R.L.R. 102.

[16] (1973) 258/102.

[17] (1973) 224/203.

[18] Compare these cases with *Watling and Co. Ltd.* v. *Richardson* [1978] I.R.L.R. 255 and *Laffin and Callaghan* v. *Fashion Industries Ltd.* [1978] I.R.L.R. 448.

[19] [1982] I.R.L.R. 85.

Resort to the general test of reasonableness permits discussion of whether a dismissal for redundancy is unfair, not only because of selection among those doing a particular job, but of selection in the entire unit. That is to say that though the special provision for unfair selection only allows the narrow test, the more general question whether an employee should have been offered alternative employment in another department, even if this meant dismissing a more junior employee in that department,[20] may be raised under the general test. The finding in *Vokes Ltd.* v. *Bear*[21] that a dismissal was unfair because of failure to consider the availability of alternative employment is particularly applicable to dismissal for redundancy.

(f) **Pregnancy**

If the reason, or principal reason, for dismissal is that the employee is pregnant the dismissal will be unfair unless one of two statutory situations pertains.

There are two principal defences to a claim for unfair dismissal on the ground of pregnancy. They are:

(a) that the reason for the dismissal is that at the effective date of termination the employee is or will have become because of her pregnancy incapable of adequately doing the work which she was employed to do;

(b) that because of her pregnancy she cannot or will not be able to continue after that date to do that work without contravention (either by her or by her employer) of a duty or restriction imposed by or under any enactment.[22]

These exceptions are remarkably widely phrased. In *Martin* v. *B.S.C. Footwear (Supplies) Ltd.*[23] an industrial tribunal held that "suitable" related to the woman's pregnant condition and health as well as to skill, experience and qualifications. "Available" means that the job should exist or be made to exist within the given staffing complement. An employer, it was said, is under no obligation to modify a woman's existing job to meet her requirements nor to create a job. The first was subject to an interesting industrial tribunal decision in *Elegbede* v. *The Wellcome Foundation Limited.*[24] The employee had been dismissed on grounds of unfitness for work due to hypertension brought on by pregnancy. The industrial tribunal held that the dismissal was due to incapacity because of hypertension and was not "because of her pregnancy" within the meaning of exception (a) above. On the other hand, the tribunal held, the dismissal was by reason of something connected with her pregnancy within the meaning of the initial provision rendering the dismissal unfair. In other words, a dismissal can be connected with pregnancy but not be because of pregnancy.

The width of the exceptions, though surprising, may well not have any very considerable effect because if they are invoked statute provides substantial protection for the employee. In the first place, even if the reason for the dismissal falls within one of the exceptions, the dismissal will still be unfair if the

---

[20] *Thomas and Betts Manufacturing Co. Ltd.* v. *Harding* [1978] I.R.L.R. 213.
[21] [1974] I.C.R. 1.
[22] s.60(1)(a) and (b).
[23] [1978] I.R.L.R. 95.
[24] [1977] I.R.L.R. 383.

employer or any successor of his has a suitable available vacancy and neglects to engage the dismissed employee under a new contract of employment in that vacant post before or on the effective date of termination. Secondly, a dismissal connected with the employee's pregnancy but rendered fair because it falls within one of the two exceptions mentioned, will not deprive the employee of her maternity rights, including the right to return to work, whatever the date at which the dismissal took place.[25]

Where an employee is absent because of pregancy or confinement a replacement will often have to be provided. The employee so absent will normally now have a statutory right to return to her former employment after the permitted period of absence.[26] It is more than ever likely that such a replacement will be regarded as temporary. If the temporary does not remain in continuous employment for 26 weeks he or she will, of course, acquire no statutory right to claim an unfair dismissal. In other cases certain modifications apply to the normal process of determination of the nature of the dismissal.[27]

Where an employer informs an employee in writing, upon engagement, that his or her employment will be terminated on the return to work of another employee who is, or will be, absent wholly or partly because of pregnancy or confinement and dismisses the first mentioned employee in order to give work to the other, then the dismissal will be regarded as having been for a substantial reason such as to justify the dismissal. This means that a claim for unfair dismissal could still succeed on the basis that, though such a substantial reason existed, it was not reasonable in all the circumstances for the employer to have treated it as a reason for dismissal. It may be suggested, for instance. that an employer with a large number of female employees might reasonably be expected to take steps to see whether another temporary vacancy which the replacement might fill in turn was imminent.

Similar provisions apply to dismissal of a temporary replacement for an employee compulsorily suspended for medical reasons.[28]

(g) Transfer of undertakings

The effect of the Transfer of Undertakings (Protection of Employment) Regulations 1981 is to produce an automatic transfer of contractual and statutory employment rights for any employee in the employment of a transferor of a commercial business immediately before the transfer[29] to the transferee of that business.

5.—(1) A relevant transfer shall not operate so as to terminate the contract of employment of any person employed by the transferor in the undertaking or part transferred but any such contract which would otherwise have been terminated by the transfer shall have effect after the transfer as if originally made between the person so employed and the transferee.

(2) Without prejudice to paragraph (1) above, on the completion of a relevant transfer—

---

[25] 1978 Act, s.33(4).
[26] *Supra*, pp. 106–109.
[27] 1978 Act, s.61.
[28] 1978 Act, s.61(2).
[29] See p. 151, *supra*.

(a) all the transferor's rights, powers, duties and liabilities under or in connection with any such contract, shall be transferred by virtue of this Regulation to the transferee; and

(b) anything done before the transfer is completed by or in relation to the transferor in respect of that contract or a person employed in that undertaking or part shall be deemed to have been done by or in relation to the transferee.

(3) Any reference in paragraph (1) or (2) above to a person employed in an undertaking or part of one transferred by a relevant transfer is a reference to a person so employed immediately before the transfer, including, where the transfer is effected by a series of two or more transactions, a person so employed immediately before any of those transactions.

(4) Paragraph (2) above shall not transfer or otherwise affect the liability of any person to be prosecuted for, convicted of and sentenced for any offence.

(5) Paragraph (1) above is without prejudice to any right of an employee arising apart from these Regulations to terminate his contract of employment without notice if a substantial change is made in his working conditions to his detriment; but no such right shall arise by reason only that, under that paragraph, the identity of his employer changes unless the employee shows that, in all the circumstances, the change is a significant change and is to his detriment.

This provision is probably wide enough to include the transfer of statutory rights and thus of the important continuity of employment essential to the maintenance of a number of statutory rights.[30] It only applies to those employees whose contracts continue to exist immediately before the transfer so that an employer may effectively dismiss before that time or an employee may effectively voluntarily terminate his employment.

Although it does not appear to have been the intention of those who framed the Directive upon which these Regulations are based, paragraph 5 seems likely to operate to transfer the contractual rights and obligations of those employees still in employment whether they like it or not. In other words, in those situations to which the Regulations apply, the rule in *Nokes* v. *Doncaster Amalgamated Collieries Ltd.*,[31] that a contract of employment is not unilaterally transferable, is abrogated. An employee thus affected could, therefore, only claim to terminate his employment by giving to the transferee the proper notice, or, according to paragraph 5(6), if the transfer involves a repudiatory breach apart from the change of identity of one of its parties. It should be pointed out that because paragraph 7 of the Regulations excludes the operation of the whole of paragraph 5 upon pension schemes an employee could not allege a change in pension provisions to constitute such a breach.

This provision, of course, destroys the possibility of dismissal arising merely by the transfer of an employee from one employer to another, so far as that occurs in the course of transfer of business. So far as rights in respect of redundancy are concerned the employee who does transfer to an employer who has taken over the business has no claim, even apart from the operation of these Regulations.[32] It seems likely, however, that the Regulations will operate to deprive the employee of the trial period he would otherwise have had.[33]

---

[30] Rideout (1982) 35 C.L.P. 233.
[31] [1940] A.C. 1014.
[32] Employment Protection (Consolidation) Act 1978, ss.84(1) and 94.   [33] *Infra*, p. 293.

The Regulations go further, however, to grant a special right to the employee who is dismissed "wholly or principally for a reason connected with the transfer."

8.—(1) Where either before or after a relevant transfer, any employee of the transferor or transferee is dismissed, that employee shall be treated for the purposes of Part V of the 1978 Act and Articles 20 to 41 of the 1976 Order (unfair dismissal) as unfairly dismissed if the transfer or a reason connected with it is the reason or principal reason for his dismissal.

(2) Where an economic, technical or organisational reason entailing changes in the workforce of either the transferor or the transferee before or after a relevant transfer is the reason or principal reason for dismissing an employee—

(*a*) paragraph (1) above shall not apply to his dismissal; but
(*b*) without prejudice to the application of section 57(3) of the 1978 Act or Article 22(10) of the 1976 Order (test of fair dismissal), the dismissal shall for the purposes of section 57(1)(*b*) of that Act and Article 22(1)(*b*) of that Order (substantial reason for dismissal) be regarded as having been for a substantial reason of a kind such as to justify the dismissal of an employee holding the position which that employee held.

(3) The provisions of this Regulation apply whether or not the employee in question is employed in the undertaking or part of the undertaking transferred or to be transferred.

It will be noted that this protection extends to employees of both the transferor and the transferee who are dismissed in connection with the transfer, and it applies whenever that dismissal occurs. Nevertheless it may be thought that paragraph 8(2) provides an easy way out of the presumption created by paragraph 8(1). Whether this is so or not depends on whether the economic, technical or organisational reason must be established as an objective fact or merely as a reasonably held view of the employer concerned. We have said that it is the second view which dominates the law of unfair dismissal. There are, however, some signs that "reorganisation" may not continue to provide an employer with carte-blanche.[34] Certainly, without such a change, paragraph 8(1) will not in practice provide effective protection against dismissal since organisational reasons will abound in the minds of the employers concerned.

It may be noted that paragraph 12 of the Regulations renders void any agreement purporting to exclude or limit the operation of paragraphs 5 or 8. An employee who agrees to transfer to a different job appears entitled to resile from that agreement and insist upon his former contract. The new employer will then be faced with the possibility of a claim for actual or constructive dismissal which he would have to defend as a reasonable response to the circumstances proved within paragraph 8(2).

(h) Other special situations

Dismissal may give rise to a claim of illegal discrimination on grounds of sex, marital status, colour, race, nationality or ethnic or national origins. We will deal with this legislation at a later stage.[35]

---

[34] See *Evans* v. *Elemeta Holdings Ltd.* [1982] I.R.L.R. 143.
[35] *Infra*, pp. 319 *et seq.*

Once a criminal conviction is "spent" after a period of time specified in the Rehabilitation of Offenders Act 1974[36] it cannot be put forward as a reason for dismissal of employees not exempt from the operation of the Act. Furthermore the employee is under no duty to disclose a spent conviction and so could not be fairly dismissed for failure to do so. In *Torr* v. *British Railways Board*,[37] however, Cumming-Bruce J. in the E.A.T. declined to extend this protection to cover a denial by the employee in his job application of the existence of an unspent conviction, observing that there was no rule of law that employers should follow the social policy of the Rehabilitation Act.

In *Property Guards Ltd.* v. *Taylor and Kershaw*,[38] however, the court declined to accept the argument that despite the existence of the Act there could be a fair dismissal where circumstances appeared to provide a justification. The two employees had failed to disclose minor offences of dishonesty when they began their employment as security guards. In both cases the offences were spent under the Act. Neill J. held that since there was power for the Secretary of State to exclude from the operation of the Act specified employments, there was no room to argue an exception where that power had not been exercised.

REMEDIES

(a) Reinstatement or re-engagement

The common law has normally refused the remedy of specific performance to the contract of employment so far as concerns a remedy by way of reinstatement or re-engagement. From this refusal developed an attitude of mind which was to the effect that enforcement was so obviously not possible that the making of anything more than an unenforceable recommendation was valueless. This attitude inhibited the consideration of available remedies when statutory provision was first made for claims in respect of unfair dismissal in 1971. Inevitably it means that the only remedy as of right continues to be monetary compensation. Though this was made much more substantial than damages under the common law the result remained that the law still failed to afford ultimate job security.

This reasoning, however, ignored the fact that no law is enforceable if a sufficient number of those subject to it refuse to obey it but that most laws are accepted and obeyed even by those reluctant to do so. The value of an order for reinstatement as against a recommendation is clear. Most employers will accept an order rather than opting for the monetary penalty which is, in the last resort, the price of disobedience.[39]

The Employment Protection Act 1975, s.71, therefore, conferred on industrial tribunals power to *order* reinstatement with the dismissing employer or re-engagement by him, his successor or an associated employer.[40] An order for

---

[36] The application of this Act is subject to numerous exceptions for specified professions and occupations—Rehabilitation of Offenders Act 1974 (Exceptions) Order (S.I. 1975 No. 1023).

[37] [1977] I.C.R. 785.

[38] [1982] I.R.L.R. 175 (E.A.T.).

[39] The effects of the statutory remedies have been stated by Williams and Lewis: *The Aftermath of Tribunal Reinstatement and Re-engagement* D.E. Research Paper No. 23 (June 1981).

[40] See now, Employment Protection (Consolidation) Act 1978, ss.68 and 69.

reinstatement is defined as an order that the employer shall treat the complainant in all respects as if he had not been dismissed. The tribunal shall, when making such an order, specify the arrears of wages and other benefits due and any rights and privileges, including seniority and pension rights, which must be restored within a specified time. In particular the complainant is entitled to be treated as if he had benefited from any improvement in terms and conditions of employment which would have applied to him had he not been dismissed. An order for re-engagement is defined as an order that the complainant should be engaged in employment comparable to that from which he was dismissed, or other suitable employment. The order must specify arrears of pay and other benefits due and restoration of rights and privileges. In this instance the order must also state the identity of the employer (he may be a successor or associate of the original employer), the nature of the employment and remuneration due. Both orders must state the date by which they must be complied with. The Act clearly indicates that the feasibility of reinstatement shall first be considered in the light of the complainant's wishes, the practicability of the employer being able to comply and the justice of such an order in the light of the complainant's contribution to the dismissal.[41] Only if it decides not to make such an order is the tribunal to consider an order for re-engagement, taking into account the same considerations.[42] In neither case is practicability to be affected by the fact that a permanent replacement has been engaged unless the employer shows that it was not practicable for him otherwise to arrange for the complainant's work to be done or that the replacement was engaged after the lapse of a reasonable period without having heard from the dismissed employee that he wished to be reinstated and that when the replacement was engaged it was no longer reasonable for the employer to arrange for the dismissed employee's work to be done without a permanent replacement.[43] A tribunal may only order reinstatement or re-engagement if the employee seeks such a remedy. On the other hand, in *Sweetlove* v. *Redbridge and Waltham Forest A.H.A.*[44] it was held that an employee who refuses an offer of reinstatement before the hearing cannot claim compensation for loss subsequent to that offer. The courts rarely discuss the elements of practicability and, if they do, tend to confine themselves to generalities such as that it requires consideration of "the industrial relations realities."[45]

It is the obvious intention of the legislation that the emphasis of the primary remedy shall move away from compensation towards reinstatement. If the employee is reinstated (or re-engaged) but the terms of the order are not fully complied with, the tribunal shall make such order for compensation as it thinks fit, having regard to the complainant's loss in consequence of the failure. If the order for reinstatement or re-engagement is not complied with the tribunal shall make an award of compensation for unfair dismissal according to the ordinary rules, taking into account as failure to mitigate any action of the employee which unreasonably prevented the order being complied with. Unless the employer satisfies the tribunal that it was not practicable to comply, the tribunal

---

[41] s.69(5).
[42] s.69(6).
[43] s.70.
[44] [1979] I.C.R. 477.
[45] *Coleman* v. *Magnet Joinery Ltd.* [1975] I.C.R. 46.

shall make an additional award of compensation of an amount of not less than 26, or more than 52 weeks' pay where the dismissal constitutes an unlawful discrimination under section 3(1) of the Race Relations Act 1968 or under the Sex Discrimination Act 1975 or is unfair as constituting a dismissal for trade union activities, or membership or unprotected dismissal under a union[46] membership agreement. In all other cases the additional award shall be of an amount of not less than 13 nor more than 26 weeks' pay.[47] The week's pay is subject to an upper limit of £135. This additional award does not count towards the calculation of the upper limit of compensation.[48] The additional award is, of course, plainly punitive and bears no necessary connection with possible loss.[49]

(b) The basic award

Although the tendency of earlier decisions upon the content of the compensatory award had been to establish something like an "irreducible minimum," founded upon the amount of wages that would have been earned during the notice period, even if the employee had secured other employment in that period, this was not applicable, for instance, to a situation in which the unfairly dismissed employee worked out his notice. The Employment Protection Act 1975, therefore, established for the first time a basic award payable in all cases of unfair dismissal irrespective of loss. Provision for this award is now contained in section 75 of the Employment Protection (Consolidation) Act 1978.

The amount of this basic award is calculated by reference to the period of continuous employment ending with the effective date of termination, reckoning backwards from that date and allowing one-and-a-half weeks' pay for each year of employment in which the employee was not below the age of 41; one week's[50] pay for each year in which the employee was below the age of 41 but not below the age of 22 and half a week's wages for each year in which the employee was below the age of 22.[51] No account shall be taken of more than 20 years of employment in this reverse reckoning. The amount due is reduced by one-twelfth for each month of the year in which the employee, if a man, is over the age of 64 or, if a woman, over the age of 59. If, however, the amount so calculated falls below two weeks' pay the award will be of two weeks' pay.

Where the reason or principal reason for the dismissal is found to be redundancy but no redundancy payment is due because of certain specified reasons[52] the amount of the basic award will be two weeks' pay only.

Where the tribunal finds that the dismissal was to any extent caused or contributed to by any action of the claimant[53] it shall, save in a case of dismissal for redundancy, reduce the amount of the basic award by such proportion as it considers just and equitable.[54] In *Devis* v. *Atkins*[55] the House of Lords held that

---

[46] See Employment Protection (Consolidation) Act 1978, s.58.
[47] s.71(2).
[48] s.75(1).
[49] *George* v. *Beecham Group* [1977] I.R.L.R. 43.
[50] There is an upper limit on a week's pay. In February 1982 this was raised to £135.
[51] Employment Protection (Consolidation) Act 1978, s.73 as amended by Employment Act 1980, s.9.
[52] s.73(2).   [53] *Infra*, p. 261.
[54] s.75(7). The previous minimum of two weeks' pay was abolished by Employment Act 1980, s.9(5). It has been suggested ((1982) 11 I.L.J. 192) that greater caution should be exercised in reducing the basic award for contributory fault than in so reducing the compensatory award.
[55] [1977] I.C.R. 662.

this provision could not apply to conduct of the employee unknown to the employer. The Employment Act 1980, s.97 amended the provision to permit reduction wherever the tribunal considers it just and equitable to reduce the amount.

Any redundancy payment actually paid whether under statutory provision or otherwise shall be deducted from the amount of the basic award.

(c) Compensation

It is provided in section 74 of the Employment Protection (Consolidation) Act 1978 that a tribunal might award such amount of compensation as is just and equitable in all the circumstances having regard to the loss sustained by the complainant in consequence of the dismissal in so far as that loss is attributable to action taken by the employer.

Compensation is based on net income.[56] Interest is not awarded on loss of future earnings or earnings capacity.[57] No deduction from earnings is made in respect of unemployment or supplementary benefit received during a period of lack of work arising from the dismissal as the Department of Employment has power to recoup such payments following an award of compensation by an industrial tribunal. National insurance sickness benefit received during this period by the employee should be deducted from an award of compensation if these payments would have been deducted from wages or if no sickness benefit would have been due had the employee still been employed.[58]

Burden of proof

The burden of proving the loss for which compensation is due falls on the claimant but it is the duty of the tribunal to raise for consideration each available head of loss.[59] Nothing which cannot be quantified in money or money's worth can be considered but, unlike the calculation of redundancy compensation, it is open to the tribunal to consider compensation for loss of anything upon which a monetary value can be placed even though the contract has not placed such a valuation upon it.

Nil award

It follows from this that if the claimant cannot show that the unfair dismissal caused him any loss a nil award should be made.[60] Such a situation will exist where it is shown that, though the dismissal in question is technically unfair, had it not occurred a fair dismissal would immediately have replaced it.[61] For the same reason loss should be confined to that incurred between the actual date of unfair dismissal and the later date on which a fair dismissal would have been likely.[62]

---

[56] *Scottish Co-operative Wholesale Society Ltd.* v. *Lloyd* [1973] I.C.R. 137. But see *Secretary of State* v. *John Woodrow and Sons (Builders) Ltd.* [1983] I.R.L.R. 11.

[57] *Clarke* v. *Rotax Aircraft Equipment Ltd.* [1975] I.C.R. 440 applying *Jefford* v. *Gee* [1960] 2 Q.B. 130.

[58] *Sun and Sand Ltd.* v. *Fitzjohn* [1979] I.C.R. 268.

[59] *Tidman* v. *Aveling Marshall Ltd.* [1977] I.C.R. 506.

[60] *W. Devis and Sons Ltd.* v. *Atkins* [1977] I.C.R. 662.

[61] *Earl* v. *Slater and Wheeler (Airlyne) Ltd.* [1972] I.C.R. 508; *Cadbury Ltd.* v. *Doddington* [1977] I.C.R. 982.

[62] *Barley* v. *Amey Roadstone Corporation Ltd.* (*No. 2*) [1978] I.C.R. 190.

Heads of loss

When the statutory system of protection against unfair dismissal was first introduced the application of the compensation provisions often led tribunals to make awards of even smaller sums than would have been recovered at common law for loss of wages during the period of notice. This resulted from concentration on the relative absence of loss of remuneration when a dismissed employee quickly obtained alternative employment. Partly to counter this and partly to produce a set of consistently applied heads of loss Sir John Donaldson laid down a set of standard considerations in *Norton Tool Co. Ltd.* v. *Tewson*[63] which remains the leading authority on this point. These heads will now be considered.

(a) *Immediate loss of wages.* Under this heading is to be included the net loss of wages during the period of notice which the employee should have received to terminate his employment. At common law, if there were sufficient misconduct on the part of the employee to constitute repudiation of his contract, no notice need be given. As we have seen, an unfair dimissal might well exist where, although such misconduct had occurred, the method of dismissal was considered unfair. In such cases, compensation would still be payable under this heading since the judgment of the court refers to the giving of notice as good industrial relations practice rather than as a matter of contract. In *Vaughan* v. *Weighpack Ltd.*[64] this was said to be the irreducible minimum of compensation.

The general obligation upon the employee to take reasonable steps to mitigate his loss[65] does not interfere with this head. The N.I.R.C. reasoned that it was concerned with justice and equity and not only with contractual rights. An employee who had received wages in lieu of notice would not be required to repay that amount if he obtained other employment during the notice period.[66]

After the period of notice, however, the duty to mitigate will apply. Moreover net earnings actually received in this period will be taken into account even if the new employment is unsuitable and would not have been regarded as requisite within the duty of mitigation.

(b) *Future loss of wages and benefits.* This second head of compensation will usually provide the major component of the total sum awarded. The amount of the loss under this heading will have to be estimated in all cases where the dismissed employee has not found further employment before the tribunal hearing. In such a situation the N.I.R.C. decided[67] that tribunals might calculate loss on a nominal period of five years. Thus the tribunal will have to estimate the time during which the employee is likely to be out of work altogether and then the difference between his former wage and the wage he might reasonably be presumed to be likely to command in future employment. This estimate will normally cover a period of five years from the date of dismissal. The method is well illustrated in the following passage from the judgment of the N.I.R.C. in the *Winterhalter* case:

---

[63] [1972] I.C.R. 501.
[64] [1974] I.C.R. 261.
[65] Employment Protection (Consolidation) Act 1978, s.74(4).
[66] See also *J. Stepek* v. *Hough* [1974] I.C.R. 352; *Hilti (G.B.) Ltd.* v. *Windridge* [1974] I.C.R. 352; *Everwear Candlewick Ltd.* v. *Isaac* [1974] I.C.R. 525.
[67] *Donnelly* v. *Feniger and Blackburn Ltd.* [1973] I.C.R. 68.

"The employee was 57 at the date of his dismissal and he was employed at an annual remuneration including commission of approximately £3,000 p.a. The tribunal arrived at the sum of £2,000 in the following way: First they concluded that it would be six months before the employee found any employment. His net loss over that period was the sum of £864. When he did find employment, the tribunal concluded, in view of his capabilities it would be at a much lower salary than £3,000 per year. They considered that his net monthly pay would be in the order of £100, rather than the figure of £194 that he had been earning with his previous employers."

In the *Norton* case the court also brought under this heading compensation for the fact that the future employment might be less secure than the previous employment. In the *Scottish Co-operative* case the court included extra liability for rent and rates, increased travelling expenses, and removal expenses. The difference between the two rates of wages, however, may not represent the true amount of loss if the tribunal concludes that the employee could have obtained more remunerative employment. Compensation under both the preceding heads will include fringe benefits quantifiable in monetary terms. Tax should be deducted before these are considered.[68] These have been held to include the monetary value of the use of a company car, subsidised housing, private medical insurance and tips received direct from customers. None of these is likely to be taken into account in assessing a normal week's wages for the purpose of calculating redundancy compensation.

(c) *Loss of job protection.* Two items may be included under this heading which may, at first sight, seem surprising. The court in the *Norton* case held that an unfairly dismissed employee was entitled to claim compensation for loss of the value of the fact that it would take him two years in new employment before he was again able to rely on the statutory provisions to claim compensation for unfair dismissal. This amount will normally, of course, be small—representing one or two weeks' wages.[69] Now that the qualifying period has been further reduced this item will be relatively insignificant in the computation of damages. Secondly, however, the court included an element of compensation for loss of entitlement to redundancy payments. This is based on the same principle that an employee with a period of, say, 10 years' service entitling him to redundancy payments will, by reason of the dismissal, lose the whole of that accrued benefit. As we have seen, however, the basic award depends on the same formula as that by which redundancy payments would have been calculated. Accordingly it is now provided[70] that the whole of the basic award due, before reduction of that award for any contributory fault, or any amount of compensation actually paid upon dismissal, should be set off against this element in the compensatory award. Normally that will totally absorb this factor in the award.

(d) *Manner of dismissal.* Before the *Norton* case there had been some speculation, originally arising at common law, as to whether compensation could be paid in respect of the manner of dismissal. The common law rule is that neither punitive nor exemplary damages are available for a breach of contract.

---

[68] *Scottish Co-operative Wholesale Society Ltd.* v. *Lloyd* [1973] I.C.R. 137.
[69] In *Brook Bros. (Petroleum) Ltd.* v. *Preece* [1974] I.C.R. 231 unreported, £750 was considered entirely out of scale for this item of loss.
[70] Employment Protection (Consolidation) Act 1978, s.74(3).

Since compensation for unfair dismissal does not depend upon contractual doctrines it might have been thought that this principle would disappear. It was, however, held that compensation should take no account of the manner of dismissal unless it could give rise to a risk of financial loss at a later stage by, for example, making the employee less acceptable to potential employers or exceptionally liable to selection for dismissal.

(e) *Pension rights.* Calculation of the amount of compensation for loss of pension rights is exceedingly complicated. The N.I.R.C. laid down what appeared to be fairly clear rules in a series of decisions.[71] Two alternative methods were suggested. If the employee is comparatively close to retirement age it was said that it would be more appropriate to work out the sum which would be required to purchase an annuity equal to the amount to which the employee would have been entitled had he remained in employment and to reduce this to take account of accelerated payment and other contingencies.[72] In other cases the employee should be compensated for loss of his own contributions to date plus loss of the benefit of the employer's contributions. Each should be increased by compound interest. On this method the employee is also entitled to compensation for loss of the prospective benefit of the employer's contributions plus the value of tax concessions on the contributions the employee would have made.[73] The E.A.T. reviewed and substantially confirmed these methods in *Smith Kline and French Laboratories Ltd.* v. *Coates*[74] but pointed out that, in view of the duty to mitigate, loss should be assessed on the basis of the length of time it might reasonably be assumed the applicant should be without pensionable employment. The introduction of the new provisions for earnings-related pensions in April 1978 will have substantially reduced this likelihood.

Neither method provides an answer to the difficult problem of the multiplier which should be applied to the annual pension. In *Powrmatic Ltd.* v. *Bull*[75] the E.A.T. held that an industrial tribunal was wrong to have applied a multiplier of 33 where an employee had 33 years to serve before retirement. The E.A.T. thought a multiplier of 15 more appropriate to such circumstances.

(f) *Expenses.* Though the statutory provisions allow compensation for expenses this is a reference to expenses incurred as a direct result of the dismissal such as the cost of looking for new employment and the reasonable cost of taking it up. The head does not include expenses of proceedings before an industrial tribunal.[76]

Deductions

The amount of compensation assessed under the above headings may be reduced by such amount as the tribunal considers just and equitable to take

---

[71] *Scottish Co-operative Society Ltd.* v. *Lloyd* [1973] I.C.R. 137; *Cawthorn and Sinclair Ltd.* v. *Hedger* [1974] I.C.R. 146; *Gill* v. *Harold Andrews (Sheepbridge) Ltd.* [1974] I.C.R. 294; *Hilti Ltd.* v. *Windridge* [1974] I.C.R. 352; *Copson* v. *Eversure Accessories Ltd.* [1974] I.T.R. 406.

[72] See, *e.g. Powrmatic Ltd.* v. *Bull* [1977] I.C.R. 469.

[73] See *Cawthorne and Sinclair Ltd.* v. *Hedger, supra; Gill* v. *Harold Andrews (Sheepbridge) Ltd., supra; Willment Bros. Ltd.* v. *Oliver* [1979] I.C.R. 378; *Manning* v. *R. and H. Wale (Export) Ltd.* [1979] I.C.R. 433.

[74] [1977] I.R.L.R. 220.   [75] *Supra.*   [76] *Nohar* v. *Granitstone Ltd.* [1974] I.C.R. 273.

account of the extent to which the dismissal may have been caused or contributed to by any action of the employee.[77] This, as the decision in *Devis and Sons Ltd.* v. *Atkins*[78] reveals, is narrower than the consideration of no-loss situations. It has, so far as the basic award is concerned, now been extended to allow consideration of actions of the employee before the dismissal notwithstanding that the employer was unaware of such actions.[79] In the case of the compensatory award where no problems arise about fixed amounts such circumstances can be dealt with on the assumption that the employee would have been dismissed when those facts came to light so that his loss only occurs in the period up to that time.

Originally the English N.I.R.C. took the view that the "contribution" provision could only be applied where the employee had contributed to the unfairness of his dismissal.[80] Relatively few situations would fall within that category. In *Maris* v. *Rotherham Corporation*[81] the English N.I.R.C. expressly reversed this approach and adopted the view, consistently taken by the Scottish N.I.R.C., that any act contributing to the dismissal could be taken into account. The statutory provision was amended by the Employment Protection (Consolidation) Act 1978 to make it clear that this was the correct view.

The conduct of the employee must be culpable or blameworthy[82] but this is wide enough to include any conduct which is unreasonable in the circumstances. Conduct involving trade union membership or activities is not to be taken into account.[83] That culpable or blameworthy action must be the action which has contributed to the dismissal.[84] There has been extensive discussion as to whether contributory fault can justify reduction by 100 per cent. In *Trend* v. *Chiltern Hunt Ltd.*[85] it was said that though such a reduction was permissible it was probably better to deal with such cases under the "no-loss" principle. Although the permissibility of a 100 per cent. reduction was confirmed by the House of Lords in *Devis and Sons Ltd.* v. *Atkins*[86] tribunals should pay careful attention to a consideration of whether, in the circumstances before them, such a reduction would be considered by the E.A.T. to be inconsistent with a finding of unfair dismissal. In *Cooper* v. *British Steel Corporation*[87] a contribution of 95 per cent. was held too high unless the element of unfairness was purely technical.

Any sum paid to the employee by the employer as a result of the dismissal, whether or not it is an *ex gratia* payment must be deducted since, of course, the

---

[77] Employment Protection (Consolidation) Act 1978, s.74(6). But this contributory conduct will not include refusal to join a trade union, pay sums of money in place of joining a union or take part in union activities: Employment Act 1982, s.6.
[78] [1977] I.C.R. 662.
[79] Employment Act 1980, s.10.
[80] *Earl* v. *Slater and Wheeler (Airlyne) Ltd.* [1972] I.C.R. 508.
[81] [1974] I.C.R. 435.
[82] *Nelson* v. *BBC (No. 2)* [1980] I.C.R. 110.
[83] Employment Act 1982, s.6.
[84] *Nelson* v. *BBC (No. 2)* [1980] I.C.R. 110 (C.A.). In *Kraft Foods Ltd.* v. *Fox* [1978] I.C.R. 311 the E.A.T. had held that an employee dismissed for incompetence could not be said to have contributed to his dismissal when he had been doing his best.
[85] [1977] I.C.R. 612 (E.A.T.).
[86] [1977] I.C.R. 662. In *Savoia* v. *Chiltern Herb Farms Ltd.* [1981] I.R.L.R. 166 (affirmed by C.A. [1982] I.R.L.R. 166) the E.A.T. affirmed that reasons must be given by an industrial tribunal in cases of reduction for contributory fault.
[87] [1975] I.C.R. 454.

employee's loss arising from the dismissal is that much less. In *UBAF Bank Ltd.* v. *Davis*[88] overruling, in this respect, *Powrmatic Ltd.* v. *Bull*[89] it was held that such payments should be deducted from the amount of compensation before that amount is reduced by a contributory factor. The maximum of £7,000 fixed for the compensatory award is the maximum amount which a tribunal can award. It is only applied, therefore, if, after all deductions and reductions, the sum arrived at is in excess of it.

The Employment Protection (Recoupment of Unemployment and Supplementary Benefit) Regulations 1977[90] provide that in assessing the compensatory award the tribunal is to ignore the amount of supplementary benefit or unemployment benefit received by the employee down to the date of the conclusion of proceedings before the Industrial Tribunal. The compensatory award has to be divided into two parts. That representing loss suffered to the date of the proceedings is known as the "prescribed element." The employer is responsible for repaying the social security benefits related to this period from this element and is required to pay the balance only to the employee.[91]

---

[88] [1978] I.R.L.R. 442.
[89] [1977] I.C.R. 469.
[90] S.I. 1977 No. 674.
[91] See *Mason* v. *Wimpey Wastes Management Ltd.* [1982] I.R.L.R. 454.

CHAPTER 6

REDUNDANCY COMPENSATION

WE have seen[1] that special statutory provision is made for unfair selection for redundancy to be regarded as unfair dismissal. Apart from this it is possible that a dismissal may be unfair on general principles even where the reason is redundancy.[2] The legislative provisions with which we shall deal in this chapter are not concerned with this situation but rather with the provision of compensation for employees who are, otherwise properly, dismissed by reason of redundancy.

Historically the passage of the Redundancy Payments Act 1965 marks the change from the era of legislative non-intervention in the employment relationship, which had lasted since the industrial revolution, to that of employee protection. In fact it was not the first example of employee protection legislation. That honour must go to the rather insignificant Contracts of Employment Act 1963. That Act cannot, however, claim to be the first of the new era since, in style, it belonged to the old. The 1963 Act sought to afford some small extra protection by tinkering with contractual concepts. The 1965 Act undoubtedly broke away from those concepts. Despite the introduction of non-contractual rights, and unfortunately for the development of the law of redundancy, the draftsman unaccountably defined redundancy by reference to the contract of employment and limited the availability of compensation by the contractual concept of dismissal.

It is interesting to speculate upon what might have been. Davies and Freedland[3] point out that it would have been possible to seize the opportunity to introduce a legislative programme for manpower planning. The truth is that technological advance had overtaken planning to deal with it in industry, the trade unions and the government. There was no time to seek out a Beveridge of labour economics to devise such a plan. Indeed, since the 1963 Act was a response to the same immediate need as the Redundancy Payment Act 1965, it is remarkable that so much progress could be made. It is nevertheless, true that much more might have been done had the objectives of so many not been so limited. Davies and Freedland[4] say that if the answer to the shortcomings of the 1965 Act is that it was really no more than a system for providing lump sum severance payments based on seniority then we may still ask why it catered for so limited a category of termination as dismissal. Such criticism is justified but does not alter the fact that among the major purposes of the legislation was the encouragement of a shake-out of under-employed labour and of acceptance of redundancy without resort to industrial action. The effects of offering lump sum compensation were well known from the experience of the Workmen's Compensation Acts and it is unlikely that the upsurge of volunteers for redundancy came as any surprise to those who conceived the scheme.

---

[1] *Supra*, p. 247.
[2] *e.g. Vokes Ltd.* v. *Bear* [1974] I.C.R. 1.
[3] p. 396.
[4] p. 395.

There can be little doubt that it was realised even before the Act had been passed that if compensation was offered for dismissal for one reason there would be growing pressure to make it available for others. It is also true that so widespread a system as the industrial tribunals is not likely to have been developed solely to deal with disputes between government and employers on the amount of Selective Employment Tax then due. Nevertheless, the details of developing employee rights have been resolved in a piecemeal fashion even if the outline was clear at an earlier stage. Had it been otherwise it would, for instance, be impossible to explain why constructive dismissal should found a claim for redundancy compensation but should not have been intended by the government to do so in claims arising from other causes.[5]

Nevertheless many of the concepts first established in the Redundancy Payments Act 1965 reappear in later employment protection legislation. Even its formula system for assessing compensation was adopted as the method for assessing the basic award for unfair dismissal. The establishment of a central fund to spread at least some of the cost of redundancy has subsequently been adopted as an equitable way of sharing the obligation to make maternity payments. In one respect the concepts have been more successful in the context of redundancy than in any other subsequent form of protective legislation. It has from the start been the purpose of such legislation to encourage, rather than suppress, the development of voluntary arrangements through collective bargaining. The various statutory systems for formally registering such agreements have not produced much response[6] though there can be no doubt that all such legislation has induced very considerable extension of voluntary arrangements. This extension has been even more marked in the development of voluntary redundancy schemes which have been absorbed into what is now a mixed voluntary and statutory system.

QUALIFICATIONS TO CLAIM

We have already dealt in general with the requisite qualifications to claim for various statutory benefits.[7] By way of reminder it should be noted that the qualifying period of continuous employment for a redundancy claim is two years.[8] In consequence the minimum fixed term period which will support a contractual exclusion of the right to claim remains at two years. The right to claim does not extend to employees of the Crown.[9] The exclusion of employees working abroad differed slightly from that applicable to unfair dismissal in that whereas an employee outside Great Britain on the relevant date is excluded unless, under his contract, he ordinarily worked in Great Britain he will be entitled to claim redundancy compensation if, on the relevant date, he is in Great Britain in accordance with instructions given him by his employer.[10] The

---

[5] See H.L. Deb., Vol. 318, cols. 1392, 1414 (May 13, 1971) and the contrary decision of Sir John Donaldson in *Sutcliffe* v. *Hawker Siddeley Aviation Ltd.* [1973] I.C.R. 560 which confirmed the practice of industrial tribunals and established unfair constructive dismissal as a judicial creation.

[6] But see the agreement in the Electrical Contracting Industry concerning dismissals.

[7] *Supra*, Chap. 3, Appendix.

[8] Employment Protection (Consolidation) Act 1978, s.81(4).

[9] *Ibid*. s.138(1).

[10] *Ibid*. s.14(4).

cut-off age for entitlement to redundancy compensation is 65, or 60 in the case of a married woman, with no alternative reference to a normal retirement age. The limitation period in which to claim redundancy compensation is six months from the relevant date (of termination) instead of the more normal three months, and the requirement will be satisfied not only if a claim is made within that time to an industrial tribunal but also if it is made to the employer.[11] The powers of a tribunal to extend this period also differ. Moreover, it appears[12] that it will be sufficient for such a claim that the application was despatched within the limitation period.

DISMISSAL

Normally only those actually or constructively dismissed may claim redundancy compensation. There has been considerable criticism of this requirement on the ground that the mechanics of termination have no relevance to the end result. The criticism is the more justified because redundancy is particularly likely to produce forms of termination which do not technically constitute dismissal.

Strictly speaking a voluntary redundancy could be treated as an agreed termination. Tribunals have, however, shown no sign of adopting such an approach which, it is submitted, would be contrary to common sense. The Code of Practice itself suggests that in the event of redundancy the first appropriate course should be for management to seek volunteers. In any case it is normal for management to assume that it has the ultimate right to reject a volunteer so that the final decision to terminate is in fact that of the employer.

It is also common to warn employees of impending redundancy. Whether such a warning in advance of decisions to dismiss is given depends on the circumstances of the business. It may well be that the continuation of trading would be placed in jeopardy if, following a warning those employees who could most easily find alternative employment left at haphazard intervals. Warnings may, however, be more than general indications of concern. They may be specific and final. If they lack a definite date for termination, however, they will probably not be treated as dismissal with notice and the risk for an employee leaving between such a warning and the statement of a dismissal date are very real.[13] The adverse effects of this situation have in the past been mitigated by the common practice of employers either formally to dismiss employees who indicate, following a warning, that they have found other work and wish to leave, or to make the redundancy payment as if the employee had been so dismissed and to hope that no questions are raised about entitlement to the rebate on this payment.

It is strange that the legislature made no attempt to deal with these common situations since it did take the trouble to extend the scope of dismissal to an extent that remains obscure. It is provided that[14]:

"Where in acccordance with any enactment or rule of law—

(a) any act on the part of an employer, or

---

[11] *Ibid*. s.101.
[12] *Nash* v. *Ryan Plant International Ltd.* [1978] 1 All E.R. 492.
[13] *Morton Sundour Fabrics Ltd.* v. *Shaw* [1967] I.T.R. 84.
[14] Employment Protection (Consolidation) Act 1978, s.93(1).

(b) any event affecting an employer (including, in the case of an individual, his death)

operates so as to terminate a contract under which an employee is employed by him, that act or event shall, for the purposes of this Part be treated as a termination of the contract by the employer."

It is clear that this will include dissolution of a partnerhip, death of an employer or winding up or receivership. What is not so clear is the extent to which it includes frustration of the contract. Frustration is a situation created by operation of law. If an employer purports to dismiss, for example for long term sickness, he has not terminated the contract where the frustrating event operated upon it some time before his action. The question then arises whether (b) above was intended to refer to frustrating events. They undoubtedly affect the employer and the way in which the provision is worded would not seem to require the effect to be *eiusdem generis* with death. On the other hand the provision does appear to suggest an intention that the primary effect should be upon the employer. It is submitted that if frustration is not included in this provision there may arguably be cases in which the very act producing the redundancy situation is sufficient to frustrate the contracts of employment so that the dismissal for redundancy is not the terminating event.

The 1965 Act also made special provision for the employee to produce a notional dismissal from a situation in which he is periodically laid off or kept on short time. The object of this was to prevent employers artificially concealing a redundancy situation by attempting to retain under-employed labour forces which shows the peculiar effect of enshrining in legislation, which is intended to be more or less permanent, temporary economic purposes.

Where the employee is laid off or kept on short time,[15] other than where that is wholly or mainly attributable to a strike or lock-out,[16] the employee must give his employer written notice that he intends to claim a redundancy payment in respect of lay-off or short time. The right only arises where the lay-off or short time has occurred in four or more consecutive weeks or in six or more weeks (of which not more than three were consecutive) within a period of 13 weeks. In both cases the notice must be served within four weeks from the last of these weeks of lay-off or short time.[17] It does not matter whether this issue concerns entirely lay-off or short time or whether the two were intermingled.[18]

If the employer serves no counter notice then a redundancy payment may be claimed in the normal way, provided that the employee leaves his employment after giving a week's notice or such longer period as is required as a minimum period of notice by his contract of employment within three weeks of serving notice of his intention to claim.[19] If the employer, within seven days of the employee's notice serves a written counter notice of intention to contest his liability the issue of liability must be determined by a tribunal.[20] In this case (unless the counter notice is withdrawn), the employee retains his right, pro-

---

[15] *Ibid.* s.81.
[16] *Ibid.* s.89(3).
[17] *Ibid.* s.88(1).
[18] *Ibid.* s.89(3).
[19] *Ibid.* ss.88(2) and 89(5)(*a*).
[20] *Ibid.* s.89(4).

vided that he leaves by the proper period of notice within three weeks of being notified of the decision of the tribunal.[21]

The purpose of the counter notice is to enable the employer to invoke the statutory "defence"[22] that, on the date of service of the employee's notice it was reasonably to be expected that within four weeks from that date the employee (if he remained in the employment) would enter into a period of not less than 13 weeks without lay-off or short time. This expectation is conclusively presumed not to be available if the employee is in fact laid off or put on short time in each of the four weeks following the date of his notice of intention to claim.[23] The work involved in the 13 weeks must be of a kind which the employee was employed to do.[24]

It should be borne in mind that some cases of lay-off or short time may amount to a breach of contract by the employer entitling the employee to claim the existence of a constructive dismissal which will render satisfaction of the above conditions unnecessary.[25] It should also be borne in mind that what looks like a series of lay-offs may be better regarded as intermittent employment.[26]

Early leaving

An employee who has received notice of dismissal from his employment and who, during the period of that notice himself gives notice to leave on an earlier date than the employer's notice is due to expire loses none of his right to claim for an unfair dismissal.[27] In the case of a claim to statutory redundancy compensation, however, the common law assumption remains effective. This is that in such a case the employee's leaving is attributable to his own actions and not those of the employer. This notwithstanding that the only reason that the employee did leave was the intimation of impending redundancy, whether it amounted to a mere warning or a dismissal.[28] In a redundancy situation it will be far more difficult to imply a variation of the leaving date, which might be a way of avoiding this difficulty, simply because an employer who is keeping employees on pending the expiry of their notice is more likely to be doing so because he needs them and is, therefore, less likely to agree to an early leaving.

A rather complicated statutory alternative is provided.[29] Under it the employee may give earlier notice in writing, but only during the minimum statutory perod of notice to which he is entitled. If the employer does not contest this notice the employee is regarded as having been dismissed for the purposes of a redundancy claim. The employer may, however, serve on the employee a notice in writing requiring him to continue in employment until

---

[21] *Ibid.* s.89(5)(c).
[22] *Ibid.* s.88(3) and (4).
[23] *Ibid.* s.89(1).
[24] *Neepsend Steel and Tool Corporation* v. *Vaughan* [1972] I.C.R. 278.
[25] See *Davis Transport Ltd.* v. *Chattaway* [1972] I.C.R. 267; *Hanson* v. *Wood* [1968] I.T.R. 14. See also the judgments in *Jones* v. *H. Sherman Ltd.* [1979] I.T.R. 63 and *Johnson* v. *Cross* [1977] I.C.R. 872; although the latter decision arrives at some startlingly improbable conclusions.
[26] *Puttick* v. *John Wright and Sons (Blackwall) Ltd.* [1972] I.C.R. 457.
[27] Employment Protection (Consolidation) Act 1978, s.55(3).
[28] *Morton Sundour Fabrics Ltd.* v. *Shaw* [1967] 2 K.I.R. 1 (N.I.R.C.); see also *Pritchard-Rhodes Ltd.* v. *Boon* [1979] I.R.L.R. 19 (E.A.T.).
[29] Employment Protection (Consolidation) Act 1978, s.85.

the expiry of the employer's notice. If the employee does not comply with this requirement he may make a reference to an industrial tribunal. This is the only way in which he may, in such circumstances, establish a claim to redundancy compensation. The tribunal may award him all, or such part, of the payment as would otherwise be due as, in all the circumstances, it considers just and equitable.

Misconduct Excluding the Right to Redundancy Compensation

Upon a claim for redundancy there arises a presumption that the dismissal is by reason of redundancy unless it is proved by some means, not necessarily by the employer, that redundancy was not the primary reason.[30] This situation is however, further affected by two statutory provisions of some complexity. In the first place:

> ... an employee shall not be entitled to a redundancy payment by reason of dismissal where his employer, being entitled to terminate his contract of employment without notice by reason of the employee's conduct terminates it either
>
> > (a) without notice, or
> > (b) by giving shorter notice than that which, in the absence of such conduct, the employer would be required to give ... or
> > (c) by giving notice (not being such shorter notice ...) which includes or is accompanied by, a statement in writing that the employer would, by reason of the employee's conduct, be entitled to terminate the contract without notice.

It will be noted that provisions (a) and (b) do not require a dismissal for any stated reason other than redundancy. An employer might, therefore, dismiss intending that dismissal to be for redundancy, accidentally giving inadequate notice, and rely on the section to exclude a claim for redundancy compensation by alleging a pre-existing cause. On the other hand if the employer gives proper notice and does not comply with provision (c), as for instance by failing to state *in writing* the reservation, the employee is entitled to a redundancy payment provided, of course, that he is otherwise entitled. The section will, of course, permit a dismissal for subsequent cause to displace a previous dismissal for redundancy by notice.

An exception to the operation of this subsection is created by section 92. This applies to exclude the operation of the preceding provision where an employer has given notice of termination by reason of redundancy or the employee has given notice by reason of lay-off or short time and the employee takes part in a strike either during the *obligatory statutory period* of notice to which he is entitled or after himself giving notice. In such circumstances the employer may, *for that reason* terminate the contract in any of the ways mentioned in (a), (b) or (c) above. If the employer does so then the exclusion from redundancy payment entitlement provided by section 82(2) will not apply but instead an application can be made to a tribunal to decide what part of the redundancy payment it thinks fit to award.

This partial restoration of the right to redundancy payment applies only where the strike follows the dismissal for redundancy and also only where the

---

[30] *Ibid.* s.91(2).

strike is given as the reason for the ultimate dismissal. In other words, for section 92(2) to apply there must be two dismissals whilst section 82(2) may apply either to a one, or a two, dismissal situation. If the employee is already on strike and is then dismissed for redundancy section 92(2) will not apply but section 82(2) might, depending on the manner of dismissal, so as to disentitle to redundancy payment. This assumes that a strike constitutes misconduct but that assumption is supported by the very lengthy consideration of the application of these provisions in *Simmons* v. *Hoover Ltd.*[31]

It is obvious that section 92 was intended to avoid a situation where a strike in protest at dismissal for redundancy would operate under section 82(2) to disentitle those participating from their redundancy payments. Unfortunately, section 92 only applies to strikes. Any other form of industrial action in protest would be caught by section 82(2) unless the argument of Mr. Sedley, which failed in *Simmons* v. *Hoover* in relation to strikes, could succeed in relation to lesser action allowing it to be regarded as constituting less than a repudiatory breach.

"REDUNDANCY"

The definitions used in the Redundancy Payments Act (and, therefore, still to be found in those parts of the 1978 Act dealing with redundancy) are intended to be more precise than those that affect principal issues on unfair dismissal. Before the intention of the unfair dismissal provisions to produce a less technical result took effect on industrial tribunals their approach to the redundancy legislation was marked by a rigidity that would seem surprising today. The legislature may well have seen itself as coping with a social and economic problem caused by the total inadequacy of legal or collective provisions for compensation for mass dismissal and by industrial reorganisation. Regrettably, it did not say so, but rather chose to define the situation by reference to unilateral change in the contractual job content.

The definition of redundancy refers separately to total shutdown of operation at the workplace and to reorganisation of that undertaking resulting in diminished job requirement.[32]

(2) For the purposes of this Act an employee who is dismissed shall be taken to be dismissed by reason of redundancy if the dismissal is attributable wholly or mainly to—

(*a*) the fact that his employer has ceased, or intends to cease, to carry on the business for the purposes of which the employee was employed by him, or has ceased, or intends to cease, to carry on that business in the place where the employee was so employed, or

(*b*) the fact that the requirements of that business for employees to carry out work of a particular kind, or for employees to carry out work of a particular kind in the place where he was so employed, have ceased or diminished or are expected to cease or diminish.

For the purposes of this subsection, the business of the employer together with the business or businesses of his associated employers shall be treated as one unless

---

[31] [1977] I.C.R. 61.
[32] Employment Protection (Consolidation) Act 1978, s.81(2).

either of the conditions specified in this subsection would be satisfied without so treating those businesses.[33]

Contractual job definition

In *Nelson* v. *B.B.C.* (*No.* 2)[33a] the Court of Appeal had clearly stated that the diminution needed to create a redundancy must be in the job content as contractually stated. Brandon L.J. said:

". . . Mr Nelson was right in law in maintaining that, because the work which he was employed to do continued to exist he was not redundant; and further right in law in asserting that the proposal which the corporation were making to him was not in reality an offer of alternative employment, but a proposal to re-assign him to other work within the scope of his existing contract of employment."

In *Cowen* v. *Haden Carrier Ltd.* [33b] Browne-Wilkinson J. stated that industrial tribunals had been asking instead whether the diminution was in requirement for employees to do the job on which the applicant was actually engaged. He expressed a preference for this approach but, referring to the two *Dixon* cases, said:

"We are unable to treat the composite effect of these two decisions of the Court of Appeal as being other than a decision binding on us that in considering s.81(2)(*b*) of the 1978 Act it is not sufficient in order to establish redundancy to show merely that the requirements of the employers for employees to carry out work of the kind on which [the employee] was actually engaged has ceased or diminished: it is necessary to show such diminution or cessation in relation to any work that he could have been asked to do."

He then went on to envisage serious problems arising from the application of this principle. It is suggested with respect that he overstated the problem when saying that it would be "exceptionally difficult" for an employer to establish a case of redundancy and would render such a conclusion very difficult in cases of "bumping." It is difficult to see why this decision should render "bumping" cases especially difficult. It is true that job descriptions often provide for flexibility—especially when a degree of latitude is sought by the employer in collective bargaining in return for increased remuneration. The decision may serve, at least, to concentrate the attention of those involved in such agreements on the potential value of flexibility to an employer. The Court of Appeal, whilst overruling this decision on the ground that the employee's job description was not so wide as to include the required change, did not distort this principle.

The Court of Appeal said[33c]:

"For these reasons: *Chapman* v. *Goonvean* was clearly distinguishable, as the EAT held, because on the facts there was no cessation or diminution of the particular kind of work which the applicants were employed to do. Further, it was an essential foundation of the decision in *Nelson* v. *B.B.C.* (*No.*1) that the court

---

[33] s.91(2) establishes a rebuttable presumption of redundancy arising from any dismissal but only for the purposes of redundancy compensation. The operation of the presumption does not supply a reason in a claim for unfair dismissal (*Midland Foot Comfort Centre* v. *Moppett* [1973] I.C.R. 219).

[33a] [1980] I.C.R. 110 (C.A.).

[33b] [1982] I.R.L.R. 225 (EAT) overruled on other grounds [1982] I.R.L.R. 314 (C.A.)

[33c] [1982] I.R.L.R. 317.

decided whether there was a cessation or diminution of the requirement under the contract of employment for employees to perform the particular kind of work that Mr Nelson was employed to do. That was necessary to the *ratio decidendi* of the decision and as the EAT held was binding upon them."

Not only does the employee (and probably the employer) tend to think of the job that is being done rather than that which may legally be required but this reliance upon the contractual job definition supposes a certainty which it is clear the contract rarely contains. This definition alone gave rise to a need judicially to construct the contract. In practice, however, that process disclosed an interesting fact about the effect of the operation of the judicial approach to that contract. If we assume an evidential vacuum then the extent of the employee's job obligations will be limited to what he is doing. It is even possible that some of that may turn out to be voluntary and not contractual.[34] If the only evidence is that of custom and practice insistence on the need for consent, even if then courts decide when consent is reasonably to be implied, will tend to operate to restrict extension of the job content by actions or assumptions of the employer[35] but may enable the employee, by consent, to entrench a change in his favour.[36] On the other hand, the sharp distinction which allows reasonableness to govern the implied terms of a contract, but excludes it wholly from express terms and partially from incorporated terms, may leave the employee with frustrated expectations when he has failed to pay attention to extensions in those aspects of his obligation extending beyond what he is actually doing.

One of the most obvious examples of this dichotomy occurs in connection with the place of work. If an employee's contractually defined place of work is more extensive than that at which he is actually working (or has ever worked) then it may be that a reduction in requirement at one point is matched by an increase at another and there is, in relation to that type of job, no redundancy situation at all. More commonly there is likely to be an overall reduction in requirement if there is a reduction at one point but the employee must show that this was the reason for the termination of his contract. If the employer is willing to continue the contract, merely transferring the work, as he is entitled to do under the contract, to another place, the employee who refuses the transfer will have his contract terminated not because of the diminution in requirement at one place but because of his refusal to move to another. This was the point in issue in *O'Brien* v. *Associated Fire Alarms Ltd.*[37] where, as we have seen, the Court of Appeal implied into the contract an obligation derived from the practice of both parties to employ and be employed only in one locality. In *U.K. Atomic Energy Authority* v. *Claydon*[38] the contract expressly provided that the employee should be available to work anywhere in the United Kingdom.[39]

---

[34] *e.g. Horrigan* v. *Lewisham London Borough Council* [1978] I.C.R. 15.
[35] *O'Brien* v. *Associated Fire Alarms Ltd.* [1968] 1 W.L.R. 1916.
[36] *e.g. Simmonds* v. *Dowty Seals Ltd.* [1978] I.R.L.R. 211.
[37] *Supra.*
[38] [1973] I.C.R. 128.
[39] See also *Sutcliffe* v. *Hawker Siddeley Aviation Ltd.* [1973] I.C.R. 560; *Stevenson* v. *Teesside Bridge and Engineering Ltd.* [1971] 1 All E.R. 296. Compare *Hawker Siddeley Power Engineering Ltd.* v. *Rump* [1974] I.R.L.R. 429. Compare *Buck* v. *Edward Everard Ltd.* [1968] I.T.R. 328 and *Shakespeare* v. *C. L. and H. L. Blundell Ltd.* [1966] I.T.R. 458 on the actual meaning of "place."

It is, however, the judicial approach to the contractual content of the job which is likely to cause most surprise to the employee. Many different influences operate in the same direction to render abnormal a situation where the contractual job obligation is defined as limited to operating a particular machine with defined materials at a specified rate. The employer will want far greater flexibility than this; the employee or his union may see any alteration of the existing elements as a matter for negotiation but will not be keen to translate them into contractual limits. The lawyer, by training, seeks to extract from them what he sees as the essential definitive boundaries. If asked to produce a contractual definition of the job, therefore, all concerned will tend to exclude from it some aspects of the job that is actually being done. The tribunals and courts have, however, gone much further than this. Not only have they excluded features which, though contractual, indicate how when and where the work shall be done but they have excluded others, which may indeed describe the job and may even be of a contractual nature, in order to arrive at a broad job type.

It is not surprising in view of this that redundancy does not deal with diminution of expectation. In *North East Coast Ship Repairers Ltd.* v. *Secretary of State for Employment*[40] the contractual job was that of apprentice. Such an employee might reasonably expect to become a journeyman, but a reduction of demand for journeymen was not a reduction of requirement for his job. The termination of his apprenticeship occurred because he had served the fixed period.

Exclusion of non-job characteristics

The distinction between terms and conditions defining the job and terms and conditions relating to other aspects of the employment is often expressed as the difference between redundancy and reorganisation. If the primary reason for declaring a redundancy is, as it often is, economic it will be clear that the employer may seek to save money either by paying wages to fewer employees or by reducing their wages, directly or indirectly. Abolition of the night shift, with the potential transfer of everyone employed thereon to the day shift, will usually save money because the normal night shift premium will disappear. Hidden in this form of cost saving may well be an expectation that the workforce will actually be reduced because some employees will not accept the new terms at all or, having accepted, will tend to leave for better pay at the earliest opportunity. If the change does not constitute a redundancy and, as a reorganisation preceded by proper consultation, is likely to lead to the conclusion that any resultant dismissal is fair,[41] no question of the change being unsuitable will arise. The employee who rejects the offer or subsequently leaves will not be entitled to compensation from either the redundancy or the dismissal legislation. The employer may, therefore, by playing upon the very technicality of the statutory definition, achieve the same purpose as by a redundancy with none of the same obligation to pay compensation. Redundancy and reorganisation are, in effect, the same situation divided by the technicality of the statutory definition of redundancy. It is for this reason that courts are able to

---

[40] [1978] I.C.R. 755.
[41] *Supra*, p. 204.

substitute one for the other as the actual reason for dismissal since they are doing no more than to change the label.

This issue is made very clear by the case of *Chapman* v. *Goonvean & Rostowrack China Clay Co. Ltd.*[42] The employers had provided a bus to bring certain employees to work. The number of employees using the bus had fallen to seven and a recession in the industry led the employers to economise by withdrawing the bus. The employees could not provide their own transport and so were unable to accept an offer by the company to retain them. They left and their places were filled by seven new employees living near the place of work. The legislation allowing claims for unfair dismissal which might have afforded a remedy was not in force at the time their contracts ended so the affected employees claimed that they had been constructively dismissed by reason of redundancy. Two previous decisions in the Divisional Court[43] had held that if in all probability a dismissal for redundancy would have been the solution adopted had it not been otherwise possible to alter the terms, then the alteration of the terms could be said to constitute a constructive dismissal by reason of redundancy. This ingenious line of reasoning was rejected in *Chapman's* case both by the N.I.R.C. and the Court of Appeal. The Court of Appeal held that it could not be implied into the definition of redundancy that the decline in requirement referred to was for jobs on the existing terms and conditions. Lord Denning M.R. justified this refusal partly on the ground that it was desirable to allow the employer to reorganise in this way. This may be so but it does not answer the question why it should be desirable to excuse the employer paying compensation thus throwing the burden of the reorganisation on the employee. That apart, however, the Court of Appeal did appreciate that the decision raises the question how far the benefit of terms and conditions—even of pay levels—could be reduced whilst still permitting the assertion that there was no diminution in requirement for employees to perform the job. Buckley L.J. said:

"Suppose, for instance, that the employment is of a kind for which there is a recognised rate for the job, and that an employer in a period of affluence and in the interests of good staff relations has been paying his employees more than that rate. If a time comes when he can no longer afford to pay his employees more than the recognised rate for the job but he is prepared to continue to employ them at that rate, there is nothing in section 1 of the Act to suggest that for the purpose of considering whether his requirement for employees to do that particular job is likely to cease or diminish he must be treated as an employer who is going to continue to pay the higher rate. This, however, as I understand Mr. Pain's argument, would be the consequence of the view which he propounds. The facts would not, it seems to me, establish that the employer's need for employees to carry out work of the particular kind was expected to cease or diminish, but only that the employer was no longer able to pay his employees on so generous a scale as before. The position would be quite different if an employer dismissed his employees because he was no longer able to pay them either the recognised rate for the job, where one existed, or a fair wage at which he could secure the services of other employees in the labour market."

There is little logic in describing as redundancy the effects of reorganisation when terms are reduced below an acceptable level save in so far as it is as good for dismissal, to contend that the employer cannot show that he reasonably held

---

[42] [1973] I.C.R. 310 (C.A.)

[43] *Dutton* v. *C. H. Bailey Ltd.* (1968) 3 I.T.R. 355; *Line* v. *C. E. White and Co.* [1969] I.T.R. 336.

the view that there was no diminution in his requirement when he must reasonably have realised that the result of his action would reduce the supply. Even if that general proposition is the basis for the suggestion of Buckley L.J. it provides a very uncertain test of "constructive redundancy," especially where the changed terms do not relate to pay and the reduction of benefit effected by them is debatable.

This distinction between a change of terms bearing upon the nature of the job and one affecting the wider "job function" was again emphasised in *Johnson* v. *Nottinghamshire Combined Police Authority*[44] where Stephenson L.J. said:

> "The difference which is alleged to 'create a redundancy situation' or make the reason for their dismissal redundancy is simply the change of working hours. You look at the task or job which the dismissed employee did (I can see that 'job' may be wider than 'task,' as the court thought, but they seem to me ancient and modern words generally used for the same thing); you look at the reason or reasons which induced the employer to dismiss him or her, and you then ask 'Is the presumption that the employee has been dismissed by reason or redundancy rebutted?': Is it proved that the reason was something else? I agree that the reason proved in this case was that in order to release police officers from clerical work the police authority required the applicants to do the same work in a different way, but that difference in method or hours did not amount to cessation or diminution. I will assume that an alteration of method or hours or of the type of person employed or of status or responsibility—or even of remuneration—may alter the work done to such an extent that it would in common sense be regarded as a different task or job so that the change required by the employer and rejected by the employee would be a change in kind. No longer would an employee be said to do the same job or the employer to require the same task to be performed. But that is not this case. If these applicants were asked 'Why did you leave your job?' they might answer 'Because it isn't the job it was.' But if asked 'Who is doing your job now?,' I doubt if either of them would reply 'Nobody. It has gone, or been done away with.' It has not. It is the same job done to a different time schedule."

In *Lesney Products and Co. Ltd.* v. *Nolan*[45] the company employed machine setters to maintain toymaking machinery. A fall in sales caused them to abolish night-shift working and to introduce a double-day shift. This resulted in a loss of overtime on the day shift. Nine machine setters who refused to accept the new system were dismissed. The employer's evidence was that there was no diminution of work for the day shift as distinct from the night shift. The E.A.T., with some hesitation, upheld the decision of the industrial tribunal that the setters had been dismissed for redundancy. There is no doubt that a redundancy situation did exist and that it was the reason for the dismissal of night-shift-workers. The Court of Appeal suggested that it was the feeling of the tribunal that this situation could not be divorced from the reorganisation of the day shift which had led it to conclude that that too was due to a diminution in requirement for employees. All the members of the Court of Appeal agreed, however, that given the clear evidence that there was no falling off of demand on the day an indication as any other of the lack of a real expectation of being able to recruit employees. It is possible, by analogy with the establishment of a reason shift the reorganisation there must be attributed to economic considerations and not to diminution of requirement.

---

44 [1974] I.C.R. 170.
45 [1977] I.C.R. 235 (C.A.).

Although we have used the term "reorganisation" as the obverse of redundancy this is only a matter of convenience. Courts and tribunals deciding that there is no diminution of requirement to suit the statutory definition of redundancy commonly use "reorganisation" to label "some other substantial reason" for the purposes of a claim for unfair dismissal. The term "reorganisation" has no technical meaning, and, as we have pointed out, it may describe the same set of facts which would give rise to a redundancy. The distinction between the two becomes a question of the manner in which the employer handles the economic situation. It follows, therefore, that a so-called reorganisation may produce a redundancy. The question is simply whether the rearrangement produces a diminution in requirement for employees to do the job or whether it effects a saving in ways which do not alter the nature of the job. In *Robinson* v. *British Island Airways Ltd.*[46] Phillips J. in the E.A.T. was prepared to find that the reorganisation had created a new job to replace two others so that the employees who held the two former jobs were dismissed for redundancy. He said:

"What has to be done in every case is to analyse the facts and to match the analysis against the words of section 1 of the Redundancy Payments Act 1965. In doing this it is of no assistance to consider whether as a matter of impression there was or was not a 'redundancy situation.' The question is whether the definition is satisfied. Complications are caused where, as in the present case, the question of redundancy arises in relation to a claim for compensation for unfair dismissal, and where the interaction of the two codes causes problems, aggravated by the fact that what is beneficial under one may not be under the other. For example, in the present case there can be no doubt that had events under consideration occurred in 1970 Mr. Sedley would have been claiming, and Mr. Jarman perhaps denying, that the employee was redundant.

There is no doubt that the employee was dismissed. To what was his dismissal attributable? It seems to us that the work done by the flight operations manager was of a 'particular kind' and that the work done by the general manager operations and traffic was of a 'particular kind,' and that each kind was different from the other. It seems to us that the work done by the operations manager was of a 'particular kind' and of a kind different from that done by the general manager operations and traffic and different from that done by the flight operations manager. Thus in our judgment it can truly be said that the dismissal of the employee was attributable to the fact that the requirements of the business for employees to carry out work of a particular kind had ceased or diminished and that each was redundant.

If this were wrong, we should be inclined to say that the circumstances constituted 'some other substantial reason of a kind such as to justify the dismissal of an employee holding the position which that employee held.' It seems to us that where there is a genuine re-organisation which has dislodged an employee who cannot be fitted into the re-organisation it must be open to the employer to dismiss him. But we prefer to think that in those circumstances he will usually be redundant, and thus entitled to a redundancy payment."

As the judgments in *Lesney* v. *Nolan* make clear it is also necessary to remember that the tests are applied to each individual affected. So what may be a reorganisation for some may produce a redundancy for others whose jobs are no longer required.[47]

---

[46] [1978] I.C.R. 304.
[47] *Wilson* v. *Underhill House School Ltd.* [1977] I.R.L.R. 475.

Change of job

It is necessary, in view of the distinction the courts have made between the job and the terms and conditions applicable to it, to consider the extent to which the courts will consider incidents of employment as essential characteristics of the job. In other words, how is "work of a particular kind" to be classified? It is already clear that if the courts can exclude from consideration of the nature of the job the fringe benefits made available in return for it and and hours at which it is performed then all other such "ancillary" factors will also be excluded.[48] What we are here concerned with is the further question how, when we have assembled the job characteristics of the former requirement and those of the new requirement we decide that the one equals the other. What, in other words, is in a name? We have seen, for instance, that in *Robinson* v. *British Island Airways Ltd.*[49] the E.A.T. was prepared to consider the new responsibilities and enhanced status of the "operations manager" to constitute that a job different from either the former "flight operations manager" or the "general manager operations and traffic." On the other hand, in *North Riding Garages* v. *Butterwick*[50] a garage manager incapable of estimating for repairs was considered to occupy the same job as any garage manager who might be required to perform this task. At what point does a change of detail cease to be merely the introduction of a new method or technique to which the employee is expected to adapt? It appears to be of no moment that the employee is necessarily unable to adapt to the new requirements. In *Vaux and Associated Breweries* v. *Ward*[51] the employers had decided to alter the image of the public house at which Mrs. Ward had been employed as a barmaid. They dimissed Mrs. Ward, who was middle aged, in order to make room for two glamorous young barmaids. Lord Parker C.J. in the Divisional Court had no doubt that the work was still that of a barmaid.[52]

These decisions should not, however, be construed as revealing a total failure of the definition to accommodate technological change. The judgment in *Vaux* reveals a court convinced not only that both jobs could be described as "barmaid" but that both involved substantially the same work. It is submitted that in view of later decisions like *Robinson* v. *British Island Airways* the surprise originally expressed at the decision of an industrial tribunal in *European Chefs (Catering) Ltd.* v. *Currell*[53] is not justified. The differences between the techniques and skills of a maker of continental pastries and a maker of eclairs and meringues are, no doubt, considerable enough to constitute two different jobs. It is, of course, possible to bring both under some such general heading as "pastrycook" but the Act did not intend excessive generalisation, which would defeat its purpose, nor do subsequent cases support the introduction of generalised categories. Accordingly in *Hindle* v. *Percival Boats Ltd.*[54] a distinction might properly have been drawn between the highly skilled work Hindle had been employed to do and which, arguably, it had never been

---

[48] *e.g. Arnold* v. *Thomas Harrington Ltd.* [1969] 1 Q.B. 312.
[49] [1978] I.C.R. 304. See also *Watts, Watts and Co. Ltd.* v. *Steeley* (1968) I.T.R. 363.
[50] [1967] 2 Q.B. 56.
[51] (1969) 7 K.I.R. 308.
[52] See also *A. W. Champion* v. *Scoble* [1967] I.T.R. 411.
[53] (1971) I.T.R. 37.
[54] [1969] 1 W.L.R. 174.

made clear to him was no longer required, and the somewhat run-of-the-mill carpentering which he was later required to perform.

The chain of causation and employer belief

Since 1971 there has normally been a double standard in the application of the law of redundancy in that since the introduction of a remedy for unfair dismissal employers, more often than not, have preferred to give redundancy as a reason wherever the facts might support it. This is no doubt partly out of kindness to the employee and partly to avoid the risk of a troublesome claim for unfair dismissal. "Redundancy" as a reason has, quite correctly, been seen almost as self-justifying. In theory the Secretary of State could have called many of these loose practical applications in question by declining to pay the redundancy rebate. Such rigid policing of the system has not been the policy of the Department of Employment which is not anxious to quibble on the technical definition when popular common sense would suggest that the loss of job should be compensated by a redundancy payment. More recently the realisation that "reorganisation" had much the same quality of self-justification whilst avoiding a liability, to which voluntary agreements might have added a burdensome multiple, has been used more extensively.

The variation in pressure upon the application of the definition of redundancy has produced an uneven and spasmodic consideration of at least one major element, namely; the extent to which the chain of causation can be stretched to conclude that the reason for a dismissal is a diminution in requirement and the associated question of the subjectivity of the reason. Lord Denning M.R., without clearly formulating this issue, has twice considered the matter. In *Hindle* v. *Percival Boats Ltd.*[55] dissenting from the other two members of the Court of Appeal he dipped into both matters without finding a firm bottom. The employer's business had changed its character. Wooden hulled sailing boats built by craftsmen had become too expensive to command a mass market. They had been replaced with fibre glass hulls. The need to sell these at competitive rates meant that even the furniture built into them could no longer be of the former high standard. The applicant could not bring himself to lower the standard of his craft and so the cost of employing him to fit out a hull was uneconomic when set against the price that could be charged. The Court of Appeal might have been saved a lot of trouble if the industrial tribunal had formulated clear views on the nature of the job upon which Hindle was employed but Lord Denning was prepared to assume that the demand for that job had diminished. He then faced the problem of deciding whether the tribunal had been right to hold that the reason for the dismissal was what the employer had in his mind as the immediate motivation. He concluded:

"In *MacLaughlan* v. *Alexander Paterson Ltd.* the *motive* of the employers in dismissing an employee was because they were reorganising their staff: and on account of that *motive* the tribunal dismissed his claim to a redundancy payment. But the Court of Session reversed the tribunal. Lord Migdail said pointedly:

'There is a distinction between "motive" and "reason." The motive was reorganisation. The reason for his dismissal was redundancy.'

---

[55] *Supra.*

The truth is that in this Act, we are concerned with the *cause* of the dismissal, and not with the employer's motives or beliefs except insofar as they throw light on the cause. To qualify for redundancy payment, the dismissal must be 'by reason of,' that is, *as a result of* redundancy, or, in other words 'attributable' to the fact; and not as a result of, or attributable to some other cause. But the presumption is in favour of a redundancy."

Although the other two members of the Court of Appeal expressed doubts about the feasibility of a distinction between reason and motive they did not really consider the possibility of extending the chain largely because they were not prepared to accept that there was a deeper seated reason for Hindle's dismissal.

Lord Denning again noted the problem of causation in *Johnson* v. *Nottinghamshire Combined Police Authority*.[56] Obviously if reorganisation is being put forward, rather than redundancy, as the reason it would be possible to argue that the reorganisation is only the immediate response to a deeper seated redundancy situation. If an employee refuses to accept a change in terms and conditions not affecting the nature of his job is it possible to go beyond the employer's immediate response of reorganisation to say that the underlying cause is a diminution of requirement? In *Johnson's* case Lord Denning preferred to avoid any deeper consideration of this question by suggesting that it would be taken care of by the need to disprove the presumption of redundancy. This, however, begs, rather than answering, that question. It is true that such proof can be derived from any source and so need not be confined to examination of the employer's belief. On the other hand a decision that the immediate cause cannot be displaced by a deeper seated reason will simply mean that establishment of an immediate cause other than diminution of requirement furnishes the necessary rebuttal of the presumption.

Had the possibility of extending the chain of causation been pursued it might have enabled the courts to adopt an objective approach to the existence of redundancy which could have overridden the technicality of the definition by enquiring whether some rearrangement which did not comply with that definition was itself the result of an underlying situation which did. In the same way it would have enabled the courts to displace an employer's belief in an immediate cause for dismissal by showing that that belief was dependent on the same underlying situation.

The line of decisions which have distinguished redundancy from reorganisation[57] necessarily contradict such a possibility, and at present it is clear that the courts will look only to the immediate cause.

Whether that enquiry enables them only to look at the employer's genuine belief in that immediate cause or to go behind it and discover a different actual cause is another matter since the answer is bound up with the question whether the diminution in requirement is, as the Act states, one of employees or, as some recent decisions have seemed to infer one of quantity of work.[58] If it is the

---

[56] [1974] I.C.R. 170.

[57] *e.g. Chapman* v. *Goonvean and Rostowrack China Clay Co.* [1973] I.C.R. 310; *Johnson* v. *Nottinghamshire Combined Police Authority, supra,* and, most particularly *Lesney Products and Co. Ltd.* v. *Nolan* [1977] I.C.R. 235.

[58] See *Ranson* v. *G. W. Collins Ltd.* [1978] I.C.R. 765; *O'Hare* v. *Rotaprint Ltd.* [1980] I.C.R. 94.

former then, as the decision of the majority of the Court of Appeal in *Hindle* v. *Percival Boats Ltd.*[59] shows, it will be difficult effectively to question that belief as providing the reason. If the latter, merely seeking or failing to seek, a replacement will provide no conclusive indication and the employer's belief may be questioned by an objective survey of the actual work requirement.

The early cases adhered strictly to the wording of the Act that the diminution in requirement should be for employees to do the work and not for the work itself. Consequently in *Brombey and Hoare Ltd.* v. *Evans*[60]—the correctness of which has never been questioned—it was held that a requirement of self-employed workers to replace employees was a reduction in requirement for employees.

This distinction is thoroughly discussed in *Delanair Ltd.* v. *Mead.*[61] The case makes the important point that it cannot be said, merely because an employee is dismissed and not replaced, that the employer believes there is a diminution of requirement for employees to do the job in question. By reasoning similar to that applied to the establishment of reasons in unfair dismissal the E.A.T. held that the employer must conduct the enquiries necessary to enable him to hold the view that his requirements had diminished. That view might be wrong in that he might, for instance, be overworking other employees in order to fill the gap. Nevertheless there would be a redundancy. On the other hand, if the employer without such enquiry had decided that he must economise by dismissing somebody that was a dismissal to save money rather than because of diminished requirement. If this appears to suggest that an employee's redundancy rights disappear if management does its job incompetently it may be pointed out that such a dismissal is very likely to be considered unfair.

It is submitted that it is entirely consistent with principle to say that the reason for dismissal is that upon which the employer thinks he is acting and that if he has no such thought it cannot be imputed to him. The dismissal of a man without replacement creates a diminution in requirement, but it is not necessarily the reason which motivated the dismissal.

> "The relevant question of fact for determination is whether the employers have shown that the decision to dispense with the services of a foreman/electrician in the maintenance department was the result of an appraisal of the requirement of the business for employees to carry out that work. If such an appraisal was made and a decision taken that the work formerly done by the employee could be redistributed over the remaining staff, that reallocation of his work brought about his dismissal on the ground of redundancy. On the other hand, if a decision was taken that a monthly paid worker had to be dismissed somewhere in the business irrespective of the queston of whether it was practicable to redistribute his work over the remaining staff, such dismissal was on the ground of economy without such regard to the requirements of the business for employees to carry out the particular type of work as to constitute redundancy within the meaning given in section 1(2)(b). We accept the criticism made by Mr. Irvine of the test apparently applied by the industrial tribunal. On its face it was the wrong test, as the industrial tribunal concentrated upon the question whether there had been a diminution in the type of work and not upon the question whether the requirement of the business for employees to carry out the type of work had diminished. . . ."

[59] *Supra.*
[60] [1972] I.C.R. 112.
[61] [1976] I.C.R. 552.

This decision, however, has a peculiar correlative effect. It is possible to say that an employer can reduce his workforce without having in his mind the reason that his requirement has diminished, then it must follow that he can increase the workforce without believing that the increase is necessary. If he never believed he needed the employees then his reason for dismissing them cannot be a belief that his need has been diminished. It may simply be a decision to save money. This is the basis of the decision in *Ranson* v. *G. W. Collins Ltd.* [62] that an assistant manager who had never been required but had been given that title while on trial as potential manager was not dismissed because of a diminution in requirement for an assistant manager but because of a decision to cut costs.

The emphasis on the employer's state of mind helps to explain the somewhat difficult decision of Kilner Brown J. in *O'Hare* v. *Rotaprint Ltd.* [63] The company, in anticipation of increased demand for its product, expanded its workforce. The demand did not materialise and it became essential to reduce costs. This was achieved by a 10 per cent. reduction of employees across the board. The reduction was made after full consultation with unions and employees and it was assumed by all parties that the dismissal was for redundancy. A claim that it was nonetheless unfair failed in the industrial tribunal. On appeal it was argued by the claimants that the dismissal was not for redundancy and was, therefore, unfair. The E.A.T. held that the dismissal was not for redundancy but was fair. It seems obvious that the second point is correct since there had been full consultation and everyone understood the factual basis of the reason which had simply been wrongly labelled. [64] The decision as to the existence of redundancy appears to be based either on the proposition that the employer had taken on employees whom he never required and so could not in his mind believe that his requirement had diminished or, alternatively, and more probably, that his decision to dismiss was not based on a reasoned response to a diminution of demand (assuming such demand had never existed) but on a simple decision to save money.

It is quite clear that none of these decisions justifies the conclusion that there is no redundancy when the diminution in requirement is foreseen at the time of engagement. [65] Just as there can be a redundancy because of a temporary diminution of requirement [66] so there can be a redundancy because of a fall off from a temporary requirement. Nor, it is submitted, do they in any way disturb the established principle that tribunals will not inquire into the factual justification for an employer's conclusion that his requirement has diminished. [67]

It is true, as Kilner Brown said in *O'Hare* v. *Rotaprint*, [68] that the state of the employer's mind is most likely to be judged by what he does. Accordingly, if he is overmanned and reduces his workforce, it will normally be assumed that this is because of a diminution of requirement. There need be nothing wrong with

[62] [1978] I.C.R. 765.
[63] [1980] I.C.R. 94.
[64] See *Abernethy* v. *Mott, Hay and Anderson* [1974] I.C.R. 323. The reasons actually adopted by the E.A.T. for this aspect of the decision seem to the present writer rather less convincing.
[65] *Lee* v. *Nottinghamshire County Council* [1980] I.C.R. 635 (C.A.)
[66] *Singh* v. *Higgs and Hill Ltd.* [1977] I.C.R. 193.
[67] *Sanders* v. *Ernest A. Neale Ltd.* [1974] I.C.R. 565; *Moon* v. *Homeworthy Furniture (Northern) Ltd.* [1977] I.C.R. 117.
[68] *Supra.*

that conclusion. The employer does not have to react immediately to a diminu-tion of requirement. The fact that he has for a long time needed fewer employees does not prevent him now making up his mind to act upon that diminution.

The problem that these decisions create, however, is one in which a decision as to the availability of redundancy compensation may depend on the state of mind of the employer. That has been true since *Hindle* v. *Percival Boats Ltd.* The extension lies in that the belief of the employer may be in exactly the same set of facts as would lead to redundancy or no redundancy. The difference lies in his state of mind as to how he proposes to deal with those facts. If the courts are to consider his thought processes as he resolves his difficulty they may conclude that he had made no decision to diminish his requirement for employees but, instead, has decided primarily to cut his costs. There is no reason why the employee should know this. The employer considers the effect of dismissals and, as Hepple and O'Higgins point out[69] this is the point at which the legislation directs attention. At the time of dismissal the mind of the employer must have decided to diminish his requirement for employees to do the job. The fact that at all earlier times he was primarily concerned to reduce costs and had not really thought about his requirement for employees is irrelevant. The courts, it is submitted, have adopted the looser approach because of the assumption that if the employer had not properly considered the matter the employee could be compensated by a claim for unfair dismissal. *O'Hare* v. *Rotaprint* reveals that this is not necessarily so. It is submitted that there is good reason in both policy and the words of the legislation to return to the original concept that if the employer dismissed and does not replace them at the time of the dismissal his requirement for employees has diminished.

ALTERNATIVE OFFERS

(a) The concept of consensual variation

Freedland[70] points out that the initiative to vary the contract of employment is almost universally a prerogative of management. As he goes on to point out the question may first have to be resolved of whether the proposal for change is merely a change of practice where both the former and the proposed new situation fall within the existing contract. This was the essential issue in *O'Brien* v. *Associated Fire Alarms Ltd.*[71] In the case of the contract of employment the resolution of such a question may involve considerable discussion of what terms might be implied into the contract.[72] Alternatively it may be necessary to interpret the contract to discover the scope of express provisions.[73] It is, of course, possible that those terms may themselves derive from some previous agreed variation. Though the courts sometimes appear over-willing to manufac-

---

[69] *Encyclopedia of Labour Relations Law*, 1–425.

[70] p. 42.

[71] [1968] 1 W.L.R. 1916.

[72] See, *e.g. McCaffrey* v. *A. E. Jeavons and Co. Ltd.* [1967] I.T.R. 636; *Stevenson* v. *Teesside Bridge and Engineering Co. Ltd.* [1971] 1 All E.R. 296; *Grace and Anderson* v. *The Northgate Group* [1972] I.R.L.R. 53.

[73] *e.g. Bex* v. *Securicor Transport Ltd.* [1972] I.R.L.R. 68; *Parry* v. *Holst and Co. Ltd.* [1978] I.T.R. 317.

ture very general implied obligations these will have little or no relevance to the issues that arise in any argument concerning variation. Such arguments, particularly when related to redundancy, mainly concern the nature of the job, the place of work and certain other specific matters such as hours and wages. In these areas it is probably fair to say that the courts are anxious to avoid too readily reaching the conclusion that the contract has been varied by agreement. In *Horrigan* v. *Lewisham London Borough Council*[74] where the E.A.T. refused to accept a long-continued practice of working overtime as evidence of any acceptance of variation of the contractual hours Arnold J. said:

> "It is fairly difficult, in the ordinary way, to imply a variation of contract, and it is very necessary, if one is to do so, to have very solid facts which demonstrate that it was necessary to give business efficacy to the contract, that the contract should come to contain a new term implied by way of variation."

Requirement of consent

This is, however, too strict a view since the basis for implication may well be evidence of acceptance which, if it exists, does not require the support of business efficacy. Browne-Wilkinson J. produced a realistic test for viewing such evidence in *Jones* v. *Associated Tunnelling Co. Ltd.*[75] when he said:

> "In our view, to imply an agreement to vary or to raise an estoppel against the employee on the grounds that he has not objected to a false record by the employers of the terms actually agreed is a course which should be adopted with great caution. If the variation relates to a matter which has immediate practical application (*e.g.* the rate of pay) and the employee continues to work without objection after effect has been given to the variation (*e.g.* his pay packet has been reduced) then obviously he may well be taken to have impliedly agreed. But where, as in the present case, the variation has no immediate practical effect the position is not the same. It is the view of both members of this Tribunal with experience in industrial relations (with which the Chairman, without such experience, agrees) that it is asking too much of the ordinary employee to require him either to object to an erroneous statement of his terms of employment having no immediate practical impact on him or be taken to have assented to the variation. So to hold would involve an unrealistic view of the inclination and ability of the ordinary employee to read and fully understand such statements.
>
> Even if he does read the statement and can understand it, it would be unrealistic of the law to require him to risk a confrontation with his employer on a matter which has no immediate practical impact on the employee. For those reasons, as at present advised, we would not be inclined to imply any assent to a variation from mere failure by the employee to object to the unilateral alteration by the employer of the terms of employment contained in a statutory statement."

The insistence on a genuine consent, which underlies the remarks of both Arnold and Browne-Wilkinson JJ., has in fact been adhered to since its first major statement in *Marriot* v. *Oxford and District Co-operative Society Ltd.* (*No.* 2).[76] There it was said by Lord Denning M.R. that the economic need to retain employment would furnish enough explanation of why an employee had remained at work for three weeks on the altered terms without any justification

---

[74] [1978] I.C.R. 15.
[75] [1981] I.R.L.R. 477.
[76] [1970] 1 Q.B. 186.

for the conclusion that this action constituted consent. In *Sheet Metal Components Ltd.* v. *Plumridge*[77] Sir John Donaldson in the N.I.R.C. said:

"It is without doubt the law that there is no dismissal where both parties to a contract of employment freely and voluntarily agree to vary its terms. This happens whenever there is an increase in rates of pay or a promotion. However, the courts have rightly been slow to find that there has been a consensual variation where an employee has been faced with the alternative of dismissal and where the variation has been adverse to his interests. As Sir John Brightman said in *Shield's Furniture Ltd.* v. *Goff*:

'What is an employee expected to do in these circumstances? He does not want to be out of a job. Nor, if he is a conscientious workman, does he want to let his employer down if this can be avoided. In most cases, therefore, he goes to the new job. He goes with an open mind. There is a period when he is uncommitted. During that period he makes up his mind whether he will accept the new employment, in which case he is not entitled to a redundancy payment; or whether he will leave or, in legal language, accept the employer's repudiation.'

We respectfully agree that this is the right approach in cases in which an employer has dealt informally with a change in the terms and conditions of employment. It is true that in *Shield's* case the time given to the employees to decide upon their attitude was much shorter than in the present case and Mr. Lyell rightly relied upon this distinction. Similarly he sought to distinguish *Marriott* v. *Oxford and District Co-operative Society Ltd.* (*No.* 2) on the grounds that there the employee went on working, but under express protest. But there are differences in degree and in the general background against which the court has to decide the question, 'Did the employer and the employee freely and voluntarily agree to vary the contract of employment?' "

Freedland[78] has cause to criticise the reasoning in *Dorman Long and Co. Ltd.* v. *Carroll.*[79] Colliery "fillers" agreed in 1943 to work an extra Saturday shift. They did so for 18 months but then gave notice to terminate the arrangement. The court characterised the arrangement as merely a method of carrying out contractual obligations leaving the contract unaltered. If this were correct then many terms and conditions of employment could be separated out of the contract as merely methods of carrying it out. Whether such methods are, or are not part of the contract is not so easily answered.[80] At the present time the obvious reluctance of the courts to imply a change of contract from a response to an emergency would be explained much more straightforwardly as implying either a purely voluntary undertaking or consent limited to that situation. That, it is submitted, is what Lord Parker C.J. meant in *Saxton* v. *National Coal Board*[81] where an employee had co-operated in working for lower wages during the run down of his job for redundancy.[82]

---

[77] [1974] I.C.R. 373. An extreme example of this reluctance to imply consent occurred in *Trevillion* v. *Hospital of St. John and St. Elizabeth* ([1973] I.R.L.R. 176) where it was found that there was no consent to vary the job description on any of several occasions where the amount of work was reduced.

[78] pp. 64–65.

[79] [1945] 2 All E.R. 567.

[80] See, *e.g. Secretary of State for Employment* v. *ASLEF* (*No.* 2) [1972] 2 Q.B. 455.

[81] (1970) 8 K.I.R. 893.

[82] Freedland, *op. cit.* criticises Lord Parker's use of the term "without prejudice."

In *Horrigan* v. *Lewisham London Borough Council*[83] the employee was engaged in 1966 to work a 40-hour week. This would mean finishing the day at 4.30 p.m. In practice he frequently did not finish his round until 5 or 6 p.m., and he was paid overtime. In 1968 this payment was formalised by agreement with the union but that agreement contained no suggestion that overtime working was obligatory. From February 1976 the employee refused to work overtime and, after warning, was dismissed. The E.A.T. held that there was, in 1966, no evidence to support the incorporation into the contract of an obligation to work overtime. Arnold J. continued:

"The next question is whether there could have been or was, by a subsequent implication a variation of that contract so as to introduce a term that the employee should, in addition to the obligations which were stated in his written contract, have the additional obligation of doing this amount of overtime. It is fairly difficult, in the ordinary way, to imply a variation of contract, and it is very necessary, if one is so to do, to have very solid facts which demonstrate that it was necessary to give business efficacy to the contract, that the contract should come to contain a new term implied by way of variation. There are a number of factors here which obviously were relevant to take into account. One factor—though not, of course, in any way conclusive—was that there was no variation of the written terms of contract, which suggests that at any rate it was not present to anybody's mind that there had been a variation in the terms of the contract. But we think more compelling than that is the circumstance that this contract, at any rate as regards February 1976 and at all times down to that date, although it did not contain any term for compulsory overtime, nevertheless was a contract under which the employee was employed, and employed in a way in which he was giving perfect satisfaction in a businesslike way to his employers; in other words, that he was doing as much overtime as was required to comply with the convenience which we have indicated without there being on the face of it an obligation so to do. We think that it is not possible to say that a variation came over this contract so as to introduce a compulsory overtime provision at any time down to February 1976; and it is as plain as a pikestaff, beccause of the attitude which was adopted by the employee, that he could not have had any intention of accepting such an implied term at any time after February 1976."

Evidence of consent

The court's relative reluctance to imply a variation owes something to the difficulty that will often be encountered, sometimes years later, of discovering reliable evidence as to the understanding of the parties. Nevertheless, although that difficulty was acute in *Simmonds* v. *Dowty Seals Ltd.*[84] the E.A.T. was prepared to hold that a transfer to the night shift had been regarded by both parties as a permanent alteration of the contract so that the employer was not entitled to require a return to the day shift four years later.

This reluctance is, for obvious reasons, not apparent when the evidence is of agreement by a trade union. In that situation the readiness of the courts to accept a variation of contract lends further emphasis to the subjection of individual choice to collective negotiation.[85] The effect of judicial thinking upon

---

[83] [1978] I.C.R. 15; See also *Hawker Siddeley Power Engineering Ltd.* v. *Rump* [1979] I.R.L.R. 425.

[84] [1978] I.R.L.R. 211.

[85] See, *e.g. Gascol Conversions Ltd.* v. *Mercer* [1974] I.C.R. 420 at 424. Compare *Joel* v. *Cammell Laird Ship-repairers Ltd.* (1969) 4 I.T.R. 206.

the different position of the individual employee when collectively represented is demonstrated by the judgment of Kilner Brown J. in *Land and Wilson* v. *West Yorkshire M.C.C.*[86] He said:

"Collective arrangements are not by themselves of any legal significance unless and until they are translated into contractual relationship between employer and employee. This may be brought about by collective agreement which, if it is to be achieved by representative process, becomes binding individually upon those who are caught by the representative process. Even if the employee is outside the representative process and is not a party to the national negotiations he may individually accept the collective agreement by agreeing to a contract which is based upon such collective agreement. Authority for these propositions is to be found in *Young* v. *Canadian Northern Railway Co.* and *Gascol Conversions Ltd.* v. *Mercer*.

By extension and analogy these principles would indicate that where a variation of, or a termination of, an existing contract is to be made based upon a collective agreement such a change can only be binding upon individuals if it is accepted individually or if they were collectively represented at the time the change was agreed upon. If the applicants had still been members of the Fire Brigades Union in October 1976 none of us would have found any difficulty in this case. If they had still been members in September 1975 we might have found a way out of a difficult problem."

Termination instead of variation

If one party makes it clear that he is not offering to vary the original contract but proposes to terminate that contract and offer a new one any consent will merely go to the establishment of a new contract and not to the question of variation.[87] This has been held to eliminate the possibility of a trial period in the new job before acceptance will be implied at common law.[88] Such a situation may also have an unexpected result upon the content of the new contract. In *S. W. Strange Ltd.* v. *Mann*[89] the defendant had been appointed manager of a bookmaking and commission agency. His contract contained a covenant restrictive of subsequent freedom of employment. He relinquished his duties as general manager and was reappointed as assistant manager of the credit department. After he had been dismissed from this post it was held that he was not bound by the restrictive covenant which was contained only in the original contract. The circumstances of the new employment will, of course, tend to imply many of the terms of the former contract into the new one but that will always be the question. If, on the other hand, there is a consensual variation it would be assumed that all the former terms, save those which could be shown to have been varied, continued to apply. It is submitted that this difference will apply no less to an agreed recision[90] as to unilateral recision even though, in the former case, the agreement may negate the existence of a dismissal.

The Court of Appeal produced a further interesting variant of the possibilities in *Land and Wilson* v. *West Yorkshire Metropolitan County Council.*[91]

---

[86] [1979] I.C.R. 452. Reversed on other grounds [1981] I.C.R. 334.
[87] *Meek* v. *J. Allen Rubber Co. Ltd.* [1980] I.R.L.R. 21.
[88] *Supra, Meek* v. *Allen.*.
[89] [1965] 1 W.L.R. 629.
[90] See *Marriot* v. *Oxford and District Co-operative Society Ltd.* (*No.* 2) [1970] 1 Q.B. 186.
[91] [1981] I.C.R. 334.

The appellants were employed as firemen for 40 hours a week. In addition they had agreed to undertake "whole-time/retained duties" under which they were paid for being on call during some periods outside their basic employment hours. Agreement was reached between employers and unions upon the abolition of these extra duties. Firemen who did not voluntarily agree to this change were given notice to vary their contracts by excluding this extra obligation. The appellants continued to work as whole-time firemen but claimed compensation for unfair dismissal. An industrial tribunal applied normal variation principles to hold that continuation in employment implied acceptance of the change. The E.A.T. applied the alternative noted above and held that the "retained duties" element was so significant a part of the contract that its withdrawal was not the offer of variation but the termination of one contract and the offer of a new one. The Court of Appeal held that the single contract of employment contained two separate parts. The retained duties part would be terminated by either party without affecting that part referring to normal full time employment.

A difficulty previously existed in explaining the contractual position if one party to the contract of employment did not accept an attempted variation by the other but nonetheless worked under the proposed new terms under protest. In *Marriot* v. *Oxford and District Co-operative Society Ltd.* (*No.* 2)[92] Lord Denning M.R. and Cross L.J. appear to have thought along the lines then current that an attempt at unilateral variation which was not withdrawn would operate to terminate the pre-existing contract. Neither of them sought to explain what would then be the legal position of the continuing employment relationship. Winn L.J. stated that such a discussion would be a waste of time and energy. Such a discussion was, however, ventured upon by counsel for the employers in *Shields Furniture Ltd.* v. *Goff.*[93] Sir John Brightman summarised his argument thus:

> "Counsel for the employers, in a forceful argument before us, submitted that redundancy payments were not due. He conceded, and indeed asserted, that the order to move to Fulham constituted a wrongful repudiation by the employers of the existing contracts of employment. This did not bring the contract of employment to an end because, submitted counsel, although employment as a status can usually be ended unilaterally, a contract as a legal relationship cannot be determined unilaterally. The employers' order to their employees placed each of them in a position where he might accept the wrongful repudiation, in which case the contract of employment terminated; or he might affirm the contract of employment, in which case it would continue until lawfully determined. The position, therefore, when the employees went to Fulham was that the contract of employment still continued, because they had not accepted the employers' wrongful repudiation; but the employers' repudiation was still capable of being accepted, in which case the contract would end, and it would be the employers who ended it so as to entitle the employees to redundancy payments. In fact, submitted counsel, the employees never did accept the employers' repudiation of the contracts. What they did was to accept the employers' offer to work at Fulham. The logical result of the acceptance of that offer was that the contract to work at Markham Street was terminated. But it was not terminated by the employer: it was terminated by mutual agreement between employer and employee. So went the argument of counsel."

---

[92] [1970] 1 Q.B. 186.
[93] [1973] I.C.R. 187.

Either this reveals a remarkable foresight or it ignores the difficulties then apparent in the rule that a repudiatory breach would terminate the contract. The N.I.R.C. chose to avoid those difficulties.

> "In our view the proper inference is that the employees did not commit themselves to working at Fulham instead of Markham Street, but accepted the employers' repudiation of the Markham Street contract. We do not think that the three weeks that the employees worked at Fulham and their two weeks' holiday was so long an elapsed period of time that one ought to assume an agreed variation or replacement of the previous contract. The employers never asked them to consider whether they wished to be discharged at Markham Street or to take on new work at Fulham. They were given no period of time in which to assess the position. The employers directed them to Fulham, which they had no contractual right to do. The employees reacted to that direction in the way that most employees would react: they went. They did not protest, but went to work and waited to see to what extent conditions would be improved. In those circumstances the time they allowed to go by was not so long as to imply the agreed substitution of a different contract. The notice which the employees gave was an acceptance of the employers' repudiation."

Nevertheless, in view of development of discussion leading to the conclusion that an employee is free to accept or reject such a breach[94] it would seem correct to say that a unilateral attempt to vary the contract will not operate as a termination. The employee who does not accept such a variation but who is permitted to continue working under protest will be working under all the terms of the old contract at least until the employer insists that he either accept the alternative offer or leaves his employment.

(b) Alternative offer as a statutory defence

Although the Redundancy Payments Act 1965 accepted the principle of the availability of compensation for loss of a job regardless of proof of actual economic loss arising from continuing absence of employment it also accepted that if the dismissing employer himself made alternative employment available such compensation should not be made. It is possible that this departure depends upon the somewhat confused situation introduced by contribution to the compensation from both the employer and central funds. Whatever the reason the establishment of a "defence" to a claim for redundancy compensation derived from the existence of a suitable alternative offer is clear. The provisions are now contained in the Employment Protection (Consolidation) Act 1978.[95]

> (3) If an employer makes and employee an offer (whether in writing or not) before the ending of his employment under the previous contract to renew his contract of employment, or to re-engage him under a new contract of employment, so that the renewal or re-engagement would take effect either immediately on the ending of his employment under the previous contract or after an interval of not more than four weeks thereafter, the provisions of subsections (5) and (6) shall have effect.[96]
> (5) If an employer makes an employee such an offer as is referred to in subsection (3) and either—

---

[94] *Supra*, p. 156. [95] ss.82(3), (5), (6), (7).
[96] This provision also applies to offers made by employers who have taken over the business (s.94(4)).

(*a*) the provisions of the contract as renewed, or of the new contract, as to the capacity and place in which he would be employed, and as to the other terms and conditions of his employment, would not differ from the corresponding provisions of the previous contract; or

(*b*) the first-mentioned provisions would differ (wholly or in part) from those corresponding provisions, but the offer constitutes an offer of suitable employment in relation to the employee;

and in either case the employee unreasonably refuses that offer, he shall not be entitled to a redundancy payment by reason of his dismissal.

(6) If an employee's contract of employment is renewed, or he is re-engaged under a new contract of employment, in pursuance of such an offer as is referred to in subsection (3), and the provisions of the contract as renewed, or of the new contract, as to the capacity and place in which he is employed, and as to the other terms and conditions of his employment, differ (wholly or in part) from the corresponding provisions of the previous contract but the employment is suitable in relation to the employee, and during the trial period referred to in section 84 the employee unreasonably terminates the contract, or unreasonably gives notice to terminate it and the contract is thereafter, in consequence, terminated, he shall not be entitled to a redundancy payment by reason of his dismissal from employment under the previous contract.

(7) Any reference in this section to re-engagement by the employer shall be construed as including a reference to re-engagement by the employer or by any associated employer, and any reference in this section to an offer made by the employer shall be construed as including a reference to an offer made by an associated employer.

Because of the rather haphazard effect upon acceptance of such an offer of common law concepts there was introduced in 1975 a statutory trial period.[97]

(3) If, in a case to which subsection (1) applies, the provisions of the contract as renewed, or of the new contract, as to the capacity and place in which the employee is employed, and as to the other terms and conditions of his employment, differ (wholly or in part) from the corresponding provisions of the previous contract, there shall be a trial period in relation to the contract as renewed, or the new contract (whether or not there has been a previous trial period under this section).

(4) The trial period shall begin with the ending of the employee's employment under the previous contract and end with the expiration of the period of four weeks beginning with the date on which the employee starts work under the contract as renewed, or the new contract, or such longer period as may be agreed in accordance with the next following subsection for the purpose of retraining the employee for employment under that contract.

(5) Any such agreement shall—

(*a*) be made between the employer and the employee or his representative before the employee starts work under the contract as renewed or, as the case may be, the new contract;

(*b*) be in writing;

(*c*) specify the date of the end of the trial period; and

(*d*) specify the terms and conditions of employment which will apply in the employee's case after the end of that period.

(6) If during the trial period—

---

[97] s.84(3)–(6).

(a) the employee, for whatever reason, terminates the contract, or gives notice
     to terminate it and the contract is thereafter, in consequence, terminated, or
(b) the employer, for a reason connected with or arising out of the change to the
     renewed, or new, employment, terminates the contract, or gives notice to
     terminate it and the contract is thereafter, in consequence, terminated.

then, unless the employee's contract of employment is again renewed, or he is
again re-engaged under a new contract of employment, in circumstances such that
subsection (1) again applies, he shall be treated as having been dismissed on the
date on which his employment under the previous contract or, if there has been
more than one trial period, the original contract ended for the reason for which he
was then dismissed or would have been dismissed had the offer (or original offer) of
renewed, or new, employment not been made, or, as the case may be, for the
reason which resulted in that offer being made.

It is obvious that apart from the technical, but important, variant of
"reorganisation" it is "redundancy" which is most likely to give rise to a radical
change of job without a change of employer. In the preceding pages it has been
suggested that where the employee agrees to such a change the common law
would conclude that the contract had been varied rather than terminated and
replaced by a new contract. The effect of this would be that there was no
"dismissal" and no statutory entitlement to a redundancy payment, dependent
as that is on the existence of such a dismissal. To have left the matter there,
however, would have been highly unsatisfactory. We have seen that the courts
are conscious of the pressures upon an employee in such situations. Had the
employee's right to redundancy payment depended upon common law distinction between variation and termination and renewal it is most likely that the
courts would have opted for the latter.

Suitable offer, unreasonable refusal

Professor Wallington[98] insists strongly on the need to keep separate the
concepts of suitable offer and unreasonable rejection. Certainly there is judicial
authority for this separation. In *Hindes* v. *Supersine Ltd.*[99] the major judicial
authorities for such distinction are considered.

"Under this subsection—as indeed, under a previous subsection—the first question that arises is, as to the suitability of the alternative employment. The second
question is whether or not the employee has unreasonably refused to carry out the
alternative employment. As to the way that this question should be approached,
Mrs. Gill referred us to two authorities; the first being *Carron Co.* v. *Robertson*.
That was a decision of the Court of Session and there are certain passages which
Mrs. Gill relied upon. There, the employee had worked as a pattern-maker in a
foundry, and when the foundry was closed he was dismissed; but he was offered
work in another foundry which he refused, because in the former foundry he had
had star status with benefits to be derived from it, whereas the new job did not
carry such status. The Lord President said:

'The peculiarity of the present case is that there are no findings in the case as to
the first of these conditions—namely, whether the offer constitutes an offer of
suitable employment in relation to Mr. Robertson. So far as the case shows,
the tribunal did not regard this condition as unsatisfied. And indeed it appears

---

98 Elias Napier and Wallington, p. 684.
99 [1979] I.C.R. 517 cited by Elias Napier and Wallington.

from the answers for Mr. Robertson that it was not maintained on his behalf before the tribunal that the offer was not suitable in relation to him. . . . It is just here that I find this case as stated to us to be difficult. The tribunal without regarding the offer as not suitable for this employee, have none the less held that his refusal of it was not unreasonable because of his loss of status and of benefits in comparison with his previous contract of employment. This seems to me to confuse the two quite separate conditions which section 2(4) provides as an answer to a claim for a redundancy payment. Suitability of employment is an objective matter, and includes questions of status and of sickness benefit, which if substantial enough could render the new employment unsuitable. This seems to me a separate issue from the reasonableness of the refusal which is intended in my view to relate to reasons personal to the employee which in fact induced him to refuse the change in his employment. The difficulty in the present case is that the decision of the tribunal on reasonableness is not based on any personal objections to the change, but on general considerations appropriate to the suitability of the new employment for this employee.'

From that dictum, therefore, which we would desire to follow, Mrs. Gill derives these requirements: first, that when considering "suitability" one must look at it in an objective way; secondly, when considering the question of reasonableness of a refusal then one must look at the personal reasons that relate to the employee. Her criticism of the way that the industrial tribunal directed their minds to the matters which we have read out and which can be seen in paragraph 7 of their reasons, is that they confused the two issues, and confused, on the question of suitability when dealing with the matter of pay, the employee's personal feelings about his being prepared to accept the differential of £10 had the job been otherwise suitable to him and had he liked the new job.

The other authority, which is of great assistance to us, is *Taylor* v. *Kent County Council.* It is a decision of the Queen's Bench Divisional Court, the leading judgment being given by Lord Parker C.J. Briefly, the facts concern the headmaster of a boys' school whose job came to an end when his school was amalgamated with a girls' school; he was not chosen as the headmaster of the new school and he was offered a post in the new school which he refused. The pay was the same but in all other respects the nature of the job differed. Lord Parker C.J. said:

'Let me say at once, suitability is almost entirely a matter of degree and fact for the tribunal, and not a matter with which this court would wish or could interfere, unless it was plain that they had misdirected themselves in some way in law, or had taken into consideration matters which were not relevant for the purpose. It is to be observed that so far as age was concerned, so far as qualifications were concerned, so far as experience was concerned, they negative the suitability of this offer, because he is going to be put into a position where he has to go where he is told at any time for short periods, to any place, and be put under a headmaster and assigned duties by him.'

In the next paragraph but one Lord Parker C.J. states the matter very plainly, and, if we may say so, with respect, very helpfully:

'But for my part I feel that the tribunal have here misdirected themselves in law as to the meaning of 'suitable employment.' I accept, of course, that suitable employment is as is said: suitable employment in relation to the employee in question. But it does seem to me that by the words 'suitable employment,' suitability means employment which is substantially equivalent to the employment which has ceased. Section 2 (3) which I read at the beginning is dealing with the case where the fundamental terms are the same, and then no offer in writing is needed, but when they differ, then it has to be put in writing and must be suitable. I for my part think that what is meant by 'suitable' in relation to the employee means conditions of employment which are reasonably equivalent to those under the previous employment, not the same, because then subsection (2) would apply, but it does not seem to me that by 'suitable employment' is meant employment of an entirely different nature, but in respect of which the salary is going to be the same.'

Therefore, there is stated there a clear way of looking at this: is the employment offered substantially equivalent to the employment which has ceased? It is plain that so far as pay is concerned the new job offered to the employee was not substantially equivalent to the job that had come to an end. Had the matter rested there, then quite clearly (as, indeed, the industrial tribunal rightly said) that would have been the end of the matter on the question of suitability, because the job offered to the employee would have been unsuitable.

Mrs. Gill, as we would understand her, would be seen to be saying that there ought not to have been taken into account the fact that, had he liked the new job, he would not have regarded the drop in pay as of importance. That is certainly a matter personal to him; but it would be our view that had the employee disregarded, without any conditions, the change in pay, then what would otherwise have been an unsuitable job, because of the drop in pay, could have been found to be suitable. But, it is plain from the facts of this case that the employee's preparedness to accept the drop in pay was conditional upon his liking the new job in all other respects. The facts also clearly show (because, from the words we have quoted, it is clear that the industrial tribunal accepted what the employee told them) that he did not like the new job and could not tolerate it for the reasons which he stated. Therefore, in those circumstances, the matter goes back to be considered on the question of suitability, namely, whether the drop in pay rendered the job unsuitable. The employee was only prepared to accept the drop in pay if he tolerated the job, and, as he did not tolerate the job, then he is not prepared to accept the drop in pay. In our view the industrial tribunal failed to look at this question in the way that they should have looked at it. It is not a matter of us expressing our view; we are saying that they have omitted to take into consideration that which should have been very much to the forefront of their consideration, namely, that the employee's acceptance of the job was conditional upon his being able to tolerate and like it in other respects. They therefore omitted to consider the vital matter of evidence and in that respect they are in error."

Though the consequences assigned by this judgment to the distinction are important it is suggested that the student may find it a counsel of perfection. The difficulty that arises in any two-stage test, where either stage operating independently can produce the same result but where different standards apply to the two stages, is to decide what matters to assign to each.[1] Both are regarded, as the above quotation reveals, as questions of fact[2] so that appellate courts are disinclined to interfere with the conclusion of an industrial tribunal. In consequence the student will find from time to time that some rather surprising

---

[1] We shall see in due course—p. 308, *infra*—that the Equal Pay Act adopts a standard of difference of "practical importance" to determine "like work" and a standard of "genuine . . . material difference" to avoid the effect of such a designation. The burden of proof of the one is on the applicant and of the other on the employer so that it must be necessary positively to assign certain considerations to one or the other. Yet "experience," for instance, whilst it may affect what the employee does is not itself part of what he does and might seem more logically considered as a material difference.

[2] See also *Williamson* v. *N.C.B.* (1970) I.T.R. 43.

conclusions as to what matters to consider under each head have passed unchallenged.[3] It is relatively easy to lay down some sort of rule such as:

> ". . . suitability should be taken to relate to the question whether or not the job as a job is suitable to the employee, bearing in mind his existing job, skills and forms of employment, whilst reasonableness concerns the question whether the particular employee, because of his personal circumstances, is justified in turning down what is prima facie suitable employment."

It is not so clear how one would decide by use of this rule to allocate the rejection of a job because the employee had a weak heart. Such distinction is obviously artificial. The question, however, is whether the distinction has significance. Although the question whether a job is suitable must be related to the individual employee[4] it may well be thought that *Hindes'* case is correct in saying that the enquiry as to suitability is objective. In this sense one may compare hours, wages, status and working conditions with those enjoyed in the previous job. "Reasonableness," however, can be regarded as a test to be applied to the personal reactions of the individual as they happen to be. At times, however, all this apparently significantly diverse approach will produce is the assignment of all subjective considerations to the second category. If, as *Hindes'* case says, suitability is confined to equating the terms of the old and new jobs then matters such as the stability of the new job will properly be considered as a question of reasonableness.[5]

It is suggested, however, that the lawyer need not worry too much about the correct classification. In practice the courts do not apply markedly objective considerations to the first or markedly subjective considerations to the second. In *Fuller* v. *Stephanie Bowman (Sales) Ltd.*[6] the alternative employment offered was in premises over a sex shop in Soho. The tribunal said that this could well be a reasonable objection in some circumstances. Individuals object to different things and many might have strong views about sex. Consequently the members of the tribunal viewed the premises and came to their own conclusions that there was nothing noticeably worse on this respect in the position of the premises than in any other site in the West End of London.

It is for the employer to prove the suitability of the offer and the unreasonableness of the refusal.[7] If no offer is made, for instance because the employer is informed, or assumes, that the employee would not be interested, then the fact that alternative employment would have been available cannot be advanced to exclude the redundancy payment.[8] The terms of the actual offer must be honoured. It is not possible to rely upon the argument that the alternative actually provided was a suitable job which it would be unreasonable to reject.[9]

---

[3] In *Johnston and Gunn* v. *St. Cuthberts Co-operative Association Ltd.* (1969) I.T.R. 137 the Court of Session affirmed as a finding of fact that an offer was suitable when it involved extra travelling time of almost two hours a day. It seems that the matter might have been better considered as one of reasonable refusal.

[4] *Executors of J. F. Everest* v. *Cox.* [1980] I.C.R. 415.

[5] *Thomas Wragg and Sons Ltd.* v. *Wood* [1976] I.C.R. 313.

[6] [1977] I.R.L.R. 7.

[7] *Jones* v. *Aston Cabinet Co. Ltd.* [1973] I.C.R. 292.

[8] *Simpson* v. *Dickinson* [1972] I.C.R. 474.

[9] *Eaton* v. *R.K.B. (Furmston) Ltd.* [1972] I.C.R. 273. The principles, if any, to be applied to a determination of the questions of reliability and unreasonableness are set out in Grunfeld, Chap. 7.

(c) The trial period

Statute provides for a standard four week trial period. The common law, as we have seen, also allows a trial period to any employee who makes this a condition of acceptance either expressly or by withholding final acceptance. The common law fixes no precise limit of time although in *Air Canada* v. *Lee*[10] the E.A.T. said that it could not last for ever but must be limited to a reasonable period in the circumstances. In this case it was accepted that the provision of the statutory trial period did not displace the common law provision. This point was developed in *Turvey* v. *C. W. Cheney and Son Ltd.*[11]; All the employees in question were accepted as having expressly or impliedly indicated that they would accept the alternative work on trial and all had worked in the new job for more than four weeks. Bristow J. said:

"It is clear law that where one party to a contract acts in such a way as to show he no longer intends to be bound, the other party can decide at his option whether or not to treat the contract as at an end. Moreover, he does not necessarily have to make up his mind at once but is entitled to a reasonable time in which to do so.

The application of this common law principle to contracts of employment is illustrated in *Shields Furniture Ltd.* v. *Goff*, where Brightman J. said that the mere fact that an employee started to work under the terms of a new contract offered him by the employer did not constitute an acceptance of the new contract so that he must be regarded as having made up his mind not to rely on the repudiation of the old contract. You have to see whether the employee is accepting the new contract by his conduct, or whether he is giving it a try to see whether he will accept it or not.

If, as in this case with the three employees, the employee says that he is giving it a trial, clearly he has not accepted the new contract simply by doing that. If having started by expressly giving it a trial he goes on working under the new terms without any more being said about it, the time will come when a reasonable time for making up his mind has expired, and he will be taken to have made a new contract or renewed the old one with variations, and he will no longer be able to . . . say: 'You dismissed me.' Each case will depend on its own facts, and it will be for the industrial tribunal to say whether or not, on the facts which it finds, a new contract has been made or the old contract has been renewed with variations. Since the answer must vary with the circumstances we will call the period which at common law the employee has to make up his mind period X. . . . [I]n the case of a dismissal in section 3(2)(a) or 3(2)(b) circumstances the employee, who has no common law protection producing period X in which he can make up his mind if he likes the new job, because no repudiation of the contract is involved, is given the section 3(5) trial period. By section 3(8), if he terminates his new or renewed contract, or gives notice to do so during the trial period and acts on the notice, or if the employer, for a reason connected with the change, does the same, the employee is treated as dismissed when the old contract came to an end or would have done had he not accepted the new job.

This is an improvement in the position of the employee who is dismissed under section 3(2)(a) or 3(2)(b) circumstances. It is also an improvement in the protection of the employee under section 3(2)(c) circumstances. He has a period X in which to make up his mind. If his decision is not to take the new job, he is treated as dismissed at the moment he brings period X to an end by leaving the new job. If his decision is to take the new job and he brings period X to an end by making a new contract or renewing the old one with variations, he then has the further trial

---

[10] [1978] I.R.L.R. 392.
[11] [1979] I.C.R. 341.

period created by section 3(5) in which to make up his mind before losing his right to say, 'You dismissed me by repudiating the old contract.' He is then in the section 3(3) situation. So he has his common law period X protection plus his statutory trial period protection."

Hepple and O'Higgins[12] suggest that it will be relatively rare in practice for an employee entitled to the statutory period also to specify for a common law period. The most likely application of this decision, therefore, is to cases where the statutory period would have been exhausted but where non-acceptance of the alternative can be implied.

It appears that the common law trial period if available will be applied first so that the statutory four week period operates on an employee entitled to a common law period after the end of that period, that is to say usually after acceptance by the employee of the new job.

As we have seen, the common law period is not available if what is offered is not a variation of contract but a termination followed by a new contract.[13] The statutory trial period can be extended beyond the normal four weeks but only by written agreement of the parties made before the start of the new job. The agreement must specify the date on which the trial period ends and the terms and conditions of employment which are thereafter to apply.

It is provided by section 84(1):

> 84.—(1) If an employee's contract of employment is renewed, or he is re-engaged under a new contract of employment in pursuance of an offer (whether in writing or not) made by his employer before the ending of his employment under the previous contract, and the renewal or re-engagement takes effect either immediately on the ending of that employment or after an interval of not more than four weeks thereafter, then, subject to subsections (3) to (6), the employee shall not be regarded as having been dismissed by his employer by reason of the ending of his employment under the previous contract.
>
> (2) For the purposes of the application of subsection (1) to a contract under which the employment ends on a Friday, Saturday or Sunday—
>
> (a) the renewal or re-engagement shall be treated as taking effect immediately on the ending of the employment if it takes effect on or before the Monday after that Friday, Saturday or Sunday, and
> (b) the interval of four weeks referred to in that subsection shall be calculated as if the employment had ended on that Monday.
>
> (3) If, in a case to which subsection (1) applies, the provisions of the contract as renewed, or of the new contract, as to the capacity and place in which the employee is employed, and as to the other terms and conditions of his employment, differ (wholly or in part) from the corresponding provisions of the previous contract, there shall be a trial period in relation to the contract as renewed, or the new contract (whether or not there has been a previous trial period under this section).

Accordingly, whenever an employee accepts an alternative offer whether suitable or not, made before his previous employment ends, there will be deemed to have been no dismissal and no claim for redundancy payment will arise. This situation also applies to offers made by employers who take over a business.[14]

---

[12] Para. 1–434/1.
[13] *Meek* v. *J. Allen Rubber Co. Ltd.* [1980] I.R.L.R. 21.
[14] Employment Protection (Consolidation) Act 1978, s.94(1) and (2).

PROCEDURE FOR DEALING WITH REDUNDANCY

Dismissal for redundancy must often be preceded by selection since it will not always be the case that every employee engaged in a particular job is surplus to requirement. We have already dealt[15] with the position in which such a selection may constitute an unfair dismissal. It should be borne in mind, however, that though the process of selection inevitably produces a secondary reason for dismissal the primary reason of redundancy may remain undisturbed and the secondary[16] reason may well provide a reasonable justification for the selection. There was an early suggestion in the judgment of the N.I.R.C. in *Sheet Metal Components Ltd.* v. *Plumridge*[17] that adoption by the employer of an unsuitable method of dealing with a redundancy situation will incline the court to permit a claim for compensation even if the statutory requirements for justifying such a claim are not precisely satisfied. The court said:

> "But sympathetic and understanding treatment is not enough. It should be coupled with a measure of formality which will concentrate the employees' minds upon the fact that they have to make an important decision. Thus they should be given formal notice of dismissal as far in advance as possible. If it is possible to offer them alternative employment, this should be the subject of a formal offer made at the same time . . . it is desirable that it should always be in writing. . . ."

The possibilities of this claim being founded on unfair dismissal have been markedly increased by the decision in *Williams* v. *Compair Maxam Ltd.*[18]

There has, for some time, been a considerable movement within the EEC to recommend special provisions for the method of dealing with collective dismissals. It is this movement which has, no doubt, inspired some relatively elementary proposals contained in the Employment Protection Act 1975 and which has led to further provisions relating to transfer of business.[19]

Consultation

These proposals centre upon two different requirements for notification and consultation. The first requires an employer to consult the authorised bargaining representatives of[20] an independent trade union recognised for the description of employees of which a potentially redundant employee is one. Recognition implies agreement.[21] If recognition is to be implied, the acts alleged to amount to recognition must be clear and unequivocal and involve a course of conduct or a period of time.[22] An isolated act which, of itself is clearly one of recognition, was treated in *Transport and General Workers Union* v. *Courtenham Products Ltd.*[23] as ineffective for that purpose since the employer

---

[15] *Supra*, pp. 247–250.
[16] See, *e.g. Cruickshank* v. *Hobbs* [1977] I.C.R. 725—E.A.T. by a majority. Compare *Forman Construction Ltd.* v. *Kelly* [1977] I.R.L.R. 468.
[17] [1974] I.C.R. 373.
[18] [1982] I.R.L.R. 83, *supra*, p. 213.
[19] Employment Protection (Consolidation) Act 1978, ss.99–107.
[20] *G.M.W.U.* v. *Wailes Dove Bitumastic Ltd.* [1977] I.R.L.R. 45.
[21] *National Union of Tailors and Garment Workers* v. *Charles Ingram & Co. Ltd.* [1977] I.C.R. 530.
[22] *National Union of Gold, Silver and Allied Trades* v. *Albury Bros.* [1979] I.C.R. 84 C.A.
[23] [1977] I.R.L.R. 8.

had not realised its general significance and the union had clearly not regarded it as indicating general recognition. In *T.G.W.U.* v. *Andrew Dyer*[24] the E.A.T. said that recognition should only be inferred from acts which were clear and unequivocal. It may be objected that it is very unlikely in practice that the employer would not so consult in the absence of a legislative duty and that it would be more important to require consultation in other cases. The difficulty, so far as this country is concerned, as against other EEC countries, is that there does not exist here any such machinery as compulsory Works Councils which would be available for consultation in the absence of recognised trade unions. Provision could, of course, be made to consult "worker representatives," *i.e.* ad hoc delegates. It is probably true to say that this was not made because of the current strength of feeling that trade union membership and, subsequently, recognition is best encouraged by granting certain rights to recognised unions only.

The consultation that is required must begin *at the earliest opportunity*[25] *and in any event* not later than 90 days before the first of a series of dismissals of 100 or more employees within a period of 90 days; or 30 days before the first of a series of 10 or more dismissals within a period of 30 days within one establishment.[26]

Though the reference is to a series, it is clear that the series must spring from one decision. The total redundancy from one of two separate decisions is not aggregated.[27] Each group is to be treated separately so that once consultation has begun for one group others are not to be added to it. Only if the employer can show the existence of special circumstances justifying non-consultation will he be able to avoid the consequences of a failure to consult within the required time.[28] There will be a breach of the statutory requirement even if, as a result of the consultations the termination date is brought forward so as to have the effect of reducing the consultative period below the minimum required.[29]

Information

The employer must disclose, in writing, to the representatives the reasons for the redundancy, the number it is proposed to dismiss and the number of employees of that description at the establishment in question, the proposed method of selection and the proposed method and period for carrying out the dismissals. It should be noted that he does not have to disclose the precise identity of those it is proposed to dismiss. The employer must consider the representations of the union and give reasons if he rejects any of them. If he

---

[24] [1977] I.R.L.R. 93.
[25] In *Union of Construction, Allied Trades and Technicians* v. *Ellison Carpentry Contractors Ltd.* [1976] I.R.L.R. 398 an industrial tribunal held that consultation becomes feasible as soon as it is clear that the next move will be a reduction of the workforce even if no definite proposals can yet be made. Ignorance of the obligation does not prevent compliance from being reasonably practicable. *UCATT* v. *H. Rooke and Son Ltd.* [1978] I.C.R. 818.
[26] These periods were amended by the Employment Protection (Handling of Redundancies) Variation Order 1979 (S.I. 1979 No. 958). On the meaning of establishment see *Barratt Developments (Bradford) Ltd.* v. *UCATT* [1978] I.C.R. 319.
[27] *T.G.W.U.* v. *Nationwide Haulage Ltd.* [1978] I.R.L.R. 143.
[28] As to what constitutes special circumstances see *Bakers Union* v. *Clarks of Hove* [1978] I.R.L.R. 366.
[29] *ASTMS* v. *Hawker Siddeley Aviation Ltd.* [1977] I.R.L.R. 418.

cannot reasonably practicably comply with any of the requirements as to consultation he must take such steps towards compliance as are reasonably practicable in the circumstances. Should he be challenged on this point it is for him to prove the reasonableness of his alternative steps. Discussion must conform with any agreed procedure.

A company or industry with its own adequate consultation scheme may seek exemption on the ground that it is at least as favourable.

There were a number of decisions holding that failure to consult in accordance with the statutory provisions constitutes a factor in unfair dimissal. In *Forman Construction Ltd.* v. *Kelly*[30] however, the Scottish division of the E.A.T. held that the statutory provisions constituted a separate procedure with its own penalty, and did not infer any right other than those specifically contained in it. This was affirmed in *Williams* v. *Compair Maxam Ltd.*[31] but it was pointed out that absence of consultation would tend towards an unfair procedure regardless of any statutory provision.

Protective award

A recognised trade union may present to an industrial tribunal a complaint of non-compliance with any of these requirements after the failure of conciliation. If the tribunal finds the complaint well founded it may[32] make a "protective award" under which every employee to whom the award relates is entitled to be paid remuneration by his employer of a week's pay for each week up to the limit of a 90-day of 30-day period according to the length of consultation due and 28 days in all other cases. This liability to pay remuneration will be reduced by any payment under the contract of employment or by way of damages for breach of that contract, and vice versa. It should be noted that compensation for unfair dismissal is not capable of being set off in this way. The actual length of the protective award in any situation is for the industrial tribunal to fix. In *Talke Fashions Ltd.* v. *Amalgamated Society of Textile Workers and Kindred Trades*[33]; the E.A.T held that the award should be commensurate with the loss suffered by the employee; the seriousness of the employer's default should not be considered. On the other hand there is no ground for saying that the original period can ever be longer than the specified statutory periods.[34] The entitlement ceases if a suitable alternative offer is made which is unreasonably rejected or which is accepted and later unreasonably terminated by the employee in respect of any period when, but for that rejection or termination, the employee would have been employed. An employee may complain to an industrial tribunal of non-observance of a protective award within three months of the last of the days to which the complaint relates.

Notification

The second type of obligation is one, in the same circumstances, but whether or not there are recognised unions, to notify the Secretary of State in writing of

---

[30] [1977] I.R.L.R. 468.

[31] *Supra.*

[32] The tribunal has the right to make no protective award—see, *e.g. ASTMS* v. *Hawker Siddeley Aviation Ltd. supra.*

[33] [1977] I.C.R. 833.

[34] *National Union of Teachers* v. *Avon County Council* [1978] I.C.R. 626.

dismissal proposals within 90 or 30 days and to give a copy of the notice to any recognised union. The Secretary of State may subsequently call for any further specified information. The sanction for failure to take this step is a reduction of the amount of the redundancy rebate by up to one-tenth or a fine, on summary conviction, not exceeding £400.

Consultation preceding a transfer of business

The elementary nature of the requirements for consultation preceding redundancy just considered is clearly revealed by the more advanced requirements contained even within the somewhat generalised requirements or the EEC Council Directive No. 77/187 upon transfer of employee's rights. In turn the way in which those requirements are enacted in the Transfer of Undertakings (Protection of Employment) Regulation 1981 reveals the reluctance of British thinking to comprehend more extensive obligations. The Regulations apply upon a transfer of business.[35]

Article 6 of the Directive requires both the transferor and the transferee employer to inform *the representatives of their respective employees affected by the transfer* in *good time* before the transfer is carried out and before the employees are directly affected as regards conditions of work of the reasons for the transfer,the *legal, economic and social implications* of the transfer for the employees and the measures envisaged in relation to the employees. Where such measures are envisaged the Directive requires the transferor or the transferee to consult his employee representatives in good time and *with a view to seeking agreement.* The U.K. Regulations[36] require the giving of information only to representatives of an independent recognised trade union and only "long enough" before the relevant transfer to enable consultations to take place. It is probably correct to say that this will be interpreted to mean that there must be time for effective consultations. It is clear that there need be no intention to agree since paragraph 6 (6) only requires the employer to consider and reply to any union representations stating his reasons for rejecting any of them. Even then a let-out clause is provided typical of similar United Kingdom legislation but such as would not be found in many other EEC member countries. It is provided[37] that if there are special circumstances which render it not reasonably practicable for an employer to perform the duties of informing and consulting he must take all such steps towards performing these duties as are reasonably practicable. If the same reasoning as to the application of this escape clause is applied as has been applied to that in section 99 of the Employment Protection Act 1975, then, as we have seen, an employer may postpone the giving of information in the hope of an improvement,[38] so long as he does not shut his eyes to the obvious,[39] until sudden disaster forces a transfer.[40] It will, however, be for the employer to prove the special circumstances.

It may be noted that in other respects the Regulations have followed and even slightly extended the Directive. The employer must inform the representa-

---

[35] *Supra*, p. 151.
[36] Para. 10.
[37] Para. 6 (7).
[38] *Hamish Armour* v. *ASTMS* [1979] I.R.L.R. 24.
[39] *APAC* v. *Kirvin Ltd.* [1978] I.R.L.R. 318.
[40] *Clarks of Hove Ltd.* v. *The Bakers' Union* [1978] I.C.R. 1076.

tives of approximately when the transfer is to take place and a transferee employer must inform the transferor employer of the measures the former proposes to apply to the employees he takes over. The restriction of the obligations to recognised unions is, however, very significant. There is no reason why the employer should not be required to inform and consult even ad hoc employee representatives. But this, like the obligation to consult with a view to agreement, would break new ground in the United Kingdom. The fact that it might be very beneficial to explore such new ground in this limited way may have to be forcibly brought home by EEC pressure to a legislature and civil service more interested in the political advantages of inertia.

The remedy for failure in either of these duties is, as might be expected, complaint to an industrial tribunal within three months of the date of completion of the transfer. If the complaint is made by the union involved the tribunal may declare the complaint to be well founded and order "compensation" not exceeding an amount equivalent to two weeks wages to be paid to any of the affected employees specified in the award. If the complaint is made by an individually affected employee the tribunal may only award him that compensation. Even this limited compensation goes towards discharging any liability of the employer for breach of contract in respect of any period falling within the protected period. It seems that it would not detract from the amount of a protective award. Appeal lies in a point of law to the E.A.T.

Special circumstances

If the employer wishes to establish a defence for failure to consult in time that it was not reasonably practicable for him to do so he must show:

(i) that there were special circumstances applicable to him;
(ii) that they did, in fact, render compliance not reasonably practicable; and,
(iii) that he took all such steps as were reasonably practicable to comply.

The Court of Appeal in *Clarks of Hove Ltd.* v. *The Bakers' Union*[41] defined special circumstances as "something out of the ordinary run of events, such as, for example, a general trading boycott." An insolvency is not on its own a special circumstance even if it is convenient for business purposes to conceal a gradual run-down until the last minute. On the other hand, the general reluctance to question management decisions suggests that this requirement may be less restrictive than it appears at first sight. In *Hamish Armour* v. *A.S.T.M.S.*[42] Lord McDonald, in the Scottish E.A.T., said that a tribunal should not seek to substitute its own business judgment for that of management in order to decide whether alleged hopes of recovery were sufficiently substantial to be justified. In that case uncertainty about the prospects of a continuing government loan were held to be a special circumstance. So was the uncertain state of a construction project in *A.S.B.S.B.S.W.* v. *George Wimpey (ME and C) Ltd.*[43] It is suggested that it is more realistic to say that uncertainty is usual[44] so that

---

[41] [1978] I.C.R. 1076.
[42] [1979] I.R.L.R. 24.
[43] [1977] I.R.L.R. 95.
[44] *G.M.W.U. (MATSA)* v. *British Uralite Ltd.* [1979] I.R.L.R. 409, I.T.

only an especial degree of uncertainty or unusual consequences of anticipating the outcome should excuse compliance with the consultation requirements.

AMOUNT OF REDUNDANCY PAYMENT

Payment is made in full by the employer but he is entitled in all cases to a 40 per cent. rebate from the central fund.[45] In *Hulland Gravel Co. Ltd.* v. *Secretary of State for Employment and Productivity*[46] no claim was made because the employees relied on the assurance of the employer that they would be paid. He eventually paid more than six months after the relevant date. The employer was held entitled to a rebate either on the ground that he was estopped from denying his current liability to pay or because the words "is liable and has paid" could be read as "having been liable and has paid." So far as the employer's loss is concerned this problem is dealt with by conferring on the Secretary of State power to pay the rebate where he thinks it would be just and equitable notwithstanding the absence of a requirement.[47] The employer will have a right to appeal to an industrial tribunal from the Secretary of State's refusal.[48]

The central fund is built up from a weekly contribution from the employer in respect of each employed person covered by the scheme. The contribution is collected as an addition to the weekly Social Security payment. Payment from the fund directly to the claimant may be made if the claimant has taken all reasonable steps, other than legal proceedings, and the employer has failed or refused to pay the whole or part of the amount due, or if the employer is insolvent and the whole or part of the amount remains unpaid.[49] In such cases, the Secretary of State for Employment whose Department administers the fund, is subrogated to the employee's rights[50] and may, in certain cases, withhold the rebate.

The amount of the total payment is based on the period of continuous employment. The scale of payment is half a week's pay for each year of employment between the ages of 18 and 21; one week's pay for each year of employment between the ages of 22 and 40, and one and a half weeks' pay for each year of employment from the age of 41. This is subject to a maximum of 20 years countable employment and to a maximum week's pay of £135. Thus a man of 61 or more who had worked with the same firm for the past 20 years or more and who was then earning £135 or more before he left, would be entitled to the maximum payment of £4,050.[51] Remembering that, in practice, there will be little examination of the details of these years of work to see whether they were continuous, few problems will be raised at this stage. The calculation which causes most difficulty is that of the week's pay which is to form the basic unit of calculation.

---

[45] An employer should generally claim this 14 days before the date of dismissal. See s.104(7), Employment Protection (Consolidation) Act 1978 for the effect of failure to do so. The rebate is calculated according to the provisions of Sched. 6.

[46] [1969] I.T.R. 110. But see, to the contrary, *Tucker* v. *Secretary of State*, 312/88 (1975).

[47] Employment Protection (Consolidation) Act 1978, s.104(3).

[48] *Ibid*. s.108(4).

[49] *Ibid*. s.106.

[50] *Ibid*. s.106(3).

[51] *Ibid*. Sched. 4.

Calculation of a week's pay

Normally, where a worker is employed on a fixed rate, the week that is taken is the last one in which he is employed. The normal rate of pay will be adopted. Where there are a fixed number of hours in a working week or other period, that fixed number constitutes the "normal working hours" even if some of these fixed hours are treated as overtime.[52] On the other hand, in the absence of a specified minimum number, the fact that overtime is paid after a given number of hours has been worked may imply that that given number is the fixed number.[53] Overtime hours over and above a basic working week are only counted if it is obligatory upon the employer to provide the hours and upon the employee to work them and that obligation is contractual.[53a] If the employee's remuneration in normal working hours does not vary with the amount of work done then the week's pay will be the amount due if the employee works throughout the normal week. In cases where remuneration does vary, the amount of a week's pay will be the average hourly rate over the period of 12 weeks preceding the calculation date, multiplied by the number of normal working hours in the week. If there are no normal hours or the rate of remuneration varies according to the time at which the work is done similar provision is made for determining an average.[54]

The effect of this provision is to concentrate attention on the contract, rather than the period actually worked. If work is, for instance, running down, unless the contract has been consensually varied,[55] the calculation will be unaffected. Even where an employee regularly works less than the number of hours specified in the contract, calculation is based on the contractual hours.[56]

"Remuneration"

All regular payment will be taken into account. So a regularly paid bonus, even if not strictly contractual, will be included.[57] A pay rise awarded after the date of dismissal but payable retrospectively to a date before the dismissal will be taken into account and a fresh claim entertained if necessary.[58] On the other hand provision is only made for "remuneration." Accordingly such benefits as free accommodation will not be given a weekly monetary value unless the contract so quantifies them.[59] A service charge paid by customers to management and subsequently divided among the staff has been held to be part of remuneration.[60] This situation is distinguishable from one in which tips are paid

---

52 *Ibid.* Sched. 14, paras. 1 and 2.
53 *Fox* v. *C. Wright (Farmers) Ltd.* [1978] I.C.R. 98.
53a *Tarmac Roadstone Holdings Ltd.* v. *Peacock* [1973] I.C.R. 273; followed in *Lotus Cars Ltd.* v. *Sutcliffe and Stratton* [1982] I.R.L.R. 381.
54 Employment Protection (Consolidation) Act 1978, Sched. 14, paras. 4–6.
55 *Saxton* v. *National Coal Board* (1970) 8 K.I.R. 893, *Basted* v. *Pell Footwear* [1978] I.R.L.R. 117.
56 *Truelove* v. *Mathew Hall Mechanical Services Ltd.* [1978] I.T.R. 65; *Saxton* v. *National Coal Board, supra; Allied Ironfounders Ltd.* v. *Macken* [1971] I.T.R. 109; *Mole Mining Ltd.* v. *Jenkins* [1972] I.C.R. 282.
57 *A. and B. Marcusfield Ltd.* v. *Melhuish* [1977] I.R.L.R. 484.
58 *Carron* v. *Pullman Spring-Filled Co. Ltd.* [1967] I.T.R. 650.
59 *Lyford* v. *Turquand* [1966] I.T.R. 544.
60 *Tsoukka* v. *Potomac Restaurants Ltd.* [1968] I.T.R. 259.

by the customer directly to the employee, since that is not remuneration from the employer.[61] Commission is also included.[62]

Considerable conflict centred on the question of inclusion of payment expressed as expenses.[63] This appears finally to have been resolved by the decision of the N.I.R.C. in *S. and U. Stores Ltd.* v. *Wilkes*[64] that the amount of any item expressed as a form of expenses such as car or accommodation allowance should only be taken into account to the extent that it represented, by an ordinary common sense approach, a profit over actual expenses.

The matter of overtime premiums is similarly referable to the contractual provision. It is clear that if the contract specifies a number, or minimum number, of hours, some of which are paid as overtime, then all the specified hours will be counted. The "extra" hours are part of the fixed week.[65] The same is true if the contract does not specify a number of hours but overtime working is contractually obligatory for both parties, *i.e.* the employer is bound to provide overtime and the employee is bound to work it.[66] Such an obligation cannot exist, however, by implication if it would have the effect of overriding an express contractual number of hours.[67] The effect is, therefore, that if a contract contains a fixed basic number of hours that constitutes the normal working hours and no additional hours can be counted even though contractually obligatory on both sides.[68] The weekly amount shall not exceed £135,[69] subject to power in the Secretary of State to vary this limit. All calculations are based on gross pay.[69a]

The amount of redundancy payment is reduced by one-twelfth for each month of a year after the employee has reached the age of 64, or 59 in the case of a woman.[70]

The Secretary of State has power by regulation to exclude, or reduce the amount of, a redundancy payment in prescribed cases in which the employee has a right or claim (whether legally enforceable or not) to a periodical payment or lump sum by way of pension gratuity or superannuation allowance payable by reference to his employment by a particular employer from the time he leaves that employment or within such period as may be prescribed.[71]

On making a redundancy payment, otherwise than in pursuance of a tribunal decision which itself specifies the amount, the employer must give the employee a written statement indicating how the amount has been calculated. Failure to comply is an offence punishable by fine.[72]

---

[61] *Wrottesley* v. *Regent Street Florida Restaurant* [1951] 2 K.B. 277 at 283.
[62] *Weersmay Ltd.* v. *King* [1977] I.C.R. 244. As to the method of calculation see *Bickley (J. and S.) Ltd.* v. *Washer* [1977] I.C.R. 425.
[63] See, *e.g. S. and U. Stores Ltd.* v. *Lee* [1969] I.T.R. 227; *N. G. Bailey and Co. Ltd.* v. *Preddy* [1971] 1 W.L.R. 796; *Barclay* v. *Richard Crittal (Electrical)* [1978] I.T.R. 173.
[64] [1974] I.C.R. 645.
[65] *Saxton* v. *National Coal Board, supra.*
[66] *Tarmac Roadstone Holdings Ltd.* v. *Peacock* [1973] I.T.R. 273.
[67] *Gascol Conversions Ltd.* v. *Mercer* [1974] I.C.R. 420.
[68] *Pearson* v. *William Jones Ltd.* [1967] 1 W.L.R. 1140; *The Darlington Forge Ltd.* v. *Sutton* [1968] I.T.R. 196.
[69] Employment Protection (Consolidation) Act 1978, Sched. 14, para. 8(1)(c) as varied.
[69a] *Secretary of State* v. *John Woodrow and Sons (Builders) Ltd.* [1983] I.R.L.R. 11,
[70] *Ibid.* Sched. 4, para. 4.
[71] *Ibid.* s.98(1).
[72] *Ibid.* s.102.

CHAPTER 7

DISCRIMINATION IN EMPLOYMENT

IT is generally regarded as beyond dispute that two principal areas of discrimination—sex and race—have had a profound effect on employment practices.[1] It is commonly accepted that a higher proportion of women than of men occupy lower paid jobs and that coloured workers have less chance of succeeding in a job application than white workers of equal ability. Coloured workers are relatively rarely promoted as foremen and women have less opportunity of securing appointments in senior management.

The Sex Disqualification (Removal) Act 1919 removed most of the legal restrictions on the appointment of women to public offices or the professions but did nothing to assist them to obtain such appointments nor to prevent discrimination in practice. The sanctity of freedom of contract ensured that employers remained free to engage, promote and dismiss on any basis they chose. Undoubtedly the decision of the Court of Appeal in *Nagle* v. *Feilden*[2] revealed a disapproval of arbitrary discrimination which had not been apparent in *Weinberger* v. *Inglis*[3] but it would be too much, even now, to have expected the common law to provide any effective disincentive to practices so endemic as those of sex and race discrimination. The entrenchment of such practices is not always the fault of those who are responsible for them. Few women earn night shift bonus because it is assumed by both men and women that it is women who should be at home when the children are there. If racial minorities are concentrated in inner city areas the selection policies of a factory on the outskirts of a city are very likely to discriminate against them. It may not be enough to eliminate "unjustified" discrimination because the very circumstances of society provide a "justification." A smaller proportion of women than men, for instance, will have 20 years' experience in a particular job. The employer who asserts that it is an advantage to have such experience may be right but he may have to forego that advantage unless it is significant or even essential. If he can be forced to forego it at the instigation of the less experienced woman she gains a positive advantage over the corresponding less experienced man.

THE EQUAL PAY ACT

The concept of equality

Much discrimination can be concealed behind some other reason. One of the areas where such concealment is most likely to be effective is that of unequal pay for equal work. Davies and Freedland[4] quote evidence which shows that

---

[1] See, *e.g.* Hepple, *Racial Discrimination in Great Britain* (2nd ed.); McIntosh and Smith, *The Extent of Racial Discrimination* (PEP 1974); Lester and Bindman, *Race and Law; Racial Discrimination* Cmnd. 6234 (1975); Phelps Brown, *The Inequality of Pay*.

[2] [1966] 2 Q.B. 633.

[3] [1919] A.C. 606.

[4] At p. 406.

women engaged on like work with men in some agricultural occupations are habitually less productive. They state, however, that the existence of such evidence is relatively rare and that most arguments as to relative value are based on assumptions lacking any factual support. It may be that the employer does not make these assumptions or even consciously know that they exist but instead responds to assumptions of what men in the same employment will tolerate in the way of sex equality. In other words, a practice may develop based on no sound reason and subsequently perpetuate itself simply because it exists. Even a response to the demands of the labour market may, therefore, be discriminatory because the practices of that market are discriminatory.

The EEC Treaty[5] provides that:

"Each member state shall during the first stage ensure and subsequently maintain the application of the principle that men and women should receive equal pay for equal work. For the purpose of the article, 'pay' means the ordinary basic or minimum wage or salary and any other consideration, whether in cash or in kind, which the worker receives, directly or indirectly, in respect of his employment from his employer. Equal pay without discrimination based on sex means: (a) that pay for the same work at piece rates shall be calculated on the basis of the same unit of measurement; (b) that pay for work at time rates shall be the same for the same job."

In *Defrenne* (*No.* 3)[6] the European Court held that this only applied to pay and not, as the Equal Pay Act, to other terms and conditions of employment.[7]

This concept was extended to provide for equal pay for work of equal value by a Council Directive of February 10, 1975[8] which stated:

"The principle of equal pay for men and women outlined in article 119 of the Treaty . . . means, for the same work or for work to which equal value is attributed, the elimination of all discrimination on grounds of sex with regard to all aspects and conditions of remuneration, in particular, where a job classification system is used for determining pay it must be based on the same criteria for both men and women and so drawn up as to exclude any discrimination on grounds of sex."

The concept of equal pay for work of equal value is also adopted in Convention No. 100 of the I.L.O. Nevertheless the United Kingdom in the Equal Pay Act 1970[9] adopted a compromise. It is provided that every contract of employment shall be deemed to contain an equality clause which will automatically modify any term of a contract of employment less favourable to a member of one sex than to a member of another, but only if both are employed (normally in the same establishment) on "like work" or "work rated as equivalent." The full provision reads:

(1) If the terms of a contract under which a woman is employed at an establishment in Great Britain do not include (directly or by reference to a collective agreement or otherwise) an equality clause they shall be deemed to include one.
(2) An equality clause is a provision which relates to terms (whether concerned

---

[5] Art. 119.
[6] [1978] E.C.R. 1365.
[7] *Burton* v. *British Railways Board* [1982] I.R.L.R. 116.
[8] Dir. 75/117.
[9] The Act came into force, as amended, in 1975.

with pay or not) of a contract under which a woman is employed (the 'woman's contract'), and has the effect that—

(a) where the woman is employed on like work with a man in the same employment—

(i) if (apart from the equality clause) any term of the woman's contract is or becomes less favourable to the woman than a term of a similar kind in the contract under which that man is employed, that term of the woman's contract shall be treated as so modified as not to be less favourable, and

(ii) if (apart from the equality clause) at any time the woman's contract does not include a term corresponding to a term benefiting the man included in the contract under which he is employed, the woman's contract shall be treated as including such a term;

(b) where the woman is employed on work rated as equivalent with that of a man in the same employment—

(i) if (apart from the equality clause) any term of the woman's contract determined by the rating of the work is or becomes less favourable to the woman than a term of a similar kind in the contract under which that man is employed, that term of the woman's contract shall be treated as so modified as not to be less favourable, and

(ii) if (apart from the equality clause) at any time the woman's contract does not include a term corresponding to a term benefiting that man included in the contract under which he is employed and determined by the rating of the work, the woman's contract shall be treated as including such a term.

(3) An equality clause shall not operate in relation to a variation between the woman's contract and the man's contract if the employer proves that the variation is genuinely due to a material difference (other than the difference of sex) between her case and his.

(4) A woman is to be regarded as employed on like work with men if, but only if, her work and theirs is of the same or a broadly similar nature, and the differences (if any) between the things she does and the things they do are not of practical importance in relation to terms and conditions of employment; and accordingly in comparing her work with theirs regard shall be had to the frequency or otherwise with which any such differences occur in practice as well as to the nature and extent of the differences.

The comparison under this Act is limited to those in the employment of the same, or an associated, employer either at the same establishment or, if different establishments, those at which common terms and conditions are observed in respect of the relevant class of employee.[10] Neither under Article 119 nor the Equal Pay Act is it possible to seek equalisation by comparison with the general industrial position. It is necessary to find a comparable worker of the other sex.[11] On the other hand the European Court has ruled that comparison may be made under Article 119 with a former employee, for instance, one replaced by a member of the other sex. It is for the applicant to choose the comparator and it is not open to the tribunal to substitute one it considers more appropriate.[12]

---

[10] See *Navy Army and Air Force Institutes* v. *Varley* [1977] I.C.R. 11; *Rice* v. *The Scottish Legal Life Assurance Society* [1976] I.R.L.R. 330 (I.T.).

[11] *Macarthys Ltd.* v. *Smith* [1981] Q.B. 180.

[12] *Ainsworth* v. *Glass Tubes and Components Ltd.* [1977] I.C.R. 347.

The Act seeks equality of conditions, not necessarily equal results,[13] but it is clear that it does not intend comparison of the pros and cons of a package of conditions to determine favourability. Each term is to be compared with its counterpart in the contract of the comparator.[14] Non-contractual conditions cannot be thus equalised. It follows that no comparison can be made if a beneficial term can have no operative contractual counterpart. In *Dugdale* v. *Kraft Foods Ltd.*[15] the E.A.T., having decided that the equivalence of work was not affected by the time at which it was done, indicated that there could be no objection to a provision in a man's contract for a night shift premium if such provision was not matched in a woman's contract because she did not work the night shift.

Like work

It is submitted that the definition of "like work" in subsection (4) of section 1 makes it quite clear that the enquiry should seek a broadly defined similarity. Initially industrial tribunals tended to look for a more or less precise equivalence.[16] This tendency was, however, reversed by two decisions of fundamental importance. *Capper Pass Ltd.* v. *Lawton*[17] was the first appeal under the Act to come before the E.A.T. Phillips J. said:

> "It is obviously difficult, in an Act intended to prevent discrimination between men and women in terms and conditions of employment to define the test which is to be applied in determining whether discrimination exists. It is easy to talk in general terms but very hard to lay down a clear test which can be applied satisfactorily in practice. One can see that it would be possible to prescribe tests of varying degrees of severity. The least favourable from a woman's point of view would be to require equality of treatment when men and women are doing the *same work*. More favourable would be to require equality where the work done by the man and woman, although different, was of *equal value*. The Act has chosen a middle course. Equality of treatment is required where the woman is employed on 'like work' with the man. And 'like work' is work which is of the *same* nature as, or of a broadly *similar* nature to, the man's work.
>
> In cases of dispute this test, imposed by section 1(4), requires the industrial tribunal to make a comparison between the work done by the woman and the work done by the man. It is clear from the terms of the subsection that the work need not be of the *same* nature in order to be like work. It is enough if it is of a similar nature. Indeed, it need only be broadly similar. In such cases where the work is of a broadly similar nature (and not of the *same* nature) there will necessarily be differences between the work done by the woman and the work done by the man. It seems clear to us that the definition requires the industrial tribunal to bring to the solution of the question, whether work is of a broadly similar nature, a broad judgment. Because, in such cases, there will be such differences of one sort or another it would be possible in almost every case, by too pedantic an approach, to say that the work was not of a like nature despite the similarity of what was done and the similar kinds of skill and knowledge required to do it. That would be wrong. The intention, we think, is clearly that the industrial tribunal should not be required to undertake too

---

[13] *Pointon* v. *University of Sussex* [1974] I.R.L.R. 119 (C.A.).
[14] See the industrial tribunal decision in *Atkinson* v. *Tress Engineering Co. Ltd.* [1976] I.R.L.R. 245.
[15] [1977] I.C.R. 48.
[16] See, *e.g.* *Brodie* v. *Startrite Engineering Co. Ltd.* [1976] I.R.L.R. 101.
[17] *Capper Pass Ltd.* v. *Lawton* [1977] I.C.R. 83 (E.A.T.).

minute an examination, or be constrained to find that work is not like work merely because of insubstantial differences.

It seems to us that in most cases the inquiry will fall into two stages. *First,* is the work of the same, or, if not, 'of a broadly similar' nature? This question can be answered by a general consideration of the type of work involved, and of the skill and knowledge required to do it. It seems to us to be implicit in the words of subsection (4) that it can be answered without a minute examination of the detail of the differences between the work done by the man and the work done by the woman. But, *secondly,* if on such an examination the answer is that the work is of a broadly similar nature, it is then necessary to go on to consider the detail and to inquire whether the differences between the work being compared are of 'practical importance in relation to terms and conditions of employment.' In answering that question the industrial tribunal will be guided by the concluding words of the subsection. But again, it seems to us, trivial differences, or differences not likely in the real world to be reflected in the terms and conditions of employment, ought to be disregarded. In other words, once it is determined that work is of a broadly similar nature it should be regarded as being like work unless the differences are plainly of a kind which the industrial tribunal in its experience would expect to find reflected in the terms and conditions of employment. This last point requires to be emphasised. There seems to be a tendency, apparent in some of the decisions of industrial tribunals cited to us, and in some of the arguments upon the hearing of this appeal, to weigh up the differences by reference to such questions as whether one type of work or another is or is not suitable for women, or is the kind of work which women can do, or whether the differences are important, and so on. These are not the tests prescribed by the Act. The only differences which will prevent work which is of a broadly similar nature from being 'like work' are differences which in practice will be reflected in the terms and conditions of employment."

The court chose to apply this standard strongly to uphold a finding of like work between a female cook in the directors' kitchen and two male assistant cooks in the works canteen. The directors' cook prepared 10 to 20 meals a day. The assistant chefs prepared some 350 meals in six sittings.

Broad similarity

The first stage of the enquiry seeking to establish broad job similarity without detailed examination relies primarily on the contractual description of the employment.[18] The second stage seeks what is actually done by the employee and not what the contract provides may be required.[19] In *Dugdale* v. *Kraft Foods Ltd.*[20] the E.A.T. considered a claim by female quality control inspectors to have their pay equated with that of male quality control inspectors. The women worked on either of two day shifts whilst the men could be required to work a night shift and might also voluntarily work on Sundays. All received the same basic rate of pay but the men received a higher shift premium for night work and overtime for Sunday work. Phillips J. said:

"It appears to us to be necessary to decide, as a matter of the construction of section 1(4), whether the first of these matters, *i.e.* the fact of doing work at a different time, falls within the words 'the things she does and the things they do.'

---

[18] *Dorothy Perkins Ltd.* v. *Dance* [1977] I.R.L.R. 226.
[19] In *Redland Roof Tiles* v. *Harper* [1977] I.C.R. 349, however, it was said that it might be relevant to look at the contract.
[20] [1977] I.C.R. 48.

To simplify the question by an example: take a factory in which a simple repetitive process of assembly takes place, employing men and women engaged upon identical work. Suppose that the men did, but the women did not, work at night and on a Sunday morning doing the same work. Undoubtedly, the women's work and the men's work would be of the same or a broadly similar nature. Prima facie, therefore, they would be employed on 'like work.' Does the fact that the men work at night and on Sunday morning, and the women do not, constitute a difference between the things which the women do and the things which the men do? It may be that either view is possible. A man, if asked what he does, might reply, 'I assemble radio components,' or he might reply, 'I assemble radio components on the night shift.' We have come to the conclusion that, in the context of the Equal Pay Act 1970 (as amended), the mere time at which the work is performed should be disregarded when considering the differences between the things which the woman does and the things which the man does. Were it not so, the Act could never apply in cases where it must obviously have been intended to apply, where the men doing the same work are engaged on a night shift.

Some support for this view is to be obtained from the judgments of the Court of Appeal in *Johnson* v. *Nottinghamshire Combined Police Authority*. That was the case of a claim for a redundancy payment. Women clerks were dismissed because they were, for good reason, unwilling to change from ordinary day work to an alternating shift system. The work which they had done was substantially the same as the work which was done by their replacements. The only difference was in the hours worked. In order to succeed it had to be established that the requirement of the employers for employees to carry out work of a particular kind had diminished. The Court of Appeal held that the change in the hours of working, without any change in the tasks performed, did not effect a change in the particular kind of work. Certainly, that case is not directly applicable, and it is true that it depends in part on the reference in section 1 of the Redundancy Payments Act 1965 to the place of employment. But it seems to us to be generally in line with our thinking on the subject. In short, in our judgment, in applying section 1(4) no attention should be paid to the fact that the men work at some different time of day, if that is the only difference between what the women do and they do."

Differences of practical importance

The subsection requires that the differences in what is actually done should be differences of practical importance. In *British Leyland Ltd.* v. *Powell*[21] it was suggested that it might be useful to ask whether the difference would affect a job evaluation. It is suggested, however, that the standard in *Capper Pass*[22] of whether differences could reasonably be expected to be reflected in different conditions of employment is both logical and workable. The type of consideration to be applied to a determination of the importance of differences is demonstrated in the following extract from the judgment in *Electrolux Ltd.* v. *Hutchinson.*[23]

"Accordingly, in our judgment, the important questions on this part of the case are: what happens in practice? How frequently are men required, in performance of the contractual obligation, to do other work? How often are they required to work on the night shift? How often are they required to work on a Sunday? On the occasions when they are required to transfer, or to work at inconvenient times or

[21] [1978] I.R.L.R. 57.
[22] [1977] I.C.R. 83.
[23] [1977] I.C.R. 252.

unsocial hours, what kind of work do they do? To what extent is it different from the work which they do during the day alongside the women? The industrial tribunal said that it was unable from the evidence given to answer these questions. Mr. Grabiner criticises this view, and says that there is to be found in the notes of evidence, and the exhibits to which the industrial tribunal did not refer, plenty of evidence, and that a witness, Mr. Froggatt, who was prepared to explain some of the exhibits, and to produce other documents, was discouraged from doing so. We cannot agree that there was plenty of evidence. If our view of the law, following the cases mentioned above, is correct, it is essential to have a reasonably accurate knowledge of how often the men work otherwise than alongside the women in performance of their contractual obligation, and what it is that they do on these occasions. We asked Mr. Grabiner to summarise the evidence which he said was not understood, or was not received, and putting it at its highest it did not seem to us to amount to a clear statement along those lines sufficient for the purpose. There is only an appeal to us on a point of law. But it was difficult to stop the applicants appearing in person from telling us something of what went on in practice: for example, no man is ever directly recruited to grade 01. The grade used is always 10. Also, there are difficulties (referred to later) in the way of women transferring to grade 10. We did not take this into account in any sense as justifying the decision of the industrial tribunal, which must stand or fall on its findings upon the basis of the evidence given to it. But we were left with the confident view that were these particular questions, which we regard as important, to be examined with complete evidence there would be a good deal to say on both sides. For present purposes, it is sufficient to say that we cannot find in the industrial tribunal's decision, or in the notes of evidence, any sure foundation on which we could come to the conclusion that the work done by the men in performance of their contractual obligation—and to which the women were not subject—would justify the conclusion, contrary to the view of the industrial tribunal, that there were here differences of practical importance in relation to terms and conditions of employment."

The decisions in *Capper Pass* and in *Dugdale* were obviously dictated by the policy of releasing the Act from the stranglehold of rigid (not to say, incorrect) interpretations so that its basic principles might be effectively applied. In *Shields* v. *E. Coomes (Holdings) Ltd.*[24] both Orr and Bridge L.JJ. said that this Act should be read together with the Sex Discrimination Act as part of a single legislative code of sex equality. It is important to bear this in mind throughout the application of the Act and particularly so in the approach to section 1(4) where the lawyer's natural tendency to formulate sub-rules to control major rules must be resisted. In *Shield's* case the Court of Appeal declined to regard the alleged security function of the male employees as a difference of practical importance because little or nothing was actually done by the men which was not done by the women. In part this conclusion was fortified by the consideration that there was no evidence that women as a class would have been less able than men as a class to respond if such a function was required.

The nature of the job

It is submitted that the requirement that the differences in work should be in what is done and also be of practical importance must be reasonably strictly adhered to. If they are not there would be a danger (which, as we shall see, exists when considering the defence of genuine material difference in subsection

---

[24] [1978] I.C.R. 1159.

(3)) of admitting common practice as an excuse for inequality. It is, for instance, common practice to pay a night shift premium. A considerably higher proportion of men than of women work night shifts and so benefit. In *Dugdale* scope was found to permit this difference in the fact that the Act only extends to comparing similar terms. So it was said that whilst basic rates could be equated a night shift premium had no similar provision in the contract of a day worker. If one is to apply such a restriction, however, there ought to be a means of containing it within the legislative principle. In other words such a difference is permissible so long as it reflects the value of the readiness to work the night shift and not a concealed form of discrimination. In *National Coal Board* v. *Sherwin*, [25] therefore, the E.A.T. picked up the point made by Phillips J. in *Dugdale* that the process of modifying the contractual terms to meet the equality clause may go so far as to render any difference not less favourable. In *Sherwin's* case this was taken to allow an increase in day rates to level off the night shift premium to 20 per cent. which the court considered reasonable in the light of common practice. Strictly speaking this would be to allow the comparison of different terms since without such consideration the night shift premium could not be brought into account. The point to make, therefore, is that even this rule of comparing like with like may be modified to avoid results obviously not in keeping the the principle of equality.

The decision in *Dugdale* might have been reached by regarding nightshift working as a "genuine material difference" within subsection (3). That approach will usually be necessary to deal with differences commonly reflected in comparable, rather than distinct, terms and conditions, such as experience. In many ways this is the more satisfactory approach since use of concepts such as "genuine" and "material" not only indicate the correctness of the view expressed in *Shields* v. *Coomes* but in turn permit the courts the latitude within which to apply the wider principles of equality. The choice between the application of the initial tests in subsection (4) and the defence in subsection (3) may seem to the student at times to be somewhat random and even misjudged. [26] There is, for instance, no real reason why the existence of greater responsibility should be assigned to one or the other. It can, as in *Waddington* v. *Leicester Council for Voluntary Services* [27] be translated into a factor giving rise to supervisory duties which affect what is done so as to fall within subsection (4). The important thing is to ensure that the choice of subsection does not produce different results. What is suggested here is that subsection (3) is more open to the application of discretion than subsection (4). This may have the advantage of allowing more scope to pursue the policy of the Act but equally give rise to more danger of influence by the adoption of common practice as a reasonable standard.

In *Maidment* v. *Cooper and Co.* (*Birmingham*) *Ltd.* [28] it was held not permissible to ignore some aspect of work because it is being separately remunerated unless that aspect constitutes a separate distinct job. In that case the male packer performed some extra work as a storekeeper. He was paid a

[25] [1978] I.C.R. 700.
[26] See, *e.g. Eaton Ltd.* v. *Nuttal* [1977] I.C.R. 272.
[27] [1977] I.C.R. 266. See also *Edmonds* v. *Computer Services* (*South West*) *Ltd.* [1977] I.R.L.R. 359.
[28] [1978] I.C.R. 1094.

supplement for this but, additionally, he received a higher rate of basic pay which the industrial tribunal had regarded as unjustified. The E.A.T. pointed out that unless there is like work (or equally rated work) no comparison can be made under the Act however unjustified a differential may otherwise appear.

Job evaluation

The Equal Pay Act provides for an alternative standard of equality from like work in "work rated as equivalent." The E.A.T. has established that this requires the existence of a properly conducted job evaluation. In *Eaton Ltd.* v. *Nuttall*[29] a valid evaluation was said to be one which was thorough and capable of impartial application not allowing management to make a subjective decision. Once there has been a valid job evaluation, it can be used as the standard even if neither employers nor unions are satisfied with the result.[30] The House of Lords confirmed this in *O'Brien* v. *Sim-Chem Ltd.*,[31] reasoning that the job evaluation activated the equality clause. It seems clear, however, that a scheme can be effectively discarded. Although this decision establishes that implementation is unnecessary the E.A.T. held in *Arnold* v. *The Beecham Group Ltd.*[31a] that the schemes must be accepted by both parties. In *England* v. *Bromley London Borough Council*[32] the E.A.T. required that to be effective the scheme should "govern the situation of the employees in that employment at the relevant time."

Job evaluation is not a precise science. Quite apart from the possibility of subjective judgment an ACAS guide on the subject[33] lists five different methods. In *England's* case the claimant was not, however, permitted to invalidate the scheme in force by showing that the evaluation study should have been carried out differently.

The two standards are not necessarily exclusive of each other.[34] Nevertheless, as was pointed out in *Eaton Ltd.* v. *Nuttall*, where there is a job evaluation the case will normally proceed on that basis and not on the basis of like work. Certainly it is true that if a job evaluation has awarded the jobs different ratings a defence of genuine material difference could be raised to a like work claim.

In practice job evaluation is not a significant alternative to like work in wide section of industry, partly because of trade union distrust of it. Some trade unions, however, favour it and it is, for instance common in local government and other related areas where NALGO acts as bargaining representative. The decision of the European Court in *Commission of the European Communities* v. *U.K.*,[34a] therefore, seems capable of producing a revolution in job evaluation as a means of achieving equal terms and conditions. The European Court held that an inevitable consequence of the right to equal pay for equal work must be the right to demand assessment of equality through a job evaluation. Hitherto

---

[29] [1977] I.C.R. 272.
[30] *Greene* v. *Broxtowe District Council* [1977] I.C.R. 241.
[31] [1980] I.C.R. 573.
[31a] [1982] I.R.L.R. 307.
[32] [1978] I.C.R. 1.
[33] Summarised in *Eaton Ltd.* v. *Nuttal* [1977] I.C.R. 272 at 278.
[34] In *Shields* v. *E. Coomes (Holdings) Ltd.* [1978] I.C.R. 1159 at pp. 1169–1170, Lord Denning M.R. introduces concepts of equal value into the consideration of like work.
[34a] [1982] I.R.L.R. 333.

job evaluation has been looked upon as a collective exercise and, therefore, normally a matter between employer and trade union. Individual intervention to compel or challenge the adoption of a job evaluation scheme could have a disruptive effect on collective bargaining. Despite the reluctance of ACAS, the CAC or the Industrial Tribunals to intervene in so controversial a matter the Government moved quickly to implement the decision of the European Court by Regulation. At the time of going to press the proposals would permit an individual to initiate a demand for a job evaluation, by normal negotiated, means with ACAS assistance. The individual would, however, be permitted to pursue his claim to an industrial tribunal if, either no scheme emerged, or he was dissatisfied with the scheme which did result.

Genuine material difference

The burden of proving like work or equal rating falls on the claimant. If he makes out a case the employer may seek to prove that:

> . . . the variation is genuinely due to a material difference (other than the difference of sex) between her case and his.[34b]

The standard of proof is the balance of probabilities.[35] As worded, this test is capable of covering most of the ground already covered by differences of practical importance in the job. As we have seen there is no hard and fast line to be drawn though the courts seem to assign terms and conditions to sub-section (4) where possible. In *Clay Cross (Quarry Services) Ltd.* v. *Fletcher*[36] Lord Denning M.R. referred to this enquiry as one into the "personal equation of the woman as compared to the man." This must not be misunderstood. The learned Master of the Rolls immediately qualifies this remark with the words "irrespective of any extrinsic forces which led to the variation in pay." Reasons personal to the employee or "economic factors" would be irrelevant. In *A.R.W. Transformers Ltd.* v. *Cupples*[37] Lord MacDonald, in the Scottish E.A.T., rejected as too narrow the suggestion that the difference must be a significant factor in relation to carrying out the job. On the other hand "material" must mean something and if one adopts the view of the Court of Appeal in *Shields* v. *E. Coomes (Holdings) Ltd.* that the purpose of the legislation is to eliminate all discrimination it is clear that only factors relevant to the employment should be taken into account.[38]

In *Jenkins* v. *Kingsgate (Clothing Productions) Ltd.*[39] Browne-Wilkinson J. in the E.A.T. sought to dispose of the risk that the standard of proof would enable an employer to support a reasonable belief in the materiality of the difference so as to rely on the justification. He said:

> "The fact that indirect discrimination is unintentional does not necessarily mean that it is lawful. Thus, under the Sex Discrimination Act 1975, indirect discrimination is rendered unlawful by s.1(1)(b) even if it is unintentional. To escape acting unlawfully, the alleged discriminator has to show that the requirement which operates in a discriminatory fashion is justifiable because, viewed objectively, the

---

[34b] Section 1(3).

[35] *Shields* v. *E. Coomes (Holdings) Ltd.* [1978] I.C.R. 1159 at 1171; *National Vulcan Engineering Insurance Group Ltd.* v. *Wade* [1978] I.C.R. 800.

[36] [1979] I.C.R. 47.

[37] [1977] I.R.L.R. 288.

[38] See *Jenkins* v. *Kingsgate (Clothing Productions) Ltd.* [1981] I.C.R. 715.

[39] *Supra.*

requirement is reasonably necessary to achieve some other purpose. The same is true in relation to racial discrimination under the Race Relations Act 1976, and under the law of the United States of America: see *Griggs* v. *Duke Power Company* (1971) 401 US 424. The question we have to decide is whether the same principle applies to s.1(3) of the Act of 1970, or whether for the purposes of s.1(3) it is enough to show that the employer had no actual covert intention of discrimination against women.

Were it not for the judgment of the European Court of Justice, we would have held that s.1(3) requires an employer to do more than disprove an intention to discriminate. The equality clause implied by s.1(2) of the Act of 1970 operates to counteract all discrimination whether direct or indirect and whether intentional or unintentional: it looks at the effect of the contractual terms, not at whether they are expressed in overtly discriminatory words or with any particular intention. S.1(3) then operates by taking out of subsection (2) those cases where the variation in the terms between men and women is 'genuinely due to a material difference (other than the difference of sex) between her case and his.' The words 'genuinely' and 'other than the difference of sex' plainly prevent an employer who is intentionally discriminating (whether directly or indirectly) from escaping the effect of the equality clause. In our view, for the variation in pay to be 'due to' a material difference it would have to be shown that there was some other matter which in fact justified the variation. It would not be enough simply to show that the employer had an intention to achieve some other legitimate objective (although this might disprove any intention to discriminate): the employer would have to show that the pay differential actually achieved that different objective.

We will assume (without deciding) that Article 119 as construed by the European Court of Justice does not apply to cases of unintentional indirect discrimination. How then are we to construe the United Kingdom statute? Although we must construe the United Kingdom legislation so as not to conflict with Article 119 and so far as possible to make it accord with Article 119, it does not necessarily follow that the United Kingdom legislation must in all respects have the same effect as Article 119. It would not contravene s.2 of the European Communities Act if the United Kingdom statutes conferred on employees greater rights than they enjoy under Article 119.[40] Since the Act of 1970 is an integral part of one code against sex discrimination and the rest of the code plainly renders unlawful indirect discrimination even if unintentional, it seems to us right that we should construe the Equal Pay Act 1970 as requiring any difference in pay to be objectively justified even if this confers on employees greater rights than they would enjoy under Article 119 of the Treaty. We therefore hold that in order to show a 'material difference' within s.1(3) of the Act of 1970 an employer must show that the lower pay for part-time workers is in fact reasonably necessary in order to achieve some objective other than an objective related to the sex of the part-time worker."

Relevance to the work situation does not imply the need for some benefit to be shown to exist. In *Methven* v. *Cow Industrial Polymers Ltd.*[41] the E.A.T. considered that a scheme for maintaining the pay of sick or disabled production workers who were transferred to clerical work was justified as derived from a genuine material difference.

Extraneous considerations

One of the most revealing applications of these principles, apart from the question of different basic rates for part time work disposed of in *Jenkins'* case,

---

[40] It should be noted that Regulations made under the European Communities Act would be *ultra vires* if they had this effect.
[41] [1980] I.C.R. 463.

arose in *Clay Cross (Quarry Services) Ltd.* v. *Fletcher*[42] where the employer sought to advance as a genuine material difference the demand of a male employee for a higher rate of pay if he was to be attracted to take the job. The E.A.T. had decided that the difference was not sex-based on the ground that men and women making such a demand would have been treated in the same way. Very shortly afterwards the same judge reached a similar conclusion in relation to the offer of a higher basic rate to attract recruits to night shift working.[43] The Court of Appeal had no difficulty in observing the serious policy drawbacks of such an approach. At its simplest it would allow an individual's objection to the policy of the Act to be used as a justification for not applying it. At only a slightly less obvious level, permitting such an approach would enable to be advanced established attitudes of mind the discriminating basis of which might be very difficult to detect. The reasoning the Court of Appeal adopted to avoid such consequences depended on the meaning given to "material" and is well illustrated in the following passage from the judgment of Lawton L.J.:

"The variation must have been genuinely due (that is, caused) by a material difference (that is, one which was relevant and real) between (and now come the important words) her case and his. What is her case? And what is his? In my judgment her case embraces what appertains to her *in* her job, such as the qualifications she brought to it, the length of time she has been in it, the skill she has acquired, the responsibilities she has undertaken and where and under what conditions she has to do it. It is on this kind of basis that her case is to be compared with that of the man's. What does not appertain to her job or to his are the circumstances in which they came to be employed. These are collateral to the jobs as such. This was the approach of the Master of the Rolls in *E. Coomes (Holdings) Ltd.* v. *Shields.* In the course of his judgment in that case, referring to s.1(3) of the Equal Pay Act, he said: 'This sub-section deals with cases where the woman and the man are doing 'like work' but the personal equation of the man is such that he deserves to be paid at a higher rate than the woman.'

For example, a woman chemist with a recently acquired doctorate who is given a job in a forensic science laboratory is not entitled under the Equal Pay Act to be paid the same salary as the man working alongside her who has the same degree from the same university but who has 25 years' experience behind him. Nor could she reasonably expect to be so paid. Their personal equations would be different. The position would be otherwise if a few months after her appointment a man with the same qualifications as hers and straight from the university were paid a higher salary merely because he asked for it and at the time there were no other applicants for the job. That is this case. When Mr. Tunnicliffe was appointed his personal equation was the same as Mrs. Fletcher's so far as the company knew or cared when employing him. After he had started work the company appreciated that he had better educational qualifications than Mrs. Fletcher and a potential for doing another kind of job and for which they were willing to train him. Had Mrs. Fletcher been a candidate for this new job her personal equation would not have been the same as his."

It will have been apparent from what has been said so far that if permission for inequality was confined to substantial differences in what is actually done there is relatively little room for indirect discrimination. Unfortunately the wider boundaries of material difference, even if limited to relevant differences,

---

[42] [1979] I.C.R. 47. But see *Albion Shipping Agency* v. *Arnold* [1982] I.C.R. 22 when economic circumstances were considered material in the case of successive employments.
[43] [1977] I.R.L.R. 259.

tend to permit inclusion of such factors as experience and seniority and the decisions have confirmed that this is so. Such grounds for differentiation are quite likely to be discriminatory in the sense that they impose a condition for the higher levels of benefit which men can more easily satisfy than women. This failure on the part of women is at least in part due to entrenched discriminatory attitudes in the domestic sphere at which legislation can only strike by means of gradual education. The source is not, however, important. What matters, as we shall see when dealing with the Sex Discrimination Act, is that the effects of the failure can be modified by prohibiting the application of conditions which women are less able to satisfy. However much the Courts say the two Acts should be taken together the judicial approach to subsection (3) does nothing to enable it to eliminate indirect discrimination. The words "other than a difference of sex" are not strong enough to prevent the application of conditions which are not themselves founded on sex difference but, nonetheless, tend to produce discriminatory results because of it.

Established practice

The passage quoted from the judgment of Lawton L.J., however, further exacerbates this legislative gap because it suggests that if the condition is part of an established scheme it will, apart from direct discrimination, virtually justify itself. In *National Vulcan Engineering Insurance Group Ltd.* v. *Wade*[44] the Court of Appeal applied the ordinary civil burden of proof of balance of probabilities to justify an employer's reliance on a genuine grading system. In *A.R.W. Transformers Ltd.* v. *Cupples*[45] a differential based on experience was considered justified because of the existence of a system of recognition of such experience.

This has been further extended by the "red-circle" decisions. Red-circling is only a formalised example of the industrial relations policy of avoiding the erosion of established differentials.[46] In *Charles Early and Marriott (Witney) Ltd.* v. *Smith; Snoxell* v. *Vauxhall Motors Ltd.*[47] the E.A.T. (sitting with five members) considered the practice of protecting an established wage differential upon renegotiation of a wage structure by placing these structures in a special category. The proportionate differential is subsequently maintained in respect of this special category in all negotiable increases. In a true red circle, however, no new employees are admitted to the special category since its sole purpose is to maintain protection for employees who had achieved a grade no longer available.[48] The practice of red-circling is quite likely to enshrine a difference between men and women. It is, for instance, not uncommon for a regrading to sweep away the highest grade of all and this may well have been achieved by those with very long periods of service. As we have said, in practice it is quite likely that all such people will be men. Phillips J. delivering the judgment of the E.A.T. expressed the justification for considering the difference to be material thus:

---

[44] [1978] I.C.R. 800.
[45] [1977] I.R.L.R. 228.
[46] See *Farthing* v. *Ministry of Defence* [1980] I.R.L.R. 402 (C.A.).
[47] [1977] I.C.R. 700.
[48] See *United Biscuits Ltd.* v. *Young* [1978] I.R.L.R. 15.

"On the employers' side there are problems also. It is seldom right or desirable or, indeed, permissible to reduce the wages of employees who are being asked to move, for reasons of economy or re-organisation or otherwise, from one sort of work to another. But if in such a case the women succeed in having their wages uplifted to be on an equality with the red circle men, other male employees, not being red circled, may then make a claim under the Equal Pay Act 1970 to have their wages uplifted to that of the women doing the same work as themselves: section 1(3). The practical problems involved are vividly illustrated in the *Trico* case, where the women, who had not taken part in the proceedings before the industrial tribunal, subsequently obtained by a prolonged strike the remedy which the industrial tribunal found themselves obliged to refuse them."

He warned, however against allowing as a justification the need to perpetuate a differential which itself sprang from discrimination.

"Putting these arguments side by side it can be seen that the solution depends upon whether, in analysing the history of the difference in treatment of Miss Snoxell and Mrs. Davies on the one hand and the red circle male inspectors on the other, one stops at the moment of the formation of the circle or looks further back to see why Miss Snoxell and Mrs. Davies were not within it. The arguments presented to us have, not surprisingly, considered questions of causation, and it has been said that the inability of Miss Snoxell and Mrs. Davies to join the red circle was, or was not, the effective cause of the current variation in the terms of their contracts of employment. It seems to us that this earlier discrimination can be said to be an effective cause of current variation. But we would put the matter more broadly. The onus of proof under section 1(3) is on the employer and it is a heavy one. Intention, and motive, are irrelevant; and we would say that an employer can never establish in the terms of section 1(3) that the variation between the woman's contract and the man's contract is genuinely due to a material difference (other than the difference of sex) between her case and his when it can be seen that past sex discrimination has contributed to the variation. To allow such an answer would, we think, be contrary to the spirit and intent of the Equal Pay Act 1970, construed and interpreted in the manner we have already explained. It is true that the original discriminaton occurred before December 29, 1975, and accordingly was not then unlawful; nonetheless it cannot have been the intention of the Act to permit the perpetuation of the effects of earlier discrimination."

In *Handley* v. *H. Mono Ltd.*[49] the E.A.T. had concluded that payment of a lower hourly rate to women was justified as derived from a genuine material difference because the women worked part-time. It took the view that the part-time employee was contributing less overall to the utilisation of equipment. This makes very clear the absence of any concept of indirect discrimination in the exclusion from the defence of sex based differences since it is quite clear that a considerably higher proportion of women than men will in practice work part-time and thus be at a disadvantage. The same issue arose in *Jenkins* v. *Kingsgate (Clothing Productions) Ltd.*[50] The E.A.T. referred the question to the European Court which held that Article 119 of the Treaty of Rome only applies to different rates of pay based on a difference of sex or on a policy designed to achieve sex discrimination. This requirement of an intention to discriminate confirms the view that Article 119 contains no equivalent of indirect discrimina-

---

[49] [1979] I.C.R. 147.
[50] [1981] I.C.R. 715.

tion capable of introduction to extend subsection (3).[50a] Nevertheless Browne-Wilkinson J. was able, in applying the decision of the European Court[51] to place some limitations on the use that can be made of part-time working as an excuse. He pointed out that the European Court had only said that a pay differential between full-time and part-time workers could be justified on economic grounds not personal to the men and women employees. From this he declared that in order to be a *genuine material* difference apart from sex the employer would have to show that it was designed to achieve some reasonably necessary objective.

It is, of course, clear that a material difference cannot be based on an asssumption about a sex difference. In *E. Coomes (Holdings) Ltd.* v. *Shields*[52] the alleged security duties would not have been permitted to constitute such a difference even had they been substantial in practice because the difference would have rested on the assumption that men were as a class more effective in deterring customers from causing trouble. In *Noble* v. *David Gold and Son (Holdings) Ltd.*[53] the Court of Appeal did not object to women being placed on light duties. Lawton L.J. said that common sense indicates that women will not be able to lift heavy loads unless of unusual physique. Though an employer must not assume that no woman is capable of doing a heavy job, if he can rely on his judgment in assessing ability it is difficult to see how the courts can expect to control the subjective application of generalised judgment.

Exclusions

Certain terms are expressly excluded from the operation of the Act. These include:

  (i) Terms and conditions affected by compliance with the law regulating the employment of women. Such statutory provisions include limitations imposed upon hours of continuous work or Sunday working by women.[54] In considering an application under section 3 of the Equal Pay Act[55] the C.A.C. concluded[56] that it had no jurisdiction to consider a claim that women should be paid for a half-hour lunch break which by statute they were required to take when men who worked that half-hour were paid for it.

 (ii) Any special treatment accorded to women in connection with pregnancy or childbirth (s.6(1)(*b*)).

(iii) Terms and conditions related to death or retirement, or to any provision made in connection with death or retirement save that equal access must be afforded to occupational pension schemes.[56a]

[50a] The European Court affirmed that Article 119 only applies to differences of pay in *Burton* v. *British Railways Board* [1982] I.R.L.R. 116.

[51] *Jenkins* v. *Kingsgate (Clothing Productions) Ltd.* [1981] I.C.R. 592.

[52] [1978] I.C.R. 1159.

[53] [1980] I.C.R. 543.

[54] Factories Act 1961, Part VI; Employment of Women, Young Persons and Children Act 1920; Hours of Employment (Conventions) Act 1936. See *Greater London Council* v. *Farrar* [1980] I.C.R. 366.

[55] See, *infra*, p. 318.

[56] Rolls Royce (1971) Ltd. and NSM. Award No. 361.

[56a] Section 6(1).

In *Worringham* v. *Lloyds Bank Ltd.*[57] the Court of Appeal (relying on *Roberts* v. *Cleveland*[58] held that this exclusion extended to provisions *about* death or retirement. The case was, however, referred to the European Court. That court considered that payments made to employees to enable them to contribute to pension schemes were remuneration and so were within the scope of Article 119.[59] The court also confirmed that Article 119 conferred rights directly enforceable in national courts without the need for national legislation and took the view that only special circumstances had justified a temporal limitation on the application of this principle in *Defrenne* v. *Sabena*.[60] The cautious form in which the European Court expressed the application of Article 119 to the facts of this case allowed the Court of Appeal to avoid deciding whether the direct applicability of that Article destroys the validity of exclusion (iii).[61] In *Burton* v. *British Railways Board*[62] the European Court held that, though Article 119 applied only to pay, Article 5 of the Directive 76/207 of February 9, 1976 on equal treatment of men and women in employment did apply to all terms and conditions of employment including, in that instance, conditions of access to voluntary redundancy payments. The Court again avoided answering the question whether this Directive had direct effect in member states so as, for instance, to override exceptions such as those mentioned above, by holding that it only contained a prohibition on direct discrimination. The indirectly discriminating effect of different retirement ages, which was itself exempt from the operation of the Directive, did not operate to produce a breach of the Directive.

Rectification of Discriminatory Collective Agreements

It is obvious that an employee may feel inhibited from making an equal pay claim against her employer. Provision is made for the Secretary of State to make such a claim on behalf of an employee.[63] Of far greater potential value would appear to be the provision in section 3 permitting reference by a party or the Secretary of State to the Central Arbitration Committee of any provision of a collective agreement applying to men only or to women only. The jurisdiction of the C.A.C. also extends to a reference by the Secretary of State of a discriminatory Wages Regulation Order made by a Wages Council or an Agricultural Wages Order made by the Agricultural Wages Board.[64]

The C.A.C. may then declare what amendments need to be made in the agreement to remove the discrimination. The effect of such a declaration will be to determine the terms of individual contracts of employment by reference to the amended collective agreement. The amendments to be made are to be such as are needed to extend to both men and women any provision applying specifically to only one sex and to eliminate any resulting duplication so as to ensure that the terms for both men and women are not less favourable than they would have been without the amendments. This means in effect that the result

---

[57] [1981] I.C.R. 558.
[58] [1979] I.C.R. 558.
[59] [1981] I.R.L.R. 178.
[60] [1976] I.C.R. 547.
[61] [1982] I.R.L.R. 74.
[62] [1982] I.R.L.R. 116.
[63] s.2(2).
[64] ss.4 and 5.

of the amendment must be to equalise upwards. The amendments may not, however, extend the collective agreement to men or women not previously falling within it.[65]

The C.A.C. pursued a policy of applying this provision whenever the result of the application of a collective agreement was discriminatory. This policy was challenged in R. v. *Central Arbitration Committee ex parte Hy-Mac Ltd.*[66] The company had introduced a revised salary structure which did not, as had its predecessor, specify different grades and rates for men and for women. The union, however, claimed that there were no women in the two highest grades of the proposed job evaluated grading whilst 70 per cent. of the women were in the two lowest grades which contained no men. The C.A.C. found that though there was no overt discrimination there had been a failure to eradicate the concept of a women's rate of pay. The C.A.C. itself fixed "reasonable salary bounds" for the grades. The Divisional Court held that for the C.A.C. to have jurisdiction there must be a provision in the agreement applying specifically to men only or to women only. Moreover the C.A.C. had no power to embark upon a general wage review. Browne L.J. stated *obiter* that the C.A.C. would not be prevented from going behind the terms of a sham agreement which in actual fact contained terms applying only to one sex.

RACE AND SEX DISCRIMINATION

The first code of anti-discrimination legislation in the United Kingdom was introduced in the Race Relations Act 1968. This Act sought to avoid the imposition of sanctions as a means of enforcement. The view was taken that this would simply produce resistance to a policy which would only work effectively in an atmosphere of consensus. Accordingly the main instrument was conciliation machinery, the Race Relations Board having only a reserve power to apply to a county court for a remedy. Direct access to the courts was, therefore, cut off and only the most dedicated complainant would pursue a claim through the Board's processes. Without a complaint there was no power of investigation. One can appreciate why enforcement was regarded as of little value when it is borne in mind that there was no parallel to the present concept of indirect discrimination. As we shall see, this concept, which is far more useful than the prohibition on direct discrimination, is essential to control even if it cannot close the major loophole of conditions which themselves produce a discriminatory result. Without control of this loophole the way out of the prohibition upon discrimination was sufficiently obvious to appeal to all but those who readily accepted the fact that the policy of the Act would produce some inconvenience.

The lessons learned by the relative failure of this measure were applied to good purpose in the Sex Discrimination Act 1975 and the Race Relations Act 1976. These two Acts were originally intended to be aspects of a single code. Consequently they are, in all but certain, rather irritating, detail virtually identical. They will, therefore, be dealt with here as a single whole. The pattern of the legislation is to define the concept of discrimination and then to specify the circumstances in which such action is illegal. Complaint lies, in employment

---

[65] s.3(4).
[66] [1979] I.R.L.R. 461.

situations, to industrial tribunals, with the Race Relations Board and the Equal Opportunities Commission retaining powers of investigation, conciliation and advice.

The definition of discrimination

Both current Acts adopt the dual concepts of direct and indirect discrimination. Together they provide the following definitions.

Direct

A person discriminates against another if, on the ground of sex, married status,[67] colour, race, nationality or ethnic or national origins he treats that other less favourably than he treats or would treat a person without such a characteristic.

Indirect

The definition of indirect discrimination involves the application to the other of a requirement or condition which applies or would apply equally to one of the other sex or to an unmarried person or to persons not of the same racial group, but:

(a) which is such that the proportion of persons of the same sex, married persons or persons of the same racial group who can comply with the requirement or condition is considerably smaller than the proportion of persons not of that category who can comply with it; and

(b) which cannot be shown to be justifiable irrespective of the sex, married status, colour, race, nationality or ethnic or national origins of the person to whom it is applied; and,

(c) which is to the detriment of that other because he or she cannot comply with it.

The comparison of the cases must be such that the relevant circumstances in the one case are the same, or not materially different, in the other. No account is to be taken in cases of direct discrimination of special treatment afforded to women in connection with pregnancy or childbirth.

Segregation amounts to discrimination within the Race Relations Act, thus excluding the principle of "equal but separate."

Victimisation

Both Acts forbid victimisation which is defined in terms of discrimination by less favourable treatment on the ground that the person victimised has:

(a) brought proceedings under either Act or under the Equal Pay Act, or

(b) given evidence or information in connection with proceedings or other-

---

[67] Note that this is not a misprint for "marital status." The Sex Discrimination Act uses the term marital status but compares it with the unmarried state thus indicating that it is talking of those who are married. Oddly it fails to make the normal provision to reverse the comparison that is made in the case of women so that the unmarried are not given a right to complain of discrimination on that ground.

wise done anything under or by reference to those Acts in relation to the discriminator or any other person; or

(c) alleged that any person has committed an act that would amount to a contravention of these Acts,

or, to the knowledge of the discriminator, intends to do, or is suspected by the discriminator of having done, any of these things.

The reader will appreciate at once that in these provisions the legislature is attempting to provide for situations where the motivation is, at the least, difficult to prove and, indeed, may not even be consciously acknowledged by the actor. It is for this reason that motive, which forms an element in direct discrimination, is omitted as a factor in indirect discrimination.

The burden of proof

The burden of proof of discrimination is upon him who asserts it. This has been criticised, especially where motive is part of the requirement, on the ground that it is peculiarly difficult to prove discrimination. The reason for such a burden of proof is the fear that if there were a presumption of discrimination wherever anyone of a specified group did not enjoy a benefit given to one not of that group discrimination would constantly be asserted in tribunals. On the other hand the existence of a presumption of unfair dismissal or of redundancy has not led to uncontrolled litigation largely because it is apparent in the vast majority of cases that such a claim will not succeed. The issue is then one of whether those against whom discrimination might be asserted should be put to the considerable trouble of adopting attitudes which render suspicion of discrimination unreasonable. The alternative is that many who reasonably suspect that they have been the subject of discrimination will take no action because they cannot prove it.

Various aids have been developed to avoid the most severe effects of this burden. Both Acts[68] make provision whereby a person who considers he may have been discriminated against may, before instituting proceedings, require the alleged discriminator to answer questions designed to reveal the existence of such discrimination. Forms have been prescribed for this purpose but there is no reason why other questions should not be asked. In *Virdee* v. *E.C.C. Quarries Ltd.*[69] the tribunal considered "equivocal and evasive" a failure to answer all but one of nine questions, making it just and equitable to infer discrimination.

Presumption of discrimination

The courts have themselves taken steps to modify the burden of proof by pointing out that the evidential burden may shift relatively easily. In *Moberly* v. *Commonwealth Hall* (*University of London*)[70] the E.A.T. held that where a difference in treatment is established between a member of one sex and a member of the other a prima facie case of discrimination exists requiring an

---

[68] S.D.A. 1975, s.74; R.R.A. 1976, s.65.
[69] *Virdee* v. *E.C.C. Quarries Ltd.* [1978] I.R.L.R. 295.
[70] [1977] I.C.R. 791.

answer from the alleged discriminator.[71] In *Khanna* v. *Ministry of Defence*[72] Browne-Wilkinson J. pointed out that affirmative evidence of discrimination will usually consist of inferences from primary facts. In that case the applicant had made 22 unsuccessful applications for promotion to the grade of principal photographer for which his commanding officer strongly recommended him. In 1979 he ran his section after the principal photographer left. He was short-listed for the permanent post. He was, however, placed third by the promotion board and the successful applicant lacked some of the relevant experience which Khanna possessed and which was required. The tribunal had found that these facts produced an unavoidable inference of discrimination requiring explanation. The explanation was, in fact, forthcoming whereupon the burden of proof shifted back to the applicant. Browne-Wilkinson J. holding that the function of the tribunal was to reach a conclusion on the balance of probabilities said:

> "In the future, we think Industrial Tribunals may find it easier to forget about the rather nebulous concept of the 'shift in the evidential burden.' . . . It has in the past been used by the Employment Appeal Tribunal in cases under the Race Relations Act and the Sex Discrimination Act. But in our view it is more likely to obscure than to illuminate the right answer. In this case the Industrial Tribunal would, we suspect, have found the case rather more straightforward if, looking at all the evidence as a whole, they had simply decided whether the complaint had been established. No useful purpose is served by stopping to reach a conclusion on half the evidence. The right course in this case was for the Industrial Tribunal to take into account the fact that direct evidence of discrimination is seldom going to be available and that, accordingly, in these cases the affirmative evidence of discrimination will normally consist of inferences to be drawn from the primary facts. If the primary facts indicate that there has been discrimination of some kind, the employer is called on to give an explanation and, failing clear and specific explanation being given by the employer to the satisfaction of the Industrial Tribunal, an inference of unlawful discrimination from the primary facts will mean the complaint succeeds. . . . Those propositions are, we think, most easily understood if concepts of shifting evidential burdens are avoided."

Evidence of discrimination

This formulation, of course, does not reveal the whole answer since it will still be necessary to decide whether the facts do suggest the existence of discrimination. Two aspects of the same problem exist, namely, whether the facts are capable of indicating discrimination and if so whether these facts influenced the decision. In *Saunders* v. *Richmond upon Thames L.B.C.*[73] a female applicant for the post of golf professional was asked questions which were not asked of men applicants and which clearly suggested doubts as to whether, as a woman, she would be able to do the job as well as a man. The E.A.T held that no inference of discrimination necessarily arose from asking men and women applicants different questions. Such questions may indeed be necessary to allow the applicant to eliminate any doubts arising from sex or race differences. In

---

[71] See also *Wallace* v. *South Eastern Education and Library Board* [1980] I.R.L.R. 193 (N.I. Ct. App.).

[72] [1981] I.C.R. 653.

[73] [1978] I.C.R. 75. In *Conway* v. *The Queen's University of Belfast* [1981] I.R.L.R. 137 (N.I. Ct. App.) it was held that a failure to interview an applicant with inferior qualifications did not raise a presumption of discrimination.

Owen and Briggs v. *James*[74] there existed facts decidedly suggestive of discrimination. A coloured Englishwoman applied for employment as a shorthand typist but was unsuccessful at the interview. Some months later she saw a similar advertisement by the same firm, applied again and was interviewed by the same partner who had interviewed her on the previous occasion. He said that there was no point in interviewing her and a hostile discussion ensued. Subsequently a white woman was offered the job despite having a shorthand speed of 35 words per minute against the applicant's speed of 80 words per minute. Allegedly the partner said to the person appointed that he could not understand why an English employer should want to take on a coloured applicant when "English" applicants were available. The E.A.T. held that it is for the tribunal to decide on the facts whether the real reason was discrimination. It is obvious that once facts of this nature have been established it will most likely be for the respondent to prove that nonetheless the decision was not substantially influenced by such considerations.

Discovery

It will be apparent that in so difficult an area of proof as that involved in discovering which facts actually did influence a decision the applicant will be at a disadvantage, despite the ready shift of the burden, if he is unable to secure certain evidence. If, for instance, it is asserted that it was not the fact that he was black but the fact of inferior qualification which produced rejection he cannot be in a position to challenge the relevance of the alleged differences unless he can examine them in detail. For this reason the development of the law relating to disclosure of documents in this field is most significant. In *Science Research Council* v. *Nasse*[75] the House of Lords confirmed the view of the Court of Appeal that there is no rule barring disclosure of confidential documents although Lord Edmund-Davies was careful to point out that confidentiality is a relevant consideration. On the other hand there is no general right of discovery in industrial tribunals. Lord Scarman said:

> "The criterion is not relevance alone, nor are general orders for discovery appropriate in this class of litigation. The true test, as formulated by the rules of court, is whether discovery is necessary either to save costs or for the fair disposal of the case. Where speed and cheapness of legal process are essential, as they are in county courts and industrial tribunals, general orders should ordinarily be avoided. And where, as will be frequent in this class of litigation, confidential records about other people are relevant, the court must honour the confidence to this extent: that it will not order production unless the interest of justice requires that they be disclosed. No hard and fast rules can be laid down: but I agree with others of your Lordships in thinking that the Employment Appeal Tribunal gave very useful guidance on the appropriate practice in *British Railways Board* v. *Natarajan*."

The House of Lords expressed approval of the approach adopted by the E.A.T under Arnold J. in *British Railways Board* v. *Natarajan*.[76] Referring to the Court of Appeal decision in *Nassé*[77] he said:

---

[74] [1981] I.C.R. 377 (E.A.T.); *affirmed* [1982] I.R.L.R. 502 (C.A.).
[75] [1979] I.C.R. 921.
[76] [1979] 2 All E.R. 794.
[77] [1979] Q.B. 144.

"Now the way in which the decision whether disclosure is essential in the interests of justice is to be made in a particular case is plainly spelled out in the decision of the Court of Appeal. The proper procedure is for the documents in question to be looked at by the judge in the county court or chairman of the industrial tribunal in order to see whether it is essential, in the interests of justice and with regard of course to the claims relevant in the cases before them, that disclosure should take place.

What does not emerge with any clarity as embodying any general principle, and what it would perhaps be impossible to embody in a general principle, is, first of all, what degree of probability has to be demonstrated before the judge or chairman performs the exercise of examination, and, secondly, at what stage in the litigious process the examination should take place. We must deal as best we can with those two matters.

We think that before deciding whether an examination is necessary, the judge or chairman of the tribunal in a case in which the matter is dealt with at first instance, or the appellate court, where the matter comes before it on review, must decide whether there is any prima facie prospect of relevance of the confidential material to an issue which arises in the litigation; put another way, whether it is reasonable to expect that there is any real likelihood of such relevance emerging from the examination. If there is not, we do not think that the exercise of examination is necessary or should take place. If there is, then to come to the second matter which we have mentioned, it is, we think, a matter of convenience in each case whether the examination should take place at the interlocutory stage of discovery or immediately the matter arises at the trial. We can conceive that there would be many cases in which, having regard to the probable way in which the material, if found relevant, would have to be treated, that it would be essential for the decision to be made at the interlocutory stage of discovery. But there are also cases where, having regard to the way in which the material would have to be dealt with, such an early examination would not be necessary. That is a matter which we think must be decided in relation to each case in which the point is relevant."[78]

Direct discrimination

Discriminatory motive

The test of direct discrimination asks the question whether the claimant has been subjected to a detriment by reason of sex, marriage or race. It directs attention, therefore, solely to an important reason for which the action was taken.[78a] It does not concern itself with the result save to the extent of requiring it to be detrimental. To assist in providing an answer to this question the courts not infrequently ask whether the person allegedly discriminated against would have suffered similarly if he or she had not possessed the race or sex characteristic. If the answer is in the negative it would seem almost inevitable that discrimination should be taken to be proved since this establishes that that characteristic must be the real cause of the detrimental action. All the question does, therefore, is to concentrate attention on the need for the reason to be clearly among those listed as constituting illegal discrimination. The question also makes it clear that if the complainant has been discriminated against for a reason other than one of those so listed there can be no direct discrimination

---

[78] The way in which these principles can be applied to sift out the relevant evidence appears clearly in *Perera* v. *Civil Service Commission* [1980] I.C.R. 699 (E.A.T.); *affirmed* [1982] I.R.L.R. 147 (C.A.).

[78a] *Owen and Briggs* v. *James* [1982] I.R.L.R. 502.

notwithstanding that that reason applies only to one sex, marital status, race, colour, etc. Between these two sets of reasons there lies an intermediate stage in which the unprotected characteristic is assumed by the alleged discriminator to attach to all possessing one of the listed characteristics. This will establish direct discrimination. So to say that an applicant has not been appointed because she cannot lift heavy weights is not to discriminate on grounds of sex. But to say that the applicant has not been appointed because women in general cannot lift heavy weights is to say that she has not been appointed because she is a woman.[78b] Accordingly, if we wish to claim that the requirement to lift heavy weights is discriminatory, although it has been applied to each applicant, because it is merely a front to exclude women who are less likely than men to satisfy it we must turn to indirect discrimination and ask whether the requirement is justified. Direct discrimination has no concern with that question.

In *Turley* v. *Allders Department Stores Ltd.*[79] the result may seem surprising but is undoubtedly correct on this basis. The discrimination was because of the complainant's pregnancy. The fact that only women can have this characteristic is irrelevant. No prohibited direct discrimination had occurred. Unless colour of skin were specified as an illegal ground in the Race Relations Act exactly the same point would apply to rejection of a West Indian because he was coloured. Equally, in *Peake* v. *Automotive Products Ltd.*[80] if the employer had been able to establish as a fact that he permitted those of less physical strength to leave early so that they would not be caught in the rush he could not have been accused of direct discrimination just because they all turned out to be women. The facts, however, indicated that he had made an assumption that women were entitled to this advantage and so the concession was based on the fact that its beneficiaries were women and not on safety.

It is submitted that it is unfortunate that the E.A.T. in *Turley's* case fell into the error of saying that its decision rested in part on the fact that there was no comparable characteristic in men. If that characteristic is attributed to the group regardless of whether it is actually possessed by any particular individual then the reason for the detriment must be membership of the group and not possession of the characteristic. That constitutes discrimination regardless of the fact that members of other groups cannot possess the characteristic in question. It will be observed that what we are saying is that the alleged characteristic is not the real reason. If in *Turley's* case discrimination had been based on rejection of women because they tend to become pregnant it is submitted that this would have constituted discrimination regardless of the fact that men cannot tend to become pregnant.

The alternative reason in *Turley's* case that no comparable characteristics existed springs from section 5(1) of the Sex Discrimination Act[81] which states that a comparison for direct discrimination must be such that the relevant circumstance in the one case are the same, or not materially different, in the other. It is submitted that once it is decided that all women are being discriminated against any allegation that this is because they tend to become pregnant is not a "relevant circumstance."

[78b] *See Horsey* v. *Dyfed County Council* [1982] I.R.L.R. 395.
[79] [1980] I.C.R. 66.
[80] [1977] I.C.R. 968.
[81] Race Relations Act 1976, s.3(4).

It is suggested that sections 5(3) and 3(4) respectively are parallel to the requirement in section 1(4) of the Equal Pay Act that a comparison should be made with work which is not different in any aspect of practical importance. If this is so it refers not to the alleged discrimination but to the surrounding circumstances in which that discriminatory factor is applied. In this light and on the facts as found the decision in *Schmidt* v. *Austicks Bookshops Ltd.*[82] may have been right but seems more likely to have been wrong. If there were different circumstances applying to women which had no comparator among men the requirement that women should wear skirts might have been incapable of being established as direct discrimination simply because no meaningful test could be applied to discover whether women were at a disadvantage. The only circumstances that seems to be different, however, is a supposed social mores that women ought to wear skirts, which is itself discriminatory. It is true that we cannot answer the question whether a man breaking such a rule would have been dismissed but, as we have seen, that is only an aid to establishing whether the cause was sex based. It is suggested that in the *Austicks* case the rule, and the assumptions from which it was derived, are clearly sex based. It was applied in similar circumstances to those in which men were employed.

The basic purity of the question asked to establish direct discrimination seems to have misled the courts into a feeling that it must be obscured by considerations similar to those of *mens rea*. This is the explanation of the aberration of the Court of Appeal in *Peake* v. *Automotive Products Ltd.*[83] The complaint was made by a male employee on the ground that female employees were allowed to leave work five minutes before male employees on every working day. The employers asserted by way of defence the existence of a "proper" motive of enabling women to leave the factory in comfort and convenience. Phillips J. admitted that the initial response of the E.A.T. was that the practice of 30 years' standing was entirely reasonable and noted that the industrial tribunal had arrived at binding findings of fact that the arrangement was in the interests of safety and was approved by the relevant trade union. He concluded, however, that the Act required the tribunal to see what was done and whether it was done because a man is a man or a woman is a woman. In the view of the E.A.T. an affirmative answer proves discrimination regardless of the absence of a discriminatory motive, that is to say, solely for some non-discriminatory reason. On appeal Lord Denning M.R. thought that the cry "women and children first" would be a demonstration of chivalry and courtesy clearly not discriminatory. Both he and Goff L.J. covered up the absence of a rational explanation for this gut reaction by falling back on the principle *de minimis non curat lex*, which subsequently was blessed by Lord Denning in *Ministry of Defence* v. *Jeremiah*,[84] thus establishing the possibility of regarding a little discrimination as not a dangerous thing.[85]

Adverse intention and adverse effect

Shaw L.J. in *Peake's* case, however, relied on the reference to discrimination against a person and applied this, not to the factual outcome but, objectively, to the nature of the act. He said:

---

[82] [1978] I.C.R. 85. See also *Horsey* v. *Dyfed County Council, supra.*
[83] [1977] I.C.R. 480 (E.A.T.); [1977] I.C.R. 968 (C.A.).
[84] [1978] I.C.R. 984.   [85] See *Schmidt* v. *Austicks Bookshops Ltd.* [1978] I.C.R. 85.

"This, to my mind, involves an element of something which is inherently adverse or hostile to the interests of the persons of the sex which is said to be discriminated against."

Whatever this might leave in theory for direct discrimination to forbid, it would result in virtual impossibility of proof and it would also result in an illogical gap between direct and indirect discrimination. It may be noted that the problem could lie, not so much in the existence of another primary reason, as in the power of that reason to obliterate its own discriminatory effect. It can, for instance, be argued that considerations of safety are neither more nor less indicative of discrimination since the assumption that men need less safety precautions than women is itself discriminatory. The effect of the Court of Appeal's decision in *Peake* would be to permit a defence of good intentions to legalise even discriminatory assumptions.

The Court of Appeal undid much of the effect of the *Peake* decision in *Ministry of Defence* v. *Jeremiah*.[86] Male and female examiners were employed in Royal Ordnance Factories. In certain shops where "colour bursting" shells were made conditions of work were particularly dirty. "Obnoxious" pay was agreed but women had refused to work in these areas because they objected to having to take showers before leaving the workplace and to the effect of the atmosphere on their hair. Jeremiah claimed that the effect of the concession to women meant that if he volunteered to work overtime he was frequently employed in such shops whereas the women were never required to work there. The E.A.T. held that the detriment was neither *de minimis* nor the result of chivalry and that the existence of extra payment could not eliminate the discrimination. On appeal Lord Denning M.R. said that the only sound ground for the decision in *Peake* was the *de minimis* principle. Brandon L.J. expressed strong doubts about the validity of the views of Shaw L.J. as to the need for adverse or hostile action. In his view the sole relevant question was whether, as a question of fact, men were subjected to a disadvantage by comparison with women because they were men. Brightman L.J. raised some interesting questions as to the nature of what might be regarded as detriment. He said:

"I do not say that the mere deprivation of choice for one sex, or some other differentiation in their treatment, is necessarily unlawful discrimination. The deprivation of choice, or differentiation, in the sort of case we are considering, must be associated with a detriment. It is possible to imagine a case where one sex has a choice but the other does not, yet there is nevertheless no detriment to the latter sex, that is to say, no unlawful discrimination. Railway carriages used to have compartments marked "Ladies Only." A lady had a choice of travelling in an ordinary compartment or in a "Ladies Only" compartment. A man had no such choice. In such a case a court would conclude that there was no sensible detriment to the men flowing from the absence of choice. A similar case might arise on factory premises where there might be two canteens with equal amenities, one canteen for men and women and the other for women only. A court would conclude, other things being equal, that there was no unlawful discrimination, though the ladies had a choice where they ate, and the men did not.

In deciding whether or not there is a detriment to a worker who complains, the court must in my opinion take all the circumstances into account. To take an

---

86 [1980] I.C.R. 13.

example from the facts of the present case, if (a) a male worker is under a duty to work in the colour bursting shop one day a fortnight and is compensated with a dirty work payment of 4p an hour and consequential pay-related pension benefits, and (b) a female worker has no such duty, and (c) a male worker complains, there is clearly discrimination based on sex. The question before the tribunal in my view would be whether a reasonable male worker would or might take the view that there was a detriment. I say "would or might," because tastes differ. Some male workers might take the view that the 4p an hour bonus, with consequent increase in pension rights, made the dirty work well worth while, and not therefore detrimental to their interests. Other male workers might take the view that it was not worth while, that it was to their detriment. It would be unrealistic to expect a tribunal to decide which group of workers were correct in their assessment. I think a detriment exists if a reasonable worker would or might take the view that the duty was in all the circumstances to his detriment. It may be said that, on this interpretation of the Act, both a male worker and a female worker might complain about the same discrimination and that both might be right. I see no anomaly in such a result. The purpose of the legislation is to secure equal treatment of the sexes so far as appropriate.

I should add that I agree with what Lord Denning M.R. has said with regard to the extra payment for work in the colour bursting shop in the present case: an employer cannot lawfully buy the right to discriminate by making an extra payment."

This decision makes it largely unnecessary to avoid the effects of the *Peake* judgment by the ingenious series of distinctions adopted by Slynn J. in *Grieg* v. *Community Industry*.[87] It is suggested that Slynn J. was clearly forced to adopt such devices and that in doing so he was not supporting, but merely following, the earlier and now avowedly incorrect judgment of the Court of Appeal. Nevertheless it is open to a tribunal to conclude that the reason which has produced a detriment has no foundation in sex-based assumptions at all. In *Seide* v. *Gillette Industries Ltd.*[88] a Jewish toolmaker was moved to the day shift because of anti-semitism among the night shift. The E.A.T. held that the employer was not motivated by anti-semitism in the way that the employer in *Jeremiah* or *Peake* had been motivated by considerations of sex. Race was merely part of the background of the case.

It is submitted that Kilner Brown J. was quite correct to hold in *Zarezynska* v. *Levy*[89] that one can be the victim of illegal discrimination notwithstanding that the discrimination is directed at others and the effects upon the complainant are incidental. In that case a part-time barmaid was dismissed for refusing to comply with instructions not to serve black customers. The E.A.T. made heavy weather of its desire to do justice but it seems clear that if direct discrimination is a question of factual detriment having nothing to do with adverse or hostile intention anyone who discriminates must be answerable for all detrimental conseqences which can be said to fall within the chain of causation.

Interaction of sex discrimination and equal pay

We have seen that in the area of employment direct inequality between men and women in terms and conditions of employment will be covered by the

---

[87] [1979] I.C.R. 356.
[88] [1980] I.R.L.R. 427.
[89] [1979] I.C.R. 184. But see *Din* v. *Carrington Viyella Ltd.* [1982] I.R.L.R. 281; *Ojutiku* v. *Manpower Services Commission* [1982] I.R.L.R. 418, *per* Eveleigh L.J.

provisions of the Equal Pay Act provided that the complainant can identify a direct comparator. The prohibitions upon sex discrimination in employment contained in section 6 of the Sex Discrimination Act expressly exclude benefits consisting of the "payment of money" regulated by the woman's contract of employment, presumably because it is assumed, wrongly, that the Equal Pay Act affords similar protection. The Equal Pay Act is in turn excluded from certain areas covered by section 6 of the Sex Discrimination Act.[90]

> (2) Section 1(1) of the Equal Pay Act 1970 (as set out in subsection (1) above) does not apply in determining for the purposes of section 6(1)(b) of this Act the terms on which employment is offered.
>
> (3) Where a person offers a woman employment on certain terms, and if she accepted the offer then, by virtue of an equality clause, any of those terms would fall to be modified, or any additional term would fall to be included, the other shall be taken to contravene section 6(1)(b).
>
> (4) Where a person offers a woman employment on certain terms, and subsection (3) would apply but for the fact that, on her acceptance of the offer, section 1(3) of the Equal Pay Act 1970 (as set out in subsection (1) above) would prevent the equality clause from operating, the offer shall be taken not to contravene section 6(1)(b).
>
> (5) An act does not contravene section 6(2) if—
>
> > (a) it contravenes a term modified or included by virtue of an equality clause, or
> >
> > (b) it would contravene such a term but for the fact that the equality clause is prevented from operating by section 1(3) of the Equal Pay Act 1970.

In *Shields* v. *E. Coomes (Holdings) Ltd.*[91] Lord Denning M.R. referred to the effect of these provisions as a jigsaw puzzle with the pieces jumbled together in two boxes.

The confusion is made infinitely worse if resort is had to EEC law in order to expand the protection of United Kingdom legislation or to avoid the effect of some express limitation thereto. As we have seen Article 119 of the EEC Treaty is directly applicable but only extends to pay—not in the limited sense of money but of any remuneration, including payment in kind.[92] The Equal Treatment Directive (76/207), which may or may not be directly applicable in Member States, applies to all terms and conditions of employment.[93]

Indirect discrimination

Indirect discrimination arises from the application of a condition which, regardless of intention, bears detrimentally on a considerably larger proportion of one protected class than on others and which the discriminator cannot show to be justified irrespective of the discriminatory ground. Many of the problems that students experience in applying this concept appear to stem from a failure to appreciate that because various forms of discrimination are deeply entrenched in society as a whole a wide range of conditions commonly applied to everyone will be substantially less capable of being met by certain groups. Racial minorities are concentrated in defined areas. Failure to recruit in such

---

[90] Sex Discrimination Act 1975, s.8.
[91] [1978] I.C.R. 1159.
[92] *Garland* v. *British Rail Engineering Ltd.* [1982] I.R.L.R. 111.
[93] *Burton* v. *British Railways Board* [1982] I.R.L.R. 116.

areas will affect everyone living there but will mean that a substantially smaller proportion of that minority can be recruited from other areas than from the majority group living therein. Discrimination against women may be bad in employment but it is worse in the domestic sphere. If an employer seeks an employee with 20 years experience he will inevitably be looking at a primarily male dominated group of people. Not all the discriminatory effect of such conditions, of course, arises from other discriminatory conditions. Protected groups may well be placed in a disadvantageous position by unavoidable circumstances. In *Perera* v. *Civil Service Comission*,[94] for instance, an age limitation was held disadvantageous to immigrants simply because a smaller proportion of them would have been in the country during the period covered by the specified ages. The answer to the degree of justification that must be shown to excuse such a discriminatory result is central to the decision as to how much indirect discrimination will escape the statutory prohibition. In order to understand the operation of indirect discrimination it must also be accepted that there is no objection to placing those against whom circumstances discriminate in a preferential position so far as remedies are concerned. To put a single illustration: the woman who complains that the circumstances of women do not permit such ready acquisition of job experience may complain of the detrimental effect upon her of a requirement for such experience. On the other hand a man who may not have such experience for some equally good reason has no ground on which to complain.[95]

This situation is clearly demonstrated in the case of *Price* v. *Civil Service Commission*.[96] The applicant complained of indirect discrimination against women arising from a requirement that applicants for the grade of executive officer in the Civil Service should be between the ages of $17\frac{1}{2}$ and 28 years of age. The E.A.T. accepted her argument that a substantially smaller proportion of women than men were on the labour market during those years because, as a fact, women were the ones who were expected to produce and look after young children, which activity tended to occur in those years of their life. In doing so the court established the important principle that the reference in the Act to the ability to comply with the allegedly discriminatory condition was not intended to produce a test of physical possibility but of practical fact. Phillips J. said:

> "Experience shows that when considering section $1(1)(b)$ it is necessary to define with some precision the requirement or condition which is called in question. Even when the facts are not in dispute it is possible to formulate the requirement or condition, usually at all events, in more than one way; the precise formulation is important when considering sub-paragraphs (i), (ii) and (iii). A fair way of putting it in the present case seems to be that candidates for the post of executive officer must not be over 28 years of age. We do not accept the submission of counsel for the Civil Service Commission that the words 'can comply' must be construed narrowly, and we think that the industrial tribunal were wrong to accept this submission. In one sense it can be said that any female applicant can comply with the condition. She is not obliged to marry, or to have children, or to mind children;

---

94 [1982] I.R.L.R. 147.
95 In *Perera* v. *Civil Service Commission, supra,* a white anglo-saxon who had been out of the country all his previous life, could not have complained that the condition was discriminatory.
96 [1978] I.C.R. 27.

she may find somebody to look after them, and as a last resort she may put them into care. In this sense no doubt counsel for the Civil Service Commission is right in saying that any female applicant can comply with the condition. Such a construction appears to us to be wholly out of sympathy with the spirit and intent of the Act. Further, it should be repeated that compliance with sub-paragraph (i) is only a preliminary step, which does not lead to a finding that an act is one of discrimination unless the person acting fails to show that it is justifiable. 'Can' is defined (*The Shorter Oxford English Dictionary,* 3rd ed. (1944) p. 255) 'To be able; to have the power or capacity.' It is a word with many shades of meaning, and we are satisfied that it should not be too narrowly—nor too broadly—construed in its context in section 1(1)(*b*)(i). It should not be said that a person 'can' do something merely because it is theoretically possible for him to do so: it is necessary to see whether he can do so in practice. Applying this approach to the circumstances of this case, it is relevant in determining whether women can comply with the condition to take into account the current usual behaviour of women in this respect, as observed in practice, putting on one side behaviour and responses which are unusual or extreme.

Knowledge and experience suggest that a considerable number of women between the mid-twenties and the mid-thirties are engaged in bearing children and in minding children, and that while many find it possible to take up employment many others, while desiring to do so, find it impossible, and that many of the latter as their children get older find that they can follow their wish and seek employment. This knowledge and experience is confirmed by some of the statistical evidence produced to the industrial tribunal (and by certain additional statistical evidence put in by consent of the parties on the hearing of the appeal). This demonstrates clearly that the economic activity of women with at least one Advanced Level falls off markedly about the age of 23, reaching a bottom at about the age of 33 when it climbs gradually to a plateau at about 45.

Basing ourselves on this and other evidence, we should have no hesitation in concluding that our own knowledge and experience is confirmed, and that it is safe to say that the condition is one which it is in practice harder for women to comply with than it is for men. We should be inclined to go further and say that there are undoubtedly women of whom it may be properly said in terms of section 1(1)(*b*)(i) that they 'cannot' comply with the condition, because they are women; that is to say because of their involvement with their children."

Although this must mean that any age limitation of which the lower age is less than, say, 45 will constitute indirect discrimination against women the proposition is obviously a correct interpretation of the legislative intention. The safety valve is justification and, as we have said, the strictness of the application of discrimination will depend on the extent to which that valve is opened. In *Clarke and Powell* v. *Eley (I.M.I. Kynoch) Ltd.*[96a] the E.A.T. approved a tribunal decision that the selection for redundancy of part-time employees discriminated against women. The E.A.T., however, held the tribunal to be wrong in its conclusion that the female complainant could have satisfied the condition by accepting full-time employment at any time in the previous six years. In view of the court the answer to the question of ability to satisfy a condition must be given by reference only to the situation at the time of the discriminating act.

Precisely the same point as was made in *Price* was applied by an industrial

---

[96a] [1982] I.R.L.R. 482.

tribunal in *Bohon-Mitchell* v. *Common Professional Examination Board, etc.*[97] to a rule that certificates of eligibility for the academic stage of the Bar examinations should be available on different terms to English speaking non-law graduates with an English degree as against those with a non-English degree. In the same way, in *Hussein* v. *Saints Complete House Furnishers*[98] an industrial tribunal held discriminatory a specification by employers that applicants for jobs should not be from the city centre of Liverpool. Evidence showed that 50 per cent. of the population in this area was coloured as against $12\frac{1}{2}$ per cent. from another area from which the employers were prepared to recruit.[99]

A difficulty in applying this principle arose in *MacGregor Wallcoverings Ltd.* v. *Turton.*[1] Women retired compulsorily at 60 whilst men did not so retire until the age of 65. This would clearly have been direct discrimination but for section 6(4) of the Sex Discrimination Act which exempts pension arrangements from the operation of the Act. A redundancy scheme was produced which provided for a higher rate of compensation for those made redundant over the age of 60. The applicant complained that this scheme was indirectly discriminatory since no woman could qualify for the higher rate of redundancy compensation. Phillips J., in a rare minority in the E.A.T., could not accept that indirect discrimination could spring from a situation expressly exempted from the operation of the Act. With respect, it is difficult to justify this hesitation. The underlying situation which gives rise to the discriminatory effect of a common condition will often be outside the operation of the Act. It is true that that underlying situation will not be the subject of complaint also because it is not created by any action of the alleged discriminator. The legislation, however, makes no point about the underlying situation save that it should exist. It is of no moment that the situation is itself legal or illegal. What is illegal is the operation of the condition upon it. Consequently it can make no difference from whence the underlying situation derives its legality.

Justification

The Presidency of Phillips J. in the E.A.T. witnessed many deliberate and important developments of the law and nowhere more obviously than in the law relating to discrimination. It is not surprising, therefore, to find that learned judge seeking, in *Steel* v. *Union of Post Office Workers,*[2] to establish a strictly limited view of the scope of justification necessary if indirect discrimination was not to be illegal. Mrs. Steel had been employed by the Post Office since 1961 but she did not achieve "permanent full-time" status until 1975 when a rule that women could not achieve this position was abolished, with the agreement of the Union. Under the terms of that agreement Mrs. Steel's seniority dated only from the attainment of permanent full-time status. Mrs. Steel applied for a "walk" which was allotted on the basis of seniority to a male employee who had had full-time permanent status since July 1973. The E.A.T. held that the rule that women could only date seniority back to August 1, 1975 was indirect

---

[97] [1978] I.R.L.R. 525.
[98] [1979] I.R.L.R. 337.
[99] See also *Thorndyke* v. *Bell Frist (North Central) Ltd.* [1979] I.R.L.R. 1; *Steel* v. *Union of Post Office Workers* [1978] I.C.R. 181.
[1] [1978] I.C.R. 541.
[2] [1978] I.C.R. 181.

discrimination against women. In dealing with justification the E.A.T. made the following points:

(i) There is a heavy onus of proof upon the discriminator to show that the discriminatory act was necessary. The condition is not that of convenience.

(ii) It is relevant to consider whether the purpose could be achieved in some other way without the discriminatory effect.

(iii) The necessity must be weighed against the discriminatory effect and not only against the needs of the enterprise.

(iv) Although the Sex Discrimination Act does not operate retrospectively it is in accordance with the spirit of the Act that it should operate so as to destroy the continuing effect of past discrimination. There is a parallel between necessity and the genuine material difference operating as a justification in section 1(3) of the Equal Pay Act.

The analogy with the Equal Pay Act has served the claimant badly because it has led to the application to them of the principle that the burden of proof is the civil standard of balance of probability.[3] It will be sufficient, therefore, for an employer to show that it was reasonable for him to conclude that the justification was necessary. In *Singh* v. *Rowntree Mackintosh Ltd.*[4] a Sikh contended that a rule forbidding employees who came into contact with food products to have beards discriminated against him. The Scottish E.A.T. took into account that moustaches and side whiskers were not forbidden and that some form of covering might be devised but held that the employer might reasonably conclude that the alternatives were not reasonable and that the rule was necessary in terms of commercial competition. The E.A.T. effectively admitted that the employer was judging not necessity but expedience but that it was reasonable for him to decide to adopt such expedience.[5] In *Kingston and Richmond Area Health Authority* v. *Kaur*[6] a Sikh woman, required by her religion to wear trousers, complained of the discriminatory effect of a requirement that State Enrolled Nurses should wear a uniform including a skirt. An industrial tribunal had held that it was reasonable to require the wearing of some uniform and the E.A.T. held that it must be justifiable to require the wearing of the only uniform permitted by the relevant statutory instrument.

The Court of Appeal expressly said that *Steel* v. *U.P.O.W.* went too far in *Ojutiku and Oburoni* v. *Manpower Services Commission*[6a] although it conceded that it was useful to indicate that the test was not one of convenience. The applicants had been refused study grants for a course leading to a Diploma in Management because they failed to satisfy the condition of possessing professional or management experience. They claimed that fewer black persons than white would possess such experience. Eveleigh L.J. said that the standard of justification was whether the requirement would be acceptable to right thinking

---

[3] *National Vulcan Engineering Insurance Group Ltd.* v. *Wade* [1978] I.C.R. 800.

[4] [1979] I.C.R. 554.

[5] In *Panesar* v. *Nestlé Co. Ltd.* [1980] I.C.R. 144 the Court of Appeal in effect confirmed this view by refusing leave to appeal in similar circumstances from a finding of justification by the E.A.T.

[6] [1981] I.C.R. 631.

[6a] [1982] I.R.L.R. 418. The training services of this and other government agencies is included by the S.D.A. 1975, ss.14 and 16 and the R.R.A. 1976, ss.13 and 15.

people as sound and tolerable. The justification, moreover, is that of the alleged discriminator in the circumstances in which he finds himself. In this case the M.S.C.'s reason for the condition was the fact that employers were much less inclined to offer employment to those in possession of the Diploma but without experience. The fact that this third party attitude might itself be indirectly discriminatory did not prevent its existence being relied upon as a justification. Whilst, perforce, accepting this standard in *Clarke* v. *Eley (IMI) Kynoch Ltd.*[6b] the E.A.T. pointed out that this placed the decision as to justification largely at the discretion of the tribunal. Browne-Wilkinson J. said, *obiter*, that if so large a discretion on so emotive an issue was to be left to so many tribunals the law should indicate the degree of importance to be attached to eliminating indirect discrimination so that doubts should not exist, for instance, as to whether a "last in—first out" formula constituted indirect discrimination or was justified.

There is no doubt that if Phillips J. had intended an objective standard of necessity it would have operated more strictly than the current requirement of a reasonable belief in necessity. It is, of course, still possible to show that the way in which an employer applies a rule which may be considered necessary may be unnecessarily wide or, in other words, that the decision as to what satisfies the necessity is itself based on discriminatory assumptions. So in *Hurley* v. *Mustoe*[7] the E.A.T. held that the necessity that employees should be reliable could not justify the conclusion that all women with young children were unreliable. The applicant might, therefore, complain of discrimination arising from such an assumption whereas there would have been no cause to complain that a proper process of investigation might statistically be likely to exclude more women than men on this ground. The possibility of arriving at different answers on this issue is clearly demonstrated by the Court of Appeal in *Coleman* v. *Skyrail Oceanic Ltd.*[8] A female booking clerk became engaged to a male employee in a rival agency. The two agencies eventually jointly considered the question of the risk of leaks of confidential information and it was decided that the lady should be dismissed because the man would be the breadwinner. The E.A.T., despite this, held that there was no evidence that the agent who employed the lady would have treated a man differently. Shaw L.J., in the Court of Appeal, supported this on the ground that once it was clear that the competing agency would not dismiss its employee the employer in question would have dismissed the employee producing the threat regardless of sex. A majority of the Court of Appeal, however, held that there was evidence to support the tribunal finding that a man would not have been treated in the same way so that the employer had, in effect, responded to the necessity to protect confidentiality by a sex-based response.

Application to employment

Having defined unlawful discrimination the two Acts proceed to apply that standard to numerous situations including employment. It is provided in section 6 of the Sex Discrimination Act[9] that:

[6b] [1982] I.R.L.R. 418.
[7] [1981] I.C.R. 490. See also *Clarke and Powell* v. *Eley (I.M.I. Kynoch) Ltd.* [1982] I.R.L.R. 418.
[8] [1981] I.C.R. 864.
[9] See corresponding provisions in R.R.A. 1976, s.4.

Offers

6.—(1) It is unlawful for a person, in relation to employment by him in an establishment in Great Britain, to discriminate against a woman—

(a) in the arrangements he makes for the purpose of determining who should be offered that employment, or

(b) in the terms on which he offers her that employment, or

(c) by refusing or deliberately omitting to offer her that employment.

Detriment

(2) It is unlawful for a person, in the case of a woman employed by him at an establishment in Great Britain, to discriminate against her—

(a) in the way he affords her access to opportunities for promotion, transfer or training, or to any other benefits, facilities or services, or by refusing or deliberately omitting to afford her access to them, or

(b) by dismissing her, or subjecting her to any other detriment.

Exclusion

(3) Except in relation to discrimination falling within section 4, subsections (1) and (2) do not apply to employment—

(a) for the purposes of a private household, or

(b) where the number of persons employed by the employer, added to the number employed by any associated employers of his, does not exceed five (disregarding any persons employed for the purposes of a private household).

(4) Subsections (1)(b) and (2) do not apply to provision in relation to death or retirement.

The Race Relations Act does not contain the provision excluding small employers.[10]

Pay

(5) Subject to section 8(3), subsection 1(b) does not apply to any provision for the payment of money which, if the woman in question were given the employment, would be included (directly or by reference to a collective agreement or otherwise) in the contract under which she was employed.

(6) Subsection (2) does not apply to benefits consisting of the payment of money when the provision of those benefits is regulated by the woman's contract of employment.

The Race Relations Act does not include this provision.[11]

Services

(7) Subsection (2) does not apply to benefits, facilities or services of any description if the employer is concerned with the provision (for payment or not) of benefits, facilities or services of that description to the public, or to a section of the public comprising the woman in question, unless—

---

[10] See R.R.A. 1976, s.4   [11] Ibid.

(a) that provision differs in a material respect from the provision of the benefits, facilities or services by the employer to his employees, or

(b) the provision of the benefits, facilities or services to the woman in question is regulated by her contract of employment, or

(c) the benefits, facilities or services relate to training.

Partnerships

A number of matters ancillary to employment are also covered, as, for instance, admission to partnerships of six or more partners, or the treatment of existing partners; the provision of services by employment agents; discrimination as to membership by professional bodies; and the provision of vocational training. Both Acts also apply to trade union membership. The Sex Discrimination Act makes special provision to exclude from its operation midwives, miners and ministers of religion.

Self employment

The word "employment" in these Acts includes self-employment (in the usual statutory sense of personal execution of work) and service under the Crown except for military service and "statutory office."[12]

It is clear that the list of items in sections 6 and 4, respectively, of the two Acts is clearly intended to be construed widely and, on the whole, the courts have done so.[13] On the other hand, reference to "benefit" and "detriment" to those already employed[14] were viewed by the Court of Appeal in *Peake* v. *Automotive Products Ltd.*[15] as subject to the *de minimis* rule.[16] It is suggested, however, that the further aspect of that decision that safety provisions made in respect of women cannot be viewed as detrimental to men must fail once it is conceded that the proper question is whether the employer was acting for reasons of safety or discrimination. If an alleged safety provision is made because of a discriminatory assumption then it must be detrimental to those who would benefit from it if such an assumption has not been made. If, on the other hand, it is properly applied to those who need it, it could be said that there is no detriment to those to whom it is not applied. In that case, however, there is no direct discrimination anyway. Accordingly it is suggested that *Peake* does not stand in the way of later decisions[17] which include any disadvantage as a detriment.[18]

---

[12] S.D.A. 1975, ss.82(1) and 85; R.R.A. 1976, ss.78(1) and 75.

[13] See, *e.g. Saunders* v. *Richmond upon Thames London Borough Council* [1978] I.C.R. 75; *Roadburg* v. *Lothian Regional Council* [1976] I.R.L.R. 283 on the scope of "arrangements for selection."

[14] S.D.A. 1975, ss.4(2) and 6(2).

[15] [1977] I.C.R. 968.

[16] See also Phillips J. in *Schmidt* v. *Austicks Bookshops Ltd.* [1978] I.C.R. 85.

[17] *Ministry of Defence* v. *Jeremiah* [1978] I.C.R. 984 (E.A.T.) and Brandon L.J. [1980] I.R.L.R. 13; *Kirby* v. *Manpower Services Commission* [1980] I.C.R. 420.

[18] The author takes the view that it must follow—contra Brightman L.J. in *Jeremiah's* case—that "Ladies only" compartments in railways carriages are a detriment to men not so much because of a restriction of choice, which might well be *de minimis,* but because of a reduction of available space.

Marriage

It should be noted that the Sex Discrimination Act section 3 unaccountably contains a serious limitation on the prohibition of discrimination on grounds of marital status by limiting it to the status of marriage.[19]

Sexual harassment

A form of workplace sexism, no doubt long recognised has, recently, been given the name "sexual harassment." For purposes of possible legal restraint two types may be distinguished.

(i) The employee is given to understand that unless she submits to some form of sexual relationship she will be placed at a recognisable disadvantage at work or may even be dismissed.

(ii) No such recognisable disadvantage is involved but sexual overtures make the working environment unpleasant.

It is sometimes said that United Kingdom law provides for neither of these situations but it is submitted that the first may constitute unlawful sexual discrimination under the Sex Discrimination Act. The only doubt that might exist is whether it can be contended that the reason for the requirement is not the fact that the employee is a woman (because only she, and not all or most other women, is selected). We have said that the reliance in *Schmidt* v. *Austicks Bookshops Ltd.*[19a] upon absence of any comparison with men is probably a misconstruction of the statutory provision. Nevertheless we have argued that direct discrimination on grounds of pregnancy is not prohibited. It may well follow that direct discrimination on grounds that the employee is sexually attractive is similarly not prohibited. Does it go too far to argue that the condition necessary to avoid the detriment is lack of sexual attractiveness and that substantially fewer women than men can satisfy that condition?

If the imposition of a recognisable disadvantage can be brought within the Act then, it is submitted, the second situation poses no problem additional to that just considered. Lawton L.J. in *Western Excavating (E.C.C.) Ltd.* v. *Sharp*[19b] selected sexual harassment as a clear example of destruction of trust and confidence constituting a repudiatory breach. The souring of the working relationship was regarded in *Isle of Wight Tourist Board* v. *Coombes*[19c] as a repudiatory breach as was the institution of the sexual relationship in *Wood* v. *Freeloader Ltd.*[19d] If such situations constitute repudiatory breach it seems inconceivable that they do not constitute a recognisable detriment.

Exclusions

Genuine occupational qualification

Both Acts contain provisions applicable to discrimination in employment and somewhat similar to section 1(3) of the Equal Pay Act exempting from prohibition the imposition of certain "Genuine Occupational Qualifications." The

---

[19] *Birk* v. *Royal West of England Residential School for the Deaf* [1976] I.R.L.R. 326.
[19a] [1978] I.C.R. 85.   [19b] [1978] I.C.R. 221.
[19c] [1976] I.R.L.R. 413.   [19d] [1977] I.R.L.R. 455.

exemption is, however, not as large as in the earlier Act but consists of specific situations which, in the case of the Race Relations Act at least, are few and narrow.

The list in the Sex Discrimination Act[20] is as follows:

7.—(1) In relation to sex discrimination—

    (a) section 6(1)(a) or (c) does not apply to any employment where being a man is a genuine occupational qualification for the job, and

    (b) section 6(2)(a) does not apply to opportunities for promotion or transfer to, or training for, such employment.

    (2) Being a man is a genuine occupational qualification for a job only where—

    (a) the essential nature of the job calls for a man for reasons of physiology (excluding physical strength or stamina) or, in dramatic performances or other entertainment, for reasons of authenticity, so that the essential nature of the job would be materially different if carried out by a woman; or

    (b) the job needs to be held by a man to preserve decency or privacy because—

        (i) it is likely to involve physical contact with men in circumstances where they might reasonably object to its being carried out by a woman, or

        (ii) the holder of the job is likely to do his work in circumstances where men might reasonably object to the presence of a woman because they are in a state of undress or are using sanitary facilities; or

    (c) the nature or location of the establishment makes it impracticable for the holder of the job to live elsewhere than in premises provided by the employer, and—

        (i) the only such premises which are available for persons holding that kind of job are lived in, or normally lived in, by men and are not equipped with separate sleeping accommodation for women and sanitary facilities which could be used by women in privacy from men, and

        (ii) it is not reasonable to expect the employer either to equip those premises with such accommodation and facilities or to provide other premises for women; or

    (d) the nature of the establishment, or of the part of it within which the work is done, requires the job to be held by a man because—

        (i) it is, or is part of, a hospital prison or other establishment for persons requiring special care, supervision or attention, and

        (ii) those persons are all men (disregarding any woman whose presence is exceptional), and

        (iii) it is reasonable, having regard to the essential character of the establishment or that part, that the job should not be held by a woman; or

---

[20] s.7.

(*e*) the holder of the job provides individuals with personal services promoting their welfare or education, or similar personal services, and those services can most effectively be provided by a man, or

(*f*) the job needs to be held by a man because of restrictions imposed by the laws regulating the employment of women, or

(*g*) the job needs to be held by a man because it is likely to involve the performance of duties outside the United Kingdom in a country whose laws or customs are such that the duties could not, or could not effectively, be performed by a woman, or

(*h*) the job is one of two to be held by a married couple.

(3) Subsection (2) applies where some only of the duties of the job fall within paragraphs (*a*) to (*g*) as well as where all of them do.

(4) Paragraph (*a*), (*b*), (*c*), (*d*), (*e*), (*f*) or (*g*) of subsection (2) does not apply in relation to the filling of a vacancy at a time when the employer already has male employees—

(*a*) who are capable of carrying out the duties falling within that paragraph, and

(*b*) whom it would be reasonable to employ on those duties, and

(*c*) whose numbers are sufficient to meet the employer's likely requirements in respect of those duties without undue inconvenience.

That in the Race Relations Act is much shorter[21]:

5.—(1) In relation to racial discrimination—

(*a*) section 4(1)(*a*) or (*c*) does not apply to any employment where being of a particular racial group is a genuine occupational qualification for the job; and

(*b*) section 4(2)(*b*) does not apply to opportunities for promotion or transfer to, or training for, such employment.

(2) Being of a particular racial group is a genuine occupational qualification for a job only where—

(*a*) the job involves participation in a dramatic performance or other entertainment in a capacity for which a person of that racial group is required for reasons of authenticity; or

(*b*) the job involves participation as an artist's or photographic model in the production of a work of art, visual image or sequence of visual images for which a person of that racial group is required for reasons of authenticity; or

(*c*) the job involves working in a place where food or drink is (for payment or not) provided to and consumed by members of the public or a section of the public in a particular setting for which in that job, a person of that racial group is required for reasons of authenticity; or

(*d*) the holder of the job provides persons of that racial group with personal services promoting their welfare, and those services can most effectively be provided by a person of that racial group.

(3) Subsection (2) applies where some only of the duties of the job fall within paragraphs (*a*), (*b*), (*c*) or (*d*) as well as where all of them do.

---

[21] s.5.

(4) Paragraph (*a*), (*b*), (*c*) or (*d*) of subsection (2) does not apply in relation to the filling of a vacancy at a time when the employer already has employees of the racial group in question—

(*a*) who are capable of carrying out the duties falling within that paragraph; and

(*b*) whom it would be reasonable to employ on those duties; and

(*c*) whose numbers are sufficient to meet the employer's likely requirements in respect of those duties without undue inconvenience.

It is often said that there are no grounds apart from this limited group which will excuse unlawful discrimination. That is strictly true. As we have noted, however, the enquiry may never reach this point because a decision resulting in discrimination is based on some established fact other than sex or race or because a discriminatory condition is justified. In *Ojutiku* v. *Manpower Services Commission*[22] for example the state of the job market effectively excused discrimination, or if one wishes to put it that way, removed the unlawful element from discrimination.

There is singularly little case law on the meaning of either of these two sections. Some of the loosest wording in either is contained in section 7(2)(*b*) which is replete with "likely" and "might reasonably object." Nevertheless in *Wylie* v. *Dee and Co.* (*Menswear*) *Ltd.*[23] an industrial tribunal interpreted them more nearly as "probably" when accepting evidence of six different ways in which a woman employed in a gents' outfitters might avoid causing objection to her taking inside leg measurements. The employer appears only to have provided an answer to one of these.

One of the most far reaching of the exceptions is contained in section 7(1)(*f*) of the Sex Discrimination Act referring to the imposition of restrictions necessary to comply with laws regulating the employment of women.[24] One of the principal examples of such statutory requirement is the provisions of the Factories Act 1961.[25] Originally the Equal Opportunities Commission took the view that it might be argued that compliance with this did not become necessary unless the employer had tried and failed to obtain a certificate of exemption.[26]

Death or retirement

The Sex Discrimination Act[27] excludes from the operation of the prohibition upon discrimination on grounds of sex or marriage any provisions in an offer of employment or any benefit or detriment applied to an employee in relation to "death or retirement." As we have seen[28] the Court of Appeal in *Worringham* v. *Lloyds Bank Ltd.*[29] followed *Roberts* v. *Cleveland*[30] in holding that this

---

[22] [1982] I.R.L.R. 418 (C.A.).   [23] [1978] I.R.L.R. 103.

[24] Despite the alleged exclusiveness of s.7, s.51 contains a similar but slightly wider provision. E.P.A. 1975, s.6(1)(*a*) has the same effect as S.D.A. 1975, s.7.

[25] s.93.

[26] The industrial tribunal in *White* v. *British Sugar Corporation Ltd.* [1977] I.R.L.R. 121 thought that the dismissal of Ted White upon the discovery that she was a woman was justified by the fact that an exemption certificate would have been needed to employ her on Sundays and this would have taken time to acquire.

[27] s.6(4)—The Race Relations Act has no parallel provision.

[28] *Supra*, p. 318.

[29] [1981] I.C.R. 558.

[30] [1979] I.C.R. 558.

exemption extended to provisions about death or retirement but that the European Court[31] had cautiously decided that differential payments made to employees to enable them to contribute to pension funds constituted remuneration required by Article 119 of the EEC Treaty to be equal. It has been noted that this caution leaves in doubt the general effect of EEC law on the death and retirement exclusion in relation to sex discrimination.[32] The Court of Appeal had considered three separate tribunal decisions on the provision in the Sex Discrimination Act.[33] In *Roberts* v. *Cleveland Area Health Authority*[34] it confirmed the decision of the E.A.T. that a requirement that women retire at 60, as against 65 for men, was covered by the exclusion. Although the Court of Appeal, somewhat surprisingly, relied on an explanatory pamphlet issued by the EEC, as Professor Wallington points out[35] this must have been the legislative intention if no attempt was made to alter the retirement provisions of Social Security legislation. In *Turton* v. *MacGregor Wallcoverings Ltd.*[36] Mrs. Turton who had been dismissed for redundancy at the age of 57 would never have qualified for an extra 10 weeks' compensation for those made redundant after the age of 60 because women were required to retire at the age of 60. Although noting that Mrs. Turton had suffered no detriment since a man dismissed at 57 would not have enjoyed the extra benefit the Court of Appeal in holding that the exclusion in relation to retirement applied, failed to observe that precisely this point meant that the operation of the redundancy scheme had nothing to do with retirement. The requirement that women should retire at 60 produced a situation in which the redundancy scheme's differential payment constituted indirect discrimination but it was not any requirement of retirement which itself amounted to discrimination so as to invoke the exclusion provision.

In the third case, *Garland* v. *British Rail Engineering Ltd.*,[37] a majority of the E.A.T. had drawn a distinction between a pre-existing benefit allowed to continue on retirement and a benefit granted *de novo* and had concluded that the former did not exist in relation to retirement. It is suggested that the Court of Appeal was right in its view that any part of a scheme of benefits upon retirement exists in relation to retirement regardless of its origin elsewhere. Before the European Court[38] it was held that Article 119 of the EEC Treaty applied so as to bring the facts of this case within the equal pay provisions and, therefore, to override the exclusion to that extent. Following this decision the Court of Appeal said that Acts of the United Kingdom Parliament should be construed so as, if possible, not to conflict with Article 119. It was, therefore, right to construe the exclusion of pension provisions narrowly.

In *Burton* v. *British Railways Board*[39] the European Court avoided overthrowing the exclusion from the Sex Discrimination Act of retirement provisions by the application of the Equal Treatment Directive (76/207). It held that that Directive did cover direct discrimination between men and women as regards any terms and conditions of employment. On the other hand the United

---

[31] [1981] I.R.L.R. 178.
[32] See also *Garland* v. *British Rail Engineering Ltd.* [1982] I.R.L.R. 111.
[33] [1979] I.R.L.R. 244.
[34] [1978] I.C.R. 370 (E.A.T.).
[35] Elias Napier and Wallington at p. 770.
[36] [1977] I.R.L.R. 249 (I.T.).
[37] [1978] I.C.R. 495.
[38] [1982] I.R.L.R. 111.
[39] [1982] I.R.L.R. 116.

Kingdom was free to determine pensionable age for the provision of social security benefits[40] and the indirect effect of different retirement ages for men and women upon a private redundancy scheme was not discrimination prohibited by Community Law. This, of course, leaves open the possibility that other discriminatory effects of retirement schemes may be contrary to Directive 76/207 and that the European Court will one day decide that that Directive is directly applicable to Member States. No doubt this view was in line with the Commission's general opposition to the existence of protective but discriminatory legislation of this sort.[41]

Discrimination provided for by the terms of any charitable instrument is exempt from the operation of the Acts[42] although there is provision to secure the amendment of the instrument. Provision is also made in both Acts[43]; to enable positive discrimination in provision of training facilities.

REMEDIES

An individual may complain of discrimination in any of the areas covered by Part II of the Sex Discrimination Act or of the Race Relations Act to an industrial tribunal[44] normally within three months of the act of discrimination or the last date of a continuing discrimination.[45] When such a complaint is made an ACAS conciliation officer must be notified[46] and he may endeavour to promote a settlement wherever requested to do so by both parties or of the opinion that he could act with a reasonable prospect of success.

If a tribunal finds a complaint well founded it may make such of the following as it considers just and equitable.[47]

(a) an order declaring the rights of the complainant and the respondent in relation to the act complained of;

(b) an order for compensation corresponding to county court or sheriff court rules subject to the upper limit currently applicable to unfair dismissal claims but including any element for injury to feelings.[48] The amount of compensation for injured feelings should be moderate in accordance with the guidance given in defamation cases.[49] No award of compensation may be made, however, where the respondent proves that indirect discrimination was not intended to result in unfavourable treatment;

(c) a recommendation that the respondent take within a specified period action appearing to the tribunal to be practicable for the purpose of

---

[40] Dir. 79/7; EEC Art. 7.

[41] For the contrary opinion see National Council for Civil Liberties Report No. 17: *Protective Laws: Evidence to the E.O.C.* (1977).

[42] S.D.A. 1975, s.43; R.R.A. 1976, s.34; *Hugh-Jones* v. *St. John's College Cambridge* [1979] I.C.R 848.

[43] S.D.A. 1975, s.37; R.R.A. 1976, s.41.

[44] S.D.A. 1975, s.63; R.R.A. 1976, s.54.

[45] The test of "just and equitable" for permitting claims out of time is somewhat more lenient than that applicable to complaints of unfair dismissal. See *Hutchison* v. *Westward Television Ltd.* [1977] I.C.R. 279.

[46] S.D.A. 1975, s.64; R.R.A. 1976, s.55.

[47] S.D.A. 1975, s.65; R.R.A. 1976, s.56.

[48] S.D.A. 1975, s.66(4); R.R.A. 1976, s.57(4).

[49] *Skyrail Oceanic Ltd.* v. *Coleman* [1980] I.C.R. 596.

treating or reducing the adverse effect on the complainant of the discrimination to which the complaint relates.[50]

A failure without reasonable justification to comply with a recommendation may lead to an award of increased compensation.

Complaint may be made of discrimination by an employer as a company but it is important to note that such complaint can be made against any person. Any person who knowingly aids another person to do an unlawful act shall himself be treated as having done an unlawful act of like description and the act of an employee or agent for whose act an employer or principal is liable shall be deemed to aid the act of the employer or principal.[51]

The Commissions

The Equal Opportunities Commission was established under the Sex Discrimination Act and the Race Relations Commission under the Race Relations Act with identical power primarily to exercise a more general function of detection and removal of discrimination than would be achieved merely by reliance on individual complaint. The Commissions have powers to promote research and education to this end.

In one particular the Commissions provide the only enforcing body. The publication of advertisements *which might reasonably be understood* as indicating an intention unlawfully to discriminate is itself unlawful; in the case of the Sex Discrimination Act only if the discrimination intended would be unlawful[52] but in the case of the Race Relations Act whether that is so or not.[53] The test is the likely response of the ordinary reader.[54] If the act complained of itself constitutes discrimination within the scope of an industrial tribunal the Commission must first secure a decision from such a tribunal that the act was unlawful before seeking an injunction from a county court. Otherwise the Commission may immediately seek such an order.

The power to conduct formal investigations on relevant matters at its own initiative or at the request of the Secretary of State into matters within its scope was, no doubt, intended as the principal effective function of each Commission. The E.O.C., however, has taken the view that the safeguards preceding the carrying out of its function render such powers of little practical value. The Commission for Racial Equality, however, habitually uses evidence of discrimination from which no individual complaint arises to guide it in the establishment of formal enquiries. It has indicated[55] that as a matter of policy it will initiate investigations in areas where equal opportunities are of proportionately high importance for the establishment of good race relations and the extent to which unlawful discrimination is a cause of significant disadvantage to ethnic minorities is itself considerable. It will also have regard to the appropriateness and effectiveness of formal investigation to eliminate discrimination

---

[50] In *Jeremiah* v. *Ministry of Defence* [1980] Q.B. 87 it was held that this did not confer power to make an order to instal showers for women.
[51] S.D.A. 1975, s.42; R.R.A. 1976, s.33.
[52] s.38.
[53] s.29.
[54] *Commission for Racial Equality* v. *Associated Newspapers Group Ltd.* [1978] 1 W.L.R. 905.
[55] Annual Report 1978.

and to the work being done by other agencies. It regards employment as a particularly suitable area for investigation.

It is intended that the power of the Commissions to issue non-discrimination notices shall provide the sanction, if such is necessary, after a formal investigation. A non-discrimination notice may require the person on whom it is served not to commit the acts in question and to inform the Commission of changes he has made which are necessary to comply with the order. He may also be required to take reasonable steps to inform other persons concerned of those steps.[56] But the Commission must first give such person notice that it is minded to issue such a notice, specifying the grounds upon which such issue is contemplated. Such person must be given an opportunity within a period of not less than 28 days specified in the notice to make representations and those representations must be taken account of. Not later than six weeks after the non-discrimination notice is served the person on whom it is served may appeal, in the case of employment matters, to an industrial tribunal which may quash any requirement which it considers to be unreasonable and substitute some other requirement in its place. A public register of final discrimination notices is kept.[57]

The Commissions may seek an injunction to prevent repeated discrimination within five years of a non-discrimination notice becoming final.[58]

Finally, it is within the powers of the Commissions to give advice and assistance to those who are actual or prospective claimants against discrimination.[59] The Commission may give advice, seek to procure a settlement, arrange for legal advice or representation or give any other assistance it considers appropriate. It has, however, no obligation, having considered the application for assistance, to grant it.

---

[56] S.D.A. 1975, s.67(2); R.R.A. 1976, s.58(2).
[57] S.D.A. 1975, s.70; R.R.A. 1976, s.61.
[58] S.D.A. 1975, s.71; R.R.A. 1976, s.62.
[59] S.D.A. 1975, s.75; R.R.A. 1976, s.66.

CHAPTER 8

COLLECTIVE INDUSTRIAL RELATIONS

As Davies and Freedland pointed out[1] collective bargaining is not, as the Webbs implied, a system whereby the power of the individual to negotiate the terms of his engagement is taken over by the group. Collective bargaining does not take place at the point of engagement of labour. Instead it is a process of making rules which will govern employment. There is, indeed, a strong element within the process in the United Kingdom of minimum rules which leave much of the freedom of individual contract-making intact. This approach not only, or indeed most obviously, allows the individual to make his own contract if he can but also permits smaller collectives to displace the original rules with others applicable to a particular location or situation within the larger group.

The Webbs seem to have regarded collective bargaining as self-justifying. The picture they paint is of inexorable growth without regard to acceptance by the employer. Indeed they seem to have thought employer opposition inevitable. They would, therefore, have been surprised that the steady movement to larger and larger bargaining units should have been reversed, failing to notice that the very freedom which characterises a system, essentially seeking to establish minimum obligations, must tend to this result. They might also have been surprised that the tendency of collective bargaining to produce uniformity, thereby removing a major cause of individual dissatisfaction, would appeal to employers.

The development of collective bargaining has made these aspects apparent. Inevitably, growing realisation of the potential of different systems has led to departures from the norm, many of which have been deliberate. Some agreements, for instance, do fix absolute standards leaving the individual or the lesser group no room to negotiate within the rules.

Kahn-Freund points out[2] that the method adopted for this rule-making process in the United Kingdom is, more often than not, by way of standing bodies rather than an ad hoc coming together of the parties to resolve a particular issue. He described these different methods as "institutional or dynamic" on the one hand and "contractual or static" on the other. The most obvious difference of effect is, of course, that under the dynamic process the scene is under constant, even organised, review. In his view, the dominance of the dynamic system in the United Kingdom to some extent accounts for the preference for devices making for flexibility such as the absence of contractual enforceability, time limits and a distinction between disputes of right (interpretation of the agreement) and disputes of interest (improvement upon its terms) which is a major aspect of the organisation of industrial relations machinery in other countries.

The popular concept of bargaining as a process of working out a *modus vivendi* between two parties in perpetual conflict is partially justified but is

---

[1] pp. 11 *et seq.*
[2] *Labour and the Law* (2nd ed.) at pp. 52–53.

345

criticised by those who refuse to accept the inevitability of conflict. The view more widely adopted by students of industrial relations is that the conflict is inevitable. There is a common purpose but the parties have different interests in it. It is incorrect to assume that there are only two parties. It is common to suggest that society has an interest which should be represented by government—rarely directly but often by precise restrictions of the freedom to negotiate for any result the "direct" parties desire. That is not the only interest which may intrude. Groups of workers may have different interests which may have little direct relevance to the dispute, as for instance where inter-union problems obtrude, and the interest of the group of workers may, on occasion, differ from that of the union which represents it. This conflict must sooner or later give rise to discussion as to the extent to which it can influence industrial organisation. In other words, how far is it to challenge management prerogative?

LOCAL AND NATIONAL BARGAINING

"Britain has two systems of industrial relations. The one is the formal system embodied in the official institutions. The other is the informal system created by the actual behaviour of trade unions and employers' associations, of managers, shop stewards and workers."[3]

It is important to realise that the strength of the local bargaining side of industrial relations is peculiar to this country and is the product of weak central trade union organisation and even weaker organisation of employers' associations. Sometimes this is seen as a strength of the system. The 1968 Royal Commission recommended emphasis on local bargaining as the most effective instrument for solving problems to which it was close and of which, therefore, it understood the issues. Some German commentators suggested at the time of the report of the Bullock Commission into employee participation in management that proposals to place employer representatives on Boards of Directors suited the atmosphere in Germany but would not have the same effect here. Similar results could be achieved they suggested, by developing the British system of largely autonomous local bargaining; particularly by supplying it with adequate information. Others point out the weaknesses of local bargaining. Inevitably, the horizons of a shop steward are more limited than those of a national official of the union. If it is regarded as desirable for government to consult trade unions—such consultation being of its nature at national level—what can be achieved by agreement if local negotiators pursue their own insular policies virtually free from central control? In terms of the national economy the inflationary and disruptive effect of local wage settlements building upon admittedly unrealistic national minima may be seen as disastrous. In the United States centrally controlled union policy often fixes a realistic national standard by an all out attack on an industry leader. The same central control then ensures a policy of bringing other employers into line. In Britain the fixing of national standards, so far as basic wage rates are concerned, is often seen as no more than the starting gun for a game of leap-frog.

Like all generalisations such conclusions are of little more value than speculation. In the public sector, for example, national agreements normally do set fixed standards for wage rates which may be no less inflationary than the sum

---

[3] Report of Royal Commission on Trade Unions 1968 Cmnd. 3623 (1968), para. 46.

total of local agreements in private industry. One can only guess at which is cause and which effect. Even in private industry national agreements lay down many standards which are closely observed, despite the fact that in some instances this produces anomalies. The length of the working week and of paid holidays and overtime, shift and weekend premium payments are often regulated nationally. In the case of premium payments this may have the unexpected result that overtime is paid at a lower rate than basic time because the premium operates in relation to the national basic rate and not the local rate—yet the agreement holds. In the same way national procedure agreements are habitually closely observed throughout an industry but they handle a diminishing number of disputes because of the development of local procedures which are not subject to the same constraint.

Effects of local bargaining

Nevertheless it cannot be doubted that the Royal Commission was right to accept the evidence of Allan Flanders that workplace bargaining is "largely informal, largely fragmented and largely autonomous" and to add[4] " . . . the shift in authority from the industry to the factory has been accompanied by decentralisation of authority in industrial relations within the factory itself." There can be little doubt that the Royal Commission was equally correct to conclude that where local bargaining existed it produced:

" (i) Fragmentation, because different groups in the same workplace competed for concessions receiving them at different times and in different degrees. To this may be added the further fragmentation between different factories of the same company.

(ii) Informality because of the lack of any incentive to enter into carefully drafted written agreements. Rarely among major industrial countries British collective agreements normally do not have legally binding force. It is important to distinguish the effect this has between procedural and substantive agreements. Procedural agreements are normally written, habitually observed and intended to last. Moreover, since the Commission reported much has been done to formalise local procedure. Substantive agreements are intended to be variable. In recent years a standard yearly interval between major revisions has tended to be fixed but minor revision takes place intermittently throughout this period."

The effect upon industrial action

It is widely asserted that this situation explains the pattern of industrial action in Britain. Characteristically that pattern may be presented by comparison with that in the United States though, again, both situations are based on generalisations. The central strength of United States unions coupled with the contractual enforceability of collective agreements results in substantive agreements based on a model agreed with a leader in the industry after a prolonged period of detailed negotiation, often accompanied by a prolonged strike. This agreement will be stated to run for two or three years before renegotiation. It will, therefore, provide a formula for periodic wage increases and will be closely linked to a procedure for interpretation of disputed provisions. Probably because it is a relatively long term treaty it will often deal with improvements in

[4] *Ibid*. para. 65.

holidays, sickness provision, pensions and severance pay, not infrequently as a package of benefits to be set against wage concessions.

In Britain, on the other hand, the agreement is rarely negotiated as a model for other employers, although it may become one. It may well be a package deal but the package will be far less complex. If the agreement is written at all the draftsmanship will be far less precise—partly because it can be renegotiated at any time, but partly as a deliberate manipulation of the flexibility allowed by non-enforceability. In order to reach a settlement the parties often consciously adopt an ambiguous form of words knowing that the understanding of each party differs as to the meaning to be given to them.

This tendency is both cause and effect. It arises from that characteristic pattern of industrial action as a succession of small stoppages on small points affecting only part of the work force which the employer, at least, desires to end as quickly and effortlessly as possible. In turn, in combination with the fragmentation mentioned above, it gives rise to that pattern. The long term picture of industrial action has not substantially changed since the Royal Commission of 1968 concluded[5]:

> "These characteristics of collective bargaining provide the explanation for the pattern of strikes in this country . . . Although the number of working days lost in strikes . . . has remained relatively low since 1926, the average number of strikes a year in the last decade has been higher than ever before . . .
>
> There is no tendency for official strikes to rise from year to year, and recently they have accounted for only five per cent of the total. The remainder are 'unofficial'; they lack the approval of the appropriate trade union authority. Almost invariably they are also 'unconstitutional,' that is, they occur before the various stages of the appropriate procedure for dealing with disputes have been able to deal with the matter, often indeed before any of the stages have been used.
>
> The overwhelming majority of these strikes are not concerned with industry-wide issues in any way. They arise from workshop and factory disputes and are settled within the workshop and factory."

It is interesting to note that, though this is correctly accepted as the current pattern of industrial relations in Britain, historically it was by no means inevitable that it should be so and it may well change again. Until the Second World War British trade unions had struggled to develop from local bargaining to District agreements with effective national agreements (subject to District variations) as their ultimate goal. In at least one instance government had responded by attempting to encourage this process with the conferment of advantages. The Fair Wages Resolution, both before that War and in its later revised version, was obviously intended to set up district agreements wherever they exist as the overriding standard of conformity. It appears that the modern dominance of local bargaining was founded during that War when the overriding need was to maintain production. This demanded speedy resolution of local disputes. Trade union leaders who had left the scene for government for a long time failed to appreciate that change was occurring, and by the 1950s it had become entrenched. If the 1978 National Engineering Agreement which attempted to set a realistic basic rate and to provide that it should not automatically be taken as a floor on which local bargaining could build was intended by those who drafted it as a tentative start of a return to effective

---

[5] *Ibid.* paras. 70–72.

national standards it shows no sign of being followed. In recent years, however, the process of company-wide bargaining has been pressed forward. It avoids much of the disadvantages of the fragmentation of local bargaining while retaining the realism desired from proximity to the causes of dispute.

STATE INTERVENTION

The State had been forced to intervene directly in the fixing of wages in the fourteenth century when a sudden acute shortage of labour occasioned by the Black Death threatened to result in what we would now describe as wage-push inflation. In the sixteenth and seventeenth centuries wages were either fixed by the justices for a district or by individual Acts of Parliament. The prohibition of combinations to alter wages was a natural consequence of this system. The Truck Act of 1831 (which has no conceptual affinity to later Acts with the same name) is one of the last examples of this intervention in wage fixing. Passed at a time when (like the Truck system itself) such intervention was doomed by the development of a complex industrial economy, it was actually never intended to do more than ensure payment of wages in coin. The courts, however, interpreted it so as to restrict deductions. Paradoxically, but not inexplicably, attempts to prohibit the growth of bargaining organisations continued for some time longer because the logical step taken by the Combination Laws Repeal Act 1824 rekindled fears of revolution born in the Napoleonic era and not yet dead. Not until the 1850s did modern trade union organisation (and, incidentally, systematic employer associations) become established.

The State responded to these changes by seeking to regularise voluntary bargaining organisations[6] and by replacing its directive role with a system designed to assist the development of voluntary bargaining.[7] This policy of assistance continued until 1980. It is, however, difficult to say with any precision what is the current situation since it is impossible to find agreement on the changes necessary to meet a situation in which international economic forces have a major effect on British industry. On the one hand government has met a new inflationary threat, owing as much if not more to various international factors as it does to wages-push or prices-pull (themselves directly affected by such factors), with intervention in the form of statutory wages policies and, more subtly, wage guidelines initially imposed on the public sector. More recently it has dismantled, or emasculated, much of the official support machinery—not always without the approval of those directly involved in negotiation.

At its peak assistive machinery included:

(a) Wages Councils.[8]
(b) The Conciliation and Arbitration Service of the Ministry of Labour ultimately absorbed into the more obviously impartial Advisory Conciliation and Arbitration Service.[9]

---

[6] Trade Union Act 1871.
[7] e.g. the Conciliation Act 1896.
[8] Now regulated by the Wages Councils Act 1979 and currently protected by international convention.
[9] See now E.P.A. 1975, ss.1–3.

(c) Statutory provision for securing recognition for employee bargaining representatives.[10]

(d) Statutory provision for securing the supply of information the absence of which would impede bargaining.[11]

(e) The Fair Wages Resolution (for government contractors) and Schedule 11 of the Employment Protection Act 1975 (generally) to provide a rudimentary system for extending collectively agreed standards for terms and conditions of employment.[12]

(f) The Health and Safety at Work, etc., Act 1974 involving representatives of recognised unions in the process of safety enforcement although the initial expectations of some union officials that safety matters would become a bargaining tool have not been realised.

It may be noticed that at no time has the machinery of assistance imposed an obligation to bargain in good faith. The EEC Directive on Transfer of Employee Rights contains an obligation to "consult with a view to reaching agreement" but even this was translated into a British regulation without the second part of the obligation. In other words, the machinery is normally restricted to avoid any form of State intervention. Apart from the ill-fated Industrial Relations Act 1971, which sought to introduce a different approach, the only exception to this policy appeared in the statutory provisions for imposing recognition for bargaining purposes which were repealed in 1980. Even in this case the Central Arbitration Committee which was constituted as the final "enforcing" body[13] declined to interpret its powers as extending to an order for recognition for bargaining purposes for a group of employees, though on occasion it was prepared to order recognition for the negotiation of individual grievances.

(a) Wages Councils

The system

Trade Boards, later renamed Wages Councils, were first created by the Trade Boards Act 1909. Initially intended to deal with sections of industry where rates of pay were unacceptably low they were, following the report of the Whitley Committee in 1917, extended to sections where trade union organisation was lacking. The underlying purpose of Wages Councils was, however, to establish a habit of bargaining which could be developed into purely voluntary bargaining. At its peak in 1947 the system provided 69 councils, including the Agriculture Wages Board covering the whole of the agricultural industry and an extensive coverage of Road Haulage and catering. By the end of 1979, however, this number had shrunk to 36 including Agriculture but no longer covering Road Haulage. Despite an extension of their powers in 1979 to cover all terms and conditions of employment the decline was part of a deliberate policy based

---

[10] E.P.A. 1975, ss.11–16, now repealed.

[11] E.P.A. 1975, ss.17–21.

[12] This system was extended, it is submitted illogically and certainly fatally, to permit the extension of "general levels" of terms and conditions regardless of their origin in collective negotiations. Sched. 11 has been repealed. The Fair Wages Resolution has shared its fate despite previous ratification of an I.L.O. convention dependent upon it.

[13] E.P.A. 1975, s.16.

largely on the feeling of both sides of industry that the system had not achieved its purpose. Only since the adverse comments of the Royal Commission on Trade Unions as to the effect of Wages Councils on union organisation[14] has there been any marked demonstration of ability to shake off a Wages Council in favour of voluntary bargaining, and those sections in which Wages Councils have operated have usually remained among the poorest paid.

With the current position as stated in the 1979 Act it may be assumed that the normal process of abolition will proceed by way of the conversion of a Wages Council to a statutory joint industrial council with or without the exclusion of groups of employers having their own bargaining procedure.[15]

In some cases abolition is obviously long overdue. When, in October 1973, the C.I.R. recommended the abolition of the Boot and Floor Polish Wages Council it had not met since 1967 and had no influence on pay of the 1,500 workers in the industry. On the other hand, when in the same month the abolition of three metalware councils was recommended it was admitted that there would remain vulnerable minorities of employees for whom some protection might be needed. It was said, however, that such protection would not be afforded by continuing the Wages Council. Rather it was hoped that it would be forthcoming from a more general consideration of the problem of low paid sections of industry. In the case of the Paper Box Wages Council[16] abolition was recommended despite the contention of the employers that no voluntary machinery existed to take its place. In both these latter cases there is obviously present an element of incentive to produce the necessary voluntary machinery.[17]

The existence of a Wages Council necessarily rests on a willingness by employers and unions at national level to bargain and so it has not been a practice recently for a Council to be established on the initiative of the Secretary of State for Employment. So far as the standard voluntary procedure is concerned, therefore, the primary difference from purely voluntary bargaining lies in the fact that the award, by becoming an implied term of the individual contract of employment, is imposed, not only on willing parties, but on employers who would not otherwise accept or apply it. It is, in other words, a permanent and automatic method of extension of agreements. That being so, it is perhaps surprising that the scope of awards has been so limited and that even in the light of the much greater sophistication one might expect of the collective bargain since 1909, the power to fix holidays with pay had been the only addition to the power to fix wages. Had the Royal Commission been less bent on destruction it might have discussed the effect that an improvement of function might have on the attitude of Wages Councils generally. The extension now contained in the 1979 Act to give power to deal with all terms and conditions of employment is likely to prove the greatest single improvement.

It is necessary to consider how these Councils fit into the voluntary framework. As Bayliss points out,[18] it was the inability of trade unions in certain

---

[14] paras. 257 et seq.

[15] s.12.

[16] C.I.R. Report No. 83 (1974).

[17] The C.I.R. also recommended that 10 Councils in clothing should be reduced to three, thereby removing 170,000 workers from their supervision.

[18] F.J. Bayliss, British Wages Councils (Blackwell 1962), p. 138.

trades to establish themselves and bargain effectively that necessitated the creation of Wages Councils by statute, initially to fix a reasonable level of wages in the "sweated" trades like bespoke tailoring. From the inception,[19] the view has been that they should be regarded as a temporary expedient, not only removing the principal impediment to trade union growth, but also providing the necessary collective experience so that a fully voluntary system could replace them. Subsequently, Wages Councils have been established which do not fit into this assumption. In Waterproof Garment Manufacturing, for instance, there was 60 per cent. unionisation when the Council was established. It is, nevertheless, true that Wages Councils were generally established where bargaining strength did not exist, if only because of numbers of small units, and where wages were relatively low.

Initially, trade unions were pleased with the added status that a Wages Council gave them and with the resultant draw towards membership, but since the 1920s there has been a constant feeling that the existence of a Council positively discourages union organisation. In evidence to the Royal Commission[20] the Transport and General Workers Union commented that the existence of a Wages Council tended to establish the idea that a system of fixing wages exists without the necessity of union membership and that the incentive to the trade union movement itself to set up voluntary machinery is weakened. In the catering and hotel industry, which is a major sector for the operation of Wages Councils, only four per cent. of employees are in trade unions. In industry generally the figures of trade union membership in Wages Council sectors are between 75 and 25 per cent. of that for employment as a whole, revealing, if nothing else, that progress towards the original objective has been either slow or non-existent.[21] Abolition or rearrangement of Wages Councils is now commonplace. Nine councils in retail distribution have been amalgamated into two new councils for food and non-food trades. In 1978 the Road Haulage Wages Council was abolished and regional bargaining established.

The Royal Commission found a remarkable similarity between the reality of the Wages Council system and the voluntary system.[22] A Wages Council, although it has power to determine rates for particular groups of workers, almost always awards rates across the board as a national minimum.[23] There is probably more adherence to this as a standard than there is to the national agreements of the better organised industries, but wherever there exists any local bargaining strength the standard will be treated as a floor from which to work upwards. A rise in the Wages Council rate will often be met automatically with a corresponding rise in actual rates which are already higher. It may also be noted that the scope of Wages Council orders has been narrowly confined.

It is doubtful whether bargaining restricted largely to wages rates can be

---

[19] Trade Boards Act 1918. Now governed by Wages Councils Act 1979 and Agricultural Wages Act 1948, as amended.

[20] Cmnd. 3623 (1967), para. 229.

[21] Bayliss, pp. 140–141, thought that these low figures had to do with the character of the trade and not the existence of the Council. This is no doubt true, but it does not alter the fact that the existence of the Council has not changed that character.

[22] Cmnd. 3623 (1968).

[23] In September 1982 new minimum *rates* fixed by Wages Councils ranged from £42 per 40 hour week in hairdressing to £64.60 in licensed residential and restaurant undertakings. In April of that year average weekly male earnings in manufacturing industry was £134.80.

considered realistic, let alone satisfactory. Consequently, the same tendency has existed for local bargaining to take on the task of effective establishment of rates and conditions wherever the position of the parties makes this possible. Bayliss[24] states that the unions in these trades concentrate their organising activities on the larger establishments. In the retail sector, one finds that in some of these establishments well organised plant bargaining machinery exists. Bayliss supports the view[25] that "the real risk of the statutory system is that it may make trade unions lazy." The unions consciously choose a part of a trade for organisation and collective bargaining knowing that the rest is protected from the worst effects of inadequate bargaining strength. This criticism is certainly too severe. Unions have the greatest difficulty, however hard they work, in organising the small unit. Relations are often too personal for any member of the staff not to feel inhibited from joining a union. Even if some do so, contact is difficult to maintain and a service difficult to offer. Specific negotiation of issues is almost impossible to organise. Wages Councils do not exist in the building industry where, of course, there is a high degree of mobility of both labour and production units, but there too, the unions have virtually abandoned attempts to organise on small sites. In contrast,[26] the policy of selective organisation in a protected atmosphere has been highly successful in the case of the Union of Shop, Distributive and Allied Workers. Quite apart from this, there are still sections of industry where the unions are so weak that conditions can only be maintained by the Wages Council system.

Establishment of Councils

It is unlikely that there will be any readiness to set up new Councils. If a new one were to be set up there are two methods still in use. (The third, by which the Secretary of State might make an order on his own initiative, had previously fallen into disuse.) The Secretary of State, either on his own initiative or following a joint application from organisations of employers and workers which habitually take part in the settlement of wages and conditions may refer the matter to the Advisory, Conciliation and Arbitration Service[27] on the ground either that there is no existing machinery for the voluntary fixing of wages, or that it is likely to cease to exist. If the Service recommends the establishment of a Council and the Secretary of State accepts the recommendation he may, after publication of his intention and consideration of any representations made to him, make an order to be laid before Parliament subject to annulment. In doing so he may make minor modifications to the draft order, but if he were to consider that major change was necessary the matter would again have to be referred to the ACAS.

---

[24] *Ibid.* p. 141.
[25] Expressed by B. McCormick and H.A. Turner, "The Legal Minimum Wage, Employers and Trade Unions: An Experiment," *Manchester School of Economic and Social Studies*, Vol. 25, No. 3, September 1957, p. 316.
[26] As Bayliss admits at p. 143.
[27] The C.I.R. was substituted for a commission of inquiry by Sched. III, para. 38 to the Industrial Relations Act 1971. This was reversed by Sched. III, para. 9(2), to the Trade Union and Labour Relations Act 1974, but s.89 of the Employment Protection Act 1975 provides for reference to the Advisory, Conciliation and Arbitration Service of all matters that would otherwise have been referred to a commission of inquiry.

Constitution

A Wages Council consists of equal numbers of representatives of employers and workmen in the industry appointed by organisations of each side, which organisations are nominated by the Secretary of State,[28] and up to three independent members, one of whom is the chairman. Voting is by sides and theoretically, therefore, the independent members would only vote when the two sides could not agree. It is obvious that upon major issues the matter would not be resolved by such a formal vote.

Wages orders

A Wages Council used to submit to the Secretary of State proposals for fixing remuneration either generally, or for groups of workers, or in particular circumstances such as the provision of a guaranteed minimum week, and also for the fixing of holidays and holiday pay, including the time at which holidays shall be taken and the conditions and time of payment.[29] The Wages Councils Act 1979 confers on Councils power to fix any other terms and conditions for workers within its scope.[30]

In section 14 of the Wages Councils Act 1979 it is provided that all terms and conditions should in future be capable of being the subject of an order made directly by the Council and without reference to the Secretary of State subject to a requirement of publication of a draft order and consideration of representations made to it as a result of such publication.

The notice of the proposals of the Council must be published to all persons affected by the proposals permitting at least 14 days for written representations. The amended proposals must be given further publicity if it appears to the Council that as a result of the modifications those affected should have an opportunity for further consideration. The order is operative from a date specified in it, not earlier than the date of the Wages Council's agreement to the proposals.[31] The orders of the Agricultural Wages Board were always made without the need for Ministerial approval.[32]

A wages regulation order may be enforced as a term of his contract by any affected worker or, on his behalf, by a wages inspector. The worker may recover by this means up to six years' back pay. Alternatively, he may be awarded up to two years' back pay in summary criminal proceedings against the employer for infringement of the order. In practice there are virtually no civil or criminal proceedings for offences of this nature but the evidence suggests that the inspectorate is active and that the absence of court actions indicates that this method of ensuring observance is satisfactory.

Abolition of Wages Councils

Efforts have been made to improve the procedure for the winding up of a Wages Council. Under the original powers a Council might be abolished, or its scope varied, by the Secretary of State on his own initiative or upon the

---

[28] Wages Councils Act 1979, Sched. 2, para. 1(2)–(4).
[29] This power was originally added by the Holidays with Pay Act 1938.
[30] s.14.
[31] s.14(5)–(7).
[32] See now E.P.A. 1975, Sched. 9.

application of a Joint Industrial Council, a conciliation board or some similar *joint* body substantially representative of organisations of workers and employers, on the ground that they jointly provide machinery which is, and is likely to remain, adequate for the effective regulation of remuneration and conditions of employment. To these powers the Industrial Relations Act 1971 added a unilateral right to apply for a winding up by any organisation of workers which represents a substantial portion of the workers with respect to whom the Council operates. The Act also substituted as the general ground for a winding up that the existence of a Wages Council is no longer necessary for the purpose of maintaining a reasonable standard of remuneration for the workers with respect to whom it operates. Both these extensions were preserved by the Trade Union and Labour Relations Act 1974.[33] The Advisory, Conciliation and Arbitration Service, to which the application for abolition is to be referred, has only to consider broadly whether such abolition is expedient. Before making the order the Secretary of State must consult the Wages Council concerned and all organisations representing a substantial proportion of the employees covered.[34]

Statutory joint council

The Employment Protection Act 1975 substantially adds to these procedural changes. The Secretary of State either on his own initiative or on the application of the employers' or workers' organisations represented in the council is given power to convert a wages council (but not the Agricultural Wages Board) into a "statutory joint industrial council" having the powers of a wages council and also having power to request the Advisory Conciliation and Arbitration Service to attempt to settle a dispute which the Council has failed to resolve. The ACAS has power to appoint an arbitrator in such a case if it is unable to bring about a settlement by other means.[35] A statutory joint industrial council will not contain independent members.

The Secretary of State has power to establish a central co-ordinating committee to operate in relation to any two or more statutory joint industrial councils. He already had such power in relation to wages councils. If the Secretary of State is of the opinion that, if a statutory joint industrial council was abolished, adequate machinery would be established for the effective regulation of wages, terms and conditions of employment, and that such machinery is likely to be maintained he may, by order, abolish the council.[36] The Secretary of State may vary the field of operation of a wages council and this includes power to exclude from that field any employer who is a member of an organisation, party to an agreement regulating remuneration or other terms and conditions of employment.[37] By this means areas of more advanced unionisation can be hived off without the need to abolish the whole council.

It has already been stated that the orders of a wages council become implied terms in the contracts of employment of those to whom they apply. This is a most interesting device capable of considerable extension into the functions of

[33] Sched. III, para. 9(3). See now Wages Councils Act 1979, s.5.
[34] Wages Councils Act 1979, Sched. I, para. 3.
[35] ss.10 and 11.
[36] s.12.
[37] s.4(3).

the bodies empowered to deal with the settlement of disputes. It has particular significance where, as generally in British collective bargaining, the collective agreement itself has no binding legal effect, since, by automatic implication it achieves this legally binding nature. The order of a Wages Council overrides less beneficial provisions previously included in the contract of employment.[38]

(b) The Central Arbitration Committee[39]

Structure and functions

A body called the Industrial Court was established by the Industrial Court Act 1919. It was never intended as a court in the normal sense of the word but it had characteristics similar to the labour courts which exist in certain Continental Western European countries. It has always been intended primarily to act as a permanent independent arbitration tribunal. It was renamed the Industrial Arbitration Board in 1971[40] and again renamed the Central Arbitration Committee in 1976.[41] In this latter guise it is formally a section of the Advisory, Conciliation and Arbitration Service. It now consists of a chairman, a number of deputy chairmen and members appointed by the Secretary of State from persons nominated by the ACAS as experienced in industrial relations. The members include those who have gained such experience as employers' or as workers' representatives.[42]

The Committee sits in any number of divisions as the chairman directs, presided over by the chairman or a deputy chairman, sitting with two other members. It may, at the discretion of the chairman, and where it appears expedient to do so, call upon the help of one or more assessors. If any division cannot reach a unanimous decision the chairman has the powers of an umpire even if outvoted by the other two members. Emphasis is, however, laid on the desirability of agreement and, though there have been a few cases in which individual members have disagreed it is believed that no decisions have been made by a chairman overruling the remainder of the committee. The former rule that when the issue concerned women at least one member should be a woman has disappeared in law and in practice.

The committee may sit in private and the practice has been introduced, initially in disputes over recognition of trade unions, whereby a preliminary inquiry may be conducted by the chairman or a deputy sitting alone. Unless the parties consent, however, a reference may not be decided without an oral hearing.

It is now extremely uncommon to find adhered to the former practice of announcing the award on the day of the hearing, although it is usual for the committee to decide the direction and main points of its award immediately following the hearing. In giving decisions it had previously been the almost invariable practice not to give reasons for the decision. Before 1977 the

---

[38] s.15.
[39] Decisions of the C.A.C. are very numerous and do not constitute binding precedent. In this section reference will normally be made to trends rather than specific decisions.
[40] Industrial Relations Act 1971, s.124(1).
[41] E.P.A. 1975, s.10.
[42] The best analysis of the work of the former Industrial Court is contained in Wedderburn and Davies, *Employment Grievances and Disputes Procedure in Britain* (California U.P. 1964).

published awards set out the arguments on either side but, apart from the statement of the award, avoided the expression of any view as to the relative merits of these arguments. This, indeed, became the standard practice in British industrial arbitration. Of it the second annual report of the C.A.C. states[43]:

> "Of recent years, the predominant view appears to have been that the giving of reasons is inadvisable. Arbitration cases usually come at the end of a long period of dispute and often follow conciliation. The parties are well aware of all the issues. What they want above all is settlement. To give reasons is to invite yet another reconsideration of the various issues—with a good chance of renewed strife. The nuances of the words chosen to express the reasons may rekindle old disputes."

This report continues, however[44]:

> "Against this view there are several strong arguments. Modern practice is tending to look to all decision makers to give reasons. Only if reasons are given can a consistent pattern be seen to emerge from the various decisions in the same or related areas. Reasons enable other disputes to be voluntarily settled or parties to disputes which are submitted to prepare their cases more effectively. These factors weighed heavily with the Committee and it decided that the parties should be given an indication of the considerations which led to the award."

Nevertheless the C.A.C. does not produce reasoned decisions as such. Of the "general considerations" the 1977 report says: "It is expected that they will be read by the parties as a guide—not as a precise legal judgment." The C.A.C. is now required to publish all the decisions arising under any of its statutory functions.

All the functions of the former Industrial Arbitration Board have been transferred to the C.A.C. Under its original jurisdiction it could deal with matters arising out of a trade dispute.[45] Part I of the Industrial Courts Act 1919 was repealed by the Employment Protection Act 1975 and this aspect of the jurisdiction of the C.A.C. is now derived from the latter Act.[46] The reference, therefore, goes to the C.A.C. from the Advisory, Conciliation and Arbitration Service, which must be satisfied that agreed procedures have first been used and have failed to result in a settlement. It has been normal for the parties to accept the award in such references but there is no compulsion to do so nor, failing such acceptance, can the award be implied into the contracts of employment of those affected.[47]

The Fair Wages Resolution

On December 16, 1982 the House of Commons resolved to rescind, after 12 months, the Fair Wages Resolution first passed at the end of the nineteenth century, amended in 1946. This decision is in accord with a policy of dismantling support machinery for industrial relations. Although the Secretary of State had said in answer to a Parliamentary question that the Government was "making sure that we do not prevent people from finding and doing jobs at prices that

---

[43] Central Arbitration Committee Annual Report 1977, para. 4.8.
[44] para. 4.9.
[45] The Employment Act 1982, Sched. 3, para. 8 provides that trade dispute shall have the same meaning as in E.P.A. 1975.
[46] s.3(1)(b).
[47] *Faithful* v. *The Admiralty, The Times*, January 24, 1964.

they think are reasonable" rescission of the Resolution ignores its basic assumption that the individual may not be free to choose to reject sub-standard terms and conditions. On that assumption it had been thought that Government, as by far the most significant dispenser of contracts, should not be seen to support such lower standards which, indeed, the provision of competitive tendering would be likely to encourage.

It may be of value to retain the outline of the operation of the Resolution which follows as one of the last surviving examples of a policy of official support for standards achieved by collective bargaining. It may be thought by some that there is little justification for a policy of sacrificing the unorganised individual to the vagaries of the labour market in order that the small employer may undercut standards established with, and observed by, employers of the majority of the labour force. The Fair Wages Resolution was not a legally enforceable provision as such,[48] but a statement of certain basic standards which ought to be binding upon all government contractors. Many local authorities and other public bodies incorporate a similar reference in their contracts. In such a case, however, enforcement will lie by way of an action for breach of contract rather than by the system of reference here described. The Resolution provided that:

1. (a) The contractor shall pay rates of wages and observe hours and conditions of labour not less favourable than those established for the trade or industry in the district where the work is carried out by machinery of negotiation or arbitration to which the parties are organisations of employers and trade unions representative respectively of substantial proportions of the employers and workers engaged in the trade or industry in the district.

(b) In the absence of any rates of wages, hours or conditions of labour so established the contractor shall pay rates of wages and observe hours and conditions of labour which are not less favourable than the general level of wages, hours and conditions observed by other employers whose general circumstances in the trade or industry in which the contractor is engaged are similar.

4. The contractor shall recognise the freedom of his workpeople to be members of trade unions.

6. The contractor shall be responsible for the observance of this Resolution by sub-contractors employed in the execution of the contract.

The contractor must furnish an assurance that he had for the previous three months complied with the resolution before he was put on the list of tendering firms. If any question arose as to non-observance, which was not settled in any other way, it would be referred by the Department of Employment for decision to an independent tribunal which was, in practice, the Central Arbitration Committee. In deciding whether to send a dispute to the Committee, the Department might listen to representations from third parties.[49] In *R.* v. *Industrial Court, ex p. A.S.S.E.T.*[50] Lord Parker C.J. said that it did not matter who brought the objection to the attention of the Secretary of State, and Wedderburn and Davies[51] state that in two out of 12 cases analysed by them the complaint had been formally submitted by individual employees.

---

[48] The obligation to observe fair standards has the force of law in other countries. See Wedderburn and Davies, *op. cit.*, p. 195.

[49] *R.* v. *Industrial Court, ex p. A.S.S.E.T.* [1965] 1 Q.B. 377.

[50] [1965] 1 Q.B. 377. In *Imperial Metal Industries (Kynoch) Ltd.* v. *A.U.E.W. (T.A.S.S.)* [1979] I.C.R. 23 the Court of Appeal held that the C.A.C. has no obligation to state a case from an application under the F.W.R.

[51] *Employment Grievances and Disputes Procedures in Great Britain*, p. 198.

The resolution acted by way of incorporation as a term of the contract with the government department.[51a] Proof of the existence of such a contract was, of course, a necessary preliminary to consideration by the C.A.C. The effect of the resolution was limited by the fact that the ultimate sanction was withdrawal of that contract, which might be economically very undesirable, and failure to provide further contracts, which might, in the case of large works, be difficult to adhere to. It is clearly established that the employee gained no rights by implication from the existence of the resolution in the sense that he might not bring an action in contract unless and until the substance of the award could be said to be implied into his contract by normal common law principles.[52] The employer need only recognise freedom to join the normally recognised unions and was not obliged to recognise every union which claimed the right to organise his workers.[53]

The C.A.C., despite the decision of the Divisional Court in relation to Schedule 11,[54] refused to construe the words "in the absence of any . . . conditions of labour so established" in paragraph 1(b) as implying that the standard of a general level might only be utilised if the standard of established terms was not available. Either of the two standards was considered to be available in the discretion of the Committee. It is not clear whether the word "established" in paragraph 1(a) should be taken for instance, to cause a nationally "recognised" rate to override a contrary practice of non-observance or whether one could argue that the contrary practice "disestablished" the rate.[55] There is little doubt that the C.A.C. wished to avoid the establishment of any rigid rules of construction either by development of a doctrine of internal precedent or by implied extension of rulings of the Divisional Court. Whereas it is difficult to contend that a statutory schedule should not be subject to statutory rules of construction, the C.A.C. probably took the view that the Fair Wages Resolution attempted to establish a standard of fairness and should be construed more as a code of practice than as a statute.[56] For the sake of consistency of this less rigid approach it did not usually seek to argue that there was any significance in the omission of reference to a district from paragraph 1(b).[56a]

Recent policies of pay restraint exempted from the effect of the restraint awards of the C.A.C. or its predecessors under the Fair Wages Resolution. This was clearly necessary if the pay policy was not to have the effect of eliminating this method of raising sub-standard conditions. The significance of this was seen by a few unions in 1974 but was not widely utilised until the subsequent pay policy in 1977. Whereas between 1956 and 1968 the Industrial Court (as it then was) heard 151 cases[57] and this number did not greatly vary between 1969 and 1976, the C.A.C., by the middle of 1977, was hearing some 80 claims per month

---

[51a] This must not be mistaken as a reference to the decision of the C.A.C. which is not incorporated into individual contracts of employment but is merely a finding as to the observance of the term incorporating the Fair Wages Resolution.
[52] *Simpson* v. *Kodak Ltd.* [1948] 2 K.B. 184.
[53] See (1964) 27 M.L.R. 600.
[54] *R.* v. *Central Arbitration Committee, ex p. Deltaflow Ltd.* [1978] I.C.R. 534. E.P.A. 1975, Sched. 11 has been repealed.
[55] See *A.U.E.W.* v. *Gloster Suro Ltd.* [1978] I.R.L.R. 271.
[56] But see *Racal Communications Ltd.* v. *Pay Board* [1974] I.C.R. 590.
[56a] See Award No. 82/17, *Dunlop Ltd.* v. *A.S.T.M.S.*
[57] *See* Wedderburn, *The Worker and the Law* (2nd ed.), p. 201. See also Wedderburn and Davies, *Employment Grievances and Disputes Procedures in Great Britain.*

many of which, although clearly within the terms of Schedule 11 or the Fair Wages Resolution, were concerned more with obtaining an improvement in terms outside the policy restraint than in improving such terms because they were sub-standard. The phenomenon of an employer openly supporting such a claim or even, under the Fair Wages Resolution, himself claiming that he was in breach of the obligation was not uncommon.

Bargaining information[58]

The Central Arbitration Committee still has a function in respect of the supply of information necessary for effective bargaining.

The Employment Protection Act 1975 deals with the question of provision of information from an employer to the representatives of his employees with whom he negotiates terms and conditions of employment. This need for information has been recognised for some time and, indeed, provision was made for it in the Industrial Relations Act 1971. The provisions of that Act never became practically operational partly for the reason that the Commission on Industrial Relations, which was charged with investigating and reporting upon the best way of making detailed provision for the supply of such information, though it did in fact report, did not really resolve the difficulties which lie in the way of the practical operation of such a scheme. The proposals in the 1975 Act appear on the face of it once more to delegate the resolution of these difficulties, since it is provided that the ACAS shall prepare a code of practice upon the disclosure of information.

The Act provides that it shall be the duty of the employer subject to certain exceptions, to disclose to the representatives of independent trade unions which he recognises, all such information relating to his undertaking as is in his possession, or that of any associated employer, and is both information without which the trade union representatives would be to a material extent impeded in carrying on with him such collective bargaining, and information which it would be in accordance with good industrial relations practice that he should disclose to them for the purposes of collective bargaining.[59] The collective bargaining to which this applies is that with the recognised independent unions in respect of those employees for which the unions are recognised,[60] or that falling within the scope of a recognition recommendation within the meaning of the 1975 legislation.

The employer is exempt from the obligation to supply information where the information:

(a) would adversely affect national security if disclosed;
(b) could not be disclosed without contravention of a statutory prohibition;
(c) has been communicated to the employer in confidence or has been obtained by him in consequence of the confidence reposed in him by another person;
(d) relates specifically to an individual who has not consented to disclosure;
(e) would, if disclosed, cause substantial injury to the employer's undertaking for reasons other than its effect on collective bargaining; or,

---

[58] The C.A.C. also hears references under section 3 of the Equal Pay Act 1970: see p. 318, *supra.*
[59] s.17(1).   [60] s.17(2).

(f) has been obtained by the employer for the purpose of bringing, prosecuting or defending any legal proceedings.

The employer also has no duty to produce or allow inspection of any document other than a document prepared for the purpose of conveying or confirming the information, or to make a copy of or extracts from any document. Nor is he required to compile or assemble any information where that would involve an amount of work or expenditure out of reasonable proportion to the value of the information in the conduct of collective bargaining. One or two obvious points may be made about this list of exemptions. In the first place, it should be noticed that the important exemption contained in (e) is qualified by the word "substantial." It seems likely that this will have a very restrictive effect on the operation of that exemption. It may also be inferred from the exemption provided for expensive compilation of information that it is not open to an employer to avoid his obligation to supply information by arguing that the information does not exist because it has not been collated or in some other way brought together. It would appear that information refers to known facts and not to any particular tangible source.

The ACAS Code of Practice gives certain examples of information relating to an undertaking which "could be relevant in certain collective bargaining situations" but admits that the list is neither exhaustive nor indicative of the fact that such information should be supplied in a given situation. It makes a similar attempt to list information which might cause substantial injury such as cost information on individual products, detailed analysis of proposed investments, marketing or pricing policies and price quotas or the make-up of tender prices. In general it states that substantial injury may occur if, for example, certain customers would be lost to competitors, or suppliers would refuse to supply necessary materials, or the ability to raise funds to finance the company would be seriously impaired. This type of guidance may be of some assistance but it must be borne in mind that the financial forecasts of a company's business are often the most useful pieces of information both a trade union and its business rivals could have.

The Code suggests that trade unions should make clear reasoned requests for specific information. In other words a fishing inquiry should not be resorted to. In turn it suggests that the aim of an employer should be to be as open and helpful as possible in meeting the request. A refusal should be explained and be capable of being supported should a claim be made to the C.A.C.

Where a trade union wishes to complain that it has not been supplied with information to which it is entitled under the statutory provisions that complaint must be made in writing to the C.A.C.[61] If the Committee is of the opinion that the complaint is reasonably likely to be settled by conciliation, it must refer it to the ACAS for this purpose. It will be observed that in this instance the C.A.C. is the initial referee rather than an arbitrator of last resort. The C.A.C. has, therefore, developed the practice of holding a preliminary hearing before a chairman alone to ascertain whether the matter must go for hearing or whether there is a chance of settlement by conciliation. If the complaint is not settled or withdrawn, and the ACAS is of the opinion that further attempts at conciliation are unlikely to result in a settlement, the ACAS must inform the Committee of

---

[61] s.19.

this opinion. Where conciliation has failed, or not been resorted to, the C.A.C. shall hear and determine the complaint and make a declaration stating whether it finds the complaint well founded wholly or in part and the reasons for its finding.[62] Any person whom the Committee considers has a proper interest in the complaint is entitled to be heard but only failure to hear the trade union and the employer directly concerned will invalidate the proceedings. The declaration must specify the information in respect of which the Committee finds that the complaint is well founded, the date on which the employer refused or failed to disclose the information, and a period of not less than one week from the date of the declaration within which the employer ought to disclose such information. At any time after that specified period, the trade union may return to the C.A.C. and present to it in writing a complaint that the employer still fails to disclose or confirm in writing information specified in the declaration.[63] At the same time, or at any time after the presentation of this further complaint, the trade union may claim in writing, in respect of one or more descriptions of employees specified in the claim, that their contract should include the terms and conditions specified in the claim.[64] Apparently the Committee's award may deal with either or both of these aspects.[65] In practice the view of the C.A.C. is that since the award becomes operative as a term of the contracts of employment it affects, it is more appropriate that it should deal with the actual terms and conditions in dispute. Generally the C.A.C. would not regard an obligation to supply bargaining information as appropriate to the contract of employment and would tend not to seek it imply such a term.[66]

Section 16 of the Companies Act 1967 dealing with additional material to be included in the directors' annual report has been extended[66a] so as to require, in the cases of companies which have during the financial year employed an average of 250 persons each week, that that report should contain certain information as to the supply of bargaining information and the availability of consultation. The matters to be dealt with concern the action taken during the financial year: to introduce, maintain, or develop arrangements aimed at:

(a) providing employees systematically with information on matters of concern to them as employees,

(b) consulting employees or their representatives on a regular basis so that the views of employees can be taken into account in making decisions which are likely to affect their interests,

(c) encouraging the involvement of employees in the company's performance through an employees' share scheme or by some other means,

(d) achieving a common awareness on the part of all employees of the financial and economic factors affecting the performance of the company.

---

[62] s.19(4).

[63] s.20(1).

[64] s.21(1).

[65] s.21(3).

[66] The provision for compulsory effect does not apply to Crown employment. It is proposed to refer any such dispute to an independent ACAS inquiry having no binding effect and without any element of C.A.C. intervention.

[66a] Employment Act 1982, s.1.

(c) Conciliation and Arbitration

The conciliation powers of the Department of Employment originated in the Conciliation Act 1896, which provided that where a difference existed or was apprehended between employers and workmen or between different classes of workmen the [Secretary of State] might:

> (i) take such steps as may seem expedient [to him] for the purpose of enabling the parties to the difference to meet together, by themselves or their representatives, under the presidency of a chairman mutually agreed upon or nominated by the [Secretary of State] or by some other person or body, with a view to the amicable settlement of the difference;
> (ii) on the application of employers or workmen interested, and after taking into consideration the existence and adequacy of means available for conciliation in the district or trade and the circumstances of the case, appoint a person to act as a conciliator or as a board of conciliation.

Though the Department could not refer a dispute to the Arbitration Board until satisfied that the agreed procedure in the industry had failed to obtain a settlement, it was in its discretion at what stage in a dispute it might introduce conciliation. In order to encourage voluntary procedure for conciliation, however, it was the practice of the Department not to intervene until the agreed procedure had been exhausted or, if there was no agreed procedure, until the parties had attempted to settle the dispute. The services of a conciliator appointed by the Department were regarded as available merely to assist the parties to find a mutually acceptable basis for settlement. To this end the conciliator had to avoid identification with either side.

Despite a general impression that these industrial relations functions of the Department had suffered badly from doubts as to its impartiality raised by a succession of government pay policies, this does not appear to have been true of conciliation.

Consent of the parties was regarded as necessary before a dispute was referred to arbitration; although if the efforts of the Department to secure settlement by conciliation failed the conciliator would attempt to persuade the parties to resort to arbitration. A number of procedure agreements include resort to arbitration as a final stage. The powers of the Department of Employment to refer a dispute to arbitration were contained in section 2 of the Industrial Courts Act 1919.[67] They might not be used until there had been a failure of the agreed settlement procedures of the industry. Apart from reference to the Arbitration Board a dispute might be referred for arbitration to one or more persons appointed by the Secretary of State, or to a board composed of equal numbers of persons (although there was usually only one person from each side) nominated by employers and by workers, and an independent person nominated by the Secretary of State. Panels of suitable persons of all three grades were maintained by the Department. Choice was, however, not limited to those on these lists.

Awards of single arbitrators, like awards of the Arbitration Board, rarely contained reasons, and are regarded as confidential to the parties so that they are not published. One of the principal advantages of the procedure was its informality and speed.

---

[67] Repealed by the E.P.A. 1975.

Boards of Arbitration

Boards of Arbitration were said only to be appointed to settle important disputes, but Wedderburn and Davies[68] suggest that all the disputes that have been referred could have gone to single arbitrators, or the Industrial Arbitration Board, had the parties so desired. The employer and worker representatives on a Board were never connected with the industry concerned,[69] nor were they involved in current disputes of a similar nature in other industries. Proceedings before the Boards were more formal than those before individual arbitrators. Again, their reports usually did not contain reasons. Although they were not published as such, however, more publicity was given to them.

A number of severe blows were dealt to the arbitration functions of the Department of Employment particularly in 1971 when guidance was issued to arbitrators upon compliance with government pay policy. As a result a strong body of opinion, particularly among trade unionists, developed in favour of a completely separate conciliation and arbitration service.

Despite the developing doubts about official conciliation the Industrial Relations Act introduced the requirement of preliminary attempts at conciliation into its procedures. It assigned the task of promoting such conciliation variously to the Department of Employment, the Commission on Industrial Relations (C.I.R.), the Industrial Court and industrial tribunals.

(d) The Advisory, Conciliation and Arbitration Service

Virtually all the previously existing machinery has been brought under a single authority known as the Advisory, Conciliation and Arbitration Service (ACAS). Initially, this service took over the conciliation and arbitration functions of the Department of Employment, together with the voluntary machinery of the Commission on Industrial Relations for the improvement of bargaining procedures.

The ACAS is headed by a chairman and a council of nine members, one third of which is nominated by the T.U.C. and one third by the C.B.I.

It will be observed that this organisation is not much more than a rationalisation of existing functions and an attempt to provide quasi-official assistance for the settlement of disputes. As already mentioned, however, it also preserves one important function of the Commission on Industrial Relations which had, otherwise, suffered from the general antipathy to all organs administering the Industrial Relations Act 1971, and which was abolished in 1974.

Advisory functions

The Royal Commission on Trade Unions had it in mind that the responsibility of the C.I.R. should be to inquire into the proper functioning of collective bargaining machinery. Its preoccupation, therefore, would be with the nature of procedural agreements, whether they should be concluded, and with whom. Procedure and substance cannot be strictly separated because the nature and effectiveness of substantive agreements depends on the adequacy of the machinery. The C.I.R. was, therefore,

---

[68] *Op. cit.*, p. 191.

[69] They might be nominated by the Secretary of State after consultation with the parties, or by the parties directly.

"the body to carry out inquiries into the general state of industrial relations in a factory or an industry such as have previously been entrusted to ad hoc committees, for example the Devlin Committee on the docks or the Pearson Court of Inquiry into the shipping industry. . . . But if it was required to arbitrate on particular disputes about terms and conditions of employment its attention would be diverted from the proper functioning of the machinery of collective bargaining to finding acceptable settlements, and from long term objectives to short term compromises."[70]

The C.I.R. was regarded, therefore, as the prime instrument in guiding the reconstruction of bargaining procedure to make it relevant to modern conditions. In this process, the Royal Commission suggested some guiding principles among which were: the importance of establishing the representative ability of the trade unions concerned; that the system must be judged by its value to the company, the factory and the workshop, so that industry-wide procedures should be confined to those methods to which could effectively be applied common national standards; that the procedure should be capable of producing precise written agreements which, in the case of pay structures, should be intelligible and coherent; that the aim of procedure should be towards productivity bargaining, *i.e.* improvements in terms and conditions should be linked to improved methods of operation; and that all procedure should be comprehensive and productive of rapid and equitable settlement of disputes. The Commission was required to examine the matter referred and to report back to the Secretary of State and any other Minister acting with him in making the reference.

The advisory function is transferred to the ACAS by section 4 of the Employment Protection Act 1975. That section gives the Service power, if it thinks fit, on request or otherwise, to provide advice on any matter concerned with industrial relations or employment policies. The section sets out a number of specific industrial relations matters and, in particular, recognition and negotiation machinery; but the generality of its provision will cover any aspect of industrial relations. The Service may also publish general advice on any matter concerned with industrial relations or employment policies. It may if it thinks fit enquire into any question relating to industrial relations generally or to industrial relations in any particular industry or any particular undertaking or part of an undertaking and publish the findings of that enquiry if it appears to it that publication is desirable for the improvement of industrial relations either generally or specifically.[71] A draft of its findings must first be sent to all parties appearing to be concerned and their views be taken into account.

These provisions are made against the background of the general duty with which the Service is charged of promoting the improvement of industrial relations and in particular of encouraging the extension of collective bargaining and the development and, where necessary, reform of collective bargaining machinery.[72]

Conciliation and arbitration

Section 2 of the Employment Protection Act 1975 provides that where a trade dispute exists or is apprehended, the Service may, at the request of one or more

---

[70] Cmnd. 3623 (1967), para. 201.   [71] s.5.   [72] s.1(2).

of the parties to the dispute or otherwise (that is to say, *inter alia* on its own initiative), offer to the parties its assistance by way of conciliation or other means with a view to bringing about a settlement. The means used may include the appointment of a person other than an officer or servant of the ACAS to offer assistance to the parties to this end. It is only provided that in carrying out this function the Service shall have regard to the desirability of encouraging use of agreed procedure for negotiation or settlement of disputes. Formal adherence to the old principle of insistence upon exhaustion is therefore removed.

Where a trade dispute exists or is apprehended, the ACAS at the request of one or more parties *and with the consent of all parties to the dispute*, may refer all or any of the matters in dispute to arbitration by one or more persons appointed by the Service or to the Central Arbitration Committee. In this instance the Service must consider the likelihood of the dispute being settled by conciliation. Where there exist appropriate agreed procedures for negotiation or settlement of disputes the ACAS should not refer a matter to arbitration unless those procedures have been used and failed to produce a settlement or unless the Service is of the opinion that there is a special reason which justifies arbitration as an alternative to those procedures.

The ACAS also has a number of other functions, some of which have already been noted. It will, for instance, provide the conciliation stage before a complaint of failure to supply information for the purpose of collective bargaining goes to arbitration by the C.A.C. It may also receive and decide disputes referred to it by statutory industrial councils (that is to say, the advanced stage of a Wages Council).[73] Section 6 of the Act gives the ACAS power to issue codes of practice containing such practical guidance as the Service thinks fit for the purpose of promoting the improvement of industrial relations. In particular, it is required to issue a code of practice on the disclosure of information and a code of practice on the time off work which is to be permitted for trade union officials to carry out their functions. Such codes of practice must be submitted in draft to the Secretary of State and, if he approves, be laid before both Houses of Parliament subject to annulment.[74]

In addition, the Secretary of State was given power in 1980[74a] to issue Codes of Practice containing such practical guidance as he thinks fit for the purpose of promoting the improvement of industrial relations. He may amend such codes from time to time and he may repeal any previous code of his own or of the ACAS which he considers to have been superseded. He is required to consult ACAS before issuing the draft of any code and to lay the code in draft before both Houses of Parliament. Such codes are admissible in evidence and, in practice, the Secretary of State has not hesitated to use them to suggest meanings for words such as "reasonable" which by statute regulate, for example, the power of a union to exclude applicants for membership in a closed shop situation.[74b]

(e) Recognition of trade unions

Organised representation of employees in the United Kingdom depends upon recognition by the employer of a particular union or a group of unions for

---

[73] s.92.
[74a] Employment Act 1980, s.3.
[74] E.P.A. 1975, s.6(4) and (5).
[74b] See Employment Act 1980, s.4.

bargaining purposes. This popular concept of recognition has, in recent years, been given a statutory significance though not a statutory definition.

Between 1975[75] and 1980[76] there existed statutory machinery whereby an independent union could seek to compel an employer to grant it recognition through an application to the ACAS. This system had itself replaced the rather more formal provisions of the Industrial Relations Act 1971[77] concerning recognition of "sole bargaining agents." It was repealed in 1980, partly because the ACAS had found it impossible to arrive at agreement on the principles which it should apply to such applications. It was the view of the then Chairman of ACAS that unless the legislature was prepared to devise new machinery no system of reference to a tripartite body such as ACAS would be capable of producing authoritative recommendations. Recognition for bargaining purposes has thus reverted to a purely voluntary status. United Kingdom law also declines to impose upon those who bargain any duty to do so in good faith. Nevertheless recognition continues to enjoy considerable statutory significance wherever the recognised union is also an "independent" trade union[78]:

Advantages of recognition

(a) Only the representatives of independent recognised trade unions are entitled to paid time off to perform their bargaining duties and receive training therein.[79]

(b) But the members of any independent trade union are entitled to unpaid time off for trade union activities.[80]

(c) Only an independent recognised trade union is entitled to appoint safety representatives under section 1 of the Health and Safety at Work, etc., Act 1975.[81]

(d) Only the representatives of an independent recognised trade union are entitled to receive pre-redundancy information under section 99 of the E.P.A.[82] This limitation also applies to the information both transferor and transferee employers are required to provide upon the transfer of a business.[83]

(e) Only the representatives of an independent recognised trade union are entitled to avail themselves of the statutory right to seek from an employer information without which they would be materially impeded in collective bargaining.[84]

(f) Only the representatives of recognised trade unions are entitled to be consulted in respect of contracting out of occupational pension schemes.[85]

---

[75] E.P.A. 1975, ss.11–16.

[76] Employment Act 1980, s.19.

[77] ss.44–60.

[78] *Infra,* p. 386.

[79] See p. 111.

[80] See p. 114.

[81] See p. 547.

[82] See p. 296.

[83] Transfer of Undertakings (Protection of Employment) Regulations 1981 (S.I. 1981 No. 1794), reg. 10.

[84] E.P.A. 1975, s.17. See p. 360.

[85] Occupational Pensions Certification of Employments Regulations 1975 (S.I. 1975 No. 1927), reg. 4.

If the practice of conferring statutory rights to information, consultation and action only upon recognised trade unions continues the gap between such practices in the United Kingdom and such practices elsewhere in the EEC will widen. In other EEC countries it is common to provide (sometimes primarily) an alternative system of employee representation by way of joint Works Councils. Where this occurs the obligation to establish such Works Councils is irrespective of recognition, let alone voluntary recognition, of trade unions. It is also common to confer on these considerably more widespread Works Councils the rights which, in the United Kingdom, are only conferred on recognised trade unions.

Definition of recognition

The definition, such as it is, of recognition[86] is linked to the definition of collective bargaining which in turn refers to a list of matters originally designed to define the limits of a trade dispute.[87]

Most of the case law on the existence of recognition has been concerned, not with any matter in this definition but with the question whether the actions and attitudes of the employer amount to a sufficient acknowledgement of the bargaining function of the union. The bulk of them have arisen in relation to the duty to consult before redundancy. In *National Union of Gold, Silver and Allied Trades* v. *Albury Brothers Ltd.*[88] the employer was a member of an employers' federation which negotiated with the union and the employer had recently discussed the rates of pay of one employee with the union's district secretary. The Court of Appeal held that there must be clear evidence of the establishment of recognition by agreement, oral or in writing, or clear and distinct conduct revealing an implied agreement. Discussion of industrial relations matters was not enough to constitute recognition by an employer, nor was membership of an employers' organisation which itself recognised the union. Eveleigh L.J. said that recognition involved not merely a willingness to discuss but also to negotiate with a view to striking a bargain. Sir David Cairns obscured this attempted distinction between consultation and negotiation by saying that "recognition" means recognition that the union is to be consulted about some of the matters listed in the 1974 Act. There are thus clearly two separate aspects of the concept; namely, that of agreement and that of the purpose of the contact between union and employer. It is submitted that the requirement of agreement is established. It is clear that the element of agreement must derive from a conscious decision of the employer to recognise the union.[89] This decision may however be inferred from a course of conduct not necessarily entirely confined to the function of bargaining.[90]

Much of the evidence in these cases, however, goes no further than to reveal consultation and it is still not clear whether the evidence of recognition

---

[86] E.P.A. 1975, s.126.
[87] See TULRA 1974, s.29(1).
[88] [1979] I.C.R. 84.
[89] *Transport and General Workers Union* v. *Andrew Dyer* [1977] I.R.L.R. 93; *National Union of Tailors and Garment Workers* v. *Charles Ingram and Co. Ltd.* [1978] 1 All E.R. 1271.
[90] *N.U.T.G.W.* v. *Charles Ingram and Co. Ltd.* [1977] I.C.R. 530; *Joshua Wilson and Bros. Ltd.* v. *Union of Shop, Distributive and Allied Workers* [1978] I.C.R. 614.

for the purpose of collective bargaining may come from a wider and more popular concept of recognition. Some discussion of this occurred, however, in *Union of Shop, Distributive and Allied Workers* v. *Sketchley Ltd.*[91] The company granted what was called "recognition" for representation purposes in respect of employees who were union members wherever the union secured a membership of 50 per cent. of the company's employees in any union District. The company allowed the appointment of shop stewards and gave them unpaid time off work. It refused to pay them for this time on the ground that no right to negotiate terms and conditions of employment had been conferred. When in January 1980 it agreed to a meeting with the union to discuss pay, it insisted that only discussion and not negotiation was to be undertaken. Subsequently a redundancy situation arose and the company's relations with the union on this question fell short of the statutory requirements in relation to a recognised union. It is well established that recognition includes partial recognition so the question before the E.A.T. was whether any recognition at all existed.

Because the items listed in section 29(1) of the 1974 Act were designed to define the limits of a trade dispute and not, originally, the limits of recognition it is possible to find a number of them which would be covered by a grievance procedure. Indeed a grievance procedure involving negotiation is undoubtedly partial recognition. The decision of the E.A.T. turns, therefore, solely on the undefined meaning of the word "recognition." It held that there was a clear distinction between one who is entitled to make representations and one who may negotiate, and that it would be contrary to industrial relations practice to conclude that the first step towards recognition constituted such recognition. The court might have been nearer the truth to say that there may only sometimes be such clear distinction between consultation and negotiation, and the remainder of its judgment demonstrates the abnormality of such a situation. It stated that the employer's later actions came close to negotiation but were saved therefrom by his insistence that no negotiation was intended. It will be much more normal to find no such careful distinction drawn and what begins as consultation will edge towards negotiation.

If conscious agreement to bargain is necessary then it is open to the employer, as in the *Sketchley* case, effectively to deny his intention to negotiate even if the evidence suggests that that is what is happening in practice. Where intention must be deduced from practice it is unlikely that any single practice will so clearly fall on one side or the other of the line between consultation and negotiation as to make any list of practices a useful guide to the distinction.

The C.A.C., which has had to consider the meaning of negotiation in relation to the duty to supply information, has shown itself more aware of the uncertain line which may divide recognition from the steps leading to it. In the light of this awareness it has been more ready to accept earlier steps as conclusive. In *Greater London Council and GLC Staff Association*[92] a tribunal chaired by Sir John Wood said:

"We do not accept the argument put forward by the Employer's Counsel that collective bargaining only arises once there has been a formal offer or request. Bargaining is a more ongoing process than such a definition would allow. In this

---

[91] [1981] I.R.L.R. 291.
[92] Award No. 79/470.

case it is clear that since 1977, when the rundown of the Department in question occurred, the parties have been in continuous (though obviously spasmodic) negotiation."

In *B. L. Cars Ltd. and General and Municipal Workers Union*[93] the employer argued that he did not recognise any union for the purpose of negotiation on the decision to cease production and that, accordingly, refusal of information on that matter could not impede the union in its negotiations. In fact, however, a great deal of information had been given to the Confederation of Shipbuilding and Engineering Unions and the Union's national officer for the Engineering Industry had been heavily involved in talks with the company and had regarded them as part of a bargaining process. The Committee concluded that discussions within the context of an agreed bargaining procedure could not be meaningfully separated into consultation on the one hand and negotiation on the other. The Committee said:

> "No doubt [the local officials of the union] understood that the existence of the [employer's plan for survival of the company] . . . would heavily influence any subsequent negotiation; but we are satisfied that the local officials did not intend to abdicate their bargaining function. Nor, we think, did the Employer assume that intention to exist. The Unions pointed out that after the adoption of the plan they were given a week to come up with alternative proposals. Had the Unions been able to do so in such a time and without adequate information negotiation upon their proposals, even if it took the form of a brief meeting in which Management made it clear that the alternative proposals were not feasible, would have been inevitable. For the reason already mentioned we do not think that such a situation could reasonably be labelled "consultation" so as to distinguish it from bargaining. It would be a use of the collective bargaining procedure agreement and not of any more limited procedure."

THE RESPONSE OF THE LAW

It is not surprising that the courts are not wholly in sympathy with the collective activities of trade unions and that even collective bargaining is to some extent at variance with the normal judicial approach. On occasion they have been heard so to confuse the judicial approach in which individual rights predominate with the approach of the unions to which such predominance would be a contradiction in terms. Classic among such misstatements is the following. Referring to his own invention of a "right to work" Lord Denning M.R. said in *Edwards* v. *SOGAT*[94]:

> "This is now fully recognised by law. It is a right which is of especial importance when a trade union operated a 'closed shop' or '100 per cent. membership'; for that means that no man can become employed or remain in employment with a firm unless he is a member of the union. If his union card is withdrawn, he has to leave the employment. He is deprived of his livelihood. The courts of this country will not allow so great a power to be exercised arbitrarily or capriciously or with unfair discrimination, neither in the making of the rules, nor in the enforcement of them . . . A trade union exists to protect the right of each one of its members to

---

[93] Award No. 80/65.
[94] [1971] Ch. 354.

earn his living and to take advantage of all that goes with it. It is the very purpose of its being. If the union should assume to make a rule which destroys that right or puts it in jeopardy . . . then the union exceeds its powers."

The shop steward

The position of the local representative—the shop steward—was most clearly and fully presented to the courts in the case of *Heatons Transport (St. Helen's) Ltd.* v. *T.G.W.U.*[95] which raised the question whether a union was, in effect, vicariously liable for the "unfair industrial practices" of its shop stewards under the provisions of the Industrial Relations Act 1971 notwithstanding its unsuccessful attempts to ensure that those shop stewards ceased such activities. On this occasion Lord Denning M.R. and Roskill L.J. in the Court of Appeal refused to imply authority from the union to the shop stewards, preferring to conclude that the shop stewards acted only on the authority of their constituents. In the House of Lords this dual source of authority was accepted but the conclusion of the Court of Appeal was reversed on the ground that the constituents *were* the union which had, therefore, authorised from one end or the other of its organisation the action taken.

Lord Wilberforce (delivering the judgment of the House of Lords) said:

"Shop stewards are elected by the membership in a defined working place and hold office for two years. Upon ratification of their election by the appropriate district committee and regional committee they are accredited officials of the union. Their credentials may be withdrawn by the regional committee or its authorised subcommittee, but only if the shop steward is not acting in accordance with the union rules and policy.

The purpose for which shop stewards are elected is described as that of 'representing membership on matters affecting their employment.' This is a phrase which is both wide and vague. No doubt their main concern is intended to be the particular industrial interests of the members of the union in the work places for which they are shop stewards. This has given rise to the suggestion that they play a 'dual role,' in that in respect of some acts done by them they are to be treated in law as agents for the union, but in respect of others as agents only for those members of the union by whom they have been elected as shop stewards. For the latter the union is said to be not responsible in law as their principal.

This concept of duality of roles is not one which would be likely to occur to trade unionists. The rules of the Transport and General Workers Union themselves provide that 'Shop stewards shall receive the fullest support and protection from the union.' Even upon the lowest basis of individual self-interest—and there is no reason to suppose that members of trade unions are actuated by this alone—it may well be thought that an improvement in the earnings or conditions of employment of any group of members will make it easier to achieve improvements for other groups and ultimately for all the members. There is thus no *a priori* reason why the members of the union should not agree that shop stewards should be authorised by *all* the members to take action to promote the interests of members employed in a particular work place.

That this is the industrial strategy of the Transport and General Workers' Union in particular is apparent from the introductory paragraph in the shop stewards' handbook issued by the union to shop stewards and from the following extract from the official journal of the union, the 'Record,' for February 1972:

---

[95] [1972] I.C.R. 308.

'Wage increases worth hundreds of millions of pounds have been won by the T.G.W.U. in the last year—and the key to this success has been the fact that the union has involved shop stewards and members in taking decisions on agreements.'

That in what they do for the purpose of representing membership in the work place shop stewards are acting on behalf of the members of the union as a whole is emphasised time and again in the Shop Stewards' Handbook.

'As a shop steward there is no doubt that the eyes of the members in your shop are upon you. You are the union as far as they are concerned. You are the agency through which come any services which our union provides for them, and through which they normally hear about us.' Again: 'Remember first of all you are an official of the union'; and again: 'As a shop steward you represent *on behalf of the union* its members in the workplace.'

The final question, therefore, is whether the evidence proves that at any time after March 23, 1972, the union withdrew from shop stewards at Liverpool or at Hull the whole or any part of their general authority and discretion to organise blacking on the union's behalf in support of its policy of reserving stuffing and stripping containers.

To be effective in law a withdrawal or curtailment of an existing actual authority of an agent must be communicated by the principal to the agent in terms which the agent would reasonably understand as forbidding him to do that which he had previously been authorised to do on the principal's behalf. One is looking therefore for some communication to the shop stewards, by some officer or committee entitled to give them instructions on behalf of the union, couched in language which they would understand as being an order by the union to stop organising the blacking by members of the union of vehicles operated by the appellant companies.

The effect of [this] evidence is summarised in the statement made by the general secretary on television already quoted: 'We don't call on shop stewards to obey the union—they are the union.' Consistently with this, so far as the evidence consisted of written communications from the head office of the union these, where they did anything more than pass on information about orders made by the court, were expressed to be by way of 'advice' only. 'Advice' and 'persuasion' were also the strongest expressions used by the permanent officers of the union in Liverpool to describe what they had said orally to the shop stewards about putting an end to the blacking of Heatons and Craddocks. What clothes a shop steward in the eyes of his fellow members with authority to act on behalf of the union and assures them that if they do what he proposes it will receive 'the fullest support and protection from the union,' is that he holds credentials given by the union. To do no more than 'advise' a shop steward as to the way in which he exercises a discretionary authority which has hitherto been vested in him by virtue of his credentials, without also intimating to him that if he does not follow that 'advice' his credentials to continue to act on behalf of the union will be withdrawn, may be reasonably understood by the shop steward as a recognition that his authority continues unaltered and that the ultimate discretion as to how it is to be exercised is still vested in him.''[95a]

Collective agreements

It is submitted that collective bargaining, including as it does the processes of applying pressure to accept a settlement, is, or can be, a sufficiently precise

---

[95a] A formalised definition of authorisation is adopted in the Employment Act 1982, s.15(3) and (4) to govern the introduction by that Act of a form of vicarious liability for the tortious acts of officials.

function to permit the application of rules of agency law. By applying an equally strict application of contractual principles the Divisional Court of the Queen's Bench reached a conclusion out of line with collective bargaining practice in *R.* v. *The Central Arbitration Committee, ex parte Deltaflow Ltd.*[96] The Transport and General Workers Union had presented a claim under Schedule 11 to the Employment Protection Act 1975[97] on behalf of employees of Deltaflow Ltd. that they were entitled to improvement of pay to bring them in line with the general level of wages established largely by local agreements. The Central Arbitration Committee made an award of such an increase on the ground that the £42 basic rate for skilled workers established by the national agreements then in force was not regarded as establishing the current minimum rate for the industry and that, therefore, there was no nationally recognised level.

Lord Widgery C.J. said:

"Is that a tenable conclusion? In my judgment, it is not. Para. 1 of the Schedule . . . deals first of all with recognised terms and conditions, and the definition in para. 2 makes it quite clear that recognised terms and conditions are terms and conditions determined by agreement. The word 'agreement' is not there accidentally. The word 'agreement' is a word which has a clear meaning in law. This is, after all, the schedule to a statute, where language is expected to be given its strict legal meaning. In my judgment it is perfectly clear that nothing can destroy or modify the provisions of the written agreement of May 1975, except some new agreement, made by competent people, the intention and purpose of which is to effect that change. The idea of a kind of tacit alteration in the terms of that central agreement derived from the fact that nobody bothered with it much for a year is not a way in which a formal document can be effectively varied. Indeed it seems to me that no sort of effective variation of the agreement of 1975 was ever made."

Occasionally judicial failure to admit the practice of collective bargaining has led them even to confuse the legal issues. The decision in *Loman and Henderson* v. *Merseyside Transport Services Ltd.*[98] might be better forgotten had it not been relied upon without examination by Lord Denning M.R. in *Gascol Conversions Ltd.* v. *Mercer.*[99] It may well crop up again since it is apparent that the courts have not satisfactorily resolved the question of the interaction of local and national agreements. In both these cases redundant workers sought to rely on local agreements specifying longer basic working weeks than the relevant national agreements. In *Loman's* case there was evidence that the local agreement "was not intended to have contractual effect." Since this is the normal position of all collective agreements in English law, varied only for a brief period by the Industrial Relations Act 1971,[1] the court's misunderstanding of the effect of this intention is extraordinary.

Lord Parker C.J. said:

"If locally legally binding agreements were made departing from the National Agreement, it would undoubtedly create demands for a complete overhaul of the national agreement. It seems to me . . . that these local arrangements are useful to iron out local labour difficulties, as under these arrangements employers, as it were, assume *ex gratia* an obligation to pay their men on the basis of a 68 hour week

---

[96] [1978] I.C.R. 534.
[97] The Schedule is now repealed.
[98] (1968) 3 I.T.R. 108.
[99] [1974] I.C.R. 420.
[1] See, *infra*, p. 378; *Ford Motor Co. Ltd.* v. *A.U.E.W.* [1969] 2 Q.B. 303; TULRA 1974, s.18.

whilst at the same time there is no obligation on any workman to work the 68 hour week. Accordingly both in law and in common sense it seems to me that the tribunal were fully entitled to come to the conclusion [that the local agreement did not vary the national agreement]."

Since it is likely that the national agreement was similarly intended not to have effect as a binding contract it is difficult to see why it should take precedence or, alternatively, from where the employee's obligation to work a basic week should be derived.

On the other hand in *Gascol* v. *Mercer* Lawton L.J. showed considerably more understanding of the varied status of collective agreements. He said:

"In my opinion the making of national agreements between unions and employers' federations does not automatically change the terms of employment of any members of the union. Whether they do or do not must depend upon the circumstances of each case. For example, in the nationalised industries the making of a national agreement would produce, I should have thought, an almost irrebuttable inference that the terms of employment had been changed, but it does not follow in other industries (particularly those in which there are large numbers of employers) that the making of a national agreement produces an inference having anything like the same effect."

It is important to realise how significant is the judicial understanding upon development not only of collective bargaining but of the individual rights springing therefrom. In *Blackman* v. *Post Office*[2] the N.I.R.C. accepted as fair the dismissal of an employee who failed to pass an aptitude test, agreed with the appropriate union as a means of preventing the employer permanently diluting the labour force, notwithstanding that the employer had no objection to the competence displayed by the employee in the job in question. One wonders how this accords with Lord Denning's understanding of the *intra vires* functions of trade unions. In *Oddy* v. *T.S.S.A.*[3] the N.I.R.C. refused to imply an obligation to represent an employee from a provision in the union rules stating that protection of interests of members was an object of the union. In *FTATU* v. *Modgill*[4] the Employment Appeal Tribunal offered no alternative remedy when the union successfully defended a claim of illegal discrimination for failing to support the efforts of a group of African Asians to receive a better wage structure by showing that it would have refused to support a group of "whites" in similar circumstances. On the other hand, if a union does choose to represent an individual in dismissal proceedings such appearance on his behalf will satisfy the requirements of natural justice apparently without enquiry as to whether it has resulted in a fair hearing.[5]

Of greatest significance, however, is the increasing tendency of the courts tacitly to accept an agency approach whereby the union member covered by a collective agreement is held to be bound to it by implication into his individual contract; and this whether he knows of the agreement or not. It is true, as Elias Napier and Wallington point out[6] that the sum of the cases in support of this

---

[2] [1974] I.C.R. 151.
[3] [1973] I.C.R. 524.
[4] [1980] I.R.L.R. 142.
[5] *Gray Dunn and Co. Ltd.* v. *Edwards* [1980] I.R.L.R. 23.
[6] p. 407.

development is small[7] but it is submitted that they represent a modern trend adopted by tribunals influenced by trade unionists and employers who clearly regard such a result as expected. The authority of Lush J. who decided otherwise in *Holland* v. *London Society of Compositors*[8] may not be as great on modern employment law as in some other areas.

The contractual enforceability of collective agreements

As the preceding discussion reveals, there are two aspects of the enforceability of collective agreements which at first appear to be separate but, on examination, are interconnected. The first is the enforceability of the agreement between the parties to it. The second is the legal effect that can be achieved once the provisions of the collective agreement are absorbed into the individual contract of employment.

The two concepts produce fundamentally different results as is apparent from the fact that trade unions are usually strongly opposed to the contractual enforceability of collective agreements but in favour of the translation of the agreement into individually binding contracts. When legislation[9] for a few years raised a presumption of contractual enforceability, employers showed no sign of being prepared to purchase trade union agreement not to remove this presumption by the insertion of an express provision that the agreement should be binding in honour alone. Most other major industrial countries, however, assign some form of contractual enforceability to the collective agreement and the alleged advantages of such a system are still canvassed in this country.

As between the parties to the collective agreement the issue of contractual enforceability primarily affects procedural agreements though this must be taken to include the frequency with which substantive agreements will be renegotiated. On the other hand it is envisaged that by conferring contractual status on substantive agreements considerable changes in bargaining technique would result.

It is assumed, for instance, that a contractually enforceable substantive agreement would necessarily have to contain a provision as to the intervals at which it was renegotiable. Such a provision could, of course, provide for renegotiation upon giving a period of notice of such a desire. It is obviously assumed, however, that at least equally common would be provision for annual or biennial review. The further assumption from this is that the parties to an agreement which was to be subject to judicial interpretation but otherwise has to stand for one or two years would take much greater care when drafting its provisions. What are known as "rights disputes" would, therefore, be less common simply because the statements of these rights were less ambiguous. "Interest disputes" would only arise when the agreement was due for renegotiation. Because of the greater permanency of the agreement such disputes might well take much longer to settle but the resulting settlement would be

---

[7] *Edwards* v. *Skyways Ltd.* [1964] 1 W.L.R. 349; *Rookes* v. *Barnard* [1963] 1 Q.B. 623; *Singh* v. *British Steel Corporation* [1974] I.R.L.R. 131; *Land and Wilson* v. *West Yorkshire Metropolitan County Council* [1979] I.C.R. 452 reversed on other grounds [1981] I.C.R. 334.
[8] (1924) 40 T.L.R. 440.
[9] The Industrial Relations Act 1971, s.34(1). Repealed by the Trade Union and Labour Relations Act 1974.

more meaningful. In other words, it is supposed by its more devoted advocates that contractual enforceability would go a long way to eliminate small disputes of either right or interest which are characteristic of British labour relations and which, by their unpredictable frequency, are disproportionately disruptive of production. They would be replaced by more intractable, more far-reaching, but far less frequent and more predictable disputes. No doubt this would result in more lengthy stoppages but such stoppages could be planned for simply because they were predictable.

So far as procedural agreements are concerned, the critical provision is the Report of the 1965–68 Royal Commission upon[10] the enforceability of a clause restricting the freedom to resort to industrial action before exhaustion of procedure. The effect of this provision and the reciprocal obligations it produces is clearly summarised by the Royal Commission[11]:

> "The 'peace' obligation is imposed upon both sides, but it is more important in practice as a remedy to assist the employers than as a remedy to assist the unions; strikes are everywhere a more significant feature of industrial relations than lock-outs. This aspect of the legal enforcement of collective agreements is therefore of special importance to protect the interest of management in the continuous flow of production. Where this interest is thus legally protected, a corresponding legal protection usually exists for the interest of the unions in the maintenance of the standards laid down in the agreement. Under such a system employers who are themselves parties to collective agreements, or members of associations which are parties, are by operation of statute prevented from contracting out of the terms of the agreement to the detriment of their employees. This means that any contract of employment within the scope of the collective agreement which is concluded by an employer bound by its term is automatically void insofar as it purports to be less favourable to the employee than the terms of the agreement; and that the corresponding terms of the agreement compulsorily become terms of the contract of employment in the place of those which, by operation of the statute, are void. The terms of the agreement thus become a compulsory code for all employers parties to the agreement or members of associations which are parties, and the agreement may by special administrative acts be extended to non-federated employers as well. These two matters, the agreement as a compulsory contract and the agreement as a compulsory code, are closely connected: the legal restriction of the freedom to strike is so to speak the consideration for the legal guarantee of the agreed minimum. The obligation to refrain from strike or other 'hostile' action is generally understood to be co-extensive with the scope of the substantive agreement: strikes are prohibited only in so far as they are intended to compel employers to consent to a change of the matters regulated in the agreement itself while that agreement is in operation, and industrial sanctions are permitted if their application is unrelated to matters dealt with in the collective agreement."

The Commission was not, however, in favour of enforceability as a means of curing the ills of the voluntary system.[12]

> "But this is not the root of the evil. As we found when seeking to identify the underlying causes of unofficial strikes, the root of the evil is in our present methods of collective bargaining and especially our methods of workshop bargaining, and it is in the absence of speedy, clear and effective disputes procedures. Until this defect is remedied, all attempts to make procedure agreements legally binding are

---

[10] Cmnd. 3623 (1967).
[11] para. 467.
[12] paras. 475–476.

bound to defeat themselves. One of the principal objects of the factory and company agreements which, according to our recommendations, should be concluded in the near future will be to develop 'joint procedures for the rapid and equitable settlement of grievances.' This is what is lacking at present, and this is the indispensable condition for reducing the number of unofficial and unconstitutional strikes. To make the present procedure agreements legally enforceable would be at variance both with our analysis of the causes of the evil and with our proposals for a remedy. It would divert attention from the underlying causes to the symptoms of the disease and might indeed delay or even frustrate the cure we recommend. It might perpetuate the existing procedures instead of replacing them by clear and effective methods of dispute settlement which at present do not exist.

Any attempt to deal with unofficial and unconstitutional strikes in isolation must be deprecated. This applies to the legal enforcement of procedure agreements as much as to the proposal to eradicate these strikes by imposing an overall obligation to give notice before resorting to a stoppage or to similar action such as go-slow, work to rule or overtime bans. None of these measures promises any success in the sense of improving our industrial relations as long as the underlying causes of these strikes have not been removed. We expect the reform of the collective bargaining system to lead to a very considerable reduction in unofficial strikes. This expectation may not be entirely fulfilled. If so, it may then be necessary to reconsider the desirability and practicability of giving some legal support to procedure agreements."

It is submitted that this assessment of contractual enforceability as the eventual consequence of stable industrial relations rather than a means towards that end is clearly correct. The multitude of factors influencing the success or failure of bargaining is well illustrated by the following classification.[13]

Environmental Factors* and Industrial Peace†

Factors	Frequently favourable circumstances	Frequently unfavourable circumstances
Industrial environment		
1. Size of plant and company	Medium-sized company	Industrial giant
2. Production pattern	Steady	Seasonal; intermittent; production crises
3. Technological advance	Moderate	Severe
4. Nature of the jobs	Skilled; responsible	Assembly-line type
5. Cost factors	Infra-marginal plant	Marginal plant
6. Market factors	Expanding; cyclically insensitive; inelastic demand	Contracting; sensitive to cycle; elastic demand
7. Locational factors	Relatively immobile plant	Relatively mobile plant
Community environment		
1. The work force	Steady; tractable	Inconstant; combative
2. Plant and Labor	Metropolitan area	One-industry town

[13] C. Kerr "Industrial Peace and the Collective Bargaining Environment," C.S. Golden and V.D. Parker (eds.), *Cases of Industrial Peace under Collective Bargaining* (Harper and Row, New York 1955), pp. 10–22.

3. Local wage levels	Low-wage community and high-wage industry	Low-wage industry and high-wage community
4. Industrial climate	"Union town"	"Open-shop town"

"Political" environment of the parties

1. The union	Secure union; secure leaders; homogeneous membership; local autonomy; pattern-following	Insecure union; insecure leaders; heterogeneous membership; external domination; pattern-setting
2. The employer	Pattern-following; in employers' association; local autonomy in non-contractual matters	Pattern-setting; lone bargainer; strong central domination of local plant
Time as an environmental factor	Origins in peaceful period; old relationship	Origins in war-like period; new relationship

* The full range of environmental conditions is not set forth in this table, but only those conditions which appear to relate to the prospects for industrial peace.

† Reference is made here to "industrial peace" developed by parties of relatively equal strength, not arising from domination by one side or by government.

Presumption of non-enforceability

In 1974 legislation in the United Kingdom favoured return to non-enforceability and because of the identification by the Royal Commission of the "peace clause" as the critical issue concentrated specifically on that. Section 18 of TULRA 1974 first reversed the general presumption of enforceability of collective agreements introduced by the Industrial Relations Act 1971 in favour of a conclusive presumption of non-enforceability unless the agreement was in writing and contained a provision stating that the parties intended it to be legally binding. It then expressly prevented circumvention of the effect of this by way of implication of a peace clause into individual contracts of employment.[14]

> (4) Notwithstanding anything in subsections (2) and (3) above, any terms of a collective agreement (whether made before or after the commencement of this section) which prohibit or restrict the right of workers to engage in a strike or other industrial action, or have the effect of prohibiting or restricting that right, shall not form part of any contract between any worker and the person for whom he works unless the collective agreement—
>
> (a) is in writing; and
> (b) contains a provision expressly stating that those terms shall or may be incorporated in such a contract; and
> (c) is reasonably accessible at his place of work to the worker to whom it applies and is available for him to consult during working hours; and
> (d) is one where each trade union which is party to the agreement is an independent trade union;

---

[14] s.18(4).

and unless the contract with that worker expressly or impliedly incorporates those terms in the contract.

(5) Subsection (4) above shall have effect notwithstanding any provision to the contrary in any agreement (including a collective agreement or a contract with any worker).

This appears to restore two separate understandings—they cannot be described much more strongly—which had existed immediately before 1971. In *Ford Motor Co. Ltd.* v. *Amalgamated Union of Engineering and Foundry Workers*[15] Geoffrey Lane J. (as he then was) reviewed for the first and only time the series of rather tenuous authorities upon the contractual status of collective agreements. Not surprisingly, he found no authority to convince him that collective agreements were contractually binding. It is clear, however, that legal authority left him equally unconvinced that they were not binding. The learned judge turned accordingly to consider the intention of the parties judged objectively by the standard of the reasonable man. He derived the evidence of intention from (i) the wording of the agreements and, particularly, their frequent resort to aspirational language, (ii) the practical problems which would arise from enforcement and (iii) the general climate of opinion, which he considered was clearly in favour of unenforceability.

The question of implication of the critical peace clause into the contract of employment thereby producing a situation very similar in ultimate effect to contractual enforceability of the collective agreement itself did not, however, have the benefit of such careful, if isolated, judicial review. The best pre-1971 assessment of the legal position is, however, contained in the following extract[16]:

"This issue of the doubtful propriety of certain collective terms for incorporation into employment contracts assumes even greater importance if we turn from clauses dealing with substantial terms of the employment to the 'procedure' clauses described in Part II. Most British collective agreements include a series of stages through which disputes and grievances are to be taken and provide that: 'Until the procedure provided above has been carried through there shall be no stoppage of work either of a partial or a general character' (Engineering Agreement); or:

The parties hereto being agreed that in the event of any dispute or difference arising between their respective members or any of them, every means for effecting an amicable settlement should be exhausted before resorting to direct action, hereby undertake not to instruct their members to strike or lockout or otherwise to take such action as would involve a cessation of work without complying with all the agreements then in existence between the parties and giving the customary notice to terminate the employment.

Do such clauses impose obligations upon the individual workers? There is no clear judicial decision on the matter. In the few cases where it has arisen, it was *conceded* without argument by the defendants that the procedure clauses in question were incorporated in full into the employment contracts; as in one where the clause said, 'The Employers . . . and the employees . . . undertake that no lockout or strike shall take place.' Such an exceptional absolute obligation never to

---

15 [1969] 2 Q.B. 303. See Selwyn, "Collective Agreements and the Law" (1969) 32 M.L.R. 377 and Clark in reply (1970) 33 M.L.R. 117.
16 Wedderburn and Davies: *Employment Grievances and Disputes Procedures in Britain* (Univ. of Calif. Press 1969), at pp. 50–51.

strike at least is clear in its meaning; and if the test be that of semantic appropriateness, then a clause that speaks of the 'employees' undertaking obligations will plainly be more readily incorporated than one that merely records the promise of the collective parties, (*e.g.* the trade union on the workers side). But a purely semantic test of this kind would produce bizarre results. For example, the standard clause quoted in the Engineering Agreement has been inserted in many agreements made by the Engineering Employers' Federation. Contrast the agreement made with the Draughtmen's Association. ('This Agreement shall apply to draughtsmen and draughtswomen members of the [union]') with that made with the Clerical and Administrative Workers Union ('The . . . Employers intimated to the Union . . . that they would be prepared to recommend the recognition of the . . . Union as representing clerical workpeople employed in engineering and allied establishments, subject to the following conditions . . . '). On a purely semantic test the 'no-strikes-until-procedure-is-exhausted' clause would, in the first case, bind individual workers; in the second, the clause would seem appropriate only as an agreement at the collective level.

It is thought that a court would not be guided only by such semantic factors but would ask whether a 'no-strike' or 'procedure' clause is in *substance* appropriate for incorporation. The worker is always in breach of his contract of employment if he strikes without giving notice to terminate employment. What can the collective term add to that? If Lord Denning's approach to the overtime clause were applied by analogy, the answer might be that the normal procedure clause obliged each worker not to *organize*, officially or unofficially, a collective cessation of work, even by means of notice of termination, while the procedure was being exhausted. This extreme interpretation is the only way to give meaning to the incorporation and thereby make procedure clauses 'normative' on each worker in the average industrial situation. Objection has been raised to this view. Professor Kahn-Freund has said that 'It goes almost without saying that neither an individual employer nor an individual employee could be bound by the agreement as a contract . . . in a recent case it was admitted that the 'no-strike' obligation had become a term of the individual contracts of employment but this must be quite exceptional.' This, too, is the view of the Trades Union Congress (T.U.C.) spokesman expressed in its oral evidence to the Royal Commission, where the Assistant General Secretary said:

> 'The procedure agreement is not part of the contract of employment, I think; the procedure agreement is really an agreement between the union or unions and the employer as to the way in which they will resolve difficulties which arise . . . Really it sets out the way in which disputes will be settled. This is not part of the contract, I think, between the employer and the employee.'"

In the United States contractual enforceability is of more recent development than is generally supposed. Until 1957 the agreements were normally regarded as common law contracts, subject to the ordinary law of contract in the various states. With so many varying systems there was still room for a theory very similar to that prevailing in this country that the agreement was similar to a treaty, enforceable only by a strike[17]; or for the agency theory by which the negotiators were considered to be agents binding the persons they represented. It was often assumed that an employer could sue employees, but not the union, for a breach of the agreement. The development of bargaining agents with the statutory right to negotiate agreements, but no statutory rights to enforce them, produced a practice, introduced by the War Labour Board in the 1940s, whereby the union concerned did in fact process a complaint of a breach of

---

[17] See Professor C.O. Gregory, "The Enforcement of Collective Labour Agreements in the United States" (1968) 21 C.L.P. 159.

agreement through the arbitration machinery. This practice was, at that time, introduced into many agreements. It was provided in the Taft-Hartley Act 1947[18]:

"Suits for violation of contracts between an employer and a labour organisation representing employees in an industry affecting commerce as defined in this Act, or between any such labour organisations, may be brought in any district court of the United States having jurisdiction of the parties without respect to the amount in controversy, or without regard to the citizenship of the parties."

In *Association of Westinghouse Salaried Employees* v. *Westinghouse Electric Corporation*[19] a union sued an employer in a federal district court for violation of a collective agreement. In the Supreme Court, Frankfurter J., writing the main opinion of the court, held that the section had only procedural significance; that is to say, it allowed unions to appear in actions if they had contracts, but it did not of itself make collective agreements contractually enforceable. Two other members of the court thought the section did have a substantive effect, but that only individual employees could sue on what were their own personal rights. Two years later, the minority view in the *Westinghouse* case prevailed[20] and the section was recognised as establishing a new substantive federal right. The basis was laid for what amounts to a new federal law of labour contracts.

In France, collective agreements are regarded as automatically incorporated into the contract of employment, replacing any term of the contract inconsistent with the agreement. They become in effect, therefore, contractually enforceable by the individual worker. Trade unions, however, do not become liable for the acts of their members but they are liable for their own acts and may, in turn, bring an action in place of an employee affected by a breach of agreement. In some cases, where the effect of a collective agreement has been officially extended, breach by an employer may lead to criminal sanctions.

In Germany, provisions of a collective agreement affecting the individual contract of employment also become part of that contract. They, like provisions which go beyond individual contractual rights, can only be enforced by the individual concerned. The right of a union to sue an employer upon a collective agreement has been expressly denied by the Federal Labour Court.[21] There is a complicated and practically ineffective procedure to sue an employers' association in order to force it to sue its member who refuses to carry out terms of a collective agreement.

Nevertheless the Collective Agreement Recommendation (No. 91) of the I.L.O. supports legal enforceability and it is a common practice in the industrial countries to make legal provision for such enforceability."

Transfer of the benefit of collective agreements

The Transfer of Undertakings (Protection of Employment) Regulations 1981[22] make provision for the transfer of recognition and other collective

---

[18] s.301.

[19] 348 U.S. 437 (1955).

[20] *T.W.U.A.* v. *Lincoln Mills*, 353 U.S. 448 (1957).

[21] See *Labour Relations and the Law*, ed. O. Kahn-Freund, Chap. 6; *The German Law*, by Professor Thilo Ramm.

[22] S.I. 1981 No. 1794.

agreements upon the transfer to another person of the whole or part of a business situated immediately before the transfer in the United Kingdom whether the transfer is by sale or by some other form of disposition. This provision does not apply to transfer of control by means of acquisition of a controlling interest in the shares of a company.

Wherever the transferred undertaking maintains, after the transfer, "an identity distinct from the remainder of the transferee's undertaking"[23] any independent trade union recognised to any extent by the transferor in respect of any description of transferred employees shall be deemed to have been recognised by the transferee to the same extent.[24] The Regulations provide enigmatically that "any agreement for recognition may be varied or rescinded" [according to existing legal principles]. United Kingdom law, as we have seen, would allow most recognition agreements to be varied or rescinded at will. The agreement itself might provide for unilateral termination by notice or, alternatively, not envisage such termination. The critical question is whether the Regulations intended to provide as a matter of law that the agreement could only be terminated according to its own terms or, in other words, to make it contractually enforceable. On the one hand it is clearly the intention of the EEC Directive that such agreements should not be compulsorily transferred merely to be rescinded at will. On the other hand it would a little surprising if U.K. law permitted most recognition agreements to be terminated at will but entrenched those recognition agreements which had passed a barrier of transfer of business.

There can be no doubt that it is permissible for legislation to provide for the contractual enforceability of a class of collective agreements even if these agreements already exist as non-binding agreements.[25] Even if the words of the Regulations were clearer, however, it is obvious that the intention to give binding effect to certain collective agreements is not apparent by any normal standard of statutory construction. It is an open question whether the obvious intention of the EEC will persuade British courts to confer that effect on these Regulations in the light of the anomalous situation in relation to other agreements which such an interpretation would produce.

The provisions relating to the transfer of other collective agreements[26] are no more clear. It is provided that wherever there is in existence in relation to any employee whose contract is transferred by reason of these Regulations a collective agreement with a recognised trade union that agreement shall have effect after the transfer as if made by or on behalf of the transferee with that trade union. Anything done in relation to that agreement by or in relation to the transferor before the transfer shall be deemed to have been done by the transferee. Any order[27] shall have effect as if the transferee were a party to the agreement.

Much of the apparent effect of this provision is unnecessary save as removing anomalous effects. The substantive parts of such agreements so far as they have individual application will almost certainly have been incorporated in the

---

[23] The EEC Council Directive 77/197 from which the Regulations spring refers to "maintenance of autonomy."
[24] para. 9.
[25] Restoration of Pre-War Trade Practices Acts 1942 and 1950.
[26] para. 6.
[27] For instance one made by the C.A.C.

contracts of employment which have been transferred. Most procedure agreements will merely be the outward manifestation of recognition. If recognition is conceded the procedure is bound to be accepted until properly amended. The doubtful points arising from this provision apply, therefore, to a small but important selection of clauses in collective agreements which are more than expressions of intention but less than matters of individual contract or recognition procedure. Perhaps the most obvious example would be union membership agreements. It seems unlikely that British trade unions will wish to fight hard for contractual enforceability of these, or any other, aspects of collective agreements and it is unlikely that the EEC will wish to bring much pressure to bear on the contractual enforceability of closed shop agreements. It seems most likely, therefore, that if there is to be an attempt to read contractual enforceability into the Regulations it will stem from the provisions as to transfer of recognition.

CHAPTER 9

INTERNAL TRADE UNION AFFAIRS

ORGANISATIONAL LEGISLATION

(a) The definition of a trade union

The Trade Union Act 1871 which first created a definition of trade unions was primarily concerned to offer some formal structure to a wide variety of industrial organisations not previously recognised by the law. Consequently, the legislature at that time had no need to distinguish between the membership of such organisations but was concerned rather to define them according to their purpose of regulating industrial relations and the conditions of the trade.[1] The resulting definition, therefore, included employers' associations and organisations of workers. So long as its principal purpose remained to define an organisation to which a particular, but not particularly restrictive, structure should apply, this caused no problems.

Only in 1971 when the legislature desired to impose more meaningful restrictions on workers' organisations was it necessary to construct a legal definition which distinguished them from industrial organisations which, though possessing the same basic purpose of regulating industrial relations, adopted methods of doing so radically different from those of workers' organisations. In practice, of course, it was this line of distinction which had long been recognised as the most significant and the popular concept of a trade union clearly separated it as a workers' organisation from the lesser known and less powerful employers' organisation. Employers are not only inclined to further their individual interests but, being more powerful as such than the individual worker are able to do so more effectively. It follows that they have less need and less reason to confer power on their own groupings, and the distinguishing features of such employers' associations and trade unions support the popular conception that the one has no practical similarity to the other.

The report of the Royal Commission on Trade Unions and Employers' Associations 1965–68[2] not surprisingly in view of the distinction recognised in its own title, recommended that the term "trade union" should be confined to organisations of employed persons. This recommendation was given effect by the Industrial Relations Act 1971. That legislation was, however, not content to enact the practical and popular understanding of the concept of a trade union because it was desired to preserve certain traditional areas of trade union activity for a particular type of organisation which accepted the imposition of certain standards of internal and external conduct. In pursuance of this policy the legal definition of a trade union was artificially confined to those organisations which registered under the new statutory procedure.

---

[1] Trade Union Act 1871, s.23 subsequently amended by Trade Union (Amendment) Act 1976, s.16 and Trade Union Act 1913, ss. 1 and 2.
[2] Cmnd. 3623, para. 766.

384

Whether or not it was the intention of this policy to do so the result was the growth of a considerable number of "trade unions" as statutorily defined, entitled to make use of the process previously exercised by all trade unions but now purportedly confined to those organisations which registered. The effect of this artificial distinction was greatly enhanced by the fact that most of the established trade unions declined to register under the new system so ceasing to be trade unions within the statutory definition.

As a consequence of this the established unions sought to ensure that in any future legislation those organisations which would not be acceptable by them as trade unions should be excluded. The basis of distinction which they advocated was that of independence from control by an employer. The current definition contained in the Trade Union and Labour Relations Act 1974[3] maintains the distinction between organisations of workers and organisations of employers. A trade union

> "consists wholly or mainly of workers of one or more descriptions and is an organisation [whether permanent or temporary] whose principal purposes include the regulation of relations between workers of that description or those descriptions and employers or employers associations."

Constituent or affiliated organisations or federations of such organisations which fulfil this requirement and their representatives may also be regarded as trade unions provided that they possess a sufficient degree of organisation.[4]

Workers

"Worker" is wider than "employee," extending to those who perform personally work or services for another person who is not a professional client.[5] So the Law Society was held not to be an "organisation of workers" under the provisions of the Industrial Relations Act 1971.[6] In *Broadbent* v. *Crisp*[7] the definition of worker was confined to those whose contracts actually obliged them to perform the work personally. This would appear to be the correct interpretation of the words used in the definition but it confines the term to those who accept an obligation which would not apply to many self-employed persons. Indeed, one of the characteristics of employment accepted in *Ready Mixed Concrete (South East) Ltd.* v. *Minister of Pensions*[8] was inability to assign performance to another.

Purposes

One of the organisation's principal purposes must be the regulation of relations between workers and employers or associations of employers. Though it is submitted that this places it beyond doubt that the definition is not intended to be exclusive of any other purpose and so disposes of any lingering suspicion that *Osborne* v. *A.S.R.S.*[9] is still the law it does have the effect of excluding

---

[3] s.28(1).
[4] *Midland Cold Storage* v. *Steer* [1972] I.C.R. 230.
[5] s.30(1) and (2).
[6] *Carter* v. *The Law Society* [1973] I.C.R. 113.
[7] [1974] I.C.R. 248.
[8] [1968] 2 Q.B. 497.
[9] [1910] A.C. 87.

organisations whose only primary purpose is to act as a pressure group.[10] An organisation merely to take industrial action in support of negotiations by others would not be a trade union.

Independent trade unions

Independence is defined[11] as denoting a trade union not under the domination or control of an employer or of a group of employers or of one or more employers' associations and

> "not liable to interference by an employer or any such group or association (arising out of the provision of financial or material support or by any other means whatsoever) tending towards such control."

In the Annual Report of the Certification Officer for 1978[12] it is pointed out that the crucial question is what is meant by "liable to interference." The certification officer there states that his office took the view that it meant "vulnerable to" or "exposed to the risk of" interference and that in considering this it was proper to consider the organisation's history, membership base, organisation and structure, finance, collective bargaining record and use of employer provided facilities. This approach was endorsed by the Court of Appeal in *Squibb U.K. Staff Association* v. *Certification Officer*[13] which rejected the test of likelihood of interference adopted by the E.A.T. in favour of the vulnerability test in the sense of subjection to a real possibility of interference. As Shaw L.J. said:

> "If the facts present a possibility of interference tending towards control, and if it is a possibility which cannot be dismissed as trivial or fanciful or illusory, then it can properly be asserted that the union is at risk of and therefore liable to such interference. The risk need be no more than one which is recognisable and capable in the ordinary course of human affairs of becoming an actuality."

The fact that it is unlikely that the employer will exploit the vulnerability is not relevant.

This sub-grouping of unions is clearly intended to exclude employer-dominated organisations from the benefit of statutory assistance to the functions of trade unions. The freedom of an employer to enforce a union membership agreement by dismissal of non-members of the appropriate union is confined to agreements made with independent unions[14] and certain statutory requirements to consult are confined to independent recognised unions.[15]

(b) The status of a trade union

The Royal Commission on Trade Unions which reported in 1968[16] recommended that trade unions be given full legal entity. There is no doubt in popular understanding that a trade union has functions and powers which give it a quality different from that of most voluntary associations. The courts, on the

---

[10] *Midland Cold Storage* v. *Steer* [1972] I.C.R. 230.
[11] TULRA 1974, s.30.
[12] para. 2.7.
[13] [1978] I.C.R. 115.
[14] TULRA 1974, s.30.
[15] E.P.A. 1975, s.99(1).
[16] Cmnd. 3623, paras. 769–785.

other hand, have been hesitant to recognise that difference as productive of different legal status.

In the leading case of *Taff Vale Railway Co.* v. *Amalgamated Society of Railway Servants*[17] only Lord Brampton said that a trade union was a legal entity, although a majority of the House of Lords permitted it to be sued in its own name. In *Kelly* v. *NatSOPA*[18] the Court of Appeal regarded the union as no more in law than a collection of individuals so that an individual member was debarred from obtaining damages for wrongful expulsion because he was either claiming against himself or had participated in authorising the wrong. On the other hand, in *National Union of General and Municipal Workers* v. *Gillian*[19] a registered union was allowed to sue for defamation of itself. The matter was not resolved by the House of Lords in *Bonsor* v. *Musicians Union.*[20] The issue was again one of the award of damages for wrongful expulsion. Although the House of Lords overthrew the decision in *Kelly's* case two of the members of that House did so on the basis of the false logic of that decision and not on the falsehood of the basic premise that a union is not an entity. The judgment of Lord Morton (with whom Lord Porter substantially agreed) comes down most strongly in favour of separate entity.

"My Lords, in my opinion the action in *Kelly's* case was an action by a member against his union as an entity recognised by the law and distinct from the individual members thereof, for breach of a contract between the plaintiff and his union. If this is so, the foundation for the refusal to award damages is gone. I base the view which I have just expressed on a line of authorities, of which the first is the well-known case of *Taff Vale Ry. Co.* v. *Amalgamated Society of Railway Servants* (1900). In that case, it was held by this House that a trade union registered under the Trade Union Acts 1871 and 1876, could be sued in tort for the wrongful conduct of its servants in the course of a strike. I find it unnecessary to set out the relevant provisions of these Acts, since they are sufficiently summarised for the present purpose in passages which I am about to quote from the judgment of Farwell J., in the *Taff Vale* case. That learned judge said:

'The defendant society have taken out a summons to strike out their name as defendants, on the ground that they are neither a corporation nor an individual, and cannot be sued in a quasi-corporate or any other capacity . . . Now it is undoubtedly true that a trade union is neither a corporation, nor an individual, nor a partnership between a number of individuals; but this does not by any means conclude the case.'

After referring to s.16 of the Trade Union Act 1876, and to an argument advanced on behalf of the defendant, the learned judge continued (*ibid.*):

'The questions that I have to consider are what, according to the true construction of the Trade Union Acts, has the legislature enabled the trade unions to do, and what, if any, liability does a trade union incur for wrongs done to others in the exercise of its authorized powers? The Acts commence by legalising the usual trade union contracts, and proceed to establish a registry of trade unions, give to each trade union an exclusive right to the name in which it is registered, authorize it through the medium of trustees to own a limited amount of real estate, and unlimited personal estate 'for the use

---

[17] [1901] A.C. 426.
[18] (1915) 84 L.J.K.B. 2236.
[19] [1946] K.B. 81.
[20] [1956] A.C. 104.

and benefit of such trade union and the members thereof'; provide that it shall have officers and treasurers, and render them liable to account; require that annual returns be made to the registry of the assets and liabilities and receipts and expenditure of the society; provide that it shall have rules and a registered office, imposing a penalty on the trade union for non-compliance; and permit it to amalgamate with other trade unions, and to be wound up. The funds of the society are appropriated to the purposes of the society, and their mis-appropriation can be restrained by injunction: *Wolfe* v. *Matthews*; and on a winding up, such funds are distributed amongst the members in accordance with the rules of the society: *Strick* v. *Swansea Tin-Plate Co.* Further, the Act of 1871 contains a schedule of matters which must be provided for by the rules.'

The Court of Appeal set aside the orders made by Farwell, J., but this House was unanimous in restoring them. . . . My Lords, in my view, the *Taff Vale* case goes far to decide the question now before your Lordships' House. It may be that Lords MacNaghten and Lindley thought that an action against the union was an action against all the individual members—indeed, that view was expressed again by Lord MacNaghten in *Russell's* case and by Lord Lindley in *Yorkshire Miners' Assocn.* v. *Howden* but I am satisfied that it has never been more than a minority view, inconsistent with the relevant authorities from the *Taff Vale* case onwards, with the solitary exception of *Kelly's* case."

Lord MacDermott (supported by Lord Somervell) equally emphatically rejected this conclusion.

"At first glance, the enabling form of s.7 [of the Trade Union Act 1981] suggests that the legislature regarded a registered trade union as an entity apart from its members which, like certain incorporated bodies, required special authority to hold land. But against this must be set the provision made in both s.7 and s.8 for the holding of union property by the union trustees which was relied on by the union as a clear indication that Parliament did not intend to make the registered trade union a juridical person, and, as such, capable of holding its own assets in its own name. Section 9 was said to point in the same direction. It provides that the trustees of a registered trade union, or any other officer who may be authorised by the rules to do so, shall be empowered

'to bring or defend, or cause to be brought or defended, any action, suit, prosecution, or complaint in any court of law or equity, touching or concern-ing the property, right, or claim to property of the trade union . . . '

If, as the appellant claims, this Act made the registered union a juridical person, in the sense in which I am using the expression, there seems no very convincing reason why it should not have been left to sue and be sued respecting its property without conferring these special powers on its officers and trustees. Section 11 makes it obligatory for the treasurer and other officers of a trade union to account and hand over balances and books in their hands when required; and, in the event of any failure to comply with these obligations, the trustees are empowered to sue for the balance due, etc., and

'. . . to recover their full costs of suit, to be taxed as between attorney and client.'

This, of course, is not in any way conclusive, but, again, it is scarcely what one would expect if the intention was to create a body which could take these steps for itself."

Lord Keith of Avonholme, who might have produced the majority, appears to conclude that whilst it would not be wrong to call a union a legal entity it was not an entity distinct at any point of time from its individual members. These two concepts are contradictory and there is no reliable indication in his judgment of what was meant by them.

It is apparent that the system of registration introduced by the 1971 Act is central to the issue of legal entity. The difference of opinion lies in whether the legislature intended, by introducing that system, to confer entity as previously it had conferred such status on incorporated companies which were also required to register. It is clear that some care was taken by the system of incorporation to separate a company from its members. The requirement of registration may well be seen as ancillary to incorporation rather than as possessing a special significance of its own. Alternatively the system of registration may be viewed less as an instrument by which legal status is conferred as a means of recognition that such separate identity has been achieved in practice. Whichever view is taken of registration the common element is that the State must confer or recognise a separate identity before it can be accepted as producing legally recognised consequences.

In the absence of any judicial consensus, legislation has taken to providing directly a more or less ambiguous answer. For a time the Industrial Relations Act 1971 suspended the argument by providing that trade unions registered under that Act should enjoy full legal entity whilst unregistered unions should not enjoy such status but should be capable of suing and being sued in their own name.[21] Trade unionists saw this as a device intended to convey an air of inferiority to the large well-established unions which declined to register whilst ensuring that the funds of all unions should be available to satisfy claims for damages for "unfair industrial practices."

The Trade Union and Labour Relations Act 1974 repealed this and provided[22]:

> A trade union which is not a special register body shall not be, or be treated as if it were, a body corporate but—
> (a) it shall be capable of making contracts
> (c) . . . it shall be capable of suing and being sued in its own name . . . in proceedings relating to . . . any . . . cause of action whatsoever.
> (e) any judgment, order or award made in proceedings of any description brought against the trade union . . . shall be enforceable . . . against any property held in trust for the trade union to the extent and in the like manner as if the union were a body corporate.

Even without so positive a statement as that contained at the beginning of this section the relegation of registration to a certification of independence not of itself conferring the sort of incidents that accompanied legal status would probably have sufficed to destroy the foundation of arguments for entity. In *Electrical, Electronic, Telecommunications and Plumbing Union* v. *Times Newspapers Ltd.*[23] O'Connor J. had no doubt that the effect of the statute was to deny any possibility of legal entity to a trade union.

---

[21] s.75. For the case law on this provision, see *Midland Cold Storage Ltd.* v. *Turner* [1972] I.C.R. 230; *Midland Cold Storage Ltd.* v. *Steer* [1972] I.C.R. 435; *Heaton's Transport Ltd.* v. *T.G.W.U.* [1972] I.C.R. 308 at 338 and 339.

[22] s.2.

[23] [1980] Q.B. 585.

"When one looks at the statute, s.1(1) is in terse and quite unequivocal terms: 'The Industrial Relations Act 1971 is hereby repealed.' Thereafter, as transitional provisions, a whole series of matters dealing with different topics in that statute were preserved in Sch. 4 to the 1974 Act. That is the end of s.1. Section 2, the side note to which reads, 'Status of trade unions,' provides:

'(1) A trade union which is not a special register body shall not be, or be treated as if it were, a body corporate . . .'

In my judgment, those are absolutely clear words. One must remember the position in law at that time. At that time, trade unions if they were registered were not necessarily corporate bodies; they were made corporate bodies. If they were on the provisional register they had the attributes of corporate bodies and could properly be called quasi-corporate associations, and the whole background of the position of trade unions until 1971 was that they were quasi-corporate bodies. It was a matter which was as much in their interest as any possible disability. Nevertheless here we find Parliament telling us what a trade union may not be: it 'shall not be, or be treated as if it were, a body corporate.'

Now it is possible that the words 'or be treated as if it were,' got into the statute because of the dislike of the decision in the *Taff Vale* case. I do not know and it is not for me to speculate. It is my task to construe the words and if I find them to be absolutely clear then, even though the result produced may be one which strikes me as being absurd, I must give effect to them. . . . It does not follow that the result which I am driven to in the present case is necessarily an absurdity, but as I have said, it seems to me that those words are absolutely clear and they are saying that a trade union is not to be a body corporate, and it is not to be treated as if it were a body corporate. That is, it is removing from the status of a trade union that which had been accorded to it from 1901 until 1971, when the matter was changed; and there it is."

Despite this a trade union is in the unusual position among voluntary organisations of being able to constitute itself a party to a contract on which it will be liable. It is suggested, therefore, that since all the evidence would suggest an intention that the contract of membership should be with the union as a party the somewhat sterile discussion as to whether a member has a series of contracts with each other member should now also be regarded as settled in favour of a single contract with the union.

(c) The legality of trade unions and their agreements

It was widely assumed, until the passage of the Trade Union Act 1871, that the rules of a trade union were in restraint of trade so as to make the contracts of the union unenforceable and its funds incapable of legal protection.[24] It is not very likely, even without statutory provision to the contrary, that a court at the present time would take such a view. Not only has the law relating to restraint of trade changed[25] in a way that would have restricted the generality of the disqualification applied to trade unions, but the attitude of the courts as to what may be considered a reasonable restraint has also changed. The power to order a member to go on strike would not now necessarily be regarded as an unreasonable restraint upon that member's freedom to offer his labour. More significantly, courts which before 1871 were anxious to deny legal protection to

---

[24] See, *e.g Hornby* v. *Close* (1867) L.R. 2 Q.B. 153.
[25] Its nature was substantially affected by the decision in *Nordenfelt* v. *Maxim Nordenfelt* [1894] A.C. 535.

a trade union, have, more recently, been anxious to assert their jurisdiction over it.

So sharp was the reversal of the judicial approach that it threatened to undermine the assumption of common law illegality upon which the 1871 Act was based, and thus to throw the legislative system into chaos.[26] The conception of a basic illegality was only re-established with difficulty in *Russell* v. *Amalgamated Society of Carpenters and Joiners*,[27] after doubt had been thrown upon it in three earlier judgments.[28] The view taken in *Russell's* case, although it may be correct, seems difficult to explain in face of such decisions as that in *Reynolds* v. *Shipping Federation Ltd.*[29] in which a combination to enforce a closed shop agreement with the compliance of the employers was held to be lawful. It may be said, with the Court of Appeal,[30] that though a closed shop is justifiable in the area in which a union operates it is, nonetheless, to be regarded as unlawful at common law, but it is obvious that to maintain that a trade union is an essentially unlawful organisation is to maintain a fiction in order to accommodate the presumptions upon which statute law was based.

So far as the validity of union rules is concerned the matter is again dealt with in the Trade Union and Labour Relations Act 1974.[31]

> The purposes of any trade union . . . shall not, by reason only that they are in restraint of trade, be unlawful, so as—
> (a) to make any member of the organisation or body liable to criminal proceedings for conspiracy or otherwise; or
> (b) to make any agreement or trust void or voidable[32];
> nor shall any rule of a trade union . . . be unlawful or unenforceable by reason only that it is in restraint of trade."[33]

In *Faramus* v. *F.A.A.*[33a] the Master of the Rolls had attempted to limit the earlier section to the protection of major purposes and to argue that agreements in pursuit of an "ancillary" purpose might still be unenforceable. This view did not commend itself to the House of Lords, but Lord Denning M.R. returned to the attack from another direction in *Edwards* v. *Society of Graphical and Allied Trades*,[34] saying that a rule allegedly entitling a union to expel a member for any, or no, reason could not be said to be *proper* to the purposes of the union.[35] The provisions of the 1871 and 1971 Acts were capable of this interpretation since they did not contain the final provision inserted in the 1974 Act.

---

[26] Kahn-Freund, *The Illegality of a Trade Union* (1943) 7 M.L.R. 202—one of the classics of academic English labour law.

[27] [1910] 1 K.B. 506 (C.A.); [1912] A.C. 421 (H.L.).

[28] *Swaine* v. *Wilson* (1889) 24 Q.B.D. 252; *Gozney* v. *Bristol Trade and Provident Society* [1909] 1 K.B. 901; *Osborne* v. *Amalgamated Society of Railway Servants* [1911] 1 Ch. 540— although it must be noted that the rules of none of the associations involved in these cases were so obviously restrictive as would now be the case with an ordinary trade union. The associations involved in the first two decisions were not even typical trade unions.

[29] [1924] 1 Ch. 28.

[30] *Faramus* v. *Film Artistes Association* [1963] 2 Q.B. 527 (C.A.); [1964] A.C. 925 (H.L.).

[31] s.2(5).

[32] Compare with the earlier provision—Trade Union Act 1871, s.3—"The purposes of any trade union shall not, by reason merely that they are in restraint of trade, be unlawful so as to render void or voidable any agreement or trust."

[33] This final provision appeared for the first time in the 1974 Act.

[33a] *Supra*, n. 30.

[34] [1971] Ch. 354.

[35] See in support of this the passage from the judgment of Sachs L.J. quoted at p. 426, *infra*.

The effect was that the validity of the individual rules, agreements or trusts, would be capable of challenge in the ordinary courts. The subjective nature of such jurisdiction is revealed only too clearly by the assumption of Lord Denning M.R. that the proper function of a trade union was to protect the right of each individual member to earn his living and take advantage of all that goes with it. Since it is obviously the purpose of any organisation to protect its members as a group rather than as individuals, to the point where the individual interest may have to suffer, and since this is the whole reason that people combine, one's confidence in judicial ability to acknowledge a proper purpose when one is observed is undermined.

The effect of the extra provision added to the 1974 legislation is to remove this method of attacking the validity of union rules. On its face it would also seem to mean that it would not be possible to argue, by analogy with the decision in *Nagle* v. *Feilden*,[36] that an attempt arbitrarily to exclude an applicant for membership was void because it was in unreasonable restraint of trade and, being neither an agreement nor trust, was still unenforceable. The new provision should make it clear that the effect of every rule of a trade union is saved from unenforceability even if it is in unreasonable restraint of trade.[37]

It is now only of historical interest to observe that section 3 of the 1871 Act was followed by a section excluding from "direct enforcement" or action for damages a number of agreements which would not have been enforceable without the provision in section 3. These included the famous provision covering an agreement between one trade union and another, which as the definition of a trade union then stood, applied to many collective agreements. It also applied to actions to enforce union rules as to the payment of benefits to members. A majority of the Donovan Commission favoured the complete repeal of this section and regarded it as bizarre to suggest that the consequence of such repeal might be that a union would seek an injunction ordering its members to come out on strike in accordance with their obligation under the union rules. The 1971 Act, which repealed the section, eliminated the reverse of this possibility by a provision which, with some amendment, is now contained in the Trade Union and Labour Relations Act 1974[38] to the effect that:

> No court shall, whether by way of—
>> (a) an order for specific performance or specific implement of a contract of employment, or
>> (b) an injunction or interdict restraining a breach or threatened breach of such a contract,
> compel any employee to do any work or attend at any place for the doing of any work.

The Trade Union and Labour Relations Act 1974 makes it quite clear that a trade union may enter into any sort of contract.[39]

---

[36] [1966] 2 Q.B. 633.
[37] To add to the chaotic state of recent legislation this effect was removed by an amendment contained in s.5(5) of the Trade Union and Labour Relations Act 1974. The Trade Union and Labour Relations (Amendment) Act 1976, however, repealed the whole of s.5 of the earlier Act thus leaving s.2(5) to have its full effect.
[38] s.16.
[39] s.2(1)(a).

(d) Amalgamation with other industrial organisations

The number of trade unions in the United Kingdom is slowly declining, almost entirely as a result of merger of two or more unions.[40] Most often such mergers involve a small union combining with a much larger union in order to offer better services to its members. Apart from this there is, in many instances, a case to be made for merger even of large and viable unions within a particular industry so as to simplify the bargaining structure and avoid duplication of services. It was, no doubt, the latter end that was in view when the Labour government proposed[41] to make grants available to assist union merger. It is certainly true that there are dangers in unplanned merger by which a group of workers goes to the highest bidder. It is probable that the Labour government also had in mind that the pace of merger should be increased, although, as this is an area where sudden suspicions are very easy to arouse, which cause severe delays in the implementation of merger proposals, the offer of money to assist was not likely to prove a catalyst.

The statutory procedure for amalgamation was not substantially affected by the Industrial Relations Act 1971, although it may be said that that Act temporarily reversed the process and gave rise to numerous splinter unions. The original statute, the Trade Union Amendment Act 1876, which had required the assent of at least two-thirds of the members of each union involved before a merger could take place was modified by the Trade Union (Amalgamation) Act 1917. This required that at least 50 per cent. of those entitled to vote should do so and that the votes of those in favour should exceed by at least 20 per cent. the votes of those against. Initially this easing of the requirement had a marked effect and a considerable number of smaller unions were absorbed. But, as today, it was very difficult in a large union to produce a 50 per cent. poll. The Trade Union (Amalgamations, etc.), Act 1964[42] has further reduced the requirement to a simple majority of those voting and eliminated that of a 50 per cent. poll.[43]

Transfer of engagements, by which the unions retained nominal identities but one transferred all its obligations and assets to the others, was easier to achieve[44] in that only the support of two-thirds of the members or delegates present at a general meeting of the transferor union, summoned for the purpose, was necessary. But the consent of not less than two-thirds of the members of the transferee union had then to be obtained unless this requirement was dispensed with by the registrar.

Procedure

The present Act requires that the members of the unions concerned draft an agreed Instrument of Amalgamation or Transfer of Engagements and submit it to the trade union Certification Officer for approval. Certain matters must be contained in the Instrument, and the Certification Officer had issued a pamphlet

---

[40] The number of unions has declined from over 1,200 to less than 600 since 1922.

[41] White Paper, *In Place of Strife* 1969, Cmnd. 3888, paras. 71 and 72, and Industrial Relations Bill 1970.

[42] The Act does not generally apply to unions registered only in Northern Ireland.

[43] This Act also applies to unincorporated employers' associations. TULRA 1974, Sched. 3, para. 10(3).

[44] Societies (Miscellaneous Provisions) Act 1940, s.6.

to guide unions in preparing the Instrument.[45] The issue of merger in the terms of the Instrument must then be put to the members of each amalgamating union. If transfer of engagement rather than amalgamation is desired, only the members of the transferor union are required to vote. The ballot on acceptance of the proposals must be without interference or constraint, and every member must be entitled to vote. A secret ballot is not actually required, the Act merely requires that a ballot paper be marked. The requirement that every member should have the right to vote extends, for instance, to apprentices and super-annuated members even if the union rules normally exclude them from voting in union affairs.[46] All reasonable steps must be taken by each voting union to secure that, not less than seven days before voting on the resolution begins, every member of the union is supplied with a notice in writing approved, for each union, by the Certification Officer.[47] The notice is designed to inform members of the proposals, and must contain either the complete Instrument or an account of it sufficient to enable those receiving it "to form a reasonable judgment on the main effects" of the proposal. In the second case the notice must state where copies of the Instrument may be inspected. A decision on the sufficiency of the notice is in the discretion of the Certification Officer. These provisions may not be altered by the rules of the union.

The manner of conducting the ballot is a matter for the governing body of the union. The decision, however, will be made by a simple majority unless the union rules expressly and in terms provide that this statutory requirement shall not apply and a different majority be required. It follows that all rules, contrary to this, made before the Act, are replaced by the statutory provision. This effect was necessary because a number of union rule books had incorporated the requirements of the earlier Act. This was being discarded as too restrictive and it would have been anomalous to have left in force equally restrictive rules based on it.

When the proposals have been approved by the required majority an application for registration of the Instrument must be made to the Certification Officer, accompanied by two copies of the Instrument, the proposed rules of the amalgamated or transferee union,[48] and by a statutory declaration signed by the general secretary of each union involved of compliance with the ballot requirements and verification of voting figures.

Objection

For six weeks from the date when the application for registration is submitted any member of a union involved in the voting has a right to complain to the Certification Officer on the following grounds:

---

[45] There is strictly speaking no need to provide for transfer of some union property. This will automatically vest in the trustees of the amalgamated or transferee union unless such transfer is excluded by the instrument. Stock in public funds of the United Kingdom is not automatically transferred.

[46] See report of an action arising from the amalgamation of the National Graphical Association and the Amalgamated Society of Lithographic Printers, *The Times*, January 15, 1969.

[47] The functions of the Registrar of Friendly Societies, briefly transferred to the Registrar of Trade Unions by the 1971 Act have now been transferred to the Certification Officer— Employment Protection Act 1975, s.7 and Sched. 16, Part IV, para. 10.

[48] In the case of a transfer of engagements the instrument itself must state whether the rules of the transferee union are to be altered and, if so, the effect of the alterations.

   (i) that every member of the union was not entitled to vote;
  (ii) that there was interference with or constraint in the voting, or that a fair opportunity to vote was otherwise lacking;
 (iii) that the ballot did not involve the marking of a ballot paper;
 (iv) that the arrangements for voting were otherwise contrary to the union rules of the procedure laid down by its governing body;
  (v) that the requisite majority was not obtained.

If it is found that the complaint was justified he may, in his discretion, declare it to be so but take no further action, or make an order specifying the steps to be taken before he will consider the application for registration. He must give reasons for his decision, orally or in writing, and he may order either the complainant or the union to pay costs. He may vary his order. An appeal on a point of law lies from any decision of the Certification Officer to the E.A.T.[49]

When the six-week complaint period has expired or, if there is a complaint, when it has been finally determined, the Certification Officer may register the merger.

The Act makes no provisions as to the political funds of amalgamating unions which transfer their engagements. This matter will normally be dealt with by the Instrument. In the case of unions which amalgamate, if one has no political fund, the statutory procedure for establishing one will have to be pursued by the new union formed by the amalgamation. Normally, if a union with no political fund transfers its engagements to a union which has a political fund the view will be taken that the members of the transferor union are in the position of new members of the transferee union and have one month to contract out. A problem may arise if a group of unions, for reasons of status, do not wish to merge with the largest of their number, but wish to amalgamate on equal terms, and some of them have, whilst others have not, a political fund. The normal way to avoid this problem, as indeed it is to avoid a number of others, would be to form a new nominal union, with or without a political fund according to the ultimate intention, and then for all the substantial unions to merge with the new nominal union.

The two methods of merger outlined above are the only methods available and a union may not provide some other method by its rules.

An interesting problem arises in connection with situations where amalgamation does not work and unions wish to separate. When it was reported[50-51] that this was the position in respect of NatSOPA and N.U.P.B.P.W. which amalgamated to form Division 1 and Division A of the Society of Graphical and Allied Trades, Division 1 issued a writ "accepting" repudiation of the contract of amalgamation brought about by the decision of Division A to stop payment into the amalgamated funds.

(e) The political fund

The British Trade Union movement has long been aware of the value of taking an active part in political activity in order to impress its views on governments and has for much of the present century been significantly success-

---

[49] E.P.A. 1975, Sched. 16, Part IV, para. 10.
[50-51] See *The Times*, October 12, 1970.

ful in this sphere. In 1900 the Trades Union Congress took positive steps to form and support the forerunner of the present Labour Party, directly to represent the views of labour, although, paradoxically, it has often been said until the present time that the union movement has found it easier to achieve adoption of its views by a Conservative government.

Political activity of any kind requires financial support. Until 1911 it was so financed from the general funds of the unions, irrespective of the opposition of minorities within the unions. This practice was confirmed in *Steele* v. *South Wales Miners' Federation*,[52] in which Darling J. rejected the argument that the financing of political activity was *ultra vires* the union. The House of Lords, however, accepted that argument three years later in *Amalgamated Society of Railway Servants* v. *Osborne*.[53] The union went further than the use of its general funds by providing that one shilling and a penny per year was to be compulsorily contributed by each member to a fund for giving financial support to the Labour Representation Committee in order to secure representation of railwaymen in the House of Commons, and to support such representatives if elected. The House of Lords held that the statutory definition of a trade union, as it then existed, was exhaustive and that it did not extend to the carrying on of political activity. Such a view would, of course, exclude a great deal more of a trade union's normal functions than merely political activities. It is fair to remark that, though ameliorating legislation only controlled political matters, the reasoning behind the judgment must now be considered to be unsound. There is no doubt that a trade union may now pursue educational objects and other purposes ancillary to its principal statutory objects and this is made plain by section 3(1) of the 1913 Act.[54]

The Trade Union Act 1913 was passed to reverse the effect of the *Osborne* case so as to permit unions to use funds for political purposes but the opportunity was taken to restrict and control this power. These statutory provisions survive the passing of the Trade Union and Labour Relations Act 1974. Any trade union may adopt "political fund" rules if their inclusion is approved, by a majority vote of those voting, in a ballot for the purpose conducted by the union by a procedure approved by the Certification Officer. The registrar[55] in practice had insisted on a second ballot after the proposal has been approved so as to approve the actual rules. Voters should receive a copy of the proposed political fund rules before this second ballot. If approved the union may then amend its rule book to include political fund rules and, if registered, must register such an amendment in the same way as any other alteration of its rules. In this case, however, the Certification Officer must approve the rules according to the requirements of the Act of 1913 before they become effective.[56]

A union with political fund rules is not necessarily obliged to make a political

---

[52] [1907] 1 K.B. 361.

[53] [1910] A.C. 87.

[54] The permissive effect of s.1 of the Trade Union Act 1913 is, therefore, no longer necessary and was repealed by the Industrial Relations Act 1971.

[55] See *supra*, note 47.

[56] At the end of 1980, 69 trade unions and two employers' associations were maintaining political funds under the statutory provisions. No applications for the establishment of new political funds has been made in that year. The total income of trade union political funds in 1980 was £5m. Some unions, in terms, commit themselves to the support of the Labour Party.

levy, although it could frame the rules so as to impose an obligation.[57] If no general obligation is imposed, then the union could collect the levy from such members as it chose. It had also been the view of the registrar that the rules themselves could provide that certain classes of membership were not subject to the levy.[58]

Application of funds

The effect of the 1913 Act is restrictive in the sense that if one now assumes that a trade union may pursue any ancillary objects it may only finance those mentioned in the 1913 Act out of its political fund, which must not be maintained in any other way save from the levy.[59] The objects covered are:

(a) payment of any expenses incurred directly or indirectly by a candidate or prospective candidate for election to Parliament or to any public office, before, during or after the election, in connection with his candidature or election;

(b) expenditure on the holding of any meeting or the distribution of any literature or documents in support of any such candidate or prospective candidate;

(c) expenditure for the maintenance of any Member of Parliament or holder of a public office;

(d) expenditure in connection with the registration of electors or the selection of a candidate for Parliament or any public office;

(e) expenditure on the holding of any kind of political meeting, or on the distribution of political literature or political documents, unless the main purpose of these is the furtherance of the union's statutory objects.

It should be noted that though these were always referred to as political objects the statement of objects covers any form of support for a candidate; even a simple appeal for support without any political overtones.[60] A union is, however, not responsible for what other organisations do with its contributions without its knowledge and consent. If a union pays its annual affiliation fee from its general funds to the T.U.C. and the T.U.C., which has no political fund, contributes to one of the specified political purposes the union will not be in breach of the Act.[61]

Payments for maintenance of an M.P. or holder of public office need only be drawn from the political fund if they are only referable to that office. The holder of a trade union office could continue to receive payment for that office from the general funds of the union whilst he was also a Member of Parliament,[62] but it might be difficult to maintain such a contention of the office holder had in fact been granted leave of absence.

---

[57] *Edwards and the National Federation of Insurance Workers.* Decision of registrar, January 21, 1949.

[58] So, for instance, when the Medical Practitioners' Union merged with ASTMS it was provided that members of the medical practitioners' section should not be required to pay a political levy.

[59] See Grunfeld, *Modern Trade Union Law*, pp. 260–262.

[60] *Forster and the National Amalgamated Union of Shop Assistants etc.*—Registrar's Report for 1925, Pt. 4.

[61] *Forster's* case, *supra.*

[62] *McCarthy and the National Association of Theatrical Kine Employees*—Registrar's Report for 1957, Pt. 4.

The expression "political meetings" is not confined to meetings in support of candidates. A meeting to support a government plan for state takeover of a private airline, for instance, should be financed from the political fund.[63] But a meeting to protest about a government prices and incomes policy would probably be considered to relate to the statutory objects of a trade union and to be open to support from general funds. It should be noted that in respect of this last specified object the word "political" is used. The registrar in *Forster's* case took the view that this must be construed narrowly in the sense of party politics. It may, however, be difficult to disentangle theoretical political issues from the support of political parties. It would appear that where a meeting or literature has a mixed content the registrar had considered its predominant character and had not required finance from the political fund unless that is political.

Although the Certification Officer is the final arbiter on the meaning of political fund rules and upon whether or not they satisfy the statutory requirements, the meaning and scope of the 1913 Act was a matter for the courts.[64] It has been held[65] that these jurisdictions could not conflict in the sense that, where union rules incorporate, as they normally do, the working of the Act, either they supersede the Act, or if this is not so, the plaintiff might elect either to take his case before the officer or before the courts. On the other hand in *Birch's* case, the issue of whether discrimination against a non-contributing member was contrary to the 1913 Act was not one for the registrar at all, since it had nothing to do with the political fund rules but solely concerned statutory prohibition.

Contracting out

When a union has adopted a political fund existing members must be informed of their right not to contribute.[66] The model rules contain a provision requiring that new members shall be supplied with a copy of the political fund rules and also a provision pointing out the right not to contribute. All members covered by the rules will, prima facie, contribute, in the case of existing members, one month after the publication of notice of the right not to contribute,[67] and, in the case of new members, one month after they have actually been supplied with a copy of the political fund rules. A member who does not give notice to contract out within that month is liable to pay until the first day of January next after he has given notice of his wish to contract out. Such notices may not be validly given before an applicant has been accepted for membership.[68]

Section 3(1)(*b*) of the 1913 Act states that:

> . . . a member who is exempt from the obligation to contribute to the political fund of the union shall not be excluded from any benefits of the union, or placed in

---

[63] *Forster's* case, *supra.*

[64] There is now an appeal from the decision of the Certification Officer to the Employment Appeals Tribunal. The meaning of the Act would still be a matter for the court—E.P.A. 1975, Sched. 16, Pt. IV, para. 10.

[65] *Forster* v. *N.A.U. of Shop Assistants etc.* [1927] 1 Ch. 539, and see also *Birch* v. *National Union of Railwaymen* [1950] Ch. 602.

[66] Trade Union Act 1913, s.5(1).

[67] See *Birns and the A.E.U.*, September 25, 1947, Reports of Selected Disputes 1938–49.

[68] *Wilson and the A.E.U.*, December 4, 1948, Reports of Selected Disputes 1938–49.

any respect either directly or indirectly under any disability or at any disadvantage as compared with other members of the union (except in relation to the control or management of the political fund) by reason of his being so exempt.

This section was considered in *Birch's* case.[69] Birch was a contracting-out member of the National Union of Railwaymen who was elected a branch chairman. The general secretary ruled that a contracting-out member could not hold this office. The registrar held that the office of branch chairman was one "involving . . . control or management" of the political fund and that as such under the union's political fund rules (as distinct from the Model Rules) the union was bound to exclude Birch. If this was contrary to the requirements of the 1913 Act the political fund rules themselves were at fault, and the registrar declined jurisdiction to consider that argument. In the High Court it was held that the approval of the registrar did not preclude the court examining the validity of the rules adopted, and that in this case it was only proper to exclude Birch from such aspects of his office as affected the control or management of the political fund. Had the office been one, such as that of general secretary, substantially involving such control or management, it seems that a non-contributor could properly be excluded from the entire office.[70]

It should be noted that the Act only gives a union member a right to complain of discrimination. It appears that an applicant who was refused admission because he indicated that he would not contribute would have no *locus standi* to complain under this Act.

TRADE UNIONS AND THEIR MEMBERS

The contractual approach

The courts control the internal affairs of many voluntary organisations including trade unions through the law of contract. The rules of the organisation, in the case of a trade union usually contained in written form in a "rule book," are looked upon as including the terms of that contract. The relation of a member to the organisation undoubtedly commences in contract but it may be that it is misleading to regard the whole subsequent course of that relationship as a matter of agreement. The rules of a trade union resemble local laws rather than terms of a contract. The group depends on the submission of its members to limitation of their freedom by rules in much the same way as the State or any other group governed by what are habitually called laws. The difference such an approach would make is surprising. Regulation by contract requires consent. Hence all the principles governing the implication of terms which we discussed in connection with the contract of employment are based on supposed consent. Regulation by law appears only to require an understanding of the purpose of the group to which the laws apply and a failure to reject its laws. Submission to group membership involves a restriction of individual freedom just as does the entry into a contract but it does not require continuous consent to that restriction.[71]

---

[69] *Birch and the N.U.R.*, November 8, 1948, Reports of Selected Disputes 1938–49; *Birch* v. *N.U.R.* [1950] Ch. 602.
[70] Grunfeld, *Modern Trade Union Law*, pp. 305–306.
[71] See A. M. Honore: *Groups, Laws, and Obedience*: Oxford Essays in Jurisprudence, Second Series (Ed. A. W. B. Simpson).

With that word of caution in accepting the contractual approach as inevitable it has to be conceded that it is, at present, dominant.

The reader who has acquainted himself with some unusual applications of contractual principle in the judicial approach to individual employment law will find, in the case of the internal affairs of trade unions, a much more strict approach to the construction of the contract of membership. Not only do the courts insist on the pre-eminence of this contract but they generally insist that its terms are exclusively to be found in the union rule book. No assistance is normally permitted from implication of other terms. Davies and Freedland[72] compare the judicial approach to asking a panel of doctors to evaluate a First Aid exercise carried out by a team of boy scouts. They go on to point out that it cannot be assumed that the courts are as sympathetic to the objectives of the trade unions as would be the doctors to those of the scouts. It is suggested, however, that the analogy would be more apt if the doctors were replaced by lawyers. For this reason complaints about the inflexibility produced by a refusal to imply terms may be misplaced. Such refusal denies the courts the most obvious opportunity to rewrite the rules of the union according to judicial concepts of reasonableness, rather than with a view to the purpose those rules are intended to serve.

The reader will find that this self-imposed disability has not been allowed to leave the courts powerless to impose upon unions certain standards of behaviour or even certain views of reasonableness. Apart from open attempts to require trade union rules not to be unreasonable,[73] more subtle but equally effective[73] interpretation of the provisions of union rules so as to produce "reasonable" results is increasingly apparent in recent cases.[74] Additionally, the courts have, for most of the time that modern trade unionism has existed, imposed upon them extra-contractual standards of fair procedure similar to the requirement imposed on administrative tribunals and based upon the judicial conception of the need to protect the individual property rights of members. It would be surprising if the judicial view of what was reasonable coincided with that of the union. The courts regard the protection of the individual as their principal purpose and have on occasion assumed that it is so self-evident that this must be the correct approach, that trade unions will take the same view.[75] In fact, however, a trade union would scarcely be a union if it did not take the view that the individual member surrenders some of his individuality in return for the protection of interests he shares with the rest of the group. The personnel of the courts have mostly grown up in an intensely individualistic working environment. The trade union member knows that management thinks more of the well-being of the organisation than of the interests of each individual working for it.

Against this background it is suggested that one may reasonably experience some surprise that the boy scouts have done so well. Despite the proximity of the issue to the interests of those comprising the internal tribunals of a trade union, there are some, but few, signs of maladministration. Davies and Freed-

---

[72] p. 513.

[73] See, e.g. Faramus v. Film Artistes Association [1964] A.C. 925, per Lord Denning M.R. in the Court of Appeal; Edwards v. SOGAT [1971] Ch. 354 (C.A.).

[74] e.g. Esterman v. NALGO [1974] I.C.R. 625.

[75] See Edwards v. SOGAT, supra, p. 391, per Lord Denning M.R.

land rightly suggest that the examining lawyers find it easy to discover irregularities of detail and most reported claims by individuals against trade unions are, therefore, successful. Yet, given the chances of success, the incidence of such claims is small. If this is thought to be explicable because of the inaccessibility of the courts to the working man it may be pointed out that conferment of a limited jurisdiction over the internal affairs of trade unions upon industrial tribunals has not yet produced any sign of a rush of litigation.

Admission to membership

The practice

As we shall see, the law has not seriously challenged the right of a union to deal with applications for admission as if they were offers by the applicant to enter into a contract. With the exception of a scattering of recent judicial pronouncements hinting at the establishment of some rights for the applicant, there has been an absence of any compulsion upon the union even to obey its rules as to admission let alone any sign of successful dictation of what those rules should be. Since 1980[76] a union is forbidden to operate unreasonable or arbitrary admission rules against an applicant who is working or wishes to work in a sector covered by a union membership agreement. Considerable "guidance" as to what ought to be considered unreasonable for this purpose is contained in a code of practice. This provision will be examined later but there has not yet been time for it to have any effect on either judicial attitudes or the attitude of unions to the drafting of rules.

The freedom this left to the rule-maker has produced a surprising similarity in union rules. Most unions merely require employment in the relevant trade as a qualification. The only widespread ground of disqualification is that of ill-health, which is presumably dictated by the function of the union as a provider of benefits to unemployed or sick members. In practice the disqualification is rarely applied. As we shall see, however, the courts may have given disqualification a significance which the somewhat discretionary approach of trade unions did not intend. Specific variations on general disqualification are a more accurate guide to union practice. So a union may provide that production of a health certificate may be made a condition of admission in individual cases. Some unions allow admission without even this condition but provide lower benefit rates for those entering in bad health.

In the craft unions the pattern is different. Apprenticeship has become less common and is, therefore, less commonly required as a condition of full membership. Some, however, seek to secure an intention to continue at the trade by requiring experience in it. Many unions, particularly in areas where the practice is common, do not object to the admission of the self-employed. In such cases, however, it is not uncommon to find a careful line drawn to exclude those who exercise managerial authority bearing on the welfare of union members. As is well known, however, unions in the printing industry[77] see things in a different light and seek to recruit management or even require them under closed shop agreements to join the appropriate union. Not all unions

---

[76] E.A. 1980, s.4.
[77] And, e.g. ACTAT.

have thought to provide for the eligibility of their own staff for membership. Of those that have some require membership of their own union whilst others see this as possibly involving difficulty in negotiating terms of employment and, accordingly, require staff to become members of another, usually specified, union. A few specialist unions provide specialised disqualification but British membership of the EEC has tended to break down the most common of these which was exclusion of foreign workers.

It is not common for British trade unions to seek by less obvious means, such as the fixing of exorbitant admission fees, to make admission more difficult than the rules appear to allow. They are, however, much less generous on the question of re-admission, some forbidding it in specified cases and many making it subject to special procedures. Almost all regard it as a privilege entitling them to expect the applicant to pay more than the usual admission fee. This is, above all others, an area where discretion is most freely exercised.

Almost all unions have more than one grade of membership. Most clearly define the grades and few allow for alteration of the structure save by the normal, and usually cumbersome, procedure for any amendment of the rules. There is no doubt that judicial insistence on the rigidity of the contractual terms has given rise to problems for unions when it is normal to place admission in the hands of branches. It appears that there is often a tendency for somewhat pragmatic solutions to individual peculiarities.

Admission procedures are most commonly elementary. Most unions require an application to be proposed and seconded, although one suspects that this is a tradition left over from their nineteenth-century history and honoured mostly as a formality. On the other hand the fact that this is not always the intended result is revealed by some rule books specifically imposing responsibility (even with penalties) on the sponsors. The admission process is normally conducted by a branch committee, or a branch meeting. It is now fairly common to require the decision of the branch to be affirmed, at least if the decision is to reject the applicant.

Legislative restriction: unreasonable rejection

Recent legislation has somewhat restricted the hitherto untrammelled freedom of the unions to admit or reject whom they choose. The Employment Act 1980[78] provides:

> Every person who is, or is seeking to be, in employment [by an employer] with respect to which it is the practice, in accordance with a union membership agreement, for the employee to belong to a specified trade union or one of a number of specified trade unions [shall have the right]
> (a) not to have an application for membership of a specified trade union unreasonably refused;
> (b) not to be unreasonably expelled from a specified trade union.

Refusal includes an implied refusal after a period within which admission might reasonably have been expected. Expulsion includes any cessation of membership upon an event specified by the rules and so includes termination for financial default—although presumably it may be reasonable in such circumstances for the decision not to involve a hearing.

---

[78] s.4.

The remedy for interference with either right is in addition to any common law remedy and is available by application to an industrial tribunal within six months of the date of refusal or expulsion or such further period as the tribunal considers reasonable in a case where it is satisfied that it was not reasonably practicable for the complaint to be presented before that time. The tribunal may make a declaration that the complaint is well founded. An appeal on either law or fact lies to the E.A.T. The matter is to be determined in accordance with equity and the substantial merits of the case. A union is not to be regarded as having acted reasonably merely because it observed its rules, or unreasonably merely because it did not.

After securing a declaration that his claim was well founded the applicant may make a claim for compensation at any time after four weeks and before six months from the date of the declaration. If at the time of the application the applicant had been admitted or re-admitted to the union the compensation application lies to an industrial tribunal. If he has not been so admitted or re-admitted the application to compensate lies to the E.A.T. In the case of an industrial tribunal the amount is subject to a limit of 30 weeks pay plus the limit for compensatory awards in unfair dismissal for the loss consequent upon the refusal of admission or expulsion. The E.A.T. has a wider power to award such sum as it considers just and equitable subject to the limit applicable to industrial tribunal awards plus 52 weeks pay.

Both awards are subject to the duty of the applicant to mitigate his loss.

This legislation was applied in unusual circumstances in *Kirkham* v. *National Society of Operative Printers, Graphical and Media Personnel*.[79] The applicant had left the trade of printing and been granted by his union an honourable discharge from membership. When he desired to re-enter the trade the appropriate union branch decided to re-admit him to a grade of casual workers it had itself defined and to which disadvantageous work opportunities applied. The E.A.T. held that this refusal would have been unreasonable had it applied to membership of the union rather than only to the branch; which latter was not specified in the membership agreement.

Discrimination

The Race Relations Act 1976[80] and the Sex Discrimination Act 1975[81] apply the prohibitions on illegal discrimination respectively contained in those Acts to "any organisation whose members carry on a particular profession or trade for the purposes of which the organisation exists." It is unlawful for such an organisation to discriminate against a person in the terms on which it is prepared to admit him; by refusing or deliberately omitting to accept his application for membership; or, if a member, in the way it affords him access to any benefits, facilities or services or by refusing or deliberately omitting to afford him access to them; by depriving him of membership or varying the terms on which he is a member; or by subjecting a member to any other detriment. The only exception applies in the case of discrimination on the grounds of sex arising from provisions made in relation to the death or retirement from work of the member.

---

[79] [1983] I.R.L.R. 70.
[80] s.11.
[81] s.12.

Judicial attempts to control admission

Every judicial attempt to find a peg on which to hang a common law action by a rejected applicant for membership of a trade union has failed. In *Davis* v. *Carew-Pole*[82] Pilcher J. suggested the possibility of a preliminary contract arising from the application and obliging the organisation to observe its rules. In *Woodford* v. *Smith*[83] Megarry J. attempted to fix receipt by the organisation of application forms as the point at which the organisation might be deemed to have made, or alternatively be estopped from denying, the existence of an offer properly to consider the application.

The right to work

A more sustained and far-reaching attempt has been made, largely by Lord Denning M.R., to establish recognition of an individual's right to work in the sense of a right not to have access to the labour market restricted. He seems first to have suggested the existence of such a right as against a trade union in *Lee* v. *Showmen's Guild of Great Britain*.[84] He followed this in a totally different context in *Boulting* v. *ACTAT*[85] and extended it to professional associations in *Nagle* v. *Feilden*[86] and *Enderby Town Football Club* v. *Football Association*.[87] In *Faramus* v. *Film Artistes Association*,[88] however, Diplock L.J. rejected the suggestion that a standard of reasonableness could be imposed on union rules.

The principal support for a cause of action alleging that exclusion from membership might constitute an unreasonable restraint of the right to work is the preliminary judgment of the Court of Appeal on the admissibility of a cause of action in *Nagle* v. *Feilden*.[89] Mrs. Nagle trained racehorses. She was, however, refused a licence to do so by the Jockey Club in pursuance of its policy of never giving such a licence to a woman. In order for her horses to be allowed to run on courses controlled by the Jockey Club the licence to train was given to her "head lad." Mrs. Nagle objected to this situation and sought an injunction to compel the Jockey Club to issue her with a licence. Her initial contention depended on the argument that a contract arose when she applied for a licence. This plea was struck out. She appealed against that decision and the Court of Appeal in considering that interim matter was concerned simply to decide whether she had an arguable case. Lord Denning M.R. (with whom Salmon and Danckwerts L.JJ. agreed)[90]:

> "I quite agree that if we were here considering a social club, it would be necessary for the plaintiff to show a contract. If a man applies to join a social club and is blackballed, he has no cause of action: because the members have made no contract

---

[82] [1956] 1 W.L.R. 833.
[83] [1970] 1 All E.R. 1091.
[84] [1952] 2 Q.B. 329.
[85] [1963] 2 Q.B. 606.
[86] [1966] 2 Q.B. 633.
[87] [1971] Ch. 591.
[88] [1963] 2 Q.B. 527 affirmed [1964] A.C. 925 (H.L.).
[89] [1966] 2 Q.B. 633.
[90] Lord Denning's derivation of public policy from the doctrine of unreasonable restraint of trade possibly derives from a remark by Lord Evershed in *Faramus* v. *Film Artistes Association* [1964] A.C. 925 that only a contract in unreasonable restraint of trade, not saved by the then existing Trade Union Act 1871, s.3 could be struck down.

with him. They can do as they like. They can admit or refuse him, as they please; but we are not considering a social club. We are considering an association which exercises a virtual monopoly in an important field of human activity. By refusing or withdrawing a licence, the stewards can put a man out of business. This is a great power. If it is abused, can the courts give redress? That is the question. It was urged before us that the members of a trading or professional association were like a social club. They had, it was said, an unrestricted power to admit, or refuse to admit, any person whom they choose: and that this was established by a case in 1825 concerning the Inns of Court. In *R.* v. *Lincoln's Inn Benchers*, Bayley J. said:

'They make their own rules as to the admission of members; and even if they act capriciously upon the subject, this court can give no remedy in such a case; because in fact there has been no violation of a right.'

'I venture to question this statement, notwithstanding the eminence of the judge from whom it fell. The common law of England has for centuries recognised that a man has a right to work in his trade or profession without being unjustly excluded from it. He is not to be shut out from it at the whim of those having the governance of it. If they make a rule which enables them to reject his application arbitrarily or capriciously, not reasonably, that rule is bad. It is against public policy. The courts will not give effect to it. Such was held in the seventeenth century in the celebrated *Ipswich Tailors' Case*, where a rule was made that no person should exercise the trade of a tailor in Ipswich unless he was admitted by them to be a sufficient workman. Lord Coke C.J. held that the rule was bad, because it was 'against the liberty and freedom of the subject.' If, however, the rule is reasonable, the courts will not interfere. In the eighteenth century, the company of surgeons required as a qualification for an apprentice an understanding of the Latin tongue. The governors rejected an apprentice because on examination they found him to be totally ignorant of Latin. Lord Mansfield C.J. declined to interfere with their decision (see *R.* v. *Surgeons' Co.* (*Master*).

There are not many modern cases on the subject, but they support the principle which I have stated. In *Weinberger* v. *Inglis* the rules of the Stock Exchange gave to the committee an absolute discretion to admit such persons as they 'shall think proper.' The House of Lords were not referred to the old cases but to the cases where directors are empowered in their discretion to refuse a transfer of shares, such as *Re Gresham Life Assurance Society, ex parte Penney*. The House were disposed to accept this analogy and to hold that, if the committee of the Stock Exchange were to act arbitrarily or capriciously, the courts could set aside their decision—see what Lord Buckmaster, Lord Atkinson and Lord Wrenbury said. Then again in *Faramus* v. *Film Artistes Association* a trade union, which kept a 'closed shop,' made a rule forbidding entry to any person who had been convicted of a criminal offence. Lord Pearce said:

'Since the respondent union have a monopoly, exclusion from membership prevents a man from earning his living in this particular profession. An absolute rule that so prevents any person who may have suffered a trivial conviction many years before is in restraint of trade and unreasonable.' "

This development was overtaken by the provision in the Industrial Relations Act 1971[91] of a statutory right to complain of arbitrary exclusion regardless of the membership agreements of the union. Subsequently, development of the concept of unreasonable restraint of trade put forward in *Nagle* v. *Feilden* was precluded by a specific statutory prohibition upon applying the doctrine to trade

---

[91] s.65(2). Repealed by the Trade Union and Labour Relations (Amendment) Act 1976, s.1.

union rules.[92] In any event it is fair to suggest that outright exclusion on arbitrary or unreasonable grounds is likely to be rare among British trade unions. Possibly because British unions are not, like their United States counterparts, operated as personal power bases the type of situation apparent in *Huntley* v. *Thornton*,[93] where the branch committee did pursue a personal vendetta, is a rare exception.

Incorrect admissions

The courts are much more likely to be asked to deal with a situation where the unions have bent their rules to meet an unexpected situation—rather as they would expect rules to be bent in negotiation of a dispute. Such a situation occurred in *Martin* v. *Scottish Transport and General Workers Union*.[94] The plaintiff had been directed to work in the docks at Edinburgh at the beginning of the Second World War. The appropriate union branch was reluctant to admit such directed labour to membership of the trade union but a compromise was eventually agreed by which such workers were classified as temporary members. Eight or nine years later when work at the docks declined the union agreed to such temporary members being laid off before ordinary members, many of whom had joined after the plaintiff. The plaintiff argued that since the rule book made no provision for temporary membership he should be considered to have been admitted a full member. The House of Lords, however, concluded that the attempt to admit him to a class of membership which did not exist was *ultra vires* and void. The strict contractual approach revealed by the following extract from the judgment of Lord Normand is typical of the judicial approach to all trade union membership cases but, it is submitted, is out of line with the normal practice of trade unions in considering such situations.

" . . . [Any] rule governing the terms on which membership is granted must apply to all admissions until it is altered by the method prescribed by the rules themselves, and I, therefore, reject the argument put forward for the respondents that *esto* the rules in August, 1940, provided only for the admission of members without any limit on the duration of their membership, some modification of the rule so as to provide for temporary membership could be brought about by an implied ratification of admissions purporting to have been made on a temporary basis. Now, r.15 contains this:

'Every person upon being admitted a member of the union shall be deemed to agree to abide by the rules of the union in every respect, and be liable to forfeit membership at any time if in the opinion of the general executive council such person has failed to abide by the rules.'

There is no rule providing for the admission of members on a temporary basis or for forfeiture for any reason except that prescribed by r.15. Rule 20 provides:

'No new rule shall be made, nor shall any rule herein contained or hereafter be made (*sic*), or amended, or rescinded except in accordance with a resolution duly passed at the annual meeting of the general executive council.'

In spite of imperfections of drafting, the sense of this rule is clear. It is common ground that r. 15 was in force in August, 1940, and that it was not thereafter altered

---

[92] TULRA 1974, s.2(5).
[93] [1957] 1 W.L.R. 321.
[94] [1952] 1 All E.R. 691 (H.L.).

by any resolution passed at the annual meeting of the general executive council. Therefore, the officials of the branch or of the union had no authority in August, 1940, or later, to admit the appellant to membership subject to a limitation of time, and when they purported to do so they acted in excess of their powers and their act had and has no validity. I agree with the view expressed by Lord Carmont that there was an attempt to create a class of member outside the provisions of the rules and that it necessarily fails. The conclusion that the appellant never was a member may be inconvenient to both parties, because it may be difficult to work out the equitable adjustment of rights, but that is not a consideration which can affect the decision of the present appeal. I would dismiss the appeal with costs."

It is not, of course, intended to suggest that trade unions should be free to manipulate rules in order to resolve a particular problem where that manipulation will affect established rights of individual members. The courts regard their principal purpose as the protection of individual rights. The trade unions regard their principal purpose as the pursuit of group interest. Instances where the two objectives are opposed are bound to occur. What is suggested is that the strict contractual approach adopted by the courts may, as in *Martin's* case, seem as unsatisfactory to the individual as it is alien to the union's ways of thinking. In *Faramus* v. *Film Artistes Association*[95] the courts noted the union's purpose of protecting the group by excluding those whose presence would endanger it but the House of Lords took no account of this purpose in strictly construing a rule providing that anyone convicted of a criminal offence should be ineligible for membership. The effect was to permit the union, admittedly in the interest of those who remained, to reduce its membership to suit a contracting industry, using the unnecessarily wide criterion of criminal conviction.

The courts have found it possible to apply the principle of estoppel to discount procedural errors in the admission process.[96] This chance discovery that estoppel is not precluded where the result it is sought to establish is *intra vires* gives a clue to the possibility of using the expectations of the parties as the source of their rights rather than strict, and often clearly unintended, interpretations of rules. A recent decision not connected with trade unions affairs indicates how this approach might develop.

In *McInnes* v. *Onslow Fane*[97] the plaintiff applied to the British Boxing Board of Control for a licence as a boxing manager. His application was rejected on more than one occasion and, finally, without hearing or reasons. He sought a declaration that this refusal was unlawful as being unfair and contrary to natural justice. Although concluding that the applicant had no right to demand a hearing or reasons the judgment of Megarry V.-C. proceeded on the basis of what he might reasonably expect.

"Where the court is entitled to intervene, I think it must be considered what type of decision is in question. I do not suggest that there is any clear or exhaustive classification but I think that at least three categories may be discerned. First, there are what may be called the forfeiture cases. In these, there is a decision which takes away some existing right or position, as where a member of an organisation is expelled or licence is revoked. Second, at the other extreme there are what may be

---

[95] [1964] A.C. 925.
[96] See *Clarke* v. *National Union of Furniture Trade Operatives, The Times*, October 18, 1957, *per* Upjohn J. The authority of this poorly reported decision is not increased by the fact that, on the evidence, the applicant had probably been properly admitted.
[97] [1978] 3 All E.R. 211.

called the application cases. These are cases where the decision merely refuses to grant the applicant the right or position that he seeks, such as membership of the organisation, or a licence to do certain acts. Third, there is an intermediate category, which may be called the expectation cases, which differ from the application cases only in that the applicant has some legitimate expectation from what has already happened that his application will be granted. This head includes cases where an existing licence-holder applies for renewal of his licence, or a person already elected or appointed to some position seeks confirmation from some confirming authority: see, for instance, *Weinberger* v. *Inglis*; *Breen* v. *Amalgamated Engineering Union*; and see *Schmidt* v. *Secretary of State for Home Affairs*; *R.* v. *Barnsley Metropolitan Borough Council, ex parte Hook*.

It seems plain that there is a substantial distinction between the forfeiture cases and the application cases. In the forfeiture cases, there is a threat to take something away for some reason; and in such cases, the right to an unbiased tribunal, the right to notice of the charges and the right to be heard in answer to the charges (which, in *Ridge* v. *Baldwin*, Lord Hodson said were three features of natural justice which stood out) are plainly apt. In the application cases, on the other hand, nothing is being taken away, and in all normal circumstances there are no charges, and so no requirement of an opportunity of being heard in answer to the charges. Instead, there is the far wider and less defined question of the general suitability of the applicant for membership or a licence. The distinction is well-recognised, for in general it is clear that the courts will require natural justice to be observed for expulsion from a social club, but not on an application for admission to it. The intermediate category, that of the expectation cases, may at least in some respects be regarded as being more akin to the forfeiture cases than the application cases; for although in form there is no forfeiture but merely an attempt at acquisition that fails, the legitimate expectation of a renewal of the licence or confirmation of the membership is one which raises the question of what it is that has happened to make the applicant unsuitable for the membership or licence for which he was previously thought suitable."

On this basis it was conceded that fairness might be expected, even in cases of application for admission alone, and the judgment picks up the point.

"Let the distinctions between this case and the authorities that I have mentioned be accepted. There still remains the question whether in this case the board's procedure is fair. Counsel for the plaintiff said with force that an obligation to be fair is not satisfied merely by being honest; or, to put it the other way round, that a person may be perfectly honest in reaching a decision, and yet be unfair. What should have been done, he said, was that if the board reached a provisional decision to reject the plaintiff's application, the board should then have adjourned further consideration of the application, and notified the plaintiff both of the gist of their reasons for the provisional rejection and of his right to attend for an oral hearing at which he could try to meet the objections. Alternatively, there should be an initial oral hearing at which those with objections could put them to the plaintiff, and then, if he lacked the materials with which to meet them, he should be given the opportunity of being heard again at an adjourned meeting. In each case, the procedure envisages that there might have to be two meetings before any final decision was reached.

Looking at the case as a whole, in my judgment there is no obligation on the board to give the plaintiff even the gist of the reasons why they refused his application, or proposed to do so. This is not a case in which there has been any suggestion of the board considering any alleged dishonesty or morally culpable conduct of the plaintiff. A man free from any moral blemish may nevertheless be wholly unsuitable for a particular type of work. The refusal of the plaintiff's application by no means necessarily puts any slur on his character, nor does it deprive him of any statutory right. There is no mere narrow issue as to his character, but the wide and general issue whether it is right to grant this licence to this applicant. In such circumstances, in the absence of anything to suggest that the board have been affected by dishonesty or bias or caprice, or that there is any other impropriety, I think that the board are fully entitled to give no reasons for their decision, and to decide the application without any preliminary indication to the plaintiff for those reasons. The board are the best judges of the desirability of granting the licence, and in the absence of any impropriety the court ought not to interfere.

There is a more general consideration. I think that the courts must be slow to allow any implied obligation to be fair to be used as a means of bringing before the courts for review honest decisions of bodies exercising jurisdiction over sporting and other activities which those bodies are far better fitted to judge than the courts. This is so even where those bodies are concerned with the means of livelihood of those who take part in those activities. The concepts of natural justice and the duty to be fair must not be allowed to discredit themselves by making unreasonable requirements and imposing undue burdens. Bodies such as the board which promote a public interest by seeking to maintain high standards in a field of activity which otherwise might easily become degraded and corrupt ought not to be hampered in their work without good cause. Such bodies should not be tempted or coerced into granting licences that otherwise they would refuse by reason of the courts having imposed on them a procedure for refusal which facilitates litigation against them. As Lord Denning M.R. said in *Re Pergamon Press Ltd.*, 'No one likes to have an action brought against him, however unfounded.' The individual must indeed be protected against impropriety; but any claim of his for anything more must be balanced against what the public interest requires."

The Bridlington Agreement

This set of rules was adopted by the Trades Union Congress at Bridlington in 1939 and is designed to govern the approach of unions to recruitment of members especially where more than one union is capable of representing a particular grade of worker. They serve to reduce the proliferation of unions operating in the same area which is characteristic of the growth of British industrial relations but which is widely recognised as detrimental to the development of orderly and stable bargaining. The Bridlington Agreement was extended in 1969 to allow the T.U.C. to intervene in disputes between employers and workers and also to extend the powers of the T.U.C. in inter-union disputes, not only about membership but also concerning recognition, demarcation and conditions of employment.

The three most significant principles of the Agreement are:

"2. No one who is or has recently been a member of any affiliated union should be accepted into membership in another without enquiry of his present or former union. The present or former union shall be under an obligation to reply within 21 days of the enquiry, stating:

(a) Whether the applicant has tendered his resignation;
(b) Whether he is clear on the books;
(c) Whether he is under discipline or penalty;
(d) Whether there are any other reasons why the applicant should not be accepted.

If the present or former union objects to the transfer, and the enquiring union considers the objection to be unreasonable, the enquiring union shall not accept the applicant into membership but shall maintain the status quo with regard to membership. If the problem cannot be mutually resolved it should be referred to the TUC for adjudication.

4. A union shall not accept a member of another union where that union objects to the transfer (see Principle 2 above), or where enquiry shows that the member is:

(a) under discipline;
(b) engaged in a trade dispute;
(c) in arrears with contributions.

5. No union shall commence organising activities at any establishment or undertaking in respect of any grade or grades or workers in which another union has the majority of workers employed and negotiates wages and conditions, unless by arrangement with that union."

It appears[98] that in adjudicating on any dispute the Disputes Committee is primarily concerned to enquire whether the procedure laid down in the Agreement has been followed, whether the recruiting union was already the dominant employee organisation in the bargaining unit and whether it has established negotiating rights. There is no doubt that the jurisdiction favours the established unions and, therefore, appears to favour the larger unions which it protects from breakaway movements.

In some ways the Bridlington Agreement operates to suppress individual freedom of choice to a degree similar to that of closed shop agreements. In *Spring* v. *National Amalgamated Stevedores and Dockers Society*[99] the effect of the order of the Disputes Committee which the court set aside would have been to compel a large number of union members to return to a union they wished to leave and in which they had little confidence. Most unions affiliated to the T.U.C. countered the effect of this decision by amendment to their rules allowing them to terminate the membership of any person recruited in breach of the Bridlington Agreement. The National Graphical Association, for example, has the following power:

> Notwithstanding anything in these rules, the National Council may by giving six weeks' notice in writing terminate the membership of any member if necessary in order to comply with a decision of the Disputes Committee of the Trades Union Congress."[1]

The judicial approach continues, however, to be at variance with that of the unions in the same two significant respects which characterise most of the membership issues. The Bridlington Agreement epitomises the union's view of the overriding importance of the group whilst the courts continue to think in terms of individual interest. Likewise, the agreement is one of the most open avowals of the unions' attitude to settling disputes without the analysis of legal issues which characterise judgments of the courts.

This conflict surfaced again in the decision of the Chancery Division in *Rothwell* v. *Association of Professional, Executive, Clerical and Computer*

---

[98] See Peter J. Kalis "The Adjudication of Inter Union Membership Disputes" (1977) 6 I.L.J. 19.
[99] [1956] 1 W.L.R. 585.
[1] Rule 17(*b*).

Staff.[2] The Association of Scientific, Technical and Managerial Staff (ASTMS) began recruiting employees of the General Accident Assurance Company. Shortly afterwards it was challenged by the newly formed "Staff Association General Accident" which subsequently merged with the Association of Professional, Executive, Clerical and Computer Staffs (APEX). Both ASTMS and APEX were affiliated to the T.U.C. ASTMS claimed that it had recruited over 20 per cent. of the staff of General Accident and that the merger accordingly constituted a breach of principle 5 of the Bridlington Agreement. The Disputes Committee upheld this claim and ordered APEX to terminate the membership of the 3,000 or so members it had acquired by the merger. APEX had a rule similar to that of the N.G.A. quoted above which would have enabled it to comply with this order. Not entirely surprisingly, Foster J. applied to the question of the validity of the Agreement reasoning similar to that of the approach of the Courts to other membership issues. He declined to resort to arguments based on public policy to invalidate the union's own rule permitting termination of membership but concluded that not only could that rule not be invoked in bad faith, or contrary to natural justice, but also that it could not provide authority to implement an award of the Disputes Committee which was itself *ultra vires*. He applied a strictly literal interpretation of principle 5 of the Bridlington Agreement and arrived at the conclusion that no valid award could be made under that principle if the complaining union did not possess membership of 50 per cent. of the employees concerned. He also concluded that it could not be *intra vires* the Disputes Committee to require a union to take action which it had no power to take. In this case APEX had already accepted a transfer of engagements from the Staff Association and could not lawfully go back on that. Similar reasoning, of course, would apply to the action required of the recruiting union in *Spring's* case. In other words the jurisdiction of the T.U.C. Disputes Committee is dependent on the active participation of the unions concerned.

The judgment of the E.A.T. (subsequently overruled by the Court of Appeal) in the later decision in *Cheall* v. *APEX*[3] is, however, sharply at variance with the normal judicial approach to any aspect of trade union membership and government, taking a non-interventionist approach to the operation of the Agreement. The facts disclose a fairly simple "Bridlington" situation of a union responding to an instruction of the T.U.C. Disputes Committee to discontinue a membership which had been granted in breach of the Agreement. The union had a rule allowing it to terminate membership, by six weeks written notice, if necessary in order to comply with a decision of the Disputes Committee. In the instant case it applied that power without giving the affected member a right to a hearing. Bingham J. seemed to experience some difficulty in explaining why there was no obligation upon the Disputes Committee to afford a hearing but less difficulty in deciding that there was equally no obligation, in the circumstances, on the union. In his view the direct relations of the T.U.C. were with its member unions. Its first object was to promote their interests. Its conduct would affect the individual who could, therefore, be said to have an interest in it. This interest, however, gave him no right against it. It might, as simply, have been said that the individual union member has no

---

[2] [1976] I.C.R. 211.
[3] [1982] I.R.L.R. 91.

relationship with the T.U.C. upon which any claim can be based. The actions of the T.U.C. are, to him, no more than an external event. The action, so far as he is concerned, can only be that of his union.

Turning to this issue, the learned judge also concluded that the union had no obligation to provide a hearing because there was no other decision which it could, in reality, arrive at than to terminate membership:

"I turn to the exercise by the Executive Council of its discretion under Rule 14. I regard it as plain beyond argument that although a discretion in wide terms was conferred it was not untrammelled but had to be fairly exercised. . . . I also accept that no trade union can give itself an unfettered discretion to expel a member without hearing him, . . . but APEX by this rule does not seek to do so. The rule is so drawn as to permit the union to give the member notice and an opportunity to be heard in an appropriate case. In some cases it might no doubt be appropriate for the Executive Council to hold an inquiry or investigation with the corollary that the rules of natural justice would fall to be observed, . . . for instance, if there were reason to doubt whether the complaining union would re-admit the member if his current membership were terminated; or if there were local negotiations, of which the member was better informed than the union, which might lead to an accommodation with the complaining union; or if the complaining union's determination to enforce its award were in question or if there were thought to be grounds for challenging the constitution of the disputes committee, or its conduct of the hearing, or the legal or factual soundness of its conclusion. In any of those cases, fairness might be held to require that the member should be told that the Executive Council was considering the operation of Rule 14 against him and invited to make any representations he wished. But would the duty to act fairly, or the requirements of 'fairplay in action' as Sachs L.J. called it in *Edwards* v. *SOGAT*, always and necessarily require that process to be followed? Might there not be cases where the Executive Council could act, and appear to act, fairly without following it? I think there might, and I think the present is such a case. Consider the facts. APEX had had ample notice of the TGWU's complaint against it. The Disputes Committee had been properly constituted and the hearing properly conducted. APEX had been given a full opportunity to put its case and had made all the points which were fairly open to it and some which were not. The result was inevitable. The factual findings inherent in the Disputes Committee's decision were unassailable. Its award was that which, in practice, always followed a finding that Bridlington Principle 2 had been violated. There was no known ground for challenging the award. The TGWU was pressing that it be enforced. The T.U.C. was indicating, politely but very firmly, that it did not intend its authority to be undermined. The chances of reaching an accommodation with the TGWU which would obviate the need for termination had, as APEX knew, receded to vanishing point. There was no reason to doubt the willingness of the ACTSS to re-admit Mr. Cheall. There was no realistic hope of respite if the matter reached the General Council. It was known to APEX that termination was highly unwelcome to Mr. Cheall, and indeed it was unpalatable to the union also. But Vauxhall Motors was not a closed shop, so termination did not mean loss of livelihood; and it left Mr. Cheall little or no worse off than he had been when of his own accord, he had left ACTSS and when, without any inducement or representation as to continuity of membership, he had chosen to join APEX. As things were turning out at Vauxhall Motors, the ACTSS were better able to represent him effectively than APEX. The ultimate alternatives to termination, namely suspension or disaffiliation from the T.U.C., would in the union's informed view have emasculated it as an industrial force and gravely weakened its ability to serve Mr. Cheall or any other of its members. In this situation, as it seems to me, APEX could not conceivably have made any other decision than to terminate, no matter what Mr. Cheall urged or argued and no matter how vehement his opposition. If any misconduct had been alleged against him it might have been different, but none was. In my view there was here no legal obligation on APEX to give Mr. Cheall notice or grant him an opportunity to be heard. To have done so in circumstances where nothing he said could affect the outcome would in my view have been cruel deception."

Significantly, he then strongly supported the view that trade unions should be permitted to regulate such relations and that a strong case of public policy would have to be made out to interfere with the method of so doing selected by them.

"I turn lastly to the expert evidence. Whether the Bridlington Principles and the model rule are on balance beneficial or detrimental to British industry and industrial relations is a very large question, the resolution of which would involve much factual research and comparative study. It would be naive to suppose that a reliable view could be formed on the basis of a couple of hours' evidence, from sources however eminent. In order that a court should find the model rule to be contrary to public policy, in the absence of other indications or authority and on the strength of factual evidence, an overwhelming case would have to be made out. It suffices to say that no such case has in my view been made out here. The practical arguments in favour of the model rule are, at the least serious and substantial. Taking all these matters together I find it quite impossible to conclude that the model rule is void as being contrary to public policy."

It is suggested that it may be unwise to rely on first impressions when reading the highly coloured judgment of Lord Denning M.R. in the Court of Appeal which, by a majority, overruled the decision of Bingham J. Lord Denning obviously rejected both that decision and the philosophy behind it, but the same cannot be said of the other majority judgment of Slade L.J.[3a]

The Master of the Rolls seized a last opportunity to reiterate many of the propositions about trade union membership which he had enunciated but which had lain dormant for long enough for hope to have begun to form that they would not re-emerge. In the forefront of these was the right for the individual freely to choose a particular union and to insist on joining it. He now founded this on Article 11(1) of the European Convention of Human Rights and pointed out that he had declared his broad interpretation a basic principle of English law.[3b] As Donaldson L.J. dissenting pointed out, the European Court of Human Rights in *Young* v. *The United Kingdom*[3c] had not committed itself on the extent of the right. The difficulty of doing so is demonstrated by the fact that Lord Denning had to rely on *Nagle* v. *Feilden*[3d] which came nowhere near to granting such a broad right as he now sought to assert. Accepting his own view of the pervasiveness of the right to join a trade union Lord Denning sought to dispose of the difficulty that such a principle was not part of the contract. Neither of the other members of the court of Appeal chose to comment on his reiteration of the far-fetched comparison between rules and bye-laws let alone on the incorrect inference that, if equivalent to bye-laws, such rules would be freely liable to be declared void as unreasonable or uncertain.

It is submitted that these elements of Lord Denning's judgment owe more to rhetoric than legal analysis and that the true significance of the decision is better determined by examination of the issues discussed by Slade L.J. on the one side

---

[3a] [1982] I.R.L.R. 362.
[3b] *UKAPE* v. *ACAS* [1979] I.R.L.R. 68.
[3c] [1981] I.R.L.R. 408. [3d] [1966] 2 Q.B. 633.

and Donaldson L.J. on the other. Both accepted that the rules of a union constituted a contract. Donaldson L.J. dissenting, however, more clearly brought out the untypical nature of that contract which, as he said, is a contract of adhesion. That being so, in his view, its interpretation depended more on the intention of the union and its pre-existing members than on that of a new member adhering to an existing agreement. From this viewpoint he was able to conclude that any implication concerning the right of the union to obey a decision of the T.U.C. Disputes Committee must depend to a considerable extent on whether its existing members could be said to have intended that it should be forced to run the risk of disaffiliation from the T.U.C. Slade L.J. accepted this view but differed in the result on the ground that not all the members of the union were likely to take the same view. That, of course, is true and it is, indeed, another good reason for not embarking on the task of implication in respect of trade union rules. It led Slade L.J. to adopt a different interpretation although, as he admitted, only a minority of the membership might have intended the rule to read as he preferred.

Donaldson L.J. substantially supported the view of Bingham J. that the appellant was a third party to the dispute between APEX and T.G.W.U. which the T.U.C. Disputes Committee had to resolve. As he said the fact that he would be affected by the outcome of that dispute could not be regarded by the courts as entitling him to participate in its resolution. He also supported Bingham J. in holding that though, when it came to his own expulsion from APEX, the appellant had a right to be treated fairly, no question of unfairness could arise in a situation in which the union took the only course feasibly open to it. The appellant must have known all along that, if it came to the crunch, the union would exclude him. Slade L.J. did not really consider these two arguments, preferring to concentrate the weight of his judgment on the somewhat arid issue of whether the union could rely in its own *wrong* in admitting the appellant in breach of the Bridlington agreement to justify its subsequent exclusion of him. Like Lord Denning M.R., who merely mentioned the point in passing, he concluded that it could not. Donaldson L.J. preferred to rely on the fact that to bring about this result it would be necessary to qualify the plain words of the union rule. Quite apart from the difficulty in reality of arriving at different results depending on whether the admission was an innocent or a guilty breach of "Bridlington" he concluded that the circumstances would suggest that anyone joining a union would accept that they would be liable to exclusion if their admission turned out to be in breach of that agreement, however that breach arose.

It is submitted that the important consideration is the extent to which the judgments of Slade and Donaldson L.JJ. support or reject the *collective reality* approach of Bingham J. Donaldson L.J. clearly supports it, but Slade L.J. does not reject it. Slade L.J. considers it necessary to support his desired qualification by looking for what he considers the real likelihood of a collective acceptance. Interestingly, Donaldson L.J. is forced to the conclusion that no implication is possible because there would be no collective consensus whilst Slade L.J. supports an implication by what he would be forced to admit might be minority intention. Slade L.J. is, therefore, assuming a presumption in favour of procedural safeguards whilst Donaldson L.J. assumes something like a presumption in favour of the accepted operation of trade union institutions. In the absence of any reasoned conclusion on this issue by Lord Denning M.R. the new approach contained in the judgment of Bingham J. can at the most be said to be in dispute. It may well survive.

Resignation and repudiation

The common law raises a presumption of a freedom to resign membership[4] but, as may be expected of the contractual approach, allows this to be rebutted by contrary provision in the rules. Statute has intervened, it is submitted, unnecessarily, by implying into every contract of membership of a trade union a term conferring on the member a right to resign on giving reasonable notice and complying with any reasonable conditions.[5]

In fact the common law rule simply accepts the inevitable, leaving the association to seek to enforce membership obligations if it can. In reality the most common system of resignation in trade unions is that whereby the individual ceases to pay his dues or ask for benefits. Unions have learned to deal with this by providing a quick procedure for removing such persons from the list of members. The courts have responded by avoiding the raising of any questions as to the invalidity of such a procedure. This compromise is now threatened by the provision in the Code of Practice on the Closed Shop that it is reasonable to expect fair procedure in all termination situations regardless of any disciplinary content.[6] Few commentators have sought to explain in terms of legal theory the current workable, if tacit, understanding. It was at one time suggested that payment of dues might be regarded as a condition precedent to the retention of membership. Alternatively it could be argued that non-payment of dues constituted a repudiatory breach which the union accepted when it deleted the individual's name from the list of members. The courts are shy of either explanation, possibly fearing to allow into this aspect of the law doctrines which might permit alternative explanations of disciplinary termination of membership.

A more realistic and less doctrinal explanation was propounded by Megarry J. in *Re The Sick and Funeral Society of St. John's Sunday School, Golcar*.[6a] The members of a long-established association decided that its object of providing sums of money for members in sickness and for the cost of members' funerals served no useful purpose in the modern welfare state. They decided, therefore, to wind up the association and distribute its assets among existing members. Certain persons who had once been members but had ceased to pay subscriptions attempted to pay these subscriptions for the period of default so as to establish their continuing membership and right to share in the distribution. Megarry J. said:

> "I should be very slow to accept that a member of a society may disregard all his obligations as a member for several years, and then, when it appears that there is some advantage in resuming his membership, assert that he is still a member because the correct procedure under the rules to terminate his membership has not been followed. The question, of course, is not one of expulsion, or of the society snatching at some trivial or short-lived breach of rules by a member to deny him

---

[4] *Finche* v. *Oake* [1896] 1 Ch. 409.
[5] TULRA 1974, s.7 as amended; replacing a more restrictive provision in the Industrial Relations Act 1971.
[6] See also *Edwards* v. *SOGAT* [1971] Ch. 354.
[6a] [1973] Ch. 51.

membership; it is a question of a voluntary disregard of the obligations of membership over a continuous period of years. There must be many instances in clubs up and down the country in which this sort of thing happens. Yet if the contentions on behalf of the four members are right, either the society or the members concerned may, if it suits them, claim that the membership is still in being. Such members might find that the society is claiming many years' arrears of a substantial subscription, or the membership might, as here, suddenly re-assert their membership when some advantage turns up.

I do not think that this can be right. It seems to me that the answer, or an answer, lies in the decision of the Court of Appeal in *Finch* v. *Oake*, which I mentioned in the course of argument. This established that a member of a society has the unilateral right, not dependent on acceptance by the society, to resign his membership at any time, even though the rules contain no provision as to resignation. In that case, the member wrote a letter saying that he desired to withdraw his name as a member of the society, and that was held to be sufficient. There can be no magic in the word 'resign,' nor in whether the resignation is written or oral. The essence of the matter seems to me to be whether the member has sufficiently manifested his decision to be a member no more. I cannot see why such a manifestation should not be by conduct instead of by words; the only question is whether the member's decision has been adequately conveyed to the society by words or deeds. In short, in addition to resignation by words, I think there may be resignation by conduct; and I do not see why in a proper case a sufficiency of inertia should not constitute resignation by conduct. The points seems to lack authority, and so I must resolve it on principle.

I am not suggesting that the mere failure to pay weekly subscriptions for a few weeks or quarterly subscriptions for two or three quarters would suffice per se; but three years and more is another matter. No reasonable man is likely to feel any real doubt about the intentions of a member of a society who for over three years has failed to make his weekly or quarterly payments, and has put forward not a word to suggest that this was due to some mistake, or that he has done some act showing an intention to continue a member. As I have indicated, among the many thousands of clubs and societies in the country there must be many cases of members whose membership has never been terminated in accordance with any provision in the rules, and yet who are regarded as still being members neither by themselves nor by the club or society. If their membership is said to have 'lapsed,' that may be another way of describing a tacit resignation. However it is described, it seems right that there should be such a doctrine, so that neither the member nor the club or society should be able to claim against the other on the basis that what has long been dead de facto still lives de jure. A moribund membership ought not to be capable of resurrection."

Discipline

The practice

Although the advent of a code of practice suggesting standards of reasonableness in admission procedures may have its influence on the attitude of industrial tribunals to legislative intervention to control union admission procedures introduced by the Employment Act 1980 the unions have not felt much pressure to adapt their admission rules to meet judicial requirements. It is otherwise with union discipline. As we shall see, the courts have consistently applied a strict contractual approach to their jurisdiction over complaints arising from such discipline. This approach has not been adapted to suit the parties' attitudes, as has the judicial view of the contract of employment, by flexible rules of implication of terms. The unions are, therefore, confronted with such clearly established principles as that no discipline is permitted unless authorised by the rules, that the courts will construe the provisions of the rule book according to judicial concepts of reasonableness which make little concession to the objectives of the union and that the courts will impose standards of reasonable procedure which, with the unexpected exception of bias, are not adapted to the amateur and informal attitudes of union branch procedure.

The most obvious sign of the union response to judicial restrictiveness is the "blanket" offence. This typically provides for discipline (usually by way of expulsion) for conduct which, in the opinion of the branch or the National Executive, is contrary to the interests of the union. This concept may be worded in different ways and because of the strictness of the courts' approach to the words used these differences may allow them to produce some surprisingly narrow constructions.[7] The intention of the unions is to cover as wide an area as possible and they would justify this approach by pointing out that it would be impossible by specification of precisely defined offences to cover all situations where it might reasonably be considered in the interest of the organisation to impose discipline. Few union rule books are without such precise offences but it is fair to say that little effort appears to have been made to ensure that they cover all the more obviously likely offences. In other words, there can be little doubt that the narrow judicial construction of what is contrary to the union's interest must surprise most of the membership. The sort of specific and blanket offences a careful union might think to include is apparent from the following extract[8] which is typical in all save the fact that it forms a single rule. More commonly this list of offences would be scattered throughout the rule book.

> 1. Without prejudice to any other grounds of expulsion herein contained any member of the Union who, in the opinion of his branch or the Executive Council, shall have injured or attempted to injure the Union, or worked or acted contrary to the interests of the Union or its members, or have attempted to break up or dissolve the Union otherwise than as allowed by these rules, or otherwise brought the Union into discredit or refused to comply with the order or decision of any Committee, Council, or conference having jurisdiction over such member under these rules or requested or taken work from any employer at any place where or when a trade dispute exists between such employer and the Union or any branch thereof, or obtained or attempted to obtain any of the benefits of the Union by means of misrepresentation, or have knowingly participated in or been a party to any fraud perpetrated upon the Union, or any misappropriation or misapplication of its funds or the funds of any branch thereof, or whose conduct shall have been otherwise inconsistent with the duties of a member of this Union or who being an officer shall have refused to perform the duties imposed upon him by these rules or any of them, may be expelled by his branch, with the approval of the Executive Council, or he may be expelled or otherwise dealt with by the Executive Council. If expelled from the Union, he shall thereupon, subject to his right of appeal as in these rules provided, cease to be a member thereof. Every expelled member shall cease to have any claim on the funds and benefits of the Union (except as provided for in Rule 27 Clause 2) and shall forfeit all right to participate in the privileges thereof. It shall be necessary to give notice to any member of the intention to proceed against him under this rule and of the grounds or matters which the branch

---

[7] See *Esterman* v. *NALGO* [1974] I.C.R. 625.
[8] A.U.E.W.

are proposing to consider, and every expelled member shall afterwards receive notice of his expulsion and the grounds thereof, and shall thereupon have the right to appeal as in these rules provided.

2. In addition and without prejudice to the foregoing if any member be satisfactorily proved to have stolen the funds or property of the Union; to have, with intent to deceive, tampered, falsified, or otherwise wilfully misused any books or other documents belonging to the Union to have, contrary to these rules, obtained possession of, or refused to give up when in his possession any books, keys, papers, or other documents or effects, belonging to the Union or any part thereof, to have refused to sign or execute any cheque, transfer, deed, or other document to which his signature or execution was required by these rules; to have refused to obey these rules, or to comply with any order by them authorised he may be fined such sum (not exceeding £5) or suspended from benefit for so long as the committee or branch meeting who have tried him may think proper.

3. Any member causing a quarrel, swearing, or using abusive language in any of the Union's meetings shall be fined 2s. 6d. Any member not obeying the president when called to order three times shall be liable to a fine not exceeding 10s.; and should he continue disorderly, he shall be expelled from the meeting, by force if necessary. Any member refusing to pay the fine, or any member conniving at or endeavouring to vindicate the conduct of a member having so offended, shall be fined 2s. 0d. Penalties prescribed in this clause shall be imposed by the president of the meeting.

4. Any member being charged with disorderly conduct while on Unemployment or Sick Benefit shall be summoned before the branch or branch committee, and, if the charge be proved, be liable to such fine, not exceeding 20s.; as the nature of the case demands. Any member finding fault with a member's conduct while on Unemployment or Sick Benefit, and not reporting him to the president or secretary of the branch to which he belongs shall be fined 5s.

5. All fines imposed by these Rules shall be applied by the branch secretary. If the branch secretary fails to apply any fine when due, he shall be liable to a fine of 1s. which shall be applied by the branch referee. All fines shall be paid within 14 weeks from the imposition of such fine, if not then paid shall be treated as arrears of contributions.

6. The General Trustees shall, under the direction of the Executive Council, prosecute, or, if more convenient, direct any branch or district officer or officers to prosecute any member or other person suspected by them of any offence, legally punishable with reference to the affairs of the union, and they may themselves institute, or, if more convenient, may direct any branch or district officer or officers to institute civil proceedings against any member or other persons refusing to give up possession of any of the Union's property or any branch property; or doing or neglecting to do any act so as to render himself or themselves liable to legal proceedings in reference to the Union's affairs, or the affairs of any branch thereof.

7. No member shall call on or write to the secretary of any branch or District Committee at the works where he is employed, under a penalty of 2s. 6d. for each offence.

8. Any member receiving money to pay for another member, or for a person proposed or desiring to be proposed to become a member, and neglecting to do so on the first meeting night, shall be fined 2s. 6d. for such neglect. He shall also be responsible for the money paid to him, and the fines incurred, if any. All such cases shall be brought before the branch or branch committee for their decision. No member so entrusting his contribution money shall have any claim upon the Union if thrown out of benefit through the person entrusted with the said contribution money failing to pay the same, but under such circumstances no member shall be expelled.

9. Should any member refuse to pay money entrusted to him as above, together

with the fine as before-mentioned, he shall be deprived of all benefit till the same be paid into the Union.

10. Any member entrusted with money from the funds, and misapplying or failing to account for the same, shall be deprived of all benefit until he has refunded the amount, and shall pay a fine of 20 per cent. on the sum so misapplied or not accounted for, such moneys to be paid to the General Office, or if so decided by the Executive Council to the money steward on a regular meeting night.

11. Any member engaged under Government auspices, by appointment or otherwise, or any member employed on the staff of any private firm, or other Trade Union, who uses the powers thus vested in him for purposes contrary to the Union's interest shall be liable to a fine of £3 or expulsion.[9]

In contrast to the relative similarity of substantive rules there is little in detail common to the rules governing disciplinary procedure. In outline such procedures do appear similar simply because the hierarchy of union tribunals follows similar patterns. Most disciplinary proceedings will be initiated before branch committees although the National Executive will very commonly be empowered to initiate such action directly. It has become much more usual to provide that expulsion should be subject to confirmation by some higher body. Not all unions allow appeals but, again, it is the usual practice to make some such provision. When it comes to the detail, however, rules seem to have grown out of what it occurred to early draftsmen to include, supplemented in a more or less haphazard fashion by later lessons from the courts. In consequence one may readily find provisions for notice of appeal much more carefully worked out than provisions for the initial branch hearing. Presumably, the unions were unwilling to impose upon the branch procedures which appeared to be unduly complex. Even the later realisation that it was at that level that errors occurred which would result in disallowance of the discipline, either on internal appeal or before the courts, will only very slowly lead to the introduction of more complex procedures.

Though surprisingly law-abiding in the conduct of their internal affairs trade unions are not over-anxious to impose upon themselves unwanted restrictions merely at the behest of the courts. There are, however, some startling examples of judicial influence. The rule book of the Musicians Union before the decision in *Bonsor* v. *Musicians Union*[10] contained what was then a very characteristic hotchpotch of offences and partial procedures. Immediately after that judgment the union thoroughly revised the disciplinary sections of the book to produce what might still be regarded by lawyers as a model. In the same way isolated pieces of guidance obviously influenced by contact with the courts often appear. The following is a good example:

"Any member summoned to appear on a charge must be notified in writing of the detailed charge made against him. This principle must be applied by the appropriate bodies to every rule where any charge whatsoever is preferred."

One of the problems that the draftsman faces is that the standard practice of

---

[9] As we have seen, in relatively recent years many unions have added to the list of causes for removal of members a provision allowing them to terminate membership in order to comply with a ruling of the T.U.C. Disputes Committee that recruitment of such a person was in contravention of the Bridlington Agreement.
[10] [1956] A.C. 104.

rule books is to define procedure committee by committee. Not only does this mean that disciplinary procedures will be scattered but it has a tendency to mean that the committee will be led to apply its normal business procedure to disciplinary matters. Even if later experience has led the union to include a special rule for disciplinary procedure it is likely to be found only to insert one or two extra details into this normal business procedure, producing thereby innumerable pitfalls. An excellent example of such a practice, together with a number of other common shortcomings appear in the following extract:

19.—Any member violating any working rules, registration, or by-laws, disseminating false statements or any rumour which tends to depreciate the organisation, its officers, or any section appertaining to the Union, or circulating any business of the Union to unauthorised persons without authority, or who is guilty of other forms of misconduct, shall be fined a sum not exceeding £10, or otherwise dealt with by the branch or authorised committee of the Union as may be deemed fit.

20.—(a) Complaints against the conduct of members may be dealt with by the branch, branch committee (where so determined by the branch), divisional committee, regional committee or the General Executive Council. A member whose conduct is the subject of inquiry shall be given notice of the complaint in writing with an intimation of his right to be present at the hearing.

(b) If a branch, branch committee or divisional committee, as the case may be, imposes a fine for misconduct, or for any of the offences specified in clause 19, the member shall have a right of appeal to the regional committee, whose decision shall be final. Notwithstanding the foregoing provision a regional committee shall have power to impose fines for misconduct provided that in the event of a fine being imposed by a regional committee, a member shall have a right of appeal to the General Executive Council, whose decision shall be final.

(c) Notice of appeal under the preceding clause (b) must be in writing and sent to the regional secretary or the general secretary, as the case may be, within fourteen days from the date of receipt of notification of the fine, and the appeal shall be heard at the first meeting of the regional committee or the General Executive Council, as the case may be, held following the receipt of such notice.

(d) Where a question of expulsion arises for misconduct, or for any of the offences specified in clause 19, the investigation shall be conducted by the regional committee who shall make recommendations to the General Executive Council. A member whose conduct is the subject of complaint, shall be given notice of the investigation in writing and afforded an opportunity of appearing before the regional committee. The General Executive Council may act upon the recommendation of the regional committee or make further investigation or take such steps as, in the opinion of the General Executive Council, seem just.

21.—Without prejudice to any other ground of expulsion contained in these rules, any member, or members, of the Union who, in the opinion of the General Executive Council shall have injured or attempted to injure the Union, or worked or acted contrary to the interest of the Union or its members, or whose conduct shall have been otherwise inconsistent with the duties of a member of this Union may be fined a sum not exceeding £10 and if holding office removed therefrom, or may be expelled by the General Executive Council from the Union and shall thereupon, subject to the right of appeal as in these rules provided, cease to be a member thereof.[11]

The judicial approach[12]

The Rule in Foss v. Harbottle

The courts from time to time express a reluctance to interfere in the domestic affairs of an association but there is little sign of such reluctance in the case of interference in the internal affairs of a trade union. The so-called rule in *Foss* v. *Harbottle*[13] springs from this reluctance. The courts state that they will not intervene where the fact of which complaint is made is *intra vires* the association so that a procedural error could subsequently be corrected. The rule was held to apply to trade unions as legal entities.[14] In *Hodgson* v. *NALGO*[15] Goulding J. held that it would not apply to an unregistered union which was not a legal entity. In the light of section 2 of the Trade Union and Labour Relations Act 1974[16] it seems likely, therefore, that trade unions are not now subject to the rule in *Foss* v. *Harbottle*. Even if it were still to apply it is not available where the act in question is an invasion of individual rights where the individuals do not sue for a wrong done to the association but in their own right to protect from invasion their own individual rights as members.[17] It might, therefore, if the courts were prepared to extend to unions the concept of a quasi-corporate status, apply to confirm the effect of the failure of an officer to carry out his duty, but the rule would not apply so as to avoid defects in disciplinary procedure.

Contractual basis of jurisdiction

When dealing with the deprivation of the contractual rights of individual members United Kingdom courts show no sign of the discretion they exercise in connection with claims for unfair dismissal to overlook procedural defects where it is apparent that the defect has not affected the outcome of the disciplinary proceeding. This is, of course, because they are not seeking to decide on the basis of what is reasonable but on the much more rigid principles of the law of contract. Even given that fact, however, they show little sign of adapting that rigidity, for instance by resort to implied terms, though they have, on occasion, *invoked* the rigidity of contractual rules to explain the exclusion of implied terms.[18] The strictly contractual approach is apparent in the judgment

---

[11] It may be pointed out that it is not at all uncommon to find the sharp contrast between a trivial fine and expulsion as the only alternatives open to a disciplinary body. The effect may be to force the union to expel for only moderately serious offences.

[12] Complaints concerning discipline normally seek either a declaration or, more commonly, an injunction. Since the union committee is most probably to be regarded as an inferior tribunal certiorari would presumably be available, *e.g. R.* v. *Thames Magistrates Courts, ex parte Polemis* [1974] 2 All E.R. 1219.

[13] (1843) 2 Hare 461.

[14] *Cotter* v. *National Union of Seamen* [1929] 2 Ch. 58.

[15] [1972] 1 W.L.R. 130; [1972] 2 All E.R. 15.

[16] *Supra*, p. 389.

[17] *Edwards* v. *Halliwell* [1950] 2 All E.R. 1064.

[18] *e.g. Bonsor* v. *Musicians Union* [1956] A.C. 104. The refusal to imply terms allowed the court to conclude that the act in this case was *ultra vires*.

of Goff J. (as he then was) in *Silvester* v. *National Union of Printing, Bookbinding and Paper Workers*.[19] The plaintiff had been censured by the branch committee for "acting to the detriment of the interests of the union" and ordered to undertake certain work he had previously refused. While his appeal to the final appeal bodies of the union was pending he was three times charged with failing to carry out the instruction. On the third occasion the secretary of the appeals committee, without authority, withdrew the appeal.

> "Whether the plaintiff could have obtained a mandatory order compelling the union to hear the case in its final appeal court or damages for the breach of the rules in not having permitted him to appeal to that body, I am satisfied that those could not be his only remedies. In my judgment, he must be entitled to say that he only submitted to be liable to be disciplined on the terms that he should have certain prescribed rights of appeal, and that upon the union refusing him those rights the sentence, albeit only of censure, and the decision that he was bound to obey the chapel committee's instructions in that matter could not stand. . . .
>
> It follows, in my judgment, that the second and third charges must be bad, despite the provisions of rules 3(12) and 24(4). If the final appeal court had heard the appeal on the first charge and dismissed it, then, of course, the second and third would have been good, but the wrongful refusal of the appeal, in my view, made the decision on the first *ultra vires*. . .
>
> I come last to what has been described as the broken thread argument, which is that the defendant union had no power to withdraw the plaintiff's appeal to the final appeal court on the first charge and that, even if it had, it could not be exercised by the secretary. This, it is said, vitiated the decision and sentence on the first charge and also the second and third. I am satisfied that the secretary had no power to withdraw the appeal. The defendants have craved in aid the principle which applies in this court, that a party who is in contempt by disobeying an order cannot appeal from it without first purging his contempt: I very much doubt whether this principle applies to the decisions of domestic tribunals where the jurisdiction and the rights of appeal depend upon contract; but even if it does, still, in my judgment, the proper authority to stay the appeal was the final appeal court, not the appeals committee or the national executive council. If, however, it was, then it was a power which the secretary was expressly enjoined not to exercise. It must, in my view, be a decision made in an appeal within the exception "in cases of appeals of any nature" in rule 3(17), and I cannot accept the argument that this was a mere executive or administrative act on his part. Then, what is the result of that? In my judgment, it must, at least, invalidate the whole of the proceedings on the first charge."[20]

Express provision for discipline

It follows from the application of contractual principles that the union has no power to discipline nor terminate the contract of membership save to the extent that such powers are conferred by the contract. In *Spring* v. *National Amalgamated Stevedores and Dockers Society*[21] the defendant union had recruited members who had previously been members of the Transport and General

---

[19] (1966) 1 K.I.R. 679.

[20] Although most other common law jurisdictions are reluctant to imply terms and adopt the same rule concerning the need for the rules to cover the offence, some are more willing to excuse minor defects, *e.g. Reilly* v. *Hogan* 32 NYS 2d 864 (1942); *Margolis* v. *Burke* 53 NYS 2d 157 (1945); *Stephen* v. *Stewart* [1944] 1 D.L.R. 305.

[21] [1956] 1 W.L.R. 585.

Workers Union. The latter union protested to the T.U.C. Disputes Committee that this practice was contrary to the Bridlington Agreement.[22] The Disputes Committee ordered the N.A.S.D. to exclude the new recruits and that union purported to do so despite their refusal to leave voluntarily. Some of the individuals affected brought an action in the Lancaster Chancery Court seeking to prohibit the N.A.S.D. from excluding them. Sir Leonard Stone V.-C. refused, on the basis of the test in *Shirlaw* v. *Southern Foundries (1926) Ltd.*[23]— the "Oh, of course" test—to imply into the individual contract of membership a provision allowing the union to act in compliance with the Bridlington Agreement.

As we have seen in considering the structure of the contract of employment this, and the business efficacy, tests are notoriously misapplied by the courts so as to allow them to achieve a result which, in their opinion, is "reasonable." It may be as well therefore that the tests are rarely applied in trade union law largely because the courts do not wish to expand the powers of the unions by implication. Nevertheless it is worth pointing out that the way in which the learned Vice-Chancellor applied the test was, probably deliberately, naive. He supposed, probably correctly, that if the plaintiff had been asked whether he intended to include a reference to the Bridlington Agreement in his contract of membership he would have asked "What's that?" The significant question, of course, is what his reply would have been when that explanation was forthcoming. The court is on firmer ground when it rejects implication of a power to expel members in compliance with the Bridlington Agreement on the ground that the Agreement is intended only as a morally binding code regulating the relations of trade unions *inter se* and that it contains no reference to a power of expulsion.[23a]

Reluctance to imply terms

On the few other occasions when they have considered the possibility of implication of terms into the contract of membership the courts have been no more adventurous. In *Radford* v. *National Society of Operative Printers, Graphical and Media Personnel*[24] the plaintiff had been made redundant under the terms of an agreement between his union and the employer which, *inter alia*, provided that those dismissed should have the choice of either receiving redundancy payment or leaving the industry altogether. The plaintiff refused alternative employment in the industry, despite an instruction from the union branch committee to take it, and claimed both a redundancy payment and the right to seek work in the industry. On hearing that he had consulted a solicitor in connection with this claim the union asked the plaintiff to produce his correspondence with that solicitor. He refused and was informed that he had taken action against the union which had "voided" his membership under a union rule stating that "Any action taken against the [union] by individual members, or members acting collectively, . . . shall be declared a wilful breach of rules, and shall void the membership of the member or members so acting." Plowman J. considered the argument of counsel that, quite apart from the express rule, the

---

[22] *Supra*, p. 409.
[23] [1939] 2 All E.R. 113.
[23a] See the judgment of Bingham J. in *Cheall* v. *APEX*, quoted *supra*, p. 412.
[24] [1972] I.C.R. 484 Ch.D.

plaintiff's action was in breach of an implied term that the plaintiff would act justly and faithfully in his dealings with the union and his fellow members thereof and would comply with all reasonable arrangements made between the union and employers and would accept all reasonable and proper directions from the union as to his dealings with employers. The learned judge continued:

> "It is not altogether clear what is the conduct of the applicant which is said to amount to a breach. In so far as it is conduct before May 23 it was in my opinion too late on May 23 to accept it as a repudiation because by treating the applicant as a member up to May 23 the branch committee must be taken to have already elected not to treat it as such. In so far as it is the applicant's conduct on May 23; in the first place that conduct is not, in my judgment, a breach of the alleged implied term. Secondly, it was not treated by the branch committee as a breach of any term of the contract except rule 20(13); and, thirdly, the branch committee was treating the contract as still alive for the purposes of applying clause 13. All this of course assumes that the contract contained an implied term such as is pleaded. In my judgment, however, no such term can be implied. In view of the very specific enumeration in rule 20 of the circumstances in which a member can be deprived of his membership by the union there is no scope or necessity for the implication of any additional obligation, for breach of which the applicant was liable to lose his membership."

This line of reasoning leaves open the possibility of implication of rules in a situation such as arose in *Abbott* v. *Sullivan*[25] where no formal rules existed at all. This situation might be considered to extend to cover matters as to which it was clear the rules made no provision but for which some substance or procedure was obviously required. "Business efficacy," if nothing else, would seem to justify implication in such a case. The courts have, with more justification, refused to imply a term to amend an express provision of the rules[26] or to permit the expression of a penalty to extend to include a lesser penalty.[27]

Substantive offences

Interpretation. The courts have consistently stated that since the jurisdiction is governed by contract they may construe the rule books which form the principal source of terms of that contract. They have also said that the rules must be construed strictly.[28] In *Lee* v. *Showmen's Guild of Great Britain*[29] the rule which was being considered permitted the Guild to fine members who were guilty of "unfair competition." The plaintiff had disregarded an instruction from the Guild to yield a site he had been allotted at the annual Bradford Fair to another member. The Court of Appeal held that this conduct was not capable of being described as unfair competition. Denning L.J. said:

---

[25] [1952] 1 K.B. 189.

[26] *Bonsor* v. *Musicians' Union* [1954] Ch. 479.

[27] *Burn* v. *National Amalgamated Labourers' Union* [1920] 2 Ch. 364; *Clarke* v. *Ferrie* [1926] N.I. 1. But compare *Santer* v. *National Graphical Association* [1973] I.C.R. 60.

[28] *Blackall* v. *National Union of Foundry Workers* (1923) 39 J.L.R. 431. In *Marley Tile Co. Ltd.* v. *Shaw* [1980] I.C.R. 72, Goff L.J. said, however, "the rules of a trade union are not to be construed like a statute. They grow by addition and amendment." He was, of course, not dealing with the rights of an individual member.

[29] [1952] 2 Q.B. 329. See also *Manders* v. *Showmen's Guild, The Times,* November 4, 1966; *Silvester* v. *N.U.P.B.P.W.* (1966) 1 K.I.R. 679.

"But the question still remains: To what extent will the courts intervene? They will, I think, always be prepared to examine the decision to see that the tribunal have observed the law. This includes the correct interpretation of the rules. Let me give an illustration. If a domestic tribunal is given power by the rules to expel a member for misconduct, such as here for 'unfair competition,' does that mean that the tribunal is the sole judge of what constitutes unfair competition? Suppose they put an entirely wrong construction on the words 'unfair competition' and find a member guilty of it when no reasonable person could so find, has not the man a remedy? I think he has, for the simple reason that he has only agreed to the committee exercising jurisdiction according to the true interpretation of the rules, and not according to a wrong interpretation. Take this very case. If the man is found guilty of unfair competition, the committee can impose a fine on him of a sum up to £250. Then, if he has not the money to pay, or, at any rate, does not pay, within one month, the man automatically ceases to be a member of the Guild: see r.14. To be deprived of membership in this way is a very severe penalty on a man. It means that he will be excluded from all the fair grounds of the country which are controlled by the Guild or its members: see. r.11(g)(ii) and r.15(a). This is a serious encroachment on his right to earn a livelihood, and it is, I think, not to be permitted unless justified by the contract into which he has entered. . . .

In most of the cases that come before such a domestic tribunal the task of the committee can be divided into two parts—(i) they must construe the rules; (ii) they must apply the rules to the facts. The first is a question of law which they must answer correctly if they are to keep within their jurisdiction. The second is a question of fact which is essentially a matter for them. The whole point of giving jurisdiction to a committee is so that they can determine the facts and decide what is to be done about them. The two parts of the task are, however, often inextricably mixed together. The construction of the rules is so bound up with the application of the rules to the facts that no one can tell one from the other. When that happens, the question whether the committee has acted within its jurisdiction depends, in my opinion, on whether the facts adduced before them were reasonably capable of being held to be a breach of the rules. If they were, then the proper inference is that the committee correctly construed the rules and have acted within their jurisdiction. If, however, the facts were not reasonably capable of being held to be a breach and yet the committee held them to be a breach, then the only inference is that the committee have misconstrued the rules and exceeded their jurisdiction. The proposition is sometimes stated in the form that the court can interfere if there was no evidence to support the finding of the committee, but that only means that the facts were not reasonably capable of supporting the finding.

My conclusion, therefore, is that the court has power in this case to intervene in the decision of the committee of the Showmen's Guild if no facts were adduced before them which could reasonably be considered to be 'unfair competition' within r.15(c) which says that

'No member of the Guild shall indulge in unfair competition with regard to the renting, taking or letting of ground or position.'"

A similar approach was adopted by Templeman J. in *Esterman* v. *National and Local Government Officers Association*.[30] The plaintiff was threatened with expulsion as being "unfit" to be a member of the union. She had disobeyed an instruction from the union by using her spare time to assist the returning officer in local government elections. The learned judge concluded that there were many good reasons why an individual might decide not to obey such an

---

[30] [1974] I.C.R. 625.

instruction or might go so far as to consider she had a public duty to disobey. The concept of unfitness, therefore, could not extend to cover her conduct.

Similar reasoning would apply to any discipline based upon an instruction *ultra vires* the union's rule. So, if the union had power to order a strike where there was an "industrial dispute" the courts would be free to interpret the meaning of that term and might well be led to adopt a definition derived from statute.[31] It is submitted that not only does this approach make no allowance for the problem solving approach of unions to the application of their rules but it runs the risk that the understanding of the parties as to the meaning of the words will be overlooked. It is interesting to note that both these dangers were avoided by Melford-Stevenson J. in *Santer* v. *N.G.A.*[32] He used the very looseness of drafting of the rules to justify a much wider view of their meaning than the courts commonly allow.

Public policy. In addition to their power of interpretation the courts have, in more recent decisions, established power to invalidate a discipline rule on grounds of public policy in exactly the same way as they have challenged admission rules. In the case of discipline, of course, this approach produces the significant difference that the successful plaintiff remains a member of the union whereas the invalidity of admission rules needs to be supported by a further development of public policy if it is to provide the desired remedy. In *Edwards* v. *Society of Graphical and Allied Trades*[33] the plaintiff was informed that his membership had automatically terminated because he was in arrears with his dues. This default had only occurred because a union official had failed to take the necessary steps to see that the dues were checked off from his wages. The union argued *inter alia* that under its rules it had power to terminate membership in its unfettered discretion. Sachs L.J. said:

> "The courts have always protected a man against any unreasonable restraint on his right to work even if he has bargained that right away, and it matters not whether the bargain is with an employer or with a society. A rule that in these days of closed shops entitles a trade union to withdraw the card of a capable craftsman of good character who for years has been a member, even if styled 'temporary' member, for any capricious reason such as (to mix conventional and practical examples) having incurred the personal enmity, for non-union reasons, of a single fellow member, the colour of his hair, the colour of his skin, the accent of his speech, or the holding of a job desired by someone not yet a member, is plainly in restraint of trade. At common law it is equally clearly unreasonable so far as the public interest is concerned. Is it then protected by either s.3 or s.4 of the Trade Union Act 1871? It cannot be said that a rule that enabled such capricious and despotic action is proper to the 'purposes' of this or indeed of any trade union. It is thus not protected by s.3 and is moreover *ultra vires*. Nor can I find any protection for it in s.4. It is thus void as in restraint of trade."

This proposition may now, however, be doubtful in the light of the admission by Lord Denning M.R. in *British Actors Equity Association* v. *Goring*[34] that he had gone too far[35] in suggesting that union rules could be invalidated if they were unreasonable.

---

[31] See *Sherard* v. *A.U.E.W.* [1973] I.C.R. 421.
[32] [1973] I.C.R. 60.
[33] [1971] Ch. 354.
[34] [1977] I.C.R. 393.   [35] In *Bonsor* v. *Musicians' Union* [1954] Ch. 479.

The normal approach of the courts leads many trade unionists to wonder whether there is any limit to the power of the courts to disallow union rules. The answer, it is submitted, must be that in the great majority of cases the issue is clear and the courts would, if the matter were brought to them, allow the union to proceed. In *Kelly* v. *National Society of Operative Printers' Assistants*[36] there can be little doubt that had the evidence established that the practice adopted by the plaintiff of undertaking two separate full time employments did constitute him a danger to his fellow printers he might properly have been expelled for conduct detrimental to the interests of the society. The problem is that the statement in *Roebuck* v. *National Union of Mineworkers*[37] that "what is or is not to the detriment of the interests of the union is a matter which is essentially within the knowledge of the members and officers of the union" is not characteristic of the actual practice of the courts. In *Esterman's* case the union would be somewhat surprised to discover that it could not reasonably consider one who refused an instruction to withdraw her labour as a person unfit for membership. The union might have argued that the court had regard to the reactions of an individual in the abstract and that if these reactions were regarded as those of a union member involved in a pay dispute the reasonableness of imposing restrictions on freedom of action becomes much more obvious. There is obviously a marked difference of opinion not only as to whether conduct unrelated to the objects of the union can bring it into discredit[38] but also as to the criterion for determining what is unrelated.

Most unions have at some time thought it worthwhile to include in their rules the provision that the existence of an offence shall be "in the opinion of" the appropriate committee. This qualification seems to have no effect on the application of the law. In *Lee's* case Somervell L.J. pointed out that in club and professional cases where a code of ethics was being considered the opinion of the body imposing that code would be dominant. This, however, seems to be a semantic distinction. The ethics of union membership are no less real for being unwritten and not attached to a profession. The only real distinction, it is suggested, is that between private clubs and organisations controlling trade. In the former, as a matter of policy, the courts may be prepared not to interfere with the members' selection of whom they associate with. Romer L.J. was, therefore, on firmer ground when he emphasised the seriousness of expulsion from a trade union and said:

> "I should require the use of clear language before I was satisfied that members of any body such as the defendant guild had agreed to leave exclusively to a domestic tribunal powers which it had neither the knowledge nor experience to use and which, if misused (however honestly), might have such serious consequences for the members."

Conversely, in what would now be the unusual case of a blanket offence not expressed to be a matter for opinion the courts would not interfere if in their view a reasonable tribunal, acting bona fide, could reach that decision.[39] This

---

[36] (1915) 31 T.L.R. 632.
[37] [1977] I.C.R. 573.
[38] See *Wolstenholme* v. *Amalgamated Musicians' Union* [1920] 2 Ch. 388.
[39] See, *e.g. Esterman* v. *NALGO* [1974] I.C.R. 625.

leaves little if any scope for the suggestion[40] that a union might reasonably reach such a conclusion even if fuller explanation might have removed the discredit.

On the other hand there has recently been some indication that the courts themselves feel they may have been too dismissive of the ability of a union properly to conduct its own affairs. In *Roebuck* v. *N.U.M.*[41] it was said that the courts should not lightly come to the conclusion that no reasonable tribunal could have reached the decision the union has arrived at. If the remarks of Denning M.R. in *British Actors Equity Association* v. *Goring*[42] that the courts should do everything they can to construe union rules as reasonable lend support to the approach adopted in *Esterman* v. *NALGO*[43] at least they also suggest the removal of invalidity as a proper purpose of such a construction. If the words of the judgment in *Cheall* v. *APEX*[44] are extended to disciplinary expulsion they would go a long way to permit the union to express a valid opinion as to what was in its own interest.

Procedure

Fairness. Although the normal principle of contract that custom may not override an express term was applied to the contract of union membership in *Bonsor* v. *Musicians' Union*[45]; it is common for customary practices to supplement disciplinary procedure. Nevertheless the courts will construe procedural rules as painstakingly as they do substantive rules. Their approach is typified in the judgment of Melford Stevenson J. in *Santer* v. *National Graphical Association*[46]:

> "Rule 38 lays down the procedure which has to be followed in the event of any contravention of the rules of the union. It says that:
>
> '(1) All allegations of contravention of these rules by a member shall be investigated by the committee of the branch to which for the time being the member belongs. The member concerned shall have the right at any such investigation to answer the charge, either in writing or in person, and call witnesses. The chapel officers concerned in the charge shall be present. The branch committee shall either dismiss the charge or, if they consider the charge proved, communicate their decision and the penalty recommended to the member and to the executive council. In so communicating their decision and recommendation, the branch committee shall make clear to the member that, provided he notifies the branch secretary within seven days of his desire so to do, he has the right to answer the charge before the executive council, in writing or in person, and to call witnesses. The executive council shall then investigate the charge and recommendation and, when the member has notified his desire to answer the charge and in fact attends with or without witnesses when called upon so to do, or sends to the executive council a written answer after hearing the member and his witnesses, if any, or considering any written answer, either dismiss the charge or impose the penalty

---

[40] See *Evans* v. *National Union of Printing, Bookbinding and Paper Workers* [1938] 4 All E.R. 51.

[41] [1977] I.C.R. 573.

[42] [1977] I.C.R. 393.

[43] *Supra.*

[44] [1982] I.R.L.R. 91.

[45] [1956] A.C. 105.

[46] [1973] I.C.R. 60; see also *Hiles* v. *Amalgamated Society of Woodworkers* [1968] Ch. 440.

recommended by the branch or any other penalty permitted by these rules as it sees fit. No penalty shall be imposed except by the executive council whose decision shall be final.'

Applying my mind as best I can to those two rules and in particular to rule 38, it is quite plain that rule 38 contemplates the formulation of a charge against a member when it appears that an offence against union rules has been committed. I can find no other explanation of the phrase in rule 38 (1) 'answer the charge,' and I think that it follows that a charge having been formulated—the rule does not say 'in writing' but it is, at least, desirable it should be—that the member has an opportunity to consider and prepare any defence he thinks he may have to the charge, and I cannot interpret the word 'investigated' in the second line of rule 38a(1) except by saying that it must contemplate an investigation by the committee in the presence of a member who has had an opportunity to prepare any answer he may wish to make to the charge formulated against him, and I am equally satisfied that in the present case the steps to which I have referred were not taken. I have no doubt that the committee did decide to recommend expulsion, but I am quite satisfied on the balance of probabilities on the evidence of the plaintiff as against the evidence of Mr. Nash and Mr. Donkin that not only did they not properly communicate their decision to the plaintiff, but that the committee did not make clear to him that provided he notified the branch secretary within seven days of his desire to do so, he had the right to answer the charge before the executive council in writing or in person, and to call witnesses. It follows that what, in my view, is a vital part of rule 38 was not observed. He was not told of his right to appeal and there was not the equivalent notice of appeal in seven days such as the rules contemplate, and there is no evidence before me to suggest (indeed, the indications are all to the contrary) that the executive council to whom the recommendation of the committee was communicated ever investigated the matter at all."

Whatever procedural rules or practices the union may apply they must observe what has traditionally been called "the rule of natural justice." More recently the courts have taken to describing this procedural requirement simply as "fairness."[47] Essentially what is required is that anybody making a decision which will directly affect an individual's rights and freedoms must give that person a fair and impartial hearing. A great deal of detail may be added to this outline which will vary with the circumstances to meet the basic concept of fairness.

The basis for the imposition of this requirement has considerably developed over the years. Originally it was attached to the concept of property rights because it originated in equitable jurisdictions which had established the principle that equitable remedies were not available to protect purely personal interests.[48] Protection of property rights became the theoretical basis of the entire jurisdiction over membership rights.[49] Following *Cooper* v. *Wandsworth Board of Works*[50] it was regarded as established that natural justice would apply to all judicial and quasi-judicial procedures. The House of Lords in *Ridge* v. *Baldwin*[51] accepted the then well-established criticism that such could not be

---

[47] See, *e.g. Breen* v. *Amalgamated Engineering Union* [1971] 2 Q.B. 175; *McInnes* v. *Onslow Fane* [1978] 3 All E.R. 211.

[48] *Gee* v. *Pritchard* (1818) 2 Swans 402.

[49] *Rigby* v. *Connel* (1880) L.R. 14 Ch.D. 482 although Jessel M.R. referred to it as a very technical ground.

[50] (1863) 14 C.B. (N.S.) 180.

[51] [1964] A.C. 40.

the test for the requirement of natural justice since all it provided was that when there was a hearing that hearing should be fair. That decision preferred to base the requirement on the existence of power to impose a penalty or deprive of a right. In its particular application to trade union discipline this principle was expressed in *Stevenson* v. *United Road Transport Union*[52] to apply "where one party has a discretionary power to terminate the tenure or enjoyment by another of an employment or an office or a post or a privilege [and] that power [is] conditional upon the party invested with the power being first satisfied upon a particular point which involves investigating some matter upon which the other party ought in fairness to be heard or to be allowed to give his explanation or put his case." In other cases the basis for the requirement had been stated even more widely,[53] but subjected to discretionary limitations inherent in so broad a concept as "fairness" and to a distinction between adjudication and administration.[54] The first instance decision in *Cheall* v. *APEX*[55] breaks entirely new ground so far as trade union affairs are concerned in suggesting that natural justice is not required when its presence is unlikely to affect the result.

Exclusion of natural justice.

It is clear, therefore, that this requirement is a rule of law.[56] Only common law courts obsessed with founding the jurisdiction on contract could have involved themselves in argument as to whether the requirement could be excluded by express provision in the contract of membership.[57] It is submitted that the rules are not implied into the contract but are extraneous to it and so cannot be excluded by it. Whether or not this is the correct explanation it is now clear that the courts deny any power to exclude "natural justice" by contract. Lord Denning M.R. has consistently so asserted and did so as early as 1949 in the case of *Russell* v. *Duke of Norfolk*.[58] In *Radford* v. *NatSOPA*[59] Plowman J. stated categorically that a rule providing for automatic forfeiture of membership as a disciplinary measure without the necessity of charge and hearing would be *ultra vires* and void.[60] Doubts expressed in earlier cases[61] and repeated as late as *Lawlor* v. *Union of Post Office Workers*[62] can now, it is submitted, be regarded as resolved.

This does, however, pose a problem. In *Edwards* v. *SOGAT*[63] the Court of Appeal applied this principle of the non-exclusion of natural justice to a case in

---

[52] [1977] I.C.R. 893.
[53] See, *e.g. R.* v. *Gaming Board for Great Britain, ex parte Benaim* [1970] 2 Q.B. 417; *Pearlberg* v. *Varty* [1972] 2 All E.R. 6; *Re Liverpool Taxi Owners' Association* [1972] 2 All E.R. 589.
[54] *e.g. Glynn* v. *Keele University* [1971] 1 W.L.R. 487; *Breen* v. *Amalgamated Engineering Union* [1971] 2 Q.B. 175.
[55] [1982] I.R.L.R. 91.
[56] See *Breen* v. *Amalgamated Engineering Union, supra, per* Denning M.R.
[57] See *Roebuck* v. *National Union of Mineworkers* [1977] I.C.R. 573.
[58] [1949] 1 All E.R. 109. See also *Lee* v. *Showmen's Guild of Great Britain* [1952] 2 Q.B. 329 at 341; *Abbott* v. *Sullivan* [1952] 1 K.B. 189 at 198; *Bonsor* v. *Musicians' Union* [1954] Ch. 479 at 485–486.
[59] [1972] I.C.R. 484. See also *Hiles* v. *Amalgamated Society of Woodworkers* [1968] Ch. 440.
[60] But see *Cheall* v. *APEX* [1982] I.R.L.R. 91 where Bingham J., at first instance would only disallow a rule compelling absence of procedure.
[61] *e.g. McLean* v. *The Workers Union* (1929) 1 Ch. 602 at 623–624.
[62] [1965] Ch. 712.
[63] [1971] Ch. 354.

which non-payment of dues was in issue. If the court will not normally consider the idea of repudiatory breach which has only to be accepted[64] they are bound to face difficulty in explaining the nature of termination for non-payment as anything but a form of discipline attracting natural justice. On the other hand, as we have seen, it is common to treat non-payment as a form of resignation, and the need to offer a hearing in each case would impose a severe burden.[65] It seems clear in practice that unions do not commonly afford a hearing in such situations. The explanation the courts might reasonably apply if they chose would be that if natural justice has become fairness there is nothing unfair in acting without a hearing on the undisputed fact of non-payment in applying the only available specific penalty of termination. This would be to go along the line developed by Industrial Tribunals when dealing with the procedural aspects of unfair dismissal. The language of some judgments suggests little acceptance of this course. So Lord Denning M.R. in *Edwards* v. *SOGAT* said:

"Just think. A man may fall into arrears without any real fault of his own. It may be due to an oversight on his part, or because he is away sick, or on holiday. It may be due, as here, to the union's own fault in not forwarding the 'check-off' slip. . . . No union can stipulate for automatic exclusion of a man without giving him an opportunity of being heard. . . ."

Nevertheless, exactly this argument was used to check but not abolish the power of tribunals to dispense with natural justice in dismissal situations in *Williams* v. *Compair Maxam Ltd.*[66]

Notice

It is quite clear that the common law requires notice of charges.[67]

Briefly, the Industrial Relations Act 1971 imposed a requirement of written notice of a charge, allowing sufficient time for the preparation of a defence.[68] With the repeal of this provision, however, the law reverts to the far less precise requirements of the common law. It is possible to argue that in certain circumstances it would only be possible to achieve fairness by a written charge but there is no reported case where writing has been required.[69] The common law, however, did require notice in time to prepare a defence although in *Stevenson* v. *United Road Transport Union*[70] it was said that there might be cases so uncomplicated that natural justice would not require particular notice of the charge.

Differing views were expressed by the members of the Court of Appeal in *Abbott* v. *Sullivan*[71] as to the necessary content of the notice. Only Morris L.J. however, was prepared to go so far as to state that a failure to communicate the essential facts to the accused, who certainly knew them already, would invalidate the procedure. Denning L.J. held that the notice was inadequate in the

---

[64] *Supra*, p. 415.
[65] But see the Code of Practice which suggests that any exclusion without procedure should be regarded as unreasonable.
[66] [1982] I.R.L.R. 83, *supra*, p. 213.
[67] *Annamunthodo* v. *Oilfield Workers' Trade Union* [1961] A.C. 945.
[68] s.65(8)(a).
[69] But see Morris L.J. in *Abbott* v. *Sullivan* [1952] 1 K.B. 189 at 211.
[70] [1977] I.C.R. 893.
[71] [1952] 1 K.B. 189.

circumstances but Evershed M.R. was inclined to regard it as sufficient.[72] In *Payne* v. *E.T.U.*[73] personal knowledge was allowed to supplement the notice as it was in *Russell* v. *Duke of Norfolk*.[74] In *Wolstenholme* v. *Amalgamated Musicians' Union*[75] Eve J. accepted a charge, in the terms of the rules, of "conduct detrimental to the interests of the union" as sufficient.

It must follow that a charge cannot be changed without fresh, and adequate, notice and the Privy Council so held in *Annamunthodo* v. *Oilfield Workers' Trade Union*.[76] In *Russell* v. *Duke of Norfolk*,[77] however, Tucker L.J., it is submitted incorrectly, excused the absence of notice of the specific charge because no specific charge had emerged before the hearing. He may, however, have been influenced by the fact that the appellant had shown himself aware of the nature of the charge.

An entirely separate aspect of notice, often apparently overlooked, is the requirement that notice must be given to all members of the tribunal. In *Young* v. *Ladies' Imperial Club*[78] the Court was uncompromising in its requirement that notice specifying the business must be sent to members if it would be physically possible for the person to attend and that failure to notify one member would invalidate an otherwise unanimous decision. It has been said that the same result will follow if notice is despatched but not received.[79]

Hearing

The hearing is the opportunity for the accused either to deny the charges or invoke mitigating circumstances. We have seen that the courts, dealing with allegations of unfair dismissal, have on occasion not enforced the requirement of a hearing when they have concluded that the accused would not be able to say anything that would alter the decision. It seems difficult, however, to say with certainty in any situation that no mitigating circumstance could be advanced.[80]

In unfair dismissal we have also seen that it is not uncommon in practice for the accused not to be present throughout the hearing and that it seems to be assumed that this absence may be excused if his "representatives" are permitted to attend, notwithstanding that they may have more than his individual interests to consider.[81]

The prima facie right to be heard before the imposition of discipline is well established in all common law jurisdictions but it is equally clear that strict judicial procedures are not required. The detailed requirements of the hearing may well vary from case to case. Wherever there is likely to be a significant dispute as to the evidence, however, it is submitted that the accused has the

---

[72] See also *Davis* v. *Carew-Pole* [1956] 1 W.L.R. 833; *Ridge* v. *Baldwin* [1962] 2 W.L.R. 716 at 734.
[73] *The Times*, April 14, 1960.
[74] [1949] 1 All E.R. 109. Strangely enough the much earlier case of *Innes* v. *Wylie* (1844) 1 Car. and K. 257 at 262–263 provided a detailed and strict requirement as to the content of notice.
[75] [1920] 2 Ch. 388.
[76] [1961] A.C. 945.
[77] *Supra*.
[78] [1920] 2 K.B. 523.
[79] *Leary* v. *National Union of Vehicle Builders* [1971] Ch. 34.
[80] *Parker* v. *Clifford Dunn Ltd.* [1979] I.C.R. 463. Compare *Conway* v. *Matthew Wright and Nephew Ltd.* [1977] I.R.L.R. 89, where it could be said to be clear that the employee did not intend to plead mitigation, with *Carr* v. *Alexander Russell Ltd.* [1976] I.T.R. 39.
[81] *Gray Dunn and Co. Ltd.* v. *Edwards* [1980] I.R.L.R. 23.

right, either personally or through his representatives, to confront his accusers.[82] On the other hand it would go too far to say that there must be a right to cross-examine.[83] Indeed, in *Breen* v. *A.E.U.*[84] it was considered that in some circumstances a purely written "hearing" would suffice.

Bias

The primary requirement of a fair hearing is that it should be before an impartial tribunal. Since all courts accept the fact that preconceptions are inevitable and look rather for evidence of a closed mind it is submitted that the test most often cited in the books[85] of whether a member could reasonably be suspected of bias goes too far. Whilst it is clear that courts look for the appearance, rather than the proved existence, of bias it is submitted that it is the appearance of a "real likelihood" rather than a suspicion which is significant. In *R.* v. *Barnsley Licensing Justices*[86] Devlin L.J. said:

"We have not to inquire what impression might be left on the minds of the present applicants or on the minds of the public generally. We have to satisfy ourselves that there was a real likelihood of bias—not merely satisfy ourselves that that was the sort of impression that might reasonably get abroad. The term 'real likelihood of bias' . . . is used to show that it is not necessary that actual bias should be proved . . . 'Real likelihood' depends on the impression which the court gets from the circumstances in which the justices were sitting . . . Bias is or may be an unconscious thing and a man may honestly say that he is not actually biased and did not allow his interest to affect his mind, although, nevertheless, he may have allowed it unconsciously to do so."

Nevertheless some conduct will inevitably incline a court to regard bias as likely. In *Roebuck* v. *N.U.M.*[87] Templeman J. said:

"In the present case, the fact that there was an overlap between the membership of the executive committee and the area council seems to me to be irrelevant. In this kind of domestic tribunal that must happen and is acceptable. But it is to be observed that the test is the likelihood of bias; in *Hannan* v. *Bradford Corporation*, Cross L.J. said,[88]

'If a reasonable person who has no knowledge of the matter beyond knowledge of the relationship which subsists between some members of the tribunal and one of the parties would think that there might well be bias, then there is in his opinion a real likelihood of bias. Of course, someone else with inside knowledge of the characters of the members in question, might say: "Although things don't look very well, in fact there is no real likelihood of bias." That, however, would be beside the point, because the question is not whether the tribunal will in fact be biased, but whether a reasonable man with no inside knowledge might well think that it might be biased.'

---

[82] *e.g. Willard* v. *N.U.P.B.P.W., The Times*, May 29, 1938; *Payne* v. *E.T.U., The Times*, April 14, 1960.

[83] See de Smith, *Administrative Hearings in English Law*, 68 Harv. L.R. at 58 (1955).

[84] [1971] 2 Q.B. 175. Compare *Payne* v. *E.T.U., The Times* April 14, 1960.

[85] Derived from *Allinson* v. *General Council of Medical Education and Registration* [1894] 1 Q.B. 750 at 758–759.

[86] [1960] 2 Q.B. 167 at 183 following *R.* v. *Tempest* (1902) 86 L.T. 585.

[87] [1978] I.C.R. 676.

[88] See Paul Jackson (1971) 34 M.L.R. 445.

That seems to me an answer to the plea of Mr. Turner-Samuels that the trial ought to take place so that one can find out exactly what happened at the relevant meetings; what the members of the various tribunals thought; what the plaintiffs, Mr. Roebuck and Mr. O'Brien thought and said; and whether in fact, despite the appearance, justice, or rough justice, was done.

As I have said already, a man before a tribunal of this kind must put up with the fact that as members of the union, and as officers, the members of the tribunal itself are rightly and properly concerned to uphold the union and its officers. But Mr. Scargill was in a different position from which the likelihood of bias was plain and evident. It is not sufficient to satisfy either the court or the (and I use Mr. Turner-Samuels' adjective) robust members of the trade union, that justice, or rough justice, was meted out to Mr. Roebuck and Mr. O'Brien. The fact is that even a guilty man is entitled to a proper tribunal and a tribunal is not properly constituted if the chairman has been personally involved and is likely to be biased, consciously or unconsciously. It is no answer to say, or prove, that Mr. Scargill in fact had no influence on the result."

In *Breen* v. *A.E.U.*[89] Lord Denning M.R. seems to have thought that vitiating bias could arise from the fact of believing incorrect evidence even if that belief is simply communicated to the tribunal by a non-voting official.

"Mr. Townsend certainly was influenced by the bad reason. He wrote it down in the letter. He repeated it later, saying to the plaintiff: 'You had the money Brother.' I expect the judge thought that Mr. Townsend's state of mind did not matter because he had no vote. But I think it mattered a lot. He was the district secretary, a paid official, there permanently. The others were elected annually. They came and went. He stayed on. He knew all about the episode in 1958. It was his job to know it. It is true that he had no vote, but he had a voice and he had a pen. The judge finds that there was little discussion at the meeting, but I would venture to ask: were there not private discussions beforehand? We know that does happen in the most sophisticated committees. Things are often decided beforehand so as to save discussion and dissension at the meeting itself."

Edmund-Davies L.J. in the majority on this question, makes it clear that this suggestion arises from the courts' belief that the person so influenced did not have an honest belief that the evidence was accurate. It is then clear that the bias in that case derived from the "well-established hostility" towards the accused. Even this proposition poses problems. In *White* v. *Kuzych*[90] the Privy Council warned of the inevitability of a certain amount of ill-feeling. What the court is really looking for is either a closed mind or significant influence from factors not relevant to the charge in hand.

"Whatever correct details may be, their Lordships are bound to conclude that there was, before and after the trial, strong and widespread resentment felt against the respondent by many in the union and that Clark, among others, formed and expressed adverse views about him. If the so-called 'trial' and the general meeting which followed had to be conductd by persons previously free from all bias and prejudice, this condition was certainly not fulfilled. It would, indeed, be an error to demand from those who took part the strict impartiality of mind with which a judge should approach and decide an issue between two litigants—that 'icy impartiality of a Rhadamanthus' which Bowen L.J., in *Jackson* v. *Barry Rly Co* thought could not be expected of the engineer-arbitrator—or to regard as disqualified from acting

---

[89] *Supra.*
[90] [1951] A.C. 585.

any members who had held and expressed the view that the 'closed shop' principle was essential to the policy and purpose of the union. What those who considered the charges against the respondent and decided whether he was guilty ought to bring to their task was a will to reach an honest conclusion after hearing what was urged on either side and a resolve not to make up their minds beforehand on his personal guilt, however firmly they held their conviction as to union policy and however strongly they had shared in previous adverse criticism of the respondent's conduct."

So it is that peculiar personal interests will almost always lead to a conclusion of disqualifying bias. This applies particularly to direct financial interest, however small.[91] The mere possibility of deriving an indirect economic advantage from a decision one way or another will not suffice[92] otherwise no trade union tribunal would ever be qualified to consider allegations of financial default. Personal interest is less common but a good example occurred in *Roebuck* v. *National Union of Mineworkers* (*Yorkshire Area*) (*No.* 2).[93] The union area president, acting on behalf of the union, had successfully sued a newspaper for libel. Two union members had given evidence for the newspaper and, at the instigation of the area president, were charged with conduct detrimental to the interests of the union. The area executive which had resolved to prefer the charges also found them proved and its decision was confirmed by the area council which had initially referred the matter to the executive. The area president was chairman of both bodies and participated in the proceedings, questioning the accused and taking part in the subsequent discussion, though he did not actually vote on the issue.

Templeman J. said:

"Mr. Roebuck and Mr. O'Brien were entitled to be tried by a tribunal whose chairman did not appear to have a special reason for bias, conscious or unconscious, against them. True it is that all the members of the executive committee and the area council, in common with all members of a domestic tribunal where the interests of their own organisation are at stake, have a general inclination to defend the union and its officers against attack from any source; this fact, every trade unionist and every member of a domestic organisation knows and accepts.

But Mr. Scargill had a special position, which clearly disqualified him from taking the part in the critical meetings of the executive committee and the area committee which he did take. I say that as a question of fact and not as a question of criticism. It is a fact that Mr. Scargill, as plaintiff, had clearly borne the heat and burden of the libel action. It is clear from the admissions that his cross-examination had been complicated and made difficult by the actions of Mr. Roebuck and Mr. O'Brien. It is clear that Mr. Scargill was a witness to what had happened and to what Mr. Roebuck and Mr. O'Brien had said and done in the course of the libel action in the High Court. Whether or not those actions of Mr. Roebuck and Mr. O'Brien, before and during the High Court proceedings, were detrimental to the interests of the union, it is quite plain that they must have been gall and wormwood to Mr. Scargill before, during and after the trial. Mr. Scargill was a plaintiff and a witness—an important witness—in the High Court proceedings. Then he reappeared as the complainant, the pleader, the prosecutor, the advocate and the chairman in the union proceedings, which followed swiftly. It is impossible to know

---

[91] *Dimes* v. *Grand Junction Canal Co.* (1852) H.L.C. 759.
[92] See *R.* v. *Barnsley Licensing Justices* [1960] 2 Q.B. 167.
[93] [1978] I.C.R. 676.

what would have happened if Mr. Scargill had recognised his impossible position and had not acted as he did. But his presence as chairman, and his conduct (admitted conduct) undoubtedly gave the impression that the dice were loaded against Mr. Roebuck and Mr. O'Brien. No amount of evidence can remove that impression, or establish affirmatively that the end result was unaffected by natural resentment and prejudice in the mind of Mr. Scargill for prolonging his cross-examination and jeopardising the success of the action which, true enough, affected the union, but in addition vitally affected Mr. Scargill as president of the union, and as a private individual, who had been libelled. Whether he recognised the fact or not, Mr. Scargill must inevitably have appeared biased against Mr. Roebuck and Mr. O'Brien. The appearance of bias was inevitable; the exercise of bias, conscious or unconscious, was probable. I am content to rest my judgment on the ground that it was manifestly unfair to Mr. Roebuck and Mr. O'Brien that Mr. Scargill should have acted as chairman, and should have played the part which he admits to have played at the relevant meetings of the executive committee and the area council.

The authorities support this approach. Although every case turns on its own facts, I can usefully adapt the words of Dixon J. in *Australian Workers' Union* v. *Bowen* (No. 2) (1948) 77 C.L.R. 601; the words which I adapt and vary slightly are at p. 631; and in the present instance would read as follows:

> 'It is not in accordance with the principles of natural justice to have as President of the tribunal a person who has promoted the charge and supports it as the prosecutor and who is inevitably biased against the accused as a result of his participation in the controversy . . .' "

The presence of a tribunal member disqualified by bias or bad faith will not invalidate the proceedings if he takes no part in them.[94]

Bad faith

Although bad faith is invariably referred to as a disqualifying element on its own there does not seem to be any reported case in which the invalidity of discipline rested on this factor without support from any other.[95] Rather, bad faith is usually a conclusion drawn from and, in turn, supporting other disqualifying defects. In the club case of *Dawkins* v. *Antrobus*[96] Brett L.J. assimilated bad faith to malice and it will be obvious that such an element is likely to appear as bias.

Appeal procedures

A large proportion of trade union rule books make provision for internal appeal. Where such provision is made the procedures must be complied with.[97] In *Silvester* v. *National Union of Printing, Bookbinding and Paper Workers*[98] the plaintiff had been censured for acting to the detriment of the union in refusing to do routine overtime which he was not contractually bound to undertake but which his chapel wished him to work. Goff J. held that since it

---

[94] *Lane* v. *Norman* (1891) 61 L.J.Ch. 149; *Leary* v. *National Union of Vehicle Builders* [1971] Ch. 34.

[95] See Lord Cooper in *Martin* v. *Scottish T.G.W.U.* 1951 S.C. 129 at 141.

[96] (1881) 17 Ch.D. 615.

[97] *Braithwaite* v. *Electrical Electronics and Telecommunications Union* [1969] 2 All E.R. 859; *Santer* v. *National Graphical Association* [1973] I.C.R. 60.

[98] (1966) 1 K.I.R. 679.

was not the clear policy of the union to encourage overtime working it could not be said to be detrimental to the union that a member should refuse to undertake such work. The plaintiff had appealed to the appeals committee of the national executive committee of the union against the instruction to do overtime. This appeal was unsuccessful and he then appealed to the final appeal court of the union. Meanwhile the plaintiff continued to disobey the instruction to do overtime and because of this failure the secretary of the appeals committee, without authority, withdrew the appeal. Goff J. held that the wrongful refusal of the right of appeal, even on one of a number of charges, placed the appellate tribunals in an impossible position from which they probably could not, but certainly did not, extricate themselves.

The unions might be forgiven for supposing that though they were bound strictly to follow their rules as to appeal procedures, the aggrieved member is not. It is logical enough to conclude that the act of appealing is not an affirmation of the union's actions. As was pointed out by the Privy Council in *Annamunthodo* v. *Oilfield Workers Trade Union*,[99] on the contrary, it is a disaffirmance. Nor, moreover, is the opportunity afforded by the appeal of a fair hearing a removal of the prejudice already suffered by the individual. It is less easy for the unions to understand, however, why, if the appeal body actually does grant a full rehearing the original basis of complaint can remain unaffected. In *Leary* v. *National Union of Vehicle Builders*[1] Megarry J. said:

"Now in the present case the hearing by the appeals council seems to me to have been in substance a complete rehearing, with the witnesses called and heard, and complete liberty of action for the plaintiff to present his case in full. Indeed, the members of the quite differently constituted branch committee might well have been put in some practical difficulty if they had been required to devote two days to disposing of the case. Nevertheless, it was not to the appeals council that the rules confided the issue of expulsion or no. It may be that the matter was properly brought before the appeals council by the combined effect of r. 2(13), r. 6(1) and the decision of the executive committee; but any such jurisdiction is merely appellate. If a man has never had a fair trial by the appropriate trial body, is it open to an appellate body to discard its appellate functions and itself give the man the fair trial that he has never had?

I very much doubt the existence of any such doctrine. Central bodies and local bodies often differ much in their views and approach; and the evidence before me certainly does not suggest that this is a union free from any such differences. Suppose the case of a member whose activities have pleased some of his fellow members in the locality but have displeased headquarters and other branches. Suppose further that in his absence, and so without hearing his explanations, a local committee is persuaded to expel him. Is it any answer to his complaint that he has not received the benefit of natural justice to say 'Never mind, one of the central bodies will treat your appeal as if it were an initial trial'? Can he not say 'I want to be tried properly and fairly by the only body with power under the rules to try me in the first place, namely, the local committee'? I appreciate that the appeals council is composed of members elected from each of the union's 12 divisions, and is not an emanation of the NEC or other central body; but I do not think that this affects the point.

That is not all. If one accepts the contention that a defect of natural justice in the trial body can be cured by the presence of natural justice in the appellate body, this

---

[99] [1961] A.C. 945.
[1] [1970] 2 All E.R. 713.

has the result of depriving the member of his right of appeal from the expelling body. If the rules and the law combine to give the member the right to a fair trial and the right of appeal, why should he be told that he ought to be satisfied with an unjust trial and a fair appeal? Even if the appeal is treated as a hearing de novo, the member is being stripped of his right to appeal to another body from the effective decision to expel him. I cannot think that natural justice is satisfied by a process whereby an unfair trial, although not resulting in a valid expulsion, will neverthe-less have the effect of depriving the member of his right of appeal when a valid decision to expel him is subsequently made. Such a deprivation would be a powerful result to be achieved by what in law is a mere nullity; and it is no mere triviality that might be justified on the ground that natural justice does not mean perfect justice. As a general rule, at all events, I hold that a failure of natural justice in the trial body cannot be cured by a sufficiency of natural justice in an appellate body."

Exclusion of jurisdiction

Equally anomalous from the viewpoint of insistence on the overriding force of the rules, but equally consistent with the judicial desire to maintain control over the nature of initial trial procedures, is the principle that the jurisdiction of the courts may not be excluded once the grievance exists, although the courts may in their discretion require internal appeals to be pursued before themselves intervening. It is clearly open to the parties to the contract of membership to make the internal tribunal the final arbiter of fact.[2] At one time it was widely thought that even if the provision of an internal appeal did not impliedly postpone the jurisdiction of the courts that effect could be achievd by an express provision. It was thought arguable that even though a contractual provision purporting to remove the jurisdiction of the courts totally would be void[3] such a provision would carry the valid implication of postponement of that jurisdic-tion. All these assumptions were destroyed by Goff J. in *Leigh* v. *National Union of Railwaymen*.[4]

"Counsel for the plaintiff concedes that he cannot, on the evidence on this motion, show cause why an express provision, if there be one, requiring that domestic remedies should be first utilised should be disregarded, and the defendants submit that the rules, and in particular r. 3(6) and r. 9(4), have that effect. I must therefore first determine whether this is so, and I am not prepared to accept that submission. The rules purport to exclude the jurisdiction of the court altogether and to that extent are void on the authority of *Lee* v. *Showmen's Guild of Great Britain*, but that is no reason for construing them as requiring recourse to the domestic tribunal first. The two things are inconsistent.

Then ought I, notwithstanding the absence of such a provision to refuse relief because the domestic remedies have not been adopted? In my judgment, on the facts of this case, I ought not. It is true that *Lawlor's* case was one of expulsion and infringment of the rules of natural justice and is therefore much stronger than the present. On the other hand, this is at least one of refusing the opportunity of election to an office of honour and profit and it is one turning on construction, which, as Ungoed-Thomas, J., observed in the passage I have quoted, is peculiarly appropriate for the court. Moreover, having regard to the decision in Bowman's case the plaintiff could not reasonably expect to succeed if at all by the domestic

---

[2] Denning L.J. in *Lee* v. *Showmen's Guild of Gt. Britain* [1952] 2 Q.B. 329 at 342.
[3] *Scott* v. *Avery* (1856) 25 L.J.Ex. 308.
[4] [1970] Ch. 326.

remedies short of an appeal to the annual general meeting, which would have meant driving the matter up to the very meeting at which the election should take place and so have left him virtually no chance of obtaining relief through the court until after the election. This would not as a matter of law prevent him from obtaining relief at all because he could apply to set it aside and for an injunction restraining the union and the successful candidate from acting on the vote, but it might well prejudice his position in fact on a subsequent election.

This in my judgment is not inconsistent with *White* v. *Kuzych*, where the Privy Council refused to act on the supposition that the domestic appellate court could not fairly try a submission that the tribunal of first instance was barred. Here the domestic tribunal is bound by the previous decision of the domestic court of appeal."

The learned judge advanced three basic propositions:
  (i) The court is not absolutely precluded by an express requirement in the rules that internal remedies should be exhausted before resort to the courts because its jurisdiction cannot be ousted. In such a situation, however, the plaintiff will have to demonstrate that the circumstances justify disregarding the contractual position.
 (ii) Where there is no such express requirement the courts may more readily intervene before exhaustion but may require the plaintiff first to exhaust internal remedies.[5]
(iii) A rule purporting to oust the jurisdiction of the courts is void and cannot be read as a valid requirement of exhaustion of remedies before resort to the courts.[6]

TRADE UNION GOVERNMENT

The attitude of the courts

Davies and Freedland[7] suggest that the legislature and the courts should seek to "maximise representativeness" of the machinery of union government. It may be in response to such a need that the legislature has made available funds to cover the expenses of conducting secret ballots in trade unions[8] and why the subsequent Code of Practice on Closed Shop Agreements and Arrangements sought[9] to confer a substantial benefit on the results of such a ballot. The two-edged nature of these provisions is clearly not what Davies and Freedland had in mind but it does reveal the proneness of such devices to influence from other factors. Quite apart from that danger there seems little justification for the suggestion that the courts should pursue any such objective. Nor, within any existing principle of law, does it appear that the courts could do so.

---

[5] These principles the learned judge extracted from the judgments in *White* v. *Kuzych* [1951] A.C. 585; *Lawlor* v. *Union of Post Office Workers* [1965] Ch. 712. The second of them was relied on in *Radford* v. *NatSOPA* [1972] I.C.R. 484 on the ground that the court was the most appropriate tribunal to decide matters concerning the construction of union rules and the sufficiency of evidence.

[6] See also Denning M.R. in *Enderby Town F.C.* v. *The Football Association* [1971] 1 All E.R. 215.

[7] At 561 *et seq*.

[8] See Employment Act 1980, s.1.

[9] See para. 54(*c*).

We have seen, however, that the purpose of the courts and that of the unions is widely at variance in the matter of regulating membership. This is partly because the courts see their function as the protection of contractual rights whilst the trade unions view the problem as one of the settlement of internal disputes. Partly it is because the courts place the interests of the individual before those of the group. A precisely similar variation of approach is seen in judicial handling of trade union government and it may well be reasonable to suggest that the pursuit of organisational efficiency, which the courts are not slow to recognise as a legitimate object of incorporated associations, could assume a more prominent place in their approach to the affairs of unincorporated associations of the importance of the modern trade union.

The present writer has suggested elsewhere[10] that there might well be value in positive legislative encouragement of particular aspects of trade union government. Again, however, it is difficult to see that much value or consistency would be derived from a similar judicial approach. Even if the courts could be supplied with sufficient information to understand the significance to the individual of the various levels of union government they would not be equipped to decide in favour of one rather than another. It may be, therefore, that the most that can be expected is that the courts should attempt to extract from the contract of membership the form of government that has been chosen and then endeavour to safeguard that choice. It is not the fault of the courts if this source fails to reveal matters vital in practice such as the unimportance of the branch and the significance of the workshop organisation.

Whatever may be the truth of this there is obviously room for a relaxation of the strict contractual approach applied to trade union affairs. In *Drake* v. *Morgan*[11] the national executive committee of a union was empowered to expend union funds to assist members in such legal matters as it deemed necessary to protect the interests of the union and in the payment of legal charges, costs and damages. That committee passed a resolution that the union would indemnify members in respect of fines imposed for picketing offences. Forbes J. resolved the matter in the following way:

> "The first argument of Mr. Melville Williams is that the resolution comes within the first sentence of rule 10(p), because (if I may abridge his argument) the N.E.C. is the sovereign authority and rule 10(1) gives them power to determine what is or what is not a purpose of the union. It is quite clear from the rules that the N.E.C. is intended to be the sovereign authority between annual delegate meetings and it is so described in rule 21(c): "Nothing in this rule shall derogate from the N.E.C.'s sovereign authority between A.D.M.'s." But as I read the first part of rule 10(1) the N.E.C. is only empowered to act on behalf of the union in accordance with the rules themselves. The committee is thus circumscribed by those rules. Indeed, in my view, the first sentence of rule 10(p) makes a deliberate distinction between the expenditure of money for union purposes, which must be purposes specified in the rules, and the expenditure for those purposes set out in (i) and (ii) over which the N.E.C. are to have an absolute discretion. I cannot find that the payment of fines for members is a purpose specified in the rules, so that the first sentence of rule 10(p) does not, in my view, cover these resolutions.
>
> Mr. Melville Williams somewhat tentatively advanced a proposition that the second sentence in rule 10(1) would cover these resolutions on the basis that by passing them the N.E.C. was effectively determining a question on which the rules

---

[10] *Power, Pickets and the Closed Shop* (1979) 32 C.L.P. at p. 212.
[11] [1978] I.C.R. 56.

were silent; but I think he virtually withdrew this point when it was pointed out that there was no evidence that the N.E.C. had ever purported to exercise an interpretative role, nor bent their intelligence to any question as to whether the rules were or were not silent on this point.

Both counsel accept that rule 10(p)(ii) cannot cover these resolutions: it refers in terms and only to legal charges, costs and damages and cannot, therefore, cover the payment of fines. But Mr. Melville Williams says that rule 10(p)(i) does cover the situation. The payment of a fine for a member must, he says, be assistance in a legal matter or proceeding and as long as the N.E.C., in its absolute discretion, deems it necessary to pay such a fine to protect the interests of the union, such a decision falls squarely within this sub-rule.

Mr. Still will not accept this. First he says you must read (i) and (ii) together and thus read (i) as a general provision which is particularised in (ii). I do not think this rule can be so read. It is clear that (i) and (ii) are intended to be two separate matters on which money can be expended by the N.E.C. in its absolute discretion. They are both concerned with legal matters and proceedings: (ii) specifically deals with legal charges, costs and damages; (i) is much wider and must be assumed to be dealing with matters other than those detailed in (ii). I can see no reason for excluding the payment of fines from the ambit of rule 10(p)(i) subject to one matter to which I shall have to return.

Mr. Still's other point is that it cannot be in the interests of the union that its members should be encouraged to break the law by having their fines paid, or that justices imposing penalties should increase them in the knowledge that the union was paying, or even impose penalties other than financial in order to hit the offender rather than the union. There is much force in this argument, but the rules, it seems to me, do not provide for intervention by the courts on this ground. A judge cannot substitute his judgment for that of the N.E.C. because the rules provide that it is the N.E.C. who shall have absolute discretion and be the sole judge of what is necessary to protect the interests of the union. It may be that if the N.E.C. decided to do that which no reasonable committee could possibly think was in the interests of the union the courts might interfere, but that is very far from being this case."

Similarly, in *British Actors Equity Association* v. *Goring*[12] the House of Lords had to consider the interaction of a rule providing for alteration of the rules by a two-thirds majority and a rule providing for the submission of any question to a referendum the majority vote in which would be binding. Lord Dilhorne stated that the purpose of the court was to construe the rules, like any other written document, so as to give the words a reasonable interpretation according with what the court thought must have been intended. Not one word of his judgment, however, indicates the consideration of evidence, other than that of the words themselves, as to this intention. Such an examination, common enough when construing the contract of employment, would have revealed a great deal of the understanding of the union and its membership as to how its structure and purpose might be served by one method or another.

Union office and elections

Administrative function

One of the principal unresolved aspects of the judicial approach to the administration of trade unions is whether, because it involves and reflects on the

---

[12] [1978] I.C.R. 791.

interests of individuals, that administration should be governed by the same extra-contractual procedural safeguards as are attached to discipline. It is obvious that many such decisions affecting individuals must be taken and that the government of the union would become impossible if all were to be subjected to natural justice. It is, therefore, perhaps surprising that the court hesitated in reaching the conclusion in *Brown* v. *Amalgamated Union of Engineering Workers*[13] that it was for the executive council to resolve the question of the length of the period of office of the plaintiff following his restoration to that office.

Walton J. said:

> "I find this a by no means easy point to resolve, but I start from this, that the rules are silent as to the date from which any successful candidate's term of office runs. That being so, the only way in which such commencement can be determined must, I think, be by the executive council in exercise of their powers under rule 15(18). In the present case on December 6, 1973, the general secretary of the union wrote to the plaintiff saying:

>> 'The executive council has now given further consideration to this matter and have decided that you should commence your three year period of office on January 7, 1974.'

> This appears to me to be perfectly valid administrative decision of the executive council which it was fully entitled to take. Accordingly, I think it means what it says, namely, that the three year term of office envisaged for the holder of the office of divisional organiser started, so far as the plaintiff is concerned, on January 7, 1974, and will therefore run until January 6, 1977. Having regard to the extremely democratic structure of the union, this was an administrative decision which might have been challenged within a period of eight weeks in the manner indicated in rule 20(2). That period having elapsed, it is now beyond challenge. I should note that Mr. Pain sought to put his case on this precise point on the question of estoppel. He said that the letter contained a representation made on behalf of the union on the faith of which his client acted to his detriment by giving up his previous employment and taking service with the union as a divisional organiser. I see the force of that, but I do not think this would have availed the plaintiff if the executive council had had no power under the rules to do what it in fact did. I do not think it is possible for a body to give itself power which it does not in fact have, via the doctrine of estoppel."

Cusack J. had had no hesitation in arriving at a similar conclusion in *Breen* v. *Amalgamated Engineering Union*[14] concerning the administrative nature of the process of approving the plaintiff's candidature for office, but the Court of Appeal overruled him and held that the decision entitled the plaintiff to be heard. Even if they do not go that far the courts will usually construe the union rules with care to ensure that the administrative action is not *ultra vires*.[15] As we have seen this may even extend to questioning the right of the union to make policy decisions. So, in *Esterman* v. *National and Local Government Officers Association*[16] it was said that:

---

[13] [1976] I.C.R. 147.

[14] [1971] 2 Q.B. 175.

[15] *Sherard* v. *Amalgamated Union of Engineering Workers* [1973] I.C.R. 421; *MacLelland* v. *National Union of Journalists* [1975] I.C.R. 116.

[16] [1974] I.C.R. 625.

"A member could take the view that action against the returning officers had never been submitted to a ballot and that whether or not a ballot was strictly necessary the national executive council, following the spirit as well as the letter of the instructions with regard to strikes, ought not to order, but rather—if they wished— to recommend, action against the returning officer. A member may have thought that such an order did not reasonably command obedience and that there was a possibility that it gave the appearance of coercing those who thought that action against the returning officers was not in the best interests of NALGO. He might take the view that, in all the extraordinary background of this case, he could not conscientiously accept an order given by the national executive council without a ballot or a fresh ballot against the wishes of the Minister and the secretary of the Trades Union Congress and in the existing national conditions, particularly since 100 per cent. obedience to the order of the national executive council would seem to imply that 100 per cent. of the members were firmly in support of the action which was being taken. A member might take the view that the national executive council order was an abuse of their powers, because, without any mandate by way of a ballot, it had the appearance, some might think, of seeking to wreck the local elections for the purpose of bringing pressure to bear on the Minister. A member might think that if the public thought that, then the reputation of NALGO might be irreparably damaged. In brief in my judgment, a member was entitled to take the view that this was an order which he might be under a positive duty to disobey. Of course, the suspicions or fears of a member that the national executive council had no power to issue the order aimed against the returning officers, or that the national executive council, even if they had the power, were misusing it and exercising it in a way objectionable to numbers of members and injurious to the reputation of NALGO, all those fears could be ill-founded. But, in my judgment, a member, faced with an order, was entitled to doubt. On the face of the order and the constitution and the rules and against all the background, there was a very large question mark hanging over the validity of the order and whether it was a proper order to issue even if there was power to do so.

Those doubts were due entirely to the insistence, as I have said no doubt bona fide and thought to be in the best interests of NALGO, but nevertheless the insistence, of the national executive council on taking a step which not only had never been put to a ballot but really was an extraordinary step to take, peremptorily ordering every member of NALGO to withdraw assistance from the local election, when what they were after dealt with London weighting allowance and they had no quarrel with the returning officers."

Elections

This extreme care is, however, erratic and piecemeal and its lack of consistent regulative effect is nowhere more apparent than in the conduct of union elections. Whereas most unions, with the exception of the printing trade unions, officially regard the shop floor organisation as an appendange of the hierarchy of union government so that most of them adopt Branch, District and National as the appropriate levels of government, there is little common detail in their rules. This is primarily because of the divergence of approach to such central issues as local autonomy and the accountability of officials. Some unions, for instance, appoint national executive officers, others elect either for relatively short periods at a time or, occasionally, until retirement. The amateur nature of local organisation undoubtedly results in a considerable amount of honest error in election procedures, much as it does in disciplinary procedure. In the case of election procedure, however, there is little or no opportunity for correcting, or even detecting, such error. The legislature has recently provided means to eliminate some of these defects encouraging resort to secret postal ballots by the provision of funds through the Certification Officer.[17] The scheme is intended to provide for reduced postal charges and the cost of printing and stationery and extends to election to any union office whether or not that office carries the status of an employee of the union. Regulation of its operation appears to be left to the chance of individual complaint in the six-week interval between application for, and payment of, the refund.

When they do deal with electoral irregularity the courts again apply to it the strict contractual approach characteristic of all their jurisdiction over the internal affairs of the unions.[18]

In *Leigh* v. *N.U.R.* the plaintiff had been nominated for office as President of his union. The general secretary refused to accept the nomination on the ground that, as a member of the Communist Party, the plaintiff would be unable to attend T.U.C. or Labour Party conferences. Goff J. said:

> "The plaintiff submits that r. 4(1) of the union's rules specifies the whole of the qualifications which a candidate for the office of president must have at the time of his nomination, and he supports this by reference to the fact that in other rules where provision is made for different offices the necessary qualifications are similarly expressly laid down. Prima facie, this appears to me to be correct, but the defendants argue that the matter is not so simple because something must be implied. First they submit that some general discretion arises under r. 4(2) from the reference there to approval of nominations. The second defendant puts it in his affidavit in this way:

>> 'Rule 4(2), imposes upon me in conformity with the general objects the administrative duty to approve the nomination and also to consider the issue of eligibility of any candidate for the Presidency of the Union.'

> The plaintiff says that I should not make any such implication and should confine the general secretary to the purely administrative and mechanical duty of checking that the nomination is correct on the face of it and that the candidate has the qualifications prescribed by r. 4(1). I accept that submission. There is not even a provision that nominations shall be approved. It is one stage removed in that circulars are not to be sent out until the nominations are approved. Moreover, once one goes beyond the narrow ground on which the plaintiff stands, I see nowhere to stop short of a discretion to review generally the suitability of the candidate, which may depend on all kinds of personal considerations. Further, this is not, as one often finds in rules of this kind, a power or discretion given to the executive committee or even a sub-committee. I do not think it would be right to make any such wide implication and I decline to do so.

> Then the defendants argue that, the duty imposed by r. 4(4) on the candidate, if elected, to attend the Trades Union Council and Labour Party conference implies that he must at the time of nomination be an individual member of the Labour Party because by its constitution unless he be such he will be ineligible to attend. Further, or alternatively, they ask me to imply that he must not be a member of any one of the large number of bodies proscribed by the Labour Party. Ought I to make any such implication? In my judgment the answer is 'No,' because it is not necessary to give to the contract contained in the rules business efficacy although it

---

[17] Employment Act 1980, ss.1 and 2 and The Funds for Trade Union Ballots Regulations 1980 (S.I. 1980 No. 1252).

[18] *Leigh* v. *National Union of Railwaymen* [1970] Ch. 326; *Breen* v. *Amalgamated Engineering Union* [1971] 2 Q.B. 175; *Watson* v. *Smith* [1941] 2 All E.R. 725.

may make it more efficient. The election does not take place for two or three months after the latest date for nominations, the successful candidate does not take office until 1st January next following, that is some six months later, and there is an interval after that before the first conference which he is required to attend. He therefore has a considerable time in which to obtain the required qualification for attendance, and he has some time before the election itself so that the electors can judge of the genuineness of his intention to join the Labour Party and the likelihood of success in that endeavour. Implication of additional requirements of eligibility over and above those expressed should not be made unless one is really driven to it, and in my judgment one is not. In my view the inability of the candidate at the moment of nomination if elected to perform his duties under r. 4(4), is a matter for the electors, not of his right to stand."

In *Brown* v. *Amalgamated Union of Engineering Workers*[19] Walton J. held that the union rules gave no power to avoid the result of an election, once that result had been declared, unless the whole election was a nullity.

Given this approach the courts are in no position to decline the application of any restrictive rule the union may possess unless they are prepared to regard the rule as ineffective or unreasonable.[20] Nevertheless they have been prepared to avoid this restriction by holding that the application of electoral rules amounts to the imposition of a penalty which may be *ultra vires* either because it is imposed by a body without disciplinary powers or because the grounds for exercise of those powers does not exist. In *Losinska* v. *Civil and Public Services Association*[21] the Court of Appeal affirmed the grant of an injunction restraining the union from publishing resolutions of the national executive committee deploring the conduct of a candidate for the Presidency. In *Breen* v. *A.E.U.*[22] the Court of Appeal supplemented the union rules as to qualification to stand for election with the requirements of natural justice.

There is little sign in this of any reflection of the judicial attitude to specific enforcement of the contract of service. It is true that the element of personal selection is missing from elected office but it seems more than arguable that where the authoritative organs of the union clearly express lack of confidence in an individual he may claim damages for any breach of contract resulting but may not seek to perform his office. Exceptionally, this was the view of Megarry J. in *Leary* v. *National Union of Vehicle Builders*.[23] The plaintiff had been full-time area organiser of the union for 14 years. At a meeting of his branch of which he had not been given notice and which he did not attend it was decided to exclude him from the union on the ground that he was more than six months in arrears with dues. Eventually, after hearing the plaintiff, the national executive committee endorsed this decision. The learned judge held that the failure of natural justice before the branch could not be cured by appeal and the exclusion of the plaintiff was, therefore, invalid. He quoted from the judgment of Buckley L.J. in the unreported case of *Shanks* v. *Plumbing Trades Union* to the effect that there was a difference between specific performance of the contract of employment and reinstatement of an officer holder removed by somebody other than those who elected him.

---

[19] [1976] I.C.R. 147.
[20] *Carling* v. *N.U.G.M.W.* [1973] I.C.R. 267. The statutory powers under which this case was decided—Industrial Relations Act 1971, s.65(4)—no longer exist.
[21] [1976] I.C.R. 473.
[22] [1971] 2 Q.B. 175.
[23] [1970] 2 All E.R. 713.

"Even if I assume that the case before me is one in which I have the power to grant the injunction sought, I feel much hesitation about whether it would be right to do so.

The union, I may say, has very properly been paying the plaintiff £20 per week under an undertaking given at an earlier stage of this motion. This comes to approximately his 'take home pay' as an area organiser. Counsel for the union has also offered an undertaking that the union will not hold an election for the plaintiff's post as area organiser pending the trial of the action. In these circumstances where does the balance of covenience lie? The union urges that there will be much embarrassment if the plaintiff is in effect restored to office. Some of that embarrassment is, I think, due to causes on which the union cannot properly rely. Counsel for the union accepts that he can place no reliance on any embarrassment due to any possible feelings of guilt within the union in having wronged the plaintiff. Further, an affidavit by the general secretary speaks of the decision to exclude the plaintiff, and ends by stating:

> 'I verily believe that most members and officials are of the opinion that the Plaintiff ought to have accepted the decision of the National Executive Committee and of the Appeal Council.'

I cannot think that embarrassment felt because the plaintiff refused to accept what I have held to be at least prima facie an insupportable decision ought to be put in the scales against him; to protest an injustice is not morally wrong.

Even so, I think that there remains considerable cause for legitimate concern by the union on the score of embarrassment. Indeed, this must be implicit in many cases in which there is any question of what in effect is akin to the specific performance of a contract of service. For myself, I should be very slow to make any such order on motion, although in a clear and compelling case there is no doubt jurisdiction to do so. I do not think that this is a case of that sort. A union must of necessity depend in large measure on the loyalty and reliability of its officers in what is plainly often a difficult and controversial field of human activity. The union in this case is attempting to remedy defects of administration in the Luton area, which the plaintiff, says the union, had done nothing to put right. He was under the control of the N.E.C."

In *Stevenson* v. *United Road Transport Union*[24] the Court of Appeal sidestepped the issue by applying the argument, usually thought to be the basis of the decision in *Vine* v. *National Dock Labour Board*,[25] that there is no objection to a declaration that a purported removal from office is *ultra vires*.

Services and benefits

It seems likely that entitlement to the services and benefits offered by the union is the matter foremost in the mind of most union members when considering the propriety of the action of the union. Of these the right to fair representation would no doubt rank high. Yet of all his rights this is likely to be least protected by the law. English law recognises no obligation to bargain in good faith. The structure of most union rule books as interpreted by the courts leads to the inference that whilst negotiation is usually a declared object of the union it does not produce a contractual obligation as between it and its members. Again, it is possible to compare this approach adversely with that adopted to the contract of employment where such a central objective of the

---

[24] [1977] I.C.R. 893.
[25] [1956] 1 Q.B. 658.

relationship would almost certainly produce the implication of a contractual obligation.

The importance to an individual's employment position of collective bargaining is obvious but the facts in *Blackman* v. *The Post Office*[26] lend it added emphasis. Difficulties had arisen in recruiting a sufficient number of post and telegraph officers. The union agreed not to object to recruiting on an unestablished basis from outside the Post Office. The agreement with the union provided that candidates whose service had been satisfactory would be expected to seek establishment in an open written examination. Subsequently it was agreed that candidates in the plaintiff's position would be allowed three opportunities to pass a special aptitude test. The plaintiff sat the test three times and only just failed the third attempt. The employer had no other cause of complaint against him but the union refused to agree to modify its agreement to permit him and others in a similar position to remain in employment and he was eventually dismissed. The union may impose very considerable sanctions upon a member by refusing him the benefit of its services as it did in *Oddy* v. *Transport Salaried Staffs Association*.[27] In that case the service in question was representation in individual negotiations with the employer. Sir Hugh Griffiths in the N.I.R.C., however, decided that no right to such representation could be construed from the declaration that it was an object of the union to protect the interests of its members.

Fair representation

Freedland and Davies[28] point out a number of ways in which the courts could provide a right to representation. They suggest that it could:

(i) be implied into the contract of membership;
(ii) be construed from the privilege a union may possess of aquiring exclusive bargaining rights, particularly where these rights are granted by some statutory machinery;
(iii) be derived from the statutory right of unions to be consulted in the interests of employees;
(iv) be regarded as a concomitant of the power derived from the closed shop situation.

So far, however, neither legislature nor courts have shown any tendency to develop these sources of implied obligation.

The only obligations towards its members arising outside the union rules are those concerning discrimination declared to be illegal by statute. In *F.T.A.T.U.* v. *Modgill*,[29] however, the fact that the union was doing no more for 16 African Asians than it was for the rest of its members at the place of work in question provided a complete answer to a claim of discrimination.

The extent to which the individual may be dependent on the efficiency of his union in affording him services is illustrated in other ways. In *Gray Dunn and Co. Ltd.* v. *Edwards*[30] Lord McDonald was ready to accept the proposition that

---

[26] [1974] I.C.R. 151.
[27] [1973] I.C.R. 524.
[28] At pp. 588–590.
[29] [1980] I.R.L.R. 142.
[30] [1980] I.R.L.R. 23. See also *Ellis* v. *Brighton Co-operative Society* [1976] I.R.L.R. 419.

an employee's right to be heard before dismissal would be satisfied by the presence at some stages only of his union representatives. There is no doubt that this makes good sense in the light of normal industrial practice. The union, however, is representing the group as much as the individual and without inferring any bad faith on its part it is almost certainly true that wider policy considerations may at times modify the case it puts forward. In *Chappell* v. *Times Newspapers Ltd.*[31] the Court of Appeal confirmed that the willingness of union members to respond to calls from their union could be effective to destroy the trust and confidence of their employer in their readiness to fulfil their obligations as employees. The dependence of the member may actually be increased by statute. In *Times Newspapers Ltd.* v. *O'Regan*[32] the E.A.T. retreated from the more lenient attitude adopted by the N.I.R.C. in *Owen* v. *Crown House Engineering Ltd.*[33] and refused to allow delay to permit negotiations to be completed to be presented to excuse the filing out of time of a complaint of unfair dismissal.

Negligence

So far the courts have acknowledged only one source of protection for the non-contractual rights of a member. The law of negligence may provide, intermittently, remedies for failure by union officials adequately to represent or provide services for union members. So far, however, even this opportunity has not been developed. In *Buckley* v. *National Union of General and Municipal Workers*[34] the discussion was limited to the application of the law of negligence to the carrying out of contractual obligations and the court was anxious not to require too high a degree of skill. In *Cross* v. *British Iron, Steel and Kindred Trades Association*[35] Salmon L.J. considered only a contractual duty of care and concluded that the obligation the union had accepted was satisfied by delegation to those reasonably thought competent.

It is suggested that the courts, which have often stated an awareness of the power of trade unions spreading far beyond the rule book, should realise that in order to provide a system of protection of a member's rights in respect of the organisation of the union they must look beyond the narrow confines of the rule book. It is essential to consider the field of action of the union, and particularly the stated purposes of the union as a source of implied obligation to the member. The almost insuperable difficulty in the way of judicial development of this line of thought, however, is that that obligation is to the member as one of a group. Discipline cases reveal no evidence of judicial comprehension of such a status.

---

[31] [1975] I.C.R. 145.
[32] [1977] I.R.L.R. 101.
[33] [1973] I.C.R. 511.
[34] [1967] 3 All E.R. 767.
[35] [1968] 1 All E.R. 250.

Chapter 10

INDUSTRIAL ACTION

INTRODUCTION

The best known form of industrial action is the strike, which so far as lawyers are concerned is defined as a deliberate and concerted withdrawal of labour. For extraneous reasons the only extant statutory definition of a strike[1] adds a limitation based on a purpose in compelling employers or others to accept or discard terms or conditions of employment. There is, however, no need to regard the meaning as thus limited. It is, in any event, largely a popular concept for which the law is increasingly forced to make provision. As we have seen it may become necessary for the law to recognise other characteristics such as the temporary nature of the withdrawal. As a broad concept it could include sub-types which are popularly regarded as separate forms of action such as refusal to work night shifts, withdrawal of overtime or attendance at union meetings.

Because the employer may, and usually does, stop payment of wages during a strike the strike as a weapon tends to combine the counter-effects of a lock-out. Full scale widespread strikes possess a built-in disincentive which leads to application of modified forms of which the selective strike of key employees is one of the most popular. It has long been apparent that short, but unforeseeable, stoppages have a disproportionately damaging effect upon production and, therefore, on supply to customers.

A good example of the failure of the law to recognise sufficient characteristics of the strike occurs in the Employment Act 1982. By imposing a defined form of vicarious liability upon trade unions which authorise action which does not enjoy legal immunity the legislation may well induce unions to abandon a system which operates as some check on hasty local responses.

For the same reason it is common to resort to forms of industrial action less than withdrawal of labour. A refusal to undertake a particular aspect of a job is popularly supposed not to lead to loss of the legal right to a part of the remuneration due for total availability within the contract. The common law has not as yet regarded such action as a partial withdrawal of labour, probably because of the impossibility of determining what portion of the remuneration would be due to it. So, in practice, wages are normally paid during most forms of industrial action other than strikes and lock-outs. It will be appreciated that as between refusal to work a shift and refusal to operate a particular machine the difference in principle is difficult to define. Other forms of industrial action are more clearly distinct. Most common among these is probably the "work to rule" or "go slow." The Court of Appeal in *Secretary of State for Employment* v. *ASLEF* (*No.* 2)[2] concluded that if the result of a work to rule was to delay or reduce production to an extent unusual in the normal run of working then the presumption is raised that the action is a breach of contract. It seems likely,

---

[1] Employment Protection (Consolidation) Act 1978, Sched. 13, para. 24.
[2] [1972] 2 Q.B. 455.

however, that many corners are cut in a day's work and (whether or not production is speeded thereby) such things as safety precautions go unheeded. In the same way, unless we accept the remark of Sir John Donaldson in *Seaboard World Airlines Inc.* v. *T.G.W.U.*[3] that, contractually speaking, an employer is entitled to demand any work load he chooses, a "go slow" does not inevitably involve a breach of contract. However much the recently recognised duties of co-operation or maintenance of trust and confidence are extended they cannot impose a contractual duty to undertake voluntary overtime.

Whereas in the past judicial dislike of industrial action centred on the element of combination and that element, by way of the criminal law, itself provided the basis for control through criminal conspiracy, the basis of modern control by means of the civil law depends on interference with contract. As we shall see, that contract need not be the contract of employment. Even where it is not, however, interference with the contract of employment often provides the illegal means rendering actionable indirect interference with commercial contracts. Breach of the contract of employment is, therefore, a significant factor in legal control of industrial action which we will consider in more detail presently.

Much of the remaining popular nomenclature surrounding industrial action has, as yet, little or no legal significance. "Unofficial action," for instance, simply denotes action not sanctioned in accordance with trade union rules, by the appropriate authority within the union. Whereas much unofficial action will be undertaken without notice that shortcoming has no significant effect on its character as a breach of contract. Much action originally unofficial and without notice, moreover, will be sanctioned retrospectively so as to become official. In the context of industrial relations "unconstitutional action" may be a more opprobrious term. Again, however, this merely connotes action in breach of collectively agreed bargaining procedures. In other countries such a distinction will often be of considerable significance. In the United Kingdom, on the other hand, voluntarism in collective bargaining has led to adoption of agreed procedures which are not legally enforceable.

A lock-out, which is the employer's counterpart of employee industrial action, in so far as there is a counterpart, is similarly likely to constitute a breach of contract. An employer may terminate the contract but he may not otherwise suspend the payment of wages (which is the essence of a lock-out) to those willing to work unless he has contractual power so to do. In practice management rarely resort to a lock-out as an initial weapon. It is usually applied as a response to employee action and, therefore, assumes the function of retaliation following the ending, or potential ending, of that action. It may, therefore, be presented as a response to a repudiatory breach by the employee. In fact it is not so since the only options are total rejection or acceptance of that breach.

"RIGHT TO STRIKE"

Sir Otto Kahn-Freund and Bob Hepple[4] ask why the law in the United Kingdom permits resort to strikes. As they point out, no one seriously advocates a total prohibition on strikes. Only one member of the Royal Commission

---

[3] [1973] I.C.R. 458.
[4] Laws Against Strikes (Fabian Research Series 305).

on Trade Unions 1965–68[5] advocated the application of criminal sanctions to any form of industrial action as such, and there is no doubt that such action is not commonly regarded as possessing the characteristics of crime. So much is this so that it is not uncommon to hear reference to the "right to strike." This right is recognised by the European Social Charter. Apart from acceptance of this charter there is no such constitutionally recognised right in the United Kingdom. The European Commission, in a report to the member states of the Council of Europe in 1970, noted that the position in relation to breach of contract in this country probably infringed the charter. Nevertheless the policy of the legislature, at least from 1906, in systematically granting immunity from civil action for industrial action in contemplation or furtherance of an industrial dispute undoubtedly creates a relatively wide freedom of such action. Kahn-Freund and Hepple's question is central to the discussion which follows, for against the answer to it must be measured every legal restriction imposed upon, or immunity granted to, such action.

Kahn-Freund and Hepple supply the answer to their question in the purpose of industrial action. First they see it as the means by which unions as bargaining agents equate their position with that of the employer. The predominating individualism of legal rules must place labour at a disadvantage as against capital. Combination is labour's answer because it concentrates the combined power of labour against the combined power of capital. Secondly, labour relations create sets of "autonomous" rules for the employment of labour in much the same way as commercial interests create their own rules for the functioning of industry. The law cannot regulate the detail of conditions of work. As legal sanctions are necessary to enforce legal rules so industrial action is the sanction used by employees to enforce rules governing the conditions of labour. Management tends to possess the initiative in applying those conditions and so the sanction is largely in the hands of labour. The third and fourth reasons are less compelling. The individual, as a matter of social ethics, cannot be forced to work and so cannot be forbidden to strike simply because he does so in concert with others. Finally, there is no doubt that the incidence of strikes increases as tension increases. This does not refer to the mental or physical stress of the work but to the stresses produced by the work environment.

It is worth pointing out that none of these factors make industrial action inevitable. By and large, the more efficient the bargaining structure the less need there will be for either side to apply its sanctions either to make or enforce the rules. If war can be said to be the sanction for breach of international law it must be admitted that it is a clumsy and inefficient one. Any legal system which did so much damage by the application of a sanction would rapidly collapse. The freedom to strike can be recognised as a part of the social ethic without the need constantly to demonstrate that freedom and tensions may be relieved more effectively by negotiation than by violence.

The law, however, can do relatively little to produce this ideal efficiency. There is no doubt that at various periods and in various countries it is achieved to a greater degree than elsewhere. On such occasions legal institutions may be seen to construct a framework but it is a framework within which the system operates rather than one which controls the system. It must follow that if it is

---

[5] Cmnd. 3623 at p. 288—Note of reservation by Mr. Andrew Shonfield.

substantially for the parties to create a workable system the law must be careful of the extent to which it disturbs the equilibrium of forces at their disposal. Indeed, as we shall see, even its conscious attempts at neutrality may disturb that equilibrium if they withdraw the support which one side but not the other needs to sustain its strength. Capital does not starve. Labour does run that risk if State support designed to prevent it is withdrawn. On the face of it, if law is to intervene at all, it would seem that the worst method it could choose would be by seeking to apply means of control designed to protect individual property interests. Conditions of work are not property and most capitalist systems do not guarantee the right to work so as to constitute that as property. Such control, therefore, must primarily benefit capital, not labour.

The extent to which this argument is accepted by lawmakers will vary. It is obviously a detailed rationalisation of what is often at best an instinctive reaction. That instinct, as the authors acknowledge, at least prevents all but a lunatic fringe from suggesting prohibition of industrial action. More significantly it inspires a feeling that industrial action is not in itself capable of being regarded as criminal. In a few cases the State may seek to protect its essential interests by the provision of criminal sanctions. People may be conditioned to accept a limited degree of application of these sanctions but without that it must be very doubtful whether acquiescence in their nominal existence as a check would extend to their use.

The History of Legal Control

Towards the end of the nineteenth century and into the early twentieth century the law turned sharply away from its previous methods of control of trade unions and industrial action. The Industrial Revolution had begun totally devoid of any thought of employee involvement in wage fixing. Since 1349 State authorities had had this function although latterly the system had been characterised more by its failure to function. The growth of industry revealed this system as totally incapable of operation but its abolition was replaced only by reliance upon the market economy. Whilst the State sought to control wage fixing it was logical that it should seek to prevent attempts by groups of workers to arrogate the function to themselves. That long period had, therefore, also been marked by statutes forbidding combinations. The common law also abhorred conspiracy not because of what it might seek but merely because of the imbalance of power which it saw inherent in any combination.

Conspiracy

Whereas the rise of industry condemned the system of statutory wage fixing, the sense of disturbance which it created (greatly assisted by the French Revolution), had for a time the opposite effect on attempts to control combinations. The Combination Act 1800 made all agreement for advancing wages or altering hours, and all attendance at meetings for such purposes criminal. Nor, as the wave of prosecutions demonstrated, was this any mere token attack. In the light of this reaction the strength of the reformist movement which secured the repeal of this legislation in 1824 is remarkable.

It is not surprising that such views were by no means those of a majority and the surge of strikes which followed led in 1825, to a reintroduction of more subtle, but equally effective, legislation designed to restrict the effectiveness of any combination of labour which it sanctioned. The sanctions which we have seen alone give labour any form of equality in bargaining were curtailed by broadly phrased offences of "threats," "molestation," "intimidation" and "obstruction" which, in the hands of a judiciary not in the forefront of the reforming movement, guaranteed the continual subjection of labour to the dominance of the employer until 1875.

In *R. v. Duffield*[6] it was held that a strike of tinplate workers against low wages constituted a conspiracy to molest and obstruct the employer. Erle J. expressed the predominant feeling that investment of capital must be protected against those who sought to restrict its supply of labour. The nominal right to strike was rendered ineffective by the requirement that such action be spontaneous, without persuasion and unaccompanied by intimations which could be described as threats. In 1857[7] Bramwell B. committed himself to the principle that all persuasion is coercive by holding non-violent picketing to be an illegal conspiracy to molest if it included anything "calculated to have a deterring effect on the minds of ordinary persons by exposing them to have their motions watched and to encounter black looks." Even after the reforms of 1871 workers who had threatened to strike to secure the reinstatement of one of their number dismissed for union activities were convicted of criminal conspiracy[8] and the judgment of Brett J. contains all the former conception of the inherence within labour combinations of interference with business amounting to "molestation." The case also acted as a reminder that the Master and Servant Acts made a breach of the contract of employment by the employee a criminal offence.

Civil conspiracy

The Conspiracy and Protection of Property Act 1875 was one in the series already begun, and destined to continue until 1913, of legislative responses to the imbalance created by the common law. It is significant because it is the first one in the series effectively to reverse that imbalance. Unfortunately it struck only at the crime of conspiracy as constituted by the act of combination alone without any other illegality. The common law responded first by extending section 7, which had been designed to deal with such extraneous illegality, to cover through the offence of "watching and besetting" the very act of peaceful picketing.[9] Subsequently the House of Lords in *Quinn v. Leathem*[10] held subject to civil liability precisely those acts of bare combination which had been given immunity from criminal law. In the same year[11] the House of Lords, having[12] first invented a new civil offence, created a new kind of defendant against whom it could be alleged by holding liable to action the funds of the trade union. The legislature responded with the Trade Disputes Act 1906 and there followed a period of apparent judicial acceptance of the relative equilibrium thus secured. Cynically, it may be suggested that such acceptance

---

[6] (1851) 5 Cox 404.

[7] *R. v. Druitt* (1867) 10 Cox 592.

[8] *R. v. Bunn* (1872) 12 Cox 316.

[9] *Lyons v. Wilkins* [1896] 1 Ch. 811; [1899] 1 Ch. 255.

[10] [1901] A.C. 495.

[11] *Taff Vale Railway Co. v. Amalgamated Society of Railway Servants* [1901] A.C. 426.

[12] Jenks: *A Short History of English Law* (1928), p. 337.

only occurred because the equilibrium was destroyed for most of the period by economic weakening of the power of trade unions.

The rest of this chapter discussing the present position of the law relating to industrial action is again an account of legislative and judicial interference with the bargaining strength of organised labour.

THE CONTRACTUAL POSITION OF INDUSTRIAL ACTION

The legal position of the individual who takes part in industrial action depends upon the effect of that action upon his contract of employment. Nowhere is the judicial approach more clearly demonstrated than in the judgment of Phillips J. in *Simmons* v. *Hoover Ltd.*[13]

"The question perhaps may be put like this: when an employee refuses to do the work, or any of it, which under his contract of employment he has engaged to do, is the employer entitled to dismiss him without notice? And, if so, does it make any difference that the refusal occurred during, and in the course of, a strike in which the employee was taking part?

There are, says Mr. Sedley, two main ways in which strikes may be organised. First, all the workers involved may give proper notice of termination of their contracts of employment, and in the early days of industrial disputes this method was often adopted. It had the advantage of avoiding any possible illegality which might then have resulted from going on strike in breach of contract. There are, however, many attendant disadvantages. For example, today, a man who gives notice will lose any possibility of making a claim for a redundancy payment or for compensation for unfair dismissal. Secondly—and this is the modern method—the strike may be organised without any employee giving notice of termination of his contract of employment. Often, however, a strike notice will be given, that is to say a notice of the intention of the employees to withdraw their labour upon a particular date unless by that time the demands which they are making have been met. In anything except the smallest firms, and the least organised strikes, some method of this kind is almost universally followed these days. The length of the strike notice may vary, but, except in the case of a lightning strike, it is usual for some notice, though not usually a long one, to be given of the intention to strike. The system of strikes, Mr. Sedley says, has now become an accepted part of industrial organisation, and neither side involved in a strike—that is to say, neither the employers nor the employees—has any expectation or wish that at the end of the strike relations between them will have been severed. There is usually an agreed procedure which has the purpose of avoiding disputes and, if disputes cannot be avoided, of regulating them. He draws attention to the agreed procedure for the avoidance of disputes in force at the employers' place of business at Perivale. The last paragraph of section 2 of the agreed procedure reads:

'Failing settlement at the joint conference'—that is the last stage in the procedure for the avoidance of disputes—'the procedure shall be regarded as exhausted and either side will give the other at least five working days' notice of any intended action.'

The whole process has become systematised, is well understood, and no one ever expects that effective dismissals will take place.

Speaking broadly, we are prepared to accept the general account given by Mr. Sedley of the way in which present day strikes are organised. The question, however, is what is the effect of a strike upon a particular employee's contract of

---

[13] [1977] I.C.R. 61.

employment? Mr. Sedley says that there are two possibilities: first, that the contract of employment is suspended, and that is his contention here; or, secondly, that the withdrawal by the employee of his labour breaks the contract of employment. If he is wrong in his submission that the contract of employment is suspended, he then turns to consider the effect of the breach caused by the employee withdrawing his labour, and submits that it is not a fundamental breach entitling the employer to dismiss him without notice. Whether it is or not, he submits, depends on the circumstances in each case having regard to the effect of the breach upon the contract of employment and the employer's business.

Of his principal submission that the contract of employment is suspended, Mr. Sedley says that it reflects the daily experience, understanding and practice of those engaged in industrial relations. No one so engaged supposes for a minute that the effect of a strike is to terminate the contract of employment. Not only, he submits, is this well recognised in practice, but it has received judicial blessing. He cites in support of this proposition the observations of Lord Denning M.R. in *J. T. Stratford & Son Ltd.* v. *Lindley* and also Lord Denning M.R.'s observations in *Morgan* v. *Fry*. He relies particularly heavily upon the words of Lord Denning M.R. in the latter case.

> 'The truth is that neither employer nor workmen wish to take the drastic action of termination if it can be avoided. The men do not wish to leave their work for ever. The employers do not wish to scatter their labour force to the four winds. Each side is, therefore, content to accept a "strike notice" of proper length as lawful. It is an implication read into the contract by the modern law as to trade disputes. If a strike takes place, the contract of employment is not terminated. It is suspended during the strike: and revives again when the strike is over.'

Mr. Sedley cites *Wallwork* v. *Fielding* and *Bird* v. *British Celanese Ltd.* as practical examples of contracts being suspended, and of the consequence flowing from suspension. So, he says, there is nothing unusual, or impossible, about a contract of employment being suspended. But even if the contract is to be treated as suspended, what is the effect of the suspension? If the employer would ordinarily be entitled to dismiss without notice, is it necessary to include among the effects of suspension the loss by the employer of that right until the suspension is lifted? The question then arises in what circumstances can the suspension be lifted? Can that be the decision of the employer alone, or does it require some further agreement between the employer and the employee?

Mr. Sedley draws attention to what he claims are some of the consequences which would flow in a time of industrial dispute if it were not possible for the mutual rights and obligations of the employer and employee to be suspended. For example, the employee must choose between terminating his contract himself and striking in breach of contract; if he adopts the former course, and gives in his notice, he will be without a job and on strike. Further, he will then lose the valuable benefits which have accrued during the period of his employment. If he chooses the latter course, and goes on strike in breach of contract, he is liable in damages to his employer. Those results, says Mr. Sedley, will be bleak, unsatisfactory and inharmonious. In answer to questions from the appeal tribunal about the effect of suspension, he accepted the logic of his submissions and conceded, or asserted, that the time would never come when the employer could lawfully dismiss the employee while on strike merely for failing to work; that, in other words, the employer could not lift the suspension and assert his right to terminate the employee's contract of employment. . . .

According to Mr. Sedley the suspension may continue indefinitely; continuity of employment is not broken; the employee can get another job; and in general the relationship of employer/employee can only be terminated at the instance of the party who brought the suspension into operation. It seems to us to be clear that before the decision of the Court of Appeal in *Morgan* v. *Fry*, no authority is to be found for the proposition that a contract of employment is suspended in this fashion during a strike. We are satisfied that at common law an employer is entitled to dismiss summarily an employee who refuses to do any of the work which he has engaged to do: see *Laws* v. *London Chronicle (Indicator Newspapers) Ltd.*—the employee has 'disregarded the essential conditions of the contract of service.' Does it make any difference that the refusal occurs during, and in the course of, a strike? In *J. T. Stratford & Son Ltd.* v. *Lindley* Lord Denning M.R. said:

> 'The "strike notice" is nothing more nor less than a notice that the men will not come to work'—or, as in this case, that they will not do their work as they should—'In short, that they will break their contracts . . . In these circumstances . . . the trade union officer, by giving the "strike notice," issues a threat to the employer. *He threatens to induce the men to break* their contracts of employment unless the employer complies with the demand. That is a threat to commit a tort. It is clear intimidation unless it is protected by statute.'

Similar observations are to be found in the cases. Thus in *Rookes* v. *Barnard* . . . Lord Devlin said,

> 'It is not disputed that the notice constitued a threat of breach of contract by the members of A.E.S.D. It is true that any individual employee could lawfully have terminated his contract by giving seven days' notice and, if the matter is looked at in that way, the breach might not appear to be a very serious one. But that would be a technical way of looking at it. As Donovan L.J. said in the Court of Appeal, the object of the notice was not to terminate the contract either before or after the expiry of seven days. The object was to break the contract by withholding labour but keeping the contract alive for as long as the employers would tolerate the breach without exercising their right of rescission.'

There are passages in some of the speeches which do not state the matter so clearly, and some which, read out of context, might suggest otherwise. But there is no doubt that it was widely believed at the time of the decisions in *Rookes* v. *Barnard* and *J. T. Stratford & Son Ltd.* v. *Lindley* that by taking part in a strike the employees committed a breach of contract, for which in many cases they were liable to dismissal. It was for this reason that section 37 of the Redundancy Payments Act 1965 amended paragraph 7 of Schedule 1 to the Contracts of Employment Act 1963 (which preserves continuity of employment where an employee takes part in a strike, except where in doing so he breaks his contract of employment) by deleting the words which we have underlined. We shall return to this provision when considering the effect of section 2(2) of the Redundancy Payments Act 1965.

One of the matters considered at length by the Donovan Commission . . . (Cmnd. 3623) was the effect of strikes on the contract of employment. In paragraph 943 of the commission's report there are enumerated some of the difficulties inherent in regarding the contract as suspended. In the end the conclusion was reached that it was not practicable to introduce such a conception into the law. Whether or not that be so, it was clearly the view of the commission that at common law a contract cannot be terminated unilaterally, and that if an employee refuses to carry on working under his contract of employment his employer has the option either to ignore the breach of contract and to insist upon performance of it, or alternatively to accept such a fundamental breach as a repudiation of the contract and to treat himself as no longer bound by it: paragraph 946. In our judgment this view was in accordance with general principle and supported by authority. In short, refusal to work during a strike did not involve 'self-dismissal' by the strikers, but left the parties to the contract hoping that the strike would one day be settled, and the contract be alive, unless and until the employer exercised his right to dismiss the employee.

The question then is whether the decision in *Morgan* v. *Fry* changed the law; that is, not merely by establishing that the tort of intimidation was not committed by threats of strike action, but also by changing the underlying law concerning the relationship between employer and employee. . . .

Morgan v. *Fry* is binding upon us, and it is necessary to try to see precisely what it is that it decides. Although *Morgan* v. *Fry* was not heard until 1968, the events in the case occurred in 1962. Thus the Trade Union Act 1965, which to some extent modified the effect of *Rookes* v. *Barnard* did not apply. The court in *Morgan* v. *Fry* not unnaturally, was reluctant to apply the reasoning in *Rookes* v. *Barnard* to the facts in the case before them. Lord Denning M.R., but not Russell L.J., was of opinion that the only way in which this result could be prevented was by holding that the effect of the strike notice was not to break the contract of employment. It is important to note that what was there being considered was the tort of intimidation. It is in this context that Lord Denning M.R. makes use of the word 'lawful' when referring to a strike notice. One can see that it would have been absurd, if the result in that case would have been different according to whether the strikers had served a notice to terminate their contracts, or a notice of their intention to go on strike on a particular date unless their demands were met. Davies L.J. agreed with Lord Denning M.R., but for a variety of reasons. He said, 'In a sense this'—the strike notice—'does amount to a termination of the existing contract and an offer to continue on different terms,' thus seeming to accept that in some sense notice was a breach of contract. Later on he said,

> 'It was a statement that in default of action by the Port of London Authority which it might lawfully take the men would withdraw their labour, which in effect I suppose would mean that the obligations under the contract would be mutually suspended.'

Though earlier in that paragraph Davies L.J. said that he was in agreement with the judgment of Lord Denning M.R., it is not clear what he meant by saying that 'the obligations under the contract would be mutually suspended.' For example, did he mean that they remained suspended indefinitely at the election of the employees, or until the employer exercised his right to dismiss? It is difficult to know.

Russell L.J. took a different approach. After reviewing the speeches in *Rookes* v. *Barnard*, he came to the conclusion that the Court of Appeal was not bound by precedent to hold in the case before them that the tort of intimidation had been committed, and that it was open to them to hold whatever was proper in the circumstances. He pointed out that in practical terms there was little to choose between a notice terminating the contract and a strike notice giving notice of intention to go on strike, and that in some respects the latter course was preferable. He continued:

> 'I would not wish in this branch of the law to establish as a proposition applicable to every case that the tort of intimidation is the intended interference with a man's employment by threat of breach of contract with his employer. I would exclude a case such as the present where exactly the same or even greater pressure could be exerted by threat of concerted due termination of such contract, and where the carrying out of the threatened breach would be preferred by the threatened party to the carrying out of a threatened termination of the contract.'

In short, he seems to have been accepting that there *was* a breach, but saying that, for the reasons given, the tort of intimidation had not been committed. . . .

We find it impossible to think that *Morgan* v. *Fry* was intended to revolutionise the law on this subject. It was a case in which, in order to avoid a particular result which would have been out of harmony with the law on intimidation, the court reached a desired result by several routes: one member (Lord Denning M.R.) was of opinion that the contract was suspended; another (Davies L.J.) gave somewhat vague support to that view, but also thought that in some sense there was a threat to terminate the contract; and the third member (Russell L.J.) founded upon a different ground and was of opinion that there was a threatened breach. It is noteworthy that Lord Denning M.R., the only member of the court unequivocally in favour of the view that the contract was suspended, although he uses the word 'suspension,' does not deal with any of the problems which arise when a contract is suspended in the sense that the obligations of the parties are suspended, such as those referred to in the Donovan Commission Report, for example, paragraph 943:

> 'The concept is not as simple as it sounds: and before any such new law could be formulated problems of some difficulty would have to be faced and solved. They include the following: (a) To what strikes would it apply? To unofficial and unconstitutional as well as to official strikes? How would strikes be defined for this purpose? (b) Would it also apply to other industrial action such as a ban on overtime in breach of contract or to a "go-slow"? (c) Would it apply to "lightning strikes" or only to strikes where at least *some* notice was given, though less than the notice required for termination of the contract? If so, what length of notice should be required? (d) Would the new law apply to the gas, water, and electricity industries, which at present are subject to the special provisions of section 4 of the Conspiracy and Protection of Property Act 1875? What also would be the position under section 5 of the same Act? (e) Would the employer still be allowed instantly to dismiss an employee for grave misconduct during the course of the strike? (Note: this is the case under French law where strikes are treated as suspending the contract of employment.) If so, what kind of acts would constitute "grave misconduct"? (f) Would "contracting out" of the new law be permissible, *e.g.* in collective bargains, or in individual contracts of employment? (g) Would strikers be free to take up other employment while the contract was suspended? If so, would any obligations of secrecy in the suspended contract be suspended too? (h) If all efforts to end the strike failed, upon what event would the suspension of the contract cease and be replaced by termination?'

Mr. Sedley, in the course of his submissions, offered answers to all these questions. Interesting, however, as they were, none of them was founded on authority; and there is no doubt that if *Morgan* v. *Fry* has introduced into the law the concept of the suspension of a contract it is in only an embryonic form, for none of the consequences has been worked out; and it is difficult to see how this could be done except by legislation.

In these circumstances, and bearing in mind the many changes in the law of industrial relations which have occurred since the decision in *Morgan* v. *Fry*, we do not feel that we are bound by that case to hold that the effect of a strike, whether preceded by a proper strike notice or not, is to prevent the employer from exercising the remedy which in our judgment he formerly enjoyed at common law to dismiss the employee for refusing to work. We accept, of course, that in most cases men are not dismissed when on strike; that they expect not to be dismissed; that the employers do not expect to dismiss them, and that both sides hope and expect one day to return to work. Sometimes, however, dismissals do take place, and in our judgment they are lawful. The Trade Union and Labour Relations Act

1974, in paragraph 8 of Schedule 1 seems to have recognised that fact. No doubt problems can arise, when a man on strike is dismissed—for example, in connection with a claim for a redundancy payment or for compensation for unfair dismissal. But these are matters which are easily dealt with by legislation; indeed, as we have pointed out, so far as unfair dismissal is concerned that has already been done. As to the effect of the dismissal of a man on strike on his entitlement to a redundancy payment, that matter has also received attention in section 10 of the Redundancy Payments Act 1965, to which we shall turn in a moment. If in the result the present statutory answers are judged to be unsatisfactory, they are easily corrected by legislation. It would, in our judgment, be far more unsatisfactory to seek to achieve a particular result by distorting the underlying law relating to employer and employee. Similarly, problems relating to continuity of employment can be, and to some extent have been regulated by statute: see Contracts of Employment Act 1972. We have considered whether any conclusions can be drawn about the legal effect of a strike upon a contract of employment from the terms of this, and other, statutes. There is obviously a limit to the usefulness of this exercise, but some indication of how the law was generally regarded before the decision in *Morgan* v. *Fry* is to be found in the language used in section 10(1) and (4) of the Redundancy Payments Act 1965. In each case the assumption seems to be that participation in a strike, or exclusion by a lock-out, is or may be repudiatory conduct entitling the employer to dismiss the employee, or the employee to terminate the contract, without notice.

We do not accept Mr. Sedley's submission that, if the contract of employment was not suspended, nonetheless the employee's action in going on strike was not repudiatory of the contract. It seems to us to be plain that it was, for here there was a settled, confirmed and continued intention on the part of the employee not to do any of the work which under his contract he had engaged to do; which was the whole purpose of the contract. Judged by the usual standards, such conduct by the employee appears to us to be repudiatory of the contract of employment. We should not be taken to be saying that all strikes are necessarily repudiatory, though usually they will be. For example, it could hardly be said that a strike of employees in opposition to demands by an employer in breach of contract by him would be repudiatory. But what may be called a 'real' strike in our judgment always will be.

For completeness, it should be said that it was not contended by Mr. Sedley that there was here an implied term of the contract that it was to be suspended in the event of a strike. There are obvious difficulties in the way of implying such a term: cf. *Cummings* v. *Charles Connell and Co. (Shipbuilders) Ltd.*, which, incidentally, tends to suggest that, in the absence of an express or implied term of the contract to the contrary, an employer, according to the law of Scotland may dismiss an employee who refuses to work because he is on strike.''

It will be observed that this quotation involves a detailed discussion of the strike as constituting a breach of the contract of employment. For the lawyer who derives the employee's rights and obligations from that contract such a consideration must be the starting point for the determination of the legality of the action. The lawyer will obviously start at the same point when considering the legality of any industrial action, from a ban on voluntary overtime to a sit-in. Normally he will be considering a claim against the organisers of the industrial action, who are most likely to be full-time officials and not employees of the claimant. The ultimate question will be whether they are liable in tort since they are unlikely to have committed a breach of contract. We shall see, however, that the most relevant heads of tort liability require the tort to have been committed by unlawful means and the lawyer will look to a breach of the contract of employment by those taking the industrial action as the most likely source of those unlawful means.

One of the most detailed examinations of the possibilities of breach of the contract of employment produced by industrial action other than strikes is contained in the judgments of the Court of Appeal in *Secretary of State for Employment* v. *ASLEF* (*No.* 2). [13a] The court was considering the legal position of those participating in a work to rule. In this particular case it had no option but to adopt that approach because the Industrial Relations Act 1971 made it a condition of the availability of emergency procedures to deal with industrial action that that action should have been in breach of the contracts of employment. But the approach is no less compulsory where the court is looking for a similar breach as the unlawful element in tortious action. Lord Denning M.R. said:

"Next I inquire into the course of conduct which the men are instructed to take. I ask whether that conduct is a breach of contract. Much of the discussion before us was concerned with the detailed instructions sent out to the men. In several respects it was said that they involved no breach of contract, and it is true to say that at any rate for the purposes of this case the Railways Board agreed that quite a number of these instructions involved no breach of contract. For instance, they agreed that no man is bound by his contract to work on Sundays, even though he is paid overtime for it. They agreed also that no man is bound by his contract to work on his rostered rest days, even though he is paid overtime for it. If this is correct, it follows that a ban on Sunday working or on rest day working is no breach of contract. But there was one specific instruction which it did seem, at all events at first sight . . . to be a breach of contract in what the NUR instructed. One of the instructions sent out in regard to non-train men was this: 'Members who are rostered for time in excess of 8 hours in accordance with existing arrangements must book off duty after 8 hours.' Apply that to the case of a signalman, who would be a non-train man. According to the rostered duty, he would be contractually bound to do 9 hours, say, in his box, of which 8 hours would be on ordinary pay and the final hour on overtime. As I read this instruction sent out, the signalman would have to leave his box after 8 hours no matter what trouble it might cause. For myself, I should have thought that did point to a breach. The instructions did tell the men in that respect to break their contracts. . . .

So much for the case when a man is employed singly. It is equally the case when he is employed, as one of many, to work in an undertaking which needs the service of all. If he, with the others, takes steps wilfully to disrupt the undertaking, to produce chaos so that it will not run as it should, then each one who is a party to those steps is guilty of a breach of his contract. It is no answer for any one of them to say 'I am only obeying the rule book,' or 'I am not bound to do more than a 40-hour week.' That would be all very well if done in good faith without any wilful disruption of services; but what makes it wrong is the object with which it is done. There are many branches of our law when an act which would otherwise be lawful is rendered unlawful by the motive or object with which it is done. So here it is the wilful disruption which is the breach. It means that the work of each man goes for naught. It is made of no effect. I ask: Is a man to be entitled to wages for his work when he, with others, is doing his best to make it useless? Surely not. Wages are to be paid for services rendered, not for producing deliberate chaos."

[13a] [1972] 2 Q.B. 455.

[13b] The obligation not "wilfully to disrupt the undertaking" has received little support though it was revised by the E.A.T. (*obiter*) in *Power Packing Casemakers* v. *Faust* [1981] I.C.R. 484. See also Lord Denning M.R. in *Chappel* v. *Times Newspapers Ltd.* [1975] I.C.R. 145 at 175.

Buckley L.J. said:

"Assuming in the appellants' favour that the direction to work to rule avoided any specific direction to commit a breach of any express term of the contract, the instruction was, nevertheless, directed, and is acknowledged to have been directed, to rendering it impossible, or contributing to the impossibility, to carry on the board's commercial activity upon a sound commercial basis, if at all. The object of the instruction was to frustrate the very commercial object for which the contracts of employment were made. It struck at the foundation of the consensual intentions of the parties to those contracts, and amounted, in my judgment, to an instruction to commit what were clearly breaches or abrogations of those contracts. These are or would be, in my judgment, breaches of an implied term to serve the employer faithfully within the requirements of the contract. It does not mean that the employer could require a man to do anything which lay outside his obligations under the contract, such as to work excess hours of work or to work an unsafe system of work or anything of that kind, but it does mean that within the terms of the contract the employee must serve the employer faithfully with a view to promoting those commercial interests for which he is employed. The contrary view is, in my opinion, one which proceeds upon much too narrow and formalistic an approach to the legal relations of employer and employee and is an approach which, I may perhaps add, seems to me to be unlikely to promote goodwill or confidence between the parties."

As we have seen that the contract of employment can be extended by implication to suit the demands of the definition of constructive dismissal so we see now that it can be extended to include similar conceptions of fair dealing between employer and employee. The courts, by the implication of terms, turn what they regard as unreasonable conduct into a breach of contract for both purposes. Whereas the employer is allowed considerable scope within the boundaries of fairness in his conduct towards the employee the outcome of the judicial approach to industrial action, as the above quotations show, may leave the employee considerably less scope for legitimate industrial action. Sir John Donaldson went further, it is submitted, than most lawyers would accept when, as President of the N.I.R.C., he said in *Seaboard World Airlines Inc.* v. *T.G.W.U.*[13c]:

"Those contracts normally would provide for the performance of broadly specified types of work for a specified period of working hours. It would not be a breach of contract by the employers to ask the clerical employees to do clerical work of any kind within those times. The fact that their actual work load increased over the working day because business improved would not be a ground for saying that the employers were in breach of contract. It might be a ground for an employee saying to the employers, 'Well now, look, this job is getting a great deal harder, I am producing a great deal more. You ought to agree to pay me an increased wage.' But there is no question of breach of contract in the employers asking the employee to do the work. It is what he has contracted to do. If the employee is unwilling to do the increased amount of work for the wage which he is being paid, his right then as an individual is to give notice terminating his contract and find another job. Collectively the employees have the right to give the appropriate strike notice and to go on strike. If they do so, or if anybody urges them to do so, they commit no breach of the Act of 1971. . . .

What no one is entitled to do is to promote by the employees a collective decision that they will do less than they have contracted to do by way of exercising industrial pressure."

[13c] [1973] I.C.R. 458.

There can be little doubt that even if courts generally do not support this view of the employee's obligations, nor that of Lord Denning M.R. concerning wilful disruption of the employer's undertaking, they are likely to regard most industrial action, with the possible exception of withdrawal of voluntary overtime and "lack of enthusiasm," as constituting breach of the contracts of employment.

It is surprising that they can be so positive as to the illegitimacy of such conduct when they take into account so few of the characteristics of industrial action in reaching that conclusion.

One of the most detailed judicial considerations ever given to the meaning of industrial action occurred in *Rasool* v. *Hepworth Pipe Co. Ltd*.[13d] Employees had engaged in a series of strikes, stoppages and other disruptive action including attendance at a number of unauthorised mass meetings. The employer informed the employees after one such meeting that by their attendance they had automaticlly terminated their employment. The tribunal considered the question whether, if this amounted to dismissal, it was dismissal at a time when employees were engaged in industrial action. Upon the meaning of that term Waterhouse J. in the E.A.T. said:

> "In order to decide this issue, the Tribunal sought to define the meaning of industrial action for itself in the absence of any express statutory definition. The majority conclusion was expressed as follows:
>
> 'It seems to this majority to be of the essence of industrial action that it is concerted action undertaken by employees with the intention of putting pressure on an employer to do something which he otherwise would not do, perhaps to coerce, perhaps to persuade him, but nevertheless to put pressure on him to resolve a grievance or demand such as an increase of wages, reinstatement of a dismissed employee, the possibilities are endless. This is to be contrasted, however, with what one might call trade union activities.'

It seems likely, or at least possible, that the majority of the Tribunal were influenced in formulating this definition by the statutory definition of 'strike' now contained in para. 24(1) of Schedule 13 to the Employment Protection (Consolidation) Act 1978, which is a provision relating to breaks in the continuity of employment.

Having defined industrial action in this way, the majority of the Tribunal went on to conclude that the action of the employees in the instant case fell short of industrial action because, if a mass meeting, albeit unauthorised, is convened for the purpose of considering the views of employees with regard to impending wage negotiations, there is no intention in the meeting to put any sort of pressure on the employer. The view of the dissenting member on the facts, however, was that the purpose of holding the mass meeting was not to discuss wages: it was a demonstration by the union shop stewards and members that they should be entitled to hold a mass meeting for whatever reason with or without authority as and when they wished. Thus, in his (Mr Hancock's) view, the holding of, and attendance at, the mass meeting was industrial action.

Mr Carr, on behalf of the employer, has criticised the conclusion of the majority on the basis that the suggested definition of industrial action is wrong in law and that the conclusion of the majority as to the purpose of the mass meeting was too blinkered or narrow in its scope on the proved facts. In the end we have reached the conclusion that Mr Carr fails on the second limb of his submission but, in deference

---

[13d] [1980] I.R.L.R. 137.

to his careful argument, it is right that we should say something about the Tribunal's definition of industrial action.

Mr Carr's basic submission is that the majority of the Tribunal were wrong to include in the definition a requirement that the concerted action by employees should be undertaken with the intention of putting pressure on an employer to achieve a specific objective of the kind described in the definition or, indeed, any specific objective beyond such familiar ones as demonstrating the solidarity of employees, their power, or perhaps, sympathy for other workers. In the notice of appeal this submission is put on the basis that industrial action includes concerted action taken by employees so as to defy an express instruction given by their employer when it is reasonably forseeable that such action will have a disruptive effect on the employer's business.

We accept that it is impermissible to import into the interpretation of industrial action in para. 7 of the Schedule to the Act of 1974 definitions contained in other statutory provisions for different purposes: (see, for example, the definition of 'irregular industrial action short of a strike' in s.33(4) of the Industrial Relations Act 1971). Moreover, the reference to strike in para. 7 does not limit the interpretation of 'other industrial action because there is no genus. Again, it is arguable that the limitation that the employees must be taking part in industrial action at the date of the dismissals is itself an important restriction upon the application of the provision so that an unduly restrictive interpretation of industrial action itself would be inappropriate. It is sufficient for us to say that it is probably incorrect to attempt to interpret the expression narrowly in terms of specific intention and that the nature and effect of the concerted action are probably of greater importance. Nevertheless, in our judgment, attendance at an unauthorised meeting for the purpose indicated by the majority of the Tribunal in the instant case falls short of 'other industrial action.' As the majority of the Tribunal found, it is more properly regarded as trade union activity, even though a degree of disruption of the manufacturing process resulted."

In *Thomson* v. *Eaton Ltd.*[13e] the E.A.T. was far less clear.

"Turning to the words of paragraph 8, two questions arise (i) were the employees at the time of their dismissal taking part in a strike or other industrial action? If so, (ii) was the reason or principal reason for the dismissal of the employees that they took part in the strike or other industrial action?

We have no doubt that the action upon which the employees were engaged was, probably a 'strike' and, if not a 'strike' was certainly 'other industrial action.' There is no doubt that the employees were collectively engaged in refusing to work and in physically preventing the employers from proceeding to prove the [new machines]. There was, therefore, an element of picketing in addition to the collective withdrawal of labour. It did not last very long, and there were other circumstances which take it out of the ordinary. However, the industrial tribunal considered all those matters, and in their decision came to a clear and reasonable conclusion that despite those matters there was here at least, 'other industrial action.' We agree.

The argument presented to us on behalf of the employees was on these lines: an essential element in a strike or other industrial action is the element of coercion on the part of those engaged in it; they must be attempting to coerce the employers; there is a difference between resisting coercion by the employers and initiating coercion themselves; so, it is not industrial action for employees to resist an unlawful coercive action on the part of the employers. The reality here, says Mr. Roberts for the employees is that these employers had unreasonably decided to

13e [1976] I.C.R. 336.

press ahead with their plan to prove the Montforts that afternoon. The industrial tribunal found that they ought to have put it off until there had been proper consultation under the agreement. Consequently, so the argument goes, the employers adopted a coercive attitude by applying the disciplinary procedure. The employees were doing no more than to stand fast against coercive action. That is not taking industrial action, he says.

In our judgment this is tantamount to saying that the provisions of paragraph 8 do not apply to a case where the employer is wholly or substantially to blame for the occurrence of the strike or other industrial action. There is no warrant for this proposition in the words of paragraph 8. Furthermore, it would introduce a test for the applicability of paragraph 8 which it would be impossible to apply in practice. It is very rare for strikes, or other industrial action, to be wholly the fault of one side or the other. Almost always there is some blame on each side. There remains the case where a strike or other industrial action has been provoked, or even engineered, by the employer in some gross manner. It seems to us very probable that in such circumstances the provisions of paragraph 8 would not apply, and that, accordingly, the difficulties and injustices which Mr. Roberts forecasts, if this appeal is dismissed, would not arise in practice. Where an employer has been guilty of such gross conduct it will probably amount to a repudiation by him of the contract of employment. If a repudiation of the contract of employment does not have to be accepted a subsequent strike will occur *after* the dismissal, so that paragraph 8 will not apply. Furthermore, in a case of gross provocation, or an engineered strike, the participation of the claimants would not be the reason, or the principal reason, for the dismissal. The reason would be the desire of the employers to be rid of the employees, which had led them to provoke or to engineer the strike."

At least this recognises that industrial action may not be the fault of the employee alone. Even if courts generally showed more readiness openly to acknowledge this it might not affect the decision that the action constituted a breach of contract, as being a response not permitted by that contract. On the other hand, such a consideration might prompt courts to enquire whether the element of employer fault itself amounted to a breach of contract. One may well ask why courts which constantly enquire into the actions of conflicting parties find it so impossible to enquire in this instance. The extent of judicial withdrawal from so vital a question is apparent in the sympathetic judgment of the E.A.T. in *Wilkins* v. *Cantrell and Cochran (G.B.) Ltd.*[13f] In that case drivers had gone on strike as a means of objecting to the frequent and unremedied practice of their employer in requiring them to take out overloaded vehicles. Kilner-Brown J. said:

"The most important point of principle in this case seems to us to centre round the precise legal and common sense position which is created by an act of withholding of labour, or in other words the act of going out on strike. If it be suggested, as it was on behalf of these men, that it was a sufficient indication of their rights to claim that there had been a fundamental breach of contract, then we unanimously come to the conclusion as a question of law, and indeed in common sense, that will not do. Probably for 150 years now, and certainly in the context of the late 20th century the whole point of men withholding their labour is so that the existing contract can be put right, so that grievances can be remedied, so that after a period in which they

---

[13f] [1978] I.R.L.R. 483.

are on strike, management will agree to their demands. Now if a man says of his employer, 'You have broken the contract of employment,' as has been clearly laid down by the Court of Appeal in *Western Excavating* v. *Sharp* the employee has to act upon the situation. He has to make it plain that he is treating the contract not only as capable of being repudiatory, but one which has been broken and which he therefore regards as at an end. It would be a disaster in our view if the going on strike were to be regarded as a termination of the contract. Indeed, the law makes it perfectly plain that it is not. In *Simmons* v. *Hoover Ltd.*, a division of this Appeal Tribunal examined in detail the numerous authorities dealing with the legal position when a strike occurs. It seems to us that whatever legal description may be given to the situation the conduct of the employees gives to the employer a right to regard the conduct of the employee as a breach of the contract and to dismiss him. Indeed, the statutory provisions clearly recognise this and entitle the employer where there is a dismissal on account of strike action to an escape from a finding of unfair dismissal. As was recognised in *Simmons'* case the nature of the strike may have to be examined and conclusions have to be reached in accordance with the circumstances of each particular case. When the men go on strike, then the responsibility passes back to the employer. He then has to decide whether the strike was justified; he then has to give due warning to the strikers, and he then has in the last resort, as in this case, to exercise his judgement in deciding whether or not to put an end to the contract by issuing notices of dismissal.

The Industrial Tribunal assessed this situation admirably. They went into it with care. They understood, as we have understood, the difficulties in which these men found themselves. They understood, as we have understood with sympathy, that these men thought that they had got their grievance rectified. When they found that they had not, they went on strike. They certainly did not go on strike as an act pursuant to a repudiatory breach on the part of the employer. They went on strike because they thought that management had let them down. They were warned. They went on with it. In the end management felt compelled to issue notices of dismissal, and the Industrial Tribunal assessed the position and came to a right answer; and, consequently, it means that these appeals must be dismissed."

Just as the courts are unwilling to include fault as an element in the legitimacy of industrial action so they have not noted many characteristics which an industrial relations expert would regard as elements in a definition of such action or have produced uncertain and conflicting views on them. In *Power Packing Casemakers Ltd.* v. *Faust*,[13g] for instance, May J. noted that there was no statutory definition of industrial action, found the cases unhelpful and ended up suggesting that motive might be a large part of the definition, but preferred not to suggest how that was to be so, leaving it to the good sense and local knowledge of the industrial tribunal. In *Coates and Venables* v. *Modern Methods and Materials Ltd.*,[13h] the Court of Appeal said that motive had no bearing on whether an employee was participating in industrial action.

Whilst courts confine themselves to a definition depending on collective coercion and find illegality in any departure from the obligations of a wide-ranging and highly flexible contract of employment they will continue to produce a one-sided result such as appeared in the remark of Lord Denning M.R. in *Chappell* v. *Times Newspapers Ltd.*[13i] The plaintiffs' union had given notice that it would resume selective industrial action which might have in-

---

[13g] [1981] I.C.R. 484.
[13h] [1982] I.C.R. 763; [1982] 3 All E.R. 946.
[13i] [1975] I.C.R. 145 at 174.

volved a call to the plaintiffs to withdraw their labour. The employers said that unless this threat was withdrawn all union members employed by them would be regarded as having broken their contracts. Lord Denning M.R. said:

> "In this case it seems to me impossible for any of the plaintiffs to say that he is ready and willing to perform his part of the contract when on the statement of his union ... he may be called upon, or other members of his union may be called upon, to take industrial action so as to bring great losses to their employers. Not being ready and willing to do their part, they cannot call upon employers to continue to employ them. They are seeking equity when they are not ready to do it themselves."

It is because of the continuing failure to define the various forms of industrial action that this form of extended liability is possible. There are a number of examples of it in the reports.[13j]

Individual actions for damages

In practice employers do not often bring actions for damages for breach of contract. This is, no doubt, primarily, because such action would have a disproportionately damaging effect on future relations. The Royal Commission on Trade Unions 1965–68[14] said:

> "It cannot be in the employer's interest to exacerbate his relations with his own men by summoning them before a court, and to do so at a time when, in the large majority of cases, the strike will be over. Whatever deterrent effect such court proceedings may have will be outweighed by the harm they are liable to do to future relations on the shop floor, on the building site, in the office. The same would in our opinion also apply if an employer deducted from wages any amount awarded to him by way of damages, a possibility referred to by the C.B.I. in its supplementary oral evidence."

There is no financial inducement to risk such a consequence. In *National Coal Board* v. *Galley*[15] the defendant had taken part in a ban on Saturday shift working. The absence of deputies meant that the shift could not be worked. It was calculated that the loss of profit on a particular shift amounted to £535 and the action claimed damages representing a share of this loss. On appeal it was held that damages must be confined to the loss caused by the individual breach of contract, namely, the cost of paying wages to a replacement. Although Galley would have been engaged on safety duties and so would not have been responsible for any individually measurable production the decision has been taken to be generally applicable to all employees.[16] The courts and the legislature have also taken steps to prevent the development of the applications of the individual breach of contract. In *Wilkins* v. *Cantrell and Cochrane (G.B.) Ltd.*[17]

[13j] e.g. *Winnett* v. *Seamarks Bros. Ltd.* [1978] I.C.R. 1240—employees on shift work are participating in industrial action as soon as they indicate an intention to do so even though they have not at that point defaulted on their obligation to report for the shift; *Williams* v. *Western Mail and Echo Ltd.* [1980] I.C.R. 366—an employee off work sick when a strike occurs may be participating in the strike. But see *Midland Plastics Ltd.* v. *Till* [1983] I.R.L.R. 9.   [15] [1958] 1 W.L.R. 16.

[16] The fact that the arithmetic is wrong in that the wages paid to the replacement would have been saved by the fact that Galley was not entitled to them has, like the absence of logic, also been ignored.

[17] [1978] I.R.L.R. 483.

the E.A.T. rejected the idea that a strike in response to a repudiatory breach of contract by the employer could be construed as an acceptance of that repudiation so terminating the employment. The legislature has effectively prevented use of an injunction against individuals to terminate a strike[18] although, in fairness, the common law had shown very little sign of venturing in this direction.[19]

Dismissal

In complete contrast to the position thus reached in practice the law freely allows the fact that industrial action constitutes a breach of contract to justify dismissal both at common law and by statute. The jurisdiction of an industrial tribunal is removed[20] wherever, during industrial action, all employees taking part in that action at the date of dismissal are dismissed (regardless of whether the strike is the reason) so long as none of them is subsequently re-engaged within three months. The E.A.T. sought to dispel the surprise that might be caused by the sudden legislative withdrawal from attempts to regulate the equilibrium in *Thompson* v. *Eaton Ltd.*,[21] although it may be noted that some of the explanation relies on the necessity under the previous statutory provision of showing that the reason for the dismissal was the strike. The effect of the removal of this requirement is to make the employee on strike something of an outlaw.

"At first sight it seems strange to find such a provision as this, so favourable to the employer, in an Act which otherwise is almost wholly favourable to the employee. The statutory predecessor of paragraph 8 is section 26 of the Industrial Relations Act 1971, the ideology and policy of which is different from the Act of 1974. Thus the provisions of paragraph 8 have found themselves in two different Acts of totally different and opposed complexions. In these circumstances we do not find it possible to derive much assistance concerning the purpose of these provisions from the other provisions amongst which they are to be found. The idea, which occurred to us, that the provisions of section 26 of the Act of 1971 were allowed to creep into the Act of 1974 per incuriam, must be wrong, for the Employment Protection Act 1975 (by paragraph 13 of Part III of Schedule 16) preserves the effect of paragraph 8, albeit with some amendments which do not affect its basic meaning.

In *Heath* v. *J. F. Longman (Meat Salesmen) Ltd.*, Sir Hugh Griffiths, delivering the judgment of the Industrial Court, said:

'It appears to this court that the manifest overall purpose of section 26 is to give a measure of protection to an employer if his business is faced with ruin by a strike. It enables him in those circumstances, if he cannot carry on the business without a labour force, to dismiss the labour force on strike; to take on another labour force without the stigma of its being an unfair dismissal. That being the overall purpose it would appear to be manifestly wrong, when an employer has been told that strike action has been called off, that he should nevertheless still be free to dismiss those who took part in the strike, without any risk of a finding that he was acting unfairly. This is a result which the members of this court would be anxious to avoid, unless the language of the section drove them to it.'

---

[18] TULRA 1974, s.16 re-enacting Industrial Relations Act 1971, s.128.
[19] *Thomas Marshal (Exports) Ltd.* v. *Guinle* [1979] 1 Ch. 227 at 243. Compare *Hill* v. *C.A. Parsons and Co.* [1972] Ch. 305.
[20] E.P.C.A. 1978, s.62 as amended by E.A. 1982, s.9. See *supra*, p. 244.
[21] [1976] I.C.R. 336.

Mr. Pardoe, for the employers, criticises this statement of the purpose of paragraph 8. He suggests that the character of the Act of 1974 is that it prevents legal recourse by anyone in respect of matters connected with a trade dispute—a situation which he describes as being one of 'collective laissez-faire.' The provisions of paragraph 8 are, he says, in the nature of a quid pro quo for the removal from the employers of any rights against an employee in respect of matters occurring during a trade dispute. The policy of the Act is to withdraw the law from the whole area of industrial disputes. So, once a strike has started, the employee is excluded from the newly created right not to be unfairly dismissed and put into a position similar to that in which he would be at common law, namely, that he would be liable to be dismissed for breach of contract. There is, says Mr. Pardoe, a close analogy with the policy whereby a man on strike is not entitled to social security benefit.[22]

It is difficult to reach any concluded view about the purpose of these provisions, particularly since (as has already been pointed out) they find themselves in two such different Acts. But, on reflection, it is perhaps not so surprising that the Act of 1974 should exclude from entitlement to compensation for unfair dismissal men who were on strike at the date of dismissal, and who were dismissed for that reason—for, otherwise, an employer must always submit to the demands of the strikers, go out of business or pay compensation for unfair dismissal. Furthermore, the problem seldom arises in practice, for it is the common expectation of employers and employees that one day a strike will end and the men return to their work. . . ."

In addition to this special statutory immunity an employer is also entitled to take into account participation in industrial action as a ground for selecting employees for redundancy.[23]

TORT LIABILITY

Since the elimination of criminal conspiracy in the late nineteenth century, the principal judicial intervention has been mounted through the medium of tort liability. As we have seen civil conspiracy was "invented" first but this has now given place largely to the tort of interference with contract which was confirmed as available for this purpose as early as 1905.[24] This form has the advantage of enabling control to be extended from employed participants to non-employed leaders of the action, and thereby, to make available a remedy by means of injunction.

(a) Conspiracy

Civil conspiracy which took the place of criminal conspiracy as a weapon to control industrial action differs therefrom primarily in that actual loss must be shown. Mere agreement is not sufficient to create liability. In *Quinn* v. *Leathem*[25] Leathem employed some non-unionists. Officials of an appropriate union asked him to dismiss them but he refused to do so. He offered to pay the union any fines and entrance fees due by these employees so that they might

---

[22] The purpose of the 1982 amendments, however, would seem unashamedly interventionist. In Debate it was stated to be the government's purpose to restore to employers "the ability to make a credible and legitimate response when they are faced with a strike"—H.C.Deb., col. 743 (February 2, 1982).

[23] *Cruickshank* v. *Hobbs* [1977] I.C.R. 725.

[24] *South Wales Miners Federation* v. *Glamorgan Coal Co. Ltd.* [1905] A.C. 239.

[25] [1901] A.C. 495.

join the union but this offer was, in turn, rejected. Leathem was then warned that one of his regular customers would be asked, under threat of strike action, to cease dealing with him. The customer was subsequently approached by the union and, rather than suffer a strike, withdrew his custom. No otherwise unlawful action was shown but the union officials responsible were held liable for the tort of conspiracy. The element of combination alone distinguished the decision from that in *Allen* v. *Flood*[26] in which the House of Lords had held that an individual, however malicious his action, was not liable for intentionally inflicting economic harm if no otherwise unlawful means were used.

If a combination to inflict economic harm were unlawful *per se* then virtually all industrial action would render the leaders and participants (and, as the *Taff Vale* case decided, the union itself) liable for damages. The legislature replied with section 1 of the Trade Disputes Act 1906.[27]

> "An agreement or combination by two or more persons to do or procure the doing of any act in contemplation or furtherance of a trade dispute shall not be actionable in tort if the act is one which, if done without any such agreement or combination, would not be actionable in tort."

Justification

This, and the economic weakening of trade unions after 1918, would have taken the pressure off development of the tort of conspiracy in the labour field. In the result the courts also retreated from the full effect of the *Quinn* v. *Leathem* stance to a point where the statutory protection became largely meaningless. Pursuit of genuine self interest, including trade union objectives, was established as a justification for that form of liability for civil conspiracy where no more than the act of combination was illegal. In *Sorrell* v. *Smith*[28] the plaintiff, a member of an association of retail newsagents, transferred his custom from one wholesaler—Ritchie—to another—Watsons—at the instance of the association. Ritchie had broken the association's policy of limiting the area in which each wholesaler traded. At Ritchie's request the defendants, as members of a committee of a newspaper proprietors' association which disapproved of this policy, threatened to cut off Watsons' supplies – and also those of his supplier—unless Watsons ceased to supply the plaintiff. Watsons did cease. Lord Cave extracted the following principles from the earlier cases:

> "(1) A combination of two or more persons wilfully to injure a man in his trade is unlawful, and, if it results in damage to him, is actionable.
> (2) If the real purpose of the combination is not to injure another, but to forward or defend the trade of those who enter into it, then no wrong is committed and no action will lie, although damage to another ensues."

In *Reynolds* v. *The Shipping Federation*[29] the pursuit of the closed shop was held to be a purpose within this second head. Sargant J. considered that the purpose was not to inflict loss but to advance the business interests both of employees and employers by securing or maintaining the advantages of collective bargaining and control existing since the establishment of the National Maritime Board.

---

[26] [1898] A.C. 1.
[27] Now TULRA 1974, s.13(4).
[28] [1925] A.C. 700.
[29] [1924] 1 Ch. 28.

Lord Cave's principles were confined to interference with trade but it is clear that the justification will extend to the private affairs of the plaintiffs. In *Crofter Hand Woven Harris Tweed Co. Ltd.* v. *Veitch*[30] the principle of justification was further extended.

> "On this question of what amounts to an actionable conspiracy 'to injure' (I am assuming that damage results from it), I would first observe that some confusion may arise from the use of such words as 'motive' and 'intention,' Lord Dunedin in *Sorrell* v. *Smith* appears to use the two words interchangeably. There is the further difficulty that, in some branches of the law, 'intention' may be understood to cover results which may reasonably flow from what is deliberately done, on the principle that a man is to be treated as intending the reasonable consequence of his acts. Nothing of the sort appears to be involved here. It is much safer to use a word like 'purpose' or 'object.' The question to be answered, in determining whether a combination to do an act which damages others is actionable even though it would not be actionable if done by a single person, is not: 'Did the combiners appreciate, or should they be treated as appreciating, that others would suffer from their action?' It is: 'What is the real reason why the combiners did it?' Or, as Lord Cave L.C. puts it: 'What is the real purpose of the combination?' The test is not what is the natural result to the plaintiffs of such combined action, or what is the resulting damage which the defendants realise, or should realise, will follow, but what is in truth the object in the minds of the combiners when they acted as they did. It is not consequence that matters, but purpose. The relevant conjunction is not, 'so that,' but 'in order that.' Next, it is to be borne in mind that there may be cases where the combination has more than one 'object' or 'purpose.' The combiners may feel that they are killing two birds with one stone, and, even though their main purpose may be to protect their own legitimate interests notwithstanding that this involves damage to the plaintiffs, they may also find a further inducement to do what they are doing by feeling that it serves the plaintiffs right. The analysis of human impulses soon leads us into the quagmire of mixed motives, and, even if we avoid the word 'motive,' there may be more than a single purpose or object. It is enough to say that, if there is more than one purpose actuating a combination, liability must depend on ascertaining the predominant purpose. If that predominant purpose is to damage another person and damage results, that is tortious conspiracy. If the predominant purpose is the lawful protection or promotion of any lawful interest of the combiners, it is not a tortious conspiracy, even though it causes damage to another person."

It is still not entirely clear how far justification will extend.[31] This aspect of the tort of conspiracy is obviously vulnerable to policy variations and it might be that the courts would not excuse a disproportionately severe injury in pursuit of a relatively unimportant interest.[32] Lord Simon in the *Crofter* case suggested, however, that such a situation would only be relevant as casting doubt on the bona fides of the purpose. Equally, it is the purpose and not the outcome which provides the justification although the purpose may be inferred from the actual consequence. It is also not entirely clear how far conspirators may pursue praiseworthy objectives in which they have no direct interest. In *Scala Ballroom (Wolverhampton) Ltd.* v. *Ratcliffe*[33] justification was held to extend to the pursuit by a trade union of opposition to racial discrimination. It may be said, of

---

[30] [1942] A.C. 435.
[31] See the *Crofter* case at pp. 446–447, 478, 492.
[32] See *Conway* v. *Wade* [1909] A.C. 506.
[33] [1958] 1 W.L.R. 1057.

course, that a union, necessarily of mixed racial membership, has a direct interest in such a policy. It seems unlikely that every pursuit of a charitable or morally justifiable purpose can justify a combination which causes injury. On the other hand much of the difficulty may be dealt with by application of the second head of the test extending to conspiracy to use unlawful means.

It remains true that the normal purposes of a trade union are likely to be held by the courts to provide justification although it must be borne in mind that there is inherent in the concept the power to declare an objective itself to be primarily injurious. This was the situation in *Huntley* v. *Thornton*[34] where members of the district committee of a trade union purported to expel, and subsequently to persecute, a union member contrary to the instructions of the union to cancel the expulsion.

Lord Cave's exposition is not exhaustive of the tort and is now recognised to contain only one aspect of it. A combination to use unlawful means constitutes the tort of conspiracy. To put it another way, if we accept that the combination to injure by unlawful means is unlawful unless justified, what we are saying here is that the employment of unlawful means eliminates the justification of self-interest, even if that self-interest is the predominant purpose. If we say that a combination is lawful unless it is proved that its primary purpose was to injure, then we must add that it is also unlawful if unlawful means were used in the pursuit of any purpose.

(b) Inducement to breach of contract

The period of judicial non-intervention ended in the early 1950s but, quite apart from statutory immunity, the courts had effectively destroyed the possibility of using civil conspiracy against industrial action involving no other element of illegality. They fell back on two other economic torts one of which had not been widely used even in commercial law and the other of which was virtually a new invention. The latter was of particular value briefly because it avoided the statutory immunity afforded to specific torts only without the need to find the absence of action in contemplation or furtherance of a trade dispute. When this avenue was closed by extension of legislative immunity the former— the tort of inducement to breach of contract—came into its own as a much more far-reaching weapon than civil conspiracy had ever been or Intimidation could become. In due course this tort was to be developed to cover any interference with contract. If it can be forgotten that "property interests" are so widespread that liability for interference with them as such would be unduly burdensome it can be said to be capable of logical extension even to protect all interference with property. Its scope, therefore, is more a matter of policy than of principle.

It will be noted that as a weapon the tort of interference with contract lacks the restriction of a developed concept of justification. The only case in which a plea of justification has succeeded would support only some concept of public policy as a defence. Moreover, as we shall see, the essential limitation of a requirement of direct intention is watered down if the only intention needed is to interfere. The further restriction upon this liability becoming oppressively wide is a requirement of knowledge of the nature of the contract. But this has almost entirely disappeared since it seems to be enough to know that there was a

---

[34] [1957] 1 W.L.R. 321.

contract if all that is necessary for liability is an intention to interfere with it. It is difficult to support the view that this steady breakdown of the inhibitions upon this tort liability developing into a monster has been accidental in view of the numerous stillborn examples of attempts which can be added to the list. For example, the attempt to substitute direct inducement through an agent for indirect inducement would remove the need for unlawful means as effectively as the equally abortive attempt directly to eliminate that requirement.

The tort stems from the long-standing common law liability for enticement of a servant to leave his service. In *Lumley* v. *Gye*[35] a strenuous effort was made to confine liability within this narrow limit. The court, however, refused to accept such a limitation in the case of an opera singer who could not have been described as a servant. From that time it was accepted that liability extended to any breach of contract. As with the tort of conspiracy, however, liability for inducement to breach of contract cannot, apparently, be attached where certain relationships exist between the inducer and the person induced.[36] The advice of an agent to his principal for instance, even though sufficient to consitute a technical inducement, would not be considered to render the agent liable to third parties for this tort.

Forms of interference

The tort has three principal forms. It may be committed directly, by the defendant approaching A and inducing him to break his contract with B. Of course, B might choose to sue A in contract. There may be many reasons why he would prefer not to do this but to seek compensation from the person most obviously responsible. The second form may be considered a subdivision of this. In it the defendant does not directly approach A, but persuades A into a breach of contract with B by an act which prevents A from performance of his contract with B. In neither of these forms is it necessary to show that the defendant adopted unlawful means to produce the effect of inducement. In the third form, however, the defendant will not be liable unless the means of inducement were unlawful in the sense of being actionable. This third form is normally referred to as "indirect inducement." Typically the defendant uses the activities of others so as to force A into a position where he breaks his contract with B. For example, a shop steward may influence the employees of A so as to place A in such a position that, either he cannot carry out his contract with B, or he is persuaded that it would be advisable for him not to carry out that contract.

Privacy

It is important to note that the action is only available to a party to the contract broken. It is not, as the tort of intimidation is, available to any third party intentionally injured by the breach who has no interest in the contract to protect. This principle, however, will necessarily disappear if the tort is extended to interference with interests other than contract, since then it will only be necessary for the party to show that he has an interest to protect.

Intention

If this development also replaces the word "inducement" by "interference" the title of the tort will much more nearly disclose its real content. The ordinary

[35] (1853) 2 E. & B. 216.
[36] See *Thomson* v. *Deakin* [1952] Ch. 646 at pp. 680–681.

meaning of inducement conveys the idea of persuading initially unwilling persons to participate in a course of action. In *Thomson* v. *Deakin*[37] Jenkins L.J. said:

"But the contract breaker may himself be a willing party to the breach without any persuasion by the third party, and there seems to be no doubt that if a third party, with knowledge of a contract between the contract breaker and another, has dealings with the contract breaker which the third party knows to be inconsistent with the contract, he has committed an actionable interference."

The last part of this statement refers to the type of situation which arose in *B.M.T.A.* v. *Salvadori*[38] where liability was incurred by a defendant who purchased the car which to his knowledge the vendor had agreed to sell to the plaintiff. Inducement can also take a negative form as in *G.W.K.* v. *Dunlop*[39] where the defendant was held liable for the removal from a car of tyres which the manufacturer was under contract to use on the car and their replacement by tyres of another make. Professor Grunfeld[40] has warned against too wide a view of inducement, saying:

"Not every communication between union officials and their members is an inducement to break a contract merely because it is followed by such a breach. To amount to technical inducement, it may be said that the communication must be both purposive and causative."

This is probably to say no more than that the defendant must intend the breach and that his conduct must be a factor in producing it. Clearly, however, there are examples of persons who take some action in the course of an inducement who cannot be said to have incurred liability for inducement. In *Thomson* v. *Deakin*[41] a messenger was said to be in this excluded category, even if he expected such a result. The facts of that case provided an excellent example of circumspection by the conveyer of the information in order to excuse his liability.

As has already been said, intention to produce the breach of contract is a necessary element in this tort. In this instance, however, the intention required is to produce the breach of contract only; there need be no intention that actual damage should result. It is sufficient that the defendant should evince a reckless indifference as to whether or not a breach of contract occurs.[42] This abrogates the former rule that in such a situation there will be no causal connection because the breach of contract could have been avoided by the party upon whom pressure was put. In *Emerald* v. *Lowthian*[43] the defendants had begun to impose pressure without any clear idea whether compliance with their demands would involve a breach of contract or could be met by a proper termination of the contract. Lord Denning M.R. said[44]:

"Even if they did not know of the actual terms of the contract, but had the means of knowledge—which they deliberately disregarded—that would be enough. . . .

---

[37] *Ibid.* at p. 694. See also *Square Grip Reinforcement Co. Ltd.* v. *MacDonald*, 1968 S.L.T. 65. But see *Camellia Tanker Ltd. S.A.* v. *I.T.W.F., The Times,* February 18, 1976, where interim injunction was refused in absence of evidence of "pressure, persuasion or procuration."

[38] [1949] Ch. 556.   [39] (1926) 42 T.L.R. 376.

[40] *Modern Trade Union Law*, p. 337.   [41] [1952] Ch. 646 at p. 686.

[42] *Emerald Construction Co. Ltd.* v. *Lowthian* [1966] 1 W.L.R. 691.

[43] *Supra.*

[44] *Ibid.* at p. 700. See also *Daily Mirror Newspapers* v. *Gardner* [1968] 2 Q.B. 768.

For it is unlawful for a third person to procure a breach of contract knowingly, or recklessly, indifferent whether it is a breach or not."

Diplock L.J. said[45] that the element of intention is sufficiently established if it is proved that the defendants intended the party procured to bring the contract to an end by the breach of it if there were no way of bringing it to an end lawfully. This seems slightly narrower than Lord Denning's proposition since it appears to leave the party procured with less discretion as to the means he chooses. Both propositions, however, go beyond the distinction attempted by Lord Pearce in *Stratford* v. *Lindley*[46] that where there is direct inducement the inducer is liable whatever the consequence; whereas in indirect inducement he is only liable if breach is the necessary consequence of his action.

Knowledge

There is no doubt that, parallel with this diminution of the element of intention, there has also been a reduction in the amount of knowledge of the contract which is required to formulate the intention. It has never been necessary that the precise terms of the contract should be known and the defendant will, in any case, be presumed to know what is common knowledge as to how a business is conducted.[47] In *Stratford* v. *Lindley*[48] Lord Pearce said:

"It is no answer to a claim based on wrongfully inducing a breach of contract to assert that the respondents did not know with exactitude all the terms of the contract. The relevant question is whether they had sufficient knowledge of the terms to know that they were inducing a breach of contract. If the pressure is continuous then the tort may be constituted at any stage during which the pressure takes effect. If, therefore, a situation occurs in which pressure continues after the time at which the defendant acquired sufficient knowledge of the contract (or, for that matter, sufficient intent) liability will arise at that point of time."

It would seem correct to say that, once the necessary intention to induce a breach of contract exists, all damage that is reasonably foreseeable at the time of the breach may be recovered. A chain reaction of liability will be prevented, in the case of this tort, by the rule that the only person who can bring the action is the person aimed at in the sense of being one of the parties to the contract. It would appear that there is a duty upon such a person to mitigate his loss, but that it is not a high standard of duty.

Illegal means

Liability for indirect inducement depends on the use of illegal means. The courts do not distinguish between illegal means used by the principal to persuade the intermediary to act and illegal action taken by the intermediary to bring about the ultimate breach desired by the principal.

Logically, the distinction between the two types of inducement is insupportable. This becomes apparent if one examines the basic authority for the distinction contained in a statement by Lord Evershed M.R. in *Thomson* v. *Deakin*.[49] He said:

" . . . the intervener assuming in all cases that he knows of the contract, and acts with the aim and object of procuring its breach to the damage of B, one of the

---

[45] [1966] 1 W.L.R. 691 at p. 704.
[46] [1965] A.C. 269.
[47] *Sorrell* v. *Smith* [1925] A.C. 700.
[48] [1965] A.C. 307.
[49] [1952] Ch. 646 at pp. 681–682.

contracting parties, will be liable not only (i) if he directly intervenes by persuading A to break it, but also (ii) if he intervenes by the commission of some act wrongful in itself so as to prevent A from in fact performing his contract; and also (iii) if he persuades a third party, for example a servant of A, to do an act in itself wrongful or not legitimate (as committing a breach of contract of service with A) so as to render . . . impossible A's performance of his contract with B."

Since there will not always be a clear distinction between direct and indirect inducement[50] some judges have had difficulty in seeing why the division between lawful and unlawful conduct should run as it does.[51] This point was taken up by Lord Denning M.R. in *Daily Mirror Newspapers Ltd.* v. *Gardner*[52]; who said:

"It seems to me that if anyone procures or induces a breach of contract whether by direct approach to the one who breaks the contract or by indirect influence through others, he is acting unlawfully if there be no sufficient justification for the interference."

He later withdrew from this advanced position, however, saying[53]:

"*Indirect* interference is only unlawful if unlawful means are used. I went too far when I said in *Daily Mirror Newspapers Ltd.* v. *Gardner* that there was no difference between direct and indirect interference. . . . This distinction must be maintained, else we should take away the right to strike altogether. . . . A trade union official is only in the wrong when he procures a contracting party *directly* to break his contract, or when he does it indirectly *by unlawful means*."

The illegality need only be trivial, although it may be that it must be sufficient to constitute a persuasive factor in itself.[54] By analogy with the rule in the tort of intimidation, it may be assumed that the illegality, despite indications to the contrary in the remarks of Evershed M.R. which have just been quoted, must amount to actionable conduct. It will suffice, however, if the conduct is actionable at the suit of any person. There are signs, however, that the rule may be becoming wider than this. In *Daily Mirror Newspapers Ltd.* v. *Gardner*[55] the recommendation to members of the federation that they should stop ordering the *Daily Mirror* was a trade restriction to which the Restrictive Trade Practices Act 1956 applied and by which it was, prima facie, deemed contrary to the public interest. A decision on whether the restriction was permitted by any special exemptions in the Act was reserved for the Restrictive Practices Court. Lord Denning M.R. took the view that the legality of the practice was within the purview of the Court of Appeal as well, and that it had not been established that such restriction was permitted by the Act. Russell L.J. concluded that the practice was one the Restrictive Practices Court would inevitably declare contrary to the public interest. This appears to introduce into the tort an element of public policy, which is already present, as we shall see, in the existence of a defence of justification. Without this, it might be said that the requirement of illegality was merely a useful device for limiting the scope of an otherwise unmanageably wide liability.

---

50 See Wedderburn, "Stratford v. Lindley" (1965) 28 M.L.R. 257.
51 See *e.g.* Viscount Radcliffe in *Stratford* v. *Lindley* [1965] A.C. 269.
52 [1968] 2 Q.B. 768.
53 *Torquay Hotel Co. Ltd.* v. *Cousins* [1969] 2 Ch. 106.
54 See Russell L.J. in *Morgan* v. *Fry* [1968] 2 Q.B. 710.
55 *Supra.*

Justification

There is undoubtedly a defence of justification to this tort. In *South Wales Miners Federation* v. *Glamorgan Coal Co. Ltd.*[56] Romer L.J. said:

"Regard might be had to the nature of the contract broken, the position of the parties to the contract, the grounds for the breach; the means employed to procure the breach; the relation of the person procuring the breach to the person who breaks the contract; and . . . to the object of the person inducing the breach."

Despite this very wide definition of justification, amounting almost to a discretion in the courts, there is very little authority on what circumstances might be held to constitute justification in this tort. It is clear that a person with a prior contract can protect that contractual right by inducing breach of a subsequent conflicting contract made with the same party. This right probably extends to a situation where, though the defendant's contract is not first in time, he had no knowledge of the plaintiff's prior conflicting contract at the time he made his own. Justification is, however, confined to protection of an existing contract and may not be used to justify an inducement in retaliation for an earlier breach.[57] This limitation apparently applies even if the way is still open for the performance of the earlier contract and the inducement is merely being used as a weapon to produce a desire for such performance. It is, of course, a justification that the inducement is produced by the exercise of statutory powers, providing they are followed closely.[58] Public interest, as a source of justification, was introduced into this tort by the decision in *Brimelow* v. *Casson*.[59] In this case the defendant had induced chorus girls to break their contracts of service with their employer in order to save them from the necessity to resort to prostitution to supplement their meagre earnings in that employment. It is clear from the cases cited, however, that public interest is not the only source of justification.

Agents

The line between direct and indirect inducement to breach of contract is blurred by the remark of Lord Denning M.R. in the *Torquay Hotel* case where he said:

"On reconsideration of the *Daily Mirror* case I think that the defendants interfered indirectly by getting the retailers as their agents to approach the wholesalers."

It is true that in the *Daily Mirror* case the Retailers' Association had taken a positive role in directing the activities of their members by sending out "stop notices" for the retailers to dispatch to their wholesale suppliers. But this is only marginally different from the normal trade union activity in calling upon trade union members employed in a factory to strike. If there is a form of direct inducement where the inducement is applied through agents, as distinct from indirect inducement applied by incited third parties, the line between direct and

---

[56] [1903] 2 K.B. 545 at pp. 574–575.
[57] *Camden Nominees* v. *Forcey* [1940] Ch. 352 at 365.
[58] *Stott* v. *Gamble* [1916] 2 K.B. 504, where licensing justices were held not liable for inducing a breach of contract by the banning of a film, for the showing of which the plaintiff had agreed to hire a theatre.
[59] [1924] 1 Ch. 302.

indirect inducement becomes impossible to sustain. The distinction will either disappear or become capable of being varied in the discretion of the courts. A trade union sued for inducement after all, may, be in some senses the agent of the third parties whom it uses to provide the inducement especially if, as is normal, they are the union members. Conversely, the decision in *Heaton's Transport Ltd.* v. *T.G.W.U.*[60] indicates clearly that, even if acting unofficially, shop stewards might well be considered to be the agents of the union. In effect the development of this form of direct inducement through an agent bypasses the insistence, in the *Torquay Hotel* case, on the need for unlawful means in cases of indirect inducement.

(c) Interference with contract

In 1966 Professor Grunfeld wrote[61]:

> "The cases unanimously make clear that the element of breach of contract lies at the heart of the tort under consideration. If no breach of contract occurs no liability ensues."

He added that the suggestion by Lord Reid[62] that the requirement of a breach was an open question was erroneous. In *Stratford's* case Lord Donovan gave what would then have been considered the correct reply to Lord Reid's suggestion:

> " . . . the argument that there is a tort consisting of some indefinable interference with business contracts, falling short of inducing a breach of contract, I find as novel and surprising as I think the members of this house who decided *Crofter Hand Woven Harris Tweed Co. Ltd.* v. *Veitch* would have done."

The suggestion was not entirely novel. It had been raised in *Quinn* v. *Leathem*[63] and had inspired the second part of the immunity afforded by section 3 of the Trade Disputes Act 1906. But the courts had subsequently rejected it, and, for 50 years, it had been considered to be dead. In *Nagle* v. *Feilden*[64] Lord Denning M.R. and the other members of the Court of Appeal in that case had expressed varying degrees of dissatisfaction that no head of liability should be found in a situation where a willing applicant for employment in a trade was excluded by the restrictive practices of the governing body of that trade. It may well be found that this decision heralds the development of liability for interference with many rights which are recognised and require protection from attack. As yet, no such far ranging development can clearly be seen. In *Emerald Construction Co. Ltd.* v. *Lowthian*,[65] however, Lord Denning remarked that some people would be prepared to hold that it would be unlawful for a third person deliberately and directly to interfere with the execution of a contract, even though he did not produce any breach of that contract. In *Daily Mirror Newspapers Ltd.* v. *Gardner*[66] he had convinced himself that the view of these people was the general rule. He said:

---

[60] [1973] A.C. 15.
[61] *Modern Trade Union Law*, p. 373.
[62] *Stratford* v. *Lindley* [1965] A.C. 269 at 324.
[63] [1901] A.C. 495.
[64] [1966] 2 Q.B. 633.
[65] [1966] 1 W.L.R. 691.
[66] [1968] 2 Q.B. 768.

"I have always understood that if one person interferes with the trade or business of another, and does so by unlawful means, then, he is acting unlawfully even though he does not procure or induce any actual breach of contract. Interference by unlawful means is enough."

Finally, in *Torquay Hotel Co. Ltd.* v. *Cousins*[67] he accepts the authority he has himself thus created for this proposition. Having referred to the long-discarded remarks of Lord Macnaghten in *Quinn* v. *Leathem*[68] to the effect that it was a violation of legal right to interfere without sufficient justification with contractual relations recognised by law, the Master of the Rolls continued:

"The time has come when the principle should be further extended to cover other 'deliberate and direct interference with the execution of a contract without that causing any breach.' "

If this line of cases were the sole authority for the development of this new head of tort liability it might, at its narrowest, be said to consist in *direct* interference, short of inducement to breach of contract, carried out by unlawful means. The development of such a head of liability was not essential to the finding in the *Torquay* case. Though no breach of contract resulted in that case this was because of the existence of a clause in the contract excluding liability for non-performance in the circumstances that occurred. Both Lord Denning M.R. and Winn L.J. said that the defendants could not protect themselves from liability for inducement to breach of contract by relying on an excuse of which they were "the mean." Alternatively, Russell and Winn L.JJ. took the view that there was a breach of contract, the protective clause only providing, as between the parties, an immunity against any claim for damages founded upon that breach. Winn L.J. however lent some support to Lord Denning's view when he said that, where there was an expectation of performance, the procuring of the exercise of an option to cease performance would suffice.

Extension of the tort of interference with contractual rights was given further impetus by the decision in *Acrow (Automation) Ltd.* v. *Rex Chain Belt Incorporated.*[69] The plaintiffs had manufactured special conveying equipment under licence from an American corporation which had patented the product. An essential part of the product was made by an American company closely associated with the patent holders. This part was supplied to the English licensees by an arrangement between the manufacturers and the patent holders. After three years the patent holders purported to terminate the licence, although the term had a further two years to run. Despite injunctions in the English courts the patent holders instructed the suppliers of the essential part in question to cease supplying it and the suppliers complied with this instruction and refused to continue to supply it to the English licensee. They said, however, that they would have been willing to continue the supply but for the patent holder's instructions. The Court of Appeal held that if one person, without just cause or excuse, deliberately interfered with the trade or business of another, and did so by unlawful means, then he was acting unlawfully and in a proper case an injuction could be granted against him.[70]

---

[67] [1969] 2 Ch. 106. See note in (1969) 32 M.L.R. 435.
[68] *Supra.*
[69] [1971] 1 W.L.R. 1676.
[70] See also *Esso Petroleum Co. Ltd.* v. *Kingswood Motors Ltd.* [1974] Q.B. 142.

The elements of this form of tort liability were most clearly expressed by Lord Denning in the *Torquay* case as:

> "First, there must be interference in the execution of a contract. The interference is not confined to the procurement of a *breach* of contract. It extends to a case where a third person *prevents* or *hinders* one party from performing his contract, even though it be not a breach. Secondly, the interference must be deliberate. The person must know of the contract or, at any rate, turn a blind eye to it and intend to interfere with it: See *Emerald Construction Co. Ltd.* v. *Lowthian.* Thirdly, the interference must be *direct.* Indirect interference will not do . . . *indirect* interference is only unlawful if unlawful means are used."

It appears from the more recent cases that the apparent contradiction in this statement between appearing to confine liability to direct interference and then suggesting that liability will extend to indirect interference by unlawful means has been resolved in favour of liability in both instances on exactly the same basis as for the tort of inducement to breach of contract. Unlawful means are, for instance, required to constitute liability for indirect interference.[71] In *Associated Newspapers Group Ltd.* v. *Wade*[72] Lord Denning suggested that unlawful means would include behaviour contrary to the public interest as, for example, interference with the freedom of the Press.

(d) Intimidation

In its industrial aspects the tort of intimidation was fashioned by the decision in *Rookes* v. *Barnard*[73] largely as a means of granting to injured persons, not party to contracts involved, a right of action.

Elements

In *Rookes'* case, Lord Devlin quoted the then current edition of Salmond.[74] Salmond said:

> "The wrong of intimidation includes all of those cases in which harm is inflicted by the use of unlawful threats whereby the lawful liberty of others to do as they please is interfered with. This wrong is of two distinct kinds, for the liberty of action so interfered with may be either that of the plaintiff himself or that of other persons with resulting damage to the plaintiff. In other words, the defendant must either intimidate the plaintiff himself, and so compel him to act to his own hurt, or he may intimidate other persons, and so compel them to act to the hurt of the plaintiff.
>
> (1) *Intimidation of the plaintiff himself.* Although there seems to be no authority on the point, it cannot be doubted that it is an actionable wrong intentionally to compel a person, by means of a threat of an illegal act, to do some act whereby loss accrues to him: for example, an action will doubtless lie at the suit of a trader who has been compelled to discontinue his business by means of threats of personal violence made against him by the defendant with that intention.[75]

---

[71] *Brekkes Ltd.* v. *Cattel* [1972] Ch. 105 at 114.
[72] [1979] I.C.R. 664.
[73] [1964] A.C. 1129; Queen's Bench Division—[1961] 3 W.L.R. 438; [1963] 1 Q.B. 623 (C.A.).
[74] *Salmond on the Law of Torts* (13th ed.), p. 697.
[75] For this proposition Salmond cited the opinion of Hawkins J., advising the House of Lords, in *Allen* v. *Flood* [1898] A.C. 1 at 17.

(2) *Intimidation of other persons to the injury of the plaintiff.* In certain cases it is an actionable wrong to intimidate other persons with the intent and effect of compelling them to act in a manner or to do acts which they themselves have a legal right to do which cause loss to the plaintiff: for example, the intimidation of the plaintiff's customers whereby they are compelled to withdraw their custom from him, or the intimidation of an employer whereby he is compelled to discharge his servant the plaintiff. . . . There are at least two cases in which such intimidation may constitute a cause of action:—

   (i) When the intimidation consists in a threat to do or procure an illegal act;
   (ii) When the intimidation is the act, not of a single person, but of two or more persons acting together in pursuance of a common intention."

This second type Salmond admits to be an aspect of the tort of conspiracy. It follows that the intimidation would have to be by threats of an unlawful act or with the intention primarily to injure the plaintiff rather than to benefit the defendants. There is, therefore, no form of actionable intimidation unless the threat is one of unlawful action.[76]

Unlawful acts

On the most significant head of liability, that of threats of unlawful action designed to produce a course of conduct injurious to a third party, there were until 1961 only two reported actions. In *Garret* v. *Taylor*[77] the threats were to mayhem and annoy by vexatious litigation customers of a quarryman so as to induce them to discontinue business with him. In *Tarleton* v. *M'Gawley*[78] the master of one slave trading ship fired at a native canoe which was about to do business with another ship similarly engaged so that the natives, in panic, ceased to do business with that ship. Some nineteenth-century actions against picketing, which might have been laid in intimidation, were, in view of the interference with free use of premises involved, brought in nuisance. In the Court of Appeal in *Rookes'* case Pearson L.J. concluded that the tort did exist, despite the argument that Salmond had invented it in the first edition of his book in 1909 by relying on an assumption, then current, that the early conspiracy cases depended on the element of threat which they contained. Pearson L.J. said:

". . . I think it does appear from the few and ancient cases, to which I am about to refer, and from the discussion of them long afterwards in the House of Lords, that where the interference takes the form of some gross illegality (such as firing a cannon at a canoe manned by natives, or threatening death or dismemberment to tenants or customers of workmen) committed by A against B with the intention and effect of deterring B from trading or otherwise dealing with C, C has a cause of action against A for the interference with his right."

Presumably it is C's freedom, rather than his right, which is interfered with. As Pearson L.J. had previously acknowledged, the third party element is a peculiarity of the tort. This explanation of the tort also confines it to grossly illegal means. Pearson L.J., like the rest of the Court of Appeal thought that those means should not extend to a breach of contract. If they did, the tort might

---

[76] *Hodges* v. *Webb* [1920] 2 Ch. 70; *Morgan* v. *Fry* [1968] 2 Q.B. 710.
[77] (1620) Cro.Jac. 567.
[78] (1793) 1 Peake 270.

outflank the doctrine of privity.[79] The House of Lords rejected this limitation. Lord Reid said:

> "It must follow from *Allen* v. *Flood* that to intimidate by threatening to do what you have a legal right to do is to intimidate by lawful means. But I see no good reason for extending that doctrine. Threatening a breach of contract may be a much more coercive weapon than threatening a tort, particularly when the threat is directed against a company or corporation. . . ."

Lord Devlin added:

> "The essence of the offence is coercion. It cannot be said that every form of coercion is wrong. A dividing line must be drawn and the natural line runs between what is lawful and unlawful as against the party threatened . . . if the intermediate party is threatened with an illegal injury, the plaintiff who suffers by the aversion of the act threatened can fairly claim that he is illegally injured."

This would eliminate the requirement of gross illegality. A modification of this is contained in the remark by Lord Denning M.R. in *Morgan* v. *Fry*[80]:

> "The new point in *Rookes* v. *Barnard* was that the threat of a breach of contract was held to be 'unlawful means.' The breach of contract in that case was of a flagrant kind. . . . If *Rookes* v. *Barnard* is carried to its logical conclusion, it applies not only to the threat of a flagrant breach of contract, such as occurred in that case, but also to the threat of any breach of contract—so long as it is of sufficient consequence to induce the other to submit."

If the person intimidated is not induced to submit, no action will lie in any event.

Russell L.J. also pointed out that Lord Devlin, in *Rookes'* case, had suggested that if the breach there had merely been the giving of a few days' less notice than was proper to terminate employment, this might have been too technical, since it would not have been the illegal means which produced the intimidation but the strike itself. He expressed no concluded view on the matter.

It is clear that the threatened wrong must be actionable. Lord Reid had doubts about this in *Rookes'* case but the general view was summed up by Lord Denning M.R. in *Stratford's* case when he said that it would be absurd that liability should attach to a threat to do something which would not be actionable if done. So special statutory protection of a particular immunity will protect the threat. This is, of course, a different matter from such illegality as arose in *Daily Mirror Newspapers Ltd.* v. *Gardner*,[81] where the illegal action was not actionable but could be enjoined by a special procedure. A threat to impose an unpermitted restrictive trade practice would, presumably, constitute the tort of intimidation because it would be a threat of action the defendant was not entitled to take.

No court has yet examined the degree of communication required to constitute a threat. If the defendant had "leaked" his threat to the Press, or some other selected intermediary, liability would, presumably, attach. Suppose, however, that the defendants had protested at the employment of a non-union

---

[79] This same point was strongly argued by Wedderburn, "The Right to Threaten Strikes" (1961) 24 M.L.R. 572; (1962) 25 M.L.R. 513.

[80] [1968] 2 Q.B. 710.

[81] [1968] 2 Q.B. 768. The principle of an inducing threat was attached to unfair industrial practices throughout the Industrial Relations Act 1971.

worker and, as soon as that man was engaged, had called a strike without proper notice or in breach of agreement. The employer may put two and two together and treat this as an indication that the strikers will continue their illegal action unless the man is dismissed. Is he entitled to regard this as a threat? It is suggested that he is not, but it is by no means easy to see where the line should be drawn.

Justification

The possibility of justification as a defence was briefly mentioned in the Court of Appeal and by Lord Devlin in the House of Lords in *Rookes'* case. It was referred to again by Lord Denning M.R. in *Morgan* v. *Fry*.[82] Lord Denning there suggested that a justification might have existed if it could have been shown that the breakaway workers were "troublemakers fomenting discord" in the docks. He admitted, however, that the place of justification as a defence in intimidation had not been established. It is suggested that it is unlikely to lie in such a direction. On the other hand, it seems that the courts were thinking in terms wider than those applicable to inducement to breach of contract.

(e) Other civil liability

Interference with trade

Once the tort of inducement to breach of contract has been extended to cover any interference with contract, especially if that is to include interference with potential contracts, the temptation to create a tort of interference with trade is obvious. Most trade, after all, is conducted by way of contract. In *Torquay Hotels Ltd.* v. *Cousins*[83] Lord Denning M.R. revived the arguments in favour of such liability first put forward in *Allen* v. *Flood*.[84]

> "I have always understood," he said, "that if one person deliberately interferes with the trade or business of another, and does so by unlawful means, that is, by an act which he is not at liberty to commit, then he is acting unlawfully, even though he does not procure or induce any actual breach of contract."

It will be realised that the Master of the Rolls is actually talking of extension of inducement to breach to cover interference with contract, but chose to describe the new liability as for interference with trade. In *Hadmor Productions Ltd.* v. *Hamilton*[85] Lord Denning, with the support of Watkins L.J., clearly asserted the existence of a separate tort of interference with business by unlawful means. Lord Diplock, with whom all the other members of the House of Lords agreed, whilst overruling virtually every other point made by the Court of Appeal, did not specifically refer to the question whether such a separate head of liability existed.[86]

If such duality does exist its implications could be alarming. "Trade" is an almost unlimited concept.[87] In *Brekkes Ltd.* v. *Cattel*[88] it was said that in this

---

[82] [1968] 2 Q.B. 710. See also *Cory Lighterage Ltd.* v. *T.G.W.U.* [1973] I.C.R. 339 at 357.
[83] [1969] 2 Ch. 106 at 139.
[84] [1898] A.C. 1.
[85] [1981] 3 W.L.R. 139.
[86] [1982] I.R.L.R. 102.
[87] See, *e.g. Nagle* v. *Feilden* [1966] 2 Q.B. 633.   [88] [1972] Ch. 105.

context it should be taken only to refer to an established course of dealing likely to lead to such contracts. It appears, however, that this is to seek to define "trade" as trade.

Duress

In *Universe Tankships Inc. of Monrovia* v. *International Transport Workers Federation*[89] union officials prevented a Liberian vessel from sailing until the operators had complied with certain demands by the I.T.W.F. These demands involved payment of a sum of money into the union's welfare funds. The plaintiffs yielded to the demands but, after the ship had been allowed to sail, claimed repayment of the money as money paid under duress. The Court of Appeal overruled the High Court decision that the plaintiffs were entitled to recover but only because the plaintiffs had accepted that if the action was in contemplation or furtherance of a trade dispute it was statutorily protected. The Court made it clear that apart from this concession, which it thought not to be based on a correct view of the law, the action for duress would have lain.

The House of Lords by a majority (Lords Scarman and Brandon dissenting) held that the statutory protection was not available. The majority took the view that the dispute in question was one as to payment of money to the fund and that this had no connection with terms and conditions of employment. Having avoided the statutory protection the majority held that the union had obtained the money by duress so that the apparent consent of the shipowner could be revoked. Lord Scarman's summary of the elements of liability for duress was not at variance with the view of the majority and is much the most clear. He said:

> "It is, I think, already established law that economic pressure can in law amount to duress; and that duress, if proved, not only renders voidable a transaction into which a person has entered under its compulsion but is actionable as a tort, if it causes damage or loss. . . . The authorities . . . reveal two elements in the wrong of duress: (1) pressure amounting to compulsion of the will of the victim; and (2) the illegitimacy of the pressure exerted. There must be pressure, the practical effect of which is compulsion or the absence of choice. Compulsion is variously described in the authorities as coercion or the vitiation of consent. The classic case of duress is, however, not the lack of will to submit but the victim's intentional submission arising from the realisation that there is no other practical choice open to him. This is the thread of principle which links the early law of duress (threat to life or limb) with later developments when the law came also to recognise as duress first the threat to property and now the threat to a man's business or trade. The development is well traced in Goff and Jones *The Law of Restitution* (2nd edn, 1978), ch 9.
>
> The absence of choice can be proved in various ways, eg by protest, by the absence of independent advice, or by a declaration of intention to go to law to recover the money paid or the property transferred. . . . But none of these evidential matters goes to the essence of duress. The victim's silence will not assist the bully, if the lack of any practicable choice but to submit is proved."

As Lord Scarman said, the issue then was whether the pressure applied by the union was illegitimate. Lord Diplock, in the majority, had argued by analogy with the protection afforded by the legislature to action in contemplation of a

---

[89] [1981] I.C.R. 129 (C.A.); [1982] 2 All E.R. 67 (H.L.). See, Wedderburn (1982) 45 M.L.R. 556 and (1982) 11 I.L.J. 156.

trade dispute that the legislature had, thereby, indicated that such activities were, broadly, legitimate. Since, in his view, the present dispute was not connected with the subject matter of a trade dispute it did not produce a legitimate object of duress.

It is, to say the least, a little surprising if industrial action to support economic demands constitutes economic duress unless the purpose can be said to be legitimate. The same does not appear to be true of the pressures brought to bear by multi-national companies where it appears that furtherance of self-interest would be regarded by the courts as a justification.[90] If it is so then it would seem necessary to have some more reliable standard of legitimacy than an argument by analogy to statutory immunity in tort.

Other straws are in the wind of an even stranger kind. In *Ex parte Island Records Ltd.*[91] a majority of the Court of Appeal held that an injunction would lie to restrain a threat to interfere with any proprietary right, including trade, by means of crime. In that case the crime was that of producing records from illicit recording of concerts contrary to the Dramatic and Musical Performers Protection Act 1958.[92] The Court declined to classify the conduct as a tort. Nevertheless it will be remembered that the tort of Intimidation was an extension from liability for threats of violence. Threats of crime would seem capable of similar extension and if that is so it seems a little difficult to deny that a tort has been created.

Breach of statutory duty

Elias Napier and Wallington[93] draw attention to the decision in *Prudential Assurance Co. Ltd.* v. *Lorenz*[94] granting an interlocutory injunction to prevent a trade union calling upon insurance agents to withhold the submission of weekly accounts to their employing companies. The agents would have been in breach of an equitable (as well as a contractual) duty to account. Statutory immunity did not cover an inducement to break the equitable duty. The learned authors show how the argument can be extended to inducement to break a statutory obligation.[95] If the supposed wrong of inducing breach of statutory duty is now a tort it is capable of considerable extension beyond individual liability. If it were a tort, it would fall outside any statutory immunity afforded to trade unions.

The legislature has acted upon the invitation to enforce statutory obligations by actions in tort.[96] It has provided that failure on grounds of union membership or exclusion from recognition to include upon a list of approved suppliers of goods and services the name of a particular person, excluding a person from a group from whom tenders are invited, failing to permit such a person to tender, otherwise determining not to enter into a contract with a particular person for such supply, or terminating a contract for such supply constitute breach of duty

---

[90] See, *Lonrho Ltd.* v. *Shell Petroleum Co. Ltd.* [1981] 2 All E.R. 456—A conspiracy case.
[91] [1978] 3 All E.R. 824.
[92] s.1.
[93] pp. 242–243.
[94] (1971) 11 K.I.R. 78.
[95] *Meade* v. *London Borough of Haringey* [1979] 1 W.L.R. 637; *Associated Newspapers Group Ltd.* v. *Wade* [1979] I.C.R. 664.
[96] Employment Act 1982, ss.12(7) and 13(4).

actionable at the suit of the person concerned or any other person adversely affected by such breach. No doubt it is the function of the legislature to determine the balance but if it is to be decided upon such piecemeal consideration it may be that breach of statutory duty is as dangerous a weapon as any forged before 1906.

LEGISLATIVE INTERVENTION

General considerations

The reader may be forgiven if he fails to see the direct relevance of any of the above mentioned heads of liability to the nature of industrial action. The ingenuity of the common law in developing an action for seduction to control modern industrial action would be admirable if it were not laughable, and would be laughable if its exacerbating effect on industrial relations could be ignored. The reader may also suspect that the history of this judicial development has been one of attempts to sidestep legislative intention to maintain a balance in favour of protection of business interests. Only during one period of unusual economic adversity did this process of boring and tunnelling cease.

The legislature, however, has been reluctant to intervene. It has, as we shall see, normally recognised the inappropriateness of the weapons we have described to the control of collective bargaining by granting far-reaching immunity to trade unions and the leaders of industrial action. It has not, however, sought to define the forms of action which it considers legitimately available to the parties in dispute as demonstrations of their relative strengths. This accords with basic constitutional principle. The definition of rights is often restrictive of a pre-existing freedom. Talk of such freedom is however meaningless if those in whose favour it exists are powerless to exercise it because of the power of those who oppose them.

If we look now at the position we have reached we may ask whether it would be possible to allow the parties to get on with the regulation of industrial relations without intervention. We shall then be in a position to consider the sufficiency of such intervention. Industrial action can only be justified as the means whereby labour acts in concert to balance the economic and, in practice, concerted power of capital. If when pitting their strength one party or the other knows that it can recoup the loss caused by the other's attack from that other by legal action the force of that attack is virtually destroyed. What has been seen of the heads of civil liability available against the organisers of industrial action makes it clear that such would be the position without legislative intervention. From 1906 to 1980 such legislative intervention was maintained and effectively avoided such a consequence. Since the Employment Act 1980 the legislature has ventured to modify the effect of statutory immunity so as to manipulate the balance of power. Detailed policy considerations are now applied and the student has to consider, for instance, the desirability, even the feasibility, of a declared policy of protecting "neutrals" by the prohibition of secondary action.

The complete contrast in relation to individual participants, as distinct from organisers of industrial action, is startling. Employer and employee are, as we have seen, left virtually free to use what legal weapons they have. The effect may well be that industrial action ceases to operate as a stage in bargaining and acts instead to stop the process. The employee who deprives the employer of his labour will be met by deprivation of wages. This may well seem a legitimate response. Indeed it is frequently suggested that the most sensible legal response to strikes would be to suspend the employment relationship or, in other words, for the law to declare its neutrality. By not withdrawing, the law tends to favour the employer. The common law never offered the employee much job protection[97] and statute, as we have seen has declined to afford to those engaged in industrial action, its extended protection against dismissal.[98] If, as the *Simmons* case suggests, this is due to a conscious decision to allow the employer to continue to hold the initiative given him by accepted management prerogative, the time may well come when the absence of such an attitude to labour disputes in other countries persuades the legislator that such a conclusion is not inevitable.

It is suggested that legislative intervention to protect the individual from his legal vulnerability (which, of course, extends to liability for the torts discussed in this chapter) would be necessary if the legal position were likely to be exploited against him. Significantly the weight of attack has always been upon the organisers of industrial action. The reasons may appear obvious and the common law has enhanced them on occasion as by the restriction of damages which may be obtained against an individual. On closer examination, it is suggested, these reasons are not compelling. Thoughts of widespread use of the injunction against organisers reveal that that weapon has its drawbacks. The extension of vicarious liability to trade union funds[98a] is an obvious attempt to counter the relative ineffectiveness of the remedies for extended liability. If these remedies continue to fail to produce change the individual participant may, for the first time, find himself the focus of attention.

The provision of State benefits

State neutrality is usually advanced to explain why social security benefits should be withdrawn from those engaged in trade disputes. Certain aspects of this withdrawal have been accepted without criticism. So, for instance, government operated "Job Centres" do not afford facilities to employers to recruit replacements for those of his employees who are on strike.

Unemployment benefit

An unemployed person is not disqualified from receiving unemployment benefit because he declines, as unsuitable, "employment in a situation vacant in consequence of a stoppage of work due to a trade dispute."[99] On the other hand there exists an equally long-standing permanent disqualification from unemployment benefit for all who are actually participating in a stoppage of work and, more controversially, for many of those affected by lay-off consequent upon that stoppage. The present provision contained in the Social Security Act 1975[1] is as follows:

---

[97] *Chappell* v. *Times Newspapers Ltd.* [1975] I.C.R. 145.
[98] *Simmons* v. *Hoover Ltd.* [1977] I.C.R. 61.
[98a] Employment Act 1982, ss.15 and 16.
[99] This long-standing provision is now contained in the Social Security Act 1975, s.20(4).
[1] s.19(1) as amended by the E.P.A. 1975, s.111.

"(1) A person who has lost employment as an employed earner by reason of a stoppage of work which was due to a trade dispute at his place of employment shall be disqualified for receiving unemployment benefit so long as the stoppage continues, except in a case where, during the stoppage, he has become bona fide employed elsewhere in the occupation which he usually follows or has become regularly engaged in some other occupation; but this subsection does not apply in the case of a person who proves—

> (a) that he is not participating in or directly interested in the trade dispute which caused the stoppage of work."

The original reason for this disqualification was that the purpose of the insurance scheme is to protect those who become unemployed through the ordinary fluctuations of trade or business rather than because of strikes or lockouts. The exceptions were introduced, extended or restricted, from time to time to avoid excessive hardship to those who were not really concerned with the dispute but who, because they worked in close relation to those who were so concerned, lost their employment accordingly. Around this basic proposition there has developed a great amount of detail the relevance of which is not always apparent.

The dispute must have occurred at the claimant's place of employment.[2] If at that place there are separate departments doing work which would normally be undertaken at separate establishments,[3] a man in one such department, who loses work because of a dispute in another, may avoid the disqualification.[4]

A question that often arises is whether the continuing unemployment is due to the dispute or whether that dispute has ended. A convenient starting point for discussion is a classic, but much misunderstood decision of the Commissioner.[5] An employee was dismissed because of a shortage of materials. Other employees complained of this and gave notice to terminate their contracts. They were, however, dismissed with wages in lieu of notice on the ground that they were troublemakers. The Commissioner said:

> "A stoppage of work [for this purpose] must be in the nature of a strike or lock-out, that is to say, it must be a move in a contest between an employer and his employees, the object of which is that employment shall be resumed on certain conditions. If a stoppage was not designed for this purpose but was a result of a decision to cease to be employed or to give employment (as the case may be), it would not in our opinion be due to a trade dispute within the meaning of the subsection, notwithstanding that this decision was because of the existence of a trade dispute. . . . The mere fact that notice to terminate employment is given is not usually significant. Such notice is commonly required by the contract of employment and the fact that it is given is not inconsistent with an intention to resume employment on fresh terms."

---

[2] Defined in s.22(6)(a). It may be wide enough, for instance, to include the car body and assembly plants at Cowley as one place of employment. See also R(U) 8/71.

[3] As to what would normally be done elsewhere, see R(U) 1/70—car trim not "normally" manufactured at separate establishments.

[4] See e.g. R(U) 24/57; R(U) 5/61; compare R(U) 3/62; R(U) 23/64; but see R(U) 1/70 —Fords of Dagenham—factory. A majority of the Royal Commission rejected the contention that the removal of disqualification should be extended to exclude the effect of disputes in any other department, whether a normally integrated part of the establishment or not—see Cmnd. 3623, para. 972.

[5] R(U) 17/52. It is interesting to compare the attitude of the Commissioners with that of the courts in relation to dismissal during industrial action. Supra, p. 244.

For some time, it was assumed that this decision meant that a stoppage due to a trade dispute would continue to be so, after settlement of the dispute, pending, for example, the resumption of full production[6]; but that a stoppage made permanent by the permanent closing of the plant, or the intended permanent dismissal of the employees to whom the claim related, would cease to be the result of a trade dispute. In a later decision, however,[7] it was said that the original decision in 1952,

> " . . . decides only that a stoppage of work which is due to dismissal is not, for the dismissed employee, due to a trade dispute . . . it affords no authority for holding that, if a stoppage of work is due to a trade dispute, a determination by either party to sever relations permanently with the other brings the stoppage to an end."

A trade dispute stoppage may come to an end without the settlement of the dispute if sufficient workers return to provide the employer with enough men to prevent work being hindered.[8] Those who remain out of work will not be disentitled to benefit unless it can be shown that a fresh dispute exists. Such a fresh dispute might arise, for example from an argument about the payment of wages during the original stoppage.[9] In one case,[10] certain printers who had taken part in a national stoppage were prepared to resume work on a specified day. By then the employer had finally dismissed them and he refused to take them back save as non-unionists. It was held that there was a fresh dispute concerning the terms of re-employment. From this it is clear that the existence of a dispute does not depend on the taking of hostile action. Claimants who had lost their work because they refused to terminate a meeting about working conditions which extended beyond the meal break were held to have been engaged in a trade dispute concerning the rejection of the claims for better conditions.[11]

A man indefinitely suspended within 12 days of a stoppage is rebuttably presumed to have lost work by reason of the dispute leading to that stoppage.[12]

With the repeal of the Trade Disputes Act 1906, and the provision by the Trade Union and Labour Relations Act 1974 of a new definition of "trade dispute," the definition of a trade dispute for the purposes of this provision becomes somewhat isolated from the rest of the law of industrial disputes. It is defined in the Social Security Act 1975 as: "Any dispute between employers and employees, or between employees and employees, which is connected with the employment or non-employment or the terms of employment or the conditions of employment of any persons, whether employees in the employment of the employer with whom the dispute arises, or not."[13] This is very similar to the old general definition but differs from the new definition of an industrial dispute in that it is less detailed. The definition has already given rise to some surprising decisions; for example, that a claimant who was prevented from working by pickets was disqualified from benefit because of the existence of a trade dispute between him and the pickets.

---

[6] R(U) 19/51.   [7] R(U) 1/65.

[8] R(U) 25/57; R(U) 11/63. Compare, *Heath* v. *Longman Ltd.* [1973] I.R.L.R. 214.

[9] R(U) 3/69; (1970) 7 K.I.R. 517.

[10] R(U) 12/60.

[11] R(U) 21/59.

[12] See R(U) 20/27—where the presumption was considered to have been rebutted.

[13] Social Security Act 1975, s.19(2)(*b*).

A claimant may seek to show that he is not participating in or directly interested in the trade dispute.[14] Of this provision the Royal Commission said[15]: "There is general agreement that a person participating in a trade dispute at his place of employment and becoming unemployed in consequence ought not to be supported by the insurance fund during such unemployment." On its face, this appears to be a reasonable attitude, but it must be pointed out that even the narrow term "participation" can be given a surprisingly wide meaning. It has been said[16] that a person participates in a dispute if he knowingly does something or refrains from doing something which contributes to the continuance of the dispute. This is somewhat inelegantly phrased but its width is borne out by the cases. In one case,[17] a colliery "repairer" lost employment due to a stoppage of "brushers." Repairers, who could be required to work as brushers, were offered such work in this instance, but refused to take it. It was held that they were participating in the dispute. Some form of active support is necessary, however, and mere failure to attend a union meeting to vote against a stoppage does not involve participation.[18] In the same way if one attempts to go to work but is prevented against one's will by the activities of pickets, it cannot be said that there is participation in *their* dispute on that ground alone.[19]

"Direct interest," like "participation," would give little cause for objection if it was narrowly construed. There are a number of decisions in which what is said to be direct interest looks somewhat indirect. It has been said that a direct interest must be a "substantial and material" one,[20] but again it has been stated that the provision is concerned with the nature of the interest and not with the magnitude of it.[21] In the latter decision the only matter in dispute which would affect the claimant was a proposal to do away with the afternoon tea-break. He was held to be directly interested in the dispute as a whole. In some cases the claimant has had no option but to be in a position where he can be said to be interested. In one such,[22] the dispute concerned the level of heating in a workshop. The platers stopped work, and a plater's helper was held to be directly interested in the dispute since he was bound to be affected by the physical conditions in the workshop. But the mere question of whether the employee should return to work does not involve a direct interest.[23]

Supplementary benefit

More recently steps have been taken to extend the exclusion from supplementary benefit entitlement. Normally supplementary benefit is payable where

---

[14] The practice is then for a test case to be taken and for the Department of Social Security to accept the result as normally applicable to all similar claimants—see *e.g.* R(U) 3/69.

[15] Report, Cmnd. 3623, para. 982.

[16] Calvert, *Social Security Law* (2nd ed.), p. 165.

[17] R(U) 41/56.

[18] R(U) 3/69—had the decision been otherwise it would have been necessary to show that *all* the members of the claimant's grade or class attended the meeting, but see, *Coates and Venables* v. *Modern Methods and Materials Ltd.* [1982] I.R.L.R. 318 (C.A.).

[19] R(U) 5/66. Compare, *McCormick* v. *Horsepower Ltd.* [1981] I.C.R. 535 (C.A.)—refusal to cross a picket line did not involve participation in industrial action in the absence of a common purpose.

[20] R(U) 18/58.   [21] R(U) 3/62.

[22] R(U) 4/65, see also *Punton* v. *Ministry of Pensions and National Insurance* [1963] 1 W.L.R 186.   [23] R(U) 3/69.

the head of a household is unemployed and the family income falls below a certain minimum level. It follows that entitlement to such benefit as a result of industrial action would only arise in the case of prolonged stoppages. Supplementary Benefit is not available in any case to the striker or person laid off in the same circumstances as those covered by the unemployment benefit provision we have just discussed.[24] In 1971 the availability of Supplementary Benefit was further restricted by treating tax rebates and strike pay as resources, subject to disregarding the first £4 per week thereof.[25] The Social Security (No. 2) Act 1980 section 6 further limits the provision. All payments (including strike pay and tax rebates) received during the period of the stoppage are to be fully taken into account and the first £4 is no longer disregarded. If, after taking account of such factors, the weekly amount due is £12 or less then no payment is made, whilst if the figure exceeds £12 that amount is deducted from it.[26] "Urgent need" payments are no longer available and additional amounts for heating and certain other specified requirements will not normally be paid where any member of the family is affected by a trade dispute.

Although the original intention of the disqualification from unemployment benefit was, no doubt, to extend neutrality to all who would benefit from selective industrial action it had been extended beyond that principle. The reduction of its scope to the present level following criticism by the Royal Commission on Trade Unions[27] may be seen as a restoration of a principle nearer to neutrality. On the other hand unemployment benefit is designed to relieve need and it may be argued that to permit such need to operate is itself a redistribution of the balance. However this may be there can be little argument about the motive for reduction of poverty relief available to a striker's family. Gennard[28] shows that previously the withdrawal of social security benefits has had little effect on the behaviour of strikers. Toughening the law relating to the provision of that benefit cannot be intended to do anything but attempt to produce some effect and, as we have seen, any disincentive to industrial action must affect the balance of power. Whatever the doubts in the past it is now clear that the State is prepared to use provision of social security benefit as a means of intervention.

Criminal sanctions

For a number of reasons, including the pursuit of neutrality, the criminal law has not, in this century, been applied to more than the periphery of industrial action. As we shall see, statute and the common law apply criminal sanctions to forms of picketing considered undesirable.[29] Members of the armed forces are not permitted to strike. Following the police strike of 1919 the Police Act made it unlawful to organise a strike of police. It is an offence to incite military

---

[24] Supplementary Benefits Act 1976, s.8.
[25] See now Supplementary Benefits Act 1976, Sched. 1, paras. 23 and 26.
[26] Since the purpose of this was to encourage trade unions to pay more strike pay Regulations have been made to prevent such higher payments merely reducing the amount of benefit due—Supplementary Benefit (Trade Disputes and Recovery of Earnings) Regulations 1980 (S.I. 1980 No. 1641).
[27] 1965–68.
[28] *Financing Strikers* (1977) p. 154.
[29] *Infra*, p. 523.

personnel or police to strike.[30] It is unlawful for a policeman to be a member of a trade union or of any association, apart from the Police Federation, having as one of its objects the control of pay, pensions or conditions of service in any police force.[31]

The Merchant Shipping Act 1894 was in a different category in imposing sanctions against seamen who went on strike in that the offences had direct links with the concept of mutiny and thus, in a way, with the former fear of combinations. These provisions were, however, modified by the Merchant Shipping Act 1970 so as to permit a seaman to leave his ship in furtherance of a trade dispute provided that he gives 48 hours' notice after the ship has reached a safe berth in the United Kingdom.[32] Selective blacking of mail by Post Office workers was considered by the House of Lords in *Gouriet* v. *Union of Post Office Workers*[33] to constitute the crime of wilfully detaining or delaying any postal packet in the course of transmission by post.[34] It appears from *Harold Stephen and Co.* v. *Post Office*[35] that the Court of Appeal considered any refusal to handle mail to be a crime but it is doubtful whether such refusal could be implied from ordinary strike action.

The Conspiracy and Protection of Property Act 1875, s.3, by rendering industrial action immune from the crime of conspiracy, undoubtedly signalled the withdrawal of criminal sanctions generally from industrial disputes. It left a small residue by providing that an employee of a gas or water undertaking[36] (to which electricity was later added) committed an offence if he wilfully and maliciously broke a contract of service with that authority knowing or having reasonable cause to believe that the probable consequence of his so doing, either alone or in combination, would be to deprive the inhabitants of the area covered by the authority of the whole or the greater part of their supply of that commodity. Despite the fact that, in evidence to the Royal Commission of 1965–68, the chairmen of the nationalised gas and electricity industries both said that they thought the sections provided some deterrent to would-be strikers although they had never been invoked, and that the Royal Commission (apparently diverted from its normal approach by this evidence) recommended retention of the provision, it was repealed by the Industrial Relations Act 1971.[37] A similar recommendation by the Royal Commission for retention in respect of a second provision was, however, accepted by the legislature. That section provided that where *any* person wilfully and maliciously breaks a contract of service *or of hiring* knowing or having reasonable cause to believe that the probable consequences of his so doing, either alone or in combination with others, will be to endanger human life or cause serious bodily injury or to expose valuable property to destruction or serious injury, that person should be liable to a fine of up to £20 or to imprisonment for a term not exceeding three months.

---

[30] Incitement to Disaffection Act 1934, s.1; Police Act 1964, s.53(1).

[31] Police Act 1964, s.47.

[32] These provisions remain anomalous in that they accept the concept of a strike by a single individual and the discarded rule that a strike terminates the contract of employment.

[33] [1978] A.C. 435.

[34] Post Office Act 1953, s.58.

[35] [1978] 1 All E.R. 939.

[36] See ss.4, 5 as extended by the Electricity Supply Act 1919, s.31.

[37] s.133.

Finally, it should be noted that it is possible than an agreement among employers to lock out workers will amount to an agreement whereby two or more persons accept restrictions "in respect of . . . the quantities or descriptions of goods to be produced, supplied or acquired." This would be subject to registration, and possible prohibition, under the Restrictive Trade Practices Act 1956.[38]

There is no doubt that this abstention of the criminal law is a wise one. The activities of the N.I.R.C. under the Industrial Relations Act 1971, in committing to prison for contempt certain leaders of pickets revealed all too clearly the undesirable effect of making martyrs of industrial activists.[38a] The Royal Commission on Trade Unions had already observed and documented this effect.[39] In 1969 the Labour Government, in order to avoid the problem of taking criminal action against strikers, had proposed a type of hybrid fine, collected by civil procedures. The unions violently objected to this and the proposal was withdrawn. There can be little doubt that criminal sanctions will have no substantial effect on an existing strike nor will they have much effect as a deterrent from striking. They derive most of their effect at this level not from the degree of penalty but from the social stigma attaching to them. If, instead, the effect is to produce acclamation of the criminal their value not only is lost, but is reversed.

Statutory immunity from civil liability

(i) *Trade unions*

The legislature responded in 1906 to the realisation by the courts that the earlier grant of immunity from liability to conspiracy was in terms confined to criminal conspiracy and the extension of liability for the newly recognised tort of conspiracy to trade unions as such. The legislature also chose the opportunity to grant immunity from the established tort of inducement to breach of contract and the somewhat hypothetical tort of interference with trade. In view of the apparent facility with which the courts were able to open new lines of liability as existing ones were eliminated, it is somewhat surprising that the legislature chose to proceed in this piecemeal fashion. Its reluctance to grant general protection to the individual organiser is even more surprising because it extended such general immunity to trade unions. Even if its decision not to limit trade union immunity to actions in contemplation or furtherance of a trade dispute can be explained as a restoration of the position as it was thought to be before the decision in *Taff Vale Railway Company* v. *A.S.R.S.*[40] it is difficult to see why it should not have granted a general immunity from actions in tort to those individuals acting in contemplation or furtherance of a trade dispute.

Immunity was granted to trade unions in wide general terms.[41]

---

[38] See s.6(1)(10); *Re The Agreement between the Scottish Daily Newspapers Society and its members,* noted in (1971) 34 M.L.R. 575.

[38a] *Churchman* v. *Joint Shop Stewards Committee of the Port of London* [1972] 1 W.L.R. 1094.

[39] See Appendix 6 of the Report: Cmnd. 3623.

[40] [1901] A.C. 426.

[41] s.4 provided:

(1) An action against a trade union, whether of workmen or masters, or against any members or officials thereof on behalf of themselves and all other members of the trade

Such extensive protection had been the subject of attack in recent years. It had earlier been said[42] that its effect was to prevent the grant of an injunction against a threatened tort, because Parliament could not have intended to allow to be forbidden a threatened activity which would not have been actionable if carried out. This obviously correct assessment of intention was questioned, by Lord Denning M.R., on the strict interpretation of the section.[43] Later still, in the judicial retreat following the Donovan Report, this doubt was withdrawn by a Court of Appeal which included Lord Denning.[44] Winn L.J., who dealt most fully with the point, said that a section which was obviously designed to protect trade unions could hardly have been intended to leave their funds open to attachment following disobedience of an injunction. The much earlier attempt to avoid the effect of the section by permitting actions to be brought against union trustees for tort under the saving clause in subsection (2)[45] would have resulted in even greater absurdity, and came to nothing.

It was, however, almost impossible to justify the width of the protection that the section afforded, and the Donovan Report recommended that it be confined to torts committed in contemplation or furtherance of a trade dispute.[46] The whole of the 1906 Act was repealed by the Industrial Relations Act 1971,[47] and section 4 was not re-enacted in any form. It reappeared in a limited form in the Trade Union and Labour Relations Act 1974.[48]

This provided that immunity should not apply to the liability of a trade union or employers' association for negligence, nuisance or breach of duty (statutory or otherwise) resulting in personal injury or, without prejudice to this general head of liability, to any liability arising from breach of duty in connection with the ownership, occupation, possession or control or use of real or personal property; so long as such liability does not arise from an act done in contemplation or furtherance of a trade dispute.

The Employment Act 1982[49] has, in part, responded to criticism of the immunity of trade unions and in part has sought, by repealing the earlier provision, to increase the effectiveness of sanctions against industrial action for which individuals may also be liable by extending liability in certain situations to union funds.

Vicarious liability

The effect of the 1982 Act is to provide trade unions with immunity from actions for interference with contract, intimidation by way of threat of inter-

---

union in respect of any tortious act alleged to have been committed by or on behalf of the trade union, shall not be entertained by any court.

(2) Nothing in this section shall affect the liability of the trustees of a trade union to be sued in the events provided for by the Trade Union Act 1871, s.9, except in respect of any tortious act committed by or on behalf of the union in contemplation or in furtherance of a trade dispute.

[42] *Ware and De Freville* v. *Motor Trade Association* [1921] 3 K.B 40.
[43] In *Boulting* v. *Association of Cinematograph, Television and Allied Technicians* [1963] 2 Q.B. 606.
[44] *Torquay Hotel Co. Ltd.* v. *Cousins* [1969] 2 Ch. 106.
[45] *Vacher* v. *London Society of Compositors* [1913] A.C. 107.
[46] Cmnd. 3623, para. 909.
[47] s.169 and Sched. 9.
[48] s.14(1).   [49] s.15. See K. D. Ewing (1982) 11 I.L.J. at pp. 218 *et seq*.

ference with contract or conspiracy where liability arises only from the element of combination, wherever an individual acting in contemplation or furtherance of a trade dispute would enjoy that immunity and also to provide trade unions with immunity where they cannot be shown to have authorised the actions complained of as defined by the section. We shall deal with individual immunity in due course. Authorisation, for the purpose of fixing liability upon a trade union is defined as follows:

[15] "(3) For the purposes of this section, but subject to subsection (4) below, an act shall not be taken to have been authorised or, as the case may be, endorsed by a responsible person unless it was authorised or, as the case may be, endorsed—

(a) by the principal executive committee;
(b) by any other person who is empowered by the rules to authorise or, as the case may be, endorse acts of the kind in question;
(c) by an official who is a regular attender of meetings of the principal executive committee;
(d) by any other official who is an employed official; or
(e) by any committee of the union to whom an employed official regularly reports.

(4) An act shall not be taken, by virtue of subsection (3)(d) or (e) above, to have been authorised or endorsed by a responsible person if—

(a) that person was, at the time in question, prevented by the rules from authorising or endorsing acts of the kind in question; or
(b) the act has been repudiated by the principal executive committee or by an official who is a regular attender of its meetings.[50]

(5) For the purposes of subsection (4)(b) above, an act shall not be treated as repudiated unless—

(a) it is repudiated as soon as is reasonably practicable after it has come to the knowledge of the principal executive committee or of an official who is a regular attender of its meetings; and
(b) the person who purported to authorise or endorse the act has been notified in writing and without delay that it has been repudiated.

(6) An act shall not be treated as repudiated, notwithstanding subsection (5) above, if at any time after the union concerned purported to repudiate it the principal executive committee or an official who is a regular attender of its meetings has taken a step which is inconsistent with the purported repudiation.

(7) In this section—

"official" means an official of the union concerned; and "employed official" means, in relation to that union, an official who is employed by it;
"principal executive committee" means the principal committee of the union concerned exercising executive functions, by whatever name it is known;
"regular attender," in relation to the principal executive committee of a union, means a person who has regularly attended meetings of that committee (whether or not as a member of that committee) and who, at the time when he purported to authorise or, as the case may be, endorse or repudiate an act had not ceased to attend its meetings;
"rules" means the written rules of the union and any other written provisions forming part of the contract between a member and the other members (or, in the case of a special register body, between a member and the body)."

---

[50] It will be noted that the effect of this is to encourage specific withdrawal of power from local levels.

This concept of authorisation was said by the government in a green paper prior to publication of the Bill, to be intended to accord with the common law principles laid down in *Heatons Transport (St. Helens) Ltd.* v. *T.G.W.U.*[51] It must be noted carefully that that case was actually dealing with liability for shop stewards. They are not included in the list of officials in subsection (3) whose authorisation will impose liability on a trade union. In other words, the 1982 Act accepts the view of the Court of Appeal as to authorisation from the top and does not extend to authorisation from the membership. It does not, however, appear to require such authorisation to be express.

Lord Wilberforce: (Delivering the judgment of the House of Lords):

"No new development is involved in the law relating to the responsibility of a master or principal for the act of a servant or agent. In each case the test to be applied is the same: was the servant or agent acting on behalf of, and within the scope of the authority conferred by, the master or principal?: *Hewitt* v. *Bonvin* and *Launchbury* v. *Morgans*. Usually a servant, as compared with an agent, has a wider authority because his employment is more permanent and he has a larger range of duties as he may have to exercise discretion in dealing with a series of situations as they arise. The agent in an ordinary case is engaged to perform a particular task on a particular occasion and has authority to do whatever is required for that purpose but has no general authority. That is the explanation of the reasoning in the case of the *Wigan Election Petition* and in *Lucas* v. *Mason*. In the former case Martin B. was stating and applying 'the ordinary rule with regard to principal and agent': that the principal 'is only responsible for that which he authorises the agent to do.' In the latter case Pollock B. said at pp. 253–254:

'In the present case there was no relation of master and servant, or of principal and general agent, or agent for such cases as might occur in the absence of the principal, but a particular direction as to a particular matter, . . . In the case of master and servant, the character and duties attaching to the employment are known and defined beforehand, the servant who is to perform them is selected accordingly. In the present case no such relationship existed in the first instance, nor did it arise during the transaction. . . . There is no such pre-existing relationship as exists in the case of master and servant, and there is, we think, no ground for extending by implication an express authority limited in its terms.'

Those two cases do not show that for the purpose of determining the responsibility of the master for acts of a servant and that of the principal for the acts of an agent different tests are to be applied. They only show that application of the same test may produce different results.

But there are cases in which an agent who is not a servant does have authority of considerable generality. He may be elected or appointed to some office or post for a substantial period and he may have to perform acts of several classes on behalf of the principal and he may have to exercise a discretion in dealing with a series of situations as they arise. The position of such an agent and the scope of his authority are very similar to those of a servant. . . .

One of the principal objects of the union is described in rule 2(2)(*b*) as

"The settling and negotiation of differences and disputes between the members of the union and employers, and other trade unions and persons, by collective bargaining or agreement, withdrawal of labour or otherwise.'

---

[51] [1972] I.C.R. 308; *Chappell* v. *Times Newspapers Ltd.* [1975] I.C.R. 145. But see *General Aviation Services Ltd.* v. *T.G.W.U.* [1976] I.R.L.R. 224.

This clearly recognises the use of strikes and other industrial action as incidental to the negotiation and settling of industrial differences and disputes; and it is conceded that the members have agreed that included in the action which the union is authorised to take on behalf of all of them is to organise 'blacking' as a means of reaching a settlement of a difference or dispute satisfactory to those members of the union who are affected by it.

What is contended is that authority to act on behalf of the union in calling for any form of industrial action by any of its members is confined to the general executive council itself or to a national or regional trade group committee or regional or district committee to whom such authority has been expressly delegated by the general executive committee. The rules, it is suggested, do not allow of such authority to be delegated to shop stewards, nor has any such delegation purported to be made.

This argument based upon the necessity for delegation of authority by the general executive council commended itself to Lord Denning M.R. and to Roskill L.J. in the Court of Appeal. There are passages in their judgments where the words 'the union' are used so as to mean the general executive council and senior permanent officers at its headquarters. But questions of delegation from 'the top,' to use the phrase adopted by Roskill L.J. do not arise if authority to take industrial action has either expressly or implicitly been conferred directly upon shop stewards from 'the bottom' *i.e.* the membership of the union, whose agreement is also the ultimate source of authority of the general executive council itself. One therefore looks first at the rule book to see what kinds of action the members of the union have expressly agreed may be taken on their behalf by shop stewards.

Shop stewards are elected by the membership in a defined working place and hold office for two years. Upon ratification of their election by the appropriate district committee and regional committee they are accredited officials of the union. Their credentials may be withdrawn by the regional committee or its authorised sub-committee, but only if the shop steward is not acting in accordance with the union rules and policy.

The purpose for which shop stewards are elected is described as that of 'representing membership on matters affecting their employment.' This is a phrase which is both wide and vague. No doubt their main concern is intended to be the particular industrial interests of the members of the union in the work places for which they are shop stewards. This has given rise to the suggestion that they place a 'dual role,' in that in respect of some acts done by them they are to be treated in law as agents for the union, but in respect of others as agents only for those members of the union by whom they have been elected as shop stewards. For the latter the union is said to be not responsible in law as their principal.

This concept of duality of roles is not one which would be likely to occur to trade unionists. The rules of the Transport and General Workers' Union themselves provide that 'Shop stewards shall receive the fullest support and protection from the union.' Even upon the lowest basis of individual self-interest—and there is no reason to suppose that members of trade unions are actuated by this alone—it may well be thought that an improvement in the earnings or conditions of employment of any group of members will make it easier to achieve improvements for other groups and ultimately for all the members. There is thus no a priori reason why the members of the union should not agree that shop stewards should be authorised by *all* the members to take action to promote the interests of members employed in a particular work place.

That this is the industrial strategy of the Transport and General Workers' Union in particular is apparent from the introductory paragraph in the shop stewards' handbook issued by the union to shop stewards and from the following extract from the official journal of the union, the 'Record,' for February 1972:

'Wage increases worth hundreds of millions of pounds have been won by the T.G.W.U. in the last year—and the key to this success has been the fact that the union has involved shop stewards and members in taking decisions on agreements.'

That in what they do for the purpose of representing membership in the work place shop stewards are acting on behalf of the members of the union as a whole is emphasised time and again in the Shop Stewards' Handbook.

'As a shop steward there is no doubt that the eyes of the members in your shop are upon you. You are the union as far as they are concerned. You are the agency through which come any services which our union provides for them, and through which they normally hear about us.' Again: 'Remember first of all you are an official of the union'; and again: 'As a shop steward you represent *on behalf of the union* its members in the work place.'

That decisions by the union must be taken only at the 'top' is specifically disclaimed in the 'Record' (May 1972) where it is said:

'to limit the ability of the union to act vigorously in the place of work or encouraging the idea that decisions have to be taken at the "top" and handed down, is merely to encourage breakaways and splits that will end in anarchy in industrial relations.'

The basic error which underlies the judgments of the two members of the Court of Appeal from whose decision Buckley L.J. ultimately did not feel he should dissent, lies in their acceptance of the necessity to find some express delegation of authority from the top—a necessity which the union itself consistently and publicly disclaims."

It should be noted that a trade union is no longer protected from torts other than those to which section 13 of the 1974 Act applies. Section 15 of the 1982 Act has no effect on liability for other torts authorised according to common law rules. We have seen that there are signs of the development of such forms of liability applicable to industrial action. In those situations it is open to a complainant to argue that the action of a shop steward has been authorised by the membership so as to make the union liable.[51a]

So far as limited vicarious liability, as defined in section 15, is concerned it was the intention of the government that such liability should attach, regardless of the fact that union rules excluded the authority. The section does not in terms impose liability for *ultra vires* acts and it is arguable that it does not change the common law in that respect. If a trade union is to escape liability for an otherwise authorised act by repudiation the section requires that repudiation to be prompt.

Damages. In any action in tort (whether under this provision or arising from ordinary principles) the liability of a trade union is limited to certain maximum sums depending on the size of the union. The Secretary of State has power to vary the sums which are currently:

£10,000 if the union has less than 5,000 members;
£50,000 if the union has 5,000 or more members but less than 25,000;
£125,000 if the union has 25,000 or more members but less than 100,000;
£250,000 if the union has 100,000 members or more.

[51a] But see, *General Aviation Services (U.K.) Ltd.* v. *T.G.W.U.* [1976] I.R.L.R. 224.

The political and provident funds of the union[52] are protected against such liability.

The potential effect of such provisions is incalculable. It is, perhaps as unlikely that an employer would seek to worsen his own industrial relations by seeking damages from union funds as by bringing actions for damages against his own employees. Even if the union in question is not one with which he negotiates he may fear the sympathetic effect of such an action upon his own unions. In a country where no provision is made for employee representation if an employer chooses not to recognise trade unions it may seem surprising that legislative provision should be made which is only likely to encourage employers who reject organised representation of their workforce to attack such representative organisation.

The possibility that they will do so, or that the practical inhibition upon organised employers will effectively be reduced is enhanced by the removal of most of the former statutory immunity from most secondary action. It is possible that the legislature seeks, by fear, to induce unions to extend their central control over officials. There would only be political reason in this if liability extended to the actions of shop stewards and that, as we have seen, applies rather by default than conscious design in this piece of legislation.

(ii) *Individuals*

The simple decision in 1906 to permit maintenance of the balance between employer and employee by removing the major legal checks upon the individuals who organised concerted action held until 1980. The most serious attack upon it in this period was the decision of the House of Lords in *Rookes* v. *Barnard*[53] that the protection did not extend to a conspiracy to intimidate. The Conservative government elected in 1979, however, had clearly concluded that this general immunity had enabled trade unions to tip the balance unfairly in their favour, particularly by pressurising the so-called "neutral" involved in secondary action. The Court of Appeal had clearly operated on this assumption for some years before that and the Master of the Rolls had publicly stated during a lecture tour in Canada that the British election was about trade union power. The result has been the introduction of complex, and as yet untried, manipulation of the balance which will be examined stage by stage.

All individual immunity is restricted to actions "in contemplation or furtherance of a trade dispute." The principal source of statutory immunity is now section 13 of TULRA 1974.

"An act done by a person in contemplation or furtherance of a trade dispute shall not be actionable in tort on the ground only—

(a) that it induces another person to break a contract or interferes or induces any other person to interfere with its performance; or

(b) that it consists in his threatening that a contract (whether one to which he is party or not) will be broken or its performance interfered with, or that he will induce another person to break a contract or to interfere with its performance.

---

[52] Employment Act 1982, s.17(2).
[53] [1964] A.C. 1129.

[(2) For the avoidance of doubt it is hereby declared that an act done by a person in contemplation or furtherance of a trade dispute is not actionable in tort on the ground only that it is an interference with the trade, business or employment of another person, or with the right of another person to dispose of his capital or his labour as he wills.[53a]]

(4) An agreement or combination by two or more persons to do or procure the doing of any act in contemplation or furtherance of a trade dispute shall not be actionable in tort if the act is one which, if done without any such agreement or combination, would not be actionable in tort."

Trade Dispute. If there is no dispute it is not possible to contemplate one. The courts have consistently held that the process of contemplation does not permit protection to be claimed by one who imagines the hypothetical possibility of a dispute arising. In *Bents Brewery Co. Ltd.* v. *Hogan*[54] it was said that the dispute must be imminent or impending. This follows the view expressed by Lord Shaw in *Conway* v. *Wade*.[55]

"My Lords, I think the argument was well founded that the contemplation of such a dispute must be the contemplation of something impending or likely to occur, and that the words do not cover the case of coercive interference in which the intervener may have in his own mind that if he does not get his own way he will thereupon take ways and means to bring a trade dispute into existence. To 'contemplate a trade dispute' is to have before the mind some objective event or situation, with those elements of fact or probability to which I have adverted, but does not mean a contemplation, meditation or resolve in regard to something as yet wholly within the mind and of a subjective character."

Lord Scarman in *N.W.L. Ltd.* v. *Woods*[56] reaffirms that despite the subjective test of furtherance of the dispute the actual existence of such a dispute must be more than merely present in the minds of those concerned. An issue which has been settled cannot be contemplated or furthered as a dispute unless raised again.[57] On the other hand industrial disputes normally develop over a period and it has been said that it is not necessary for the parties to be locked in combat before a dispute will be held to exist.[58] Presumably the raising of a claim can be implied from the reasonable conclusions an employer would attach to union actions.

Now that disputes between workers and workers have again been excluded from the definition of a trade dispute[59] the question will once more arise of the extent to which an employer can remain aloof and claim that he is not in dispute. Such a possibility had been the basis of the decision in *Larkin* v. *Long*[60] and its possibility was accepted in *Crofter Hand Woven Harris Tweed Association* v.

[53a] This subsection was repealed by the Employment Act 1982, Sched. 4.
[54] [1945] 2 All E.R. 570.
[55] [1909] A.C. 506 at 522. See also *Crazy Prices (Northern Ireland) Ltd.* v. *Hewitt* [1980] I.R.L.R. 396 (N.I. Ct. of App.).
[56] [1979] I.C.R. 67 quoted *infra*, p. 503.
[57] *Sherard* v. *A.U.E.W.* [1973] I.C.R. 421. See also *J.T. Stratford and Son Ltd.* v. *Lindley* [1965] A.C. 307; *B.B.C.* v. *Hearn* [1977] I.C.R. 685.
[58] *Beetham* v. *Trinidad Cement Ltd.* [1960] A.C. 132.
[59] Employment Act 1982, s.18(2)(*b*).
[60] [1915] A.C. 814. Compare *Brimelow* v. *Carson* [1924] 1 Ch. 302.

Veitch.[61] In *Cory Lighterage Ltd.* v. *T.G.W.U.*[62] certain tugmen had refused to work with a man whose union dues were in arrear. The employer acquiesced in their attitude and sent the man home on full pay. The Dock Labour Board, however, refused permission to dismiss the man and the employer sought to relieve the pressure on him by injuction against the union and its officials. The Court of Appeal held that no dispute existed with the employer. Lord Denning M.R. said:

> "Since the decision in *White* v. *Riley* there have been many cases in which union men have refused to work with a non-union man. They have threatened the employers that unless the non-union man is dismissed, they will stop work. It has always been accepted that a dispute on those lines as to union membership is a 'trade dispute.' Such was *Rookes* v. *Barnard* and *Morgan* v. *Fry*. The reason is plain. It was because the dspute fell exactly within the words of the Act of 1906 as a dispute 'between workmen and workmen' which is connected with the employment or non-employment of any person.
>
> Now among the many changes made by the Industrial Relations Act 1971, there is one very significant one. It omits the words 'between workmen and workmen.' So all the cases which rested on those words since *White* v. *Riley* onwards must be put on one side. A dispute as to union membership is a typical dispute between workmen and workmen. It does not fall within the new definition of industrial disputes.
>
> A parallel can be drawn from a demarcation dispute. This, too, in its inception is a dispute between workmen and workmen. The employers may afterwards get involved in it, much against their will. But that does not make them parties to the dispute. The point was specially considered by the *Royal Commission on Trade Unions and Employers' Associations* 1965–1968 presided over by Lord Donovan. Their report says:
>
> > 'The following members of the commission, namely, Lord Robens, Sir George Pollock and Mr. John Thomson, are of the opinion that demarcation disputes between trade unions in which the employer is neutral (that is, is indifferent as to which of the contending parties' members do the particular job) should be excluded from the statutory definition of trade dispute and that this should be achieved by deleting the words "or between workmen and workmen." They point out that the dispute they have in mind is not of the employer's making, that he can do nothing to resolve it and that in these circumstances it is unjust that he should be debarred from exercising legal remedies which might otherwise be open to him.'
>
> The remaining members of the Royal Commission did not agree with the deletion of the words. 'To do so' they said 'would, in any event, not solve the dispute: it would merely leave the employer free to sue for damages in certain cases where he cannot sue now.'
>
> Yet Parliament, with the report before them, did delete the words 'or between workmen and workmen.' The omission must have been deliberate. Parliament must have intended that a dispute between workmen and workmen should be subject to the ordinary law unless the employer was, or became, a party to it on his own account."

It should be noted that Lord Denning here distinguishes between later becoming involved in the dispute and later "becoming a party on [the employer's] own account."

---

[61] [1942] A.C. 435.
[62] [1973] I.C.R. 339.

The particular situation arising in this case was subsequently covered in part by statute which now provides[63]:

> "An act, threat or demand done or made by one person or organisation against another which, if resisted, would have led to a trade dispute with that other, shall, notwithstanding that because that other submits to the act or threat or accedes to the demand no dispute arises, be treated for the purposes of this Act as being done or made in contemplation of a trade dispute with that other."

It should be noted, however, that the position of acts subsequent to that submitted to is not covered. It would seem easy enough to draw an employer into a dispute by making a demand upon him which it is known he will not resist. That demand will be deemed in contemplation or furtherance of a dispute. No action or threat apart from this is covered, however. That which is not a dispute only becomes a dispute so as to protect the unresisted demand. The fact that the act has been deemed to be protected does not mean that the employer has been deemed to be drawn into the dispute so as to make it a trade dispute.

Before 1982 it was commonly assumed that a trade dispute could be raised solely by outside intervention without the participation of the employees whom it concerned.[64] This indeed was the assumption behind the argument in a series of cases dealing with intervention by the International Transport Workers Federation to raise the level of pay and other terms and conditions on ships sailing under flags of convenience.[65] In most of these cases the crews affected had obviously been willing to accept the sub-standard conditions. The Employment Act 1982[66] however, now requires that the dispute must arise initially between workers and their employer. Once the dispute has arisen outsiders may contemplate and further it but in future it will be necessary to find a disaffected employee before a trade union can intervene. A dispute between two employers has never been within the scope of the immunity.[67]

In 1974 the definition of a trade dispute had been extended to matters occurring outside Great Britain.[68] The 1982 Act restricts this to situations where the outcome of the dispute outside the *United Kingdom* is likely to affect the person taking action within the United Kingdom in one or more of the matters constituting a trade dispute.

Subject matter of trade disputes. These matters are set out in section 29 of TULRA[69]

> " . . . 'trade dispute' means a dispute between *workers and their employer which relates wholly or mainly* to one or more of the following, that is to say—
>
> (a) terms and conditions of employment, or the physical conditions in which any workers are required to work[70];

---

[63] TULRA 1974, s.29(5).

[64] *Beetham* v. *Trinidad Cement Co. Ltd.* [1960] A.C. 132.

[65] See: *N.W.L. Ltd.* v. *Woods* [1979] 3 All E.R. 614; *Midland Cold Storage Co. Ltd.* v. *Turner* [1972] I.C.R. 230.

[66] s.18(2)(a).

[67] *Larkin* v. *Long* [1915] A.C. 814.

[68] TULRA 1974, s.19(3).

[69] As amended by Employment Act 1982, s.18, TULRA 1974, s.29 is now re-enacted as s.126A of E.P.A.—Employment Act 1982 Sched. 3, Part II, para. 13(3).

[70] In *Hearn* v. *B.B.C.* [1977] I.C.R. 685 Lord Denning M.R. said that the reference to terms and conditions did not require that those should be contractual terms. The claim need only refer, therefore, to working practices and need not require variation of the contract.

    (b) engagement or non-engagement, or termination or suspension of employment or the duties of employment, of one or more workers;

    (c) allocation of work or the duties of employment as between workers or groups of workers;

    (d) matters of discipline;

    (e) the membership or non-membership of a trade union on the part of a worker;

    (f) facilities for officials of trade unions; and

    (g) machinery for negotiation or consultation, and other procedures, relating to any of the foregoing matters, including the recognition by employers or employers' associations of the right of a trade union to represent workers in any such negotiation or consultation or in the carrying out of such procedures.

Principal and ancillary purposes. In *Hearn* v. *B.B.C.*,[71] the Court of Appeal required that the dispute should have direct reference to one or more of these matters. It sought on this basis to distinguish coercive action from a trade dispute if the coercion made no reference to terms and conditions of employment. Quite apart from the fact that this seems to ignore the existence of some of the heads in the list it also goes against previous interpretation of the words "connected with." These words were used from 1906 to 1971 and again from 1974 to 1982 applied to a more or less wide concept of terms and conditions of employment. In the interval the words "related to" were substituted but no issue arose in which the difference was discussed by the courts. The words "related wholly or mainly to" have now been introduced to eliminate the effect of the decision of the House of Lords in *N.W.L. Ltd.* v. *Woods*[72] setting aside the effect of the decision in *Hearn's* case, that any connection with the above matters, however ancillary to the main issue, would suffice. Lord Diplock said:

"It was submitted on behalf of the shipowners in the instant cases, as it had been in *The Camilla M*, that the real object of the ITF is to drive 'flags of convenience' (as they define them) off the seas, so that every vessel is entered on the registry of the nation to which her beneficial owner belongs; and that, it is suggested, is a political and not what Lord Denning M.R. in *The Camilla M* described as 'a legitimate trade object.' It may well be that this is indeed the ultimate object of ITF's campaign of blacking vessels sailing under flags of convenience unless their crews are engaged on ITF standard articles at ITF rates of wages; but this, in my view, would not prevent the immediate dispute between ITF and the shipowners in which the interlocutory injunctions are sought, from being a dispute connected with the terms and conditions of employment of those workers who were or might become members of the *Nawala's* crew. Furthermore in a case originating in the commercial court it would be carrying judicial anchoritism too far if this House were to feign ignorance of the fact that, apart from fiscal advantages, one of the main commercial attractions of registering vessels under flags of convenience is that it facilitates the use of cheap labour to man them. So even the ultimate object of ITF's campaign is connected with the terms and conditions of employment of seamen. . . .

My Lords, I would accept that there may be cases where strikes are called or refusals to perform contracts of employment in some particular respect are ordered by trade unions for political reasons that are unconnected with any of the subject

---

[71] [1977] I.C.R. 685.
[72] [1979] I.C.R. 867.

matters described in section 13(1). *British Broadcasting Corpn* v. *Hearn* provides an example of this. Union officials threatened that their members would refuse to allow the BBC to televise the cup final in such a way that it could be seen by viewers in South Africa. This was not a dispute connected with the terms and conditions of employment; but it could readily have been turned into one by a demand by the union that the contracts of employment of employees of the BBC should be amended to incorporate a term that they should not be obliged to take part in the transmission of sporting events to South Africa.

My Lords, if a demand on an employer by the union is about terms and conditions of employment the fact that it appears to the court to be unreasonable because compliance with it is so difficult as to be commercially impracticable or will bankrupt the employer or drive him out of business, does not prevent its being a dispute connected with terms and conditions of employment. Immunity under section 13 is not forfeited by being stubborn or pig-headed. Neither, in my view, does it matter that the demand is made and the dispute pursued with more than one object in mind and that of those objects the predominant one is not the improvement of the terms and conditions of employment of those workers to whom the demand relates. Even if the predominant object were to bring down the fabric of the present economic system by raising wages to unrealistic levels, or to drive Asian seamen from the seas except when they serve in ships beneficially owned by nationals of their own countries, this would not, in my view, make it any less a dispute connected with terms and conditions of employment and thus a trade dispute, if the actual demand that is resisted by the employer is as to the terms and conditions on which his workers are to be employed. The threat of industrial action if the demand is not met is nonetheless an act done in furtherance of that trade dispute. I do not regard *The Camilla M* as distinguishable from the instant case. In my view it should be treated as overruled . . . ."

Lord Scarman confirmed this view.

"The dispute is, upon its face, connected with the terms and conditions of employment not only of the crew of the *Nawala* but of all seafarers, many of whom are members by affiliation of the union. The union objects to the practice of shipowners making use of flags of convenience to secure cheap labour on their ships. The evidence certainly suggests that the union also has other objections to flag of convenience ships. But, unless one gives words whatever meaning one chooses (and judges, unlike Humpty-Dumpty, are not permitted this freedom), the dispute is connected with the terms and conditions of the employment of workers (including the crew of the *Nawala*) in the shipping industry. It is, therefore, apparently covered by sub-paragraph (a) of the subsection [s.29(1)]. The appellants concede this much. Their case is, however, that the dispute is not really about the terms and conditions of employment of this particular crew at all but part and parcel of a campaign being waged all over the world by the ITF against flags of convenience. The 'predominant motive' of the union, it is said, is political, not industrial. They rely upon *Conway* v. *Wade* and *The Camilla M* for the proposition that an extraneous motive, if it be the predominant motive, will prevent a dispute from being a trade dispute even though it appears to fall within the subsection.

I totally reject the legal foundation of this case. If there be a conflict between the decision of this House in *Conway* v. *Wade* and the language of the subsection construed in the light of the purpose (or policy) of the legislation, I have no doubt that it would be the duty of this House to reject *Conway* v. *Wade*. If the decision of the Court of Appeal in *The Camilla M* is (as I believe) inconsistent with the subsection, it is wrong and must be overruled.

All that the subsection requires is that the dispute be connected with one or more of the matters it mentions. If it be connected, it is a trade dispute, and it is immaterial whether the dispute also relates to other matters or has an extraneous, *e.g.* political or personal, motive. The connection is all that has to be shown.

Does it follow that *Conway* v. *Wade* must now be treated as wrongly decided? I confess that I find it a difficult case to understand. Section 5(3) of the Act of 1906 was basically the same as section 29(1) of the Act of 1974: all it required was that a dispute be connected with one or more of the matters it mentioned. On the face of it, the dispute in the case was so connected. But the facts were very special. The jury found as a fact that it was a case of personal animosity or grudge, and nothing else, as also was *Huntley* v. *Thornton* decided by Harman J. No connection was, therefore, proved in either case.

The continuing importance of *Conway* v. *Wade* is that it remains good authority for the proposition that the connection required by the subsection must be a genuine one, and not a sham. The mere pretext, or 'specious cover,' of a trade dispute will not do: see *J.T. Stratford & Son Ltd.* v. *Lindley per* Lord Pearce. But *The Camilla M* was, in my view, wrongly decided . . .

It is only if the alleged connection is a pretext or cover for another dispute which is in no way connected with any of the matters mentioned in the subsection that it is possible to hold that the dispute is not a trade dispute. The facts in *British Broadcasting Corpn* v. *Hearn* illustrate the sort of case in which there may be no connection—an objection by workers to apartheid leading to a decision to black the transmission to South Africa of the television showing of the cup final."

There is no doubt that this represented a broader approach to the meaning of the words "connected with" than had been adopted in earlier cases. The decision in *J.T. Stratford and Son Ltd.* v. *Lindley*[73] was not only based on the assumption that the courts were required to ask what the matter was about but also seems to have assumed that the subject of enquiry was the actions rather than what caused them to give rise to a dispute. The decision of the House of Lords in the *N.W.L.* case would leave very few practical possibilities of action being unconnected with trade disputes. A strike wholly in protest at legislation having no connection with industrial matters would be excluded because the government would not be involved in its capacity as an employer.[74] It is easy to see from the facts of *B.B.C.* v. *Hearn*[75] how political objection to the policies of the government of South Africa could have been given the necessary trade connection by a demand that the employer should agree to variation of the contract of employment so as to provide that employees could not be required to assist in broadcasting to that country. In *General Aviation Services* v. *Transport and General Workers Union*[76] the N.I.R.C. accepted that concern about the policy of the British Airports Authority (as such and not as an employer) to contract out certain functions was a dispute connected with the security of employment.

Only a handful of cases such as *Huntley* v. *Thornton*[77] are left in which the courts might have been prepared to hold the predominant purpose—in that instance the pursuit of a personal vendetta—so dominant as to exclude any

---

[73] [1965] A.C. 307.
[74] *Associated Newspapers Group Ltd.* v. *Flynn* (1970) 10 K.I.R. 17; *Sherard* v. *Amalgamated Union of Engineering Workers* [1973] I.C.R. 421.
[75] [1977] I.C.R. 685.
[76] [1974] I.C.R. 35.   [77] [1957] 1 W.L.R 321.

ancillary trade aspect. In the *N.W.L.* case Lord Scarman was prepared to treat the decision in *Conway* v. *Wade*[78] as demonstrating that the dispute must be genuine. With respect it is difficult to see how that factor could be determined but it is possible that the facts in that case might also be taken to demonstrate only the motive of jealousy. The House of Lords whilst regarding its view as the only reasonable construction of the words "connected with" took care to indicate that this did not imply agreement with the policy of so wide an immunity. In *Universe Tankships of Monrovia Ltd.*v. *I.T.F.*[79] Lord Diplock appeared to be on the way to avoiding some of the more sweeping consequences of his earlier approach. The House of Lords was concerned to consider the statutory immunities as affording, by analogy, legitimacy to the purposes for which economic duress had been applied.

Lord Diplock said:

> "'Connected with' also is a wide expression, but it, too, has its limits. In my view, it is not enough in order to create the necessary connection between a dispute relating to terms and conditions of employment of employees of a particular employer, and a demand made on the employer by a trade union acting on its own behalf and not on behalf of employees working for the employer, that the demand should be made at a time when the trade union is negotiating a collective agreement relating to the terms and conditions of employment of those employees, and the employer's yielding to that demand is made a condition precedent to the lifting of the blacking additional to the condition precedent that the employer should also agree to the terms of the collective agreement insisted on by the trade union. To take an extreme example, if a trade union were to demand as a condition precedent to lifting a blacking that the employer should make a contribution to a particular political party favoured by the union, or to a guerilla group in some foreign country, such a demand whenever it was made would not, in my opinion, have the necessary connection with any dispute about terms or conditions of employment in furtherance of which the blacking was imposed."

Lord Scarman, in the minority, clearly adhered to the earlier wider view:

> "It is a necessary part of the immediately preceding argument that payments to the union for the fund were made on behalf of crew members and were intended to be for their benefit. The fund is governed by rules which the I.T.F., if it acts in accordance with the rules, can amend. The objects of the fund, as defined by the rules, are very wide ('promoting . . . by any such means as the Executive Committee in their absolute discretion may decide, the interests of seafarers': see r.2); and there is no legal principle to prevent the ITF, if it acts constitutionally, from winding up the fund and transferring its substantial cash assets to itself. But the fund does exist; it is used to provide amenities in many ports for seamen; there is no indication that the union has any present intention other than to maintain the fund in the interests of seafarers; and without contributions obtained from owners there would be no fund available for their welfare. I am not prepared, on the evidence, to find that the payment of contributions to the fund is not of benefit to seafarers in general, or to the crew members of this ship, even though I recognise that some may never benefit from it."

The legislature, however, preferred the policy represented by the narrower view adopted by the Court of Appeal in looking for the primary purpose. The

---

[78] [1909] A.C. 506.
[79] [1982] 2 All E.R. 67.

Employment Act 1982 has accordingly replaced "connected with" by the words "which relates wholly or mainly to." It is difficult to speculate at all accurately upon the likely effect of such a major change. It seems likely, however, to cause difficulty wherever a union is pursuing a particular dispute as part of a wider policy since it would appear that both the immediate and the wider object must fall within the list of items. Suppose, for instance, that the policy of the union is to oppose racial discrimination as in *Scala Ballroom Ltd.* v. *Ratcliffe.*[80] This may produce justification or "legitimacy" but if, in respect of other purposes, it does not the incidental effects of the dispute upon employment will cease to provide immunity.

Contemplation or furtherance. In a remarkable series of attacks upon the legislative immunity between 1976 and 1980 the Court of Appeal advanced a considerable number of proposed limitations based upon restriction of the meaning of "contemplation or furtherance." They may be summarised thus:

(i) One must consider the motive of the action to decide whether it is in contemplation or furtherance of a trade dispute. A dislike of flags of convenience, for example, might provide a non-trade motive notwithstanding that it was advanced by attacks on terms and conditions of employment.[81]

Making demands in connection with terms and conditions which the person against whom they are made cannot meet is evidence that securing agreement to them is not the motive of those who put them forward. There must be established a genuine intention to enter the dispute.[82]

(ii) Not every consequence of a trade dispute is in furtherance of it[83]—the remoteness test.

(iii) The action must be objectively capable of furthering the dispute.[84] The words "contemplation or furtherance" are not synonymous with "in the belief of furtherance." So the blacking of one product or customer cannot be said to be in furtherance of a dispute with an employer other than such a customer or one using that product.

All these limitations were destroyed by two decisions of the House of Lords although legislation has since reintroduced the substance of some of them either generally or in relation to secondary action.

In *N.W.L. Ltd.* v. *Woods*[85] the House of Lords held that it was immaterial that non-trade matters provide the predominant object. A predominantly political motive does not prevent a connection with terms and conditions of employment and so there can be an ancillary furtherance of the trade aspects of the dispute.[86] The immunity is not forfeited because it is impossible to comply with the demands. In *Express Newspapers Ltd.* v. *McShane*[87] an even stronger reversal of the views of the Court of Appeal occurred. A trade dispute had

---

[80] [1958] 1 W.L.R. 1057. But an existing trade dispute may be furthered by those who also pursue other objectives.
[81] *Star Sea Transport Corporation of Monrovia* v. *Slater* [1978] I.R.L.R. 507; *Associated Newspapers Group Ltd.* v. *Wade* [1979] I.C.R. 664; *P.B.D.S. (National Carriers) Ltd.* v. *Filkins* [1979] I.R.L.R. 356.
[82] *McShane* v. *Express Newspapers Ltd.* [1979] I.R.L.R. 79.
[83] *Beaverbrook Newspapers Ltd.* v. *Keys* [1978] I.C.R. 582, *per* Denning M.R.
[84] *McShane* v. *Express Newspapers Ltd., supra.*
[85] [1979] I.C.R. 867.
[86] This, as we have just seen, has been reversed by the Employment Act 1982, s.18(2).
[87] [1980] I.C.R. 42.

arisen between the National Union of Journalists and the Newspaper Society which represented the proprietors of provincial newspapers about the pay of journalists employed on those newspapers. These journalists were called out on strike and a strike was also called of journalists working for the Press Association which supplied news to both national and provincial papers. Not all P.A. journalists obeyed the strike call so union members working for *national* newspapers were instructed to black P.A. copy. The proprietors of the *Daily Express* sought an injunction to prevent N.U.J. officials from inducing the breach of contract by journalists employed by them in refusing to handle P.A. copy.

Lord Wilberforce pointed out that a subjective approach to "furtherance" would enable a person to gain immunity merely by proving his genuine belief in the possible effectiveness of his action. He continued:

"In the first place I do not find it to be excluded by the words of the section. It is clear enough that 'in contemplation . . . of' are not words exclusively subjective. It cannot be enough for someone to depose, in general terms, which cannot be proved, that he had a trade dispute in mind. The words, to me, presuppose an actual or emerging trade dispute as well as the mental contemplation of it. Similarly, 'in . . . furtherance' may quite well include, as well as an intention to further, an actual furtherance (help or encouragement) or the capability of furtherance. Secondly, so to construe the phrase is not to impose upon it a limitation. There is much in the cases to the effect that 'the words must be given some limitation' and to this the appellants object. The words, they say, and I agree, must be given their natural meaning and the courts must not approach them with a disposition to cut them down. But it is always open to the courts—indeed their duty—with open-ended expressions such as those involving cause, or effect, or remoteness, or in the context of this very Act, connection with (*cf. British Broadcasting Corpn* v. *Hearn*) to draw a line beyond which the expression ceases to operate. This is simply the common law in action. It does not involve the judges in cutting down what Parliament has given: it does involve them in interpretation in order to ascertain how far Parliament intended to go.

If there is to be an objective test what should it be? The Court of Appeal found difficulty in this: Lord Denning M.R., through various revisions, finally settled, I think, upon practical effect. This I think with respect goes too far: it involves judging the matter by results (at what time?), a very uncertain process in the complex, and sometimes irrational world of industrial relations. He did, as I read his judgment, take into account the actual effect of the action as he saw it. But one cannot use hindsight to interpret or apply the expression; the act must be appraised when it is done. Lawton L.J., and Brandon L.J. agreed, did not go so far: the acts done, pursuant to the genuine intention, must in his view be reasonably capable of achieving the objective: it is not necessary to prove that what is done *will* achieve the objective. The test involves, necessarily, finding some connection between the action taken, or proposed, and the result, and to that extent is a test based on remoteness. In my opinion this test is in line with sound accepted principle and I find myself able to accept it. In applying it the court must take into account the belief of the initiators of the action as to the capability of that action to achieve the objective. If these are, as in most but not all cases they will be, experienced trade union officials; if they express a clear opinion as to the 'capability' of the action; and if there is no evidence the other way, the court will or should be very reluctant to substitute its own judgment for theirs. The court may have to form its own judgment, either if there is no such clear expression of opinion (*cf. United Biscuits (UK) Ltd.* v. *Fall*) or it comes for a source less fitted to form a judgment, or, rarely, if the conclusion suggested is so implausible, or the connection between the action called for and the objective so remote and tenuous that the court feels justified in disregarding it. This it should do directly rather than by the indirect device of questioning the initiator's belief."

Lord Diplock was of the same opinion:

"My Lords, these tests though differently expressed, have the effect of enabling the court to substitute its own opinion for the bona fide opinion held by the trade union or its officers, as to whether action proposed to be taken or continued for the purpose of helping one side or bringing pressure to bear upon the other side to a trade dispute is likely to have the desired effect. Granted bona fides on the part of the trade union or its officer this is to convert the test from a purely subjective to a purely objective test and for the reasons I have given I do not think the wording of the section permits of this. The belief of the doer of the act that it will help the side he favours in the dispute must be honest; it need not be wise, nor need it take account of the damage it will cause to innocent and disinterested third parties. Upon an application for an interlocutory injunction the evidence may show positively by admission or by inference from the facts before the court that the act was not done to further an existing trade dispute but for some ulterior purpose such as revenge for previous conduct. Again, the facts in evidence before the court may be such as will justify the conclusion that no reasonable person versed in industrial relations could possibly have thought that the act was capable of helping one side in a trade dispute to achieve its objectives. But too this goes to honesty of purpose alone, not the reasonableness of the act, or its expediency."

Lord Scarman tried, somewhat ineffectively, to reserve something for the judicial function.

"Upon the first question, *i.e.* the interpretation of section 13(1), I find myself in agreement with my noble and learned friend, Lord Diplock. The words, 'An act done by a person in contemplation or furtherance of a trade dispute' seem to me, in their natural and ordinary meaning, to refer to the person's purpose, his state of mind. The court must satisfy itself that it was his purpose, and, before reaching its decision, will test his evidence by investigating all the circumstances and applying the usual tests of credibility: that is to say, it will ask itself whether a reasonable man could have thought that what he was doing would support his side of the dispute, or whether the link between his actions and his purpose was so tenuous that his evidence is not to be believed. But, at the end of the day, the question for the court is simply: is the defendant to be believed when he says that he acted in comtemplation or in furtherance of a trade dispute?

I accept that this construction limits the extent of judicial review. But it does not exclude it. An effective judicial review remains. 'To "contemplate a trade dispute" is to have before the mind some objective event or situation . . . but does not mean . . . something as yet wholly within the mind and of a subjective character': Lord Shaw of Dunfermline in *Conway* v. *Wade*. Likewise, to further a trade dispute presupposes that a dispute exists. In either case, the court must ask itself whether a trade dispute as defined in section 29 of the Act is either imminent or actual: and, unless it is, it cannot be said that the defendant acted in contemplation or furtherance of it. A fanciful suggestion of a dispute will not do: the defendant must have in mind an 'objective event or situation.' The effectiveness of this objective factor in the exercise of judicial review is well shown by *British Broadcasting Corpn* v. *Hearn*, a decision of the Court of Appeal to which I was a party and which I continue to think was correctly decided.

It follows, therefore, that, once it is shown that a trade dispute exists, the person who acts, but not the court, is the judge of whether his acts will further the dispute. If he is acting honestly, Parliament leaves to him the choice of what to do. I confess that I am relieved to find that this is the law. It would be a strange and embarrassing task for a judge to be called upon to review the tactics of a party to a trade dispute and to determine whether in the view of the court the tactic employed was likely to further, or advance, that party's side of the dispute. And the difficulties which have beset the Court of Appeal in their attempts to formulate a test are a persuasive argument for keeping his act of judgment in the industrial area and out of the judicial forum. Without going further afield than the present case, Lord Denning M.R. has made two attempts to formulate a test—'remoteness' and 'practical effect.' Lawton L.J. and Brandon L.J. have favoured one of seeing whether the act done is reasonably capable of achieving the party's objective in the dispute. It is, not surprisingly, a case of 'quot praetores, tot sententiae.' It would need very clear statutory language to persuade me that Parliament intended to allow the courts to act as some sort of a backseat driver in trade disputes. . . . "

The Court of Appeal remained reluctant to accept the destruction of all its efforts[88] and the House of Lords was forced to confirm that it had meant to destroy both the objective test and the remoteness test.[89] The Court of Appeal had attempted to distinguish two separate disputes so as to conclude that one aspect was not connected with trade but the House of Lords held that even if there were two disputes one would support the other.

Most of the effect of the House of Lords decisions will be destroyed not by legislative interference with the meaning of "contemplation or furtherance" but by the new legislative requirement that trade matters must be the predominant element. Whereas it is still true that it is enough that the person concerned genuinely believed that to be his predominant motive the remoteness test would seem to be partially reinstated since objectives which would be too remote cannot be primarily connected with the dispute. In *Hadmor Productions Ltd.* v. *Hamilton*[90] the Court of Appeal had discounted alleged fears of redundancy as part of the motivation for a dispute on the ground that such fears were without substantial foundation. The House of Lords, however, held that such fears were a reality and were one among a number of matters falling within section 29 of TULRA.[91] But once such primary motivation exists, outsiders may further the dispute so long as the trade purpose is among their motives.

(iii) *Secondary action*

There seems no doubt that secondary action has been greatly extended in recent years. Typically, a union resorts to secondary action where it is in a strong position to bring pressure to bear on a party not in dispute who, in order to avoid that pressure, will use his position as customer or supplier to pressurise the employer who is in dispute to reach a settlement. Secondary pressure may also be used to prevent the effects of primary pressure from being undermined. During a coal-miners' strike, for instance, it may be considered desirable to picket oil-fired electric power stations to prevent them replacing losses of electricity caused by the shortage of supplies to coal-fired stations. Such an example of what might be called "tertiary" action occurred in *United Biscuits (UK) Ltd.* v. *Fall.*[92] A dispute existed between the Transport and General

---

[88] *Duport Steels Ltd.* v. *Sirs* [1980] I.C.R. 161.
[89] [1980] I.C.R. 161.
[90] [1981] I.C.R. 690.
[91] [1982] I.R.L.R. 102.
[92] [1979] I.R.L.R. 110.

Workers Union and the member companies of the Road Haulage Association. In order to further this dispute the union sought to restrict the supply of goods by and to other employers not involved in the dispute. Vehicles owned by United Biscuits Ltd. were sent to collect supplies of edible oil from Loders and Nicoline Ltd. Neither company was involved in the dispute. These vehicles were turned back by pickets at the latter's premises. Although an injunction was granted it is clear that since the decisions of the House of Lords which we have discussed such action would have been considered to be in contemplation or furtherance of a trade dispute. Such, indeed, would be its primary purpose.

If we were to list the heads of enquiry so far the stages would be:

   (i) Does liability arise under one of the statutorily protected heads of tort?
  (ii) Is there a dispute between employers and their employees?
 (iii) Is that dispute primarily related to a "trade" matter within the meaning of section 29 of TULRA?
 (iv) Is the action of the individual whom it is sought to make personally liable or for whom a trade union may be made vicariously liable under the terms of the Employment Act 1982 in contemplation or furtherance of a trade dispute?

The Employment Act 1980 adds a further question.

  (v) Is the attack upon contracts of supply between employers upon which the claim in question is founded directed at an employer not party to the dispute through interference with his contracts of employment? This is the only form of action defined as secondary action by section 17(2). (An employer who is a member of an employer's organisation which is a party to that dispute will only himself be regarded as a party to that dispute if the association represents him in the dispute.)

     It will be observed, therefore that action directed against a supplier of labour in order to bring pressure on the contractor for such labour with whom a dispute exists will not constitute secondary action within the meaning of this provision.

If the answer to question (v) is affirmative then prima facie any immunity which would otherwise have been available under section 13 of TULRA will be removed so far as concerns attack upon a contract of supply of goods or services. Immunity will not be removed as regards the (probably) direct interference with contracts of employment by which that attack was mounted.

The immunity from tortious liability for interference with the contract of supply will not be removed despite the existence of secondary action if the secondary action comes within one of the specific exceptions laid down in sections 17(3), (4) or (5) of the Employment Act 1980. A final question may, therefore, need to be asked as regards secondary action:

 (vi) Is the attack on the contract of supply in question within one of the following exceptions?

    "(3) Secondary action satisfies the requirement of this subsection if—

       (*a*) the purpose or principal purpose of the secondary action was directly to prevent or disrupt the supply during the dispute of goods or services between an employer who is a party to the dispute and the employer under the contract of employment to which the secondary action relates; and (*b*) the secondary action (together with any corresponding action relating to other contracts of employment with the same employer) was likely to achieve that purpose.

(4) Secondary action satisfies the requirements of this subsection if—

(*a*) the purpose or principal purpose of the secondary action was directly to prevent or disrupt the supply during the dispute of goods or services between any person and an associated employer of an employer who is a party to the dispute; and

(*b*) the goods or services are in substitution for goods or services which but for the dispute would have fallen to be supplied to or by the employer who is a party to a dispute; and

(*c*) the employer under the contract of employment to which the secondary action relates is either the said associated employer or the other party to the supply referred to in paragraph (*a*) above; and

(*d*) the secondary action (together with any corresponding action relating to other contracts of employment with the same employer) was likely to achieve the purpose referred to in paragraph (*a*) above.

(5) Secondary action satisfies the requirements of this subsection if it is done in the course of attendance declared lawful by section 15 of the 1974 Act—

(*a*) by a worker employed (or, in the case of a worker not in employment, last employed) by a party to the dispute, or

(*b*) by a trade union official whose attendance is lawful by virtue of subsection (1)(*b*) of that secton.

(6) In subsections (3)(*a*) and (4)(*a*) above—

(*a*) references to the supply of goods or services between two persons are references to the supply of goods or services by one to the other in pursuance of a contract between them subsisting at the time of the secondary action; and

(*b*) references to directly preventing or disrupting the supply are references to preventing or disrupting it otherwise than by means of preventing or disrupting the supply of goods or services by or to any other person."

The situation described in subsection (3) is best explained diagrammatically.

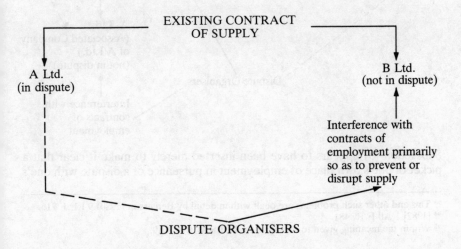

EXISTING CONTRACT
OF SUPPLY

A Ltd.
(in dispute)

B Ltd.
(not in dispute)

Interference with
contracts of
employment primarily
so as to prevent or
disrupt supply

DISPUTE ORGANISERS

It will be observed that this exception accounts for the most usual form of secondary action. Why, after all, should dispute organisers attack B Ltd. unless he is linked to A Ltd. by lines of supply. It must be remembered, however, that the section requires supply under existing contracts. The tort of interference with contract may extend liability beyond interference with such a situation.[93] In *Marina Shipping Ltd.* v. *Laughton*[94] the Court of Appeal had to consider a situation in which a dispute existed between the International Transport Workers Federation and certain shipowners. In furtherance of this dispute employers of the Port Authority at Hull were persuaded to break their contracts of employment to prevent one of that shipowner's ships leaving the Port. The contract of supply of harbour services had been made between the Port Authority and shipping agents who had arranged the berth. In doing so, the Court held, the shipping agents were acting as principals. The attack was made, therefore, on a contract of supply which was not made by or with the employer in dispute and consequently subsection (3) did not operate to afford immunity.

It will also be observed that whereas immunity is available under section 13 of TULRA upon a subjective test of furtherance, once that immunity is applied to secondary action it can only be retained if, *inter alia*, it is shown that the action is objectively likely to achieve the purpose of disrupting the contract of supply. It does not, however, have to be shown that that disruption is in turn objectively likely to further the dispute.

Section 17(4) extends the immunity preserved by section 17(3) to an attack upon contracts of supply which are substituted for such contracts with the party in dispute but only where one of the parties to the substitute contract is an associated company[95] of the employer in dispute. Diagrammatically the situation covered may be represented thus:

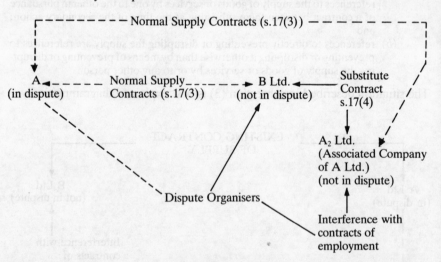

Subsection (5) appears to have been inserted merely to make it clear that a picket of one's own place of employment in pursuance of a dispute with one's

93 This and other such problems are dealt with in detail by Bercusson (1980) 9 I.L.J. 216.
94 [1982] 1 All E.R. 481.
95 Within the meaning given to that term by TULRA 1974, s.19.

own employer is not affected by section 17(2). A picket at one's own place of work may be within section 15 of TULRA[96] but it will not be protected from liability for the torts covered by section 13 of TULRA if it constitutes secondary action within section 17(2) of the 1980 Act and outside the saving exceptions of sections 17(3) and 17(4).

In order to continue to enjoy immunity the principal purpose of the secondary action must be the disruption of the supply. In the *Duport Steels* case we saw that the Court of Appeal attempted to avoid the multiple purpose test of the House of Lords by dividing the issue into separate sections one of which might be said not to have a trade purpose. Conversely it might be possible to argue that the secondary action was in fact a series of actions each with a separate principal purpose. In order to enjoy immunity the attack must be on supplies under a subsisting contract.

In view of the extension of the tort of interference with contract to cover interference with potential contracts it is possible that an actionable interference might arise which was precluded from immunity by section 17(2) and not saved by either subsections (3) or (4). The operation of the subsections will in any case be haphazard since, as the facts of *J. T. Stratford and Co.* v. *Lindley*[97] reveal, organisers of industrial action may be in no position to know the state of an employer's contracts.

On the other hand, it would have seemed likely in 1981 that there would be little difficulty in raising a primary dispute in order to support what was in reality secondary action. Since 1982 it will be possible to contend that such a dispute is not primarily concerned with a trade matter. Bercusson[98] also raised the possibility of developing "hot cargo" clauses whereby employees are permitted under their contracts of employment to take secondary blacking action. Inducing them to do so would then not constitute secondary action under section 17(2) so as to deprive them of immunity for interfering with contracts of supply.

Possibly because of its failure to cover the more usual areas of secondary action, or because of the uncertainty as to its meaning, or because of the apparent inadequacy of the remedies available, the reduction of immunity by section 17 of the 1980 Act did not result in much litigation. The incidence of "tertiary" action, however, appears to have fallen significantly and there is no doubt that trade unions often preferred to avoid creating situations which might afford the courts an opportunity to explore the potential of the section.

The Employment Act 1982, in pursuit of one of its principal aims of curtailing the scope of the closed shop, also limits the availability of section 13. It is there provided[99] that the immunity granted by that section does not apply to inducement or attempts to induce another to incorporate a union membership or recognition clause in a contract for the supply of goods or services. The protection of section 13 is also removed from inducement or attempt to induce failure to include the name of a supplier on an existing list of approved suppliers, to terminate a contract of supply, otherwise to determine not to enter into a contract of supply or to exclude a person from a group of tenderers or fail to permit a person to submit a tender.

---

[96] As amended by Employment Act 1980, s.16.
[97] [1965] A.C. 269.
[98] (1980) I.L.J. at 219.
[99] s.14.

Section 13 immunity is also withdrawn from inducement to break a contract or interference with a contract of employment or a threat thereof where the main reason for so doing is that work to be done in connection with the supply in question has been, or is likely to be, done by a person other than an employee of an employer whose contracts of employment are interfered with and who are, or are not, members of a particular trade union.

The same withdrawal of immunity applies where the action is aimed at contracts of employment and one of the reasons for so doing is that a supplier, other than that employer does not, or is not likely to recognise, negotiate or consult with a trade union.

The scope of immunity

If section 13 of the 1974 Act does afford protection that protection is confined to a group of specific torts. The restrictive effect of this largely unnecessary limitation was demonstrated very clearly in *Rookes* v. *Barnard*.[1] The appellant, who had been a member of the Draughtsmen's and Allied Technicians' Association, had become disillusioned with the effectiveness of the union and had terminated his membership, thereby destroying the 100 per cent. union membership at his place of work. The union members who worked there threatened, through their shop stewards and a full-time district official of the union, that they would strike unless Rookes was dismissed. They were covered by a collective agreement which contained a prohibition of the taking of industrial action prior to negotiation of an industrial dispute. It was conceded (probably incorrectly), at first instance, that this prohibition was an implied term in their contracts of employment. The two shop-stewards, therefore, were threatening to break their own contracts of employment and, together with the district official, were also threatening to induce the other employed union members to break their contracts of employment.

Specific torts

The House of Lords concluded that the protection afforded by section 3 of the 1906 Act was intended only to protect from liability where the actual ground of action was the tort of inducement to breach of contract. Lord Hodson said:

> 'It would seem . . . very unlikely that . . . Parliament could have intended to go so far as to give protection to members of trade unions in every case where the *consequences* of that act, whether the act is lawful or unlawful, were that a breach of contract has been induced or that a person's employment has been interfered with.'[2]

From this follows the conclusion, expressed by Lord Devlin, that the words "on the ground only that . . . " were:

> " . . . not used to define an ingredient in a tortious cause of action but to define the whole tort by reference to the essential ground by which the tort is usually described. Inducing a breach of contract is descriptive of a tort which comprises all

---

[1] [1964] A.C. 1129. See Kahn-Freund, "Rookes v. Barnard—and After," 14 *Federation News*, April 1964; Wedderburn (1961) 24 M.L.R. 572; (1962) 25 M.L.R. 513; (1964) 27 M.L.R. 257; Weir, "Rookes, Stratford—Economic Torts" [1964] Camb. L.J. 225.

[2] Author's italics. The import of the last nine words has been dealt with at pp. 477–479.

the elements of knowledge, malice, inducement and damage. If the means of inducement are honestly persuasive and nothing more, the inducer commits the tort of inducing a breach of contract and nothing more. But if the means are slanderous or deceitful, he may commit also the tort of defamation or of deceit. Then if an action is brought, it will not be only on the ground of inducing a breach of contract but also on the ground of slander or deceit, and the section will not prevent it."

It only needs to be pointed out that these extra available causes of action do not have to be made the subject of the action, so long as they exist.

It will be noted that the separate torts here mentioned are complete in themselves. The only relevance to them of the consequence that they are a means of inducing a breach of contract is that this supplies the source of injury. It is true that most torts are actionable only upon proof of injury so that this can be said, in a sense, to be an element of the tort. Lord Hodson said the legislation must be taken to have been dealing with immunity from particular forms of action and not broad sources of injury.

Unlawful elements

The tort of intimidation requires, as we have seen, a threat of unlawful means. The majority of the House took the view that if one threatened to do what the statute protected from action, one threatened only what was lawful. So the essential element of the tort of intimidation had been removed, and no action could be brought under that head. As Lord Denning pointed out in the Court of Appeal in *Stratford* v. *Lindley*,[3] it would be strange if it was unlawful to threaten to do something which would not be actionable if done. On the other hand, since the section does not deal with the source of injury an induced breach of contract remains available to form that element of the tort.

Lord Reid, in the minority, went a stage further. In his view, the protection of the section did not apply where action could be brought under any other head of tort whatsoever, even if one of the essential elements of that tort was the illegality involved in the inducement to breach of contract, which illegality the section purported to remove. So, a *threat* to induce a breach of contract was, for him, actionable as intimidation despite the statutory protection available to the illegal act which was threatened.

Lord Reid, again in a minority, also argued that "not actionable" did not mean "lawful" so that, even if he was wrong on the first point, the threat of unlawful action would remain so as to constitute the complete tort of intimidation. The majority did not accept that once the right of action had been withdrawn the essential unlawfulness could remain, although in some instances in the law, where a particular person has a special immunity, the act committed by him has been said to remain unlawful. The effect of providing, not that an act "shall not be actionable," but that it "shall not be actionable in tort," introduction in 1971,[4] remains unexplored. It is clearly arguable that this leaves a sort of residual illegality although, on the other hand, it is difficult to define the nature of that residue if the only action was in tort.

---

[3] Reported together with the judgments of the House of Lords in [1965] A.C. 269.
[4] Industrial Relations Act 1971, s.128. The second phrase was first used in the Trade Disputes Act 1965.

Finally, Lord Reid infers that there might be something essentially unlawful in the use of threats which would override the statutory protection. This, on all available authority, is plainly not so.

At the other extreme, Lord Evershed argued that "actionable" meant "actionable at the suit of any specific person," inferring that to remove the statutory protection the unprotected right of action would also have to be available to the person who could have sued for inducement to a breach of contract. The majority view would mean that indirect inducement, which requires the use of unlawful means, would always be outside the statutory protection. Lord Evershed's view would be that that protection was only not available if the unlawful means were also actionable at the suit of the party who could sue for inducement.

Immunity in tort

Finally, Professor Grunfeld argues that "actionable" must have implied civil liability so that if the inducement is inducement to commit a crime it would not have been protected. On the face of it the view of the House of Lords could be said to extend to any head of liability specifically under the name of "inducement to breach of contract," whether liability was criminal or civil. If one considers, as did the House of Lords, the framing of the 1974 Act as a whole, and the legislative intention, Professor Grunfeld's does seem to be the correct view. It appears that the statutory protection[5] would not have been available if the activity constituted an unfair industrial practice. Probably the words "actionable in tort" were put in section 132 of the 1971 Act to achieve this effect. They were strictly unnecessary for this purpose and, as we have seen, may have wider implications.

Most of the problems that Lord Reid foresaw about the existence of threats were removed by the special additional protection for threatened inducement which was introduced by the Trade Disputes Act 1965 and is continued in the 1974 Act.

An attempt was made in the 1974 Act also to remove the underlying availability of breach of contract as the unlawful means necessary to constitute other torts.[6] It was provided that:

> "For the avoidance of doubt it is hereby declared that—
>
> (a) an act which by reason of subsection (1) or (2)[7] above is itself not actionable;
> (b) a breach of contract in contemplation or furtherance of a trade dispute;
>
> shall not be regarded as the doing of an unlawful act or as the use of unlawful means for the purpose of establishing liability in tort."

The first part of the provision undoubtedly affirms the majority view in *Rookes'* case that if a particular tort is not actionable it cannot form the unlawful element necessary to constitute other torts. The second part of the provision, however, removed no doubts, but provided a wholly new immunity. It had never been judicially questioned that a breach of contract should not provide the unlawful element in such torts. Once constituted by such an unlawful element one then

---

[5] TULRA 1974, s.13 as amended by the 1976 Act.
[6] s.13(3).
[7] Repealed by the Employment Act 1982, Sched. 4.

had to consider whether the actors were immune from liability for that tort as a whole, but no attempt had ever been made to provide immunity for a breach of contract. It is undeniable that breach of contract forms the most usual unlawful element in industrial action.

This subsection was repealed in 1980.[8] In *Hadmor Productions Ltd.* v. *Hamilton*[9] Lord Denning M.R. had held that the effect of the repeal could not have been intended to recreate the uncertainty canvassed in *Rookes* v. *Barnard* concerning the application as unlawful acts of actions granted immunity by section 13. In his view, the legislature intended to make it clear that such immune actions—in this case inducement to breach of the contract of employment—were available to constitute the unlawful element in the tort of interfering with the trade or business of a third party. This reasoning is somewhat extraordinary. Section 13(3) spoke of the removal of doubt. The majority opinion in *Rookes* cannot have been overturned by the *failure* of the legislature to make contrary provision. In the House of Lords the Court of Appeal decision in *Hadmor* was overruled on almost every point including this one.[10] Lord Diplock pointed out that suggestions in *Stratford* v. *Lindley*[11] and *Rookes* v. *Barnard*[12] that section 13 only granted immunity from actions at the suit of the employer had been rejected by Lord Denning M.R. in *Morgan* v. *Fry*[13] and Templeman J. in *Camellia Tanker Ltd.* v. *I.T.F.*[14] Lord Diplock also pointed out that the interpretation placed on the repeal by Lord Denning would render the immunity retained by sections 17(3) and (4) of the 1980 Act ineffective. In his view a provision which made intimidation not actionable must have the effect of destroying it as the unlawful element in another tort. If it were otherwise the immunity granted by sections 13(1) and (2) of the 1974 Act would itself be overridden by the unlawful element necessary to the heads of liability there covered.

Interference with trade

It had been further provided, by section 3 of the Trade Disputes Act 1906, that:

> "An act done by a person in contemplation or furtherance of a trade dispute shall not be actionable on the ground only . . . that it is an interference with the trade, business or employment of some other person, or with the right of some other person to dispose of his capital or labour as he wills."

At the time when *Rookes* v. *Barnard* was decided it was generally assumed that there was no head of tort liability known as "interference with trade." So it was contended that even if the first part of the section referred to a specific tort the second part could not do so. It was argued that it must have the effect of removing liability wherever the *source of damage* was such interference, whatever the means or the particular torts used to effect that end.

---

[8] Employment Act 1980, s.17(8) and Sched. 2.
[9] [1981] I.C.R. 690.
[10] [1982] I.R.L.R. 102. The outstanding exception is the failure of the House of Lords to disapprove liability for interference with trade.
[11] [1965] A.C. 269.
[12] [1964] A.C. 1129.
[13] [1968] 2 Q.B. 710.
[14] [1976] I.R.L.R. 183.

In *Rookes'* case the House of Lords, it is submitted quite correctly, held that both parts of the section referred only to specific torts. The fact that no such tort as was envisaged in the second part had then emerged did not preclude the feeling of Parliament, in 1906, that it might have done so. The intention was to afford protection if such liability did emerge. At that time there was considerable reason to suppose that such liability might grow out of the emerging tort of conspiracy. Such a view of the legislative intent seems wholly reasonable. Indeed, it may again be found in those provisions of the 1974 Act which have just been considered,[15] since it will be observed that they introduce, for the first time, in the provision of immunity, reference to a tort of interference with contract which, as has been noted, was at most only in the formulative stage. Both in 1971 and 1974, therefore, the legislature chose to adopt the same cautious approach to the possibility of liability for a tort of interference with trade. The provision is identical in both Acts[16]:

> "For the avoidance of doubt it is hereby declared that an act done by a person in contemplation or furtherance of a trade dispute is not actionable in tort on the ground only that it is an interference with the trade, business or employment of another person, or with the right of another person to dispose of his capital or his labour as he wills."

As we have seen, the House of Lords in *Hadmor Productions Ltd.* v. *Hamilton* failed to deal with the clear assertion of the existence of a tort of interference with trade by Lord Denning M.R. in the Court of Appeal. Most commentators seem to accept that the appearance of such liability is therefore, inevitable. The door having been forced the legislature withdrew the guards by the total repeal of this subsection in 1982. The question must be asked whether the withdrawal of a provision designed to avoid doubt is effective to impose liability. In this instance it may well be so since the doubt was not as to whether there was immunity but as to whether the tort existed. If repeal does have the effect of withdrawing immunity precisely when it was required, that consequence may be alarming. It could be said that the primary intention of trade unions engaged in industrial action is to interfere with trade.

Combination

The protection afforded by section 1 of the 1906 Act is repeated[17] with some small amendments and a troublesome addition. It now reads:

> "An agreement or combination by two or more persons to do or procure the doing of any act in contemplation or furtherance of a trade dispute shall not be actionable in tort if the act is one which, if done without any such agreement or combination, would not be actionable in tort."

In *Rookes* v. *Barnard* the question of the existence of an actionable conspiracy was vital in the case of the district official—Silverthorne—who had not threatened to break his contract and, in the view of the majority, would have been protected from an action for threatening to induce a breach of contract. Lord Reid, who would consider him to be unprotected in respect of the tort of

[15] s.13(1).
[16] Industrial Relations Act 1971, s.132(2); replaced by TULRA 1974, s.13(2).
[17] TULRA 1974, s.13(4).

intimidation involved in this latter activity, did not have to consider his case further. Of the remainder, only Lord Devlin dealt in detail with his liability for conspiracy with the shop-stewards to threaten that *they* would break *their* contracts of employment. The majority of the House, therefore, entirely ignored the difficulty that in such a case the liability of Silverthorne would arise solely because he had combined with others in an unlawful act which he himself could not commit. Lord Devlin took the view that since it is clear that one can be liable for conspiracy, even though one does not take part in the unlawful acts, it followed that it was only necessary to show that the statute failed to protect certain members of the conspiracy. All those joining with them would then be unprotected however much, as individuals, their actions would have been unobjectionable. If the section, then or now, had spoken in terms of the tort of conspiracy such a view would have been supportable, but it speaks rather in terms of an agreement or combination. A conspirator, who commits no illegal act himself, only becomes liable for the unlawful acts of his fellows by reason of his combination or agreement with them. Silverthorne would seem to offer the classic example of someone the legislature intended to protect from liability arising only from this act of combination.

Both the old and the new protective provisions relieve of liability where no otherwise unlawful act has been committed and the conspiracy would have been of the variety that used lawful means with the primary intent of causing injury. Since 1906 it has become clear that the pursuit of trade union objectives in contemplation or furtherance of a trade dispute is likely to be considered to be justified by self interest. Where those combining do in fact intend primarily to injure it is almost certain that this intent, and not the contemplation or furtherance of such a dispute, would be considered to be their aim. So the section would, in any event, afford no protection that was not already available to this form of conspiracy.[18]

Where unlawful means were used the conduct would be actionable on other grounds, and so the protection would not apply. In fact, only application of the protection to the sort of situation in which Silverthorne found himself would give the section any effect at all. The apparent absurdity of yet another provision with no practical effect is to be explained in the same way as the last. In 1906 it was not clear that conspiracy would develop in such a way that the self-interested aims of trade unions, pursued by lawful means, would be considered to be justified.

Nevertheless, in the face of the apparent absurdity, counsel for the defendants attempted to establish a wider effect. It was argued that as none of the torts in question were actionable *per se* without proof of damage individuals could not have committed them, since, as such, they would not have had the strength to produce the injury. The torts, therefore, only became actionable as a result of the combination. Lord Reid countered this argument, which would have given the protection a very wide scope, by saying that one must ask whether there would be liability for the nearest available act to that of combination; that is to say, to a situation where all the members of the combination acted in precisely the same way but wholly independent of each other. In such a situation a series of individual threats with the same purpose would have

---

[18] See particularly *Huntley* v. *Thornton* [1957] 1 W.L.R. 321.

produced sufficient coercive effect, with or without the element of combination, to produce the injury.

The amended provision, first introduced in 1971, contains a second, puzzling, use of the limitation introduced by the words "would not be actionable in tort." It is this use that we have referred to as the introduction of a limitation within the elements of the tort against which protection is afforded. The agreement or combination is not to be actionable in tort if, without the element of combination, it would not have been actionable in tort. Suppose, therefore, that the means used by the conspirators are actionable only in contract. It would seem that in such a case the immunity from tort action will apply and an injured party will only be able to seek any available remedy in contract. This appears anomalous in the light of the fact that, had the means been separately actionable in tort then the whole immunity would disappear and an action for conspiracy would become available. It is probable that these last few words were introduced in 1971 to make it clear that if the means used were unlawful as an unfair industrial practice they should not destroy the immunity, otherwise it would have been theoretically possible to bypass the N.I.R.C. by an action in the High Court for conspiracy. This still leaves unexplained the failure to add the words "or contract" so as to limit this effect solely to this suggested purpose. Moreover a new provision had appeared in the 1971 Act whereby, in any proceedings in tort in respect of an agreement or combination to do or procure any act in contemplation or furtherance of an industrial dispute, where the protection just discussed was not available, the court might stay proceedings if proceedings under the Act had been, or could be, brought in the Industrial Court or an industrial tribunal.[19] As it transpired,[20] the High Court evinced a strong desire to have nothing to do with these matters and so there was, in fact, very little danger of such a conflict of jurisdiction. Now that all such danger has gone it seems unnecessary to retain the apparent distinction between conspiracy involving other actionable tortious means (which is not protected) and conspiracy involving means actionable under any other head of liability than tort (which is protected).

The Labour Injunction

In the period between the two World Wars the judicial injunction was extensively resorted to in the United States of America as a means of restraining industrial action. From this use sprang the name "labour injunction." Although a party alleging injury from industrial action may have available an action for damages and may also have self-help weapons such as non-payment of wages, lock-out and even dismissal what he most desires is a means to stop the action. In English, as American, law this purpose is usually achieved by means of an interlocutory injunction. The person seeking such an injunction is not normally concerned with his chances of success in any ultimate decision on the merits since it is well known that it is difficult to revive industrial action on a dispute which has gone cold.[21] The possible effect of interlocutory procedures is well demonstrated by the *Duport Steels* case where the application for an injunction

---

[19] s.132(4). The Industrial Court had no jurisdiction in tort—s.136.
[20] *Midland Cold Storage Ltd.* v. *Steer* [1972] I.C.R. 435.
[21] See for instance *B.B.C.* v. *Hearn* [1977] I.C.R. 685.

was heard on Friday in the High Court. The Court of Appeal confimed the grant of the injunction on Saturday. The strike was called off by the union on the following Tuesday. Leave to appeal to the House of Lords was granted on Thursday and the House of Lords set aside the injunction a week after it had been granted. It had, however, secured most of the effect desired for it.

In *American Cyanamid Co.* v. *Ethicon Ltd.*[22] the House of Lords held that the question the court has to consider is not primarily the relative legal merits of the claims by each side but the balance of convenience as between the harm done if the injunction is granted and the likely harm to the plaintiff if it is not. In *Harold Stephen and Co. Ltd.* v. *The Post Office.*[23] Geoffrey Lane L.J. (as he then was) based his judgment in the Court of Appeal upon the proposition that only in the most exceptional circumstances should a court interfere by way of mandatory injunction in an industrial dispute. Such an attitude is not common.

In *Hubbard* v. *Pitt*[24] Forbes J. said:

"On the material I have, and even on the basis of accepting nearly everything in the defendants' affidavits where there is conflict with the plaintiffs', it seems to me that the plaintiffs would still be entitled to an injunction if this were the trial of the action. The basis on which the court will grant interlocutory injunctions is well settled. The principle is usually referred to as that of the balance of convenience, and is covered by the note to R.S.C., Ord. 29, r. 1, in the *The Supreme Court Practice* (1973). Mr. Hoolahan draws my attention to some words of Kay L.J. in *J. Lyons & Sons* v. *Wilkins*:

"in all these cases of interlocutory injunctions where a man's trade is affected one sees the enormous importance that there may be in interfering at once before the action can be brought on for trial; because during the interval, which may be long or short according to the state of business in the courts, a man's trade might be absolutely destroyed or ruined by a course of proceedings which, when the action comes to be tried, may be determined to be utterly illegal; and yet nothing can compensate the man for the utter loss of his business by what has been done in that interval."

What is the advantage to the plaintiffs in obtaining an interim injunction? Clearly, the preservation of their business and the restoration of unimpeded access to their premises for their staff and customers. What of the defendants? If an injunction were granted they would have to suspend operations outside the plaintiffs' offices. But they would still be free at some other place, and by legitimate means, to bring their dislike of the plaintiffs' actions before the public. Mr. McEnery, one of the defendants, in the course of an able and persuasive argument, suggested that it was important to demonstrate one's dislike of someone's conduct at the place where that conduct was occurring, otherwise, he said, it would lose impact. But the loss of impact seems to me a small weight to be cast in the balance against the possibility of injury to the plaintiffs' business if the picket continues. In those circumstances, it is right that an interlocutory injunction should issue."

The courts seem much more prepared to take note of assessments of actual economic loss to the employer than of the equally real but less provable loss resulting from even temporary diversion of the union's bargaining strength. An employee is unable to obtain an injunction to restrain the employer from terminating his employment. The converse may appear to be the statutory

---

[22] [1975] A.C. 396.
[23] [1978] 1 All E.R. 939.
[24] [1975] I.C.R. 77 at 93.

prohibition[25] upon the grant of an injunction to enforce, or order specific performance of any contract of employment so as to compel an employee to do any work or attend at any place for the doing of any work. This link is, however, deceptive. The strength of the employer is his economic independence enabling him, for instance, to retaliate by dismissing not one but all his employees. The union's strength derives not from the freedom of the individual but from the ability to organise concerted action.

The only formal safeguard against these disadvantages is contained in section 17 of TULRA.

> (1) Where an application for an injunction or interdict is made to a court in the absence of the party against whom the injunction or interdict is sought or any representative of his and that party claims, or in the opinion of the court would be likely to claim, that he acted in contemplation or furtherance of a trade dispute, the court shall not grant the injunction or interdict unless satisfied that all steps which in the circumstances were reasonable have been taken with a view to securing that notice of the application and an opportunity of being heard with respect to the application have been given to that party.
>
> (2) It is hereby declared for the avoidance of doubt that where an application is made to a court, pending the trial of an action, for an interlocutory injunction and the party against whom the injunction is sought claims that he acted in contemplation or furtherance of a trade dispute, the court shall, in exercising its discretion whether or not to grant the injunction, have regard to the likelihood of that party's succeeding at the trial of the action in establishing the matter or matters which would, under any provision of section 13, 14(2) or 15 above, afford a defence to the action.

There is little evidence that in practice this provision has delayed the grant of interlocutory injunctions.

In the light of these effects it is significant of the strength of the rule of law in industrial relations that labour injunctions are obeyed often beyond their actual terms. The undesirability of ultimate enforcement by way of proceedings for contempt was demonstrated in *Midland Cold Storage* v. *Tanner*.[26] The injunction as a weapon against secondary picketing is limited by the need to identify the individuals against whom it is sought. Only those individuals are restrained and others may take their place. Surprisingly such "defiance" of the intention rather than the letter is rare.

PICKETING

Picketing, which is, for some unexplained reason, an activity best known in the English speaking world, is regarded in the United States of America as protected by the free speech provisions of the Constitution. As this indicates, it is, and should be regarded as, primarily a means of communication, persuasive though that communication may be.

In this country, however, it is not protected by any such fundamental right. The activities involved in picketing, in the absence of any special statutory immunity, fall, therefore, to be judged according to the ordinary law. A person or a group of people, whether they be pickets or not, is free to stand on a street

---

[25] TULRA 1974, s.16.
[26] [1972] I.C.R. 130.

corner or outside a building and communicate information or persuade others to adopt a certain course of action. Such persons have no inalienable right to do so and are subject to all the ordinary laws of obstruction, assault, nuisance, trespass, conspiracy and the like, and to the risk that their activities may induce in the police reasonable anticipation of a breach of the peace.[27]

The so-called law relating to picketing is in practice, therefore, a consideration largely of the special immunities (if any) that may be claimed for pickets and, for that reason, is dealt with at this point. It is true that a few criminal provisions, and in particular those of section 7 of the Conspiracy and Protection of Property Act 1875, have a particular relevance to the activities of pickets, but there is no illegality which peculiarly attaches to those activities.

Criminal liability

As we have seen, the early law of picketing was largely concerned with the discovery of criminal conspiracies. In abolishing this liability the legislature retained the criminal sanction against certain forms of wrongful action. It was provided by section 7 of the Conspiracy and Protection of Property Act 1875, that[28]:

"Every person who, with a view to compel any other person to abstain from doing or to do any act which such other person has a legal right to do or abstain from doing, wrongfully and without legal authority,
   (1) uses violence to or intimidates such other person or his wife or children, or injures his property;
   (2) persistently follows such other person about from place to place;
   (3) hides any tools, clothes or other property owned or used by such other person, or deprives him of, or hinders him in the use thereof;
   (4) watches or besets the house or other place where such other person resides or works or carries on business, or happens to be, or the approach to such house or place; or
   (5) follows such other person with two or more other persons in a disorderly manner in or through any street or road,
shall on conviction thereof by a court of summary jurisdiction, or on indictment as hereinafter mentioned be liable to pay a penalty not exceeding £20, or to be imprisoned for a term not exeeding 3 months. . . . "

In *J. Lyons & Sons* v. *Wilkins*[29] the Court of Appeal held that pickets who sought to persuade people not to enter into the plaintiff's employment were doing more than this provision permitted and were "watching and besetting" within the criminal provisions of the rest of the section.[30] In the second hearing before the Court of Appeal, Lindley M.R., who was not noted for sympathy towards trade union objectives, said:

"The truth is that to watch or beset a man's house with a view to compel him to do or not to do what is lawful for him not to do or to do is wrongful and without lawful

---

[27] See, *Hubbard* v. *Pitt* [1975] I.C.R. 77 (Q.B.); [1975] 3 All E.R. 1 (C.A.) which contains a very useful survey of the picketing cases by Forbes J. and a strong statement of the case for the basic legality of picketing by Lord Denning M.R.
[28] This part of the section was repealed by s.2(2) of the Trade Disputes Act 1906.
[29] [1896] 1 Ch. 811; [1899] 1 Ch. 255.
[30] *Infra*.

authority unless some reasonable justification for it is consistent with the evidence. Such conduct seriously interferes with the ordinary comfort of human existence and ordinary enjoyment of the house beset, and such conduct would support an action on the case for a nuisance at common law."

It will be observed that the Master of the Rolls here makes two points:

(i) that "watching and besetting" outside the protection mentioned is itself wrongful;

(ii) that in the circumstances what happened was common law nuisance.

It is, of course, the first of these which is of greatest significance. Chitty L.J. supported it by pointing out that in the section the description "wrongful" was applied to all the subsections and, since it applied equally to violence, intimidation and injury to property and to watching and besetting, it must follow that this last was regarded as equally unlawful with the first three. In *Ward, Lock & Co.* v. *Operative Printers' Assistants' Society,*[31] however, a different view was taken. The words "wrongfully and without legal authority" were regarded as intended to make it clear that the crimes specified in section 7 would only be committed where the conduct was otherwise unlawful so as to give rise to a civil remedy. Fletcher Moulton L.J. said of the section:

> "It legalises nothing, and it renders nothing wrongful that was not so before. Its object is solely to visit certain selected classes of acts which were previously wrongful, *i.e.* were at least civil torts, with penal consequences capable of being summarily inflicted."

In contra-distinction to the tort of "intimidation," criminal intimidation appears to be confined to threats of personal violence[32] but actual fear need not be proved.[33] It is sufficient if the act in question would have been enough to produce fear in men of normal courage. The exhibition or threat of force or violence without their use, will suffice.[34] "Persistent following," as an offence, raises some problems. In *Smith* v. *Thomasson*[35] it was said that the offfence does not require proof of actual or threatened violence nor, in view of the offence in the fifth head, does it require disorderliness. Yet this would suggest that persistent following is rendered wrongful *de novo*, since there is no civil liability merely for following a person about from place to place. It is suggested that this decision is incorrect and that, as in the case of the fifth head (where the element of disorderly conduct was described in *R.* v. *McKenzie*[36] as "the gist and pith of the offence") disorderly conduct, or some other illegal element, is also necessary to provide the unlawful element in the offence. The distinction between the second and fifth head, therefore, is simply that liability under the second head, in respect of following by a single person, will only arise if that following is persistent.

In the same way, the hiding of tools, clothes or other property will not be criminal under this section unless accompanied by measures which are other-

---

[31] (1906) 22 T.L.R. 327; followed in *Fowler* v. *Kibble* [1922] 1 Ch. 487. But see now *The Mersey Dock and Harbour Co.* v. *Verrinder* [1982] I.R.L.R. 152 *infra.*
[32] *Gibson* v. *Lawson* [1891] 2 Q.B. 545.
[33] *Agnew* v. *Munro* (1891) 28 S.L.R. 335.
[34] *R.* v. *Jones and Others* [1974] I.C.R. 310.
[35] (1891) 62 L.T. 68.   [36] [1892] 2 Q.B. 519.

wise wrongful. Very commonly, of course, such means would be constituted by the trespass upon the property hidden; but in *Fowler* v. *Kibble*[37] a colliery lampsman had been persuaded, by lawful means, to refuse to issue lamps to certain non-union miners before they went down the mine. The lampsman might be said to have been induced to break his contract of employment by this act, but because of the effect of what was then section 3 of the Trade Disputes Act 1906, such inducement would not have been actionable. There was, therefore, no unlawfulness in the activity concerned and it was held that no offence had been committed under section 7.

"Watching and besetting" is simply a description of certain forms of picketing. It seems to follow that once the prerequisite that the watching and besetting is otherwise wrongful is established the criminal offence under the section is made out, provided that its object is that specified in the section.[38] Apart from these special statutory provisions, picketing is particularly likely to give rise to general types of criminal conduct. In *R.* v. *Jones*[39] the indictment against six pickets contained 42 counts. The first three charged them all with conspiracy, unlawful assembly and affray. The remaining 39 charged offences under section 7, as well as damaging, attempting to damage or threatening to destroy property, threatening behaviour and assault. Pickets may also be guilty of criminal offences of unlawful assembly and even, in some situations, of affray.[40]

Civil liability

The Trade Disputes Act 1906,[41] in revising the protective clause in the 1875 Act, did not add anything in support, save that, in expressly permitting persuasive measures, it might be said to have made it clear that more than lawful inducement was required for the offence of watching and besetting. This lent support to the view that to constitute unlawfulness it was necessary to demonstrate unreasonable interference amounting to nuisance. Section 2 provided:

> "It shall be lawful for one or more persons, acting on their own behalf or on behalf of a trade union . . . in contemplation or furtherance of a trade dispute, to attend at or near a house or place where a person resides or works or carries on business or happens to be, if they so attend merely for the purpose of peacefully obtaining or communicating information, or of peacefully persuading any person to work or abstain from working."

Of this section Professor Grunfeld[42] has said:

> "[It] would appear to add nothing new to the position at common law, at least, if the view taken of the common law in *Ward, Lock & Co.* is the correct view. Section 2, today, merely makes the legality of such reasonable interference with access to strike-bound premises doubly sure. So section 2 of the 1906 Act neutralises trespass to the highway[43] and makes clear beyond doubt that peaceful persuasion, etc., does not itself render picketing an unlawful nuisance, provided it is not done in an unreasonably obstructive way."

---

[37] [1922] 1 Ch. 487.
[38] See *Farmer* v. *Wilson* (1900) 69 L.J.Q.B. 496.
[39] [1974] I.C.R. 310.
[40] *Ibid.*
[41] s.2.
[42] *Modern Trade Union Law*, p. 444.
[43] On this aspect, see *Ferguson Ltd.* v. *O'Gorman* [1937] I.R. 620.

Apart from a few minor amendments made by the Industrial Relations Act 1971 this position was maintained until 1980. The majority of the Court of Appeal in *Hubbard* v. *Pitt*[44] upheld the injunction granted by Forbes J. at first instance.[45] He had based that injunction on the probability that picketing not protected by statutory immunity was unlawful. Upon the freedom to use the highway he said:

"The true position, therefore, is that whether passing or repassing, or, exercising the reasonable extension spoken of by Collins L.J., the user has to be ordinarily and reasonably incidental to the exercise of a right of passage, otherwise it becomes a trespass and therefore unlawful.

Now, even then, such user must be reasonable in extent. The tired pedestrian or the motorist with the breakdown can only rest for a reasonable while. Those who queue for theatre tickets or stop to watch window displays must do so reasonably and in such a way as not unduly to obstruct other users. If a use of a highway, though incidental to the right of passage, is unreasonable in extent, it goes beyond the purpose for which the highway was dedicated. If it is not incidental to the right of passage at all, it also goes beyond that purpose.

One may therefore define the right of the public to use a highway as a right to use it reasonably for passage and repassage and for any other purpose reasonably incidental thereto. . . .

[The] second proposition is effectively that a use of the highway which goes beyond these public rights is a trespass unless such use is covered specially by the dedication or authorised by some statute. . . . [T]his proposition, . . . seems to me to be well settled law. Of course, the trespass is only actionable at the suit of the owner of the soil of the highway. So much for the first general question—what is the nature of the public right in the highway.

The second general question is, what conduct in relation to a highway constitutes a public nuisance? . . . The term 'unreasonable' can only be interpreted in a context, and the context in this case is the law of highways. What Lord Gifford is really saying is that his clients were behaving reasonably in the sense that they were not resorting to violence or intimidation and did not station themselves so as completely to obstruct the footpath or the entrance to the plaintiffs' office. But one is not here considering what is the behaviour to be expected of a reasonable picket (whatever that may be) but whether or not the behaviour of these pickets amounted to an unreasonable user of the highway. And whether or not a use of a highway is reasonable can only be determined by reference to the fact that the purpose of dedication is that the public may pass and repass, a subject I have already dealt with earlier."

Later he considered the effect of the statutory protection upon this position and concluded that without this immunity an unreasonable use of the highway was unlawful.

In *The Mersey Dock and Harbour Co.* v. *Verrinder*[46] Judge Fitzhugh sitting in the Chancery Division at Manchester granted an interlocutory injunction on the ground that it was likely that picketing which had purposes beyond those rendered lawful by section 15 of TULRA would constitute a nuisance. In his view not only violence but intimidation would constitute a nuisance. So also would the existence of an intention to regulate and control traffic to and from industrial premises. If this is true it leaves very little of *Ward, Lock* and

---

[44] [1975] I.C.R. 308.
[45] [1975] I.C.R. 77.
[46] [1982] I.R.L.R. 152.

substantially reinstates *Lyons* v. *Wilkins* since most picketing will have such interventionist purposes.

Scope of statutory declaration of legality

The limitations of the immunity existing before 1980 were very clearly brought out in *Tynan* v. *Balmer*.[47] Forty pickets, under the direction of the appellant, had begun to walk in a circle blocking a service road, which was part of the public highway and which gave access to the main entrance to a factory. It was inferred that one of their purposes was to seal off the entrance so as to prevent supplies being delivered to the factory. The appellant was arrested after he had declined to disperse the pickets when requested to do so by a constable, and he appealed against his conviction for obstruction of the police in the execution of their duty. In convicting him the Recorder of Liverpool had said:

> "If the Trade Disputes Act 1906 confers any right to produce what would otherwise be an obstruction in a public highway (and it may be that it does) it only does so to the extent that attendance at a place for the purpose of peacefully obtaining and communicating information or of peacefully persuading people to abstain from working cannot reasonably take place at all without producing that result."

As a statement of principle this would seem correct. Its effect entirely depends on whether picketing is to be declared unprotected just because, for example, two men instead of four could reasonably have communicated the information.

On appeal, a Divisional Court, though not dissenting from this statement, took another and even more restrictive point. Widgery J. said:

> "What in my view one must do is to look carefully at section 2 [of the Trade Disputes Act 1906] and see exactly what it authorises. It authorises in its simplest terms a person to attend at or near one of the places described if he does so merely for the purpose of peacefully obtaining or communicating information. . . . The recorder has found as a fact that the pickets in this case were not attending merely for the purposes described in the section. . . . In my judgment that finding of fact is quite enough to require this court to say that as a matter of law the recorder's judgment in this case should be upheld."[48]

Lord Parker C.J. seemed to suggest that this view, that section 2 offers no protection if any purpose of the picket is outside section 2, will apply even if those purposes are, in the circumstances, necessary to the communication. It would seem that a picket may, within the protection, walk alongside a pedestrian talking to him but that a picket has no protection if he obstructs a vehicle to talk to the driver. Picketing for other purposes than those covered by section 2 might still contain no unlawful element, apart from the technical trespass to the highway, but will be unprotected if the means used go beyond what is reasonable.[49]

Two major decisions at the end of 1973 and the beginning of 1974 should, therefore, have come as no surprise. In *Hunt* v. *Broome*[50] the House of Lords

---

[47] [1967] 1 Q.B. 91.
[48] See also on this approach *Toppin* v. *Feron* (1909) 43 I.L.T.R. 190.
[49] *Bird* v. *O'Neal* [1960] A.C. 907.
[50] [1974] I.C.R. 84. In *Kavanagh* v. *Hislock* [1974] I.C.R. 282 at 290, Widgery C.J. appears to suggest that there was something novel in the decision.

held that a picket has no right to obstruct the highway while attempting to persuade a lorry driver to turn back. The defendant, a strike picket, during an industrial dispute, stood holding a placard in front of a lorry urging the driver not to work at a nearby site and actually preventing him from driving along the road. The picket was charged with obstruction of the highway. The magistrates had taken the view that his action was reasonable and so fell within the statutory immunity. The Divisional Court had, however, reversed this decision. With a rare display of resort to Hohfeldian jurisprudence Lord Reid said:

" . . . I see no ground for implying any right to require the person whom it is sought to persuade to submit to any kind of constraint or restriction of his personal freedom. One is familiar with persons at the side of the road signalling to a driver requesting him to stop. It is then for the driver to decide whether he will stop or not. That, in my view, a picket is entitled to do. If the driver stops, the picket can talk to him but only for so long as the driver is willing to listen.

"That must be so, because if a picket had a statutory right to stop or to detain the driver that must necessarily imply that the Act has imposed on those passing along the road a statutory duty to stop or to remain for longer than they choose to stay. So far as my recollection goes it would be unique for Parliament to impose such a duty otherwise than by express words, and even if one envisages the possibility of such a duty being imposed by implication the need for it would have to be crystal clear."

Lord Salmon said:

" . . . it is nothing but the attendance of the pickets at the places specified which is protected; and then only if their attendance is for one of the specified purposes. The section gives no protection in respect of anything the pickets may say or do whilst they are attending if what they say or do is itself unlawful. But for the section, the mere attendance of pickets might constitute an offence under section 7(2) and (4) of the Act of 1875 or under the Highways Act 1959 or constitute a tort, for example, nuisance. The section, therefore, gives a narrow but nevertheless real immunity to pickets. It clearly does no more."

The Royal Commission on Trade Unions, 1965–68,[51] concluded that the law of picketing was satisfactory. It is suggested that the practice may be satisfactory, in that there are relatively few cases before the courts arising from picketing. The conduct of most pickets is reasonable, even if it technically steps beyond the bare essentials presumed to be within the statutory protection on either of the above grounds, and the subjects of the picketing accept it as such.

Police powers

The same practical justification applies to the power of the police to disperse pickets. In *Piddington* v. *Bates*[52] eight employees were, at the time, at work in the premises of the Free Press Ltd. during the major printing stoppage of 1959. The company employed non-union labour and was owned by an organisation generally regarded as anti-union. A party of 18 pickets arrived in two vehicles. Two pickets were stationed at the front gate and four at the rear gate. A constable arrived and informed the pickets at the rear gate that two pickets were sufficient there. Two of them departed. The constable made his way to the front gate and, on his way, passed the appellant, who was clearly going back to the

---

[51] The Government White Paper *In Place of Strife,* 1969, Cmnd. 3888, also suggested this.
[52] [1961] 1 W.L.R. 162.

gate. The constable told the appellant several times that two pickets would be enough there, but the appellant asserted that he knew his rights and could stand at the back gate if he chose. He attempted to push past the constable and was arrested and charged with obstructing a policeman in the exercise of his duty. It was alleged that the duty involved was the prevention of a breach of the peace which the constable reasonably anticipated. The court held that, in the circumstances, it would not say that the constable had no reasonable grounds for such anticipation. Lord Parker C.J. indicated the existence of a considerable protection against abuse of the powers of the police which may not, in practice, exist:

> "The law is reasonably plain. First, the mere statement by a constable that he did anticipate that there might be a breach of the peace is clearly not enough. There must exist proved facts from which a constable could reasonably have anticipated such a breach.
>
> "Secondly, it is not enough that his contemplation is that there is a remote possibility of a breach of the peace. Accordingly in every case it becomes a question whether, on the particular facts, there were reasonable grounds on which the constable charged with this duty reasonably anticipated that a breach of the peace might occur."

It is fairly obvious, however, that a court will not be over-anxious to discard the assessment of a policeman on the spot.

An attempt was made in *Kavanagh* v. *Hiscock*[53] to restrict this police power by asserting a right to picket. The divisional court, following the decision in *Hunt* v. *Broome*[54] confirmed that immunities did not amount to rights. May J. said:

> "Both before the stipendiary magistrate and in this court the defendant contended that section 134 of the Industrial Relations Act 1971[54a] gave him a right, in the sense of a positive entitlement, to picket peacefully, that is to seek peacefully to persuade the driver of the coach to cease carrying the electricians who were not on strike. In my judgment this is not the effect of section 134(1) nor what, by its plain terms, it enacts. Section 134 merely provides, as did its statutory predecessors, that the activity specified in subsection (1), which may loosely be described as peaceful picketing, shall not, of itself, and these words require to be stressed, constitute a criminal offence or a civil wrong."

Picketing which, by reason of the application of excessive means, does not fall within the statutory protection, is usually referred to as "non-peaceful" picketing. This must not be taken necessarily to refer to the existence of violence.[55]

The amendments introduced by the Employment Act 1980 were intended to deal with what the government saw as two serious weaknesses in the control exercised by the law. In the first place, whereas it was admitted that the provisions of the criminal law were adequate to control the manner of picketing[56] there was dissatisfaction with the extent to which that law was enforced. Secondly, the criminal law could not operate to deter people from picketing but

---

[53] [1974] Q.B. 600.
[54] *Supra*.
[54a] Which at that time contained the statutory protection for picketing.
[55] See, *e.g. Ryan* v. *Cooke and Quinn* [1938] I.R. 512—placards bearing gross misrepresentations.
[56] Standing Committee A, March 20, 1980, col. 1411.

could only control the way in which the picketing was conducted. Three separate forms of amendment were, therefore, adopted.

  (i) Protection from "technical liability" was withdrawn from "secondary" picketing (that is to say, picketing other than at the place of work of those picketing);
 (ii) A code of practice was issued effectively inviting the police to take a more restrictive view of what would amount to criminal intimidation;
(iii) All protection from civil liability was withdrawn from picketing not at the place of work of the pickets which was made unlawful even if only because it was no longer protected from the "technical" liability for unreasonable user of the highway.

As we have already seen an otherwise lawful picket within section 15 will be protected from civil liability even if his picketing of his own place of work constituted secondary action from which immunity was normally withdrawn by section 17(2) of the 1980 Act.[57]

Withdrawal of immunity from secondary picketing

The Employment Act 1980[58] inserts a revised section 15 into the TULRA 1974.

"**15.**—(1) It shall be lawful for a person in contemplation or furtherance of a trade dispute to attend—

  (*a*) at or near his own place of work, or
  (*b*) if he is an official of a trade union, at or near the place of work of a member of that union whom he is accompanying and whom he represents,

for the purpose only of peacefully obtaining or communicating information, or peacefully persuading any person to work or abstain from working.

(2) If a person works or normally works—

  (*a*) otherwise than at any one place, or
  (*b*) at a place the location of which is such that attendance there for a purpose mentioned in subsection (1) above is impracticable,

his place of work for the purposes of that subsection shall be any premises of his employer from which he works or from which his work is administered

(3) In the case of a worker who is not in employment where (a) his last employment was terminated in connection with a trade dispute, subsection (1) above shall in relation to that dispute have effect as if any reference to his place of work were a reference to his former place of work or (b) the termination of his employment was one of the circumstances giving rise to a trade dispute.

(4) A person who is an official of a trade union by virtue only of having been elected or appointed to be a representative of some of the members of the union shall be regarded for the purposes of subsection (1) above as representing only those members; but otherwise an official of a trade union shall be regarded for those purposes as representing all its members."

Bercusson[59] has pointed out in detail the problems of definition in this provision.

---

[57] Employment Act 1980, s.17(5). But the dispute must be with his employer.
[58] Employment Act 1980, s.16(1).
[59] "Picketing, Secondary Picketing and Secondary Action" (1980) 9 I.L.J. at pp. 220 *et seq.*

—Where is the place of work on large multi-plant sites or complex plants? (It is clear that "attending at . . ." does not permit entry to the place).

—Is the place defined by the contract of employment or the practice of the picket?

—To what extent can a person be said normally to work otherwise than at one place? When is it "impracticable" to picket a place and, in both cases, what is the limit of permission to picket elsewhere?

—When do employees cease to be in the employment of the employer picketed?

The purpose of permitting union officials to attend derives from the view of the police that they exercise a controlling influence. But when are they accompanying members of their union entitled to picket and how many of them are able to claim representative functions? It should be noted that for the purpose of this provision the trade union need be neither independent nor permanent.

The Code of Practice

It is doubtful whether the Code is correct to say "the law gives the police discretion to take whatever measures may reasonably be considered necessary to ensure that picketing remains peaceful and orderly."[60] A disorderly picket protected by the statutory immunity does not seem to commit any offence (nor even incur civil liability) merely by reason of that fact, and it is submitted that not all disorderly conduct can reasonably be foreseen as likely to provoke a breach of the peace. In the same way it is not the fear of disorder among the pickets that entitles the police to limit their numbers.[61] These provisions seem designed to suggest to magistrates that it is an offence for a picket to refuse to obey the request of a policeman to move.

Is a "disorderly" picket one not supervised according to paragraph 32?

"An experienced person, preferably a trade union official who represents those picketing, should always be in charge of the picket line. He should have a letter of authority from his union which he can show to police officers or to people who want to cross the picket line. Even when he is not on the picket line himself he should be available to give the pickets advice if a problem arises."

More significantly, the Code contains the following guidelines.[62]

"Large numbers on a picket line are also likely to give rise to fear and resentment amongst those seeking to cross that picket line even where no criminal offence is committed. They exacerbate disputes and sour relations not only between management and employees but between the pickets and their fellow employees. Accordingly pickets and their organisers should ensure that in general the number of pickets does not exceed six at any entrance to a workplace; frequently a smaller number will be appropriate."

It is important to realise that the powers of the police and the provisions of the criminal law are indeed very extensive.[63] The difference between tolerable levels of control and oppression of freedoms that are part of the freedom of

---

[60] para. 26.
[61] para. 28.
[62] para. 31.
[63] See, *e.g.* para. 24.

speech is, in the area of picketing, very much dependent on the way the police exercise their powers. The distinction between instructions and guidelines is no doubt real but the Code comes perilously close to governmental instruction to the police to regard six pickets at any one point as the normal permitted maximum.

Withdrawal of civil immunity

By far the most important effect of the 1980 Act upon picketing is not produced by limitation upon the scope of statutorily declared legality. As we have seen that in itself does not amount to much since it leaves the criminal law intact and only excludes civil liability which would be inherent in the very act of attendance. Hitherto all industrial picketing has been able to rely on the normal immunity available to all action in contemplation or furtherance of a trade dispute. This immunity is very important to pickets the purpose of which is usually some form of interference with contract. If both the statutory immunity and the legalising effect of section 15 of TULRA are removed then the attendance itself will provide the necessary unlawful means to make the unprotected interference actionable.

Section 16(2) of the Employment Act 1980 provides

> "(2) Nothing in section 13 of the 1974 Act shall prevent an act done in the course of picketing from being actionable in tort unless it is done in the course of attendance declared lawful by section 15 of that Act."

The effect of this is that all picketing not at the place of work of the picket renders the organisers and participants liable in tort for interference with contract, regardless of whether they would otherwise be contemplating or furthering a trade dispute. Moreover, as soon as picketing at the place of employment of the participants takes on some unlawful characteristic it loses the immunity from liability for the economic torts which it would previously have continued to enjoy notwithstanding that characteristic. A picket which, for instance, uses means excessive to the purpose of communication or persuasion might well not thereby commit any extraneous tort previously capable of destroying the immunity offered by section 13 "on the ground only" of the economic torts. Nevertheless that excessive measure will mean according to *Tynan* v. *Balmer* that it no longer falls within the protection of section 15 and so loses the benefit of section 13. The economic torts themselves are not declared lawful by section 15 so their presence in picketing appears to be capable of destroying the immunity from liability for them granted by section 13.

If employees picket their own employer but in support of a dispute with another employer it might be said to have a purpose in addition to communication or persuasion to work or not to work. Even if this is not so, such action is not exempt from the destruction of section 13 immunity. The only picketing so exempt is picketing by an employee of his place of work when he is also employed by a party to the dispute. In other words picketing of those not in dispute is in a worse position as regards lack of immunity than any other industrial action.

SPECIAL AND EMERGENCY PROVISIONS

Virtually all industrial countries possess some legislative provisions to protect essential services, or to deal with the problem of the termination of supplies or the withdrawal of the means of supply by reason of industrial action. Until 1971, and again after 1976, Great Britain (as distinct from the United Kingdom) has possessed little legislation of this type. It was considered necessary in 1919[64] to make it a criminal offence to seek to cause disaffection among, or a withdrawal of services by, the police. Members of the police force were prohibited from membership of a trade union. No restriction has, however, been placed on the right of civil and other public servants to withdraw their labour, although such restrictions exist in the United States of America and a number of other countries. A general criminal offence capable of commission by any worker who breaks a contract of service or of hiring having reasonable cause to believe that the consequence will be to cause serious bodily injury or injury to valuable property has existed since 1875[65] and survived the widespread repeal of earlier provisions by the Industrial Relations Act 1971. It has been little used.

Apart from this it has been argued that a purely political strike would be unlawful,[66] although it is difficult to see what civil or criminal offence would necessarily be committed.[67] It seems only open to argument that if the strike had given rise to actionable torts it would not attract the statutory protection available to actions in contemplation or furtherance of a trade dispute.

For 50 years, with the almost unused intervention of the Trade Union Act of 1927, this gap was filled only by the provisions of the Emergency Powers Act 1920.[68] Under this Act, the Queen in Council may declare a state of emergency if it appears that "there have occurred, or are about to occur, events of such a nature as to be calculated, by interfering with the supply and distribution of food, water, fuel or light, or with the means of locomotion, to deprive the community, or any substantial portion of the community, of the essentials of life." Upon the declaration of such an emergency Parliament, if not in session or due to reconvene within five days, must be recalled and the proclamation communicated to it. The state of emergency may last for one month, although one has never done so, and this period may be extended by the same procedure. During such a state of emergency Orders in Council may be made as deemed:

> " . . . necessary for the preservation of the peace, for securing and regulating the supply and distribution of food, water, fuel, light and other necessities, for maintaining the means of transit, or locomotion, and for any other purposes essential to the public safety and the life of the community."

Such orders must be laid before Parliament as soon as may be after being made and will last for seven days at a time. These orders may not, however, forbid strikes or peaceful picketing, nor introduce compulsory military service, nor order persons to return to work. Existing criminal procedure may not be changed, nor may fines or imprisonment be imposed without trial.

This appears to be a rather ponderous machinery although actually it is a reasonably efficient form of supervised direct government. It is obvious, how-

---

[64] Police Act 1919, see now Police Act 1964.

[65] Conspiracy and Protection of Property Act 1875, s.5.

[66] *National Sailors' and Firemen's Union* v. *Reed* [1926] Ch. 536 at 539–540. *Sed contra*, Goodhart, *Essays in Jurisprudence and the Common Law*, Chap. 11.

[67] See Wedderburn, *The Worker and the Law* (2nd ed.), pp. 392–393.

[68] As amended by the Emergency Powers Act 1964. The Industrial Relations Act 1971 introduced extensive emergency control of industrial action but this was all repealed in 1974.

ever, that it is a short-term solution, resting for its principal effect upon its shock effect. To maintain this it must be used sparingly and it has only been applied in the General Strike of 1926, when orders were made under the proclamation, and seven times since 1945, orders being made on six of these occasions.[69] A change was introduced in 1964 which, though small in appearance, could have considerable significance. Without a declaration of emergency:

"The Admiralty, the Army Council or the Air Council may, by order, authorise officers and men of Her Majesty's naval, military or air forces under their respective control to be temporarily employed in agricultural work or such other work as may be approved in accordance with instructions issued [by the appropriate authority] as being urgent work of national importance, and thereupon it shall be the duty of every person subject to [the discipline of such forces] to obey any command given by his superior officer in relation to such employment. . . . "

This effectively makes permanent the relevant provisions of defence regulations first made in 1939. The powers seem to have been used three times in peace-time, including one occasion when a state of emergency had been declared. Such power is obviously more effective as a way of getting work done, but its exercise may deter the return to work which a declaration of a state of emergency is usually designed to promote. On the other hand it does not seem quite so inflammatory as the device of Presidential seizure which is, more commonly, resorted to in the United States.[70]

The history of the emergency provisions contained in the Industrial Relations Act 1971,[71] which, briefly, between 1972 and 1974 extended emergency powers to allow for orders having the effect of requiring the industrial action to cease, is the story of the litigation surrounding *Secretary of State for Employment* v. *ASLEF.*[72] That experience certainly does not encourage the supposition that such interdiction will be attempted again.

---

[69] The dock strikes of 1948, 1949 and 1970, the railway strike of 1955, the seamen's strike of 1966, the miners' strikes of 1972 and of 1973–74.

[70] Blackman, *Presidential Seizure in Labour Disputes* (Harvard, 1967).

[71] ss.138–145.

[72] [1972] 2 Q.B. 455.

CHAPTER 11

PROTECTING HEALTH AND SAFETY AT WORK

Introduction

At the risk of greatly over-simplifying the situation it must be explained that there are two radically different ways of viewing the law relating to safety and health at work. First, it can be looked at primarily as an instrument to secure forms of compensation for the employee in which the rules governing liability are formulated and interpreted largely after the event to determine fault and then to assign damages or other forms of compensation according to the measure of the injury. Secondly, it can be viewed as a set of rules defining duties meant to be imposed so as to reduce risk.

Clearly the common law duty of care, breach of which will entitle the injured person to bring an action for damages, is of the first type. It is true that the risk of having to pay damages may act as an incentive to safety. No satisfactory answer as to the extent to which this is so has ever even been attempted although it is clear that employer's liability insurance, the premiums for which become a cost of production, will tend to reduce the deterrent effect. Whatever this effect may be, however, the law is primarily concerned to assess fault after injury and not to advance safety. Perhaps surprisingly, however, much legislation before 1975, the intention of which undoubtedly fell within the second category, was primarily applied by lawyers as if it came within the first category. The tort of breach of statutory duty made possible the argument that because a legislative duty to advance safety had been broken an action for damages lay from that breach. There seems to be no objection to the provision of duties as to safety and health at work performing a dual function. Indeed, they could in theory operate less haphazardly to provide compensation than the duty to take reasonable care. Objection may, however, be taken when the primary mental reaction is not to ask what should be done to secure safety but whether one will be liable to an action for damages if a particular course of conduct is, or is not, adopted and how large that liability will be.

In these chapters we shall consider three separate systems relating to risks to health and safety at work. The first, based on the Health and Safety at Work Act 1975, is designed to lead to sanctions of enforcement rather than compensation although the effect of the latter consideration will probably never be entirely excluded. The second, based on the action in tort for damages, plainly pursues the second primary objective though there may, as already stated, be some residual effect on safety. This second system has absorbed the duties laid down in much pre-1975 safety legislation and used those duties to determine liability to compensation, thus inevitably tending to obscure their primary intention. The third has no significant link with the rules applied by the other two nor any pretension to seek to secure standards of safety. It is concerned with the provision of social security benefits to ameliorate the economic effects of physical or mental injury or damage to health and its rules are solely designed to govern the assessment of that benefit and not at all to define any duty in respect of the working environment.

535

Inevitably a question has long been raised as to whether there is any theoretical justification for the second of these systems which, ideally, would seem merely to supplement provision made after the event by the third system; such supplementation being available largely fortuitously if someone is found to be at fault and having the disadvantage of tending to an attitude of mind which considers paying for the injury rather than preventing it. The need for compensation, it is pointed out, does not depend on whether or not there has been a failure in a duty. The object of the imposition by law of a duty ought to be that it should be observed. This falls within the first system in that all one needs is effective enforcement of preventive measures and adequate provision for the injured when that enforcement fails to prevent injury. Although the Pearson Commission[1] rejected the argument for abolition of the tort system of compensation for injury, either in industry or, generally, so that that system may be said to be undiminished in its operation, only some outlines of its operation will be given in this book, not so much as an indication of support for arguments favouring its irrelevance as because it is not peculiar to labour law and, in its general application, would require much more extensive treatment than is possible here.

Safety legislation in general

The first Act to regulate the conditions of work in factories was passed in 1802.[2] It has been described as more an extension of the Poor Law than a forerunner of modern factory legislation and was concerned rather with cleanliness, clothing, hours of work and religious instruction, than with safety. The restriction of the Act to textile manufacture has been said to be due to the unusually bad conditions in those factories, but, in practice, it set a pattern of piecemeal provisions that was to last until 1974.[3] The Act may also be considered less a triumph of philanthropy than of another example of the alliance between philanthropic and economic interest. It may, in part, have been an attempt by the textile finishing trades to reduce the flow of raw textiles, much of which could not be handled in this country, but was finished on the Continent and re-imported to undercut home finished cloth. It is clear that nineteenth-century employers believed, or purported to believe, in the restrictive effect of safety measures upon production. In providing for religious instruction, the 1802 Act might be supposed to take up valuable productive time, and so there may be partial truth in this rather cynical explanation of this legislation.[4]

Much effort was devoted to reducing the effectiveness of the enforcement of the early Acts. It has been suggested that it was this desire which underlay the introduction in 1819 of the forerunner of modern inspection replacing enforcement by visitors appointed by justices of the peace. This is, however, unlikely

---

[1] Royal Commission on Civil Liability and Compensation for Personal Injury 1978: Cmnd 7054.

[2] Act for the Preservation of the Health and Morals of Apprentices and others employed in Cotton and Other Mills and Cotton and Other Factories, 42 Geo. 3, c. 73.

[3] Hutchins and Harrison, *A History of Factory Legislation*.

[4] I am deeply indebted to Dr. R. E. Dickson of Birmingham Polytechnic for pointing out to me both that Sir Robert Peel who was responsible for the first Act was the leading employer in the cotton printing trades, and, to the contrary that the system then existing in the finishing trades would not generally have been considered a factory system. Such a term would have been reserved for textile manufacture.

since the nineteenth-century employer would hardly volunteer for official inspection on any pretext and the visitors, appointed as they were, were much more likely to have proved satisfactory to the employers.

Safety provisions first appeared in legislation in 1844. The Factory and Workshop Act 1878 was the first attempt to consolidate the numerous statutes and regulations which had grown up, ad hoc, to meet new situations. It was in that year that the duty to fence dangerous machinery was re-imposed and made absolute. Ad hoc regulation was replaced by more generally applicable provisions in 1901. Even then, however, the statutory requirements were specific and open to restrictive construction. Safety in agriculture, shops, offices and railway premises, mines and quarries, and in merchant ships is still the subject of separate legislation. Safety in mines was first regulated in 1842, but the first two classes have only been dealt with in the past few years.[5]

The Factories Acts continued to be the primary source of industrial safety standards until the passing of the Health and Safety at Work Act 1974 although they were supplemented by the specialised provisions of a number of Acts relating to particular sections of industry or industrial processes.[6] The pattern of this legislation was criticised by the Robens Committee on Safety and Health at Work[7] because it laid down no general standard of care but dealt with particular abuses. The fragmentation produced by the specialised legislation simply enhanced this effect. Even the area of operation of the legislation was fragmented. None applied to all working environments but each statute defined its area as, for instance, "factories," "shops, offices and railway premises," "mines and quarries" or agriculture. Duties were imposed on "occupiers" and "contractors" but rarely on "employers." Systems of enforcement varied, most notably with the establishment of separate inspectorates (sometimes not even having informal links with each other) under the supervision of different government departments. Worst of all, the piecemeal applications of standards of care were nonetheless defined with relatively precise detail. Not only was it possible to argue on a strict application of its language that a section governing the fencing of machinery did not apply to something that might be described as a vehicle or to a machine produced, as distinct from in use, in the factory but it was also common to find a different standard of duty applying according to whether what was in question was the provision of a fence or the maintenance of a stairway. When this inconsistent mass was used as a standard for the assessment of liability to pay damages the proliferation of fine judicial distinctions meant inevitably that both lawyer and employer were more concerned with the application of words than the attainment of reasonable safety. Certainly there was little in the legislation to promote the feeling of total involvement in the promotion of safety which the Robens report[8] saw as the necessary prerequisite to success.

---

[5] The Agriculture (Safety, Health and Welfare Provisions) Act 1956; the Offices, Shops and Railway Premises Act 1963. The problem in offices and shops is, of course, far less. In each year there are well over 300,000 factory accidents reported, but less than 20,000 reportable accidents in offices and shops.

[6] Those that are still to some extent operative are listed in an appendix to this Chapter at pp. 566–567.

[7] Cmnd. 5034, para. 22 (1972).

[8] See para. 59.

The Health and Safety at Work Act 1974

The 1974 legislation is intended as a set of basic outline duties round which to group more detailed regulation and guidance. It adopts, with one obvious exception, a single standard of care—that of reasonable practicability. Some of the earlier legislative requirements, and most notably the fencing section[9] of the Factories Act 1961 had adopted the apparently more severe standard of absolute liability. Superficially, it may appear surprising that a less rigorous requirement should be imposed, but strict liability suffers from at least two major defects. In the first place it does nothing to assist the promotion of safety or involvement in its attainment that one should be required to do the impossible. In the second place, partly because they recognised this and partly from a desire to appear, if only to a magistrates' court, to be behaving reasonably, the inspectorate only enforced the duty by criminal prosecution where conduct could be said to be unreasonable. In addition a part of a machine could only be said to be dangerous so as to require fencing when some danger could reasonably be foreseen.

Meaning of "reasonably practicable"

The word "practicable" has been regarded by the courts as meaning something less stringent than "physically possible." In *Adsett* v. *K. and L. Steel Founders and Engineers Ltd.*[10] Parker J. said that it implied possibility in the light of current knowledge and invention. So reasonable practicability is more than reasonable care[11] but use of the qualification "reasonable" introduces into consideration such factors as the cost of preventive action when weighed in the balance against the risk of injury and the possible extent of that injury should it occur. The word "reasonably" only serves to qualify "practicable." The standard is not one of what is reasonable *and* practicable.

Though reasonable practicability requires something more than reasonable care, in determining the standard it is right to take into account such matters as expense and trouble and whether they are disproportionate to the result to be attained. The courts will, however, not be unduly sensitive to the effect of expense upon profits.

In *Coltness Iron Co. Ltd.* v. *Sharp*[12] Lord Atkin said:

> "The time of non-protection is so short, and the time, trouble and expense of any form of protection is so disproportionate, that I think the defence is proved."

The implication is of a requirement of considerable disproportion. The most acceptable definition of the term to date is contained in the judgment of Asquith L.J. in *Edwards* v. *National Coal Board*[13]:

> "'Reasonably practicable' is a narrower term than 'physically possible,' and seems to me to imply that a computation must be made by the owner in which the *quantum* of risk is placed on one scale and the sacrifice involved in the measures necessary for averting the risk (whether in money, time or trouble) is placed on the

---

[9] s.14.
[10] [1953] 1 All E.R. 97.
[11] See *Edwards* v. *National Coal Board* [1949] 1 K.B. 704 at 709 and *Marshall* v. *Gotham Co. Ltd.* [1954] A.C. 360.
[12] [1938] A.C. 90.
[13] *Supra.*

other, and that, if it be shown that there is a gross disproportion between them—the risk being insignificant in relation to the sacrifice—the defendants discharge the onus on them."

The manner in which this may be applied is evident in the words of Lord Reid in *Marshall* v. *Gotham Co. Ltd.*,[14] where he said:

". . . as men's lives may be at stake, it should not lightly be held that to take a practicable precaution is unreasonable. . . . The danger was a very rare one. The trouble and expense involved in the use of the precautions, while not prohibitive, would have been considerable. The precautions would not have afforded anything like complete protection against the danger, and . . . adoption would have had the disadvantage of giving a false sense of security."

Practicability itself involves taking measures which are feasible.[15] The layman in applying these terms to his duty must be honest with himself. He has no right to substitute for the word "impracticable" expressions such as "difficult," "not too easy" or "inconvenient."[16] It will be realised, for example, that though it may satisfy a standard of reasonable care that a danger should be clearly indicated and lit, practicability may require the removal of that danger even though to do so is inconvenient.

In deciding what is practicable, the state of knowledge at the time is obviously an important consideration.[17] It is not practicable to take measures against an unknown danger, unless, indeed, it was reasonably practicable to suppose that one should have known of it.[18] In the same way, it cannot be said that there has been a failure in the duty when what was omitted was not available at the time of the accident.[19] A standard of reasonable practicability has considerable advantages over a strict liability which some of the provisions of previous legislation have sought to impose. It will, for instance, permit the taking into account of special circumstances inherent in the operations, and it is capable of comprehending all the detailed exclusions from strict liability which would otherwise have to be inserted to permit the removal of safety devices during such operations as cleaning and servicing.

A subjective approach

It is the policy of the Health and Safety Executive to seek to establish, as it were, a minimum standard. Those who claim they cannot reasonably attain this standard should be regarded as unfit to engage in the activity. However, more affluent employers will be expected, on a subjective application of reasonable practicability, to achieve a standard higher than the minimum.

Workplaces

The Act imposes duties not so much in relation to a place, as did previous legislation, but in relation to the broadly defined situation of being "at work."

---

[14] *Supra.*
[15] See, *e.g. Boynton* v. *Willment Bros. Ltd.* [1971] 1 W.L.R. 1625—the fact that risks caused by a handrail would exceed those resulting from its absence did not make its erection impracticable.
[16] *Schwalb* v. *Fass (H.) & Son Ltd.* (1946) 175 L.T. 345.
[17] On this see, *Cartwright* v. *G. K. N. Sankey Ltd.* (1972) 12 K.I.R. 453; *Wright* v. *Dunlop Rubber Co. Ltd.* (1973) 13 K.I.R. 255.
[18] *Richards* v. *Highway Ironfounders (West Bromwich) Ltd.* [1955] 1 W.L.R. 1049.
[19] *Adsett* v. *K. and L. Steel Founders and Engineers Ltd.* [1953] 1 W.L.R. 773.

Where it is necessary specifically to impose a duty relating to premises,[20] premises is defined to include any place. More particularly it is said to cover any vehicle, vessel, aircraft or hovercraft; any installation on land or offshore or any other installation and any tent or movable structure.[21] There is little room for any of the fine distinctions built upon the lengthy and detailed definition of a factory in the 1961 Act or its predecessors. In particular the need to show that the principal purpose of the undertaking is commercial profit disappears. It is obvious that adoption of a concept of covering everyone at work in any place will involve overlap with other legislation. The reference in the definition of premises to vehicles is one example of this since vehicles on public roads are regulated by the Road Traffic Acts. Failure to take reasonably practicable steps to check the brake fluid pipes on a road tanker so that they became corroded would produce a dangerous condition constituting an offence under both sets of legislation. Theoretically, therefore, both police and factory inspectorate might prosecute. In practice the factory inspectorate normally take the view that they will not intervene if the matter is more appropriately covered by other legislation.

Employer's general duty

Appropriate duties are laid on everyone connected with the work situation but in the nature of things it will, no doubt, be usual to expect most from the employer. The duty imposed on an employer[22] is, in the scope of its requirements, in sharp contrast to the specific requirements of earlier legislation. It is provided that:

> "(1) It shall be the duty of every employer to ensure, so far as is reasonably practicable, the health, safety and welfare at work of all his employees.
> (2) Without prejudice to the generality of an employer's duty under the preceding subsection, the matters to which that duty extends include in particular—
>> (a) the provision and maintenance of plant and systems of work that are, so far as is reasonably practicable, safe and without risk to health;
>> (b) arrangements for ensuring, so far as is reasonably practicable, safety and absence of risks to health in connection with the use, handling, storage and transport of articles and substances;
>> (c) the provision of such information, instruction, training and supervision as is *necessary* to ensure, so far as is reasonably practicable, the health and safety at work of his employees;
>> (d) so far as is reasonably practicable as regards any place of work under the employer's control, the maintenance of it in a condition that is safe and without risks to health and the provision and maintenance of means of access to and egress from it that are safe and without such risks;
>> (e) the provision and maintenance of a working environment for his employees that is, so far as is reasonably practicable, safe, without risks to health, and adequate as regards facilities and arrangements for their welfare at work."

It should be emphasised that the duty is contained in subsection (1). Subsection (2) merely provides some examples of that duty. Nevertheless there will be a tendency to treat the latter as laying down sub-rules if only because those with the responsibility of preparing prosecutions will tend to frame everything that

---

[20] As for instance in s.4.
[21] s.53.
[22] s.2.

might lead to such a prosecution in the more specific format of subsection (2), feeling that courts will tend to react against invocation of too undefined a duty. It is essential that the duties specified in subsection (2) should not, because of this, come to be regarded as a comprehensive breakdown of the general duty. To this end it is perhaps unfortunate that subsection (2)(c) actually modifies the general duty by purporting to require only such reasonably practicable steps as are necessary. No doubt this is a sensible limitation on what training and instruction should be provided but it does infer an element of reasonableness on its own.[23]

Despite continuation of a rate of prosecution somewhat over 2,000 per year,[24] very few cases have been reported which provide guidance upon the interpretation of the provisions of the 1974 Act. The experience of the inspectorate varies considerably with the approach of magistrates' courts, for instance to the question of bringing a charge under both sections 2(1) and 2(2). One of only two major reported cases shed some valuable light on the interpretation of section 2. In *R. v. Swan Hunter Shipbuilders Ltd.*[25] a serious fire had broken out in the destroyer H.M.S. Glasgow while it was under construction. A welder had struck his arc with his torch. The resultant fire burned fiercely and spread rapidly because the atmosphere was enriched with oxygen due to the negligence of sub-contractors who had failed to turn off the supply of oxygen the previous evening. The shipbuilders were well aware of the danger of fire in such circumstances and had laid down for their own employees a system by which all oxygen valves were shut off at the end of the day and all hoses returned to the upper deck. They were, however, charged with a breach of section 2 particularly with reference to subsections (2)(a) and (c). They were also charged with a breach of section 3 in failing to conduct their undertakings so as to ensure, so far as reasonably practicable, that persons not in their employment were not exposed to safety risks.

The Court of Appeal held that though the sections constituted penal provisions the examples in section 2(2) had to be construed sufficiently widely to accord with the purpose of the general duty in section 2(1). Since the safety of the shipbuilders' own employees depended on the provision of information and instruction as to potential dangers to the employees of other contractors the shipbuilders had a duty to give such information and instruction. The Crown had argued that such a construction would not extend the duties imposed by the Act beyond those already accepted by the common law duty of care.[26]

Dunn L.J. said:

"We accept the submissions of Mr. Potts so far as the construction of the section is concerned. In our view the duties are all covered by the general duty in subsection (1) of section 2: 'It shall be the duty of every employer to ensure, so far as is

---

[23] If it is not always easy to apply the provisions of section 2 to protection of health it is often impossible to formulate the boundaries within which "welfare" should be governed. All that can be said is that there is little sign in the foreseeable future of enforcement of the Act as a regulator of standards of welfare. The inspectorate have a handful of specific items, such as the provision of hot water in wash rooms, which they list as welfare.

[24] A total of 2,323 informations were laid by HMFI in 1980 resulting in 2,137 convictions. The average penalty was £179. The factory inspectorate issued 4,385 improvement notices and 1,585 prohibition notices of which 223 required immediate prohibition—Health and Safety: Manufacturing and Service Industries 1980, Table 6.

[25] [1981] I.C.R. 831 (C.A.). See Brenda Barrett (1982) 45 M.L.R. 338.

[26] See *McArdle* v. *Andmac Roofing Co.* [1967] 1 W.L.R. 356.

reasonably practicable, the health, safety and welfare at work of all his employees.' As the judge said, that is a strict duty. If the provision of a safe system of work for the benefit of his own employees involves information and instruction as to potential dangers being given to persons other than the employer's own employees, then the employer is under a duty to provide such information and instruction. His protection is contained in the words 'so far as is reasonably practicable' which appear in all the relevant provisions. The onus is on the defendants to prove on a balance of probabilities that it was not reasonably practicable in the particular circumstances of the case."

Control of the undertaking

The same standard of reasonably practicable protection is extended by section 3 to those not in the employment of the employer but who may, by the conduct of his undertaking, be affected by being exposed to risks to their health and safety. A similar duty is owed to those likely to be affected by the conduct of an undertaking by a self-employed person. Both employers and the self-employed may be required, in prescribed circumstances, to give persons other than their employees who may be affected by the way in which they conduct their undertaking prescribed information about aspects of that conduct which might affect those persons' health and safety.[27] The inspectorate do not antici-pate that use of the words "conduct of his undertaking" will prove restrictive of the scope of these provisions.

The specific reference in section 3(3) to a duty to provide information led to the argument in the *Swan Hunter* case that the more general provisions of section 3(1) and 3(2) should be read as limited to exclude an obligation to provide information save so far as sub-section (3) required it. The Court of Appeal adopted the words of Boreham J. at first instance:

"So far as section 3 is concerned we cannot do better than reproduce the words of the judge, when he gave his ruling on the submission. He said:
'In my judgment subsection (3) does not impinge upon nor does it limit in any way subsection (1) of section 3. Subsection (3) is dealing with a very limited class and a very limited number, namely, the prescribed cases where only prescribed information is to be given. If subsection (1) were to be subject to subsection (3), why then I should expect it to say so, but the words in my judgment in subsection (1) are wide enough to include the giving of informa-tion and instruction to employees other than one's own employees. For that and for reasons which I have already given in dealing with the other submis-sion indeed it would be in my judgment crucial, particularly in the circum-stances of this case or in similar circumstances, that such information should be imparted. It would seem a strange thing in my view if information is only to be given in the prescribed cases that there have not yet been any cases prescribed. In my view count 6 is well founded.'"

Safety of premises

The primary purpose of the Factories Acts was to impose duties on occupiers of premises. Although this duty, in common with all similar statutory duties, could not be assigned, occupation of premises could be so assigned, thus transferring the burden of the duty. This not infrequently occurred where, for

---

[27] s.3(3).

instance, part of factory premises was transferred into the temporary occupation of a construction company engaged in building a further part of the factory. Quite apart from the tendency to produce a lack of involvement in safety measures this might well have the effect of excluding from protection considerable numbers of people likely to be directly affected by the work done in the assigned portion. Section 4 of the 1974 Act eliminates much of the shortcoming of this situation which has not already been removed by imposition of the principal duty on the employer. It provides a duty upon each person who has, to any extent, control of premises or the means of access to or egress therefrom, other than domestic premises, made available to those not in his employment as a place of work or as a place where they use plant or substances provided for their use, or to other premises used in connection therewith. The duty is to take such measures as it is reasonable for a person in his position to take to ensure, so far as is reasonably practicable, that the premises, all means of access to or egress therefrom available for use by persons using the premises, and any plant or substance in, or provided for use in, the premises is or are safe and without risks to health. Whereas it is possible to find more than one person in occupation of a place for the purposes of the Factories Act[28] adoption of the concept of "control to any extent" clearly involves almost everyone having any right in respect of the property. The landlord, the head tenant, any sub-tenants and almost everyone with a licence to use the premises will have some rights of control, even if only temporary. There is no opportunity of assignment without abandonment of the interest. It is, of course, clear that the right of control may range from a very real power to a merely nominal residue. In actual practice the incidence of liability will obviously depend on the area of control in which the risk falls. Recognition of the fact that section 4 will produce a considerable number of people with varying degrees of duty appears in subsection (3) which provides in the case of any person who has a contractual obligation to maintain or repair the premises or in relation to the safety or absence of health risks arising from plant or substances in the premises that that person "shall be treated . . . as being *a person* who has control of *the matters to which his obligation extends.*"

Employee's duty of care

It is the duty of every employee, while at work, to take reasonable care for the health and safety of himself and of other persons who may be affected by his acts or omissions at work.[29] It is also his duty while at work to co-operate with his employer so far as is necessary to enable the employer to perform or comply with any duty or requirement in any of the relevant statutory safety and health provisions. A provision somewhat similar to the first aspect of this duty has been contained in industrial safety legislation for some time. It clearly includes a requirement that the employee should make use of safety devices supplied for his benefit. It will be the duty of the employer under section 2 to take reasonably practicable steps to ensure that the employee knows how to use the device and does use it.

---

[28] See, *e.g. Weavings* v. *Kirk and Randall* [1904] 1 K.B. 213; *Fisher* v. *Port of London Authority* [1962] 1 All E.R. 458.
[29] s.7.

If this section is to some extent designed to transfer the burden of an employer to an employee who blatantly disregards safety provisions the question naturally arises whether an employer such as Swan Hunter could transfer the primary liability to a subcontractor who had similarly disregarded safety obligations.[30] It is relatively rare that the employee should be prosecuted for breach of his duty to take care. Nevertheless, where there exists a clear example of an employee endangering himself or others by failure to take *reasonable care* prosecution is possible.

A general duty is laid on everyone[31] not to interfere with or misuse, intentionally or recklessly, anything provided in the interests of health, safety or welfare in pursuance of any statutory duty.

Atmospheric pollution

There are contained in the specification of general duties two somewhat more specialised provisions. The first has distinct environmental implications and may seem slightly out of place in relation to the others with which we have dealt. It is provided[32] that it is the duty of the *person having control* of any premises of a class prescribed as emitting noxious or offensive substances into the atmosphere to use the *best practicable* means for preventing that emission and rendering such substances as may be emitted harmless and inoffensive. The precedent for this provision stems largely from regulation of alkali works and the peculiarity of the language used to explain the nature of the duty stems therefrom. In practice it is not anticipated that the standards of "best practicable means" will differ materially from "reasonably practicable steps" although it must be acknowledged that, on a strict interpretation of the words there appears to be a considerable difference.

Designers and suppliers

The duty in respect of design, manufacture, importation or supply of articles for use at work is new and is undoubtedly the most interesting provision in the 1974 Act. It is provided[33] that it is the duty of any person who designs, manufactures, imports or supplies *for use at work* any article or substance:

(a) to ensure, so far as is reasonably practicable, that the article is so designed and constructed as to be safe and without risks to health, or the substance is similarly safe and without risk, when properly used;

(b) to carry out or arrange for the carrying out of such testing and examination as may be necessary for the performance of the duty imposed in (a) above;

(c) to take such steps as are necessary to secure that there will be in connection with the use of an article at work adequate information about the use for which it is designed and has been tested, and about any conditions necessary to ensure that when put to that use, it will be safe and without risks to health and, in the case of a substance, similar steps in connection with its use and adequate information about tests carried out and conditions necessary to ensure an absence of risk.

It is also provided that it is the duty of any person undertaking design or manufacture of any article for use at work to carry out, or arrange to be carried

---

[30] See s.36.
[31] s.8.
[32] s.5.
[33] s.6.

out, any necessary research with a view to the discovery and, so far as is reasonably practicable, the elimination or minimisation of risks to health and safety to which the design of the article may give rise. It would appear from this that the duty to undertake necessary research is an absolute one. The reference to reasonable practicability apparently does not qualify the institution of the research but merely its objective. It is difficult to see, however, how this can be so in practice since no one can tell how much research is necessary to discover a risk until the risk has revealed itself either during research or after research has ended. The amount of research necessary would appear only to be capable of definition according to standards of reasonableness. A similar duty is imposed on anyone who undertakes the manufacture of any substance for use at work. The section also imposes a duty to take reasonably practicable steps to ensure safety and an absence of risks on any person who erects or instals any article for use at work in premises where that article is to be used by persons at work so far as regards the way it is erected or installed.

All these provisions are clearly designed to avoid the failure of earlier statutes to cover the situation in which the employer had been able to say that he could not reasonably take any steps to avoid a risk derived from the way that a machine was designed or from faults in its manufacture or from the qualities of a substance which had not been disclosed to him. It was of course true that such a defence would not, in theory, be available to the imposition of an absolute duty. In practice, however, though it is possible to penalise someone who is not at fault for a dangerous situation it is not possible to secure the desired improvement of that situation unless penalties and remedial requirements can be imposed at the source of the danger. Section 6 will, therefore, be of great value in enabling a fault to be traced back to its source and rectified there.

It is probable that section 6 was not intended, and certain that it will not be operated, so as to require a manufacturer to disclose a trade secret involved in the manufacture of an article or substance, but the qualities of a substance which may produce risk must be revealed. Some express limitations are, in addition, imposed on the operation of the duty:

(a) There is no requirement on any person to repeat any testing examination or research carried out other than by him or at his instance in so far as it is reasonable for him to rely on the results of that testing, etc.;

(b) the duty only applies to things done by a person in the course of his trade, business or other undertaking (whether carried on for profit or not) and to matters within his control;

(c) the duty of the designer or other person covered by the provisions relating to articles is transferred to the person for whom that task is carried out wherever the work is done on the basis of a written undertaking by the person for whom it is done that he will take specified steps sufficient to ensure, so far as is reasonably practicable, that the article will be safe and without risk to health when properly used. This exemption does not apply to substances. This distinction may seem surprising since it is quite likely, for instance, that a substance will only be safe if regularly tested. Presumably, however, it would be feasible to conclude that reasonably practicable steps had been taken by one who drew this need to the attention of the person supplied, and that that person was at fault if he failed to perform those tests.

(d) the effective supplier and not the ostensible supplier bears the duty in the case of supply under a hire-purchase agreement, conditional sale agreement or credit sale agreement.

Other safety legislation

The basic legislative duties imposed by the most recent legislation which is designed progressively to take over from the earlier and more specific legislation are, thus, contained in a few sweepingly general provisions. Round them will still cling for many years much of that earlier legislation. The whole package is referred to as "the relevant statutory provisions," and until the earlier legislation is repealed it will continue to provide duties enforceable equally with these more general obligations. In many instances the two forms of duty will cover the same ground. In some instances it may be felt that the earlier duty is more effective because, for instance, it is absolute. In practice it has appeared that the principal inhibition on the application of the 1974 Act rather than earlier more restricted legislation has been the very uncertainty of its scope. The inspectorate likes to know whether it can succeed upon a prosecution. Narrower though the scope of earlier legislation may be, where it is applicable this is now usually much clearer than the answer to whether a course of action will be regarded as reasonably practicable.

Regulations and codes of practice

It is envisaged that in the course of time specification will appear in regulations and codes of practice and not in the body of statute law, largely because the latter is too rigid and too capable of being rendered impotent by restrictive construction. Statute may also be not sufficiently subject to speedy processes of change. The Secretary of State has power to make regulations either to give effect to proposals of the Health and Safety Commission or independently of such initiative.[34] The regulations may deal with any matter relating to the general purposes of Part I of the 1974 Act but a more particular list of subjects is contained in Schedule 3 to that Act. As was the case under the Factories Act and other safety legislation the regulations may repeal or modify any of the existing statutory provisions[35] or may exclude or modify the effect of sections 2 to 9 in relation to any specified class of case. So, for example, regulations governing experiments in genetic manipulation extend to all those conducting such experiments even if the work is merely a hobby. These regulations require prior reporting of the experiment irrespective of any established risk. Regulations also may specify the persons or classes of persons who, in the event[36] of contravention of a requirement or prohibition are to be guilty of an offence and may provide for the availability of any specific defence. It follows that a regulation, once properly made, stands in place of the statutory requirement

---

[34] s.50.
[35] s.15(3)(*a*).
[36] s.15(6).

which it may lessen or increase and is in no sense subject to any overriding standard.

A code of practice, on the other hand, does not replace the provision either of statute or regulation but merely provides guidance as to how a duty may be fulfilled. The provision of a code cannot be relied on, therefore, if it is either more or less extensive than the legislative duty. Except as regards matters relating exclusively to agricultural operations the Commission may, for the purpose of providing practical guidance on any relevant statutory provision or regulation, approve a code of practice issued from some other source or issue its own approved codes,[37] and may issue or approve any revision of such a code. With the consent of the Secretary of State it may withdraw approval of any code and indicate by written notice the effective date of such withdrawal of approval.[38] It is provided that failure to comply with a code will not, of itself, render any person liable to civil or criminal proceedings but, in the case of criminal proceedings for contravention of a requirement or prohibition, any relevant provision of a code is admissible in evidence.[39] This would seem to be true of any code of guidance whether approved or not. In the case of an approved code, however, the section goes on to provide that a failure to observe any provision of the code is conclusive proof of contravention of the requirement or prohibition to which it relates unless it is proved to the satisfaction of the court that there was compliance by some other method.

In practice it is quite common to add to the hierarchy a further lower stage by way of notes of guidance.

Enforcement

Safety representatives

For many years there had been considerable advocacy of the need for safety representatives at the place of employment. In earlier days it had commonly been alleged in answer to this that such provision would be worse than useless because the representatives would be induced by fear of dismissal to avoid offending senior management. That answer was felt to be largely negated with the introduction of protection from unfair dismissal. Increasingly strong local union organisation enabled the possibility of linking the representative to the trade union rather than the management structure. It is provided, accordingly, in section 2 of the 1974 Act that the Secretary of State may make regulations providing for the appointment by recognised trade unions of safety representatives from amongst the employees to represent the employees particularly in consultation with the employers. "Recognition" has the same meaning as under the Employment Protection Act 1975. The provision is operative in all cases where one or more persons is employed by an employer who recognises a union, with the exception of those employed in a mine within the meaning of the Mines and Quarries Act 1954.[40] It is clear that there is no parallel with the appointment of a shop steward whereby the employer could indicate dis-

---

[37] s.16.
[38] s.16(5) and (6).
[39] s.17.
[40] S.I. 1977, No. 500, cl. 3(1). British Actors Equity Association and the Musicians Union are also excluded—cl. 8.

approval of the person appointed. As soon as the employer has been notified of the appointment the safety representative may proceed to exercise his or her functions.[41] So far as reasonably practicable, however, the representative shall have two years' experience with that or a similar employer. Normally the representative will act on behalf of a particular group but the notes of guidance accompanying the regulations indicate that there is no objection to a representative acting for more than one group by agreement among the unions concerned or raising general matters affecting employees as a whole.

Investigation

In addition to his function of representation of employees in consultation with the employer the safety representative is entitled:

(a) to investigate, and make representations to the employer upon, potential hazards and dangerous occurrences and to examine the causes of accidents at the workplace;

(b) to investigate, and make representations to the employer upon, complaints by any employee he represents relating to that employee's health, safety or welfare at work.

(c) to make representations to the employer on general matters affecting the health, safety or welfare at work of the employees at the workplace;

(d) to carry out inspections of any or all of the workplace upon giving the employer reasonable notice in writing, provided that he has not inspected it or that part of it in the previous three months. This is subject to an exception where there has been a substantial change in working conditions. He may, by agreement with the employer, carry out more frequent inspections.

It is difficult to see how the limitations upon this right of "general" inspection are expected to operate in view of the powers under (a) and (b) above. Inspection of the scene of an accident is unlikely in practice to be regarded as precluding general inspection for a further three months[42] and exercise of the function of pursuing a complaint may well lead to inspection indistinguishable from a general inspection. On the other hand, when carrying out general inspections the representative is entitled to be provided with such facilities as he may reasonably require, including facilities for independent investigation and private discussion. In all aspects of inspection of the workplace, however, the employer or his representative is entitled to be present. The same duty to provide facilities attaches to the ad hoc inspection of the part of the workplace concerned in any notifiable accident, occurrence or disease or any other part of the workplace inspection of which is necessary to determine the cause thereof.[43]

(e) to represent employees he was appointed to represent in consultations at the workplace with inspectors of any enforcing authority and to secure information from inspectors under section 28(8) of the 1974 Act;

(f) to attend meetings of the safety committee in his capacity as a safety representative.

---

[41] Cl. 3(2).
[42] Cl. 6.
[43] Cl. 6.

Information

For all these functions a safety representative is entitled to necessary time off with pay, as is also the case when undergoing such training in aspects of these functions as is reasonable in all the circumstances. A safety representative is also entitled, on giving the employer reasonable notice, to inspect and take copies of any document relevant to the workplace or to the employees he represents which the employer is obliged to keep under any of the relevant safety legislation, except a document consisting of or relating to any health record of an identifiable individual.[44] The employer must also make available to the representative information within the employer's knowledge necessary to enable the representative to fulfil his functions unless that information falls within the usual specified exceptions.[45]

Safety committees

If at least two safety representatives so request in writing the employer must establish within three months of the request a safety committee in consultation with the representatives who have requested it and representatives of the recognised trade unions in the workplace concerned.[46]

These safety committees have the general function of keeping under review the measures taken to ensure the health and safety at work of the employees. The notes of guidance state that an objective should be the promotion of co-operation between employers and employees in instigating, developing and carrying out measures to ensure the health and safety at work of the employees. The Robens Report had seen the attainment of safety as a matter ultimately for negotiation. There is no doubt that at the time of the institution of safety representatives in October 1978 many trade union officials saw the situation much more as one in which they were entitled to demand implementation of measures and standards supported by the threat of industrial action if the demands were not complied with.

Subject to the power of the Health and Safety Commission to grant exemption from any requirement imposed by the regulations, a safety representative, normally within three months of the date of the failure, may complain to an industrial tribunal, that the employer has failed to permit him the appropriate time off to perform his functions or has failed to pay him for that time off.[47] The tribunal, if it finds the claim well-founded, may so declare and may award such compensation as it considers just and equitable in all the circumstances.

Inspectors

If the institution of workplace representatives is, as yet, an untried method of enforcement, the institution of safely inspectors is as old as industrial safety legislation. As has been said, before the passing of the 1974 Act there existed a number of separate inspecting authorities almost all of which have now been brought within the control of the Health and Safety Executive. It is provided, however[48] that the Secretary of State may, by regulation, make local authorities

---

[44] Cl. 7.
[45] Cl. 7(2).
[46] s.2(7) and S.I. 1977, No. 500, cl. 9.
[47] Cl. 11.
[48] s.18(2).

responsible for the enforcement of prescribed provisions of the relevant statutory provisions. Local authorities have habitually dealt with fire regulations and, since 1963, with safety in shops and offices.

Powers of inspectors

Any inspector appointed by an enforcing authority has rights of entry to premises and a right to make necessary examination or inspection for purposes within the field of responsibility of his enforcing authority. The inspector has power to direct that any part of any premises which he has power to enter be left undisturbed for as long as is reasonably necessary for the purpose of examination or investigation. He may take samples and may cause any article or substance appearing to him to have caused or be likely to cause danger to be dismantled or subjected to tests or detained in his possession. Any person the inspector has reasonable cause to believe to be able to give information relevant to any investigation or examination may be required to answer such questions as he thinks fit to ask and to sign a declaration of the truth of his answers. The inspector has the right to require to inspect and copy any entry in any book or document required to be kept under the relevant legislation or which it is necessary for him to see for the purposes of any examination or investigation. Any person may be required to afford him such facilities and assistance within that person's control or responsibility as are necessary for the exercise of any of these powers. Where, in any premises which he has power to enter an inspector finds an article or substance which he has reasonable cause to believe to be a cause of imminent danger of serious personal injury, he may seize it and cause it to be rendered harmless whether by destruction or otherwise.[49] Finally, if these specific powers do not suffice, the inspector is given any other power which is necessary for the general purpose of carrying into effect any of the relevant statutory provisions within the field of responsibility of his enforcing authority.[50]

Improvement notices

If an inspector is of the opinion that a person is contravening one or more of the relevant statutory provisions or has done so in circumstances that make it likely that the contravention will continue or be repeated he may serve on him an "improvement notice."[51] The notice must state the provision or provisions as to which the inspector is of opinion that there has been a contravention, and require the person on whom it is served to remedy the contravention or the matters occasioning it within a specified period not shorter than the period in which an appeal against the notice may be lodged. Failure to comply with the notice after the expiration of the specified date constitutes an offence for which a fine may be imposed for each day of non-compliance. The person on whom the notice is served may appeal to an industrial tribunal which may cancel the notice or affirm it with or without modification. The bringing of the appeal suspends the operation of the notice until the appeal is finally disposed of or withdrawn.[52]

---

[49] s.25.
[50] s.20.   [51] s.21.
[52] s.24. See *Tesco Stores Ltd.* v. *Edwards* [1977] I.R.L.R. 120 in which the tribunal added a requirement to the notice.

The Commission regards the notice as part of a range of approaches and has made it clear that failure to comply will always be followed up with a view to prosecution. On the other hand notices are not regarded as appropriate where they can readily or quickly be complied with or where they would merely repeat an existing obligation. Once a notice has been complied with it is spent and further breach would have to be met with further notice. A notice will not be issued if the general attitude of the employer calls for immediate prosecution but it should be borne in mind that the issuing of a notice does not preclude resort to simultaneous prosecution in respect of matters leading up to the notice.[53]

Prohibition notices

If, as regards an activity being, or about to be, carried on by or under the control of any person, which is one to which any of the relevant statutory provisions apply, an inspector is of the opinion that it involves or will involve a risk of serious personal injury he may issue a "prohibition notice."[54] This notice must state that the inspector is of that opinion as regards specified matters. It should be noted carefully that there is no precondition to the issue of the notice that there shall have been any breach of any statutory requirement, although if, in the inspector's opinion, there has been such a breach he should specify that provision. In other words, the prohibition notice is available to deal with certain dangerous situations which no amount of reasonably practicable precautions will eliminate or reduce. Introduction of this remedy, therefore, is an attempt to deal with the situation which is regarded as inherently dangerous and beyond effective remedy and which, in the past, has, for this reason, often been permitted to continue to exist. The notice, as its name implies, forbids the continuation of the activity unless the matters specified have been remedied. This prohibition will take immediate effect if the inspector states it as his opinion that the risk of serious personal injury is or will be imminent. In every other case the prohibition will take effect at the expiration of a period specified in the notice. There is, again, a right of appeal[55] to an industrial tribunal but in this case the bringing of the appeal will only postpone the operation of the notice if, and when, the tribunal so directs.[56]

Offences

It is a criminal offence to fail to discharge any of the general duties that have been mentioned as falling within sections 2–8 of the 1974 Act, to contravene any health or safety regulation or any improvement or prohibition notice. A considerable number of other offences, particularly in connection with the giving of information or the obstruction of an inspector, are also specified.[57] A person guilty of any such offence is liable on summary conviction to a fine, not

---

[53] From January 1, 1975, to August 1978, 15,983 improvement notices were issued by factory inspectors from an overall total of 26,770 by all enforcing authorities.

[54] s.22.

[55] s.24.

[56] 9,808 prohibition notices were issued by all enforcing authorities between January 1, 1975, and August 1978. 208 appeals were lodged against improvement and prohibition notices, of which 12 were upheld although some others led to variation of the notice.

[57] s.33.

exceeding £1,000. In the case of some of the more serious offences there is the possibility of conviction on indictment which carries a maximum penalty of two years' imprisonment and/or a fine of £1,000. Where a person has committed an offence due to the act or default of some other person that other person is guilty of the offence and may be charged whether or not proceedings are taken against the first person.[58] Where an offence is committed by a corporation and is proved to have been committed with the consent or connivance of, or to be attributable to any neglect on the part of, any director, manager, secretary, or other similar officer of the corporation or anyone purporting to act in such a capacity, both that person and the corporation will be guilty of an offence. In *Armour* v. *Skeen*[59] the Court of Session held the Director of Roads for Strathclyde Regional Council liable, under this provision, for failure to have a sound safety policy or to train employees in safe working practices. The court held that "neglect" referred to any neglect of duty and was not to be confined to neglect of duty under this, or any other, authority and its neglect was sufficient to render him directly liable. The court took the view that though the Director of Roads was not a "director" in the sense referred to by that word in section 37, he came within the ambit of the class of persons referrred to. Although a manager of a supermarket had, under a similar provision[60] been held not to be a "manager" within the meaning of that provision[61] the Scottish Court took the view that the issue was one of the parts played by the person concerned within the organisation.

In any proceeding for an offence of failure to comply with a duty or require-ment to do something so far as practicable, or so far as reasonably practicable or to use the best practicable means it is for the person accused to prove that it was not practicable or reasonably practicable to do more than was done.

CIVIL LIABILITY FOR BREACH OF STATUTORY DUTY

By Jacqueline Dyson

Principles

Even under the older type of safety legislation, the intention was to ensure safety rather than to define a duty of care in order to fix the incidence of compensation for injury. Unfortunately, the operation of this type of legislation tended to lend greater emphasis to compensation after the event rather than prevention. It was not only lawyers who thought primarily in terms of employer's liability. Management tended, in many instances, to measure their safety effort by the yardstick of the consequences of accidents. It is, of course, true to say that the imposition of civil liability for breach of statutory duty may be a valuable sanction to ensure observance of safety standards designed to prevent that liability arising. Some of the value of this sanction, however, is removed by the almost universal practice of insurance. It cannot, therefore, be

---

[58] s.36.
[59] [1977] I.R.L.R. 310.
[60] Trade Descriptions Act 1968, s.37(1).
[61] *Tesco (Supermarkets) Ltd.* v. *Natrass* [1972] A.C. 153.

too often repeated that this emphasis on employer liability was considered by the Robens Committee to be wrong. The object of the 1974 legislation is to remove from the field of legislative duty the question of civil liability and to provide a system of safety involvement which does not depend on any form of sanction operative only after an injury. It is provided accordingly[62] that nothing in the general duties of sections 2–8 of the 1974 legislation shall confer any right of action in civil cases. Right to civil action arising from existing safety legislation remains unaltered, however. A right to civil action arising from statutory regulation will depend on the existing legislation. It is, therefore, still important to examine the question of civil liability. In this connection the section most commonly invoked in the past has been section 14 of the Factories Act 1961. Examination of the interpretation of that section will also afford a useful comparison with the new legislation.

The student will find that safety legislation commonly does not mention the question of civil liability. He must be very careful, for instance, to note that when a safety statute provides defences, it is providing defences to criminal sanctions and that these defences will only have an indirect effect on damages for the civil action of breach of statutory duty. The possibility of this civil action arising stems solely from the operation of common law. The existence of a separate action for breach of statutory duty appears to have been finally recognised by the Court of Appeal in *Groves* v. *Lord Wimborne*[63] in which the plaintiff's hand had been crushed in the unfenced gear wheels of a steam winch in the defendant's factory. Although the action was brought both in negligence and for breach of statutory duty, only the latter aspect was in issue before the Court of Appeal. A. L. Smith L.J. said:

> ". . . unless it could be found from the whole 'purview' of the Act that the legislature intended that the only remedy for a breach of a duty created by the Act would be the infliction of a fine upon the master, it seemed clear that upon proof of such a duty and of an injury done to the workman, a cause of action was given to the workman against the master."

Vaughan Williams L.J. stated the proposition more generally in this way:

> "It cannot be doubted that, where a statute provides for the performance by certain persons of a particular duty, and someone belonging to a class of persons for whose benefit and protection the statute imposes the duty is injured by failure to perform it, prima facie, and if there be nothing to the contrary, an action by the person so injured will lie against the person who has so failed to perform the duty."

The question, therefore, is always whether there has been a breach of a statutory duty causing injury to a person whom the duty was designed to protect. If the answer to this is in the affirmative, an element of fault is not always necessary.[64] The terms of the statute alone will define the degree of responsibility.

The first of these aspects of this form of tort is well illustrated by the decision in *Phillips* v. *Britannia Hygienic Laundry Co. Ltd.*[65] where McCardie J., in the Divisional Court, had said that a breach of a statutory obligation to keep motor vehicles in good repair did not afford a cause of civil action, but only provided

---

[62] s.47.
[63] [1898] 2 Q.B. 402.
[64] *London Passenger Board* v. *Upson* [1949] A.C. 151 at 168.
[65] [1923] 2 K.B. 832; *Booth* v. *National Enterprise Board* [1978] 3 All E.R. 624.

evidence of negligence, because it was not enacted for the benefit of any particular class of persons. The Court of Appeal had no doubt that a class of persons could be so wide as to include everyone using the highway. Nor was it doubted that a statute which contained its own full machinery for definition and enforcement of the duty could, nonetheless, be the source of a civil action of this type. The sole question with which the court concerned itself was whether it could be said that the intention of the legislature in this situation was to provide for a duty owed to an aggrieved individual as well as to the State. The court concluded that since the duty was framed in terms of absolute liability it could not have been the legislative intention to impose such an obligation for the benefit of every individual using the highway.

As already indicated, however, this must not lead us to suppose that where a statute imposes absolute liability, this is necessarily incompatible with a right on the part of individuals to bring civil proceedings for damages for breach of statutory duty. The terms of some of the more significant requirements of the Factories Act 1961, for instance, clearly impose absolute liability. Theoretically, and without the benefit of modifying regulations, the well-known duty in section 14 of the Act to fence dangerous machinery imposed a duty completely to encompass a dangerous part of a machine by a fence, notwithstanding that the existence of such a fence could make it impossible to use the machine. It followed from this that where an inadequate fence was provided, leaving space through which material could be introduced into the machine, civil liability would arise if, instead of the material, the operative introduced a portion of his own anatomy, which was thereby injured. Obviously there is room in this type of decision for the introduction of a considerable element of policy.

The plaintiff must, of course, also show that he suffered an injury within the general class of risk to which the statutory provision was directed and that he was one of the persons protected by that provision.[66]

There is no doubt that an action for damages for breach of statutory duty lies in respect of the duties imposed by most pieces of industrial safety legislation. In the case of the Factories Act 1961 this seems to extend to the health provisions. Following *Ebbs* v. *James Whitson and Co. Ltd.*[67] Redgrave[68] concludes that "the preponderance of authority is . . . now strongly in favour of allowing a civil right of action for breach of a health provision of the Act." No similar general statement can as yet be made concerning the welfare provisions, however.

This duty is so much an inevitable outcome of such legislation that it has been necessary in the Health and Safety, etc., at Work Act 1974 specifically to exclude the implication of such a civil action arising from the provisions for safety, health and welfare. The reason for the exclusion in this particular case is that, as we have seen, the expressions of the duty are in such general terms that they would normally add little to the common law duty to take reasonable care for the safety of employees at work. There is no point in having two largely parallel systems.[69] It has become apparent from the operation of civil liability

---

[66] *Donaghey* v. *Boulton & Paul Ltd.* [1968] A.C. 1 at 16 and 25; *Curran* v. *William Neill and Son (St. Helens) Ltd.* [1961] 1 W.L.R. 1069.

[67] [1952] 2 Q.B. 877.

[68] *Health and Safety in Factories*, p. 17.

[69] See, *e.g. Stanley* v. *Concentric (Pressed Products) Ltd.* (1971) 11 K.I.R. 260 where reasonable practicability was said to impose the same duty as reasonable care.

under previous legislation that there may be little point in having two systems which operate separately and produce different results. As the operation of the 1974 Act works to phase out the earlier legislation, so the action for breach of statutory duty in relation to injury at work will either give place to the single cause of action at common law for negligence which is examined in the next chapter, or will spring solely from breach of the detailed regulations issued under the Act. For the time being, however, it will be possible not only to bring an action under this general head, but also to continue to bring actions for breach of statutory duty under the safety legislation preceding that of 1974. Criminal actions under this earlier legislation will probably disappear fairly quickly when regulations become available to give substance to the legislation. The same will not be true of civil actions which will continue to offer a chance in particular cases to obtain compensation by an action based upon the statutory duty where ordinary common law negligence would not provide a remedy, or vice versa.

It is important, therefore, for the student to appreciate the complexity of construction of detailed safety requirements when used as a basis for civil claims for compensation for injury. Though it is the purpose of the new safety legislation, by specifying offences in general terms, to eliminate such technicality from the process of enforcement of statutory safety provisions there is no indication that such simplification will, or can, appear in the civil law. It is impossible in this book to consider the construction of regulations. Such an exercise would, in any event, tend to reveal as much of the absence as of the existence of judicial authority. In order, therefore, to provide some indication to the student of the type of exercise which must be undertaken we shall, as in the first edition of this book, examine the sections of the Factories Act 1961 requiring the fencing of dangerous machinery. These are, of all safety legislation, the most completely subject to judicial construction in civil cases. It must be emphasised, however, that they are only considered here as an example of a very much more extensive area of the law.[70]

The obligation to fence

(i) "Machinery"

The Factories Act 1961 provides rules for the fencing of three separate categories of machinery. Section 12 provides that moving parts and flywheels of any machine which provides mechanical energy from any source, termed a "prime-mover," must be securely fenced, wherever the prime-mover is situated. There is, in effect, a conclusive presumption that these parts are dangerous. Section 13 provides that every part of "transmission machinery," that is to say, any device such as a drum, pulley, clutch or driving belt, by which the motion of the prime-mover is carried to the productive machine or appliance, must, likewise, be securely fenced, unless it is in such a position or of such construction as to be safe to every person employed or working on the premises as it would be if securely fenced. In the case of other machinery the obligation to fence only applies to a "dangerous part" and is again excused if the

---

[70] See Munkman, *Employer's Liability* (9th ed); Redgrave, *Health and Safety in Factories*.

part is safe by position or construction.[71] By section 16, all such fencing is required to be of substantial construction, constantly maintained, and kept in position while the parts required to be fenced are "in motion or in use," except where those parts are necessarily exposed for examination and for lubrication and adjustment, shown by examination to be immediately necessary.

These sections appear to form a comprehensive code for the fencing of machinery. However, the restrictive interpretation by the courts has reduced the protection afforded to employees.[72] The word "machinery" is not defined in the Act, but one limitation on its meaning is to be found in the decision in *Parvin* v. *Morton Machine Co. Ltd.*[73] The House of Lords held that the Act only applied to machinery used as plant in the factory and not to machinery manufactured in the factory even if it was being tested there. Lord Normand said:

> ". . . I cannot find that any of the provisions of Part II of the Act apply to any machinery except machinery which is part of the factory and used in the manufacturing processes, and I think that none of them applies to machines made in the factory."

The House seems to have taken the view that use of the words "*the* transmission machinery" in section 13, indicated not any such machinery but only that in use in the factory. It followed that the other sections should be similarly limited. This view is open to question. It is unlikely that the legislature would have shown an intention to exclude a whole class of machinery by the haphazard use of a definite article in one place only. Even if such rigid adherence to the words of the Act is to produce this result it should be maintained consistently so that, however odd the result, the failure to use the same form in other sections should have precluded the same construction. In any event, there is no reason why the legislature should not have intended to include all accidents in factories arising from the operation of machinery.[74]

The distinction was applied again in *Ballard* v. *Ministry of Defence*[75] a case concerning a factory in which engines were being repaired. The Court of Appeal held that a fan which was attached to an engine for testing purposes should be treated as a product of the factory. It was argued that the fan was part of the equipment of the factory as it would be used for testing another engine. Lawton L.J. rejected this argument:

---

[71] s.14. "Every dangerous part of any machinery other than prime movers and transmission machinery, shall be securely fenced unless it is in such a position or of such construction as to be as safe to every person employed or working on the premises as it would be if securely fenced."

[72] See list given by Lord Hailsham in *F. E. Callow* v. *Johnson* [1970] 3 All E.R. 639 at 641.

[73] [1952] A.C. 515.

[74] The strange effect of the construction in this case was already on record because, in *Thurogood* v. *Van Den Berghs and Jurgens Ltd.* [1951] 2 K.B. 537, the Court of Appeal had classified as machinery within the act an electric fan which normally operated in a ventilator of one of the rooms of the factory but which had been taken to the maintenance shop and was being tested there. A further refinement was introduced in *Irwin* v. *White, Tompkins and Courage Ltd.* [1964] 1 W.L.R. 387. Although regulations such as those for building operations may impose safety requirements on unfinished buildings—*Corn* v. *Weir's Glass (Hanley) Ltd.* [1960] 1 W.L.R. 577—it is clear that machinery as yet incompletely installed in a factory is not within the fencing requirements. In *Irwin's* case, however, it was held that once it had been installed, and provided that it was in motion the section applied even though it was not, and had never been, used for factory purposes.

[75] [1977] I.C.R. 513.

"Products of the factory have to be tested before they can be sent out from the factory. In order to test, there must be a fan attached to the engine in order to keep the engine cool when running. When this reverse thrust fan was fixed on this engine it was fixed on that which was under test and which was a product of the factory. Until it was fixed on the engine it was not a dangerous part: it was static, inert. It only became a dangerous part when it was on a product of the factory. For that simple reason, in my judgment, it was not a dangerous part of machinery for the purposes of section 14(1) of the Factories Act 1961."

A further example of the restrictive interpretation of the word "machinery" is to be found in *Mirza* v. *Ford Motor Co. Ltd.*[76] The plaintiff's finger was trapped by part of a safety hook on a hoist. Ormrod L.J held that the section only applies to machinery or a part of machinery to which the concept of fencing is apposite. The other judges simply held that the safety hook was not part of the machinery of the hoist.[77]

The decision in *Parvin's* case was illogically extended in *Cherry* v. *International Alloys Ltd.*[78] by the Court of Appeal. In that case a mechanic was injured when adjusting the engine of a petrol driven truck used in a factory. Pearce L.J. said that *Parvin's* case indicated that the Act did not include machinery of every kind, and so thought that a distinction could be made between "machinery" and vehicles. *Parvin's* case had not imposed a distinction based on the type of machinery, but on its use. If one were to apply this distinction based on use, it would follow that the motor truck being considered in *Cherry's* case, since it was plainly in use for the purpose of the factory, came within the fencing requirement. Other approaches were available. It was possible to say that the danger produced by the vehicular character of the truck as distinct from its mechanical aspect was outside the contemplation of the Act. Alternatively, following the strict approach adopted in *John Summers* v. *Frost*[79] it could have been said that its dangerous parts should have been fenced so producing a different result. In terms of compensation this would have done no great harm. In any event the injury in question had arisen from contact with the engine fan which was a part eminently capable of fencing, and which would have required fencing had the truck been stood on the floor without its wheels. This objection to *Cherry's* case was precisely spelled out by the House of Lords overruling that decision in *British Railways Board* v. *Liptrot*.[80] In that case a mobile crane was being operated in a scrap-yard. The jib and body of the crane revolved upon a chassis, thus creating, with each 90 degree turn, a nip between the largely rectangular body and the rectangular chassis. Without giving warning to the driver, a slinger dodged into this gap to remove a piece of wire and was caught by the nip as the crane rotated. The majority of the Court of Appeal[81] held that the crane was not just a vehicle. Had it been rotating on a fixed base it would plainly have been a machine and its nature did not alter because it had wheels.[82] The House of Lords went further to hold, as was suggested to be the

---

[76] [1981] I.C.R. 757.
[77] See also *British Railways Board* v. *Liptrot* [1976] 2 All E.R. 1072 at 1077.
[78] [1961] 1 Q.B. 136.
[79] [1955] A.C. 740.
[80] [1969] 1 A.C. 136. There was a limited question for consideration in the House of Lords.
[81] [1966] 2 Q.B. 353.
[82] The question of whether thin air between two dangerous parts of a machine can be considered part of the machine does not, as the majority of the Court of Appeal appeared to think, arise. It is the parts which are dangerous by reason of their proximity.

proper approach in *Cherry's* case, that the question is whether the danger is mechanical or vehicular. As Lord Reid explained:

> "Section 14 is dealing with parts of machinery where danger arises from their not being fenced and is obviated by fencing. So it appears to me that the fact that vehicles in motion creates a kind of danger which does not exist with stationary or fixed machinery is no reason for not requiring the fencing of parts of the machinery in vehicles which are dangerous whether the vehicle is in motion or not."

Viscount Dilhorne disregarded the classification altogether and relied on the limitation in the section to dangerous parts to make feasible the application of the section to vehicles.[83]

It is to be hoped that the decision in *Liptrot* will make it impossible to follow the Court of Appeal in *Quintas* v. *National Smelting Co. Ltd.*[84] The plaintiff had been knocked off the flat roof of a building by one of the heavy metal buckets slung on an overhead cableway. No fence or other method of defining the path of the buckets over the roof was used. Sellers L.J. (with whom Danckwerts L.J. agreed) classified the bucket as plant rather than machinery. A bucket, in his view, was a bucket even when moving, and only the movement made it dangerous. It is, of course, usually movement that makes a part of a machine dangerous and although there are some parts like cogs, which are typically mechanical, a considerably adapted bucket is no different from many other common things which are adapted to form parts of machines. The starting point of Lord Justice Sellers' difficulty lay in his refusal to recognise the entire combination as a machine. As Willmer L.J., dissenting, said, the mere fact that a thing is on a large scale should not alter its character as machinery. In *Liptrot's* case Lord Hodson agreed with this dissenting view that the cableway was a single piece of apparatus of which a part could be dangerous.

(ii) "*Part*"

The duty is to fence a dangerous *part* of a machine and there is no statutory duty to fence dangerous material in the machine. This remains so however dangerous the nature of the material, or even if it only becomes dangerous by being moved by the machine.[85]

In *Eaves* v. *Morris Motors Ltd.*[86] the operative had injured his hand on the sharp, rough edge of a bolt he was milling. The Court of Appeal was clearly bound by *Bullock's* case[87] and held there was no breach, but Holroyd Pearce L.J. said:

> "If a moving arm of the machine does not project and is therefore safe when the machine is empty, but projects dangerously when the machine is supplied with its proper material, it can obviously be labelled as dangerous machinery. And if it creates a dangerous nip when supplied with its normal material and when working normally (or in a foreseeable manner) I see no reason in principle why the court

---

[83] Before the decision of the House of Lords in *Liptrot* it had been held in *Lovelidge* v. *Anselm Olding Ltd.* [1967] 2 Q.B. 351 that a distinction could not be made between a hand power tool and machinery.

[84] [1961] 1 W.L.R. 401.

[85] *Bullock* v. *G. John Power (Agencies) Ltd.* [1956] 1 W.L.R. 171—wire being drawn through machine on to drum—see also *Sparrow* v. *Fairey Aviation Co. Ltd.* [1964] A.C 1019.

[86] [1961] 2 Q.B. 385.

[87] *Bullock* v. *G. John Power (Agencies) Ltd.*, *supra*.

cannot consider the machinery dangerous, even if that nip is only created by a juxtaposition of material and machinery. For in that case it is not the nature of the material and it is not the material itself which causes the danger. The danger is caused by the design of the machine itself working normally with harmless material."

Confirming this view in *Midland and Low Moor Iron and Steel Co. Ltd*. v. *Cross*[88] Lord Reid said that it would be surprising if the Act had in mind the operation only of empty machines. It will be noted that the above quotation limits the principle to danger caused by the normal operation of the machine. This arises because, as we shall see, "dangerous" is defined by the courts in terms of foreseeability. So the machine need not be acting normally when only dangerous parts are involved, and even in the case of material there will be a duty to fence against the danger caused by the foreseeable but abnormal act, provided that it is within the area of the machine's normal operation.[89]

In *Hindle* v. *Joseph Porritt & Sons Ltd*.[90] an assize court declined to extend liability to a situation in which an essentially safe part of a machine (a stationary blunt projection) had caused injury to the operative's arm which had been drawn against it by the action of moving material in the machine with which his arm had come in contact. This decision seems to be a return to the idea that a part is, or is not, inherently dangerous in itself and reveals clearly the danger of that approach.

The matter was reconsidered by Lord Hailsham L.C. in *F. E. Callow (Engineers) Ltd*. v. *Johnson*.[91] The respondent was machining on a lathe a stainless steel workpiece, which was itself rotating at 30 revolutions per minute round a boring bar. The bar moved, almost imperceptibly, towards the interior of the workpiece. There was an automatic cooling system but it was not necessary to use it when cast-iron workpieces were being machined, and for a single job on stainless steel the operatives were in the habit of avoiding the trouble of having the system's sump cleaned out by squirting coolant by hand from an ordinary plastic "squeezie" bottle. The appellant knew of this practice but regarded it as hazardous and disapproved of it. While the respondent was applying the coolant manually his hand was, in some unexplained fashion, caught in the nip between the boring bar and the interior of the workpiece. It was held by a majority (Viscount Dilhorne dissenting) that, in the context, it was foreseeable that the nip could cause an accident of the type that occurred. The boring bar created a dangerous nip when the machine was in use and so the whole constituted a dangerous part capable of being fenced even though in itself the part was not so. Lord Hailsham said that he would be reluctant to enlarge the gap left in the protection of the Act by the decisions on section 14 and went on:

". . . in considering whether a part of the machinery is dangerous within the meaning of section 14 one must have regard to the operation of the part while the machine is doing its ordinary work and not when it is stationary. It may therefore be that a part can be dangerous because of its juxtaposition to another part of the machine or because of its juxtaposition to a moving workpiece or the material

---

[88] [1965] A.C. 343.
[89] *Ibid*. at pp. 365 and 372.
[90] [1970] 1 All E.R. 1142.
[91] [1971] A.C. 335.

notwithstanding that in isolation it would not be dangerous and notwithstanding that when the machine is not in use the part itself would be innocuous."

So in some situations the part of the machine may be combined with the material in the creation of a composite danger. The duty to fence may arise even though the material is itself not dangerous. In *Wearing* v. *Pirelli Ltd.*[92] the House of Lords was again unwilling to give a restrictive interpretation to the Act where not compelled to do so. The injury was not caused by direct contact with the dangerous part, a revolving drum, but with the rubber fabric covering it. Although contact was only with material there was liability as it was the dangerous part of the machine which imparted the danger to which the rubber covering contributed nothing. The proposition does not extend to a danger created by a juxtaposition between the part and objects extraneous to the machine.[93] It may be difficult to draw the line. In *Irwin* v. *White, Tompkins and Courage Ltd.*[94] an operative's head and shoulders were caught in the nip between the descending bar of a sack hoist and the sill of a "window" through which sacks were to be taken off the hoist. The sill was treated as part of the machine.

(iii) *"Dangerous"*

The definition of danger within the Act has been left to the courts. In *Close* v. *Steel Company of Wales Ltd.*[95] the House of Lords finally put beyond question the acceptance of the test of reasonable foreseeability of danger. This test originated in the judgment of Wills J. in *Hindle* v. *Birtwhistle*.[96] It was explained by du Parcq J. in *Walker* v. *Bletchley Flettons Ltd.*[97] in the following terms:

> ". . . I would say, and I think I am saying nothing inconsistent with what the learned judge said, that a part of machinery is dangerous if it is a possible cause of injury to anybody acting in a way in which a human being may be reasonably expected to act in circumstances which may be reasonably expected to occur."

This explanation was slightly qualified by Lord Reid in *John Summers* v. *Frost*[98] and has often been applied. In *Close's* case Lord Denning pointed out that there had been an intervening period when the courts were inclined to accept the view that a part might be dangerous in fact. No doubt this approach would produce liability where there was such a part and it could only be, and was, approached from an unforeseeable angle. In many cases, though, a part can only be described as neutral, even when moving, and one would then have to go a step further to say "The part actually proved to be dangerous by producing an injury." So the happening of the accident would become proof of danger. It is said in support of this approach that if the foreseeability test had been intended there would have been no need to provide exemption from fencing for those parts which were safe by position or design, but it could equally be said of the

---

[92] [1977] I.C.R. 90 (H.L.).
[93] *Pearce v. Stanley-Bridges Ltd.* [1965] 1 W.L.R. 931, where the object was another stationary machine.
[94] [1964] 1 W.L.R. 387.
[95] [1962] A.C. 367.
[96] [1897] 1 Q.B. 192.
[97] [1937] 1 All E.R. 170.
[98] [1955] A.C. 740.

factual approach that the exemption would be meaningless, because no part would ever be safe by position or design.

In *Close's* case Lord Denning took the view that the foreseeability test had been re-established in *Carr* v. *Mercantile Produce Co. Ltd.*[99] and it has subsequently been accepted unquestioningly in both the Court of Appeal and the House of Lords.[1] The Court of Appeal, in *Eaves* v. *Morris Motors Ltd.*[2] having waited for the decision in *Close's* case, revealed some of the tortuous ways into which it could lead. In that case the operator of a horizontal milling machine injured his hand when he pulled it away from the traversing part of the machine which had, unexpectedly, begun to move in the reverse direction. There was no proof that the machine had done this before although it seems that it would not be unusual in this type of machine. Redgrave[3] suggests a difference between foresight of ordinary, and of abnormal, behaviour. A reasonable man, in his view, would be reluctant to anticipate incorrect behaviour from one or two previous aberrations. Whether or not this is what foresight means the Court of Appeal seems to go further than this. Willmer L.J. said:

> "An employer may reasonably be expected to foresee and guard against dangers likely to arise in the course of the normal operation of the machinery. But no man could be expected to foresee and guard against the almost unlimited possibilities of danger that might arise from a machine going wrong or operating in a way that it was never designed to do."[4]

It is to be noted that though one cannot be expected to foresee a machine behaving abnormally, it is "not open to doubt" that the unreasonable action of a human being may be foreseeable.[5] Once it is established that a part is dangerous and should be fenced, foresight is no longer material. Liability will then exist for injury arising even from wholly unforeseeable circumstances, provided that the injury would not have arisen but for the want of a fence.[6] This restrictive construction of the term "dangerous" has resulted in a serious gap in the protection afforded to employees by the law in respect of injury caused by dangerous machinery. This was clearly recognised by Holroyd Pearce L.J. in *Eaves* case. He said:

> "Now dangerous machinery is only required by Section 14 to be fenced against danger of a particular and limited kind, namely danger from workmen coming into contact with the machine. There is no protection under s.14 against a class of obvious perils caused by dangerous machinery, namely, perils which arise from a dangerous machine ejecting at the worker pieces of the material or even pieces of the machinery itself. Thus, there is now left a gap which neither logic nor common sense appears to justify."

---

[99] [1949] 2 K.B. 601.
[1] *Pearce* v. *Stanley-Bridges Ltd.* [1965] 1 W.L.R. 931 (C.A.); *F. E. Callow (Engineers) Ltd.* v. *Johnson* [1971] A.C. 335.
[2] [1961] 2 Q.B. 385.
[3] *Health and Safety in Factories*, p. 55.
[4] In view of the remarks of Holroyd Pearce L.J. at p. 396, it does not seem possible to explain the decision in *Eaves'* case by saying that there was foresight of the activity but not of the resultant injury.
[5] *Smith* v. *Chesterfield and District Co-operative Society Ltd.* [1953] 1 W.L.R. 370.
[6] *Millard* v. *Serck Tubes Ltd.* [1969] 1 W.L.R. 211. See (1969) 32 M.L.R. 438.

(iv) *"Securely fenced"*

These words appear in all three sections. A strict interpretation of secure means fencing to prevent any contact. Lord Morton in *John Summers & Sons Ltd.* v. *Frost*[7] favoured this view when he said:

> "What is contemplated, in my view, is that there shall be complete protection against contact for every person employed or working on the premises."

Lord Reid plainly preferred the view of Somervell L.J. expressed in *Burns* v. *Joseph Terry & Sons Ltd.*[8] that the balance of authority was against a requirement to provide an adequate fence against "improbable and unforeseeable" circumstances. Lord Simonds seems to support this same view because he says that a dangerous part is not securely fenced so long as:

> ". . . in the ordinary course of human affairs danger may reasonably be anticipated from its use . . . not only to the prudent, alert and skilled operative intent upon his task, but also to the careless or inattentive worker whose inadvertent or indolent conduct may expose him to risk of injury or death from the unguarded part . . ."

It is not entirely clear whether the majority of the House supported this view. If it is the law that a secure fence is one which protects against reasonably foreseeable dangers and the initial duty to provide a fence at all depends on reasonable foresight of some danger, then the courts have moved some way from interpreting section 14 as imposing absolute liability.

A more difficult problem is whether the machine must be taken out of use if reasonable foresight leads to the conclusion that the machine is dangerous and no fence can be devised to protect from reasonable risk. Some sections of the Act do use such words as "so far as is reasonably practicable" to modify the extent of the duty but the fencing sections contain no such limitation. This situation arose in *John Summers & Sons Ltd.* v. *Frost*.[9] An employee in a factory was injured when his thumb came into contact with a revolving grindstone. Although there was a hood over the grindstone the protection was not total as this would have rendered the machine unusable. The House of Lords held that the grinding wheel was not securely fenced although it was clearly aware that the machine would be commercially unusable following the decision. Lord Keith stated this emphatically.

> ". . . I see no escape from the view that, as matters at present stand, the destruction of the machine as a working unit if it is completely fenced, is no answer to the mandatory words of the statute."

The problem will normally be overcome by modification of the extent of the duty by regulation.[10]

The next question is whether, whatever the extent of the duty to provide a secure fence, that fence must cope with every foreseeable cause of injury. There was at one time reason to suppose that this was so. In *Dickson* v. *Flack*[11] the

---

[7] [1955] A.C. 740 at 757. See also Lord Porter in *Carroll* v. *Andrew Barclay & Sons Ltd.* [1948] A.C. 477.

[8] [1951] 1 K.B. 454.   [9] [1955] 1 All E.R. 870.

[10] s.76—special regulations may modify or extend the requirements. It is suggested that this is the answer to any suggestion that the House of Lords should itself have modified the duty to meet with practicability.

[11] [1953] 2 Q.B. 464.

Court of Appeal had to consider the fencing of a vertical moulding machine. This is one of the most dangerous machines in use in modern factories because of the real danger of the rotating cutter throwing off broken blades with great force. Denning L.J., who on this point agreed with the majority, took the view that any part which might be expected to throw off a loose part of itself ought to be securely fenced against such a risk. A bare majority of the House of Lords rejected this approach in *Close* v. *Steel Company of Wales Ltd.*[12] and held that the duty was to provide a fence to keep people from contact with the machine and not to prevent parts of the machine from flying out and coming into contact with people.[13] There is, of course, a good deal of policy in such a decision since the type of fence required to keep machines in would, in many cases, of which this was an example, be impossible to provide.

If the duty is only to keep the worker away from the machine the further point is raised of the extent of the duty when something he is holding comes into contact with a dangerous part. In *Johnson* v. *J. Stone & Co. (Charlton) Ltd.*[14] the plaintiff was manoeuvring a heavy casting into position on the table of a band-saw when the top of the casting struck the fast moving pulley at the top of the band, fracturing its bearings and causing the pulley to drop on to the plaintiff's hand. Streatfield J. held that the injury arose from the breach of a statutory duty to fence against such an eventuality, but Hinchcliffe J. refused to follow this in *Sparrow* v. *Fairey Aviation Co. Ltd.*[15] The facts of this case are more complicated. The plaintiff was machining a rough burr off a metal disc clamped to the revolving face of a lathe. To carry out the task he had to insert a tool into a hole in the centre of the disc. There was only one-sixteenth of an inch clearance between the disc and the jaws of the chuck which held it in position. As one would have thought almost inevitable, the tool slipped, touched the jaws and flung the plaintiff's hand against the disc or the face of the lathe. It was pleaded only that the jaws of the chuck and not the lathe face were dangerous and a majority of the House of Lords held, therefore, that no part of the plaintiff's body having come in contact with a dangerous part of the machine, the injury had not arisen from a breach of the statutory duty.[16] The revolving material did not produce a danger capable of being fenced within the meaning of interaction developed in *Midland and Low Moor* v. *Cross.*[17] Something of the policy behind the decision is reflected in the words of Lord Reid: " . . . a line must be drawn somewhere and I could not distinguish between a small tool as used in this case and anything else which a man might be holding in the course of his work." Lord Morris reserved the question of whether some form of equipment might be so attached to an operative that it could be regarded as part of him, and it seems clear that the courts will not go to the length of distinguishing between a man and his clothing.[18]

It is not enough to provide a guard that will be adequate if left alone,[19]

---

[12] [1962] A.C. 367.

[13] Although Lord Guest treats this point as the ratio of the decision and Redgrave, *Health and Safety in Factories*, p. 58, so refers to it, it is apparently *obiter* since all the members of the House of Lords held that the risk of injury was not foreseeable in the circumstances. The authority of the decision is not, however, in question on this point.

[14] [1961] 1 W.L.R. 849.

[15] [1961] 1 W.L.R. 844.

[16] [1964] A.C. 1019.

[17] [1965] A.C. 343.

[18] See *Lovelidge* v. *Anselm Olding & Sons Ltd.* [1967] 2 Q.B. 351.

[19] Hilbery J. in *Charles* v. *S. Smith & Sons (England) Ltd.* [1954] 1 W.L.R. 451.

although guards are not expected to be proof against intentional misuse. This is largely overtaken by the provision in section 16 that the guard must be constantly maintained and kept in position while the parts requiring a fence are in motion or in use. Though an employer may escape criminal liability under section 155 he will retain civil liability if the guard is not in position, irrespective of the reason.

(v) *"In motion or in use"*

Section 16 requires that all fencing shall be of substantial construction, constantly maintained and kept in position while the parts are in motion or in use, save for permitted removal of guards for servicing.[20] The words "in motion or in use" have been considered in a series of recent cases. It is possible to limit the words "in use" to "in normal use," but it is straining the language to say that "in motion" means not "movement" but "running as it would normally run."[21] In *Richard Thomas and Baldwins Ltd.* v. *Cummings*[22] the plaintiff had trapped and injured his hand while pulling on a disconnected driving belt so as to turn a part of a grinding machine. The question was whether the part of machinery was "in motion or in use." The House of Lords held that there was no breach. As Lord Reid explained:

"... I do not think that one would naturally say of a man moving parts of a machine round to a required position that he had set the machine or its parts in motion. The phrase 'in motion' appears to me more apt to describe a continuing state of motion lasting, or intended to last, for an appreciable time."

Lord Tucker arrived at the same result by holding that the belt and pulley were not transmission machinery. There is a hint in his judgment of the need for the application of mechanised energy for transmission machinery to be in motion.

Such mechanical power was provided in *Knight* v. *Leamington Spa Courier Ltd.*[23] where the rollers of a printing press were being inched round under power using a device designed for that purpose. Holroyd Pearce L.J. said: "the words 'in motion or in use' connote the substantial movement of its normal working or, if it is not at the time achieving its normal purpose, some movement reasonably comparable to its normal working." Upjohn and Donovan L.JJ. also followed *Baldwin's* case holding that the rollers were not in motion although mechanical energy was used. In *Mitchell* v. *W. S. Westin Ltd.*[24] the Court of Appeal considered similar facts. The plaintiff needed to move the collar to tighten some screws. It was possible to do this by hand but instead he switched the machine on and off very quickly catching his finger in the moving gear wheel. The Court of Appeal held that since there was only intermittent movement in order to repair or adjust the machinery, there was no breach. Pearson L.J. thought that "regard should be had to the character of the movement more than to its purpose."

---

[20] The conditions under which a fence may be removed for such purposes are laid down in the operations at Unfenced Machinery Regulations S.R. & O. 1938 No. 641.
[21] A machine may of course, be in motion but not in use as where it is started accidentally— *Horne* v. *Lec Refrigeration Ltd.* [1965] 2 All E.R. 898.
[22] [1955] A.C. 321.
[23] [1981] 2 Q.B. 253.
[24] [1965] 1 All E.R. 657; see *Mackay* v. *Ozonair Engineering Co. Ltd.* (1981) 131 N.L.J. 481.

If this were to mean considering whether the character of the movement is dangerous in fact it might produce a different result. If the question of danger is to be limited by foresight the difference will normally be one of degree, especially as Pearson L.J. suggests in order to establish danger "the factors to be taken into account include the speed of the movement, its duration or the method of starting the machinery." The duration of the movement would not seem relevant to danger. It is not surprising that as a final factor he admitted that to some extent and in some cases one would have to take into account the purpose of the movement.[25] Salmon L.J. felt the grammatical difficulty arose from the fact that motion and movement are the same, but thought that the circumstances of industry required a more narrow view. This is almost the same as saying that there are risks which the employee must be taken to accept; although, as we shall see, very much the same is true of liability for negligence. If so much emphasis is to be put upon the aspect of compensation in the Factories Act it is unfortunate that the argument cannot be taken the whole way, so that there is liability to compensate for injury arising from recognisably dangerous processes irrespective of the practicality of prevention.

Prior to 1961 cleaning had been allowed while the machine was in motion and the guards removed, but this is now excluded. The Act goes further to forbid any woman or young person to clean any prime mover or transmission machinery while it is in motion, or any part of any machine if to do so would expose such person to a risk of injury from a moving part of that or an adjacent machine.[26] Despite the restricted meaning given to "in motion" in section 16 it has been held that a "moving part" is a part which may at any time move, whether it was doing so at the time of the accident or not.[27] A part which is "in motion" must be a "moving part" so that the first part of this section imposes a duty irrespective of the foreseeability of injury whilst the second requires such foresight.

---

[25] *Horne* v. *Lec Refrigeration* [1965] 2 All E.R. 898.
[26] Note the effect on this of the Sex Discrimination Act 1975, s.55.
[27] *Kelly* v. *John Dale Ltd.* [1965] 1 Q.B. 185.

HEALTH AND SAFETY AT WORK ETC. ACT 1974

SCHEDULE 1

EXISTING ENACTMENTS WHICH ARE RELEVANT STATUTORY PROVISIONS

Chapter	Short title	Provisions which are relevant statutory provisions
1875 c. 17.	The Explosives Act 1875.	The whole Act except sections 30 to 32, 80 and 116 to 121.
1882 c. 22.	The Boiler Explosions Act 1882.	The whole Act.
1890 c. 35.	The Boiler Explosions Act 1890.	The whole Act.
1906 c. 14.	The Alkali, &c. Works Regulation Act 1906.	The whole Act.
1909 c. 43.	The Revenue Act 1909.	Section 11.
1919 c. 23.	The Anthrax Prevention Act 1919.	The whole Act.
1920 c. 65.	The Employment of Women, Young Persons and Children Act 1920.	The whole Act.
1922 c. 35.	The Celluloid and Cinematograph Film Act 1922.	The whole Act.
1923 c. 17.	The Explosives Act 1923.	The whole Act.
1926 c. 43.	The Public Health (Smoke Abatement) Act 1926.	The whole Act.
1928 c. 32.	The Petroleum (Consolidation) Act 1928.	The whole Act.
1936 c. 22.	The Hours of Employment (Conventions) Act 1936.	The whole Act except section 5.
1936 c. 27.	The Petroleum (Transfer of Licences) Act 1936.	The whole Act.
1937 c. 45.	The Hydrogen Cyanide (Fumigation) Act 1937.	The whole Act.
1945 c. 19.	The Ministry of Fuel and Power Act 1945.	Section 1(1) so far as it relates to maintaining and improving the safety, health and welfare of persons employed in or about mines and quarries in Great Britain.
1946 c. 59.	The Coal Industry Nationalisation Act 1946.	Section 42(1) and (2).
1948 c. 37.	The Radioactive Substances Act 1948.	Section 5(1)(a).
1951 c. 21.	The Alkali, &c. Works Regulation (Scotland) Act 1951.	The whole Act.

1951 c. 58.	The Fireworks Act 1951.	Sections 4 and 7.
1952 c. 60.	The Agriculture (Poisonous Substances) Act 1952.	The whole Act.
1953 c. 47.	The Emergency Laws (Miscellaneous Provisions) Act 1953.	Section 3.
1954 c. 70.	The Mines and Quarries Act 1954.	The whole Act except section 151.
1956 c. 49.	The Agriculture (Safety, Health and Welfare Provisions) Act 1956.	The whole Act.
1961 c. 34.	The Factories Act 1961.	The whole Act except section 135.
1961 c. 64.	The Public Health Act 1961.	Section 73.
1962 c. 58.	The Pipe-lines Act 1962.	Sections 20 to 26, 33, 34 and 42, Schedule 5.
1963 c. 41.	The Offices, Shops and Railway Premises Act 1963.	The whole Act.
1965 c. 57.	The Nuclear Installations Act 1965.	Sections 1, 3 to 6, 22 and 24, Schedule 2.
1969 c. 10.	The Mines and Quarries (Tips) Act 1969.	Sections 1 to 10.
1971 c. 20.	The Mines Management Act 1971.	The whole Act.
1972 c. 28.	The Employment Medical Advisory Service Act 1972.	The whole Act except sections 1 and 6 and Schedule 1.

CHAPTER 12

CIVIL LIABILITY FOR INJURY AT WORK

By Jacqueline Dyson

THE FORMS OF LIABILITY

Historical development

The development of employer's liability in the law of tort has produced a complicated, perhaps even a chaotic, mixture of concepts. In the first case in which a servant sued his master for personal injuries received at work,[1] Lord Abinger displayed great apprehension of the consequences of unrestricted acceptance of the view that the master, as principal, is liable for the negligent acts of his servants as if they were his own, provided those acts were committed within the scope of the servant's employment. This form of liability, which later came to be known, misleadingly, as "vicarious liability," was well established in the common law.[2] But the decision in *Priestley* v. *Fowler* culled from the nineteenth century god of freedom of contract the concept of common employment, whereby it was presumed that the servant voluntarily undertook the risk of the negligence of his fellow servants. Thirteen years later, in *Hutchinson* v. *York, Newcastle and Berwick Rail Co.*[3] this pervasive defence was firmly established on its contractual basis and it survived until 1948,[4] though its worst effects were somewhat alleviated in later decisions. An almost concurrent development, from the same root of acceptance of risk, was the doctrine of *volenti non fit injuria*, which might exclude liability for any type of risk.

At this time the concept of the master's personal liability to take care not to expose his servant to unreasonable risk was barely apparent. How wide this concept was is open to doubt. Lord Abinger, in *Priestley* v. *Fowler*[5] had admitted that the master was bound to provide for the safety of his servant if the master knew of the danger, but Alderson B., in *Hutchinson* v. *York*, confined it to a duty to provide ordinary competent fellow servants and "to furnish them with adequate materials and resources for the work." As industrialisation increased and the master became a more remote figure, or even merely a combination of higher servants of an impersonal company, the doctrine of common employment tended completely to obscure this type of liability. The courts refused to take the view that the acts of the servant should be looked upon as the acts of the master, holding rather that the acts of the master were acts of servants, thus preventing recovery.[6]

---

[1] *Priestley* v. *Fowler* (1837) 3 M. & W. 1.
[2] See *McManus* v. *Crickett* (1800) 1 East 106; *Boson* v. *Sandford* (1690) 2 Salk 440; *Middleton* v. *Fowler* (1698) 1 Salk 282.
[3] (1850) 5 Exch. 343.
[4] Law Reform (Personal Injuries) Act 1948.
[5] See also: *Brydon* v. *Stewart* (1855) 2 Macq. 30; *Tarrant* v. *Webb* (1856) 25 L.J.C.P. 261; *Roberts* v. *Smith* (1857) 26 L.J.Ex. 319.
[6] See *Wilson* v. *Merry* (1868) L.R. 1 Sc. & Div. 326.

A further obstacle to recovery was the development of the defence of contributory negligence so that the courts came to regard almost any contributory negligence on the part of the plaintiff as destroying the causal relationship between the fault of the defendant, however obvious that might be, and the injury.[7]

In order to avoid the harsh effects of common employment, Lord Wright, in *Wilsons and Clyde Coal Co. Ltd.* v. *English*,[8] took from *Wilson* v. *Merry* what is generally regarded as the basis of the "direct" liability of the employer. He had to create new categories of duty apparently separate from the master's vicarious liability for negligence of his servants. These duties were: (i) to select competent fellow servants, (ii) to provide proper and adequate machinery, (iii) to provide a proper system of working. However, this new basis of liability tended to be distinguished from that attaching to other relationships by establishing a higher standard for the employer and a lower standard of care for his own safety by the employee,[9] a divergence which was forced upon the courts by the need to avoid the restrictive effect of contributory negligence.

Present position

At first sight, therefore, it appears that the common law has developed two forms of liability for the master:

(i) a personal liability, apparently divided into a number of separate categories;

(ii) vicarious liability for the negligence of his employees.

(i) In fact, once legislation had abolished the defence of common employment[10] and rationalised that of contributory negligence[11] it was possible to see the duty of the employer as simply one of reasonable care for the safety of his employees. This approach was clearly demonstrated in the judgment of the House of Lords in *Davie* v. *New Merton Board Mills*.[12] Viscount Simonds referring to the doctrine of common employment said:

> ". . . the determination to avert, or at least to reduce, the consequences of that decision led to a great deal of artificiality and refinement which would have been otherwise unnecessary. The shadow of it is still on us. But we can at least return to the simple question which is at the bottom of it all: 'Has the employer taken reasonable care for the safety of the workman?' a question which can only be answered in each case by a consideration of all its circumstances."

The categories are merely a convenient form to express that general duty of reasonable care.[13] If the duty is not carried out, the employer is responsible. The employer's activities are normally and necessarily carried out by

---

[7] *e.g., Caswell* v. *Worth* (1856) 5 E. & B. 849.

[8] [1938] A.C. 57 at 80.

[9] See *Caswell* v. *Powell Duffryn Associated Collieries Ltd.* [1940] A.C. 152.

[10] Law Reform (Personal Injuries) Act 1948.

[11] Law Reform (Contributory Negligence) Act 1945.

[12] [1959] A.C. 604. For discussion of facts see *infra.* See also *Wilson* v. *Tyneside Window Cleaning Co.* [1958] 2 Q.B. 110 at 113.

[13] See, *e.g. Thompson* v. *National Coal Board* [1982] I.C.R. 15. As to the dangers of treating the categories as anything but useful methods of exposition, see *Cavanagh* v. *Ulster Weaving Co.* [1960] A.C. 145 at 166.

employees, who may neglect to carry out such reasonable duties as the provision of proper machinery and a safe system of work. In the same way the employer is liable if the work is carried out by third parties. The question again is simply whether the employer has taken reasonable care for his employee's safety. That being so, it is possible to see employer's liability as no more than a specialised form of the general duty of care. In principle his liability to an independent contractor is precisely the same. It is still said that an employer owes no duty to an independent contractor such as he owes to his own employees,[14] but the difference lies only in the degree of care.[15] This is not to say that one does not find many explanations of this difference cast in terms of the former classifications. In *Inglefield* v. *Macey*,[16] for instance, the fact that no master/servant relationship existed was held to preclude a duty to provide a safe system of work, and, as the claim was founded on this basis, liability was held not to exist. The only justification for this type of decision, however, must lie in the reasonableness of expecting an independent contractor to provide his own system of work.

(ii) The "vicarious liability" of the master for the torts of his servant is really a vicarious duty of care, but it may still be thought to differ from the personal duty of the master, albeit delegated as in *Davie* v. *New Merton*, since it will not suffice for the master to prove that *he* has exercised all reasonable care. It is, in a sense, therefore, strict liability for the fault of others. In practice, however, the distinction is becoming less and less apparent, at least in relation to fellow servants, because there is now something approaching a *res ipsa loquitur* whenever the employee is injured at work. Alternatively, it can be said that the duty of the employer is now put so high that whenever a workman is injured at work one looks for an explanation, and if none is forthcoming, negligence is presumed.[17] Vicarious liability, in turn, is being divested of the substance of its former distinctions, and the courts are assuming that the servant's actions were in the course of employment if the events took place on the employer's premises, during normal working hours. The result of these trends is as Danckwerts L.J. observed in *Kay* v. *I.T.W.*[18]: "when one considers the position in this way of the vicarious liability of employers and the provisions of the Factories Act 1961, it seems to me that the employers's life is a somewhat hazardous one. Indeed, it appears that it would be a good deal safer to keep lions or other wild animals in a park than to engage in a business involving the employment of labour." An employer may not still be liable vicariously, when he would not be so directly (or vice versa, for an employee may be incompetent but not negligent), but it does mean that liability or non-liability depends less and less on the classifications that were once regarded as so meaningful.

When one compares the liability of an employer to that of any other person, one finds such a difference of degree that it is easy, as *Inglefield* v. *Macey*[19]

[14] See, *e.g. Norton* v. *Canadian Pacific Steamships Ltd.* [1961] 1 W.L.R. 1057; *Baxter* v. *Central Electricity Generating Board* [1965] 1 W.L.R. 200.
[15] See *McArdle* v. *Andmac Roofing* [1967] 1 W.L.R. 356; *Smith* v. *Vange Scaffolding and Engineering Co. Ltd.* [1970] 1 W.L.R. 733; *Smith* v. *A. Davies and Co. (Shopfitters) Ltd.* (1968) 5 K.I.R. 320. See also *Field* v. *E. E. Jeavons and Co. Ltd.* [1965] 1 W.L.R. 996.
[16] (1967) 2 K.I.R. 146.
[17] See *Mason* v. *Williams and Williams and Thomas Turton & Sons* [1955] 1 W.L.R. 549.
[18] [1968] 1 Q.B. 140.
[19] (1967) 2 K.I.R. 146.

shows, to continue to speak as if differences of principle existed. The employer's duty is no longer a series of separate obligations,[20] but practitioners and writers are still apt to resort to them for easy reference.[21]

PROOF

A person proved to have been convicted of an offence will be taken to have committed it unless the contrary is proved.[22] In other cases, however, it is for the plaintiff to prove the tort, so that for example the plaintiff must prove negligence and that the negligence is attributable to the defendant or to someone for whom the defendant is vicariously liable. This task usually involves proof of acts or omissions which can be regarded as negligent. In certain cases, however, the courts will be prepared to infer from the immediate circumstances of the injury a chain of facts leading back to the conclusion that the defendant had been negligent. It will then be for the defendant to seek to rebut this inference.

This principle, normally referred to as *res ipsa loquitur*, is usually said to have originated in the dictum of Erle C.J. in *Scott* v. *London and St. Katherine Docks Co.*[23]

> ". . . where the thing is shown to be under the management of the defendant or his servants, and the accident is such as in the ordinary course of things does not happen if those who have the management use proper care,[24] it affords reasonable evidence, in the absence of explanation by the defendants, that the accident arose from want of care."

It must be borne in mind that not everything that happens at a workplace can be said to be properly within the control of the employer.[25] An employer may be vicariously liable for the intervening acts of employees.

In *Lloyde* v. *West Midlands Gas Board*[26] Megaw L.J. explained the principle.

> "I doubt whether it is right to describe *res ipsa loquitur* as a 'doctrine.' I think that it is no more than an exotic, although convenient, phrase to describe what is in essence no more than a common-sense approach, not limited by technical rules, to the assessment of the effect of evidence in certain circumstances. It means that a plaintiff prima facie establishes negligence where: (i) it is not possible for him to prove precisely what was the relevant act or omission which set in train the events leading to the accident; but (ii) on the evidence as it stands at the relevant time it is more likely than not that the effective cause of the accident was some act or omission of the defendant or of someone for whom the defendant is responsible,

---

[20] *Cavanagh* v. *Ulster Weaving Co. Ltd.* [1960] A.C. 145 at 164. See, *e.g. Winfield and Jolowicz on Tort* (11th ed.), ed. W. V. H. Rogers, at pp. 173 *et seq.*

[21] This has its dangers when lawyers attempt to force new situations into one of the old categories. See *Williams* v. *Grimshaw* (1967) 3 K.I.R. 610—stewardess of sports club injured in abortive attempt to rob her of takings on way home—no breach of duty of care not to expose her to unnecessary risk of injury—see also *Houghton* v. *Hackney Borough Council* (1961) 3 K.I.R. 615.

[22] Civil Evidence Act 1968, s.11.

[23] (1865) 3 H. & C. 596.

[24] *Res ipsa loquitur* is not necessarily excluded merely because there has been the possibility of outside interference with the thing—*Lloyde* v. *West Midlands Gas Board* [1971] 1 W.L.R. 749.

[25] See, *e.g. Easson* v. *L. & N.E. Railway Co. Ltd.* [1944] 2 K.B. 421.

[26] [1971] 1 W.L.R. 749 at 755.

which act or omission constitutes a failure to take proper care for the plaintiff's safety . . . The plaintiff must prove facts which give rise to what may be called the *res ipsa loquitur* situation. There is no assumption in his favour of such facts."

When the facts are sufficiently known they must be proved. Under modern industrial conditions, however, it is often very difficult for the injured employee to ascertain how the accident occurred. Winfield and Jolowicz[27] suggest that the plaintiff can himself raise the maxim by calling expert evidence as to what normally does not happen without negligence. In *Mason* v. *Williams and Williams Ltd.*[28] Finnemore J. allowed the plaintiff merely to prove the facts as he knew them.

> "What the plaintiff says here is:—'This is your chisel: you made it and I used it in the condition in which you made it, in the way you intended me to use it, and you never relied on any intermediate examination; therefore, I have discharged the onus of proof by showing that this trouble must have happened through some act in the manufacture of this chisel in your factory, which was either careless or deliberate, and in either event it was a breach of duty towards me, a person who, you contemplated, would use this acticle which you made, in the way you intended it to be used.' If that is right he would be entitled to succeed against the second defendants (manufacturers)."

Once *res ipsa loquitur* is raised[29] the defendant can rebut the presumption by positively disproving the case established. Although it is not sufficient for the defendant merely to counter with an acceptable explanation of how the injury might have occurred without negligence the presumption can be rebutted other than by positive disproof. The position of the defendants was explained by Lord Guest in *Colvilles Ltd.* v. *Devine*.[30]

> "They are absolved if they can give a reasonable explanation of the accident and show that this explanation was consistent with no lack of care on their part."

In that case a violent explosion in a steelworks caused the plaintiff to suffer injury when he jumped from a platform where he was working. He successfully raised the presumption. The defendants presented a plausible explanation for the fire which caused the explosion but failed to fulfil the second requirement, namely to prove that there was no negligence on their part.

The Pearson Commission[31] considered and rejected the formal reversal of the burden of proof for work injuries. A factor which influenced this conclusion was the existing favourable treatment of those injured at work. It has already been suggested that the duty of care in employers' liability cases is so high that in practice there is almost a presumption of negligence and strict proof of negligence is not required. The effect is that the employee does not need to rely on the maxim.

---

[27] *Tort* (11th ed.), p. 102.

[28] [1955] 1 W.L.R. 549, quoted with approval in *Taylor* v. *Rover Co. Ltd.* [1966] 1 W.L.R. 1491. See also *Ward* v. *Tesco Stores Ltd.* [1976] 1 All E.R. 219.

[29] It is unnecessary expressly to plead the doctrine, see *Bennett* v. *Chemical Construction (G.B.) Ltd.* [1971] 1 W.L.R. 1571.

[30] [1969] 1 W.L.R. 475.

[31] Royal Commission on Civil Liability and Compensation for Personal Injury 1978. Cmnd. 7054 (1978).

ELEMENTS OF LIABILITY

(a) Foresight

The employer's duty of care is founded in tort, but it can also be expressed as an aspect of the contractual relationship if this is advantageous.[32] The action in contract is rarely used, largely for procedural reasons and because the basis of assessment of damages is less beneficial. Munkman,[33] suggests that the contract of employment merely fixes the class of those between whom the duty of care exists.[34] The point is apparently wholly one of procedural convenience since the substantive aspects of a contractual claim are largely the same as those of an action in tort.[35]

It is most important when considering an employer's liability in tort to realise that it has nothing to do with contract and is certainly not limited to those with whom he has a contract.[36] The duty of an employer arises because that employee entered into work for the employer and not because of the contract.[37]

The duty of the employer is not limited to those occasions when the employee is acting in the course of his employment. Provided the circumstances are sufficiently within the control of the employer, as such, he will be liable even if the employee was on a frolic of his own.[38] No doubt there is a limit to the scope of an employer's duty, but it is not a limit imposed by the course of employment but by the reasonable responsibility of the employer. An employer's duty extends to the premises of third parties on which he sends his employees; if they go there in working hours, but on a frolic of their own, it would probably be said that the employer was not liable because, in such circumstances, he would not be expected reasonably to foresee the risk.[39]

The basis of the test of duty of care is generally accepted to have been laid down in its modern form in the dictum of Lord Atkin in *Donoghue* v. *Stevenson*.[40]

> "You must take reasonable care to avoid acts or omissions which you can reasonably foresee would be likely to injure your neighbour. Who, then, in law is my

---

[32] *Matthews* v. *Kuwait Bechtel Corporation* [1959] 2 Q.B. 57.

[33] *Employers' Liability* (9th ed.).

[34] See also Salmon L.J. in *Quinn* v. *Burch Brothers Builders Ltd.* [1966] 2 Q.B. 370.

[35] There is some suggestion of substantive advantage in a contractual action in *Wright* v. *Dunlop Rubber Co. Ltd.* (1973) 13 K.I.R. 255 where it was said that though an employer had no duty in tort to rescue an employee from a situation caused by the negligence of a third party he had a contractual duty of care which would extend to dangers enhanced by his own failure.

[36] See, *e.g. Grant* v. *Australian Knitting Mills Ltd.* [1936] A.C. 85.

[37] *Winfield and Jolowicz on Tort* (11th ed.), by W. V. H. Rogers at p. 69.

[38] *Davidson* v. *Handley Page Ltd.* [1945] 1 All E.R. 235; *Uddin* v. *Associated Portland Cement Manufacturers Ltd.* [1965] 2 Q.B. 582; *Allen* v. *Aeroplane and Motor Aluminium Castings Ltd.* [1965] 1 W.L.R. 1244; *Westwood* v. *The Post Office* [1973] 3 All E.R. 184. *Davidson's* case mentions only ancillary matters, such as tying a bootlace or washing a teacup, but the others, although themselves dealing with statutory liability, extend to common law negligence and go beyond such examples. The Employer's Liability (Compulsory Insurance) Act 1969, which came into effect on January 1, 1972, only requires insurance to cover acts which are in the course of employment.

[39] In this respect Munkman's earlier suggestion (6th ed.), pp. 89—91—that a broader concept of course of employment operates in employers' liability cases, as distinct from vicarious liability cases, was misleading.

[40] [1932] A.C. 562 at 580.

neighbour? The answer seems to be persons who are so closely and directly affected by my act that I ought reasonably to have them in contemplation as being so affected when I am directing my mind to the acts or omissions which are called in question."

This formulation enabled the courts to commence to develop a duty extending beyond particular categories of relationship and specialised duties to formulate what is a minimum standard of care applicable now in almost every situation. So for instance, it was possible to conclude that if A owed a duty to B, then A was liable to C if C was endangered by his attempt to rescue B from an imminent peril caused by A.[41]

Liability depends on the absence of reasonable care to prevent reasonably foreseeable dangers. However remote the employer may be in practice he is expected, usually through those acting for him, to apply his mind to think about the consequences of the situation he has created. The case of *Carmarthenshire County Council* v. *Lewis*[42] is an excellent example of the process which takes foresight step by step towards the ultimate source of risk in the light of experience and the known or foreseeable peculiarities of the actors or their behaviour. Consequently it may move to the stage where anything might happen or anyone become involved. The facts were that a teacher at a county council nursery school prepared two children for a walk and left them unattended in a classroom whilst she went elsewhere to get ready. She was delayed and before her return one of the children wandered eventually on to a busy road. A lorry driver swerved his lorry to avoid the child, struck a telegraph pole and was killed. Lord Reid dealt with the argument on foreseeability:

> "Was it foreseeable by an ordinary reasonable and careful person that a child might sometimes be left alone in the nursery school for a short period? I think it was. I see nothing very extraordinary in the circumstances which caused these children to be left alone. Was it, then, foreseeable that such a child might not sit still but might move out of the classroom? If I am right in my view that it is not safe to make assumptions about the behaviour of such young children, again I think it was. Was it then foreseeable that such a child might go into the street, there being no obstacle in its way? I see no ground for assuming that such a child would stay in an empty playground when the gate was not more than 20 yards or so from the classroom. And once the child was in the street anything might happen."

The county council was thus held liable for the absence of the teacher.

Where all those involved are within the area of employment there would appear to be a distinct tendency to extend the field of vision of reasonable foresight. This is partly because reasonable foresight depends heavily on experience and a common employment is an obvious breeding ground for extensive experience.[43] It is, for instance, common experience that employees will, on occasion, behave carelessly, forgetfully and even stupidly. As Lord Oaksey said in *General Cleaning Contractors Ltd.* v. *Christmas*[44]

---

[41] *Haynes* v. *Harwood* [1935] 1 K.B. 146. This has since been extended to impose liability on A in respect of the rescue even if A owed no duty to B—*Videan* v. *British Transport Commission* [1963] 2 Q.B. 650.

[42] [1955] A.C. 549.

[43] *e.g. Nicholls* v. *Austin Leyton Ltd.* [1946] A.C.493.

[44] [1953] A.C. 180 at 189-190; *Field* v. *Jeavons* [1965] 1 W.L.R. 996; *Charlton* v. *The Forrest Printing Ink Co.* [1980] I.R.L.R. 331.

"It is, I think, well known to employers, and there is evidence in this case that it was well known to the appellants, that their workpeople are very frequently, if not habitually, careless about the risks which their work may involve. It is, in my opinion, for that very reason that the common law demands that employers should take reasonable care to lay down a reasonably safe system of work."

In *Griffiths* v. *Arch Engineering Co. Ltd.*[45] a director of company A borrowed a grinding machine from a director of company B and lent it to one of A's employees C. C in turn lent it to a fellow employee D. D used the machine with a grinding wheel with too large a diameter to allow it to be operated safely at the speed at which it rotated. D also held the machine in one hand and the workpiece in the other whereas it was intended that the machine should be held in both hands and presented to a firmly clamped workpiece. The grinding wheel shattered and D's hand was severely injured. It was held that the director of company B who held himself out as a qualified engineer should have foreseen or ascertained the risk of the machine being used at the wrong speed in relation to the size of the grinding wheel. He should also have foreseen that a borrower might pass the tool to another who would use it without examination.

It is true that courts have said that the employment relationship is not to be viewed in the same light as that of pupil and teacher[46] or, as Viscount Simonds put it in *Smith* v. *Austin Lifts Ltd.*[47] the duty is not that of nurse to imbecile child. Thus the Court of Appeal in *Black* v. *Carricks (Caterers) Ltd.*[48] found it was not foreseeable that the employee would expose herself to injury where she had been left with no assistant in a bread shop and interpreted orders from the employer to get on as best she could to include lifting heavy trays which caused her injury. Nevertheless the degree of foresight required by an employer is undoubtedly high.[49] The employee is entitled to depend on the employer. So, for instance, departure from a previous practice will tend to induce the conclusion that thought would have produced foresight that an employee would rely on its continuance. Nervous shock is as likely in employment as in other relationships[50] and the relationship of one employee to another is almost certain to be close enough to establish foresight. The degree of relationship necessary was considered by the House of Lords in the recent case of *McLoughlin* v. *O'Brian.*[50a]

Foresight is to be measured in the light of knowledge and experience possessed or reasonably expected at the time of the alleged negligence.[51]

(b) The duty of care

Although the employer has no general duty, arising from the tort of negligence, positively to act for the benefit of his employees, this does not mean, however, that he can create a dangerous situation and stand by to await

---

[45] [1968] 3 All E.R. 217.
[46] *Withers* v. *Perry Chain Co. Ltd.* [1961] 1 W.L.R. 1314 at 1319.
[47] [1959] 1 W.L.R. 100.
[48] [1980] I.R.L.R. 448. They also held there was no liability under Offices, Shops and Railway Premises Act 1963, s.23.
[49] See, *e.g. Smith* v. *National Coal Board* [1967] 1 W.L.R. 871.
[50] *e.g. Dooley* v. *Cammell Laird and Co. Ltd.* [1951] 1 Lloyd's Rep. 271.
[50a] [1982] 2 W.L.R. 982.
[51] *Roe* v. *Minister of Health* [1954] 2 Q.B. 66.

the consequences with impunity. If the employer creates a danger, however lacking in fault he may be in such creation, he has a duty to remedy it.[52]

The duty is that of a reasonable man. But a reasonable man does not hold himself out to have specialised skills without expecting to be judged according to the standards of each representation. As we have already seen from the judgment in *Griffiths* v. *Arch Engineering Co. Ltd.*[53] an engineer is expected to show the standard of care to be expected of a reasonably competent engineer. The common law is, therefore, in principle, even-handed. A large company with plenty of funds for research will not be required to show a higher standard of care before marketing its products than the small and impecunious company engaged in a similar activity.[54]

The standard of care required is judged by the state of knowledge at the time in question.[55] If the danger is unknown at the time then it will not be foreseeable.

However, with advances in scientific knowledge the standard of care required will change. As Lord Denning put it: "The standard goes up as men become wiser."[56] Once the danger is widely known the employer will be liable if he fails to take precautions.[57] The employer is expected to use specialised skill and knowledge which he has or ought to have. This includes the growing amount of advisory material available in various industries.[58] These provide a guide to the expected standard.[59]

Balancing risk against precautions

The degree to which care must be exercised depends on a balancing of the risk against the precautions necessary to offset it. The risk is measured not only in terms of frequency but also of seriousness. All the facts of the case are taken into account not least the particular sensibility of the plaintiff. So, in *Paris* v. *Stepney Borough Council*[60] the plaintiff who had only one good eye was employed in dismantling motor vehicles. It was not normal practice to provide goggles and they were not provided on this occasion. Whilst he was removing rusty bolts a metal chip entered the plaintiff's good eye causing him almost total blindness. The argument proceeded on the assumption that the normal practice was normally reasonable. However, Lord Normand said in the House of Lords:

"... the judgment of the reasonable and prudent man should be allowed its common every-day scope, and it should not be restrained from considering the

---

[52] *Johnson* v. *Rea Ltd.* [1962] 1 Q.B. 373.
[53] [1968] 3 All E.R. 217.
[54] But see to the contrary *Stokes* v. *Guest Keen and Nettlefold (Bolts and Nuts) Ltd.* [1968] 1 W.L.R. 1776 at 1783 and 1786.
[55] *Tremain* v. *Pike* [1969] 3 All E.R. 1303—farmer not expected to know of Weil's disease carried by rats as no warning issued by health authorities.
[56] *Qualcast* v. *Haynes* [1959] 2 All E.R. 38 at 45.
[57] *Wright* v. *Dunlop Rubber Co. Ltd.* (1972) 13 K.I.R. 255.
[58] *e.g.* Health and safety executive leaflets, codes of practice on health and safety matters issued under Health and Safety at Work Act 1974, s.16.
[59] *Stringer* v. *Automatic Woodturning Co.* [1956] 1 W.L.R. 138—mere observance of regulations under Factories Act or similar legislation will not raise implication of exercise of reasonable care. *Sheridan* v. *Durkin* (1967) 111 S.J. 112—refusal to regard fact that regulations had subsequently required the provision of goggles during the hand cutting of glazed earthenware pipes as indicating that an employer's common law duty of reasonable care previously extended to such provision.
[60] [1951] A.C. 367.

foreseeable consequences of an accident and their seriousness for the person to whom the duty of care is owed."

Here it was held to be negligent to fail to supply goggles to a workman known to be subject to a risk of injury so severe as that faced by Paris.

A good example of the balance between risk and expense is contained in the reasoning in the judgment in *Latimer* v. *A.E.C. Ltd.*[61] In that case a factory had been flooded by rainwater produced by an exceptional storm. The flood water had mixed with a greasy coolant which was normally carried in ducts in the floor. As the mixture subsided a greasy film was deposited on the floor. Forty men were set to clean up and spread three tons of sawdust—the whole of the available supply. Despite this, part of the floor remained untreated. The appellant slipped on an untreated portion and was injured. The decision of the trial judge that the factory should have been closed if it could not be made safe was rejected by both the Court of Appeal and the House of Lords and the defendants were held not to be liable. The proper question according to Lord Tucker[62] was:

> "Has it been proved that the floor was so slippery that (further) remedial steps not being possible, a reasonably prudent employer would have closed down the factory rather than allow his employees to run the risks involved in continuing work?"

Conversely, of course, if a high level of benefit will be derived from a safety device, for instance, then it may be held reasonable to expect the employer to incur considerable expenditure to instal it.[63]

The risk is to be examined in the light of the importance of the object to be attained. This proposition would be open to serious objection on grounds of policy if the common law of negligence were to be considered primarily concerned to secure safety. Accordingly, as we have seen in the field of industrial safety, this balancing exercise has often been discarded in favour of absolute liability or, more recently, the granting of power to prohibit an activity even in the absence of any breach of duty. The law of negligence is designed to provide compensation, and it does so by a balancing of interests. So the purpose to be attained may permit the taking of a risk which in other circumstances would be impermissible.[64]

Attributes of employee

The employer must, of course, take the worker as he finds him. So if he can foresee some injury the peculiar susceptibility of the plaintiff will not excuse him.[65] The employer is, in turn, entitled to rely on the particular employee's skill, experience and knowledge.[66] So far as statutory duties are concerned it

---

[61] [1953] A.C. 643; see also *Powley* v. *Bristol Siddeley Engines Ltd.* [1966] 1 W.L.R. 729—ice on office steps in early morning.

[62] At p. 659.

[63] See *Toronto Power Co.* v. *Paskwan* [1915] A.C. 734.

[64] *Watt* v. *Hertfordshire County Council* [1954] 1 W.L.R. 835. Compare *Gaynor* v. *Allen* [1959] 2 Q.B. 403.

[65] See, *e.g. Robinson* v. *The Post Office* [1974] 1 W.L.R. 1176.

[66] *Qualcast (Wolverhampton) Ltd.* v. *Haynes* [1959] A.C. 743; *McWilliams* v. *Sir William Arrol Ltd.* [1962] 1 W.L.R. 295; *Boyle* v. *Kodak Ltd.* [1969] 1 W.L.R. 661; see R. W. L. Howells (1970) 33 M.L.R. 89; *Richardson* v. *Stephenson Clarke Ltd.* [1969] 1 W.L.R. 1695.

may be necessary to give instructions even to an experienced man.[67] Even in common law negligence a fully experienced man, knowing what should be done, may, for example, foreseeably use inadequate equipment if the proper plant is not readily available.[68] Experience is not, of course, general, and must relate to the work in hand,[69] although a job may be so straightforward that it is reasonable to leave it to an unskilled man, without instruction.[70] On the other hand, a perfectly suitable system of work may be insufficient because it has not been communicated to an employee.[71] Where a system has been communicated to an employee but is ignored, the employer will not be liable. In *Charlton* v. *The Forrest Printing Ink Co.*[72] the Court of Appeal held the employer was not in breach of duty to an employee injured by robbers whilst collecting wages from the bank as instructions on varying the route and method of collection had been given but ignored.

Under statutory provisions requiring the taking of "all practicable measures" it has been held that there is a duty to induce people to wear safety masks.[73] So far as the law of negligence is concerned, the duty to warn of danger depends upon what is considered reasonable, rather than what is practicable.[74] The common law, therefore, has hesitated long to place upon an employer a duty to exhort an employee to use a safety device.[75] In *James* v. *Hepworth and Grandage* a notice was displayed in the factory warning of the need to wear protective clothing, which was available. The plaintiff, a West Indian worker who apparently was unable to read, did not wear the clothing and was injured. The employer was held to have taken reasonable care.

It is obvious that the employer's duty is not limited by considerations of what may happen to the employee while at work as a result of the conduct of that work. In *McGhee* v. *National Coal Board*,[76] for instance, the employee had to cycle home caked with sweat and dirt because no washing facilities were provided. The House of Lords held that the employer was liable even if other factors might have contributed to the contraction of dermatitis.

In *Jones* v. *Lionite Specialities Ltd.*[77] it was held unreasonable to require an employer to go to the extent of dismissing an employee in order to protect him from the risks attendant on the employee's addiction to trichlorethylene vapour from a tank in the degreasing plant. In *Withers* v. *Perry Chain Co. Ltd.*[78] the Court of Appeal went further to hold that there was no duty to transfer to yet another department a female employee who contracted severe dermatitis from

---

[67] *Boyle* v. *Kodak Ltd.* [1969] 1 W.L.R. 661.

[68] *Machray* v. *Stewarts and Lloyds Ltd.* [1965] 1 W.L.R. 602.

[69] *Ross* v. *Associated Portland Cement Manufacturers Ltd.* [1964] 1 W.L.R. 768; *Byers* v. *Head Wrightson & Co. Ltd.* [1961] 1 W.L.R. 961; *Rands* v. *McNeil* [1955] 1 Q.B. 253.

[70] *Vinnyey* v. *Star Paper Mills Ltd.* [1965] 1 All E.R. 175.

[71] *Beer* v. *Wheeler* (1965) 109 S.J. 133—method of securing bull in pen.

[72] [1980] I.R.L.R. 331.

[73] *Crookall* v. *Vickers Armstrong Ltd.* [1955] 1 W.L.R. 659; *Clarkson* v. *Modern Foundries Ltd.* [1957] 1 W.L.R. 1210—see (1967) 30 M.L.R. at 460–461.

[74] *Qualcast (Wolverhampton) Ltd.* v. *Haynes* [1959] A.C. 743.

[75] *McWilliams* v. *Sir William Arrol & Co. Ltd.* [1962] 1 W.L.R. 295; *James* v. *Hepworth and Grandage* [1968] 1 Q.B. 94.

[76] [1973] 1 W.L.R. 1.

[77] (1961) 105 S.J. 1082.

[78] [1961] 1 W.L.R. 1314.

the grease used in her job. This despite the fact that no protective devices were effective and she had been transferred on a previous occasion.

Sellers L.J. expressed the view that in bringing the action the employee showed ingratitude. He concluded:

". . . I think there is no duty at common law requiring an employer to dismiss an employee rather than retain him or her in employment and allow him or her to earn wages because there may be some risk. The duty of the defendants in this case was to take all reasonable care for the plaintiff in the employment in which she was engaged including a duty to have regard to the fact that she had had dermatitis previously."

General and approved practice

There is no rule of law that to follow normal practice is conclusive of the absence of negligence as the normal practice may be unsafe.[79] Conversely, it does not necessarily follow that an employer is negligent for failing to adopt a usual practice.[80] However, as Lord Reid said in *General Cleaning Contractors Ltd.* v. *Christmas*:[81]

"A plaintiff who seeks to have condemned as unsafe a system of work which has been generally used for a long time in an important trade undertakes a heavy onus. If he is right, it means that all or practically all the numerous employers in the trade have been habitually neglecting their duty to their men."

The burden of challenging normal practice is, therefore, a heavy one.[82]

Care on premises of another

The employer's duty of reasonable care extends to activities for which he is responsible upon another's premises, although, of course, the extent of what he can reasonably do may be small. In *General Cleaning Contractors* v. *Christmas*[83] a window cleaning company sent one of their employees to clean the windows of a building belonging to a customer. The window cleaner stepped out on to the window sill, holding on to the open sash window, but lost his grip, and his balance, and fell when one of the sashes, which moved at the slightest touch, came down on his fingers. A safety belt was provided but could not be used because no hooks were fixed to the premises. The occupiers of the building were held, by the Court of Appeal,[84] not to be liable as this was not an unusual danger, but one against which window cleaners might be expected to provide. In considering the liability of the employer, Lord Reid in the House of Lords, said that he was satisfied that none of the alternatives to the "window sill method" was reasonably practicable. Since the window sill method was dangerous if no precautions were taken, it called for a proper system which the

---

[79] *Paris* v. *Stepney Borough Council* [1951] A.C. 367.
[80] *e.g. Brown* v. *Rolls Royce Ltd.* [1960] 1 All E.R. 577.
[81] [1953] A.C. 180.
[82] See, *e.g. Barkway* v. *South Wales Transport Co. Ltd.* [1950] A.C. 185; *Morris* v. *West Hartlepool Steam Navigation Ltd.* [1956] A.C. 552; *Cavanagh* v. *Ulster Weaving Ltd.* [1960] A.C. 145; *Sexton* v. *Scaffolding (Great Britain) Ltd.* [1953] 1 Q.B. 153; *Brown* v. *John Mills and Co. Ltd.* (1970) 8 K.I.R. 702.
[83] [1953] A.C. 180.
[84] [1952] 1 K.B. 141.

employer was bound to devise. Even though, in this case, the employee was an experienced man, it was not sufficient to leave the devising of a system to him. As Lord Oaksey pointed out[85]:

> "Employers are not exempted from this duty by the fact that their men are experienced and might, if they were in the position of an employer, be able to lay down a reasonably safe system of work themselves. Workmen are not in the position of employers. These duties are not performed in the calm atmosphere of a boardroom with the advice of experts. They have to make their decisions on narrow window sills and other places of danger, and in circumstances in which the dangers are obscured by repetition."

Upon very similar facts, however, in *Wilson* v. *Tyneside Cleaning Co.*[86] the employee's claim failed, not upon the absence or impracticability of a duty of care on the premises of others, but on this last point that the employee, as an experienced man, could be expected to take care of himself.

The decision of the House of Lords in *Smith* v. *Austin Lifts Ltd.*[87] followed the same principle and was only different in outcome because the employers had been informed of the danger a number of times. The appellant was employed by the first respondent, who had contracted with the second respondent to maintain a lift in the second respondent's premises. The appellant had paid many visits to the machine house, and his reports to his employer that its doors were dangerous had been passed on to the second respondent. On one occasion the appellant had found the lower hinge of one of the doors to be broken, and had tied the two doors together to keep them shut. On his next visit he found that someone else had jammed the doors in order to keep them shut. While trying to force them he fell off the metal ladder leading to the doors. Lord Denning, delivering the most positive judgment, held that the first respondent was at least under a duty to inspect the premises to see whether a known defect had been put right. Three other members of the House of Lords, though more doubtful, on the facts, that there had been failure by the first respondent to take reasonable care, did not dissent.[88] Lord Reid did dissent, again on the ground that it would have been reasonable to leave the appellant to make up his own mind about the extent of the danger.[89] Clearly, therefore, the employer's duty of care upon the premises of others is most likely not to be broken where it can be said that the experienced employee, himself present on the premises, is expected on his own account to exercise reasonable care. There is an obvious danger that, in forcing the employee's responsibility for his own safety into the area of his employer's obligation, the law may find that it has, in another form, introduced something like the principle of *volenti non fit injuria*.

The duty of care of the employer on premises of others may even extend to those who are not his own employees. For example, in *McArdle* v. *Andmac*

---

[85] But "where the operation is simple and the decision how it should be done has to be taken frequently it is natural and reasonable that it should be left to the foreman or workman on the spot"—*Winter* v. *Cardiff Rural District Council* [1950] 1 All E.R. 819.

[86] [1958] 2 Q.B. 110.

[87] [1959] 1 W.L.R. 100.

[88] Much may go wrong between one inspection and another. Satisfaction of the duty of reasonable care will depend on the frequency of inspections in all the circumstances— *Braham* v. *J. Lyons & Co. Ltd.* [1962] 1 W.L.R. 1048.

[89] A workman might even reasonably be left to effect simple repairs—*Pearce* v. *Armitage* (1950) 83 Ll.L.Rep. 361.

Roofing Co.[90] there was held to be a duty on a main contractor to co-ordinate operations at the place of work to ensure the safety not only of his own employees but also the employees of sub-contractors.

There is no reason to talk, as in *Baxter* v. *Central Electricity Generating Board*,[91] of the need to "hold that the [employer] owed generally to persons engaged on work within this building the special employer's duty which is owed to their own employees." As has been said the "special" nature of this duty is only a matter of degree of care. In *Baxter's* case no liability was found to attach to the non-occupying employer. The plaintiff who was employed by the owners of the building (the C.E.G.B.) was helping an employee of a company installing machinery to detect a fault in a fan heater. He lost two fingers while attempting to make an adjustment after the motor had been started. Ashworth J. held that the installation company had no reason to contemplate the involvement of the plaintiff. This appears to be a decision that no duty was owed to him simply because he was not in the area of foresight. Such a decision, of course, does not depend on the distinction between one employee and another. Though an employee will in his working time almost inevitably be within this foresight, so too might the plaintiff in this case had the facts of his intervention been only slightly different.

Performance of the duty of care by others

The employer must normally make use of third parties, whether or not his employees, to carry out his duty of care. As has been said, if they are his employees, the issue may be resolved by asking whether they have been negligent and holding the employer vicariously liable. The question does sometimes arise of whether an employer who has, probably necessarily, delegated the carrying out of his duty can be said to have exercised all reasonable care. Delegation may be the means of carrying out the duty. It should be noted that no such question can arise in the case of an absolute statutory duty, where the inquiry will be solely as to whose breach caused the accident. In common law negligence, however, although it is equally impermissible to delegate the duty itself, reasonable care, not being absolute, may be shown to have been taken; the fault being that of another.

In *Davie* v. *New Merton Board Mills Ltd.*[92] the House of Lords held that the employer had carried out his duty. He had bought from a competent supplier a metal drift which was apparently in good condition. His system of maintenance and inspection was not at fault, but the drift had a latent defect, which only an X-ray might have detected. When the appellant struck it a piece flew off it and blinded him in one eye. The drift had, in fact, been negligently case-hardened so as to have a brittle edge. Clearly the employer was under a duty to take reasonable care to supply proper tools, which duty he could not delegate.[93] As Viscount Simonds said, however, to make him liable for the negligence of a manufacturer with whom he had no connection would be to impose an absolute liability. Lord Reid said:

> "On the one hand it appears that an employer is liable for the negligence of an independent contractor whom he has engaged to carry out one of what have been

---

[90] [1967] 1 All E.R. 583; see also *R.* v. *Swan Hunter Shipbuilders Ltd.* [1982] 1 All E.R. 264.
[91] [1965] 1 W.L.R. 200.   [92] [1959] A.C. 604.
[93] See, *e.g. Riverstone Meat Co. Pty. Ltd.* v. *Lancashire Shipping Co. Ltd.* [1961] A.C. 807.

described as his personal duties on his own premises and whose work might normally be done by the employer's own servant. . . . On the other hand . . . I am of the opinion that he is not liable for the negligence of the manufacturer of an article which he has bought, provided that he has been careful to deal with a seller of repute and has made any inspection which a reasonable employer would make."

Almost the same facts occurred in *Taylor* v. *Rover Co. Ltd.*,[94] with the interpolation of a supplier of defective steel and the fact that the employer's foreman had discovered the defect but kept the drift in use. It was held that the manufacturer was not guilty of any failure to take reasonable care in respect of the supply of steel, but that the employer had been negligent. It was his failure to withdraw the tool which caused the injury.

It seems correct to regard *Davie's* case, therefore, as one in which the duty of care within the area of responsibility remained unassignable but the area of responsibility was not limitless. The employer may run an undertaking, and that undertaking may in turn depend on the functions of other undertakings without the employer becoming responsible for the performance of those functions.

In *Sumner* v. *William Henderson & Sons Ltd.*,[95] the employer had engaged an independent contractor to modernise his department store, the normal work of which was continuing. Consultant engineers had specified an electric cable which was installed by electrical contractors. Either the cable or its installation was faulty, and because of this a fire broke out. The fire spread rapidly, possibly owing to negligent building work carried out by a firm of building contractors under the supervision of architects. Some employees at the store died in the fire. It is difficult to follow the reasoning of Phillimore J. in the court of first instance, but he appears to say that on the basis of *Davie's* case the employer discharged his duty of care as regards the provision of a suitable material, namely an electric cable, but that he was in breach of the duty to provide safe premises.

The principle of *Davie's* case is not in doubt, but in its particular application it was felt to impose an unfair burden on the employee, who had to proceed against the supplier, who might be difficult to identify or bankrupt, or lose his remedy. The Employer's Liability (Defective Equipment) Act 1969,[96] applies to employers engaged in business (including the Crown). It provides that where an employee suffers personal injury *in the course of his employment* in consequence of a defect in equipment provided by his employer for the purposes of the employer's business, and the defect is attributable wholly or partly to the fault of a third party, the injury should be deemed to be also attributable to negligence on the part of the employer. This allows the employee primarily to proceed against his employer, leaving the latter to seek a contribution from the supplier. It is perhaps unfortunate that the provision is limited to injury in the course of employment, whereas normal employer's liability is not so confined. "Equipment" is defined in section 1 as including "any plant and machinery, vehicle, aircraft and clothing" though, again, only if provided for the purposes of the employer's business. It follows that domestic servants, gardeners, chauffeurs and the like are not normally included within the statutory extension. It appears also that the provision of "equipment" does not cover materials, nor such things as dangerous oils or abrasive powders. The manufac-

---

[94] [1966] 1 W.L.R. 1491.
[95] [1964] 1 Q.B. 450, set aside by the Court of Appeal on other grounds [1963] 1 W.L.R. 823.
[96] See Hepple, 1970 C.L.J. 25.

turer retains his liability both to the employer and to the employee. No agreement may effectively exclude the employer's personal liability,[97] so that there is no room for the operation of the defence of *volenti non fit injuria* which is based on implied contractual acceptance.

The student is often confused between the type of liability we have been discussing and vicarious liability, and the confusion is not resolved by some of the loose language of the courts.[98] The highly specialised statutory liability just mentioned is a form of strict liability, but even this can hardly be regarded as vicarious in any normal sense. The common law liability for the negligence of a delegate bears even less resemblance to vicarious liability. As has been pointed out, the employer is directly liable for a failure to discharge the duty of reasonable care which is imposed upon him personally. This confusion was explained in *Salsbury* v. *Woodland*.[99] An independent contractor had been engaged to fell a tree in the front garden of a house. By what Sachs L.J. described as a "near miracle of incompetence" the contractor felled the tree in such a way that, in falling, it brought down telephone wires across the road. The plaintiff, a bystander, was removing these wires when he saw a car approaching at considerable speed. He threw himself on the grass verge of the road to avoid the car, but because of a spinal defect, suffered severe injury. Widgery L.J. explained the distinction in the type of liability:

> "It is, of course, trite law that an employer who employs an independent contractor is not vicariously responsible for the negligence of that contractor. He is not able to control the way in which the independent contractor does the work and the vicarious obligation of a master for the negligence of his servant does not arise under the relationship of employer and independent contractor. I think it is entirely accepted that those cases—and there are some—in which an employer has been held liable for injury done by the negligence of an independent contractor are in truth cases where the employer owes a direct duty to the person injured, a duty which he cannot delegate to the contractor on his behalf."

The householder could not be vicariously liable as the employer of an independent contractor. There was no direct duty to ensure that care was taken as this situation was not one of the exceptional cases referred to by Widgery L.J., such as the commissioning of an extra-hazardous act[1] or the creation of a danger on the highway.[2] The court declined to extend this latter category to a danger near the highway so as to place a duty of care directly on the occupier.

(c) Causation

The courts must from all the "causes" which have led to the injury establish whether the negligence of the defendant can be said to be the "operative" cause. Many words are used in place of operative but none is more than a shorthand heading for the conclusion reached by the application of the principles of causation. "Causation," said Lord Shaw in *Leyland Shipping*

---

[97] s.1(2).
[98] See, *e.g. Wilson and Clyde Coal Co. Ltd.* v. *English* [1938] A.C. 57, *per* Lord MacMillan.
[99] [1970] 1 Q.B. 324.
[1] *e.g. Honeywill and Stein Ltd.* v. *Larkin Bros. (London's Commercial Photographers) Ltd.* [1934] 1 K.B. 191.
[2] *Holliday* v. *National Telephone Co.* [1899] 2 Q.B. 392.

Co. v. *Norwich Union Fire Insurance Society*,[3] is not a chain, but a net. . . . It is for the judge as upon a matter of fact to declare which of the causes thus joined at the point of effect was the proximate and which was the remote cause." In *Wayne Tank and Pump Co.* v. *Employers' Liability Corporation*,[4] for instance, the plaintiffs supplied to a company certain equipment which was unsuitable and likely, when operated, immediately to cause a fire. An employee of the company switched on the equipment and then negligently left the premises. It was held that the predominant cause of the resultant fire was the supplying of the equipment. Not all the aspects of causation can be considered here but some of these most relevant to employment will be dealt with.

Sole cause

It is, of course, normal for an industrial injury to be the result of negligence of a number of individuals, often linked by contract but otherwise independent tortfeasors.[5] In such a case the injured employee can bring an action against any or all of the tortfeasors for the whole of his damages, leaving the defendant to seek contribution from the other tortfeasors.[6] In many cases, however, it will be the injured employee who has been partly at fault and this situation is covered by the apportionment of blame under the doctrine of contributory negligence. Occasionally, however, the argument is advanced that though both employer and employee have been negligent, or in breach of a statutory duty, it was entirely the employee's breach of duty that caused the injury.

In *Stapley* v. *Gypsum Mines Ltd.*[7] S and D had been instructed jointly to bring down an unsafe roof. Both gave up the attempt and returned to their normal work. Subsequently the roof fell and killed S. The Court of Appeal held, that either the cause of the accident was the fact of S returning to work under the unsafe roof so that the causal negligence was not that of D at all—that is to say, the return of S was a *novus actus interveniens* breaking D's link with the injury—or, alternatively, that without the negligence of S the accident would not have happened, so that that negligence was the sole cause of the injury. No member of the House of Lords accepted this second argument. The majority took the view put clearly by Lord Tucker:

> ". . . so far as causation is in question it can make no difference whether Stapley or Dale was the person injured, nor can it matter whether Stapley was one of two, or one of a hundred men who acted in disobedience to the order. Each of them was guilty of a separate and independent act of negligence and breach of statutory duty which was a contributory cause of the accident."

The plaintiff was, in the result, held to be 80 per cent. to blame for the accident. The concept of the plaintiff being responsible for the sole cause of his injury was successfully advanced in *Ginty* v. *Belmont Building Supplies Ltd.*[8] In that case the defendant had provided crawling boards for roof work but they had not

---

[3] [1918] A.C. 350 at 369.
[4] [1974] Q.B. 57.
[5] See, *e.g. Clay* v. *A. J. Crump & Sons Ltd.* [1964] 1 Q.B. 533—followed in *Driver* v. *William Willett Ltd.* [1969] 1 All E.R. 665; *McArdle* v. *Andmac Roofing* [1967] 1 W.L.R. 356.
[6] Civil Liability (Contribution) Act 1978.
[7] [1953] A.C. 663.
[8] [1959] 1 All E.R. 414; See also *Kearney* v. *Eric Waller Ltd.* [1967] 1 Q.B. 29.

been used. Not only was the defendant under a duty to provide them, but both he and the plaintiff were under a duty to see that they were used. Although the failure to use the boards was entirely due to the plaintiff, the defendant had, therefore, broken precisely the same statutory duty as the plaintiff. Pearson J. said:

> "If the answer to that question [viz.: Whose fault was it?] is that in substance and reality the accident was solely due to the fault of the plaintiff, so that he was the sole author of his own wrong, he is disentitled to recover. But that has to be applied to the particular case and it is not necessarily conclusive for the employer to show that it was a wrongful act of the employee plaintiff which caused the accident. It might also appear from the evidence that something was done or omitted by the employer which caused or contributed to the accident; there may have been a lack of proper supervision or lack of proper instructions; the employer may have employed, for this purpose, some insufficiently experienced men, or he may in the past have acquiesced in some wrong behaviour on the part of the men. Therefore, if one finds that the immediate and direct cause of the accident was some wrongful act of the man, that is not decisive. One has to inquire whether the fault of the employer under the statutory regulations consists of, and is co-extensive with, the wrongful act of the employee."

He held that though the employer, through the employee, failed in his duty to use the boards, there was no other fault on his part. His fault, therefore, was entirely co-extensive with the causative fault of the employee and it would be wrong to impose any liability on him. This assessment was regarded by the Court of Appeal[9] as having been approved by the House of Lords in *Ross* v. *Associated Portland Cement Manufacturers Ltd.*[10] Certainly it recurs in a rather alarming form in *Horne* v. *Lec Refrigeration Ltd.*,[11] in which a toolsetter had been killed while working on a press which was insecurely fenced, in breach of the employer's duty under the Factories Act 1961. The toolsetter had failed to carry out the safety drill and this failure was held to be the sole cause of the accident. In this case it can hardly be said that the two breaches were co-terminous in the sense used in *Ginty's* case.[12] The writer suggests that, even more strongly than in *Ginty's* case, there is cause to hold that both breaches contributed to the injury, and that damages should have been apportioned.

Fault was plainly not coterminous in *Ross's* case although, surprisingly, both the court of first instance and the Court of Appeal had held that it was. Not only was proper equipment not supplied, as it had been in *Ginty's* case, but the employee had not been properly instructed, as had occurred in *Horne's* case, in the unusual job he was required to do. The effect of *Ross's* case upon sole cause is highly doubtful. The same cannot be said of the decision of the House of Lords in *Boyle* v. *Kodak Ltd.*[13] Once again both lower courts had held the plaintiff to be the sole cause of his injury, and once again the House of Lords

---

[9] *McMath* v. *Rimmer Bros. (Liverpool) Ltd.* [1962] 1 W.L.R. 1.
[10] [1964] 1 W.L.R. 768; see also *Boyle* v. *Kodak Ltd.* [1969] 1 W.L.R. 661; note in (1970) 33 M.L.R. 89—R. W. L. Howells.
[11] [1965] 2 All E.R. 898; see also *Quinn* v. *Green (Painters)* [1966] 1 Q.B. 509.
[12] In *Leach* v. *Standard Telephones and Cables Ltd.* [1966] 1 W.L.R. 1392; this was admitted but it was said that the accident, as distinct from the breach, was entirely the fault of the plaintiff.
[13] [1969] 1 W.L.R. 661.

affirmed the continuing existence of a defence of sole cause. In the light of the application to the facts, however, it seems that it will, in future, rarely succeed. The plaintiff had fallen off a ladder while painting the inside of an oil storage tank 30 feet high. He had actually been climbing up the ladder to secure it at the top when it slipped. Both he and his employer were under a duty[14] to see that the ladder was properly secure. The plaintiff could have carried out this duty by going up a fixed ladder on the outside of the tank and securing the inside ladder therefrom. Lord Reid said:

> "In my opinion . . . once the plaintiff has established that there was a breach of an enactment which made the employer absolutely liable, and that that breach caused the accident, he need do no more. But it is then open to the employer to set up a defence that in fact he was not in any way in fault but that the plaintiff employee was alone to blame."

He went on to say that a skilled practical man might easily fail to appreciate that he should have used the outside ladder and the employer should have given instructions to this effect. Lord Diplock pointed out that the mere fact that failure to give such instructions was not negligent did not mean that they were not necessary in fulfilment of the employer's statutory duty. It was, in his view, essential to the defence of sole cause that the plaintiff should know which precautions to take, and to this end, it made a vital difference whether the danger was obvious or not.

An example of what may remain of the principle of sole cause occurred in the earlier decision of *Quinn* v. *Burch Brothers (Builders) Ltd.*[15] which, because of the degree of knowledge involved, may have survived. The plaintiff was a sole contractor engaged on building work for the defendants. An implied term (the existence of which Sellers L.J. doubted) in his contract provided that the defendants should supply any necessary equipment. They failed to supply a step-ladder and, to avoid loss of time, the plaintiff used a trestle, which he knew to be unsuitable unless "footed." The trestle was not footed and it slipped. The defendant's foreman admitted that it was foreseeable that, in the absence of a ladder, the plaintiff might use an unfooted trestle, but it was held that the breach of the contractor's duty merely provided the occasion for the injury. The cause was entirely the omission of the plaintiff.[16] If the doctrine does survive where the plaintiff has sufficient knowledge and experience to avoid the effect of the employer's negligence but fails to do so, the law has again touched upon a reactivation of the doctrine of *volenti non fit injuria*.

Hypothetical cause

The search for causation has, however, thrown up a more dangerous proposition than that of sole cause. A number of decisions have accepted the proposition that the fault of the defendant was not the cause of the accident, which would have happened in precisely the same way without the default, because the plaintiff would not have taken advantage of the fulfilment of the defendant's duty. The decision about the plaintiff's possible actions is normally a speculative

---

[14] Imposed by regulation 29(4) of the Building (Safety, Health and Welfare) Regulations 1948.

[15] [1966] 2 Q.B. 370.

[16] Whatever may remain of sole cause the principle obviously does not apply where the employer is in independent breach of duty—*Stocker* v. *Norprint Ltd.* (1971) 10 K.I.R. 10.

one since, even if he is still alive, he is unlikely to admit that he would not have used a safety device had it been provided. In such circumstances, in *Roberts* v. *Dorman Long & Co. Ltd.*[17] the Court of Appeal held that, as safety belts had not been "provided" within the meaning of the statutory duty, it could not be said by the defendants that they would not have been used even had they been available. As the plaintiff had not been given a chance to elect, it could not be said that he was likely to elect only one way. The judgments were, however, cast in terms suggesting that, even had evidence been available, the defendants, having failed in their duty, would not be permitted to adduce it. In *McWilliams* v. *Sir William Arrol & Co. Ltd.*[18] the House of Lords approached the matter as one to be dealt with on the evidence. The plaintiff's husband, a steel erector, fell 70 feet to his death from an overhanging section of a steel tower that he was building. A safety belt would have prevented the fall but these had been removed from the site two or three days before the accident. The deceased had not been instructed, nor exhorted, to use a safety belt by the defendants, and it was not the practice of steel erectors to wear safety belts, even on work of this type. The trial court found that it was highly improbable that the deceased would have worn a belt had it been provided. Lord Reid said: "If I prove that my breach of duty in no way caused or contributed to the accident I cannot be liable in damages. And if the accident would have happened in just the same way, whether or not I fulfilled my duty, it is obvious that my failure to fulfil my duty cannot have caused or contributed to it." Viscount Kilmuir reached the same conclusion in *Wigley* v. *British Vinegars Ltd.*[19] despite the fact that the first instance judge in that case had inclined to the view that the window cleaner who was killed by the accident might have worn a safety belt had it been provided. Another example of the approach followed by the courts is to be found in the judgment of Sellers L.J. in *James* v. *Hepworth and Grandage Ltd.* He said[20]:

> "If everything had been done that could possibly have been done, if individual attention had been given to the workman and he had been asked to make his choice expressly whether he would wear spats or not, what are the probabilities as to what he would have done? Looking at the evidence as charitably as I can, and having regard to what others were doing and the fact that the workman himself did not inquire as to what the notice, which was there, said . . . and did not make any inquiries of his fellow-workmen who were wearing spats as to what they were for and why they wore them, and having regard to the large number who did not wish to wear spats, I think that on the probabilities . . . it is unlikely that the workman would have been wearing spats at the time."

The plaintiff was available in this case. Where he is not this process can rarely be given a more dignified title than guesswork.[21] In *Ross'* case[22] it was held that there was insufficient evidence to support an inference of non-user but, with

---

[17] [1953] 1 W.L.R. 942. See also *Nolan* v. *Dental Manufacturing Co. Ltd.* [1958] 1 W.L.R. 936—awarding damages despite a lack of evidence that goggles would have been worn if provided.

[18] [1962] 1 W.L.R. 295.

[19] [1964] A.C. 307. See also *Hay* v. *Dowty Mining Equipment Ltd.* [1971] 3 All E.R. 1136.

[20] [1968] 1 Q.B. 94 at 104.

[21] Proof of probability of use was accepted in *Baker* v. *White's Window and General Cleaning Co. Ltd., The Times,* March 1, 1962.

[22] [1964] 1 W.L.R. 768; see also *Herton* v. *Blaw Knox Ltd.* (1969) 6 K.I.R. 35.

respect, this is not a correct way of avoiding the injustice. Legally it is for the plaintiff to prove causation and so, if the issue is raised, he must prove that he would have made use of the safety precaution had it been available. In practice, however, it is most likely that the courts will tend to reverse the provisional burden of proof by accepting at its face value a contention that the safety measure would have been used.

(d) Remoteness

In questions of statutory liability it is sufficient to show a breach of duty, which caused or contributed to the injury. In negligence, however, the defendant is only liable if it can additionally be shown that it was reasonably foreseeable that his breach of the duty of care would lead to the type of injury which resulted.[23] What otherwise may be a *novus actus* can be foreseen as a stage in this process.[24] In any event, however, it seems that *The Wagon Mound* principle has been extended. In *Hughes* v. *The Lord Advocate*[25] the extent of injuries resulting from the negligence could not have been foreseen, save by the most vivid imagination, but they were injuries of a foreseeable type; namely, burns, and this was held sufficient. Likewise, in *Smith* v. *Leech Brain & Co. Ltd.*[26] a negligently caused burn from molten metal, splashing onto an employee's lip, set up cancer in tissues which already had a pre-malignant condition. The fatal effect of the cancer was held to be merely an extension of the injury foreseeably caused by the burn, and against which inadequate protection was provided and the plaintiff recovered damages. It is clear that this approach can extend to a situation where the foreseeable injury would not normally be regarded as injury at all. In *Bradford* v. *Robinsons Rentals Ltd.*[27] foresight would only have extended to discomfort from a low temperature and the contraction of a cold. Frostbite actually set in. This was held to be injury of the same kind so that damages were recoverable.

This reasoning must not be taken too far. In *Doughty* v. *Turner Manufacturing Co. Ltd.*[28] cauldrons of liquid metal were used in the defendant's factory to heat metal parts of machinery under construction. These cauldrons were covered with lids, made of asbestos cement, purchased from a reputable dealer. An employee accidentally knocked one of the covers into its cauldron. No one moved from the vicinity because no one realised, nor apparently could have realised, the likely consequence. The subjecting of asbestos cement to intense heat released moisture, and this moisture, rising to the surface of the cauldron, caused an eruption of the molten metal out of the cauldron, injuring the plaintiff

---

[23] *Overseas Tankship (U.K.) Ltd.* v. *Morts Dock and Engineering Co. Ltd.* [1961] A.C. 388; reaffirmed in *The Wagon Mound (No. 2)* [1967] 1 A.C. 617.
[24] See, *e.g. Hyett* v. *Great Western Rail Co.* [1948] 1 K.B. 345—protection of employer's property; *Baker* v. *T. E. Hopkins & Son Ltd.* [1959] 1 W.L.R. 966—doctor risking life to save another negligently endangered; *Billings & Sons Ltd.* v. *Riden* [1958] A.C. 240—respondent's knowledge did not absolve contractors who had blocked exit. Compare *Taylor* v. *Rover Co. Ltd.* [1966] 1 W.L.R. 1491.
[25] [1963] A.C. 837.
[26] [1962] 2 Q.B. 405.
[27] [1967] 1 W.L.R. 337.
[28] [1964] 1 Q.B. 518; see also *Tremain* v. *Pike* [1969] 1 W.L.R. 1556 which, it is suggested, is an incorrect application of the principle to the facts of the case.

who was standing nearby. The Court of Appeal considered it to be unrealistic to describe what happened as a type of foreseeable splash when the lid fell into the liquid.

DEFENCES

(a) Volenti non fit injuria

The defence of *volenti non fit injuria* is based on the principle that a plaintiff is prevented from complaining of the effects of a risk he has freely agreed to run. It springs from that contractual argument which produced the doctrine of common employment and beset the nineteenth century development of employer's liability.[29] There must be acceptance of the likelihood of a tortious act, not merely, nor indeed at all, of danger. So far as the law of employment is concerned, however, *volenti* did not have a long run. The defence was allowed in *Thomas* v. *Quartermaine*,[30] but immediately after, in *Baddeley* v. *Earl Granville*,[31] Wills J. expressed a doubt about its general applicability and established that it could not apply where the employer was in breach of his statutory duty.[32] In *Smith* v. *Baker & Sons Ltd.*[33] the majority of the court hesitatingly denied its application, but in a strong and typical dissenting judgment Lord Bramwell said:

> "It is a rule of good sense that if a man voluntarily undertakes a risk for a reward which is adequate to induce him, he shall not, if he suffers from the risk, have a compensation for which he did not stipulate. . . .
>
> It is said that to hold the plaintiff is not to recover is to hold that a master may carry on his work in a dangerous way and damage his servant. I do so hold, if the servant is foolish enough to agree to it. This sounds very cruel. But do not people go to see dangerous sports? Acrobats daily incur fearful dangers, lion tamers and the like. Let us hold to the law. If we want to be charitable, gratify ourselves out of our own pockets."

The cautious majority took the view that the plaintiff, assuming he appreciated the danger, did not, merely by continuing in work imply acceptance of the risk. On the strength of this view it is commonly said that this decision abolished *volenti* as an available defence in the ordinary employment situation. Lord Bramwell's analogies are only apposite to the implication of acceptance of ordinary risk. The acrobat accepts the ordinary risks of his job, which are high, but even he does not impliedly accept the enhancement of those risks by negligence. Further, he volunteers at the point of entry into employment and at that point has no idea of an injury through the employer's negligence. Knowledge of the risk is clearly essential.[34] However, knowledge alone does not imply acceptance of the risk.[35] In *Smith* v. *Baker*, however, the plaintiff

---

[29] *Clarke* v. *Holmes* (1862) 7 H. & N. 937.
[30] (1887) 18 Q.B.D. 685.
[31] (1887) 19 Q.B.D. 423.
[32] In *Wheeler* v. *New Merton Board Mills Ltd.* [1933] 2 K.B. 669, the Court of Appeal followed this decision. It was a view shared by Lord Pearce in *I.C.I.* v. *Shatwell* [1965] A.C. 656—but Lord Reid queried the position where the employer's statutory liability springs solely from the employee's wrongful act.
[33] [1891] A.C. 325.
[34] *Merrington* v. *Ironbridge* [1952] 2 All E.R. 1101.
[35] *Thomas* v. *Quartermaine* (1887) 18 Q.B.D. 685.

worked in a quarry at a spot where a crane swung heavy boulders above his head. He was occasionally showered with dirt and small stones from this operation and complained to the foreman, but went on working there. So the question of acceptance arose at a later stage when the negligence was known and his contractual "choice" was not to decline the job but to leave it. In the particular circumstances of that case it could hardly be said that the mere continuance of work implied acceptance, despite the other signs of non-acceptance. The same is true of *Bowater* v. *Rowley Regis Corporation*[36] which, however, is much stronger authority against the application of *volenti*. Scott L.J. said:

> "For the purpose of the rule, if it be a rule, a man cannot be said to be truly 'willing' unless he is in a position to choose freely, and freedom of choice predicates, not only full knowledge of the circumstances on which the exercise of choice is conditioned, so that he may be able to choose wisely, but the absence from his mind of any feeling of constraint so that nothing shall interfere with the freedom of his will. Without purporting to lay down any rule of universal application, I venture to doubt whether the maxim can very often apply in circumstances of an injury to a servant by the negligence of his master."

Such a principle could be construed narrowly. Lord Reid seemed to be doing this when in *Staveley Iron and Chemical Co. Ltd.* v. *Jones*[37] he suggested that the defence might have succeeded, if pleaded, in *Stapley* v. *Gypsum Mines Ltd.*[38] As we have seen earlier in this chapter a strict construction of the early part of this statement could let in those situations when the plaintiff had the knowledge and experience and the opportunity to avoid the effect of his employer's negligence, but neglected to do so. Generally, however, litigants have accepted the test in the spirit in which Scott L.J. applied it.[39] It may be that the long period of the eclipse of *volenti* can also be partly explained by the election of a plaintiff, in doubt about the application of *volenti*, to bring his action under the Workmen's Compensation Acts and abandon his right to sue at common law.

The availability of the defence was dramatically demonstrated, however, in *Imperial Chemical Industries* v. *Shatwell*.[40] The respondent was one of a team of three shot-firers. His employer had issued instructions that testing of detonating wires should be done from a place of shelter. This was in accordance with statutory regulations, which imposed a similar duty on the shot-firers themselves. One of the team went to obtain a longer cable so that it would stretch to the shelter, but the respondent and the respondent's brother, in his absence, decided to go ahead and test the circuit in the open. They were both injured by an explosion. The respondent brought an action against the employer claiming that he was vicariously liable for the negligence of the brother. The House of Lords pointed out that had the employer himself been in breach of his statutory duty, he could not have been allowed effectively to delegate it by pleading the

---

[36] [1944] K.B. 476.
[37] [1956] A.C. 627 at 644.
[38] [1953] A.C. 663—miners of equal status instructed to bring down unsafe roof left it and returned to work.
[39] *Taylor* v. *Sims and Sims* [1942] 2 All E.R. 375, where Lewis J., for no obvious reason, found *volenti* to exist, did not depend on this finding because the case revealed no negligence.
[40] [1965] A.C. 656.

implied contractual acceptance of the breach inherent in *volenti*. Had sole cause been used as an answer, or any form of apportionment for contributory negligence, the employer would inevitably have been liable to an action by the other brother vicariously for the assessed proportion of liability of the respondent.[41] Lord Pearce said:

> "The defence should be available where the employer was not himself in breach of statutory duty through the neglect of some person who was of superior rank to the plaintiff and whose commands the plaintiff was bound to obey (or who had some special and different duty of care, *e.g. National Coal Board* v. *England*,[42] where a miner was injured by the shot-firer firing the charge), and where the plaintiff himself assented to and took part in the breaking of the statutory duty in question. If one does not allow some such exception one is plainly shutting out a defence which, when applied in the right circumstances, is fair and sensible."

The judgment bristles with considerations of policy, some of them misconceived, as is that of Viscount Radcliffe who said that if the respondent and his brother were to be entitled to some damages this would deprive the employer of any reason to be vigilant, and the employee of a useful stimulus to prudence. In practice, few employees would be less careful because they thought they would receive compensation, let alone, say, one-fifth of that compensation, if injured, and management seems to be either safety conscious, or not, entirely irrespective of any payment of damages.

Unfortunately the intitial reaction of the courts to *Shatwell* seemed to be that the door of *volenti* had been opened again. It was allowed as a defence in one case,[43] and in another the judge would have done so had it been necessary. There are those who fear that if *volenti* became again well established as an available defence in this field all of the doctrine of common employment could be re-introduced in another form. If policy is to be openly considered it might be pointed out that employment does give rise to situations in which two employees spur each other on to negligence in order to take a short cut. Neither can be said to be entirely to blame and there is little reason in policy why the employer's insurance company should not bear some of the liability. It is suggested that this crack in the exclusion of *volenti* from the field of employment has been cured to some extent by the decision of the Court of Appeal in *Burnett* v. *British Waterways Board*,[44] that a lighterman sent by his employer to the defendant's dock had not freely and voluntarily incurred the risk of negligence despite his knowledge of a notice which said that he brought the barge in at his own risk.

The Unfair Contract Terms Act 1977 now prevents the exclusion or restriction of liability for death or personal injury resulting from negligence by any contract term or by a notice given to persons generally or to particular persons.[45] This only applies in a business context which will be the case in the field of employment law. The Act also expressly reinforces the principles of *volenti*

---

[41] The language used by Lord Pearce almost infers that this would have imposed total 100 per cent. liability on the employer but it is, of course, 100 per cent. out of 200 per cent.

[42] [1954] A.C. 403.

[43] *Bolt* v. *William Moss & Sons* (1966) 110 S.J. 385; *The Times*, April 29, 1966. *O'Reilly* v. *National Rail and Tramway Appliances Ltd.* [1966] 1 All E.R. 499 at 504.

[44] [1973] 1 W.L.R. 700.

[45] s.2(1).

by providing "where a contract term or notice purports to exclude or restrict liability for negligence a person's agreement to or awareness of it is not of itself, to be taken as indicating his voluntary acceptance of any risk." In other words, the defence of *volenti* is still theoretically available; but is not to be inferred merely from an employee's agreement to or awareness of the risk: there must be some other evidence of his voluntary acceptance of it.

(b) Contributory negligence

The Law Reform (Contributory Negligence) Act 1945[46] provides that where the fault of the person injured and of another contribute to the injury, the claim shall not be defeated but the damages recoverable shall be reduced to "such extent as the court thinks just and equitable having regard to the claimant's share in the responsibility for the damage." For the defence of contributory negligence there is no necessity for any breach of duty owed by the plaintiff to the defendant. The defendant need prove only that the plaintiff failed to take reasonable care for his own safety. Contributory negligence is a defence both to negligence and breach of statutory duty.

Standard of care

Just as the courts have insisted that in the determination of liability too strict a standard of care should not be asked of the workman[47] so they apply an even more moderate standard when determining whether there is contributory negligence. It is apparent from a number of decisions that an injured employee may be excused many errors of judgment, carelessness or inadvertence.[48] The courts take into account the pressures in an industrial situation.[49] In *Caswell* v. *Powell Duffryn Associated Collieries Ltd.*, a case concerned with breach of statutory duty, Lord Wright said:

"What is all important is to adapt the standard of what is (contributory) negligence to the facts, and to give due regard to the actual conditions under which men work in a factory or mine, to the long hours and the fatigue, to the slackening of attention which naturally comes from constant repetition of the same operation, to the noise and confusion in which the man works, to his preoccupation in what he is actually doing at the cost of some inattention to his own safety."

No such allowance can be made:

"where there is no evidence of workpeople performing repetitive work under strain or for long hours at dangerous machines."[50]

Before the 1945 Act the position at common law was that any degree of contributory negligence defeated a plaintiff's claim. For this reason, the courts were reluctant to find contributory negligence, and demanded of a plaintiff only a low standard of care in his own conduct. The standard required now is that of a

---

[46] See Fagelson (1979) 42 M.L.R. 646. "The Last Bastion of Fault? Contributory Negligence in Actions for Employers' Liability."

[47] See *Staveley Iron and Chemical Co. Ltd.* v. *Jones* [1956] A.C. 627 at 648; *Quintas* v. *National Smelting Co. Ltd.* [1961] 1 W.L.R. 401 at 408–409.

[48] *Caswell* v. *Powell Duffryn Associated Collieries Ltd.* [1940] A.C. 152.

[49] *Boothman* v. *British Northrop* 13 K.I.R. 112—employee on piece work.

[50] *Staveley Iron and Chemical Co. Ltd.* v. *Jones* [1956] A.C. 627, *per* Lord Tucker.

reasonable employee in all the circumstances but this does still, in practice, result in a reluctance by the courts to find contributory negligence. The employer is required to insure against liability for injuries to his employees.[51] If the defence of contributory negligence succeeds the plaintiff, who is unlikely to be insured will have to bear the reduction in damages personally. This, perhaps, is a factor which explains the low standard of care required of employees.[52]

An example of the attitude of the courts was provided in *Mullard* v. *Ben Line Steamers Ltd.*[53]

> "What he did . . . when stepping from a lighted into a dark compartment, with all the difficulties that can ensue when one goes from one state of light to another, was a momentary error, not to be judged too harshly when balanced against the defendants' flagrant and continuous breach of statutory duty. What happened was indeed exactly of the nature intended to be guarded against by the precautions prescribed by the regulations; and when a defendant's liability stems from such a breach the courts must be careful not to emasculate that regulation by the side wind of apportionment. However, the more culpable and continuing the breach of the regulation, the higher the percentage of blame that must fall on the defendant."

In the same way, in *Westwood* v. *The Post Office*[54] the majority of the House of Lords held that the employee was not guilty of contributory negligence (a) because he was a trespasser, or (b) because a notice forbade his presence, since the notice gave no warning of danger. In general, it was said, an employee was entitled to assume that the employer had complied with statutory obligations.

Apportionment

In assessing the degree of contributory negligence the court need not adopt a strictly mathematical approach but should take into account the degree of blameworthiness of the plaintiff. So in *Williams* v. *Port of Liverpool Stevedoring Co. Ltd.*[55] the plaintiff was one of six employees who all disobeyed orders and were thus equal contributors to the accident but the employer's vicarious liability for the other five was reduced by half.

Where the court finds that the plaintiff contributed to the injury it cannot use its discretion to make no reduction in the damages. As Stephenson L.J. explained in *Boothman* v. *British Northrop Ltd.*[56]

> "The words of section 1(1) of the Act of 1945 do not seem to leave much room for an application of the *de minimis* principle. But they certainly do not encourage and I very much doubt if they permit not a reduction to such extent as just and equitable but no reduction."

On the other hand the court may assess a 100 per cent. contributory negligence

---

[51] Employers' Liability (Compulsory Insurance) Act 1969.

[52] See Atiyah, *Accidents, Compensation and the Law* (3rd ed.) at p. 144; Fagelson (1979) 42 M.L.R. 646 where it is suggested that only the damages intended to compensate the employee himself should be reduced and not those for the employee's family.

[53] [1970] 1 W.L.R. 1414, *McPhee* v. *General Hotels Ltd.* (1970) 8 K.I.R. *McGuiness* v. *Key Markets Ltd.* (1973) 13 K.I.R. 249.

[54] [1974] A.C. 1.

[55] [1956] 1 W.L.R. 551.

[56] (1972) 13 K.I.R. 112 criticising previous dicta in *Hawkins* v. *Ian Ross Castings Ltd.* [1970] 1 All E.R. 180 and *Stocker* v. *Norprint Ltd.* (1971) 10 K.I.R. 10.

against the plaintiff if it considers that the employer should not bear liability for a purely technical breach.[57]

It has also been held to be within the principle of contributory negligence that the plaintiff, though in no way contributing to the accident has by his negligence, contributed to the degree of injury.[58] This is, of course, of considerable significance in the light of the large number of industrial injuries which are enhanced, or even wholly sustained, because of a failure to use safety devices.[59]

Discounting industrial injury benefits

In 1948 a compromise between the wishes of trade unions and those of employers was accepted whereby damages for negligence should be reduced by 50 per cent. of social security benefits arising as a result of the injury. It is proposed, to raise this discount to 100 per cent. after April 1984.

LIMITATION OF ACTION

The Limitation Act 1980[60] consolidates the law of limitation. It is provided by section 11 of the Act[61] that in an action for damages for personal injuries arising from negligence, nuisance or breach of duty the limitation period is three years from:

 (a) the date on which the cause of action accrued; or
 (b) the date of knowledge, if later, of the person injured.[62]

Personal injuries include any disease and any impairment of a person's physical or mental condition. When the person injured dies before the expiration of the three year period then the period of limitation in respect of an action for the benefit of his estate[63] is three years from the date of death or, if later, the date of knowledge of the personal representatives.[64] There is a similar provision for an action under the Fatal Accidents Act 1976.[65]

Date of knowledge

The cause of action in negligence accrues when the damage is suffered. This caused injustice in the case of plaintiffs who suffered damage from disease, such as pneumoconiosis, which did not become apparent for many years.[66] The "date of knowledge" provision is designed to remedy this injustice.[67] The date

---

[57] It will be rare to have 100 per cent. contribution where there has been a breach of statutory duty by the defendant: *McGuiness* v. *Key Markets Ltd.* (1973) 13 K.I.R. 249 but see *Cope* v. *Nickel Electro* [1980] C.L.Y. 1268.

[58] See, *e.g. O'Conell* v. *Jackson* [1972] 1 Q.B. 270—failure to wear a safety helmet; *Froom* v. *Butcher* [1975] 3 All E.R. 520—failure to wear a safety belt. These cases both concerned safety devices in road accidents. See also Gravells 93 L.Q.R. 581.

[59] *e.g. McWilliams* v. *Arrol* [1962] 1 All E.R. 623.

[60] The Act came into force on May 1, 1981.

[61] The Act must be pleaded for reliance to be placed on it: R.S.C. Ord. 18, r.8.

[62] Davies 98 L.Q.R. 249 *Limitations of the Law of Limitation* suggests replacing fixed periods with a complete discretion for the courts.

[63] Law Reform (Miscellaneous Provisions) Act 1934, s.1.

[64] s.12.

[65] s.13.

[66] *e.g. Cartledge* v. *Jopling* [1963] 1 All E.R. 341; applied in respect of property damage in *Pirelli* v. *Oscar Faber & Partners* [1963] 2 W.L.R. 6.

[67] It was first introduced by the Limitation Act 1963.

of knowledge is defined in section 14 of the Act as the date on which the person concerned first knew:

(a) that the injury in question was significant; and
(b) that the injury was attributable in whole or part to the act or omission which is alleged to constitute negligence, nuisance or breach of duty; and
(c) the identity of the defendant; and
(d) where it is alleged that the act or omission is that of some person other than the defendant, the identity of that person and the additional facts supporting the bringing of an action against the defendant.[68]

Knowledge that the acts or omissions did, or did not, as a matter of law, involve negligence, nuisance or breach of duty is irrelevant. Knowledge is extended to constructive knowledge as it includes knowledge which might reasonably be expected to be acquired from facts observable or ascertainable by the plaintiff or ascertainable with medical or other expert help which it would be reasonable to expect the plaintiff to seek. In *Simpson* v. *Norwest Holst Southern Ltd.*,[69] the plaintiff had no actual knowledge of the identity of the defendant employer where the company was one of a group and had given the plaintiff an incorrect name on payslips. The Court of Appeal held that he could not reasonably have been expected to acquire knowledge of the identity of his employer. Knowledge of a fact ascertainable only with the help of expert advice is not attributed to a person so long as he has taken all reasonable steps to obtain and to act on the advice.[70] An injury is treated as significant if the plaintiff would reasonably have considered it sufficiently serious to justify his instituting proceedings against a defendant who did not dispute liability and was able to satisfy a judgment.[71] Financial significance is important; personal factors are not treated as relevant as appears from *McCafferty* v. *Metropolitan Police Receiver*[72] where Geoffrey Lane L.J. said:

"It seems to be that sub-s. (7) (now s.14(2)) is directed at the nature of the injury as known to the plaintiff at that time. Taking *that* plaintiff, with *that* plaintiff's intelligence, would he have been reasonable in considering the injury not sufficiently serious to justify instituting proceedings for damages? I do not consider that it is permissible under s.2A (now s.14(2)) to look into such problems as whether it would have been politic in the circumstances for the plaintiff to sue his employers at that time for fear of losing his job."

A plaintiff's desire not to sponge on his employer was also held not a relevant factor in determining the significance of the injury.[73]

Discretion

Section 33 of the Act (first introduced by the Limitation Act 1975) gives a discretion to the court to override the time limits if it appears to the court that it would be equitable to do so having regard to the degree to which:

(a) the provisions of section 11 or 12 of this Act prejudice the plaintiff; and

---

[68] *e.g.* where the defendant is an employer who is vicariously liable so the additional facts might concern the scope of employment.
[69] [1980] 2 All E.R. 471.
[70] *Leadbitter* v. *Hodge Finance Ltd.* [1982] 2 All E.R. 167. [71] s.14(2).
[72] [1977] 2 All E.R. 756.
[73] *Buck* v. *English Electric Co. Ltd.* [1978] 1 All E.R. 273.

(b) any decision of the court under the subsection would prejudice the defendant.

In deciding whether to exercise this discretion the court is to have regard to all the circumstances of the case and in particular to[74]:

(a) the length of, and reasons for, the delay on the part of the plaintiff[75];
(b) the extent of loss of cogency of evidence because of the delay[76];
(c) the conduct of the defendant after the cause of action arose[77];
(d) the duration of any disability of the plaintiff after the cause of action arose;
(d) the extent to which the plaintiff acted promptly and reasonably once he knew he might have an action for damages;
(f) the steps, if any, taken by the plaintiff to obtain medical, legal or other expert advice and the nature of any such advice he may have received.

As Lord Diplock observed in *Thompson* v. *Brown*[78]: "These six present a curious hotchpotch." The delay referred to in (a) and (b) is the delay after the expiration of the primary limitation period.[79] The effect of the length of the delay depends on the type of injury. Apart from the six criteria expressed in the Act other factors may be taken into account. One which has been accepted as relevant is the existence of a right of action by the plaintiff against a third party; for example a possible action for negligence against solicitors.[80]

The availability of the discretion has given rise to a spate of recent cases. One question was whether the discretion was available in all cases or only in limited and exceptional cases. In *Firman* v. *Ellis*[81] the Court of Appeal had held that the statute:

"Confers on the Court an unfettered discretion to extend the three-year period in any case in which it considers it equitable to do so."

However, the House of Lords in *Walkley* v. *Precision Forgings Ltd.*,[82] limited the discretion to exclude cases where the plaintiff had commenced a first action wihin the normal limitation period. Lord Wilberforce said:

"He brought his first action within the normal limitation period, and if he has suffered any prejudice, it is by his own inaction and not by the operation of the Act."

Accordingly the discretion could not be exercised. This decision was followed by the Court of Appeal in *Chappell* v. *Cooper*[83] who applied *Walkley's* case to a

---

[74] See *Firman* v. *Ellis* [1978] 2 All E.R. 851 at 859 for background to this section.
[75] e.g. *McCafferty* v. *Metropolitan Police Receiver* [1977] 2 All E.R. 756; *Buck* v. *English Electric Co. Ltd.* [1978] 1 All E.R. 273; *Davies* v. *British Insulated Callendar's Cables Ltd.* (1977) 121 S.J. 203.
[76] *Walkley* v. *Precision Forgings* [1979] 1 W.L.R. 606; *Simpson* v. *Norwest Holst Southern Ltd.* [1980] 2 All E.R. 471.
[77] This conduct includes that of the defendant's advisors *Thompson* v. *Brown* [1981] 2 All E.R. 296.
[78] [1981] 2 All E.R. 296.
[79] *Ibid.*
[80] *Firman* v. *Ellis* [1978] 2 All E.R. 859; *Liff* v. *Peasley* [1980] 1 All E.R. 623; *Thompson* v. *Brown* [1981] 2 All E.R. 296.
[81] [1978] 2 All E.R. 857.
[82] [1979] 2 All E.R. 548.
[83] [1980] 2 All E.R. 463.

situation where a first writ had been issued but not served. The general availability and unfettered nature of the discretion, as expressed in *Firman* v. *Ellis*,[84] was reinstated in *Thompson* v. *Brown Construction*[85] by the House of Lords. The result is that the present state of the law is that once the plaintiff has shown prejudice by virtue of the primary three-year limitation period the court has an unfettered discretion to consider all the circumstances of the case.

With increased understanding of causes of long term injury suffered by employees at work the provisions of the Limitation Act have become of particular importance. The three tiers of rules provided for by the legislation are seen in action in the decision in *Buck* v. *English Electric Co. Ltd.*[86] The deceased had been employed between 1947 and 1957 in an iron foundry. Throughout that employment he knew of the existence of dust and the inadequacy of the masks provided to counteract it. He left that employment in 1957 because he was suffering from shortness of breath. In 1959 he was certified as suffering from pneumoconiosis. He first realised he had a cause of action in 1963 but as he was then in full-time employment and receiving a 20 per cent. disability pension he did not then consider a claim worthwhile. Between then and 1975, as his condition progressively worsened, he knew that claims had been brought against the employer by other employees whose circumstances were similar. In 1973 he was assessed as 100 per cent. disabled and had to give up work. He issued a writ in February 1975 and died in April 1975. The court held that a decision not to sponge upon his employer was not a legally valid reason for delay but that the extreme delay was not itself a reason to refuse to exercise the residual discretion to allow the action to proceed. The deceased had acted reasonably in not instituting proceedings but there was a presumption of prejudice to the defendants from a delay of more than five years. That presumption was, however, rebutted by the fact that the defendants had had to deal with a number of similar claims between 1963 and 1976 in that they had the evidence to enable them to defend the action. Accordingly it would be equitable in all the circumstances to allow the action to proceed.

VICARIOUS LIABILITY

It is well established that where an employee acting in the course of his employment injures another by tortious act, both employee and employer are liable for that tort.[87] It will be observed that since most employees are now employed by corporate bodies which usually act through other employees, the principle of vicarious liability comprehends virtually all an employer's liability to his employees. In some cases, where an employee is injured by reason of the negligence of another employee, the same set of facts may give rise both to direct liability and vicarious liability on the part of the employer. There are, however, many cases where it would be artificial to seek to impose liability on another employee so that the employer could in turn carry it.

Theoretical basis of vicarious liability

In a significant work (*Vicarious Liability in the Law of Torts*; Butterworth (1967)) Professor P. S. Atiyah examines the theoretical basis for vicarious

---

[84] [1978] 2 All E.R. 857.
[85] [1981] 2 All E.R. 296.   [86] [1978] 1 All E.R. 273.
[87] Civil Liability (Contribution) Act 1978 for contribution between them.

liability. He points out that there is not necessarily a lack of causal connection between the tortious act of the employee and the liability of the employer, since the latter will normally have created at least the basic situation from which the injury arises.[88] The doctrine, however, imposes liability without any necessary element of fault on the part of the employer. Any theory which tended to imply the employer's involvement in the sense of being in some way at fault, therefore, would be misplaced and would reduce the present scope of the doctrine. In the same way it would be wrong to look for the necessity for any authorisation, implied or otherwise, for the act which causes the injury, as distinct from the setting for that act. Nor does the doctrine rest on the contention that he who controls, or can control the activity must bear the liability for it. This would be an attractive conclusion since, as we have seen, control used to be the dominant aspect of the definition of a contract of service, which, throughout the whole of the second half of the nineteenth century was largely concerned with determining on whom to fix this liability. We shall see, moreover, that even today, where an employee is lent to another, vicarious liability more readily attaches to the person who actually controls the employee's actions than he with whom the contract of employment exists, whichever definition of that contract is applied. If control were the principal reason for the imposition of vicarious liability, however, the doctrine should extend to parents, teachers and many independent contractors, none of whom, at present, bears such liability.[89]

A number of other reasons for the doctrine have been discussed from time to time, including the concept that he who takes the benefit of a situation must assume the risk of liability arising from it. In *Ilkiw* v. *Samuels*[90] Diplock L.J. spoke in terms of delegation. "If he delegates the performance of the acts which give rise to this duty to his servant he is vicariously liable if the servant fails to perform it. In this sense he may be said to delegate the duty though he cannot divest himself of it, as his continuing vicarious liability shows." This seems a highly improbable basis for the doctrine of vicarious liability since it applies equally to direct liability for negligence. Again, it has been said that as the employer has the power of dismissal he must assume liability, if he does not acquaint himself with the position and apply necessary sanctions. Much vicarious liability arises, however, from the unforeseeable act of a thoroughly reliable servant for whom, even after the event, dismissal would not be a practical remedy. In any event the decision to dismiss is dependent on so many factors that the social implications of linking it to vicarious liability would be very undesirable. Finally, a significant jurisprudential concept of group liability based on group enterprise is advanced for making group funds liable. This is more realistic, but Professor Atiyah rejects each of these reasons in turn. He suggests that together they provide a satisfactory theoretical basis for the doctrine even if no one or more of them has consistently and consciously been adopted by the courts as a legal explanation. Perhaps, however, Willes J. was not far wide of the real reason for the doctrine when he said[91]:

---

[88] In *Rose* v. *Plenty* [1976] 1 All E.R. 97 at 103 Scarman L.J. spoke of the employer putting things in motion.

[89] See, *e.g. Morgans* v. *Launchbury* [1973] A.C. 127 in which the doctrine was held not to apply as between the owner of a car and the driver who drove it negligently.

[90] [1963] 1 W.L.R. 991 at 1005.

[91] *Bayley* v. *Manchester, Sheffield and Lincolnshire Railway* (1872) L.R. 7 C.P. 415.

"A person who puts another in his place to do a class of acts in his absence, necessarily leaves him to determine, according to the circumstances that arise, when an act of that class is to be done, and trusts him for the manner in which it is done; and consequently he is held answerable for the wrong of the person so instructed either in the manner of doing such an act, or in doing such an act under circumstances in which it ought not to have been done; provided that what was done was done, not from any caprice, but in the course of employment."

Whatever the theoretical basis, as Atiyah says, there is plenty of practical justification for the doctrine. If the individual employee had alone to bear liability for his torts in the course of employment he would be forced to insure himself. The cost of this would presumably be reflected in his wages, so that the employer would indirectly be paying the premium, as he now does directly. However, the process of separately insuring numerous units would not only be less economic but would certainly require a statutory system of enforcement in the interests of the injured party, such as prevails in the case of motor vehicles at the present time. Under the influence of vicarious liability the employer is almost invariably sued in preference to the employee, despite the extra burden of establishing that the tort was committed in the course of employment. In consequence, as a matter of sound business practice, the employer generally carries adequate insurance. He is required by statute to insure against liability to his employees.[92] Before the Act was passed some small and impermanent employers failed to insure.[93]

Finally it may be noted that there are good reasons for not extending liability to most of the various relationships to which one or other of the above theoretical arguments might equally apply. In the case of independent contractors operating under a business contract,[94] however almost all these arguments apply with as much force as they do in the case of the employer/employee relationship, provided that one is prepared to take a broader and more realistic view of control such as has been applied to determine the existence of employment. It is suggested that there is a good case for extending vicarious liability to a main contractor for his sub-contractor and, in turn, the sub-contractor's employees.[95] The present practice is to impose liability on a sub-contractor, but not on a main contractor. This gives rise to many practical problems, such as difficulty of identification of the tortfeasor and lack of insurance.

It should be noted that, whatever the logic of confining liability to an employee/employer or similar situation, the opportunity to extend the doctrine was decisively rejected by the House of Lords in *Morgans* v. *Launchbury*.[96]

---

[92] Employers' Liability (Compulsory Insurance) Act 1969, *infra*.

[93] *Donaghey* v. *Boulton & Paul Ltd.* [1967] 2 All E.R. 1014.

[94] See *Ormrod* v. *Crosville Motor Services Ltd.* [1953] 1 W.L.R. 1120, where liability was imposed for an "agent" who was effectively an independent contractor. See also the discussion on this point in *Nottingham* v. *Aldridge* [1971] 2 Q.B. 739. Vicarious liability for an independent contractor was said in *Jolliffe* v. *Willmett & Co.* [1971] 1 All E.R. 478 not to exist.

[95] The real difficulty, in practice, would be to know how to define the conditions in which the contract was to be considered to be in the course of the business of the main contractor rather than a purely private arrangement upon whch vicarious liability would be unduly burdensome.

[96] [1973] A.C. 127; owner of car not vicariously liable for driver.

Transfer of liability

It is said that vicarious liability will follow the relationship of employer and employee. It is not proposed to discuss again the tests for establishing this relationship.[97] In the rare case alleging vicarious liability, where the issue arises of whether the original tortfeasor was an employee at all, similar tests will be applied. Nor can the employer avoid liability by an arrangement with the employee, or anyone else, since that cannot be binding on an injured person.[98]

Questions concerning which of two possible employers is the actual employer who should bear vicarious liability usually arise when a person, normally employed by A, commits a tort whilst working for B, to whom A has lent his services. Students often become confused at this point, imagining that the courts require a change of the parties to the employment relationship to be shown to have occurred. In reality, however, the question is not whether A or B is, in legal terms, the employer, since almost always the primary employer will retain that relationship.[99] Rather, the issue is whether the borrower has placed himself in such a position that he, instead of the primary employer, should bear liability.[1] In the leading case of *Mersey Docks and Harbour Board* v. *Coggins and Griffith Ltd.*[2] three of the members of the House of Lords make it plain that this was what they were concerned to determine, although in *Garrard* v. *Southey (A. E.) & Co.*[3] Parker J. appeared still to be looking for a transfer of employment. The liability in the *Mersey Docks* case arose from the negligent operation of a crane and the question for the purpose of vicarious liability was taken to be who controlled the manner of performing that operation. As Lord Uthwatt said:

> "The workman may remain the employee of his general employer, but at the same time, the result of the arrangements may be that there is vested in the hirer a power of control over the workman's activities sufficient to attach to the hirer responsibility for the workman's acts and defaults and to exempt the general employer from that responsibility."

In this case such control was held not to have passed because, when lending a crane, A would expect to retain control over the manner of its operation, and so over the operative. This approach received strong support in *Denham* v. *Midland Employers' Mutual Assurance Ltd.*[4] Denning L.J. pointed out that in *Nokes* v. *Doncaster Amalgamated Collieries Ltd.*[5] it had been held that the contract of employment is personal and cannot unilaterally be assigned, so that

---

[97] See Chap. 1.

[98] He can, of course, contract with another for an indemnity in the event of his being sued vicariously—see, *e.g. Arthur White* v. *Tarmac Civil Engineering* [1967] 1 W.L.R. 1508.

[99] In *Smith* v. *Blandford Gee Cementation Co. Ltd.* [1970] 3 All E.R. 154, a Divisional Court said that the evidence needed to show a new contract is not as heavy as that needed to show a transfer of employment. This was a redundancy case. Assuming that by transfer of employment was meant the transfer necessary for purposes of vicarious liability it seems that the proposition should be reversed.

[1] These two sentences were quoted with approval by the E.A.T. in *Cross* v. *Redpath Dorman Long (Contracting) Ltd.* [1978] I.C.R. 730.

[2] [1947] A.C. 1.

[3] [1952] 2 Q.B. 174; see also McNair J. in *Johnson* v. *A. H. Beaumont and Ford Motor Co.* [1953] 2 Q.B. 184.

[4] [1955] 2 Q.B. 437, followed in *Gibb* v. *United Steel Co. Ltd.* [1957] 1 W.L.R. 668.

[5] [1940] A.C. 1014.

it would be necessary for the employee to consent to the formation of a new contract. He took the view that any question of transfer was merely a convenient explanation for the fixing of liability. He said:

"I see no trace of a contract of service with [the borrower] except the artificial transfer raised by the law so as to make [the borrower] liable to others for his faults or liable to him for their own faults; and I do not think the artificial transfer so raised is 'a contract of service' within this policy of assurance."

In *Chowdhary* v. *Gillot*[6] Streatfield J. said that there was a presumption against transfer of employment, as distinct from the use of services, apparently inferring that the first would, but the second would not, carry vicarious liability. This would seem incorrect, and the statement is in any event unhelpful. It is worth observing, however, that in *Century Insurance Co. Ltd.* v. *Northern Ireland Road Transport Board*[7] the House of Lords, though looking for a transfer of control, spoke as if they were doing so in order to discover a transfer of the master/servant relationship.[8] The onus of proof that there has been a sufficient transfer of control lies with the primary employer.[9] It is clear that this burden is a heavy one.[9a] In *Bhoomidas* v. *Port of Singapore Authority*[10] the Privy Council held that the burden on the Port Authority, the primary employer, had not been discharged. It was not proved that the employee whose services had been hired out to a shipowner came under the entire and absolute control of the shipowner.

It may be noted that if the injury is caused by the execution of authorised orders given by borrowers they would probably become liable. This liability would be direct not vicarious.[11] In *Savory* v. *Holland*[12] Lord Denning M.R. added that, where a servant is lent with a machine or is sent out as a skilled man to do work for another, the general rule is that he remains the servant of the general (primary) employer throughout. Presumably this would be because an employer lending his own equipment would not wish to transfer sufficient control of the operator.[13] In the case of a skilled man, evidence of the passing of a sufficient degree of control for the purpose of establishing vicarious liability, could not be adduced simply because, in practice, no such control was exercised even by the primary employer. In other words, the rule that vicarious liability passes when control passes has run into the usual difficulties, experienced in determining employment, about the existence of the reality of control. It is difficult to see, however, what else could replace control as an indication of the passing of vicarious liability, as distinct from the passing of the employment relationship. At least this approach avoids the need to talk of "master and servant *pro hac vice*," as if some magic transference lay in those words, or,

---

6 [1947] W.N. 267.

7 [1942] A.C. 509.

8 See particularly the judgment of Lord Wright.

9 *Gibb* v. *United Steel Co. Ltd.*, *supra*.

9a *O'Reilly* v. *I.C.I. Ltd.* [1955] 1 W.L.R. 1155; *Mersey Docks and Harbour Board* v. *Coggins and Griffith Ltd.* [1947] A.C. 1.

10 [1978] 1 All E.R. 956.

11 See *Mersey Docks and Harbour Board* v. *Coggins and Griffith Ltd.* [1947] A.C. 1.

12 [1964] 1 W.L.R. 1158 at 1163.

13 *i.e.* the existence of a loan of machinery is evidence of an intention not to transfer control as MacKenna J. said in *Ready Mixed Concrete Ltd.* v. *Minister of Pensions and National Insurance* [1968] 2 Q.B. 497.

perhaps, to cover the fact that control is being used for a purpose other than establishment of the employment relationship.[14] At least a test of control has some meaning in practice, unlike the question of whose business the servant is engaged upon, when plainly he is normally on the business of both lender and borrower; unless it were possible to develop this logically to hold both vicariously liable.[15]

In *Garrard* v. *Southey (A. E.) & Co.*[16] Parker J. was concerned with determining direct liability of an employer for the safety of his servant. He suggested that a different test should apply where a third party is injured and seeks to establish vicarious liability, since the duty lies on the general employer in this case to provide a skilled man, whereas, when the workman himself is injured, liability rests on him who controls the work and so could have stopped the injury. This shows that the burden of proving transfer of control in the first situation is a heavy one, nevertheless, the distinction is not a valid one. In the case of vicarious liability one is not attempting to discover which of two possible employers owed a duty to the injured third party and, conversely, in the case of direct liability, there would be little the general employer could reasonably do even if he still owed a duty, as indeed he probably does. The better view of the modern trend is that it is inclined to bring direct and vicarious liability together rather than to produce insubstantial distinctions to separate them.

The more valid criticism of the confusion the above cases reveal is that, though, for whatever reason, it is well established that vicarious liability depends on the existence of a master/servant relationship, there is no real reason why the courts should assiduously have searched for such a relationship in those cases dealing with direct liability, unless we are to perpetuate the idea that negligence liability depends on a classification of relationships. The search should not be for which of two *employers* owe a duty of care but for which of two people owe such a duty. This is the same process as that which does apply when considering questions of direct liability. In *O'Reilly* v. *I.C.I.*,[17] it seems to have been assumed that a finding that there was no master/servant relationship between plaintiff and defendant automatically meant that there was no duty of care.[18] But this attitude cannot now be supported. It may well be that the same tendency to render the actual technicalities of the relationship unimportant should, and will, spread to vicarious liability.

It would follow from the presumption against transfer that Lord Macmillan was wholly correct to suggest[19] that *Donovan* v. *Laing, Wharton and Down Construction Syndicate*,[20] in which it was held that a hirer who gave instructions on how the work was to be done assumed vicarious liability, will not now be followed. On the other hand, some of the economic effects of this very severe test, by which the company who control the site and the method of work may appear not to be liable for those working on it, have recently become apparent. In the case in point, they were avoided because the person injured was also working on the site, so that the plaintiff recovered against the hirer on the basis

---

[14] See Diplock L.J. in *Savory* v. *Holland, supra,* at 1163.
[15] Atiyah advances this solution.
[16] [1952] 2 Q.B. 174.
[17] [1955] 1 W.L.R. 1155.
[18] See Diplock L.J. in *Savory* v. *Holland* [1964] 1 W.L.R. 1158 at 1163.
[19] In *Mersey Docks and Harbour Board* v. *Coggins and Griffith Ltd., supra.*
[20] [1893] 1 Q.B. 629.

of the hirer's direct but not vicarious liability. It would be much more difficult to apply this solution to injury to parties who are not employed by, nor working for, any of the defendants. In *McArdle* v. *Andmac Roofing*,[21] on a site under the supervision of P's building department and owned by P, employees of N, a labour-only sub-contractor, were laying joists and boards over part of a roof originally covered by skylights. They were working ahead of the plaintiff, an employee of A, who was a specialist sub-contractor, and who was laying felt and bitumen over the boards. N's employees, without warning went for their lunch break leaving a portion of the roof uncovered and unguarded. The plaintiff, necessarily walking backwards pouring bitumen from a bucket, fell through this hole, sustaining very severe injuries. Sellers L.J. said that N's employees were as nearly the employees of P as they could be without there being a temporary transfer, but that the requisite heavy burden of proof prevented a finding that there had been the necessary degree of transfer. He suggested that the House of Lords in the *Mersey* case might not have understood sufficiently the economic advantages of permitting the easier recognition of such a transfer. As it was, the Court of Appeal was able to hold that P had retained control of the operations, and so owed a direct duty of care to workmen engaged on them. It will be possible for the court to extend this form of direct liability a long way into transfer situations so long as the injury takes place on the transferee's premises, or to some extent, outside them. This prompts the question whether the continued widening of negligence liability will not eventually render vicarious liability unnecessary.[22] In effect, therefore, both employers (or rather, in this case, all three), were held liable on varying grounds. Atiyah[23] suggests that the obvious solution to the problem of transfer would be to hold both employers to be vicariously liable, but he agrees that it is clearly established in this country that this will not be done. As he later suggests,[24] this failure throws the burden of inquiry on to the injured workman, rather than permitting him to get compensation from one or other, leaving them to apportion liability between themselves. Against this must be set the fact that the cost of hire probably includes a sum for the general employer's insurance so that, in practice, if the hirer is made liable he will have to pay twice. It may be remarked that he probably now pays twice in some cases, since, unless his lack of liability is certain, he will, in practice, insure himself as well. In any event such a problem merely begs the question of who should bear which of the burdens of carrying out an industrial process. Talk of paying twice because of insurance, even though that insurance may be compulsory, is irrelevant.

"Course of employment"

Having established who is to bear the vicarious liability, it is then necessary to show that the tortious act was committed "in the course of employment," inasmuch as an employer will not be held vicariously liable unless it is. The test stated in *Salmond on Torts*[25] is as follows:

> ". . . the master is responsible for acts actually authorised by him; for liability would exist in this case, even if the relation between the parties was merely one of

---

[21] [1967] 1 W.L.R. 356; but compare *Baxter* v. *Central Electricity Generating Board* [1965] 1 W.L.R. 200.

[22] See *Smith* v. *Vange Scaffolding and Engineering Co. Ltd.* [1970] 1 W.L.R. 733.

[23] *Vicarious Liability in the Law of Torts,* pp. 156–158.

[24] *Ibid.* p. 163.   [25] (18th ed.), pp. 437–438.

agency, and not one of service at all. But a master, as opposed to an employer of an independent contractor, is liable even for acts which he has not authorised, provided they are so connected with acts which he has authorised that they may rightly be regarded as modes—though improper modes—of doing them. . . . On the other hand, if the unauthorised and wrongful act of the servant is not so connected with the authorised act as to be a mode of doing it, but is an independent act, the master is not responsible; for in such a case the servant is not acting in the course of his employment, but has gone outside of it."

It is unfortunate that Salmond uses the word "act" to describe both the situation authorised by the employer and the wrongful act of the servant within that situation. Nevertheless, the passage makes clear the two separate stages of the inquiry. At the first stage it must be asked what the employer has expressly, impliedly or apparently authorised. At the second stage it must be asked whether the action of the employee which caused the injury was a mode of carrying out the authorised conduct, even though a wrongful mode.[26] The act of the employee will rarely be authorised and may even be directly contrary to his employer's instructions, but authorisation of this stage is irrelevant. So the decision in *Poulton* v. *London and South Western Railway*[27] is based on misleading considerations. It was there held that a railway company, whose powers depended on statute and did not include a power to arrest for non-payment of sums due for carriage of goods, could not be vicariously liable when its station master detained a passenger on suspicion that the latter had not paid for transporting a hourse to an agricultural show. The court assumed that the act for which authorisation was required was the arrest. In fact, at its narrowest it was probably the collection of unpaid fares, the arrest being merely a wrongful manner of carrying out the authority.

Prohibitions

An express prohibition going to the sphere of employment will, therefore, prevent vicarious liability. If the prohibition relates only to the mode of performance, the employer will remain liable. An example is to be found in the case of *Rose* v. *Plenty*[28] in which a milkman was employed. He was expressly prohibited from engaging children to assist him on his milk round and also from giving lifts on the milk float. Scarman L.J. considered the prohibitions and held:

> "There was nothing in those prohibitions which defined or limited the sphere of his employment. The sphere of his employment remained precisely the same after as before the prohibitions were brought to his notice. The sphere was as a roundsman to go round the rounds delivering milk, collecting empties and obtaining payment. Contrary to instructions, this roundsman chose to do what he was employed to do in an improper way. But the sphere of his employment was in no way affected by his express instructions."

It follows also that the question of whether the act is in the employer's interest is not of primary importance. If the underlying situation has nothing to do with

---

[26] Compare, *e.g. Morris* v. *C. W. Martin & Sons Ltd.* [1966] 1 Q.B. 716 with *Leesh River Tea* v. *British India Steam Navigation Co. Ltd.* [1967] 2 Q.B. 250.

[27] (1867) L.R. 2 Q.B. 534.

[28] [1976] 1 All E.R. 97; *Stone* v. *Taffe* [1974] 1 W.L.R. 175.

the employer's interest it is unlikely to be regarded as authorised. If it has, and is authorised, an act within it but completely contrary to the interest of the employer or entirely for the servant's benefit will, nevertheless, render the employer vicariously liable. Diplock J. in *Hilton* v. *Thomas Burton (Rhodes) Ltd.* [29] even foresaw that the authorised situation could arise from permission to do something solely for the benefit of the employee. An act in the employer's interest is not conclusive evidence of the existence of the underlying authority necessary for vicarious liability. [30] Nevertheless it has long been accepted that the existence of action in the employer's interest is evidence of an apparent authority, [31] and as we shall see the existence of such an interest is now taken virtually to raise a presumption of action in the course of employment.

Possibly because of the fact that everything turns, not on the immediate act, but on whether the act is within the permitted sphere of employment, one finds a widely divergent approach by the courts in individual cases to the question of the extent of the permitted scope of the employment. If, at the present time, the courts are appearing to favour a very wide scope indeed, it is worth remembering that such an approach was adopted in the early case of *Limpus* v. *London General Omnibus Co.* [32-33] but was not, subsequently, consistently maintained. In *Limpus'* case the defendant's bus driver, in the days when the horse-drawn buses of competing companies raced from stop to stop for custom, had caused an accident by deliberately driving his vehicle across the path of that of the plaintiff, despite the fact that he had been expressly forbidden to cause an obstruction by his manner of driving. A remark of Willes J. about secret instructions suggests that the court may have been influenced by a feeling that the prohibition was more apparent than real, but the case was decided solely on principle. The driver was employed to drive to convey passengers and that is what he was doing, however wrongful the manner adopted.

At one extreme it could have been said that he was employed to drive and that did not include obstruction, thus excluding from the authorised situation the act in question. The authorised situation could have been narrowly limited, as it was later in *Joseph Rand* v. *Craig.* [34] Certain carters were employed to take rubbish to the contractor's dump. They were expected to take three loads a day and were paid a bonus if they took a fourth. They were strictly forbidden to tip the rubbish elsewhere than on the dump. Some of the carters turned off the road on the way and deposited their load on the plaintiff's land, adjacent thereto. At first instance it was held that they were not in the course of their employment because what they did was entirely for their own benefit and without any regard to, or intention of, carrying out the job for which they were employed. As has been said, the second part of this proposition is not in itself a sufficient basis to establish absence of a course of employment.

The Court of Appeal upheld the decision but placed it on the sound but narrow ground that the carters' authority was not to transport rubbish, but

---

[29] See *Century Insurance Co. Ltd.* v. *Northern Ireland Road Transport Board* [1942] A.C. 509.
[30] See *Performing Right Society* v. *Mitchell and Booker (Palais de Danse) Ltd.* [1924] 1 K.B. 762.
[31] *Rose* v. *Plenty* [1976] 1 All E.R. 97; *Kooragang Investments Ltd.* v. *Richardson & Wrench Ltd.* [1981] 3 All E.R. 65 P.C.
[32-33] (1862) 1 H. & C. 526.
[34] [1919] 1 Ch. 1.

solely to transport it from and to defined places. The actual decision, though apparently too restrictive, may be correct in that, though employed, the carters were engaged on a casual basis and one would not expect the employer to vest in them the degree of discretion which might normally be allowed to an employee.

Extent of implied authority

At the other extreme the authority may be considerably added to by implication. In *Ilkiw* v. *Samuels*[35] the authority of a lorry driver was held to cover not only driving but also looking after his lorry. In allowing another person into the cab to drive the lorry he was negligently carrying out his authorised employment.

The extent of authority to exercise discretion will, of course, vary with the type of job. In theory one might also expect that it would vary with the quality of the employee, but there is little sign that the courts consider this as a relevant factor. In *Smith* v. *Martin and Kingston-upon-Hull Corporation*[36] Fletcher Moulton L.J. said that a school teacher would have a wide discretion in small matters, arising out of her quasi-parental position to her class, so that it was in the course of her employment to send a child to poke the fire in the staff room. In *Weaver* v. *Tredegar Iron and Coal Co. Ltd.*[37] Lord Porter emphasised that there was such an area of discretion in most employment: "The man's work," he said, "does not consist solely in the task which he is employed to perform, it includes also matters incidental to that task. Times during which meals are taken, moments during which the man is proceeding towards his work from one portion of his employer's premises to another, and periods of rest may all be included. Nor is his work necessarily confined to his employer's premises."[38]

In view of the above, the decision on assize, in *Crook* v. *Derbyshire Stone Ltd.*[39] is, perhaps, another of those which would have been better not reported. A lorry driver, implicitly permitted to stop for food on long journeys, was held not to be in the course of employment when he was re-crossing the road to a café for breakfast after having retrieved the keys from the dashboard of his parked lorry. The court held that he had no further duty to perform on his master's account until he returned to the lorry. It appears from this that the court in *Staton* v. *National Coal Board*[40] were correct to distinguish *Crook's* case on the ground that the relevant fact was that the crossing of the road was not in the employer's interest. As we have seen, when considering the actual act, this should not be a decisive factor and one would have thought that, if Crook was employed to transport goods for the defendant, having breakfast was an incidental act within the discretionary area of his authority. In *Staton's* case, the plaintiff was cycling on his employer's premises to collect his pay. The employer has a duty to see that an employee receives his pay, but to draw a line based on the existence of such a duty would be highly impractical. Presumably, if Crook

---

[35] [1963] 1 W.L.R. 991.

[36] [1911] 2 K.B. 775; see also *Bayley* v. *Manchester, Sheffield and Lincolnshire Railway Co.* (1873) L.R. 8 C.P. 148.

[37] [1940] A.C. 955 at 990.

[38] But see *Vandyke* v. *Fender* [1970] 2 Q.B. 292 where Lord Denning M.R. emphasised that going to or coming from work along a public road would not be considered in the course of employment unless there was an obligation to travel in the particular vehicle.

[39] [1956] 1 W.L.R. 432.

[40] [1957] 1 W.L.R. 893.

had carelessly left his engine running he would, if such a consideration were all important, have remained in the course of employment.

The continuing attempts of textbook writers to accommodate this decision by strained explanations must be deplored as confusing. *Crook's* case stands entirely alone in its severity, if not in the irrelevance of the basis on which it was decided. As the courts move to adopt wider approaches it becomes so isolated as to be best forgotten. The narrow decision in *Crook's* case could not possibly be reconciled with the width of the scope of employment found by the Court of Appeal in *Navarro* v. *Moregrand Ltd.*[41] In that case the landlord's agent demanded a premium of £225 for the grant of a lease without having either actual or ostensible authority. The payment of the premium was illegal by statute. The landlord was held liable to return the premium as the demand was merely an improper method of letting the property. Denning L.J. held:

> "He had no actual or ostensible authority to do an illegal act. Nevertheless, he was plainly acting in the course of his employment because his employers, the landlords, had entrusted him with the full business of letting the property, and it was in the very course of conducting that business that he did the wrong of which complaint is made."

In *Hilton* v. *Thomas Burton (Rhodes) Ltd.*[42] the plaintiff's husband was one of a party of demolition workers who had the use of a van to travel from the firm's base to a particular site. On the day in question they had done singularly little work but had used the van for several journeys to a public house some miles from the site. The accident in which the plaintiff's husband was killed occurred through the van driver's negligence on the way back from the last of these journeys to the site to pick up one of the gang before returning to base. It is unfortunate that the court thought that the employer was being kind when he said that they had his authority to use the van in this fashion and so, despite its willingness to take a broad view, held that the negligence was no part of the authorised employment. In fact he was probably speaking only the truth since, in some sections of the demolition industry, the employer fixes a certain time limit for the destruction of a building and is not greatly concerned when the job is done within that time, nor what happens meanwhile.

The court apparently did not realise that the industry in question permitted a wholly exceptional latitude far outside the normal range of discretion as to working time, but otherwise was prepared to take a very broad view. It was with reluctance therefore, that Diplock J. felt constrained to dismiss the claim.

The modern approach

All these decisions, however, were outstripped by that in *Kay* v. *I.T.W. Ltd.*[43] It is obvious that no decision on whether an act is committed during the course of employment can be arrived at by merely taking the act in question and the description of the employment and comparing the two.[44] All the elements

---

[41] [1951] 2 T.L.R. 674.
[42] [1961] 1 W.L.R. 705; see also *L.C.C.* v. *Cattermoles (Garages) Ltd.* [1953] 1 W.L.R. 997; *Nottingham* v. *Aldridge* [1971] 2 Q.B. 739.
[43] [1968] 1 Q.B. 140; followed in *East* v. *Beavis Transport* [1969] 1 Lloyd's Rep. 302.
[44] See *Harvey* v. *O'Dell Ltd.* [1958] 2 Q.B. 78. What a man has a contractual obligation to do, and to do carefully, may be much more narrow than the course of his employment.

of the authorised employment and of the act itself are relevant to the decision, and in a large number of cases such matters as that the employee was on his employer's premises and that the act was in his employer's interest have been considered relevant.[45] In *Kay's* case, one Ord was employed in a warehouse to drive trucks and small vans. He was returning to the warehouse intending to leave in it the fork-lift truck that he was driving when he found a five-ton diesel lorry standing on the ramp leading up to the warehouse doors, with its back against those doors. The plaintiff was standing at the back of the lorry helping to unload it. Ord entered the cab of the lorry, intending to move it out of his way. When he started the engine, the lorry moved backwards because the normal driver had left it in reverse gear to prevent it running down the slope if the handbrake failed to hold. The plaintiff was injured. Sachs L.J. said:

> "Once, however, it is conceded that Ord was doing something in his working hours, on his employers' premises, and when seeking to act in his employers' interests, and that, moreover, his act had a close connection with the work which he was employed to do, it seems to me that the onus shifts to the employers to show that the act was one for which they were not responsible."

This decision in turn appears to have been overtaken by *Compton* v. *McClure*.[46] The defendant, who was late for work, drove his car too fast on the wrong side of the factory road and injured the plaintiff who was emerging from a doorway opening on to that road. The employer had taken all reasonable precautions to prevent accidents of this type but was held vicariously liable because the defendant was on the employer's premises for the employer's purposes.

The emphasis on the act of the employee being for the purpose of the employer's business seems to have been the principal factor leading a majority of the Court of Appeal in *Rose* v. *Plenty*[47] to decide in favour of the existence of vicarious liability. A milk roundsman had been expressly prohibited from employing children to perform his job and from giving lifts on the milk float. Contrary to these instructions he invited a boy aged 13 to assist him. The boy was injured due to the negligence of the milkman and brought an action against the employer. Lord Denning M.R. said:

> "In considering whether a prohibited act was within the course of employment it depends very much on the purpose for which it is done. If it is done for the employer's business, it is usually done in the course of his employment."

In *Stone* v. *Taffe*[48] the manager of a public house was held to be acting in the course of his employment at 1 a.m., two and a half hours after his licensed closing time, when he negligently failed to see that a stairway was properly lighted for a customer who had only recently finished drinking. This suggests that if an employee, without the knowledge of his employer extends his working hours he may remain within the scope of his authority, provided, at least that he is performing his ordinary work in that extended time.

This brings us to a position akin to that created by the doctrine of *res ipsa loquitur* in virtually establishing from certain facts a presumption of activity

---

[45] *e.g. Staton* v. *N.C.B., supra; Weaver* v. *Tredegar Iron and Coal Ltd., supra; Kay* v. *I.T.W. Ltd., supra. cf. Nottingham* v. *Aldridge* [1971] 2 Q.B. 739.
[46] [1975] I.C.R. 378.
[47] [1976] 1 All. E.R. 97.   [48] [1974] 1 W.L.R. 175.

within the course of employment. In the recent case of *Kooragang Investments Pty.* v. *Richardson & Wrench Ltd.*[49] the facts did not lead to this conclusion. The Privy Council held that the employee, Rathbone, acted outside the scope of his employment in making valuations. Lord Wilberforce considered the factors.

> "In the present case, the respondent did carry out valuations. Valuations were a class of acts which Rathbone could perform on their behalf. To argue from this that any valuation done by Rathbone without any authority from the respondents not on behalf of the respondents but in his own interest, without any connection with the respondent's business, is a valuation for which the respondents must assume responsibility is not one which principle or authority can support. To endorse it would strain the doctrine of vicarious responsibility beyond breaking point and in effect introduce into the law of agency a new principle equivalent to one of strict liability."

Assaults by employees

That there is still a point at which implied authority stops is, however, demonstrated by the decision of the Privy Council in *Keppel Bus Co. Ltd.* v. *Sa'ad bin Ahmed.*[50] A bus conductor had been rude to an elderly lady who wished to get off the bus and the respondent had remonstrated with the conductor. Although restrained by the other passengers from coming to blows, the conductor continued to abuse the respondent who, at one point, stood up to ask the conductor to stop being insulting and then sat down again. Thereafter the conductor struck the respondent with his ticket punch causing loss of sight in one of the respondent's eyes.

The Privy Council held that a jury would only be entitled to find that an act had been done in the course of employment if the employee's act had been done within his delegated authority as part of his duty to the employer. It was accepted by the court that the keeping of order among the passengers was part of the duties of a conductor but the Privy Council held that the conductor was not acting within his authority.

> "Their Lordships are of the opinion that no facts have been proved from which it could be properly inferred that there was present in that bus an emergency situation calling for forcible action, justifiable on any express or implied authority with which the appellants could be said on the evidence to have clothed the conductor."

There are also dicta to suggest that vicarious liability will not be established where the plaintiff knows or should know, of the limits of the employee's authority.[51] It appears that this proposition is limited to a restriction on the scope of authority. It could not logically extend to a limitation as to the manner in which authorised work should be done. If so confined, however, the proposition appears to be unexceptionable.

It is often said[52] that the excessiveness of the wrongful act may be sufficient to take it outside the class of authorised action. In *Poland* v. *Parr.*[53] where a carter

---

[49] [1981] 3 W.L.R. 493.
[50] [1974] 1 W.L.R. 1082.
[51] *Iqbal* v. *London Transport Executive* (1974) 16 K.I.R. 329; *Stone* v. *Taffe* [1974] 1 W.L.R. 1575.
[52] See Scrutton L.J. in *Poland* v. *Parr and Sons* [1927] 1 K.B. 236 at 243; see also *Pettersson* v. *Royal Oak Hotel Ltd.* [1948] N.Z.L.R. 136.   [53] [1927] 1 K.B. 326.

going home from work struck a child he believed to be stealing sugar from his master's cart, causing the child to fall under the wheel of a following cart, the act was held not so excessive. In *Daniels* v. *Whetstone Entertainments and Allender*,[54] it was held, on the other hand, that there had been sufficient excess. The plaintiff, a visitor to a dance hall, had been struck by a steward inside the hall because the steward mistakenly thought that the plaintiff had first struck him. The dispute was pursued outside the hall until the manager ordered the steward to return to his duties. Instead of doing this the steward first pursued someone else up the road, and then, returning, again struck the plaintiff, who was talking to a young lady. The question of assault by someone employed *inter alia* to maintain order has been considered in two well-known Commonwealth cases.[55] It is much easier to construe such an act, even if motivated by a desire for private vengeance, as within the course of employment than was the assault in *Warren* v. *Henleys Ltd.*,[56] which again was an act of private vengeance, but which had no connection with the work of a petrol pump attendant.[57] In *Daniel's* case, however, though the first assault was almost certainly in the course of employment, the court took the view that the steward's conduct immediately before the second assault was so excessive as to remove that assault from the course of his employment. This is not to say, however, that skylarking may not and indeed frequently will be, in the course of employment.[58] Atiyah[59] points out that this exception is illogical since once a situation is in the course of employment the excessiveness of the employee's response cannot remove it. If it was otherwise the whole basis of vicarious liability for unauthorised or forbidden acts would be attacked.

One commentator[60] has distinguished cases of employees' assault from all other areas of vicarious liability, and has shown that though an employer's vicarious liability is very wide where the employee has authority to use force, it is very narrow where he has no such authority. This, as the writer concedes, begs the question of when force may be considered to be authorised. The question is often one of the extent to which the act which forms the basis of the complaint can be separated from the performance of his employment. Clearly an assault at work by an employee upon his wife's lover (Mr. Rose's example) is more easily treated as an act separate from the employment than the lighting of a match in order to smoke a cigarette while pouring petrol for his employer.[61]

The correct approach

A warning should be given concerning a confusion that arose between vicarious liability and the duties of care in the two cases of *Twine* v. *Bean's Express Ltd.*[62] and *Conway* v. *George Wimpey*.[63] In view of the clarifying

---

[54] [1962] 2 Lloyd's Rep. 1.
[55] *Pettersson* v. *Royal Oak Hotel Ltd.* [1948] N.Z.L.R. 136—barman throwing glass at customer; *Carlson* v. *Hotel West Ltd.* [1950] 2 W.W.R. 129—bar waiter hitting back at drunk customer.
[56] [1948] W.N. 449. Compare *Dyer* v. *Munday* [1895] 1 Q.B. 742.
[57] It might have been otherwise if the attendant had still thought that the van driver had not paid for his petrol.
[58] See *Baker* v. *Snell* [1908] 2 K.B. 825.   [59] *Vicarious Liability*, p. 212.
[60] F. D. Rose, "Liability for Employee's Assaults," (1977) 40 M.L.R. 240.
[61] *Century Insurance Co. Ltd.* v. *Northern Ireland Road Transport Board* [1942] 1 All E.R. 491.
[62] [1946] 1 All E.R. 202.
[63] [1951] 2 K.B. 266.

remarks in *Young* v. *Edward Box & Co. Ltd.*,[63a] it is suggested that these cases could best have been forgotten.[64] Most textbooks have, however, devoted disproportionate space to them, even fitting them into a theory of liability and, at the risk of doing the same thing, it seems necessary to dispose of them. Both cases concerned the unauthorised giving of a lift to a third party. In *Twine's* case the driver although expressly prohibited from doing so gave a lift to the plaintiff. Uthwatt J., at first instance, stated as the basis of the plaintiff's claim that the employer owed the plaintiff a duty of care, and that this duty was to be performed by the employee driver. It was then a short step to hold that the driver could not extend the duty so as to cause it to be owed to an unauthorised person, otherwise the employer's duty would verge on one to the world at large. Uthwatt J. expressed the duty in these terms:

> "The general question in an action against the employer such as the present is technically—'Did the employer in the circumstances which affected him owe a duty?'—for the law does not attribute to the employer the liability which attaches to a servant."

This approach and the decision that the driver was not in the course of his employment, were affirmed by the Court of Appeal.[65] The case is, therefore, concerned with an entirely different theory of vicarious liability, namely, that the fact that a servant's liability is usually the same as the employer's is purely a coincidence, which really depends on the assumption that the master himself commits a tort. It is suggested that the end result may frequently be the same, but *Twine's* case is an indication that such a theory will sometimes lead to confusion.

In *Conway's* case the only detailed consideration was given in the judgment of Asquith L.J. He adopted the same attitude of considering whether it was within the scope of the driver's employment to bring unauthorised persons within the employer's duty of care. He concluded:

> ". . . I should hold that taking men other than the defendant's employees on the vehicle was not merely a wrongful mode of performing an act of the class which the driver in the present case was employed to perform, but was the performance of an act of a class which he was not employed to perform at all."

It should have been obvious when his logic led him to this conclusion, that he was on the wrong track, since the act of taking the man into the vehicle was not the cause of the injury.

It may be argued jurisprudentially that vicarious liability is a recognition of the employer's own duty. The confusion introduced by these two cases indicates that, whether this should be the case, it is not so. Vicarious liability, it is suggested, does not depend on any breach of a duty of care by the employer, but on a breach of a duty of care by the employee,[66] for whom the employer

---

[63a] [1951] 1 T.L.R. 789 (C.A.).

[64] They were considered yet again in *Rose* v. *Plenty* [1975] 1 C.R. 430 and form the basis of the difficulty experienced by Lawton L.J.   [65] (1946) 62 T.L.R. 458.

[66] This is not always made very clear: *Electrochrome Ltd.* v. *Welsh Plastics Ltd.* [1968] 2 All E.R. 205; Rose (1977) 40 M.L.R. at 430 suggests that vicarious liability could now readily be ignored when the employer is in contractual relationship with the plaintiff. This, of course raises the age-old problem of the forms of action. Vicarious liability arises in the course of an action for the tort of the employee. There may well be an action in contract against the employer upon an implied duty of care just as there may be an action directly against the employer for his own negligent breach of a duty of care. To confuse the three, it is suggested, will lead to complete uncertainty in the law.

assumes liability. This is seen in the judgment of Denning L.J.[67] where he resorted to the standard explanation of the basis of vicarious liability which is to be preferred:

> "In every case where it is sought to make a master liable for the conduct of his servant the first question is to see whether the servant was liable. If the answer is yes, the second question is to see whether the employer must shoulder the servant's liability."

This, it is submitted, was the basis of the decision in *Rose* v. *Plenty*,[68] and the result of that case is that the appoach in neither *Twine's* case nor *Conway's* case will be applied in future. Lawton L.J. (dissenting) opined that insurers had proceeded on the basis that these two cases were properly decided and it would be unfortunate if the Court of Appeal departed from them save on good and clear grounds. It is submitted that there can hardly be a clearer ground than their inherent illogicality. In this respect it is unfortunate that neither Denning M.R. nor Scarman L.J. was prepared to declare the earlier decisions wrong. Scarman L.J. indeed, seems to have been in danger at one point of similar illogicality when he distinguished the situation of Rose by saying that *he* was on the float to assist the milkman in his job.

Liability of employer occupier

There is, of course, no reason why a case against an employer should not also involve his liability as an occupier, just as it may involve direct liability for negligence, but neither of these was an issue in these three cases. Very little difference exists, however, in the duty to those lawfully on the premises.[69] In the case of those not lawfully there the House of Lords, in *British Railways Board* v. *Herrington*[70] held that the duty was that of common humanity, a lower standard of care than the ordinary negligence standard of reasonable care. As Lord Reid said:

> "An occupier's duty to trespassers must vary according to his knowledge, ability and resources. . . . It would follow that an impecunious occupier with little assistance at hand would often be excused from doing something which a large organisation with ample staff would be expected to do."

Rather oddly it seems that the servant of an occupier,[71] not being himself the occupier, appears to owe a duty of reasonable care to a trespasser, as distinct from the duty of common humanity. His employer would be vicariously liable for a breach of that higher duty.[72] The position is unclear following *Herrington's* case as doubt was cast on this refusal to take into account the status of a trespasser.[73]

---

[67] [1951] 1 T.L.R. 789 at p. 793. He adheres to this simple distinction in *Rose* v. *Plenty* [1975] I.C.R. 430 but refrains from declaring the previous decisions to be wrong.

[68] [1975] I.C.R. 430.

[69] Occupiers' Liability Act 1957.

[70] [1972] 1 All E.R. 749.

[71] The same would apply to a contractor.

[72] See *Genys* v. *Matthews* [1966] 1 W.L.R. 758; *Davis* v. *St. Mary's Demolition Co. Ltd.* [1954] 1 W.L.R. 592; *Buckland* v. *Guildford Gas Light and Coke Co.* [1949] 1 K.B. 410 and compare *Mourton* v. *Poulter* [1930] 2 K.B. 183.

[73] By Lords Wilberforce and Pearson.

Compulsory insurance

The Employers' Liability (Compulsory Insurance) Act 1969[74] requires that every employer (except a nationalised industry or local authority) carrying on any business in Great Britain shall maintain insurance against liability for bodily injury or disease sustained by his employees arising out of and in the course of their employment in that business in Great Britain. The penalty for failing to comply is a fine of £500 a day which also falls on any director, manager, secretary or other officer of the company with whose consent or by whose connivance or facilitation the offence has been committed.

Regulations made under the Act[75] prohibit the inclusion in such policies of certain specified clauses excluding the liability of the insurer.[76]

The required amount of cover is £2 million for claims relating to one or more employees arising out of any one occurrence. Copies of the certificate of insurance must be displayed at the place of business and may be inspected by authorised inspectors.

Lord Wilberforce in *Jobling* v. *Associated Dairies*[77] was willing to take into account the fact of insurance.

> "In the present case, and in other industrial injury cases, there seems to me no justification for disregarding the fact that the injured man's employer is insured (indeed since 1972 compulsorily insured) against liability to his employees. The state has decided, in other words, on a spreading of risk."

---

[74] The Act came into force on January 1, 1972 (S.I. 1971, No. 1116).
[75] S.I. 1971, No. 1117.
[76] *i.e.* the requirement that some specified thing to be done or omitted to be done after the happening of the event giving rise to a claim under the policy; the policy holder taking reasonable care to protect his employees in the course of their employment; compliance by the policy holder with the requirements of any safety statute; the keeping by the policy holder of specified records or the availability to the insurer of information therefrom.
[77] [1981] 1 All E.R. 752 at 755.

CHAPTER 13

INDUSTRIAL DISABLEMENT BENEFIT

ALTHOUGH legislation may seek to induce safety consciousness so as to reduce the risk of injury at work it is unlikely that it will succeed in eliminating that risk. As we saw in the last chapter lump sum compensation by way of damages will be available if fault can be established. This leaves the question of making a reasonably comprehensive provision for all who are economically dependent on their ability to earn wages in return for work.

The first Workmen's Compensation Act of 1897 imposed on the employer an obligation to pay compensation in respect of industrial injury to his employees without the necessity that fault should be shown, and ultimately, in some instances, obliged him privately to insure against the risk of having to do so. The injured worker, however, had to elect between accepting this compensation and pursuing a common law claim. The amount of compensation payable on total or partial incapacity was expressed as a weekly sum, based on average earnings during the previous 12 months or such lesser period as the workman had been with that employer. The workman was entitled to compromise a disputed claim in return for a lump sum payment. It was alleged that this allowed numerous unwise compromises and that the resultant lump sum, which seemed to many workers at first to be large, was often misapplied. Although the compromise sum was carefully scrutinised, it was alleged that the amount was often inadequate.

In the event of the death by industrial injury of a workman his dependants might claim a lump sum compensation, which was not to exceed £700.

The system, which operated through the county courts in the event of a dispute, tended generally to provide reasonably speedy payment of compensation. The involvement of insurance companies, however, gave rise to a great deal of case law on appeal from those courts. Arbitration was always subject to review on a point of law. There was immense scope for litigation upon the provision that was made in such words and phrases as "accident" and "arising out of and in the course of employment."

The risks covered were similar to those now provided for in Chapter IV of the Social Security Act 1975. There is no doubt that the legislation of 1946 represented a compromise between conflicting views as to what scheme of accident insurance was desirable. It avoided complete abolition of fault-based liability and failed to include within the scope of national insurance the consequences of all accidents.

The Report of the Royal Commission on Liability for Injury[1] published in 1978 reveals that there is still no significant official move towards consideration of a system of total insurance. That Report recommended extension of the national insurance scheme to road accidents but expressed itself as satisfied in general with a dual system of national insurance and fault-based compensation. The recommendations in the field of industrial injury insurance amount to little more than the alteration of some details.

---

[1] Cmnd. 7054.

Benefits

The two principal classes of benefit available under this system before 1982 were industrial injury benefit and industrial disablement benefit. The first covered a period of absence from work because of an industrial injury which was no different in kind from absence from work due to sickness. There is a lot to be said for maintaining the distinction. Sickness is a common hazard whereas industrial injury, by definition, is linked to work. Originally it had been intended to maintain a marked distinction in rates of benefit but by 1982 industrial injury benefit was only 12 per cent. more than sickness benefit. In 1982, therefore, industrial injury benefit was abolished[2] and measures introduced to eliminate differences in the rules applicable to sickness and injury benefit. [2a] The Statutory Sick Pay scheme introduced in April 1983 provides for payment of rates of benefit, dependent on earnings bands, for any day of incapacity for work. A day of incapacity for work is any day when the employee is, or may be deemed to be, incapable, by reason of some specific disease or bodily or mental disablement, of doing work which he can reasonably be expected to do under his contract.[3] No payment is due for the first three days of incapacity.[3a] Thereafter the employer will be responsible for making the payments for the first eight weeks.

Disablement benefit is not available until after 90 days (disregarding Sundays) beginning with the date of the relevant accident.[4] Before 1982 an employee would transfer to disablement benefit if and when he established that he was permanently disabled, and in any case after 156 days. The reduction constitutes 90 days not only as the maximum, but also as the minimum, qualifying period so that a claimant will have to rely on sick pay for that period notwithstanding permanent disablement. Disablement benefit is assessed on the basis of a table of deemed percentage loss. It is proposed in 1984 to withdraw benefit from those with less than 10 per cent. disablement and to reduce amounts available for loss of less than 40 per cent., while increasing amounts above 60 per cent. A lump sum is paid for less than 20 per cent. disablement. A weekly pension is paid for 20 per cent. disablement and over.[5] Entitlement to disablement benefit has normally followed upon entitlement to injury benefit—though this is not necessary. Presumably the same will remain true of entitlement to sickness benefit.

Industrial Death Benefit is currently payable to a widow or dependent widower either previously residing with a person who has died as a result of an industrial accident or prescribed disease or to one who was receiving, or entitled to receive, periodical payments from such a person.[6] A widow's but not a dependent widower's—entitlement ceases on remarriage when she receives a gratuity of 52 times her weekly entitlement.[7] It is proposed to abolish this benefit from April 1984.

---

[2] Social Security and Housing Benefits Act 1982.
[2a] *e.g.* Social Security and Housing Benefits Act 1982, s.39 inserting a new section 50A into the 1975 Act.
[3] *Ibid*. s.1.   [3a] *Ibid*. s.5(1).
[4] Social Security and Housing Benefits Act 1982, s.39.
[5] Social Security Act 1975, s.50(2).
[6] *Ibid*. s.67. In the latter case the amount of benefit shall not exceed the amount of such payments.
[7] *Ibid*. s.67(2).

These entitlements may be supplemented by allowances for children, wives and dependent relatives. Industrial disablement benefit may be supplemented either by an *unemployment supplement* or a *special hardship allowance*. The first is available where, as a result of the loss of faculty, the claimant is, and is likely to remain, incapable of work yielding earnings of more than a specified amount.[8] The second is available where the claimant, though not incapable of any work, is incapable of following his regular employment or a suitable occupation of an equivalent standard.[9] "Regular employment" does not include a former ancillary occupation but it does include a prospect of advancement.[10] Where disability is assessed at 100 per cent. and the claimant requires constant attendance a *constant attendance allowance* may be added to the disability benefit[11] and an *exceptionally severe disablement allowance* is also payable.[12]

A claimant will be disqualified from benefit while absent from Great Britain or detained in legal custody. He also may be disqualified, usually for a maximum of six weeks, for behaving in such a manner as is calculated to retard his recovery, or for failure to give certain notifications within the specified time,[13] or for failure without good cause to comply with the requirements of relevant regulations,[14] or for wilful obstruction of, or misconduct in connection with, any examination or treatment required under regulations.[15] Claims for disablement and death benefit must be made normally within three months.[16]

Industrial disablement

Benefits are payable in respect of an employed earner who has "suffered personal injury caused . . . by accident arising out of and in the course of his employment,"[17] or where such a person suffers from any of a number of diseases prescribed by reference to specific industrial operations which are likely to give rise to them.[18] There is a rebuttable presumption that an injury in the course of employment arises out of employment. Nevertheless it will become apparent that not every accidental loss of earning power will produce entitlement to benefit. There is a surprising degree of legalism in provisions which were designed simply to compensate for inability to work.

Personal injury

A personal injury must be one to the living body. "Damage to some artificial appendage, such as spectacles, false teeth, a wig or an artificial limb, may well

---

[8] s.59.
[9] s.60(1).
[10] s.60(3). If it does so the supplement should begin on the date of the anticipated advancement and not at the date of onset of the disablement R(I) 10/63. On the question of what constitutes a less advantageous job see R(I) 10/73.
[11] s.61.
[12] s.63.
[13] s.90(1).
[14] s.90(1)2(*a*).
[15] s.90(2)(*b*). See also National Insurance (Industrial Injuries) Hospital In-Patients Regulations 1971 (S.I. 1971 No. 1440).
[16] Claims and Payments Regulations, para. 13 and Sched. I; a late claim involves loss of benefit for days outside these periods, unless good cause for the delay can be shown.
[17] s.50(1).
[18] ss.76–78. In examining Commissioners' decisions the student must realise that the absence of a system of precedent produces a wholly different and more flexible approach. In respect of almost any "rule" that is formulated, what would be considered in law to be inconsistent decisions can be found.

cause incapacity for work, but such damage cannot . . . constitute 'personal injury.'"[19]

Accident

An accident is consistently defined as "an unlooked-for mishap or an untoward event which is not expected or designed" by the person injured. Moreover, "it signifies an event which, although it may be one of several similar events, is capable of being reasonably clearly identified as the cause of the trouble."[20] Very often, of course, the existence of an injury will reveal that there has been an accident, but this is not always so.[21] It is possible, however, to register the happening of an accident even if no ill effects arise.[22] It was pointed out in the decision just cited that whereas there need be no external mishap, nor even an unusual incident, but merely an internal physiological change (a confusion again of accident and injury), there must be a particular moment of occurrence, whether or not such a moment can be pinpointed in time. Talk of a particular moment, however, must not be taken too strictly. Lord Porter in *Roberts* v. *Dorothea Slate Quarries*, said[23]: "There must . . . come a time when the indefinite number of so-called accidents and the length of time over which they occur take away the element of accident and substitute that of process." Thus, whether the injury results from the development of a situation or a series of situations, the time necessary to establish the process is, as a matter of practice, regarded more as a matter of weeks than of minutes. It may be noted that this word by word approach to interpretation of the formula is not inevitable. There is no reason why it should not have been construed as referring to an "accidental injury" thus concentrating attention on the development of the incapacity rather than the events which produced it. It is submitted, however, that the balance of authority on this particular point is against this construction. It appears from the judgment of Lord Macnaghten in *Fenten* v. *Thorley and Co.*[24] that though he referred to accident and injury as interchangeable and as constituting a compound expression this has only been applied so as to permit the existence of injury to raise the presumption of an accident. In *Brinton Ltd.* v. *Turvey*[25] for instance, the House of Lords took contraction of anthrax as indication of an accident but still found it necessary to pinpoint the occasion on which that accident occurred as an event separate from the incapacity. This approach inevitably meant that an approach of injury which was undeniably gradual would not qualify for benefit.[26]

It is clear that a series of identifiable events, such as the frequent lifting of heavy weights, may constitute an accident, or perhaps a series of accidents, each being a contributory factor in the eventual injury.[27] Lack of identifiability will tend to indicate a process. This has been taken to such a point that if it cannot be said whether the injury resulted from one of a series or the series as a whole it

---

[19] R(I) 7/56.
[20] R(I) 52/51.
[21] See R(I) 7/73.
[22] National Insurance Act 1972, s.5(2)(*b*).
[23] [1948] W.N. 246; adopted in C.I. 257/49.
[24] [1903] A.C. 443.   [25] [1905] A.C. 230.
[26] See, *e.g. Steel* v. *Cammell, Laird Ltd.* [1905] 93 L.T. 357.
[27] C.I. 29/49; R(I) 31/56.

may be said to be the result of a process.[28] Contraction of the muscles of the hand as the result of persistently gripping a knife and chisel has been held to be the result of a process,[29] as has the development of disease from unhealthy working conditions.[30] There has developed, however, a tendency to reduce the operation of this distinction between process and accident by extending the period of time over which an accident may be considered to occur.[31]

There is often a tendency, having drawn such a distinction as that between "accident" and "process," subsequently to behave as if that distinction were embodied as part of the statutory definition. Thus tribunals and courts have on occasions been led to define the word "process."[32] The Pearson Commission, however, whilst making some suggestions for minor extensions of the concept of industrial disease propose no fundamental improvement of this exercise in legalism.

Sometimes it is possible to pick a point of time in a disabling process which can be said to be the point of disablement and, therefore, an accident. So a claimant, issued with wellington boots which were too small, found that they rubbed his ankle. After two weeks the skin over an old injury there broke, and he was incapacitated by the development of an ulcer. It was held that the accident was the breaking of the skin.[33]

If there are two succcessive accidents, the second of which produces the disability and is not an industrial accident, it may still be shown that the second accident is merely an outcome of the first, industrial, accident. It will not, however, suffice to show merely that it was a contributory cause.[34]

Even with these general principles in mind, it may seem that the line dividing some of the decisions on the happening, or otherwise, of an accident is fine. At the extreme end of the list, one can see that murder, or indeed any unprovoked assault, is an accident from the claimant's point of view.[35] Suicide is plainly not so, although it may be shown that it is a consequential injury arising out of an accident.[36] Incapacity caused as a result of a vaccination is not the result of an accident because the vaccination is not unlooked for.[37]

Since the resulting injury may consist of any physiological change, such as nervous debility as a result of witnessing an accident at work,[38] or strain,[39] or even heart disease, if its cause can be identified,[40] the question is raised of the distinction from a process.

"Arising out of and in the course of employment"

An "industrial" accident is defined as one arising out of and in the course of employment. The definition, which is taken directly from the law of workmen's

---

[28] C.I. 83/50—tuberculosis.
[29] C.I. 125/50.
[30] C.S.I. 21/49.
[31] R(I) 43/61; R(I) 4/62.
[32] See, e.g. R(I) 31/52; R(I) 54/53; R(I) 49/52.
[33] R(I) 70/50.
[34] C.I. 114/49.
[35] R(I) 47/51.
[36] C.I. 172/50.
[37] R(I) 12/58.
[38] R(I) 49/52. Loss of faculty includes disfigurement—s.5.
[39] C.I. 27/49; C.I. 29/49.
[40] C.I. 39/49; R(I) 31/56.

compensation, constitutes the most difficult aspect of the application of this legislation. As Lord Denning M.R. has said[41]:

> "I think it is right to say, as (counsel for the insurance officer) said, that those words are so very like the words of the old Workmen's Compensation Act that it is legitimate to look for guidance to the decisions of the courts in the old days. But I would make it subject to the qualification that we do not fall into the errors which the courts did then."

It has been said that, while it may be useful to take the phrase "out of and in the course of employment" in two parts (as has been done so far in this chapter), ultimately a decision must rest upon it as a composite whole.[42] This is true in that each part has a bearing on the other. According to the wording of the statute, it is the accident that must both arise out of and in the course of employment, rather than the claimant who must be in the course of employment and suffering an accident arising out of it. Equally, it has been recognised[43] that the question of whether an accident arises out of employment is one of causation. It is not a question of whether the employment exists so as to set the scene, but of whether it was an effective cause of the accident. It is submitted that whatever may be said about the whole nature of the test, it is this second aproach which indicates the common practice; to set the scene by consideration of the course of employment and then to examine causation, if it is in question, by a consideration of the source of the injury, which tends so often to be called the source of the accident. It may be unfortunate that "course of employment" is thereby more often taken to refer to the claimant rather than the accident. Any examination of the decisions will reveal that this is so and that it is actually the rare case where it may help to take the test as a whole.[44]

Not only the decisions, but the legislation itself, constantly distinguish the two parts of the test. It is provided[45] that "an accident arising in the course of an insured person's employment shall be deemed, in the absence of evidence to the contrary, also to have arisen out of that employment." The strange provisions of section 55[46] are wholly concerned with the effects of the distinction.

If no such distinction is made one finds such statements as:

> "In order that the accident may be one arising out of employment, it must be shown that it was brought about by an act which the claimant was authorised by his employers, expressly or impliedly, to perform, or was an act so closely incidental to that which he was authorised to perform that it was reasonably necessary and proper for him to do it."

This is the test of course of employment. It cannot limit the meaning of the words "out of employment" since they may refer entirely to the conduct of third parties or events and apply whether or not those third parties are themselves in the course of their employment. The same confusion led to the decision that the claim of an employee who had been poisoned by eating ham sandwiches bought at a colliery canteen should be disallowed. He was not employed to eat ham

---

[41] R. v. *Industrial Injuries Commissioner, ex p. A.E.U.* [1966] 2 Q.B. 31. Followed in R(1) 3/67.

[42] R(I) 14/51.

[43] R(I) 2/63; Wedderburn, *Cases and Materials*, p. 769.

[44] See R(I) 3/67.

[45] Social Security Act 1975, s.50(3).

[46] First introduced by Family Allowances and National Insurance Act 1961, s.2.

sandwiches, so that the accident did not arise out of his employment.[47] This decision was overruled in 1963[48] in a case where the claimant had suffered injury from a piece of glass in some toast bought from a trolley, provided under contract with the employer to supply food during the mid-morning break. On the principles already discussed, the accident plainly arose in the course of the claimant's employment. An entirely separate question arose of whether the circumstances of the accident were sufficiently closely connected with employment to be said to arise out of employment, or whether eating poisoned food could be said to be a common risk similar to being knocked down in the street.

So also an accident can arise in the course of employment but out of a wholly extraneous circumstance, such as provocation by the plaintiff. There is no doubt that the conjoint test could be used to say that *the accident* suffered by an employee who had called a colleague a lazy swine was not in the course of employment because it did not arise out of employment.[49] To do so, however, would not allow us to distinguish a case where the employment does produce such a risk, as by attracting particularly violent and quarrelsome fellow workers, but the claimant goes out of his way to offer more than ordinary provocation.

Very often, however, the fact that an accident is in the course of employment will undoubtedly facilitate a decision that the statutory presumption that it arises out of employment should not be rebutted by an extraneous element.[50]

Course of employment

The scope of a concept such as "course of employment" can be appreciated when it is compared to the much narrower concepts, such as job content, used in other legislation. The concept of "course of employment" depends on a number of factors, some of which have little direct connection with "time." "Place" is the most obvious of these. The further point must be made, however, that for some inexplicable reason "course of employment" is applied more narrowly in industrial injury law than in the law of vicarious liability. The view that has prevailed is that once the employee arrives on his employer's premises he is at his place of work and the course of employment has begun but states that this must be qualified by the requirement that the employee be doing something reasonably incidental to his employment.[51]

In *Culverwell's* case[52] the claimant was entitled to a 10 minute tea-break. Smoking was not allowed in the workshops. So it was common to smoke during this break, and a small booth was set aside for the purpose. On the occasion in question the booth was full and Culverwell squatted in the passage outside to wait for a place. While he was there, and having already overrun the permitted break by five minutes, he was run into and severely injured by a negligently

---

[47] R(I) 90/53.

[48] R(I) 3/63; Wedderburn, *Cases and Materials*, p. 772.

[49] See C.I. 5/50.

[50] See R(I) 1/64—telephone engineer assaulted while repairing telephone; C.I. 51/49—woman driver who called for her employer each morning scalded with boiling water thrown by employer's daughter-in-law; R(I) 3/72—injury to home help going down common stairs of a block of flats. In course of employment. Only permitted use of stairs was for access to flats. Compare R(I) 21/58—bus conductor attacked by youths who boarded bus with intention of assaulting anyone they encountered, risk general and not peculiar to employment.

[51] See *R. v. National Insurance Commissioners, ex p. East*. Appendix to R(I) 16/75.

[52] [1966] 2 Q.B. 31.

driven fork-lift truck. Any decision as to course of employment in this connection is bound to owe something to the similar concept governing the incidence of vicarious liability. The Master of the Rolls said that for insurance purposes also a man is only to be considered to be taken outside the course of his employment when he is doing something of a kind different from anything he was employed to do.

> "I would agree," he said, "that in the ordinary way if a man while at his place of work, during his hours of work, is injured by a risk incidental to his employment, then the right conclusion usually is that it is an injury which arises out of and in the course of the employment, even though he may not be doing his actual work but chatting to a friend or smoking or doing something of that kind. But he may take himself out of it if he does something of a kind entirely different from anything he was employed to do. That is what the commissioner found here. This man was overstaying his tea-break for so long that he was taking himself out of his employment."

The principle stated here is more appropriate to determination of the vicarious liability of an employer for acts for which he cannot be held responsible. The view of the facts is as restrictive as that of the law. The statement that he had overstayed his tea-break "for so long" even if taken to refer to the fact that he showed no sign of returning, rather than to the actual period of five minutes, is unrealistic in the light of the reasonably wide view that, as the passage quoted indicates, has been, and is to be, taken of the meaning of course of employment. It is almost unbelievable that so restricted a view of both fact and law should be taken in relation to provision of national insurance benefit.

In other decisions the principle has been applied more liberally. It was said in one decision[53]: ". . . acts which are natural to the worker, which are not (or would not be) objected to by the employer, and which do not to any significant extent interfere with the performance of the worker's duty will [not] be regarded as interrupting the course of employment." It is also clear that the pattern of decision, as in the case of vicarious liability, has changed. The decision that handing a sweet to a colleague during a lull in work was not in the course of employment is unlikely to be followed.[54] Certainly it would be wrong now, if it was not always so, to say:

> "Of course certain purely personal and private acts, though strictly not acts which an employee is required by his employment to perform—such as having a meal on his employer's premises, or going to relieve nature, or drying clothes at his work place and so forth—may be held to arise out of his employment, if they are so reasonable and necessary in the circumstances *that the employee may be taken as having an implied authority from his employer to perform them.*"[55]

The point of objection is that such implied authorisation of the act in question is not necessary. This does not mean that in many cases it will not prove a significant factor. A fireman who was required to keep fit and was encouraged to play volley-ball in a recreational period was held to be in the course of his employment whilst playing this game.[56] On the other hand, permission to make tea at any time was held to have been overstepped by the employee who did so

---

[53] R(I) 17/63; see also R(I) 3/67—smoking in corridor with permission.
[54] R(I) 41/56; Compare R(I) 71/52; R(I) 46/53; R(I) 17/63; see R(I) 2/68, at para. 10.
[55] R(I) 71/52. Author's italics.
[56] R(I) 13/66.

within 10 minutes of arriving at work,[57] although the Commissioner must have overlooked the fact that this is standard practice in many outdoor occupations.

As with the common law, it may be significant that what the claimant was doing assists, even indirectly, his employer.[58]

Whatever may be said of specific examples, there is undoubtedly a large element of consideration of what is reasonable.[59] Thus an instinctive move, however personal the purpose, may be in the course of employment,[60] whilst a similar, but calculated move, for much the same sort of purpose may not be.[61] Where the whole situation has to be considered, rather than the position of an isolated reaction, the decisions reveal some more surprising conclusions. It has been held that travelling back from a post office after cashing the money order by which wages had been paid was not in the course of employment,[62] but it appears from a number of decisions that travelling to draw wages is within that course.

The performance of personal acts for third parties are considered on the same principle, even if the other is a superior servant who requests, or orders, the performance of the act. In one case[63] a general labourer was injured whilst attempting to remove a brush from the chimney of his foreman's private house, which the latter had asked him to sweep. The habit of performing such odd jobs was known to the employers, who neither authorised, nor objected, to it. The Commissioner said[64]:

"I appreciate. . . that it is difficult for an employee to refuse a request of this kind from his immediate superior; quite apart from the fear of possible injury to his prospects . . . an employee would naturally desire to be co-operative in such a matter as this. But anxiety about his career or a desire for popularity or pure good nature may prompt a man to do work which is clearly outside the scope of his contract of service; when this happens the work will not be done in the course of the man's employment unless it can be shown that it was done in response to an order or request made by or with the authority (actual or ostensible) of the employers[65] and that it was the express or implied intention of both parties that the work should be done under the contract of service and not merely as an act of good nature or friendship . . ."

Even in this statement there again appears the idea that the act itself should be authorised whereas, as we have seen, in the case of vicarious liability it is only the situation in which the act takes place which requires such authorisation. Could it not be said that the employer had impliedly authorised a general situation in which the course of employment might extend to such acts as took place here?[66]

---

[57] R(I) 34/53.
[58] R(I) 13/68.
[59] See R(I) 13/68, at para. 7.
[60] R(I) 32/53—recovery of tobacco tin which had dropped into funnel of machine.
[61] R(I) 78/52—movement of billiard slabs to recover lost coin.
[62] R(I) 34/52. In this case the accident probably did not arise out of the employment.
[63] R(I) 8/61; Wedderburn, Cases and Materials, p. 767.
[64] Relying on R(I) 36/55.
[65] This is not to imply that an order or request is required in all cases—R(I) 13/66 and [1966] 2 W.L.R. at 104 and 107.
[66] This distinction was adopted in R(I) 1/70.

The whole position of incidental acts was dealt with by Lord Denning M.R. in the *Amalgamated Engineering Union* case. He said[67]:

"Take the first class where 'a man goes away from his work for purposes of his own.' An illustration is where a man goes from one end of a factory to the other to compare notes on football pools. He is not acting in the course of his employment. It would be different if he went to get a tool or to go to the lavatory.

Now take the next class, where a man, 'at his place of work does something which has nothing to do with his employment.' An illustration was given by Lord Atkin in *Noble's* case.[68] If the guard of a train takes it on himself to drive the train and is injured while driving, he is outside the course of his employment . . .

Take the third class where 'being away from his place of work, he does not return to it when he should.' An illustration can be taken from *Knight* v. *Howard Wall Ltd.*[69] Suppose the boy in the canteen, instead of going back to his work at the end of the meal, had stayed on for half an hour or an hour playing darts with the rest of the men in the canteen. By overstaying his visit to the canteen he would be taking himself completely out of the course of his employment, because he would be doing something of a kind different from anything he was employed to do."

This still seems to be applying to insurance benefit a more severe test than the common law would apply to vicarious liability. Fortunately such severity does not always appear from the decisions of the Commissioner. A lorry driver who was required to assist in the unloading of bricks from his lorry was held to be in the course of employment when he helped to move a cement mixer on the building site.[70] A worker who, with his employer's permission, attended a lunch hour union meeting relating to the terms of his employment was also within his employment.[71] A machine operator who acted at his place of employment as a collector for a firm of pools promoters was held not to have interrupted his employment when he stooped to recover some money dropped while being paid to him in this capacity. In the process he dislodged a heavy spanner which fell on his hand. It was held that this was an ordinary risk of employment.[72]

It was said in a case concerning injury while assisting another in difficulty on the highway that, to be within the course of employment, there must be a similarity of function between the helper and the person helped.[73] If this were to mean that a travelling salesman could help another salesman but could not, within his employment, help a different type of employee, the point of distinction would appear to be irrelevant. It seems, however, that the Commissioner meant to look at the position from the point of view of the claimant. If it is taken to mean that an employee engaged to travel may help any traveller, the statement may be justified on the ground that his function particularly exposes him to the risk of being expected to be helpful in such cases. This must have been the basis of the decision that a security guard on night patrol was in the course of his employment when he was asked by a policeman to help him to

---

[67] *R.* v. *Industrial Injuries Commissioner*, *ex p. Amalgamated Engineering Union* [1966] 2 Q.B. 31. See also *R.* v. *National Insurance Commissioners*, *ex p. East*, *The Times*, November 1, 1975, where the Divisional Court held an employee in the course of his employment whilst changing into his working clothes in the staff canteen before clocking on.
[68] *Noble* v. *Southern Railway Co.* [1940] A.C. 583.
[69] [1938] 4 All E.R. 667.
[70] R(I) 11/56.
[71] R(I) 63/51.
[72] R(I) 4/73.
[73] R(I) 52/54.

investigate a light in a building he was not employed to guard. At most, the policeman only suspected a felony, so there was no duty on the guard to render such assistance. He was undoubtedly subject to a special risk of being asked to do so.[74]

Before dealing with some situations which are the subject of special provisions, it may be worth concluding this examination with a few general examples on either side. The following acts have been held not sufficiently incidental to be in the course of employment:

> Long distance lorry driver who took a broken-down lorry to the manufacturers for repair was found lodging for the night and was injured in the morning while leaving to collect the lorry.[75]
> Post Office worker who was injured whilst putting up Christmas decorations at a post office. His employers did not object and he had been asked to do so by his immediate superior.[76]
> Claimant who was injured whilst going, with her employer's permission, to the telephone room to make a telephone call about the non-delivery of fruit and flowers to a sick colleague.[77]
> Bus conductor who was going to deposit his ticket machine at his employer's office before going to the canteen. He was forbidden to take the machine into the canteen.[78]
> Insurance agent who was injured whilst taking home a prospective client after an interview with him.[79]

The indication of an interest primarily on behalf of the employee is apparent in all these.

The following acts have been held to be in the course of employment:

> Claimant playing non-obligatory volley-ball, which he was encouraged to do to keep fit.[80]
> A school teacher attending a Christmas party after school hours but as a normal incident of her duties.[81]
> Fireman injured whilst performing in the brigade's agility team for recruiting and publicity purposes. Once he had voluntarily joined the team he was obliged to work with it as required.[82]
> Factory worker who was injured by the treatment given to him in the company's ambulance room.[83]
> Mother injured whilst taking her child to a nursery provided by her employers at her place of work.[84]

---

[74] R(I) 62/51.
[75] C.S.I. 3/49.
[76] R(I) 36/55.
[77] R(I) 53/56.
[78] R(I) 38/59, distinguished in R(I) 4/67.
[79] R(I) 8/52.
[80] R(I) 13/66.
[81] R(I) 62/52.
[82] R(I) 72/52. But note that obligation is not necessarily a limiting factor—R(I) 2/68. But see R. v. *National Insurance Commissioner, ex parte Michael* [1977] I.C.R. 121 adopting a much more restrictive attitude.
[83] R(I) 3/54.
[84] R(I) 53/54.

Colliery worker going to the canteen to purchase a replacement bootlace which was necessary before he could start work.[85]

Claimant calling at her employer's office to hand in a medical certificate and discuss her return to work.[86]

Apprentice on day release course at local Technical College. Attendance was voluntary but if he had not gone he would have been expected to report for work.[87]

Doubt has, however, again been thrown on this wider application by a further example of the strangely restrictive attitude of the courts. In *R*. v. *National Insurance Commissioners, ex p. Michael*[88] the Court of Appeal held that a policeman was not in the course of his employment when he sustained injury whilst playing football for his force against another force at a time when he was off duty and unpaid. The evidence showed that he was expected by his superiors to play but was not compelled to do so. A certain amount of time off with pay was allowed but the expectation extended to off duty unpaid time. It was pointed out that the words "normally incidental to employment" were a judicial gloss upon the statutory requirement of course of employment and it was said that they should only be applied to injury during an interruption of work.

It is provided by the Social Security Act 1975[89] that so long as an act is done for the purposes of, and in connection with, the employer's trade or business, and would have been considered to be within the course of employment but for an infringement of statutory or other regulations or orders, such contravention will not take the act outside the course of employment for the purposes of the Act.[90] It is difficult to see exactly what effect this is meant to have, since it appears to be enacting the common law rule that an act within the scope of an authorised situation shall not be considered to be outside employment merely because it is a wrongful or illegal way of carrying out that authority. If that is so, one may ask whether the very existence of section 7 indicates that the meaning of "course of employment" in this legislation was intended to differ from the common law meaning.[91]

Travel to work

The failure to cover all accidental injury but rather to develop a concept of industrial accidents has forced the legislature to attempt to draw artificial lines to distinguish common accident situations even where they occur to an employee in connection with his work.

Accidents which occur in the course of travel to work are the subject of such statutory provisions.[92] Such an accident is to be deemed to arise out of and in

---

[85] R(I) 72/54.
[86] R(I) 48/56.
[87] R(I) 2/68.
[88] [1977] I.C.R. 121.
[89] s.52.
[90] See *R*. v. *D'Albuquerque, ex p. Bresnahan* [1966] 1 Lloyd's Rep. 69—doubted on general meaning of course of employment in *Kay* v. *I.T.*W. [1968] 1 Q.B. 140.
[91] Calvert, *Social Security Law* (2nd ed.), p. 332, suggests that the section does have the effect of extending benefit since a common law approach to this type of situation would exclude entitlement. This, it is submitted, is not correct.
[92] s.53.

the course of employment if it occurs while the claimant is, with the express or implied permission of his employer, travelling[93] as a passenger[94] to or from his place of work in a vehicle operated by, or on behalf of, or by arrangement with, his employer, and not in the ordinary course of a public transport service; provided that had the employee been obliged so to travel, the accident would have been considered so to have arisen.

In line with what it is submitted is the usual misapprehension as to the purpose of this legislation this provision is construed strictly. It has been said that as a normal rule the old workmen's compensation principle that such travel is not in the course of employment will be applied.[95] This, however, is most likely to have been the product of a need to limit the scope of a private insurance scheme. Nevertheless, it is quite possible for travel to or from work to be considered to be ordinarily within the course of employment, although it is difficult to formulate any clear rule from the decisions. It has been held that if a workman is travelling in response to a special summons on a particular occasion to deal with an emergency, his employment will begin at the time he leaves home.[96] This may be so even if he is only paid from the time that he "clocks-in," which, because of the accident, he never does.[97] The exception does not apply where there is no emergency and the claimant was, for example, travelling to work in the normal way, but an hour earlier as requested.[98] Payment for travelling time does not prove that the travel was in the course of employment.[99]

The question of travel on the employer's premises to the place of work has been raised in a number of decisions.[1] The Chief Commissioner has said[2] that the tenor of the cases reveals that course of employment is always wider than the immediate place of work.[3] He went on to point out the difficulty of marking a point in the employee's progress when he could be said to be near enough, and decided that the general conclusion from the cases is that a man is in the course of employment when, on his way to work, he leaves the area used by the public.

A different position arises where, rather than travelling to or from work, the claimant was travelling on duty.

In a number of cases the travel has disrupted a course of employment which has begun. The test is very much the same as that applied to decide whether an act is incidental to employment. So a school inspector who used his house as his base was injured whilst travelling home to lunch after a conference and before going on to visit some schools. It was held that the travel was part of his employment and it was immaterial that the journey would be done in two stages.[4] It has been explained, however, that the decision did not depend on the

---

[93] Which for this purpose includes boarding and alighting from transport—C.I. 182/49—but not crossing a road to board—R(I) 79/51; R(I) 1/53.

[94] Which does not include the driver R(I) 9/51—motorcycle.

[95] *Vandyke* v. *Fender* [1970] 2 Q.B. 292. Applied in R(I) 3/71—a distinction between long and short journeys is not practicable.

[96] R(I) 36/57.

[97] R(I) 21/51.

[98] R(I) 36/57.

[99] C.I. 148/149; R(I) 16/58; R(I) 3/71.

[1] A number of them are considered in R(I) 5/67.

[2] R(I) 5/67.

[3] As to this see R(I) 13/68.

[4] R(I) 59/53.

fact that his home was his base,[5] but solely on what he was employed to do.[6] So a journey from one's home and base *preparatory* to work is sometimes held not in the course of employment.[7]

A bus driver who was allowed no specific breaks but was permitted to have a cup of tea during an 11 minute interval at the end of the run, was held to be in the course of his employment whilst walking to a café, partly because he was still required to keep his eye on the bus.[8] But in 1967 a tribunal of three Commissioners confirmed this decision partly on the consideration that the claimant was required in the course of his work to travel upon the highway, which he was still using for an intended purpose when injured.[9] In this later decision it was said that the same result might not emerge if the break was longer. This reservation is certainly supported by earlier decisions, in one of which a coach driver, employed to be available at the call of the coach party and injured whilst going with some of them to have a meal, was held not entitled to claim because the course of his employment was temporarily suspended.[10]

Such an approach could, in its turn, produce difficulties about the restarting of employment. In one such case, a commercial traveller returned home for his mid-day meal and was injured whilst getting his car out of his garage after the meal. It was held that he must have re-entered his employment at the latest when he re-entered the garage.[11]

There is no doubt that the statutory provisions work best in the case of the type of employee they have primarily in mind, that is to say, one who has defined times and areas of operation. The more discretion that is allowed to the employee to fix his own times and areas, the greater latitude must be allowed in the concept of "course of employment." The problems are, surprisingly, largely unexplored.[12] Professor Wedderburn cites two cases[13] in which such latitude was permitted. In the first case a female civil servant who preferred to arrive at the office at 7.00 a.m., rather than 8.30 a.m., so that she might avoid the rush hour, and who filled in the time by reading, was held to be in the course of her employment in that time. The second decision concerned a miner who might be said to have less latitude in choosing his hours but who was, nevertheless, held to be in the course of his employment whilst, for the same reason, he waited in the canteen for a later bus home.

Normal meal breaks

Where travelling does not enter into consideration, the meal break taken within the ultimate limits of the workplace and between two spells of work is

---

[5] R(I) 18/55.
[6] R(I) 2/67.
[7] In R(I) 2/67 it was said that each case must be decided on its facts—home help travelling to first call. See R(I) 4/70—employee, whose work involved outside visits, in course of employment when travelling to first visit of the day.
[8] R(I) 20/61.
[9] R(I) 4/67, see para. 6.
[10] R(I) 10/52.
[11] In R(I) 2/67 it was said that "there is a clear distinction between the case of a man such as a commercial traveller who has no fixed hours of work and no precisely ascertainable place of employment and that of a person who has definite hours and a fixed place of work each day."
[12] But see Mrs. J. Reid (1966) 29 M.L.R. 389.
[13] R(I) 3/62 and R(I) 1/59. Wedderburn, *Cases and Materials*, p. 766n.

normally regarded as incidental to employment.[14] A meal taken after work may be necessary to life, but it is not considered necessary to employment. The act of purchasing food before work begins is also not in the course of employment.[15]

Even if the canteen is not on the premises, meal breaks may still come within the course of employment if the facility is provided by arrangement with the employer.[16] The distinction between this and going home to lunch appears to be illogical, and even unfair, if regarded simply in the light of what is reasonably incidental to employment. There is, however, no doubt that some of the thinking on the provisions of these Acts is influenced by insurance practice and by the concept of the scope of the insured risk. It would have seemed preferable, had that been so, however, to have based the refusal to grant benefit on the fact that in most cases of injury on the way to or from home it could be said that the injury did not arise out of employment. It is this element which should really serve to distinguish certain sources of injury from the industrial context. In practice, it is not unusual to find "course of employment" judged by whether the *risk* is one peculiar to an employee or to the general public.[17]

Causation

It must be shown that the disabling injury arose from the accident. A miner who received a severe blow on the chest from a wire haulage rope took to his bed and died several months later from chronic congestive heart failure due to arteriosclerosis. It was held that though the injury and shock were indirect causes, they were not operative causes of the death.[18] In another decision the insured person, employed for 18 years in the blasting department of a chemical factory, was exposed to certain chemicals which investigation had shown to be capable of causing sudden death. Records revealed that such deaths usually occurred after short periods of absence from work and so, frequently, upon a Monday morning. The deceased's death, for which there was no explanation, had occurred on a Monday morning. It was held that the death was caused by the employment although not by an accident.[19] With these two may be contrasted the case of the gardener who soaked his trousers with sodium chlorate whilst spraying weeds. Such treatment renders the material, when dry, highly inflammable. The trousers did, in fact ignite when the gardener lit a cigarette at home. It was held that the accident arose not from employment but from the lighting of the cigarette.[20]

The outcome of claims relating to accidents which occur after the normal hours of work but whilst the claimant is doing something connected with, or incidental to, his normal employment, will depend on the usual considerations of the closeness of the connection.[21]

---

[14] C.S.I. 6/49; C.I. 120/49; R(I) 17/60.
[15] R(I) 11/54.
[16] R(I) 11/53.
[17] See R(I) 1/68.
[18] R(I) 14/51.
[19] R(I) 7/66. The decision reveals some of the inadequacy of the system of prescribed diseases.
[20] R(I) 4/58.
[21] C.I. 374/50—nurse on call, claim allowed; R(I) 49/51—resident cook on call, though unlikely to be required, claim allowed; R(I) 64/51—sub-postmistress doing accounts in her living room in the evening, claim allowed; R(I) 46/59—civil servant locking up following after-hours meeting of staff association—claim not allowed.

The introduction of a causal connection is, of course, necessary given acceptance of a concept of compensation linked solely to the existence of employment. Whilst it does not imply that the accident must arise from a risk directly connected with the work it has been said to involve a "superficial nexus."[22] The test seems to be connected with the place of the accident and the question that is asked is whether the requirement of his work caused the person injured to be at that place. The question whether this means that the secretary who goes out specifically to post letters intending subsequently to return to the office is covered should he or she suffer a road accident whilst the contrary is true of the secretary who takes letters to post on the way home serves to emphasise the artificiality of the entire limitation of industrial injury rather than any avoidable fault of draftsmanship.

A presumption is now provided by statute[23] that "an accident arising in the course of . . . employment shall be deemed, in the absence of evidence to the contrary, also to have arisen out of that employment." This enacts what had in many instances developed as a practice in decisions of the Commissioners. The effect of the provision is considerably reduced by the note that "evidence to the contrary" is presumptively constituted where known facts justify the inference that the accident did not arise out of the employment.[24]

This further example of a word by word approach no doubt derives its greatest impetus from the case of *Weaver* v. *Tredegar Iron Co.*[25] in which Lord Wright distinguished the two limbs of the basic test as indicative of causation and time.

Misbehaviour

The distinctive feature of cases of assault, skylarking and the like, which may be said to be in the course of, but not arising out of, employment, has been considerably reduced since 1961 by the provision which now appears as section 55 of the 1975 Act[26]:

> An accident . . . shall be treated . . . as arising out of an employed earner's employment if—
>
> (a) the accident arises in the course of the employment; and
> (b) the accident either is caused by another person's misconduct, skylarking or negligence, or by steps taken in consequence of any such misconduct, skylarking or negligence or by the behaviour or presence of an animal (including a bird, fish or insect), or is caused by or consists in the employed earner being struck by any object or by lightning; and
> (c) the employed earner did not directly or indirectly induce or contribute to the happening of the accident by his conduct outside the employment or by any act not incidental to the employment.

This is intended to comprehend the relatively large number of cases where the claimant has been injured by some force extraneous to his employment, or by

---

[22] R(I) 16/61.
[23] See now Social Security Act 1975, s.50(3).
[24] See *R.* v. *National Insurance (Industrial Injuries) Commissioner, ex p. Richardson* [1958] 1 W.L.R. 851.
[25] [1904] 3 All E.R. 157.
[26] Social Security Act 1975.

the misconduct of his fellow workers, where the happening can be said to be a risk common to all persons and so not arising out of his employment, or where the risk, although obviously confined to the employment situation, has no necessary connection therewith. It remains a mystery, however, why it should have been thought proper to introduce into a system where liability is not founded on fault the idea of a contributory cause acting as a total disqualification.

There is little doubt that many of the decisions before the introduction of this provision were unreal. An apprentice injured whilst trying to avoid the customary Shrove Tuesday "blacking" was held to be entitled to claim because his employment specially subjected him to the risk.[27] So was a girl injured by a nut fired at her "in play" by a fellow employee who used a compressed-air gun for the purpose. The provision of such equipment was said to enhance the risk by suggesting the notion.[28] On the other hand, the presence of a tin of trichlorethylene has been held not to provide such a temptation to throw it.[29]

Our predecessors might have found it difficult to see why a caravan missioner, who was struck by lightning, had not suffered an accident arising out of his employment, whilst a farm labourer, the object of a similar display of wrath, had. A workman travelling in a lorry in the course of employment and struck by a stone thrown by a boy at the roadside was held to have suffered an accident arising out of his employment, since boys are well known to be apt to throw stones at moving vehicles and so a causal connection with employment had been shown.[30]

That the Commissioner no longer has to seek to provide rational explanations for acts of God or of those mortals with perverted senses of humour will be an improvement, but some of the efforts that must be made under the new provision are equally difficult. In one decision[31] a workman, plainly of a sober mien, was struck by a snowball. He pursued the thrower for a matter of two steps in order to remonstrate with him. His fingers were lacerated as they went through a glass door slammed by the retreating culprit. It was held that the workman came within section 55 and, since he was not in pursuit for the purposes of retaliation, he had not contributed to the accident. The contributory act will only disqualify if it is not incidental to employment.[32]

Prescribed diseases

It is plain that since most diseases are the result of a process they would not come within the meaning of an industrial accident. The Act[33] makes provision for benefit to be paid for incapacity due to certain diseases which are prescribed in relation to the industrial process which is known, frequently, to cause them. Many of these relate to the use of chemicals and to the various respiratory diseases which occur in processes producing dust from coal, asbestos, and

---

[27] C.I. 334/50.
[28] R(I) 63/52.
[29] R(I) 75/54. Surely this cannot be a correct way of determining what arises out of employment?
[30] C.I. 88/50; see also R(I) 71/53.
[31] R(I) 3/67.
[32] See R(I) 2/63; Wedderburn, *Cases and Materials*, p. 769.
[33] Pt. II. Chap. V.

similar substances. The bald statement leaves much unexplained. The process of prescription is a slow one, and considerable problems arise from the system of fixing the onset of the disease and its disabling effect. None of these numerous problems can be dealt with here, but the question is plainly posed of whether the two classifications are necessary at all or whether benefit should not be payable for all disabling injury which can be traced to employment. The formula would, of course, be difficult to devise and would again encounter the problem of disease which could not always be satisfactorily traced. The Pearson Commission however recommended that benefit should be payable in all cases where disease could be shown to have arisen out of employment.

The most common types of disease currently presented are those involving poisoning as a result of a particular risk of an industrial process. Lung cancer and tuberculosis are prescribed for certain occupations whereas it is established that they are inherent in a considerable number of others for which there is no prescription.

Claims

Questions of right to benefit and of disqualification are determined initially by an insurance officer, who may either allow or disallow the claim or refer it to the local tribunal. If the claim is not allowed in full, the claimant is given a written notification of the decision and the reasons for it. He may appeal to the local tribunal. In a case where the decision of the insurance officer depends entirely upon a previous determination by the Minister, the permission of the tribunal chairman is necessary before the claim may proceed. Written notice of the intention to appeal must be given to the local office of the Ministry within 21 days of the decision, unless the chairman of the local tribunal allows further time, upon the showing of good cause for the delay.

From the decision of the local tribunal either the insurance officer who originally dealt with the claim, or the claimant, or any association which exists to promote the interest and welfare of its members and of which the claimant is, or was before his death, a member, may appeal to the National Insurance Commissioner within three months (or such longer period as the Commissioner may "for special reasons" allow). An insurance officer or, on reference from him, a local tribunal has power to review any decision in the light of fresh evidence or changed circumstances. If the Commissioner feels that the appeal involves a question of law of special difficulty, he may direct that instead of a hearing by the Commissioner, or one of his deputies, sitting alone, the claim shall be heard by a tribunal of them, which decides by a majority. If a question of fact of special difficulty is involved, he may appoint one or more assessors to sit with him or his deputy.[34]

The decision of a tribunal is regarded as binding on single Commissioners.[35] There is no way of disposing of it save by an action for *certiorari*. The jurisdiction of the ordinary courts is entirely excluded.[36] As to the binding effect of decisions of individual Commissioners it has been said[37]:

---

[34] As to test cases, see R(U) 7/71.

[35] R(U) 15/62.

[36] *Punton and Croxford* v. *Minister of Pensions and National Insurance* [1964] 1 W.L.R. 226. Certiorari for error on the face of the record was granted in *R.* v. *Industrial Injuries Commissioner, ex p. Langley* [1976] I.C.R. 36.   [37] C.S. 414/50.

"The reported decisions of the Commissioners are printed for the guidance of insurance officers and local tribunals. The trouble and expense involved would be futile if members of local tribunals in general were to ignore the principles explained in those decisions when dealing with cases to which they are clearly applicable . . .

But

"The position is different in relation to the Commissioner . . . [He] normally follows an earlier decision of the Commissioner. In view, however, of the difficulty of getting rid of the erroneous decision of the Commissioner it is right, if error is not to be perpetuated, that the Commissioner should not hesitate in a proper case to decline to follow an earlier Commissioner's decision if completely satisfied that it is erroneous."[38]

In *R.* v. *Deputy Industrial Injuries Commissioner, ex p. Moore*[39] it was stated in the High Court that the Commissioner had an almost unfettered discretion as to how he will proceed. Willmer L.J. said:

"He is not bound to hold any hearing at all, even where the claimant has asked for one. . . . If there is a hearing, witnesses may or may not be called, and, if called, may or may not be sworn. It is to my mind abundantly clear that Parliament intended that there should be a minimum of formality. . . . Where so much is left to the discretion of the commissioner, the only real limitation, as I see it, is that the procedure must be in accordance with natural justice.[40] This involves that any information on which the commissioner acts, whatever its source, must be at least of some probative value. It also involves that the commissioner must be prepared to hear both sides, assuming that he has been requested to grant a hearing[41] and that on such hearing must allow both sides to comment on or contradict any information that he has obtained. This would doubtless apply equally where a hearing had been requested but refused, for in such a case it would not be in accordance with natural justice to act on information obtained behind the backs of the parties without affording them an opportunity of commenting on it."

Medical questions, such as relate for instance to the extent of the disability, go before a local medical tribunal, with appeal to a medical appeal tribunal,[42] and in certain cases, finally, to the Commissioner. The relationship between the "statutory authorities" and the medical authorities, which has proved to be a point of difficulty, has been considered in two recent cases.[43] In the first of these a labourer had suffered pain on lifting a heavy flagstone and was awarded injury benefit as suffering from hiatus hernia. Later he claimed disablement benefit. The medical authority ruled that hiatus hernia could not possibly have been caused in this way. The House of Lords held that such a decision inevitably meant that there had not been an industrial accident, whereas the finding of the statutory authorities that there had was binding on the medical authorities. Lord Morris said that if the latter started with the finding that there had been an

---

[38] R(G) 3/62.
[39] [1965] 1 Q.B. 456.
[40] See R(1) 4/71; R(I) 2/72; *R.* v. *National Insurance Commissioner, ex p. Viscusi* [1974] 1 W.L.R. 649.
[41] This should presumably read: "assuming that he has agreed to grant a hearing."
[42] Which must conform with natural justice—R(I) 6/67.
[43] *Minister of Social Security* v. *Amalgamated Engineering Union*; *Re Dowling* [1967] 1 A.C. 725; *Jones* v. *Secretary of State for Social Services* [1972] 1 A.C. 944.

industrial injury caused by accident, they could not say that there had been no such injury. This conclusion derives its support from the statutory provision for the finality of the decision of each set of authorities within its own area.

In the second case the appellant, a fitter, lifted a heavy piece of metal during the course of his work and felt a pain in his back. In hospital he was diagnosed as having myocardial infarction. A local appeal tribunal allowed his appeal from the decision of the insurance officer that he had not suffered injury caused by an accident. As a result he was allowed injury benefit. Later he claimed a disablement benefit. The medical board, to which was referred the question of assessment of disability, found that he had suffered two separate disabilities, a strained chest and myocardial infarction, but that only the former was caused by the work which he had been doing before he became ill. This decision, resulting in rejection of his claim, was confirmed by the medical appeal tribunal. The Commissioner held that it was not erroneous in law.

All seven members of the House of Lords refused to distinguish *Dowling's* case on the ground of difference between one and two injuries. Three members held that it was rightly decided. Lord Simon of Glaisdale joined these three in holding that, though he thought the decision wrong, the House should not, on this occasion, overrule itself. A bare majority was thus in favour of following *Dowling's* case[44] and compelling the medical authorities to accept the prior decision of the statutory authorities that the injury arose from an accident in the course of employment. Viscount Dilhorne (dissenting), however, pointed out that if the decision of the medical authority within its proper field came first the view of the majority would inevitably mean that the statutory authorities were bound by it. So, if the medical authorities first decided that the injury was not due to an accident the statutory authority could not reverse this. If a local officer had so decided the medical board must follow him. On a subsequent appeal from the local officer the local appeal tribunal would be bound to follow the inevitable decision of the medical board. On appeal from the medical board the medical tribunal would be bound to follow the local appeal tribunal. The Commissioner would be bound to follow the medical appeal tribunal. As Lord Diplock said, the intention of the legislature might be assumed to be that the initial decision, which necessarily must be made quickly, should be subject to later correction by a medical board who had the time and expertise thoroughly to examine the matter. The matter is different where a medical board makes a finding different to a previous medical board.[45] In *R. v. National Insurance Commissioner, ex parte Viscusi*[46] it was pointed out that where a decision was made with reference only to a future specified period a different decision could be arrived at with reference to a subsequent period. If it was sought to alter an assessment for the self-same period the proper procedure would be to seek a review of the previous decision on the ground of fresh evidence, which would include anything the claimant could not reasonably have been expected to produce at the previous hearing.

Finally, any decision of a statutory authority may be reviewed by an insurance officer or, upon his reference, by a local appeal tribunal, on the

---

[44] Followed in *R. v. National Insurance Commissioner*, *ex p. Herbert Maiden*, reported as a note to R(I) 1/173.
[45] See R(I) 1/73.
[46] [1974] 1 W.L.R. 646.

ground that it was given in ignorance of, or was based on a mistake as to, some material fact.[47] If the original decision was made by a Commissioner, there must be fresh evidence to support this contention. Similar review can be based on the fact that there has been a change of circumstances, or that the original decision was based on a decision of the Minister which he has himself subsequently revised. The medical authorities can, and normally do, periodically review their decisions as to the degree of disability.

---

[47] s.104.

INDEX

ACTION, JOINDER IN,
action short of dismissal, concerning,
122
branch union as defendant, 228, 238
ACTION SHORT OF DISMISSAL,
"action," 118–119
activities of trade union,
appropriate time for, 119–120
authorisation, 120–121
employer consent to, 121
industrial action as, 119–120
meetings, mandatory, as, 120
reason for, as, 117
recruitment as, 120
safety complaint, as, 120
tea-break, during, 121
complaint of, 121–122
Great Britain, employment in, 153
non-membership of union, 122
promotion, failure of, as, 119
proof of, 118
qualification to complain, of, 118
reasons, prohibited, for, 117
union rights, deprivation, as, 118–119
ADVISORY CONCILIATION AND ARBITRATION
SERVICE,
Central Arbitration Committee connected
with, 356
codes of practice, issue of, 366
conciliation, bargaining information
claim, in, 361–362
constitution of, 364
establishment of, 364
recognition, application for, 367
statutory industrial council, reference by,
366
wages councils,
abolition of, 355
establishment of, 353
AGE,
children, employment of, 22
discrimination based on, 330–331, 341
qualification for statutory rights, 134–135,
265
ALIENS,
employment of, 23
ALTERNATIVE EMPLOYMENT,
continuity, 145
ALTERNATIVE OFFER. See GUARANTEE
PAYMENT, MATERNITY RIGHTS,
REDUNDANCY.

APPEAL. See also DISMISSAL.
disciplinary, 226–227
fresh hearing as, 227
industrial tribunal, from, 194–195
mitigation by, 227
rectification of defects by, 227
APPORTIONMENT. See WAGES.
APPRENTICE, 20–22
common law implications, 20
continuity of employment of, 145
discipline of, 21
dismissal of, 21, 170
enforcement of contract, 21
intolerable conduct of, 170
minor as, 20
partnership, to, 21
personal relation of, 20
premium, repayment of insolvency,
123–124
redundancy of, 272
statutory rights of, 21
termination of, 21
termination by dissolution of partnership,
180
trade union membership conditional on,
401
ARBITRATION. See also CENTRAL ARBITRATION
COMMITTEE.
Board of, 364
consent to, 363
reasoned awards, 357
reference to, 363
ASSOCIATED EMPLOYER,
definition, 150
local authorities as, 150
return of employee, preserving
continuity, 144
transfer of employment affecting
continuity, 150–151
ASSOCIATION, FREEDOM OF. See CLOSED
SHOP.
ATTACHMENT OF EARNINGS. See WAGES.

BALLOT,
union membership agreement, to
approve, 233–234
closed shop, to approve, 232, 233–234,
237
BARGAINING AGENCY, 32
BREACH OF STATUTORY DUTY,
defences, statutory, to, 553

635

BREACH OF STATUTORY DUTY—*cont.*
elements of, 553–554
health, 554
liability for, 535
liability for,
  safety, promoting, 552
origin of, 553
safety requirements precluded from, 553,
  554
sole cause, 584–586
BRIDLINGTON AGREEMENT. *See* TRADE
  UNIONS.
BUSINESS EFFICACY. *See* CONTRACT.

CENTRAL ARBITRATION COMMITTEE,
awards,
  publication, 357
  reasoned, 357
bargaining information,
  award concerning, 362
  preliminary hearing, 361
complaint to, 361–362
constitution of, 356
equality in collective agreements, 318–319
Fair Wages Resolution. *See* FAIR WAGES
  RESOLUTION.
origins of, 356
recognition,
  award of, 41
  enforcement of, 350
  meaning of, 369–370
  preliminary hearing, 356
trade disputes, arbitration in, 357, 366
CERTIORARI,
dismissal, to challenge, 16
CHECKWEIGHING, 131–132
CHILDREN. *See* MINORS.
CIVIL SERVANT,
Crown Servant, as, 17
CLOSED SHOP,
admission to union, right of, 402–403
agency shop, 231, 233
agreed procedure, 236–237
ballot to oppose, 232, 233–234, 237
code of practice, 238
conscientious objection to, 232, 237–238
contract to maintain void, 239
contractors, compulsion to accept,
  484–485
contractors,
  enforcement against, 239
  restriction open, 513–514
definition of union membership
  agreement, 231
degree of compliance, 236
employer's belief, 236
enforcement by dismissal, 231–2
exceptions to obligation, 232–233,
  237–238
independent trade union, 386
individual contract, 31–32

CLOSED SHOP—*cont.*
inducement to agree, 513
international restrictions on, 240–242
legality of, 391
notice of agreement, 235
objection to, 232, 237, 238
objectives of, 231
practice of observing, 234–235
pressure to observe, 228
professional ethics exempting, 238
restraint of trade, as, 234
scope of, 230–231
statutory duty relating to sub-contracts,
  484–485
T.U.C. independent review body, 242
trade dispute concerning, 502
transfer of, 383
CODES OF PRACTICE,
ACAS, issue by, 366
closed shop, on, 238
dismissal,
  guidelines, as, 215
  influence of, 206
  warnings, 216–217
picketing, 530
repeal of, 366
safety, 546–547
Secretary of State, issue by, 366
time of, 111, 112, 113, 115
union membership, 401, 415, 416, 439
  ballots, 439
  dues, non-payment of, 415
COLLECTIVE AGREEMENT/BARGAINING,
advice concerning, 364–365
agency of union, 32
  specific employees, for, 34
amendment by C.A.C. of, 319
amendment to, 38–39
aspirational characteristics of, 379
bargaining information,
  code of practice concerning, 360, 361
  company annual report containing, 362
  Crown, by, 362n
  duty to disclose, 360
  protection from disclosure, 360–361
binding effect of, 373–381
  France, in, 381
  Germany, in, 381
  I.L.O. recommendation, 381
  United States, in, 380–381
"Bridlington Agreement," affecting, 410
closed shop. *See* CLOSED SHOP.
company wide, 349, 370
contents of, 347–348
contract of employment,
  express incorporation in, 35–36
  non-unionists, of, 34
  peace clause, in, 514
contractual effect of, 356
contractual enforceability,
  effect of, 375–376

COLLECTIVE AGREEMENT/BARGAINING—cont.
contractual enforceability—cont.
  presumption against, 378–381
  presumption of, 375
contractual enforcement of, 31
disciplinary procedure, 38, 224–226
discriminatory provisions in, 318
employment protection by, 100
enforceability of, 347
  statutory provision for, 382
expectation of, 32
extension of, 350
flexibility of, 345
function of, 345
good faith, bargaining in, 350, 446–448
government control of, 346
growth of, 100
guaranteed employment, as to, 39
guaranteed pay, 104
incorporation into contract, 28, 29, 31
individual acceptance as binding, 32–33
individuals applicability to, 36
individual rights in, 447–448
individually binding effect, 31–32
individual contract,
  agency implying 32, 33
  custom and practice implying, 32
industrial action,
  influence on, 348
  restricting, 32
information concerning, to recognised
  union, 367
intention to honour, 31
interpretation of, 38–40
judicial view of, 373–375
local, 36, 346–349
  effect of, 347
  wages council awards, following, 353
manning agreements, 114
mobility allowance, 95–96
national, 36, 346–347, 373–374
  pre-eminence on local, 373–374
  standards, 346–347
patent rights, affecting, 92
peace clause in, 376, 378–380
policy statements in, 37
procedure,
  industrial action in breach of, 450
  trade dispute concerning, 502
public sector, in, 346–347
recognition. See RECOGNITION.
redundancy, 37, 100, 249
  selection, 37, 249
re-instatement, as to, 137
revocation of, 373
rule making by, 345
successful bargaining, 377–378
time-off for. See TIME-OFF.
transfer of, 382
travelling time, 40
variation by, 284

COLLECTIVE AGREEMENT/BARGAINING—cont.
written statement referring to, 28
COMBINATION ACTS. See TRADE UNIONS.
COMPANY REPORT,
annual report, bargaining information,
  362
assets for employee benefit, 124–125
consultation, annual report concerning,
  362
disabled persons, annual details, 24
group, industrial relations within, 112
transfer of, 147, 151
  hiving down, 151–152
  share control, by, 151
winding-up termination of employment
  by, 180–181
CONCILIATION,
statutory provision for, 363
exhaustion of procedure preceding, 363
CONFIDENCE. See TRUST.
CONFIDENTIALITY, 73–88
acceptance, implied, if, 80
contractual foundation of, 73–74
disclosure, public interest in, 81
discriminatory protection of, 334
documents, of, 323–324
dual employment endangering, 92–93
duration of, 82, 158
equitable foundation of, 73
express statement as to, 74
faithful service as basis of, 74
fiduciary relationship, 82, 88
fresh employment affecting, 79–80
implied term as to, 74
injunction to protect, 92
knowledge by recipient, 76, 80
management, duty of, 82
misconduct, affecting, 81
patents, inapplicable to, 76
personal knowledge, 79–80, 82, 85
personal skill distinguished from, 75
public domain, information in, 76
public interest in disclosure, 81
public policy, 79, 85
secrecy, relative, 76
secret information, attaching to, 76
special relationship, 82
"spring-board" test of, 77–78, 85
termination of employment intending, 74
third party disclosure, 78–79
trade secret, similarity of, 76
trivial information, 76–77
unlawful acquisition of information,
  81–82
CONSPIRACY,
criminal, 452–453
elements of, 468–469
immunity from, 469, 492, 494, 498, 499,
  518–520
justification, 519
justification as defence, 469–471

CONSPIRACY—*cont.*
trade union as, 391
unlawful element in, immunity for, 516–517
CONSTRUCTIVE DISMISSAL,
alternative offer as, 190
anticipatory breach as, 191
appeal, defect as, 226
breach of contract causing, 189
breach of contract constituting, 73, 118, 156, 267
common law basis of, 186
definition of, 185–186
early reaction to, 185, 189–190
lay-off as, 267
notice, by, 185
reason for, absence of, 191
repudiatory breach as, 187–189
resignation as, 192
seriousness of breach, 188
unreasonable conduct as, 187
committal for, 492, 522
CONTINUITY OF EMPLOYMENT,
alternative employment, pending, 145
associated employer, transfer to, 150–151
fixed term contracts, 154
hours, reckonable, 139–140
interruption of,
custom, by, 141, 144–145
maternity, by, 141
pregnancy, by, 139, 140
sickness, by, 139, 140
temporary cessation, by, 141–144
maternity leave, during, 106–107
normal week, 139, 147
notice period as, 145
notice period, extension by, 166–167
qualification for statutory rights, as, 137–138
redundancy payment affecting, 145
statutory statement of, 43
strike affecting, 145
transfer of business, 146–152
death, upon, 146
gap between, 146–147
partial, 146, 151
partnership, between, 146
associated employer, to, 150–151
characteristics of, 147–150
date of, 152
goodwill, 148
hiving down, by, 151–152
CONTRACT,
advertisement as terms of, 42
agreement to, implied, 27
alternative employment under, 190
amendment of collection agreement affecting, 38–39
anticipatory breach, 191
appeal procedure as, 226
apprenticeship, of, 20–22, 145

CONTRACT—*cont.*
assignment of, 251–252
associated employer, return to, 144
breach,
criminal, 491
damages for, 176–177
dissolution of partnership as, 180
immunity clauses, effect of, 478
incompetence as, 170
industrial action, as, 243–244
lock-out as, 450
lock-out following, 192
measure of damages for, 466
motive affecting, 54, 71
reluctance to sue for, 466
strike, as, 454–459
waiver, 169–170
withdrawal of criticism as, 450
work to rule as, 449–450, 460–461
warning of dismissal as, 184
business efficacy,
as reason for implied term, 37, 99
incorporation of documents as, 42
care, duty of, 49, 96–97, 573
carriage, of, 8
collective agreement,
acceptance by parties as binding, 32–33
express incorporation, 28, 29, 31, 35–36, 188
non-unionists, binding, 33–34
competence, warranty of, 96, 170
confidentiality, duty of. *See* CONFIDENTIALITY.
consideration, wages as, 57–58
continuation, industrial tribunal by, 230
continuity of. *See* CONTINUITY OF EMPLOYMENT.
co-operation, duty of, 54, 71–73
Crown servant, of, 18
custom and practice, implication of, 32, 33
damages,
assessment of, 176–177
notice period, limited to, 176–177
punitive, 176
discipline, 502
disruption of undertaking, 54, 71
documents, incorporation of, 41–42, 44
drafting of, 13
duality affecting continuity, 139–140
equality clause, 304–305
estoppel,
action, founding, 155
creating, 42
express term,
interpretation of, 30
priority of, 29, 30
statutory statement as, 29–30
false statement in, 31
fixed-term, 154
expiry as dismissal, 185

CONTRACT—*cont.*
  frustration, 177–179, 191
    automatic effect of, 178
    dismissal for redundancy, as, 266
    imprisonment, by, 179, 191
    repudiation confused with, 158, 159
    seamen, 19
    self-induced, 179
    sickness, by, 178
  fundamental breach, 158–159
  good faith in performance, 72
  Great Britain, employment in, 152–154
  illegality of, 25–26
    public policy, 25
    severance of, 26
    Truck Acts, under, 25, 130
  implied term,
    bargaining information, as to, 362
    bargaining procedure as, 380
    breadth of, 46, 72
    business efficacy as test of, 48–49, 56,
        70, 99, 445
    collective agreement as, 514
    contract, detailed, of, 51–53
    custom and practice as, 51, 55–56
    equipment, supply of, 586
    evidence of, 33
    Fair Wages Resolution affecting, 359
    French collective agreements as, 381
    German collective agreements as, 381
    intention of parties, 48, 49
    knowledge of, 32–33
    necessity of, 49, 56
    new contract, transferred to, 52–53
    notice, permitting, 171–172
    "Oh, of course" text, 423
    peace clause as, 378–380, 514
    precedent establishing, 51
    reasonableness of, 50, 56, 63, 72
    sources of, 28
    statute, by, 40–41
    suspension by strike, 459
    trade union rules, in, 421–422, 423–424,
        444–445
    trust and confidence. *See* TRUST
    wages, as to, 63–64
    wages council orders as, 355–356
  incorporation of written sources, 41–42,
      46, 56
  informality of, 27
  insurance, duty of, 99
  interpretation of, 39–40, 56–57
  invention, disposing of, 91
  job content, 54–57
    flexibility of, 272
  letter of appointment as terms of, 42
  maternity rights, 106
  membership of trade union, 399–401
  minors, of, 20, 24–25
  misdescription of nature, 31
  mitigation, 161–162, 176–177

CONTRACT—*cont.*
  mitigation—*cont.*
    acceptance of repudiation, as, 161,
        162
  mobility, 40
  negligence liability, exclusion of, 591–592
  notice to terminate, statutory statement
      of, 43
  overtime, consideration, as, 52, 57–58
  place of employment, 95–96
  policy statements as, 37
  purpose, primary, of, 8
  reciprocity, 172, 174
  redundancy selection procedure as, 37
  recognition clauses in, 37–38
  repudiation of, 10, 190–192
    acceptance of, 157, 190, 192
    affirmation following, 164, 189–190
    constructive dismissal, creating, 156,
        187–189
    date of termination, fixing, 167
    dismissal justifying, 169, 191
    effect of, 156–165, 188–192
    notice, by, 185
    reduction of job content as, 58, 190
    series of faults constituting, 169
    serious breach, by, 47–48, 188, 192
    test of, 157
  restrictive covenant in. *See* RESTRICTIVE
      COVENANT.
  revocation of collective agreement
      affecting, 39
  seamen, of, 1, 19
  secondary blacking permitted by, 513
  series of, 10
  severance test of, 87–88
  signature to, 30
  services, for, 1
  service, of, 1, 2, 4–14
  sources of, 28
  specific enforcement, 21, 156, 160,
      173–177, 254
    apprenticeship, of, 21
    negative covenant, 176
    nullity, to declare, 175–176
    statutory prohibition of, 175, 392
    trade union office, of, 445–446
    trust and confidence affecting, 174
    loss of trust disentitling, 69
    office-holder, 15
  statute, exclusion by, 30–31, 155, 253
  statutory implication, 40–41
  statutory statement not, 44
  supply, of, in membership clause, 513–514
  suspension by strike, 455, 457, 458
  termination,
    agreed, 184
    date of, 135n; 163, 164, 165–169, 267
  date, variation of, 185
    death, by, 179–180, 266
    dissolution of partnership as, 180, 266

CONTRACT—*cont.*
  date, variation of—*cont.*
    employee, by, 191–192
    exclusion of notice of, 171–172
    nullity of, 175–176
    variation, distinguished from, 285–286
    winding up of company as, 180–181
  terms of, wages councils fixing, 351
  trade union, by, 389, 391
  trade union,
    discipline, 416, 421
    membership application constituting,
      404
    natural justice in, 430–431
  transfer of rights, 151, 251–252
  Truck Act invalidating, 130–131
  uncertainty of implied terms, 47, 56, 72
  unenforceability of, 24–25
  unfair, 591–592
  unfair dismissal, relevance to, 216
  unwillingness to perform, 174
  variation,
    agreement to assumed, 49, 267
    collective agreement, by, 284–285
    consent to, 282–283
    consent evidenced by continuing
      employment, 286–287
    consideration for, 184
    date of termination by, 185
    dismissal, displacing, 283
    guarantee payment, affecting, 103–104
    job content of, 54–55
    management initiative, 281
    parties, change of, 146
    refusal to accept, 204
    reluctance of courts to comply, 36, 267,
      282
    statutory statement as evidence, 44–45
    trial period preceding, 285
    unilateral, 252
  vicarious liability, indemnity for, 600
  void, 25–26
    terms in, 30–31
    union membership term as, 239
  wage-work bargain, 53–69
  work,
    extent of obligation, 461
    nature of, 54–57
    provision of, 57–59
    incomplete performance of, 53, 449
  written, 19, 28, 29
  written statement of terms, 28
CONTRACTORS,
  closed shop, statutory duty towards,
    484–485
  Fair Wages Resolution affecting, 358
  low standards of employment among, 240
  union membership among, 239–240
CONTROL,
  apprentice, over, 21
  employment, as test of, 2, 4–6, 9, 11

CO-OPERATION. *See* CONTRACT.
CROWN,
  bargaining information, supply by, 362n.
  discrimination by, 336
  enforcement of contract against, 18
  servants of, 17–18
  statutory rights of employees against, 18
  statutory statement not required by, 154
  wages, obligation to pay, of, 18
CUSTOMERS,
  solicitation of, 85–86

DEATH,
  discriminatory provisions concerning,
    340–342
  dismissal, constituting, 180
  provisions for equal pay, affecting, 318
  termination of contract by, 179–180
  dismissal for redundancy, as, 266
  transfer of employment upon, 146
DELEGATION OF EMPLOYMENT,
  employee, by, 7–8
DISABLED PERSONS, 23–24
  dismissal of, 24
  inadequate protection of, 24
  quota, 23
DISCIPLINE,
  appeal from,
    code of practice, 226
    notification of procedure for, 43
  collective agreement as to, 38
  procedure, agreed, 224–226
  seamen, of, 19–20
  shift transfer as, 117
  statement of rules of, 43
  warning as, 223
DISCRIMINATION,
  advertisements, 343
  age limits as, 330–331, 341
  charitable organisation, by, 342
  collective agreements, in, 318–319
  comparable characteristics, 325–326
  compensation for, 342–343
  complaint of, 342–343
  conciliation, 342
  conditions invoking, 330
  courtesy as, 326
  Crown, by, 336
  death, provisions concerning, as,
    340–342
  de minimis, 326, 327, 336
  detriment, 327–328
  different treatment as, 322
  direct, 320
  discovery of documents, 323–324
  effects of, 303
  employment agents, by, 336
  employment, application to,
    benefits of, 335, 336
    offer of, 335
  equality clause, effect upon, 329

DISCRIMINATION—*cont.*
　Equal Opportunities Commission,
　　343–344
　Equal Pay Act, interaction with, 329
　evidence of, 322–323
　good intentions irrelevant, 327
　household, private, in, 335
　indirect, 329–334
　　conditions, ability to comply with,
　　　331–332
　　definition of, 320
　　effect of prohibition on, 319–320
　　justification, 320
　intention, detrimental, 327–328
　investigation of, 343–344
　justification, 332–334
　　expediency as, 333–334
　　occupation qualification as, 338–340
　　proof of, 333
　　subjective test of, 333
　　third party attitudes as, 334
　marriage as reason for, 320, 337
　motive, relevance of, 321, 324–326
　partnership, by, 336
　part-time employees, 331–332
　payment, affecting, 329, 335
　pension, inapplicable to, 332, 335
　presumption of, 322
　proof of, 321–322
　Race Relations Commission, 343–344
　reasons for, prohibition on, 320
　remedies,
　　injunction, 344
　　non-discrimination notice, 344
　remedies for, 342–344
　sanctions against, 319
　segregation, by, 321
　self-employed protected, 336
　seniority affecting, 333
　services, related to, 336
　sexual harassment as, 337
　small employer, by, 335
　statutory, 317, 339
　third party, affecting, 328
　trade unions, by, 336
　　representation, 447
　　union membership, 403–404
　training, in, 335, 336, 342
　United Kingdom, outside, 339
　victimisation, definition of, 321
　wages, affecting, 329, 335
DISMISSAL,
　agreed, 184
　ambiguity in, 183
　appeal against, termination postponed by,
　　168
　apprentice, of, 21
　avoidance of, by successful appeal, 168
　care, duty of requiring, 578–579
　constructive. *See* CONSTRUCTIVE
　　DISMISSAL.

DISMISSAL—*cont.*
　criminal offence for, 254
　Crown, by, 18, 266
　death as, 180, 266
　deemed, 265–267
　definition of, 3, 4–14
　disabled person, of, 24
　discrimination, as, 253
　early leaving as, 185, 267–268
　employee breach, following, 191–192
　employer, by, 183–185
　fixed term, expiry, as, 185
　intention, 183
　national security, 18
　notice,
　　permitted by, 170–172
　　precise, 183–184, 265
　　statutory minimum, 172–173
　pregnancy for, 106, 250–251
　reasons for,
　　statement of, 153
　　subsequent to, 196–197
　　written statement of, 195–196
　redundancy, for, 263–269
　repudiatory breach justifying, 169
　　series constituting, 169
　　sufficiency of breach, 169–170
　　waiver, 169–170
　right of, 10
　statutory definition of, 183–192, 265–268
　strike, for, 458–459, 467–468
　variation, contractual, replacing, 283
　voluntary leaving before, 185, 265
　wrongful, 169–173
DISSOLUTION OF PARTNERSHIP,
　apprenticeship, affecting, 21
DOCK WORKERS,
　guaranteed payments, exclusion from,
　　102
　registration, 175
DOCUMENT,
　discovery of, 323–324
DURESS, ECONOMIC,
　elements of liability for, 483
　justification, 484

EMERGENCY PROVISIONS, 532–534
　armed forces, use of, 534
　industrial action, cessation of, 534
　state of emergency,
　　declaration of, 533
　　duration of, 533
　　Orders in Council, 533
　　picketing during, 533
　　strikes during, 533
EMPLOYEE,
　abuse of, 47, 70
　account, duty to, 97–98
　admonition of, 46
　assault by, 109
　assets of company, benefit from, 124–125

EMPLOYEE—*cont.*
authority of, 46
canvassing of customers by, 75
care, duty to, 96–97
carelessness of, foresight of, 574–575
competence, warranty of, 96–97, 170
constructive trustee, as, 98
consultation, company annual report
concerning, 362
control of, 601
conviction, disclosure of, 254
criminal liability, transfer of, 252
delegation by, 7–8
director, as, 3
disclosure to employer by, 82, 88–90
duties of, trade dispute concerning, 502
fiduciary, as, 82, 88, 98
good faith, duty of, 89
helpfulness of, 94
illegal contract of, 25
indemnity, duty of, 97, 99
information concerning, disclosure to
employer of, 90
information to,
maternity leave, concerning, 104–105,
107, 108
inventions, property in, 90–91
notice to terminate contract, 172
obedience,
duty of, 93–96
instructions to, 41, 159
place of work, as to, 95–96
trade union instructions affecting, 94
on call, 140
other employers, working for, 9
part-time, discrimination against, 331–332
property, care of employer's, 97
replacement, unfair dismissal affecting,
255
safety, duty of, 543–544
secret profit by, 98
interest upon, 98
social surveyor as, 3, 10
status of, 59
statutory rights of, 2
sub-postmaster as, 3, 11–12
third party, working for, 92–93
tools, ownership by, 9
trade dispute, involvement in, 501
trust and confidence,
maintenance of, 46–47, 70, 170
trade union instructions affecting, 448
welfare of, 541
work, unlimited, by, 461
worker distinguished from, 385
EMPLOYER,
abuse by, 47, 70
care, duty of, 96–97. *See also*
NEGLIGENCE; SAFETY.
contract, in, 573
dismissal to satisfy, 578–579

EMPLOYER—*cont.*
care, duty of—*cont.*
origins of, 568
courtesy, duty of, 46, 70
criminal liability, transfer of, 252
determination of, 600–603
indemnity, right to, 97, 99
information by,
entitlement to receive, 82, 88–90
insolvency, upon, 124
reasons for dismissal, 195–196
redundancy, concerning, 296–297, 299
redundancy payment, as to, 302
wages, upon attachment of, 133
insolvency. *See* INSOLVENCY.
insurance,
negligence liability against, 573n, 593
statutory duty of, 613, 614
inventions, property in, 90–91
notice to terminate contract, 172
obedience to, 93–96
occupier, liability for negligence as, 612
property of, care by employee, 97
requirements, reasonable, of, 102–103
safety,
non-employees, obligation to, 542
statutory duty of, 540–542
strikes, protection from, 467, 468
trade dispute, involvement in, 500–501
training by, 113
trust and confidence,
maintenance of, 46, 70, 170
trade union instructions affecting, 448
EMPLOYMENT,
agreement to, 156
aliens of, 23
alternative offer. *See* GUARANTEE
PAYMENTS; MATERNITY RIGHTS;
REDUNDANCY.
application for, 254
assignment of, 7–8, 11, 252, 600
base of, 153–154
benefits of, discrimination affecting, 335,
336
businessman not in, 9, 10, 11–12
children. *See* MINORS.
commencement, date of, 43
conflict of interest in, 92
continuity of. *See* CONTINUITY OF
EMPLOYMENT.
continuous character of, 10
control,
as test of, 2, 4–6, 9, 11
transfer of, 600–603
co-operation in, 156, 161
course of,
indemnity for expenses in, 99
invention in, 91
liability, as test of, 603–612, 620–628
definition, 5–14
parties, by, 3, 13–14

EMPLOYMENT—*cont.*
  disabled persons, of, 23–24
  domestic service, as, 180
  economic advantages of, 4
  forms of, 1–2
  Great Britain, in, 152–154, 264–265
  Great Britain, outside, not affecting
      continuity, 139
  hours of, 22–23
  illegal contract of, 25–26
  inconsistent contracts, 8, 10–11, 12
  information relevant to, disclosure of,
      88–92
  job security, 182
  loss, risk of, 8, 9, 10, 11–12
  multiple elements of, 7–14
  night, 23
  notice, statutory mimimum to terminate,
      172–173
  offer of, discrimination, as, 335
  ordinary course of, 153
  "organisation" test of, 6–7
  personal nature of, 173, 179
  place of, 50, 52, 55, 95–96, 626–627
  probationary, 190
  profit, chance of, 8, 9, 10, 11–12
  property right in, 176
  re-engagement, 174–175
  re-instatement, 174–175
  relationships of,
      continuous, 10, 14
      non-contractual, 156
      parties to, 10–11
  resignation,
      constructive dismissal as, 192
      employer by, 191–192
  status, as, 156, 176
  statutory rights confined to, 134
  termination. *See also* CONTRACT.
      trade dispute concerning, 502
  terms and conditions, trade dispute
      concerning, 502
  time off, 10
  women. *See* WOMEN.
  yearly hiring, 171
EMPLOYMENT APPEAL TRIBUNAL,
  function of, 192–195
EMPLOYMENT PROTECTION, 100–133
ENTERTAINMENT,
  children employed in, 22
EQUAL PAY,
  comparison, 305–306
      former employee, with, 306
  discrimination, interaction with, 329
  equality clause, 304–305
  EEC obligation, 304
  EEC provision for, 318
  exclusion, grounds of, 317–318
  genuine material difference, 312–317
      beneficial effect, absence of, 314
      established practice justifying, 315–317

EQUAL PAY—*cont.*
  genuine material difference—*cont.*
      experience as, 315
      market forces as, 314–315
      part-time working as, 316–317
      personal characteristics as, 312, 314
      qualifications as, 314
      reasonable belief in, 313
      "red circle" as, 315–316
      sex based assumptions, 317
  intention to discriminate, 313
  job evaluation,
      equality, as standard of, 305, 311
      like work, excluding standard of, 311
      obligatory, 312
      validity of, 311
  like work,
      broad similarity, 306–308
      common practice, 310
      contractual definition, 307
      differences of practical importance,
          308–309
      excessive value of differences, 310
      experience, 310
      job content, 308
      separately remunerated aspects, 311
      statutory definition of, 305
      supervisory duties, 310
      time, 308, 310
  non-contractual conditions, 306
  statutory standard of, 305
  time limit to claim, 135
  value of work, 303–304
ESTOPPEL,
  incorporation of documents in contract,
      42
  statutory statement effecting, 43, 155
EUROPEAN ECONOMIC COMMUNITY,
  discrimination, prohibition, confined to
      remuneration, 329, 341
  works councils in, 368

FACTORIES ACTS,
  application, area of, 537
  danger, foresight of, 560–561
  "factory," 540
  fencing,
      carelessness, against, 562
      danger, reasonable foresight of, 538
      ejection of pieces, against, 561–562, 563
      impracticability of, 562
      machinery, 537
      machinery, dangerous part, of, 555–556
      maintenance of, 564
      material, 558
      normal operation, during, 559
      prime movers, of, 555
      security of, 556, 562–564
      tools, against, 563
      transmission machinery, of, 555
      workman, against, 561–562, 563

FACTORIES ACT—*cont.*
  inspection to enforce, 536–537
  machinery, 537, 556–569
    cleaning, 565
    factory, in use in, 556
    mechanical nature of, 557, 558
    testing of, 556–557
    motion or use, in, 564–565
    moving part of, 565
    normal operation of, 559
    vehicle distinguished from, 557–558
  motion or use,
    mechanical power creating, 564
    normal, 564
    purpose of, 564–565
  moving part, 565
  origin of, 536
  part of machine,
    inherent danger of, 559
    juxtaposition of, 557, 559–560
    material combined with, 560
    safety of, 558–559
  piecemeal approach of, 536, 537
FACTORY,
  children employed in, 22
  textile, 131
  wages in, 131–132
  women employed in, 22
FAIR WAGES RESOLUTION, 348, 350, 358–360
  awards exempt from pay policy, 359–360
  enforcement of, 358, 359
  general level of wages, 358, 359
  organisation, freedom of, 358
  provisions of, 358
  purpose of, 358
  references under, 358
  rescission of, 357–358
FIXED TERM CONTRACT, 154
Foss v. *Harbottle,* Rule in, 421
FRIENDLY SOCIETY, 132
FRUSTRATION. *See* CONTRACT.

GREAT BRITAIN,
  employment in. *See* EMPLOYMENT.
GUARANTEE PAYMENT, 101–104
  alternative work, offer of, 102
  collective agreement for, 39, 104
  complaint of non-payment, 104
  continuity of employment as qualification, 138
  days of entitlement, 101
  deductions from, 104
  employer requirements, compliance with, 102–103
  excluded categories of employment, 102
  Great Britain, employment in, 153
  holidays, 101–102
  industrial action excluding, 102
  payment for, 2, 61
  period of, 103–104

GUARANTEE PAYMENT—*cont.*
  priority of, 123–124
  suspension of, 39
  time limit to claim, 135
GRIEVANCE PROCEDURE,
  notification of, 43–44

HEALTH AND SAFETY AT WORK. *See* SAFETY.
HIVING DOWN,
  employment, effect on, 180–181
HOLIDAY,
  guarantee payment not available, 101–102
  pay, priority on insolvency, 123–124
  statutory statement of, 43
  wages councils fixing, 351
HOURS,
  basic, 60
  continuity, for. *See* CONTINUITY OF
    EMPLOYMENT.
  on call, 140
  overtime, 52, 55, 57–58, 284
  short time, guaranteed payment, 101–104
  statutory statement of, 43
  women, of, discrimination, justifying, 340

ILLEGALITY. *See* CONTRACT.
IMMUNITY, STATUTORY. *See* TRADE DISPUTE.
INCOME TAX,
  fraud, 25–26
  self-employed, assessment of, 3
  sickness payment deducted from, 69
INDEMNITY, 97, 99
INDEPENDENT CONTRACTOR. *See also* CLOSED
    SHOP, SELF-EMPLOYMENT.
INDUSTRIAL ACTION,
  agreement to exclude, 378–379
  authorisation,
    membership of trade union, by, 497
    shop stewards, by, 495–497
    trade union, by, 494–495
  balance of power, as, 485–486
  breach of contract, as, 243–244
  cessation, order of, 534
  collective agreement restricting, 32
  collective bargaining, influence of, 348
  conspiracy, civil, as, 453–454
  conspiracy, criminal, as, 453
  constitutional right to, 451
  control, legal, 450
  criminal sanctions, 451, 490–492
    advocacy of, 451
    breach of contract, against, 491
    drawbacks of, 492
    gas, water and electricity workers,
      against, 491
    postal workers, against, 491
  definition, 242, 462–466
  dismissal for, 244–247
  emergency provisions relating to. *See*
    EMERGENCY PROVISIONS.
  establishment, separate, 246, 247

INDUSTRIAL ACTION—*cont.*
fault, 464–465
forms of, 449
guarantee payment, disqualification from, 102
immunity, individual, 498–514. *See also* TRADE DISPUTE.
  conspiracy, 492, 493–494, 499
  criminal actions, 516
  inducement to breach of contract, 492, 493–494, 498–499
  interference with trade, 492, 517–518
  intimidation, for, 499. *See also* TRADE DISPUTE.
  picket, of, 532
  threats of action, 493
  trade unions, of, 492–498
  union membership agreements, 513
  unlawful element in tort, covering, 516–517
individual liability, reluctance to enforce, 466
injunction to restrain, 520–522
lock-out, breach of contract as, 450
motive, 465
organisers, liability of. *See* CONSPIRACY; DURESS; IMMUNITY; INTIMIDATION; STATUTORY INTERFERENCE WITH CONTRACT.
overtime, withdrawal of, 450
peace clause affecting, 376, 378–380
picketing, immunity of, 532. *See also* PICKETING.
pressure to dismiss by, 228
prohibition of during emergency, 533, 534
protected union activity, as, 119–120
purpose of, 451, 462–464
re-instatement after maternity, 109
repudiation of, by trade union, 494, 495
restriction upon non-contractual nature of, 40–41
safety obligations, to ensure, 549
secondary, 509–514
  contractual disruption by, 513
  contractual permission for, 513
  definition, statutory, of, 510
  immunity dependent on contract, 512
  immunity, removal of, 510
  immunity, retention of, 510–514
  primary dispute ancillary to, 513
  purpose of, 509–510
selective illegality, 242
social security benefits during, 486–490
threats of, immunity, 493
time off for, 115
tortious liability for. *See* CONSPIRACY; DURESS; INTERFERENCE WITH CONTRACT; INTIMIDATION.
trade union liability for, 497–498
trade union pressure, 122

INDUSTRIAL ACTION—*cont.*
unconstitutional, 450
union meeting as, 246
unofficial, 450
work to rule, breach of contract, as, 449–450, 460–461
INDUSTRIAL COURT. *See* CENTRAL ARBITRATION COMMITTEE.
INDUSTRIAL DISABLEMENT BENEFIT,
accident,
  definition of, 617–618
  foresight of, 618
  process distinguished from, 617–618
authorised conduct, 619, 621
availability of, 615
causation in, 618, 619, 628–630
claim to benefit, 631–634
common risks, 620, 628, 630
commissioner, appeal to, 631
commissioner, procedure before, 632
constant attendance allowance, 616
course of employment, 620–628
  contributory negligence affecting, 629–630
  emergency as, 626
  incidental acts, 621, 623
  meal breaks as, 627–628
  misbehaviour in, 629–630
  negligence in, 629–630
  place of accident, affecting, 626–627
  provocation causing, 620, 630
  reasonable conduct as in, 622
  recreational activities in, 624–625
  resumption of, 627
  third parties, assistance of, 623–624
  travel to work, 625–627
  vicarious liability, comparison with, 620
damages for negligence, discounted against, 594
death benefit, 615
decisions,
  binding, 631–632
  review of, 633–634
disqualification from, 616
exceptionally severe disablement allowance, 616
injury, 616–617, 618, 620
insurance officer, determination by, 631
local appeal tribunal, 631
medical authorities,
  review by, 634
  statutory authorities, bound by, 632–633
medical questions, 632–633
out of employment, presumption of, 616, 620, 629
out of ... course of employment, 618–620
Pearson Commission, the, 614, 618, 631
prescribed diseases, 630–631
special hardship allowance, 616

INDUSTRIAL DISABLEMENT BENEFIT—*cont.*
  supplements to, 615–616
  unemployment supplement, 616
INDUSTRIAL INJURY BENEFIT,
  abolition of, 615
  employee, available to, 2
  incomplete provision for, 614
  origins of, 614
  sickness benefit, assimilation to, 615
INDUSTRIAL RELATIONS,
  fair practice, 194
  group of companies, within, 112
  scope of, 112–113
  training in, 113–114
INDUSTRIAL TRIBUNAL,
  appeal from, time limit for, 136
  appeal to,
    non-discrimination notice, from, 344
    safety orders, against, 550, 551
    time limit for, 136
  complaint to,
    action short of dismissal, 121–122
    discrimination, of, 320, 342
    guaranteed payment, 104
    insolvency, non-payment upon, 124
    maternity pay, 105
    medical suspension, payment during, 123
    re-instatement after maternity, 110–111
    safety representation, by, 549
    time for. *See* LIMITATION OF ACTION.
    time-off, refusal of, 114, 116, 117
    trade union membership, 403
  continuation of contract by, 230
  discretion of, 192–195
  discrimination, complaint of, 320
    discretion as to, 334
  error of law by, 193–195
  interim relief by, 229
  jurisdiction,
    estoppel not extending, 155
    strikes, dismissal during, 244–247, 467
  perverse decision by, 193–195
  protective award by, 297
  redundancy payment,
    early leaving, following, 268
    justification for, 248
    lay off, upon, 266–267
    strike affecting, 268–269
  redundancy rebate, 300
  re-engagement, order for, 255–256
  reinstatement, order for, 254–256
  safety,
    improvement notice, appeal from, 550
    prohibition notice, appeal from, 551
  time off for, 115
  unfair dismissal, subjective standard, 201–205
INFORMATION. *See also* CONFIDENTIALITY.
  attachment of wages, upon, 133
  bargaining, statutory requirement for, 350

INFORMATION—*cont.*
  disclosure to employer of, 88–90
  insolvency, upon, 124
  redundancy proposals, 296–297, 298–299
  redundancy, Secretary of State, 297–298
INJUNCTION,
  contempt, proceedings for, 522
  contract of employment, to enforce, 392
  industrial action, to restrain, 520–522
  interlocutory, 520–522
    balance of convenience in, 521
    statutory restriction upon, 522
  picketing, to prohibit, 526
INJURY AT WORK. *See also* BREACH OF STATUTORY DUTY; NEGLIGENCE; SAFETY.
  compensation, statutory duty of, 614
  liability for, multiplicity of actions, 555
INSOLVENCY,
  complaint of non-payment upon, 124
  Great Britain, employment in, 153
  hiving down, 151–152
  information from employer upon, 124
  maternity pay, 111
  preferential rights in, 2
  priority of claims, 123–124
INSURANCE,
  contractual duty of, 99
  indemnity, duty of, affecting, 99
INTERFERENCE WITH CONTRACT,
  ancillary participation in, 473
  breach of contract, 477–478
  damage, mitigation of, 474
  direct, 472
  direct interference through agent, 471
  elements of, 479
  illegal means, 472, 474–475, 479
    persuasive effect of, 475
  immunity from liability for, 492, 493–494, 498, 499, 514, 517–518. *See also* TRADE DISPUTE.
  indirect, 472
  inducement to breach, 471
  industrial action, control of, 450
  intention, 471, 473–474
  justification as defence, 471, 476–477
  justification, 472
    prior contract, to protect, 476
    public policy, 476
    statutory obligation, 476
  knowledge of contract, 471, 474
  origin of, 472
  picket, by, 532
  potential contracts, 513
  privacy in, 472
  relationships immune from liability, 472
  right of action, 472
  trade, extension to, 482
  unlawful element in, immunity, 516–517
  unlawful means, 479
  willing response to, 472–473

INTERFERENCE WITH TRADE,
  interference with contract, connection
    with, 482
  limits of, 482–483
INTERNATIONAL CONVENTION,
  closed shop, restrictions upon, 240–242
INTIMIDATION,
  coercion by, 481
  communication of, 481–482
  elements, 479–480
  immunity from liability for, 498, 499, 516.
    See also TRADE DISPUTE.
  justification, 482
  picketing, during, 523, 524
  submission to, 481
  unlawful action,
    breach of contract as, 481–482
    threat of, 480
  unlawful element in, immunity, 516–517
  unlawful means, immune actions as,
    515–516
INVENTION,
  course of normal duties, in, 91
  disposal of, 91
  employer's property, as, 53
  employment, scope of, within, 90
  payment for, 91–92
  property of employer, derived from,
    90
  property in, 89
    statutory definition of, 90–91

JOB,
  content of, 54–57, 190, 271–272
  equality of. *See* EQUAL PAY.
  reduction of, 55, 58, 190
  security of, 182
  title, statement of, 43, 44
JOINDER. *See* ACTION, JOINDER IN.
JUSTICE OF THE PEACE,
  time off to act as, 115

LAY OFF,
  dismissal for redundancy, as, 266–267
LIMITATION,
  extension of time, 136–137
  industrial tribunal, appeal to, 136
  industrial tribunal, claim to, 135–136
  negligence, for. *See* NEGLIGENCE.
  redundancy claim for, 165
  unfair dismissal, 448
LOCK-OUT,
  breach of contract, following, 192
LOCAL AUTHORITIES,
  associated employers, as, 150
  children, control of employment,
    22
  job evaluation by, 311
  safety inspection by, 550
  time off to serve, 115
LUMP, THE, 1

MATERNITY RIGHT,
  alternative employment, 107–108
  continuity of employment as qualification,
    138, 141
  contractual, 106
  dismissal affecting, 109–110
  information to employer, 104–105, 107,
    108
  medical certificate, 105, 108–109
  pay, 105
    employee, available to, 2
    industrial tribunal, complaint to, 105
    non-payment of, 111
    refund, 105
    set off against, 105
  period of leave, 107
    extension of, 108–109
    industrial action extending, 109
  pregnancy, dismissal for, affecting, 251
  qualification for, 104–105
  redundancy, date of dismissal for, 109
  reinstatement, 106–110
    alternative offer, 107–108
    employee, available to, 2
    enquiry by employer, 108
    exclusion of right, 107–108
    failure as unfair dismissal, 108
    postponement of, 108–109
    redundancy affecting, 107
    terms of, 106
  replacement,
    employment of, 110, 251
    dismissal of, 110
  time limit to claim, 135
MEDICAL CERTIFICATE,
  confinement, date of, 105
  sickness following maternity, of, 108–109
MERCHANT SEAMEN. *See* CONTRACT SEAMEN.
MINE,
  children employed in, 22
  discrimination affecting, 336
  safety in, 537, 547
  safety representatives in, 547
  women employed in, 23
MINOR,
  age of employment, 22
  cleaning of machinery by, 565
  contract of, unenforceability of, 24
MITIGATION,
  reinstatement, affecting, 255
  wages during notice, 258

NATIONAL INSURANCE,
  contributions,
    deduction from sick pay, 68
    self-employed, by, 3
  employment, definition in, 7
  reference to High Court, 7
  sickness benefit, 65–67. *See also* SICKNESS.
    industrial injury benefit assimilated to,
    615

NATIONAL INSURANCE—*cont.*
  unemployment benefit,
    compensation for dismissal, affecting,
      257, 262
    employee, available to, 2
NATURAL JUSTICE. *See also* TRADE UNION.
  employment relationship, application to,
    16
  office-holder, application to, 15
NEGLIGENCE,
  causation, 583–588
  compensation, justification for, 536
  course of employment, relevance of, 573,
    582
  damages,
    industrial injury benefit discounted, 594
    reduction by contribution of, 592,
      593–594
  danger, creation of, 575–576
  defective equipment, 582–583
  defences,
    common employment, 568
    contributory apportionment of blame,
      584
    contributory, assessment of, 593–594
    contributory negligence, 569, 592–594
    contributory, standard of care in,
      592–593
    volenti, 568, 589–592
      abolition of, 589
      knowledge affecting, 589–590
      re-appearance of, 591
      sole cause as, 586
      statutory exclusion of, 583, 592
  delegation, 581–583
  dismissal to avoid liability, 578–579
  election, Workmen's Compensation Acts,
    under, 590
  elements of, 573–589
  employer's liability for,
    categories of, 569–570
    origins of, 568
  exclusion of liability for, 591–592
  exhortation, 578
  experience, reliance upon, 577–579, 580
  fault, 586–588
  foresight, 573–575
    carelessness of employee, 574–575
    nature of injury, of, 588–589
  generality of liability for, 574
  instructions, disregard of, 578
  insurance against, 573n, 593, 599, 613,
    614
    statutory duty of, 613, 614
  knowledge, standard of care affecting,
    576
  limitation of action, 594–597
    discretion, judicial, 595–597
    knowledge affecting, 594–595
    period of, 594
  nervous shock, 575

NEGLIGENCE—*cont.*
  normal practice as, 579
  novus actus interveniens, 584
  performance by others, 581–583
  premises, third party, 573, 579–581
  presumption of, 570, 572, 582
  reasonable man, duty of, 576
  remoteness, 588–589
  res ipsa loquitur, 570, 571–572
  risk,
    balanced against cost, 577
    subjectivity of, 576–577
  safety device, failure to use, 586–588
  safety, promotion of, 552
  sole cause, 584–586
  standard of care,
    knowledge affecting, 576
    reasonable man, of, 576
    small company of, 576
  sub-contractors, duty to, 580–581
  sub-contractor, of, 541
  trade union, of, 448
  trespassers, duty to, 612
  vicarious liability, absolving, 602–603
  vicarious liability for. *See* VICARIOUS
    LIABILITY.
  warnings, 578
NOTICE,
  claim for unfair dismissal during, 137
  continuous employment, as, 145
  Crown, by, 154
  damages confined to period of, 162
  date of termination, affecting, 135n
  dismissal permitted by, 170–172
  fixed term contracts, in, 154
  length of employment affecting, 138
  period of, 172–173
  period of, voluntary leaving during, 185
  precise, 183–184
  presumption of right to give, 171
  repudiatory breach by, 185
  rights during, 173
  statutory minimum, 172–173
    termination, 166
  statutory right to, Crown bound by, 154
  statutory statement of, 43
  unfair, dismissal, irrelevant to, 182, 216
  variation of, 185
NUISANCE,
  picket as, 524

OBEDIENCE. DUTY OF. *See* EMPLOYEE.
OFFICE, 15–16
  definition, 15
  ministers of religion, 16
  natural justice applied to, 15
  specific performance, 15
  status, as, 15
ORGANISATION,
  employment, as test of, 6–7
OVERTIME. *See* HOURS.

PARTNERSHIP,
  apprentices, 21
  change of, continuity of employment on,
    146
  discrimination by, 336
  dissolution,
    dismissal for redundancy as, 266
    termination of employment as, 180
PATENT. *See also* INVENTION.
  confidentiality not applicable to, 76
  payment for, 91–92
PEACE CLAUSE. *See* COLLECTIVE AGREEMENT.
PENSION,
  compensation for loss of, 260
  consultation concerning, recognised
    unions, with, 367
  discrimination, inapplicable to, 332, 335,
    340–342
  equality of provision for, 318
  insolvency, payments upon, 124
  notification of terms of, 43
  redundancy payment, affecting, 302
  restraint of trade, conditions in, 86
  transfer of, 252
PICKETING,
  breach of peace, provoking, 523, 529, 531
  code of practice as to, 531–532
  conspiracy, criminal, as, 453
  contempt, committal for, 492
  criminal liability for, 523–525
  excessive means, 527
  freedom of speech affecting, 522
  freedom to, 523, 528, 529
  illegality, inherent, of, 523–524, 528
  immunity,
    limit of purposes attracting, 527, 528
    place of work, limited to, 530
  immunity from liability of, 525–528, 532
  injunction prohibiting, 526
  interference with contract by, 532
  nuisance, as, 524, 528
  number of, 532
  obstruction of highway, as, 526, 528
  obstruction of police, 527, 529
  place of work, at, 530–531
  police control of, 528–530
  secondary, 532
    definition of, 530
    immunity not available to, 530
  state of emergency, during, 533
  statutory offences, 453
  tortious liability for, 523, 528
  trade union officials participating, 530
  trespass to highway, as, 525–526, 528
PIECE WORKERS. *See* WAGES.
POLICE,
  assistance to, course of employment, in,
    623–624
  disaffection among, 533
  obstruction of, 527, 529, 531
  office holders, as, 16

POLICE—*cont.*
  picket, control by, 528–530, 531
  strike among, inducing, 533
  unfair dismissal not applicable to, 154
POST OFFICE,
  blacking of mail, 491
  discrimination by, 333
PREGNANCY. *See also* MATERNITY.
  continuity not affected by, 139, 140
  dismissal by reason of, 250–251
  equal pay, affecting, 318
  replacement during, 251
  sickness benefit during, 65
  time off, ante-natal care, 117
  unfair dismissal for, 137–138
PRODUCTIVITY. *See* WAGES.
PROOF,
  burden of,
    action short of dismissal, 118
    discrimination, of 321–323
    inadmissible reasons, of, 230
    negligence, of, 571–572, 588
    pre-redundancy procedure, 297
    reasonable dismissal, 201
    reasonably practicable safety
      requirements, 552
    safety standards, of, 542
    shift of, 322
    transfer of control of servant, 601, 602
  discovery of documents, by, 323–324
  discrimination, justification for, 333
  genuine material difference, of, 312–313,
    315, 316
  interrogatories, 321
  loss, of, 257
  negligence, of, 571–572, 586–588
  safety,
    codes of practice facilitating, 547
    conclusive of, 547
    employee unlikely to apply, 586–588
  vicarious liability, of 601, 602, 608
PUBLIC DUTIES. *See* TIME-OFF.
PUBLIC POLICY,
  contract contrary to, 25

RACIAL DISCRIMINATION. *See also*
    DISCRIMINATION.
  action short of dismissal, 117
  dismissal as, "additional award"
    following, 256
  time limit to claim, 135, 136
RAILWAYS,
  normal operation of, 56
RECEIVER,
  agent, as, 180, 181
  appointment, termination of employment
    by, 180–181
  voluntary distinguished from compulsory,
    180–181
RECOGNITION,
  advantages of, 367

RECOGNITION—*cont.*
  award, contractual implication of, 41
  business efficacy not requiring, 49
  C.A.C., preliminary hearing by, 356
  consultation distinguished from, 368,
       369–370
  enforcement of, 350
  grievance procedure as, 369
  individual contract, 31–32, 37
  intention, 369
  meaning of, 295–296, 368–370
      C.A.C. view of, 369, 370
  safety representation following, 547
  statutory machinery for, 367
  statutory provision for, 350
  transfer of, 382
  voluntary, 367
  withdrawal, 37
RECTIFICATION,
  statutory statement, of, 45–46
REDUNDANCY,
  age limit at claim, 134–135, 265
  alternative offer, 288–292
      statutory provision for, 287–288
      suitability, 289–292
      trial period following, 288, 293–294
      unfair dismissal affecting, 250
      unreasonable rejection, 289–292
  apprentice, of, 272
  basic award, affecting, 256
  collective agreements, 100
  compensation,
      employee, available to, 2
      expenses, 302
      normal week's pay, 301
      notice in period of assessment, 166
      overtime premiums, 301, 302
      pension affecting, 302
      period of service for, 165
      rebate, 300
  continuity of employment as qualification,
       138, 264
  Crown, application to, 154, 264
  date of, maternity leaving, during, 109
  definition,
      classification of jobs, 276
      contractual basis of, 270–271
      expectations, 272
      job content, 270–271
      job, scope of, 272
      motivation for dismissal, as, 277–281
      place of work, 271
      strict construction, 269
      temporary diminution, 280
      terms of employment not included,
          272–275
  dismissal,
      early leaving following, 267–268
      frustration as, 266
      lay-off as, 266–267
      motivation for, 277–281

REDUNDANCY—*cont.*
  dismissal—*cont.*
      short-time as, 266–267
      terminating events as, 265–266
      volunteers, 265
      warning of, 265
      presumption of, 180
  economy, as, 272–274
  fixed term contract excluding, 154–264
  Great Britain, employment in, 153, 264
  information as to payment, 302
  justification for, 248
  management prerogative to declare, 182
  maternity leave, reinstatement following,
       107
  misconduct displacing, 268–269
  payment, continuity affecting, 145–264
  pre-redundancy procedure,
      consultation with trade union, 295–296,
          298–299
      notification to Secretary of State,
          297–298
      protective award, 297
      recognised union, information to, 367
      selection, 295
      special circumstances excusing, 299–300
  presumption of, 268
  procedure,
      customary, 248–249
      "last-in," "first-out," 249
      selection for, 37
  qualifications to claim, 264
  rebate, 300
  redundancy fund, 300
  reorganisation distinguished, 272, 275
  scheme of compensation, 263–264
  selection for, 214, 247–250
  selection,
      grade of employee, 248
      procedure for, 214, 247
      prohibited reasons, 118
      reason for, 200
      strikers, of, 468
  strike following notice for, 268–269
  strikers, selection among, 249
  subjectivity of, 278–280
  time limit to claim, 135, 136, 265
  time-off pending, 116
  transfer of business affecting, 252
  unfair dismissal for, 263
  voluntary, agreed termination as, 265
  warning of, 194, 214
RE-ENGAGEMENT. *See also* EMPLOYMENT.
  industrial action, following, 246, 247
  refusal, increase of compensation for, 238
REGISTRATION,
  dockworker, of, 175
RE-INSTATEMENT. *See also* EMPLOYMENT;
      MATERNITY RIGHTS; UNFAIR
      DISMISSAL.
  refusal, increase of compensation for, 238

RELIGION,
  ministers of, 16
    discrimination among, 336
REMUNERATION. *See* WAGES.
REPUDIATION. *See* CONTRACT.
RESIGNATION. *See* EMPLOYMENT.
RESTRAINT OF TRADE,
  closed shop, 234
  expulsion from trade union as, 392
  trade union in, 390, 391
  trade union membership, denial of, 404
  trade union rules in, 426
RESTRICTIVE COVENANT,
  competition, restraining, 86
  enforcement of, specific performance, as,
    176
  extent, geographic, of, 85, 86
  general knowledge, restraining, 85
  period of, 85
  personal skills, affecting, 84
  proprietary interests protected by, 84
  public policy affecting, 83, 84, 86–87
  purpose of, 82
  reasonableness of, 83–85
  severance,
    invalid provisions, of, 87–88
    remainder of contract, from, 87–88
  solicitation of customers, against, 85–86
  third party challenge to, 83
  trade secrets, protecting, 84
  variation of contract by, 204
RESTRICTIVE TRADE PRACTICE, 81
  employer acceptance of, 95
  industrial action as, 492
RETIREMENT,
  normal age of, 134
RULE BOOK, COMPANY,
  contractual nature of, 41–42

SAFETY,
  appliances, interference with, 544
  assignment of duty of, 544, 545–549
  "at work," 539–540
  breach of statutory duty, causing, 554
  burden of proof of, 542
  civil liability assisting, 552
  codes of practice of, 546–547
  commission, codes of practice by, 546–547
  committees, 548, 549
  complaint concerning, as union activity,
    120
  conclusive proof of absence, 547
  controller of premises,
    duty of, 543
    pollution, duty of prevent, 544
  designers, duty of, 544–546
  early statutory provision, 537
  employee's duty of, 543–544
  employer's duty of, 540–542
  experiments, reporting of, 546
  fines, 552

SAFETY—*cont.*
  importers, duty of, 544–546
  improvement notice, 550–551
  individual liability, 552
  industrial tribunal, 549, 550, 551
  information concerning, 541–542, 544–546
    inspector, to, 550
    representative, employee, to, 549
    trade secrets, 545
  inherently dangerous situations, 551
  injury, compensation for, 535
  inspection,
    local authority, by, 550
    origins of, 536–537
    representatives, employee, by, 548
  inspectors, 549–551
    powers of, 550–551
    prosecution by, standard of, 538, 539
    seizure by, 550
  legislation affecting, 566–567
  manufacturers, duty of, 544–546
  negligence liability as incentive, 535, 591
  non-employees, duty to, 542
  occupiers, duty of, 542–543
  place of work, of, 540
  plant, of, 540
  pollution, atmospheric, 544
  premises, 542–543
  prohibition notice, 551
  proof, reasonable practicability, of, 552
  prosecution, 546, 551, 552
    corporation, officer of, 552
    improvement notice, non-compliance
      with, 550–551
    success of, 546
  regulations, 546–547
  "relevant statutory provisions," 546,
    566–567
  representatives, 350, 547–549
    inspection by, 548
    investigation by, 548
    qualification for, 548
    recognised union, appointment by, 367
    time-off, 111–112, 549
    training of, 549
  research, 545
  Robens' Report on, 537, 549, 553
  self-employed, duty of, 542
  standard of care in, 538
  standard of reasonable practicability,
    538–539
  strict liability for, 538
  sub-contractors affecting, 541–542
  substances, of, 540
  suppliers, duty of, 544–546
    hire purchase agreement, under, 546
  system of work, of, 540
  testing for, 544–546
  tort liability arising from, 535
  training in, 540, 541
  vehicles, 540

SAFETY—cont.
  vicarious criminal liability, 552
  welfare, 541n
SALARY. See WAGES.
SEAMEN,
  articles of association, 19
  contract of, 1, 19
  disabled, 24
  discipline of, 19–20
  Great Britain, employment in, 153
  non-characteristic position of, 19
  strike by, 491
  terms and conditions of employment, 502,
    503, 505
SECONDARY ACTION. See INDUSTRIAL ACTION.
SELF-EMPLOYMENT,
  employee, distinguished from, 1, 2
  individual choice of, 13
  safety, duty of, 542
  taxation of, 3
SENIORITY,
  sick pay linked to, 65
SERVICE. See CONTRACT.
SEX DISCRIMINATION. See also
    DISCRIMINATION.
  action short of dismissal, 117
  dismissal as, "additional award"
    following, 256
  time limit to claim, 135, 136
SEXUAL HARASSMENT. See DISCRIMINATION.
SHIP,
  children employed on, 22
  disabled employed on, 24
  flag of convenience, 502–503
  master, 19, 20
SHOP,
  employment in, 23
  factory, attached to, 23
SHOP CLUBS, 132
SHOP STEWARD,
  functions of, 371–372
SHORT TIME,
  dismissal for redundancy, as, 266–267
SICKNESS,
  continuity not affected by, 139, 140
  dismissal,
    consultation preceding, 222
    hearing concerning, 224
  frustration by, 178
  guaranteed pay during, 104
  maternity leave, during, 107
  medical certificate, 68–69
  national insurance sickness benefit,
    compensation for dismissal, affecting,
      257
    deemed incapacity, 67
    disqualification from, 67
    incapacity, evidence of, 65–66
    intermittent incapacity, 66
    misconduct disqualifying, 67
    normal work, 66

SICKNESS—cont.
  national insurance benefit—cont.
    pregnancy, during, 65
  notification of, 43, 69
  suspension during, statutory requirement
    of, 122–123
  S.S.P. scheme,
    appeal from refusal to pay, 68
    contractual payments satisfying, 69
    deductions from payments, 68, 69
    disputed entitlement, 68, 69
    employer's obligation, 67–68
    excluded categories, 68, 69
    notification requirements of, 43
    period of payment, 65, 68
  qualifying days, 68
    rate of benefit, 68, 69
    self certification, 69
    waiting days, 68
  statutory statement of terms, 43
  wages during, 61–65
    private schemes for, 64–65
    reasonableness of, 63
    seniority, linked to, 65
SIGNATURE. See CONTRACT.
SOCIAL SECURITY,
  supplementary benefits,
    entitlement to, 490
    strikers, availability to, 490
  unemployment benefit,
    disqualification from, 486–490
    participation in trade dispute, 489
    strikers disqualified from, 487–489
    strikes during, 486–489
    workers affected by strike, disqualified,
      487–489
STATUS,
  employment as, 27, 156
STATUTORY DUTY. See also SAFETY; TORT.
  union membership,
    enforcement upon contractors, 239
STATUTORY RIGHTS,
  contractual exclusion of, 30–31
STATUTORY SICK PAY SCHEME. See SICKNESS.
STATUTORY STATEMENT. See also CONTRACT.
  collection agreement, as evidence of
    incorporation, 35
  contents of, 43
  contractual nature of, 44
  evidence of acceptance as binding, 35
  Great Britain, employers in, 153
  obligation to issue, 42
  period of employment entitling, 138
  qualification for, 166
  rectification of, 45–46
  reference to other documents, 44, 45
STRIKE,
  armed forces, by, 490
  breach of contract, as, 454–459
  conspiracy, criminal, as, 453
  continuation after dismissal, 246

STRIKE—*cont.*
continuity of employment, affecting, 139, 145
definition of, 242, 449
dismissal for, 244–247, 458–459, 467–468
dispute connected with, 487–488
general, 534
incitement, among armed forces, 490–491
incitement, among police, 491
injunction against, 466
misconduct, as, 269
notice of, 454, 456, 457
organisation of, 454
organisers, liability of. *See* CONSPIRACY; DURESS; INTERFERENCE WITH CONTRACT; INTIMIDATION.
police, by, 533
police, organisation among, 490
political, 533
protection of employer from, 467, 468
public service, in, 533
redundancy, following notice for, 249, 268–269
replacement workers, recruitment of, 486
right to, 450–452
seamen, by, 491
social security benefits during, 486–490
state of emergency during, 533
suspension of contract by, 455, 457, 458
SUSPENSION,
compulsory, 122–123, 251
medical grounds, on, 122–123, 251
priority on insolvency, 123–124
Truck Acts affecting, 129
wages, of obligation to pay, 62

TIME-OFF WORK,
ante-natal care, for, 117
Code of Practice concerning, 111, 112, 113, 115
Great Britain, employment in, 153
payment for, 114, 116, 117
priority of claim in insolvency, 123–124
public duties, for, 115–116
reasonable conditions for, 113–114, 115–116, 117
recognised union, in respect of, 367
redundancy, pending, 116
refusal of, 113
safety representative, for, 549
time limit to claim, 135
training, for, 113–114
reasonable limits to, 113–114
union member, for, 114–115
unpaid, 114–116
TORT. *See* BREACH OF STATUTORY DUTY; CONSPIRACY; DURESS; INDUSTRIAL ACTION; INTERFERENCE WITH CONTRACT; INTIMIDATION.
damages, trade union, against, 497–498

TORT—*cont.*
immunity from, 498–514. *See also* TRADE DISPUTE.
specific torts, limited to, 514–515
interference with proprietary right, 484
joint tortfeasors, 584
miscellaneous categories, trade union liability for, 497
new developments, 482–484
statutory duty, inducing breach of, 484–485
statutory development of, 484–485
unlawful element, immunity extended to, 516–517
TRADE DISPUTE,
arbitration arising from, 357, 366
conciliation in, 366
contemplation of, existing dispute, 508
contemplation or furtherance of,
existing dispute, 499, 508
immunity limited to, 498
motive as, 506
objective test of, 506–509
remoteness of, 506
union membership agreements, 239
definition of, 499–506
social security purposes, for, 488
disqualification during, from statutory sick pay, 68
direct interest in, 489
employees, non-involvement of, 501
employer involvement in, 500–501
employers' association party to, 510
injunction, restrictions upon, 522
participation in, 489
union meeting as, 489
personal animosity as, 504, 505
political purpose as, 502, 503
purpose of, 502–506
separation into two, 509, 513
strike connected with, 487–488
subject matter of, 501–506
termination of, 487, 488
third party involvement in, 501
United Kingdom, outside, 501
unresisted demands as, 501
workers and workers, between, 499
TRADE SECRET. *See* CONFIDENTIALITY.
safety, affecting, 545
wage rates as, 131
TRADE UNION,
action against, 387
activities of,
action short of dismissal for, 117–122
"additional award," 256
dismissal for, 117
protected from dismissal, 228–230
time off for, 114–115
administrative decisions by, 442
admission, 401–415
branch meeting, by, 402
"Bridlington" conditions for, 409

TRADE UNION—*cont.*
  admission—*cont.*
    discretionary, 405
    natural justice inapplicable to, 408
    political fund contributions affecting, 399
    procedural errors, 407
    ultra vires, 406–407
  agency, bargaining, of, 33–35
    individual members, affecting, 374–375
  amalgamation of, 393–395
    objection to, 394–395
    political fund, affecting, 395
    procedure for, 393–394
    registration of, 395
  appeal, internal,
    affirmation of hearing, as, 437
    failure to hear, 422
    refusal of, 437
    re-hearing, as, 437–438
  authorisation of industrial action, 494–495
    damages, 497–498
    membership, by, 495–497
    shop stewards, by, 495–497
    ultra vires, 494, 495
  ballot,
    amalgamation, for, 393, 394
    financing of, 439, 444
    industrial action, preceding, 443
    political fund, for, 396
  bargaining information,
    complaint of non-receipt, 361, 362
    supply to, 360
  benefits, discrimination in, 403
  branch,
    disciplinary procedure in, 419, 420, 428
    secretary, 131
  Bridlington agreement, 409–415
    implication in rules, 423
    natural justice applicable to, 411–414
    power to comply with, 410, 411
    recruitment, 409
    ultra vires action, 411
  certification officer, 386, 393, 394, 395,
      396, 398
    ballots, financing of, 444
  collective approach of, 370, 374
  combinations, prohibition of, 452–453
  conspiracy, as, 391
  consultation, redundancy, preceding, 214,
      295–296, 298–299
  contract of membership, 399–401
    rule book containing, 400
    specific performance, 9, 445
  contracts of, 389, 390, 391
    legality of, 391
  defamation of, 387
  definition, 384–386
  discipline,
    appeal, 429, 436–438
    bad faith, 436
    bias, 433–436

TRADE UNION—*cont.*
  discipline—*cont.*
    blanket offence, 417, 423
    charge, 429
    customary procedure, 428
    discretion to impose, 426
    investigation, 429
    judicial approach to, 416–417, 421–439
    judicial review, exclusion of, 438–439
    leaving, 429
    natural justice, 429–436
    opinion, subjective, 427
    penalty, 424
    procedure, 419, 420, 428–433
    restraint of trade, as, 426
    rules concerning, 416–421
    ultra vires, 422–423, 426
  discrimination by, 336, 447
  disputes committee, 410
  dues,
    check-off, 128–129
    procedure on non-payment, 415
    resignation by non-payment, 415–416
  election,
    candidates, selection of, 445
    diversity of, 443
    eligibility for, 444–445
    natural justice applied to, 408, 445
    nullity of, 445
    right to participate, 445
  employee of, authorisation of industrial
      action by, 494
  employers' associations distinguished
      from, 384
  entity, as, 386–390
    Foss v. Harbottle, applicable to, 421
    statutory creation of, 389
    statutory denial of, 389, 390
  executive committee, authorisation of
      industrial action, 494
  Foss v. Harbottle, rule in, 421
  funds, transfer of, 394n
  government,
    inadequate provision for, 440
    judicial attitude to, 440–441
  immunity from liability, 492–498
    restriction of, 493–498
    threatened action, for, 493
    trustees, of, 493
  independent, 385, 386
  individual representation in disciplinary
      procedure, 225
  individual rights, representation of, 374
  industrial disablement claim by, 631
  instructions of, 94
  inter-union disputes, 409
  job protection by, 182
  joinder as defendant, 228, 238
    action short of dismissal concerning, 122
  judicial understanding of, 370, 374
  law enforcement by, 126

TRADE UNION—*cont.*
legality of, 390–392
meetings,
course of employment, in, 623
industrial action, as, 246
protected activity, as, 120
member/membership,
action short of dismissal for, 117–122
application constituting contract, 404
apprenticeship as condition, 401
Bridlington agreement, 409–415
code of practice, concerning, 401, 415, 416
compensation for denial of, 403
contract of, 416–417, 421, 422, 428
discretion to grant, 409
discrimination, 403
dues as condition precedent, 415
expectation of, 407–408
expulsion, unreasonable, 401
freedom of, 358
management, 401
police, 491
protected from dismissal, 228–230
public policy as to, 413, 426–428
re-admission, 402
reason for rejection, 408–409
representation of, 446–448
resignation, 415, 416
resignation by estoppel, 415–416
right to, 413
right to work affecting, 404
time off work, 114–115
trade dispute concerning, 502
trade union staff, 401–402
unreasonable exclusion from, 401, 402–403
unreasonable expulsion from, 401, 402–403
"workers," of, 385
natural justice,
absence of not affecting decision, 412–413, 421
basis for, 429–430
bias, 433–436
bias, evidence of, 433–435
bias, financial, 435
bias, personal, 434, 435–436
bias, test of, 433
charge, amendment of, 432
charge, disciplinary, 429, 431–432
content of, 408
election, applied to, 445
exclusion of, 430–431
hearing, 432–433
notice to committee, 432
negligence of, 448
office,
declaration of right to, 446
political fund affecting, 399
specific performance of, 445–446

TRADE UNION—*cont.*
officers,
duties of, 444
official, authorisation of industrial action by, 494
definition, 111
duties of, 111, 112
job protection for, 117
picket, organising, 530
time off work. *See* TIME-OFF.
trade dispute concerning facilities, 502
organisational rights, deprivation, 118–119
political activities of, 395–396
ultra vires, 396
political fund,
admission, refusal, 399
amalgamation affecting, 395
application of, 397–398
ballot for, 396
contracting out, 395, 398
discrimination concerning, 399
jurisdiction concerning, 398
levy, 397
protected from tort liability, 498
T.U.C., contributions to, 397
pressure to dismiss by, 228
property of, 389
provident funds, protected, 498
purposes of, 385–386
recognition of,
advantages of, 367
evidence of, 295–296
meaning of, 368–370
safety representative appointed by, 547
statutory machinery for, 367
voluntary nature of, 367
recruitment, protected activity, as, 120
registration of, 385
entity, creating, 387–389
representation by,
good faith, in, 446–448
individual grievance, in, 447
repudiation of industrial action, 494, 495
notification of, 494
restraint of trade, in, 390
rules,
admission, 401–402
amendment of, 441
appeal, disciplinary, 429
contract, as, 400, 414
disciplinary charge, 429, 431–432
election, 444–445
expulsion, for, 392
hearing, disciplinary, 429
implication of, 400, 414, 444–445
inadequacy of, 440
industrial action, empowering authorisation of, 494
interpretation of disciplinary, 424–426
interpretation strict, 407, 414, 421

TRADE UNION—*cont.*
rules—*cont.*
investigation, disciplinary, 429
judicial influence on, 417, 419
legality of, 391
procedure, disciplinary, 419, 420,
428–433
reasonableness of common law,
404
restraint of trade, as, 406
unreasonable, 413, 426, 428
safety representatives, 547–549
shop stewards,
authority of, 371–372, 495–497
functions of, 371–372
status of, 386–390
suit against, 389
transfer of engagements, 393
trustees, liability of, 493
ultra vires acts of, 391–392
political activities, 396
wages councils, attitude to, 352
winding up, rights in, 415–416
TRADES UNION CONGRESS,
Bridlington agreement, 409–415
ultra vires action, 411
independent review body, 242
training, approval by, 113
TRAINING,
discrimination in, 335, 336, 342
employer, by, 113
safety, in, 540, 541
safety representative, of, 549
time-off for. *See* TIME-OFF.
T.U.C. approval of, 113
TRANSFER OF UNDERTAKINGS. *See also*
CONTRACT CONTINUITY OF
EMPLOYMENT.
collective agreements, 382
consultation preceding, 298–299
dismissal, as, 181
recognition, 382
TRANSPORT,
children employed in, 22
TRUCK ACTS,
amount of payment, 128
calculation of wages unaffected, 129,
130
check-off of union dues, 128–129
cheque, payment by, 127
contract contrary to, 130–131
criminal offences under, 130
deductions, control of, 128–130
fines and deductions, 129–130
illegal contracts, 25
inspection, 126
method of payment, 126–127
suspension without pay, 129
truck system, 125–126
wages, definition of, 127
"workman," application to, 127

TRUST,
behaviour destroying, 70
intolerable conduct destroying, 71, 72
maintenance of, 46–47, 69–73, 170
test of repudiatory breach, as, 69

UNEMPLOYMENT BENEFIT. *See* NATIONAL
INSURANCE.
UNFAIR DISMISSAL,
age limit to claim, 134–135
agreed procedures, departure from,
224–226
appeal, 226–227
disadvantages of internal, 226–227
fresh reasons upon, 198
apprentice of, 21
basic award,
notice period, 166
period of employment, 165
priority on insolvency, 123–124
closed shop, to enforce. *See* CLOSED
SHOP.
compensation,
contribution, unknown factors as, 197
union membership, for, 238
continuity of employment as qualification,
137–138
contribution by employee to, 261
disobedience, improper orders, to, 95
explanation, opportunity for, 207
failure to reinstate as, 108
fairness, standard of, 192–195
fixed term contract excluding, 154
Great Britain, employment in, 153
gross misconduct, 220
hearing, 207
conduct of, 212
consultation replacing, 216, 221
lack of, reasons for, 224
mitigation of offence, 213
police investigation affecting, 212
sickness, concerning, 224
trade union representation, 225
industrial action, 244–247
industrial relations practice, failure to
follow, 194
interim relief, 229
contractual authorisation by, 230
priority of award on insolvency,
123–124
investigation of reasons for, 198–199
notice, irrelevance of, 182, 216
police, not applicable to, 154
pregnancy, for, 106, 251
presumption of, rebuttal by reason, 191
procedure,
collective agreement, 224–226
effect on decision, 209–215
employer practice as to, 215
exceptions to need for, 207, 215
full time official, attendance of, 212

UNFAIR DISMISSAL—*cont.*
procedure—*cont.*
  pre-redundancy consultation, 297
  reason, dependence upon, 206
reason,
  age, 200
  belief in, 199
  date of dismissal at, 196–197
  dishonesty, 212
  down grading, 215
  economy, 200
  gross misconduct, 220–221
  homosexuality, 203
  inadmissible, 228
  investigation of, 198–199
  multiplicity, 200
  objectivity of, 253
  permissibility of, 197–198, 199, 200
  presumption rebutted by, 195, 197
  primary, 197
  redundancy, 200, 247
  reorganisation, 204–205
  self-justifying, 205
  suspicion as, 198
  transfer of business, 253
  variation, refusal of, 204, 205
reasonableness,
  arbitrary action as, 202
  balance of probability, 213
  burden of proof, 201
  common practice as test, 203–205
  different views as to, 203
  employee's view as to, 205
  standard of employer, 201–205
redundancy, for, 263
  alternative offer affecting, 250
  consultation preceding, 247
  procedure to select, 214
  selection for, 247–250
remedies,
  "additional award," 256
  basic award, 256–257
  basic award, deducted from
    compensation, 259
  basic award, reduction of, 256–257
  compensation, basic award as, 259
  compensation, calculation of, 257–262
  compensation, increased expenses, for,
    259
  compensation, sickness benefit, 257
  compensation, unemployment benefit,
    257, 262
  expenses, 260
  job protection, loss of, 259
  manner of dismissal, 259–260
  mitigation affecting, 255
  mitigation during notice period, 258
  nil award, 257
  pension rights, loss of, 260
  practicability of, 255
  reduction of compensation, 260–262

UNFAIR DISMISSAL—*cont.*
remedies—*cont.*
  re-engagement, 255–256
  reinstatement, 254–256
  replacement employee affecting, 255
  set off, 261–262
  specific enforcement, 254
replacement during maternity leave, 110,
  251
size of employer, 201, 206, 208
time limit to claim, 135, 136–137
trade union activities, for, 117
transfer of business, upon, 253
warning,
  absence of, 208
  cancellation of, 223
  code of practice, 216–217
  different reasons for, 223
  gross misconduct displacing, 220–221
  implied, 218
  purpose of, 217–218, 221–222, 223, 226
  standing, 221
  successive, 223
UNION MEMBERSHIP. *See* CLOSED SHOP.
UNION PRESSURE. *See* INDUSTRIAL ACTION.

VARIATION, CONSENSUAL. *See* CONTRACT.
VICARIOUS LIABILITY,
  assault producing, 609–610
  authorisation affecting, 603–604
  authorisation, implied, 606–607
  control establishing, 596, 601–602
  control, transfer of, 600–603
  course of employment,
    establishing, 603–612
    presumption of, 605, 608
    skylarking included in, 610
    test of, 603–604
  delegation distinct from, 583
  direct liability absorbing, 602–603
  discretion of employee, 606–607
  dual, 602
  duty of in, 611
  elements of, 570
  employer, determination of, 600–603
  employment relationships, confined to,
    599
  extended hours, during, 608
  incidental acts, 606–607
  indemnity for, 600
  insurance, need for, affecting, 599
  interest of employer affecting, 604–605,
    608–609
  justification for, 599
  misunderstood, 610–612
  modern role of, 607–609
  origins of, 568
  presumption of, 605, 608
  prohibition affecting, 604–606
  site, control of, affecting, 602–603
  strict liability distinguished from, 609

VICARIOUS LIABILITY—cont.
sub-contractors, 599
theory of, 598–599
trespassers, in relation to, 612
width of, 607–609
VICTIMISATION. See DISCRIMINATION.

WAGES,
ability to work, return for, 61–62
apportionment, 61
arrears, priority on insolvency, 123–124
attachment of, 132–133
details of earnings, 133
method, 132–133
purposes, permitted, 132
calculation, Truck Acts affecting, 129, 130
check weighing affecting, 131–132
cheque, payment by, 127
collection agreement fixing, 31
collection, course of employment, in, 622
compensation related to, 256, 257
Crown, obligation to pay, 18
definition, 127
discrimination in, 329, 335
duty to pay, 606
Fair Wages Resolution protecting, 358
fixing of, 452
forms of, 59–61
general level of, 358, 359
guaranteed. See also GUARANTEE
PAYMENTS.
statutory provision for, 2, 61
withdrawal of, 204
interim relief from dismissal, following,
230
itemised statement of, 153
medical suspension, during, 123
minimum rates of, 59–60
normal week's pay, 301
notice, during, 258
obligation to pay, 57
outworkers, of, 131
overtime, for, 302
particulars of, 131–132
"pay," EEC definition of, 304
pension contributions as, 318, 341
piece-rates, 58, 59
Truck Acts affecting, 130
policy, Fair Wages award exempt,
359–360
policy, government, 349
productivity, linked to, 60–61
"red-circle" to maintain, 315–316
remuneration,
expenses as, 302
meaning of, 301–302
salary distinguished from, 59, 61
sickness, during, 61–65
flat rate schemes, 64
statutory control of. See TRUCK ACTS.
statutory fixing, 349

WAGES—cont.
statutory statement of, 43
suspension of, 62
tax fraud, involving, 25
time off, during, 114, 116, 117
Truck Acts. See TRUCK ACTS.
wage-work bargain, 53–69
WAGES COUNCILS, 41, 349, 350–356
abolition of, 351, 352, 354–355
agriculture, 354
awards,
contractual implication of, 41
contractual term, as, 351
constitution, 354
contractual terms fixed by, 351, 355–356
decline of, 350–351
establishment of, 353
holidays, fixing of, 351
local bargaining affecting, 353
origin of, 350, 352
purpose of, 350
statutory industrial council, 366
statutory joint industrial council, 355–356
temporary nature of, 352
trades unions attitude to, 352
wages orders, 354
WOMEN. See also DISCRIMINATION.
cleaning of machinery by, 565
employment below ground, 23
employment of, 23
Sunday work by, 317
WORK,
co-operation in, 54
equal value of, 303–304
incomplete performance of, 53
injury at. See BREACH OF STATUTORY
DUTY; INJURY AT WORK; NEGLIGENCE;
SAFETY.
order to, 392, 466
place of, 50, 52, 53, 271, 626–627
picket at, protected, 530–531
practice affecting obligation, 55–56
pregnancy affecting, 250
provision of, 57–59
safety at. See SAFETY.
temporary cessation of. See CONTINUITY
OF EMPLOYMENT.
time-off. See TIME-OFF.
travel to, 625–627
wage-work bargain, 53–69
WORKER,
definition of, 16–17, 385
WORKING HOURS. See also HOURS.
tea break as, 121
WORKMEN,
definition, Truck Acts, in, 127
Workmens' Compensation Acts, 590, 614
WRITTEN STATEMENT. See CONTRACT.

YOUNG PERSONS,
hours of employment, 22–23